D1713452

A Reference Guide to Modern Armenian Literature, 1500–1920

A Reference Guide to Modern Armenian Literature, 1500–1920

With an Introductory History

Compiled and with an Introduction by

Kevork B. Bardakjian

Wayne State University Press • Detroit

04 03 02 01 00 5 4 3 2 1

Library of Congress Cataloging-in-Publication Data

Bardakjian, Kevork B.
A reference guide to modern Armenian literature, 1500–1920 : with an introductory history / Kevork B. Bardakjian.
p. cm.
Includes bibliographical references (p.) and index.
ISBN 0-8143-2747-8 (alk. paper)
1. Armenian literature—To 1800—History and criticism.
2. Armenian literature—19th century—History and criticism.
3. Armenian literature—20th century—History and criticism.
4. Armenian literature—Bio-Bibliography. 5. Armenian literature.
6. Armenian literature—Translations into English. 7. Armenia–Intellectual life. I. Title.
PK8505.B37 2000
891'.99209—dc21 98-43139

The preparation of this volume was made possible by a grant from the Program for Research Tools and Reference Works of the National Endowment for the Humanities, an independent federal agency. This assistance is most gratefully acknowledged.

Grateful acknowledgment is also made to the Armenian General Benevolent Union for financial assistance in the publication of this volume.

Մի եղէց անպտուղ ի փոքր վաստակոյս
իբր ապաջան սերմանող անբերրի երկրի

Նարեկ, բան Բ

To
Ani and Nayiri

Contents

Acknowledgments

When Robert W. Thomson and I jointly undertook this project, originally conceived as a single volume, *A Reference Guide to Armenian Literature,* we were fortunate to enjoy the support and encouragement of a host of friends, colleagues, and interested persons.

The initial impetus for the book came from Dr. David H. Partington, then head of the Middle East Division of the Harvard College Library. A two-year grant (1979–81) from the National Endowment for the Humanities enabled us to gain the services of Geoffrey Goshgarian from UCLA. He spent two years at Harvard, amassing bibliographical information and preparing drafts for many of the entries. The groundwork he prepared was of fundamental importance, as was his intelligent analysis of a vast amount of material. But finishing touches to the project were delayed, and Robert and I decided to bring up the cut-off date for the material from 1980 to 1990. A most generous grant from the Armenian General Benevolent Union enabled us to accomplish the task. Helen Greene-Quigley of the Middle East Division of the Harvard College Library gathered material in Western languages. Manya Babayan and Emma Babayan, both senior bibliographers at the National Library in Erevan, assiduously and expeditiously collected an extensive amount of material from Armenian and Russian sources, enabling us to close the ten-year gap in critical literature in the existing manuscript. In September 1993, by which time both Robert and I had left Harvard, we agreed to make this project into two separate books. His part, published under *A Bibliography of Classical Armenian Literature to 1500* AD (Brepols, 1995; *Corpus Christianorum*), covers the fifth to the fifteenth centuries. This volume includes authors born between 1500 and 1920.

To Robert, an old friend and colleague, I owe a profound debt. His role and experience in initiating and planning this project has been indispensable, his contribution vital, and his support kind throughout.

The generous assistance given by many friends, colleagues, and students I acknowledge collectively and with gratitude. Edmond Y. Azadian, Rev. Father Krikor Maksoudian, Ronald G. Suny, Robert W. Thomson, and Khachig Tölölyan made helpful comments on the Introduction. I am indebted to the staff of the Middle East Division of the Harvard College Library, where the project took shape; and to the authorities and staff of many institutions in whose collections I worked at various stages of the project: the Mekhitarist Congregations of Venice and Vienna; the National Library of Armenia; the Matenadaran; the Manuk Abełyan Institute of Literature of the Academy of Sciences of Armenia; the Library of the Academy of Sciences of Armenia; the Ełiše Charents Museum of Art and Literature in Erevan; the Library of the State University of Erevan; Bibliothèque Nubar in Paris; Krikor and Clara Zohrab Information Center of the Diocese of the Armenian Church of America in New York; and the H. Hatcher Graduate Library of the University of Michigan. Thanks are due to Arzo Computers, Inc., of Southfield, Michigan, for designing special fonts and for related technical assistance. Alice Nigoghosian, Jennifer Backer, and Kathy Wildfong of Wayne State University Press and Kathy Wilson meticulously helped prepare the manuscript for publication. Art Chartow elegantly designed the book. A most generous subvention from the Armenian General Benevolent Union made the publication of this volume possible.

This book owes its completion to the solicitous support of my wife and our two daughters, and to their delightful suspension of disbelief for many long years.

KBB
2 August 1995, Ann Arbor

Preface

As its title indicates, this guide is designed to provide reference to texts and secondary literature as a starting point for further study of the works of Armenian authors born between 1500 and 1920. Although the reader may encounter occasional references to writings in manuscript form, this book is a guide to *Armenian* texts in *printed* form only. Authors of Armenian descent writing in other languages have been excluded.

The term "literature" has been employed in its broader sense for the years 1500 to 1800; so historians, for instance, have been included. But for the nineteenth and twentieth centuries, the focus has been strictly on belles-lettres. It is important to remember that in Armenian, as well as in many other systems of periodization, the Middle Ages conclude with the eighteenth century. One could, then, argue for the validity of designating the period covered by this book as the "late medieval and modern" era. In fact, internal chronological divisions and accompanying commentary in many ways reflect the traditions of Armenian scholarship. But, for a number of reasons, such as familiarity and convenience, I chose to adhere to the more formal and common, though by no means universal, periodization of history.

Of the five principal parts of this volume, the first consists of two sections: a brief background to each of the six periods into which the modern era has been divided, followed by a cursory glance at the works of some of the authors born between 1500 and 1920. In addition to this general evaluation, an effort has been made to point to some similarities, characteristics, and trends in the works of both modern and earlier writers, and to some external influences. On occasion, certain biographical details have been introduced to elaborate a point; but fuller portraits are to be found in the second, bio-bibliographical part, followed by a list of a given author's works and their translations, and a section on critical literature.

When this work was planned as part of the larger project, the amount of time allotted and the resources available to us had to be apportioned and employed in a practical fashion. This meant two things. Firstly, cut-off dates had to be set for both the authors and sources (1920 and 1990 respectively). Secondly, the sources had to be reduced to a manageable quantity while maintaining their chronological sequence and continuity. Many secondary sources, dailies, weeklies, and periodicals of general nature, as well as a number of post–World War II journals published in the Middle East, Europe, and the United States, have thus been left out. Reviews, as a rule, have been excluded for major authors, but this rule has been disregarded especially in the case of lesser writers on whose life or work such pieces remain the only source of criticism and information. Both the traditional and reformed systems of orthography have been maintained. A question mark in square brackets renders the Armenian question mark which, as is known, is always placed on the interrogative form. Periodicals are cited by year of publication followed by issue number. Volume numbers, when used, appear first and are followed by year of publication and issue number.

I alone bear full responsibility for all imperfections, and all faults of omission or commission in this first attempt ever of its kind. I put my shoulder to the wheel in the hope that this introductory guide will be of benefit to reader, student, and scholar alike. If it arouses interest in Armenian literature, and if it leads the general reader on to more books, the beginner on to more advanced research, and the scholars of neighboring traditions on to comparative studies, my efforts will have been worthwhile.

Transcription of Armenian

ա	բ	գ	դ	ե	զ	է	ը	թ	ժ	ի	լ
a	b	g	d	e	z	ē	ě	tʻ	ž	i	l
խ	ծ	կ	հ	ձ	ղ	ճ	մ	յ	ն	շ	ո
ḥ	tz	k	h	dz	ł	č	m	y	n	š	o
չ	պ	ջ	ռ	ս	վ	տ	ր	ց	ւ	փ	ք
ch	p	j	ṙ	s	v	t	r	ts	w	pʻ	kʻ
օ	ֆ	ու									
ō	f	u									

The alphabetical sequence always follows that of the Latin script. Diacritical marks and phonetical values of Armenian have been disregarded (thus *ēš*, for instance, comes before *ez*); and the four ligatures fashioned for this system (*CH-Ch-ch; DZ-Dz-dz, TS-Ts-ts, TZ-Tz-tz*) have been treated as separate letters (*dēz-dzayn-dzuk; tseḥ-tsōł-tsolkʻ; tʻuz-tzapʻ-tziran*).

Abbreviations

A	*Ararat.* Vałaršapat.
AAP	Arutiunian, S., and Kirpotin, V. *Antologiia armianskoi poezii s drevneishikh vremen do nashikh dnei.* Erevan, 1940.
AASL	Poteian, S., and Balasan, V. *Antologiia armianskoi sovetskoi literatury.* Erevan, 1957.
ABS	Veselovskii, Iu., and Berberian, M. *Armianskie belletristy.* 2 vols. Moscow, 1893, 1894.
AD	Leist, A. *Armenische Dichter.* Berlin and Leipzig, 1912.
AFT	Khachatrianz, I. *Armenian Folk Tales.* Philadelphia, 1946.
AHPT	Akinean, N. *Hing panduḥt tałasatsner.* Vienna, 1921.
AL	Arnot, R. *Armenian Literature.* London and New York, 1901.
ALG	"Armenische Lieder und Gedichte" in Paul Rohrbach, *Armenien.* Stuttgart, 1919. Pp. 116–44.
ALP	Boyajian, Z. *Armenian Legends and Poems.* London and New York, 1916. Reprinted 1958.
AM	*Arewelean mamul.*
AMH	Akinean, N. *Matenagrakan hetazōtutʻiwnner, kʻnnutʻiwn ew bnagrer.* 6 vols. Vienna, 1922–64.
AN	Chatschatrjanz, J. *Armenische Novellen.* Berlin, 1949.
ANA	*Anahit.*
AND	*Andastan.*

AP Blackwell, A S. *Armenian Poems.* Boston, 1917. Reprinted New York, 1978.

APA Navarian, A. *Anthologie des poètes arméniens.* Paris, 1928.

APAS Lerena Acevedo de Blixen, J. *Antología de poetas armenios.* Montevideo, 1943.

AQ *Armenian Quarterly.*

ARAS Shklovskii, V. *Armianskie rasskazy.* 2 vols. Erevan, 1953.

Armeniaca *Mélanges d'études arméniennes.* Venice, 1969.

ARPO Shervinskii, S. *Iz armianskoi poezii.* Erevan, 1966.

AZA *Azatamart.*

B *Bazmavēp.*

BAI *Bulletin de l'Académie impériale de St. Pétersbourg.*

BEH *Banber Erevani hamalsarani.*

BM *Banber Matenadarani.* (First two issues under *Gitakan nyutʻeri žołovatzu*)

BPA Briusov, V. *Poeziia Armenii s drevneishikh vremen do nashikh dnei v perevodakh russkikh poetov.* Moscow, 1916. 2d ed., Erevan, 1966.

Brosset, *Col.* Brosset, M. *Collection des historiens arméniens.* 2 vols. St. Pétersbourg, 1874, 1876.

CHE Chōpanean, A. *Hay ējer, mer naḫneats banastełtzutʻiwnn u aruestě.* Paris, 1912.

CPA Marcel, L.-A., and Poladian, G. *Choix de poèmes arméniens.* Beirut, 1980.

CR *Caucasian Review.*

DILS Safrazbekian, I. *Dorogie imena, lyubimye stranitsy. Stikhi i novelly.* Erevan, 1965.

DLA Achrafian, J., *Diciotto liriche armene.* Rome, 1939.

E *Europe* (monthly, 39, February–March, 1961).

EJ *Ējmiatzin.*

EPA Eremean, A., *Parskahay ašułner.* Tiflis, 1930.

EPNA	Eremean, A., *Parskahay noragoyn ašułner.* Vienna, 1925.
FPA	*Festival de poésie et de musique arménienne.* Paris, 1945.
HA	*Handēs amsōreay.*
Hayapatum	Ališan, K. *Hayapatum, patmichkʻ ew patmutʻiwnkʻ hayots.* Venice, 1901.
HG	*Hay grakanutʻiwn.*
HGP	*Handēs grakan ew patmakan.*
HK	*Hayrenikʻ.* Boston.
HNV	Manandean, Y., and Ačaṙean, H. *Hayots nor vkanerĕ (1155–1843).* Vałaršapat, 1903.
IZAP	Ter-Akopian, A. *Iz zapadnoarmianskoi poezii.* Erevan, 1979.
JM	Missakian, B. *Au jardin des muses de la littérature arménienne.* Venice, 1961.
KAL	*Kavkazskii al'manakh.* St. Petersburg, n.d.
KHAN	Khachatriants, Ia. *Armianskie novelly.* 2 vols. Moscow, 1945, 1948.
KNS	Safrazbekian, I. *Komochek nezhnogo serdtsa.* Erevan, 1973.
KNZ	Kostaneants, K. *Nor žołovatzu, mijnadarean hayots tałer u otanaworner.* Four parts. Tiflis, 1892, pts. 1, 2; 1896, pt. 3; 1903, pt. 4.
KV	*Kavkaz i Vizantiia.*
L	*Lraber.* (Earlier *Tełekagir*).
LM	*Le Muséon.*
LPA	Melik, R., ed. *La poésie arménienne.* Paris, 1973.
LPAM	Cianascian, M. *La poesia armena moderna.* Venice, 1963.
LS	*Lettres soviétiques.* (Earlier *Œuvres et opinions*).
M	*Masis.*
MA	*Mélanges asiatiques.*
MKH	Miansareants, M. *Kʻnar haykakan.* St. Petersburg, 1868.

Manr žamanakagrutʻyunner	Hakobyan, V. *Manr žamanakagrutʻyunner.* Two vols. Erevan, 1951, 1956.
MPT	Mkrtchyan, M. *Hay mijnadaryan pandḥtutʻyan tałer (XV–XVIII dd.).* Erevan, 1979.
OO	*Œuvres et opinions.* (Later *Lettres soviétiques*).
PA	Tcheraz, M. *Poètes arméniens.* Paris, 1913.
PAAM	Tchobanian, A. *Poèmes arméniens anciens et modernes.* Paris, 1902.
PAM	Marcel, L.-A. "Poètes arméniens modernes." *Cahiers du Sud,* 45 (1957): 169–217.
PBH	*Patma-banasirakan handes.*
PCN	Arsharuni, A. *Pod chuzhim nebom.* Moscow, 1967.
PHA	Palean, T. *Hay ašułner, żołovrdakan hay ergichner ew tałasatskʻ.* 2 vols. Smyrna, 1911, 1914.
PHG	Połarean, N. *Haygrołner, v–xvii darern.* Jerusalem, 1971.
RA	*La roseraie d'Arménie.* 3 vols. Paris, 1918, 1923, 1929.
RAN	Rachian, Kh. *Armianskie novelly.* Erevan, 1962.
REArm	*Revue des études arméniennes.*
ROC	*Revue de l'orient chrétien.*
Roseraie	See *RA.*
S	*Sion.*
SAP	Kudian, M. *Soviet Armenian Poetry.* London, 1974.
SBAL	Gor'kii, M. *Sbornik armianskoi literatury.* St. Petersburg, 1916.
SG	*Sovetakan grakanutʻyun.*
SHA	Sahakyan, H. *Hay ašułner XVII–XVIII dd.* Erevan, 1961.
SHAP	*Armianskie poety v per. S. Ia. Sharti.* Tiflis, 1917.
SL	*Soviet Literature.*
SOV	*Sovetskaia armianskaia literatura. Sbornik poezii i prozy.* Erevan, 1953.

SUM Sahakyan, H. *Uš mijnadari hay banastełtzutʻyunĕ (XVI–XVII dd.).* 2 vols. Erevan, 1986, 1987.

T *Tełekagir.* (Later *Lraber*).

TA Tchobanian, A. *Les trouvères arméniens.* Paris, 1906.

TFA Antreassian, J. *Tales from the Armenian.* New York, 1955.

TH Tēvkants, A. *Hayerg: mełedikʻ, tałkʻ ew ergkʻ.* Tiflis, 1882.

THG Tʻarverdyan, G. *Hay gusanner.* Erevan, 1957.

Trouvères See *TA*.

TZ *Tzałik.*

UDS Umanets, L., and Dervish, Ar. *Sovremennye armianskie poety.* Moscow, 1903.

VAM Veselovskii, Iu., and Khalatiantz, G. *Armianskaia muza. Sbornik.* Moscow, 1907.

VER *Veratznund.*

WM Glagoleva, F. *We of the Mountains: Armenian Short Stories.* Moscow, 1972.

Z *Zuartʻnots* (amsatʻertʻ; amsōreay; eṙamseay; taregirkʻ).

1

A General History of Armenian Literature, 1500–1990

What follows is an introductory history that sketches out in the form of individual portraits nearly five centuries of Armenian literature in six chapters. Each chapter begins with a discussion of some relevant aspects of the political, social, and cultural realities prevailing in the homeland and the Armenian communities abroad, followed by a brief and general outline of the literature of the age and some of its characteristics. Each part is arranged chronologically (and whenever possible by genre, or thematically), but such sequence in general and within each part is neither wholly consistent, nor has it been possible to follow strictly, especially for the sixteenth through the eighteenth centuries. In addition to similar divisions, nineteenth- and twentieth-century authors have been also distinguished in four categories: Eastern, Western, Soviet Armenian, and post-genocide Dispersion literatures. When no exact dates have been available for the writers of a particular century, an effort has been made to group them thematically. Authors whose dates overlap the chronological units imposed here have been assigned, somewhat arbitrarily, to the era most consonant with their outlook, age, or productivity (nineteenth- and twentieth-century authors and survivors of the genocide in particular).

The Sixteenth Century

An Overview of the Armenian Realities of the Age

Following the fall of the Kingdom of Cilicia to the Mamluks of Egypt in 1375, the Armenians lost statehood until 1918. Armenia proper, deprived of independence since the eleventh century, in the sixteenth century became a battlefield for two Muslim but mortal enemies, the Ottoman and Safavid empires. Their violent rivalry had devastating consequences for Eastern Anatolia's economic, social, cultural, and demographic realities, and many Armenians sought safety beyond the homeland. But long before such setbacks, they had been dispersed in large numbers in neighboring and distant lands. The rise of Armenian Cilicia was but an eloquent expression of the magnitude of such displacement. Most of those who had left or had been made to leave Armenia in the tenth and eleventh centuries had gone in a westerly and a northwesterly direction, settling in Russia and later in Crimea and in southern and eastern Europe (in regions now known as Bulgaria, Rumania, Ukraine, Hungary, and Poland). Special mention should be made of the old Armenian community of Constantinople, which grew rapidly after the fall of Byzantium and was destined to exercise a formative influence on Armenian realities in the ensuing centuries. These settlements were active in the sixteenth century and would soon form a belt of communities, the largest ever in the history of Armenian Dispersion, extending from southeast Asia to western Europe and from St. Petersburg to northern Africa and Palestine. Needless to say, the dominant Armenian element in the homeland dwindled due to such adverse circumstances. And as newcomers from the East (Turkic elements) and the South (Kurds) settled in the region, its demographic make-up altered dramatically, with pernicious consequences for posterity.

There were by the sixteenth century six hierarchies within the Church of Armenia: the Catholicosate of All Armenians at the Mother See of Ējmiatzin; the Catholicosates of Cilicia (or Sis), Ałt'amar, and

Gandzasar (the former Church of Ałuankʻ, i.e. Caucasian Albania), all three with limited regional jurisdiction; the Patriarchate of Jerusalem; and the bishopric of Constantinople, which slowly evolved into an universal patriarchate for the Armenians of the Ottoman Empire. Although conflict among these centers, with rivalry, corruption, ignorance, and superstition within each, seriously weakened the Church's authority and administrative unity, it still remained the most important and influential institution, the sole custodian of Armenian culture and, together with trade and the mother tongue, the strongest national bond holding her flock together. In the absence of national political structures, the Church's power transcended the religious realm; it now played a greater political role, representing her adherents before local rulers, kings, shahs, and sultans. Such aspects of the Church's activities slowly and imperceptibly rendered the Church into a symbol of nationhood, seriously rivaling faith and religion as the essence of her mission.

Perhaps the gravest concern for Church leaders were the activities of Catholic missionaries. Close contact between the two churches had been initiated in Cilicia in the twelfth century as a result of the powerful leverage the Pope and the Latin principalities held in local and regional politics. The Church of Armenia in Cilicia had indeed on occasion recognized papal supremacy, despite the failure of most Armenian historians to admit to such union, and some considerable Roman Catholic influence proved inevitable. But the astonishing frequency with which communion with Rome was reaffirmed must call its effectiveness into question. Those who adhered to it sincerely came largely from the ranks of the clergy and were very few in number. Many Armenians looked upon the idea of papal supremacy as a political expediency, but most fiercely resisted it, especially those who resided in the homeland. For the latter, the national church still embodied their ancestral faith and identity. Attitudes toward Rome continued to be a divisive issue in the sixteenth century as well. Some Cilician patriarchs, like many of their predecessors, adhered to a pro-Catholic line in sharp contrast to those of Ējmiatzin, who in general keenly guarded the integrity and autocephalous state of the Church of Armenia. It was precisely for this reason that the seat of the Catholicosate of All Armenians had been moved from Sis back to Ējmiatzin, barely two years after the Council of Florence (1439), where, yet once more, an attempt had been made at cementing union with Rome.

Ironically, the Church of Armenia, twice in the sixteenth century, helplessly pinned her hope on the person of the Pope and his influence throughout Europe to have her flock delivered from Muslim yoke. It is believed that Stepʻanos V, Salmastetsi, Catholicos of Armenia, roamed western Europe in the late 1540s, presumably to submit to papal supremacy in return for some practical, if undefined, European support for Armenian aspirations. His successor, Mikʻayēl I, Sebastatsi, convened a secret meeting in Sebastea (Sivas) in 1562, and a plenipotentiary by the name of Abgar Tʻoḥatʻetsi (or Ewdokatsi, d. c1572), believed to have descended from ancestors born in the purple, was sent to the West for the same purpose. Reliable details are lacking. What is certain, though, is that both attempts bore no fruit.

That the supreme patriarch of Armenia should resort to such rather credulous steps, despite the strained relationship between the two churches, spoke clearly of the desperation that had gripped the Armenian ecclesiastical hierarchy and its willingness to accommodate Roman Catholic terms. As Armenia suffered under Turks and Persians fighting to control the region, the leadership placed some hope in Christian solidarity, most probably in the form of a new crusade. There were some very shaky grounds for such optimism. Nersēs Šnorhali's expectations for a new crusade in his lament in the wake of the fall of Edessa (1144) had indeed been fulfilled (although Edessa itself was never recovered), with some benefits for the Armenians of Cilicia. Pope Pius II's efforts, albeit abortive, to generate European support for a new crusade after the fall of Constantinople and the Council of Florence may or may not have been fresh in Armenian memory, but a document doctored in Cilician Armenia certainly was. This was the *Dašants tʻułtʻ* (a "pact," or a "letter of concord"), allegedly concluded between Grigor Lusaworich (Gregory the Illuminator) and King Trdat the Great of Armenia on the one hand and Emperor Constantine and Pope Sylvester I on the other, during a visit of the former two to Rome. The redactions of this forgery granted the Church of Armenia ecclesiastical autonomy in the East (or a standing at least equal to that of the Patriarchate of Antioch) and promised Western political-military support for Armenia in the future. Not only was a copy of the text submitted to Rome by Abgar Tʻoḥatʻetsi, but the promise it held for assistance was entertained by some sixteenth-century authors. According to some travel accounts, some ordinary Armenians also anticipated help from Western Christendom. A more pious expression of popular belief, with its roots deep in the early period of Christianity in Armenia and echoed by many Armenian authors, held that their plight was a visitation of God for their sins. There is a long record of ordinary Armenians choosing death over apostasy, the ultimate betrayal of ancestral faith. Although the much longer list of those who under duress renounced their faith has not been handed down, martyrdom also had its roots in the Christian ethos. All this, together with a host of various factors, long failed to shake Armenian optimism in Christian solidarity, which most Armenians seem to have distinguished from submission to Constantinople or Rome, and hindered, in no small measure, political imagination and intellectual creativity.

As for the written word and wisdom, several famous scriptoria and monastic schools had been active in Cilicia. In Armenia proper, Nor Getik (founded by Mḫitʻar Goš, and later known as Gošavankʻ), Aṙakʻelots vankʻ near Muš, Gladzor (1290s–1330s), Tatʻew (1370s–1400s), and Metzopʻ (1390s–1440s) had been some of the renowned centers of learning. Since the twelfth century, illustrious (and mostly itinerant) teachers had taught and trained students converging upon such schools from all parts of Armenia, at once disseminating knowledge and establishing channels of transmission to posterity. It was in such schools that the dogma of the Church of Armenia was fortified against Catholic penetration. The effort almost completely consumed the intellectual energy of the learned few. Added to the problem posed by the pro-union line of the Church in Cilicia was that of the Franciscans and Dominicans, who established missions in Iran and Nakhichevan in the fourteenth century and gave rise to the Armenian *Fratres Unitores* (Ełbarkʻ Miabanołkʻ, i.e., Uniate Brothers), a group of clerics given to extreme zeal that was eventually absorbed into the Dominican Order. As will be seen from this introduction, the conflict between the two camps continued for a very long time, assuming larger proportions and social-political significance. It should be noted that for the Armenians the confrontation was not one between "pro-western" and "anti-western" or "pro-eastern" orientation, nor between progressive and conservative elements. For there was no "eastern" (in this case Islamic) or "anti-western" alternative for the Armenians, and most of those who defined the Armenian position were reasonably well versed in Latin traditions. In fact, much of the intellectual vigor of the period was generated by the activities of the Catholic missionaries. In essence, then, the question was one of identity and loyalty to the ancestral religious tradition, embodied by the Church of Armenia.

By the tenth century, Classical Armenian had long ceased to be the spoken language but continued, in a progressively corrupt form, to be the vehicle of expression for learned poetry and certain ecclesiastical texts for many more centuries. Middle or Cilician Armenian became the standard in Cilicia, and with certain variations it prevailed as the literary medium in Armenia and in the Armenian communities abroad. It introduced two new letters (*ō* and *f*) to the original script and exhibited considerable deviations from the Classical tongue (in the phonetical system and the formation of compounds; some new forms of inflexion and the plural, etc.). What little uniformity Cilician society brought to Middle Armenian disappeared with the fall of the kingdom. Dispersion and the decline of city life in the homeland further diminished such features. Dialectal and spoken patterns prevailed, and the amount of loan words from Persian, Arabic, and Turkish increased rapidly. Since Middle Armenian was used for non-religious or "profane" expression, it would not be at all unreasonable to suggest that the distinction in some ways added to the veneration in which Classical Armenian is still held by many Armenians. From about the sixteenth century, it also marked, along with other factors (such as literary genres, thought, social habits, and attire, etc.), an almost complete break with many aspects of the old tradition, as the Armenians found themselves amid a sea of Muslim nations and overlords.

Armenian printing ushered Armenian letters into the sixteenth century. It began with the publication of five books in Venice by a priest known only by his name, Yakob, to which the sobriquet *mełapart* (sinner) was later attached. *Urbatʻagirkʻ* (Friday book, essentially a medical collection), *Pataragatetr* (missal), *Ałtʻarkʻ* (a collection pertaining to astrology, the horoscope, and medicine), *Parzaytumar* (a compendious calendar), and *Tałaran* (songbook, with works by Nersēs Šnorhali, Frik, Yovhannēs Tʻlkurantsi, Mkrtich Nałaš, and others) are the first five books that appeared in Venice in 1512 and 1513. More than half a century lapsed before Abgar Tʻoḥatʻetsi printed the next batch of books: two in Venice (1565, 1566) and five or six in Constantinople (1567–69), where he had returned shortly after printing his second book, leaving his son, Sultʻanšah, behind. Next, Yovhannēs Tērzntsi (a priest, whose dates are unknown) and Sultʻanšah translated Pope Gregory XIII's Gregorian Calendar and published it in Rome in 1584. In 1587, Tērzntsi published a *Sałmosaran* (Psalter) in Venice.

Armenian printing gathered momentum in the seventeenth century. In the mid-1630s, a printing press was set up in Nor Jułay (New Julfa, Isfahan), the first in Iran, to print the Armenian Bible when the Pope forbade the printing in Catholic Europe of any version but the Vulgate. The plans for printing the Bible did not materialize, but a number of books of a religious and moral nature were published. After a very long hiatus following Abgar Tʻoḥatʻetsi's short-lived activities, Armenian printing was revived in Constantinople in the 1680s, and a number of distinguished printers (Grigor Marzuanetsi, whose exact dates are unknown, Astuatzatur Kostandnupolsetsi, d. c1748, Pōłos Arapean, 1742–1835, Yovhannēs Miwhēntisean, 1810–91, who designed Turkish type faces as well) made invaluable contributions to Armenian printing. A large number of titles were published in Rome and Venice, particularly in the eighteenth century, including textbooks and reference works to facilitate Catholic propaganda among the Armenians. Armenian publishing in Amsterdam is held in particular distinction for printing non-religious books and the first Armenian Bible. It was in March 1666 that the Armenian Bible began to roll off the presses in the land of the "heretical Dutch," who had allowed and helped its printing, bringing a long-standing Armenian dream true. It was published by Oskan Erewantsi (1614–74), from the Bible (1295) of King Hetʻum II of Cilicia, but with additions and changes to the old canon of the Armenian Bible (e.g., Oskan added the Fourth Book of Esdras, the Book of Sirach, and Epistle of Jeremiah). Mḫitʻar Sebastatsi (q.v.) and a few others based their edition on Oskan's, but Yovhannēs Zōhrapean (1756–1829) reinstated the old canon in his 1805 edition. Even though Oskan moved his press to Livorno and then to Marseilles, some members of the Vanandetsi family (from the village of Vanand in the old Armenian region of Gołtʻn, i.e., Naḫijewan) carried on his mission in Amsterdam, printing some twenty books by the second decade of the eighteenth century. In Armenia proper, the first press was set up in Ējmiatzin in 1771 by Catholicos Simēon Erewantsi (q.v.). There followed other centers of printing from Madras (where *Azdarar,* the first Armenian periodical, appeared, 1794–96) to Constantinople (in first place with some 350 titles to 1800) and to western Europe, and from St. Petersburg to Jerusalem and Cairo. In the nineteenth century there were over a hundred Armenian printing presses in Constantinople alone. An estimated one thousand titles appeared between 1512 and 1800, and fifteen thousand titles appeared between 1801 and 1920. It is interesting to note that printing initially supplemented rather than supplanted manuscript copying, which continued well into the nineteenth century.

With its origins deeply rooted in antiquity and nurtured by Iranian civilization, Hellenistic culture, and Christian literature in Greek and Syriac, the new *written* phase of Armenian tradition began with the invention of a script by the monk Maštots around the year A.D. 400. The enterprise was undertaken in large part with a view to boosting the sluggish progress of Christianity in Armenia. Immediately, important religious texts were rendered into Armenian. The Bible, patristic, liturgical, and similar texts in Greek and Syriac were made available in Armenian. In due course, the movement encompassed a larger number of languages (Arabic, Old French, Latin, etc.) and a wider range of fields: theology, philosophy, grammar, rhetoric, science, homiletic and exegetical writings, commentaries, martyrologies, natural sciences, medicine, law, etc. There was a long hiatus in the fifteenth and sixteenth centuries, but this venerable tradition subsequently resumed with renewed zeal.

Almost simultaneously an original literature was developed, expressed in many a genre and mirroring a wide range of Armenian interests and concerns. Historiography stands out as both popular and influential. It was in such writings that historians with a strongly pronounced Christian orientation formulated the new ethos. Thus, Agatʻangełos spoke of the miraculous conversion of Armenia and the glorious beginnings of her Church. Depicting a single episode, the Armenian revolt of 451 against Iran, Ełišē in an eloquent, dramatic, and inspiring narrative sanctified the two principal pillars on which the Armenian collective self rested: absolute loyalty to ancestral faith and fatherland. Movsēs Ḥorenatsi, whose date and person are some of the most controversial issues in Armenian historiography, wrote the first comprehensive history; provided his fellow countrymen with an elaborate biblical pedigree, filling in the missing links in the works of Christian genealogists and Armenian sources; placed Armenia in a much larger regional and international context; promoted patriotism; and recorded for posterity some precious relics of oral pagan lore. Many a notable historian followed in the footsteps of these masters, writing regional or short accounts or histories of particular noble families. In addition to established patterns of historiography, especially after the tenth century, chronicles become a common format, and increasingly elaborate colophons supply reliable local and regional information.

Not surprisingly, prayers and hymns were composed in abundance. Although restricted in purpose, imagery, and imagination, they nonetheless came closest to literary expression. But poetic utterance found its greatest master in the person of Grigor Narekatsi (tenth century), whose *Book of Lamentation* (also referred to as *Narek,* or *Book of Prayers*) laments the separation of the mystic from God. Its style is convoluted in many instances, but its spontaneous, torrential flow, allied with the author's spiritual anxiety and burning desire to attain communion with God, simply overwhelm the reader. Its solemn mood and diction contrast with the lighter, festive colors and tone of his poems, allegorically reflecting spiritual and certain aspects of human and natural beauty. Following Narekatsi's death at the turn of the eleventh century, Armenian literature underwent some profound changes. The rise of cities in Bagratid Armenia, international trade and travel, Byzantine policy in Armenia, the appearance of the Turks in the region, demographic changes (both voluntary and involuntary), the arrival of the Crusaders, the rise of Armenian Cilicia, and some other factors accounted for new trends in Armenian letters.

The intense antagonism between the two churches notwithstanding, Armenian interest in Greek learning was revived in the eleventh century (Grigor Magistros, Grigor Vkayasēr). The cosmopolitan population of

Cilicia (Greeks, Syrians, etc., and the numerous monastic communities on the Black Mountain near Antioch) and immediate contact with the West had a tremendous impact on Armenian thought. Cilicia gave birth to one of the giants of Armenian literature: Catholicos Nersēs IV, Klayetsi, more commonly referred to as Nersēs Šnorhali (c1100–73), who is remembered for his earnest efforts to remove the rift between the churches of Eastern Christendom and for his hymns, commentaries, theological, and literary writings. He seems to have been among the first authors to write riddles and to use acrostic patterns and rhyme (following Grigor Narekatsi and Grigor Magistros). Of his numerous poems, the lament (*ołb*) on the fall of Edessa is particularly memorable. The origins of this genre may be traced to Movsēs Ḥorenatsi's prose lament at the conclusion of his *History* and to Dawt'ak K'ert'oł's abecedarian elegy on the murder of Juanšēr (seventh century). Another noteworthy Cilician clergyman, Nersēs Lambronatsi (1153–98), commemorated the death of Nersēs Šnorhali with an elegy, while Grigor IV, Tłay (c1133–93) grieved over the fall of Jerusalem. In Greater Armenia, Aristakēs Lastivertsi and Ḥachatur Kechaṙuetsi (also Kechaṙetsi) bewailed the misfortunes that befell Armenia, as did the historian Step'anos Ōrbēlean (thirteenth century) in his elegy on the Cathedral of Ējmiatzin, in which he longed for the revival of Greater Armenia as the overall homeland and Ējmiatzin as the overall spiritual center. The fall of Constantinople was yet another occasion that at least two authors mourned: Abraham Ankiwratsi and Aṙak'el Bałišetsi. Mḥit'ar Goš, who also compiled the secular law code, and Vardan Aygektsi wrote the earliest fables; Ḥachatur Kechaṙuetsi renewed Armenian interest in the *Alexander Romance*.

From about the thirteenth century onward, Armenian authors touched upon a wider range of topics. Frik, a layman, who suffered under the Mongols and wrote in Middle Armenian, spoke of social injustice and inequality. Yovhannēs Erznkatsi Pluz, a widely traveled *vardapet,* was one of the originators of the genre of *ḥrat* ("advice," usually on moral topics, a common genre in the region), who wrote with regret of the transience of human life. Kostandin Erznkatsi offered advice and wisdom, sadly noted the impermanence of life, and excelled in his hymns to the spring and the sun, to love and light, and made use of the allegorical device of the rose and the nightingale. Aṙak'el Siwnetsi was attracted to the story of Adam and Eve, which he recast with a certain degree of originality in many a dainty line. Mkrtich Nałaš wrote religious and didactic poems, but his poignant songs of the exile, about languishing away from home and friends, helped establish a new trend in Armenian poetry. Yovhannēs T'lkurantsi (also T'ulkurantsi), enamored of life and fearful of death, composed impassioned poems of love. Intoxicated with amorous sentiments, Grigoris Ałtʻamartsi, Catholicos of Ałtʻamar, wrote his poems celebrating life and love, with a bursting passion unusual for a monk. He also rendered into Armenian the story of the *City of Copper* from *One Thousand and One Nights.*

Among the literary forms that were in circulation by the sixteenth century, mention should be made of a form of anonymous poem called *hayrēn* (presumably from *hayerēn*, i.e. 'in Armenian'), dealing with a variety of topics pertaining mainly to urban life, which surfaced in the thirteenth century but was abundantly attested from the fifteenth to the eighteenth centuries. M. Abełyan (*Hin gusanakan žołovrdakan erger,* Erevan, 1931) believes that *hayrēns* evolved from old Armenian folklore, more specifically from the tradition of *gusan* folk songs. A variation of the *hayrēns* is the *antuni* ("homeless," in the sense of being away from family or ancestral home), recorded from the sixteenth century. Unlike the simple eloquence of *hayrēns, antunis* are usually in a florid style, with the plight of the *panduḥt* (exile) as one of their most common subjects. *Kafa* (from the Arabic *qāfiyah*) originated in the eleventh century and fell into disuse after the sixteenth century. An eight-line stanza, it is attached to the end of a chapter or an episode in texts, usually in prose or translations (e.g. *The Alexander Romance; The Story of King Pʻahlul*), as a peroration, interpretation, or meditation, mostly on moral issues.

Scattered far and wide and subject to diverse influences, the Armenians at home and abroad mirrored trends of both creation and emulation in their literature. Secular themes, with a steadily growing range of topics, were articulated in Middle or Cilician Armenian. The imitation of old masters was poor and pale, especially in the religious realm, but their imposing presence lingered on nonetheless. So did some of their concerns, particularly their preoccupation with human fate after the trump of doom had sounded. Not surprisingly, therefore, choosing between the temptations of this world and the awards of the next posed a sad and serious dilemma for a number of Armenian authors. Although certain didactic purposes still prevailed, some authors now stood on firmer ground on this planet, with earthly rather than celestial concerns; a few of them even wrote for joy and entertainment.

The sixteenth century was an age of transition and regrouping rather than one of doom and gloom, as is commonly held. What with political and economic instability, dispersion, demographic shifts, and the eclipse of centers of learning, the ties linking the Armenians weakened considerably and the old tradition was forgotten. Islamic elements surfaced in more ways than one. Religious persecution was by no means uncommon. Yet the monastery of Ḥndrakatar in Bałēš (Bitlis), for instance, showed considerable activity. Efforts to collect, repair, and copy manuscripts began in this century. Bridges were extended to the past. The Mamikoneans, military leaders in the past, were periodically remembered. Grigor Lusaworich was featured prominently in literature. One of the earliest references to the Armenian national epic *Sasuntsi Dawiṫ* (*David of Sasun,* consisting of four cycles, but generally identified by the name of the hero, David, of the third cycle) was made in this age. Faith in Christian solidarity and in Western assistance persisted. While some writers looked at earthly life with apparent disdain, expounded themes of faith and piety, composed "passions" of martyrdom, and bewailed their "sinful" fellow countrymen, many poems were written in praise of wine and love. Humor was not lacking, nor was allegory. Above all, whether in allegorical poems or in works of nostalgia for the past, there was definite hope for a revival.

A Survey of the Literature of the Age

Some of the themes discussed above are also found in the work of **ZAK'ARIA** *Episkopos* **GNUNEATS**, Bishop of the old Armenian region of Gnunik', north of Lake Van. The exact dates of this sixteenth-century author are not known. He hailed from the Armenian princely family Př̄ōsean and may have been a distant relative of Ḥachatur Kechaṙuetsi and a student of Grigoris Ałt'amartsi.

There is one more link that brings these authors together and that is their common attraction to the *Alexander Romance.* Interest in the old Armenian translation of this work was renewed by Ḥachatur Kechaṙuetsi, and dozens of manuscripts, written in various Armenian communities from Europe to India, attest to its continued appeal well into the nineteenth century. The purpose was to cloak Alexander in Christian garb. Zak'aria visited Constantinople in the mid-1540s, where he copied and illustrated this celebrated story at the request of his friend, patriarch Astuatzatur. At an unknown date, he made another illuminated copy of the same in Rome for one of his teachers by the name of Esayi, of whom nothing is known. Ḥachatur Kechaṙuetsi, as well as Grigoris Ałt'amartsi and Zak'aria, all wrote *kafas* to sum up, interpret, or meditate on Alexander's career, emphasizing the vanity of life, the fleeting nature of glory and wealth, and other moral points. Although most of their *kafas* have been distinguished, it is still difficult to decide with absolute certainty the authorship of some of them.

There is a similar uncertainty regarding a number of poems attributed to Zak'aria. Of five poems (on the Blessed Virgin, Christ, and some religious themes, published in *Bazmavēp* in 1910), Nersēs Akinean (1883–1963) found four to be of doubtful origin. On the other hand, he ascribed to Zakʻaria some anonymous poems of whose authenticity he himself was skeptical. One of these is dedicated to the luminous apparition of the Holy Cross to a hermit at the celebrated monastery of Varag, near the city of Van. The other noteworthy poem deals with the plight of emigrants (*łarip* or *łarib,* from the Arabic *gharīb*) and shares imagery and many verbal affinities with similar verse by Mkrtich Nałaš. The story of the rose and the nightingale found expression in three poems, all comparable in some respects to similar poems by Kostandin Erznkatsi. Only in one of them did Zakʻaria see the matter as a religious allegory and fashioned it, unlike the other two, in good Classical Armenian. Zakʻaria could not resist the temptation of using simple acrostic devices, popularized by Nersēs Šnorhali, which (in numerous other forms such as mesostich, telestich, alphabetical, or abecedarian, etc.) were widely employed by subsequent Armenian authors. Despite such limitations, Zakʻaria on the whole wrote in a fine style, noteworthy for its warmth and spontaneity.

If one is to judge by the colophons of some of the manuscripts he copied or repaired, **KARAPET BAŁIŠETSI**, a native of Bałēš (Bitlis), seems to have spent most of his life in the old Armenian province of Tarōn to the west of Lake Van. His dates are not certain (d. c1520?), nor is the short list of his poems. N. Akinean has attributed some of his work to Karapet Pʻarḫndetsi and has made him the author of a poem by a namesake, Karapet *vardapet,* titled "Tał araratzots" (On mankind). It depicts the descendants of Sem, Ham, and Japheth; provides topographical, economic, and political information on the respective regions in which they dwelt; and concludes with the sorrowful state of the Armenians, evoking some glorious Armenian figures and expressing hope for deliverance. This as yet dim sentiment, devoid of political connotations, is echoed in his poem on Lazarus's rise from the dead where he supplicates the Virgin to intercede on behalf of all nations, but most of all on behalf of the Armenians.

The deliverance he sought was from the conquerors and invaders of his country, as illustrated by his poem opening with "Pʻaṙkʻ anełin astuatzutʻean" (Glory unto the Uncreate God), to which N. Akinean gave the title "Ołb i veray aršawanats Šah Ismayēli" (A lament on the invasions of Shah Ismayel). This poem speaks of the rise of shah Isma'il I (1501–24), his initial conquests and defeat of Alvand, grandson of Uzun Hasan and the sultan of the Ak Koyunlu ("White Sheep," Turkmen tribes that controlled Eastern Anatolia in the fifteenth century), but focuses mainly on the siege and capture of Bitlis. The local Kurds, Karapet says, went on a looting rampage, confiscated and stored provisions in their fortifications and burned everything else before Isma'il's forces arrived. After this ordeal, the Armenians suffered heavy taxes, cruel treatment, and dispersion at the hands of the Qizilbash ("Red Head," Turkmen tribes that initially supported Safavid Iran) when Bitlis fell to them. His fellow countrymen were victims of a conflict they had nothing to do with. Yet Karapet, like almost all of his predecessors, interprets these calamities as a manifestation of God's displeasure with the sinfulness of the Armenians. His wrath engulfs the guilty and the innocent alike, just as the sun rises for all, the rain falls for plants both useful and unuseful, and the fire burns both the wet and the dry. A despondent Karapet sees no hope for the Armenians in this long lament (236 lines), which flows rapidly and smoothly but lacks the emotional depth and tragic streaks of his old masters.

Karapet finds himself to be as unrighteous as his errant nation (in "My God, Jesus Christ"), and seeks, on their behalf as well as his own, God's protection against satanic wiles and His mercy on the terrible day of the Last Judgment. His vision of salvation through piety, sense of pride in the Church of Armenia, and belief in Christian solidarity crystallize in his hymn to Grigor Astuatzaban (theologian, i.e. Gregory Nazianzenus). He begins with the Creation and brings his narrative down to Jesus Christ, the Apostles, and the church fathers, among whom were Basil of Caesarea, his colleague Gregory Nazianzenus, and the latter's equal ("hamanman") and namesake, Grigor Lusaworich (Gregory the Illuminator), whose Cappadocian connections obviously were not lost on Karapet. There follows a brief biography of Nazianzenus as the militant but quintessential Christian, whose intercession and help Karapet seeks.

One instance of the rare insights we get into the aesthetic standards of the time is Karapet's unsophisticated, spontaneous poem on singing, written in a limpid and succinct manner, and remotely echoing similar views expressed by Vardan Areweltsi (cf. Vardan Areweltsi, *Meknuťiwn ќerakani,* Erevan, 1972, p. 78). The jarring rendition of a chanter could conceivably have prompted him to state his preference for "sweet" and "thin" (i.e., fine and subtle) voice. But equally important for him was the fluency of recitation; for hesitation or inability to read rendered a song an "extinguished lamp" and made the singer an object of ridicule for the multitude. One needs, Karapet averred, two oxen to a plow and to cut straight furrows in soil, just as a bird needs two wings to fly. The third element, the melody, gave a song its harmonious appeal. Another poem ("Ḥrat tał ergeloy," Advice on singing a poem), exhorting singers to handle and maintain manuscripts with utmost care, reinforces the reader's image of Karapet as a passionate man of letters.

Only two poems by **GRIGOR VANETSI**(16th–17th c.) have come down to us. One is an exhortation to spend this short life in a manner pleasing to the Lord, so as not to be caught napping at the unannounced arrival of death and the day of retribution. The other, titled "A spiritual and allegorical advice on a cart" ("ḩrat hogewor ew ařakawor vasn sayli"), is one of the best poems of the period, with vanity of life and conceit as its central concerns. It is a carefully crafted creation, dramatic and engagingly nonchalant, with alluring imagery and a lingering atmosphere of helpless nostalgia for life.

A wider range of topics such as love, historical and moral-meditative poems, and the calendrical system are covered by **YOVASAPʿ SEBASTATSI**, a sixteenth-century poet and scribe born c1510. The date of his death is not known. He was a married deacon with some education but with little or no reputation among his contemporaries. His father, Tʿadēos, also a scribe, taught him the art; though Yovasapʿ put it to good use, his penmanship remained inferior to his father's. Only a few manuscripts Yovasapʿ copied and illuminated are extant, including a collection of his own work and a copy of the *Alexander Romance* (1535). Nothing is known of him after 1564, the date of a colophon inconclusively attributed to him. V. P. Gevorgyan's monograph (introduction and texts) leaves out fifteen unpublished pieces.

Seven love poems form a cycle that he said he wrote "for joy," and may wine-drinkers delight in their hearts so as to remember and speak well of him. His imagery is colorful, his sentiments warm and disarming. He is overwhelmed by a woman's fiery disposition; her eyes are as large as a sea, and her graceful body is likened in one instance to a palm tree and in another to a pomegranate tree. He desires her, and she is prepared to become his "slave"; yet Yovasapʿ repels his amatory temptations and their charming source. Like some of his great predecessors, whose robust passion he lacked, he concludes by renouncing mundane pleasures and extolling spiritual love and piety.

This contradiction, which has been expressed by many authors in many forms, is not so dramatic and central to Yovasapʿ as it is to some other poets, whose rejoicing–and rejection in their next breath–of fleshly feelings has been viewed by some Soviet Armenian critics as a contrivance to cover up or mitigate their worldly sentiments, or to placate the ubiquitous and heavy-handed control the Armenian Church supposedly exercised over intellectual life. In fact it was a genuine conflict between human needs and religious tenets that elicited varying reactions from Armenian poets faced with changing realities.

For an unquestioning Yovasapʻ, who reconciled himself with the inevitability of death with equanimity, hope in salvation lay in piety and the Lord's mercy. Man, whom Yovasapʻ casts in the metaphor of a city with five gates, is vulnerable to satanic tricks through his five senses; hence, his call for spiritual and moral vigilance. Some of his best *kafas* elaborating on this theme are impressively succinct, limpid, and serene in tone. Birth and death, he observes, form a cycle through which life maintains a balance and assures continuity to itself on earth. This image, if not the thought, comes from Yovhannēs Erznkatsi Pluz, who compares life to a carpenter and a wheel, as does Ḥachatur Kecharuetsi in some of his *kafas* on the *Alexander Romance* (they had both been anticipated by Omar Khayyam). Just as a certain spot on a turning wheel now goes up and now down, so a carpenter makes both cribs and caskets for those who arrive and those who depart. There is a similar thought in one of the episodes of the History of King Pahlul (*Patmutʻiwn yałags Pʻahlul tʻagaworin,* Tiflis, 1857, pp. 57–58), and its first line becomes the opening refrain for each of Yovasapʻ's *kafas* in octastichs: "Such is life" ("ašḥarhis sahmann ē hants"). It is a "house of pains" and of satanic wiles, where life is but a dream, happiness a fleeting second, and aspirations vain and all but unattained since Adam. Piety and prayer, humility and integrity, and constant mindfulness of one's mortality and the day of reckoning are sure steps to please the Almighty.

Nersēs Šnorhali and, to a lesser degree, Grigor Narekatsi left their mark on Yovasapʻ's religious poetry. His poem on the voluntary beggar Yovhannēs is an extensively abridged adaptation of "Varkʻ eranelwoyn Yovhannu ordwoy Ewtropiosi" (cf. *Varkʻ srbots harants ew kʻałakʻavarutʻiwnkʻ notsin,* Venice, 1855, i, 126–38). His elegy on the martyrdom of Kokča, a victim of vicious calumny who is tortured to death when he refuses to convert to Islam (reproduced in Manandean's and Ačaṙean's *Hayots nor vkanerě,* pp. 373–75), is similar to the martyrdom of Paron Loys of Caffa, mourned by Vrtʻanēs Sṙnketsi (q.v.). He also has a poem commemorating the Forty Martyrs of Sebaste and an elegiac *kafa* on the death of his brother Grigor at age thirty-two.

Of the historical poems Yovasapʻ wrote, two reflect the rebellion of Alqas Mirza against his brother Tahmasp I and his collaboration with the Ottomans, the ensuing Ottoman attack on Persia, the short-lived capture of Tabriz, and Tahmasp's retaliatory strikes in 1548, during which he laid waste, according to Yovasapʻ, eastern Anatolian cities such as Muš, Erzurum, Erzinjan, Derjan, and Bitlis. A fearful Yovasapʻ found much consolation in the fact that his native Sebastea (Sivas) was spared by the grace of God and the Forty Martyrs of Sebaste, but he lamented the destruction of churches and innocent Christians in neighboring towns.

Two historical poems glorify the fourth-century military leader Mušeł Mamikonean. Alarmed by the forlorn state of his nation and the devastation and hardship caused by the Perso-Ottoman clashes, Yovasapʻ recalls with pride and nostalgia how the forefathers of the Persians "shuddered" before the magnanimous Mamikonean and suffered military setbacks at his hands. Yovasapʻ claims that the Armenians were then a "happy" lot under King Pap and Patriarch Nersēs the Great, and admonishes his "foolish" fellow countrymen for killing Mušeł and poisoning the Patriarch.

A flicker of Yovasapʻ's patriotism and his naive concept of a world flourishing in peace as a result of the anticipated eventual triumph of Christianity over Islam are outlined in his poem on the vision of Nersēs the Great, Patriarch ("Catholicos") of Armenia. The prophecy is only one of many such traditions of prescience and originates in the history of Pʻawstos Buzand (i.e., *The Epic Histories,* as rendered by N. Garsoïan). According to this text, Nersēs called down curses upon the Aršakuni (Arsacid) kings of Armenia and foretold their destruction. In an embellished version, written by Mesrop Vayotsdzoretsi and found in a twelfth-century manuscript (cf. *Patmutʻiwn srboyn Nersēsi Partʻewi,* Venice, 1853, "Sopʻerkʻ haykakankʻ," vi; and other editions), Nersēs also divines the Byzantine control of Armenia; the fall of Jerusalem to the Persians; the decline of Byzantium and the destruction of Armenia by the "archers" (the Mongols); and, in an optimistic conclusion, the revival of Christendom through "frankish" military might, the final defeat of the infidels, and the restoration of a reign of peace, justice, and prosperity. This new, blissful world, however, would come to an end with the appearance of an Antichrist. The story grows taller with new additions, but its rosy prospects–also found in Nersēs Šnorhali's lament on the fall of Edessa–and its basic elements, with some omissions, changes, and a greater role envisaged for Armenian kings and forces, provided the model for Yovasapʻ's account. Yovasapʻ may have benefited from the Armenian version of Mesrop's source and from Stepʻanos Ōrbēlean's history (*Patmutʻiwn nahangin Sisakan,* xxxii).

Was Yovasapʻ aware of the efforts undertaken at this point by Armenian Church leaders to generate "frankish" interest in Armenia? It seems unlikely that he was, given the surreptitious nature of the contacts initiated with the West. But his poem on Nersēs the Great's malediction unmistakably shows that he and perhaps many around him shared the dream and considered renewed crusades by the "Franks" to be a distinct possibility.

AZARIA JUŁAYETSI (16th c.?), to be distinguished from the Catholicos of Cilicia bearing the same name and from another namesake, expressed a burning desire to be a tenant of Paradise, that eternally luminous abode, as he envisioned it, with luxuriant trees and colorful and fragrant flowers. In two poems, one on the Nativity and Epiphany and the other on Paradise, a sinful but repentant Azaria hoped to be among the chosen on the terrible day of the Last Judgment. Although filled with apprehension, his fears were in many ways lighter than those that seized the earlier masters. Grigor Narekatsi in his *Lamentation* envisioned his death, the cataclysmic collapse of the universe, the day of reckoning, and appealed to the Lord for mercy, all with blazing agony and formidable imagination. Nersēs Šnorhali, in *Jesus the Son* (*Yisus Ordi*), described the day of retribution and sought mercy almost as powerfully, but with awe rather than agony and with melancholy rather than pain. Yovhannēs Tʻulkurantsi dreaded death (he visualized decomposition of the body) as a bitter end, but still more bitter was Hell. Ḥachatur Kecharuetsi, in his simple but dramatic style, resented death but lamented the evanescence of life, holding one's soul, rather than body, responsible for one's fate (he likened the body to a horse and the soul to its rider). The tragic drama of life and death, of this life and the next, though still a painful concern, gradually lost its petrifying, macabre impact.

Azaria's namesake, Catholicos Azaria I, Jułayetsi (1534–1601, reigned 1584–1601) of Cilicia, accepted the Roman Catholic creed in 1585 to the dismay of most Armenians. This was part and parcel of futile attempts to secure European help through the good offices of the Holy See. Since Azaria's exact dates are unknown, we may only assume that his poem dedicated to Grigor Lusaworich may have been a reaction to Azaria I's pro-Catholic stand. This short poem is an assertion of the Apostolic origin and autocephalous state of the Church of Armenia and narrates the mission and martrydom of Thaddæus in Armenia and the succession of his illustrious heir, Grigor Lusaworich, the God-sent illuminator of Armenia.

Azaria wrote with greater verve on the monastery of Julfa and on wine, holy and immaculate, which held the promise of absolution for sinners through confession and communion. He called for moderation and control of tongue and temper, warning against the consequences of intemperance; physical decline and excessive weight, he observed, made one too lazy to pray or go to church. Azaria is also known for his calendrical works.

VRTʻANĒS SṘNKETSI (16th c.) wrote some of the earliest "epistles" in Armenian literature. Four private letters (the author alternately calls them *ťulť,* "epistle," and *namak,* "letter"; and once, *nomos*) in verse are extant. They are addressed to a Grigor, presumed to be Grigor Varagetsi (also Vanetsi), then Archbishop of the Armenians of Lemberg (now L'viv, Ukraine). By calumny and gossip, some unknown and unnamed enemies caused estrangement between these two old (and now aged) friends, and Vrtʻanēs is beseeching with tenacity to forgive and forget. He heaps all the blame on himself, while with touching humility showering his erstwhile friend with pious praise. His hurtful anxiety comes to an end in his fourth letter, in which we learn that peace and friendship have been reestablished between them.

Vrtʻanēs has a poem on the famine of 1560 in Caffa, focusing on the misery suffered by its inhabitants. He interprets the disaster in terms of their impiety and views it as a warning by God, rather than a retribution, for the population to come to their senses. But perhaps Vrtʻanēs's best piece is his derision of an illiterate but possessive owner of a book who is unwilling to lend it to others; a case of "a dog in the manger" par excellence. A little protracted by the numerous analogies it draws, the poem speaks of its author's belief in sharing and disseminating wisdom. In Caffa in 1567, Vrtʻanēs witnessed the martyrdom of Paron Loys and interred his remains. Ill-wishers imputed apostasy to this eighteen-year-old. When Muslims sought to confirm it, Paron Loys denied the allegation and was decapitated. With sorrow but controlled emotions, Vrtʻanēs marked the sad occasion in verse and prose (reproduced in Manandean's and Ačaṙean's *Hayots nor vkanerě*), venerating and taking pride in the martyr who, he maintained, derived fortitude from Grigor Lusaworich.

Praise of the Holy Trinity, the sad business of life, vices, and repentance are only some of the themes expounded by a group of four poets all hailing from Tokat: Minas, Tʻadēos (Tʻatʻos), Stepʻanos, and Yakob. **MINAS TʻOḤATʻETSI** (c1510–?), a scribe, copied, illuminated, and repaired many an Armenian manuscript. He was the secretary at the Armenian Archdiocese at Hačkatar Monastery and the registrar of the Armenian court register (in Kipchak) in Lemberg (L'viv, Ukraine) during the tenure of Grigor Vanetsi (or Varagetsi). It is believed that the Grigor to whom Minas dedicated an encomium is the same Grigor Vanetsi who also appears in Minas's humorous poem spirited by his passionate love for *harisa.* We are told by Minas that this most popular national dish was the staple food of the epic hero Sasuntsi Dawitʻ (David of Sasun) and that its original recipe was created by Grigor Lusaworich! In three other poems, Minas approves of the competence of the twelve Armenian judges of Lvov (N. Akinean believed these were an introduction to the Armenian court-register in Lvov); bemoans his loneliness at old age; and, wondering how short life can be, especially when spent merrymaking, repents and asks for prayers to allay his fears of the eternal blazes.

Minas's better known work is his elegy on the persecutions the Armenians of Wallachia (Rumania) suffered at the hands of Stefan Raresh VII (1551–52), who forcibly imposed Greek Orthodoxy on them. Stefan, a "Chalcedonian," and his underlings desecrated the Church of the Blessed Virgin in Seczow (Suczawa), confiscated the utensils and decorations, sealed up this and all the other churches, and imprisoned the priests. The next day his artillery pounded the same church, and as the Armenians fled the city, Stefan made a bonfire of their religious texts. Then they were forced to be rechristened and were made to wear Wallachian attire; Armenian priests were "defrocked" and Wallachian priests were sent to their homes. Neither Valens, Julian, nor the pharaohs, Minas noted with smoldering anger, had committed such cruelties.

Both Yakob Tʻoḥatʻetsi and **TʻADĒOS TʻOḤATʻETSI** (16th c.?) wrote, the former in a more trenchant style, of sins and piety, repentance and salvation, and hymns to the Father Almighty and Jesus Christ. Some influence by Grigor Narekatsi and Nersēs Šnorhali is noticeable on both authors. Tʻadēos (whom N. Akinean identified with Tʻadēos Kołonatsi) wrote a rhymed narrative from the Creation to the Resurrection, a dialogue between his body and his soul, and about the Last Judgment, all with simple spontaneity.

In order fully to understand his poem on the Nativity, the brief discussion above of the *Dašants tʻułtʻ* must be complemented with some details. According to this twelfth-century concoction, the Pope consecrated Grigor Lusaworich as a patriarch equal to the rank and primacy of those of Jerusalem, Antioch, and Alexandria, and the emperor crowned Trdat the Great as King of Armenia. Constantine requested (and Trdat obliged) three hundred valiant "Armens" to serve at his court and predicted the future fall of Armenia and its regeneration with the assistance of his successors (i.e. the "frankish" kings). A related prophecy, named after Agatʻon or Agadron, the "invincible philosopher," tells us that the four dignitaries went on a pilgrimage together to Jerusalem. Constantine built the Holy Sepulchre, and Trdat the Nativity in Bethlehem. Then they all returned to Rome, accompanied with sixty-four thousand Armenian troops (or seventy thousand, cf. Aṙakʻel Bałišetsi's *Lament on the Fall of Constantinople,* "Ołb mayrakʻałakʻin Stampōlu"), of whom Constantine retained two hundred before seeing his allies off to their country. It was from among these soldiers that a new Constantius would rise and come to the rescue of the Armenians. A very short and garbled conflation of these two stories is integrated by Tʻadēos Tʻoḥatʻetsi in his poem on the Nativity (a sort of Christmas carol). Thrilled to have seen Golgotha with his own eyes, he in essence praises his nation's orthodox creed and glorifies Grigor Lusaworich.

In his *Encyclical* (*Tułtʻ ěndhanrakan*), Nersēs Šnorhali speaks of clerics engaged in wine growing and wine making. Wine has always been popular in Armenia, but Šnorhali's is among the earliest written references to clergymen for whom, it seems, wine had by now become new wine in old bottles. Still, Yovhannēs Tʻlkurantsi spoke of wine as the symbol of Christ's blood. On the few occasions he wrote of wine in a social context, he called for temperance, viewing wine as the mother of all evil and calling on all those who loved God to "hate" wine and whores–not to wench, that is. In the sixteenth century, sacramental wine was still solemnly revered as a symbol of Christ's blood, celebrated on the altar as well as in literature. But now wine was also distinguished as a favorite tipple. **ASTUATZATUR** (16th c.?), known only by his name and for a single poem on vineyards, grapes, and wine, makes his case eloquently. He views wine in its biblical and Christian context as a life-giving symbol of absolution (i.e. wine consecrated in the Eucharist). He then describes the beauty and charm of vines and grapes in vivid colors and how they are made into wine. Whether wine had anything to do with this poem's smooth flow, it is not possible to say with certainty, but Astuatzatur, fully aware of the unpleasant consequences of toping, leaves it to his readers' discretion to decide how to enjoy wine, which is good for prince and peasant alike.

SARKAWAG BERDAKATSI (16th c.), also remembered by a single poem on wine, similarly projects it as a God-given gift beneficial for all (including kings, the poor, the blind, the dumb, the sick, the sinners, and mourners). His subtle and sensitive description in luscious colors brings the grapes to life and adds sparkle to the wine. He too fortifies his reasoning by upholding the religious symbolism of wine, and his poem rejoices in the "cup" (i.e. the chalice with wine consecrated in the Eucharist) that illuminates souls. In these two poems, wine as a sacred symbol and wine as such are equated, since it is earthly wine that is elevated to divine symbolism. If as a spiritual symbol it appeals to and inspires the spirit, then as wine it appeals to the palate and inspires the mind.

MARTIROS ḤARASARTSI (16th c.?), who may have been a married priest, was a veritable devotee of Bacchus. His poems, written in a rather slipshod style, employing numerous forms of acrostics and commonplace imagery, betray a lively, unsophisticated character for whom social-religious events (weddings, christenings, etc.) turn out to be occasions for carousal. He has a panegyric on the Armenians of Caffa and a few love poems, one of which is in four languages (a sort of "macaronic verse"); the first line of each quatrain is in Armenian, the second in Turkish, the third in Greek, and the fourth in Persian.

ŁAZAR SEBASTATSI (16th–17th c.) should not be confused with a number of contemporary namesakes. He was a priest of whom only a few love poems survive. Not distinguished for their diction and teeming, not surprisingly, with Persian, Arabic, and Turkish loan words, their special character lies in his boiling passion, unusual for a clergyman. A strikingly uninhibited soul, he finds the only meaning of life in love, more specifically, in a particular woman's manners, walk, figure, and intimate body parts. Oblivious of his vocation and the day of reckoning, he finds the light bursting out of her bosom to be as bright as that emanating from the Holy Sepulchre.

A native of the village of Aparankʻ in the old Armenian province of Mokkʻ (south of Lake Van), **SIMĒON APARANETSI** (d. 1615?), "Metzn" (i.e. the elder), studied at the Ḥndrakatar monastery in Bałēš (Bitlis) and attained fame both as a poet and a peripatetic teacher in monastic schools in Armenia proper. With pride and sadness, he wove a poem on the cross and religious relics brought to the monastery of Surb Nšan in his birthplace. The story had been told by Grigor Narekatsi, but Simēon, following the great master, rephrased the story in verse, adding nothing to the older narrative either by way of information or inspiration.

A deeper and more spontaneous sense of regret and forlornness inspired his elegy on Metzopʻ, once a flourishing monastic school and scriptorium (1330s–1440s) where bright figures such as Grigor Tatʻewatsi, Mḫitʻar Sasnetsi, Yovhannēs Metzopʻetsi, Grigor Ḫlatʻetsi Tzerents, and Tʻovma Metzopʻetsi had taught. Simēon likens it to Athens as a center of wisdom and learning admired by many a nation, both neighboring and distant, and notes with regret that when sins accrued and evil prevailed, it was trampled by Turks and Kurds, who turned it into a stable. Although he calls on the Armenians to bewail its decline, he expresses hope that with God's grace the place may be renewed and may even shine brighter than before.

Simēon observes many an event in historical perspective, and it is in this context that his patriotism must be seen. In a poem on the occasion of the Ottoman conquest (under Osman pasha) of Tabriz in 1585, Simēon reflects on the tribulations of the Armenians at the hands of the Ottomans and interprets Persian defeat as Providential dispensation. The Persians fled before the Ottomans like foxes before a lion, and they got a taste of the bitterness and agony which they themselves had perpetrated on Vardan Mamikonean and his comrades-in-arms and the Armenians in the middle of the fifth century. Unbearable though the situation of the Armenians was, spring, Simēon hoped, would soon arrive.

In his poem dedicated to King Trdat's summer residence in Gaṙni (southeast of Erevan), Simēon with decorum makes a loud appeal to sister churches and the "Japhethian" nations to mourn in Christian solidarity the fall of the Armenian nation. His heart aches, and his tears inundate his ink pot at the sight of the ruined palace, as he ponders the inescapable fate of the mighty king that built it. In view of its abrupt end, one is left with the impression that the poem is incomplete.

Simēon recapitulated in rhyme and rhythm a *History* often referred to as that of Łazar P'arpetsi. Although Simēon makes no reference to Movsēs Ḥorenatsi, he owes him a profound debt for the earliest part of his history. Simēon begins with the Creation and goes on to narrate Xisuthros's voyage to Armenia, Zruan's tyranny and his conflict with Titan and Yabet', Hayk and Bel, Aram, Ara and Šamiram (Semiramis), the descent of the "Pahlawunik'" (or "Palhawunik'") from Abraham and the arrival of the Mamikoneans from Čenastan, and concludes with the appearance of the Arabs. Simēon was certainly inspired by Nersēs Šnorhali's "Vipasanut'iwn," a versification of Armenian history with particular emphasis on the "Pahlawuni" family from Grigor Lusaworich to Catholicos Grigor Vkayasēr. While Šnorhali wrote the poem to glorify his family and ancestors (some 150 years later the story was updated by Vahram Rabun to the year 1275), Simēon wrote his for the joy and amusement of his readers at the request of two of his students, Kirakos Ayraratetsi and Anania Naḥavkayetsi. Writing in a simple style, Simēon certainly pursued some didactic, mnemonic, and patriotic purposes (invoking some proud moments of past triumphs). The poem has generated a keen interest on the part of historians and philologists in view of the numerous sources it draws upon.

Historiography, traditionally a main genre in Armenian literature, seems to have been totally neglected in the sixteenth century. There are simply no historians from this age; at least, no histories are extant. The gap is partly filled by colophons and chronicles, which by this time emerge as important supplementary sources, particularly for regional and local history. From the more usual format consisting of date, place, name of scribe and Mæcenas, and title of copied manuscript, colophons after the tenth century gradually expand into detailed and generally trustworthy records of political, social, and cultural events. V. Hakobyan has published a two-volume collection of chronicles, and many volumes of colophons have been and are still being published.

An important chronicle is that by **YOVHANNISIK TZARETSI** (c1560–?), covering the years 1572–1600, which Aṙakʻel Dawrižetsi (q.v.) integrated into his *History.* There are two people with this name, and V. Hakobyan in *Manr žamanakagrutʻyunner* (Minor chronicles) distinguishes Yovhannēs Tzaretsi, son of Jhanšah (d. 1583), from Yovhannisik Tzaretsi, son of Melkʻon, a distant relative of the former and the actual author of this chronicle. He was from Tzar (in Artsaḥ), belonged to the brotherhood of the monastery of Tʻadē, and studied at the feet of Nersēs Gnunetsi (or Hetewak, or Hetiotn, or Amketsi) and his namesake, Yovhannēs Tzaretsi. Of the numerous monasteries bearing the name Tʻadē, the one in Artaz (Maku, Persarmenia), also known by the name Tzortzor, is certainly the most celebrated. Although the tendency is to affiliate him with Tʻadē in Artaz, Yovhannisik, as a native of Artsaḥ, could have been a monk of the Tʻadē monastery (better known as Dadivankʻ) in Artsaḥ. True to the best traditions of some of his fellow monks, Yovhannisik copied, renovated, collected, and commissioned the copying of manuscripts. His chronicle, which has no title, describes some major events in Transcaucasia, such as the Ottoman campaigns (1578–90) and the Georgian-Ottoman clashes.

ḤACHATUR EWDOKATSI (16th–17th c.) has a verse description of Venice that captures a fleeting moment in the city's history sometime between the end of the sixteenth century and the beginning of the seventeenth century. A keen observer with an artistic bent and a vivid style, Ḥachatur was enchanted by the beautiful and bounteous Serenissima. Its economic prosperity, magnificent edifices, mechanical devices, and public discipline left him aghast. He witnessed the carnival and the Holy Week. So many candles were lit on Good Friday that the streets seemed to him to have been covered with snow, while at night the entire sea surface undulated with their light. But certain aspects of their lifestyle violated his social-moral norms. Most were venial violations, but some were incomprehensible or disagreeable. He disapproved of women's dress, the public display of affection between lovers, and Venetians' tolerance for prostitutes. He was astonished to see women use urine for cosmetic purposes and the Venetians eating almost anything that came out live from the sea. Although he marveled at the services dogs performed, he was struck by the Venetians' passion for pets and by the sight of a woman breast-feeding a puppy.

The Seventeenth Century

An Overview of the Armenian Realities of the Age

The seventeenth century opened with disastrous calamities. The maelstrom of Jelali rebellion continued to rage, bringing devastation to Armenia. Although the revolts had begun much earlier, they erupted with renewed force in the concluding years of the sixteenth century and in the first decade of the seventeenth century. Similarly destructive were the Perso-Ottoman clashes and the policy of scorched earth pursued in the region. In the late autumn and winter of 1604, Shah Abbas I ordered the Armenian population of Julfa and neighboring regions in Eastern Armenia to be driven to Iran and resettled in his new capital, Isfahan, and its vicinity. Contemporary accounts speak of the heart-rending suffering the ancestors of the large Armenian community of Iran endured en route to their destination. At long last the treaty of Zuhab in 1639 put an end to the hostilities between the two empires and brought peace to Armenia.

Plagued by rivalry, disunity, and corruption, the Church experienced one of the most turbulent phases in her history. It was by no means uncommon for any given hierarchy to have more than one incumbent office-holder at the same time. But the most serious internal threat was that posed by Bishop Ełiazar Aynt‘aptsi, who created an anti-catholicosate (1664) to wrest from Ējmiatzin the overall spiritual authority it held over the Armenian hierarchies of the Ottoman Empire. In addition to such internal challenges, the Church had to combat the Catholic missionaries now active throughout the Ottoman Empire and Iran. Their renewed zeal provoked strong reactions from the Armenian Church and her apologists, and an unrelentingly hostile attitude long gripped both parties. Such confrontation also took place in some communities abroad. A case in point was the Armenian community of Poland, which was manipulated by what turned into a religious conflict and was forcibly converted to Roman Catholicism in the middle of the century.

Ironically, the Armenians still looked to Rome and to her favorite daughter, France, and her Sun King for liberation from Muslim domination. There is some evidence of a vague initiative inspired by the war of Candia and of contacts (both during the siege and after the fall of Crete to the Ottomans) with Louis XIV, regarding the liberation of Armenia, but the period has not yet been fully explored. Similarly uncertain and controversial is the role played by some of the leaders who conceived of and pursued the plans for restoring Armenia (Yovhannēs vardapet Areweltsi, also known as Tiwtʻiwnči, d. 1703, who for two very short terms became Patriarch of Constantinople; Ełiazar Ayntʻaptsi; Ḥachatur III, Gałatatsi, Catholicos of Cilicia, etc.). The last attempt in this century was made by Yakob IV, Jułayetsi, Catholicos of Armenia, who convened a secret meeting in Ējmiatzin in 1677, with a view to approaching the West for assistance. He is believed to have coordinated his political scheme with the Georgians and to have corresponded with Poland's John III, Sobieski, among others. The Catholicos, already an octogenarian, left for Europe via Constantinople, where death overtook him in 1680.

Despite adversity, learning and scholarship were revived in the seventeenth century thanks to some monastic schools (often referred to as "universities") in Armenia and Iran. Of the four monasteries in and near Bałēš (Bitlis), those of Ḥndrakatar and Amlordi (also known as Amrdol, Amrtol) attained prominence, the first in the sixteenth century and the second in the seventeenth century. Some scholars trace the origins of the Bałēš tradition of learning to students of Grigor Tatʻewatsi (1346–1409). In Bałēš, particular attention was paid to collecting, repairing, and copying old manuscripts. Such efforts proved to be of incalculable value, as the texts of some early Armenian historians have survived in these copies. Amlordi flourished particularly under Vardan Bałišetsi (d. 1705), and among some of its better known students were Yovhannēs Bałišetsi Kolot, the future patriarch of Constantinople (1715–41), and Grigor Širuantsi Šłtʻayakir, the future patriarch of Jerusalem (1717–49). The school eclipsed after Vardan Bałišetsi's death.

When Bishop Sargis (also known as Sargis Parontēr, or Sałmosavanetsi, or Amberdtsi) and the priest Kirakos Pontatsi (or Trapizontsi) met in Jerusalem and had occasion to hear from the historian Grigor Daranałtsi (q.v.) about monasticism, especially in Egypt, they at first thought of founding an hermitage in the region (there is no *written* indication that they were mindful of Catholicos Grigor II, Vkayasēr's visits and activities). But soon they had second thoughts, returned to Armenia, and organized an hermitage c1610, the Siwneats Metz anapat (the Great Hermitage of Siwnikʻ) or Harants anapat, at a remote spot near Tatʻew in the region of Siwnikʻ. Known for its discipline and asceticism, the hermitage rekindled learning through distinguished men of religion such as Movsēs Tatʻewatsi (later Catholicos of Armenia, 1629–32), Melkʻisetʻ Vžanetsi, Pōłos Mokatsi, Nersēs Mokatsi (or Bełlu, q.v.), Ḥachatur Kesaratsi (founder of the monastic school in Nor Jułay), and others. The hermitage led to the rise of similar centers in Yovhannavankʻ, Ējmiatzin, Sewan, and elsewhere. In 1622 Nersēs Mokatsi left it for the islet of Lim in Lake Van, where he set up a new school. His successor, Stepʻannos Mokatsi (or Šataḥetsi), was instrumental in founding a similar school on Ktuts, also an islet in Lake Van.

Students trained at the Siwneats Metz anapat carried the torch to various centers of learning in Armenia and beyond. The aforementioned Ḥachatur Kesaratsi (1590–1646) established a school at the Amenapʻrkich monastery in Nor Jułay in the 1630s. In due course there were set up a scriptorium, a library (still in existence with some six hundred manuscripts), and a printing press (c1638), the first in Iran, where a number of books of a religious and polemical nature were published. Apart from the traditional topics, a few subjects of practical relevance to mercantile activities were also taught. There developed a particular style of architecture and painting (especially murals), and there took place a considerable degree of cultural interaction between Iranian and Armenian civilizations.

Most of these schools and some lesser ones gradually lost their initial momentum or were short-lived, but there is every reason to consider the age as one of "awakening." Peripatetic teachers played an important role. The seeds of learning had been sown, and education's benefits had been observed. Not only did these teachers serve a most valuable purpose, but they also helped some learned Armenians to see Armenian realities in perspective. Understandably, and perhaps inevitably, they spent much effort on restoring, emulating, and providing continuity to the received tradition. Hence the broader approach to culture and the renewed interest in certain traditional disciplines (e.g. philosophy), heretofore in regress. In this and in other instances, Armenian men of learning in the homeland drew upon accumulated wisdom. But they must have also realized, no matter how vaguely, that certain aspects of the tradition had exhausted themselves. Grigor Tatʻewatsi had long since sealed an entire epoch. Peace in the region underscored the need for viable structures, cultural and otherwise. Armenian communities abroad, travel, extensive mercantile activities, contact and conflict with Catholic missionaries, and the challenges posed by Islam and its culture all had an invigorating effect on Armenian letters, dictating the need for fresh approaches.

While some able supreme patriarchs of Ējmiatzin, such as Movsēs III, Tatʻewatsi, Pʻilippos I, Ałbaketsi and Yakob IV, Jułayetsi, had the foresight to undertake reform and renovation, with an emphasis on education and learning, historians, who outnumbered poets in this century, revived historiography. What these historians created—chronologies, chronicles, and travel accounts reflecting Armenian as well as non-Armenian realities—was a far cry from the works of their classical masters. But the upsurge of interest in history, in sharp contrast to the previous century, was indicative of a slowly but surely growing sense of national awareness, unity, and a shared present, especially among men of learning. The cultural, chronological, and other distances now separating them from their ancestral tradition were greater than ever, and they almost exclusively focused on contemporary events, highlighting the urgent need to respond adequately to challenges and threats posed to a dispersed nation by changing times and superior adversaries. Polemical works continued to appear as the sole weapon to counter Roman Catholic claims (e.g., the work of the Theatine missionary and Orientalist Clemens Galanos, *Conciliationis Ecclesiae Armenae cum Romana*).

In literature there was a preponderance of secular themes and thematic variety. Besides the laments occasioned by the calamitous Jelali rebellions, one finds many poems dedicated to nature (flowers were a favorite), love, and merrymaking; verse in a satirical-humorous vein; anti-clerical criticism; elegies on the death of family members; and a few poems echoing national pride and some as yet general political aspirations. Individual martyrologies and religious themes were still common. Some of these themes were taken up by writers in the Crimea whose Armenian population increased with the arrival of refugees fleeing the Jelalis. The community here made many valuable contributions to Armenian culture in this age through its schools, scriptoria, and writers. In sharp contrast to the sixteenth century, during which only a few works were rendered into Armenian, the seventeenth century witnessed a revival of the art, thanks to the efforts of a small group of translators such as Yovhannēs Holov (1635–91) and, perhaps the most prolific of them all, Stepʻanos Lehatsi (d. 1689). The Armenians of Ukraine and Poland left a vast amount of literature (a very considerable part of which is made up of court records) in Armeno-Kipchak (Kipchak in Armenian script), dating from the sixteenth and seventeenth centuries, which has been the subject of more serious studies since about the middle of the twentieth century.

A Survey of the Literature of the Age

NERSĒS MOKATSI (c1575–c1625) was an illustrious figure and celebrated itinerant teacher in the educational network that rapidly expanded in the early seventeenth century. It would therefore be most fitting to start with his poem marking, in learned and graceful style, the founding of the Siwneats Metz anapat by four luminous figures whose efforts the poem elaborates with elation. Of these, the only layman was "prince" Haykazn (son of Haḥnazar from Nor Jułay), a soldier honored and given local power in Siwnikʻ by Shah Abbas I and a generous Christian who took the hermitage under his wing. Nersēs lionized him as a giant who, while equal in strength and skill to the legendary Tigran Haykazn, the slayer of Aždahak (cf. Movsēs Ḥorenatsi's *History*), was of even greater exaltation by virtue of his belief in the triune Godhead. Nersēs then paid tribute to Pōłos Mokatsi, a peripatetic preacher and teacher, revered for his saintly character, stamina, and pious defiance of the persecutions of Catholicos Melkʻisedek, who usurped the patriarchal throne briefly (1618–23) but disrupted church and communal life for long decades. The two actual founders, however, were Sargis, a bishop, and Kirakos Pontatsi, a priest (cf. the discussion above of the Siwneats anapat). For Nersēs, all four were the very embodiment of God's grace on Armenia and the Armenians, who promoted piety and wisdom, leaving the nation with a great legacy and disciples to carry on their worthy cause. Their death he likens, with inspiration and imagery from Grigor Narekatsi, to a ship wrecked by a sudden storm.

Six more poems are known to have been penned by Nersēs. Of these, the elegy on the fall of Jerusalem to Saladdin is an adaptation of an older version in the vulgar tongue ("gełjuk bar̄iw"), which Nersēs "animated" and "added" to. In the poem, Nersēs avers that the failure to reclaim Jerusalem was preordained by the Lord as a punishment inflicted on the arrogant and sinful crusaders. As usual, his style is neatly polished and his emotions impressively controlled. It is difficult to say whether Nersēs was familiar with an elegy Grigor IV, Tłay composed on the same occasion more than four centuries earlier, as no distinct influences are discernible in his poem.

Nersēs is the author of only one fourth of a poem 1,572 lines long (completed by Stepʻanos Mokatsi or Šataḥetsi, founder of the monastic school on the islet of Ktuts in Lake Van) celebrating the Assumption of the Blessed Virgin and transportation of her image to "Hogeats vankʻ," a monastery near the Kordukʻ mountain to the south of Van (Nersēs's native region). This is a well known traditional account (cf. "Patasḥani tʻłtʻoyn

Sahakay . . . ," attributed to Movsēs Ḥorenatsi in the Venice edition of his *Matenagrutʻiwnkʻ;* Nersēs Lambronatsi's "Nerbołean i verapʻoḥumn amenōrhneal Astuatzatznin" in H. Oskean's *Matenagrakan kʻnnutʻiwnner,* Vienna, 1926; and Aṙakʻel Dawrižetsi's *History,* where he basically follows Movsēs Ḥorenatsi's version), which holds that St. Bartholomew, who had been away at the time of the Virgin's Assumption, is given her image, which he carries to a spot known as Darbnakʻar in the region of Andzewatsikʻ southeast of Lake Van, where it is housed in a chapel later built into a magnificent shrine by Grigor Lusaworich.

The story of an Armenian priest by the name of Andrēas who declined to renounce his faith and was put to death by the Persians during a visit in 1617 of Shah Abbas I to Agulis, Naḥijewan, was greatly appealing to Nersēs (the story is also recorded in Aṙakʻel Dawrižetsi's *History,* XXVII; is reproduced in Manandean's and Ačaṙean's *Hayots nor vkanerě;* and is the basis for a short novel, *Andrēas Erēts,* by Muratsan, q.v.). The elegy is written in short, five-syllable lines, limpid and mellow, and flows rapidly sobbing out the author's grief at the death of a martyr who rekindled the flame of faith.

In two poems Nersēs engages in self-flagellation, requesting the prophets' and patriarchs' intercession in one, and heaping sins upon himself in the other. It is in the latter poem that his impressive command of the classical tongue and his vivid imagination find eloquent expression.

There are some doubts about the authorship of the sixth poem dealing with an intriguing theme: the contest of heaven and earth (a device in various forms common to old neighboring traditions). It was Łewond Ališan (q.v.) who first attributed it to Nersēs Mokatsi without any elaboration of his sources. This has been accepted by many critics, including A. G. Doluḥanyan, author of the monograph on Nersēs Mokatsi. Garegin Yovsēpʻean (1867–1952) has pointed out (in an article in *Ararat,* 1898) that the theme was popular in Mokkʻ and that Nersēs was the first author to write an adaptation of it. A number of versions are found in As. Mnatsakanyan's collection of medieval Armenian songs (*Haykakan mijnadaryan žołovrdakan erger,* Erevan, 1956). It is written in pseudo-Classical Armenian, employing quite a few Persian, Arabic, and Turkish loan words. The contest ends with the triumph of earth over heaven; for earth is where ordinary mortals live and are interred. And it is on earth that the Church was founded, prophets and apostles were born, and where the Lord will descend for the Last Judgment. There seems to be some ground here to question the authorship of the poem, since in both manner and matter it does not seem to square with Nersēs's outlook and style; judged by his other writings, he was too devout a monk to busy himself with such literary exercises. True, Nersēs did rework the poem on the fall of Jerusalem (wherein, incidentally, he is recognized as just Nersēs, not Nersēs Mokatsi), but given its theme and style, the Jerusalem piece was in line with, not alien to, Nersēs's literary bent and habits. Still, the quaint contest of heaven and earth for superiority, despite its limited imagery, is a lively and lovely exchange.

A number of writers dwelt on the consequences of the Jelali ravages with regret and alarm. **AZARIA SASNETSI** (d. 1628), a gentle, devout soul (his sobriquet "hlu" means "obedient") from Sasun, composed a 532-line lament on Jelali turpitude in "the eastern provinces and Armenia." It is a mini-history of the Jelalis, the initial depredations of Kara Yazıcı and his brother Deli Hasan from Urfa to Janik. Azaria then tells us that Deli Hasan received the sanjak of "Tmshuar" from the sultan but that the latter had him killed two years later. Hasan's troops dispersed, crossed over to the Asiatic part of the empire, and converged in Armenia. There follow brief sketches of ten Jelali leaders and the destruction of Armenia at their hands. The story ends with Shah Abbas I reclaiming (1603–07) from the Ottomans Armenia and the eastern regions of Tabriz, Ganja, Derbend, Shamakhi, Erevan, Kars, etc.; the resettlement of Eastern Armenians in Persia; and the forcible return of Armenian refugees from Constantinople and neighboring cities to their original homes in the provinces (described in detail by Grigor Daranałtsi, q.v., in his *Chronology*).

With profound pain expressed in a somewhat terse and simple style, Azaria speaks of the havoc the Jelalis wrought in the region. His major concern is for his country, now completely destroyed, and its population, a headless flock, entirely uprooted. Even though he attributes all this to sinful Armenian conduct, Azaria at the same time incisively observes that it was due to corruption, economic hardship, and the very short tenure of pashas appointed at brief and overlapping intervals to the same position in the provinces. Azaria himself barely escaped death at the hands of Jelali brigands and found refuge in Constantinople, which attracted him for yet another reason: Armenian law codices. He had heard that Grigor Kesaratsi, the Armenian patriarch of Constantinople (for three terms 1601–09, 1611–21, 1623–26) had a fine copy in his possession. Grigor Kesaratsi became his teacher and consecrated him *vardapet.* Azaria knew Italian (N. Akinean claimed that he at one point visited Italy) and translated a commentary of Ptolemy's *Geography* into Armenian. This and his calendrical, astronomical poems as well as his church canons remain in manuscript form. The historian Grigor Daranałtsi (q.v.) who had an extremely unfavorable view of patriarch Grigor Kesaratsi, maintained that the patriarch treated Azaria badly. So much so, Grigor Daranałtsi claims, that when Grigor Kesaratsi ascended the patriarchal throne for a third time, Azaria decided to flee to Egypt and boarded a ship at Antioch. He died aboard the ship of thirst and the cold weather and was buried at sea. Grigor Daranałtsi reported that pious Maronites (who surmised from his haircut that he had been a priest) interred him when his body washed ashore near Tripoli.

STEPʻANOS TʻOḤATʻETSI (b. 1558–?), a priest and a scribe, repaired and copied a number of manuscripts and completed at least one manuscript left incomplete by his brother when death carried him off at the age of thirty-five. Stepʻanos remembered him as a devout priest dedicated to his flock in a somewhat verbose but affectionate elegy. His other laments are less impressive. One is a standard "keen," with the deceased's name left blank to be filled in by would-be mourners as part of the obsequies. The second, written by request, commemorates a young merchant. The third mourns the murder by Russian pirates of a merchant from Erzinjan, who bought goods in Marzuan (Merzifon) and shipped them to Caffa from Trebizond. The latter two contain a number of phrases, even stanzas, lifted verbatim from Stepʻanos's monody on his brother. Much livelier, both in form and content, are his two facetious poems: one, a persiflage on the priests of Caffa (personal weaknesses and appearance); the other, a comical attack on fleas and flies. Stepʻanos manages to prove to his readers that a flea bite is really more than just a flea bite, especially at night.

His talent finds its fullest expression in his lament on his birthplace, Tokat ("Ołb . . . i veray Ewdokia metzi kʻałakʻin"). Stepʻanos had escaped death by the skin of his teeth at the sacking of Tokat by the Jelalis in 1602. He was caught by seven of them, who at first wanted to lynch him, then shoot him, but they ended up beating him up and leaving him for dead. He fled to Constantinople and thence to Caffa. Stepʻanos chose to omit this close encounter with death, and he crafted his poem with a good eye for the picturesque and a sharp sense for contrast. First, he with deep pain and genuine concern described the unmerciful ransacking of churches and, indeed, the entire prosperous city of Tokat. Then, he imaginatively restored Tokat to its former charm, amid its splendid natural surrounding, with its bustling life, commerce, and material wealth, magnifying, in a moving fashion, the enormity of the loss.

Almost as memorable is **YAKOB TʻOḤATʻETSI**'s (c1560–1660s?) lament on the same occasion. Yakob, though, sees the Jelali destruction of Tokat as an expression of Providential wrath: its inhabitants are sinful and indifferent to Divine warnings, such as an earlier famine. He also wails the misfortunes of the Armenians of Wallachia (Rumania), particularly those of Yash-Bazar, who were victims of the political intrigues and military confrontations of the early 1590s, which pitched the Wallachians, the Cosacks, the Turks, and the Poles against one another.

Yakob wrote touchingly of human decrepitude, but this world for him, just as for Yovhannēs Erznkatsi Pluz before him, was a place for beasts. He found confidence, consolation, and courage in his unalloyed love for the Redeemer and believed in the rewards awaiting the just in the afterlife. This outlook permeates his two eulogies for his teacher Yakob Ayvatʿents, whom he generously characterizes as a wise, just, learned, and humble priest. No less sagacious than his teacher was Yakob, who translated the *Seven Sages* from Latin and sought knowledge in accordance with his belief that God in His mercy laid the mysteries of knowledge before human beings for self-knowledge and for them to recognize their Benefactor.

Traditional patterns are still dominant in the verse of some poets such as **ASAPOV** (17th c.), presumed to have been a blind native of Isfahan. Five of his seven extant poems, written in a reasonably good style, are dedicated to the Blessed Virgin as an encomium or supplication for intercession and salvation. **YAKOB SSETSI** (17th c.), from the Ajapahean family (custodians of Grigor Lusaworich's right arm reliquary) was presumably a native of Sis, Cilicia (now Kozan, Turkey), who on the death of his wife became a *vardapet* and later could possibly have been created bishop. Noteworthy among his few poems are his simple but interesting elegy on the death of his wife; his poem heaping reproaches upon Armenian clergymen from patriarch down to deacon, local lay leaders, and the public at large for corruption and arrogance, and for smoking tobacco and "afyun" (i.e., *afyūn,* opium); and his brief and general description of Gharasu (Belogorsk, the Crimea).

No biographical details are available for **ANDRĒAS ARTZKETSI** (17th–18th c.), save that he had studied at the feet of the celebrated *vardapet* Vardan Bałišetsi of Amrdol. In two of his poems, the second and fourth lines in each quatrain are in Armeno-Turkish (Turkish in Armenian characters). He has two poems on the subject of *panduḥt* (exile) and both are rather maudlin and lugubrious. His other two poems on the theme of the rose and nightingale are inferior to the accomplishments of the older masters. What stands apart in his poetry is his description in enumerative verse of a long list of a very large variety of foods and fruits at a banquet, a *grande bouffe,* which very likely would have satisfied the passion of Archestratos for rare and varied foods. The dishes are served all at one time in a manner reminiscent of *service à la française* (rather than *service à la russe*), but the participants in the feast and for the breakfast next morning savor quality and variety rather than indulge in gluttony.

ḤACHATUR ḤASPĒK ERĒTS KAFATSI (1610–86), a native of Caffa, studied under a priest by the name of Yovhannēs and learned the art of copying and illuminating manuscripts from a deacon by the name of Galust. Numerous samples of his handwriting have survived. Contemporaries speak of him with respect and with appreciation for his musical talent. He spent a couple of decades (1640s–60s) in Gharasu (Belogorsk, the Crimea), a few years in Constantinople (1668–71) and at one point became a married priest. His commemoration of the martyrdom of a Sargis in 1642 in Gharasu is written with sympathy and simplicity. His four poems on the Virgin Mary display some originality and a skillful, sometimes innovative use of previous imagery. One of them ("Gluḥ hanur azgin kanants," First among womankind) is a particularly detailed and imaginative interpretation of the colors, shapes, and allegory of a portrait of the Virgin with the Child. One immediately wonders if this could have been the same portrait as that placed at the alter of the St. T'oros Church in Caffa in 1620 (cf. Ḥachatur Kafayetsi's chronicle, *Manr žamanakagrut'yunner,* i, 209).

Ḥachatur's praise of love and merrymaking is attractive for its simplicity and naivete. It uses the theme of the rose and the nightingale, but with no symbolic coloring; this sets it apart from most other poems elaborating this story. Spoken Armenian forms are preponderant in this as well as his poem dedicated to flowers—his best. It is an ethereal description of the rose and some other fragrant flowers, with a refrain, internal rhyme, phrases, and imagery in spoken Armenian, all put to effective use.

DAWIT' SALADZORETSI (17th c.) was an orphan from the village of Saladzor in Erzerum. In two separate letters written on 7 August 1718, Ełia Mušełean (q.v.) reported that an earthquake shook the region of Erzerum on 7 July 1718 and that the village of Saladzor was one of the four villages that "sank" totally (*Ełia Karnetsu divaně,* pp. 37–38). Dawit', whose birthdate is not known (c1630?), would in most likelihood have written something had he survived the earthquake, but the date of his death still remains unknown. He lived away from his birthplace at least for a while. He was a deacon, but there are no indications that he ever became a priest or a *vardapet.*

Dawit''s most celebrated poem "Govasank' tzałkants" (in praise of flowers) opens with the author as a frail person, sunken into sadness and darkness, seeking wisdom and ability from the Almighty to praise "a few things" and to distinguish good from evil. His general debility is in sharp contrast to the fascinating feast of colors he describes with exuberant imagination. Dawitʻ sees parallels between the four elements, the four major units of time (day, week, month, year), the four principal stages in human life (infancy, childhood, old age, and death), and the four seasons. It is in the month of March that the Everlasting orders mother earth to wake up from its slumber and let the plants out, and for dew to be showered down from the clouds. Heaven and earth rejoice, and the "fragrance of immortality" suffuses the earth as hundreds of thousands of flowers appear, each more beautiful than the next. Then, treading on air, Dawitʻ speaks of some eighty flowers, each with its particular color or character, and there unfold before the eyes of the reader mountains and valleys flowering, "clapping," and undulating in myriad of colors. Dawitʻ likens the flowers he describes to the stars, good and beautiful, and his sinful self to a short-lived flower ("nanir") that germinates in the morning and withers in the evening. (As an adjective, "nanir" means vain, useless; although this meaning would also fit the context, it seems that Dawitʻ used it as a name for an unidentified flower, which, according to unsubstantiated accounts, has a dawn-to-dusk lifespan and which kings reportedly kept in sight as a constant reminder of the vanity of life.) Dawitʻ modestly concludes that he praised only a few flowers and that many are left for future masters to describe, but no one yet has appeared in Armenian literature to complement Dawitʻ's fascinating floral tableau.

His two poems for Husniḥan, the woman he loved, are forceful and dignified, and have a lingering appeal partly explained by his effective employment of refrains, his winning sincerity of emotions, and a touch of drama. His poem to a "ḥanum" gone astray (i.e., converted to Islam) is a powerful plea to return to the fold. Dawitʻ felt that she brought shame upon the Armenians and that she would no doubt end up in the lower regions. But most interesting is his unflagging loyalty to the faith of Grigor Lusaworich (Gregory the Illuminator) and his national identity: like tiny but precious stones, small yet as dearly cherished is the Armenian nation (an image that would find a fuller expression in Gevorg Ēmin's poem, "Menkʻ," in *Kʻsanerord dar*). Although composed with characteristic verve, somewhat less impressive are his other poems on émigrés, his eulogy for the Virgin, and his poem on the Creation.

The death of Dawitʻ's daughter, Nṙanay, cut him to the heart. A world-weary Dawitʻ believed this was a visitation from the Supreme Being for his impiety. Dawitʻ was inconsolable. There was no one or nothing around him from which to derive solace. Every object Nṙanay touched or used—her room, the cellar, the domestic animals, the fields, hills, valleys, and streams—mourn her in multiple voices of lament. Sad and sonorous, this threnody flows quietly from Dawit‘'s "clouded heart," arousing tender sympathy in the reader.

MARTIROS ŁRIMETSI (d. 1683) was at the very center of some dramatic events in the second half of the seventeenth century. He was born at Caffa, studied at the feet of Step‘anos T‘oḥat‘etsi (q.v.) and Patriarch Astuatzatur Tarōnetsi of Jerusalem (three terms: 1645–64, 1665–66, 1668–71). Martiros himself became patriarch of Constantinople (1659–60), bishop of the Armenians of Crimea (1661–64), and patriarch of Jerusalem twice (1668–71, 1681–83), even though during the first term Astuatzatur held office nominally. He was early associated with Ełiazar Aynt‘aptsi (d. 1691), an ambitious and dynamic character, who held the patriarchal thrones of both Jerusalem and Constantinople and eventually became Catholicos of Armenia (1681–91).

The first cause Martiros fought for in league with Patriarch Astuatzatur and Ełiazar Aynt‘aptsi was the serious confrontation in the 1650s that pitched the Armenians against the Greeks over the St. James monastery and Ethiopian presence in the Holy Places. This was only one, albeit major, battle in the perennial conflicts between the three principal custodians of the Holy Places: the Armenians, the Greeks and the Latins.

Martiros turned against Ełiazar Aynt‘aptsi when the latter created a hierarchical schism within the Armenian Church. In 1664 in Aleppo, Ḥachatur III, Gałatatsi, Catholicos of Cilicia (1657–74?), consecrated Ełiazar Catholicos of the Armenians of the Ottoman Empire, and many communities recognized him as their pontiff. Ełiazar's move posed a serious threat to the unity of the Church of Armenia, and Martiros immediately left Crimea to head the opposition to topple him. Having spent much effort and pelf, Ełiazar managed in 1671 to impose himself as both Catholicos of the Armenians of the Empire and Patriarch of the Holy City. Ousted from Jerusalem, Martiros returned to the Ottoman capital and until 1679 held the nominal title of patriarch or prelate of Jerusalem.

Meanwhile, Yakob IV, Jułayetsi, Catholicos of Armenia, arrived in Constantinople on his way to Europe. Here, two of Yakob's confidants were Martiros and Eremia K‘ēōmiwrčean (q.v.), a well-known and a highly respected figure. Martiros was dispatched to Jerusalem with plans to remove the rift between the two hierarchies. Martiros and Ełiazar buried the hatchet, and Ełiazar left Jerusalem but returned to his seat when, half way through his journey, he learned of Yakob's death in Constantinople in

August of 1680. In July of 1681, Ełiazar himself was elected Catholicos of Armenia, and the rival seat he had forged seventeen years earlier was thus abolished.

Embroil himself though he did in many a conflict, Martiros found time to copy and commission the copying of some manuscripts and to compose a number of literary pieces. A. A. Martirosyan, author of *Martiros Łrimetsi* (*E.,* 1958), enumerated but excluded fifteen pieces, four poems in Armeno-Turkish, and a number of letters by Martiros found in a manuscript collection in Jerusalem containing letters by seventeenth- and eighteenth-century figures. Of the sixteen or so published poems, seven deal with married priests, and all but one are distinguished by their satirical vein. His satire is caustic and at times not averse to vulgarity, especially when dealing with priests violating the tenets of their vocation. Such profane practices were common at least to some celibate priests (*vardapets* and bishops) as well, but Martiros kept them at a safe distance from his whip. The priests' pettiness, gluttony, and inefficiency he treated in a teasing banter. And he wrote affectionately of the sad plight of a widowed priest, who was forbidden to remarry in observance of the customs of the Church of Armenia. In a few poems marking certain occasions such as merrymaking and Mardi Gras, Martiros called for temperance.

Martiros has a history in verse of Crimea with particular emphasis on Armenian emigration to the peninsula. It has a certain historical value despite the fact that it is based on oral traditions rather than historical accounts. Attributing the dispersion of the Armenians to their sinful conduct, Martiros begins its history with the destruction of Ani and traces the routes along which Armenian emigration branched off to Julfa and Van, and along the Caspian to an "insignificant place" called "Aḥsaray," whence to Caffa and Wallachia, Poland, etc. Armenians fleeing the Jelali disturbances formed the second major wave of emigration to the Crimea.

Martiros Łrimetsi's rhymed chronology of Armenian kings ("Karg ew t'iw t'agaworats hayots") begins with Hayk and concludes with the fall of Cilicia. Movsēs Ḥorenatsi was his source for the earlier period; as for the later period, it seems that he benefited from a similar text by Nersēs Palients ("Išḥanut'iwnk' ew t'agaworut'iwnk' Hayots" in V. Hakobyan, *Manr žamanakagrut'yunner,* ii, 196–206). Martiros Łrimetsi's work is a purely descriptive poem, which, he says, he wrote for the Armenians to emulate and derive consolation from, and he concludes with deep regret for the western half of his fellow countrymen languishing under the "haughty nation of Turks."

A historian, poet, and man of high station, **EREMIA** *chēlēpi* **K'ĒŌ-MIWRČEAN** (1637–95) was a moderating force in the ecclesiastic imbroglio referred to above. He was intimately associated with Ełiazar Aynt'aptsi, Martiros Łrimetsi, Yakob IV, Jułayetsi, and Abro ("Aprō," i.e. Aprōyean) Chelebi (1621–76), an entrepreneur with vast commercial undertakings in Europe and the Ottoman Empire and a most influential banker to the grand vizier Köprülü-oğlu Ahmed. This was the group that in many ways pulled the strings of contemporary Armenian affairs, and Eremia often found himself in awkward situations created by these powerful personalities. On the whole he seems to have been motivated by overall national interests, not to have minced matters and to have mediated adroitly. When Ḥachatur III, Gałatatsi, Catholicos of Cilicia on a visit to Constantinople to stave off threats by an aspirant to his seat intimated Eremia of Ełiazar's plan to create a rival catholicosate, Eremia, appalled by the disclosure, traveled to Aleppo in a futile attempt to dissuade Ełiazar from his design. He later (together with Abro Chelebi) appealed to Yakob IV, Jułayetsi to show flexibility and share authority with Ełiazar, but Yakob politely and persistently refused to compromise. Earlier, he had been the only one to dare accompany Ełiazar to gaol, when the latter was arrested in his secret residence in the vicinity of Constantinople, barely a few months after his escape from the rebellious associates of Abaza Hasan in Asia Minor. Ełiazar had appealed to them for assistance to restore Armenian control over the St. James monastery in Jerusalem, and he was forced to stay at their camp for almost a year.

Eremia was the son of a priest, and his two younger brothers were also ordained into priesthood. His daughter and son, a *vardapet,* died young. He did not live long enough to witness the tragic decapitation in 1707 of his youngest brother, Komitas, whom Armenian Catholics regard as a martyr of their faith and whom Małak'ia Ōrmanean considers a faithful son of the Armenian Church. Komitas was certainly associated with Catholics and was influenced by Catholic principles at least to some degree. His death came as a result of the somewhat still obscure fate of Patriarch Awetik' Ewdokatsi (1657–1711) of Constantinople, who at this time was reportedly abducted by the French and sent to Mont Saint Michel in Brittany. (Patriarch Awetik' has been identified by some as The Man Behind the Iron Mask.) According to Ōrmanean, Komitas was among the detractors of Awetik' and when the Ottoman government, incensed by Awetik''s disappearance, arrested a number of Catholic Armenians, Komitas was among them. Unlike his colleagues, who all professed Islam to save their skins, Komitas paid the ultimate price for his Christian creed.

Eremia was a secretary at the Armenian Patriarchate in Constantinople, and his counsel was eagerly sought by Armenian leaders both within and without the Patriarchate. He was well versed in scribal art and, apart from his native tongue and Turkish, is said to have had a good command of Greek, Persian, Arabic, and Hebrew. He set up a very short-lived printing press with, it seems, the help of Abro Chelebi. His extensive travels in the Ottoman Empire and in Transcaucasia must have in some ways contributed to his enlightened approach to church and religion.

Eremia was a prolific author who wrote in Armenian and in Turkish. A considerable part of his *Nachlass* is unpublished and some works are presumed lost. He translated into Turkish the New Testament and parts of the Old Testament, the *Alexander Romance,* and a good many other writings all from Armenian sources. Other pertinent details are found in Avedis K. Sanjian's extensive introduction in *Eremya Chelebi Kömürjian's Armeno-Turkish Poem "The Jewish Bride."*

Noteworthy among his historical work but non-extant is a history of Armenia, which he reportedly translated into Turkish (cf. Mik'ayēl Chamchean, *History,* iii, 723). Eremia used Movsēs Ḥorenatsi for the earlier part of this history that he concluded with Cilicia. It has been suggested that the historian Münedjdjim Bashı relied on Eremia's narrative for his account of the origin and history of the Armenians in *Ṣaḥā'if al-akhbār.*

An important but unpublished manuscript is his "Taregrakan patmut'iwn" (Annals), based in part on his *Ōragrut'iwn,* and which covers the years 1648–90 in three parts: the first part reports fires and natural disasters in Constantinople and the Asiatic provinces; the second part tells of a local history of the Ottoman Empire with references to its wars in Europe; and the third part examines contemporary Armenian realities with a close scrutiny of rivalries among Armenian hierarchical sees.

His *Ōragrut'iwn* (Diary) encompasses the years 1648–62. Eremia began to commit his thoughts and observations to paper at age eleven. His initially short entries expanded to include detailed notes on his daily routine and his family; his involvement in and observations of the Armenian and Ottoman scenes social, political and otherwise; intrigue and the rise and eclipse of politicians in the Ottoman Empire; visits of dignitaries; janissaries and their disorderly conduct in the capital; sultans' unannounced tours in disguise; obituaries and funerals; fortifications in the city against possible attacks by rebels; religious issues; and a number of other aspects of contemporary life.

Similarly detailed is his rhymed history of Constantinople, made up of eight long chapters. Eremia started writing this poem in 1661, put it aside for twenty years, and completed it in 1684. It is a description, not inclusive, of Constantinople beyond the walls of the old city, where Eremia, acting as a guide to a friend identified as Vardan (who could conceivably be the celebrated Vardan Bałišetsi of Amrdol), tours the city and its vicinity by sea and land. A lively panorama of Constantinople emerges with minute geographical and topographical information, along with information on government edifices, churches and mosques with particular traditions, Catholic Orders and churches, embassies, historical references and Byzantine connections, Armenian and Greek Gypsies, various ethnic groups, bakeries, food and cuisine, accounts of traditional Ottoman ceremonies, economic realities, exports and imports, the seaport and quays, comical episodes, etc. Although the history is written in Classical Armenian, Eremia's style teems with modern forms and Persian and Turkish loan words and phrases. The historical value of this straightforward descriptive poem is greater than its artistic merits. But it reads well, and it is light in tone, peppered with some humor and facetious, trivial, episodes. In the three-volume publication of this history by Vahram Tʿorgomean (1858–1942), the poem takes up only about one fourth of the first volume, the rest of the volume and the second and third parts comprise annotations to the text. Read against the commentaries and background provided by Tʿorgomean, Eremia's poem brings alive the "Armenian" city of Constantinople of old with its churches, institutions, and famous figures.

Eremia is the author of the first Armenian history of the Ottoman Empire (*Patmutʿiwn hamaṙōt*). It begins with Osman I and concludes in the year 1678 during the reign of Mehmed IV (1648–87). The only extant manuscript was commissioned by Abraham III, Kretatsi (q.v.), Catholicos of Armenia, 1734–37, and was copied by Ḥachko Galipoltsi. The history itself was originally commissioned by Catholicos Yakob IV, Jułayetsi, and was completed in the years 1675–78, in the form of a rhymed narrative made up of 1,811 couplets in Classical Armenian contaminated by a good many Turkish words and phrases. It covers four centuries of Ottoman history, with the dates in either Hijrī or the Armenian era. For the period down to the accession of Mehmed IV, Eremia drew upon Turkish and Armenian sources; for the last thirty years he relied on himself as a witness and contemporary to current history. Eremia seems to have been familiar with 'Ashık-Pasha-Zāde's *Tawārīkh-i āl-i 'Uthmān,* Mehmed Neshrī's *Djihān-nümā,* Luṭfī Pasha's *Tawārīkh-i āl-i 'Uthmān,* Kātib Čelebi's *Fedhleke,* and the work of other historians. In addition, Eremia made use of old as well as seventeenth-century historians (Grigor Daranałtsi, Aṙakʿel Dawrižetsi, q.q.v.), chronicles, colophons, and eyewitness accounts.

Despite his belief in the Omnipotent as the arbiter of human destiny, Eremia interprets historical events in the light of economic, political, and military factors. To his way of thinking, there were some disconcerting aspects to Ottoman rule: wars, violence, and sacking; destruction or conversion of churches to mosques; instances of forcible apostasy; and corruption and rivalry in the Ottoman Palace and officialdom, with dire consequences for the population. His mood darkens when outlining setbacks suffered by Christendom at the hands of the Ottomans, who were newcomers to the region (e.g. the fall of Constantinople and Candia). Unlike many an Ottoman historian, Eremia does not delight in Ottoman might, nor does he see eye to eye with them. Eremia also includes a great deal of information on the Armenians (especially of Constantinople), the Greeks, and the Jews and their relationship with the central government.

Eremia's literary work for the most part is in the form of poetry. His longest poem, titled "Vasn ēkʻmēkʻchi aṙnawut Timōyi umemn or sireats załjik mi hrēi Mrgatay anun . . ." ("On the Albanian baker Dimo who fell in love with a Jewish maiden by the name of Mrkada . . ."), has as its plot a love story, but is in fact a thinly veiled attempt to establish the superiority of Christianity over Judaism. At least one critic has suggested that in view of Eremia's sympathetic disposition towards Jews in this poem and elsewhere in his works, Islam had been Eremia's intended target but that he for obvious reasons depreciated the Jewish faith instead. A Turkish version, again by Eremia, and twice as long as the Armenian, was discovered by A. K. Sanjian at the New York Public Library; the title "The Jewish Bride" had been "arbitrarily employed" to identify the text. We learn from the editors of this text (Avedis K. Sanjian and Andreas Tietze) that the story has an anonymous Greek version as well, first published at Venice in 1668.

Eremia composed numerous occasional poems, elegies, and letters. Some of his laments betray the detached and firmly controlled contemplation of a thinking poet. This is not to say that they lack spontaneity altogether (his sincere sorrow is all too evident in poems mourning the death of his parents and the six-year-old daughter of Abro Chelebi, for instance). Entirely different in nature are his two elegies on the death of Catholicos Yakob IV, Jułayetsi. This was an occasion for Eremia to take stock of Armenian realities with pain and pessimism, patriotism and pride, but with very little else. Movsēs Ḥorenatsi's famous lament and Nersēs the Great's curse had both come true, he averred: The original royal (Arsacid) and patriarchal (Grigor Lusaworich) families had disappeared and their successors had been unworthy leaders; the Armenians since the battle of Awarayr in 451 had been vanquished and dispersed. He noted with satisfaction, however, that more recently some saintly figures had appeared: Catholicos Movsēs Tatʻewatsi and his successors Pʻilippos Ałbaketsi and Yakob Jułayetsi.

A number of encomiums and some thirty letters (six in Turkish) by Eremia are extant. Of his eulogies noteworthy for its anti-Ottoman undertones is his panegyric for John III (Sobieski) of Poland, in which he wishes that the Armenians had been under the protection of this Christian king. Eremia's letters do not shed much light on his life, either public or personal. To be sure, no billets-doux are to be found among them, but the ones he addressed to Ełiazar Ayntʻaptsi are interesting and informative. Astonishing, to say the least, is one particular letter he wrote to Ełiazar on the death of Abro Chelebi, their erstwhile protector and benefactor, casting him as a villain of the blackest dye.

Eremia was one of the major figures of his age with many links to the old traditions yet also forward-looking in many ways. His historical writings are of much value. Some of his literary pieces betray affinities with Armenian *ašułakan* literature (minstrelsy), already popular by this time, while others unmistakably attest to the meticulous attention this urban poet paid to the formal aspects of poetry—a trend which continued well into the nineteenth century.

Born c1600 in Julfa, **SIMĒON JUŁAYETSI** (d. 1657) was as a child among the Armenians who were forcibly resettled in Isfahan by Shah Abbas the Great. He studied under Ḥachatur Kesaratsi (1590–1646), one of the learned *vardapets* of the time and founder of the monastic school in New Julfa. The *Girkʻ hartsmants* of Grigor Tatʻewatsi Simēon copied in 1623 had a notable influence on his thought. His interest in learning was to receive impetus from unlikely quarters in Poland, where he had gone in 1629 in the company of his teacher, Ḥachatur Kesaratsi. Here, in encounters and disputes with Catholics, both pupil and professor were badly bruised in matters grammatical. Determined to do something about the flaws in their education, they (and Oskan Erewantsi) sat in on lectures by Melkʻisetʻ Vžanetsi, who had replaced his teacher, Nersēs Mokatsi (q.v.), as the leading authority on "artakʻin" (i.e. non-religious, profane) sciences. It was a brief course, as death overtook Vžanetsi at the end of 1631, but Simēon carried on through disciplined self-instruction and soon made a name for himself as the expert on the subject. Simēon taught at New Julfa and assisted Ḥachatur Kesaratsi in his efforts to establish what was to be the first printing press in Iran. By the request of Catholicos Pʻilippos Ałbaketsi, Simēon was teaching at Yovhannavankʻ by the early 1640s, and then at Ējmiatzin a little later, attracting a number of serious students, such as Ařakʻel Dawrižetsi (q.v.) and others.

As he taught, Simēon felt the need for some practical materials. He first wrote his grammar of Armenian in a clear and concise fashion, making an effort to rid it of the artificial patterns of Latin. The favorable reaction of some contemporaries and the abundance of extant manuscript copies of the work lead one to conclude that it was a fairly well-known and extensively used grammar. Similarly well received was his textbook on logic, *Girkʿ tramabanutʿean,* written c1650, which he said was based on Aristotle's work. Pałtasar Dpir (q.v.) published it in Constantinople in 1728 with his own comments on its sources (there are textual differences between this and the 1794 edition). Simēon also has an unpublished commentary on *Šałkapkʿ astuatzabanakankʿ* (*Elements of Theology*) of Proclus ("Diadochus"), a fifth-century Neoplatonist philosopher. H. Mirzoyan, the author of a monograph on Simēon, offers a comprehensive analysis of Simēon's philosophical views and talks at some length of the Georgian translations of this as well as his other two works, maintaining that they left their mark on Georgian thought.

Another eminent representative of the New Julfa school was **YOVHANNĒS JUŁAYETSI** (1643–1715, nicknamed *Mrkʿuz,* also *Mrguz,* i.e., "worthless"), a scholar and theologian who studied under Bishop Dawitʿ, father-superior of the Armenian monastery in New Julfa. Yovhannēs persistently declined ecclesiastical preferment offered by his former school fellow, Catholicos Ałekʿsandr I, Jułayetsi (q.v.). But he was not as popular with some of his "envious" fellow monks who burnt a number of his manuscripts and whose hostility forced him to abandon his monastic cell. The historian Ḥachatur Jułayetsi (q.v.) in his history of Persia devotes sixty-five pages to Yovhannēs's work, extant and non-extant. We learn from him that Yovhannēs held theological discussions with Shah Sulaiman (Safi II, 1666–94) and Shah Sultan Husain (1694–1722), and that the respect he commanded at the Safavid Court enabled him to spare his fellow countrymen forced conversion. His skills in horology and painting (some of the paintings attributed to him have survived) must have also been appreciated by the rulers of Iran. He was fluent in Persian and Arabic (which he studied in "Arabia") and translated the New Testament into both languages (so says Mesrop Tʿałiadean, q.v., in the periodical *Azgasēr,* Calcutta, 1845/12, 94, adding that the manuscript of this translation into Persian in Armenian characters was given to the Bishop's College in Calcutta).

Jułayetsi's *Hamaṙōt kʿerakanutʿiwn* is a very brief treatise on logic and the grammar of Classical Armenian. His *Girkʿ hamaṙōt vasn iskapēs . . .* is an apologetic work on the orthodoxy of the Church of Armenia as well as an attack on Chalcedon and the dogma of the Roman Catholic Church. His *Girkʻ patmutʻean* is essentially a summary of the theological discussions he conducted with the shahs and Muslim theologians, which promotes and elaborates the biblical tradition and Christian tenets. We again learn from Mesrop Tʻaɫiadean (*Azgasēr,* 1845/12, 94) that the original manuscript was in both Armenian and Persian and that it too was given to the Bishop's College in Calcutta. The published text of his major work *Srbaznagortzutʻiwn,* dealing with the sacrament of communion as interpreted by the Church of Armenia, represents less than half the original manuscript.

AŁEKʻSANDR I, JUŁAYETSI (d. 1714) was a childhood friend, fellow student, and a brother in Christ of Yovhannēs Juɫayetsi (q.v.), whose anti-Catholic zeal he also shared. When Aɫekʻsandr ascended the throne in Ējmiatzin (late 1706), the conflict between the Armenians on the one hand and the Armenian Catholics, the Catholic missionaries, and the French ambassador on the other had been raging intensely. Patriarch Awetikʻ Ewdokatsi of Constantinople had reportedly been banished to Mont Saint Michel and thence to the Bastille. The Armenians of Constantinople wrote to Aɫekʻsandr requesting that he write to the Pope to demand the release of Awetikʻ, that he appoint Yovhannēs *vardapet* Zmiwṙnatsi as Patriarch of Constantinople, and that he excommunicate a number of Armenian Catholics and sympathizers whose names they appended to their letter. Aɫekʻsandr wasted no time. He immediately dispatched Yovhannēs and wrote to both the Pope and the grand vizier, Çorlulu Ali Pasha (1706–10). The latter acted promptly, had a dozen or so suspects arrested, tried, and sentenced to death. All but Komitas Kʻēōmiwrčean, brother of Eremia Kʻēōmiwrčean (q.v.), turned apostates and saved their lives. As mentioned earlier, Komitas was decapitated in October, 1707.

Aɫekʻsandr wrote to Pope Clement XI to protest the inimical activities of Catholic missionaries, who labeled the Armenians as "schismatic" and "heretics." Contrasting the benevolence of Muslims (especially those of Persia) to the unrelenting antagonism of the Catholic missionaries, Aɫekʻsandr demanded, in a conciliatory spirit, that an end be put to the trials and tribulations of his flock at the hands of the Pope's subordinates. But Aɫekʻsandr wrote a second letter to the Pope (cf. Tēr Yovhaneants, Y., *Patmutʻiwn Nor Juɫayu or yAspahan,* ii; and Galēmkʻearean, G., *Kensagrutʻiwnner erku patriarkʻneru . . . ,* Vienna, 1915). Apart from the conclusions, the differences between the two texts are negligible. The former corresponds more or less to what has already been outlined. The second concludes with an interesting paragraph regarding Israyēl Ōri

(1659–1711). Ałekʻsandr informs the Pope that his envoy, Israyēl Ōri, has arrived in Ējmiatzin, that he is rewriting his earlier letter in the hope of deriving solace in these troubled times, and that Israyēl Ōri will personally convey to the Pope many of Ałekʻsandr's confidential thoughts. It has been suggested that Ałekʻsandr may have written the second letter at the urging of Israyēl Ōri, who was acting as a papal envoy to Persia and was anxious to promote peace and harmony between the Armenians and Rome to secure success for his plans for the liberation of Armenia.

Ałekʻsandr had much earlier assailed Roman Catholicism in his *Girkʻ or kochi atenakan vičabanutʻiwn.* In it, he elaborates on the three Councils (Nicaea, Constantinople I, and Ephesus) recognized by the Church of Armenia and launches a fierce attack on Chalcedon, the Council that "destroyed the world" (*ašḫarhakortzan*). He then defends the Christological position of the Church of Armenia and challenges the supremacy of Rome. His *Grkʻoyk or kochi ałōtʻamatoyts* is a collection of prayers to be said at mass and during various times of the day, with explanations of the officiating priest's vestment and the symbolism and mystery of mass.

STEPʻANOS DAŠTETSI (17th–18th c.) was an articulate opponent of both Yovhannēs and Ałekʻsandr Jułayetsi, but his polemical works against theirs are still in manuscript form. He was the son of a priest, but it is not known when or under what circumstances this audacious and venturesome merchant, who roamed half the globe from India to Holland, defected to Catholicism and became its ardent propagator and defender of "the nation of the Franks." He could conceivably have done so while studying at Rome.

Daštetsi has also written poems in a satirical vein. He has particularly harsh words for the pugnacious bigwigs of New Julfa, who honor the "mullas" but dishonor the "patri," and who are notorious for their bad and disorderly conduct, hypocrisy, and corruption. His anti-Armenian invective includes the *vardapets,* who to him are ignorant and preach and teach things they know nothing about. He has caustic remarks for the speakers of the dialect of Julfa, who consider themselves and their dialect superior to all other dialects and their speakers. In his bitter criticism of a renegade it is not possible to say whether the apostate abandoned Catholicism for another Christian denomination or for Islam. He is outraged by his treatment at a prison in Livorno but we do not know exactly how he ended up there.

Daštetsi's moral poems, most of which he wrote in *tajnīs* (pun, "paronomasia"), are far less impressive. His good and flexible command of Classical Armenian is still evident, and his style (he also wrote in the New Julfa dialect) on the whole contains much useful linguistic information of historical value. But a number of his poems lack emotional depth and display a touch of pedantry and impenetrable obscurities and allusions. Some of his poems do not match the mold of his mind or style, leading one to question their authorship and underscoring the need for a closer examination of his somewhat enigmatic personality and work.

Historiography is revived with vigor in the seventeenth century, responding to and promoting a sense of national awareness. **GRIGOR DARANAŁTSI** or **KAMAḤETSI** (1576–1643), a native of Daranałik‘ (southeast of Sebaste), studied under a hermit by the name of Paron in the Sepuh mountains and at the monastery of Sałmosavank‘ (north of Aštarak, Armenia), where he met bishop Sargis Parontēr (also Sałmosavanetsi or Amberdtsi), one of the founders of the Siwneats Metz anapat. He was created *vardapet* soon after copying the *History* of Kirakos Gandzaketsi and made his first pilgrimage to Jerusalem via Egypt in 1604 (he made a second trip in 1616, a third in 1625). There he again met bishop Sargis Parontēr and Kirakos Pontatsi (or Trapizontsi), and all three (and some others) agreed to return to Armenia and establish an hermitage. While Sargis and Kirakos left for Siwnik‘, Grigor hastened to Constantinople to help his half-sister and her daughter. Here he met Grigor Kesaratsi, the patriarch of Constantinople, but the two became lifelong enemies. This certainly accounted for Daranałtsi's hostile view of Kesaratsi, who is otherwise recognized as an able and learned *vardapet* with a long record of unrelenting anti-Catholic labor.

One reason for this inimical relationship was the issue of refugees fleeing the Jelali ravages. Daranałtsi claimed that they had been treated rather poorly by Kesaratsi. His supporters managed to obtain an Ottoman *berat* proclaiming Daranałtsi as the religious head of all Armenians from Erzerum residing in Constantinople (1607–09). Daranałtsi was intimately involved in the subsequent rivalries over the patriarchal throne, collaborating with two other contenders, Yovhannēs Ḥul (patriarch for four terms: 1600–01, 1610–11, 1621–23, and 1631 to his death in 1636) and Zak‘aria Vanetsi (patriarch for two terms: 1626–31 and 1636–39), despite his intolerance for their pro-Catholic views. When an Ottoman edict forced the Armenians to return home, Daranałtsi led a group of seven thousand refugees to their ancestral homes in Marzuan (Merzifon), Kamaḥ (Kemah), etc. In about 1609, Daranałtsi became the prelate of Rodosto (Tekirdağ) and remained in office presumably to his death in 1643; very little is known of him after 1628.

Drawn into the vortex of national affairs, Daranałtsi was in a perfect position to observe the contemporary scene. His work is, in fact, a detailed chronology that he started recording in 1634 and completed in Rodosto in 1640. The first part, covering the eleventh through the sixteenth centuries, is a compilation of little value. The second part is the account of a passionate and partisan observer, who often finds himself in the thick of the action he describes; the work is a diary in many ways. It is a panorama of national-ecclesiastical history embracing the Ottoman Empire from Rodosto to its easternmost provinces and is set against a background of the history of the empire itself. It is a mine of information on religious leadership and centers (Ējmiatzin, Constantinople, and Jerusalem); on demographic changes, the era being marked by instances of forcible resettlement of Armenians; on the founding of the Siwneats Metz anapat; on the martyrdom of three Armenians; and on profiles of celebrated *vardapets* such as Małakʿia Derjantsi, Srapion Uṙhayetsi (or Edesatsi), Nersēs Hetewak (or Hetiotn, or Gnunetsi, or Amketsi), Simēon Aparanetsi (q.v.), Barseł Bałišetsi, Azaria Sasnetsi (q.v.), and many other figures and events that shook and shaped Armenian realities. He wrote in a corrupt mixture of Middle and Classical Armenian, teeming with loan words and dialectal forms. But his testimony, with his belief in miracles left to the discretion of the reader, is on the whole trustworthy, and it is one of the earliest texts heralding a spiritual revival, a renewed interest in learning, and a greater awareness of national identity.

Such aspirations and concerns are more forcefully embodied in the *Histories* of **AṘAKʿEL DAWRIŽETSI** (d. 1670), arguably the most important historian of the age. It was commissioned in 1651 by Catholicos P̔ilippos I, Ałbaketsi (1632–55), on whose death Dawrižetsi interrupted his work, only to resume in 1658 at the urging of Catholicos Yakob IV, Jułayetsi (1655–80), bringing it to a successful conclusion in 1662. Oskan Erewantsi (1614–74), a celebrated cultural figure and the first publisher of the Armenian Bible (1666–68), printed Dawrižetsi's manuscript in 1669 in Amsterdam, making him the first Armenian author ever to see his work in print (although Ōrmanean, *Azgapatum,* ii, 1527, gives the distinction to Yovhannēs T̔ulkurantsi, whose many poems appeared in the *Tałaran* printed by Yakob Mełapart).

Dawrižetsi's work covers a period of sixty years (1602–62), but it is not a closely knit narrative. Rather, it is a compilation made up of fifty-seven chapters, some of which were written by different hands at different times. So it lacks internal unity; its general framework is one of time and scope only. Nor is it free of tautology. He wrote it in Classical

Armenian, but many elements of Middle or Cilician Armenian crept into his account. As for textual accuracy, some have maintained that Oskan may only have had a preliminary version of Dawrižetsi's *Histories* at his disposal. Not to put too fine a point on it, but he seems to have made some arbitrary changes such as omitting certain sections; conflating or rephrasing others; making stylistic changes so as to bring Dawrižetsi's style into conformity with Classical Armenian but in fact Latinizing it instead; and, last but not least, by adding to the original manuscript two chapters penned by him, an autobiography and a philosophical piece. A long-overdue critical text appeared in Erevan in 1990.

A genuine desire to revive and disseminate learning and an inspired patriotism and uncompromising loyalty to the Church of Armenia (the Catholic Church moved swiftly to suppress the dissemination of his book) permeate Dawrižetsi's *Histories,* which mirror almost all contemporary principal events: the Jelali nightmare, the ordeal of the Armenian community of Poland with Nikol Tʻorosovich as a central hero, corruption and decline in Ējmiatzin under Catholicos Melkʻisedek, the forcible resettlement of the Armenians in Iran by Shah Abbas I and its aftermath, the founding and history of famous monastic schools such as Amrdol (or Amlordi) in Bałēš and Siwneats Metz anapat in Siwnikʻ, biographical sketches of the learned *vardapets* of the time (e.g. Simēon Jułayetsi, q.v., Melkʻisetʻ Vžanetsi, Stepʻanos Lehatsi), numerous martyrdoms (including that of Andrēas Aguletsi, also mourned by Nersēs Mokatsi, q.v.), four chapters dealing with contemporary Georgian history, a chapter on the Jews of Isfahan and their forced conversion to Islam, another chapter on Shabbetai Ẓevi, and so on. Dawrižetsi was a devout Christian who believed in and reported miracles. His history, based on the accounts of his contemporaries and detailed colophons, has proved to be reliable.

SIMĒON LEHATSI (b. c1584–?), also known as **ZAMOSTSATSI,** was a cheerful traveler who at once indulged his curiosity and provided practical information for pilgrims. From an early age, he says, he had a desire to tour "foreign and unknown regions" and go on pilgrimages to Jerusalem, Rome, and Muš, where the monastery of Surb Karapet (saint or holy forerunner, i.e. St. John the Baptist) had been a most venerated place of pilgrimage. In 1608 he left Lvov for Constantinople, where he spent a year and a half visiting Armenian refugees along the shores of the Marmara and the Aegean. For six months he was hosted by Patriarch Grigor Kesaratsi (of whom he speaks very highly), during which time he met the famous *vardapet* and future Catholicos Movsēs III, Tatʻewatsi (1629–32) and Azaria Sasnetsi (q.v.), for whom he copied the *Datastanagirk‘* of Mḫit‘ar Goš. In 1611 he left for Rome with Zak‘aria Vanetsi, a contender for the patriarchal throne and future ally of Grigor Daranałtsi (q.v.). After a two-month stop in Venice, he continued on to Rome via Ancona and was received by Pope Paul V. After nine months in Rome, he returned to Venice (1612), whence he went on to Smyrna and to the monastery of Surb Karapet via Brusa, Marzuan, Amasia, Tokat, Sebaste, Malatia, Harput, and Muš. He then spent a year in Constantinople copying manuscripts to raise money for his trip to Jerusalem, where he arrived in 1615 via Alexandria, Cairo, and Gaza. In 1616 he took the overland route back, arriving in Constantinople in 1618 (via Aleppo, Marash, Frnuz, Zeitun, Kayseri, Engürü, Konia, Sivrihisar, Karahisar, and Izmit). Two months later he returned to Lvov, married in 1620, and moved back to Zamostsa (Zamosc, Poland), his birthplace, where he was met with open and rather nasty hostility and was told that by playing truant he had forfeited his right to become the local priest. In 1624 he took up a teaching position in Lvov. It is now believed that he made a second trip to the Middle East in the years 1632–36, but nothing at all is known of him after 1636.

Simēon is not the first Armenian author to write of foreign lands, but his account is the most detailed on both the countries he visited and the Armenians they hosted, and it is written in a reasonably lively, if somewhat poor, blend of Middle and Classical Armenian. He is a naive observer and faithful recorder who complements the work of historians by describing peoples, places, lifestyles, and traditions. For the benefit of pilgrims he provides distances, outlines holy places and traditions associated with them, and describes the main buildings and whatever else that catches his eye. He has detailed descriptions of Constantinople, Venice, Rome, Cairo, Jerusalem, Lvov, and some other cities. One encounters rare and intriguing information, for instance, on the two-hundred Armenian families who fled the Jelalis and settled in Cairo, on the few Jewish families in Tokat who spoke Armenian, and on the "Arewordik‘" near Merdin. One also comes across visions and miracles. Simēon was a believer whose elation upon crossing the Ottoman borders over to Europe (Christendom!) and realization that he is beyond the grip of the hated "ḥondk‘ar" (the sultan) is memorable for more reasons than one.

ḤACHATUR or **ḤACHGṘUZ KAFAYETSI**'s (c1592–1659?) chronicle records historical, social, and religious events as well as natural disasters in Crimea in the years 1608–58. In addition, it sheds light on the succession and conflicts of khans among themselves and with neighboring regions, with occasional references to the Ottomans, and comments more extensively on local economic issues, politics, and Armenian realities. Three simple, even simplistic, but sincere poems are attributed to him, dealing with the vanity of life and salvation. He is credited with handing down to posterity some twenty Armenian songs that he had been taught as a boy, which seems to be the first collection ever of such songs.

YOVHANNĒS KAMENATSI's (16th–17th c.) history (*Patmutʻiwn paterazmin Ḥotʻinu*) focuses on a single event, the Polish-Ottoman war in Hotin (now in Ukraine). It is made up of eighteen chapters depicting the war from its beginning to the armistice and to the strangling of Osman II in Constantinople in 1622. The history, written six years after the war, is a significant complement to similar Polish and Turkish materials. Although an eyewitness to certain stages of the conflict, Kamenatsi gathered some of his information from firsthand sources and based the larger part of it on the account of Ōkʻsent, an eyewitness to the war, whose chronology in Armeno-Kipchak covers the years 1611–21 (cf. Ł. Ališan, *Kamenits,* pp. 68–112). Tēr Yakob, brother of Ōkʻsent, compiled the initial years of this chronology.

YAKOB KARNETSI (1618–?), the son of a priest and himself a priest, is the author of a topography of "Upper" Armenia (*Tełagir Verin Hayots*), which largely concerns the province of Erzerum. In the 1903 edition of the text, Karapet Kostaneants (1853–1920), the owner and publisher of the now non-extant manuscript, left out certain "repetitious" material. The text published by V. Hakobyan in *Manr žamanakagrutʻyunner* (Minor chronicles) differs considerably from this and other manuscripts. Although a topography, the work, written in 1668, also deals with many geographical, economic, political (Perso-Ottoman wars, Ottoman internal policy), and ethnographic issues, and contains accounts of Armenian churches in the region with traditional stories of their founding. The author wrote with verve in simple, tolerable Classical Armenian. He used and acknowledged works by Movsēs Ḥorenatsi, Nersēs Šnorhali, etc., but also benefited from Agatʻangełos, Pʻawstos Buzand (*The Epic Histories,* as rendered by N. Garsoïan), and others.

As part of this same text, K. Kostaneants also published the story of twelve Turks who broke into an Armenian church in Karin (Erzerum) and stole precious utensils. The pasha hunted them down and had them so severely punished that all twelve died.

Yakob is the author of two more pieces: a chronology (1482–1672), with the years 1627–1672 authentically mirroring Ottoman and local Armenian realities; and a short biography of his father, Gēorg, for purposes of edification.

A reflection of Armenian mercantile activities at this time is **ZAKʻARIA AGULETSI**'s (1630–91?) *Ōragrutʻyun,* i.e. diary, covering the years 1664–91. Zakʻaria was a native of Agulis (Naḫijewan), a merchant who traveled widely in the Ottoman Empire and Iran and made a trip to western Europe that took him to Italy, Holland, and Spain. His diary, in dialectal Eastern Armenian, is made up of three parts: the first gives geographical distances in units of "mil" and "ałaj"; the third is a history of his own family, the Kʻrdunts; and the second, the main body of the text, is a record of business transactions, economic realities, pilgrimages, renovation of churches, local religious leaders, and his birthplace and its immediate vicinity. The Erevan edition of this work was prepared and annotated by Tʻ. Avdalbegyan (1885–1937), but was published anonymously in 1938, by which time Avdalbegyan had already been eliminated during the Stalinist purges.

ZAKʻARIA SARKAWAG KʻANAKʻEṘTSI's (1627–c1699) *History* in three parts in some ways reminds one of Aṙakʻel Dawrižetsi (q.v.), whose person and work Zakʻaria respected and benefited from. But Dawrižetsi had a critical-analytical approach and a distinct ability to organize his material. Not so in Zakʻaria's case. His *History,* also based on oral sources, has many merits indeed, but the material is disorganized and unsifted. He conveys to the reader every bit of hearsay he has heard from the fantastic to the puerile. He even has a chapter of witty entertainment for the intellect.

The first part is an interesting repository of Persian traditional stories on some shahs, such as Abbas I. The second contains important historical information on some people and events contemporary to Zakʻaria: the capture of Erevan by Murad IV in 1635 and its recapture by the Persians in less than a year; the three bishops who ascended the patriarchal throne in Ējmiatzin, Pʻilippos I, Ałbaketsi, (1632–55), Yakob IV, Jułayetsi, (1655–80), and Nahapet I, Edesatsi, (1691–1705); numerous martyrdoms, etc. The third part is the history of the founding of Yovhannavankʻ (which he traces back to Grigor Lusaworich), the premises of the complex, inscriptions, and a list of fathers-superior and prelates. The aforementioned are some of the most valuable parts of Zakʻaria's work.

MINAS AMDETSI (also **AMTʻETSI, HAMDETSI,** c1630–1704) was the Armenian Patriarch of Jerusalem for about ten years (with interruptions) and died in office in 1704. He traveled widely in western and eastern Armenia and managed to publish Grigor Narekatsi's *Matean ołbergutʻean* and homilies, to copy Samuēl Anetsi's chronicle and Mḫitʻar Goš's *Datastanagirkʻ,* and to write two works of historical nature. His *Azgabanutʻiwn . . . Hayots . . .* (a genealogy of Armenian kings) is an insignificant compilation of lists of Armenian rulers (Arsacids, Bagratunis, Rubenids, based on Movsēs Ḥorenatsi for the earlier period) and emperors (Roman, Byzantine, etc.) with some brief commentaries. His more important work, "Ōragrutʻiwn" (Diary), is unpublished (a very brief outline is to be found in M. Nšanean's *Ōragrutʻiwn Eremia chēlēpi Kʻēōmiwrčeani . . .*, Jerusalem, 1939). This manuscript was written at various places (Jerusalem, Constantinople, Ējmiatzin, Tokat, Erzerum, Aleppo, etc.) and contains brief but valuable autobiographical and topographical references as well as information on contemporary Armenian realities.

The Eighteenth Century

An Overview of the Armenian Realities of the Age

The appeal for help made to the papacy, initiated by Catholicos Stepʻanos V, Salmastetsi, emulated by Mikʻayēl I, Sebastatsi and subsequently taken up by Yakob IV, Jułayetsi in the seventeenth century, is now carried on by laymen too. Among Yakob IV Jułayetsi's companions headed for Europe via Constantinople was a young man by the name of Israyēl Ōri (1659–1711). When Yakob died in Constantinople in 1680, his delegation returned home, with the exception of Ōri, who left for Europe to pursue the dream of liberating Armenia. In Düsseldorf he first approached Johann Wilhelm of the Palatinate, and the idea of involving the Holy Roman Emperor Leopold I, the grand duke of Tuscany, and the Pope was entertained. Ōri then turned to Peter the Great for similar assistance, since the would-be liberators of Armenia would have hastened to the Perso-Ottoman border via Poland, Russia, and the Caucasus. None of Ōri's fantastic plans materialized.

In the mid-1720s there was a short-lived uprising to clear Siwnikʻ (in the southeastern part of modern Armenia) from Persians and Ottoman Turks. The defiant elements were led by an Armenian professional soldier, Dawitʻ Bek (d. c1728), from the ranks of the Georgian military, and Mḥitʻar Sparapet (d. 1727), who, with considerable help from the Armenians of Artsaḥ (Karabagh) and inspired by the Russian advance into Darband, initiated a series of successful military operations against the Persians and the invading Ottomans. An account of this rebellion is found in *Patmutʻiwn łapʻantswots* . . . (q.v.). This early episode of armed struggle in modern Armenian history inspired the historical novel *Dawitʻ Bek,* by Raffi (q.v.); an opera, *Davitʻ Bek,* by Armen Tigranyan (1879–1950); and another historical novel, *Mḥitʻar Sparapet,* by Sero Ḥanzadyan (q.v.). Movses Arazi wrote an eponymous novel based on Israyēl Ōri's political orientation and plans.

Israyēl Ōri's vision inspired Yovsēpʻ Ēmin (i.e., Joseph Emin, 1726–1809), who initially pinned his hope on Great Britain, but like Ōri appealed to Russia for military assistance when the British showed no enthusiasm for his patriotic schemes. The Russians proved to be as indifferent as the British. Ēmin then tried to organize armed resistance in various Armenian regions from Artsaḥ to Muš and to forge an alliance with the Georgians, but neither plan generated any practical external support. Ēmin's autobiography in English details his activities.

At some point in the early 1770s, Ēmin established contact with the Armenians of Madras and found them to be receptive to his political and patriotic ideas. This as well as other Armenian communities in India had seen an influx of Armenians leaving an increasingly intolerant Persia towards the end of the seventeenth century. A printing press was established in 1772, and a priest by the name of Yarutʻiwn Šmawonean (1750–1824) published the first Armenian periodical, *Azdarar* (1794–96), and a number of books. As British trade gradually dislodged Armenian merchants from their powerful positions in the Indian trade, the support and protection a homeland, an empire, and a mighty fleet extended to its citizens became glaringly apparent to the Armenians. Inspired by patriotism, by economic realities and interests, and by Ēmin, a group of Armenians took a closer and collective interest in politics.

The revival of Armenian statehood was contemplated and made public in two books. *Nor tetrak or kochi yordorak,* of uncertain authorship (Yakob Šahamirean and Movsēs Bałramean have been suggested), outlines a history of Armenia and probes into the causes that led to its downfall. It is also, as its title proclaims, an exhortation for young Armenians to shake off apathy and lassitude and to liberate their country. (The Madras group envisaged the active participation of the Armenian *melikʻs* of Artsaḥ, the alliance of the Georgians, and the assistance of the Russians with the blessing of Ējmiatzin to bring about the restoration of Armenia. But Catholicos Simēon Erewantsi (q.v.), a conservative and circumspect monk loyal to established authority, repudiated the book, called for making a bonfire of its copies, and severely reprimanded its authors). This call for struggle was complemented by a book titled *Girkʻ anuaneal orogaytʻ pʻaṙats* (The snare of glory) and published in the late 1780s, and not in 1773, as the title page indicates. Inspired by the French Enlightenment, it projects a detailed political, legislative, and judiciary system for the future independent republic of Armenia.

In view of the geographical proximity of Russia, a Christian power, and its expansion and wars with the Ottoman Empire, a Russophile orientation inspired the Armenians with some hope, despite the strong disinclination of the Russians to act in any manner other than that dictated by their own interests. Russia's pretension to being the guardian of Christians in the Ottoman Empire boosted such hopes. A plan for the liberation of Armenia (that of Movsēs Sarafean, a merchant, whose project called for the restoration of Armenia through Russo-Georgian-Armenian military action against the Ottoman Empire and Iran) was submitted to the Russians in 1769, and a plan for the revival of the Armenian monarchy under Russian patronage was promoted by Archbishop **YOVSĒPʻ ARŁUTʻEAN** (1743–1801) in 1783. The Archbishop was well placed to keep Ōri's and Ēmin's dream alive by virtue of his close connections to the imperial family and the religious positions he held in Russia. (His eminence was instrumental in the founding in 1780 of the Armenian town of Nor Naḫijewan, next to Rostov na Donu, for the Armenians emigrating from Crimea, and the founding in 1792 in Moldova of the town of Grigoriopol(is) for Armenian refugees from Moldova and Bessarabia). Both Count Grigory Potyomkin and Count Alexander Suvorov were involved in these plans. Such efforts, despite the fact that they bore no immediate fruit, continued and intensified as many Armenians looked to the northern giant with anticipation as it inched its way south to Transcaucasia.

But the absolute majority of the Armenians were still under Persian and Ottoman domination. If in the upper echelons of Armenian leadership in Russia, India, and to some extent Persia, pro-Russian sentiments had been in the ascendant, such was decidedly not the case with the western Armenians, who were subjects of the Ottoman Empire. The deadly Perso-Ottoman wars, political animosity between the two empires, political expedience and circumspection, Ottoman internal policy, and a number of other factors restricted the overall authority of Ējmiatzin and propelled the Patriarchate of Constantinople into a position of preeminence in the Ottoman Empire. Its standing gained in power and prestige in the eighteenth century, especially under Patriarch **YOVHANNĒS BAŁIŠETSI KOLOT** (1715–41). He was still a *vardapet* and only thirty-seven years old when he was coaxed into accepting the position.

Kolot brought stability and added luster and dignity to the Patriarchate. He was instrumental in the election of a fellow monk, Bishop **GRIGOR ŠIRUANTSI ŠŁTʻAYAKIR** (i.e., the "Chainbearer"), as Patriarch of Jerusalem (1717–49), who similarly established peace and prosperity in his insolvent see, vexed by a multitude of problems. Kolot was tactful in his dealings with the Catholics and a period of relative restraint characterized Armenian-Catholic relations in Constantinople after the stormy years of Patriarch Awetikʻ Ewdokatsi. Both Yovhannēs and Grigor had studied at the feet of the celebrated Vardan Bałišetsi *vardapet* at Amrdol in Bałēš (Bitlis). Kolot left his imprint on the history of Armenian letters at this juncture, and his cultural activities ushered in an era of educational and intellectual renewal. In practical terms he sponsored numerous publications, the translation of many books (mainly from Latin), and personally collected and commissioned the copying of manuscripts. He also set up a school and a library at the Armenian church at Kumkapu and saw to it that worthy disciples carried on the torch. Indeed, his administrative abilities and cultural initiatives consolidated Constantinople as the major Armenian center in the Ottoman Empire.

Far more organized and far greater in impact in the cultural realm were the efforts of **MḤITʻAR SEBASTATSI,** a contemporary of Kolot. Mḥitʻar founded a Catholic order (Mḥitʻarean Miabanutʻiwn) in Constantinople, which later (1717) moved to the islet of St. Lazarus in Venice and has since, with its split-branch in Vienna (1811), made invaluable contributions to Armenian culture. Mḥitʻar's vision was to bring about a religious and cultural revival among the Armenians, which he and his followers set out to accomplish through periodicals, printing, translations, a network of schools, and painstaking research into Armenian language, literature, and history. At the same time they channeled Western thought and progress into Armenia. So thorough was their influence that it went beyond Mḥitʻar's original scope and control and constituted one of the main factors that stimulated change and progress in Armenian realities in the eighteenth and, particularly, the nineteenth centuries.

Mḥitʻar's enterprise and abilities are too great to be judged by what he committed to writing. Teaching and attending to his congregation left him with little time for creative compositions. Yet he managed to write twenty or so books. The overwhelming majority is of religious-moral nature (hymns, prayers, commentaries, etc.), and a high value is still attached to his commentary on the Gospel of Matthew. He has grammars of Classical and Modern Armenian, the latter being the first attempt to describe (in Turkish) the structure of Modern Armenian in its rudimentary stages. Mḥitʻar took the lead in the field of Armenian lexicography as well; his dictionary of the Armenian language, *Bařgirkʻ haykazean lezui* (surpassed by another monumental Mekhitarist accomplishment, the *NBHL,* i.e. *Nor bařgirkʻ haykazean lezui,* Venice, 1836–37), is the first scientifically compiled Armenian dictionary.

Mḥitʻar's movement helped bring the thorny and ultimately divisive issue of national identity into sharper focus. The distinction he made between his national and religious allegiances was irrelevant and unacceptable to most Armenians, for whom national and religious issues formed an inseparable fusion, symbolized by their non-evangelistic national church. Any threat to her unity was a threat to the unity of the Armenian people, especially since a subject's identity or status in the Ottoman Empire was determined by his religious affiliation rather than ethnic-national background. Dispersion and the lack of a political focus had further reinforced the Church's position as the only national institution, as yet irreplaceable. Not surprisingly, therefore, friction and outright hostility between the Armenian Church on the one hand, and the Catholic missionaries and the French embassy on the other, continued unabated throughout the century, giving rise to a number of polemical works.

Armenian cultural relations were not confined to the West alone. A telling indication of interaction between Armenian and Islamic cultures was the birth of a new genre, that of the *ašułakan* poetry (minstrelsy). The word *ašuł* derived from the Arabic *'āshiq* (lover), and despite the limitation implied by the word, it denoted an itinerant poet-musician who sang in public on a very broad range of themes. The genre, common in Middle Eastern (including Transcaucasian) literatures, initially arose under Islamic-Persian impact, with the first *ašułs* emanating from Nor Jułay. The extent of such Islamic influences and the elements of Armenian popular poetry that shaped the tradition have been studied neither adequately nor dispassionately. It was by no means uncommon for Armenian *ašułs* to write in non-Armenian languages, especially Turkish. Sayeatʻ-Nōvay (q.v.), in whose work the art attained its finest expression, wrote in Armenian, Georgian, and in what in more recent times has been called Azeri-Turkish. The *ašułs* employed local dialects, teeming with Persian, Turkish, and Arabic loan words. But Jiwani (q.v.), who is recognized as the founder of the "national school" of minstrelsy, used the written standard. In the second half of the twentieth century, the appellation *ašuł* was discarded; the old Armenian *gusan,* by which Armenian minstrels were known in olden times (and which despite some fanciful etymologies is almost certainly an Iranian loan) was revived.

In matters intellectual and literary, certain trends emerge more clearly in the eighteenth century. The Mekhitarists channel Western thought methodically and in various forms, such as by way of encyclopedic compilations and books for practical purposes, the use of Western sources and methodology, and translations, literary and otherwise, never neglecting the fundamentally religious and educational essence of their mission. Unlike the western Armenian communities, political aspirations dominate the thoughts and activities of a number of prominent Armenians and ecclesiastic leaders in Transcaucasia and Russia, as well as India. The *ašułakan* genre reigns supreme. In western Anatolia, Armenian poets pay a greater attention to form within the confines of traditional verse. They are still unaffected by European trends, but in general take a much closer look at Europe. The publication in Armeno-Turkish of some books of essential national significance (religious and historical) and the writing of verse in Turkish clearly indicate the gradual rise of a Turkish-speaking stratum in Armenian communities well to the west of Erzurum. As the Armenian Patriarchate in the Ottoman capital consolidated its power, it acquired the semblance of a central national authority for the western Armenians. A reformist catholicos will a little later in the century add luster to Ējmiatzin. The latter's spiritual supremacy would not be challenged, but rivalry between the two seats would continue unabated. Perhaps most important of all, M. Chamchean's lavishly embellished history of Armenia would completely recover an idealized past. It would have a tremendous impact generating romantic visions and expectations. Such sentiments would, especially in the first half of the nineteenth century, be heightened by the publication of the works of early Armenian historians.

A Survey of the Literature of the Age

Nothing is known of **SARGIS APUCHEḤTSI**'s (17th–18th c.) life save that he was from the village of Apucheḥ near Akn (Eğin, now Kemaliye, Turkey). He is believed to have flourished in the first half of the eighteenth century. His poems sing of nature and love and elaborate on some religious themes (the Virgin, Jesus Christ, and John the Baptist). Like all his other verse, his compositions treating the latter theme are subdued in tone, sparing of words, but sincere in belief and expression. Similarly gentle is his voice in his descriptive songs dedicated to the awakening of nature in spring with the splendor of its colors and flora. But nature is a distant world and no threads seem to link him to it. Much closer to the real world are his words of affection for a woman who seems to have caused him a great deal of tribulation and doubt. Unlike Yovnatʻan Nałaš (q.v.), he sings not of the joys of love, which must have remained a dream, but of its indispensability for mutual happiness, as illustrated in his poem fashioned in the traditional pattern of the rose and the nightingale.

Yovhannēs Karnetsi (q.v.) knew **GRIGOR ŌŠAKANTSI** (c1756–98) personally and sketched his biography (still in manuscript form) with some help from the elderly members of the Ējmiatzin congregation. From an early age, Grigor was sent to Ējmiatzin, where Catholicos Simēon Erewantsi (q.v.) ordained him a celibate priest, and Catholicos Łukas Karnetsi (1722–99) a bishop. He was sent as nuncio ("nuirak" in Armenian) to several Armenian communities including that of Karin (Erzurum), where a plague claimed the life of his brother and later, his own. An able preacher, Grigor enjoyed respect for his immaculate character, modesty, and devotion to his flock. Grigor has left a number of poems and inscriptions at various churches and monasteries, all of which have been collected in a single manuscript.

Grigor's twenty or so inscriptions are of some social and historical value. Quite a few of his poems are commonplace, with acrostic patterns and lyrics composed to certain popular tunes doing most of the damage to his art. But he has a number of poems, such as those dedicated to Grigor Lusaworich, Christ and the Virgin, and friends since separated from him, which memorably reveal his poetic gift. Equally enjoyable are his poems on the four seasons, particularly those on the summer and autumn, which capture the colors of nature with a spirited subtlety and a touch of melancholy. His poem on the summer in a way anticipates Daniēl Varužan's (q.v.) *Hatsin ergě* with its grasp and glimpses of life in the countryside. Grigor is among the earliest Armenian poets to sing of Mount Ararat as the resting place of Noah's Ark (in his poem on winter).

PAŁTASAR DPIR (c1683–c1768) is among the last poets of the native tradition whose work is untouched by Western concepts that were then slowly penetrating Armenian letters. His verse is polished, much like that of Eremia K'ēōmiwrčean (q.v.), but with a greater attention to rhyme. Pałtasar introduces variety to form with a sensitivity to euphony and with a view to enhancing the artistic merits of his verse. He employs numerous schemes of repetition, echo, and mosaic rhyme, though not always successfully. Aware of the monotony repetition might generate, he hastens to alert the reader that such lyrics were composed to be sung. The device is particularly common in his love poems, which refer to a number of unidentifiable objects. This poses a problem of sorts, especially in view of his note to the readers that his poems of "love and longing" concern the spiritual sphere of human life, not the physical. This cannot be entirely true. Alongside some poetry of a general and personal, meditative nature, some of his lyric poems with their elegiac tone and impassioned, if controlled, sentiments are unmistakably intended for an individual from whom he has been long separated.

In half a dozen or so poems, the rose and the nightingale appear as symbols of unrequited love; though their conventional story is not told. "I nnjmanēd ark'ayakan . . ." ("From your royal repose"), the best in the cycle, is one of his memorable poems and certainly his most popular song. Also among his best are the ones on Mammon, gold, wine, and some of his meditative pieces on life in general, himself, and his tribulations caused by unidentified ill-wishers. He has a few macaronic poems (Armenian and Turkish) and a praise for two contemporary patriarchs: Grigor Šłtʻayakir of Jerusalem and Yovhannēs Kolot of Constantinople (not for the "theologians Georg and Yakob" as surmised in *Pałtasar Dpir,* Erevan, 1958, p. 253). Pałtasar writes in a simple Classical Armenian, almost free from Persian-Arabic-Turkish loans, as well as in the emerging Modern Armenian (in works such as his Grammar of Classical Armenian). What makes Pałtasar one of the important men of letters of his age is not just his good poetry.

Pałtasar studied at the feet of Astuatzatur *vardapet* Jułayetsi (nicknamed Aławni), a nuncio of Ejmiatzin in Constantinople. What he exactly learned from Astuatzatur, a man known for promoting printing, is not certain, but we can safely assume that his teacher instilled in him or encouraged his passion for books and printing. For Pałtasar was for decades actively engaged in printing books by himself as well as by other authors. Of his own books, *Grguks šahawēt* . . . is devoted to Christian tenets; *Grkʻoyk . . . tsankgirkʻ* . . . is sort of a concordance for the New Testament; *Krtʻutʻiwn kʻristonēakan* . . . (Turkish in Armenian characters) also concentrates on Christian principles; *Pu patmutʻiwn girkʻi* . . . (Turkish in Armenian characters), is the story of the conversion of Armenia; *Parzabanutʻiwn kʻerakanutʻean* . . . is a grammar of Classical Armenian, as is *Girkʻ kʻerakanutʻean* (in Modern Armenian); and *Ōrinakkʻ barewagrats* is a letter-writing manual.

There is practically no biographical information regarding **PETROS ŁAPʻANTSI** (d. 1784), an eighteenth-century *vardapet* and poet, save that he acted as nuncio of Ējmiatzin in the Crimea, Rumeli, and Nicomedia (Izmit, Turkey) and spent many years in the Ottoman capital, far away from Łapʻan, if that was his native region. Internal evidence gleaned from his poetry lead one to believe that he lived to a ripe old age and that he composed his poetry in the last decades of his life. There is some ambiguous evidence to this effect in the author's preface to the publication in 1772 of his *Grkʻoyk or kochi ergaran.* Be that as it may, we are dealing with one of the more prominent poets of the age with a keen eye for nature, a sensitive ear for euphony, and a noteworthy skill to manipulate form to reinforce content. Sharply articulate, he is engagingly capable of swinging between extreme moods from the lightheartedly jubilant to heart-rending ululations. Some of his songs (the first thirty-six poems in his *Grkʻoyk* are songs) have been very popular; a few are still sung today.

The interpretation of Łapʻantsi's allegorical poems is not yet satisfactorily resolved. Š. Nazaryan, author of the monograph on Łapʻantsi, has tried to refute earlier views that Łapʻantsi sang of love. In her view, the poems are all of a patriotic nature. There is certainly much to be said for her theory, and she is probably right; but more evidence will be needed for such conclusions to become convincing. These are some of Łapʻantsi's most passionate poems; and if the titles of some of them clearly establish them as a praise for the *Patria,* the allegorical nature of many others, especially where the allegory of the rose and nightingale is employed, render it difficult to determine whether Łapʻantsi's sentiments are for a person or the personified fatherland.

A considerable number of Łapʻantsi's poems are on occasional topics. He writes in a simple but eloquent Classical Armenian, which is not entirely free from elements of Modern Armenian. There are certain instances, notably in his longest poem dedicated to Constantinople, in which Łapʻantsi violates his own normative prescription to maintain a sense of proportion. But he has a distinct ability to make most effective use of rhyme, rhythm, and meter, which allied with his spirited sentiments, place his work among the best of the age.

YOVNATʻAN NAŁAŠ (1661–1722), founder of the celebrated Yovnatʻanean family of artists, distinguished himself as both a poet and painter. His jovial poems light up the concluding decades of the seventeenth century and usher in the eighteenth century. There are many elements of the *ašułakan* genre in his lyric pieces, some of which he himself set to music. One can also glean certain aspects of the lyric tradition shaped by masters such as Kostandin Erznkatsi, Yovhannēs Tʻulkurantsi, and Grigoris Ałtʻamartsi, but no trace whatsoever of the duality that tormented them. His sensual poetry shows greater affinities with the *hayrēns* attributed to Nahapet Kʻuchak, embraces the secular spirit with glee, and paves the way for the distinct and distinguished art of Sayeatʻ-Nōvay (q.v.).

Yovnatʻan composed love, moral-religious, satirical, elegiac, and mirthful poetry. In both his moral and satirical works, clergymen are one of his targets for their laziness, avarice, ignorance, and hypocrisy. He teased banteringly fishwifely, headstrong, superstitious, slovenly women, and the impious; but expressed disgust for egocentric men. Definitely a man of urban tastes, he had a low opinion of the then squalid Erevan. The artist stood tall in him, as he dismissed the importance attached to money and derided those who subordinated to Mammon, the creations of artists and artisans. In poems published by S. Simonean (1914–86, q.v.),

Yovnatʻan has a description of the water blessing on Epiphany; of Armenian churches in Šoṙotʻ and Agulis, and praise for the benefactors of the former; and elegies on the death of two clergymen and a certain *mahtesi* (i.e., from the Arabic *maqdisī,* one that had made the pilgrimage to Jerusalem), Šahbaz Ērzrumetsi.

Apart from satire, eulogy, and elegy, Yovnatʻan's fame lies principally in his poems of love and merrymaking, the vivid and convivial expressions of a frolicsome soul. Many a mixed metaphor, some haste, repetition, and at times a slipshod style, tell us of a sprightly man carried away by the visible and attainable, colors and nature, women and wine, kindness and fraternity, all of which gave this transient life its meaning. Mortifying the flesh was an alien concept to him; he praised the Lord, called for compassion, but relished the delights of the temporal. Yovnatʻan and his descendants, who made noteworthy contributions to Armenian art and literature, were receptive to Persian and other Middle Eastern influences. His son, Yakob (d. 1757), a painter and minstrel who wrote in Armenian, Georgian, and Turkish, mourned his father's death in an elegy that remains the principal biographical source for Yovnatʻan.

In a little over half a century after his murder during the Persian invasion of Tiflis in 1795, **SAYEATʻ NŌVAY**'s (1722?–95) poetry was partly recovered in an 1852 Moscow edition of his poems by Gēorg Aḫverdean (1818–61). Research into Sayeatʻ Nōvay's life and work has since been conducted continuously, bringing him an ever-growing popularity. Especially in the last decades of the Soviet regime, his poetry was promoted as a symbol of fraternity for the Transcaucasian republics of Armenia, Georgia, and Azerbaijan.

There are a number of uncertainties about Sayeatʻ Nōvay's life and work. His birth date is unknown, though 1722 seems to be gaining ground. There is some doubt concerning his birthplace too, but most biographers consider him a native of Tiflis. His mother's family were *qmani* (Georgian for serfs), and his immigrant father, having married into that family, must have become a *qma* too. It follows that Sayeatʻ Nōvay himself was a *samkvidro qma* ("hereditary" serf). He seems to have served his apprenticeship with a weaver. His formal education, if any, did not go beyond the elementary, and his knowledge he owed to self-instruction. Apart from Armenian, Georgian, and Turkish, he probably knew some Persian and may have had a rudimentary knowledge of Arabic. Even though he copied Grigor Narekatsi's *Lamentation,* he had only a smattering of Classical Armenian. It is presumed that his teacher in the *ašułakan* art was Dosti, an *ašuł* from Tiflis. It is also presumed that he was captured in his early teens during a raid and was sold into slavery in the Ottoman Empire, that in 1741 the future king Erekli II (Irakli) of Georgia ransomed him, and that during his years of slavery he likely saw many countries, including India. The story of Sayeatʻ Nōvay's travels was probably a *topos* common to minstrels and so were a number of related issues, all of which need more evidence to be taken seriously.

Most critics agree that Sayeatʻ Nōvay became a resident musician at the Georgian court. Here he fell in love with Anna Batonishvili, a daughter of Taimuraz, king of Kartli (1744–62), and a sister of Erekli II, then king of Kakheti. This affair between an ordinary mortal and a noble woman led to Sayeatʻ Nōvay's fall from favor and his eviction from court some time in the early 1750s. He was readmitted a few years later but was thrown out of the royal court for good c1759. Not only that, he was sent into exile and the priesthood. Although central to understanding one of the dominant themes of Sayeatʻ Nōvay's poetry, unrequited love, this story needs further evidence. He married a certain Marmar who bore him two sons and two daughters. Upon his wife's death (1768) he became a celibate priest, a member of the brotherhood of the Hałpat monastery.

For the historians of Armenian literature, the Middle Ages conclude with the eighteenth century. Sayeatʻ Nōvay is seen as the last poet of the age and as the greatest Armenian *ašuł*. In many ways, the Soviets had good reason to promote him as a symbol of fraternity: he wrote in all three major languages of Transcaucasia, Armenian, Georgian, and Azeri Turkish; his poems are totally free of even the slightest hue of nationalism; and he was a classic victim of class conflict. One hundred and twenty of his poems are in what is now referred to as Azeri Turkish, seventy or so in Armenian, and about thirty in Georgian. There can be very little doubt that he began by writing in Turkish and Georgian and began writing in Armenian in his thirties. Turkish was the prevalent vehicle for the genre, and Georgian the local standard; together they gave him a much wider audience and the opportunity to compete with other *ašułs*. It has been noted that his poems in Turkish more faithfully reflect the traditional Islamic patterns of the genre in terms of style and devices. Interestingly, it is in these poems that he most frequently speaks of his religious loyalty and religiosity. He had a good command of colloquial Georgian, which emerges as a flexible medium in his poems, especially the ones written in a humorous vein. But most of all, he was at home in his mother tongue, the Armenian dialect of Tiflis.

The patterns of rhyme, rhythm, and meter he employed all derive from the established practice of the tradition, the most intricate of which he used in his Turkish poems. His imagery and literary references reflect Armenian and Middle Eastern folklore and many common traditions (Majnūn and Laylā, Farhād va Shīrīn, Rustam, the rose and the nightingale, the *Alexander Romance,* etc.). Certain descriptive patterns of women's appearance bear resemblance to those used by Kostandin Erznkatsi, Yovhannēs Tʻulkurantsi, Grigoris Ałtʻamartsi, and, particularly, Nałaš Yovnatʻan (q.v.). His imagery is somewhat restricted; the object of his love is most frequently likened to the rose, or to precious stones and metals.

Sayeatʻ Nōvay is an original *ašuł,* head and shoulders above all his confrères. Despite his use of features common to the tradition, his lyric verse stands out with its effusiveness, spontaneity, and dramatic force. Oblivious of the world, he is consumed by his unrequited love, which inspires his contemplative philosophy, his views of the human condition and social inequality, his aesthetic principles, and the values he upheld. His noble sentiments, majestic suffering, stoical optimism, and charming sincerity in large measure account for the continuing popularity of his songs, which are practically free from bilious emotions, despite the unhappy course of his life. The verbal forms he tends to use endow his verse with momentum and energy. And his long lines (sixteen syllables) do not at all slow the pace of his rhythm; each foot is almost complete, self-contained, and the reader feels the prolonged progression of his smoldering agony.

Distilled in Sayeatʻ Nōvay's verse are the accomplishments of Armenian minstrels. It simultaneously refracts and marks the apogee of longstanding, though not so profound, Islamic literary influences on Armenian poetry. The imprint of neighboring traditions is most conspicuous in the *ašułakan* verse and finds expression in form, prosody, appellation, and certain standard phrases and imagery. Sayeatʻ Nōvay absorbed and blended the best in Islamic minstrelsy with Armenian traditions and created his own profile with inimitable distinction.

EŁIA MUŠEŁEAN (1689–?), a restless and adventuresome character, was caught in the murky world of international intrigue and conflicting interests. He was born in the village of Krman, near Ḥotorjur in the region of Erzerum, to a wealthy merchant father. He was sixteen when his father died and his paternal uncle consigned him to a Jesuit who made an ardent Catholic of him. Ełia, fond of the "Franks" and full of desire to study in their country, preached Catholicism for a while. He also engaged in trade, which took him to numerous parts of the Ottoman Empire, Iran, and Russia; he later joined British and Dutch companies working for the

East India Company at its Tabriz branch from 1718–20. We later find him in Isfahan, breaking through the Afghani siege line, and a little later as the French consul in Mashhad. By now well-known and well-connected to the Persian ruling circles, Tahmasp dispatched him to Europe with letters for its monarchs and the Pope. But he was arrested by the Russians and incarcerated for thirteen years (1724–36).

Ełia blamed his personal foes, French intelligence, and Catholic missionaries for his detention. But further details come to light in his unpublished manuscript *Patmutʻiwn imn karčařōt i veray andzkutʻeants Ełiayis Astuatzaturean Mušełeants, zors kretsi i azgēn frankats, man-awand i ḥabebay krōnaworats notsa ew i surb eḥpayrts ew barekam kochetselots* (On his tribulations at the hands of the nation of the Franks, their treacherous clergymen, the holy brothers and so-called friends). It transpires that both the Armenians and Georgians accused him of obstructing Russian assistance to them; the Turks suspected him as an agent of Persia; Nadir and Tahmasp distrusted him as a partisan to the other; the "Franks" feared that he might seek vengeance to retaliate for their mistreatment of him; and the Armenian Catholics despised him for his return to the fold of the Armenian Church. But Ełia claimed that the Capuchins were his deadliest enemies, who denounced him and masterminded his imprisonment. When the Russians finally released him, Ełia headed for Europe in the hope of finding assistance from former friends. This being a fruitless journey, he returned to Constantinople and spent some time in Tiflis. From 1740 to 1744 he was back in Persia with a view to recovering his position and restoring his business. This, too, proved unsuccessful, and Ełia returned to Karin in 1745, where he died c1751, in utter poverty and obscurity.

Ełia spoke in his papers of his desire to meet Peter the Great for a Russian effort to liberate Armenia. But there are no details concerning his actual plans nor the extent of his participation, if any, in the liberation movement of the time. Such references are not to be found in his *Divan* either. Published in this volume is a selection of Ełia's correspondence in the years 1718–24. Ełia was in the habit of keeping copies of his letters and summaries of the ones he received. He was in touch with wealthy and influential merchants, high-ranking clerics, political figures, and diplomats (e.g., the French ambassador to the Porte), and discussed contemporary economic and political realities in the region. There is thus a great deal of historical information here on almost all the countries of the Middle East (e.g., the Lezghis, political upheavals in Iran, Russo-Persian diplomatic relations, Catholic missionaries, Ottoman and French policy in the region, political events in Transcaucasia, etc.) and the Armenian communities. Such economic aspects of the region as trade, industry and production, prices, transportation costs, and the effects of European imports on local markets are also covered, at times in minute detail.

Most of Ełia's other works are unpublished. These include translations of two medical treatises; an astronomical text; a treatise on crafts; a collection of songs, *Girkʻ ḥałits,* in Azeri Turkish in Armenian characters by seventeenth- and eighteenth-century authors whose works appearing here are not known from any other source; works by Armenian minstrels who also wrote in Turkish such as Miran, Majnun, Łazar, Sargis, Kʻuchak, and Mirakʻ; an old version of Kʻyoṙ Ōłli; translations from French of fables; and a drama. Ełia has compiled Armenian-French, Armenian-Persian, and Armenian-Russian glossaries. His Turkish-Armenian dictionary was published in Erevan in 1986 by B. L. Chugaszyan. This was compiled before his arrest in 1724 and contains some two thousand entries, mostly on trade terminology, the crafts, means of transportation, precious stones, weights and measures, plants, animals, etc., with some instances of incorrect translations from Turkish. In the Armenian explanations there are some dialectal words and loans from Pahlavi, Persian, Arabic, and Turkish not found in the standard Armenian dictionaries. Reportedly among his non-extant manuscripts were works on the Jesuits in Tabriz and Isfahan in the years 1717–21, French policy in the region, trade in India, and other writings.

PETROS DI SARGIS GILANENTS (d. 1724) was educated at the Armenian monastery at Nor Jułay (New Julfa) and spoke a number of languages. He was intimately involved in plans for liberating Armenia through Russian assistance, and he himself recruited and led a squadron in Russia's campaign for the Caspian. His chronicle, consisting of 133 sections in two major parts and written in the dialect of New Julfa, provides information on the political, military, and social aspects of the region. Gilanents also relied on a number of informants, but he compared and sifted the material before integrating it into his chronicle and forwarding it to Bishop Minas Tigranean (c1658–1740), a staunch proponent of Russian orientation and a close collaborator of Israyēl Ōri, who in turn passed the information on to the Russian authorities.

ABRAHAM EREWANTSI (18th c.) is the author of a history that surveys political events in Transcaucasia, Iran, and the Ottoman Empire in the years 1721–36, from about the time of the Afghan invasion to Nadir's coronation at Mughan. It provides very detailed and mostly reliable information on the Perso-Ottoman-Afghan wars that raged in the region for the control of Erevan, Ganja, Shamakhi, Tabriz, Hamadan, etc., with accounts on local rulers, conflicts, alliances, and Armenian realities. It is a continuous narrative in the Eastern Armenian dialect.

The text as first published in Erevan in 1938 is now of little value. (M. Avdalbegyan has maintained that her father, T'adevos Avdalbegyan [1885–1937], prepared this edition and that a "critical" text of the history is found in his papers, but she gives no further details in her article discussing Zak'aria Aguletsi's case.) It is believed that the Erevan edition was based on a copy made by the historian Leo (q.v.) of an altered version of the original manuscript by Abraham Erewantsi. The author's manuscript found its way to St. Lazarus, where a monk, Matt'ēos Ewdokiatsi Garagašean (1691–1772), somewhat liberally edited Abraham's text, rewriting it in Classical Armenian, expanding or expunging certain passages and restoring traditional forms of names or suppressing them altogether. The 1977 Venice edition by S. Čemčemean includes both the authentic and doctored versions by Garagašean.

ABRAHAM III, KRETATSI, Catholicos of Armenia (1734–37), is the author of an interesting history, in many ways a memoir, of his reign and his relations with Nadir Shah. There are sketchy biographical details about Abraham. We know that he was primate of the Armenians of T'rakia (Thrace, i.e. Rodosto = Tekirdağ) from 1709 to 1734. He made a pilgrimage to Jerusalem at one point and in 1734 fulfilled his hope of visiting popular monasteries in Armenia proper. At Ējmiatzin, Catholicos Abraham II, Ḥošabetsi (1730–34) detained Abraham Kretatsi longer than he wished to stay, and in the event long enough to preside over Abraham II, Ḥošabetsi's funeral. Within a few days, Abraham Kretatsi was proclaimed Catholicos, despite his unwillingness.

Abraham met Nadir for the first time in May of 1735 near the town of Aparan. From this point on there developed a warm relationship between them. Nadir honored him as a "father," readily acceded to his requests regarding the needs of the Catholicosate, and frequently sought his company and counsel. They met for the last time at the Plain of Mughan a few days before Nadir was proclaimed Shah. Abraham left before the actual ceremonies, but a priest from his entourage who had remained behind provided him with a description of the festivities. Abraham's narrative deals with the military campaigns of this period, his encounters with and observations of Nadir and his activities, the Persian court, and such contemporary information. Abraham also has a history of Ani (attached to the 1870 Vałaršapat edition of his *History*), which ascribes the destruction of the Bagratid capital to the wrath of Providence aroused by the corrupt lifestyle of its inhabitants.

Only a few details are known of **ḤACHATUR JUŁAYETSI**'s (18th c.) life. A native of Nor Jułay, Isfahan, he studied at the local Armenian monastery. He died in Basra on his way to India. His *History of Persia* was written at the request of a friend by the name of Yarutʻiwn Isahakean Ałanureants (who was born in Basra, died in Bombay, and left both prose and verse writings, all unpublished). Yarutʻiwn Tēr Yovhaneants mentioned in his *History of New Julfa* (*Patmutʻiwn Nor Jułayu or yAspahan*) that Mikʻayēl Chamchean (q.v.) wrote to Ałanureants in 1787, requesting a chronology of Persian rulers. It is presumed that Ałanureants approached Ḥachatur for the task, although the latter makes no reference either in his dedication or introduction to Chamchean's request.

The history was to be in two volumes, but apparently death overtook him before he could complete the second. The extant volume is divided into two parts, the first dealing with Iranian history from the earliest times to Karim Khan Zand, and the second dealing with Karim's career to his death. He begins with the earliest dynasties, relying on biblical, Armenian, and unspecified Persian sources: Cyrus to Darius; the "Aršakuni" dynasty, from Aršak to the murder of Artawan by Artašir, son of Sasan; the Sasanians; the Arab period with a chronology of Arab rulers; the Seljuks; the "Tʻatʻars," i.e., the Mongols; Tamerlane; and the Safavid. By far the longest sections on Persian rulers are those on Shah Abbas I and Nadir Shah. Ḥachatur leaves out Nadir's exploits in India, referring the reader to an unnamed English historian's work (which was almost certainly Jonas Hanway's *An Historical Account of the British Trade over the Caspian Sea . . .*, London, 1753, the fourth part of which dealt with Nadir and was translated into Armenian by P. Mirzaean as *Patmagrutʻiwn varutsn ew gortzots Nadr šah tʻagaworin parsits,* Madras, 1783). Ḥachatur is unaware of Abraham III, Kretatsi's history; he moves from Nadir to Ali Mardan Khan to Karim Khan Zand and concludes with a list of rulers of Iran.

From the outset, Ḥachatur includes his fellow countrymen in his account, but the volume of such information increases following their forcible resettlement by Shah Abbas the Great. Some of the most valuable parts of his history are those dealing with the Armenians of Persia in the seventeenth century (unfavorable treatment by the successors of Shah Abbas, the printing press in New Julfa, and portraits of famous monks such as Ḥachatur Kesaratsi, Dawitʻ, father-superior of the local monastery, etc.). There is a very long section on Yovhannēs Jułayetsi (q.v.) with paraphrased summaries from his disputes with the shahs. Ḥachatur's earlier history of Iran is of little value as it duplicates Armenian sources. The closer he gets to his own time, the greater the importance of his account becomes. But it is difficult to pinpoint his sources for eighteenth-century Persia. Ḥachatur writes in a turgid Classical Armenian, with mistakes and tautologies, and with little sympathy for Muslim Persia.

Not all historians of the age had Persia as the sole concern of their compilations. **STEPʻANOS ṘŌŠKʻA** (or **KAMENITSATSI, STEPʻANOS STEPʻANOSEAN,** etc., 1670–1739) was an author with a wider range of interests. A native of Kamenits, he studied at the college De Propaganda Fide (1691–c1700), where Ḥachatur Ērzrumetsi (or Karnetsi, q.v.) was one of his fellow students. He was acquainted with Mḫitʻar Sebastatsi (q.v.) and corresponded with him. Holding religious positions in Poland, he served the Armenian communities of Kamenits and Stanislavov, first as a *decanus* and later as an *oficial.*

Ṙōškʻa's *Žamanakagrutʻiwn kam tarekankʻ ekełetsakankʻ* (i.e., Chronicle or Annales ecclesiastici) is a record of the Roman Catholic Church, with a brief, complementary, and concurrent history from a Catholic point of view, including the chronology of the Armenian "heretics," namely the Church of Armenia. It begins with the birth of Christ and concludes with the year 1739. The format records the year, the reigning Pope, emperor (Roman, Holy Roman, etc.), head of the Armenian Church, and Armenian king, followed by pertinent ecclesiastical-religious and political information. There is much on the Armenians of Poland and an emphasis on the wayward doctrinal deviations of the Armenian Church. His entries expand as he deals with events closer to his own time. Ṙōškʻa used a limited number of Armenian sources and a large number of non-Armenian sources (of which there is a detailed discussion in H. Oskean, *A.-Stepʻanos v. Ṙōškʻa b.-Mattʻēos v. Julayetsi,* Vienna, 1968). Not surprisingly, his most reliable guide is the *Conciliationis Ecclesiae Armenae cum Romana* by C. Galanos. H. Oskean's Vienna edition selects the parts pertinent to Armenians, narrated in a rather poor Classical Armenian. The Chronicle is important. H. Oskean somewhat generously qualified it as an "unique" work, presumably in view of its inclusion of parallel events and the use of a large number of sources.

Ṙōškʻa is the author of a number of unpublished works, originals and translations, mostly of a religious and philosophical nature. His Armenian-Latin (comprising three-fourths of the text) and Latin-Armenian (taking up one-fourth of the manuscript) dictionary has been of some interest and controversy. According to Łewond Ališan (q.v.), who compared it with *Nor baṙgirkʻ haykazean lezui,* it has 4500–5000 words not listed in the *NBHL;* his etymologies are imaginary; and the passages he claims to be translations from Greek or Latin are unverifiable, as are those he supposedly extrapolated from Armenian sources. Mesrop Čanašean (1908–74) has made an attempt to mitigate some of this criticism.

SIMĒON I, EREWANTSI, Catholicos of Armenia (1763–80), is remembered as one of the bright figures in the modern history of the Armenian Church. He reorganized Ējmiatzin, invigorated its spiritual authority and cultural force, and boosted its economic prosperity and political standing. Simēon set up a printing press in Ējmiatzin (1771), the first ever in Armenia, and systematized the archives of the Catholicosate.

Jambr̄ (from *chambre,* which Simēon used for record or archives) is a mine of information on the Supreme Patriarchate of Ējmiatzin. This is the work of a patriot-administrator-reformer, keen on strengthening the central authority of the Church of Armenia, its independence and particular character. The historical part begins with the apostolic origins of the Armenian Church and the building of Ējmiatzin, and moves on to the return of the Mother See from Cilicia, followed by biographies of his predecessors from Movsēs III, Tatʻewatsi onwards (with a stinging attack on Yovhannēs Bałišetsi Kolot, whose "machination," he averred, forced Ējmiatzin to deal with the Ottoman authorities through the Patriarchate of Constantinople, rather than independently) to his own biography, which was sketched by a different hand. Then comes a detailed description of the jurisdiction of Ējmiatzin and other Armenian hierarchies, tithe and taxation, property owned by Ējmiatzin, the irrigation system and water resources, etc. There follows a list of Persian *raqams, farmāns* and such documents with summaries of their contents, and a list of Ottoman *fermans* and similar formal records. The final, twenty-fifth chapter enumerates Armenian monasteries in the region of Erevan with their jurisdiction and properties.

His *Yišatakaran* (published by G. Ałaneants in *Diwan Hayots patmutʻean,* vols. 3, 8, 11) is a record of the correspondence conducted by the Mother See of Ējmiatzin in the years 1763–79 (compiled, with major lacunae, by Archbishop Isahak Gełamatsi and Yovhannēs *vardapet*). It is a comprehensive record of Ējmiatzin's relations with the Armenian sees (in Russia, Iran, Georgia, the Ottoman Empire, India, etc.) and local chieftains, rulers, and dignitaries. It covers such matters as pilgrims to Ējmiatzin, especially from the Ottoman Empire; disciplinary measures (defrocking, etc.); nuncios ("nuirak," in Armenian) and their activities; Armenian Catholic communities (especially in Akhaltsikha); personal letters; modes of operation and channels of communication maintained by Ējmiatzin; finances of the Catholicosate; transfer of moneys across borders in coded messages; regional politics and appropriate bribes; the printing press in Ējmiatzin; Simēon's furious opposition to novel ideas emanating from Madras to liberate Armenia through armed struggle; and his request to shut down the printing press and burn all the copies of *Nor tetrak or kochi yordorak.* In a word, it paints a detailed picture of the Armenian realities of the time, and of Simēon and his activities, with most useful information on Transcaucasia, the eastern provinces of the Ottoman Empire, northwestern Iran, and certain parts of India. Simēon also maintained a special file for his encyclicals and bulls, which is not extant.

Perturbed by his Church's vulnerability to Catholic inroads, Simēon sought to introduce certain protective measures. In fact, most of the steps he took were reactions to Catholic activities. He made changes in the Armenian calendar of feasts (*Tōnatsoyts*) to counterbalance that published by the Mekhitarists of Venice, and to ensure uniformity of observation, he prepared a calendar for a cycle of 532 years. He moved the feast days for Nersēs the Great, Trdat the Great, Sahak Partʻew, Maštots, the Translators, and others to Saturdays and called for solemn celebrations. He also replaced a number of non-Armenian saints with Armenian saints, some of whom had been unwavering defenders of the Armenian dogma (e.g. Yovhannēs Ōdznetsi, Yohan Orotnetsi, Grigor Tatʻewatsi).

His prayer book, *Girkʻ ałōtʻits . . . ,* radiates piety and patriotism. The prayers, meant for various occasions, express his solicitude for his flock and their monasteries, abandoned or trampled by heathen overlords. But it is in his praise for Ējmiatzin that his religious-national creed crystallizes. Ējmiatzin to him is a God-built, luminous church; the Armenians a nation "cleansed" through the passion of Grigor Lusaworich; and the Armenian alphabet a God-given script. Very popular and still sung in churches, especially on solemn days and in times of uncertainty, is the first stanza of one of his songs opening with, "Rise, O God of our fathers" ("Ari Astuatz hartsn merots").

The last great historian of Armenian traditional historiography and its first major modern figure is **MIKʻAYĒL CHAMCHEAN** (1738–1823), a Venice Mekhitarist. No Armenian historian since Movsēs Ḥorenatsi had ventured to undertake what Chamchean accomplished in a grand, magisterial fashion: a three-volume history of Armenia (*Patmutʻiwn Hayots*) from the Creation to the year 1784, narrated with exuberant imagination and exultant pride. Each of the three parts consists of two books, representing Chamchean's system of periodization: the era of the Armenian ancestors, the Aršakuni (Arsacid) dynasty, the era of "marzpans and ostikans" (the Arab period), the Bagratunis, the Rubenids (Cilicia), and the era of vanished statehood and anarchy (*anišḥanutʻiwn,* used in both senses).

Chamchean listed in his introduction some of the difficulties he encountered: the inaccuracies, interpolations, and inconsistencies in Armenian sources; the unreliability of non-Armenian sources; the discrepancy between the two materials; and a general lack of specific chronology. He compared Armenian variants, sifted the material, and used non-Armenian sources to fill the gaps. For the earliest stages of Armenian history, Chamchean (with some inspiration from Josephus) emphatically asserted the primacy and absolute authenticity of Armenian histories (which meant Movsēs Ḥorenatsi's sources), assaulting all other information (especially early Greek and Latin historiography and literature) as fanciful and, therefore, unreliable. One of the simple reasons for this was that no historian of either tradition gave a record of his own Greek or Latin forebears and their descent from Noah. As for a veracious system of dates, Chamchean used biblical chronology and well-established histories of famous figures and events as signposts for his chronology. The initial part of Chamchean's history, then, has no solid historical basis and is a traditional account at best.

Chamchean consulted a very large number of sources, more than twenty Armenian and over sixty non-Armenian accounts, apart from countless documents such as colophons and letters. No critical editions of the Armenian texts existed yet, and a number of records were still unavailable to him. In some instances he relied on later historians for earlier periods and wrote from a Roman Catholic perspective. Frequently, the reader finds no clear or complete indication of Chamchean's sources, some of which are now undetectable or untraceable. As the first modern attempt at writing a comprehensive history of Armenia, the work has many merits indeed, and it is of extraordinary significance for the seventeenth and the eighteenth centuries. It was also a labor of love on the part of a patriotic monk, for whom the Garden of Eden and Mount Ararat (the resting place of Noah's Ark) were both found in his homeland, Armenia, the cradle of mankind before and after the Flood.

Chamchean held that the Roman Catholic Church never anathemized the Church of Armenia. This line of thought, which Małakʻia Ōrmanean (1841–1918) considers a major, if not overt, characteristic of the Mekhitarists of Venice, prevails in Chamchean's history and other works. Ōrmanean (*Azgapatum,* ii, 2165) avers that Chamchean, with the approval of his Order, prepared a work titled *Vahan hawatoy* (Shield of the faith), theoretically to justify and tactfully to promote this concept that did not sit well with Latin and Latinizing quarters in Rome and elsewhere. This is not to say, however, that Chamchean or his fellow monks retreated from the Roman Catholic dogma by so much as a hair's breadth; they simply reinterpreted and reconciled the Armenian position with that of Rome. Being opposed to the creation of a separate Armenian Catholic community and to direct confrontation, they emphasized similarity and union rather than dissimilarity and schism. Chamchean's position would have had far-reaching consequences (e.g., Armenian Catholics frequenting Armenian churches and receiving sacraments), but it was one of the few practical ways in which they hoped gradually to forge a rapprochement between the two churches. In fact, in the early nineteenth century Chamchean was personally involved in unofficial talks in Constantinople to bring about a reconciliation.

Of great importance was Chamchean's grammar of Classical Armenian, which went through fifteen editions in little over half a century. In order to reinstate its earlier structure, Chamchean tried to refute the patterns of Latin fancifully imposed on Classical Armenian—a trend that was carried further by subsequent Mekhitarist linguists of both the Venice and Vienna Orders. Among his published works, special mention should also be made of his ten-volume commentary on the Psalms, with comparative references to Greek, Syriac, Latin, Arabic, and other versions. Still unpublished are some of Chamchean's works including a Latin-Armenian dictionary and an account of his travels.

ḤACHATUR ĒRZRUMETSI (1666–1740) was educated in Rome and in Catholic circles and was held in high esteem by them, becoming a monk, a theologian, a philosopher of vast erudition, and a prolific author. Unlike Mḥitʻar Sebastatsi (q.v.), with whom he was intimately acquainted, Ḥachatur seems to have been a man of reflection rather than action. He has a grammar, a rhetoric, a book of sermons, and at least two works in Latin, one on Christianity and the other on theology, both of which were translated into Armenian by Mariam Kʻarakʻašean and published in Venice.

But perhaps his most practical contribution is his compendium on philosophy, which made some aspects of the accomplishments of European thought in many a field accessible to his fellow countrymen. Brought together in two thick volumes in verse (not without some artificial rhyming) are large sections dealing in detail with topics in the humanities and the sciences, with each major field (e.g., poetry, rhetoric, logic, metaphysics, music, physics, mathematics, geometry, medicine, plants, etc.) divided into subsections. Although Ḥachatur misses no opportunity to inject his interpretations with a goodly dose of Catholic doctrines, his encyclopedic scope is quite unique to his age. One of the largest sections treated seriously is on astrology; it drew fierce criticism from an implacable opponent, Gēorg Mḥlayim (q.v.).

ARSĒN DPIR KOSTANDNUPŌLSETSI's (18th c.) exact dates are not known. His family had its roots in Kayseri, but he was born in Constantinople, where he became a student of Patriarch Yakob Nalean (1702–64). He is remembered for his "encyclopedia." The printing of this book began when Nalean was still Patriarch (1741–49, 1752–64), but must have been completed when Patriarch Minas Aknetsi (1749–51, later Catholicos of Armenia, 1751–53) had succeeded Nalean. Strictly speaking, his encyclopedia is a book of about twelve hundred definitions of concepts, facts, and phenomena of a theological, natural, moral, and political nature, based on the works of "theologians" and "philosophers," as he put it. It opens with an introduction elaborating man's natural aspiration to desirable ends, such as knowledge which dispels ignorance, endows man with wisdom, and makes him an heir to eternal life. There follow two prayers seeking mercy, grace, and inspiration from the Virgin. The main body of the text concludes with a short section made up of forty-three descriptive entries for animals ("bark' kendaneats"), which is believed to have been taken from Łukas Vanandetsi's *I ĕzbosans haykazuneats ("bark' omants kendaneats").* Especially extensive are headings for spiritual, religious, or ritual significance. Occasionally, the Greek and Latin roots are given, and sometimes synonyms in Greek, Latin, Arabic, and Turkish are also noted. Although in certain ways his work reflects some aspects of Western advances, especially in the fields of science and natural phenomena, Christian tenets and traditional Armenian interpretations dominate Arsēn's approach.

ŁAZAR JAHKETSI (d. 1751), an inspired opponent of Roman Catholicism, came from Jahuk (now in Naḥijewan), a stronghold of Catholic Uniates. He was not the leading candidate to succeed Abraham III, Kretatsi (q.v.) to the throne of Grigor Lusaworich, but Grigor Šłt'ayakir, the Patriarch of Jerusalem, declined, as he had on a number of occasions before, to head the Church of Armenia. Following this, the choice fell upon Łazar, who was then at Smyrna as a nuncio of Ējmiatzin. Mik'ayēl Chamchean (q.v.) reckoned that Łazar's trip from Smyrna to the Mother See with his entourage was the most extensive and expensive procession by an elected Catholicos. Łazar was rich, enjoyed pomp and ceremony, and was not at all averse to traits of vanity and tyranny. Although a man of many gifts, he was in thrall to his passions.

He wrote his theology (*Girk' astuatzabanakan . . .*) at the request of Catholicos Abraham (most probably Abraham II, Ḥošabetsi, 1730–34), to counter Catholic claims that the Armenians had no independent tradition. Made up of twenty chapters, the treatise is a blistering attack on

Chalcedon, the Roman Catholic Church, and such figures as Nestorius, Eutyches, Pope Leo I, the Great, Albertus Magnus, C. Galanos, and others, with supporting quotations from Clement of Alexandria, Athanasius, Gregory Nazianzenus, John Chrysostom, Grigor Tatʻewatsi, and others in defense of the dogma of the Armenian Church and her apostolic origin. The twentieth chapter is a review of the Armenian tradition. He begins with the story of Hayk and Bel, i.e. the origins of the Armenian nation and Armenia (from Movsēs Ḥorenatsi), and moves on to Grigor Lusaworich and Trdat the Great (Agatʻangełos, Movsēs Ḥorenatsi). He sketches an outline of the Armenian Church, beginning with Thaddaeus and Bartholomew; a history of the four hierarchies (Ējmiatzin, Cilicia, Ałtʻamar, Gandzasar); an outline of the "translators and theologians" and "pillars of the Church of Armenia," from Maštots to Yovhannēs Orotnetsi, Grigor Tatʻewatsi, and Yovhannēs Jułayetsi (q.v.); and a list of Armenian historians to Aṙakʻel Dawrižetsi (q.v.), Eremia Kostandnupolsetsi, and Łukas Vanandetsi (c1650–?). He concludes with a garbled version of Abraham III, Kretatsi's *History of Ani,* with the references to Yovhannēs Erznkatsi Pluz.

Łazar's prayer book (*Girkʻ ałōtʻits . . .*) is a collection of Psalms, chapters from Grigor Narekatsi's *Lamentation, šarakans,* a few poems by Łazar himself, one piece by Yovhannēs Gaṙnetsi, another by Mḥitʻar Goš (abridged), and Nersēs Šnorhali's most popular "Hawatov ḥostovanim" ("With faith do I confess"). His song book, (*Girkʻ noraboys . . .*), includes his poems inspired by biblical themes, Ējmiatzin, Grigor Lusaworich, Nersēs the Great, Sahak Partʻew, Maštots, and other great figures and saints, and three poems marking his trials and tribulations. Unlike his forcefully and passionately apologetic work on the Church of Armenia, his poems do not convey any originality.

Purely polemical are the works of **GĒORG MḤLAYIM** (18th c.), a native of Constantinople and a *vardapet,* a student at the "Royal School" (Collège Louis-le-Grand?) in Paris (1706–11?), and a prisoner in one of the gaols of the French capital (1711–13?). It has been speculated that he may have been incarcerated for attempting to contact or rescue Patriarch Awetikʻ Ewdokatsi. Gēorg's great-grandfather was killed in Sivas during the Jelali disturbances. He is known to have toured Armenia at some point and to have spent some time in Kayseri and Tokat after his return from France. He knew Greek, Latin, French, and Turkish.

To prove the validity of the Armenian Christological position, Gēorg culled "Testimonies from Church Fathers . . ." in the "writings of Latins" (*Vkayutʻiwnkʻ hayrapetats yałags mioy bnutʻean Kʻristosi . . .*), which are very brief and paraphrased extracts from Clement of Alexandria, Athanasius, and Gregory the Theologian (Nazianzenus), with a heavy emphasis on the Council of Ephesus and passages from Grigor Narekatsi, Nersēs Šnorhali and Grigor Tatʻewatsi. In the introduction to his "The true meaning of Catholicity" (*Čšmarit nšanakutʻiwn katʻułikēutʻean*), Gēorg felt that C. Galanos's work (*Miabanutʻiwn . . .*, i.e., *Conciliationis Ecclesiæ Armenæ cum Romana . . .*) must not be left unanswered. Having explained the origins and true meaning of the Universal Church, he expounds on ten signs or characteristics (*nšankʻ*) distinguishing the "schismatic" (Roman Catholics). Up to this point, the content of this work is, with slight stylistic variations, the same as the first eighty-three pages of his dispute against the Dyophysites (*Girkʻ vičabanutʻean ěnddēm erkabnakats*), which makes up the first part of this book in two sections. This part is basically a diatribe (especially against Catholic practices of proselytizing), with some explanation of the Armenian version of the *Trisagion* (the addition of "who were (was) crucified for us" in the "thrice holy") and a sarcastic criticism of Ḥachatur Ērzrumetsi (q.v.) for his inclusion of a section on astrology and the horoscope in his Philosophy (*Hamaṙōtakan imastasirutʻiwn . . .*), which he condemns as an un-Christian piece of sorcery. The second part of this book, titled "Yałags pahots," is a justification of the Armenian position on fasting and even includes an Armenian translation by Gēorg ("Tʻułtʻ s[r]boyn Ōgostinosi, Aṙ Kasulanos ērētsn, ěnddēm hṙōmayetswoy urumn. or greal ēr v[a]s[n] paheloy zawurs šabatʻu") of St. Augustine's letter on fasting on the Sabbath (cf. *Epistola XXXVI,* "Augustinus Casulano presbytero . . . dissertationem pro sabbati jejunio . . . ," in J.-P. Migne's edition of Augustine's *Opera Omnia,* vol. ii, 136–51, *Patrologia Latina, xxxiii*).

Gēorg's homily on the Nativity, the Passion, and Grigor Lusaworich's vision (*Čaṙ amenamakʻur Tznndean . . .*) was popular at the time and went through eight editions. It is in Turkish in Armenian characters (but with some passages and many words in Armenian) and reflects the position of the Church of Armenia (e.g., justification of Armenian observation of Christmas and Epiphany on 6 January). All passages from the Gospels are in Armenian. The Crucifixion contains laments in verse in both Armenian and in Turkish. The vision of Grigor Lusaworich is accompanied with commentary.

MANUĒL DPIR KOSTANDNUPOLSETSI (18th c.) was also absorbed and motivated by the Armenian-Roman Catholic confrontation. The main purpose of his *Girkʻ or kochi lutzich tarakusanats* is to dispel doubts about the Church of Armenia. It was commissioned by a barber from Agulis by the name of Yovhannnēs, who converted to Catholicism at age seven or eight, and in his late teens agitated against the national church by encouraging many to renounce it. Yovhannēs was "deservedly punished" by Patriarch Yakob (Nalean, two terms: 1741–49, 1752–64); he returned to the fold of the Mother Church soon thereafter and collected many writings. He then supplicated Manuēl to make the truth public in this book. It deals in the main with some of the controversial issues that separate the two churches: baptism, communion, the Eucharist, mixing water with the wine, the Holy Chrism, the *Trisagion,* etc. In his "The foundation of authenticity" (*Girkʻ or kochi himn stugutʻean*), Manuēl discusses the Universal Church, feasts, rites, liturgy, and the Councils, and launches an assault, not free from vulgarity, on C. Galanos and Mḫitʻar Sebastatsi and his followers, who to him are *nerayinkʻ* and not *merayinkʻ* ("they belong to Antichrist, not to us"). His *Girkʻ or kochi akn lusatu* contains a similar onslaught in Turkish on Chalcedon, the papacy, Albert the Great, Yovhannēs Holov (1635–91, an Armenian Catholic grammarian and translator educated at Rome), Mḫitʻar Sebastatsi (q.v.), and others.

The Nineteenth Century

An Overview of the Armenian Realities of the Age

The annexation in 1828 of the Khanate of Erivan by Russia eventually proved to be a fateful political event with momentous consequences. The Russians created a new administrative unit, called the Armenian Region (*oblast'*), which comprised the Khanates of Erivan and Naḫijewan and the province of Ordubad. Although the unit was abolished and the Khanate of Erivan integrated into a new administrative structure in 1840, the roots of modern Armenian statehood lie in this stretch of territory, formally recognized as Armenian for the first time in modern history. Thus, what had remained of the historically much-larger Eastern Armenia entered the orbit of Russian-Slavic civilization. The Armenians now belonged to two distinctly hostile camps, the Russian and Ottoman empires, with two different political systems and civilizations. This entailed a number of crucial implications.

As Ottoman sultans and rulers tried to hold their tottering empire together, they instituted a number of reforms. Two such schemes were adopted in 1839 and 1856. The latter sanctioned the reorganization of the non-Muslim communities in the empire. The Armenians, who had themselves been agitating for reform, were quick to take advantage of the legal bases this document provided. For some years, the public had been disenchanted with the arbitrary government of the patriarchs and their unofficial partners, the *amiras,* men of enormous means and of almost unrestricted influence within the community. Students returning from France and Italy and some educated local elements formed a loose group of liberals, who in due course informally organized the public into a vociferous movement of protest, calling for reform in the administration of the community. A "constitution" was drafted within the framework provided by the Ottoman scheme, the final version of which the Porte promulgated in 1863. This set of regulations sanctioned the formation of a National Assembly and various councils to help the patriarch run the community.

The "constitution" (which in fact institutionalized the *millet* system) was created to regulate the *internal* affairs of the community, not the inter-communal relations in the empire. But complaints poured into the Patriarchate about oppression and misgovernment in the Armenian provinces. A detailed report of the conditions was submitted to the Porte by the administration of Patriarch Mkrtich Ḥrimean (q.v.), but it fell on deaf ears. Rebellion shortly broke out in the Balkans, and amid talk for reform in the region, the Armenians approached the Porte for a similar plan for the entire empire. (According to some very sketchy and unsubstantiated claims in the Records of the Armenian National Assembly, i.e., *Atenagrutʻiwnkʻ Azgayin žołovoy,* the central Ottoman authorities themselves orchestrated the Armenian request.) Indeed, the Ottomans soon proclaimed their own constitution, formally doing away with the need for regional or local reforms. The document did not prevent the Russians from going to war to rescue their Slav brethren. The defeated Ottomans and their despised northern adversary in 1878 signed the Treaty of San Stefano, which included an article (16) on certain measures in Armenia. The treaty was revised at the Congress of Berlin, and the new Armenian article (61) vaguely and inconclusively alluded to the need for the amelioration of conditions in Armenia. An indifferent Europe and an unwilling Porte thus effectively shelved the issue of reform in the Armenian provinces. Very soon, in the 1880s, the Armenian political parties came into existence, one after the other. The century concluded with the Armenian massacres of the mid-1890s.

The inimical relations between the Armenian and Roman Catholic Churches continued well into the nineteenth century. After some well-intentioned, if overly optimistic, attempts at reconciliation, the final rift came in 1831, when the Porte, under pressure from some European powers, recognized the Armenian Catholics as a separate community. Proponents of Latinization and ecclesiastic administration of the new *millet* clashed with the proponents of semi-secular and autonomous local leadership, and the conflict soon rent the community apart for many decades. The whole problem reflected negatively on the conciliatory attitude of the Mekhitarists of Venice, who were eventually rebuked into conformity with directives from Rome. By the closing decades of the century, then, passions had died down considerably, and a peaceful phase marked the relations of the Church of Armenia with Armenian Catholics.

The nascent Armenian Protestant community was granted formal recognition by the Porte in 1850. Small and well-organized, the community contributed its share to the dissemination of secular concepts of government and to the emergence of Modern Armenian as the national standard. Here too, after a stormy relationship from about the 1870s, reason and tolerance prevailed in the Armenian-Armenian Protestant relations. By the middle of the century, then, the Armenian population of the empire was divided into three formally recognized religious communities. The Church in Russia suffered no such rupture and disunity, but experienced severe restraints on the nature and extent of her national mission.

In 1836 the Russians promulgated the *Polozhenie* ("Statute") to regulate the affairs of the "Armenian Gregorian" Church (this designation, intensely resented by the Armenians, originated in this document) in the Russian Empire. The regulations severely restricted the overall rights and authority of the Mother See of Ejmiatzin. Unlike the Ottoman Empire, the Armenians here were not regarded as a separate religious community, and questions of personal status were dealt with by the Russian bureaucracy. The Church was stripped of her social-political and—to a large extent—her cultural functions; her role being confined in the main to the spiritual sphere and parochial schools. The Western Armenians on a number of occasions unsuccessfully tried to modify the method of electing the Catholicos of All Armenians to secure the elevation to the throne of their own candidates. The hope was that their protégé would have the *Polozhenie* revised for the better. Such timid and haphazard attempts invariably met with failure.

The Western Armenians moved in the opposite direction. Their constitution to a certain degree secularized the Patriarchate of Constantinople; the overwhelming majority of deputies to the National Assembly ("Azgayin žołov") were laymen and the various councils (Judicial, Educational, etc.), except for the Religious Council, were made up of laymen. But the system, it must be emphasized, served a formal purpose. The sultan still recognized the patriarch as the sole head of the Armenians of the empire. The Patriarchate espoused, in a tactful and flexible way, the cause of reform in Armenia to be implemented by the Porte in a peaceful fashion. In this spirit, Patriarch Mkrtich Ḥrimean (1869–73) unsuccessfully tried to revise the constitution, in effect envisioning executive powers for the Patriarchate. His successor, Nersēs Varžapetean (1837–84), during his ten-year tenure (1874–84), personally pursued the cause of reform, but his efforts were in vain. After Varžapetean's death, no patriarch raised the issue. It was left to the political parties, the rivals of the Church; and the parties attracted many Armenian writers into their ranks. But some conclusions were drawn from the experience long before the death of Varžapetean and the birth of the Armenian parties. Commenting on the redrawn Treaty of San Stefano in Berlin, Mkrtich Ḥrimean, who had been called upon to head an unofficial delegation to the Congress, unequivocally illustrated to his audience at the Armenian Cathedral in Constantinople that the old adage, "might is right," was still valid.

European nationalism, and similar concepts flowing from Europe to Armenian circles in Constantinople, underscored for a number of enlightened Armenians the importance of practical communication with the population at large. A dispute, mostly of a theoretical and academic nature, over whether Classical or Modern Armenian should be the national standard intermittently continued from the 1840s to the 1880s. Modern Armenian had long since been used in inscriptions, chronicles, and books. More recently, it had been used by Catholic (especially the Mekhitarists) and Protestant missionaries, the Armenian Church, and the periodical press, above all for purposes of religious propaganda. Its ascendance alarmed the traditionalists and prompted the reformists to hasten to its defense in the early 1850s. The Armenian Church, the Mekhitarists, and conservative elements stood up for Classical Armenian, the scriptural tongue of the ancestors, which to them was a fully developed, uniform vehicle of expression and, possibly, a unifying bond for the Armenians dispersed far and wide who spoke various, often mutually unintelligible, dialects. For this informal coalition, Classical Armenian was an end in itself, an abode of cultural nationalism that most of the time replaced the physical homeland. By contrast, they held, there were many forms (i.e., dialects) of Modern Armenian, a rudimentary and vulgar language, contaminated with numerous loan words from Turkish, Persian, and Arabic. For the youthful liberals on the other hand, Modern Armenian was a readily available means that afforded them direct access to the public, and reviving the Classical idiom among a dispersed nation was well-nigh impossible in their view. The dispute, ostensibly a "linguistic-cultural" disagreement, in addition reflected the ideological-political clash of the two camps. But life dictated its own, and the dialect spoken in Constantinople, itself an amalgam of dialectal elements introduced by "local" and "immigrant" Armenians, was in the second half of the century developed into a flexible tool, the Modern Western Armenian standard. There was a similarly passionate controversy in Transcaucasia, but it was short lived; the Eastern Armenians were in smooth waters as they made the transition to Modern Eastern Armenian in the 1860s.

In every sense of the word, the nineteenth century marked a new phase in Armenian realities. "Renaissance" and its synonyms have been used to describe the age. By the middle of the century the Armenians had fully recovered an idealized past and were poised to pursue some as yet dim aspirations. The superficial Islamic influences were discarded and the

Armenians briefly looked back for inspiration. But soon they were in a race against time to catch up with Europe; their current identity, although valid in many respects, had to be revised and renewed. Many factors opened education to the public, increased its awareness, enhanced its solidarity, and sharpened its sense of purpose. Various institutions and individuals set up a vast network of schools in Europe (Mekhitarist schools in Padua, Venice, Paris), the Ottoman Empire (e.g., Smyrna, Constantinople, etc.), the Russian Empire (e.g., the Ałababean in Astrakhan, 1810, the Lazarean in Moscow, 1815, the Nersisean in Tiflis, 1825, and various other schools in Erivan, Šuši, Alexandrapol, etc.), India (the Mardasirakan in Calcutta, 1821), and elsewhere. There existed a printing press in almost every Armenian community and in many of the schools. Periodicals increased in number, especially in the second half of the century. *Bazmavēp* of the Mekhitarists, still being published, was launched in Venice in 1843. Some of the more important ones that followed were *Hayastan* (1846–52, absorbed by *Masis,* 1852–1908, with interruptions), *Mełu* (1856–65, 1870–74), *Tʻatron* (1874–77), *Arewelkʻ* (1884–1913, continued under different names), *Hayrenikʻ* (1891–96), all published in Constantinople. *Čṙakʻał* (1853–62) and *Hiwsisapʻayl* (1858–62, 1864) were published in Moscow. *Ararat* (Ējmiatzin, 1868–1919), *Mełu Hayastani* (1858–86), *Mšak* (1872–1921), *Nor dar* (1883–1916, irregular and infrequent after 1903), and *Murč* (1889–1907) were published in Tiflis. *Arewelkʻ* (1855–56) and *Arewmutkʻ* (1859, 1864–65) were published in Paris. *Arewelean mamul* (Smyrna, 1871–1909, 1919–22) and *Handēs amsōreay* (Vienna, 1887, still being published) were important periodicals of the day as well. Numerous cultural and educational societies promoted knowledge throughout the Armenian communities. The translation of Western authors into Armenian continued with a feverish zeal. A worthy competitor to the Mekhitarists, who were selective in their approach, was a group of translators in Smyrna, who in the second half of the century translated more than two hundred volumes, mostly from French and a few from English, German, and Italian. The writings of many old Armenian historians were rendered into European languages, and Armenian was established as an Indo-European language by European linguists and historians who now took a closer interest in Armenian studies. Grammars of Armenian (both Classical and Modern) and non-Armenian languages, dictionaries (Armenian, especially the celebrated *Nor baṙgirkʻ haykazean lezui,* Venice, 1836–37, and multilingual), histories, and geographical and topographical works were published in abundance. Of the several histories and surveys of Armenian literature that appeared in Italian, German, Russian, and Armenian, Garegin Zarbhanelean's *Patmutʻiwn hayerēn dprutʻeants* (2 vols., 1865, 1878) should be singled out. Numerous valuable collections of folkloric and ethnographic material and studies were made public, helping the Armenians restore continuity to their tradition. In this respect, particularly noteworthy was the impact of the theater.

The theatrical presentations of Mekhitarist students were emulated in other schools in Constantinople. Local talents organized performances in the middle of the century, and the first Western Armenian professional theater ("Arewelean tʻatron") was established in Constantinople in 1861. Artists trained in this theater formed the Gedikpaşa ("Osmaniye") Theater under Yakob Vardovean (c1840–98?, better known in Turkish sources by the Turkified form of his name, Güllü Agop), who in 1868 was given a ten-year monopoly on Turkish performances. The Armenian theater of Tiflis originated almost simultaneously. When Abdulhamid II suspended performances at the outbreak of the Russo-Ottoman War of 1877–78, a most talented group of actors and actresses from Gedikpaşa revived the Armenian theater of Tiflis. The repertoire, most of which is non-extant, was made up of translations of the works of the giants of European theater and original plays in Armenian.

A vast corpus of literature in the form of books, periodicals, and pamphlets in Armeno-Turkish (Turkish in Armenian characters) appeared in the eighteenth and nineteenth centuries. The practice was put to extensive use by Catholic and Protestant missionaries and by the Church of Armenia in counter-propaganda literature of religious nature. But in the second half of the century, numerous works by European authors (mainly French) were rendered into Armeno-Turkish. Of the few books originally created in Armeno-Turkish, the novel *Agapi* (i.e., Agape, Constantinople, 1851) by Yovsēpʻ pasha Vardanean (1815–79) should be mentioned. The tradition continued well into the twentieth century but was totally confined to religious literature.

By the end of the century, most of the usual European genres were being emulated by Armenian authors. Beginning in the middle of the century, literary reviews, at times in the form of extensive essays, began to appear in the periodical press, which initially also hosted a great many literary pieces. But it was only in the 1890s that criticism acquired some semblance of sophistication and professionalism. Gradually, small circles of readership were formed, especially in big cities such as Constantinople and Tiflis, and clearer perceptions of literature as belles-lettres emerged. These urban centers were inundated with translations, Venetian editions of early Armenian historians, and some work of original composition. The latter, poems long and short, were mainly of a patriotic nature in the first half of the century and were dominated by Mekhitarist literary theory and verse, which does not merit attention here. Classicism, jejune and removed from life, is what the Mekhitarists preached and practiced. But it was one of them, Łewond Ališan (q.v.), who broke the mold and helped accomplish the transition to romantic verse in Western Armenian literature. The volume containing this cycle of poems appeared in 1858, and although exact dates are generally unhelpful in tracing the evolution of literary trends, it so happened that the year saw the publication of two other books: "Hayk the Hero" (*Hayk Diwtsazn*) by Arsēn Bagratuni (q.v.), a senior fellow monk of Ališan; and the "Wounds of Armenia" (*Vērkʻ Hayastani*) by Ḥachatur Abovean (q.v.). The former, a poem more than twenty-two thousand lines long, a noble effort indeed, was stillborn and at once signified the apogee of the age of classicism and its demise. Abovean's creation, on the other hand, proved to be an epoch-making novel that pointed to the future path of Eastern Armenian literature.

Mention has been made of the periodical press's hosting a great many literary works. This led to a certain degree of confusion, polarization, and monopoly, especially in Eastern Armenian literature. On the one hand, the periodical press helped disseminate and promote literature; on the other it confined literature to social-political issues, reducing it to a tool almost completely devoid of purely literary and aesthetic aspects. This certainly contributed to the already prevailing view of the tendentious nature of literature. Secondly, a spirit of *parti-pris* gripped a number of writers who identified with the outlook of certain authoritative papers (soon to be replaced by political parties). This blurred the fine line separating partisan from tendentious literature. Hence, some writers greeted the appearance in the 1890s of purely literary journals in Eastern Armenian with a deep sigh of relief. In terms of literary "schools," V. Hugo was immensely popular; Zola, too, had by this time become a household name, and the distinction between realism and naturalism was an overriding concern. In Western Armenian prose, with Paronean's satire and the appearance in the mid-1880s of realist writers around the daily *Arewelkʻ* (A. Arpʻiarean and his circle), a more or less swift transition to realism had taken place. But romanticism lingered on in Eastern Armenian prose throughout the 1880s (Raffi) and beyond (Muratsan). At the same time, and especially on into the 1890s, realists (e.g., Širvanzade) made their literary debut.

We now come to the larger cultural context enveloping both literatures. The duality between East and West in Armenian tradition that had manifested itself in political, social, cultural, religious terms, and in various other forms since the dawn of Armenian history had more or less corresponded to the geographic division of Armenia proper into such parts. Perennially, Armenia was a field where the two civilizations clashed, competed, or fused with no grave or permanent threat to its overall cultural unity. But the Armenians faced new realities in the nineteenth century, and political factors (Russo-Ottoman antagonism), geographical distances, religious-hierarchical disunity, the formation of mind under different circumstances and influences (e.g., Eastern Armenian students attended Russian and north European, primarily German, universities, while Western Armenians went to Latin Europe, mainly France), and the rise of two national standards rendered the growing gap between the Eastern and Western Armenians somewhat unbridgeable. This happened despite some conscious efforts on the part of such writers as A. Arp̓iarean (q.v.) to build bridges between the two literatures, and despite the immense popularity of Y. Paronean and Tzerents among Eastern Armenian readers and Raffi's reputation among Western Armenian readers. (Though hard evidence is lacking, it is quite tempting to those familiar enough with the era as to capture its "mood" by putting the pieces together, to speculate that a few Western Armenian intellectuals with affection and nostalgia reflected upon the idea of Cilicia as their homeland. One of the eloquent and indeed evocative testimonies is Nahapet Ṙusinean's moving and still-popular poem, "Kilikia," i.e., Cilicia, an adaptation surpassing the original model, "Ma Normandie," by Frédéric Bérat, a French poet-musician, 1801–55. Initially, the wish may have been father to the thought, but the dream was pursued in the wake of World War I, under entirely different circumstances.) Moreover, in the second half of the century, Russia witnessed social and political turmoil and underwent profound cultural changes, all of which had an immediate and widespread impact on Eastern Armenian literature and political thought. Such was not the case in the Ottoman Empire, where the Armenian provinces (the easternmost part of what is today called Turkey) were a particularly stagnant region. The Armenians had nothing to learn from their overlords, except, perhaps, to master the art of survival under oppression and maltreatment, a result of the very nature of the Ottoman political system. They looked up to their newly formed leadership stationed in far away Constantinople to ameliorate their conditions. Here, the situation was very different from that in the provinces, and at least one intellectual (Grigor Ōtean, i.e., Krikor Odian Efendi, 1834–87) participated in the Ottoman constitutional movement. But it soon became glaringly apparent to Armenians and non-Armenians alike that Ottoman imperialism had no prospects of survival as a multi-ethnic and multi-religious system. The Eastern Armenians, now subjects of a Christian power and soon of cultural oppression, focused their attention on delivering Armenia from the Ottoman yoke. They pinned their hope on the Russians to remove the borderline that separated the two halves of the Armenian people. Literature played a prominent role in this and all other national affairs.

By the middle of the century, cultural conditions were in place in Constantinople for a new era in the long history of Armenian literature. The tradition had not been interrupted, and there were new stimuli, emanating mainly from the West, a new impetus generated by the clash of the old and the new and an inspiring sense of renewal and anticipation. There was a small reading public and an audience whose taste for the theater had been cultivated by European troupes. The Armenian theater needed, and was indeed provided with, a native repertoire. Much groundwork was done by a number of public figures, literati, and intellectuals. Nikołos Palean (1826–58), Nikołos Zōrayean (1821–59), Nahapet Ṙusinean (1819–76), Grigor Ōtean (1834–87), Servichēn (Serovbē Vichēnean, 1815–97), and a few others played a vital role in the cultural, educational, and social-political activities of the time. Resistance to novel ideas came from the conservatives and their theorist, Karapet Tēroyents (also known as Tēr Karapetean and Chamurčean, 1801–88), an erudite and polyglot Christian apologist, who saw mainly ritual differences between the Armenian, Greek, and Latin churches that together formed the Catholic Church to the exclusion of the Protestants. The Mekhitarists, conservative in matters religious, cultural, and political, certainly contributed their share by popularizing European translations. In the early 1850s, they published a two-volume collection of their own verse (*Tałkʻ mḥitʻarean vardapetats,* Poems of the Mekhitarist Fathers), followed by A. Bagratuni's poem *Hayk Diwtsazn,* all in conformity with the norms of classicism. But their poetic output (with the exception of Ališan's) had a limited scope and influence.

One of the earliest prose pieces was a penny dreadful novel (Y. Hisarean's *Ḥosrov ew Makʻruhi,* 1851). But together with Łewond Ališan (q.v.), whose fame and influence lingered on, romantic poets and playwrights (M. Pēšiktʻašlean, P. Durean, q.q.v.) led the way. Y. Paronean (q.v.) dominated the 1870s with his satire, and Tzerents (q.v.) wrote the first historical novel. In the early 1880s, S. Tiwsab (q.v.) in her novels called attention to the plight of women, a concern echoed by a number of woman writers in the 1890s (e.g., Mariam Ḥatisean, Mari Svačean), whose work is yet to be explored. The decade saw the rise to prominence of a younger generation of writers, the realists (A. Arpʻiarean, T. Kamsarakan, G. Zōhrap, q.q.v., et al.), who in their novels and short stories looked at the social realities of the community in Constantinople and the dismal predicament of migrants from the provinces. The massacres of the mid-1890s concluded the era as Armenian authors, fleeing the carnage, sought safety in Europe and elsewhere, and just as fresh voices were beginning to mirror life in the Armenian provinces.

The development of modern Eastern Armenian from a dialect into a literary standard owes much to the Lazarean and Nersisean schools. Both had printing presses and both in the late 1820s published the initial literary experiments (verse in Classical Armenian) of their students. In some ways, the Armenian communities of India, which had always maintained active channels of communication with Eastern Armenia, helped promote progress, providing additional impetus to belles-lettres. The first serious effort in prose, in the form of novels, was made by M. Tʻałiadean (q.v.), for whom India was a second home. Here as well as in Western Armenian literature, the initial novels lacked originality and were mostly adaptations. But the laurel has been given to Ḥ. Abovean (q.v.) as the father of modern Eastern Armenian literature, though some critics have unjustifiably proclaimed him to be the founder of modern Armenian literature in general. His work, with an emphasis on active patriotism, the homeland, and the Armenian ethos, inspired many subsequent writers. From the middle of the century on, Russian social, political, and literary realities exercised an eminent influence on Armenian thought and letters. Not only did Armenian authors (most of them graduates of Russian universities) admire the magnificent accomplishments of Russian literature, they also lived much closer to the homeland, which similarly felt the weight of the radical changes sweeping Russia. *Narodnichestvo* ("populism") resonated in some Armenian political and intellectual circles, as did its cry, *khozhdenie v narod* (to go to the countryside, to the people). Not surprisingly, then, there took shape a socially committed literature, with poets (Ṙ. Patkanean, S. Šahaziz, q.q.v.) far outnumbered by writers of prose. Sundukean's talent shone in vaudevilles and comedies mirroring the Armenian community of Tiflis. The intellectual battles between various currents of thought (revolutionary-democrats, liberals, conservatives, and in Soviet Armenian terminology, "clerical-feudalistic" circles) were fought in the periodicals where many a literary piece was originally published. Apologists for the traditional and proponents of change passionately disagreed on the national standard, the nature and role of literature, the elements of Armenian identity, and the part the Church was to play in it. The land reform in Transcaucasia, the arrival of the railway and telegraph, and the Baku oil fields transformed rural Armenia rapidly and profoundly. For many a writer the disintegration of Armenian peasantry meant the destruction of traditional society and moral degeneration. At the same time as impoverishment struck the countryside, the Armenian bourgeoisie, the wealthiest in Transcaucasia, attained a dominant position in the economy of the region. Things soon took a turn for the worse when, in the wake of the Russo-Ottoman War, Russian chauvinism raised its head and a ruthlessly rigid censorship stifled Armenian intellectual creativity. Heretofore, the Armenians had looked up to Russia expecting, with euphoria before the outbreak of the war, the liberation of Western Armenia from Ottoman domination. Instead, abandoning all tactful appearances, the Russians now openly and in a hostile fashion pursued a policy of Russification and colonization. The intelligentsia turned inward in an attempt to maintain the precarious unity of their nation, Church, and culture, which was now subject to the severest political, cultural, and economic repressions in both empires. Younger patriots founded the political parties. Ṙ. Patkanean with his declamatory patriotic verse, Sundukean with his theater, and Pṙōšean, Ałayean, and Raffi with their novels and short prose examined the social-political conditions and turned to history and the magic world of folk tales to reflect and react to these challenges. A romantic Muratsan clung to traditional values and invoked the past. Širvanzade analyzed the ravages of industrial capitalism, Nar-Dos explored the psychological effects on the alienated individual, and H. Hovhannisyan, with his fresh, lyrical poems, conquered a new frontier in Eastern Armenian verse, paving the way for the next generation of poets.

A Survey of the Literature of the Age

YOVHANNĒS SEBASTATSI (d. 1830) has left a history of the monastery of Surb Nšan (Holy Cross) in Sebastea (Sivas), published in Erevan in 1974 by B. Chugaszyan under the title *Patmutʻiwn Sebastioy.* It is essentially a history of the monastery from its building in 1021 to 1829, with a list of the Armenian prelates of the area, cast against a background of abundant information on the region about government and governors, economy, demography, Armenian craftsmen, Armenian *amiras,* fourteen martyrologies, events in and around Sebastea, and many other useful and reliable information. Yovhannēs drew upon the work of Grigor Magistros, Mattʻēos Uṙhayetsi, Samuēl Anetsi, Vardan Areweltsi, Kirakos Gandzaketsi, and others for the earlier period of his history, and on Mikʻayēl Chamchean (q.v.) and various chronologies, bulls, inscriptions, colophons, crosses, ornaments, and such religious utensils and furniture for the more recent and contemporary period of his history. Some of the religious-moral poems and epitaphs he composed are found in his *Nerbołakan nuagerguťiwnkʻ* . . . (Tiflis, 1825).

YOVHANNĒS ŁRIMETSI (Pʻotʻišantsi, d. 1848) is the author of a history of the monastery of Hałpat to 1827. It is a topographical, geographical, and historical record of the monastic complex and churches in Hałpat and its neighborhood, and of famous monks, fathers-superior, and local dignitaries and leaders. Among the sources he used for the earlier period are Vardan Areweltsi, Kirakos Gandzaketsi, Stepʻanos Asołik, Stepʻanos Ōrbelean, and inscriptions.

A native of Gümüşhane, **MANUĒL KIWMIWŠḤANATSI** (1768–1843), is the author of an "autobiography," *Andznakan patmuťiwn Manuēl Kiwmiwšhanatsi vardapeti, Alťuneani kam Šahinovi.* The published part concludes with the year 1836, and the work is a detailed description of himself and of his travels and work in St. Petersburg, Crimea, Tiflis, Ējmiatzin, and Sewan. He deals extensively and at times colorfully with the pastoral positions he held in Armenia and Crimea. There are interesting parts on the conquest of Erevan, for instance, by the Russians (1828), when he was the librarian of Ējmiatzin and made laudable efforts to repair and preserve old manuscripts; his role in recruiting students for the celebrated Lazarean Institute (established in Moscow in 1815 and in 1827 renamed the "Lazarevskii institut vostochnykh iazykov"), to which he donated his collection of manuscripts; and the Dawitʻ-Daniēlean imbroglio over the succession to the throne of Ējmiatzin, in which Russia and Persia were closely involved.

Kiwmiwšḥanatsi has a history of the monastery of Sewan (*Patmut'iwn antsits antselots Sēwanay vanuts*). Following Movsēs Ḥorenatsi, he begins with etymologies of toponyms (Gełam, etc.), the building of the chapel allegedly erected by Grigor Lusaworich and Trdat the Great, and a curious popular etymology for the name "Sevan" (from "sa ē van," i.e., this is [a] monastery). He then moves on to the Arab period, the building of the complex, renovations and traditions (with some criticism of Mikʻayēl Chamchean's "Chalcedonian" views), inscriptions, the founding of the hermitage, the succession of fathers-superior (one of whom, fearing the wrath of Catholicos Simēon Erewantsi (q.v.) on the eve of his visit to Sewan, threw into the lake some old, disintegrated manuscripts and records!), and a list of relics and utensils with their donors or provenance.

Kiwmiwšḥanatsi also has a *Lutz armatoyn meroy* (literally, The yoke of our root) on fasting. The "root" is Adam, from whom emanates the tradition of fasting, which Kiwmiwšḥanatsi promotes with supporting material from the Old and New Testaments, Basil of Caesarea, Ambrose,

Jerome, Augustine, Nectarius, Grigor Narekatsi, Nersēs Šnorhali, and many other Armenian and non-Armenian authorities, guided by the maxim "fasting is the mother of all virtues, gluttony is the mother of all vices." The book concludes with a poem by his "spiritual father," Yovhannēs Sebastatsi Cherkʻezean (d. 1796), archbishop of Amasia and Marzuan (Merzifon), and one-sentence quotations against drinking from Seneca, Ambrose, Jerome, and others.

YOVHANNĒS KARNETSI (c1755–1820s?) is remembered as a scribe, a celebrated teacher in Karin (Erzurum), and a poet whose verse (still mostly in manuscript form) is yet to be fully evaluated. His manuscript on the life and work of Grigor Ōšakantsi (q.v.) is not extant, but two later copies of the original have survived. His love poetry shows influences from Turkish poetry and would certainly be a good case for the study of Armeno-Turkish literary relations at this juncture. A considerable part of his work consists of translations from Turkish into Armenian and vice versa. His poem on the famine of 1813 in Karin (Movsēs Ḥorenatsi and Dawitʻ Anyałtʻ, "the Invincible," figure among the city's founders!), which had devastating social and economic consequences, is of a descriptive nature. His imagination and verve are memorable in his poems on the occasion of the martyrdom of Sahak manuk (Sahak Měšěr Karnetsi) in 1778; Yarutʻiwn Karnetsi in Smyrna in 1806; Łazar in Baberd in 1809; and those of Dvnik (a village near Karin) in 1810, with Varvaṙē as the central heroine. Like most other martyrs, these too die for their ancestral faith and identity, and like many other poems written on similar occasions, they have a social and political significance in that they highlight, among other things, the ways in which conversion to Islam was at times imposed on Armenians.

ŁUNKIANOS (d. 1841?), born probably in Erzurum, moved at a young age to Tabriz with his father where he learned Persian. He was then sent to the Antonean Catholic monastery in Lebanon, but he never took the vows of celibacy. He spent some years in Egypt, where he learned Arabic, engaged in trade, and lost his fortune aboard a ship destroyed by the Greek fleet. He lived in Aleppo for a brief period and moved to the Crimea in 1828. He returned to Loṙi, Armenia, via St. Petersburg and Tiflis, by the time the Armenians of Karin had retreated with the Russian Army to Širak, where he spent some time teaching. He journeyed to Constantinople on several occasions, but spent most of his time in Akhalkalak, where he died.

He wrote in Armenian and Turkish, but only his Armenian poems on religious themes have been published. He wrote "divānī," "ilāhī," "destan," "dū-baitī," and in other forms. The central theme is the Blessed

Virgin. He sings of her as a lover would sing of his love, and as H. Thorossian has with good reason suggested in his *Histoire de la littérature arménienne,* he may have had carnal love in mind. He is tired of this life and longs for the next. Although sincere, Łunkianos is monotonous and lacks depth. He also has a few pieces of occasional poetry, such as the one on the dispute between "baḥt and ḥelkʻ," where Fortune and Intelligence eventually agree that only he who possesses them both may succeed in life. He writes in a Western Armenian mixed with elements from the Širak dialect.

A native of Van, educated at the hermitage at Ktuts (an islet in Lake Van) and at Constantinople, **YOVHANNĒS VANANDETSI** (1772–1840) lived chiefly in Smyrna, where he became a priest and taught at the famous Mesropean school. Well-versed in Armenian letters, he also knew Turkish and taught himself Arabic and Persian. But he knew no European languages and his training, the best the Armenian educational system could offer, was inferior to that of a Mekhitarist monk or to European standards. Although a gifted poet, his lack of sophistication in literary craftsmanship decidedly limited the artistic appeal of his poetry. Not only that, he had no masters to learn from as he composed three long poems, seminal in many ways and pointing to two dominant topics for subsequent authors: piety and patriotism. This partly emanated from the themes he tackled, but the Greek War of Independence and Russian expansion and victories against the Ottoman Empire could have alerted him to the urgency of national identity, unity, and pride.

In Vanandetsi's *Arṙiakan Hayastani* (i.e., the celestial or luminous age of Armenia), narrated in nearly ten thousand lines, is Agatʻangełos's *History* in verse (including St. Gregory's Teaching), which employs a certain degree of poetic license. Needless to say, Grigor Lusaworich is the central hero, and here, as in his other poems, Armenia is considered the cradle of mankind with a pronounced emphasis on the orthodoxy and primacy of the Church of Armenia. It concludes with Grigor Lusaworich laboring over his *Yačaḥapatum čaṙkʻ* ("multifarious homilies"), a work, in fact, of uncertain authorship.

His *Tesaran handisitsn Haykay, Aramay ew Arayi* (a review of the brave deeds of Hayk, Aram, and Ara) is based on the first part of Movsēs Ḥorenatsi's *History,* in which the origins of the Armenians and the exploits of their legendary forefather and his successors are narrated. Vanandetsi does not adhere to Ḥorenatsi's chronology, but in his master's spirit he sings, in some six-thousand rhymed lines, of their valor and virtues and castigates the "lascivious" Šamiram (Semiramis) with an elegy for Ara, a victim of his innocence and handsome appearance.

Oski dar Hayastani (The golden age of Armenia) is a history in verse (nearly fifty-six hundred lines long) of Armenia beginning with Adam and descending down to the modern times. It is a conflation of facts and fiction culled from Armenian historians and traditions, with a resounding patriotic message and a stream of invective against American missionaries mentioned just as an afterthought. This marks the initial stages of a new front of battles with the missionaries, who professed to have arrived in the region with a view to reforming the "corrupt" and "degenerate" Church of Armenia from within, but who soon helped establish a new, separate Armenian community: the Protestants. Vanandetsi, for one, looked at them with grave suspicion; he thought that they should have taken their proselytizing zeal to un-Christian lands, such as China and Japan.

There are some very good parts in all three of Vanandetsi's poems, illuminated by the bright flashes of his poetic talent. He was among the earliest writers to introduce political elements into poetry; to exhort his fellow countrymen to be patriotic and pious, deriving inspiration from the past splendor of their country; to promote knowledge and learning; and to resort to self-defense should they or any aspect of their identity be threatened by hostile forces.

Although belles-lettres as such was not a primary concern for the Mekhitarists, **ARSĒN BAGRATUNI** (1790–1866), a gifted poet and an erudite man of letters, stands out among the few who engaged in literary activities. He is acclaimed as the best representative of Armenian Classicism, with a few more feathers in his hat as a linguist, translator, and teacher. The occasional poems he wrote to elegize or eulogize certain dates or figures and his two posthumously published plays call for no special attention here. But there is a clue to understanding his magnum opus, *Hayk Diwtsazn* (Hayk the hero), in the fact that Bagratuni remained a staunch supporter of Classical Armenian to the very end of his life.

Bagratuni had a passion for all things classical. He loved his Greek and Latin, and imitating Homer and Virgil, he created the Armenian classical epic, *Hayk Diwtsazn.* It is perhaps the longest poem in Armenian literature, made up of more than twenty-two thousand lines, and embodies his cherished dream to glorify the origins of his people. His choice for a hero naturally fell upon Hayk, who for well over a millenium had been lionized as the legendary forefather of the Armenians. Whatever the original content and contour of the pagan myth, the so-called *Primary History* had placed Hayk's story in the biblical context; Movsēs Ḥorenatsi had worked out an elaborate pedigree for Hayk as a descendant of Japheth, and Mikʻayēl Chamchean (q.v.) put the finishing touches to the myth in his *History.* Pushing poetic license beyond its limits, Bagratuni fleshed out the story into an intricate plot with a resounding message of piety and patriotism.

Briefly told, the Lord chooses Hayk to fight His battles against the ungodly Bel. The latter makes three requests for Hayk to worship him as god, to recognize his political supremacy, and to give his daughter to him for wife. Hayk rejects all three demands (the first two are later dropped), and hostilities follow. Bel is aided and abetted by forces of evil, Hayk by the goddess Astłik, biblical patriarchs, saints, and a celestial host. There follow numerous clashes and sea battles, and conflicts and clashes of personalities within Hayk's camp. Haykak, son of Hayk, is killed in action; Hayk is wounded, but an attempt on his life is foiled. Many other events lead to the Almighty's displeasure and, therefore, to a state of disastrous flux. Here, Noah intercedes with prayers, and as Heaven triumphs over the forces of evil, Hayk downs Bel with his arrow.

Bagratuni is heavily indebted to Homer, Virgil, Ovid, Tasso, Milton, Chateaubriand, and many others for the form and structure of his eponymous poem. The basic elements of the story he borrowed from Armenian historians, but the elaborate plot was the brainchild of his own imagination. He must have been familiar with a play bearing the same title by another Mekhitarist monk, Ełia Tʻomačean, either through reading it in manuscript form or attending its performance at St. Lazarus in 1805. He must have also been aware of *Tesaran handisitsn Haykay, Aramay ew Arayi* by Yovhannēs Vanandetsi (q.v.). Both works may have inspired the conception of Bagratuni's poem, but the plots, save the traditional outline of the myth, bear no resemblance to it. Bagratuni's greater gift, skill and eloquence, make his poem distinctly superior to either model.

Yet, despite Bagratuni's masterful command of Classical Armenian, his fertile imagination, the putative appeal of his message, the magnificent Armenian customs and traditions he created, and the splendid triumph of Hayk, the poem was met with total indifference. A number of factors accounted for this. First and foremost, very few Armenians could read Classical Armenian. Secondly, the religious-biblical aspects were so overwhelming that blending them with a decidedly heroic, pagan past turned the poem into a toyland where, in a sort of *deus ex machina* fashion, nothing moved without divine dispensation. This religious thrust did not resonate with the political aspirations of the Armenians; there was, for instance, no real threat to the faith of the Armenians at the time. Thirdly, the microcosm he created was not recognizably Armenian and seemed distant and unrelated to the Armenian ethos, past and present. Last but not least, the poem suffered from numerous technical flaws: protraction, harangues, and many an excursus in a frequently convoluted style. It was a monumental effort, indeed, with many attractive passages, which has forced the historians of Armenian literature to regard it as the masterpiece of Armenian Classicism. But both this school and its best expression arrived rather late in the day; not surprisingly, it had few readers and still fewer imitators.

YARUTʻIWN ARARATEAN's (1774–1830s?) memoirs cover the years 1751–97. He was well connected to a number of influential Russians and Armenians in St. Petersburg, and his story is an imaginative and at times imaginary account of his own life, intimately woven into a background of contemporary events. Somehow, things are either black or white to him as are the portraits he depicts. Particularly negative is his attitude towards the rich, the military, local rulers, and men of religion. His positive profiles, on the other hand, are bestowed with an angelic character; his indulgence in self-aggrandizement, therefore, comes as no surprise. A proponent of Russian orientation, Araratean supported the Russian advance in Transcaucasia, fully expecting that it would bring relief to his people and country.

GABRIĒL PATKANEAN (1802–89, father of Ṙapʻayēl Patkanean, q.v.), was a savant who made contributions to many aspects of Armenian cultural and social life. Although his literary output was mainly composed in the first half of the nineteenth century, much of it was published decades later, and much still remains in manuscript form. In addition to teaching, translating, and editing, he wrote a number of works in prose and an even greater number in verse. There is a touch of suspense to some of his prose writing, and the bulk and best of his poetry invokes figures from the pagan past and mythology. He was one of the earliest writers to employ modern Armenian in almost all of his oeuvre, making his own modest contribution to Armenian literature at this period of transition, which according to most Armenian scholars signals the beginning of the modern era in Armenian letters.

YARUTʻIWN ALAMDAREAN (1796–1834), a priest, poet, patriot, and teacher, was closely associated with three famous Armenian schools in the nineteenth century that have left their mark on generations of Armenian students: Łababean in Astrakhan (1810), the Lazarean Institute in Moscow (1815), and the Nersisean School in Tiflis (1825). He studied under Serovbē Patkanean (1769–1836), father of Gabriēl Patkanean (q.v.) and grandfather of Ṙapʻayēl Patkanean (q.v.), and became a teacher himself before completing his studies. He was then invited to Moscow and taught at the Lazarean for almost ten years. The Nersisean in Tiflis opened its doors in January, 1825, with Alamdarean as its principal at the request of Catholicos Nersēs V, Aštaraketsi (1843–1857), then primate of the Armenians of Tiflis. Here, under the supervision of Nersēs himself, he was active in recruiting men and support for the Russian Army in its wars against the Persians and Ottomans in the late 1820s, which brought Eastern Armenia under the czar's control. In conjunction with his teaching activities, Alamdarean prepared a number of primers on Armenian and Russian and Russian dictionaries, most of which (with the exception of his Russian-Armenian dictionary, Moscow, 1821) remain unpublished.

Some thirty poems and an incomplete play have secured a niche for him in the history of Armenian literature. He is a poet of transition, associated with previous verse in some ways, but departing from it in others, a fact that has led many critics to see him as a representative of Armenian classicism. Religious concerns and love nurture his imagination. The single most important event inspiring him was the death of his wife, reincarnated in his poetry as a beautiful woman in both body and soul. It is the grief of her untimely departure, which leaves him inconsolable, that informs his sentiments on love and companionship. His pain grows all the more deeper following his banishment to the monastery of Hałpat (1830), which he soon left to become father superior of the monastery of Holy Cross in Nor-Naḥijewan (Rostov-na-Donu). He writes in elegiac but simple Classical Armenian, with a warm imagination and sincerity that made some of his poems popular. His use of the "rose and nightingale" device, unlike earlier practice, is in a lucid Classical Armenian free from Persian imagery and words and holds no hope for the nightingale: no spring will ever bring the rose to life again.

Western Armenian Literature

ŁEWOND ALIŠAN (1820–1901) was both a voluminous and luminous author who commanded profound respect among his fellow countrymen and enjoyed wide recognition in European scholarly circles. What initially brought him popularity was the collection of his poems, *Nuagkʻ,* published in 1857–58, and *Yušikkʻ hayreneats hayots,* a collection of inspiring portraits and episodes from Armenian history. There followed his massive volumes on the history, geography, topography, and flora of Armenia (*Širak, Sisuan, Ayrarat, Sisakan, Hay busak,* etc.); works of historical and philological nature (*Hay-Venet, Šnorhali ew paragay iwr, Hayapatum,* etc.); and the publication of numerous texts, including the series titled *Sopʻerkʻ haykakankʻ.* Ališan made a number of translations such as Canto IV from *Childe Harold,* Schiller's "Die Glocke," and a collection titled

K'nar amerikean (i.e., American Lyre with works by N. P. Willis, Andrews Norton, Bryant, J. G. Whittier, and others).

Nuagk' appeared in five volumes. The first volume, *Mankuni,* includes prayers and religious exhortations for children. The second contains a number of occasional verse of little value, but also some of his better, reflective poetry, as well as his still better poems dedicated to nature. The third volume, *Hayruni,* represents his patriotic songs, including the cycle of eleven poems subtitled "Ergk' Nahapeti" (i.e., Songs of the patriarch), long recognized as the crown of his verse. Volume four, *Tēruni,* is made up of poems on religion, religious feasts, and saints. Volume five, *Tḥruni,* has human suffering, death, and the plight of émigrés as its main subjects.

Religion, faith, and patriotism dominate Ališan's work. Any search for dissension from Christian tenets on the Creator, the Creation, and human behavior would be a futile attempt. He cared, he said, not a whit for life on this planet, especially his own; but earthly concerns such as the misfortune of his fellow countrymen always troubled his compassionate soul. This frail and frugal monk himself in his early thirties extinguished the brilliant fire fueling his creative imagination, forever silencing the poet in him. His lavish poetic gift and his passionate disposition combined to create a formidable force, too dangerous for a monk. He marked the occasion with a moving poem bidding farewell to the muse ("Husk ban aṙ Ogin nuagahann," *Nuagk',* v) and wishing eternity would immediately swallow him up.

Save for the cycle titled "Patriarch's Songs," all of his poetry is in Classical Armenian and has since been inaccessible to the public at large. Mekhitarist theorists are not entirely alone in their contention that Ališan is at his best in the ancient tongue. What has been appealing to them has been his subject matter (religious, moral, and meditative) and his form and style (classical, majestic). The influence of Chateaubriand, Lamartine, Hugo, Goethe, Schiller, and Byron has been noted as beneficial. Those who read Classical Armenian will most likely agree that his talent does indeed shine in many poems, though the quality is strikingly uneven overall and much of it is difficult to salvage. The "Patriarch's Songs" are overrated and overemphasized by Soviet Armenian critics and somewhat berated by Mekhitarists as the *ašułakan* strain in Ališan's verse.

Most of Ališan's patriotic songs as well as his "Patriarch's Songs" appeared in the third volume of his verse titled *Hayruni.* Figures and episodes from Armenian history sparked his imagination (King Trdat the Great; the military leaders Mušeł, Vardan, and Vahan Mamikonean; King Ašot II, Erkat'; the Aršakuni [Arsacid] dynasty; the battles of Dziraw and

Vardanank', etc.). The boisterous noise in some of his poems often seems to replace, or cover up, rebellious sentiments unutterable by a monk. His best poems, though few in number, are memorable. Of particular note are the ones dedicated to nature, to the heroes of the battle of Awarayr, and to the sad fate of his fatherland, in which he ponders over or thunderously complains of the afflictions befallen his people, in a tone of glowing pride and patriotism.Ališan's patriotism, it must be noted, despite its not-so-infrequent militant strains, was a cultural and in many ways a passive patriotism. It nonetheless had an enormous impact on the reading public, arousing a sense of unity, pride, and patriotism throughout the 1860s.

Ališan is among the earliest authors to write romantic verse (of nationalism and nature) in Modern Armenian, and thanks to this he has clinched a permanent niche in the history of Armenian literature. Ironically, he was a profound admirer of Classical Armenian and considered it far superior to the spoken idiom. His fame has far outlived his influence, for he has had some impact on a number of contemporary writers in terms of style, as well as topics he chose from Armenian history.

MKRTICH PĒŠIKT'AŠLEAN (1828–68) found himself in the midst of some dramatic developments in the 1860s. In 1862, Zeitun (now Süleymanlı, Turkey) erupted against the local Ottoman authorities. Pēšikt'ašlean marked the occasion with a cycle of poems, but suggestions that he was involved in organizing this bold act of defiance seem to be unsubstantiated. Soon thereafter the so-called Armenian "constitution" was promulgated (1863), generating unrealistic expectations of a political nature. Both events, allied with the theater and patriotic poetry of the period, account for much of the romantic euphoria of the 1860s, to which Pēšikt'ašlean himself contributed to some degree.

Pēšikt'ašlean was active in organizing some of the earliest theatrical performances and in founding two societies: *Hamazgeats* ("National") and *Baregortzakan* ("Beneficent"), both of which promoted education and agricultural work. One of the loudest cries heard at this juncture was the call for unity transcending religious-denominational boundaries as the Armenian Catholics and Armenian Protestants had by now been formally recognized by the Ottoman government as separate communities. Pēšikt'ašlean's "We are brothers" ("Ełbayr emk' mek'") echoed and embodied such sentiments and brought him popular acclaim. His transient glory also partly rested on his dramas, some of which he acted in himself.

Sensing public dissatisfaction with the performances he staged in Classical Armenian (original and translations), Pēšikt'ašlean increasingly relied on the emerging new vernacular, but never fully shed the influence of the Mekhitarists. His first play, *Koṙnak* (which he called a tragedy), is in Modern Western Armenian, as are his other three plays. It takes place in fourth-century Armenia (in the wake of King Trdat the Great's death) and depicts a deadly conflict between unselfish patriots and treacherous traitors. His second tragedy, *Aršak [II],* is only one of the numerous interpretations of the intriguing story of this enigmatic king. Very popular throughout the decade, it too revolves round unity and selfless patriotism. In both *Vahan [Mamikonean*] and *Vahē,* the clash of personal and national interests is illustrated. Similar preoccupations seem to have led Pēšiktʻašlean to translate Voltaire's *La Mort de César* and Alfieri's *Saul* among others.

In many ways, Pēšiktʻašlean's tragedies conform to principles of Classicism, yet in other ways they depart from the canon. His are among the earliest in Modern Armenian, and at the time they intrigued and illuminated, delighted and inspired enthusiastic audiences. But his tragedies, like many of his poems, have not withstood the test of time.

Most of Pēšiktʻašlean's poems are in Classical Armenian, and besides occasional elegies, eulogies, epitaphs, etc., they primarily express the patriotism and love sentiments of a sad, sensitive soul. The four poem cycle on Zeitun was and still is popular, as are his "Tzern Vanay" (The old man from Van), "Ełbayr emkʻ mekʻ" ("We are brothers"), and particularly, "Garun" (Spring; beginning "Oh, inch anuš ew inchpēs zov . . . ,'' believed to have been put to music by Tigran Chuḥačean, 1837–98). Two of the Zeitun poems are adaptations: one of Hugo's "L'Enfant" from *Les Orientales* and the other of Charles Wolfe's poem "The Burial of Sir John Moore." Pēšiktʻašlean has made some other adaptations and a noteworthy translation of a popular romance, "Ma Normandie" (rendered as "Erg hayreni," A song of the homeland), by Frédéric Bérat, a French poet-musician (1801–55), which inspired a far more popular and enduring adaptation by Nahapet Ṙusinean ("Kilikia," Cilicia). Few though they are, Pēšiktʻašlean's best poems are attractive for their sincere emotions and lyricism, sympathetic concerns, and subtle and occasional humor, and are among the earliest exemplars heralding the rise of the Romantic tradition in modern Armenian literature.

PETROS DUREAN (1851–72), a poet, playwright, and aspiring actor, broke new ground in Armenian poetry. In many ways, the modern lyric tradition originates in his work; both in manner and matter it is removed from the then prevalent Mekhitarist patterns. Despite flaws in the technique, it is unfettered by conventions and concerns, and thus it is innovative and splendidly spontaneous. His imagery and metaphors are fresh and eloquent, his immediacy charming, and his diction limpid. Beneath his predominantly elegiac and seemingly subdued style, there lurks a tempestuous soul, eagerly but vainly trying to cling to a life sadly cut short by consumption. In his slim collection of verse shines some of the best lines ever uttered in Armenian.

Durean's patriotic sentiments forcefully manifest his genuine concern for his fellow countrymen and their uncertain fate. Unlike Łewond Ališan (q.v.), he is preoccupied with their present and future, and in a burst of rebellious sentiments, he urges them to protest. In another instance he calls on the sultan either to curb disorder and depredations or to allow the Armenians to carry arms for purposes of self-defense. He knew that his death was imminent and expressed regret that his contribution to national aspirations would be as short-lived as his life. Unrequited love and personal agony, failing health and unfulfilled dreams, intense feelings of loneliness and forlornness, and his own life so quickly slipping through his fingers inspired his lyrical poetry. He exploded in an awesome protest ("black torrent") against God for his cruel fate in one poem, and mitigated in repentance with calm and pride in the next. Despite his regret he did not expunge the former poem from the record.

The Armenian theater in Constantinople fascinated Durean. Despite his father's opposition, he frequented performances and engaged in acting. Given the financial hardship his family suffered at the time, practical purposes may also have been one of the factors attracting him to the theater. He collaborated with the leading theatrical figure of the time, Yakob Vardovean (later also referred to in Turkish sources as Güllü Agop). Most of his plays were staged in his own lifetime, bringing him instant recognition that was to be sustained and multiplied by his poems after his death. Durean's plays, too, departed from established molds. His *Vard ew Šušan . . .* (Rose and lily . . .) is an intensely emotional melodrama in the earlier sense of the term. His second play, *Artašēs ašḫarhakal* (Artashes [II] the Conqueror], a historical play on the founder of the Artaxiad dynasty in Armenia, mostly conforms to the rules of classicism. *Sew hoɫer . . .* (Black soil, but the word figuratively could also mean "tomb"), his most frequently staged tragedy, illustrates patriotism against a background of Tamerlane's destructive raids. Durean transcends the limitations of classicism in *Ankumn Aršakuni . . .* (The fall of the Aršakuni dynasty), which depicts the end of the Aršakuni royal line as a result of the treachery of Armenian *naḥarars* (nobles). Another historical play of intrigue and betrayal is *Aspatakuťiwnkʻ parskats i Hays . . .* (Incursions of the Persians into Armenia, or the destruction of the Bagratid capital of Ani). Durean's last play, *Tatron kam ťšuařner* (Theater or wretched people), tackles social injustice and moral corruption through the story of two lovers, who as actors commit suicide on stage. These plays are reckoned to be among the earliest works of romantic drama. They enjoyed wide popularity and certainly had an impact on the rising tide of patriotism at the time. But they were the initial experiments of a teenager, and even though they occasionally glisten with his genius, they have not worn well.

MATTʻĒOS MAMUREAN (1830–1901) was a writer, translator, educator, public figure, celebrated editor and publicist, and one of the more prominent representatives of the Armenian community of Smyrna, the second largest center of Armenian culture in the Ottoman Empire. He was well-versed in English and French letters, and played an important role in promoting Western literature and cultivating a readership. He also contributed to the emerging Western Armenian standard. His *Angliakan namakani* (English letters) highlights patriotism and the cause of enlightenment in Armenia and the dire consequences of emigration. *Haykakan namakani* (Armenian letters) focuses on the contemporary Armenian scene, especially the issue of the so-called Armenian constitution and constitutionalism, and portrays some of the well-known public figures of the time, including Grigor Ōtean (Krikor Odian Efendi) among others. His *Sew leṙin mardě* (The man of the black mountain) remained incomplete. The background to the novel is the Russo-Persian War of 1826–28. The novel is intensely anti-czarist, partly because of the failure of the Russians to compensate in tangible political terms the assistance the Armenians had given them during the campaign in Transcaucasia. In his popular monthly, *Arewelean mamul,* which he founded in 1871, Mamurean covered a very wide range of social, cultural, literary, educational, and political issues of considerable importance.

YAKOB PARONEAN (1843–91) is the first great master of sweeping satire, vivid humor, and comedies of unsurpassed popularity. An ethical purist and a self-appointed arbiter of the social scene, this expert of demolition left hardly any contemporary person or issue of import untouched. If the public respected him, many of his victims looked daggers at him, and some denounced him. The periodicals he published, although popular, never paid the bills as the not-so-numerous copies sold circulated among wider circles of non-subscribers. No source of supplementary income ever enabled him to free himself of the clutches of poverty. This and the failure of his campaign to reform society through whiplash words seem to a certain degree to have affected the mood and mode, if not pertinacity, of his satire.

Paronean's political criticism is found in his minor journalistic pieces and columns, particularly in "Ksmitʻner" ("Pinches," published in *Tatron*) and "Im dzeřatetrě" ("My notebook," published in *Pʻordz* of Tiflis). In the early 1870s, he threw his unqualified support behind Patriarch Mkrtich Ḥrimean (q.v.) and his efforts to have the Armenian constitution revised. From Europe he chose Don Carlos (1848–1909) and the Carlist risings (1872–76) to poke fun at freely, with no restrictions imposed by the Ottoman censorship. But both issues receded from his sight as he exposed the consequences of maltreatment and inequality in the Armenian provinces of the Ottoman Empire, arising from the corruption and inefficiency of Ottoman officialdom and the nature of the Ottoman political system. As the Balkans erupted in rebellion, leading to the Russo-Ottoman War of 1877–78, which in turn gave rise to the Armenian Question as an international issue, Paronean punctured the pious pretensions of the European powers in pithy chronicles and with biting sarcasm. He ferociously attacked Ottoman internal policy, especially with regard to the Armenians. No contemporary Armenian observer has so perspicuously evaluated the diplomatic entanglements and political rivalries of the time, maintaining all along that the very foundation of such selfish policies was the same old adage: might is right.

The *National Big-Wigs* (*Azgayin jojer*) contains some of Paronean's brightest satirical pages. Paronean owes its conception to the biographies published in the French periodical *Le Polichinelle* rather than to Plutarch's *Lives* or Mattʻēos Mamurean's *Haykakan namakani* (Armenian letters). Some writers such as Ōtean and Zōhrap (q.q.v.) benefited from Paronean's experience in their satirical and non-satirical biographies. All biographies begin with the birth of a given celebrity and evaluate the negative aspects of his activities. Except for a few, all portraits are critical. Some are written with annihilating satire. The portraits include figures active in public affairs, priests, editors, artists, writers, and celebrities. There were some omissions, such as Grigor Ōtean (Krikor Odian Efendi, 1834–87), Yarutʻiwn Tatean (Artin Pasha Dadian, 1830–1901), and Servichēn (Serovbē Vichēnean, 1815–97), who all served the Ottoman government. All portraits are cast against a background of contemporary Armenian realities that come alive in these lives. There are portraits with some protraction and verbosity, and a reading of them without appropriate annotation of the contemporary scene is difficult. But overall they are highly original, despite the obscurity of their circumstances, and they scintillate with wit or elicit sardonic smiles with their devastating satire.

Paronean's comedies mark the earliest stages of the genre in modern Armenian literature. His first experiment seems to have been *Erku tērov tzaṙay mě* (A servant of two masters), a comedy with a very simple plot, inspired by the second and third acts of Goldoni's work of the same title. His next comedy was a musical (in the European sense) called *Atamnaboyžn arewelean* (The oriental dentist), and it bears much brighter marks of his comical genius. It ridicules quacks as well as the predictable consequences of incompatible marriages. *Šołokʻorťě* (The flatterer), lacking a concluding scene, was later completed by Eruand Ōtean (q.v.). The structure of this comedy and some of its protagonists echo Molière's *L'Avare* and also reflect Paronean's continuing search for his own comic characters. This he accomplished some fifteen years later with his best comedy, *Pałtasar Ałbar* (Uncle Balthazar).

Pałtasar Ałbar is a most, if not the most, popular play in the Armenian comic repertoire. Not surprisingly, Balthazar has been interpreted both as a stupid wealthy man, who is made a laughingstock, and as a simple honest person worthy of sympathy. The former is the result of the considerable resemblances this work bears to Molière's *Georges Dandin* and is typical of the Western Armenian theatrical tradition; the latter is a tendency one observes among the Eastern Armenians, which, ideological changes and pursuits notwithstanding, has found expression in the acting of such celebrated Soviet Armenian actors as Hrachya Nersisyan (1895–1961) and Mher Mkrtchyan (1930–93). Nersisyan accentuated the tragic aspects of this character, and Mkrtchyan stressed the comical ones. Balthazar is decidedly not a replica of Georges Dandin; nor is he, to be sure, a tragic figure. He is a victim of many a circumstance and a comical hero derided for many a reason, despite Paronean's express aim to lampoon the Armenian Judicial Council for its incompetent handling of divorce. The whole work is an enduring tribute to Paronean's vibrant wit, so brilliant that it alone sustains the third act, despite its insignificant relevance to the plot.

Paronean was the first to introduce satirical biography, and the laurel for the first satirical novel goes to him, too. There can be little doubt that Molière's *Les Fâcheux* prompted the form of Paronean's *The Most Honourable Beggars* (*Metzapatiw muratskanner*). Both works are collections of portraits, but their similarity ends there. Paronean wrote the novel to illustrate the misery of the men of letters and the cruel indifference of the wealthy to literature. No sooner does Abisołom Ała, the central figure of the novel, arrive in Istanbul from Trebizond in search of a wife, than the "intellectuals" stand in a long queue to pay him their respect and pilfer money from him. Most of the characters disappear after making a memorable appearance. Paronean had sympathy but no kind words for most of the intellectuals, particularly the poet, whose portrait, along with the numerous excursuses Paronean makes in the novel, reveal many aspects of Paronean's literary views. No less well-liked than Uncle Balthazar, the text of *The Most Honourable Beggars* has been tampered with in Soviet theaters in Moscow and Erevan for political purposes. Both the Eastern and Western Armenians have converted this work of rich dialogues into an ever-popular comedy.

A greater sense of urgency and an unrestrained invective characterize most of Paronean's works written in the 1880s. *Ptoyt mě Pōlsoy ťałerun mēj* (A walk in the quarters of Constantinople) is a detailed description of thirty-four city districts, touching nearly upon all social, cultural, and economic realities of the Armenian community. *Tzitzał* (Laughter), it has been suggested, was conceived under the influence of Casti's *Gli Animali Parlanti,* but the two works have nothing in common besides animal characters. *Tzitzał* is a collection of fables tackling social and moral issues against an exclusively Armenian background. *Aḥtabanuťiwn baroyakan* (Moral pathology) is an incomplete portrayal of Hypoptos (suspicious), Stenokardos ("narrow-hearted," impatient) and Philargyros (avaricious). Paronean's *Ḥōsaktsuťiwnkʻ meřelots* (Dialogues of the dead) appeared after he had translated parts of Lucian's work. He drew on the Greek author's work only for the form of his allegorical work. Personified here are virtues such as Compassion, Truthfulness, Charity, and Merit who have assembled in the World of the Dead to analyze aspects of moral decline that resulted in their banishment from the World of the Living. *Kʻałakʻavaruťean vnasnerě* (The disadvantages of courtesy) sparkles with Paronean's wit and shows in uproarious dialogues the inconveniences a polite person suffers for the impoliteness of others. Paronean also published a periodical, *Tiyatro* (1874–75), in Ottoman Turkish, treating mainly issues of social nature pertinent to the Ottoman public at large.

Almost simultaneously with Raffi (q.v.), **TZERENTS** (1822–88) inaugurated the genre of the historical novel. Armenian history had captured his imagination at St. Lazarus, where the Mekhitarist monk and playwright Petros Minasean (1799–1867) taught him history. If Minasean instilled in him a love for Armenian history, what he saw in Constantinople in large measure gave shape to his interpretation of that experience. Particularly in the 1850s and the 1860s, tension, to put it mildly, ran high between the Armenian Apostolic community on the one hand and the Armenian Catholics and Armenian Protestants on the other. The former two were also rent apart by internal strife. The Catholics were divided into two camps: a Latinizing faction that called for direct control by the Holy See, and a more "nationalistic" faction that demanded a say in running the affairs of the community. This is often referred to by historians as the "haka-Hasunean," i.e., anti-Hasunist, movement (after Cardinal Anton Hasunean, or Hasun, 1809–84). Tzerents was a Catholic and he soon found himself heading the anti-Hasunist faction. So he was well-positioned to observe the ravages of denominational disunity. Unity became an agonizing concern and an elusive dream–a dream that he shared with an intimate friend, Mkrtich Pēšiktʻašlean (q.v.).

Tzerents wrote three historical novels. The first, *Tʻoros Lewoni* (Toros [son] of Lewon), appeared in 1877. It recounts the restoration and expansion in the mid-twelfth century of Armenian political power in Cilicia by Tʻoros II, Ṙubinean, son of Lewon I. The second, *Erkunkʻ T. daru* (Ninth century travail), focuses on the anti-Arab rebellion in Armenia proper in the middle of the ninth century, one of the leaders of which was Yovnan from Ḥoytʻ to the south of Muš, who was beheaded for declining apostasy (cf. Tʻovmay Artzruni, *Patmutʻiwn Tann Artzruneats = History of the House of the Artsrunikʻ,* iii, 11, translated into English by R. W. Thomson). The third novel is titled *Tʻēodoros Ṙštuni,* so named after the commander-in-chief of the Armenian Army and marzpan ("viceroy") of Armenia (approximately 630s–54). The country is threatened by Byzantium and the Arabs, and the Armenian nobility, divided by conflicting political orientations and interests, is indecisive amid the uncertainty. Tʻēodoros Ṙštuni's efforts to forge unity ultimately bear no fruit.

The episodes and protagonists Tzerents lifted from critical periods in Armenian history gave much food for thought to his contemporaries. The vital importance he attached to strong and dedicated leaders, his fierce denunciation of centrifugal forces, and above all, the emphasis he laid on national unity–a concern that runs almost like an ostinato throughout his work–resonated with the patriotic fervor and political expectations of the time, making his novels (*Erkunkʻ,* in particular) very popular. Despite this, his work is flawed. His Armenian heroes distinguish themselves by extraordinary feats of prowess, but some of them are barely distinguishable from one another. Elements of *deus ex machina* appear here and there, as does artless propaganda in his last book. Still, the novels are interesting, reasonably well-built, and are written with verve in a tidy modern Armenian; they progress at a good pace and make for enjoyable reading.

SRBUHI TIWSAB (c1841–1901) embraced the cause of emancipation of women. Educated in a French school, she reclaimed her national roots under the tutelage of Mkrtich Pēšiktʻašlean (q.v.), her tutor in Armenian language and literature. Her mother was active in the fields of education and charity and in some ways left her imprint on her views. But the impetus for the cause and some of the themes she chose seems to have come mainly from George Sand. She launched her career with a few poems in the 1860s (including one dedicated to Arsēn Bagratuni and another to Mkrtich Pēšiktʻašlean, q.q.v.), only to realize quickly that she was not made to be a poet. After a long silence (during which she attended to her family), her work appeared again in the early 1880s in the periodical press, flashing signals of the tone and scope of her novels to come. Indeed, she soon wrote three books declaiming against social prejudice that reduced women to "serfs" or to objects "owned" by their spouses.

Mayta, a romantic epistolary novel, outlines the plight of a helpless widow. Totally dependent on her husband before his death, Mayta is now kept in fetters in an unequal and intolerant society and is unable to have a life of her own. She corresponds with Sira, an advocate of full freedom for women and essentially a mouthpiece of Tiwsab. The novel polarized the Armenian intellectuals. Some authors unequivocally supported Tiwsab, others (e.g., Grigor Zōhrap, q.v.) questioned the social and moral premise of the novel, and still others (e.g., Yakob Paronean, q.v.) criticized its form and style. Pointing to elements of *deus ex machina,* for instance, when Mayta is rescued *in extremis* by a total stranger, Paronean argued that the plot was unconvincing. As the debate lingered on, Tiwsab published her second novel, *Siranoyš,* casting the character of yet another victim deprived of free choice, love, and identity. She too, like Mayta before her, is unable to break through the barriers of convention and meets a tragic end. Not so Arakʻsia, the heroine of Tiwsab's third and last novel, *Arakʻsia kam varžuhi*; she is lucky enough to marry the man she loves. Despite some serious flaws in both form and content, Tiwsab's romantic vision of women was the spirited expression of a genuine concern that Armenian writers could no longer ignore.

MKRTICH ḤRIMEAN (1820–1907), affectionately recognized as "Hayrik" (Armenian for "father," with the endearing dimunitive "ik") was a luminous religious and political figure throughout the second half of the nineteenth and early twentieth centuries. But he has been given a spot in this introduction for his literary effort, which in the history of Armenian literature is distinguished on two accounts. He was among the earliest writers to turn his attention to the soil of Western Armenia proper, rather than to the communities in the Armenian Dispersion. Thus, he paved the way for a generation of authors who mirrored life in the homeland (Sruandzteants, Tʻlkatintsi, Ṙ. Zardarean, q.q.v., and others).

Of his two long poems in Classical Armenian, *Hrawirak araratean* tells of the land of Ararat, and his *Hrawirak erkrin aweteats* tells of the Holy Places. He lamented the deliberate burning of the Armenian section of Van in *Vangoyž,* and the anti-Armenian atrocities in the 1877–78 Russo-Ottoman War in his *Haygoyž. Draḥti ěntanikʻ* (A family of paradise) reflects his concerns for the family. *Sirakʻ ew Samuēl* offers words of wisdom for the young on a wide range of topics. His *Papik ew tʻoṙnik* (Grandfather and grandchild) speaks with profound love of land and husbandry and of the interdependence of man and land (and homeland). In a sentimental and romantic frame of mind he cast himself as the continuator of Movsēs Ḥorenatsi's lament in his *Ołbatsoł Ḥorenatsin* (The mourning Ḥorenatsi) and promoted peace and prosperity for all nations, big and small, in his *Tʻagaworats žołov* (A meeting of kings).

GAREGIN SRUANDZTEANTS (1840–92) is the author of a number of poems and two historical plays, all of which are insignificant except for the poem dedicated to the "Martyrs of Awarayr," the Vardanankʻ (beginning "Tʻē hayreneats psakadir . . ."). But his efforts to attract the attention of observers, literary and otherwise, to the realities of life in the Armenian provinces of the Ottoman Empire, and perhaps more importantly, his boundless diligence in collecting and introducing Armenian folklore materials, have been of inestimable value. In a span of ten years (1874–84), he published five collections containing topographical, ethnographic, and statistical information, as well as folk tales, songs, riddles, customs, excerpts from manuscripts, colophons, and other such material that has had a noteworthy impact on the course of Armenian literature. There followed a generation of Armenian writers who wrote from life in Armenia proper, rather than life in big cities to the west (e.g., Constantinople) or north (e.g., Tiflis) of the country, and writers such as Tʻumanean and Ałayean (q.q.v.) wrote adaptations of many of the folk tales he published. The first and one of the best versions of the oral Armenian epic tale, *Sasuntsi Dawitʻ kam Mheri duṙ* (David of Sasun), recited in the dialect of Muš, was published by Sruandzteants in 1874.

ARPʻIAR ARPʻIAREAN (1851–1908) owes his popularity as much to his oeuvre as to his literary and cultural activities. He has come to symbolize Armenian realism as both the mentor of the generation of realist writers and as one of the earliest authors to write in a realist vein. Initially, the forum was the daily *Arewelkʻ* (East or Orient) founded in 1884, and the new prose found expression predominantly in the new genre of the short story, called *noravēp,* the equivalent of nineteenth-century French *nouvelle* or *conte* (Flaubert, Maupassant), or in novels appearing in *Arewelkʻ,* and later in *Masis* and *Hayrenikʻ* under Arpʻiarean's editorship and intellectual leadership. His image of a writer was that of a clairvoyant who faced reality in all its ugly and painful aspects, met the needs of society and the challenges of change and progress, and put literature to practical and aesthetic use. He regarded language as a means rather than an end and was, not surprisingly, unequivocally in favor of Modern Armenian.

Compulsive and communicative, Arpʻiarean wielded public influence with passion and compassion, boldly raising issues of common interest in public forums. His favorite form was the journalistic *chronique* (the Armenian form being "kʻronik"), which he developed into an effective vehicle for social and political criticism and to extend bridges between the Eastern and Western Armenians, their literatures, concerns, and aspirations. A genuine warmth, a consuming interest in all aspects of life, and a spare, unadorned style radiating with subtle irony account for the charm of his *chroniques* (especially his "Ōruan keankʻě," a sort of "daily life," or "goings-on in a day," which have yet to be collected in a single volume).

His short stories are of uneven quality. Although the romantic streak, plainly visible in his early work (e.g., *Erazi mě gině,* The price of a dream), diminishes considerably, it never quite vanishes. He wrote from life, mainly from that of the urban middle and poor classes, highlighting the consequences of economic hardship, moral degeneration, old customs (e.g., pre-arranged marriages), snobbish class-consciousness, and the vain aping of European mores that struck at the very roots of the family. His stories usually end on an unhappy note, but happy endings are by no means uncommon. James Etmekjian, in his *The French Influence on the Western Armenian Renaissance,* noted a few common traits in both Daudet and Arpʻiarean.

One of Arpʻiarean's better stories is *Oski aprjan* (Golden bracelet), which is a recast version of his earlier short story, *Ḥndamolik ałjikě* (The gleeful gal), and which in a number of ways typifies his concerns. Armik, an orphan adopted by Łukas, is to marry the unemployed Artʻakʻi, who hopes to start his own business with Armik's dowry, consisting of a number of railway company shares. But Łukas is soon laid off, and he is forced to sell the shares to feed his family. Artʻakʻi annuls his engagement to Armik, who becomes heartbroken, succumbs to illness, and dies.

Karmir žamuts (The crimson offertory) is Arpʻiarean's best short novel. It illustrates the clash of two opposing philosophies held by two strong personalities: Hayrapet Efendi and Tēr Yusik, a priest "from Armenia" (i.e., the Armenian provinces). Hayrapet, the acknowledged leader of the Armenians of his quarter in Istanbul, is extremely careful not to provoke suspicion or reprisals on the part of the police chief. The priest, who has more faith in Jehovah than Christ, believes in and has devoted himself to organizing self-defense. This was a grave dilemma that haunted all Armenians from the 1890s to 1915. In a crisp and elegant style, Arpʻiarean, in this absorbing narrative, delves deep into the mentality of both protagonists who, mindful of the deadly threats looming overhead, develop two different strategies for survival. Through Arpʻiarean's detailed analysis, Hayrapet acquires an imposing and yet sympathetic presence. What endears Tēr Yusik to the reader is the calm, matter-of-fact approach of a man of strong convictions facing matters of life and death, and the significance of the mystery shrouding the sketchy details of his life and activities. He comes through as the personification of something larger than his self: his people.

TIGRAN KAMSARAKAN (1866–1941) at the age of twenty-two rose quickly to fame with his novel *Varžapetin ałjikě* (The teacher's daughter). Referring to this work, he once revealed that it was only after reading Daudet's *Fromont jeune et Risler aîné* and *Jack* that he was tempted to write his artistically "weak, naive," but "so very spontaneous" novel. The work generated a good deal of controversy. Kamsarakan's comrades-in-arms, the realists, hastened to his assistance, praising it and defending him against his detractors. Judging the novel now from a chronologically and ideologically safe distance, it is very difficult fully to justify Kamsarakan's modesty. True, the plot is simple, and there are certain flaws to the structure. But the story is true to life, so very real and typical of the period, that the flaws are nearly indistinguishable in the flow of the narrative, which Kamsarakan ably darkens and deepens, as his authentic characters, drawn with moving affection, bring alive the Armenian community of Constantinople of the 1880s.

The novel is a profoundly touching story of a sort of mésalliance. The characters are inextricably indigenous to the variegated and faithfully encompassed setting, and Astłik, the angelic heroine, meets an inescapable though predictable end. This is why the novel, despite certain shortcomings, romantic strains, and a few instances of mawkishness, was hailed as a first-rate expression of the nascent realist tradition. Although anticipated by many novels, *Varžapetin ałjikě* was head and shoulders above them all, and it challenged Armenian novelists to new standards of excellence.

Kamsarakan's tendency, not so clearly perceptible at this stage, to ponder over human bondage in the form of general contemplation, rather than in specific or localized expression through plot and characters, emerged as a preponderant feature of his short novels. *Yarō, Hovkul,* and *Ěnkuzin kołově* (The walnut basket) written in a refined style free from Classical Armenian forms, illustrate the point and stand out as some of the best short novels to mark the concluding part of his literary career. During the Armenian massacres of the mid-1890s, like so many of his colleagues, he fled Constantinople, never to return. He contributed to *Masis* and *Arewelkʻ* from abroad, and in 1910 he wrote a drama jointly with Mikʻayēl Kiwrčean (q.v.), *Pʻrkankʻ* (Ransom), about a marriage of convenience that does not materialize when the dowry is lost. Regrettably, to his death almost three decades later, Kamsarakan abandoned literature for business.

GRIGOR ZŌHRAP (1861–1915), acclaimed as the prince of *noravēp* by Aršak Chōpanean (q.v.), sought insight into the unusual and unexplored realms of human behavior, especially that of women. He began his literary career as a polemicist, composed some poetry, launched his notorious attack on Srbuhi Tiwsab's views of women's emancipation, and wrote one of the earliest novels. But it is with his shorter novels and stories that he made a permanent name for himself. Allied with his literary fame was a bright public side to this man of shining intellect, tempestuous emotions, and impeccable appearance and manners, which put him in the limelight as one of the foremost, if not the leading, writers and public figures from the early 1890s onward. He practiced and taught law, and was an articulate and outspoken member of the Ottoman Parliament and the Armenian National Assembly. He was active in promoting the Armenian Question, particularly immediately before World War I. Shortly after hundreds of Armenian intellectuals had been rounded up on 24 April 1915, Zōhrap too, despite his close connections to some of the highest ranking members of the Young Turk clique, was arrested, shipped to the interior, and put to death in a most brutal fashion somewhere between Diyarbekir and Urfa. (One prominent Young Turk, Halil Menteşe, claimed to have attempted to arrange for Zōhrap's return from the interior, while another, Sait Halim, spoke of his protest, cf. *Harp kabinelerinin isticvabı* [The interrogation or rather "hearings" of the wartime cabinets], Istanbul, 1933, 214–16, 295–96).

His earliest poems are of no memorable merit, and the few he wrote much later had an almost lubricious touch to them. *Anhetatsatz serund mě* (A vanished generation), his first and last novel (since *Nardik* remained incomplete), reckoned to be the first novel in a realist vein, was well received. It tackles the issue of unalloyed love as the foundation of happy marriages. The theme was not new, but Zōhrap's approach was. Although he himself qualified it as an unsuccessful experiment, a mixed bag of romantic and realist sensibilities, it was nonetheless unmistakably a very promising beginning. His bright talent, though, would blossom in his short novels, *noravēps,* three dozen or so in number. When Srbuhi Tiwsab (q.v.) published her *Mayta* and raised the question of women's emancipation, Zōhrap, then in his early twenties, countered the novel with a vitriolic attack denying women equality. He believed that the happiness promised by a woman was nothing but an illusion women exploited to gain power. Furthermore, he believed that women were a source of misery and misfortune in social life. Echoes of this negative attitude are audible in some of his prose. In a number of his *noravēps,* Zōhrap deliberately sought out anomalous positions and exceptional, or rather untypical, characters, which shocked some of his readers, especially those with deep-seated convictions who were impervious to change, inquiry into the unexplored, and taboos. His sinewy style–simple, direct, precise, dispassionate, and often laced with irony–was yet another element contributing to such rejection. Moreover, Zōhrap's work generally exhibits a disdain for the conventional, a sense of boredom on the part of a man for whom life seems to have no more veiled secrets, and an anxious search for the more fulfilling aspects of existence. But that Zōhrap conceded no social role to women, and that he saw their beauty as their greatest charm is an undeniable fact. Yet it is also true that in most of his work, women, whether good or wicked, weak or strong, fleshly or decent, are of pivotal importance and are paradoxically depicted with profound sympathy.

Many other themes attracted Zōhrap's attention: the Armenian establishment (i.e., the Patriarchate and the rich), the victims of economic hardship, the plight of immigrants from the provinces, poverty, the shift in moral standards, religion, feigned piety, and so on. All this he wove into an economical prose that delved into the human soul in a limpid and elegant Modern Western Armenian, with little or no attention to context and plot. He was intimately versed in French culture, which had a formative and lasting impression on his thought. In forging the Armenian tradition of *noravēp*, Zōhrap creatively assimilated the accomplishments of A. Arpʻiarean (q.v.), Maupassant, and to a lesser degree, those of Zola and Daudet.

Ējer ułewori mě oragrēn (Pages [or Excerpts] from the diary of a traveler) is an intellectual annotation to his own world view, occasioned by his travels in Germany and France. A keen power of observation, disarming wit and reason, and a noteworthy ability to sketch characters in a few broad strokes distinguish his collection of seventeen portraits of contemporary or newly deceased public figures, titled *Tzanōtʻ dēmkʻer* (Familiar names). Still scattered in the periodical press are most of his literary reviews and articles of diverse nature, bursting with energy and informed by a critical spirit, in support of the cause of progress and public interest.

LEWON BAŠALEAN (1868–1943) was recruited into journalism early. Together with A. Arpʻiarean (q.v.), but somewhat overshadowed by him, he was the moving spirit behind *Arewelkʻ, Masis, Hayrenikʻ,* and *Nor keankʻ,* the first three of which pioneered and propagated the realist movement. In his articles and *chroniques,* he covered with lucidity and intensity the whole gamut of topical issues, making ceaseless efforts to rid his diction of Classical Armenian forms. For the 1880s witnessed a revival of sorts in the usage of Classical elements and phrases with ideological (i.e., conservative), rather than linguistic, undertones. These writings form an essential part of his literary heritage and embody, as do his short stories and *noravēps,* his realist credo of literature as a mirror of human life.

There is, though, a glowing, romantic touch to some of his short, uncomplicated stories, lit up by his talent in bright but brief emissions. Here he is at his best, writing with precision and grace. He was among the earliest authors to focus almost exclusively on working-class and poor people, their trials and tribulations and lifestyle, in the closing decades of the nineteenth century. A call for spiritual fortitude permeates his work, of which the following comprise some of the best aspects of his literary effort: "Nor zgestě," "Łalatʻioy Ṙestʻě," "Kałand," "Tsełin dzayně," "Siwzēni varpetě," "Ays ē ełer," and "Hmayatʻapʻě." He engaged in business in the last forty years of his life, completely disengaging himself from literature.

EŁIA TĒMIRČIPAŠEAN (1851–1908) was a popular and gifted writer. He was frail and eccentric; the death of his father, his younger brother, and particularly his mother precipitated his mental derangement, and clear symptoms of insanity appeared by 1900. A somewhat schizoid recluse, Tēmirčipašean maintained that Goethe's *Die Leiden des jungen Werthers* was one of the greatest influences of his life as was Positivism (Auguste Comte, Herbert Spencer). Above all, however, Emile Littré was a demigod for him. He devoted his energy entirely to literature and literary journalism. Many of his works are still scattered in the periodical press.

"Ełia," as he was affectionately referred to by his contemporaries, wrote both verse and prose (short stories, literary criticism, articles, essays, diaries, etc). His poems (personal anguish, death, love, nature, philosophical contemplation) are of a descriptive-analytical and often cerebral nature and have been written with little imagery, but with imagination and in a distinct style. Pain and occasional elation contrast sharply, and many elements of Symbolism, though not musicality, are found in his subjective poetry. His prose, similarly subjective and often egocentric, suffers from technical flaws; it has no characterization, construction, reasonable plot, or denouement. Yet it is highly charged with emotion and permeated by his dreams and visions, his thoughts and everchanging mood, and a romantic sentimentalism. His language is heavily overburdened by Classical Armenian, and maudlin feelings and expressions often mar his still highly regarded oeuvre, parts of which have had an enduring appeal.

Eastern Armenian Literature

MESROP T'AŁIADEAN (1803–1858), a native of Erevan, spent most of his life in Calcutta, India. Endowed with an inquisitive mind, an adventuresome disposition, and a yearning for learning, his desire to study in Paris never materialized. Instead, he satisfied his intellectual curiosity at the Bishop's College in Calcutta, with financial and moral support from Bishop Reginald Hebert (1773–1833). The college also had an Armenian press, where for a while T'ałiadean worked as a compositor. Before making India his second home, T'ałiadean had studied at Ējmiatzin at the feet of Pōłos *vardapet* Łaradałtsi (Nersisean) and had toured his fatherland extensively on two occasions. The deep affinity he felt with the land of his ancestors moved his pen, and his intellectual contacts with non-Armenians inspired his imagination.

In his travels and sojourns abroad, T'ałiadean came into daily contact with the British in India and Iran and American missionaries in Constantinople. He was always suspected of pro-Protestant tendencies, and this caused him a great deal of inconvenience, especially in Constantinople, where at the time of his visit in the late 1830s the relations between the Armenians and the small community of Protestant Armenians were extremely inimical. But his most fruitful years were spent in Calcutta. From 1845 to 1848, he published the periodical *Azgasēr,* which ceased with the death of his friend, who was the publication's benefactor. T'ałiadean then launched another periodical, *Azgasēr araratean* (1848–52). He also set up a school for girls in Calcutta. Besides his journalistic activities, he was also engaged in printing some of his own work and the work of other Armenian and non-Armenian authors.

T'ałiadean's thoughts and activities were geared towards enlightenment. Although he spared no unworthy cleric, he was a Christian and a deacon of the Armenian Church and regularly read scripture. He was obedient to God and ruler. He fought superstition, promoted enlightenment, and believed that a heightened sense of duty and responsibility would result in prosperity for society with the family as its basic cell. He was full of envy of educated foreigners and urged his fellow countrymen to emulate them. Education, learning, and "love and unity" were the keys to political and economic advancement. He had a special fascination with English literature. He translated and published his mentor's (Reginald Hebert) "Palestine" in Armenian, along with a good many pieces by Shakespeare, Milton, John Locke, Alexander Pope, and Robert Burns. Other translations and publications by him included a considerable amount of Chesterfield's "Letters" to his son Philip Stanhope, many works by Byron (his favorite poet), and Legh Richmond's *The Young Cottager* (published posthumously in *Diwan,* 1979). He also translated from Latin and published Hugo Grotius's *Čšmartutʻiwn kʻristonēakan hawatoy* (*De Veritate Religionis Christianæ*).

Tʻaɫiadean has a history of ancient India; a comprehensive history of Persia, with information on the Armenian communities; a selection of fables and anecdotes translated from the Persian; a pamphlet on the education of girls; a booklet on mythology; primers of Armenian and English; a short grammar of Armenian; a pamphlet on the martyrdom of St. Sanduẖt and another against the Roman Catholic Church (*Hreštak azdetsutʻean . . .*); a concise glossary of about two-hundred mostly dialectal words (first published in *Diwan,* 1979); descriptions of his travels in Armenia and Persia; a "diary" (first published in *Diwan,* 1979) of his travel to Armenia (via Dhaka, Calcutta, Ceylon, Bushehr, Shiraz, Isfahan, Teheran, Tabriz, Erevan, and Ējmiatzin); and a number of minor works.

Tʻaɫiadean's novel *Vēp Vardgisi T[eaṙ]n Tuhats* is among the earliest samples of modern Armenian fiction. Vardgēs is known in ancient Armenian history and lore as the husband of the sister of King Eruand I and as the builder of a town he named after himself. In the second century, King Vaɫarš I rebuilt and renamed it Vaɫaršapat (now Ējmiatzin). But Tʻaɫiadean's plot has very little in common with this story, because it is an adaptation with minor changes of Heinrich Zschokke's *Abällino, der grosse Bandit,* which Monk Lewis had translated into English (*Abællino, The Bravo of Venice*). Tʻaɫiadean is illustrating loyalty to king, national unity, and personal integrity in his work. The latter theme, along with persistence, industry, and self-reliance are the leitmotifs of his other novel, *Vēp Varsenkan,* which is fashioned after a tale common in Middle Eastern traditions. Both novels exhibit a good deal of action and suspense while propagating the author's purposes.

Tʻaɫiadean's adaptations and translations illustrate some of the ways in which the earliest experiments in novel writing were conducted in the history of Armenian letters. He was familiar with the work of British novelists and was fond of Gothic novels. One may venture to suggest that he was familiar with M. G. Lewis's own work, too. His novels speak to this, and from his introduction to *Vēp Varsenkan,* it is obvious that he wittingly strove to combine entertainment with practical purposes. His effort to cultivate a love for reading among the Armenians was a challenge for many contemporary and subsequent writers.

The epigrams he wrote are witty, and his subtle and warm poetry reflects trends of romanticism. Love and patriotism are central themes to him, and religious motifs are not found in his work. Most of his long poems are incomplete. The best, perhaps, is *Sōs ew Sondipi,* in which the central figures' love transcends national and ethnic boundaries, and healthy patriotism promotes harmony. Tʻaḷiadean's passage from classicism to romanticism is best illustrated in this poem written in Classical Armenian, structured in accordance with the norms of Classical poems, and has gods among its heroes. It also has an adventuresome plot with action and suspense; it uses short, lyrical lines; and it probes the individual's inner life.

ḤACHATUR ABOVEAN (c1809–48) has been placed on a pedestal as the father of modern Armenian literature. Although there is much to be said for this posthumous veneration, many have questioned the wisdom of such zealous ranking in literature and other fields of culture. This is not an uncommon practice, but it was carried to extremes, especially during the Soviet years, leaving many worthy contemporaries in the shadow of the chosen "fathers" or "masters." At the very least, such rigid adoration easily turned into a sort of cult and precluded objective evaluation and revisionism. Abovean, an original, prolific, and multifarious writer, did indeed usher in a new era in Eastern Armenian literature. But it is not possible to speak of any palpable influence on his part on Western Armenian literature, especially in its formative stages. With much of his work (books, essays, articles, and collections of a historical, educational, linguistic, ethnographic, and folkloric nature) published decades after his death, its implied impact remains open to question. His *chef d'œuvre, Vērkʻ Hayastani* (Wounds of Armenia), alone, also published posthumously in 1858, is good enough to recognize him as the founder of modern Eastern Armenian literature.

Abovean launched his literary career by writing verse in Classical Armenian. Patriotism, love, nature as well as meditative themes preoccupied him initially. He jettisoned the traditions of classicism and gradually wrote in a romantic mood, especially during his years at Dorpat (Tartu, Estonia). There his exposure to European, especially German, culture and literature came to inform his poetry and dramatically exposed the appalling backwardness that prevailed in his fatherland. The duality in his work in these same years was a reflection of his encounter with the West, as he simultaneously composed poetry akin to that of Armenian minstrels. His satirical bent found its best expression in "Hazarpʻešen" (a sort of wine pitcher), in which he criticized the Russian bureaucracy. *Parap vaḥti ḥałalikʻ* ("Pastime," or "Entertainment for spare time") he reportedly adapted from notes he took in public gatherings. It is a collection of fables in verse, written in a lucid style with many dialogues that castigate moral degeneration, vice, injustice, and the corrupting power of money. Classical Armenian gradually gave way to Modern Armenian, well stocked with dialect and slang, which eventually emerged as the literary standard for the Eastern Armenians.

His use of the spoken dialect, especially in his Wounds of Armenia, has been one of the predominant factors Armenian critics have cited to justify his exalted position. What emboldened Abovean to challenge tradition was his desire to reach "hundreds of thousands" of people, as he put it in his preface to the novel. But two points must be emphasized here: he was not the first author to use Modern Armenian; and like many of those who supported the modern vernacular, he looked upon it as a temporary means or as a stage of gradual transition to Classical Armenian. But his immediate concern—to bring knowledge to the masses—totally submerged this distant and somewhat impractical expectation.

Abovean considered the vernacular and faith as the very pillars of the Armenian ethos. The Wounds of Armenia is, among other things, a hymn to the Armenian language, whose loss, Abovean averred, would be tantamount to losing national identity. His concern for the fate of his people was inextricably intertwined with that for the mother tongue. But there were other factors in addition, concepts and aspirations that could be conveyed only through this cherished national idiom.

Vērkʻ Hayastani is a heart-to-heart dialogue between the author and his people. Abovean, who unlike many of his colleagues was born and spent most of his life in what was left of Armenia, fully understood and shared the mentality of his people and grasped all too well the consequences of ignorance and corruption within the ranks of Armenian priesthood. The political plight of his fellow countrymen under the Persian khans was profoundly painful to him. And the survival of his nation against overwhelming odds throughout its history was a delightful source of pride and respect for Abovean. All this inspired him to write a novel that extolled patriotism, loudly justified self-defense, castigated ignorance and illiteracy, and called upon his fellow countrymen to break away from their ignoble lassitude to restore Armenian statehood.

Vērkʿ Hayastani, one of the earliest novels in Armenian literature, has a simple plot. Its idealized central hero, Ałasi, the first rebel in modern Armenian literature, fights and dies for the liberation of his country. In this case it was the annexation of the Khanate of Erevan by Russia in 1828, the background against which the novel is set. This was the deliverance from Persia that many Armenians, Abovean among them, had been waiting for with great anticipation. So excessively zealous is Abovean's praise for Russia that one might be tempted to mistake his gratitude for undignified cringing. The fact is that Abovean was already disillusioned with Russian policy in Armenia when he wrote the novel in the early 1840s. In 1836 the Russians had instituted the *Polozhenie,* which imposed severe restrictions on the Church of Armenia. In 1840 they had abolished the *Armianskaia Oblast'* (Armenian Region) as an administrative unit and were now interested in an Armenia without Armenians. Was Abovean being faithful to his intoxicated sentiments some fifteen years earlier? Probably. He would most likely have moderated his tone had he written the novel a year or two before his disappearance, when his attitude toward Russia had turned openly and bitterly hostile. He had envisaged the Russian presence in Armenia as the first step towards the revival of Armenian statehood under the wing of the northern power. By then, that vision must have vanished into thin air.

Despite its flaws, such as didactic digressions and protracted dialogues and descriptions, the novel's sustained intensity, animated style, colorful imagery, patriotism, and overwhelming outpouring of sincere emotions have made it a highly popular novel that has had considerable impact. Historically speaking, it tackles a burning issue, that of the future of his people, and depicts rebellion against foreign domination in sharp contrast to Christian Armenian traditions of pacifism and passivity. It captures a momentous period in Armenian history; true, one imperialist was being replaced with another, but Russian annexation proved beneficial in the long run in that, unlike their brethren in the Ottoman Empire, the Eastern Armenians were physically safe. Understandably, then, much was made of Abovean's political orientation later in Soviet Armenia, and his disappearance added a touch of mystery to an unfortunate life given to lofty ideals. Nonetheless, his retrospective aggrandizement, well-deserved in many respects, was often unnecessarily tainted with ideological motivation. Wounds of Armenia, his cri du cœur, is a gem in the Armenian literary tradition with or without such idolization.

MIKʿAYĒL NALBANDEAN (1829–66) was an impassioned author and a propagandist of reform and renewal. His travels widened his horizon, and his entanglement in national and political affairs led to conflicts with local Armenian dignitaries and religious authorities and eventually with the czarist government. He met some of the leading publicists of the day abroad, including Stepʻan Oskanean (1825–1901), the editor of the biweekly *Arewmutkʻ* (Paris), and Yarutʻiwn Sěvačean (1831–74), the founder and editor of *Mełu* (Constantinople). He also came in close contact with the so-called "London Propagandists," notably Alexander Herzen and Nikolay Ogaryov, and with Mikhail Bakunin and Ivan Sergeyevich Turgenev. He was arrested in his birthplace in 1862 and found guilty of association with the "Propagandists," of disseminating their literature in Russia, and of inciting anti-government sentiments among the Armenians. After his initial internment in St. Petersburg, he was exiled to Kamyshin in the region of Saratov, where he died within months of his arrival.

Nalbandean attracted attention as an outspoken publicist and polemicist whose lively and bold style, at times crude and arrogant, was almost invariably laced with irony or sardonic in tone. Early on, he collaborated with Stepʻanos Nazarean (1812–79), a bright intellectual and founder of a new and influential periodical, *Hiwsisapʻayl* ("the northern lights," aurora borealis, 1858–62, 1864), in which Nalbandean published some of his prose. In both his literary and journalistic pieces, Nalbandean emerges as an unrelenting champion of freedom and equality; a fearless opponent of despotism, imperialism, and serfdom; an interpreter of human life from materialistic positions; a tireless propagandist of enlightenment, science, and scientific approach; a believer in agriculture as the key to prosperity and independence; uncompromisingly anti-clerical; and a zealous supporter of Modern Armenian. A large body of literature and evidence, amassed by Soviet Armenian critics, establishes him as a revolutionary democrat.

His writings are not extensive in number or volume. His short novel *Minin hōskʻ miwsin harsn* (i.e., a bride promised to one but given to another) negates superstition and promotes enlightenment. *Meṙelahartsuk* (Necromancy) is among the earliest urban novels, but is incomplete; it would likely have dealt with ignorance had it been finished. His popular *Yišatakaran . . .* (something akin to a journal) deals, in a sarcastic and sometimes polemical fashion, with a very wide spectrum of topical issues of a social, political, and cultural nature. His literary views are distilled in his criticism of Perč Pṙōšean's novel, *Sōs ew Varditʻer.* For him literature was a vehicle for reform, a harmonious amalgam of the natural with the creative, brought together with a sound unity and structure and skillful characterization. He called for the creation of a national literature (reflecting the realities of a given nation and its concerns and aspirations), good examples of which were Ḥ. Abovean's *Vērkʻ Hayastani* and P. Pṙōšean's *Sōs ew Vardiṫer.* Of his non-literary prose, mention should be made of *Erkragortzuṫiwnĕ orpēs ułił čanaparh* (i.e., Agriculture as the right path, published under the pseudonym Simēōn Manikean), which summarizes his views on economic, social, and political injustice and disparity, on nationalism and nationhood, on Armenian emigration and inter-communal and international relations, and on the 1861 reform in Russia.

Nalbandean has a small number of poems, with the earlier ones in Classical Armenian, fashioned mainly in a patriotic-political, satirical, or reflective mood. He has poems dedicated to Apollo, Mesrop Maštots, and Rousseau, among others. But his poems in praise of liberty and his "Song of the Italian girl" brought him enduring fame and found some imitators. The latter, believed to be an adaptation, was adopted with some textual patch-up as the national anthem ("Mer hayrenikʻ") of the Third Republic of Armenia.

ṘAPʻAYĒL PATKANEAN (1830–92) was a compatriot of Nalbandean who believed, like his confrère, in the utilitarian role of literature. Encouraged by Nikolay Karamzin's views, he chose to use the spoken vernacular for poetic expression; learning from Nikolay Nekrasov he strove to become a "poet-citizen." This descendant of a family with a distinguished tradition in Armenian letters combined teaching with writing–a dual role characteristic of some of the authors of the age, including Ḥ. Abovean, S. Šahaziz, P. Pṙōšean, and Ł. Ałayean (q.q.v.). As part of his literary mission, he sought to bring enlightenment to his fellow countrymen and to ignite their patriotism. He had no time for poetic form or craftsmanship. He felt that it was a time for immediate action on what he perceived as essential needs of a people in distress. Although too many of his poems read like rhymed speeches, his sincere and emotional patriotic appeal resonated with the prevailing mood. Some of his better poems brought him wide public acclaim and propelled him to the forefront of poetry for a number of decades.

Launching the initial phase of his career with a series of merrymaking and drinking songs in the best traditions of the Armenian students at Dorpat (Tartu, Estonia), Patkanean formed a literary coterie in Moscow with two colleagues for the purpose of publishing their own literary works. The group called itself Gamaṙ Kʻaṫipa (a combination of the initial letters of their first names with the vowel *a* inserted between them: *G*ēorg, *M*natsakan, *Ṙ*apʻayēl; and the first two letters of their last names:

*K'A*nanean, *T'I*murean, *PA*tkanean). Patkanean soon assumed the group's name as his pen name, as the overwhelming majority of poems published in the series (in five parts, 1855–57) were written by him. Following this and the appearance of his collection in 1864, there occurred a hiatus in Patkanean's literary career.

But by then he was a well-established name. Two poems in particular met with immediate success and have been among his few enduring pieces. "Arak'si artasuk'ě" (The tears of the river Araxes) is a dialogue between the poet and the river. The river is in an utterly despondent mood in view of the misery and dispersion of its children, and has avowed to remain in mourning until the causes have been removed. Personification and dialogue generate an intimate dynamism; grief and a sense of irretrievable loss, which never quite explode into anger, convey an unspoken yet audible sense of optimism and sustain the appeal of this song. The other poem, titled "Vardan Mamikoneani mahě" (The death of Vardan Mamikonean), owes something to Łewond Ališan (q.v.) and to his poem on Vardan Mamikonean ("Plpuln Awarayri") for its conception. This time it is the moon that narrates Armenian history, down to the Battle of Awarayr that pitched the Armenians against the Persians in 451. One of the more popular parts of this long poem is "Vardan's Song" (Vardani ergě), a call to arms against the treacherous oppressors of Armenia.

Patkanean expressed his contagious patriotic enthusiasm in a number of other poems, attacking clergymen for lulling the faithful into inaction, castigating the apathetic to national concerns, and condemning the formal, impractical aspects of national identity and its detractors. But there is frustration, anger, and embittered sarcasm in the poems he wrote following the Russo-Ottoman War of 1877–78. Often crude in diction, these poems capture the mood of utter disappointment that gripped the Armenians in the wake of the Treaty of San Stefano and the Congress of Berlin. The cause of reform in the Armenian provinces of the Ottoman Empire, whether through direct appeals to the Ottoman government or through European pressure upon the sultan, was now dead. As the maltreatment of the Armenians worsened, Patkanean was among the first to express sympathy for the Western Armenians in the heartland around Muš and Van. Echoing Ḥ. Abovean and M. Nalbandean and paving the way for Raffi (q.q.v.), Patkanean urged his fellow countrymen to resort to self-defense, a trend that gathered rapid momentum. Europe got a piece of his mind too; he denounced it in harsh and contemptuous terms for selfishly abandoning the Western Armenians.

Patkanean's social and patriotic concerns found expression in the verse (*Nor Naḫijewani k'nar*) and prose (mainly short stories from life in his birthplace and a few set in St. Petersburg and Moscow) he wrote in his native dialect of Nor Naḥijewan. One frequently encounters his satirical vein and biting impatience in these writings that deal with dehumanizing social and political injustice, incompetent and corrupt local officials, wicked and greedy merchants, illiterate and incompetent priests motivated by material rather than spiritual ends, and a degenerate youth.

A junior contemporary of Patkanean and Nalbandean, **SMBAT ŠAHAZIZ** (1840–1907) was of a more modest talent. His first collection of verse (in Modern and Classical Armenian) touched on historical and patriotic themes, nature, and love. His second collection was markedly better than his first and mirrored his social concerns and patriotic aspirations. The dominant piece in this collection is his long poem "Lewoni viště" (Levon's grief), a distillation of his literary vision, notable for expounding a contemporary theme. It is the story of a young patriot dedicated to the welfare of his homeland. He sets out from Moscow and arrives in Armenia through Nor Naḥijewan and Tiflis. Throughout, the reader hears Lewon's observations regarding superstition and ignorance, intellectual, moral, and religious decline, servility, corrupt leadership, etc. Lewon's fervent wish is to do away with all such evils and brighten the skies of Armenia with enlightenment and progress. Even though the poem concludes without the reader ever seeing Lewon engage in any kind of action to bring about change, and despite its lack of drive and action, passion, and punch, it was very well received and certainly left its mark on its readers. Although Šahaziz ascribed the birth of the poem to the "reformist" atmosphere in Russia of the 1860s, which we have no reason to disbelieve, and despite the fact that he received his intellectual nourishment mainly from Russian writers (Pushkin, Lermontov, Nekrasov, etc.), Byron looms large in the formal aspects of the poem's conception.

Šahaziz the journalist dealt with a variety of topics: from literature to the plight of the Armenians in the Ottoman Empire and from imperialism and China to an evaluation of self-centered European civilization (he once branded it as an intellectual "syphilisation"). In his articles as well as in his romantic poetic output, Šahaziz's style is sluggish and his technique gauche. He saw himself as a servant to the cause of enlightenment and liberty through a literature expressed in simple (simplistic, in fact) language. His poetry did serve its purpose at the time, and together with the work of M. Nalbandean and Ṙ. Patkanean (q.q.v.) it paved the way and set the agenda for the next generation of poets. Very few of his poems are now remembered. Of these "Eraz" (Dream; opening line: "Es lsetsi mi anuš dzayn" = I heard a sweet voice . . .) will most certainly outlast them all and seems destined to remain an all-time favorite.

GABRIĒL SUNDUKEAN (1825–1912) set new, remarkable standards for the Armenian stage. His student years at St. Petersburg must have given him a foretaste of the theater. He knew French, Georgian, Italian, Latin, and Russian (and may have had a passive knowledge of Tatar or what is now called Azeri Turkish, and Persian, since his dissertation at St. Petersburg was on Persian prosody). Some of these languages opened up before him the splendid world of theater. There is at least one note from V. Hugo in response to his letter; he met Dumas *fils* in Paris, and he came to know Alexander Ostrovsky personally in Tiflis. Some striking similarities between the art of Sundukean and Ostrovsky (characters, situations, and the use of colloquial speech) suggest that Ostrovsky may have prompted and inspired Sundukean with some guidance.

Nonetheless, Sundukean created his own theater, a microcosm all his own. With no noteworthy native tradition to draw upon and the emergent Armenian repertoire still largely limited to translations and to plays of a historical, religious, and moral scope, Sundukean turned to contemporary issues afflicting his own community in the cosmopolitan city of Tiflis. He wrote comedies in the sense of French *comedie* and *drame.* He employed the local Armenian dialect, adding touches of authenticity, dynamism, and appeal to his characters, the likes of whom the audience encountered daily in the Armenian quarter of Hawlabar or Sololak(i) in Tiflis. For all this, Armenian critics see in him the first master of realistic theater.

Sketched in *Ḥat̕abala* (Trouble; or, "A can of worms") is his first memorable negative protagonist, Gerasim Yakulich Zambaḥov, a merchant with an uncomely spinster daughter. Zambaḥov, a traditionalist tyrant at home and a cringing wretch before the bureaucracy, is unable to marry off his daughter for all his monetary prowess and scheming. The worship of Mammon, feigned piety, moral degeneration, and the clash of old and new are issues common to this and to most of Sundukean's other plays. In *Ēli mēk zoh* ("Yet another victim"; initial version titled *Maḥlas*), a father unsuccessfully tries to force his son to marry a wealthy girl instead of the woman the son is in love with. This open rebellion against patriarchal authority in violation of long-standing traditions, a clash of "fathers and sons" as other observers put it, aroused a good deal of controversy. The conservatives saw it as an artificial conflict irrelevant to Armenian society and damaging to its fabric and the unity of the family. While such concern may have had some legitimate aspects, what they did not like was what they saw of themselves in the mirror Sundukean held up to them in this and in his other plays.

Sundukean's next work, *Pēpō,* has been acclaimed since its first performance as the crown of his literary labor. Sundukean himself was of like mind. He dictated the work with elation to Gēorg Chmškean (1837–1916), an actor (who played the title role in *Pēpō*'s premiere) and a friend and amanuensis whose counsel he held in high esteem. He also left a description in his will of the statue of Pēpō he hoped would be built in the future. Mutatis mutandis, the theme of this play is similar to that of Sundukean's major comedies. The wealthy merchant Arutʻin Zimzimov, aware that proof has disappeared, willfully denies the debt he owes to Pēpō's family. Following an altercation during which Pēpō humiliates Zimzimov, and just before the former is arrested by police, the promissory note is recovered. Zimzimov is now prepared discreetly to cough up even more than the amount he owes, but Pēpō heads for jail anticipating a public showdown with his famous enemy. Sundukean judiciously left the conflict unresolved, a fact that has added so much to its continuing appeal. Unlike his other comedies, here two powerful adversaries speaking for two very different social groups clash, endowing the play with dynamism, gripping power, and revealing depth. So colorfully real in both speech and behavior are its characters, so deep did Sundukean probe into their minds, that the play conquered the hearts of multi-ethnic audiences in Transcaucasia.

Kʻandatz ōjaḥ ("A shattered family," 1873), the last of this series of four attractive plays on money, marriage, and mores, was followed by a long hiatus. *Amusinner* (Spouses, 1890), Sundukean's first play in the literary standard, focuses on divorce, moral decline, and, as the author confided to a contemporary, on rather dimly delineated political and patriotic aspirations. His last two plays, *Sēr ew azatutʻiwn* (Love and freedom, 1910), which deals with biased divorce rules favoring men, and *Ktakě* (The will, 1912), which depicts a rich merchant bequeathing his wealth to charity and the ensuing conflict among his heirs, are dull and very poor in craftsmanship. The only short story he wrote, *Varinki vecherě* (An evening at Varinka's), is an impressive piece on the misery of the downtrodden. His numerous "maslahatʻ" (a sort of "heart-to-heart talk"), published in the periodical press, tackle mainly topical issues of a social nature. Sundukean had earlier written a number of vaudevilles that were quite popular. But what truly lit up his imagination was a particular category of characters, whose colloquial speech and way of life were masterfully animated in his first four comedies. His *Pēpō* remains one of the best Armenian plays of all time.

PERČ PŘŌŠEAN (1837–1907) profoundly admired and derived inspiration from Ḥ. Abovean (q.v.), but he had neither his master's scope nor his impact. His prose was prolix and often plain. His first novel, *Sōs ew Varditʻer* (proper names), brought him fame and prompted an important critical review by Mikʻayēl Nalbandean (q.v.). This love story revealed his power of observation, his fascination with ethnographic and "national traditions," and an as yet dim awareness of some changes affecting rural Armenia. Only sixteen years later did his second novel appear. Titled *Křuatzałik* ("A bone of contention"; two men competing for the same woman) and mirroring the closing decades of the eighteenth century, it speaks of Persian maltreatment, makes a faint call for self-defense, criticizes local Armenian dignitaries and clergymen, echoes social biases and inequality, and pictures an ideal village reconstructed by traditionalists. Being fond of the traditional lifestyle in the countryside, Přōšean dreaded urban life. He recorded faithfully and regretfully its disintegration under the impact of some evil factors to which he never reconciled himself (Soviet Armenian criticism has seen in him a writer immune to class consciousness), but he hoped that decent, thoughtful, and enlightened men might still salvage the vanishing world of his childhood and dreams.

Three years later, Přōšean penned his masterpiece, *Hatsi ḥndir* ("A matter of bread," i.e., struggle for survival). The novel, qualified as realistic, documents the destruction of traditional lifestyle and changing economic and social values in rural areas due to the penetration of monetary relations and mores. The novel is head and shoulders above all else Přōšean wrote; it reads well and has enriched Armenian literature with a few memorable characters (notably Mikitan Sakʻo). Similar in theme and structure and almost as good was his fourth novel, *Tsetser* (tsets = moth, i.e., "parasites"). His next novel, *Błdē,* also has some merits, such as a certain degree of psychological insight into Błdē's criminal obsession with money. His *Yunon* is a kind of Armenian Robin Hood and in many respects marks a departure from some of his literary patterns. Přōšean has two more novels and numerous short stories. As a respected teacher, he made valuable contributions to the cause of education; as an individual endowed with considerable administrative skills, he lent much support to the Armenian theater.

Few modern Armenian writers can rival the impact and appeal of **RAFFI** (c1835–88). He began with poetry of no particular merit save for one popular poem, "Dzayn tur ov tzovak" (Respond, O, Lake), which is reminiscent of Łewond Ališan's personification of the moon and Řapʻayēl Patkanean's personification of the river Arakʻs. A romantic to the marrow, he moved on to prose and captured his readers' imagination and, arguably, the foremost spot in the genre with some of his historical novels. His numerous short stories and short novels of a social nature are set mainly in Iran (depicting both Armenian and Persian realities) and Tiflis and are a savage attack on the social injustices, predatory landowners and merchants, tyrannical bureaucrats, moral corruption, superstition and ignorance, tradition and submission that account for the sad life of the trampled and dispossessed. Perhaps his best works focusing on such concerns are *Oski akʻałał* (Golden rooster) with its protagonist, a petty bourgeois who is a slave of money and the quintessence of such vices as fetishism and cruel inhumanity, and *Ḥachagołi yišatakaranĕ* (The memoirs of a robber), in which poverty drives men into criminal conduct. In Raffi's view, human behavior is shaped by its milieu; removing or improving bad conditions will transform human character for the better. Hence his firm conviction that enlightenment and education is an all-powerful recipe for social and moral progress. Only such enlightened individuals, collectives, or nations can sue for political justice.

When the Russo-Ottoman War of 1877–78 broke out, the Eastern Armenians expected Russia to wrest Western Armenia from the Ottoman Empire. Though the Russian victory brought bitter disappointment to the public, the war and its aftermath ignited Raffi's imagination. Responding to political situations in a string of historical novels, he formulated his vision of the ultimate mission: the gradual liberation of Armenia. *Jalaleddin* is named after a Kurdish chieftain who drowned Armenian villages and towns in blood with impunity. Raffi pits sons and fathers against one another; Sarhat, the central hero, blames his father for not opposing evil and dies fighting for his family and country. Raffi's disapproval of all religions, particularly Christianity (as a "passive" creed) and Islam (as an "aggressive" religion), his intolerant criticism of Armenian clergymen as ignorant parasites who preached blind obedience to oppressors, and his promotion of self-defense as a legitimate right form some of the basic elements of his political thought and are reinforced in all his novels.

Having faith in neither Europe nor Ottoman nor Russian imperialism or in the Armenian leadership and organizations, Raffi looked up to the "crowd," the educated and well-informed masses, to bring about radical change. Part of his mission was to cultivate a readership, because the reading public was so small. The elements of suspense, mystery, and adventure that occasionally appear in his work are meant to sustain interest in reading and thereby feed the public with new concepts of social and political justice. Social reform, as said, would breed reformed individuals, and reformed individuals would build a new blissful world.

This and certain elements of his ideology of liberation are the two essential messages conveyed to readers by Raffi's *Ḥentʻě* (The fool), whose plot unfolds during the Russo-Ottoman War of 1877–78. Raffi never quite called for armed rebellion; the Armenians were not ready for that yet. But he zealously promoted self-defense as the most dignified and legitimate human right. This and a myriad of ideas pertaining to the unenviable plight of his fellow countrymen in the Ottoman Empire, along with possible ways of bringing political relief, are raised and discussed in Raffi's *Kaytzer* (Sparks), which many an observer have considered the bible of the modern Armenian liberation movements. Indeed, its impact on contemporary political thought and action has been enormous. Although not a novel in the conventional sense, it is the story of a group of students (including a number of characters who also appear in *Ḥachagołi yišatakaraně*) who work in or visit Western Armenia. They observe and analyze the Armenian realities under the Ottoman yoke and explore options and possible ways of alleviating the plight of their fellow countrymen.

Next, Raffi turned to the latest episode of self-defense, still fresh in Armenian memory: Dawitʻ Bek's successful, short-lived struggle in Siwnikʻ, Armenia. This was a more sophisticated novel and brought into sharper focus two elements in Raffi's thought: that disunity had been a major factor in the downfall of Armenian statehood, and that treachery had been a national trait. He interrupted *Dawitʻ Bek* and delved into his "melikdoms" of Khamsa (*Ḥamsayi melikʻutʻiwnnerě*), a study of the history and fall of local Armenian rulers in Artsaḥ-Karabagh, who had been autonomous well into the nineteenth century. The project was undertaken with a view to collecting additional material for *Dawitʻ Bek* and to reviving and evaluating the latest manifestation of Armenian political power in the region. Soon thereafter, Raffi completed his *Paroyr Haykazn* (i.e., the rhetorician Proaeresius, A.D. 276–367/8), a short prose work contrasting Movsēs Ḥorenatsi's dedication to the progress of his own nation with Paroyr Haykazn's contribution to the progress of an alien society.

On the surface, the 1880s looked strikingly tranquil and uneventful. Following the failure of the Armenian Question, the Armenians and their hopes seemed to have sunk into a miasma of despair. In fact, it was a pregnant tranquility. The Armenian political parties were born, and major shifts marked a new course for Armenian literature, most notably the rise of realism. What came as a sudden and painful jolt was the re-emergence of Russian chauvinism, one of the ominous consequences of which was the closure of Armenian schools. *Samuēl* was Raffi's response to this unjudicious Russian measure. Construing the Russians' acts as a devastating attack on the Armenian language, which in his eyes was comparable to an attack on the very essence of the Armenian ethos and the sole bond of unity for a nation in dispersion, Raffi recalled the specter of a similar threat by Persia in fourth-century Armenia.

Armenian historians speak of Samuēl, the central hero, in only a few terse phrases. He was a descendant of the venerable Mamikonean family and killed his own father, Vahan Mamikonean, for apostasy. Raffi expanded this act of patricide into an extensive novel cast against the background of a massive Persian campaign to supplant the native tongue and culture with their own. The novel illustrates selfless patriotism; transforms the abstract concept of Armenia into a geographical and topographical entity, a peopled land bustling with traditions and collective experiences; promotes national unity; restores continuity to Armenian identity by viewing the Christian tradition as both a modified version and a continuation of the pagan Armenian lifestyle; and endorses militant action in defense of country and identity.

Raffi publicly complained that Armenian authors had no clear picture of the Armenian society of old. He was envious, he said, of such writers as Sir Walter Scott and Georg Ebers (whose *Eine ägyptische Königstochter* and *Samuēl* share certain remote resemblances), who were fortunate to have ample historical material at their disposal. (Actually, Ebers himself collected much of the information he used in his novels.) To create a semblance of fourth-century Armenia, Raffi relied on his own imagination, on whatever information he could glean from Armenian sources, and on lifestyles he observed in remote regions, especially in Iran where change would have crept in rather slowly, he contended. It may never be possible to determine how close or off the mark Raffi was in his re-creation of daily life in fourth-century Armenia. Given the benefit of the doubt, it may be assumed that he was satisfactorily imaginative if not altogether authentic. But his reading of this very intricate era in Armenian history is revealing. He was one of the earliest writers, perhaps the earliest, to peer at the realities of the time and make incisive observations on a number of issues: the decentralized nature of political power in Armenia, the negative effect centrifugal forces had on Armenia, and the bloodstained conflict between church and state in the fourth century.

There are a number of instances of anachronism and protraction in this work, but some of the lateral connections are of practical importance. Raffi's women are virtuous patriots, and Meružan Artzruni, whom we know to have been a powerful political personality, comes through as a rather petty quisling. Raffi removes Samuēl from the thick of action for a long stretch of time to illustrate the calamities the traitors and the Persians inflict on the country and to justify Samuēl's inescapable decision to commit patricide amid harrowing mental agony. This renders Samuēl's character somewhat remote. But as the novel races to its dramatic conclusion, he re-emerges as a heroic, if tragic, patriot owing much of his charm and force to the character of Vahan Mamikonean, his own father and arch enemy, whom Raffi portrays in masterful strokes as an intelligent and determined man of strong convictions. Raffi wrote in an excellent Modern Eastern Armenian.

ŁAZAROS AŁAYEAN (1840–1911), endowed with an energetic talent, was a multifarious writer but not as voluminous as some of his contemporaries. There is something utopian about the sum total of his work. He liked Edward Bellamy's projection of a new social and economic order and translated the initial parts of Bellamy's *Looking Backward: 2000–1887* into Armenian. When admonished by his younger colleague and protégé, Yovhannēs Tʻumanean (q.v.), he replied that Bellamy made much more sense than Marx and Engels. Like Bellamy, he particularly liked to juxtapose the idealized future with the ugly present and longed for the disappearance of private enterprise and the appearance of some kind of a communal lifestyle. His adaptations of Armenian folk tales, well-suited to his own edifying purposes, inaugurated a trend emulated by Y. Tʻumanean, A. Isahakyan, and later by S. Zoryan (q.q.v.). They also illustrated his belief in well-rounded education and the importance of acquiring dexterous skills or practical crafts (e.g., his folk tale titled "Anahit"). He prepared numerous popular textbooks and taught tirelessly. He thoroughly enjoyed teaching children and took the lead in creating wonderful poems and rhymes for them, many of which are still fondly recited. His best piece in verse is his adaptation of the tale of Torkʻ Angeł (from Movsēs Ḫorenatsi), whom he recast into a patriot and a loving, gentle giant in a community of a similarly colossal creatures, but one where there are no masters and slaves.

His first novel, *Arutʻiwn ew Manuēl* (proper names, 1867; revised and supplemented 1888–93), is actually an autobiographical collection of vignettes. Elaborating on his use of the form "Arutʻiwn" for "Yarutʻiwn" (resurrection, John), he said it stood for the Armenian word *arutʻiwn* (courage, fortitude) and not for the popular or corrupt form of Yarutʻiwn. From these sketches emerge the sad childhood and early years of Ałayean, who launches a "courageous" assault on old ideas and teaching methods. His next work was a shorter novel titled *Erku kʻoyr* (Two sisters). It is the unhappy love story of two sisters, a cry for social justice, equality of men and women, and the problem of land-tenure in the Armenian realities of the 1870s. Like Ṙ. Patkanean (q.v.) before him, he tried an incomplete adaptation of K'yoṙ-Ōłli (Köroghlu, a bandit, or perhaps a Jelali rebel, and central character of a romance, reminiscent of older accounts of a hero avenging the blinding of his father; these older accounts, it has been suggested, are also echoed in the story of Aršak II, King of Armenia; cf. H. Pērpērean, *Aršak B. ew K'eōṙōłlu,* [Paris, 1938]). But unlike Patkanean, he wrote it in prose and portrayed K'yoṙ-Ōłli not as an Armenian patriot, but as a hero with no specific ethnic identity, who wages wars against oppressors, rulers, and sultans to protect the poor and champion the cause of freedom.

Ałayean has numerous articles discussing various aspects of the emerging literary standard. He was carefully attentive to language and the subtleties of its use and wrote in a neat, simple, and flexible Eastern Armenian, providing a model for his younger colleagues to emulate and improve into a fine tool. But the charm of his idiom is only one of the elements making his literature attractive. In questions of form and substance, literary values and approaches, his literature was distinct from that of his contemporaries and certainly illuminated a more clearly delineated path for the future of Eastern Armenian letters.

The Twentieth Century: The First Two Decades

An Overview of the Armenian Realities of the Age

As the twentieth century turned, Armenian letters were still subject to unrelentingly harsh censorship in both the Ottoman and Russian empires. Both tyrannies made a conscious effort to subdue and terrorize their Armenian subjects. Some cataclysmic events with catastrophic consequences soon shook both the Eastern and Western Armenians. In 1903 the Russian government confiscated Armenian Church properties and closed Armenian parochial schools. Protest and defiance forced the government to reconsider its decision in two years, but there followed the "Tatar [Azeri]-Armenian" clashes (1905–06) and the Stolypin repressions in the aftermath of the first Russian revolution. Despite their anti-Armenian domestic policy, the Russians revived the issue of reform in the Armenian provinces of the Ottoman Empire shortly before World War I. But the outbreak of the war enabled the Young Turk clique to cancel such arrangements and to implement a premeditated state policy of resolving the issue once and for all by eliminating the Armenian population of the empire. When Lenin called home the Russian troops, the Caucasian front disintegrated, and the Ottoman Army, recovering the eastern provinces, marched east in pursuit of the Pan-Turanian fantasy. The Armenians made a last stand in May of 1918 and were able to stop the Turkish onslaught, but not the massacre of the Armenians of Baku. Immediately after the fateful battle of Sardarapat and following the example of Georgia and Azerbaijan, Armenia declared its independence. It survived for only thirty months and became a Soviet republic at the end of 1920.

In the Ottoman Empire, Abdulhamid II's repressive anti-Armenian policy continued until the Young Turk coup of 1908, which, amid joy and jubilation, promised a new start for all elements of the empire. But Armenian hopes and lofty ideals of equality and fraternity were drowned in the bloodbath in Adana (1909). The Young Turks had their own imperialistic fancies and pursued a policy of Turkification now that neither Ottomanism, Islam, nor any other artificial common identity imposed from above could hold the empire together. Shortly after the Balkan wars, the militants and fanatic ideologists in the government and the Committee of Union and Progress (*Ittihad ve Terakki*) managed to drag the country into a war it could not fight. But it provided the leadership with a pretext and cover for the genocide they perpetrated against the Armenians. Deportations began in March, and it was on the night of 24 April 1915 that the Armenian intelligentsia was rounded up and shipped to the interior. Slaughtered in a most brutal fashion were the glories of Western Armenian literature: G. Zōhrap, D. Varužan, Siamantʻō, Eruḥan, Ṙ. Sewak, M. Kiwrčean (Hrand), Ṙ. Zardarean, Tʻlkatintsi, A. Yarutʻiwnean, T. Chēōkiwrean, S. Biwrat, G. Barsełean, and hundreds of intellectuals. A precious few either survived (E. Ōtean), dodged capture and eventually slipped away (Y. Ōšakan), or happened to be abroad on the night of the simultaneous arrests (V. Tʻēkʻēean). But for all intents and purposes, Western Armenian literature was extinguished in 1915.

In the early 1880s it became clear to the Armenians that Abdulhamid II had an implacable aversion to reform and progress and that Europe had its own interests. The rise of the Armenian political parties was partly due to a desire on the part of young Armenians to take matters into their own hands. The "sick man of Europe" though it was, the empire was still a deadly tyranny, especially for the Armenians. Abdulhamid and the Young Turks had proved this in no uncertain terms. The Armenians in Russia fared no better, save that there had been no threat to their lives. Perplexing anxiety is perhaps what best describes the state of mind that prevailed at first. But soon the Armenians realized that things were coming to a head. Frustration, compounded with a sense of despair and impotence, set in as they pondered their uncertain future. All this, in varying forms and degrees, resonated in the works of contemporary authors, amid feverish scholarly and cultural activities.

In the field of Armenian studies, European linguists (e.g., A. Meillet, J. Karst) continued their remarkable contributions, inspiring a new generation of Armenian scholars (H. Ačaṙyan, 1876–1953; M. Abełyan, 1865–1944). Critical editions of old Armenian texts appeared, as did collections and studies of Armenian folklore. Professional inquiries towards reconstructing a more detailed and factual history of Armenia were more actively pursued (Leo, q.v.; N. Adonts, 1871–1942). Tʻ. Tʻoramanyan (1864–1934) shed new light on the monuments of Armenian architecture. Komitas *Vardapet* (Sołomon Sołomonean, 1869–1935) popularized

Armenian folk songs, enchanting large audiences. The Armenian theater and the arts in general enlivened the scene. Literary activities were revived with relative freedom after the return of most of the writers from exile in the wake of the Young Turk coup. New periodicals were published, some of a purely literary character. At public gatherings the latest creations of Armenian writers were discussed. Finally, after decades of groundwork, a discerning reading public and a fine infrastructure was in place. Literary criticism and history made an impact. Criticism developed from popular journalistic reviews to more intricate critique and to monographs, mostly on contemporary writers. A. Chōpanean, A. Yarutʻiwnean, and the most famous of them all, Y. Ōšakan (q.q.v.), forged the canon in the West; a promising Vahan Nalbandean (1876–1902), Nikol Ałbalean (1873–1947), Simeon Hakobyan (1880–1942), Arsen Terteryan (1882–1953), Harutʻyun Surḥatʻyan (1882–1938), Tsolak Ḥanzadyan (1886–1935), and Połos Makintsyan (1884–1938) formulated the Eastern Armenian critical creed. Held in high esteem later in Soviet Armenia were also a number of prominent Bolsheviks who practiced criticism from a Marxist point of view: Stepʻan Šahumean (1878–1918), Suren Spandarean (1882–1916), Alekʻsandr Myasnikyan (1886–1925), etc. Their views reflected a very wide range of conflicting or complementary convictions and diverse influences. A number of histories were written on both eastern and western literatures, taking stock of their accomplishments.

If prose, both long and short, had dominated the concluding three decades of the nineteenth century, poetry ruled supreme in the opening decades of the twentieth. A constellation of poets, the likes of which Armenian letters had not experienced before, adorned Armenian verse with exquisite work in form and content: Siamantʻō, D. Varužan, M. Metzarents, and V. Tʻēkʻēean in the west, and Y. Tʻumanean, A. Isahakyan, V. Tērean, and E. Charents in the east. Certain aspects of symbolism, naturalism, and futurism left their mark on the work of some of these poets who tried to keep abreast of literary trends in Europe and Russia. H. Hakobyan and Š. Kurłinyan in their *engagé* verse founded the proletarian style. In short lyrical prose pieces, a few writers contemplated life in a philosophical mood; others, in similarly short but allegorical writings, gave expression to some concerns and aspirations. Drama was revived in Širvanzade's and L. Šantʻ's plays.

This was a time when the politically doomed Western Armenians found their spiritual fortitude. There was a return to the pagan past, when aesthetic beauty and physical prowess were extolled. The movement generated a good deal of controversy and was denounced by some Eastern Armenian writers. Nonetheless, it was a firm bridge of legitimacy and continuity that extended into antiquity, above and beyond the very symbols that defined the status of Armenians in the empire, namely, the Church and Christianity. This was yet another attempt to foster the political element in the Armenian self-image. Abovean had long since proclaimed language and the Church as two of the most fundamental pillars of the Armenian ethos, and many writers were of like mind. But Raffi, and now Siamantʻō and Varužan, placed much emphasis on pre-Christian Armenian culture, the homeland, and the vernacular. A number of short-lived periodicals, such as *Nawasard* and *Mehean* (both published in Constantinople on the eve of World War I), promoted national and literary rejuvenation and similar concepts. *Nawasard* covered literature and the arts in general. *Mehean* focused on literature, and, proclaiming its allegiance to the Armenian-Aryan spirit, called for a cultivated, purified Armenian as the vehicle for a new literature, free from politics and the ravages of journalism. But the most striking literary expression of such shifting values at this juncture was Siamantʻō's poem "Mesrop Maštots," published just as the Armenians in Constantinople celebrated with pomp and pride, before the envious eyes of the Young Turk leadership, the fifteen-hundredth anniversary of the invention of the Armenian script and the four-hundredth anniversary of Armenian printing.

A Survey of the Literature of the Age

Western Armenian Literature

ARŠAK CHŌPANEAN (1872–1954), a prolific and multifarious author, wrote both poetry and prose (*noravēps,* short stories, prose poems, etc.), as well as essays, articles, and literary criticism. With unflagging determination, he promoted the literary and artistic accomplishments of his nation through lectures, studies, and translations from Armenian into French and vice versa. He also founded and edited the celebrated literary-cultural periodical *Anahit,* cited extensively in this work. So wide was his embrace that he left barely any topical issues untouched. Such activities, conducted in an almost missionary zeal, may indeed have drained his creative, literary energies.

Nonetheless, Chōpanean remains an important figure in the history of Armenian literature, particularly verse. His poetic oeuvre is adorned with few first-rate poems, but as a whole it helped pave the way for subsequent Western Armenian poets. Counterbalancing the treacly clichés of sentimental poetry and the rigidity of formal poetry, Chōpanean emphasized the significance of image and emotion and supplanted the excessively flowery, convoluted expression, often mistaken for sophistication, with a simple and at times ordinary diction. In this sense, he played for Western Armenian verse a role somewhat akin to that played by Hovhannes Hovhannisyan (q.v.) for Eastern Armenian poetry. He was also among the earliest poets to take to Western forms, taste, and sensibilities, channeling such aspects and accomplishments into Armenian letters. In a similar vein, he emerged as the central figure in forging the formative stages of literary criticism. His studies of Grigor Narekatsi, Nahapet K'uchak, Nałaš Yovnat'an, Mkrtich Pēšikt'ašlean, Petros Durean, and others laid the groundwork for the tradition.

Personal sentiments, universal suffering, love, nature, and patriotism are some of the themes he sang in his poems in a warm, spontaneous style. He was well-versed in world, especially French, literature. And Yakob Ōšakan (q.v.) has seen traces of influence of the Romantics, the Parnassians, and the Symbolists in his work. His short prose pieces tackle social themes pertaining principally to the lower and poor classes.

SIAMANT'Ō's (1878–1915) verse is unique in a number of ways. Thematically, it has a very limited range; almost exclusively it tells of the horrors suffered by his nation. In terms of form, it has been suggested that his free verse (which is not quite that) owes something to Verhaeren's *vers libre* and Paul Fort's experiments in poems in prose and the emphasis he placed on cadence. The suggestion needs further elaboration, but it is true inasmuch as Siamant'ō wrote in free verse. In the 1890s and 1900s, many Armenian writers searched for and experimented in new ways of expression.

Siamant'ō's first work, a slim cycle of poems, *Diwtsaznōrēn* (Heroically), in effect prefigured his poetic world. It speaks of centuries-old persecution and butchery of his people (particularly the massacres of the mid-1890s), and evokes and justifies the espousal of defiant aspirations for the ideal, the dream, and the sacred aim. Long-dead martyrs for the cause of freedom rise from their tombs and triumphantly pursue the struggle with the still oppressed crowd. Morbid images (akin to "deep images") and scenes, ghosts, apparitions, and selflessly fighting masses mingle to create an atmosphere of haunting hyperbole. The abstract symbolic forces of fighters for freedom are replaced by contemporary heroes in his next collection, *Hayordiner* (Armenians), made up of three cycles. The background is once again the gruesome images of death and destruction, blood and corpses, and chilling terror that deny mercy and laxity, nurture vengeance, and urge unceasing struggle until victory. The poet calls on the "masters of thought" to come out of their "halls of dream" to sow the seeds of heroism and on the "hooded mystics" (the monks) to arm themselves with the arms of the shattered cross, all while pouring bitter contempt on the hypocritical West. There are tender moments that bring the gloom into even darker focus. But the author never lets go of the thread of hope. Amid unbearable anguish, his apocalyptic voice thunders messages of determination, self-reliance, and relentless pursuit of the ultimate dream.

His third collection, titled *Hogevarkʻi ew yoysi jaher* (literally, Torches of dying breath and hope; i.e., something like Flickering flames of death and hope), is also a threnody on the carnage of his people, but one that lacks the exhortations to revenge and rebellion he had made in his previous collection. The slaughter of Armenians in Adana (Cilicia) in 1909 prompted his next book, *Karmir lurer barekamēs* (Red news from my acquaintance, i.e., Bloodstained reports from a friend). It consists of twelve reported episodes, which Siamantʻō recast in his own style into deeply disturbing narrative poems (e.g., in "Parĕ," The dance, naked women are made to dance to exhaustion and then burnt alive). On a visit to the United States in 1909, he wrote and published his last collection, *Hayreni hrawēr* (An invitation to [return to] the native land, 1910). In twelve moving pieces, in a lyrical style not always entirely free from sentimentalism, Siamantʻō admonishes his fellow countrymen residing abroad, making an impassioned, heartfelt appeal for them to return to their families and the homeland they have abandoned.

In the early 1910s, Siamantʻō very slowly moved away from the realm of pain and darkness. The theme must have seemed to have run its course, and new sources of spiritual fortitude had to be explored. Siamantʻō turned to pagan Armenia, like Daniēl Varužan, in whose *Hetʻanos erger* (Pagan songs) the trend found its fullest expression. Having rejected Christian tenets of pacifism and passivity, Siamantʻō in his poem dedicated to Anahit, the goddess of fertility, supplicates her to give birth to a new invincible god, begotten by the sun. His last major poem was an effusive encomium for Maštots, originator of the Armenian script, commemorating the fifteen-hundredth anniversary of its invention. (Nersēs Mezpurean, 1841–80, and Stepʻanos Nazarean, 1812–79, had earlier written odes to *Mayreni lezu,* i.e., mother tongue, sharing similarities so striking as to suggest a common source of inspiration or adaptation, but neither had the impact nor the symbolic significance of Simantʻō's poem). As usual, Siamantʻō wrote these two poems in an epic breath and a sonorous style. But they both lacked the emotive power of his formidable imagination, his foremost strength in his earlier collections. On the whole, his work suffers from a certain amount of verbosity and repetition, declamatory patterns, mixed metaphors, and a lack of depth. Today, many of his poems make for difficult, monotonous, and uneasy reading. It is difficult to say in what new spheres his imagination would have hovered, had he not been silenced at age thirty-seven in a conflagration unlike any he described.

MISAKʻ METZARENTS (1886–1908) is one of a handful of Armenian poets who redefined and refined the Armenian poetic canon with vision and finesse at the turn of the century. His two collections, *Tziatzan* (Rainbow) and *Nor tałer* (New songs), published in the spring and autumn of 1907, were met by some with harsh, if distasteful, criticism claiming, among other things, that his work was infested with Symbolism, an alien malaise unacceptable to Armenian traditionalists. A larger army of admirers went to the other extreme, refusing to acknowledge all traces of Symbolism in his art.

Metzarents knew by his early teens that his years were numbered (he suffered from consumption), but unlike Petros Durean (q.v.), he neither allowed the black specter of death visibly to color his utterances, nor did he defy fate rebelliously. Nor did he escape into Vahan Tērean's distant visions, undulating in the mist of melodic melancholy. There was an air of elevated and deeply moving insouciance about the way in which he touched upon his destiny, women, and love. The real world was the abode of his noble sentiments, refracted in a bright, but never dazzling, interplay of colors. This is to say that he read nature particularly well, viewing its vitality with a discerning eye and listening to its rhythm with a musical ear. A heartening optimism mitigated his profound sorrows, channeling them away into the light enveloping him, and grief gave him renewed strength to carry on with the business of life. He worshipped the sun–as a flame, not as a massive conflagration–and caught the infinite manifestations of light, releasing them in varying shapes and shades into many of his poems, including the nocturnal ones. His unalloyed, boundless altruism, now in the form of the wind touching everybody on the forehead in sympathy; now as the cuddlesome evening descending upon all; and now as a hut awaiting the arrival of weary travelers, was at once a source of inspiration and solace for him. His amatory expressions are dreams, prompted by a heart languishing in an unquenched thirst for love. This is perhaps best illustrated in one of his most popular poem-songs "Gišern anuš ē . . ." ("Sweet is the night . . . ," titled "Sirerg" = Lovesong) where the author, inundated with kisses from the sea, air, and the light embracing him, longs for the "only" kiss, the ultimate seal of happiness.

Like his predecessor, Petros Durean, and his contemporaries Tʻumanean, Isahakyan, Siamantʻō, Varužan, and Tērean (q.q.v.), Metzarents formed new compound words and endowed some old words with new nuances. He paid meticulous attention to form and wrote effortlessly, in a crystal clear, elegantly compact Western Armenian with fresh, vibrant imagery all his own.

DANIĒL VARUŽAN's (1884–1915) first collection of verse, titled *Sarsuṙner* (Sensations, or *Frissons*), is a small volume that expresses some social concerns. His next book, *Tsełin sirtĕ* (Heart of the race, i.e., nation), deals with a much wider variety of concerns and aspirations. It opens with a poem dedicating it to the fatherland, the Armenian émigrés (*panduḥt*), the victims of sword and fire, his home and parents, and the Armenians fighting for the national cause. There follows a prologue titled "Nemesis," depicting the carving of a statue of the goddess of retribution. Varužan calls on his people to worship the goddess, but to destroy her statue and cult as soon as tyranny is abolished. Having set the tone to the entire collection, Varužan then groups his poems under three headings: "Baginin vray" (on the altar of sacrifice), "Krkēsin mēj" (in the arena), and "Diwtsaznavēper" (epic poems). With passion and verve, Varužan asserts in the first part that his fellow countrymen have long been victims of Ottoman religious fanaticism and chauvinism. He juxtaposes some of the darkest moments in the Armenian experience with spiritual vitality and moral strength (e.g., the poems on the ruins of Ani, the spirit of the fatherland, the red soil, the massacres of the mid-1890s and Adana, 1909), while he unceremoniously buries "the God of Lusaworich [Gregory the Illuminator] and Nersēs [the Great, A.D. fourth century]." In the second and third parts, he amplifies the theme of spiritual fortitude: e.g., Revival ("Veratznutʻiwn"), The Victor ("Yałtʻołĕ"), etc.; invokes the god Vahagn for his prowess and calls on him to make peace with his "renegade" people; and promises justice and liberty to the Armenian victims of the Armenian-Tatar (i.e., Azeri) clashes of 1905–06.

Enamored of pagan life, many elements of which are found in this collection, Varužan wrote a whole new cycle of poems, *Hetʻanos erger* (Pagan songs). The second part is titled *Gołgotʻayi tzałikner* (Golgotha flowers), and in contrast to the first it is a bitter indictment of the machine age and its devastating consequences of cruel exploitation, poverty, moral corruption, and other manifestations of human degradation in ugly, monstrous urban centers. The first is a splendid, if controversial, hymn to life in luscious (and at times even lascivious), glittering imagery, fusing the colors of the East and the art of the West. Širvanzade (q.v.) attacked it (the poem "Ov Lalagē," in particular) as pornography, but numerous colleagues and critics came to Varužan's rescue. He is singing, in innocent elation, of passion and sensual sensations and the beauty of the female body, at times in somewhat suggestive settings. It is the concept of fertility and cycle of life, the inextricable intermingling of pleasure and pain, that endow the collection with a putative air of eroticism. It is decidedly not pornographic, though in an instance or two Varužan does sing of Eros rather than Agape. Nor is there on the part of Varužan a call to return to an era he brought to life in such bright colors as in the narrative poem, "Harčē" (The concubine), the collection's brightest jewel. Varužan's intention was to unveil and liberate the pagan tradition, perceived by him as an age of prowess, valor, and the aesthetically beautiful, to undermine the bleak aspects of Christian tenets that clipped the wings of human spirit, and to shape and solidify the will to live. The influences of E. Verhaeren, M. Maeterlinck, Rig-veda, and the rich colors of the Flemish masters have been pointed out. To these influences one should perhaps add Parnassian poetry, with its emphasis on formal and visual, rather than emotive, aspects.

Varužan's last collection was *Hatsin ergĕ* (The song of bread), which tells the entire story of obtaining flour, from ploughing the land to the water mill. The cycle is believed to be incomplete, lacking the six poems that would have put the baked bread on the table. The manuscript was confiscated at the time of his arrest by Ottoman Turkish police on 24 April 1915, but it was recovered after his murder and published in 1921. Bucolic poems of an idyllic setting, ablaze with the colors of sunrise and sunset and various other hours of the day, recount the routine of industrious peasants engaged in the "sacred" labor of producing bread. It opens with the poet's appeal to the muse to teach him all about bread, followed by twenty-eight poems, interspersed with songs, romantically idealizing a tranquil, blissful lifestyle. This is the fatherland in its simplest, most precious form. Popular expressions, sparingly applied, add charm and authenticity to his style. He conjures up delightful images infused with light, colors, and warmth–one of the most celebrated, enduring, and endearing aspects of his poetic genius.

ṘUBĒN SEWAK's (1885–1915) output is small in quantity but contains a good many impressive pieces in both verse and prose. His *Karmir girkʿĕ* (The red book), made up of three poems inspired by the Armenian massacres in Adana, was the only collection to appear in his lifetime. He was not in the same league as his great contemporaries, but his warm, sincere, and spontaneous poetry, like theirs, marked a turning point in the history of Armenian verse in a modest way. Social inequality and injustice, corruption, human bondage, the transience of life, and issues of universal harmony and the aesthetically beautiful emerge as some of his major concerns. His sentiments are rebellious in poems (which seem to have been born in a hasty outburst), protesting, with a tinge of pessimism, the brutal way in which his fellow countrymen were treated.

The short pieces he published in the periodical press were put together posthumously as a volume under the title *Bžiškin girkʻēn pʻrtsuatz ējer* (Pages, or Extracts from the diary of a physician). It is an uneven medley of short stories, *noravēps,* articles, and narratives that speak of the observations of a physician who encounters matters of life and death daily. The theme was new, as was the setting for many of the sad episodes. One of Sewak's intentions was to show that death could be delayed or defeated if certain conditions were met (change in personal lifestyles, removal of ignorance, etc.). Sewak's immense sympathy for those in affliction, his thoughtful reflections on human life, and his rapid narrative style make some of these writings enjoyable reading.

ARTAŠĒS YARUTʻIWNEAN (1873–1915) attained fame as both an influential literary critic and as a gifted poet who sang of love, dreams, and nature with a vexed heart. But his poetic glory faded as rapidly as it had risen, some years before his life was brought to an end in 1915, and it is his critical sketches of contemporary authors and analyses of particular literary works that are still of value. An incisive observer, with a subtle artistic discretion, he wrote short reviews that are distinguished for their insight, wit, and élan, never mincing matters and never shying away from giving his detractors some of their own medicine in terms of temperamental responses and repartee in the periodical press of the day. To him, the role of a critic was to detect, publicly appreciate, and, if need be, propagate the intrinsic values of a literary piece as a consummate individual creation. He designed the famous survey, published in the form of a questionnaire in the literary periodical *Masis,* on the future of Western Armenian literature. Looking at literature as a repository and as a reflection of the past and present experiences of his people, expressed in and consonant with the particular and paramount aesthetic-literary character of the Armenian people, Yarutʻiwnean publicly raised a long-standing concern regarding the future of Armenian literature. More to the point, the question he asked the Armenian intellectuals was whether Constantinople (an alien, cosmopolitan home of an Armenian community) or the eastern provinces (the original homeland and thus a "purer" Armenia) of the Ottoman Empire were the genuine and, therefore, the more fertile ground for Armenian letters. Yarutʻiwnean unequivocally favored the latter. The response to the questionnaire was disappointingly meager. But regardless of the answers, no power would have deflected the course of this natural trend, which was initiated by Mkrtich Ḥrimean (q.v.). Were it not for 1915, "provincial" literature, it seems, would have rivaled and complemented that produced in Constantinople as an indispensable part of the national tradition.

It is difficult to say in what other ways Yarutʻiwnean's flair for criticism would have manifested itself had his life run its normal course. But what we have from him is a string of short evaluations confined to contemporary literature, lacking the sweeping grasp of canon-shapers, such as that of his close friend, Yakob Ōšakan, or that of Aršak Chōpanean (q.q.v.), the forerunner of them both and chief originator of the tradition. For all three, intellectual sustenance and guidance came mainly from French sources. Yarutʻiwnean had a masterful command of French, and according to Ōšakan, he contributed to French periodicals under a pseudonym. Ōšakan also mentioned that Yarutʻiwnean read seldom but deeply. Based on what the former has recorded and on what one can glean from Yarutʻiwnean's own writings, Yarutʻiwnean was familiar with Kant, Heine, Schopenhauer, and, particularly, Nietzsche; Byron and H. Spencer; and among French philosophers, the writers and critics Joachim du Bellay, Ronsard, A. Comte, V. Cousin, H.-F. Amiel, Littré, Leconte de Lisle, Gabriel Tarde, A. France, the French Symbolists, and especially Remy de Gourmont. He read the *Mercure de France* religiously, but had no particular interest in Bergson and chose to disregard Taine, maintaining that his influence had already waned.

VAHAN TʻĒKʻĒEAN's (1878–1945) army of admirers is probably outnumbered by those indifferent towards his art. His first collection produced two sharply contrasting reviews but mainly went unnoticed. The second appeared when Metzarents, Siamantʻō, and Varužan had already published their best work. When his third book saw the light of day, the Armenians were still mortified by the harrowing and continuing trauma of 1915. No new aspects of his talent shimmered in his fourth and fifth volumes. The aforementioned poets struck a chord with their readers, who basked in optimism. Tʻēkʻēean's second book, arguably his best collection, appeared in a tense atmosphere on the eve of World War I. Perhaps his technique had something to do with it, too. Most of his verse lacks internal rhyme and abounds with enjambment and grammatical inversion, often requiring a second reading to fathom the depth of his contemplation. Ironically, he was a painstaking perfectionist when it came to form and precision of words, meter, and rhyme and invariably revised (often repeatedly and over long periods of time) the initial forms of his inspiration. Yakob Ōšakan (q.v.) proclaimed him to be the most original poet of the Armenian Dispersion.

He was off to a rough start with his first collection, which brought to light his youthful dreamy anxieties and aspirations. But his second and third (*Hrašali yarutʻiwn,* Wonderful rebirth; *Kēsgišerēn minchew aršaloys,* From midnight to dawn), firmly established him as a first-rate poet. The identity of the object of his affections, which deeply agitated his heart and mind, remained mysteriously ambiguous. Unrequited and privately cherished love, haunting memories, unattainable dreams such as fathering a son, and terrible blows of fate, all gnawing at his heart, are major themes in the latter two volumes. More or less the same topics, expressed in an uneven voice, make up the next book, *Sēr* (Love). Patriotic sentiments and Armenia predominate his penultimate collection, titled *Hayergutʻiwn* (Songs on, or a celebration of, Armenia and the Armenians), which brings together numerous poems culled from his earlier work, those interspersed in the periodical press, and a considerable number of new ones. *Tałaran* (Songbook) contained the poems, mostly sonnets, he wrote in the twilight of his life (he is often referred to as the Armenian Prince of Sonnets).

In his patriotic lyrical verses, many of which were inspired by his two visits to Armenia, Tʻēkʻēean sought the spirit of his nation, rather than its splendor, and echoed its aspirations, old and new (e.g., "Zuartʻnots tačarin mēj" = At the Zvartnots Cathedral). He was one of the few intellectuals fortuitously to escape 1915, because he happened to be in Jerusalem on the night of April 24 when the Armenian intellectuals were rounded up. The destruction of the Western Armenians remained a bleeding wound to the end of his life and gave rise to a number of commemorative, tryingly painful, indignant but dignified poems (e.g., "Kʻsan kaḥałanner" = in memory of the twenty members of the Hnchakean Party sent to the gallows in June of 1915; "Suetia"; "Epʻrat" = Euphrates; "Ahawor ban mě . . ." = Something terrible . . . ; "Erb ōrě gay verjapēs = When the day finally comes; "Garnan gišer" = A spring night; "Ov Hayastan" = O, Armenia; "Piti ěsenkʻ Astutzoy" = We shall say to God; etc.).

Tʻēkʻēean's poetry was on the whole cerebral, austere yet poignant, subtle and elegiac, distressful yet lyrical and dignified. There was something of the stoic in him; personal love remained elusive, and only dreams and hopeful anticipation of reciprocal affection periodically illuminated his otherwise sad life. His mental and artistic steadfastness was remarkable. His attractive verse was expressed in an elegant and meticulous Armenian, with a voice all its own.

MATTʻĒOS ZARIFEAN (1894–1924) published two collections of poetry in his lifetime. The Beirut edition of his collected works, edited jointly by Siran Seza (sister of Zarifean) and Vahē-Vahean (q.v.), contains unpublished poems, diaries, and letters not found in his two poetry collections. His diaries cover mainly his days of service in the Ottoman Army (1916–18), with two very short sections on his days as interpreter in the British Army and teacher at the Pērpērean School. His two verse collections made him a celebrity overnight; his poems struck a responsive chord particularly in the hearts of young readers. For, although the war had long since ceased, what was left of the Ottoman Empire was still in turmoil, and the fate of the Armenians was still uncertain.

Death overtook Zarifean before he could refine his poetic gift into a distinct style. His romantic poetry is intensely subjective and revolves around unrequited sentiments in matters of the heart, mental anguish, unfulfilled dreams, and a yearning for tranquility. He faced death with courage, although in many a poem sentimentality and self pity are a touch too obvious. Nature and the night, the sea, trees, and a certain locale in Istanbul form the basic elements of his imagery. His poems suffer from a number of imperfections. But they are written with genuine sincerity, simplicity, and a good feel for rhyme by a sensitive soul enamored of life.

AHARON TATUREAN (1886–1965) became a familiar name to the Western Armenian reading public in the years 1908–15 through his poems published in the periodical press. His fame lingered briefly after the Armistice of Mudros, but rapidly dissipated after the early 1920s. The publication of his first collection in 1938 revived his reputation to a certain degree. Although more collections followed, Aharon, as he was often called, never regained the modest prominence he had achieved in the pre-genocide era. His poetry was uneven, and much of it was outdated or irrelevant. But a few poems, particularly from his first two collections, stand out for the elegance of their style, the vividness of their imagery, and the intensity and spontaneity of his emotions. From his first collection, *Magałatʻner* (Parchment), the cycle "gehenakankʻ" (Infernal [songs]) is written with verve; the cycle "Sirts karmir varderov" (My heart with red roses) is a spirited hymn to love; and the cycle "Giwłi siwkʻer, earoj erger" (Country breezes: songs for the beloved) is a fascinating imitation of folk-style poetry. From his second collection, *Pohemakankʻ* (Bohemian [songs]), so named after a cycle he wrote while a student in Prague), the cycle "Hogis čermak varderov" (My soul with white roses) speaks of love in mellow and melancholic lines that run deep.

ERUḤAN (1870–1915), a junior contemporary of the realist writers, wrote *noravēp*s and novels conforming to the literary creed of his senior colleagues. Like most of them, he also contributed to the periodical press and taught, but he never enjoyed as wide a recognition as they had, despite the fact that his *Amirayin ałjikě* (Amira's daughter) is considered by many as the best realist novel. That was perhaps due to the fact that realism had outlived its age by the early twentieth century; prose was gradually relegated to a secondary position by poetry, and authors explored new literary realms. Nonetheless, he is reckoned to be one of the important prose writers of his age.

Like Eruḥan himself, many of his characters (fishermen and fishmongers and poor people of humble origin who owe to Eruḥan their existence in Armenian literature) came from the district of Hasköy in Istanbul, which at one point had also been the home of some *amiras* (self-made dignitaries in the service of sultans and the higher echelons of Ottoman bureaucracy, who wielded considerable power within the Armenian community). There are no variations in craftsmanship in his short stories, which almost exclusively deal with the inner life and external appearance of a neglected class of people. He is both unquestioning and unmindful of their social standing or realities; in an unembellished fashion and with vigorous strokes, he paints little action and pays even less attention to the world they inhabit.

Amirayin ałjikě (initially titled *Meržuatz sēr,* Rejected love, or A jilted lover, which better describes the plot of the novel) is in fact the story of an *amira's* grandchild by the name of Aršak, a quack given to self-indulgence. He abandons Sofi, his servant, and takes off to Paris, returning with a French woman. The latter abandons Aršak when he shows renewed interest in Sofi, who sought out an old admirer of hers, Hambik, while Aršak was gone. As Aršak and Sofi revive their relationship, Hambik goes insane. Far more interesting than the central protagonist are the secondary characters, who are mostly sincere, simple, poor, though not always pure, and whose well-drawn profiles testify to Eruḥan's intimate familiarity with such people. In his other novel, *Harazat ordi* (Legitimate son), a dissolute and impotent husband, Beniamin, commits suicide upon realizing that his child has been fathered by someone else. In addition to unnecessary epithets that encumber his novels as well as his shorter works, the former also suffer from excessively prolonged description of tedious details. His best pages are those that captured for posterity what society and other writers had disregarded: the particular group of the poor and forgotten he knew best.

MELK'ON KIWRČEAN's (1859–1915) work is limited in scope but original in many respects. There was in Constantinople a large number of immigrants who had left their families and homes in Armenia in quest of employment and security. A new influx of such young men poured into the

Ottoman capital immediately after the Russo-Turkish War of 1877–78. They lived in squalid conditions, were mostly shunned by the established community, and engaged in menial jobs, many of them working as porters. A number of contemporary writers had touched upon their plight, but with inspiring encouragement from Arpʻiar Arpʻiarean (q.v.), Kiwrčean made it the central theme of his literary output. As a provincial Armenian, Kiwrčean had firsthand experience of their lives and mentality; he is said to have closely associated with them.

There were some dramatic aspects and consequences to this phenomenon. Migration destroyed families and sapped the strength of the Armenian people in the provinces, somewhat altering the demographic balance in the region. Insecurity, extreme economic hardship, and separation for uncertain periods of time were all profoundly painful for those who remained behind and those who emigrated to the Ottoman capital, where many of them died of starvation, illness, or emotional distress. Kiwrčean movingly chronicled their wretched existence in his *kʻroniks* (*chroniques*), short stories, and vignettes, reviving and enriching in prose the long-standing tradition of émigré verse. His talent shone in his *kʻroniks,* each of which captures the bare essence of contemporary realities and mentality in an austere, economical, and down to earth manner. It is difficult to speak of full-fledged characters in his work; they are, rather, authentic portraits, sketched with sensitivity, spontaneity, and wistful concern. His Armenian, limpid and flexible (though he was never able fully to jettison the influence of Classical Armenian, the passion of his early years), captures in its rapid flow a lifestyle that perished with its chronicler in 1915.

TʻLKATINTSI (c1860–1915) introduced to Armenian literature the distinct flavor of his native region, Ḥarberd (Harput), and its environs. Mkrtich Ḥrimean and his student, Garegin Sruandzteants (q.q.v.), had already provided a glimpse into life in Armenia proper, but it was Tʻlkatintsi who turned his attention fully to native Armenians. This grew into a warmly received trend in the works of his students and emulators (e.g., Ṙ. Zardarean, B. Nurikean, and Hamasteł, q.q.v.), which enriched Armenian literature in more ways than one and has often been referred to as the authentic expression of the soul and soil of Armenia. Although Tʻlkatintsi had read some European literature in translation and was up to date on the literary output and activities in Constantinople, Tiflis, and elsewhere, the content of his writings, if not the form, was virtually free from influences. He wrote with spontaneous pride of the noble aspects of the lifestyle he was born to, but pounded with unforgiving alacrity its vices, failings, and pompous detractors, in a sinewy and vivacious style permeated with lyrical sadness, contagious humor, and a biting sarcasm. Although some of his pieces are verbose, on the whole he had a good sense of proportion and a very fine feel for the beautiful. He employed standard Western Armenian for most of his work, but wrote a few pieces (especially plays) entirely in, or peppered with, his native dialect. The Armenian massacres of 1915 claimed not only his life but also most of his unpublished manuscripts.

Tłkatintsi wrote half a dozen poems (all in 1908) imitating the popular folk style, and three *noravēps: Mutʻ ankiwnnerē* (From dark corners), *Gawatʻ mě miayn* (Only one glass [drink]), and *Es kataretsi im partkʻs* (I fulfilled my obligation). These are well-written short novels dealing with the very sad plight of women, nuptial infidelity, and religious antagonism (actually, anti-Protestant sentiments). But the bulk of his work falls under the genre of *chronique.* Many contemporary masters (e.g., A. Arpʻiarean, q.v.) had been using the form skillfully. Tłkatintsi developed his own approach of writing profiles, pictures, scenes, short stories, and childhood reminiscences, where customs and traditions, daily routine and lifestyle, along with a wide range of characters, sad and funny, cruel and tender, ugly and attractive, capture an authentic moment in Armenian life in the town of Ḥarberd and the neighboring villages. Topical issues, for instance, were the often-tragic consequences for young women shipped to the United States as wives for men they had only seen photographs of, the rapidly increasing rate of emigration to America, and certain aspects of the activities, religious and educational, of American missionaries. His *Gełi namakner* (Village letters) revolves around village life. The second letter is a detailed description of village dwellings and daily life in the countryside.

In the play *Ēndi dēmēn* (From the other world), a dead man returns to the world of the living to solicit recommendations to alleviate his suffering in the nether world, but makes his journey back with empty hands. *Zalěm tłan* (The cruel boy) is a more complicated story. An Armenian returns home to marry a local girl. But he abandons her and sets sail for America, and his would-be bride dies amid scandalous monetary and moral corruption. *Ktakě* (The will) is a one-act play highlighting the clash of heirs to the wealth and property of a dying man. *Dēpi artasahman* (Going abroad) in two scenes illustrates the disintegration of the family due to emigration to America.

ṘUBĒN ZARDAREAN's (1874–1915) *Tsaygaloys* (Twilight or, twilit night) was his first and last collection. From about 1908 to his murder shortly after he and the Armenian intelligentsia were arrested on the night of 24 April 1915, he wrote very few pieces, giving himself almost entirely to editorial work instead. The volume brought him immediate acclaim and secured him a visible spot in the modern Armenian canon as one of the brightest stars of a generation of writers (Ḥrimean, Sruandzteants, Tʻlkatintsi, and others) whose literature placed an increasingly greater emphasis on life in Armenia proper, instead of the Armenian Dispersion (e.g., the Armenian community of Constantinople). Folk tales, prose poems, and short stories make up the bulk of his output.

His literary vision had certain affinities with the work of a number of contemporaries with otherwise diverse aesthetic principles: Siamantʻō, Metzarents, Varužan, and Šantʻ (q.q.v.). He shared their belief in spiritual renewal and fortitude, especially in view of the ravages of ignorance, religious superstition, social lassitude, fatalism, and a demoralizing sense of servitude. He averred that a relentless pursuit of lofty ideals–selfless but healthy patriotism was one such virtue–was what rendered existence meaningful and fit for human beings; he paid a warm tribute to noble souls who rose above petty ends, braved deadly odds, rebelled against tyranny, and pointed the way to human dignity, freedom, and progress. His folk tales reverberate with these themes and an unmistakable political undertone, as do his prose poems, which are also cloaked in allegory. This was a congenial device, but one that also enabled him to avoid the suffocating restrictions of Ottoman censorship. The title of the collection was in fact a reference to Abdulhamid II's reign before 1908, a nightmare that the Logos ("ban"), as Zardarean put it in his preface, barely survived. His short stories offer saddening insights into the drab, rotten, and dehumanizing realities in the Armenian provinces (principally in the Ḥarberd, or Harput, region).

Aspects of authentic Armenian life in many of Zardarean's works come alive through local color, mores and mentality, customs and traditions, captured and drawn skillfully. The lack of action or characterization is compensated for by a contemplative and dramatic symbolism, expressed in vivid yet austere imagery, with a lyrical touch and elegantly controlled emotions. Personification and abundant descriptions of nature play a significant role in achieving effective contrast. He wrote in a felicitous and sumptuous, inornate, Armenian.

TIGRAN CHĒŌKIWREAN (1884–1915) wrote a number of short novels and stories, of which *Herosě* (The hero) and *Vankʻě* (The monastery) brought him recognition as a promising writer. While the former with irony and a tinge of sarcasm revives a certain mood in Constantinople at the turn of the twentieth century, the latter in the form of a diary narrates the temptations and tribulations of a celibate priest as the principal of an orphanage sheltering children who have survived the Armenian massacres of the mid-1890s. Here, as well as in some of his other short stories, his prose is economical and immediate, warm and subtly melancholic. Yakob Ōšakan, in his *Hamapatker,* noted the influence on *Herosĕ* and *Vankʻĕ* respectively, of Maupassant's *Boule-de-suif* and L. Andreev's *Krasny smekh* (The red laugh), both of which Chēōkiwrean translated into Armenian.

ERUAND ŌTEAN (1869–1926) was a prolific and popular satirist, novelist, and editor-publicist, with a considerable amount of writing scattered in the periodical press. His celebrated predecessor, Yakob Paronean, had just died when Ōtean started his literary career in the early 1890s. Ōtean stood on Paronean's shoulders, but their styles and scopes were dissimilar in many respects. Paronean's spontaneous wit sparkled brightly, and his sweeping satire was annihilating; Ōtean's satire was distinguished by subtlety. The former roared with laughter, often through tears, and was embittered when his whiplash words failed to bring people to their senses; the latter smiled, frequently provoked a good laughter, and lacked his elder colleague's reformist tendencies. Paronean focused almost exclusively on the Armenian community in Constantinople; Ōtean's purview, by virtue of his nomadic life, encompassed wider geographical areas and a greater variety of characters. Paronean concentrated on humor and satire alone, while Ōtean also wrote novels and short stories. As contributors to and editor-publishers of periodicals (almost a mania for Ōtean), they both wasted a good deal of their time and talent on topical issues, and had neither the time nor desire, it seems, to revise their writings.

His novels dealing with social themes depict Armenian realities in Constantinople and frequently have merchants as their protagonists. *Ĕntanikʻ, patiw, baroyakan* (Family, honor, morality), *Tałakanin knikĕ* (Wife of the parish council's chairman), *Mijnord tēr papan* (The matchmaker priest), are some of his better known works. The first is the story of an immoral man, hiding behind the values making up the title of the novel, who wants those words for his epitaph after Sister Atropos has cut off the thread of his life. In the second book a termagant, Satʻen, wife of the wealthy Margar, feels terribly insulted when the wife of the chairman of the parish council is offered a chair at church while she is disregarded. She runs off to her husband, plots her revenge for this outrage, and the chairman is eventually forced to resign. The third novel shows the unscrupulous ends to which a priest goes to make money through matchmaking. Ōtean has raised more or less similar concerns in numerous well-knit and rapidly moving short novels and stories (e.g., "Vačaṙakani mě namaknerě kam katareal mard ěllalu aruestě" = The letters of a merchant, or the art of being a perfect [i.e., successful] person).

Ōtean wrote some of the earliest detective stories. The novel *Aptiwl Hamit ew Šerlokʻ Holms* (Abdulhamid and Sherlock Holmes), which he categorized as a contemporary historical novel, has as its sequel *Saliha haněm kam banakě bṙnaworin dēm* (Miss Saliha or the army against the tyrant), a novel of "Ottoman revolutionary life." Action, suspense, and all the other usual elements and devices are used by Ōtean to highlight multinational political opposition to sultan Abdulhamid II. In *Matniché* (The traitor), yet another *roman feuilleton,* a handful of Armenians are seen pursuing similar aspirations. Mention should also be made of *T'iw 17 ḥafiēn* (Spy number seventeen), despite the fact that it is not a purely detective story. The backdrop is the Young Turk regime, World War I, and the wholesale slaughter of the Armenians in 1915–16.

Most critics regard Ōtean's "socialist" tri-part novel as his masterpiece or at least as one of his best works, made up of *Aṙakʻelutʻiwn mě i Tzaplvar* (A mission to Tzaplvar), *Ěnker Pʻanjuni Vaspurakani mēj* (Comrade Panchuni in Vaspurakan), and *Ěnker Pʻanjuni taragrutʻean mēj* (Comrade Panchuni in exile). There is much room under this umbrella for some other works, such as some of his short novels and novels (e.g., *Es drsetsi chem aṙner* = I shall not marry an outsider, a central theme of which is the contempt in which the provincial Armenians were held by the "indigenous" Armenians of Constantinople, a deep-seated and multifaceted attitude with a long history) and *Yełapʻoḥutʻean makaboytznerě* (Parasites of the revolution). Ōtean, as a witness to the rise and activities of the Armenian political parties and as one who intimately knew many of their leaders and followers, derided, in his tri-part novel referred to above, the extreme expressions of formalism and mechanical approach to political theory. Described here are the activities, actually the ravages, of Pʻanjuni (pronounced Panchuni in Western Armenian, a kind of malapropism for Armenian *ban* [pronounced *pan*] *chuni* = brainless), a Marxist propagandist who audited social sciences at Geneva, returns to Constantinople and, finding the field crowded, sets himself the destructive task of mobilizing the Armenian proletariat against the bourgeoisie and capitalists, none of which truly existed in the Armenian provinces, especially the rural areas. There is neither passion nor bitterness nor alarm to Ōtean's narrative, which exposes the absurd activities of his bizarre character through caricature. In this and in a number of other respects, it bears some resemblance to *Don Quixote,* though it lacks such depth and tragicomic elements. Also, unlike the Knight of the Lions, one feels no degree of sympathy for P‘anjuni; yet one does not detest him either. He is pernicious because he is thoughtless. As Ōtean parodies the confusion of socialist terminology with theory, its broader misinterpretation and misapplication, hyperbole puts certain parts of the novel beyond the realm of the real and fosters in the reader a benevolent intolerance for anything leading to such absurdities.

Yełap‘oḫut‘ean makaboytznerě (Parasites of the revolution) strings together brilliant satirical portraits of a number of charlatans who pose as revolutionaries to benefit from the respect and hospitality accorded to such activists by the public. *Mer eresp‘oḫannerě* (Our deputies) is a collection of profiles of some of the deputies to the Armenian National Assembly. With humor and sarcasm and some help from Paronean, Ōtean has handed down to posterity an amusing and incisive commentary on the intelligentsia and Armenian realities of the period. *Tasnerku tari Polisēn durs* (Twelve years spent away from Constantinople, i.e., 1896–1908) is an intimate, spirited, and humorous account covering half a dozen years or so of Ōtean's peregrination in Europe and Egypt, his encounters with Armenian intellectuals (most of whom, like the author himself, had fled the Armenian massacres of the mid-1890s), and interesting anecdotes, episodes, and events. As usual, Ōtean writes in excellent Armenian, with a light, delicate touch and a broad smile ("the divine laughter" as he put it "free from grudges and hatred"), entertaining no illusions about the power of satire and humor to transform human life.

ZAPĒL ASATUR (1863–1934) emerged in the 1890s as the leading woman writer at a time when Srbuhi Tiwsab (q.v.) maintained long years of silence to her death in 1901. Asatur wrote both verse and prose (*noravēps,* short narratives and a novel), the bulk and best of which was published by the early 1900s. She launched her career with her only novel, *Ałjkan mě sirtě* (The heart of a girl), which was well received. This is the story of a girl who acts on the prompting of her heart, but is abandoned and wastes away in desolate grief. Asatur's short stories highlight mothers and motherhood, the temptations women find themselves exposed to, their vanity, and what women expect from men—namely love, attention, and dedication. Although her craftsmanship was less distinguished than some of her celebrated contemporaries, Asatur's prose bears witness to the mores and mentality of the times.

Asatur's early poems were overburdened by a heavy dose of Classical Armenian, which she discarded over a relatively short period of time. A considerable part of her verse is made up of narrative poems and concentrates on the sadder aspects of women's lives and on nature. Contemplative and retrospective elements of a general nature come to govern her vague poetic energies a little later in her life. A romantic to the marrow of her bones, Asatur paid meticulous attention to form and diction. And it is in this realm that she made her modest contribution to Armenian verse, in some measure anticipating the accomplishments of the greater talents who were about to burst onto the literary scene.

INTRA's (i.e., Indra, 1875–1921) two volumes, one in prose and the other in verse, stood outside the mainstream of literature of the day. Their appearance generated a good deal of controversy and still await a credible interpretation, especially of the sources that inspired them. The first collection, *Nerašḥarh* (Inner world, i.e., Inner self), is a prose narrative in which the author speaks in first person of impressions, ideas, symbols, states of mind, and of spiritual, mystical, and metaphysical sensibilities. In an attempt to escape the real world by defining his relationship to society, nature, love, and the "eternal," he longs for the "light" and the "infinite." Beside excellent passages there are some nonsensical ones. His ability to articulate abstract ideas is remarkable. His Armenian, employed with unusual flexibility, is replete with calques, new compounds and syntactical patterns, reinterpretation of words, colorful images, and intricate metaphors. There is a certain degree of lyricism to his style, but it is often circuitous, repetitive, and tortuous. Both Theosophy and Gongorism, along with a score of other movements, have been suggested as possible sources of influence. Certain trends of Theosophy (Mme Blavatsky's version) seem to be plausible. As for the latter, though unlikely, it may partly explain some aspects of his book, particularly the intricate metaphors, vivid images, and strangeness of language.

His *Nočastan* (A cypress grove) is a collection of verse (sonnets) spoken in Intra's distinct voice. They have been composed in an intellectual vein and lack warmth and immediacy. Rhyme and meter seem to have restricted the flight of his imagination. Still, his very own senses and sensibilities, his fine receptiveness for sound and shades of color, images, and his unmistakable identity set this not-so-popular volume apart from the verse of his contemporaries.

ZAPEL ESAYAN (1878–1943) holds an illustrious place in the front rank of modern Armenian prose. She attained fame early, and her attractive literature generated much critical interpretation. She contributed to the periodical press, too, though it is not only her writings that kept her in the limelight; she was also very active in public life. She championed the cause of women's emancipation in numerous articles, pressing for a radical and comprehensive re-evaluation of women's standing in society and conjugal life. Of similar central importance for Esayan were a number of social-cultural issues and the destiny of her people.

The sophisticated exploration of the human spirit in general, and that of women in particular, is a favorite domain of Esayan's, and the most charming, original, and enduring aspect of her short novels and stories. Introspection (but not introversion); fulfillment through self-expression, literature, and the arts; and communion with others and mother nature, all against a background of the human condition, are some of the elements that inspired adulation of her work. Esayan's ebullient journeys into the human psyche, needs, and aspirations are expressed in a simple but elegant, trim and trenchant, style aglow with warmth. Her short pieces that appeared in the first decade of the twentieth century consolidated her growing fame and attested to the wide embrace of her shimmering talent. *Spasman srahin mēj* (In the waiting room) analyzes the sad plight of a young mother; *Skiwtari verjaloysnerě* (Scutari twilights) is a delightful description of nature intertwined with some literary and aesthetic concerns; *Hlunerě ew ěmbostnerě* (Conformists and dissidents) deals with some socio-political issues under Abdulhamid II's oppressive rule; *Šnorhkʻov mardik* (Decent people) exposes the degenerate Armenian bourgeoisie; and *Kełtz hančarner* (Phoney [i.e., unrealized] geniuses) castigates, though with regret, ignorance in some circles of Armenian society and the slothful arrogance of some Armenian writers, principally the precocious Intra (q.v.).

There followed *Aweraknerun mēj* (Amid the ruins), a soulful record of the aftermath of the 1909 massacres of the Armenians in Adana and neighboring towns. Esayan toured the area on a relief mission, observed the devastation, and met with survivors. The motives for the calamity were beyond her scope, and her account is free of political or racial-religious commentary. Beside slain and charred bodies, houses, and churches, Esayan's testimony with dramatic sensitivity articulated the anguish of those who witnessed the carnage, mainly women and elderly people. Many of the victims had come from the Armenian provinces in the East. Having fled the Armenian massacres of the mid-1890s, some of them had settled in the region, and some had come in search of temporary or seasonal employment. Although Esayan portrays a number of defiant Turks, the unavoidability of self-defense dawns upon some of those who had been taken by surprise or had shunned the idea of resistance before the carnage. But perhaps Esayan's greatest triumph was her optimism, generated by her people's wonderful resilience, with which she illuminates her disquieting narrative.

Verjin bažakě (The last cup) and *Hogis ak'soreal* (My soul in exile) are among Esayan's best pieces. The former lays bare the sentiments and sensations of a woman, unhappy after a somewhat hasty marriage. Esayan explores in a luminous prose the power of unalloyed love as an expression of perhaps the only freedom one can attain, and the clash of individual liberties with social duties and conventions. *Hogis ak'soreal* is a sophisticated discussion of the intricate universe and relationships of individuals with one another on the one hand, and with the arts and literature, society, and the homeland on the other. War, love, cultural influences, glimpses into the frame of mind of Turkish women, and Armeno-Turkish relations are touched upon in *Meliha Nuri Haněm.* Traits of the latter's cold-blooded character appear in Ewp'imē, the heroine of *Erb aylews chen sirer* (When they no longer love), who banishes her original love for another in anticipation of a marriage of convenience.

Esayan wrote a number of other outstanding short novels and stories before settling in Soviet Armenia. She also published "Žołovurdi mě hogevark'ě" (A people in the agony of death), the testimony of a survivor of the genocide; *Nahanjoł užerě* (The retreating forces), a novel of political nature; and *Promet'ews azatagruatz* (Prometheus unchained), her very sympathetic impressions of a visit to Soviet Armenia. In the last, Soviet phase of her literary career, Esayan created two exquisite works: *Krake šapikě* (A shirt ablaze) and *Silihtari parteznerě* (The gardens of Silihdar; an incomplete work), both of which are reminiscences of an autobiographical nature. *Barpa Ḥachik* (Uncle Ḥachik), an extensive novel, appeared posthumously and suffers from a number of flaws. Had she supervised its publication, Esayan would undoubtedly have made substantial revisions to it.

SURĒN PART'EWEAN (1876–1921), a writer of short prose pieces, editor, publicist, and a spirited polemicist, in the main reflected the effects of the Armenian massacres of the 1890s and that of Adana on the Armenian Dispersion. Passionate and partisan, somewhat cantankerous and condescending, Part'ewean nonetheless made a name for himself early in his literary-journalistic career. To a large extent, he owed this to his short stories, vignettes, and short prose forms, which encapsulated the physical agony and mental anguish of the survivors who were left with a hollow life devoid of human and national identity. His otherwise confident and forceful style is now and then marred by rhetorical elements and contrived eloquence.

ARAM ANTONEAN (1875–1951), primarily an editor-journalist, was also a historian, critic, and the author of a considerable number of prose pieces, both large and small. His non-literary volumes are important but beyond the scope of this brief survey. What clinched him a spot in the history of Armenian letters was his small collection of short stories, titled *Ayn sew ōrerun* (During those dark days). Antonean was among the Armenian intellectuals deported in 1915. He fortuitously escaped certain death and recorded a number of episodes he had witnessed on the trek of deportation and death across the Syrian desert. Narrated in a direct and simple style, the stories capture in an unembellished fashion some chilling instances of man-made tragedy.

YAKOB ŌŠAKAN (1883–1948) is a celebrated novelist and a key figure to understanding both modern Western Armenian literature and that of the Dispersion. No serious study of the former can be undertaken without his extensive literary survey, *Hamapatker arewmtahay grakanutʻean* (A panorama of Western Armenian literature). His own novels, some of which rank among the best, added a new dimension to Armenian prose and signified a principal, albeit inimitable, trend in the literature of the Dispersion. Aspiring after originality, he, together with Kostan Zaryan (q.v.) and Gełam Barsełean (1883–1915), founded the short-lived literary periodical *Mehean,* devoted to innovative approaches to Armenian literature. The bloodbath of 1915 claimed Barsełean's life and radically altered the outlook of those very few writers who fortuitously escaped it. Ōšakan and Zarean were among the survivors. But these erstwhile colleagues of like mind in quest of innovation pursued their literary experiments in very different ways.

Ḥonarhnerě (The humble), Ōšakan's first collection of short stories, depicts marginal characters from his native village in the vicinity of Iznik (the Nicaea of olden times). In a limpid and trenchant style and with soulful sympathy, Ōšakan probes the psychological depths of his protagonists, almost all of whose passionate yearnings remain unfulfilled. They eventually lose their sanity, soul, or life to unrequited love and passion. It was in this collection that one of Ōšakan's fundamental tenets took a clear-cut shape: that the libido was the most potent driving force behind human behavior. Despite the fact that the reader can easily discern the effects of poverty, ignorance, and traditions, such social issues were in themselves of no concern at all to the author, who maintained that the sole domain of literature was the human soul.

A thematic kinship, indeed oneness, marks his novels wherein there emerges in varying shades one other cardinal element central to Ōšakan's creed: "blood," by which he meant heredity, atavistic patterns, customs, myths and traditions, and overall racial characteristics. As he once put it in his self-portrait, for him the elements of true art are derived from blood. This concept informs his analysis of human behavior, including that of the perpetrators of the genocide. Not surprisingly, the massive butchery of his nation haunted him throughout his life (on several occasions he had escaped death by the skin of his teeth). Before his very eyes, the pre-1915 intellectual substratum had been destroyed, and its architects, the glories of Western Armenian literature, most of whom Ōšakan knew intimately, had been slaughtered in cold blood. A lifestyle, a culture, and its monuments had perished and a homeland lost. His people were decimated and dispersed. And the Dispersion that arose offered him but cold comfort. Ōšakan had always felt that the response of Armenian writers to the massacres of the mid-1890s, those of Adana, and the inferno of 1915 had been, with few exceptions, inadequate. Now a new generation of writers, many of whom were orphaned by the calamity, turned inward, rejected old Armenian ways and values, and tried, albeit unsuccessfully, to circumvent the genocide. Ōšakan believed that he had to help Armenians and non-Armenians understand this crime against humanity—lest it strike mankind again—especially in view of the apathy of the West and Turkish denials of this wholesale slaughter, in which, he averred, the Turkish masses had actively and extensively taken part. The key to understanding this man-made tragedy, Ōšakan held, lay in the Turkish psyche. Overwhelmed by the enormity of the loss and consumed with wrath, he delved into the Turkish soul in search of the roots of the terrible evil, as he put it, that gripped it during and after the massacres of the mid-1890s. He did so with unforgiving passion.

Siwlēyman Ēfēnti (Süleyman Efendi), perhaps the least successful of his novels, is an attempt to project his image of the Turk. The protagonist, a man of unspeakable cruelty, utter corruption, and base instincts, rises rapidly to eminence, power, and wealth. His son, totally unlike his ghoulish father, is a decent young man (taking after his mother, who came from a fine urban family) with enlightened political views. He disowns and kills his father and is sentenced to 101 years in prison. *Hači Aptullah* (Haji Abdullah), a far better work, is the sad and lurid story of Abdullah, who has two wives: one of whom bears him five children that all die in infancy. Misled and inspired by his superstitious and fanatical father-in-law, Abdullah commits ghastly murders. He too, is sentenced to 101 years in prison. In the same gaol, the reader meets Haji Murad, the Armenian protagonist of *Hači Murat,* a lone wolf unjustly wanted for murder. Recruited by Armenian revolutionaries, Murat is eventually disillusioned with them. He falls for a Circassian woman and is dragged to prison straight from her bed. *Tzak ptukě* (The incontinent woman; the moral-traditional context of this idiomatic phrase is not possible to capture in a single English word) is arguably Ōšakan's best novel. There is much more to it than just the dramatic life and demise of a lascivious young woman. In this novel, as well as in *Hači Murat* and some earlier works, including *Kayserakan yałt'ergut'iwn* (Imperial exultation; a series of five abstract and rather dull stories), Ōšakan outlined certain trends, factors, and metamorphoses in Turkish mentality on the eve of World War I, all of which were to have been amplified in his grand novel, *Mnatsordats* (acclaimed by almost all observers as his chef-d'oeuvre), which remained incomplete.

Mnatsordats is the classical, genitive-dative plural form of *mnatsordk'* (i.e., remnants, relics, fragments and, hence, *Paralipomena*), and the Armenian appellation (as in the Greek version, *1* and *2 Paralipomenon*) of the two books of Chronicles. But Ōšakan, despite some very obvious parallels (e.g., destruction and exile), makes no reference to the books of Chronicles and simply uses the word in the nominative, in the sense of "remnants," "fragments" or "relics." The reader is left to surmise on the basis of the extant version and Ōšakan's comments on the unwritten parts of the plot that what he principally had in mind was not so much the survivors, as the collective self of those who perished in 1915. He wished to perpetuate as many traits of this identity as he could, in a manner creatively adapted from Proust. The period he planned to cover stretched from about the 1850s to 1915, but the published text brings the story of some Armenian peasants and urban Turks up to the early 1900s, well within Abdulhamid II's reign. The third, *inachevé,* volume, was to deal with the crime in Bursa and Çankırı, the final destination of some of the luminous intellectuals rounded up on the night of 24 April 1915, concluding the narrative in the Syrian desert.

The novel juxtaposes the Armenian mentality and Turkish psyche and illustrates the corrupting effects of the latter on the former, according to Ōšakan's lights. It shows, at a certain locale near Bursa, the transformations in Armenian character under oppression and terror. As in the Armenian, so in the Turkish case: Ōšakan resorts to psychological analysis to probe the metamorphoses in the Turkish soul, tracing its genetic characteristics, social and political structures, music and architecture, and the rise of atavistic patterns among German-educated leaders (Ōšakan firmly believed in German complicity in the genocide), which, he averred, also seized the Turkish masses and gave rise to a pervasive state of mind that conceived and carried out the genocide. There is little action in the novel, but its intriguing plot, penetrating analyses, and the torrential flow of Ōšakan's narrative make for gripping reading. Such, however, may not be the case for readers (of Ōšakan's prose in general) unfamiliar with his style, which has been severely criticized for its unconventional patterns and studied complexity. In fact, unusual syntax, ellipsis, inversion, periphrasis, and parallelisms are common, as are exceedingly short nominal sentences, tortuously long sentences, vague interrogative phrases, new semantic nuances, and unorthodox punctuation. He argued convincingly that his sophisticated style was unstudied and urged the first-time reader to be patient. In addition, Ōšakan's dissection of human behavior from his own perspective has not been popular with some readers. As more and more of his works are made available to the public, there is a growing recognition of his experiments, his contribution to the genre, and of his novel as one of the remarkable accomplishments in twentieth-century Armenian literature. Although Ōšakan named three contemporary Armenian writers (cf. his *Hamapatker,* vol. 10, 133–34) and certain factors to explain his failure to complete the novel, one should look elsewhere for such mitigating circumstances. In all likelihood, what clipped his wings and crippled his mental stamina was of a technical, structural, and emotional nature.

The Armenian theater had forged a remarkable tradition by the time Ōšakan appeared on the literary stage. Nonetheless, he found the accomplishments of playwrights, including those of the most celebrated, Širvanzade and Šantʻ (q.q.v.), to be unsatisfactory, particularly in content. According to him, the former resorted to cheap effects and vulgar realism; the latter paid excessive attention to form, and his plays were removed from life and rather cinematic. (From what one can glean from sporadic comments, Ōšakan had no taste for the cinema.) The plays he fashioned were to expose the inner recesses of the human soul and to imitate human life in a genuine fashion. Although he never said as much, they also partly illustrated his criticism of his colleagues. He wrote a number of plays and many a *kʻnaraḥał,* (literally, a "lyrical play"), which, he once said, were meant to be read and staged. They are interesting and mostly enjoyable to read as the expression of a different and creditable experiment. But they all suffer from technical flaws that call into question their suitability for stage and their power to convince. Ōšakan relied on the utterances of his characters to unveil human drama, conflicts of base instincts, sexual drive, etc.; yet styling effective dialogues was not one of his foremost strengths. In some cases his characters lack credibility, and intensity withers in protracted, repetitious conversations. One of his best "lyrical" plays remains *Stepʻannos Siwnetsi,* a most attractive *kʻnaraḥał* in verse, based on the life of Stepʻanos Siwnetsi (d. 735), metropolitan of Siwnikʻ, who was killed by a harlot and whose life is related by a number of historians (Movsēs Kałankatuatsi or Dasḥurantsi, Kirakos Gandzaketsi, Mḥitʻar Ayrivanetsi, and Stepʻanos Ōrbelean.) Having been shunned, privately as well as in public, by the metropolitan, Ōšakan's Princess of Siwnikʻ (replacing the historical harlot) commits a crime of passion. Three plays of Ōšakan's were published in 1990: *Nor psakě* (The new wedding) deals with love and loving in wedlock; *Knkʻahayrě* (The godfather) is the story of a wealthy old man who "charitably" unites a couple in matrimony, only to use the bride as his mistress and the husband for public appearances; and *Akʻloramartě* (The cockfight) illustrates love and patriotism and juxtaposes, in the catastrophic days of World War I, those who sink deep into the mire of utter corruption and dishonor to save their skin with those who face death with courage and dignity.

Ōšakan attached no importance to literary criticism, regarding it as an ephemeral effort with no appreciable impact on literature (he once called it a "parasitic genre"). Yet with his critical thought molded by Sainte-Beuve, Taine, Jules Lemaître, and Remy de Gourmont, among others, he wrote a monumental panorama of Western Armenian literature, which has since become an indispensable tool for its history, from its birth in the 1840s to its extinction in the wake of its man-made eclipse in 1915. It is a gallery of some fifty portraits drawn against a background of the period, with unique insights into the person, life, and work of the authors. Such sharp perception Ōšakan owed not only to his bright intellect, keen memory, and erudition, but also to his active participation in Western Armenian literary-cultural life in the early twentieth century and to his personal acquaintance with most of the illustrious and the not-so-illustrious writers of the period. Given his propinquity to them, Ōšakan took pains to maintain exacting standards of objectivity–one of the main merits of this work. Vastly improving the tradition initiated by Aršak Chōpanean and Artašēs Yarutʻiwnean (q.q.v.), Ōšakan developed his highly personal approach to literary history and criticism. He recreated the era as seen through his own eyes, and he forged the complex environment that nourished its own literature, bringing to life multitudes of characters and colors, texts and tools, ideas and idiosyncrasies, impressions and impulses, and national moods and spirits. The work certainly took the pulse of Armenian intellectual life and, together with elements of inquiry and judgment (such as analysis, comparison, craftsmanship, simplicity, sincerity, and depth), and what he considered national ethnic features, has been an interesting and unique touchstone by which to judge the accomplishments of Western Armenian authors. Still, many have disagreed and will undoubtedly continue to disagree with some of his principles and pronouncements, though never without help from Ōšakan himself. His sweeping, if audacious and candid, generalizations and criticism are at times parochial, contradictory or naive. But the chief reason for discord lay in Ōšakan's definition of literature and his principles of critique. And when it came to that, both he and his opponents took intolerant and intransigent stances. An extra element of contention and recrimination was Ōšakan's almost total failure to appreciate Eastern Armenian verse, whether pre-Soviet or Soviet. In truth, Ōšakan was similarly censorious towards Western Armenian poets, but in the final analysis, he did indeed have a bias in favor of Western Armenian poetry and criticism. If one looked at the larger picture, such polarity ultimately reflected the cleavage between the Eastern and Western Armenian mentality and outlook.

YAKOB MNDZURI (1886–1978) was already a septuagenarian when his first collection of short stories and prose pieces appeared in 1958. He has since been ranked among the chief masters who have chosen the Armenian countryside as the setting for their literature. A fine tradition had been gradually shaped in the works of Ḥrimean, Sruandzteants, Tʻlkatintsi, Ṙ. Zardarean, Hamasteł (q.q.v.), and many others. What Mndzuri revealed to his readers was a new and enchanting tiny universe that had all but vanished in 1915. To age thirteen, Mndzuri had lived in his native village of Armtan (Armudan, Turkey). He then spent nine years in Constantinople and returned to his birthplace in 1907. He taught in the winter and worked in the fields the remainder of the year. In 1914 he left his wife and four children behind for medical treatment in Istanbul. As World War I broke out within a short period of his departure, he was unable to return home. In the meantime, his entire family perished in 1915. Mndzuri settled in Istanbul, remarried, and took odd jobs to earn a living. And he set forth quietly on a long, nostalgic journey to his native village and its vicinity in the years 1890–1914, recreating its era and aura in short stories and in short descriptive pieces.

Mndzuri must have led a double life; his mind fled his body, an exile resident of Istanbul, a kind of pied à terre, for total immersion in the routine of his native village. The chronological and geographical distances that stood between him and his cherished home were reduced to almost nil. His image of his birthplace is one large, detailed, and variegated picture, where people, places, nature, and animals are painted as an organic whole. But even to the naked eye, certain details of the larger canvas look fuzzy. In many a piece, Mndzuri left the denouement (actually, "conclusion" would be a more appropriate word) unresolved; they come to an abrupt and uncertain end. This helps explain one cardinal facet of his literary postulate. He was interested in recalling real life, as he had lived and remembered it, with a view to saving it from oblivion. And if a particular scene or event was devoid of drama or conflict, it still revealed certain details that contributed to the larger picture. Hence, it seems he was indifferent to the niceties of literary devices and plot, since the overwhelming majority of his pieces do not conform to conventional definitions of the short story.

In adhering to the tenet of recreating true life, Mndzuri closely courted the danger of mechanically descriptive reproductions. But he was able to bring his characters to life. They are seen in their habitat and quaint customs, in their intimate relations to nature and animals, in their follies and foibles, in their affectionate desires and infidelities, in their failures and triumphs, in mourning and feasting. Many of them are non-Armenians (Kurds, Syrians, Qizilbash, etc.), but they all belong to and are shaped by the same milieu; they are invoked with the same tender love by the author, who was and remained one of them to the end of his life. He saw them through their own eyes and employed their own modes of thought, but his descriptions of them are those of a lavishly gifted narrator. The universe he recreated was not one of consuming passion, though it lacked neither drama nor conflict. Mndzuri sought out no class-consciousness, class conflict, or explicit instances of social and political injustice. But his prose is subtly infused with such complications and implications. The author made no deep excursuses into the psyche of his characters; their telling behavior and curt utterances speak volumes to the reader. He wrote in the spoken tongue (using dialect abundantly, especially in his dialogues), in a taut, concise style that is unusual in many ways; a single complex sentence is often loaded to the full capacity of a paragraph or a whole page, rapidly leading the reader from one point of culmination to another, with graceful simplicity and a sensitive touch of melancholy and humor. Some of his best characters, the last of a vanished world, leap out of his pages with memorable vivacity and veracity, setting his art apart from that of other acknowledged masters of the genre in terms of style and treatment.

Eastern Armenian Literature

HOVHANNES HOVHANNISYAN's (1864–1929) melancholic poetry, though small in quantity, set the tone for a number of major poets. His wistful, impersonal yearning that captured the mood of the age was a marked change from the patriotic poetry of Ṙapʻayēl Patkanean (q.v.) and that of his teacher, Smbat Šahaziz (q.v.). Nature, love, patriotism, exhortation for his nation not to be given to despondency, some historical figures, and the Armenian massacres of the mid-1890s inspired Hovhannisyan's gentle, lyrical verse. Some observers have found some correlation in mood between Hovhannisyan and the Russian poet Semyon Nadson (1862–87). Hovhannisyan's diction is purer and more flexible than that of his predecessors, and contains elements of vivid popular expressions and idioms thrown into some of his better known songs. Hovhannisyan also distinguished himself by his sensitivity to form–an early experiment that was built upon by subsequent masters.

ALEKʻSANDR TZATUREAN's (1865–1917) work has affinities with both his generation of writers and the work of his junior contemporaries, who were soon to emerge as the pre-eminent poets of the age. Love, nature, the countryside, emigrants, patriotism, the plight of the unfortunate and the working class, and his championing of the truth and the beautiful inspired his imagination. His imagery is ordinary and his work, popular at the time, lacks an overall strong note of authenticity, but his winsome sincerity and lively style add charm to some of his poems, of which half a dozen or so have been put to music and gained popularity, as have his humorous-satirical poems. He seems to be the only author to have written a series of marine poems (notably the cycle "Łrimi albomits, 1896–1898," i.e., From the Crimean album, 1896–1898), which, it is tempting to note (however unfair the comparison may be) have been overshadowed by the marine paintings of his senior contemporary and fellow countryman, I. K. Ayvazovski (1817–1900).

YOVHANNĒS TʻUMANEAN (1869–1923) is one of the most popular writers of the twentieth century. His poems, epic and lyric, his short stories, tales, and folk tales are all drawn from the soil of Armenia, especially the region of Loṙi, where he spent his childhood feasting his eyes on its pristine nature and listening to haunting tales and the fury of the elements dinning in his ears. His Armenian is a luminous, unadorned idiom, felicitous and dynamic in flow. There is an Olympian calm to his tone, particularly in his contemplative stanzas, and bare drama in his longer poems of epic nature. The unobtrusive presence of the elegiac is always felt, and a mourning mood pervades some of his monodies and his "Hogehangist" (Requiem) inspired by the grief of his nation. But overall, an unflinching optimism subtly illuminates his whole work, written with unstudied charm. Tʻumanean was initially under the spell of Ṙ. Patkanean and Ł.Ališan, but later felt closer affinities with H. Hovhannisyan and A. Tzaturean (q.q.v.). He considered Shakespeare and Pushkin the greatest masters, and he certainly owed the latter something for the craftsmanship in which he fashioned his delightful, homespun tradition.

A serious social concern provides the context for some of his best narrative poems: the devastating consequences of superstition, ignorance, and long-standing customs. “Maron,” “Loṙetsi Sakʻon,” and *Anuš* (or *Anoyš*) eloquently illustrate this point. Unable to tolerate her forced marriage, Marō sets herself free, but is cruelly shunned and snubbed by friend and foe alike, driving her to utter desperation. Despite skepticism on the part of some critics, “Loṙetsi Sakʻon” is a convincing and poignant psychological probe into the anguished soul of an ignorant, superstitious Sakʻō, whose imagination magnifies and multiplies imaginary beings, sounds, and threats that drive him insane. *Anuš,* the most popular opera (put to music by Armen Tigranyan, 1879–1950), is considered Tʻumanean’s masterpiece by most critics. Until the breakup of the Soviet Union, the Armenian national opera house inaugurated and concluded its annual season performing *Anuš.*

Anuš has a simple plot. Sarō and Mosi are friends, and Anuš, sister of Mosi, and Sarō are in love. Catching Mosi off guard at a traditional wrestling match, Sarō topples him to the ground with the rashness of an unreasoning lover. Mosi hunts down and shoots Sarō dead, avenging his public humiliation; Anuš goes out of her mind. Surprisingly, some have construed the poem (and a number of other works dealing with similar themes) as a nostalgic elegy for yesteryear. If there is any nostalgia here on the part of Tʻumanean, it is for noble love and the moral puṙity that characterized the peasantry. In all other respects, it is a total negation of outdated and disastrous notions of honor and tradition. In *Anuš,* as in other works revolving around similar subjects, Tʻumanean’s characters are entrapped by convention; they have no life of their own beyond the long-standing code of behavior, and are thus victims of ineluctable fate. Any act of defiance entails a deadly or tragic punishment. This has been seen as a manifestation of Tʻumanean’s realism, which assumes even greater sophistication when it documents the ravages of money and industrialization in this essentially backward and conservative society.

Tʻumanean congenially tapped the wellhead of Armenian folklore, especially folk tales, legends, and popular accounts. His adaptations are as vivid and varied in approach as the original material. In some cases he made only minor changes, leaving the plot untouched; in other instances he made major modifications, and on a number of occasions he blended his stories into a synthesis of varying details. Dawitʻ in “Sasuntsi Dawitʻ” is a composite character, with details of his portrait taken from the various recensions available to Tʻumanean. The poem, left incomplete, recreates the third cycle of the Armenian national epic and illustrates what Tʻumanean thought were the essential aspects of Dawitʻ’s character: a relentless struggle against invaders and despots, and the promotion of peace and friendship.

The "wandering" *ašuł*'s account recorded in E. Lalayeants's ethnographic collection, *Jawaḥkʻi burmunkʻ,* is the subject of *Tʻmkaberdi aṙumě* (The capture of Tmkabert), a poetic hymn to love and prowess, and the sad story of a woman's fickleness. The evil aspects of human nature and the power of love found expression in "Aḥtʻamar," an Armenian echo of *Hero and Leander.* A traditional account of faith and patriotism, and perhaps an allegorical commentary on Armenian resilience, is the essence of "Aławnu vankʻě" (The dove monastery). "Pʻarvana" (i.e., *parvāneh* = moth) illustrates the elusive nature of happiness and how lofty aspirations often remain unattainable. "Mi katʻil mełr" (A drop of honey), taken from *Ałuēsagirkʻ* (a medieval collection of fables), mocks the stupid aspects of human behavior, petty parti-pris, rash action, and mob mentality. Tʻumanean wrote a few yarns and adaptations of some twenty Armenian fairy tales and translated nearly as many into Armenian, mainly from German.

The mysteries of the universe and life claimed a good deal of Tʻumanean's thoughts. His long poem "Dēpi anhuně" (Journey to infinity) and his quatrains, close to seventy in number, explore such concepts in relation to time and space, revealing something of the cosmic pantheist in him. To him, the soul was immortal; it merged in eternal union with the only immutable constant–time–just like the wavelets of a tributary river with the ocean. The vanity of life, the joy of giving, altruism and lofty human values, and "the biography of his soul" are vividly framed in his philosophical quatrains, in effortless and rhythmic lines. Not surprisingly, the elegiac mood in his patriotic verse ("Hayots leṙnerum," "Mer uḥtě," "Hayots viště," "Hayrenikʻis het," etc.) is free from chauvinism or extreme partisanship, and though at times overwhelmed by grief, racial and racist distinctions are inundated by his opulent spirit.

Of his short stories, "Erkatʻułu šinutʻiwně" (The construction of the railway) laments the negative consequences the train carried in its train into rural areas, spoiling nature, polluting the air (and driving the deer away), and precipitating industrialization, thus drastically changing the moral and social fabric of society. "Nesoyi kʻarabałnisě" (Neso's steam bath) is the sad story of victims of ignorance. In "Im ěnker Neson" (My friend, Neso), cruel social conditions transform Neso from a kind soul into a villain. And "Gikʻor," wherein the boy of the title is uprooted from his native village only to wither away in the big city, is an exquisite accomplishment, the crown of his short stories.

AVETIKʻ ISAHAKYAN's (1875–1957) first poems and verse collection, *Erger u vērkʻer* (Songs and wounds), were greeted with acclaim, as were his subsequent collections. If Loṙi was T'umanean's source of inspiration, then Širak, with its landscape and lifestyle, was Isahakyan's. Even though T'umanean, the brightest star of his generation, had only just made his promising appearance, heralding the arrival of a new generation, Ṙap'ayēl Patkanean and particularly Hovhannes Hovhannisyan (q.q.v.) were still the dominant poets. There were some innovative qualities to Isahakyan's literary effort in both form and content, instantly acknowledged by the public and recognized by the historians of Armenian literature. A far more emotional, fiery, and transparent lyricism than that found in H. Hovhannisyan's verse distinguished Isahakyan's poetic profile. He sang of love, often juxtaposing its ineffable joys with its rejections, sorrows, and deep pain. There was drama and color to his poems, of which a few (a greater number than any of his predecessors) celebrated mothers, motherly love, and devotion–a theme later picked up by Hovhannes Širaz (q.v.). Some of his songs were so sorrowful that they bordered on maudlin sentimentality. He used the spoken dialect of his native region, which was flexible, simple but highly idiomatic, and richly adorned with popular expressions of native provenance, along with many non-native phrases that originated in neighboring Islamic traditions. Thus, aspects of his style and facets of his sensibilities reveal a certain affinity with the art of the Armenian *ašułs*. Isahakyan had an excellent feel for rhyme and rhythm. He frequently used compound adjectives (somewhat akin to the Homeric epithet), incremental repetition, and, particularly, internal rhyme to impressive effect. On some occasions this led to monotony and repetition, but on the whole it introduced musicality to his stoically melancholic poems. This, perhaps, explains why a large number of his poems were put to music.

Isahakyan wrote numerous narrative poems, fables, and legends on a wide variety of topics: love, patriotism, liberty, selfless maternal dedication, and human values and virtues. Such verse was rendered in a lyrical, contemplative mood, employing the literary standard, as in the case of almost all of his non-amatory verse. He also wrote short fiction, a kind of prose poem blended with elements of poetic prose. He was attracted to and recast legends and traditional stories of various countries from Finland to Arabia, from Serbia to Iran, India, and China. One cannot help likening him to a wayfarer with an insatiable appetite, in search of the bright moment, the fleeting second of happiness; for life for him was "the fleeing shadow of a cloud." It is on this premise and a few other philosophical concerns that his long poem, *Abu-Lala-Mahari* (named after the celebrated Arab poet-thinker, Abū al-'alā' al-Ma'arrī, 973–1058), rises.

The poem opens with a brief prologue followed by seven *sūrahs* (so named are the chapters in the *Qur'ān*) and a final *sūrah.* The numeral seven (which has many symbolic values), the camels (symbolizing humility, prudence, but also nymphomania), the palm trees (a symbol of triumph), and the sandy desert, all frequently visible in the poem, do not seem to convey a pronounced symbolic significance. The word *sūrah* (*surah* in the poem) and a number of other Arabic words are interspersed in the text for purposes of characterization. There is no story to narrate; Abu Lala Mahari is seen at night fleeing Baghdad in disgust and baring his soul to the reader in a soliloquy of morbid damnation and vituperation against society. The great Arab poet's profound pessimism, his denunciation of society, women, worldly pleasures, and the unstoppable reign of evil in the world all resonate in the poem. In the harshest terms, Isahakyan also condemns women and dismisses man-made laws, friendship and loyalty, evanescent glory, wealth, power, cities and urban life, the masses, tyrants, and corruption. There is some repetition and verbosity as his breath occasionally falls short of loading to capacity the twenty-syllable lines, which serve his purposes well and help him hammer his message home. Human beings incur Isahakyan's wrath for their failure to grasp and appreciate in practical terms the transience of human life and evanescence of beauty, pursuing instead petty ends and rendering life an insufferable experience for all. Soviet Armenian critics have seen the poem as a reaction to the abortive Russian revolution of 1905. There may be some truth to this, but Isahakyan had also been following European (especially German) philosophy and studying world religions. These obviously suggest alternative or at least complementary sources of influence and inspiration.

VAHAN TĒREAN's (1885–1920) distinct poetic voice ranked him among the elite of Armenian writers at the turn of the twentieth century. Both Tʻumanean and Isahakyan warmly greeted his first collection (the latter had earlier taken him under his wing), which differed so very much from their poetry and ushered in a new approach to verse. Titled *Mtʻnšałi anurjner* (Twilight or crepuscular reveries), it appeared in 1908 and reappeared in a 1912 volume bringing together his subsequent series, written between the two dates: *Gišer ew yušer* (Night and recollections), *Oski hēkʻiatʻ* (Golden fairy tale), and *Veradardz* (Return). These collections, containing a good dose of romanticism, established the Symbolist tradition in Armenian verse, traces of which were already perceptible in Isahakyan's work.

Fairy tales were very much a part of Tērean's childhood. The magic fantasy in them, unreal and distant yet palatable and palliative, must have strongly impressed his mental disposition. During his student years in Moscow (at the Lazarevskii or Lazarean Institut and the university) and St. Petersburg, he avidly and in the original read Baudelaire, Mallarmé, Verlaine, Verhaeren, and the Russian Symbolists: F. Sologub, K. Balmont, V. Ivanov, V. Briusov, and A. Blok. Receptive to impulses from these poets, Tērean's poetic genius invented an *état d'âme,* all autumnal music. His bitterness, he once said, resulted from the incompatibility of his inclinations with the circumstances of life around him. The realm where his fancy and sensibilities fused is a distant one, set mostly in the twilight, where his imagination, transcending objective realities, conjures up misty visions of memories and a mystical experience of love, in rapidly changing moods; a fleeting second of perceived exaltation is instantly submerged in sadness, agony, disillusionment, forlornness, and nostalgia. He felt that the remote and the unreal were peaceful and attractive shelters for his indefinite sensations. He found "eternal liberty" in death, a tranquil realm of reprieve where he would feel relatively free of the burden of his emotions and anguish, which, together with love, he averred, were the only links bonding human beings together. In the poems where Tērean has given himself up completely and blissfully to gloom and pain, some Soviet Armenian critics have seen a miasma of despair and a plunge into decadence.

In the early 1910s, Tērean wrote a number of articles (in particular, "Hay grakanutʻean galikʻ ōrě" = The future of Armenian literature, and "Hogewor Hayastan" = Spiritual Armenia, both in 1914) severely criticizing the parochial aspects of Armenian intellectual life, the political parties, and the creation in nineteenth-century Armenian literature of a romantic and material (as opposed to cultural) Armenia. Every aspect of social, political, and cultural life, he held, was geared solely towards the political future of the Western Armenians. It was time the Armenians stopped gazing expectantly at the summit of Mount Ararat and at the ramshackle dome of Ējmiatzin and turned their sights to the revolution brought about by capitalism, the bustling cities, the machine age, and the crumbling of the barriers separating national cultures. It was important that a spiritual Armenia be created, bringing her out of her languorous and debilitating insularity into the mainstream of civilization by shattering the fetters of chauvinism and thoroughly assimilating European civilization. Although somewhat harsh and one-sided, there was much truth to Tērean's observations, which also offer clues to understanding his series titled *Erkir Nairi* (Land of Nairi), the mythical, spiritual homeland, conceived in his heart and projected in his visions as a magnificent apparition.

Echoing Lermontov, who loved the land and people of Russia rather than its glory ("Rodina" = Homeland, 1841), Tērean sang Armenia's soul and songs, misery and prayers, the sad sound of her tolling bells and the dim light of her huts, not the dazzle of her ancient glory. This, he felt, illustrated how his approach contrasted with backward looking "traditional" patriotism and its symbols of Armenia. He sought through his art to release and ennoble the soul of Armenia, to brighten the prospects of her survival. The land of Nairi, as spiritual Armenia incarnate, and his heart and mind mingle into one entity, simple yet mysterious, drowned in blood yet invincible. What is perhaps more important still, despite the grief, gloom, and the black mist shrouding Nairi, is that an uplifting optimism aesthetically and emotionally informs the poems, most of which were written during World War I, when the Armenians looked death in the eye. (It is interesting to mention here that Tērean had been politically active since his student days. A Social-Democrat, he became a Bolshevik in 1917 and served in the higher echelons of the Soviet government. As the voice of Armenia, he met with Lenin on several occasions, went to Brest-Litovsk with Trotsky, and worked under Stalin at the Nationalities Commissariat.)

There is splendor and captivating mystery to Tērean's lyrical style. Limpid and elegant, it flows melodiously, in pulsating rhythm and rhyme. He employed synesthesia, onomatopoeia, assonance, and alliteration (with an abundance of sibilants) to impressive musical effect and formed new compound words. Although Armenian verse is syllabic, he experimented stress patterns, and introduced forms such as the triolet and ghasel (ghazal).

AWETIS AHARONEAN's (1866–1948) literary output consists of short stories, reminiscences, travel notes, plays, some poetry, and ethnographic studies. Among his better works are his short stories and novelettes set in his native province or in other parts of Armenia proper. He received immediate recognition for his initial works such as *Patkerner* (Scenes), in which he depicted refugees fleeing the Armenian massacres of the mid-1890s, and *Azatutʻean čanaparhin* (On the road to freedom), which became a part of the revolutionary canon, depicting the activities of Armenian revolutionaries. Portrayed in his other short novels and stories are peasants clinging to traditional values in a world where they are treated as second-class subjects. In this gloomy and cruel microcosm, sometimes characterized by massive scenes of destruction, Aharonean's anguished characters, often given to fatalism, almost invariably meet a tragic end. His main preoccupation here lies not so much with the reasons for his heroes' misery as with psychological analyses probing the tortured depth of the human soul.

Given entirely to imagination, Aharonean pays hardly any attention to characterization or construction–flaws that are characteristic of even his best short stories. His solicitude for his fellow countrymen and for human suffering are revealed in his haunting descriptions, which are further dramatized by his notable skill in depicting nature. His style, highly emotional throughout, is often marred with mawkishness, but is colorful and flows smoothly. His lyricism and analytical abilities have led some critics to draw parallels between him and the Russian writer Leonid Andreev. It has also been noted, more appropriately perhaps, that his patriotism and style are more in tune with those of one of his celebrated masters: Ḥachatur Abovean (q.v.).

MURATSAN (1854–1908) was one of the few leading authors who swam against the tide of progress and reform sweeping the Armenian intelligentsia in the closing decades of the nineteenth century. With little or no regard for socioeconomic and political factors, he saw the responsible, mature, and inward-looking individual, and the subordination of the personal to the common good, as the basis for human prosperity. Appalled by the secular and enlightened nationalism of the liberals and the irreparable damage he claimed it caused to Armenian solidarity, Muratsan appeared on the literary scene as a convinced conservative and a staunch proponent of national unity, tradition, and religion.

The debate since the 1840s between the Russian westernizers and Slavophiles, and its subsequent manifestations, stimulated similar disputes over Armenian identity and the role of the Church of Armenia in defining and perpetuating the national ethos. Unlike the Armenian liberals, Muratsan held that loyalty to the Church of Armenia was of utmost importance. Three of his short novels illustrate the point in an intolerant fashion. *Hay bołokʻakani ěntanikʻě* (The family of an Armenian Protestant) elaborates how the conversion of an Armenian to Protestantism leads to the destruction of his family and his own demise. *Im katʻolik harsnatsun* (My Catholic bride-to-be) is an attack on Roman Catholicism, as is *Andrēas Erēts* (Andreas the priest), which is based on the story of Andrēas, a martyr whose death is commemorated in an elegy by Nersēs Mokatsi (q.v.) and recounted by Aṙakʻel Dawrižetsi (*History*, xxvii).

The countryside occupied a prominent place in Muratsan's thought, because he believed a purer form of life and the best elements and traditions of nationhood had been preserved there, holding the only hope for a bright future. And Muratsan sounded the alarm at its decline. It was also partly in response to the then prevalent calls for young people to go on missions of enlightenment in rural areas that he wrote three of his better known novels. *Ḥorhrdawor miandznuhi* (A mysterious sister) is the story of Sister Anna, who has moved away from the city to promote literacy and religious zeal in the countryside. In *Noyi agṙawě* (Noah's raven), a peasant educated in Tiflis and St. Petersburg refuses to return to his needy parents in his native village. In *Aṙakʿealě* (The missionary), an inspired volunteer determined to illuminate and serve the peasantry flees back to the lap of luxury from the very first village on the shores of lake Sewan.

One of the attractive qualities of Muratsan's literature is his attempt to probe the depths of human behavior, the sole domain where human destiny takes shape, almost independently of objective factors. His creed that the individual ego should be submerged to achieve social harmony found its best expression in his historical novel, *Gēorg Marzpetuni,* whose eponymous character is a military leader. Action unfolds in the first half of the tenth century, the twilight of Arab rule, with King Ašot Erkatʿ and Catholicos-historian Yovhannēs Drasḥanakerttsi as two of the more prominent characters in the novel. Muratsan plunges the reader into a dramatic situation, where all but the central hero are in thrall to their passions and personal ends. King Ašot Erkatʿ is in love with a noble's wife and has thus alienated her husband as well as his own queen, father-in-law, and a number of other powerful and vengeful figures, while he, the desperate king, is in a state of agony and debilitating apathy. It is Gēorg Marzpetuni, Muratsan's ideal character, a patriot at peace with himself and motivated only by overall national interests, who tries to keep the country together. The work, certainly one of the best historical novels, makes for a tense and gripping reading, in a flexible Eastern Armenian with a good deal of Classical Armenian forms.

Širvanzade (1858–1935) is one of the pre-eminent masters of prose and drama. He is a chronicler, with a cold clear eye and probing psychological insight, of the Transcaucasian cities, large and provincial, and the profound economic and social changes that propelled the region into an era of bustling economic activities and attendant consequences, particularly after oil fields lit up the skies of Baku, attracting capitalists and workers alike. Abiding by the tenets of realism as he saw it (he detested naturalism), he held his heroes hostage to the socioeconomic conditions enveloping them. Traditional values crumbled, bringing down with them all those individuals and families who clung to them, while simultaneously opening up opportunities for agile entrepreneurs with little or no regard for anything but wealth and power. He shed no tears for the old, but observed and negated the new with forceful skepticism. His sympathy certainly lay with the victims of economic oppression and social injustice, but even the slightest expression of sentimentality was always firmly held in check. There occur in his narrative at times annoying instances of hollow aloofness. His somewhat inflexible objectivity as an author might be one of the factors accounting for this. His belief in reproducing the unadorned truth might be another. And the occasional unevenness of his aesthetic feel for the language might be the third element. For he never had formal instruction in Armenian, and initially, if very briefly, he wrote for Russian periodicals. Yet the sweep of his work is so broad, evincing so many merits, and his insight into human character and actual realities is so incisive that his exalted position among the shapers of the canon is permanent.

Širvanzade began by contributing to the periodical *Mšak* of Tiflis on the oil fields of Baku and wrote his first, touching short narrative on the degradation and worthlessness of workers in the oil fields (*Hrdeh nawtagortzaranum*). *Namus* (Honor, or good repute), his first major novel, was widely recognized. It takes place in Shamakhi, the author's birthplace, and is artistically documented by his intimate familiarity with the local mores and mentality. The two heroes, Susan and Seyran, fall victim to circumstances generated by uncompromising adherence to traditional customs and concepts of personal dignity, poverty, moral degeneration, and the power of money. Fatma and Asad (in *Fatman ew Asadě*) meet a similar fate for more or less identical reasons. *Arambin* (A married woman), with elements of romanticism, deals with the issue of divorce. Varvara, the heroine, is abandoned by her husband and subjected to cruel intolerance. She is unable and unwilling to remarry due to rigid divorce laws, and to avoid "staining" her father's honor, she wastes away.

The 1890s were a productive decade for Širvanzade. Of his many works, *Zur yoyser* (Vain hopes), *Arsēn Dimaksean*, *Tsawagarě,* or *Char ogi* (The epileptic, or evil spirit) stand out and precede his masterpiece, *Kaos* (Chaos). The first is an intriguing novel in which the hopes and expectations of lovers and aspirants dissipate in the moral, social, and economic confusion of the time with dire consequences. Arsēn Dimaksean, a dedicated social educational reformer but a physically unattractive character, faces mighty foes with murky ends and fails in matters of the heart. Mesrop Čanašean (1908–74) in his history of modern Armenian literature, *Patmutiwn ardi hay grakanutean,* has seen in the situation arising from Arsēn's ugly appearance a possible parallel with E. Rostand's *Cyrano de Bergerac*. The unfortunate epileptic is Sona, a wonderful, innocent young woman, who meets a violent fate in an evil and superstitious society.

Kaos is set in Baku at the end of the nineteenth century, by which time the oil industry had done away with all the hues and colors of a backward, indolent society, repainting it starkly in black and white. It is the story, or rather the chaos, the savage feud over money, that rends Markos Alimean's family apart after his death. Markos, an oil magnate, has designated his son, Smbat, to oversee the execution of his will, which calls on Smbat to rectify the mistake he committed by marrying a Russian (as opposed to an Armenian) woman and to extricate his brothers Mikʻayēl and Aršak from the mire of dissipation. The discord in Smbat's own family, the passion he shares with his brother Mikʻayēl for the same woman, Šušanik, and a doctored will provide the main springs of action and suspense in the novel. Numerous other characters and families form part of the conflict, which Širvanzade blends into the larger social picture in a magisterial fashion, as his memorable protagonists undergo profound transformations under the impact of industrial capitalism.

A number of shorter works followed *Kʻaos*. *Melania* is the sad story of a beautiful young woman bursting with life, married to an older, physically incapable man who attempts to maim her to ward off potential suitors. Širvanzade had shown his ability to explore the inner recesses of women's soul in an earlier short story, *Ōriord Liza* (Miss Liza), in which Liza, in sharp contrast to Melania, responds to the promptings of her heart rather than her mind. It must be remembered, though, that the situations in both stories are very different and that Liza was an unmarried woman when she promised to marry a person she loved, before succumbing to the mysterious charm of another. *Artistĕ* (The artist) tells of an ebullient teenager, Lewon, intoxicated by his love for music and the theater, and of the eventual collapse of his dreams and his suicide in a society where money, not art, sets standards and priorities. In sharp contrast to Lewon, another teenager, Vardan of *Vardan Ahrumean,* which Širvanzade wrote in a semi-satirical vein a year after *Artistĕ,* is obsessed with money like his father and is groomed, under his tutelage, as a would-be vampire.

Širvanzade also enjoys fame as one of Armenia's leading playwrights. His *Ewginē* attracted much attention, despite his as yet unfocused views on women. Ewginē, an innocent soul, is in agony for having loved someone else at one point in her teen years, and eventually bares her heart to her husband. Mihran, after an almost violent reaction, forgives her, recalling his sinful associations before his marriage to Ewginē. *Unēr irawunkʻ [?]* (Was she right?) is a far more sophisticated discussion of women's emancipation. Hersilē, artistically gifted and a believer in women's independence, is pitted against an older husband who thinks of her as only a wife and mother. She wittingly avoids the traditional, self-defeating denouement (suicide) and walks away from him. Of a piece with this drama is *Armenuhi,* in which the title character, who is all "poetry," is captive to her dull, tyrannical husband, Samson. With her husband's unexpected consent and with assistance from her admirer, Armenuhi is able to begin a new life.

Patui hamar (For honor; or, A debt of honor) had its premiere in Baku in 1904, and it has been a most popular drama ever since. It sketches conflicting characters in a family, the Ēlizbareans, who are on the verge of disintegration amid the social, economic, and moral disorder afflicting a society, usually defined as bourgeois by Soviet Armenian critics. Margarit, a genuine champion of truth and honesty, pays dearly for her principles in a deadly conflict with her father, Andrēas Ēlizbarean, who has amassed wealth and gained social standing by ruthlessly trampling partners and rivals alike. The characters, victims all of the changing rules of the business of life, drift helplessly to a sad confrontation, some driven by their passion for money and desire to maintain their public reputation, and some (Margarit, Artašēs) by an inbred sense of integrity.

In a way, *Awerakneri vray* (On the ruins) is a sequel to *Patui hamar.* It chronicles the collapse of a family, in this case due to the inability of a traditional merchant-businessman to compete with a new breed of sophisticated capitalists and the nouveaux riches whose enterprises rise on the ruins of the old. *Arhawirkʻi ōrerin* (In the days of terror) takes place near the borders of "Turkish Armenia" and depicts one aspect of the Armenian massacres and deportations: the participation of Armenian volunteers in the initial Russian thrust and withdrawal at the outset of World War I. The play reflects the hopes the Armenians pinned on Russia for deliverance from certain death and concludes with the retreat of the Russians and Armenian refugees. *Morgani ḥnamin* (Morgan's in-law) is Širvanzade's only full-length comedy (the other being *Šaṙlatanĕ,* The charlatan; or, Humbug, a one-act comedy, 1908), which he wrote after Armenia had become Soviet. It derides wealthy émigrés who fled the Bolshevik Revolution and settled in Paris, but who are still bent on maintaining their corrupt lifestyle by trafficking in cocaine and dreaming about selling off the oil fields and property they left behind to wealthy Americans. The main characters are Petros Mintʻoyean and his son Žorž (Georges), who is heavily in debt and bamboozles his father into believing that he is about to marry the niece of [J. Pierpont] Morgan. Of great literary and historical significance is Širvanzade's memoirs, *Keankʻi bovits* (From the crucible of life), a lively and insightful account of people, places, and events.

LEO (1860–1932), a prominent cultural figure with remarkable impact on Armenian intellectual activities, is best known for his history of Armenia, a vibrant account in a most engaging style. He is also known for his history, documents, and ideology of the Armenian Question; studies of the life and work of outstanding individuals, religious, and intellectual leaders (Mesrop Maštots, Catholicos Yovsēpʻ Arłutʻean, 1743–1801, Stepʻanos Nazarean, 1812–79, Grigor Artzruni, 1845–92); history of certain schools in Karabagh and Erevan; history of Armenian printing and merchants (ḥojas), etc.; and many other works still in manuscript form. After Armenia became a Soviet republic (Leo was invited to lecture at the State University of Erevan), he revised some of his views and works. It was a hasty revisionism with unconvincing results.

Leo also engaged in literary activities as an adherent of the school of realism. He wrote some literary criticism; sketched the portraits of some eighteenth- and nineteenth-century Armenian writers; introduced Russian, French, and English authors to Armenian readers; wrote a history of Eastern or Russian Armenian literature from its origins to the 1900s; and formulated his own literary vision in the form of short stories, novels, and plays, almost all of which he wrote at the earlier stages of his career. Armenian rural regions, sad and squalid, impoverished and forlorn, where superstition, ignorance, and old traditional values had a strong hold over peasants, make up the central theme of some of his short works, which are narrated in a lively style. His stories in an urban setting depict innocent victims of the "monstrous" bourgeois system. But a large part of the blame for many a misfortune Leo placed on religious (i.e., Christian) passivity and pacifism, despite the occasional, favorable stance he had for similar traditional values. Artsaḥ (Karabagh) forms the backdrop, either partially or wholly, to a few of his short stories and his patriotic novel *Melikʻi ałjikě* (The Melik's daughter).

LEWON MANUĒLEAN (1864–1919) tried his hand in poetry, plays, and prose. His verse, covering such issues as honesty and the defense of truth, the Armenian massacres, social and other topical concerns, bears the marks of H. Hovhannisyan's influence and now mostly seems rather turbid. Shakespeare was his idol and he wrote drama and "dramatic poems," as he called them, which are thought-provoking and have a greater appeal than his collection of poems. "Tigranuhi," based on Movsēs Ḥorenatsi's account (Tigranuhi, sister of Tigran and wife of Aždahak), illustrates the clash of personal and public interests. In "Galiley ew Milton," a Dominican (i.e., the Inquisition), science, and free thought (Galileo and Milton) confront one another (Manuēlean must have been aware of Milton's *Areopagitica*). In "Pʻotʻorik" (Storm), an indomitable poet, Diagoras of Melos, is seen rebelling against the gods. "Sasuntsi Dawitʻ ew Msray Melikʻ" illustrates one episode from the Armenian epic. Similarly,

"Dēpi ver" (Upward climb) represents a dramatic stage in Ḥ. Abovean's life. Manuēlean's novels (*Chalabineri aršawankʻě,* The Chalabi invasion, and *Ḥortakuatz keankʻ,* A shattered life) are insignificant. His dramas, which, broadly speaking, tackle the dangers threatening the family, were staged in many cities. His *Ṙusahay grakanutʻean patmutʻiwn* (A history of Russian Armenian literature) covers the nineteenth century and was for a while used as a textbook.

VRTʻANĒS PʻAPʻAZEAN (c1866–1920) was a prolific writer despite his constant peregrinations in the Armenian communities of the Caucasus, Iran, and the Ottoman Empire. Perhaps this was partly due to the reputedly Armenian gypsy blood running in his veins and may to a degree explain his attraction to the wide range of topics and lifestyles he covered in his short stories, tales, allegories, novels, plays, essays, literary criticism, and ethnographic and social articles. He made the first attempt to narrate the history of Armenian literature from its origins to his own time. His contributions to both Eastern and Western Armenian periodicals brought an even greater degree of public familiarity with Armenian affairs on both sides of the Russo-Ottoman border. His first short stories and narratives revolve around social injustice and inequality, usury, excessive taxation, moral decline, and economic hardship in the Armenian provinces of the Ottoman Empire. These stories are uneven and often characterized by verbosity, yet they contain some of his better works.

There was a marked turn in Pʻapʻazean's literary style and approach, and some formerly vague trends became more pronounced after his return from a nearly four-year sojourn as a student in Geneva. While his prose became more economical, his embrace grew wider, and he raised issues of broader regional and universal importance in Persian, Kurdish, or Armenian settings and short allegorical works. In his blistering attack on old values and stagnation (*Ĕmbost erger,* Rebellious songs), some saw the influence of Nietzsche, which Pʻapʻazean vehemently, but not altogether convincingly, rejected. But he readily admitted his admiration for and the influence of Ibsen (*Brand* and *The Master Builder,* in particular), which was embodied in his heroes, whose drive and aspirations (and eventual destruction) distinctly recall some of Ibsen's unusual characters. Among some of his better shorter works, most of which conform to the principles of realism, while some are in the romantic mold, are: "Nkariche̊," "Enicheri," "Laloy," "Beram," "Ṙašid," "Hatʻ Saba," "Mi gišer Karachobanum," "Lur-da-lur," "Ayiša," "Anna," "Ḥentʻě," "Santʻoy," "Ĕmbosti mahě," and "Višap." His novel *Ēmma* discusses currents of thought and Armenian life in Transcaucasia; *Asi* is dedicated to Luristan's rebellion against Nasreddin Shah; *Alemgir* is about the turbulent Teheran in the 1890s (following the granting of tobacco monopoly to the British), and in its sequel, *Azerfeza,* the "worshippers of Mithra" are told to use fire to consume or eradicate corruption and tyranny.

Of P'ap'azean's plays, *Žayṙ* (Rock) was well received after its premiere in 1905 and was quite popular in Erevan for a few decades after World War II. Beyond a shadow of a doubt, ideological considerations played a role in staging this production, and Gurgen Janibekyan's (1897–1978) interpretation of Grigor Ała's role much enhanced its popularity. Indeed, Grigor Ała, a vast landowner and a ruthless usurer, is a powerfully drawn character, who manages to frustrate the efforts of an inspired young man bent on defeating the system and restoring justice in a provincial Caucasian town in czarist Russia. As in much of his later work, so in this drama, P'ap'azean observed and exposed the old world order in good and frequently elegant Eastern Armenian and portrayed (despite Soviet Armenian claims of his inability to grasp the pivotal role of the proletariat) individuals, groups, and masses struggling for a better life.

Wide public recognition was slow in coming to **NAR-DOS** (1867–1933), who belonged to the conservative circle of Armenian intellectuals and contributed to their mouthpiece, the periodical *Nor dar.* His moderate outlook, it has been suggested, led some to consider him and his confrères less talented than the liberal intellectuals. Although he witnessed the Sovietization of Georgia, all of his work except for a few insignificant additions belongs to the pre-Soviet era.

In his prose, in the form of short stories, short novels, and novels, Nar-Dos is concerned mainly with the psychological profiles of his heroes rather than plot and action. All his protagonists are contemporary types, and almost all appear as fully developed characters. Although they may at times seem simple, transparent, and somewhat indistinguishable, they are complex and subtly dissimilar. Conflict and action spring from the irreconcilable nature of their mentalities, which was what attracted Nar-Dos most.

Through his tendentious literature, Nar-Dos sought to mirror life "as it was," to offer psychological analysis, and to inspire and guide. In his early pieces, his heroes subordinate the personal to public interests. The unhappy and the poor, the illiterate and the superstitious, the consequences of drinking and uncivil behavior, and similar topics make up the main themes in his series titled *Mer t'ałě* (Our quarter). With his *Anna Saroyean,* Nar-Dos began to chart the depths of human emotions. This is the tragic story of a sensitive soul, Anna, and the impoverishment and destruction of her formerly wealthy family. But his *Spanuatz aławni* (Slain dove), *Payk'ar* (Struggle), and *Mahĕ* (Death) are among his best.

When Nar-Dos converted his *Spanuatz aławni* into a play, there were suggestions in the Russian press that it might have been inspired by Chekhov's *The Seagull.* Nar-Dos went on public record to refute the suggestion and maintain that it was based on his own work published years earlier. Nevertheless, despite his assertion, there are certain similarities common to both works but not enough, perhaps, to claim a formative influence by Chekhov. Sar̄a, whose honor and innocence have been violated by T'usean, is now married to Sisakean. Sar̄a's obsession with revenge is an expression of her insistence on respecting the rights of individuals, the flagrant violation of which is glossed over by society. T'usean believes in unrestricted, egotistical freedom and acts on his principles. Sisakean is the spineless and spiritless husband unable to understand, let alone respond, to his wife's emotions, concerns, and humiliation.

Payk'ar is about the clash of the old and the new. The representatives of the modern reflect the formal aspects of change, denying the traditional as totally incompatible with the progressive. Caught between these two tides is the heroine (Manē), who, although not a conservative, is not prepared to sacrifice the better aspects and accomplishments of the old for the falsehood and formal sophistry of newfangled concepts. The novel was partly inspired by the rivalry between the conservative periodical *Nor dar,* to which Nar-Dos contributed artistically and administratively, and the liberal periodical *Mšak.*

Mahĕ was to echo the rising patriotic sentiments among the Eastern Armenians in the 1890s, but with changes forced by the czarist censorship, it was transformed into a psychological novel with only vague references to the movement. The central theme, as the author himself saw it, was that of life and death seen from the perspectives of active optimists and passive pessimists, which remotely echoed some of the serious dilemmas facing the Armenians at the time.

LEWON ŠANT' (1869–1951) wrote prose, verse, and drama. A few of his poems were popular in his time, but almost all of his poetry is now part of his less-read oeuvre. This is also true of his novels. Drawn to universal values and Symbolism, Šant' increasingly looked beyond the immediate Armenian scene, receiving his intellectual and aesthetic nourishment from Europe and giving shape to his distinct literary approach largely in his plays. There is something of Greek tragedy, Nietzsche, Ibsen, G. Hauptmann, and Maeterlinck in his work. Many, if not most, of his characters are brought to life from within, with little or no attention to the locale, mores, action (with the exception of his plays), or other means of characterization. They are, especially his *dramatis personae,* individualistic and passionate; they symbolize and cling to certain concepts, pursue lofty aspirations, dream in ever changing moods, and suffer in dignity as they search for the meaning and mode of their existence. Herein, perhaps, lies the disquieting charm and intellectual elegance of some of his work.

His novel *Dursetsinerě* (The outsiders) illustrates the clash of public interests with personal interests. Similarly, *Derasanuhin* (The actress) elaborates the conflict of individual aspirations in personal relations. *Dardzě* (The conversion) outlines the contrast of religious and mundane philosophies, which foreshadows one of the main themes in his *Hin astuatzner* (Ancient gods). His last work, *Hoginerě tzarawi* (Thirsty souls), deals with marriage, family, and fidelity. His first three plays were variations on the aforementioned themes. *Esi mardě* (The man of the I) deals with the issue of national and personal ends through the characters of a revolutionary and a traitor. *Uriši hamar* (For others) is the story of a woman sacrificing her own happiness for that of her father, brother, and sisters. And *Čambun vray* (On the road) depicts a fighter who has given his life to his country, submerging his own happiness and aspirations.

To many, *Hin astuatzner* is his best drama. It marked a fresh phase in his creative work in that Šantʻ now turned from the real world to the realm of ideas. It revived, in a new form, the clash of body and soul, a long-standing dilemma in Armenian literature. The leading characters, Vanahayr (Abbot) and Abełay (Deacon), have turned away from the world, the flesh, and the devil. With the financial assistance of an old flame, the princess, Vanahayr has erected on the islet of Sewan (now a peninsula!) a new church on the ruins of an old temple as a monument to their old love, but also as an irrevocable renunciation of worldly life. Seda, niece of the princess, falls off the boat taking them to the monastery for a visit and plunges into the waters of Lake Sewan. Abełay rescues her, gives her a new life, but fatally compromises his own as fleshly desires tear him apart. To eradicate his past root and branch, Vanahayr envisions replacing the church he had built with a new one.

Kaysrě (The emperor; literally, The caesar) portrays the reigns of emperors Nicephorus II Phocas (d. 969) and his successor John I Tzimisces (d. 976), who was of Armenian stock, and their drives for power and fame. A timid Nicephorus ascends the Byzantine throne with the help and prodding of an ambitious and adventurous John, who shortly thereafter overthrows Nicephorus with the help of Empress Theophano, consort to Nicephorus. John, "the emperor," is a restless character, who thrives on danger and challenge, and for whom life is but a game. He abandons Theophano, but his love for Hanna, although mutual, remains unattainable. Hanna, a forceful and interesting character, shuns evanescent glory and sentiment, withdrawing to a monastery with her love for John intact and immune to all threats and temptations.

Nominally, the person referred to in *Šlťayuatzě* (The chained one) is Artawazd I, son of King Artašēs I. According to a traditional story, Artawazd is bound in chains in a cave in Mount Masis (Ararat) with his two dogs gnawing at his shackles to free him. There are two interpretations to this legend, both of which are articulated by characters in this play. Eznik Kołbatsi sees Artawazd in a somewhat positive light: He will one day emerge and rule the world. But Movsēs Ḥorenatsi relates that he will destroy the world. In the play, the fictitious events take place in Ani. The mob rises against its ruthless rulers and seizes power, but this bold initiative brings no advantages to the simple folk. The play illustrates the corrupting effects of power and the futility of attempting to gain freedom with the help of others or external forces. Symbolically, therefore, the title of the play is a reference to all human beings in whose chest there lives a tyrant whom the individual must kill if he is to be free. Yakob Ōšakan (q.v.) found this play to be reminiscent of G. Hauptmann's *Die versunkene Glocke.*

Inkatz berdi išḫanuhin (The princess of the fallen fortress) has Cilicia as its background and pits a prince, Goł Vasil, against Princess Anna. Vasil kills Anna's husband and children and captures their fortress with an eye towards possessing her too. Bent on revenge, Anna weaves a web of intrigues that eventually lead to grisly crimes, including the murder of Vasil's two sons by their own father and Anna's suicide. *Ōšin Payl*'s plot echoes some sad events in Cilicia in the 1320s. Prince Ōšin, Lord of Kořikos, and Ṙita, daughter of Prince Smbat, admire one another, but Cilicia is rent apart by religious strife of political significance between those faithful to the national church and the followers of the papacy. Putting national interests above all else, Ōšin becomes regent and tries to restore peace in the land, but his efforts are frustrated. He declines Ṙita's assistance to rescue him from gaol, and they both meet a tragic end.

KOSTAN ZARYAN (1885–1969) abandoned French for Armenian at a time when a search for new aesthetic and national values was already under way. After the 1915 slaughter of most of the explorers and innovators, Zaryan carried on the mission with intriguing experiments. If the originators of the pagan movement (Varužan, Siamanťō, et al.)

raked up their roots in polytheist Armenia, Zaryan sought to uncover the essence and mystery of the Armenian soul. Steeped in Western culture and contemporary literary trends, Zaryan embarked on a literary journey that was at once aesthetic, metaphysical, contemplative, and cultural. Armenian letters was enriched by his craftsmanship, style, and interpretation of the artistic, the beautiful, and the mysteries of the human soul. Like that of any committed writer, Zaryan's oeuvre indeed has its flaws and failures, but his detractors have no leg to stand on.

An acquaintance of many contemporary European giants of the arts and literature, Zaryan was respected by some Armenian intellectuals but shunned by others and never attained widespread popularity. All his works were listed in the Soviet Index and prohibited until the early 1960s, when he returned to Soviet Armenia after a forty year exile; only a few were published thereafter. Many of his writings, especially those of the 1920s and 1930s, appeared in installments in the periodical press and still remain inaccessible to the public at large, though quite a few have been recently disinterred. His literary commentary on the human condition and his own nation attracted sophisticated readers, but few others. Since the 1970s there has been a revival of interest in his work. That his art was shaped under the formative influence of Western thought is beyond the slightest shadow of doubt. Although some of the sources of this influence are clearly evident to the informed reader, no detailed scrutiny has yet been undertaken to pinpoint them in a more specific and comprehensive fashion.

Zaryan's first collection of verse in Armenian was *Ōreri psakě.* (It is difficult to say what exactly he had in mind by the Armenian word *psak,* which has numerous meanings: crown, prize, circle, accomplishment, wreath, garland, halo, etc. Perhaps he meant something like the "crown" in the sense of "circle," or "course of the days," since poems 1, 5, and 10 in the series of poems for which the collection is named are titled "Morning," "Noon" and "Evening," respectively.) The cycles making up the collection express varying and contrasting moods, captured with vivid imagination through sensations and impressions of light, color, and sound. The collection was a bold experiment with words, imagery, form, and style, but it suffered from repetition, infelicity, instances of studied effect, and choppy sentences (which, in this case, was not an expression of Zaryan's favorite tenet of omitting details to put the reader's imagination to work). But Zaryan's poetic talent found its best expression in a long poem titled *Tatragomi harsě* (The bride from Tatragom), one of his two best known works and which still generates controversy. It is the story of a newly married young man, Yovan, who shortly after his marriage joins Armenian guerilla fighters (*hayduk* or *fidayi*) to defend their village against Kurdish attacks. He leaves behind his wife, Sana, who for long years hears nothing of her husband and, overpowered by her carnal desires, succumbs to a Kurd, a man from the ranks of the mortal enemy. Yovan's comrades-in-arms decide that Sana must die and that Yovan must carry out the verdict. Written with verve in a laconic and eloquent style, this exquisite poem mingles epic elements and symbols with bare drama, offers revealing insights into the hearts and minds of its heroes, and boldly raises a host of sensitive issues and values of a political, social, and cultural nature. Sana's frailty and fate, seen in the wider context of national and Ottoman issues of the 1900s, has been the subject of sharply conflicting and unsettled interpretations.

Zaryan's prose is a rewarding chronicle of countries and cultures that he came to know intimately as the wandering Armenian. Such observations and analyses are invariably suffused with keen insights into the Armenian experience both in Armenia and abroad. Himself an émigré par excellence, Zaryan incessantly pursued his quest for the underground roots of Armenian vitality and the spiritual forces of the nation. He had candid criticism for the failings of his fellow countrymen: the obsessive importance they attached to tradition, which Zaryan regarded as merely a graveyard; their tendency to adapt and imitate rather than discover and invent; their obliviousness to universal principles and values; and their shallow approach to culture. Yet, he identified with this very culture even as he sought to transform it by impressing on the Armenians the need for introspection in the search for the intrinsic national values that made up the Armenian quintessential self.

In *Antsordě ew ir čampʻan* (The wayfarer and his route), Zaryan depicts the Armenian atmosphere and mentality in Istanbul, then under Allied occupation, shortly before his departure for Armenia in 1922. He then speaks of his three-year sojourn in Soviet Armenia, under rather rough and rigid terms, and his return to Europe. Conditions in Armenia, the Armenian community of Tiflis, repatriated Armenians in Armenia, Armenia-Diaspora relations, Armenian hopes vainly pinned on Europe, anti-Russian sentiments, flashbacks to his childhood, and reminiscences of colleagues put to death in 1915 are some of the moments and elements Zaryan masterfully captures in his eloquent and engaging narrative. *Bankoopě* (i.e., *banvorakan kooperativě*) *ew mamutʻi oskorneřě* (The bancoop [i.e., workers' cooperative] and the bones of the mammoth) brings together Soviet Armenian impressions and reminiscences, along with descriptions of Turkey, Greece, Italy, France, Switzerland, and Spain. Here too, Armenia, Armenians, Armenian culture, the search for the Armenian soul, philosophical reflections, writers, literature and society, irreconcilable conflict between religion and science, and nations and nationalism are topics that Zaryan discusses in an illuminating and entertaining fashion. Similarly, *Kłzin ew mi mard* (The island and a man) consists of a string of meditations on man and his alienation from himself, the earth, and the universe (written on the island of Corfu, where the author made the acquaintance of Lawrence Durrell). It also concerns the intricate relationship between man and nature and the latter's powerful impact on the former's thought, countries, art and literature, and many of the topics mentioned above. Continuing his effort to unravel the mysteries of universe and man, Zaryan suggested, in these and in other works not discussed here, that man would find much gratification if he restored the old bonds that once linked him to the earth.

One of Zaryan's best known works is his novel *Nawě leran vray* (The ship on the mountain). Ara Herean, the central hero, is a professional sailor, who is intent upon operating a boat in Lake Sewan as his contribution to the rebuilding of Armenia in the years 1919 to 1921. He purchases a ship in Batumi but is unable to transport it beyond the heights of K'anak'eṙ, to the north of Erevan, due to the political situation. When Zaryan settled in Soviet Armenia in 1962, he expunged the anti-communist and anti-Russian aspects from a revised edition of the novel and added an epilogue enabling Herean to realize his dream with the help of the newly established Soviet regime. It was a regrettable and, perhaps more importantly, unnecessary redaction. Some critics, particularly Soviet Armenian ones, have seen the ship, stranded on the heights of K'anak'eṙ, as an indictment of the pre-communist system of Armenia. The revamped version lent much support to this interpretation. But political orientation may not have been Zaryan's foremost concern, as he was also critical, if less bitterly, of the political chaos in the first Republic of Armenia. The ship embodied one of Zaryan's principal remedies for the revival of Armenia and Armenian spirit: self-reliance. Ara Herean's ship was not built in Armenia. By contrast, another character in the novel, Mik'ayēl T'umanean, builds a boat on the very shores of Lake Sewan and uses it for military purposes. Hence, it seems that Zaryan's sympathy lay with the enterprising local and national elements, with no pronounced concern for their political persuasions. The novel, certainly one of the best in the Armenian literary tradition, masterfully encompasses most of the vital aspects of the Armenian realities of the day, giving a large role to Armenians of the dispersion. As usual, Zaryan provides incisive, provocative, and at times controversial analyses of cultural, social, political, and philosophical nature.

The Twentieth Century: 1920–1990

Soviet Armenian Literature

An Overview of the Soviet Armenian Realities

Armenia became Soviet at the end of 1920. Initially, together with Georgia and Azerbaijan, it made up the Federal Union of Transcaucasian Republics , which in 1922 was replaced by the Federalist Soviet Socialist Republic of Transcaucasia. In 1936, all three republics were individually incorporated into the USSR. The events that led to the collapse of the Soviet Union, the rise of the Armenian National Movement, and the emergence of Armenia as an independent republic are well known. As a sovereign state, Armenia elected as its first president in October, 1991 Dr. Levon Ter-Petrosyan, a prominent scholar of Armenian studies. With his tenure there began a new era for Armenia, which is beyond the scope of this introduction.

In the early twenties, Armenia appealed to Armenians abroad for assistance. The Committee to Aid Armenia (*Hayastani ōgnutʻean komitē*) was set up in 1921 (and was dissolved in 1937), with branches in Armenia as well as abroad (Greece, France, Germany, Bulgaria, the United States, Iran, Rumania, England, etc.). Many intellectuals responded to the appeal of the government to return and help rebuild the country. Between the years 1921 and 1982, an estimated two hundred thousand Armenians were repatriated from the Middle East, Europe, and the United States. Some of them, along with tens of thousands of local Armenians, lost their lives to the Stalinist terror, as did scores of intellectuals and some of the best writers. Hundreds of thousands of Armenians were killed fighting against Nazi Germany, and the Church experienced a catastrophic period of persecution. Only after the last wave of terror in the late forties and the death of Stalin in 1953 did Armenia slowly recover relative freedom in matters cultural and intellectual.

Soviet Armenia's relations with the Armenian Dispersion were governed by politics and ideology. The twenties saw a relatively open relationship with the Dispersion, which was not the case in the following decade. During World War II, Armenia appealed to Armenians everywhere to help defeat the Nazis. The Dispersion responded immediately and generously, raising considerable monetary funds to help the Red Army war effort. During the cold war era, Armenia maintained practically no relations with the Dispersion. The sixties saw a rapid thaw and activation of relations: Armenia sent books and textbooks, dance ensembles, writers, and soccer teams abroad and offered free higher education to Armenian students from abroad. At first rigidly selective, such exchanges acquired a flexible, broader scope in time, but they were never entirely free of political considerations.

The Church of Armenia was fortunate indeed to have Archbishop Georg Chorekʻchyan (1868–1954), a student of philosophy and theology (Leipzig, 1889–94), as *locum tenens* (1941–45) at a most dramatic and fateful period in her history, following the murder of Catholicos Ḥoren I, Muradbegyan (1873–1938, supreme patriarch from 1932). A sagacious administrator endowed with a keen mind, he seized upon a number of favorable circumstances in the concluding years of the war, rallied the Armenians of the Dispersion to the Soviet war effort, and initially took part in abortive Soviet diplomatic moves to reclaim Armenian territory from Turkey. Unanimously elected Catholicos (Georg VI, 1945), he actively promoted the repatriation movement (1946–48), reopened the theological seminary and the printing press in Ējmiatzin, launched the periodical *Ējmiatzin,* and securely placed the Church on an irreversible, though slow and limited, course of regeneration.

Soviet rule was in many ways beneficial to Armenian culture. A centralized system, despite its many serious drawbacks, and substantial state subsidies helped create within a relatively short period of time a solid cultural infrastructure in an utterly destitute Armenia. Armenian was proclaimed the state language. A policy to obliterate illiteracy was adopted in 1921, the orthography was reformed in 1922, and elementary education was made mandatory in 1930. The state theater, the national public library, and the state museum were established in 1922 and were followed by the film studio, the conservatory (1923), the national opera (1933), the Academy of Sciences (1943, in existence since 1935 as the Armenian section of the Academy of Sciences of the USSR), the repository of manuscripts (1959; the Matenadaran, named after Mesrop Maštots on the basis of the Ējmiatzin holdings), and numerous other centers and institutions of culture, education, and research. Anniversaries of writers and cultural figures were observed. Books were published in massive runs to meet the needs of a cultured and demanding reading public. Annual literary prizes named after Y. Tʻumanean, A. Isahakyan, D. Demirčyan, G. Sundukean, M. Nalbandean, and S. Zoryan (q.q.v.) were instituted, all in 1980. Anniversaries of major figures and events (such as the millennial of the epic *Sasuntsi Dawitʻ,* David of Sasun, in 1939) were observed locally, by Moscow, and at times throughout the republics of the Soviet Union.

Literatures of the peoples of the Soviet Union, especially Russian, were rendered into Armenian, and Armenian literature was made available to a much wider audience through translations into Russian. Most of the leading writers and intellectuals visited Armenia: M. Gorky, A. Akhmatova, N. Tikhonov, M. Shaginian, V. Shklovsky, A. Lunacharsky, A. Fadeev, K. Fedin, V. Kaverin, S. Gorodetskii, Vyacheslav Ivanov, A. Bely, O. Mandelshtam, V. Grossman, I. Erenburg, K. Simonov, E. Evtushenko, and many others. Armenian literature was rendered into Russian by, to name but a few, Gorodetskii, S. Marshak, Akhmatova, B. Pasternak, Tikhonov, M. Svetlov, A. Tarkovsky, I. Selvinsky, N. Grebnev, Evtushenko, V. Zviagintseva, and M. Petrovykh. Earlier, V. Briusov and M. Gorky had published anthologies of Armenian literature. As for Western literature, thought, and culture in general, Moscow was the sole arbiter; it selected and disseminated what it saw fit. For many long decades, Western literature was rendered into Armenian from Russian translations.

The assumption was that the Soviet Revolution was to bring in its wake a new way of life and, therefore, a new kind of art and literature. Old traditions were to be discarded. The twenties was a decade of experiments; the old was rejected with enthusiasm, and the search for the new was intense, bringing fresh approaches to literature both in form and content. Lyric poetry was neglected; instead, general or universal values and sentiments were embraced. A feverish preference for depicting daily life, the building of irrigation canals, mechanization, electrification, and other such changes that characterized Soviet economic policy, as well as a strong sense of solidarity with the "anti-imperialistic" East (Muslim countries from Algeria to Iran), inspired some Armenian writers. On the other hand, Ełiše Charents (q.v.) and many others realized the importance of the past and aesthetic and technical aspects of poetry; they knew they could contribute to world civilization only through Armenian culture.

With no literary theory yet firmly formulated by the Party, things were in a state of flux in the twenties. An overriding concern was the nature and role of the new "proletarian" literature and how to create a literature that was national in manner but socialist in matter. Borrowing certain elements from the Russian futurists (especially V. Mayakovsky), the imagists, and the principles of "proletarian culture" ("proletkult"), three writers, E. Charents, A. Vštuni, and G. Abov, proclaimed a manifesto (14 June 1922, since known as the Declaration of the Three). They rejected the pre-revolutionary literature, which they claimed was a dying tradition, afflicted by such maladies as nationalism, romanticism, pessimism, and symbolism, and infected by such concepts as the "fatherland," "immaculate love," "desert and loneliness," "twilights," "oblivion and dreams," and the like. They saw themselves as "disinfectors" who wished to bring in fresh air and to counterbalance bourgeois nationalism with "proletarian internationalism" and immaculate love with "healthy instinct." They also sought to bring literature, heretofore immured in "salons," out into the streets and to the masses, and to focus on subjects of actual importance, such as class struggle, all in a style and imagery characteristic of the new lifestyle.

The group disbanded quickly, with E. Charents disowning its nonsensical creed. But the Association of Proletarian Writers of Armenia came into existence at the end of 1922, and extreme views led to acrimonious disputes. The Party, while recognizing the importance of a free atmosphere for literature to develop, denounced insularity and parochialism and called for an universal socialist literature in 1925. In April of the same year, G. Mahari (q.v.) and others formed a splinter group in Gyumri, named *Hoktember* (October), to oppose the appalling rigidity of the Association's members. That autumn, E. Charents initiated *Noyember* (November), and members of the short-lived *Hoktember* joined the group. There were at least two other literary associations, including the circle of *ułekits* ("companion") writers (D. Demirčyan, V. T'ot'ovents, S. Zoryan, et al.), who steered clear of these bitter partisan clashes. But the lines of battle were drawn. Although the two warring parties merged into the Union of Proletarian Writers of Armenia (1926), they failed to bury the hatchet. The members of the former Association continued to adhere unimaginatively and stubbornly to dogma and violently attack and denigrate Charents and his camp. The gap widened and the two groups became implacable foes even after the Party had decreed the Union of Soviet Writers of Armenia (1932, actually founded in 1934) and had defined its literary theory. In due course, Armenian writers unions were established in Georgia, Azerbaijan, and Nagorno-Karabagh.

This most pernicious confrontation continued into the thirties. The central concept for Charents and his circle was that the local or national proletariat was the concrete basis of literature, not the abstract and "homeless" international proletariat. In other words, national traditions and literature formed the foundation on which an "internationalist" literature would rise. One of the bizarre aspects of the situation was that their opponents, the Proletarians, by form understood mainly the language, which they also rejected as the former vehicle of capitalist values. Having no substitute, they vulgarized the literary standard, using the spoken idiom, a dialectal mishmash with a strange phraseology. A far more ominous problem was the relationship between a writer's ideology and the topics he chose to illustrate; the choice of the latter, they held, clearly mirrored his political profile. He who wrote, for instance, about the past was denounced as a propagandist of the old, stigmatized as an enemy of the Revolution, and called a "class enemy," a "people's enemy," "nationalist," "individualistic," "bourgeois," and so on. Thus, the Party amassed much "ideological" ammunition to justify the ruthless annihilation of the intelligentsia in the late thirties. From the mid-thirties to the early forties, the arena was left to political propagandists and "political minstrels," literally and figuratively speaking, who sang Stalin's praises in dreadful poems. The war period brought a torrent of patriotic, rhetorical propaganda and some satire. To fuel patriotism, Moscow winked at local manifestations of national pride as expressed in historical novels.

But restrictions were reinforced and reprisals ensued immediately after the war. In the second congress of the Union of Soviet Writers of Armenia (1946), works dealing with the past and written in the concluding years of the war were condemned: Demirčyan's *Vardanank̔*, it was pointed out, overemphasized the role of church and religion in the national liberation movement; King Pap in Zoryan's eponymous historical novel was lionized as a democrat; Zaryan's *Ara Gełetsik* idealized the past; and Širaz was sternly warned that he was following an extremely pernicious path by making excessive use of religious, mystical references, and imagery, and by elaborating only on national themes. During this period, literature depicted Soviet society as being free of conflicts; the only conflict was the one between man and nature. Repatriation and repatriated Armenians and Mount Ararat as a symbol of lost territory and culture were also fairly common themes.

The post-Stalin era in Armenia began with Anastas Mikoyan's speech in a meeting with his "electorate" in Armenia on 11 March 1954. Ṙ. Patkanean, Raffi, E. Charents, A. Bakunts (q.q.v.), and others were rehabilitated. There followed a period that witnessed the gradual return of lyric poetry and the exploration of human behavior. The next phase in Soviet Armenian literature was the drive launched by a new generation, spearheaded by Paruyr Sevak (1924–71) and others, to broaden the thematic scope beyond love, nature, and patriotism, to destroy the shackles of parochial insularity, and to explore the universal context of the human condition in this age of sweeping changes and giant technological advances. The trend, existing side by side with the traditional, was taken up by yet a younger generation, excluded from this book.

Armenian literature developed under considerable influence from Soviet Russian literature. In general, especially after the war, socialist realism set the tone. Love, patriotism, humanitarian concerns, World War II, Soviet solidarity and fraternity, and Soviet routine (which only suffered from "correctable" and "temporary" flaws) were some of the prevalent themes. The basic premises of ideology, Party, and government were believed to be faultless and were never questioned. With the exception of pro-Soviet, pro-peace praise, and anti-imperialistic propaganda, political criticism was a taboo, as was the genocide. Noteworthy changes began to appear in the mid-sixties, especially in the wake of the massive demonstration in Erevan, commemorating the fiftieth anniversary of the genocide. Historians and writers alike elaborated on this manmade tragedy, and the past, both immediate and distant, became a popular theme. In fact, the historical novel had not been discontinued after the war, and Armenian authors continued to evoke historical figures and events, which they invariably reinterpreted and often embellished beyond recognition. Earlier, a number of literary experiments had been introduced by Charents in rhyme and rhythm, prosody, and literary devices and technique. There were other changes. The term "ballad," for instance, acquired a new meaning in Soviet Armenian literary terminology. It became, especially for Charents, a kind of Soviet martyrology. It depicted the heroics of contemporary heroes, most of whom had served the cause of the Revolution.

Eastern Armenian underwent the influence of Russian, too. The dramatic increase in Russian schools in the sixties was a factor. But overall, Russian was simply indispensable for communication, education, learning, career and social advancement, information, and daily routine. An extreme but telling case of the ravages of Russian was that of the newspaper *Sovetakan Hayastan,* the Party organ, which daily translated leading articles and official texts from the central organs, such as *Pravda.* Lack of time was obviously a difficult challenge to overcome, but religious faithfulness to the original resulted in some absurd words, expressions, and patterns that were alien to Armenian, bringing to mind some parallels, often remote, from the long history of the Armenian tongue (e.g., Hellenizing Armenian, or the arbitrary application of the patterns of Latin). As said, this was an extreme case, but Russian patterns of expression slowly and imperceptibly penetrated the literary standard as well. Loan words and place names that were borrowed "through" Russian were calques or simply Russian forms, reflecting their endings and gender. Eastern Armenian was regulated by a number of academic committees.

A Survey of Soviet Armenian Literature

Damned and banned since the mid-thirties, **EŁIŠE CHARENTS** (1897–1937) was rehabilitated following Anastas Mikoyan's speech on 11 March 1954, delivered at a meeting in Erevan. Soon thereafter, Soviet Armenian criticism restored him to the foremost position in the Soviet Armenian literary canon. He is often thought of (with Mayakovsky as the leading originator) as one of the principal founders of Soviet verse. His works are now seen as signposts and symbols of his time, and his turbulent life, cut short at forty, as a record of both literary and political developments in the opening decades of Soviet rule in Armenia. Some of his fiery propaganda verse (e.g., his "Leniniana"), embodying the sincere hopes millions of people pinned on the October Revolution, now have only a historical value. Such poems are considerable in number, and although ideology resonates through most of his work, it contains a great many of the brightest pages of literature ever written in Armenian.

Traditionally, critics associate the origins of Soviet Armenian literature with Hakob Hakobyan and Šušanik Kurłinyan, the first to write "proletarian" literature. But the laurel for forging a new literary tradition must be given to Charents, who labored passionately to fashion an aesthetic realm for the Red Regime, for which he fought with word and weapon. It was a tortuous, somewhat erratic, and eventually fatal process. There was the pull of his national identity. It had of late, especially since the beginning of the twentieth century, given rise to visions of a homeland: the remote, misty land of Nairi that fed romantic political expectations. Charents was given to such dreams until his shocking march in 1915 in the ranks of Armenian volunteers supporting the Russian war effort against the Ottoman Empire. It inspired his long poem "Dant'eakan aṙaspel" (Dantesque legend), wherein Charents leads the reader through the Armenian inferno of 1915. Death, devastation, and innocent optimism contrast sharply in the poem. A little later, in his "Vahagn" (whom some contemporary poets had invoked triumphantly), Charents buried the remains of this old god, humiliated and slain by Armenia's enemies. The symbolic end of Vahagn's myth marked the beginning of a new phase in Charents's political orientation. He soon committed himself, body and soul, to Bolshevik Armenia.

But charting his own literary course was not to be as simple a task. The great masters of Armenian literature, past and present, crowded his path. Particularly in his early years, he was under the spell of Vahan

Tērean's poetic output (e.g., "Erekʻ erg tḥradaluk ałjkan," Three songs for a pale girl). He repudiated Tērean's art, only to repent many a time. He was then attracted to the Russian symbolists (e.g., his collection "Tziatzan," Rainbow). Seized by revolutionary fervor, he wrote two long poems in 1918, "Soma" and "Ambohnerě ḥelagarvatz" (The frenzied masses), while fighting for Tsarytsin in the ranks of the Red Army. Both were sheer dynamite, an indictment of the old world order and a romanticized panegyric of the revolution and the power of the masses. These were followed by his "radio-poems" and the first of his three celebrated "visions" of death. The latter took shape in the autumn of 1920, during the Turkish onslaught on Armenia. In it, Charents offers himself as the ultimate sacrifice in hopes of sparing his country further suffering. There followed his "Amenapoem" (a sort of "Everyone's poem," sharing certain similarities with Mayakovsky's "150.000.000"), a reflection of the fateful events of the time, and "Charents-name," an autobiographical poem intertwined with contemporary realities to 1921.

By the early twenties, Charents had certain obvious affinities with the principles of the Russian *Lef* (Left front of art). Furthermore, Armenia had become Soviet and the matter of re-evaluating or discarding the old literature and fashioning a new one had emerged as an imperative. Although he had already introduced some innovative trends, Charents, with G. Abov and A. Vštuni, issued in June of 1922 the "Declaration of the Three," totally rejecting old Armenian literature. This brought him much closer to the Russian futurists. But as always, Charents rapidly shifted between extreme moods and remained a knotty bundle of contradictions. As an artistic expression of the new principles (class struggle, sexual instinct, iron, technology, the color red, style, movement, rhythm, speed, etc.), Charents wrote the long poem "Ṙomans anser" (Loveless romance), a brilliant vulgarity. In the same nihilistic vein he worked on his novel, *Erkir Nairi,* and soon completed his "Tałaran" (Songbook).

Erkir Nairi placed Charents in the thick of the most pernicious controversies and the most painful dilemmas of the day. It was meant to deliver the *coup de grâce* to an ailing romantic mentality that, as he saw it, had turned into a demoralizing malaise, epitomized by an amorphous, nonexistent fatherland, Nairi. He went all out to define and destroy the inebriating myth of Nairi as a web of associations of antiquity, legitimacy, national vainglory, parochial patriotism, indolent nostalgia, debilitating insularity, and unfulfilled rosy dreams. Ever since the annexation of the Khanate of Erivan by Russia in 1828, the issue of reviving historic Armenia had by the 1870s slowly risen to the top of the national agenda, reducing almost all other concerns into insignificant issues. An intense, dramatic period of alternate hopes and utter disappointments had begun with the Balkan Wars, only to end with the cataclysm of 1915. And the first Republic of Armenia had survived for barely thirty months. For Charents, these setbacks spoke loudly of the ineffectiveness of Armenian mentality, identity, and, above all, leadership that he saw unfit for attaining national aspirations in this rotten, odious old world. Now that a new world was on the rise, with Armenia a part and parcel of the larger historical processes, it was time to jettison, once and for all, the old legacies that weighed down heavily on the Armenian spirit, impeding its wholesome progress.

Erkir Nairi is a politically charged satirical novel. Kars, a provincial city, is the setting, just before the outbreak of World War I. Though not a novel in the conventional sense, it ably captures the atmosphere in Charents's birthplace. In a rapid tempo, in short and sharp sentences, Charents describes Kars, a typical Nairian town, ramshackle and squalid with a deadly dull routine–a far cry from the romanticized vision of Nairi. In the second part of the novel, Kars and its leadership are seen during the war; in the third part, the fall of Kars and the destruction of the dream are described. The tragic backdrop to all this is the heinous crime perpetrated against the Armenians during the "imperialistic" war, with Charents plunging into unforgiving criticism of the leadership for its incompetence, naivete, and petty bourgeois romanticism. But the author looked forward to the remaining tiny stretch of Nairi, now a Soviet Socialist Republic, where the country was being built anew. This unusually dynamic experience of soul searching, sustained throughout with an invigorating honesty, was controversial. Charents's demolition work, some of his views and generalizations, and his technique (caricature, hyperbole, a sarcastically cutting style, etc.) have all been seen by some as unnecessarily extreme.

As *Erkir Nairi* appeared in installments in the periodical press, Charents completed the cycle "Tałaran" (Songbook), a collection of lyric poems. This was an abrupt return to the moods and modes of the old literature he repudiated, an imitation in many ways of Sayeatʿ-Nōvay's style. But the series bore the imprint of Charents's artistic character and appeared at a time when a trend to banish lyric poetry was restricting the imagination of Soviet Armenian authors, who were now entirely given to the political and economic agenda of the new system. The collection concluded with a most popular poem, "Es im anuš Hayastani arevaham barn [or bařn] em sirum" ("I love the sun-drenched fruit [or name] of my sweet Armenia"; there is some uncertainty as to which of the two words Charents used, but the academic edition of his works opted for *bar*). No Armenian poem treating the same theme in modern times seems to be as popular as this poem, whose figurative and connotative epithets powerfully and memorably evoke Armenia's spirit and story. At this juncture, Charents wrote poems for Lenin and other politically motivated works (*Poezozuṙna, Kapkaz ťamaša, Komalmanaḥ*), still rejecting the legacy of the past.

In late 1924 Charents left for a seven month tour of Europe (mainly Italy, Germany, and France). The West had a benevolent impact on his thought. Qualifying his literary position as vulgar and erroneous in letters from abroad, Charents noted that the great masters of the past had faithfully but creatively echoed their respective epochs, and the mentality of the ruling classes reverberated in their work. The new proletarian literature, he went on, lamentably lacked this essential quality and had become a lifeless literature in the form of pitiable *agitkas*. Having set aside "the drum of the *Lef,*" he was now ready to imbibe imaginatively the art of the masters and, maintaining the highest professional and aesthetic standards, to fashion a new literature as a mirror of the socialist mentality and lifestyle. Two of the memorable poems born during the trip were "Stambol," which to the author was an "international prostitute" and stood as a symbol of bloody conquests, decadence, and anti-communism, and "Ēlegia grvatz Venetikum" (Elegy written in Venice), evaluating the political and poetic stance toward Soviet Armenia of Avetikʻ Isahakyan (q.v.) and like-minded Armenians in the Armenian Dispersion.

In 1926, having shot and wounded a sixteen-year-old girl, Mariana Ayvazyan, Charents ended up in the Erevan House of Correction. (It has been suggested that Charents committed this violent act to draw the party's attention to his insupportable plight. Cf. A. Zakʻaryan, ed., *Ełiše Charentsi datavaruťyuně,* Erevan, 1995 [*Banber Hayastani arḥivneri*, 1995/1].) He published his sympathetic diaries under the title *Hišołuťyunner Yerevani ułłich tnits.* He attained a high level of artistic creation with his "Ḥmbapet Šavaršě" (Captain Shavarsh), which offers revealing psychological insight into the life of a soldier against a background of the harrowing events of the day. By now, Charents had ruefully made peace with his predecessors and had outdistanced a very talented group of young contemporaries. His only quarrel now was with a host of rigid adversaries (e.g., Nairi Zaryan, q.v., and the critics Gurgen Vanandetsi, 1898–1937, and Norayr Dabałyan, 1904–55), who similarly aspired to chart a fresh literary course. In the early twenties, especially after the appearance of his two volumes in Moscow (1922), Charents had already come under venomous attacks that denounced him as a nationalist-bourgeois-chauvinist-individualist-egotist-pornographer-reactionary, among other things. The gap grew ever wider as Charents unequivocally adhered to his losing proposition that the national tradition was the irreplaceable premise on which a new literature with universal dimensions and international significance would rise.

In *Ēpikʻakan lusabats* (Epic dawn, 1930), which consisted of the poems he wrote in 1927–30, Charents evaluated his maturing art. He passed harsh judgment on his wayward experiments and paid tribute and aspired to the art of Yovhannēs Tʻumanean, Vahan Tērean (q.q.v.), and Pushkin—a genuine echo of their own time that was distinguished by dazzling sophistication and amazing simplicity. Charents continued his public polemic against his antagonists, who paradoxically advocated the same principle. But most of them were mere versifiers who barely touched the inner world of their contemporaries, and who shunned lyricism and sang in a bombastic version of the spoken dialect the praises of metal, tractors, vulgar physical love subordinated to instinct and ideology, communist solidarity, revolutionary figures, the Muslim East, and North Africa and the Orient as rising anti-imperialistic powers (especially in the early and the mid-twenties). Alternating between a lyrical and epic tone in this collection, Charents contemplated Armenia's immediate and revolutionary past, and the various stages of his life and accomplishments, always predicated on the contemporary history of his fellow countrymen.

His last collection, *Girkʻ čanaparhi* (The book of the road), was printed in 1933, but its distribution was delayed. Additions and revisions were forced before it was made available to the public in 1934, at a most unpropitious period in the history of the Soviet Union. Its content provided much ammunition for ill-wishers, rivals, and critics, who, as before, unleashed a heavy barrage of hostile criticism for his ideological failures. Broadly speaking, in this book Charents summed up his bold revisionist views on some fundamental aspects and epochs of Armenian history, thought, and letters; offered wisdom and guidance to generations yet to come; and ruminated in a lyrical vein on the meaning of life, the human soul, and the elements of abiding artistic creation.

The cycle of historical pieces in largely chronological order evaluates the principal stages in the Armenian experience. It begins with the long poem "Sasuntsi Davitʻě," in which Charents claims that obsequiousness and conformity accounts for the hazy and gloomy past of his country. (He made Dzenov Ōhan into a pusillanimous and cringing character and released Pʻokʻr Mher from his captivity to destroy the forces of evil, an unmistakable reference to the advent of communism.) His attack on the Armenian ruling classes is particularly virulent in the next poem, "Patmutʻyan kʻaṙułinerov" (Along the crossroads of history). Charents heaped all the blame on them for the misery of his people. In "Depi lyaṙě Masis" (Heading for Mount Masis), Charents imaginatively recreated Ḥ. Abovean's last night before his disappearance. Abovean is seen reviewing his papers and life, dismissing renewed doubts–doubts that have been gnawing at his heart for a long time now–and questioning his political orientation. In thinly veiled critical allegory, "Mahvan tesil" (Vision of death) assesses the views of writers, intellectuals, and other figures (e.g., Ł. Ališan, P. Durean, Ṙ. Patkanean, Raffi, D. Varužan, q.q.v., and others) who shaped Armenian mentality in the second half of the nineteenth century and the early part of the twentieth. The break with the sad, uninspiring past, both distant and immediate, and adherence to the new revolutionary era and the Soviet regime occurs in "Zrahapat 'Vardan Zoravar' " (The armored car 'General Vardan'), thus completing Charents's sweeping review of the Armenian experience.

The second cycle ("Tałer ev ḥorhurdner") is made up of poems for the travelers, the sick, the illuminators of manuscripts, the dead, masons and architects; it counsels future generations, city builders, tillers, and song makers. This is followed by "Arvest k'ert'ut'yan" (The art of poetry) and "Girk' imatsut'yan" (Book of the intellect), made up of *ṙubaiyat,* distichs, and other poems, and which includes the famous "Patgam" (message) that alerts the Armenians that their only salvation lies in their unity (literally, "collective power"). A wide range of topics is covered under these subtitles, including words of wisdom, philosophical contemplation, literature as art, polemical lines, politics, history, cultural topics, and self-evaluation. Some critics have suggested that Charents was aware that this would be his last book (based on his line "Du gites, or k'o matyann ays verjin. . . ." "You know, that this last book of yours. . . ." However, the Armenian for "last" could also mean "latest"). There is clearly a pervasive sense of urgency and anxiety and a good many parting words to lend support to this suggestion. Charents, who sang the new as the old crumbled around him, now saw the new degenerate into cruel totalitarianism. That he was disillusioned with the central leadership and apparatus (Beria had already embarked on his monstrous mission) is beyond doubt, but whether or not he was disillusioned with the lofty ideals of the new political philosophy cannot be said with certainty.

The book is among the very best collections and is unrivaled in many respects. Not only does it distill the contributions (new patterns of meter and rhyme, rhythm and cadence, and genre and diction) of a genius who had just begun to mature, it is the brightest reflection of the latest, albeit thorny, phase of the Armenian experience. Here, as elsewhere in his work, Charents unveiled new aspects to the Armenian soul and audaciously explored fresh grounds for a new literature and identity with cruel but salutary honesty. There is some noise and rhetoric in some of his works, but such flaws are far outweighed by the better part of his oeuvre, which remains one of the best responses yet to calls made by Vahan Tērean and other contemporaries to elevate Armenian literature to a higher plane of universal significance.

AKSEL BAKUNTS's (1899–1937) life was cut short at the terribly young age of thirty-eight. The usual array of ideological charges were brought against him, including chauvinism, idealization of the past, rejection and alienation from socialist society, and so on. Such attacks were unleashed early in his career and intensified immediately after the appearance of his first collection of short stories, *Mtʻnadzor.* The eighteen pieces included here set the tone, scope, artistic principles, and interests of the author. The majestically mountainous region of Zangezur was one of the principal settings, and life in this remote, primitive rural area came under his artistic scrutiny. Out of the drama and anguish of the individual, whether inflicted by the harsh rules of fellow individuals, religion, custom and tradition, political upheavals, or nature, sad stories come to light of suffering that speak of the brutal truth in a context free from feelings of pity or maudlin sentimentalism. This proved to be a bitter pill to swallow. It was obvious that Bakunts, despite treating the topic in his own way, was not going to proclaim loudly and falsely the advent of a new lifestyle. The latter had as yet had no effect on the countryside, and Bakunts was not prepared to swallow the blanket ideological prescriptions hook, line, and sinker. Nor was he prepared to give up his uplifting aesthetic principles, the in-depth exploration of the human soul, or his literary creed and freedom.

The stories dealing with the Soviet period far outnumber those focused on the pre-revolutionary era. In the opening decades of the new regime, no changes were visible in the remote parts of the Armenian countryside (in Bakunts's "Mrots," for instance, some families are still celebrating the pagan Armenian New Year, *Nawasard*). This was Bakunts's domain. With keen eyes, he looked deep into the inner world of the Armenian peasant and into the complex relationships with his fellow human beings and nature. His aim, emanating from his literary creed, was to capture the essence of all this—a task which in his better stories he accomplished brilliantly.

A tragic picture of the Armenian peasantry emerges from Bakunts's artistic accounts. "Alpiakan manušak" (Alpine violet) brings together some of the finer aspects of Aksel's craftsmanship and literary-aesthetic principles. It has a simple plot. An archaeologist and a painter visit a remote village, where they encounter a beautiful woman whose picture the artist paints. The woman's husband returns from the fields after the visitors depart and, in a rage of jealousy, hits his wife with a club. Night falls, and another day in their lives comes to a close. The author concludes the story by describing a beetle, intoxicated by fragrant pollen, who seems to think that the world is an alpine violet. Out of these bare elements, Bakunts fashions a dramatic story on the rough life in inaccessible and forgotten villages, the ugly plight of beautiful women, and the still-existing gap between rural and urban areas, which looks beyond deceptive appearances in search of the deformities and beauties of the human soul.

"Namak ṙusats tʻagavorin" (A letter to the king of the Russians) is the story of a saintly old man whose son is in exile in Siberia. In infinite faith and hope, he writes a letter to the czar to have his son released. After a long wait, he is told to appear at the police station. He is beaten and thrown out, his mouth bleeding. Yet he still awaits a reply, and on his dying day he requests his wife to announce the good news at his grave as soon as she hears from the czar. In "Bruti tłan" (The potter's son), the peaceful and creative life of a potter is shattered and his wife dies when their son is killed fighting for the Bolsheviks. Dilan dayi and Sona of "Mirhav" (Pheasant) have an unspoken love, but she is married off to someone else and dies within a year. Dilan dayi sustains himself into old age with memories of his unalloyed and unfulfilled love. The characters in "Tzirani pʻoł" (The apricot wood flute; *pʻoł,* here, is a flute-like wind instrument) are survivors of the Armenian massacres and deportations in Sasun who have settled in Eastern Armenia. Pining for home in the mountains of Sasun, Hazro, the central character, plays his instrument to alleviate the painful longing that smolders in his heart. In "Spitak dzin" (The white stallion), horses are requisitioned from the villagers. To save his horse, Simon cuts a wound in its back. The horse is taken away anyway and remorse cuts Simon deeply. "Mtʻnadzor" is a dark story of the evil aspects of human nature.

Kyores (i.e., the city of Goris, Armenia) is a work of biting satire, a kind of chronicle that has no plot or individual characters in the true sense. It deals with the clash of the old and the new before the Soviet era, and it is close in tone and intent to Charents's monumental *Erkir Nairi* (The land of Nairi), which seems to have sparked Bakunts's imagination, and Gurgen Mahari's *Ayrvoł aygestanner* (Burning orchards), which was written long after Bakunts's death. This work was an expression of Bakunts's desire to try his hand at novels. His first attempt, *Karmrakʻar,* remained incomplete; only its initial part was published. The central theme was to be the changes that reshaped social life in rural areas at the turn of the twentieth century. Bakunts undertook extensive research into the life and work of Ḥachatur

Abovean before embarking on a novel dedicated to him, of which only fragments have been published.

Certain elements of Gogol's "Nevsky prospekt" are found in Bakunts's "Provintsiayi mayramutĕ" (The sunset of the province). His work shares certain similarities with that of Knut Hamsun and the Russian Mikhail Prishvin (1873–1954), whom Bakunts knew personally, but neither seems to have had a formative influence on him. Although he learned much from both Armenian and non-Armenian masters, he fashioned his own distinct tradition. Bakunts's nature imagery is fresh, epic, and hauntingly beautiful. His lyricism is vibrant, and his touch is delicate in his exquisite observations of the innermost realms of human nature, its drama, frailties, defeats, and triumphs. Modern Armenian prose attained crystalline elegance in his best stories.

VAHAN T'OT'OVENTS (1894–1938) tried his hand at verse early on, but later emerged as one of the notable masters of Soviet Armenian prose. Although he wandered far and wide before settling in Armenia, he was a prolific author of short stories, novels, plays, essays, and articles in the periodical press. The latter dealt with topical issues of importance in the early Soviet years of Armenia. His short novel, *Doktoṙ Burbonyan* (original title *Hayastani Ton-K'išot'ĕ,* The Armenian Don Quixote) is a satirical writing with a hallucinating caricature of a windbag political propagandist as its central character. The novel owes something of its structure to Eruand Ōtean's similar works. His impressions of life in the early twentieth-century United States, articulated in the form of short stories, scenes, and personal experiences, appeared under the title *Amerika.* Perhaps the only bright note in this collection is his heartfelt sympathy for the plight of black people, which is demonstrated in three of the twelve stories making up the cycle. The remaining pieces are a bleak commentary on the "gilded" dirt of capitalism and its dehumanizing effects on society. A similar condemnation of capitalist and bourgeois lifestyles is found in his most extensive novel, *Bak'u,* an attempt to depict the proletariat and its struggle at the turn of the century. The novel suffers from a number of major flaws and confirms that T'ot'ovents excelled in more compact formats. Of his shorter works, *Hovnat'an ordi Eremiayi* (Jonathan, son of Jeremiah) is an impressive piece. Through the life of a potter-sculptor, it sings the praises of human creativity and industry, art and liberty, and deplores outdated values, views, and religious shackles. One of his best works in this category is *Bats-kapuyt tzałikner* (Light blue flowers), which was made into a film by Armenfilm in Erevan (Henrik Malyan, 1980), titled "Ktor mĕ erkink'" (A piece of sky). It is the touching story of an unconventional marriage between a prostitute and an orphaned young man in a remote region steeped in conservative traditions. His best play, which met with great success at the time, remains his *Nor Byuzandion* (New Byzantium). It won an all-Union prize, was translated into several languages, and was performed on many stages both inside and outside Armenia. The plot unfolds in Constantinople immediately after the 1819 beheading of the male members of the celebrated Tiwzean Armenian Catholic family (more commonly known as Duzian, its Western Armenian pronunciation) on the orders of the sultan (Mahmut II, 1785–1839). Survival, rivalry, revenge, and intrigue sustain a chilling sense of turpitude, dramatically illustrating the precarious fate of individuals and societies under arbitrary rule in an atmosphere of religious fanaticism.

T'ot'ovents's unsurpassed effort was his *Kyank'ĕ hin hřovmeakan čanaparhi vra* (Life on the old Roman highway). Consisting of fragmented memories of his birthplace, the work is written with broad strokes in robust colors and sharp contrasts. The locale, the small circle of characters, and the constant presence of the author endow the narrative with a considerable degree of unity. In a trenchant, warm style, sparingly laden with lyrical metaphors and imagery, with thinly veiled nostalgia, poignant emotions, humor, and sarcasm, he evokes a quotidian routine, mores, intriguing characters and events, and glimpses into the mentalities of ruler and ruled, Turks and Armenians. In form and scope, the novel is very different from the autobiographies of S. Zoryan (*Mi kyank'i patmut'yun*) and G. Mahari (*Mankut'yun; Patanekut'yun*). But this is not its only distinction, nor does it explain its immense popularity. Besides its historical value as an absorbing record of a lifestyle that has all but vanished, the book is an illuminating inner and geographical journey by a candid pilgrim with a keen eye for the bleak and the beautiful in human life.

DERENIK DEMIRČYAN (1877–1956) began his literary career long before the Bolshevik Revolution, but flourished after the establishment of the Soviet regime in Armenia. At first he wrote verse, but he later moved on to prose, writing comedies, dramas, short stories, novels, art reviews, and essays in the periodical press on various topics. He was thus a prolific and multifarious writer, touching on a wide range of topics, but until the twenties he was outshone by the younger glories of Armenian literature such as Y. T'umanean, A. Isahakyan, V. Tērean, and E. Charents (q.q.v.). Ideological considerations were yet another barrier. Demirčyan was one of the leading figures of the so-called "companion" writers who adhered to neither of the two main factions of writers competing to set the tone for the new Soviet Armenian literature. At least for a while, he tried to steer clear of politically motivated literature, and official criticism was more often than not unfavorable towards him. Another factor was the uneven quality of his literature. Although a re-evaluation of his oeuvre (as well as those of all other Soviet Armenian authors) would be a timely review, it would in all likelihood still sustain the prevailing judgment.

Demirčyan was given to philosophically analyzing his topics of interest and to probing the depths of human behavior and its infinite manifestations, rather than characterization. This is true of many of his writings, with the notable exception of his best works, for which he gained a bright and permanent standing in modern Armenian literature. His comedy, *K'aj Nazar* (Nazar the brave), finally brought him wide popular acclaim. This was a rather bold undertaking on his part, because some famous authors (T'umanean, Isahakyan, and others) had already written adaptations of this folk tale. Strictly speaking, Nazar was more than just an adaptation; Demirčyan fleshed out its bare plot with new details and episodes, creating a remarkably witty comedy. The main concept was to show the catastrophic consequences of the incompetent despots and timid, cringing rulers who held arbitrary power. Social realities and some philosophical tenets were also satirized. The denouement (Nazar's fortunes eventually eclipse) proved to be somewhat controversial, especially in view of the fact that other versions of the story end with Nazar's triumphant reign. There can be no doubt that the Armenian political leadership and parties were one of Demirčyan's main targets, but some critics have sensibly argued that many political arbiters of human destiny are exact replicas of Nazar. A telling example of such political terror was the fate that befell Demirčyan's comedy, *Napoleon Korkotyan,* which, in a story reminiscent of Gogol's *Revizor,* mercilessly exposed corruption at a *sovkhoz,* a new economic institution created by the new system. Official criticism shot down the play as a distortion of the bright realities of Soviet life.

The history (old and new, e.g., the drama *Hovnan metzatun* on 1915 and its impact) and destiny of his own people were among the dominant themes in Demirčyan's work. This took on a more pronounced importance in the thirties, when (from positions of "vulgar socialism") the past and patriotism were still seen as expressions of "bourgeois nationalism." Demirčyan's *Girk' tzałkants* (The book of flowers), a short piece of prose written with inspiration from Kostandin Erznkatsi, told its readers about some of the creative principles and continuities in Armenian culture. What exactly Demirčyan meant by the title is difficult to say with certainty. He may have had in mind a very special kind of *florilegium,* a repository of some of the facets of Armenian culture. But it is also an unmistakable reference to the illuminated manuscript created by the abbot of a monastery, a novice by the name of Zvartʻ, and a scribe named Tʻade. The abbot, a former architect, writes an illustrated treatise on creating and building as two elements of vitality in life. Inspired by him, Zvartʻ composes a poem on flowers as symbols of eternal beauty and revival, and Tʻade illuminates the manuscript with floral patterns. The manuscript survives for centuries through overwhelming odds and is at last salvaged at a market in Damascus. The work was a synthesis of Demirčyan's views of the intellectual and artistic creativity of his people, a hymn to those often anonymous monks, creators of the tradition, and to the touching ways in which such treasures were fostered and handed down to posterity.

In 1938 Demirčyan wrote an enthusiastically received (and splendidly staged) drama, *Erkir hayreni* (Fatherland), about eleventh-century political life in Armenia. King Gagik II, the central hero, is seen fighting for his country and crown against deadly Byzantine threats. But the jewel of Demirčyan's literary endeavor is *Vardanankʻ,* an extensive historical novel that he completed in about four months in 1943. The event (the battle of Awarayr, A.D. 451) and the theme are well known from the work of the historians Ełišē and Łazar Pʻarpetsi. Successive Armenian historians have also elaborated on the episode, and more recently playwrights have invoked it on stage. The Armenians' resolve to die rather than renounce their Christian faith has emerged as one of the fundamental aspects of the Armenian self-image. Nonetheless, the purpose for which the war was fought and the course advocated by the two most influential figures of the time, Vardan Mamikonean (commander in chief of the Armenian forces) and Vasak Siwni (*marzpan,* i.e., "viceroy" of Armenia), have been reinterpreted.

While faithful to historical accounts, Demirčyan placed a far greater emphasis on the political rather than the religious interpretation of the battle of Awarayr; the Armenians, he averred, fought to maintain their national identity. Vasak Siwni remained a traitor to Demirčyan, who explained but did not mitigate Vasak's betrayal. He held that Vasak had a carefully considered political agenda that called for compromise, a line that brought him into a collision with Vardan Mamikonean, who favored ourtright confrontation with Ctesiphon. Furthermore, Vasak's two children were held hostage at the Persian court. Therefore, as a father and as an ambitious and vainglorious politician, Vasak, his name now synonymous with treason, had a limited range of choices. (A more or less similar explanation is found in Stepʻanos Ōrbelean's *Patmutʻiwn nahangin Sisakan.*) The plot revolves round essentially one minor and two major conflicts: Armenia-Persia, the partisans of Vardan and Vasak, and the disenchanted masses and their rulers (the *naḫarars,* the nobles) in Armenia. The novel is written with gripping verve, in an excellent Eastern Armenian with appropriate Classical Armenian forms for purposes of characterization. The initial parts are protracted, there is some repetition, and certain social aspects are covered in an inadequate fashion. But Demirčyan ably recreated the political and cultural atmosphere of the era that generated wide support for the Armenian military by the public at large.

STEPʻAN ZORYAN's (1889–1967) prose reflects the changes that shaped Eastern Armenian realities in the opening decades of the twentieth century. His initial short stories, permeated with melancholy and subtle humor, tell of the mentality of ordinary people, dispirited by the harshness of a dull life. Zoryan chooses ordinary situations and seemingly insignificant events, and viewing his subjects from fresh angles, opens up the inner life of his heroes with penetrating details. These are sad people, enslaved to the circumstances surrounding them, living by inertia with no awareness or prospects for a brighter present or future (notably his first collection, *Tḫur mardik,* Sad people). His subsequent short stories deal with a wider variety of characters, good and bad, honest and dishonest. The clashes here occur for monetary considerations or for apparently unimportant issues, with serious, sometimes fatal, consequences. His lyrical but detached tone adds to the inner drama, especially in his portraits of rebels who refuse to tolerate or give in to corruption and moral decline. Zoryan was unable to match these fine accomplishments in his works that mirrored the dramatic events of the years 1918–21. His *Hełkomi naḫagahě* (Chairman of the revolutionary committee), for instance, is somewhat shallow. A better work, though still inferior to his earlier achievements, was *Amiryanneri ěntanikʻě* (The Amiryan family), which pitches fathers against sons, the traditional and the parochial against the new and progressive, all against a revolutionary background. Zoryan's eloquence in the short story owes something to Chekhov and, to a lesser degree, Dostoevsky.

When Moscow unofficially relaxed restrictions on literature during World War II, Zoryan seized the opportunity, as did D. Demirčyan, to write his historical novel *Pap tʻagawor* (King Pap [c368–c374]). This was followed by *Hayots berdě* (The fortress of Armenia) in 1960 and by *Varazdat [Aršakuni, ca. 374–378]* in 1967. In terms of historical chronology, *Hayots berdě* dealt with the earliest period of this trilogy. It depicts the reign of King Aršak II (c350–c367), father of King Pap. The novel focuses on Aršak's policy and the building of Aršakawan, a city of refuge. Zoryan's purpose was to reinterpret the extremely unfavorable view Armenian historians held of Aršak. Indeed, Zoryan believed that Aršak initiated a centralized and independent policy (vis-à-vis Rome and Ctesiphon) in an attempt to consolidate the hold of the monarchy over the country and the centrifugal tendencies of the *naḥarars.* Aršak, Zoryan reasoned, embarked on the building of Aršakawan with a view to making it into an impregnable fortress for *all* of Armenia, a fortress that was to be far stronger than those of the *naḥarars,* and an effective focus of loyalty and unity. But foes from within and without disabled Aršak and destroyed his plans.

As Zoryan saw it, Pap of *Pap tʻagawor* shared his father's concerns and adhered to his political principles. But unlike his father, who never hesitated to put to the sword entire houses of *naḥarars,* Pap tried to appease them and to win them over. Pap also attempted to curb the immense power of the Church of Armenia while at the same time trying to make her an independent national church. In *Varazdat,* the concept of self-reliance is propounded. This novel lacks the flare and depth of the former two. In all three works, Zoryan on some occasions wanders away from the historical record and in many instances reinterprets the received tradition. To him, as to many of his contemporaries who surveyed the scene of Armenian history and its bitter lessons, the future of a prosperous Armenia lay in its unity. In these novels, the masses and representatives of social classes emerge, in the best traditions of socialist realism, as one of the most vital, indispensable forces shaping the destiny of Armenia. Almost all of his characters are lively and skillfully sketched; save for some dull ideological passages, the novels, especially *Hayots berdě,* rank with the best in the genre. Zoryan wrote in a vivid, incisive, and limpid style.

GURGEN MAHARI (1903–69) was one of the writers forging a new literary tradition in the twenties and thirties. After a brief association with the proletarian writers, he collaborated with Charents. Mahari came under mauling attacks and was twice exiled for long years. Yet, the corpus of his literature is considerably large and contains some of the luminous pages of twentieth-century Armenian literature.

Going through the usual phases, by the early thirties Mahari had found his own voice. His rhymed lines, in the form of both short and long poems, were at first pessimistic in tone. Seized by the fervor generated by hopes pinned on the new system, Mahari, in the manner of all his contemporaries, sang songs of steel and the color red and wrote *agit-operets* ("operettas") and *agitkas* (propaganda in various short literary forms) from positions of Russian futurism and the *Lef* (Left front of art). But soon, swimming against the tide in the company of daring souls, he turned to lyric poetry, arguing for and asserting his own literary creed. He excelled in short forms of verse, distinguished by refined sensibilities, bright and captivating colors, an enchanting sense of humor, and a serene, dreamy nostalgia. He wrote of love and nature and of the childhood he was forced to leave behind in the city of Van, his birthplace. Throughout Mahari's life and work, this beloved city remained a hovering presence and a focus of identity, lit up by fond memories or scarred by indelible scenes of death and destruction. Even though his longing for his birthplace was never touched by chauvinism, pessimism, or idealization, it occasioned fierce criticism by his ideologically motivated adversaries, among whom was Nairi Zaryan (q.v.), ironically also from the region of Van and who had similarly experienced and survived the 1915 massacres and deportations.

From the early twenties, Mahari simultaneously tried his hand at prose, which some critics believe better suited his talent and temperament. Love, the family and its structure (a burning issue at the time), and the independence of the individual within society attracted Mahari's attention. He established himself as one of the masters of Soviet Armenian prose with a cycle of short novels: *Mankutyun* (Childhood); *Patanekutyun* (Adolescence, 1930); and *Eritasardutyan semin* (On the threshold of youth), published a quarter of a century later. The next anticipated part, *Eritasardutyun* (Youth), remained unfinished. The first novel once again took him to his native Van; the second depicted the flight of the Armenians of Van to Eastern Armenia in the Russian Empire; and the third illustrated Mahari's first years in Armenia and certain parts of Transcaucasia. All three reflect the harrowing ordeal and its devastating impact on the Armenians. From 1937 to 1954, Mahari was exiled and forced into silence.

After his rehabilitation, Mahari put together a collection of verse and his *Lṙutyan dzaynĕ* (The sound of silence, 1962), a collection of short stories from life in the early decades of the Soviet regime and in Siberia. Perhaps the best short novel of the Siberian exile cycle is *Tzałkatz pšalarer* (Barbed wire in bloom). This work was first published in 1988, though its smuggled manuscript had been serialized much earlier in Beirut. It tells of the author's trial in Erevan and the years of exile he spent at a camp in Vologda, north of Moscow. Mahari's last novel was *Ayrvoł aygestanner* (Burning orchards), which immediately aroused indignant criticism for "distorting" certain aspects of recent Armenian history (the revised version appeared posthumously in 1979). The novel concentrates on Van, especially the year 1915, and illustrates its self-defense and eventual fall. It is an indictment of Ottoman Turkish policy towards the Western Armenians in general and the Armenians of Van in particular. But it is also critical of Armenian political leadership, hence the hue and cry when the book first appeared. All this takes place against a vividly detailed background of social, political, and cultural realities in the city of Van.

Many of Mahari's works appear fragmented and seem to lack unity and meticulous plot. The author appears to be narrating in a kind of relaxed stream of consciousness, seeking and revealing the truth as he saw it. Prescriptions, guidelines, and genres never really restricted either the flight of his imagination or the inquisitiveness of his mind. Sparkling wit, teasing humor, and biting sarcasm are characteristic of his unconventional style, as are his lyricism and emotive powers. A spontaneous optimism renders his work memorably charming.

MKRTICH ARMEN (1906–72) was actively involved in the search during the twenties and thirties for a new literature to rise from the ashes of the old. His collections in verse echo such concerns, prevalent at the time when praise of technology and iron emerged in the works of many writers as a politically, socially, and aesthetically predominant theme. His initial short stories also elaborate on the rise of a new mentality, new criteria for human relationships, and new economic and socio-political realities. Among his better short novels are *Skaut No 89* (Scout no. 89), a criticism of the institution he came in touch with during his years at the American orphanage in Alexandrapol (Leninakan, now Gyumri); *Gagatneri ergĕ* (The song of the summits); and *Erg kałaki masin* (A song for the city), both of which depict the conflict of the old and the new and illustrate Armen's pronounced preference for urban life. One of his earliest novels was *Yerevan,* a juxtaposition of the old and the newly rising Erevan. (The plan for rebuilding Erevan was then a burning issue, and almost all the writers expressed their views on the architectural future of the capital.)

Armen was among the intellectuals exiled to concentration camps during the Stalinist purges and one of the very few to return home in the early fifties. His observations took shape in a collection titled *Patviretsin handznel dzez* (roughly, "I was requested to deliver this to you"), which contains a few brilliant sketches about the shockingly tragic life at camps in the freezing north. This was followed by a novel titled *Žirayr Glents,* the story of a victim returning to his family after his release from a concentration camp. But Armen's best and enduring work remains his short novel *Hełnar ałbyur* (Heghnar fountain), one of the finer accomplishments in Armenian prose. Ultra-orthodox communist writers such as Nairi Zaryan (q.v.) were inflexible and fiercely denounced the work, but the public and most critics greeted it warmly. The plot unfolds in Alexandrapol, Armen's birthplace, and illustrates the destruction of some honest, ordinary people by the formidable powers of traditional values and religious intolerance. Love, wedlock, the family, individual dignity, and contributions to society as the ultimate personal fulfillment are the basic issues presented in this moving piece. His characters are original, good-hearted, and lively natives of Gyumri-Leninakan, a provincial town with an authentic Armenian lifestyle. Armen knew its dialect (it was his own) and put it to excellent use. Drama, lyricism, an incisive analysis of the heroes' behavior, and a spare but forceful style all combine to make this work a rewarding read.

A good deal of controversy surrounds the life and work of **NAIRI ZARYAN** (1900–69), the censorious literary crusader of the pre–World War II period. He was the most prominent, passionate, and talented writer of the Association of Proletarian Writers of Armenia, a hotbed of the "Proletkult" (Proletarian culture), or the "Left," and the informal leader of the relentless opposition (with devastating, sometimes deadly, consequences) to some of the greatest authors of the Soviet era: Charents, Bakunts, Mahari (q.q.v.), and others. Zaryan called for a new, ideologically motivated literature that was epic in tone, international and universal in character, and focused on the rebuilding of the country and people of the Soviets. He found lyric poetry to be abominable, untimely, and therefore unacceptable; employed a bombastic rhetorical style; and paid very little attention, if any, to the aesthetic and artistic aspects of form. Zaryan made extended visits to many a *kolkhoz* and *sovkhoz,* factory and construction site, for inspiration and authenticity in depicting the rise of the new communist world. In his verse of the twenties, Zaryan described, mostly in the spoken language, the changing economic picture (irrigation, hydraulic power plants, etc.), the unrest and conflicts in Armenia from 1918 to 1921, the revolution and its heroes, and the might and promise the new regime held.

His long poem *Ṙušani k̇araṗě* (1935), named after a stretch of land (a kind of frontage), was considerably original and marked a turning point in his literary career. It depicted the early stages of collectivization and its attendant problems. Unlike his earlier works, many of his characters here are lively and credible, as are his imagery and his description of the countryside. A number of critics suggested, and the author agreed, that there is something of Ṫumanean's style in this poem. Shifting to prose, in 1937 Zaryan published the first part of his novel *Hatsavan* (a village in Armenia), which in a way was a sequel to *Ṙušani k̒arap̒ě* in that it dealt with covert resistance to collectivization by former landowners and saboteurs. Here again, most of Zaryan's characters grow out of circumstances and are deeply affected by the new economic order. If the first part of *Hatsavan* was a noteworthy accomplishment, its second part (1947) left much to be desired. In the thirties, Zaryan also wrote humorous and satirical verse, mostly tackling literary matters.

World War II inspired Zaryan to change the manner and matter of his verse. Stalin received his fair share of panegyric and so did the soldiers of the Red Army, Armenian and non-Armenian. He had earlier dismissed Grigor Narekatsi and other old glories, but now he turned to them and to Armenian history, language, and culture (e.g., his *Dzayn hayrenakan,* Voice of the fatherland) to inspire his fellow countrymen at home and on the front. But his best effort remains *Ara Gełetsik* (Ara the fair, 1944), an adaptation for stage of Movsēs Ḥorenatsi's account of the legend. Writing in a solemn style and an epic breath, Zaryan made many changes in Ḥorenatsi's version. For instance, Ara and Šamiram (Semiramis) are mutually attracted; Nuard, wife of Ara, plays an important role as a patriotic mother and a devoted wife; and the whole atmosphere in the drama is politically charged (there are echoes of German-Soviet relations, such as the emphasis on the abrogation by Šamiram of the peace treaty between Urartu and Assyria). A patriotic and faithful Ara is eventually able to rise above personal ends in order to fight and die for his country. Some aspects of the denouement and characterization have been criticized, but the play has been popular since. Zaryan was prolific after the war too, writing many plays and lyric poetry, some of which casts a retrospective glance at his past and clarifies some of his extreme views.

SERO ḤANZADYAN (1915–1998) was one of the prominent Soviet Armenian novelists of the post–World War II era. Ḥanzadyan early abandoned his initial attempts in verse and wrote a large number of short stories, short novels, and novels of contemporary life in Armenia, the past, and World War II (during which he fought in the ranks of the Red Army). He elaborated on the latter theme in novels such as *Mer gndi mardik* (The men in our battalion) and *Erek̒ tari 291 ōr* (Three years and 291 days). Some of his novels tackled contemporary social, economic, and agricultural issues, including *Hołě* (The land), *K̒ajaran,* and *Sevani lusabatsě* (The dawn of Sevan). What spread his fame far and wide, however, was his first historical novel, *Mḥit̒ar Sparapet* (Mekhitar, commander-in-chief), an extensive book illustrating the struggle of the Armenians of Siwnikʿ and Artsaḥ in the 1720s under the leadership of Dawitʿ Bek and his successor, Mḥitʿar. The novel was a labor of love, a record of valor, dedication, patriotism, and not-so-subtle praise for Russian might, assistance, and the fraternity of the two peoples. Despite Ḥanzadyan's gripping style, the novel is protracted and suffers from a number of flaws.

Ḥanzadyan's next historical novel, *Ḥosekʿ, Hayastani leṙner* (Speak, you mountains of Armenia), focuses on the Armenian genocide during World War I. Apart from depicting death and destruction, the work is an indictment of the Young Turk leadership as well as German leadership (for its complicity in the crime perpetrated against the Armenians by the Young Turk regime). The novel also highlights the pro-Russian orientation of the Armenians and their resistance despite disunity and dispersion. In *Tʿaguhin hayots* (Queen of the Armenians), Ḥanzadyan zooms backwards from the twentieth century into obscure periods of Armenian history to prove that the Armenians were indigenous to Armenia and that their origins as a unified nation occurred much earlier than is generally assumed. The setting is Hayasa in the fourteenth century B.C. under Huganna (i.e., Hukannas) and his heir Karanni[s] and the Hittite Empire under Mursilis II. It is the aim of Karanni[s] and particularly his wife, Mari-Luys, to unite the Armenian tribes and introduce monotheism into Hayasa-Armenia. For his fiction, Ḥanzadyan may have relied on I. M. D'iakonov's *Predistoriia armianskogo naroda* (The pre-history of the Armenian people) and, since there are a number of parallels, on the history of Egypt under Akhenaton (Amenhotep IV).

Ḥanzadyan's *Andranik* had been suppressed for years before its publication in 1989. It appeared as the Soviet Union raced towards its collapse and the movement for Karabagh and independence gathered momentum in Armenia. With General Andranik (Ōzanean, 1865–1927) as its central hero, the novel analyzes the course of events in the recent history of Armenia, illustrating the plight of his small nation and its inability to control its destiny, despite its heroic struggle and military contributions to the war effort on the side of the Allies. Ḥanzadyan has nothing but furious contempt for Western apathy to the predicament of his nation and disdain for czarist Russian policy during World War I. He dwells at some length on British disapproval of Andranik's plans for military assistance to the Armenians of Artsaḥ (Karabagh), implying that the map and fate of both Armenia and Artsaḥ would probably have been very different had Andranik been allowed to extend military assistance to his fellow countrymen in 1918. Despite his anti-communist statements in the late 1980s, Ḥanzadyan called in this novel for self-reliance and alliance with Bolshevik Russia. Some lurid scenes, verbosity, haste, and infelicities mar this novel. Such shortcomings are found in many of his extensive works, but Ḥanzadyan was an experienced craftsman who wrote with verve and imagination.

HOVHANNES ŠIRAZ's (1915–84) first collection of verse was met with wide and warm acclaim. Amid rhymed euphoria for steel, tractors, industrial technology and the like, he delighted his readers with his lyrical microcosm, ablaze with dazzling colors of nature. This was shortly followed by *Siamant'o ev Ḥjezare* (also *Ḥačezare,* or *Ḥčezare*), perhaps his most popular narrative poem, which has an Armenian shepherd and a half-Armenian, half-Kurdish girl as the central characters of a tragic love story. In more ways than one, it established his style and foreshadowed some of the themes that would fascinate him most: love, human destiny, nature, and patriotism. Širaz's first book unfolds for the reader the natural beauty of his native region, Širak, in Eastern Armenia, and his poem has as its backdrop the area around Lake Van in the historical Armenian province of Vaspurakan in Western Armenia. In the context of Armeno-Kurdish relations, land and landmarks, oppressive traditions and history, religious and social injustices are all fused into one with Siamant'o's suffering and unhappy fate, in a powerfully emotional and highly romantic style adorned with an endless string of fresh, vivid metaphors and imagery. The topographical and geographical designations that emerge as appealing symbols still in captivity under Ottoman rule would have an even greater presence in his verse composed after the fifties.

Many threads in Širaz's art intimately linked him with folklore, popular mentality and expression, Avetik' Isahakyan, Sayeat' Nōvay (q.q.v.), and the minstrelsy. But Širaz, like most of his predecessors, had his own distinct literary personality. He once said that he felt the tumult of the "white element of Niagara" in his chest and that the colors of the rainbow made up the strings of his lyre. Indeed, passion and emotional lyricism are the two salient features of his verse through which he sought to unravel the secrets of eternity, human character, fate, virtues, and the aesthetically beautiful. For Širaz, man was the master of his own destiny; although still imperfect, he held the potential and promise of becoming perfect ("Bibliakan," A biblical poem). Made up of divine and "satanic" elements, human beings could elevate themselves to impeccable standards by renouncing their devilish ways ("Bnut'yan gluḫgortzotsĕ," Nature's masterpiece). Moral rectitude and unalloyed love were essential; for vain ambitions would lead to corruption and hinder human happiness

("Siraname," a love story, originally published as *Ṙusťavtsi Šoťan ev Ťamarě,* Shota of Rustavi and Queen Tamar). Perhaps no other Armenian author has so reverently worshipped mothers and motherhood (*Hušardzan mayrikis,* A monument to my mother, and many other poems). But, to put it mildly, Širaz had a rather poor and traditional view of women; he distinguished only between mothers (always saintly) and other women (frequently satanic). In terms of style, Širaz's love poetry has a number of affinities with Middle Eastern literary traditions and his confrères, old and new. Eyes, eyebrows, cheeks, and lips are common in his imagery. Redeeming features of his work include the frequent flash of his sterling talent, demonstrated by sudden fresh epithets and images, and sincere sentiments bursting with emotion.

Patriotism accounted for much of Širaz's immense popularity. It nettled the establishment, but the establishment never grasped the nettle. Many criticized Širaz for repetition, worn-out platitudes, and narrow-minded nationalism. But Širaz continued unperturbed, and his entourage of young admirers recited his censored patriotic poems at literary events and public gatherings. He furiously rejected taboos and restrictions placed on political topics, toponyms, and symbols that covered up historical facts and expunged associations in compliance with Soviet central policy. Širaz invoked many an old Armenian figure, event, and toponym to highlight his numerous concerns. Held in the highest esteem is Mesrop Maštots, the genius who invented the Armenian script, ("Hayots hrašk'ě: Mesrop Maštots," The marvel of Armenia: Mesrop Maštots), an indestructible shield for the mother tongue and national identity. The most frequently cited symbol in all of his poetry is Mount Ararat. It epitomizes Armenia and Armenian suffering and aspirations, especially the consequences of the 1915 genocide: almost total annihilation, loss of a unique culture and land (including cities such as Ani and Van), and an implicit determination never to recognize the new political borders. Numerous poems, short and long, have been inspired by each of these and similar topics; for instance, the genocide is commemorated in short works and a long poem, *Hayots danťeakaně* (The Dantesque inferno of the Armenians). The heroes of the Armenian liberation movement (e.g., General Andranik Ōzanean, 1865–1927), the worldwide dispersion of the Armenians, their future and their ties to the homeland, unity of the Armenian people, prosperity of Armenia, and visions of a bright future are also a part of his patriotic verse. The opinion, whether motivated by ideology or artistic refinement, that Širaz was becoming repetitive was undoubtedly valid. It was reinforced by Širaz's own disinclination to experiment with new forms of expression. He felt that good poetry was that which touched the reader's heart. And many of his vibrant, impassioned poems of love and his concern for peace and the destiny of his people struck a responsive chord in his readership.

HAMO SAHYAN (1914–93) wrote traditional poetry but in a voice all his own. From an initially rhetorical style, he refined his verse into a delicately fashioned world of warm sentiments, fine impressions, deep colors, scents, and sounds, all infused with a gentle sense of nostalgia and drama. With a fascination for nature up hill and down dale in his native region of Zangezur, Sahyan refracted through his soul nature's awesome forms and formations, seasons and elements, trees and twigs, breeze and brooks, to reveal his own state of mind and unrequited, elusive moods. His communion with his birthplace was such that he at times felt he was nature incarnate. With his native landscape as nearly the only mise en scène for his verse, Sahyan did indeed court monotony, and dangerously so. But more often than not, especially in his mature years, his eloquent and subtle imagery, resembling a fine embroidery, along with his unalloyed sentiments and dignified simplicity endowed many of his poems with charm.

Sahyan himself once stated in one of his poems that he was neither Sayeatʻ-Nōvay nor Nahapet Kʻuchak; unlike those deep seas he was just a simple lake. Neither passion nor passionate love are found in his poetry. Instead, loneliness and an intoxicating, languorous longing for his vanished youth and an unsettling ambiguity permeate his lyrical verse, in addition to a subtle tension and a sense of unfulfillment. Although fully aware of his colleagues' experiments, he showed no interest in innovative trends. He remained faithful to traditional patterns and wrote in a tidy, unadorned, and unobtrusive style. This and his austere, intensely personal sentiments distinguished him from other traditionalist writers. The fresh angles he discovered as he contemplated the inseparable affinities human beings shared with nature distinguished him from all other Soviet Armenian poets.

SILVA KAPUTIKYAN (1919–) made her literary debut on the eve of World War II, but published her first major collection in 1945. Included in it is "Ḥoskʻ im ordun" (A word to my son), which is still her most popular poem. An exhortation for her son not to forget his mother tongue, the poem concerns one of her two major themes, national identity. (Her other favorite theme is lyric poetry.) National identity is symbolized in the poem by Mount Ararat, the capital Erevan, the Armenian language, and figures and events of the past and present and inspire her devotion to her homeland. Her nationalism is enveloped in the larger context of Soviet patriotism, which brought her All-Union popularity and laurels (such as the USSR State Prize for Literature in 1952). The unhappy course of her people's history left a profound mark on her poetry, as did the revival of Armenia as a Soviet republic and, particularly, the protection the USSR afforded Armenia. Her patriotism is free from chauvinism and extremism, and her poetry places much emphasis on peace and prosperity. In poems commemorating the genocide (e.g., *Mtorumner čanaparhi kesin,* Reflections at the halfway point), despite her unallayed wrath, she found the survival of her nation, the rebuilding of Armenia, and its rosy future to be the most eloquent and most promising response to the attempt to destroy her people.

Although Kaputikyan's first collection was met with adverse criticism by some, she was soon recognized as one of the gifted poets of her generation and as the leading poetess of Armenia. Her preeminence owed much to her candid lyric verse. Youthful sentimentalism disappeared fast, and her love poetry blossomed into tender yet proud sentiments and sensibilities. Hers was an unrequited emotional affection. Hence her disappointments, handled delicately and ingenuously; hence also her charming sense of anticipation and poignant longing, all of which add a light touch of drama to her verse, making it vibrate with life and lofty feelings of love.

Kaputikyan wrote two well-known travel books. The first, *K'aravannerĕ deṙ k'aylum en* (The caravans are still on the move) is a description of her visit to Middle Eastern Armenian communities. The second, *Ḥčankar hogu ev k'artezi guynerits* (A mosaic composed of the colors of the soul and the map), is an account of her visit to North American Armenian communities. While the former is a highly emotional encounter with the descendants of the survivors of the genocide of 1915, the latter is a sober scrutiny of the Armenians of the United States and Canada. Both have historical value as records of the Armenian realities in two very different regions seen through the keen, if biased, eyes of a Soviet Armenian observer. Both are eloquent testimonies to Kaputikyan's excellent prose, written with verve in an attractive Eastern Armenian.

GEVORG ĒMIN (1919–1998) was inclined from the outset to avoid the trodden path of poetry. But like so many of his generation, Ēmin was subjected to fierce attacks for wayward ideological and artistic failures. There was amid all this senseless criticism some validity to the observation that Emin's style was somewhat careless and his love poetry rhetorical. The blend of sentiment and intellect he sought remained elusive. In the mid-fifties as the Stalinist rigidities loosened somewhat, Ēmin and his colleagues spoke loudly of the need for exploring the complexities of human character and relations. A decade later, he cast his net even wider to capture the concerns and aspirations of generations who had experienced Dayr al-Zūr (the final destination of the deportations during the genocide), the Gestapo, and Auschwitz. Such thoughts and the negative aspects of technological advances, alienation, the cold war, the nuclear arms race, and the devastating effects of the inequal economic order in the West all preoccupied Ēmin's imagination. These issues found their way not only into Ēmin's thought and imagery, but also into the hearts and minds of his readers, sharpening their alertness to world peace and overall human concerns. His intellectual poems rejected parochialism and mediocrity, bombastic and vain patriotism, and paralyzing traditional styles and mentality. Instead, they promoted wider, universal perspectives and are among his most attractive works, ranking him among the leading poets whose work has introduced innovative trends into Soviet-Armenian verse.

During World War II, Ēmin wrote sorrowfully of agony, devastation, and the senseless loss of human life. Repatriation (*hayrenadardzuťyun*) of Armenians to Armenia from abroad was another theme that engaged his attention in the aftermath of the war. As he charted his own course, Ēmin made no attempt to conceal his contempt for hackneyed poems, produced en masse in the late thirties and forties, in a vulgar imitation of the art of minstrels and folkloric formulae. Wit, irony, and sarcasm sharpened the edge of his rhymed commentary. In the same vein, Ēmin often humorously stripped his love poetry of its romantic veil. He saw himself and all poets as citizens, not so much in the Soviet style, but rather as prompters, always on the qui vive; for despite immense progress, little had changed in human character. Profoundly proud of his national heritage, he has sought to interpret the defeats and unhappy destiny of his people with pride and dignity, allegory and wit, hope and renewal; he has sung, in an affectionate tone, the praises of his homeland in prose (e.g., *Yoť erg Hayastani masin,* Seven songs about Armenia).

Literature of the Post-Genocide Dispersion

An Overview of the Realities of the Post-Genocide Armenian Dispersion

Dayr al-Zūr, in the Syrian desert, was the final destination of the survivors of the Armenian genocide of 1915. Few returned from this town, but those who had been driven to larger cities in western Syria, from Aleppo to Damascus, stood a much better chance of survival. Some of them settled in Syria, some in Lebanon, some went farther south to Palestine and Egypt, and some to Greece, France, the United States, and South America, giving rise to a new Dispersion. From the fifties there occurred some substantial shifts in the demographic distribution of the Dispersion. Many Armenians left Egypt following the overthrow of the monarchy, and a considerable number left Syria for Lebanon in the early sixties (as Egypt and Syria merged to form the United Arab Republic). Almost at the same time, many thousands of Armenians left both countries for Kuwait, the United Arab Emirates, and Australia. In the mid-seventies, some Cypriot Armenians fled the Turkish invasion of the island and settled in the United Kingdom, and a little later, during the Lebanese civil war, many more sought safety in France, Canada, and the United States. The latest large exodus was caused by the Iranian revolution, while the Persian Gulf war displaced many as well. In the eighties, large numbers of Armenians left Soviet Armenia, mainly for California.

In the wake of the genocide and the French withdrawal from Cilicia, the Catholicosate of Cilicia (with its seat at Sis, now Kozan, Turkey) went into exile in Syria, and within a few years permanently relocated in Ant'ilias (Antelias), then a village immediately to the north of Beirut. In 1916, the Young Turk government arbitrarily dismissed Patriarch Zawēn Ełiayean, *Pałtattsi,* of Constantinople (two terms, 1913–16, 1919–22) from office and sent him into exile in Baghdad. In a similarly high-handed fashion, the government abolished the Armenian National Constitution and placed the Patriarchates of both Constantinople and Jerusalem and the Catholicosate of Ałt'amar under the jurisdiction of the Catholicosate of Sis, whose incumbent head, Sahak II, Ḥapayean (1849–1939, reigned 1902–39), was appointed Catholicos-Patriarch of all Armenians of the Ottoman Empire, with his seat in Jerusalem. Gabriēl Archbishop Čēvahirčean (d.1923) sat in Constantinople as "patriarchal" *locum tenens* (1916–18). Although it retained its title, the Patriarchate of Constantinople in Turkey was in effect reduced to a see overseeing the Armenians of Istanbul and a few very small communities in Turkey that had survived the genocide. The Catholicosate of All Armenians in Ējmiatzin was severely suppressed, but after World War II gradually regained some of its rights.

The post-genocide Armenian Dispersion is a complex reality that defies definition in precise and absolute terms. Scattered far and wide and subject to diverse influences, no two communities abroad are alike, and no attempt will be made here to describe any such entity in any specific detail. In general terms, what seems to be common to all the communities is the existence of a number of institutions that represent and organize them: the Armenian Church; the political parties; charitable organizations; the periodical press; cultural, social, and compatriotic societies; an educational network; and to a lesser extent, athletic clubs. These organizations neither exhaust the list nor are they characteristic of every community. Broadly speaking, most refugees and emigrants belonged to one of two camps: pro-Soviet Armenian or anti-Soviet Armenian. Attitudes towards Soviet Armenia, the genocide, and an all-out effort to perpetuate Armenian identity defined the characteristic aspects of the Dispersion.

None of the traditional political parties folded after the Bolshevik takeover of Armenia. The Armenian Revolutionary Federation (the Dashnak party), driven out of Armenia in 1920, tried to entrench itself firmly in the Dispersion and embraced an unremittingly anti-Soviet line. An independent and united Armenia was still the dream, as was the party's wish to return to power some day. The Social Democratic Hnchakean party supported the new regime, as did the Armenian Democratic League (the Ṙamkavar party), despite the wide ideological gaps separating them. Hence, a point worthy of note: Support for Soviet Armenia on the whole did not emanate from Marxist convictions (the Armenian communists were a tiny minority), but rather from a belief that Soviet Russia afforded Armenia solid protection against Turkish designs, and from a wish to see this last stretch of land flourish as a viable entity. This divergence of views manifested itself in various forms and in varying degrees of intensity. The parties by no means shied away from violence (including assassinations) against each other in the United States and, particularly, Lebanon, whose confessional system allowed a greater degree of ethnic-religious autonomy and enabled the parties to exercise a greater control over the community. But Armenian communities elsewhere enjoyed no such autonomy, and the Church remained by far their most influential institution. In an effort to strengthen its hold over the Dispersion, the Dashnak party in the mid-fifties seized full control of the Catholicosate of Cilicia in Ant'ilias, Lebanon. The latter now began to expand its jurisdiction either by wresting sees from Ējmiatzin (e.g., that of Iran, a traditional pillar of support for Ējmiatzin throughout its history) in the Middle East, Europe, and the Americas, or by creating new ones. This hierarchical schism, allied with a number of other factors, rent the Armenian communities apart throughout the length and breadth of the Dispersion. For a while, such was the degree of fanatical partisanship that in certain circles and in certain communities, one was born to a party rather than one's ethnic roots.

These organizations, one and all, regarded the fostering of Armenian identity as their foremost mission. It was their response to the genocide, the ungodly crime that haunted their collective memory, and at once impeded and inspired their intellectual and mental energies. The Dashnak party was particularly active in this realm, not only for patriotic reasons, but also because its future hinged upon that of a vibrant Dispersion. Ideological and geographical distances, Soviet Armenian insularity and hostility to Armenian "bourgeois, nationalist" political organizations (especially the Dashnak party), the cold war, and a greater degree of integration into the host countries accentuated the differences between a divided and estranged Dispersion and Soviet Armenia. In the post-Stalin era, a thaw began in the late fifties. Students from the Dispersion were offered scholarships to study in Soviet Armenian institutions, cultural exchange intensified, and Dashnak attitudes mellowed towards Soviet Armenia (beginning in the seventies). But the new ties were selective and partisan in nature and limited in scope. Furthermore, the Dispersion, now prosperous and with deep roots in host countries, had many faces and spoke in multiple voices due to some major economic, social, cultural, and political shifts. And Armenians' perceptions of their own self-image exhibited striking variations in national values. If language, for instance, was the most essential element in the Middle Eastern Armenian identity, it was of little or no importance for most Armenian-Americans, and it even became a source of muffled tension between the latter and new immigrants from the Middle East. A fragmented Church, torn between its religious-spiritual and national-cultural missions and further weakened by a general decline in religiosity, was no longer as effective as before. The United States and France ceased to play a leading role in literature and culture in general. Younger Armenians in increasing numbers began writing in English and French, and a new identity began to take shape in the West. The unspoken truth, long discerned by perceptive observers, now became apparent to most Armenians: The Dispersion was to be a permanent reality.

But a new era was taking shape as the old died. From the sixties onward, cultural activities were renewed with unprecedented zeal in the Middle Eastern communities, which assumed a leading position in the Dispersion. But not for long. The Armenian-American community, which had been showing signs of revival since the fifties, established its superiority in the late seventies. Several factors accounted for this, but a fresh impetus for both communities came from unlikely quarters: Soviet Armenia. The massive demonstration in Erevan commemorating the fiftieth anniversary of the genocide not only introduced new perspectives for the Armenians in the homeland, but it also provided a new élan for a languishing cause: to gain international and Turkish recognition of the forgotten genocide in more effective ways. The effort towards this end took various forms, including acts of violence, and was launched and supported by both the traditional organizations and some new cultural, professional, and political structures. With the outbreak of the Artsaḥ-Azerbaijani war, the earthquake, the collapse of the Soviet Union, and the birth of an independent Armenia, there began a new phase in Armenia's relations with the Dispersion. When local forces led Armenia to independence and the traditional political parties, especially the Dashnaks, tried to participate in Armenia's political life and vied for power, some substantial differences in outlook and mentality, hitherto neglected and still unacknowledged, that set Armenia and the Dispersion apart (and divided the Diaspora itself) became glaringly apparent.

The post-genocide literature took shape in the Armenian communities of the United States, France, and the Middle East. The first had been an active center, particularly in the wake of the massacres of the mid-1890s, with numerous periodicals (Boston taking the lead) and fierce political rivalries. This activity abated somewhat after 1908, when some intellectuals, in exile since the 1890s, returned to Constantinople after the Young Turk coup. The literature produced here by the more important writers was essentially of a retrospective and nostalgic nature. Most of the masters had been born in the "old country," in or near Ḥarberd (Harput), where Tlkatintsi (q.v.) had reigned supreme. But while they reminisced about the immediate past, life in the New World was not lost upon them; the effects of American society on Armenians transplanted to or born in the United States were almost as central to their literature as the destroyed lifestyle they restored for posterity. Some writers tackled the social and political problems afflicting American society at large, and echoes of Armenian politics reverberated in many a work. But disruptive political infighting (sometimes intensified by external factors, such as World War II or the cold war) found its fiercest expression in journalism and in attitudes towards Soviet Armenia and the Church. Armenian authors in the United States adhered to traditional patterns, and no literary experiments or innovative trends distinguished their output. William Saroyan and Leon Surmelian inaugurated Armenian-American literature in English, which, of course, is a different story.

In sharp contrast to the United States, France witnessed profound transformations and experiments in Armenian literature. There, the "Desert Generation," the shocked and confused survivors (some of them orphans) of the genocide, faced a superior and sophisticated culture beside which their own tradition paled, giving rise to serious, tormenting questions as to its validity and viability. Adaptation almost invariably meant assimilation. Although overwhelmed by it, they also perceived a moral, social, and economic crisis damaging the fabric of Western civilization between the two wars. Renewal was the key. The literature they created was a tortuous quest for clues to fresh values and a new self-definition. It was nihilistic; it rejected the past (just as some Soviet-Armenian writers had earlier, but under entirely different circumstances and for entirely different ideological and aesthetic purposes) and showed the "retreat" (i.e., assimilation, alienation, or fall) of the first generations. The short-lived periodical *Menkʻ* (We) appeared as the mouthpiece of a similarly short-lived literary coterie by the same name, made up of fifteen young writers (Š. Šahnur, V. Šušanean, Z. Orbuni, N. Sarafean, H. Zardarean, N. Pēšiktʻašlean, B. Tʻōpʻalean, Pʻ. Mikʻayēlean, Š. Narduni, and others) who put their signatures to a manifesto initiating this revisionist approach and espousing the cause of literary and intellectual reform. Compared to the *Mehean* group, the *Menkʻ* circle was far more modest in tone, ambition, and style. They sought to cultivate camaraderie and solidarity among their members, thereby creating bonds among young writers scattered in four corners of the earth, which in due time would give rise to a common creed that would recognize the individuality of writers along with national threads and concerns common to them all. The credo was stated briefly and in general terms—an early indication, perhaps, of the disparity in the views of its founders and, hence, the temporary nature of their association. Some of these authors looked more sympathetically to Soviet Armenia. A smaller but vociferous group of writers, some of whom were communists, pragmatically concentrated on the present and saw the problem in a much larger context. Capitalism was the culprit, but it became the lesser evil when fascism raised its head. They took up arms and died for France fighting against the Nazi armies.

The writers who survived the genocide were active at cultural institutions in Egypt, Palestine (the seminary at the Patriarchate), Cyprus (the Melgonean, i.e., Melkonian, School in Nicosia), Lebanon (the Nšan Pʻalančean, Yovakimean-Manukean, Daruhi Yakobean, and Sahakean in Beirut), and Syria. Following the death of the last great writers in the forties (e.g., Tʻēkʻēean, Ōšakan) and the founding of schools, Lebanon and Syria, now with larger Armenian communities than any other Arab countries, set the tone for the cultural initiatives in the entire Middle East and North Africa. Although political orientation polarized the community, and most writers took clear positions vis-à-vis Soviet Armenia, the rich literature developed here was of a traditional character, devoid of innovative trends and almost free from crises of identity. There were no threats to the language, religion, cultural institutions, or autonomy of this entirely Armenian-speaking community, at least until the sixties, when certain restrictions were imposed on political and cultural activities and the teaching of Armenian language and history at schools in some Arab countries. The Armenians of Iran, a most vibrant community, also contributed their share to Armenian literature and culture.

A Survey of the Literature of the Post-Genocide Dispersion

HAMASTEŁ (1895–1966) is usually referred to as a "giwłagir" (a compound word made up of the Armenian for village "giwł," in the sense of countryside, and the word for letter or writing, "gir," in the sense of a writer), a term that has acquired the full force of convention, but does no justice to Hamasteł, who cast his net beyond the generally accepted definition of the designation. In much the same way, identifying the era and group of writers he belonged to is somewhat difficult and can be arbitrary; for there seems to be equal ground to assigning him to the last phase of Western Armenian literature or to the nascent tradition forged by writers of the new Dispersion. Properly speaking, since no characters born and brought up in the Armenian Dispersion appear among his protagonists, Hamasteł belonged to the last generation of Western Armenian authors, with senior colleagues such as V. Tʻēkʻēean, E. Ōtean, and Y. Ōšakan, who had fortuitously escaped the nightmare of 1915. But he has also been recognized as one of the writers of the post-genocide Armenian Dispersion. Geographically, chronologically, and (to a certain degree) thematically speaking, this makes much sense. After all, his literature, as a chronicle of a microcosm that had all but vanished shortly after he had left it in 1913, in many ways documented the inestimable loss suffered in 1915.

Hamasteł wrote short stories, a novel, plays, prose poems, and some verse. Of his two plays, the one titled "Hayastani leṙneru srngaharě" (The flutist from the mountains of Armenia) is about the hold the spirit of the homeland exercises over the hearts of its children, especially for the early emigrants abroad (in this case, those living in the U. S. state of Maine) who, unwilling and unable to assimilate, immure themselves in a world of dreams, a mental replica of their former homeland, with an almost demented nostalgia as their only spiritual sustenance. The novel *Spitak dziaworě* (The white horseman), contrived as a grand novel, proved to be a failure. Hamasteł's intention was to flesh out the spiritual and heroic aspects of the Armenian quintessential self against the backdrop of recent Armenian history. His premise was built upon preconceptions, such as that the Armenians are a people of romantic sentiments, faith, and heroes. The result was a curious mixture of fact and fantasy, hyperbole, legend, and epic that lacked coherence and genuine characters.

In contrast, Hamasteł was at his best in his short stories, which grew out of a lifestyle he knew and identified with intimately. The setting is primarily the Harput area, but some of his heroes are transplanted onto American soil. The latter, mainly peasants, are unable to shed their old lifestyle or to adapt themselves to the new environment; thus, they lead an insular life with an undying yearning for their homeland. But Hamasteł is in his element depicting fellow countrymen in their original habitat. Here he brings the region to life, describing its everyday routines, customs, and superstitions, along with a host of memorable characters, drawn in masterful strokes, in a colorful and most engaging diction. Some are mean, crude, or brusque, but most are good-hearted, honest, and simple-minded people with entrenched values and a profoundly moving attachment to the soil. With subtlety, discretion, and penetrating skill, Hamasteł lays bare their soul and mentality before the reader. He does so in an eloquent and detached manner, radiating his immense love in a vibrant, unadorned, and splendidly spontaneous style. It is these works that rank him among the masters of short prose in twentieth-century Armenian literature.

VAHĒ HAYK (1896–1983), in bright colors and a lyrical style, initially contemplated his impressions of his native region, its magic and majesty, the spell it cast on him, and allegorically narrated its sad fate. All this revealed some of the affinities he shared with a master he admired, Ṙubēn Zardarean (q.v.). But soon Hayk shifted his emphasis onto the Armenian realities in the United States, occasionally stealing retrospective glances at his birthplace as if it were an entrancing dream. Hayk wrote with some social awareness of the clash of traditional Armenian attitudes with American values, the alienation renting the Armenian family apart, the power of money, the rapid retreat the Armenian language suffered as English began to replace it, and the bleeding wounds afflicted by 1915. With few exceptions, his characters are Armenians, rich and poor, good and evil. With a sense of urgency he emphasized, as did most of his colleagues, the importance of maintaining the vernacular as the most important pillar of Armenian identity, whose roots went deep into the now ravaged native soil, but whose memory and distant hope of regeneration Hayk now saw in his image of Soviet Armenia. Hayk also wrote some works of a historical and philological nature.

BENIAMIN NURIKEAN (1894–1988) made a conscious effort to capture for posterity images of life in and around his native village. His prose, economical and simple, consists of short stories and also of vignettes and profiles of real people and events that added a touch of authenticity and verisimilitude to his account of his birthplace. Its enchanting landscape dominated by two mountains, its customs, mores, and details of daily routine are all part of the picture Nurikean painted for the reader. Nurikean also echoed what he saw as the emotional and economic hardship and the cultural distress that the survivors of 1915 experienced in the United States, where the specter of assimilation seriously threatened the Armenian identity. Soviet Armenia was a symbol of survival and a source of hope for some of these characters and for Nurikean himself. He was the principal founder and editor of a literary periodical, *Nor gir,* which for over fifteen years played a vital role in promoting Armenian letters in the United States.

ANDRANIK ANDRĒASEAN's (1909–96) prose covers a wide range of topics: from the Spanish Civil War and the struggle of Ukrainian partisans, to the plight of African Americans and academic life in the era of McCarthyism; from the Armenian genocide and his sad days at orphanages at Corfu, to scenes from Armenian life, social injustice, and racism in America and the destructive appeal of an utterly corrupt Hollywood. He paid little attention to the artistic aspects of his literary output, which suffers from protraction and pontification. As an ideologically motivated writer, the ravages of capitalism, poverty, economic disparity, discrimination, and concern for the peace and prosperity of his homeland and mankind are central to his work.

YAKOB ASATUREAN (1903–) wrote poetry at first, but he later turned to prose. His novel *Yovakimi ťořnerě* (Joachim's grandchildren) remains his best literary effort. It is a journey back to his childhood and teenage years, recreated in a simple and spontaneous style, with his birthplace and the catastrophic carnage of 1915 as its background. Although somewhat disjointed, the novel is an unadorned record of the harrowing ordeal he and his resilient fellow countrymen experienced, and makes for sober reading. After a long hiatus, Asaturean published *Yovakimi ťořnordinerě* (Joachim's great-grandchildren), a kind of sequel to his first novel. Here Joachim's posterity is seen in the United States, caught between conflicting (old and new) loyalties, memories, and challenges. *To lač tnawer* (Thou, homeless lad) is a literary account of a visit he paid to his native region, which vividly evoked a painful past.

SURĒN MANUĒLEAN (1906–80) covered a variety of topics, but his pages evoking his birthplace and childhood remain his best. The collection *Argawand akōsner* (Fertile furrows, as the author translated it) chronologically depicts portraits and episodes of his fellow compatriots against the landscape of his native region, the horrors of the genocide, his years at orphanages, and his and his fellow countrymen's early days in the United States. The volume concludes with wartime stories repudiating jingoism and the dehumanizing nature of war. Manuēlean is in his element, especially in the first part of the book, which he narrates with spontaneous élan, heartfelt emotions, and in a sharp style mixed discriminatingly with elements of his dialect. A few similarly impressive pieces are found in his other collection of short stories, *Dgal mě šakʻar* (A spoonful of sugar).

ARAM HAYKAZ (1900–86) feigned apostasy, and unlike his family, survived the 1915 wholesale slaughter and deportations. As a Muslim (and having been renamed "Muslim"), he was adopted by a Turkish family and lived mostly among Kurds for nearly four years (1915–19). A goodly part of his prose touchingly recalls various aspects of this experience: the harrowing agony of the nightmare and its impact on Armenian orphans forcibly or willingly converted to Islam to escape certain death; and penetrating glimpses into the lifestyles of Armenians, Kurds, and Turks. The genocide also looms large in his other writings and permeates his outlook, especially his views vis-à-vis Turks and Kurds. Longingly and lovingly narrated recollections of his birthplace; impressions of Armenian realities in Constantinople under Allied occupation, where he spent a short while before crossing the Atlantic; and interesting descriptions of and searching reflections on his Armenian and non-Armenian neighbors in New York, invariably seen in their ethnic context, constitute the principal topics of his literary output. His sympathetic impressions of a visit to Soviet Armenia are included in his volume *Karōt* (Longing). Autobiographical and subjective elements are ever-present in Haykaz's writings, most of which are in the form of vignettes, recollections, and episodes from real life. His immense love for nature and his inquisitive look into innocent and seemingly simple aspects of life enabled him to observe certain aspects of human behavior, some sad and some delightful. Although at times repetitive or protracted and chatty, Haykaz's prose is on the whole limpid, disarmingly frank, and engagingly humorous.

ŽAG YAKOBEAN's (1917–) earliest work was greeted favorably by established poets such as Vahan Tʻēkʻēean and critics such as Nikol Ałbalean (1873–1947). The latter noted the limpid and vivid qualities of Yakobean's verse and the distinctness of his expression. Tʻēkʻēean had earlier expressed similar ideas, but had also observed the limited realm of Yakobean's inspiration and its lack of force and depth. Neither of the two eminent men of letters was mistaken in recognizing in Yakobean a fresh voice; in time he emerged as one of the visible poets of the post-genocide verse of the Dispersion. Echoes of M. Metzarents's and V. Tērean's poetic visions have already been discerned in Yakobean's poetry; to these one must add the influences of Siamantʻō, D. Varužan, H. Širaz, S. Kaputikyan (q.q.v.), and Paruyr Sevak (1924–71). Yakobean skillfully assimilated impulses from these poets and fashioned his own world, where songs of piety and patriotism abruptly relegated almost all else to a negligible position, conveying to his readers a message of "hope and light," as Yakobean put it in one of his poems ("Im ergers," My songs, in his collection *Ulunkʻašar,* String of beads). In tender and calm lines, Yakobean sings of Christ with exaltation and takes pride in the Church of Armenia and her fathers and saints, such as Grigor Lusaworich, Grigor Narekatsi, and Nersēs Šnorhali. After initially jejune pieces, Yakobean's religious poetry improved rapidly, and it always remained closest to his heart. But an equally cherished theme for Yakobean was his patriotism, which pulsated with extraordinary zeal. It covered a wide range: historical figures, events, toponyms, pride in Soviet Armenia as the homeland (whose official atheism was his greatest disappointment), a profound concern for the Armenian Dispersion and language, and the threat of assimilation. Yakobean eschewed political entanglements and refused to face the reality of a fragmented Dispersion. His patriotism is often naive, shrill, and almost invariably opens up the wounds the genocide inflicted on the souls of the survivors in general and the writers in particular. Repetition and verbosity take much away from his verse, especially his longer pieces. But his better poems, although smaller in number, are written in a fresh voice, with distinct diction and energetic emotion.

ŠAHAN ŠAHNUR (1903–74) attained immediate fame with his novel Retreat without Song (*Nahanjě aṙants ergi*), which still stands out as perhaps the most powerful landmark of Armenian Dispersion literature, epitomizing its turbulent emergence. The context, indeed the entire plot, revolves around the crestfallen love story of Petros, turned Pierre, with a French woman, Nenette. To a certain degree, the main theme is an encoded elaboration of the subtext, the dissolution of Armenian identity, exemplified by a number of secondary characters, who are assimilated into French society in varying ways. As a whole, the novel is a subliminal reaction to the genocide, illustrating its consequences.

The hue and cry raised over the novel, though understandable in some ways, cannot be taken seriously. Pornography and other such accusations were hurled at the author, who had in fact dared to question established authorities and assumptions, puncturing some outdated sensibilities, both ethnic and ethical. The novel does suffer from a number of flaws. The author himself pinpointed its shortcomings: instances of infelicity in diction, simplicity of construction, sporadic sentimentality and pathos, and an "imperfect acquaintance" with "national history." However, it was not so much the facts as the spirit that the critics assailed. Yet the very merit of this novel is the élan it derived from an honest, unencumbered probing into Armenian realities. As for the attempts of antagonists and apologists alike to cite the author's age at the time he wrote this work (he was twenty-six), the game is not worth the candle, as the saying goes. This novel stands on its own merits. It is the gem of the literature of the Dispersion; it set a world on fire with its tormenting self-scrutiny, its tenderly memorable characters, and its riveting narrative, which is written in a forceful style and forthright tone.

Šahnur's second work, *Yaralēznerun dawačanutiwnĕ* (The treason of the gods) is a collection of seven short stories. Three of these are about life in Istanbul; two depict first-generation emigrants to France; one is set at a sanatorium; and another, the story that lends its title to the collection, is a reflection on Armenian political inaptitude, disunity, and failure. The first three show the dull, inane routine of ordinary Armenians. The ones set in Paris show Armenians on the horns of a dilemma: either resisting assimilation or becoming absorbed into the French system and finding themselves in a cul-de-sac. This collection can be seen as a sequel to the novel. For cultural and political reasons, Šahnur suggested that the present and future of the Armenian Dispersion was bleak.

Shortly after the appearance of the aforementioned collection, a crippling illness forced Šahnur to spend his remaining years bedridden in hospitals or sanatoriums. For long years, especially in the forties, he wrote in French and only occasionally in Armenian. He slowly returned to Armenian literature, committing to paper reflections and recollections, essays, short stories, and literary criticism, brilliantly living up to expectations raised by his return. Although his critical attitude towards Armenian institutions, political and otherwise, remained unchanged, a certain amount of optimism came to characterize his outlook. (We learn of his debilitating physical agony and occasional despondency only from the letters he wrote to French friends, no traces of which are found in his literature.) He remained faithful to his old, healthy credo, that "Armenianism" was a finite topic, but that the Armenians themselves offered an infinite realm for literary reflection of universal importance. His incisive observations and reflections, his aesthetic views, his artistic sincerity and integrity, and the dynamism of his literature, all expressed in an eloquent and vigorous style with trenchant wit and dignity, rank him among the best writers of the twentieth century.

VAZGĒN ŠUŠANEAN's (1903–41) work resonates with deep yet tender echoes of the genocide of 1915. Of his poems, the longest, titled "Erkir yišatakats" (A land of memories), merits special mention. It reflects in a raw, unpolished, and emotive touch the deportation of his family (parents, brother, and sister), their death, and his brief return home. The bulk of his prose that has been collected (a considerable corpus of writing is still scattered in the periodical press) has appeared in the form of letters, diaries, reminiscences, and novels. The latter almost invariably suffer from technical imperfections and verbosity. But what redeems his prose and may explain his rising popularity since the fifties is his lust for life, which characterizes his spontaneous and candid narrative, sketched in robust colors with sensuous hues, affectionate sentiments, and warm-hearted concern for mankind, the lower and working classes in particular. Amid the dismal uncertainty and utter despair that seriously threatened Šušanean's generation in the years immediately following the nightmare of 1915, his voice refreshingly sang of impassioned love, nature, moral and intellectual integrity, and political regeneration. Despite his markedly leftist tendencies, he was not a class-conscious author; his political convictions were instead motivated by his concern for his country rather than international solidarity. He never really came to grips with some of the political, cultural, and moral tenets of his adopted country or with the loss of his immediate family, which is a common thread in all of his work. Yet neither hatred nor vengeful rhetoric mars his recollection of the tragedy and its consequences for uprooted Armenians, now scattered far and wide under foreign skies. He reacted with alarm to intellectual stagnation, and although he looked back to the days of his childhood with yearning, he was essentially a forward-looking writer concerned with the culture and spiritual rejuvenation of his fellow countrymen. In many an instance, pagan values revived by senior colleagues (D. Varužan, et al.) inspired his definition of love.

Among some of his better works are the novels *Ōrerĕ gełetsik chen* (The days are not attractive), *Čermak Varsenik* (White Varsenik), both of which are set in the countryside, and *Amran gišerner* (Summer nights), written in the form of a diary. The central characters in *Garnanayin* (Vernal) exchange letters on love and social-cultural topics. In his *Siroy ew arkatzi tłakĕ* (Of loving and adventurous youngsters), Šušanean reminisced with gushing affection about a love affair that had begun in Tiflis and concluded in Batumi. The setting was his unhappy stay in Armenia, which he recalled in a few flashbacks and with some political commentary as part of the Armaš Agricultural School that had been relocated in Armenia for eight months in the years 1920–21. (Leon Z.

Surmelian speaks of the same episode in his *I Ask You Ladies and Gentlemen.*)

ZAREH ORBUNI's (1902–80) first short novel, *P'ordzĕ* (The attempt), was one of his best accomplishments. It deals with the quandary of a family of four genocide survivors stationed in Marseilles. Narrated in a simple, wry style, it tells of the impact of displacement and disintegration on the new Armenian Dispersion in France. This emerged as one of the dominant themes in his other short novels and stories, where, taking his cue from contemporary European and French literature, Orbuni delved deeper into the psychology of his characters, much to the disapproval of some Soviet Armenian critics. His characters, usually poor and humble, are led into a state of confusion and moral disarray by their mental anguish, in an environment whose moral and social aspects Orbuni decidedly disapproved. The unobtrusive, subtle presence of the genocide is felt throughout, as its children, deracinated and dispirited, are held hostage to tradition and the burden of identity and struggle to survive. His short stories do not fully fit the traditional definition of the genre. The external world does not play a large role in these pieces, in which the author delves into the hidden realms of the self in an economical prose, with bright imagery and a distinct ability to articulate abstract thoughts and impressions. Variations in the mood and tone of his first-person narrative are by no means unusual. At times he speaks in stream of consciousness and at others in a discursive manner, with Kafkaesque and surrealistic touches here and there. Some of Orbuni's non-Armenian characters appear in his cycle of ten short stories, subtitled "I ḥorots srti" (From the bottom of the heart), wherein Orbuni recalls his experience as a prisoner of war in a Nazi camp. Of this series, "Penthesilea, Penthesilea" and related stories of human turpitude, hubris, and haughtiness are hauntingly memorable.

ŠAWARŠ NARDUNI (1898–1968) was a journalist, a studious but amateurish philologist, and a prolific author, who preferred short prose pieces, chiefly in the form of tales, stories, recollections, observations, and reflections. His work is uneven in quality. Save for his best (and they are small in number), many of his writings, though distinguished for their eloquent locution and imagery, are shallow, weak in structure, and lacking in focus. His best is found mainly in his book *Mełediner, mełediner . . .* (Melodies, melodies . . .). Perhaps the relative abundance of phrases, quotations, images, and topics from Classical Armenian texts as well as from the Bible (especially the Old Testament) are partly due to the awe in which Narduni held the Armenian language (always associated with what many consider the mysterious appeal of Classical

Armenian) and to his penchant for the traditional, the mythical, and the mystical. Narduni characterized the aforementioned collection with a sensuality through which, he said, he sought fulfillment by fathoming agony. Such sentiments resonate in most of the stories, in which Narduni, with idealized nostalgia and melancholy, recollects his birthplace and its enchanting nature and retells with wistful elegance local folk tales, stories, and vignettes of human love, amatory sentiments, and turpitude. Narduni had an excellent command of Armenian. In this regard, he shares an affinity with A. Bagratuni (q.v.) and, to a certain degree, Y. Ōšakan (q.v.), in matters related to the sensual realm.

HRACH ZARDAREAN (1892–1986), son of Ṙubēn Zardarean (q.v.) and a noted novelist, is remembered chiefly for his two novels, both of which took stock of a rapidly deteriorating Diaspora. *Mer keankʻě* (Our life) juxtaposes two brothers; the elder is the embodiment of a traditional Armenian outlook, but is at the same time the denunciation of some elements of that mindset. He has both fallen heir to a legacy of passivity, timidity, and cringing before the Turk, which has deeply bruised his soul, and is the beneficiary of his fathers' virtues. So, in the murky world of business, governed by the law of the jungle, he is barely able to eke out a wretched existence and is bereft of any fulfillment. By contrast, his younger brother is a cold-blooded pragmatist, an observer of *raison,* and a worshipper of Mammon. Zardarean's second novel, *Orbatsoł mardik* (Orphaned men; the Armenian title employs a present participle for the past participle used here, giving the word a sense of continuity), is the story of a musician who is determined to remain faithful to the gods of his forefathers. He struggles amid a sea of people who, in the name of individual liberties and independence, are denying parents and rejecting ethnic-national loyalties, the homeland, and the arts. Although Zardarean, like some of his colleagues (e.g., Š. Šahnur, q.v.), dismissed certain recent manifestations of the Armenian experience, he felt, unlike some of them, that the Dispersion was not beyond redemption. Moral integrity and a fervent allegiance to the national ethos, the mother tongue, the ancestral land, the national church, and genuine piety were the most important factors. Zardarean's third volume, *Žamanak ew ḥorhurdkʻ iwr* (Time and its mysteries), is made up of short reflections on things philosophical, ethical, social, literary, and cultural. Instances of prolixity mar his otherwise animated and lucid style, in which some of his best characters illuminate the depths of the self.

NIKOŁOS SARAFEAN (1905–72) has been slowly gaining the recognition he deserves as a writer of note. Acceptance has been slow in coming for a number of reasons. An intellectual gap, the author once observed, separated him from his fellow Armenians in the Dispersion as well as from those in Soviet Armenia. The latter were not even aware of his existence. "Official" criticism in the Dispersion had been initially unfavorable to his work; its heaviest gun, Y. Ōšakan, had dismissed Sarafean's first two collections for contrived originality and insincere expression. Furthermore, his work is difficult to understand, let alone to accept and assimilate; his imagery and ideas are not always clear or comprehensible. Sarafean's bold new approach, which defied conventional definitions of identity and showed his alienation not only from himself but also from his compatriots (both in the Dispersion and in Soviet Armenia) and from the host society, seemed manufactured and was unacceptable to many a reader. It transpires from some of his essays that he was familiar with the work of St. John of the Cross, Kierkegaard and *Existentialisme,* and French literature of the nineteenth and twentieth centuries, especially *Symbolisme* and *Surréalisme.*

Three of his collections in verse, *Anjrpeti mě grawumě* (*anjrpet* means a partition, boundary, or a gap, space; *grawum,* from *grawel,* is to conquer, to occupy, to seize; hence, The conquest of a boundary or an expanse; or, Filling up a void), *Tełatuutʻiwn ew makěntʻatsutʻiwn* (Ebb and flow), and *Mijerkrakan* (Mediterranean), and his prose piece of reflections, *Vēnsēni antařě* (i.e., *Bois de Vincennes*), form a complementary cycle and the original part of his work. It is important that the reader be mindful of Sarafean's peregrinations and his experiences in Russia in his teens, because the indelible mark they left on his outlook find a manifest expression in these works. In the age of cogwheels and conveyors, the author sees himself as a rootless voyager on an endless journey into uncertain realms, and he is unwilling to look back lest he suffer the fate that befell Lot's wife. There arise two paths: one that splits him off from his childhood, and another that separates him from city and society. These two do not always run parallel, but instead criss-cross over his embattled identity. And the farther he goes from his point of departure, the emptier he feels. Lonely and sad, the poet is in both internal and external exile in a world that lacks love and compassion. In order to reconstitute his soul, fragmented in its agonizing search for a spiritually gratifying realm, the poet recalls his childhood through a number of symbols and metaphors (e.g., ships, trains, railways, the propeller, the motorcar), in this case water and trees, which he eventually replaced with the sea (the Black Sea and the Mediterranean) and the wood (*Bois de Vincennes,* southeast of Paris). In this region of his split personality, Sarafean makes no connections to his Armenian origins. The reference to King Artawazd of Armenia, whom tradition has kept in fetters for over two millenia now, shows how time has been unkind to Sarafean and like-minded people awaiting spiritual liberation.

Still afflicted by the same malaise, Sarafean comes full circle in his second collection. Nature, the wood and the sea in particular, become the poet's intellectual habitat. The motorcar, symbolizing technical progress and new ideas fathomed against time and space, helps the poet accomplish more than effects of dynamism; it at once creates and reflects the distances within the poet and those between him and society. It also casts him as a perennial traveler or explorer. As the car hurtles through a wood at night, the trees recede and disintegrate into the darkness left behind; out of this tenebrous realm the well-lit road springs forward, like a phoenix rising from its ashes. Similarly, all falsehood, old convictions, and connections die away in the recesses of the author's soul, signifying the demise of his youthful hopes for a bright future and his faith in the West. From this chaos emerges the author's state of mind. Idle and bored, he feels no affinity with either the cruel world around him or his homeland, which he at one point had loved with an "idiotic zeal." Alienation breeds destructive urges, but early recollections forge a new perspective. The author rejoices in his childhood, which he likens to the sandy ground revealed by the tide receding on an ebb. But this proves to be a delusion, since his childhood conjures up memories at once joyful and painful. The circle repeats itself as the tide starts to come in, drowning visions of his early years. When these old dreams die, the author feels reborn for a fleeting second. Then he realizes that he is carrying the sea within him, along with its eternal ebb and flow. Nonetheless, he concludes on an optimistic note; as a citizen of the world, he is inspired by the efforts of mankind to conquer the future.

Sarafean continued his inner journey in his prose writing *Vēnsēni antaṙě*. Here, in the form of observations, associations, descriptions, and sensations, he touched upon a wider range of topics, including war, politics, the destiny of his nation, Soviet Armenia, and repatriation to Soviet Armenia, all viewed from his own angle. The same sense of isolation prevails. An ideological barrier separates him from the homeland, where, he believes, he would have felt "more foreign and less free." But some striking changes transformed the author's outlook in the two decades preceding the publication of his last collection, *Mijerkrakan,* wherein he makes peace with his nation. He identifies with its trials and tribulations for enlightenment and spiritual accomplishment. He and his people are now on the same elevated plane of intellectual and universal values. Although the gap between them is gradually bridged, it is never fully closed.

Some of Sarafean's other works complement or amplify the themes discussed above in a different style and temperament. *Išḥanuhin* (The princess) is the distressing story of a Turkified Armenian girl married to a *pasha* and that of her brother. Narrated in a lyrical tone and interspersed with passionate passages, it sharply contrasts with Sarafean's other works, in which his equanimity and restrained emotions camouflage his eerie unease. A short novel with a weak structure, the work is a sadly helpless, fulminating revenge on paper for the unacknowledged genocide. Excruciating pain overwhelms the author in his long poem *14,* made up of reflections occasioned by *14 Juillet.* Flotsam in a French sea, he speaks of blood as a symbol of both life and death and as the highest price paid for progress that never materializes. Revolutions, he avers, never serve their purposes. The passion and jubilation with which the French marked the fall of the Bastille disturbed him for two reasons. Firstly, such passion bred violence, and the author speaks with concern, though without specific references, of imminent bloodshed in Europe. Secondly, the French remembered only *their* dead, overlooking the poet's nation, its sacrifices, and accomplishments. He professed to have no homeland, yet he could not sever his ties, forged at an early age, with an unsympathetic France as the land of promise. Hence his agony. But therein lay his hope and consolation: Life, he postulated, renewed itself through pain.

ANDRANIK TZAṘUKEAN (1913–89) attracted fame as both a writer and a journalist-publicist, whose periodical *Nayiri* (1941–83) remains an indispensable record for students of the Armenian Dispersion. He published only one collection of verse, *Aṙagastner* (Sails), and bade farewell to poetry in a long poem titled *Tułtʻ aṙ Erewan* (A letter addressed to Erevan). His imagination was fired by a scurrilous attack of a political nature, launched by the Soviet Armenian poet Gevorg Abov ("Menkʻ chenkʻ moṙatsel," We have not forgotten). As the self-appointed target of Abov's criticism, Tzaṙukean responded in Eastern Armenian and in a style, technique, and vocabulary reminiscent of Soviet Armenian verse, particularly that of Ełiše Charents (q.v.). The thrust of his poem is to forge a sense of unity with Soviet Armenia by transcending or glossing over the irreconcilable ideological differences that stand between himself and the homeland. Indeed, making some sweeping generalizations, Tzaṙukean patches up the political disunity and rancor that bedevils the embattled Armenian Dispersion and its relations with Soviet Armenia, projecting the floodlights instead on a common ground: that of the *patria* and patriotism. He does so in a highly effective dramatic style that, though not always free of sentimentality and self-pity, attains a bewitching power in the concluding parts of the poem in which Tzaṙukean, with contagious spontaneity, pledges his selfless loyalty to Soviet Armenia.

The poem reverberates with echoes of the 1915 holocaust, as do Tzaṙukean's other works, since he himself was a survivor of the calamity. *Mankutʻiwn chunetsoł mardik* (Men deprived of childhood) sketches a series of intimately knit episodes from Tzaṙukean's own childhood and that of other orphans, innocent children lacking parental affection and care. There is something cruel about the atmosphere in which these orphans grow up, alienated from themselves and society at large, and given willy-nilly to their instincts for survival. Narrating with verve and poignant sorrow, Tzaṙukean recalls memories of the saddest phase in his life, one that he believed should have been the happiest. In certain ways, *Erazayin Halēpě* (Charming Aleppo; literally, Dreamlike) is a sequel to the former and shows the author and some of his friends at a slightly later phase in their lives. With delight and nostalgia, Tzaṙukean draws portraits of Armenian friends, characters, and local dignitaries and captures aspects of Armenian realities in Aleppo. *Verjin anmełě* (The last innocent) is a political novel. It delves into the character of a political activist, whose mentality and political outlook are shaped by his father and are out of touch with reality. The larger picture of this novel deals with the relations between Soviet Armenia and the Dispersion; the subtext deals with the activities and attitudes of certain political leaders and elements, including father and son, the two central heroes. There seem to be many authentic elements to this novel which, like Tzaṙukean's other works, is written in a trenchant and eloquent style with revealing insights into the inner world of his characters. Tzaṙukean's last novel, *Sērě Ełeṙnin mēj* (Love and genocide, 1987), concerns the bloodthirsty destruction in 1915 of the Western Armenian intelligentsia, its flower and flower-bed alike. More specifically, it encompasses the last year in the life of the poet Ṙubēn Sewak (q.v.), one of the intellectuals rounded up in April of 1915. The novel discusses his banishment to Çankırı and his murder, together with Daniēl Varužan (q.v.) and others, on the way to Ayaş. Tzaṙukean's age must have taken its toll; the novel is a hasty and shallow sketch, flawed in structure and technique, and lacking the vigor and zest of his style.

VAHĒ-VAHEAN's (1907–1998) poetry, especially his first collection, *Arew-andzre*w (Sun-rain), bears the imprint of the genocide, which he survived as a child. Under a pervasive mood of anxiety and occasional pessimism there lurk painful memories of irretrievable loss, uncertainty accentuated by concern for the fate of mankind, and antiwar sentiments. His introspection, though in the main cerebral, is blended with a good deal of lyricism. Vahē-Vahean derived some inspiration from Petros Durean, Misak‘ Metzarents, DaniēlVaružan, and Vahan T‘ēk‘ēean (q.q.v.), but spoke in his own voice throughout. Soviet Armenia, a cardinal theme, is celebrated with deep affection as a safe, peaceful, and prosperous land, betokening the revival of the Armenian people. These same themes—patriotism, altruism, melancholy and despondency, love and longing, and a greater sense of stoicism and optimism—preoccupy the poet in his second collection, *Oski kamurj* (Golden bridge), as well as his subsequent collections, in which a number of bridges are extended between the past and present and the personal and public. From the ashes of a grievous implosion, Vahē-Vahean's optimism emerges triumphantly in his fourth collection, *Yušardzan Vahramis* (A memorial to my Vahram), written in memory of his younger son, Vahram (1944–76), who was tragically killed in a car accident. Two contrasting moods characterize Vahē-Vahean's verse. World War II, the Lebanese civil war, the fragmented Armenian Dispersion with an obscure future, and concern for society at large aggravate his harrowing memories of World War I. The rebirth of Armenia, lofty ideals, and a personal determination not to yield to bleak sentiments and situations nourish his optimism. He writes in an eloquent and felicitous Western Armenian, with meticulous attention to structure, rhythm, and rhyme. His emotions are balanced by his intellect, radiating the solicitude of a concerned human being.

MUŠEŁ IŠḤAN (1913–90) wrote prose and verse. His prose consists of two novels, a short novel, and an autobiographical work, *Mnas barov mankut‘iwn* (Farewell, childhood), which recalls the flight of his family from his birthplace to Damascus before the advancing armies of Kemal Atatürk. His plays bear no marks of distinction. Some are curious and naive experiments: *Mer̄nilě ork‘an džuar ē* (Dying is so difficult); *Sar̄naranēn elatz mardě* (The man who came out of the refrigerator); *P‘ostal* is an adaptation of G. Zōhrap's famous short story bearing the same title; *Paroyr Haykazn ew Movsēs Ḥorenatsi* (Paruyr Haykazn [i.e., the rhetorician Proaeresius] and Movsēs Ḥorenatsi) elaborates on the same idea advanced by Raffi in his novel *Paroyr Haykazn,* that is, the importance of serving one's own nation before anyone else's; *Mardorsě* (The sniper) depicts a ruthless arms dealer; and *Kilikioy ark‘an* (The king of Cilicia), perhaps his best, underlines the significance of keeping national ideals alive in the face of adversities. But Išḥan excelled as one of the well-known poets of the Dispersion. Although his cherishing love for home and the homeland manifests itself in various forms, it is mainly a spiritual bond expressed in tender, deep sentiments and quietly smoldering longing. His mother tongue, loyalty to national and traditional values, dreams, ideals, prayers, and aspirations often form a spiritual abode for him. The genocide remained a bleeding wound in the form of sad memories and unhappy survivors, as did the fate of Armenians under foreign, albeit hospitable, skies. His call for shielding Armenian identity from the threats of assimilation was gentle but firm and sincere. Poems of disappointment and despondency are found in his work, as are poems of altruism and a general concern for mankind. He wrote with heartfelt sympathy for the downtrodden, the poor, and the neglected. Universal suffering, personal grief, vanity of life, and certainty of death are themes that are found in almost all of his collections of verse. But almost equally prevalent are Išḥan's warm hymns to life, composed in a traditional style, yet with glowing warmth and sincerity.

Mirrored in **EDUARD PŌYAČEAN**'s (1915–66) literature, particularly his prose, are some aspects and impact of the dolorous fate that befell the inhabitants of the six Armenian villages in the vicinity of Musa Dagh (then in the region of Alexandretta, now Hatay, Turkey). Faced with certain death in 1915, they accomplished an extraordinary feat of self-defense against superior Turkish forces, a tour de force that inspired Franz Werfel's acclaimed novel, *Die vierzig Tage des Musa Dagh.* Evacuated to Port-Said, Egypt, aboard French and British warships, they returned to their homes after the armistice of 1918. By a cruel twist of fate, they unwillingly abandoned the region for the last time when French imperialism ceded it to Turkey in 1939. Most of them moved to the village of Aynčar in Lebanon, and many of them settled in Soviet Armenia in the forties.

Pōyačean composed poetry, but he never quite found his own poetic voice. Still, passion and vigorous diction endow a few of his poems with distinction. Dreams, songs, and love formed the essence of life for him. He sang of unrequited love, human suffering, and lofty ideals, with sadness and occasional pessimism. In some instances, he mistook a convoluted style for sophistication and verbosity for spontaneity, especially in his verse glorifying his birthplace. In other cases his sentiments were rather vague. His Letter to my children (*Tułt̒ zawaknerus*) contains a few bright passages (particularly the one on Šamiram's love for Ara) along with conventional counsel on his preference for moral-social and intellectual values over the material aspects of life. But it is his other prose pieces that more elegantly represent the original and enduring aspects of his literary output.

In his best pages, bitterness, anxiety, and a strong sense of disappointment mingle with tenderness and elegance to characterize the tone of Pōyačean's sinewy style. His protagonists, drawn from real life, are ordinary mortals with both good qualities and bad. Some are naive and some superstitious; some are topers and some maniacs; some are mean swindlers but most are honest. What they all share in common is a pining for home in Jabal Mūsa: its mountains in the proximity of starry skies, its lush nature, its invigorating air, and their gardens and houses perched high on cliffs. Dying away from home becomes a greater agony than fear of death. Thus, most of them lose interest in living and simply peak and pine. In a robust style with subtle humor and irony, Pōyačean captured a number of interesting characters and created some memorable stories in which his sympathy and concern touched upon certain values of universal appeal. Although Pōyačean refused to reconcile himself to the defeat inflicted upon his fellow compatriots and himself (he was only a few months old at the time of the fabulous self-defense of Musa Dagh), he had little hope beyond the will power to survive in anticipation of better days. Such days must have seemed distant. He was an anti-Bolshevik and pinned no hope on Soviet Armenia. And he was a passionately partisan observer of his people's Diaspora, rent apart by political stances on Soviet Armenia, the conflict within the Armenian Church, and the Lebanese civil war.

SIMON SIMONEAN (1914–86) highlighted the consequences of the genocide and its impact on survivors from Sasun, some of whom found refuge in Aleppo. His finest short stories revolving around this subject, indeed some of his best works, narrated in a crisp, dramatic, and often pungent style, are found in *Leṙnakanneru verjaloysě* (The twilight of the mountain dwellers [*montagnards*]), a poignant depiction of the gallant Armenians from Sasun, written with pride, passion, and fondness for his fellow compatriots. (Simonean's forefathers reportedly emigrated from Sasun to Aintab, now Gaziantep, Turkey.) It is almost a documentary record in that the author knew most of his heroes from childhood, historical figures one and all, who languished under foreign skies, away from their ancestral mountainous habitat. Wit and sarcasm are typical of Simonean's style, as are verbosity and an excessive use of puns and similar associations. Such is the case, for instance, in some of his short stories dealing with Soviet Armenia and its relations with Moscow and the Armenian Dispersion, and with his stories highlighting Armeno-Turkish relations.

His first literary effort was a satirical piece, *Kě ḥndrui . . . ḥachadzewel* (Please . . . organize conflicting functions; or, Please . . . boycott [the festivities marking the ten-thousandth anniversary of the birth of the Armenian people]). The title is an allusion to Armenian disunity. The text examines, in a straightforward fashion, certain aspects of Armenian history, national traits, and political parties (e.g., Bel blaming Hayk, the eponymous forefather of the Armenians, for migrating to the north, thereby injecting the Armenian character with a nomadic strain and abandoning an oil-rich region!). The concept offered intriguing possibilities, but the narrative, although amusing, rather hastily touches upon a few topics and is obviously incomplete. Simonean's sense of purpose is diffused in exciting or unusual events and details, and his strokes are uneven. One is left with a similar impression by Simonean's next novel, *Anžamandros,* despite its extensiveness and far better structure. Reflecting Simonean's own independent thinking, the narrative is anti-capitalist, anti-bourgeois, anti-communist, and anti-revolutionary, with topical allusions to some political issues and concerns. The author explained the compound title as made up of *anžamanak* (Armenian for timeless, eternal) and the word *andros,* man ([*sic*]; the genitive of Greek *anēr,* man). It is a novel within a novel; thus, Anžamandros is the protagonist of a novel by the architect Arsēn Zamanean (from *zamān,* time, presumably in the sense of transient and mortal, in contrast to the timelessness of Anžamandros), who is the central character of Simonean's novel. Anžamandros, punished for loving instead of warring, is condemned to reappear on earth after a 9999-year slumber. His life at his second coming and that of the other characters (an architect and revolutionaries) bear certain resemblances, but they are also dissimilar in many ways. What Simonean sought to illustrate was the lure of the unknown; more importantly, the elusive nature of love and happiness, the only true and imperishable bond between human beings, a dream relentlessly pursued since the time of hirsute, quadrupedal ancestors. Furthermore, he held that unfulfilled sentiments and unattained goals rendered human life tragic; hence the beauty and attraction, at times fatal, of the unreachable.

2

Bio-Bibliographical Entries: Authors Born between 1500 and 1920

ABOV, GEVORG (1897–1965)

Pen name: Gevorg Abov.

Born Gevorg Abovyan in Tiflis and educated at the local Nersisean school. Writer, translator, and literary critic. With E. Charents and A. Vštuni (q.q.v.), he made up the rebellious literary group that wrote the famous "Declaration of the Three" (1922), inspired by the new political system in Armenia. The declaration rejected the past and called for a new Armenian literary tradition. Abov was the secretary of the Association of Proletarian Writers of Armenia (1925–31), director of the Armenian State Theater (1928–31, named after Gabriel Sundukyan in 1937), director of the Matenadaran (1940–52, the national repository of manuscripts and a research institute named after Mesrop Maštots in 1962), and editor of *Tełekagir* (renamed *Lraber* in 1966) of the Academy of Sciences of the Armenian SSR (1961–64).

Texts

Miayn kinĕ. (Tiflis, 1919). (Poetry).
Danakĕ bkin. (Moscow, 1923). (Poetry).
Edini front, kʻałakʻakan agitka. (Moscow, 1924). (Poetry).
Patmvatzkʻner. (Erevan, 1928). (Stories).
Čakatum ev t'ikunkʻum. (Erevan, 1943). (Prose).

Other works

Dašnaktsutʻyunn antsyalum ev ayžm. (Erevan, 1929; Vałaršapat, 1930).
Siro ev ardarutʻyan metz ergichĕ, Sayatʻ-Novan. (Erevan, 1945).
Khachatur Abovian. Zhizn' i tvorchestvo. (Erevan, 1948).
Gabriel Sundukyan, kyankʻn u gortzuneutʻyunĕ. (Erevan, 1953).
Gabriel Sundukian. Zhizn' i tvorchestvo. (Erevan, 1956).

ABOVEAN, ḤACHATUR (c1809–1848)

Born in Kʻanakʻeṙ, near Erivan, now a suburb of the Armenian capital. Educated at Ējmiatzin (1819–22) and at the Nersisean school in Tiflis (1824–26). In 1829 he scaled Mount Ararat with Friedrich Parrot (1791–1841; a professor of natural philosophy at Dorpat University and a Russian imperial councilor of state), who later arranged for a Russian state scholarship for Abovean to study at Dorpat (now Tartu, Estonia). Upon his return, Abovean accepted an appointment as supervisor of the Tiflis district school (1837–43), a position that he also held in Erivan from 1843 to shortly before his mysterious disappearance on 2 April 1848.

Collections

Tēr Sargsean, S. *Erker.* (Moscow, 1897).
Zaryan, Ṙ. *Ĕntir yerker.* 3 vols. (Erevan, 1939–40).
Šahaziz, E. *Divan Ḥachatur Abovyani.* 2 vols. (Erevan, 1940–48).
Erkeri liakatar žołovatzu. 8 vols; 2 suppl. vols. (Erevan, 1947–61).
Felekʻyan, H., and Hakobyan, P. *Erker.* (Erevan, 1984).

Texts

Naḥašawił krtʻutʻean i pēts noravaržits. (Tiflis, 1838, 1862; Erevan, 1940). (Textbook).

Vērkʻ Hayastani, ołb hayrenasiri. (Tiflis, 1858; Baku, 1908; Constantinople, 1931; Erevan, 1939, 1955, 1959, 1975, 1978, 1981, 1984). (Novel; 1984 edition illust. by G. Ḥanjyan; adaptations and selections published in Tiflis, 1912; Erevan, 1948, 1957).

Parap vaḥti ḥałalikʻ. (Tiflis, 1864). (Fables; includes the play *Fēodora*).
Antip erker. (Tiflis, 1904). (Unpublished works).
Hazarpʻešen. (Tiflis, 1912; Erevan, 1941). (Poem).
Abrahamean, Ṙ. "Ḥachatur Aboveani antip namaknerě." *HA,* 1929/43, 395–407. (Letters).
Bayatʻiner. (Erevan, 1939, 1941). (Poetry).
Aṙakner. (Erevan, 1941). (Fables).
Banastełtzutʻyunner. (Erevan, 1941). (Poetry).
Zrutsaran. (Erevan, 1941).
Ĕntʻertsaran. (Erevan, 1941).
Turkʻi ałjikě. (Erevan, 1941). Also published as *Turkʻi aḥchikě.* (Erevan, 1984). (Story).
Mankakan banastełtzutʻyunner. (Erevan 1941). (Poetry for children).
Harutʻyunyan, G. "Ḥachatur Abovyani antip dambanakan čaṙě." *EJ,* 1948/7–9, 56–60. (Funeral oration).
Hakobyan, P. "Ḥachatur Abovyani zatkakan kʻarozě, artasanvatz Moskvayi hayots ekełetsum, 1836 tʻ. marti 29-in." *EJ,* 1986/5, 30–35. (Sermon on Easter).

Translations

FRENCH ANTHOLOGIES

LPA, 159–63.
PAAM, 75–79.

GERMAN

Erkeri liakatar žołovatzu, Vol. 7. (Erevan, 1947–61).

RUSSIAN

Shervinskii, S. *Stikhotvoreniia.* (Erevan, 1948).
———. *Rany Armenii. Vopl' patriota.* (Erevan and Moscow, 1948).
———. *Rany Armenii. Skorb' patriota.* (Erevan, 1971, 1984).
———., and Gevorkian, M. *Izbrannoe.* (Moscow, 1948).

Bibliographies

Akopian, P. *Khachatur Abovian, 1805–1955. Kratkaia bibliografiia.* (Erevan, 1956). (Armenian and Russian).
Babayan, A. *Ḥachatur Abovyan: asuytʻner ev bibliografia.* (Erevan, 1948).

Criticism

Abełean, A. "Abovean ew Hakʻsthauzēn." *HK,* 5 (1926–27/1), 115–26; 2, 82–89; 3, 131–45.
———. "Bodenštēdt Hayastanum." *HK,* 5 (1926–27/5), 75–85; 6, 98–111.
———. "Fridrih Parrot Hayastanum." *HK,* 9 (1930–31/6), 107–18; 7, 135–47.
———. "Ḥachatur Aboveani tznndean tarin." *B,* 106 (1948), 252–54.
———. "Čakatagri haruatznerě ew Aboveani vaḥčaně." *HK,* 28 (1950/5), 51–61.
Abov, G. *Khachatur Abovian. Zhizn' i tvorchestvo.* (Erevan, 1948).
Abrahamyan, H. "Nyutʻer Abovyani masin." *BM,* 1 (1941), 189–94.
Adonts, N. "Ḥachatur Aboveani vaḥčaně." *Vēm,* 1 (1933/1), 5–13.
Aivazian, S. *Predvestie zari: Roman o Kh. Aboviane.* (Moscow, 1983). (Translated by V. Dolukhanian).
Akopian, P. "Khachatur Abovian i obshchestvennye deiateli Estonii 30-kh godov XIX veka." *T,* 1960/5–6, 157–72.
———. *Khachatur Abovian.* (Erevan, 1968).

———., et al. *Khachatur Abovian: Problemy tvorchestva i lit. sviazei.* (Erevan, 1987).
Asatryan, A. "Abovyani grakan žaṙangutʻyan patmutʻyunits." *T,* 1948/9.
Atʻanasyan, Ł. "Im hušers Ḥachatur Abovyani masin." *EJ,* 1952/8, 44–48.
Awdalbēgean, Tʻ. "Ḥachatur Abovean." *A,* 1910, 555–63, 643–51, 735–43, 867–74, 965–72.
———. *Ḥachatur Abovean, patmakan-grakan verlutzutʻiwn.* (N.p., 1910).
Bakunts, A. *Ḥachatur Abovyani anhayt batsakayumĕ.* (Erevan, 1932).
Bałdasaryan, A., and Abrahamyan, G. "Ašḥarhagrutʻyunĕ Ḥachatur Abovyani ašḥatutʻyunnerum." *T,* 1957/9, 132–33.
Bazyan, S. *Abovyani grakan žaṙangutʻyunĕ.* (Erevan, 1966).
———. *Abovyani banastełtzakan ašḥarhĕ.* (Erevan, 1977).
Čanašean, M. "Ḥachatur Abovean, S. Nazareants, G. Dodoḥeants, Dorpati hamalsaranin diwanakan vkayatʻułtʻerun hamadzayn." *B,* 106 (1948), 16–20.
Chōpanean, A. "Ḥachatur Abovean." *ANA,* 1 (1898–99), 50–62.
———. "Aboveani hariwrameakin aṙtʻiw." *ANA,* 1906/1–2, 1–12.
Chrakʻean, Kʻ. "Ḥachatur Abovean." *B,* 61 (1903), 33–37.
Chubarean, V. "Mi aknark Ḥachatur Aboveani grakan ew hasarakakan gortzunēutʻean veray." *Lumay,* 10 (1905/2), 64–72.
Dar'ian, V. *Voskhozhdenie Khachatura Aboviana na Ararat.* (Erevan, 1980).
Eritsean, A. "Ḥachatur Aboveani kensagrutʻean hamar nor niwtʻer." *Pʻordz,* 1880/8–9, 191–98.
Eritsyan, L. *Ḥachatur Abovyani tun-tʻangaranĕ.* (Erevan, 1984, 1988).
———. *Metz lusavorchi žaṙangnerĕ.* (Erevan, 1987).
Ezekyan, L. " 'Verkʻ Hayastani' vepi šarahyusakan mi kʻani aṙandznahatkutʻyunnerĕ." *BEH,* 1990/1, 190–98.
Ganin, Ž. "Ḥachatur Abovyani kʻartezagrakan ašḥatankʻnerĕ." *PBH,* 1979/1, 271–74.
———. *Ḥachatur Abovyanĕ ašḥarhagrutʻyan usutsich.* (Erevan, 1986).
Gasparyan, G. *Baṙaran Ḥachatur Abovyani erkerum gortzatzvatz barbaṙayin ev ōtar baṙeri.* (Erevan, 1947).
Grigoryan, A. "Abovyani očĕ ev očakan hnarnerĕ." *T,* 1948/9.
"Ḥachatur Abovyan." *EJ,* 1948/7–9, 34–39.
Ḥachatur Abovyan: grakan-banasirakan hetazotutʻyunner. (Erevan, 1948).
"Ḥachatur Abovyani mahvan 100-amyakĕ." *EJ,* 1948/7–9, 40–55.
" 'Ḥachatur Abovyanĕ ev SSHM žołovurdneri grakanutʻyunĕ' tʻemayov hamamiutʻenakan gitakan konferans nvirvatz Ḥ. Abovyani tznndyan 175-amyakin." *L,* 1984/2, 81–83.
Ḥachikyan, Y. "Ḥ. Abovyani gełagitakan hayatskʻneri bnutʻagrman šurjĕ." *PBH,* 1959/2–3, 211–17.
Hakobyan, P. "Ḥachatur Abovyanĕ ev ṙusakan aṙajavor kulturan." *T,* 1952/5, 31–44.
———. "Ḥachatur Abovyani ukrainatsi barekamnerĕ." *T,* 1954/2, 65–74.
———. "Antzanotʻ ējer Ḥachatur Abovyani kyankʻits u gortzuneutʻyunits." *T,* 1955/10, 69–88.
———. *Ḥachatur Abovyani 'Verkʻ Hayastani' vepi stełtzagortzman patmutʻyunĕ.* (Erevan, 1956).
———. "Orn ē 'Verkʻ Hayastani'i himkʻum ĕnkatz irakan depkʻĕ?" *T,* 1958/5, 45–52.

———. "Abovyanagitakan hetaḥuzumner." *PBH,* 1960/2, 121–27.
———. "Abovyani kievyan dzeṙagirě." *T,* 1962/9, 49–64.
———. "Grakan ēt'ikayi antesman mi p'asti masin." *T,* 1965/10, 99–101.
———. *Ḥachatur Abovyan. Kyank'ě, gortzě, žamanakě (1809–1836).* Vol. 1. (Erevan, 1967).
———. "Antzanot' namak Tp'łisi 1795 t'vakanin averman masin ev Ḥachatur Abovyani 'Dzayn ałałaki . . .' banastełtzut'yuně." *L,* 1969/7, 69–80.
———. "Avelord ēj Abovyani ev Sundukyani kensagrut'yan mej." *SG,* 1971/11, 159–63.
———. "Abovyani 'Parap vaḥti ḥałalik'i' stełtzagortzakan patmut'yunits." *BEH,* 1972/1, 69–88.
———. "Ḥachatur Abovyani ṙusakan kołmnorošman akunk'nerě." *L,* 1972/4, 14–23.
———. "Abovyani verjin verelk'ě Ararati gagat'." *PBH,* 1972/1, 127–44.
———. "Ḥachatur Abovyani etverk'yan t'argmanut'yunnerě ('Agnes,' 'Feodora')." *L,* 1973/4, 15–34.
———. "Ḥachatur Abovyani 'Parap vaḥti ḥałalik'' žołovatzun." *L,* 1976/3, 59–78.
———. " 'Verk'i mi antesvatz hratarakut'yun (Polis, 1930)." *BEH,* 1976/1, 194–98.
———. "Ḥachatur Abovyani anhaytatsman hin varkatzi nor 'meknabanumě'." *L,* 1977/5, 61–86.
———. "Abovyani masnavor dprotsě ev aṙajin ašakertě." *BEH,* 1978/1, 157–73.
———. "Ḥachatur Abovyani bayat'inerě." *BEH,* 1979/2, 50–70.
———. "Ḥachatur Abovyani 'Achk'i luys jan, dard mi anil . . .' banastełtzut'yan patmut'yuně." *L,* 1979/8, 69–80.
———. "Norits Ḥachatur Abovyani tznndyan t'vakani masin." *PBH,* 1979/4, 199–209.
———. "Abovyaně ev Bakuntsě." *BEH,* 1980/2, 47–61.
———. "Abovyaně ev Ṙusastaně." *L,* 1980/6, 16–27.
———. "Mi tari Ḥachatur Abovyani etdorpatyan kyank'its (1837t')." *L,* 1981/11, 30–46.
———. *Verelk'. Vaveragr. patm. aṙajin angam Ararati gagat' bardzranalu masin ěst F. Parroti ev Ḥ. Abovyani champ'ord. not'eri ev namakneri.* (Erevan, 1982).
———. "Ḥachatur Abovyani kyank'i ev stełtzagortzut'yan hartserits." *BEH,* 1984/3, 16–39.
———. "Ḥachatur Abovyani usumnasirut'yuně Dorpatum" *L,* 1984/11, 9–20.
———. " 'Naḥašaviłi' koratz ējerits." *BEH,* 1987/3, 86–107.
Hambardzumyan, V. "Hamadrakan baładrut'yunnerě Ḥachatur Abovyani 'Nor tesakan ev gortznakan k'erakanut'yan' mej." *PBH,* 1986/2, 66–75.
Harut'yunyan, G. " 'Ḥachatur Abovyani ev S. Nazaryani kensagrut'yan šurjě stełtzvatz aṙeltzvatzi lutzumě." *EJ,* 1947/7–8, 61–69.
Hovakimyan, B. "Ḥachatur Abovyaně ev adrbejaneren lezun." *T,* 1964/4, 60–74.
Hovhannisyan, A. *Abovyan.* (Erevan, 1933).
Hrand. "Ḥachatur Abovean." *HG,* 1911/5, 4–9.
Irazek. "Ḥachatur Aboveani ṙusasirut'iwně." *HK,* 13 (1934–35/1), 67–85.
Jrbašyan, Ēd. "Ḥachatur Abovyani avanduyt'nerě ev Hovhannes T'umanyaně." *PBH,* 1984/4, 3–19.
———. "Ḥachatur Abovyani grakan žanrerě." *BEH,* 1989/1, 47–59.

K'alant'aryan, Ž. "Ḥachatur Abovyanĕ arevmtahay k'nnadatut'yan gnahatut'yamb." *BEH,* 1984/3, 40–55.

Karapetyan, H. *Ḥachatur Abovyani "Verk' Hayastani" vepi patmakan akunk'nerĕ Hovh. T'umanyani usumnasirmamb.* (Erevan, 1982).

Karapetyan, N. *Ḥachatur Abovyanĕ ev sovetahay patmavepĕ.* (Erevan, 1988).

Khachatur Abovian: Probl. tvorchestva i lit. sviazei. (Erevan, 1987).

Kudu, E. "Spisok knig, prochitannykh Kh. Abovianom v biblioteke Tartuskogo universiteta." *T,* 1956/1, 93–94.

Kurdoev, K. "Ḥachatur Abovyanĕ orpes k'rdaget-azgagraget." *T,* 1955/10, 89–100.

Łanalanyan, A. *Abovyanĕ ev žołovrdakan banahyusut'yunĕ.* (Erevan, 1941).

———. *Ḥachatur Abovyan.* (Erevan, 1948).

Łazaryan, V. "Ḥachatur Abovyani 'Verk' Hayastani'i gałap'arakan bovandakut'yan mi k'ani hartser." *PBH,* 1966/1, 139–54.

———. "Ḥachatur Abovyanĕ ev tsarakan grak'nnut'yunĕ." *T,* 1967/9, 49–62.

———. "Patmagrut'yan tirapetoł ułłut'yan k'nnadatut'yunĕ Abovyani kołmits." *L,* 1967/6, 20–27.

———. "Abovyani t'iflisyan gortzuneut'yan hartsi šurjĕ." *PBH,* 1973/2, 211–26.

———. "*Ḥachatur Abovyan (hasarakakan gortzuneut'yunĕ).* (Erevan, 1979).

———. "Ḥachatur Abovyani tznndyan t'vakanĕ." *PBH,* 1979/2, 231–40.

Manukyan, A. "Ḥachatur Abovyani 'Dorpatyan ōragrerĕ'." *T,* 1955/10, 101–6.

Margaryan, A. *Ḥachatur Abovyanĕ ev ašḥarhabarĕ.* (Erevan, 1958).

———. "Ḥachatur Abovyani lezvagitakan hayatsk'nerĕ." *T,* 1976/12, 65–80.

Melik'set'-Bek. "Nor nyut'er Ḥachatur Abovyani masin." *T,* 1948/9.

Muradyan, H. *Žamanakakitsnerĕ Ḥachatur Abovyani masin.* (Erevan, 1940).

———. *Sovremenniki o Khachature Aboviane.* (Erevan, 1941).

———. "Ḥachatur Abovyani 'Verk' Hayastanin'." *T,* 1948/9.

———. *Ḥachatur Abovyan.* (Erevan, 1955, 1963).

Muradyan, N. " 'Verk' Hayastani' vepi gałap'arakan ēut'yunĕ." *PBH,* 1972/2, 45–60.

———. " 'Verk' Hayastani' vepi gortzoł andzants patmakan henk'ĕ." *PBH,* 1974/4, 171–83.

———. "Abovyani očĕ ev greladzevĕ." *SG,* 1975/6, 141–50.

———. "Abovyani ułegrut'yunnerĕ." *BEH,* 1975/3, 69–78.

Nanumyan, Ṙ. "Ḥachatur Abovyani poezian." *T,* 1955/10, 53–68.

Nersisyan, M. "Ḥachatur Abovyani aṙajin hraparakakan eluyt'ĕ." *T,* 1976/6, 107–12.

Ōrdiḥan, J. "Ḥachatur Abovyanĕ k'rderi masin." *SG,* 1960/1, 154–58.

Partizuni, V. *Ḥachatur Abovyan.* (Erevan, 1952).

Šahaziz, E. *Ḥachatur Abovyani kensagrut'yunĕ.* (Erevan, 1945).

———. "Ḥachatur Abovyanin veraberoł noragyut mi vaverakani aṙt'iv." *EJ,* 1948/5–6, 43–48.

———. "Im gragrut'yunĕ ēstonatsi doktor Paul Aristei het Ḥachatur Abovyani masin." *EJ,* 1950/5–6, 27–28.

Šahnazarean, Y. *Ḥachatur Aboveani hasarakakan ew grakanakan gortzunēut'iwnĕ.* (Moscow, 1899).

Šahuni, V. "The Soviet Interpretation of Khachadour Abovian." *CR,* 2 (1956), 105–9.

Sant'rosyan, M. *Hay metz lusavorich-mankavarž Ḥachatur Abovyan.* (Erevan, 1953).

———. *"Khachatur Abovian–vydaiushchiisia armianskii pedagog.* (Moscow, 1957).

Saruḥanyan, N. "Ḥachatur Abovyani azgayin-k'ałak'akan mtatzołut'yan hartsi šurjě." *SG,* 1971/10, 131–36.

Seid-Zade, A.-A. "Nor tvyalner Ałasu andznavorut'yan masin." *T,* 1957/5, 83–94.

———. *Khachatur Abovian i ego sviazi s peredovymi predstaviteliami Azerbaidzhana XIX veka.* (Baku, 1960).

Sevyan, V. "Ḥachatur Abovyani p'ilisop'ayakan hayatsk'neri hartsi šurjě." *T,* 1967/1, 17–28.

Shaginian, M. "Khachatur Abovian." *SL,* 1956/1, 134–40.

Simonyan, P. "Ḥachatur Abovyani mi antip k'erakanakan ašḫatut'yan masin." *T,* 1952/1, 107–10.

Šlepchyan, S. "Ḥachatur Abovyani 'Verk' Hayastani' vepi het kapvatz mi čštum." *T,* 1956/1, 89–92.

T'amrazyan, H. "Ḥachatur Abovyani grakan-k'nnadatakan hayatsk'nerě." *BEH,* 1984/3, 3–15.

T'arverdieva, K. *Abovyaně ev Aḫundově.* (Erevan, 1958).

Tēr Astuatzatreants, H. *Ḥachatur Abovean.* (Tiflis, 1905).

Tēr Karapeteants, N. "Ḥachatur Abovean." *Lumay,* 1 (1896/2), 145–92; 2 (1897/1), 49–96; 2 (1897/2), 145–86.

———. *Ḥachatur Abovean.* (Tiflis, 1897).

Terteryan, A. *Abovyani stełtzagortzut'yuně.* (Erevan, 1940).

Yarut'iwnean, I. "Zgatsmunk'neri ašḫarh (Ḥachatur Aboveani Erkeri ařt'iw)." *Lumay,* 3 (1898/1), 273–320.

Zaryan, Ř. "Abovyani anhayt šrjagayut'yunnerits." *T,* 1948/9.

———. *Abovyani kyank'ě.* (Erevan, 1939, 1954).

———. "Nor nyut'er Abovyani kensagrut'yan hamar." *T,* 1948/4, 31–46.

ABOVYAN, ANUŠAVAN (1862–1938)

A native of Uzunlar (now Ōdzun), a village in T'umanyan, Armenia. A schoolmate and a friend of Yovhannēs T'umanean (q.v.). He received his elementary education in Jalalōłli (now Step'anavan, Armenia), and spent most of his life in Tiflis. The main theme of his prose is life in Eastern Armenian villages.

Texts

Patkerner (giwłakan keank'its). Book 1. (Tiflis, 1906).

Lewoni hēk'iat'ě. (Tiflis, 1916).

ABRAHAM EREWANTSI (18th c.)

No biographical details are available for this eighteenth-century historian, who describes the Perso-Ottoman military confrontations in Transcaucasia and Iran in his "History of the Wars, 1721–1736."

Texts

Patmut'iwn paterazmatsn 1721–1736 t'. (Erevan, 1938; Venice, 1977). (Edited by S. Čemčemean; edition also includes an edited version of the text by Matt'ēos Ewdokiatsi, a Mekhitarist monk).

Translations

GEORGIAN

Davlianidze, L. *Omebis Istoria.* (Tbilisi, 1976).

RUSSIAN

Istoriia voin 1721–1736 gg. (Erevan, 1939).

ABRAHAM III, KRETATSI, Catholicos of Armenia (d. 1737)

Also known as Ṙotostʻotsi, Tʻēkʻirtałtsi, or Tʻrakatsi. Abraham was born in Candia (Crete) to a Greek mother and an Armenian father. He was the prelate of the Armenians of Rodosto (Tekirdağ) 1709–34, and was elected Catholicos of Armenia in 1734. A close acquaintance of Nāder Shāh (1688–1747), he wrote a history of the wars the Persian ruler fought in Transcaucasia in 1734–36.

Text (history)

Patmutʻiwn antsits teaṙn Abrahamu srbazan katʻołikosin hayots Tʻēkʻirtałtswoy aṙ Natršah arkʻayin parsits. (Calcutta, 1796). Second edition, *Patmagrutʻiwn antsitsn iwrots ew Natr-Šahin parsits.* (Vałaršapat, 1870; includes *Patmutʻiwn Ani kʻałakʻin:* "A History of the City of Ani," and an encyclical). Third edition, *Patmutʻyun.* (Erevan, 1973; a critical text with Russian translation, *Povestvovanie,* by N. Korganian [i.e. N. Łorłanyan]).

Other works (encyclicals)

"Kondak i veray Tʻekʻirtału." *S,* 1877, 50–53, 73–77.

Galamkʻearean, G. *Kensagrutʻiwn Sargis arkʻep.-i Sarafean ew žamanakin hay katʻołikeaykʻ.* (Vienna, 1908), 160–66.

Patmutʻyun (Erevan, 1973), 179–86. (Also found in *Patmagrutʻiwn antsitsn iwrots ew Natr-Šahin parsits*).

Translations

FRENCH

Brosset. *Col.,* Vol. 2, 257–335. ("History," "History of the City of Ani" and encyclical).

RUSSIAN

Patmutʻyun. (Erevan, 1973). (A critical text of history with Russian translation, *Povestvovanie*, by N. Korganian [i.e. N. Łorłanyan]).

Criticism

Babayan, L. "Abraham Kretatsi." *PBH,* 1977/4, 115–25.

"Dzeṙagir tʻiw 1749: 'Patmutʻiwn Ani kʻałakʻi'." *A,* 1888, 85–89.

Ter-Avetisyan, S. "Abraham Kretatsu Hišatakaranĕ (tzotsi tetrakĕ). Abraham Kretatsu Hišatakarani patmakan aržekʻn u nšanakutʻyunĕ." *Erevani petakan hamalsarani gitakan ašḫatutʻyunner,* 13 (Erevan, 1940), 285–309.

AČĒMEAN, ARSĒN (1899–)

A poet born in Oduṙ, a village near Divriği (Turkey). He was educated in Constantinople and at the Sorbonne, and taught in the Armenian communities of the Middle East.

Collections

Ambołjakan erker: banastełtzutʻiwnner (1920–1940), (1940–1960). 2 vols. (Venice, 1959, 1961).

Texts

Siroy ew hayreni erger. (Lyon, 1927).
Gasa-Bella. (Beirut, 1942).

AČĒMEAN, MKRTICH (1838–1917)

Born in Constantinople and educated in the local Armenian schools and at the Murat-Rapʻayēlean of Venice (1852–58), where Łewond Ališan (q.v.) was one of his teachers. Upon his return to his birthplace, he worked for the telegraph company and wrote poetry in his spare time.

Texts (poetry)

Žpitkʻ ew artasukʻ. (Constantinople, 1871).
Vahagn: diwtsaznergutʻiwn. (Constantinople, 1871).
Loys ew stuerkʻ. (Constantinople, 1887).
Garnan hover. (Constantinople, 1892).
Trtʻṙun yanger, ḥunki burumner, loys ew stuerkʻ, garnan hover. (Constantinople, 1908).

Translations

French
APA, 45–46.

Russian
AAP, 403–5.

Spanish
APAS, 123–25.

Criticism

Gamēr. "Uruagitzner–Mkrtich Ačēmean." *M,* 1903/16, 250–51.
Mamikonyan, K. "Mkrtich Ačemyan." *BEH,* 1974/3, 181–90.
Nemtsē, G. "Mkrtich Ačēmean." *B,* 94 (1936), 294–96.
Sargsyan, G. "Mkrtich Ačemyani stełtzagortzakan kyankʻi vał šrjanĕ." *T,* 1963/8, 77–88.
Sewan, A. "Mkrtich Ačēmean." *HK,* 6 (1927–28/10), 127–36.
Y. A. "Mkrtich Ačēmean." *B,* 59 (1901), 181–84.
Yarutʻiwnean, A. "Mkrtich Ačēmean." *AM,* 1902, 497–504.

ADAM, AZBAR (1816–1846)

A native of Pʻarakʻar, a village near Erevan. A self-taught minstrel (*ašuł*).

Poetry

MKH, 399–403; 415–16; 460–63; 526–27.
PHA, 1, 49–75.
THG, 74–78.

Criticism

MKH, 588.
PHA, 1, 46–48.

ADĒLEAN, AZARIA (1871–1903)

Pen name: Azaria Adēlean.

Born Azaria Daniēlean in the village of Mełri, Armenia. Educated in his birthplace, in Baku, and at the Riga Polytechnic, where he studied chemistry (1892–1901). Taught in Erevan and in his birthplace until his early death of consumption. His prose deals mainly with social problems in rural areas.

Collections

Erkeri žołovatzu mek hatorov. (Erevan, 1950).

Texts

Skesurě. (Tiflis, 1899).

Translations (Russian)

Kavkazskaia zhizn', Book 1, (Tiflis, 1896), 27–50.

Criticism

Ałbalean, N. "Łochałě ibrew tip hay vipagrutʻean mēj." *Murč,* 1897/7–8, 1060–69; 1897/9, 1247–63.

Danielyan, S. *Azaria Adelyan.* (Erevan, 1964).

AFRIKEAN, GĒORG (1887–1918)

A teacher by profession, the poet Afrikean, nephew of Avetikʻ Isahakyan (q.v.), was educated in his native Alexandrapol (later Leninakan and now Gyumri) and in Šuši, Artsaḥ (Karabagh).

Poetry

Gevorg Afrikyan, Isahak Isahakyan, Art. Ter-Martirosyan, erekʻ kʻnar. (Erevan, 1963), 19–68.

AGAPEAN, ARŠAK (c1860–1905)

Born in the village of Lali (now Nor Lala, Ijevan, Armenia). A cousin of Harutʻyun Čułuryan (q.v.). Attended the Nersisean school in Tiflis, but there is conflicting information as to whether he completed his studies at the school. He taught before attending the Tiflis Institute for Teachers (1882–86), following which he resumed his teaching career in various places in Transcaucasia. His prose deals with life in the countryside.

Collections

Erkeri žołovatzu. (Erevan, 1934).

Erker. (Erevan, 1966).

Texts

Musini gangatě. (Tiflis, 1890).

Criticism

Danielyan, S. *Aršak Agapyan.* (Erevan, 1968).

AHARONEAN, AWETIS (1866–1948)

Born in the village of Igdirmawa near Iğdır (Eastern Turkey). Attended the Gēorgean Seminary and audited courses at Lausanne (1898–1901) and at the Sorbonne (1901–02). After his return from Europe in 1902 as an already well-known author, he emerged as an active political figure. In 1917 he was elected chairman of the Executive Council of the Armenian National Council in Tiflis.

In 1918 he led the Delegation of the Armenian Republic to Istanbul for talks on the Treaty of Batum, and in the following year he headed the delegation of the Armenian Republic to the Paris Peace Conference. In that same year he became president of the Armenian Parliament in Erevan, and in 1920 he signed the Treaty of Sèvres on behalf of Armenia, which was later replaced by the Treaty of Lausanne. He lived in France after the establishment of Soviet regime in Eastern Armenia.

Collections

Žołovatzu erkeri. 10 vols. (Boston, 1947–1951). (Vols. 7 and 9 have imprint Venice, St. Lazarus).

Texts (short stories, novels, travel accounts)

Bašon. (Tiflis, 1899).
Patkerner. (Moscow, 1899; St. Petersburg, 1909).
Ḥełčerě. (Tiflis, 1902).
Italiayum. (Tiflis, 1903).
Keankʻi dasě. (Tiflis, 1903).
Mrrki surbě. (Tiflis, 1903).
Arazě. (Tiflis, 1904).
Mayrerě. (Tiflis, 1904).
Artsunkʻi hovitě. (Baku, 1907).
Gaylerě oṙnum ēin. Ašnan gišerin. (Tiflis, 1907).
Azatutʻean čanaparhin. (Tiflis, 1908; Boston, 1926; Teheran, 1956).
Keankʻi vēpě. (Tiflis, 1908).
Lṙutʻiwn. (Tiflis, 1909; Boston, 1924).
Andundě. (Tiflis, 1910).
Ḥawari mēj. (Tiflis, 1910).
Partuatzner. (Constantinople, 1912).
Astzu krakě. (Tiflis, 1912).
Šveytsarakan giwłě. (Tiflis, 1913).
Hayrenikʻis hamar. (Boston, 1920).
Čambordě. (Boston, 1926).
Karōt hayreni. (Boston, 1927). (Poetry).
Katʻuškě. (Cairo, 1927).
Im girkʻě. (Paris, 1927, 1931).
Menutʻeans mēj. (New York, 1938).
Im bandě ew erazneris ašḫarhě. (Boston, 1943).

Other works

Hṙō kině. (Tiflis, 1897).
Kʻristapʻor Mikʻayēlean. (Boston, 1926; Buenos Aires, 1945).
Sardarapatits minchev Sewr ew Lōzan. (Boston, 1943).

Translations

English

Ashjian, S. "The Symbol." *Nor ašḫarh* (Paris), 1962/4, 4; 1962/5, 4; 1962/6, 4.
Kelikian, H. "The Blind Minstrel." *Ararat* (New York) Fall 1961, 40–41.
Mahdesian, A. "Honor." *Outlook,* 111 (October 13, 1915), 357–59. Also in *The New Armenia,* 8 (1915/1), 11–13.

"The New Year of a Revolutionist." *The New Armenia,* 8/3 (1916), 43–44.
Serpouhie. "Over the Mountains." *Kochnak,* 17 (June 9, 1917), 719–21.
"That Night." *Armenia* (Boston), 4 (1910/4), 11–14.
Torossian, A. "Death Knell." *The Armenian Herald,* 1 (1917–18), 387–89.
———. "Homage to Thee." *The Armenian Herald,* 1 (1917–18), 503–5.
———. "John's Grief." *The Armenian Student,* 5 (1934/4), 5–17.
Wingate, J. "The Night Watchman." *The Golden Book Magazine,* (New York), January, 1928.

French

Altiar and Sarkissian. "Dans les ténèbres." *Oeuvres libres,* August, 1925/50, 299–380.
Altiar, E. "Les loups hurlaient." *La Revue,* June 15, 1912, 509–25.
Chamlian, M. "Le nouvel an d'un Haïdouk." *Hayastan* (Paris), 1964/96, 4.
Chamlian, M. and E. Altiar. *Vers la liberté* and *L'Abîme.* (Paris, 1912). (F. Macler, ed. Petite bibliothèque arménienne, 19).
"Le chêne séculaire." *La semaine littéraire* (Geneva), July, 1, 1911.
Der Merguerian, R., and Ketcheyan, L. *Sur le chemin de la liberté.* (Roquevarie, 1978).
"Les deux aveugles." *Bibliothèque universelle,* (Lausanne), September, 1912.
"Eclipse-toi, lune." *Revue chrétienne,* May 1, 1911.
"L'Honneur." *Hayastan* (Paris), 1963/37, 4; 1963/38, 4.
Macler, F. "Djavo. Nouvelle." *REArm,* 4 (1924), 207–14.
———. "Le Cavalier noir." *REArm,* 10 (1930), 201–12.
"Les Massis." *Revue bleue* (Paris), August 24, 1912.
"Les mères." *Hayastan* (Paris), 1964/52, 4; 1964/53, 4; 1964/54, 4.
"Nuit d'automne." *Mercure de France,* February, 15, 1911.

French anthologies

APA, 101–5.

German

Finck-Gjandschezian. *Armenische Erzahlungen.* (Leipzig, 1909).
Smbatiantz, A. *Bilder aus Turkisch-Armenien.* (Ējmiatzin, 1910).

German anthologies

ALG, 139–44.

Italian

Il Silenzio. (Milan, 1932).

Russian

Dolina slez'. (Tiflis, 1907).
Materi. (Moscow, 1913). (*Armianskie pisatseli*, ed. M. Gorky).
Rasskazy. (Moscow, 1912). (Universal'naia biblioteka, 712).

Spanish anthology

APAS, 163–66.

Criticism

Aharonean, V. *Yišataki handēs nuiruatz Awetis Aharoneanin.* (Beirut, 1948).
Awagean, Y. *Yobelean Awetis Aharoneani kʻaṙasnameay grakan gortzunēutʻean, 1890–1930.* (New York, 1930).
Baluean, H. "Awetis Aharonean: keankʻn u grakanutʻiwnĕ." Z (eṙamseay) 1947/1, 31–42; 1947/2, 136–43.

Berberean, Ṙ. "Handipumner A. Aharoneani ew G. Kiwlpēnkeani het." *HK,* 26 (1948/1), 6–19.
Čanašean, M. "Awetis Aharonean." *B,* 128 (1970), 46–54; 129 (1971), 72–81; 130 (1972), 114–21.
Engibarean, G. "Grakanakan aknarkner, A. Aharoneani erkerě." *Lumay,* 2 (1903), 171–83.
Erewantsean, P. "A. Aharonean ibrew banahawakʻ." *HK,* 8 (1929–30/6), 87–96.
Ḥachaturean, A. *Awetis Aharoneani het.* (Beirut, 1968).
Hamasteł. "A. Aharoneani mahuan aṙtʻiw." *HK,* 26 (1948/7), 72–74.
Hayrapetean, E. "Aharoneani grakan gortzunēutʻean aržēkʻě." *A,* 1916, 599–606, 704–72, 867–72; 1917, 156–61.
Kʻiwfēčean, Y. "Ṙusahay grakanutʻenēn–Awetis Aharonean." *HG,* 12 (1912), 56–61.
Siruni, Y. "Aruestagētě Awetis Aharoneani mēj." *HK,* 8 (1929–30/9), 89–105.
Varandean, M. "A. Aharonean." *HK,* 8 (1929–30/7), 67–79.
———. *Banastełtz, hraparakaḥōs Awetis Aharoneani grakan gortzunēutʻean kʻaṙasnameay yobeleani aṙtʻiw.* (Paris, 1930).

ALAMDAREAN, YARUTʻIWN (1796–1834)

Born Gēorg Alamdarean in Astrakhan and educated at the local Ałababean School. He was ordained a married priest in 1814, and spent the years 1813–24 in Moscow organizing the newly founded Lazarean Institute. He became the first director of the newly established Nersisean School in Tiflis (1824–30), and took the vows of celibacy (1828) before his exile to Hałbat (1830) by the Russian authorities for his nationalist views and activities and his close ties with Catholicos Nersēs V, Aštaraketsi (1770–1857). In the early 1830s, Alamdarean was appointed Father Superior of the Monastery of Surb Ḥach in Nor Naḥijewan, where he was killed under somewhat mysterious circumstances. Among the better-known students of this poet, playwright, and teacher were Ḥ. Abovean (q.v.) and S. Nazarean (1812–79), a celebrated journalist, critic, orientalist, and founder of the periodical *Hiwsisapʻayl* (i.e., the northern lights, *aurora borealis*).

Collections

Patkanean, kʻ. *Chapʻaberakankʻ.* (St. Petersburg, 1884). (Poetry).

Texts

Hamaṙōt baṙaran i ṙusats lezuē i hay. (Moscow, 1821). (Russian-Armenian Dictionary).

Poetry

MKH, 103–5, 110, 445, 507–8, 511–12, 535–36.
PHA, 1, 78–79.

Other works

"Aṙak: Aṙiwtz ew ēš." *BM,* 1 (1941), 188. (Fable).

Criticism

Ēskičyan, M. "Harutʻyun Alamdaryan." *EJ,* 1955/2, 42–46.
Gevorgyan, Ē. "Harutʻyun Alamdaryani poezian." *L,* 1973/10, 49–60.
———. "Harutʻyun Alamdaryani antip draman." *SG,* 1974/7, 161–64.
———. *Harutʻyun Alamdaryan.* (Erevan, 1977).

Inčikyan, A. "Harut'yun Alamdaryani grakan žarangut'yunĕ." *T,* 1957/9, 63–73.
Nazaryan, Š. "Harut'yun Alamdaryani gortzuneut'yan moskovyan tarinerĕ." *BM,* 5 (1960), 177–97.
Šahaziz, E. "Harut'yun vrd. Alamdaryan." *EJ,* 1945/5, 27–38.
T'erzibašyan, V. " 'Hramizd ev Zenobia' patmakan dramayi masin." *T,* 1956/3, 57–68.
Vantsean, G. "Hayer bošanerits." *Murč,* 1897/10, 1394–1403.
Zak'aryan, H. "Norahayt p'aster Harut'yun Alamdaryani veraberyal (1793–1813 t't'.)." *BEH,* 1984/2, 131–39.

AŁASYAN, VARSENIK (1898–1974)

Born in Jahri, a village in the region of Nakhijewan. She received her secondary education in Tiflis. Worked for the Armenian daily *Komunist* and the Armenian radio program, both in Baku. Except for a few plays, she wrote verse.

Collections

Hatĕntir. (Baku, 1955).

Texts

Banastełtzut'yunner. (Tiflis, 1926).
Ōreri ergĕ. (Baku, 1933).
Mayrakan huyzer. (Baku, 1937).
Erjanik mankut'yun. (Baku, 1938).
Tzitiki ḥindĕ. (Erevan, 1940).
Tonatzaṙ. (Erevan, 1941).
Banastełtzut'yunner. (Baku, 1947).
Banastełtzut'yunner. (Erevan, 1948).
Garun. (Erevan, 1952).
Žpitner. (Baku, 1957).
Nver ereḥanerin. (Erevan, 1958).
Banastełtzut'yunner. (Erevan, 1959).
Lirika. (Baku, 1964).
Mayramutis šołerov. (Erevan, 1971).

AŁAVNI, (1911–1992)

Born Ałavni Grigoryan in Taylar, a village in the region of Kars, and educated in Leninakan (now Gyumri). As an editor and journalist, she worked for Soviet Armenian periodicals, Armenian radio, and other organizations. She wrote both prose and poetry.

Collections

Erker. 2 vols. (Erevan, 1981–82).

Texts

Arteri lirikan. (Erevan, 1930). (Poetry).
Mant'aš. (Erevan, 1934). (Poetry).
Banastełtzut'yunner. 2 books. (Erevan, 1936, 1939). (Poetry).
Kak'avadzor. (Erevan, 1937).
Arevatzałik. (Erevan, 1937).
Abuzeyt'. (Erevan, 1938).

Pavlik Morozov. (Erevan, 1940).
Ordin. (Erevan, 1942).
Partizan Vasyan. (Erevan, 1942).
Ṙazmi erger. (Erevan, 1942). (Poetry).
Vanka oskedzeṙikě. (Erevan, 1943).
Frunzei tłan, Tʻimurě. (Erevan, 1943).
Zruyts germanakan generali ev chaltik akʻlori masin. (Erevan, 1944).
Im tałaraně. (Erevan, 1944). (Poetry).
Erg amaṙnamuti. (Erevan, 1947).
Inch tesel em u sovoreł, akanj arekʻ patmem dzez ēl. (Erevan, 1947).
Sakravor Sakʻon. (Erevan, 1948). (Poem).
Hayrenikʻi hamar. (Erevan, 1950).
Erevanyan erger. (Erevan 1951). (Poetry).
Mer bakayin čambarum. (Erevan 1952).
Širak. (Erevan, 1954, 1957, 1963 [2 books], 1973). (Novel).
Hayreri mankutʻyuně. (Erevan, 1959).
Iriknamut. (Erevan, 1962).
Nra mtermakan ašḥarhum. (Erevan, 1975). (Reminiscences about Avetikʻ Isahakyan).
Čampʻaneri łołanjě. (Erevan, 1977). (Stories).
Bari luys, Areg. (Erevan, 1980). (Novel).
"Ḥłči datastaně." *SG,* 1980/3, 39–77. (Play).
"Maro Vardani." *SG,* 1983/3, 10–21. (Story).
Mišt kanchoł dzayner. (Erevan, 1983).

Translations

GERMAN

Movsessian, L. "Herbstaufgang." *Armenische Grammatik* (Vienna, 1959), 282–83.

RUSSIAN

Sadovskii, A. *Shirak.* (Moscow, 1956).
Sadovskii, A., and Dudintsev, V. *Shirak.* 2 vols. (Moscow, 1960–64, 1967).

Criticism

Ałababyan, S. "Artzvnaki-Aregi hasunutʻyuně." *SG,* 1981/3, 129–31.
Darbni, V. "Ḥoskʻ Ałavnu masin." *SG,* 1981/9, 63–67.

AŁAYEAN, ŁAZAROS (1840–1911)

Born in the village of Bolnis Ḥachen (now Ḥachen, in the region of Bolnisi, Georgia). Received his elementary education in his birthplace and attended the Nersisean school in Tiflis for one year (1853). He worked as a compositor in Tiflis, Moscow, and St. Petersburg (1861–67); edited the periodical *Ararat* (1869–70); and taught in Armenian schools in Transcaucasia (1870–82). Suspected as a member of the Hnchakean party, Ałayean was banished to Nor Naḥijewan and Crimea (1898–1900). Died in Tiflis.

Collections

Ěntir erker. (Erevan, 1939).
Inčikyan, A., and Asatryan, A., eds. *Erker.* 4 vols. (Erevan, 1939–1950).
Ěntir erker. (Erevan, 1956).

Erkeri žołovatzu. 4 vols. (Erevan, 1962–63).
Erkeri žołovatzu. 3 vols. (Erevan, 1973–74).
Erkeri žołovatzu. 4 vols. (Erevan, 1979–).
Erker. (Erevan, 1981).

Texts

Arutʻiwn ew Manuēl: azgayin vēp. Vol. 1 (Tiflis, 1867). Vols. 1–3 (Tiflis, 1888–1893). (Novel).
Erku kʻoyr. (Tiflis, 1872, 1892, 1916; Erevan, 1962). (Novelette).
Anahit. (Tiflis, 1881, 1891, 1903; Erevan, 1944, 1973, 1983; Beirut, 1971). (Story).
Sring hovuakan. (Tiflis, 1882). (Poetry).
Aregnazan kam Kaḥardakan ašḥarh. (Tiflis, 1887; Beirut, 1955; Erevan, 1984). (Folk tale).
Torkʻ-Angeł ew Haykanoyš Gełetsik. (Tiflis, 1888). (Poem).
Banastełtzutʻiwnner. (Tiflis, 1890, 1903). (Poetry).
Im keankʻi glḥawor dēpkʻerě. (Tiflis, 1893; Erevan, 1955). (Reminiscences).
Žamanakakits atenaḥōsutʻiwn. (Tiflis, 1898).
Hēkʻiatʻner. 2 vols. (Tiflis, 1904). (Folk tales).
Hekʻiatʻner. (Erevan, 1937, 1952, 1959, 1968). (Folk tales).
Kʻēōṙōłli. (Tiflis, 1908; Constantinople, 1924). (Prose).
Banastełtzutʻyunner. (Erevan, 1938). (Poetry).
Antaṙi manukě. (Erevan, 1966, 1984). (Folk tale).
Hazaran blbul. (Erevan, 1983). (Folk tale).
Mankakan patmvatzkʻner. (Erevan, 1983). (Tales for children).
Manušak. (Erevan, 1983). (Poetry).
Aslan bala. (Erevan, 1986). (Folk tale).

Translations

French

LPA, 174–75.

Russian

Anait. (Erevan, 1983).
Aregnazan: Skazka. (Erevan, 1988).
Areknazan ili zakoldovannyi mir. (Baku, 1902).

Russian collections

Izbrannoe. (Erevan, 1941).
Skazki. (Erevan, 1952).
Skazki. (Erevan, 1989).

Russian anthologies

ABS, 471–518.
BPA, 297–98.
KHAN, 2, 213–28.

Bibliographies

Ḥanzadyan, Pʻ., and Adyan, G. *Łazaros Ałayan (1840–1911): matenagitutʻyun.* (Erevan, 1972).

Criticism

Abēl Sarkawag. "Łazaros Ałayean, nra yišatakin (1840–1911)." *A,* 1911, 605–12, 700–6, 786–92.

Asatryan, A. *Łazaros Ałayan, kyankʻn u gortzuneutʻyunĕ.* (Erevan, 1940).
———. "Łazaros Ałayani gełarvestakan ardzakĕ." *T,* 1961/8, 49–64.
———. *Łazaros Ałayanĕ žamanakakitsneri hušerum.* (Erevan, 1967).
Astvatzatryan, V. *Pedagogicheskaia deiatel'nost' G. Agaiana.* (Erevan, 1941).
———. *Ł. Ałayanĕ mankavarž.* (Erevan, 1957).
Avtʻandilyan, A. "Łazaros Ałayani pʻilisopʻayakan ev sotsiologiakan hayatskʻneri šurjĕ." *PBH,* 1962/3, 165–72.
———. *Łazaros Ałayani ašḥarhayatskʻĕ.* (Erevan, 1983).
Čanašean, M. "Łazaros Ałayean ew ir 'Erku kʻoyr' vēpĕ." *B,* 110 (1952), 49–54.
Eremean, S. "Łazaros Ałayean, gragētĕ." *B,* 61 (1903), 306–19.
Ērukʻyan, Ž. "Łazaros Ałayanĕ hušagir." *L,* 1970/7, 76–84.
Harutʻyunyan, G. "Łazaros Ałayani kensagrutʻyanĕ veraberoł pʻastatʻłtʻer." *EJ,* 1949/3–4, 58–63.
Jrbašyan, Ēd. "Ałayan-Tʻumanyan grakan žaṙangutʻyan hartsi šurjĕ." *PBH,* 1990/2, 41–61.
Muradyan, H. *Łazaros Ałayan.* (Erevan, 1941).
Raffi. "Paron Ł. Ałayeantsi hastsēin." *Ardzagankʻ,* 6 (1887/39), 615–16; 6 (1887/47–48), 741–42.
Šahaziz, E. "Im hušerits: Łazaros Ałayanĕ." *EJ,* 1948/10–12, 73–79.
Sargsyan, Ḥ. " 'Arutʻyun ev Manveli' erku hratarakutʻyunnerĕ." *T,* 1964/2, 47–56.
Širvanzadē, "Łazaros Ałayeants." *HK,* 2 (1923–24/9), 46–50.
Stepʻanean, Y. "Łazaros Ałayeants." *HK,* 12 (1933–34/5), 46–55; 6, 49–64; 7, 70–76; 8, 61–72; 9, 59–65; 10, 69–78; 11, 68–79.

ALAZAN, VAHRAM (1903–1966)

Pen names: Vahram Alazan, Hordzankʻ.

Born Vahram Gabuzyan (also Garbuzyan), in Van. Fled his native city during the Armenian genocide of 1915 and settled in Erevan. Editor of the periodical *Tpagrakan banvor,* 1922–30; chairman of the Association of Proletarian Writers of Armenia, 1923–32; editor of *Grakan tʻertʻ,* 1932–36; and secretary to the Union of Writers of Armenia, 1933–36. Siberia looms large in some of his verse and prose. Although exiled for many years, Alazan survived the Stalinist purges.

Texts

Tarineri ḥałĕ. (Erevan, 1922). (Poetry).
Hrabḥapoezia; žaytʻkʻum aṙajin. (Erevan, 1923). (Poetry).
Ašḥatankʻayin. (Erevan, 1924). (Poetry).
Gyułi gišerĕ. (Erevan, 1925). (Poetry).
Ōriord Ōlga. (Erevan, 1925). (Story).
Poem gyułi masin. (Erevan, 1926). (Poem).
Dasalikʻĕ. (Erevan, 1927, 1934). (Story).
Kʻsanvetsĕ. (Erevan, 1928). (Poetry).
Čanaparhin. (Erevan, 1928). (novel).
Patmvatzkʻner. (Vałaršapat, 1929). (Stories).
Erger kaṙutsman ev haltʻanaki. (Erevan, 1930). (Poem).
Poem paterazmi, ḥałałutʻyan ev hngamya plani masin. (Erevan, 1931). (Poem).
Eṙaguyni u mahi erkrum. (Erevan, 1931). (Prose).
Tʻłtʻi ev arčiči herosnerĕ. (Erevan, 1933).
Makʻaṙumner. (Erevan, 1933). (Poetry).

Vatʻsunerord horizonum. (Erevan, 1934). (Prose).
Darĕ dari dem. (Erevan, 1936). (Poetry).
Banasteltzi sirtĕ. (Erevan, 1954). (Poetry).
Žołovrdi kamkʻĕ. (Erevan, 1955).
Hyusisayin astł. (Erevan, 1956, 1958). (Novel).
Horizonner. (Erevan, 1957). (Poetry).
Lusełenn u karotĕ. (Erevan, 1962).
Antip erger. (Erevan, 1972). (Poetry).
Dirkʻerum. (Erevan, n.d.).
Łazarean, V. "Zapēl Esayeanĕ ew Vahram Alazanĕ Vahan Tʻēkʻēeanin." *Haykazean hayagitakan handēs,* 10 (1982–84), 299–308.

Other works

Hay fašistnerĕ grakan andastanum. (Erevan 1932).
Tasnerku tari (Sovetakan Hayastani 1920–32i mšakutʻayin kyankʻi notʻagrutʻyun). (Erevan, 1933). (Jointly with Vałaršak Norents).
Kulturayi paštpanutʻyan mijazgayin kongresi ardyunkʻner. (Erevan, 1935).
Dłyakner ev orjer (tpavorutʻyunner artasahmanits). (Erevan, 1936).
Hušer. (Erevan, 1960, 1967).

Translations (Russian)

Makintsian, A. *Severnaia zvezda. Roman.* (Erevan, 1960).
Na shestidesiatom gorizonte. Roman. (Tiflis, 1935).
Serdtse poeta. Stikhi. (Moscow, 1958).
Vek protiv veka. (Moscow, 1934).
Zviagintseva, V., et al. *Stikhi.* (Moscow, 1935).

Criticism

Aristakesyan, A. "Vahram Alazan." *SG,* 1963/6, 149–51.
Arzumanyan, S. "Vahram Alazan." *SG,* 1959/6, 147–58.

AŁEKʻSANDR I, JUŁAYETSI, Catholicos of Armenia (d. 1714)

No biographical details are available for this author, save that he had been Abbot of the Monastery of Amenapʻrkich in Nor Jułay (New Julfa, Isfahan, 1697–1706) before ascending the throne of Ējmiatzin, as Catholicos of Armenia (1706–14). Died in office and was buried in Ējmiatzin.

Texts

Girkʻ atenakan or asi vịčabanakan. (New Julfa, 1687). Later edition, *Girkʻ or kochi atenakan.* (Constantinople, 1783).
Grkʻoyk or kochi ałōtʻamatoyts. Published in *Gandzaran uḥtakanutʻean, ałōtʻamatoyts ew zbōsaran.* (Nor Naḥijewan, 1790). Later edition, *Ałōtʻamatoyts, gandzaran uḥtakanut'ean, ałōtʻamatoyts ew zbōsaran hogewor . . .* (Moscow, 1840).
Azgasēr araratean, 1848/12, 91–95. (Text of his first will).
Letter to Pope Clement XI. Second recension. In *Maseats aławni,* 1856, 114–23. Also in *Pʻaros,* 1873/2, 6–14.
Letter to Pope Clement XI. First recension. In *Aršaloys araratean,* 1857/554 and 555. Also in *Patmutʻiwn Nor Jułayu or yAspahan,* Y. Tēr Yovhaneants, Vol. 2 (New Julfa, 1881), 38–46. Also in *B,* 1922, 354–57.

Encyclical to the Armenians of Burvar, and Encyclical to the Armenians of Šrškan. In *Patmut'iwn Nor Jułayu or yAspahan,* Y. Tēr Yovhaneants, Vol. 2, (New Julfa, 1881), 102–3, 309.
Letter to the Bishop Movsēs of the Monastery of Amenap'rkich in New Julfa. In *Patmut'iwn Nor Jułayu or yAspahan,* Y. Tēr Yovhaneants, Vol. 2, (New Julfa, 1881), 35–36.
Text of second will. In *Patmut'iwn Nor Jułayu or yAspahan,* Y. Tēr Yovhaneants, Vol. 2 (New Julfa, 1881), 36–37.
Letter to Pope Clement XI. First and second recensions. In *HA,* 1914, 539–52. Also in *Kensagrut'iwnner erku hay patriark'neru ew tasn episkoposneru ew žamanakin hay kat'ołikeayk',* G. Galēmk‘earean. (Vienna, 1915), 196–215.
Letter to Peter I of Russia. In *Hay-ṙus ōrientatsiayi tzagman ḥndirě,* A. Yovhannisean. (Ējmiatzin, 1921), supp. pp. 13–15.
"A. Kondak Ałek‘sandr A. Jułayetsi kat‘ołikosi (1706–1714)." *HA,* 1942, 108–10.
"B. Kondak Ałek‘sandr Jułayetsi kat‘.i." *HA,* 1942, 110–13.
"G. Kondak Ałek‘sandr Jułayetsi kat‘ołikosi." *HA,* 1942, 113–15.

Translations (Russian)

Ezov, G. A. *Snosheniia Petra Velikogo s armianskim narodom.* (Petersburg, 1898), xliv–xlv. (Translation of his letter to Peter I).

Criticism

Ayvazovski, G. "T‘ułt‘ Ałek‘sandr kat‘ołikosi aṙ Papn Hṙovmay Kłemēs ŽA." *Maseats aławni,* 1856, 110–23.
Galēmk‘earean, G. "Yovakim v. Jułayetsi, ark‘episkopos Ējmiatzni (1666–1720)." *HA,* 1914, 532–62.
———. "Yovakim v. Jułayetsi, ark‘episkopos Ējmiatzni (1666–1720)." *Kensagrut'iwnner erku hay patriark'neru ew tasn episkoposneru ew žamanakin hay kat'ołikeayk'.* (Vienna, 1915), 183–234.
Eritsean, A. "Ałeklsandr A. kat‘ołikos hayots anirawatsi ambastanwatz." *Ardzagank',* 11 (1892/80, 84–87).
Set‘eants, M. "Haykaban vardapet mi Yisusean." *B,* 1922, 299–303, 326–28, 354–57; 1923, 3–5.

ALIK‘SANEAN, AWETIS (1910–1984)

Born and educated in Istanbul, Alik‘sanean published several periodicals in Istanbul and in Paris, where he settled in the 1950s: *Kit'aṙ* (1928), *Amsuan girk'ě* (1930), *Patker grakanut'ean ew aruesti* (1930), *Patker* (1932–40), *Aysōr* (1947–48), *Luys P'arizi* (1957), and *Lusałbiwr* (1959). In 1960 he launched another periodical in Paris, *Ašḥarh.* Most of Alik‘sanean's literary works are still scattered in the periodical press.

Texts (prose)

Anuně Masis drink'. (Paris, 1964).
Erjankut'iwn. (Paris, 1966).
Anuně Masis drink'. (Erevan, 1968). (Includes selections from the two above).

Translations (Russian)

KNS, 187–215.

ALIŠAN, ŁEWOND (1820–1901)

Ališan (from Ottoman Turkish âlişan, "illustrious," etc., itself a loan from Arabic 'aliyy al-sha'n, through Persian 'alī-shān) received his elementary education in his birthplace, Constantinople. In 1832, he joined the Mekhitarist Congregation of Venice and became a monk upon completing his studies in 1840. He subsequently held administrative positions at the Monastery of St. Lazarus and taught and supervised at Mekhitarist schools in Paris and Venice. He edited *Bazmavēp* briefly (1849–51) and embarked on a European tour in 1852–53, which took him to England, Austria, Germany, France, Belgium, and Italy. After 1872, by which time he had established himself as a popular poet, Ališan devoted himself entirely to research. His scholarly contributions provided an impetus to Armenian studies and brought him recognition from European scholars, learned societies, and academic insitutions.

Collections

Štikyan, S. *Erker.* (Erevan, 1981).

Texts (literary)

Nuagkʻ. 5 vols. (Venice, 1857–58, 1867–1886). (Poetry). Selections published as *Nvagner.* (Erevan, 1957).

Yušikkʻ hayreneats hayots. 2 vols. (Venice, 1869–70; 1920–21, 1946). (Prose).

Ěnd ełewneaw yamayutʻean batsavayri ḥorhrdatzutʻiwn. (Venice, 1874). (Prose).

Čaṙkʻ hogeworkʻ vasn miandzants. 2 vols. (Venice, 1904–27).

Texts

Varkʻ s. Gēorgay Zōravarin. (Venice, 1849).

Sopʻerkʻ haykakankʻ. Vols. 1–22. (Venice, 1853–1861).

Hawakʻumn patmutʻean Vardanay Vardapeti. (Venice, 1862).

Kirakosi vardapeti Gandzaketswoy hamaṙōt patmutʻiwn i Srboyn Grigorē tsawurs iwr. (Venice, 1865).

Labubneay diwanagri dpri Edesioy Tułtʻ Abgaru yełeal yasorwoyn i dzeṙn s. tʻargmanchats. (Venice, 1868).

Ḥosrov Andzewatsi. Meknutʻiwn ałōtʻits pataragin. (Venice, 1869).

Varkʻ ew vkayabanutʻiwnkʻ srbots. 2 vols. (Venice, 1874).

Ansiz Antiokʻay. Assises d'Antioche. (Venice, 1876). (Armenian and French).

Girkʻ vastakots. (Venice, 1877).

Sahman benediktean vanats. (Venice, 1880).

Abusahl Hay, Patmutʻiwn ekełetseats ew vanoreits Egiptosi. (Venice, 1895, 1933).

Kamenits. Taregirkʻ hayots Lehastani ew Ṙumenioy hawastcheay yaweluatzovkʻ. (Venice, 1896).

Vasn vanoreits or i s. kʻałakʻn yErusałēm ěst naḥneats merots gałłiarēn tʻargmanutʻeamb. (Venice, 1896).

Other works (historical and topographical)

Kʻałakʻakan ašḥarhagrutʻiwn nkaratsoyts patkerōkʻ. (Venice, 1853).

Tełagir Hayots Metzats. (Venice, 1855).

Le Haygh, sa période et sa fête. ([Paris], 1860; Venice, 1880).

Physiographie de l'Arménie. (Venice, 1861, 1870).

Nšmarkʻ haykakankʻ. (Venice, 1870).

Šnorhali ew paragay iwr. (Venice, 1873).

Geonomia Armena. (Venice, 1881).

Haykakan ašḥarhagitutʻiwn. (Venice, 1881).

Širak. (Venice, 1881).
Tableau succinct de l'histoire et de la littérature de l'Arménie. (Venice, 1883).
Skewṙay vankʻ, vanakankʻ ew Srbarann. (Venice, 1884).
Sisuan. (Venice, 1885).
Ayrarat. (Venice, 1890).
Sisakan. (Venice, 1893).
Hay-busak kam haykakan busabaṙutʻiwn. (Venice, 1895).
Hin hawatkʻ kam heṫanosakan krōnkʻ hayots. (Venice, 1895).
Hay Venet kam Yarĕnchuṫiwnkʻ hayots ew venetats i ŽG-D ew ŽE-Z dars. (Venice, 1896).
Aršaloys kʻristonēuṫean hayots. (Venice, 1901).
Hayapatum. (Venice, 1901).
Zardankarkʻ Awetarani Mlkʻē ṫaguhwoy. (Venice, 1901).
Hayastan yaṙaj kʻan zlineln Hayastan. (Venice, 1904).
Štikyan, S. *Namakner.* (Erevan, 1969).
———. "Łewond Ališani norahayt namaknerĕ." *Banber Hayastani arḫivneri,* 1981/2, 45–57.

Translations

English

Blackwell, A. "The Lily of Shavarshan." *Armenia* (Boston), 1/8 (1905), 17–19. Also in *The New Armenia,* 8/12 (1916), 188; 21/2 (1929), 24–25.
———. "The Easter Has Come." *Armenia* (Boston), 4/11 (1911), 16.
———. "The Exiles." *Armenia* (Boston), 7/1 (1913), 17. Also published in *The New Armenia,* 9 (1917/8), 136.
———. "A Song of Fatherland." *The New Armenia,* 9 (1917/19), 298; 21/2 (1929), 24.
———. "The Nightingale of Avarair." *The New Armenia,* 10 (1918/2), 31; 21/2 (1929), 25–26.
Kitabjian, V. "The Night Thrush of Avarair." *Kochnak,* September 14, 1918, 1503–1504.
———. "Easter Song." The New Armenia, 20 (1928/1), 2. Also in *The Armenian Church* (New York), March, 1964, 1.
Boyajian, Z. "The Nightingale of Avarair." *The New Armenia,* 11 (1919/3), 35.
———. "Moon in the Armenian Cemetery." *The New Armenia,* 21 (1929/2), 26.
Picturesque Armenia. (Venice, 1875).

English Anthologies

AP, 95–114.
ALP, 37–40, 108–9.

French

L'Arménie pittoresque. (Venice, 1872).
Ayas, son port et son commerce et ses relations avec l'Occident; extrait du "Sissouan" ou l'Arméno-Cilicie. (Venice, 1899).
Bayan, G. *Léon le Magnifique, premier roi de Sissouan.* (Venice, 1888).
Dulaurier, Ed. "Topographie de la Grande Arménie, par le R.P. Léonce Alischan." *Journal Asiatique,* 13 (1869), 385–446.
Hékimian, M. J. *S. Théodore le Salahounien, martyr arménien.* (Venice, 1872).
Minassian, J. "Le jugement de Vassag." *La Patrie,* 1910/89, supplement. (Reprinted separately, Constantinople, 1910).

Sirounian, Ed., and Issaverdentz, J. *Sissouan ou l'Arméno-Cilicie, description géographique et historique avec cartes et illustrations.* (Venice, 1899).

French anthologies

LPA, 164–65.

German

Das pittoreske Armenien. (Venice, 1893).

German anthologies

AD, 29–31.

Italian

L'Armeno-Veneto, compendio storico e documenti delle relazioni degli Armeni coi Veneziani. 2 vols. (Venice, 1893).

Elia d'Alessandro, insigne artista manufatturiere armeno-veneto, e la Famiglia Alessandri. (Venice, 1876).

Teza, E. *Il Giglio di Sciavarscian.* (Venice, 1897). (Armenian and Italian).

Vardan il Grande. (Venice, 1875).

Modern Western Armenian

Yovhannēsean, V. "Ełewinin tak." *B,* 87 (1930), 35–38, 60–66, 124–31, 186–90, 271–72; 88 (1931), 39–41, 85–86. (Published separately in Venice, 1944).

———. "Hayastani ogin." *B,* 95 (1937), 207–8.

———. "S. Hṙipʿsimēin." *B,* 95 (1937), 294.

———. "Hetʿumi ołbě ir zawaknerun vray." *B,* 97 (1939), 308.

———. "Kʿajakorov Mušełě Dzirawi čakatamartin mēj." *B,* 97 (1939), 170.

———. "Aṙandzar Sepuh Amatuni gntapet haykakan hetzelazōrin." *B,* 98 (1940), 22.

———. "Hayots ahełazōr Trdat tʿagawori mahě." *B,* 102 (1944), 82–86.

———. "Vasak Sepuh." *B,* 104 (1946), 186–88.

———. "Aṙuakin," "Lusině," "Agaraki ěnkuzenin," "Moṙtsir všterd inchpēs antsnoł alikʿnerě," "Karōt," "Erkar pandḫtutʿiwn." *B,* 109 (1951), 296–305.

———. "Datastan Vasak matnichi." *B,* 109 (1951), 267–74.

Pʿechikean, E. "Garun," "Amaṙ." *B,* 88 (1931), 268–69.

———. "Hayreni erg." *B,* 88 (1931), 332.

———. "Panduḫti ḫōskʿer." *B,* 88 (1931), 500.

———. "Matnich Vasaki datastaně." *B,* 93 (1935), 21–24.

———. "Antsealě," "Apagan." *B,* 95 (1937), 292–93.

Tʿomačean, Tʿ. "Matnich Vasaki datastaně." *B,* 97 (1939), 20–25.

Russian anthologies

AAP, 387–88.

BPA, 427–28.

VAM, 143–46.

Russian bibliographies

Shtikian, S. "Gevond Alishan v russkikh perevodakh." *Literaturnaia Armeniia,* 1962/1, 131–33.

Criticism

Aliḫanean, A. "H. Łewond Ališan" *B,* 128 (1970), 398–404.

Antonean, Ṙ. "Andradardzutʿiwnner Ališani 'ṙomantizmi' masin 'Kʿnar amerikean'i aṙitʿov." *B,* 128 (1970), 376–80.

Aproyean, E. "H. Ališani ełbayrě, mēk tʿłtʿikě u kʿertʿuatzě." *B,* 93 (1935), 34–35.

Aslanyan, A. "Łevond Ališan." *L,* 1970/9, 85–94.
Biwzandatsi, N. *K'nnadatut'iwn Haybusaki.* (Vienna, 1925).
Čanašean, M. "H. Łewond Ališan, nahapet hayots." *B,* 128 (1950), 297–302.
Čemčemean, S. "Ališani 'Sisuan'ě." *B,* 128 (1970), 323–35.
———. "Ališani dēpi Ewropa čambordut'iwně." *B,* 129 (1971), 226–67.
———. "H. Łewond Ališan tesuch P'arizi Muratean varžarani." *B,* 134 (1976), 316–40; 136 (1978), 381–449; 137 (1979), 309–35.
———. *H. Łewond Ališan tesuch P'arizi Muratean varžarani.* (Venice, 1980).
Chrak'ean, K'. "Hayr Ališani 'Hogewor čaŕk'ě'." *B,* 77 (1920), 362–63.
———. Yušers h. Ališani masin." *B,* 119 (1961), 268–70.
Chōpanean, A. "H. Łewond Ališan." *ANA,* 4 (1902), 69–80.
Erkat', Arsēn, "Hayr Łewond Ališan ibrew k'ert'oł." *B,* 72 (1914), 462–64; 73 (1915), 75–77; 74 (1916), 27–29.
Eremean, S. *Kensagrut'iwn h. Ališani.* (Venice, 1902).
Ḥanpekean, M. "Ališan, metz hayrenasērě." *B,* 119 (1961), 249–52.
Hatsuni, V. "Ališani het." *B,* 83 (1926), 337–43.
Jrbašyan, Ēd., "Łevond Ališani 'Ergk' nahapeti' banastełtzakan šark'ě ev nra gełarvestakan miasnut'yuně." *BEH,* 1982/2, 22–46.
K'iparean, K. "Hayr Łewond Ališan ew ir Bnunin." *B,* 77 (1920), 359–61.
———. "H. Ališan Tḥruniin mēj." *B,* 84 (1927), 146–50.
———. "H. Łewond Ališan." *B,* 128 (1970), 314–22.
Makvetsyan, E. "Ališani 'Sisakan' ašḥatut'yan ałbyurnerě." *BEH,* 1970/1, 168–74.
Nazarean, T. "Anzugakan erkuoreak hayrenatench hayr Łewond Ališan (1820, Yulis 18) ew Ḥrimean Hayrik (1820, April 17)." *B,* 77 (1920), 373–75.
S. G., "Nahapetin viště." *B,* 119 (1961), 253–59.
Sak'isyan, S. *Ališan.* (Erevan, 1978).
Srapean, A. "Ališan banastełtz." *B,* 119 (1961), 246–48.
Štikyan, S. "Ališani ardzakě." *T,* 1958/12, 39–50.
———. *Łevond Ališani hayrenasirakan poezian.* (Erevan, 1959).
———. "Ališani poeziayi mi k'ani motivnerě." *T,* 1960/2, 41–52.
———. "Ališaně ev Peterburgi hneabanakan ěnkerut'yuně." *T,* 1964/2, 79–82.
———. *Ališani gełarvestakan stełtzagortzut'yuně.* (Erevan, 1967).
———. "Łevond Ališan." *PBH,* 1970/2, 13–26.
———. "Metz eraḥtavorě." *SG,* 1970/7, 127–30.
———. *Ališaně žamanakakitsneri hušerum.* (Erevan, 1974).
———. "Ališani anstoragir gortzerě 'Bazmavepi' ējerum." *PBH,* 1978/2, 81–92.
Tēr Łazarean, E. "Ališani 'Sisuan'ě." *B,* 119 (1961), 260–61.
T'omačan, T'. "Yušer ew nišer h. Łewond Ališani nerk'in keank'ēn, uḥtadrut'ean hariwrameakin aŕit'ov (1838–1938)." *B,* 97 (1939), 37–47, 122–30.
Yovhannēsean, E. "Nahapetě iwr tełagrut'eants mēj." *B,* 77 (1920), 363–69.
Yovhannēsean, M. "Ališani 'Ayrarat'ě." *B,* 119 (1961), 262–64.
Yovhannēsean, V. "Aŕants šrjanaki." *B,* 119 (1961), 229–41.

ALLAHVĒRDI, AŠUŁ (1820–c1890)

Born in the Armenian village of Livasean in the district of Chahar Mahall, Ishafan, Iran. Learned the art of minstrelsy from *ašuł* Yart'un Ōłli (q.v.). He made the traditional pilgrimage to the monastery of Surb Karapet in Muš to seek divine grace in his art, and as an itinerant *ašuł,* he traveled widely in Iran, Iraq, and the Caucasus. He wrote in both Armenian and in what is now called Azeri Turkish.

Poems

EPNA, 40–74.
THG, 43–44.

Criticism

Eremean, A. *Parskahay noragoyn ašułner.* (Vienna, 1925), 22–74.

ALPʻIAR, YARUTʻIWN (1864–1919)

Pen names: Kʻrizantʻēm, Ṙatamēs.
Born in Smyrna and educated in Constantinople. A journalist and writer of humor. He lived in Europe and Egypt, where he published a periodical titled *Pʻaros.* A considerable part of his writings is still buried in periodicals.

Texts (prose)

Fantʻaziō, ardzak ew hamardzak grakanutʻiwn. (Constantinople, 1913).
Šog-mog. (Constantinople, 1915).
Kʻmaykʻi tzałikner. (Constantinople, 1917).

AMIR ŌŁLI (c1740–1826)

Born to an affluent and well-known family in Burvar, Isfahan, Amir Ōłli at an early age settled in Nor Jułay (New Julfa), then a center for Armenian minstrels. Fascinated by them and learning their art, he followed their path and soon made a name for himself as a popular *ašuł.* He, too, traveled to the monastery of Surb Karapet in Muš, where Armenian minstrels traditionally sought divine grace in their art.

Poems

SHA, 142–53.
THG, 37–38.

Criticism

Eremean, A. *Ašuł Amir Ōłli.* (Venice, 1930).

ANANYAN, VAḤTʻANG (1905–1980)

Pen names: For a list of pen names used by this author see B. Melyan's *Vaḥtʻang Ananyan (matenagitutʻyun).* (Erevan, 1980), 18–19.
Born in Pōłoskʻilisa (a village, renamed Šamaḥyan, and now well within the confines of the city of Dilijan, Armenia) and educated in Dilijan. He fought in the ranks of the Soviet army in World War II, and practiced journalism before and after the war. Hunters, hunting, nature, and wildlife are featured widely in this author's short stories and novelettes. His best writings have been translated into more than two dozen languages.

Collections

Orsordakan patmvatzkʻner. 8 parts. (Erevan, 1947–77).
Patmuatzkʻner orsordakan keankʻē. (Beirut, 1955).
Hayastani kendanakan ašḥarhě. 5 vols. (Erevan, 1961–75).

Erker. 6 vols. (Erevan, 1968–71).
Erker. 4 vols. (Erevan, 1984).

Texts (stories and novels)

Och mi gayl mer handerum. (Erevan, 1930).
Krake ołaki mej. (Erevan, 1930).
Patkerner kolḥozayin dašterits. (Erevan, 1931).
Payk'ar bambaki ankaḥut'yan hamar. (Erevan, 1932).
Dali t'ap'a. (Erevan, 1934).
Ors. (Erevan, 1934).
Manišakaguyn bardzunk'nerum. (Erevan, 1935).
K'arandzavi bnakichnerě. (Erevan, 1936).
Džoḥk'i dṙan gałtnik'ě. (Erevan, 1945).
Marti dašterum. (Erevan, 1946).
Paterazmits heto. (Erevan, 1947).
Sevani ap'in. (Erevan, 1951, 1953, 1961, 1987; Cairo, 1960–61).
Fermayi mardik. Part 1. (Erevan, 1951).
Mankut'yuně leṙnerum. (Erevan, 1954).
Yovazadzori gerinerě. (Beirut, 1955; Erevan, 1956; Cairo, 1959).
Orsordi ordin. (Beirut, 1955).
Leṙnayin katzannerov. (Erevan, 1956).
P'ok'rik mayrer. (Erevan, 1958).
Karmraḥayt. (Erevan, 1960).
Leṙner hayreni. (Erevan, 1963).
Andzrev. (Erevan, 1963).
Komunarě. (Erevan, 1970).
Artzuak'ar. (Paris, 1972).
Ḥutsup sari arjerě. (Paris, 1972).
P'asianner. (Paris, 1972).
Zarmank'. (Paris, 1972).
Anlezu mayrer. (Paris, 1973).
Ełniki dzagě. (Paris, 1973; Erevan, 1979).
Es inchpēs or kam. (Paris, 1973).
Loriknerě. (Paris, 1973).
Ururi boyně. (Paris, 1973).
Arak'si jrern ijneluts yetoy. (Paris, 1973).
P'aḥstakanner. (Paris, 1973).
Hin vrani p'ok'rik bnakichě. (Erevan, 1978).
Ur en tanum katzannerě. (Erevan, 1980).

Other works

Zorašarž. (Erevan, 1931).
Bambaki frontě payk'ari front. (Erevan, 1931).
Bolševikoren lutzel msi problemě. (Erevan, 1931).
Koltntesut'yan šinararut'yan himnakan ōłakě. (Erevan, 1932).
T'e inchpes aṙołjanum ē manr erkragortzi hogebanut'yuně. (Erevan, 1932).
Erkri veratznundě. (Erevan, 1935).

Translations

English

Bobrova, R. *The Steep Paths.* (Moscow, 1958). (Short stories translated from the Russian).

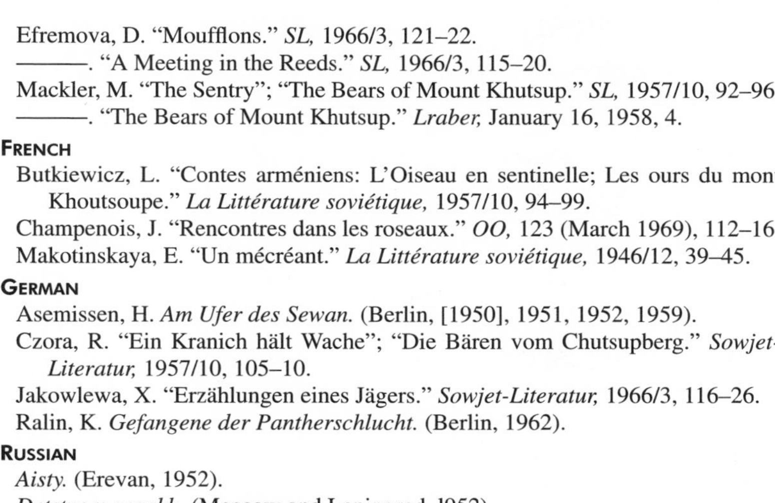

Efremova, D. “Moufflons.” *SL,* 1966/3, 121–22.
———. “A Meeting in the Reeds.” *SL,* 1966/3, 115–20.
Mackler, M. “The Sentry”; “The Bears of Mount Khutsup.” *SL,* 1957/10, 92–96.
———. “The Bears of Mount Khutsup.” *Lraber,* January 16, 1958, 4.

French

Butkiewicz, L. “Contes arméniens: L’Oiseau en sentinelle; Les ours du mont Khoutsoupe.” *La Littérature soviétique,* 1957/10, 94–99.
Champenois, J. “Rencontres dans les roseaux.” *OO,* 123 (March 1969), 112–16.
Makotinskaya, E. “Un mécréant.” *La Littérature soviétique,* 1946/12, 39–45.

German

Asemissen, H. *Am Ufer des Sewan.* (Berlin, [1950], 1951, 1952, 1959).
Czora, R. “Ein Kranich hält Wache”; “Die Bären vom Chutsupberg.” *Sowjet-Literatur,* 1957/10, 105–10.
Jakowlewa, X. “Erzählungen eines Jägers.” *Sowjet-Literatur,* 1966/3, 116–26.
Ralin, K. *Gefangene der Pantherschlucht.* (Berlin, 1962).

Russian

Aisty. (Erevan, 1952).
Detstvo v gorakh. (Moscow and Leningrad, 1952).
Giul’-Nazariants, A. *Rasskazy okhotnika.* (Moscow, 1947).
———. *Na beregu Sevana.* (Moscow and Leningrad, 1950, 1951, 1953; Erevan, 1952; Leningrad, 1953; Novosibirsk, 1953; Moscow, 1953, 1953, 1959, 1965).
———. *Rasskazy okhotnika.* (Moscow, 1951).
———. *Rasskazy.* (Moscow, 1952).
———. *Okhotnich’i rasskazy.* ([Moscow], 1953).
———. *Rasskazy.* (Moscow and Leningrad, 1953).
———. *Plenniki Barsova ushchel’ia.* (Moscow, 1956, 1961; Novosibirsk, 1963).
———. *Po gornym tropam. Rasskazy.* (Moscow, 1956).
———. *Nebylitsy i byli armianskikh gor.* (Moscow, 1957).
———. *U “Volch’ikh vorot”.* (Moscow, 1957).
Mkrtchian, K. *Olenenok. Rasskaz.* (Erevan, 1984).

Spanish

Uribes, V. “Cuentos de caza.” *Literatura Sovietica,* 1966/3, 103–9.

Bibliographies

Melyan, B. *Vaḥtʻang Ananyan (matenagitutʻyun).* (Erevan, 1980).

Criticism

Gardišyan, L. “Vaḥtʻang Ananyan.” *SG,* 1961/6, 88–100.
Gyulnazaryan, Ḥ. *Vaḥtʻang Ananyan.* (Erevan, 1963).
Karapetian, L. *Pevets prirody i cheloveka.* (Erevan, 1987).
Karapetyan, L. “Bnašḥarhi ergichě.” *SG,* 1973/7, 129–33.
———. *Vaḥtʻang Ananyan, kanach ašḥarhě.* (Erevan, 1975).

ANAYIS, (1872–1950)

Pen name: Anayis.

Born Ewpʻimē Awetisean and educated in Constantinople. She spent the latter part of her life in Bulgaria, Rumania, Switzerland and her final years in Paris. She published her literary works in the leading periodicals of the time (*Arewelean Mamul, Biwzandion, Masis,* etc.), but published them in book form only in the 1940s.

Texts

Ułetsoyts hay ałjkan. (Paris, 1940).
Ayg u verjaloys. (Paris, 1942). (Poetry).
Yušers. (Paris, 1949). (Autobiography).

Translations (French anthologies)

APA, 125–26.

Criticism

Chōpanean, A. "Anayis kʻertʻołuhwoyn yobeleanĕ." *ANA,* 15 (1949/1), 39.
Ḥondkarean, A. "Yušers." *HK,* 29 (1951/7), 110–12. (Review).

ANDRĒAS ARTZKETSI (17th–18th c.)

Andrēas is presumed to be a seventeenth- or eighteenth-century author.

Poems

"Awał ankay ōtar yerkir amayi." *MPT,* 53–54.
"Awał andzn im yoyž trtmeal ē." *MPT,* 55.
SUM, 2, 527–41.

ANDRĒASEAN, ANDRANIK (1909–1996)

Born in Hazari, a village near Çemişgezek (Turkey). A writer of short stories, novels, and journalism. During the Armenian massacres of 1915, he found shelter in orphanages in Transcaucasia and Greece, and after a short stay in France (1924–28), he sailed for New York in 1928. In the course of his long career in journalism, he was editor of the organs of the Armenian Democratic League: *Nor ōr* of Fresno (1937–57) and *Paykʻar* (Baikar) of Boston (1957–69). Moved to Los Angeles in 1970.

Collections

Spitak ardarutʻyun. (Erevan, 1960).
Dařnutʻyan bažakĕ. (Erevan, 1984).

Texts

Spitak ardarutʻiwn. (Fresno, 1938). (Stories).
Karmir aspataki ōragrēn. (Boston, 1947). (Stories).
Verjin kayanĕ. (Beirut, 1956). (Stories).
Ḥoher. 3 vols. (Beirut, 1961; Los Angeles, 1976–80). (Reflections on contemporary issues).
Spʻiwřkʻĕ ew hayrenikʻĕ. (Beirut, 1962) (Reflections on the Diaspora and Soviet Armenia).
Haykakan datin nor hangruanĕ. (Beirut, 1967). (On the Armenian Question).
Taragir erkinkʻi tak. (Boston, 1967). (Stories).
Erkar gišerin mējēn. (Beirut, 1974). (Novel).
Anmarmin sērĕ. (Los Angeles, 1983). (Stories).
Gerezman ew yarutʻiwn: vēp Metz Ełeřni šrjanēn. (Los Angeles, 1985). (Novel; second volume in a projected trilogy, titled *Pʻluzum ew veratznund*).
Grakanutʻean ew grołneru masin. Datumner ew gnahatumner. (Los Angeles, 1988). (On literature and writers).

Translations

English

Antreassian, J. *The Cup of Bitterness.* (New York, Ashod Press, 1979).

———. *Death and Resurrection: A Novel of the Armenian Massacres.* (New York, 1988).

Russian anthologies

KNS, 176–86.

PCN, 18–28.

Criticism

Eagupean, G. *Andranik Andreasean: grakan-hasarakakan gortzunēut̔ean 45ame-aki yobelean.* (Los Angeles, 1976).

Danielyan, S. "Andranik Adreasyanĕ ev k̔nnadatakan r̄ealizmi nor verelk̔ĕ." *L,* 1989/7, 57–67.

ANOYŠ, ARMĒN (1907–1958)

Pen name: Armēn Anoyš.

Born Armēn Marašlean in Urfa and educated in Aleppo and Beirut. A survivor of the genocide of 1915, he grew up in a French orphanage in Aleppo, where he eventually settled and taught after a brief sojourn in Damascus.

Texts

Ōrerun het. (Beirut, 1933). (Poetry).

Srteru ergĕ. (Beirut, 1938). (Poetry).

Ayruatz k̔ałak̔i mĕ patmut̔iwnĕ. (Aleppo, 1948). (Novel).

Erkir ḥr̄ovk̔i. (Cairo, 1956). (Poetry).

Et̔ē apri. (Teheran, 1957). (Poetry)

Arean čanaparhov. (Aleppo, 1959). (Autobiographical novel).

ANTONEAN, ARAM, (1875–1951)

Pen names: A. A., Aybayb, Ētlvays, Mara, Mērsētēs.

Born and educated in Constantinople. A novelist and journalist. Witnessed the genocide of 1915 and later depicted his experiences in his literary collection titled *Ayn sew ōrerun.* He also published the texts of Ottoman Turkish telegrams transmitting ciphered orders for carrying out the Armenian massacres and deportations of 1915. Edited a number of literary and satirical periodicals (*Tzałik, Loys, Kar̄ap̔nat, Ḥarazan*) and a daily, *Surhandak,* and assumed the directorship of the A. G. B. U. Nubar Library in Paris from 1928 to 1951. He is also the author of textbooks and historical accounts. Many of his writings published in periodicals are yet to be collected.

Texts

Čšmartut̔iwnĕ, vipak. (Constantinople, 1909). (Story).

Kawē ardzanner. (Constantinople, 1910). (Satire).

Yarut̔iwn Šahrikean. (Constantinople, 1910).

Širvanzadē: kensagrakan nōt̔er ir grakan gortzunēut̔ean yobeleanin ar̄t̔iw. (Constantinople, 1911). (Biography of Širvanzade).

Gandzaran. (Constantinople, 1912). (Textbook).

Patkerazard ĕndardzak patmutʻiwn Palkʻanean paterazmin. 5 vols. (Constantinople, 1912). (A history of the Balkan wars).
Ayn sew ōrerun. (Boston, 1919). (Reminiscences of the Armenian genocide).
Metz očirĕ: haykakan verjin kotoratznerĕ ew Tʻaleatʻ pʻaša; paštōnakan heṙagirner. (Boston, 1921). (The Armenian massacres and Talât Pasha, official telegrams).

AṘAKʻEL DAWRIŽETSI (d. 1670)

A native of Tabriz, Iran. Studied at the feet of Pʻilippos I, Ałbaketsi, Catholicos of Armenia (d. 1655), and took holy orders in Ējmiatzin. Was held in high esteem by his contemporaries as a learned *vardapet.* In his formal capacity as nuncio (*Nuirak*) of the catholicos, he traveled in Greece and the Middle East (Isfahan, Aleppo, Jerusalem, Athens, etc.). Began writing his celebrated history in 1651 at the request of his tutor and mentor, Catholicos Pʻilippos I, Ałbaketsi, and completed it in 1662. He is believed to be the first Armenian historian to have been published in his lifetime. Died in Ējmiatzin.

Texts of his History

Girkʻ patmutʻeants. (Amsterdam, 1669). (First edition).
Patmutʻiwn Aṙakʻel vardapeti Dawrižetswoy. (Vałaršapat, 1884, 1896). (Second edition).
Girkʻ patmutʻeants. (Erevan, 1990). (Critical edition).

Poems

"Tał vasn mahramayi." *A,* 1868/69, 116.
KNŽ, 2, 38–40.
SUM, 2, 256–59.

Translations

Modern Armenian

Antʻosyan, S. "Hatvatzner 'Patmutʻiwn Aṙakʻel vardapeti Dawrižetswoy' grkʻits ašḥarhabar tʻargmanutʻyamb." *EJ,* 1970/5, 36–39.
Aṙakʻelyan, V. *Patmutʻyun.* (Erevan, 1988).

French

Brosset, M. "Livre d'histoires." Brosset, *Col.* I, 267–608.

Russian

Patkanov, K. P. *Dragotsennyie kamni, ikh nazvaniia i svoistva po poniatiiam armian v XVII veke.* (Petersburg, 1873). (Chapter 53 of his history).
Khanlarian, L. *Arakel Davrizhetsi, Kniga istorii.* (Moscow, 1973).

Criticism

"Aṙakʻel vardapet Davrižetsi." *EJ,* 1970/5, 6–7.
Aṙakʻelyan, V. "Aṙakʻel Davrižetsi," *PBH,* 1970/3, 33–45.
Danełyan, L. *Aṙakʻel Davrižetsu erkĕ orpes sefyan Irani XVII dari patmutʻyan skzbnałbyur.* (Erevan, 1978).
Eremean, A. "Aṙakʻel vardapet Dawrižetsi," *S,* 1970, 332–38.
Ḥanlaryan, L. "Aṙakʻel Davrižetsu ałbyurnerits mekĕ." *PBH,* 1984/2, 82–86.
Hatityan, A. "Yałags norogutʻean lusakaṙoyts srboy atʻoṙoyn Ējmiatzni." *EJ,* 1970/5, 22–35.
Kʻiwrtean, Y. "Aṙakʻel vardapet Dawrižetsii gortzatzatz mēk yišatakaranĕ ew yarakits niwtʻer." *S,* 1970, 313–21.

K[ostaneants], K. "S. Lusaworchi ajě. 'I veray Ajoyn ew Ējmiatzni amenayn azgn hayots kapeal kan.' Aṙakʻ. Dawrižetsi." *A,* 1896, 215–22, 265–72.
Leo. "Aṙakʻel vardapet Davrižetsi," *EJ,* 1970/5, 12–14.
Melkʻonyan, E. "Aṙakʻel vardapet Davrižetsu 'Patmutʻyan' erekʻ hratarakutʻyunnerě." *EJ,* 1970/5, 40–44.
Minasean, L. "Aṙakʻel Dawrižetsi ew ir patmagrutʻiwně." *S,* 1970, 328–31.
Mirzoyan, H. "Aṙakʻel Davrižetsu Patmutʻyan aṙajin hratarakutʻyan masin." *BEH,* 1971/2, 190–97.
Müller, Fr. "Geschichte Ar'aqel's von Tebriz." *Wiener Zeitschrift für die Kunde des Morgenlandes,* 2 (1888), 259–62. Translated into Armenian in *HA,* 3 (1889), 139–41.
Ṙuben vardapet. "Aṙakʻel Davrižetsi." *EJ,* 1944/10–12, 36–41.
Sukʻiasyan, K. " 'Andreas Aguletsu vkayabanutʻyuně' ev nra hełinakě." *PBH,* 1976/1, 199–202.

ARAKʻS, (1903–1978)

Pen name: Arakʻs.

Born Arakʻs Avetisyan in Łarakʻilisa (later Kirovakan, now Vanadzor, Armenia) and educated at the Mariamean-Yovnanean school for women in Tiflis. She pursued her higher studies at the State University of Erevan (1930) and the Institute of Communist Journalism in Moscow (1933), and subsequently worked as a journalist for various publications and organizations. Short stories were her favorite form of literary expression, and she wrote many of them for children.

Collections

Erker. (Erevan, 1954).
Erker. (Erevan, 1965).

Texts

Erekʻ patmvatzkʻ. (Tiflis, 1926).
Patmvatzkʻner. (Erevan, 1926).
Ēs jurn ira čamptʻov kgna. (Erevan, 1928).
Alvan. Nargo. (Erevan, 1928).
Zimmi. (Erevan, 1931, 1973).
Komerituhu namaknerě. (Erevan, 1934).
Hrašali savaṙnakě. (Erevan, 1937).
Mankakan patmvatzkʻner. (Erevan, 1937).
Tzałkadzortsi Tʻaṙikě. (Erevan, 1939, 1972.
Lauriki arkatznerě. (Erevan, 1941).
Lipo. (Erevan, 1942).
Taptʻastani aṙyutzě. (Erevan, 1942).
Nṙnakakir ałjikě. (Erevan, 1942).
Amenakrtserě. (Erevan, 1944).
Azatutʻyan hrtʻiṙner. (Erevan, 1945).
Karmir tzałikner. (Erevan, 1945).
Hpart ser. (Erevan, 1947).
Karmir droš. (Erevan, 1949).
Zvartʻ dzayner. (Erevan, 1951).
Bibi. (Erevan, 1956).

Pataniner. (Erevan, 1960).
Arevatzinner. (Erevan, 1977).
Pʻotʻorkits heto. (Erevan, 1980).

Translations

Russian

Shatirian, M. et al. *Druz'ia. Rasskazy.* (Erevan, 1956).
Schastlivye passazhiry. (Erevan, 1952).
Shatirian, M., and Ostrogorskii, V. *Snova zhizn'* (*Rasskazy*). (Erevan, 1952).

ARAKʻSMANYAN, ALEKʻSANDR (1911–1982)

Pen name: Alekʻsandr Arakʻsmanyan.
Born Alekʻsandr Manukyan in Alexandrapol (Leninakan, now Gyumri, Armenia) and educated in Tbilisi. A playwright, novelist, and critic. He taught in various places before settling in Erevan in 1943. From 1968 to 1973, he was editor of the periodical *Ēkran,* for the cinema.

Collections

Manukyan, Ēm. *Hrdeh.* (Erevan, 1984).

Texts

Gyazbel leṙan gałtnikʻě. (Erevan, 1942). (Story).
Čanaparh depi Kamišin. (Erevan, 1945). (Novel).
Čanaparhordutʻyun apaku ašḫarhum. (Erevan, 1951).
Azatutʻyunn akʻsorakan. 2 vols. (Erevan, 1954–55, 1979). (Novel).
Erkunkʻ. (Erevan, 1961). (Plays).
Čampʻaner, čampʻaner. (Erevan, 1964). (Novel).
Pater andundi ezrin. (Erevan, 1974). (Plays).
Hrdeh. (Erevan, 1976). (Novel).
"Pʻšrvatz Afrodite (Vipak-ełelutʻyun)." *SG,* 1981/12, 5–8.
Ostayn. (Erevan, 1982). (Story).

Other works (portraits of actors of the Soviet Armenian theater)

Davitʻ Malyan. (Erevan, 1957).
Arus Asryan. (Erevan, 1964).
Varduhi Varderesyan. (Erevan, 1972).
Arev Bałdasaryan. (Erevan, 1973).
Tʻatroni arahetnerov. (Erevan, 1976).
Eranosyan, H. *Alekʻsandr Arakʻsmanyan* (*Hodvatzneri žołovatzu*). (Erevan, 1981). (Essays on the theater).

Translations (Russian)

Asoiants, T. *Mnogo dorog, mnogo . . . Roman.* (Moscow, 1968).
Giul'-Nazariants, A. *Svoboda v izgnanii. Roman.* (Moscow, 1958).
Mikael Nalbandian. (Erevan, 1952; Moscow, 1953).
Mnatsakanian, M. *Trudnaia liubov'. Povest'.* (Erevan, 1956).
Ogon' tvoei dushi. P'esy. (Erevan, 1981).
Sagratian, A. *Pozhar. Roman.* (Moscow, 1981).

Criticism

Hunanyan, A. "Dramaturgi ułin." *SG,* 1962/7, 142–47.

ARAMUNI, VAHAN (1914–1966)

A poet and novelist born in Kars. In 1934, he completed his studies in Armenian language and literature at the State University of Erevan and began working as a journalist.

Texts

Aṙajin p̕ordzer. (Erevan, 1932). (Poetry).
Kanach erger. (Erevan, 1938). (Poetry).
Erger. (Erevan, 1939). (Poetry).
Baleniner. (Erevan, 1945). (Poetry).
Banastełtzut̕yunner. (Erevan, 1948). (Poetry).
Garnanayin ōrer. (Erevan, 1952). (Poetry).
Im ašḥarhě. (Erevan, 1955). (Poetry).
Hayastann im srtum. (Erevan, 1958).
Garunn im aygum. (Erevan, 1962).
Hasmik, nerir indz. (Erevan, 1965). (Novel).
Leṙnayin amrotsnerum. (Erevan, 1966). (Story).
Šat ban chem uzum. (Erevan, 1968).

ARAMYAN, VALTER (1909–)

A novelist and translator born in Vałaršapat (now Ējmiatzin). He worked at the Matenadaran upon his graduation from the department of Armenian language and literature of the State University of Erevan (1932).

Texts (stories and novels)

Taygayi ōrenk̕ě. (Erevan, 1955).
Patmvatzk̕ner. (Erevan, 1956).
Ṙusa, ordi Argišti. (Erevan, 1957).
Mardě. (Erevan, 1959).
Vałě norits lvatsk̕ kp̕ṙen. (Erevan, 1959).
Mardu serě. (Erevan, 1962).
Ěnkatz tzaṙě. (Erevan, 1964).
Mit̕e bolorě hoł dardzan[?]. (Erevan, 1970).
Ḥełč mardě. (Erevan, 1970).
T̕anak̕aguyn tzałikner. (Erevan, 1973).
Arahetner. (Erevan, 1976).
Veradardz. (Erevan, 1983).
Zarmanali tariner. (Erevan, 1985).
Ḥotorjurtsiner. (Erevan, 1987).

Translations (Russian)

Zakon Taigi. (Moscow, 1957).

Criticism

Bałdasaryan, A. "Grołi azniv grichě." *SG,* 1984/6, 112–14.

AṘANDZAR, (1877–1913)

Pen name: Aṙandzar.

Born Misak̕ Guyumčean in Talas (near Kayseri, Turkey) and educated at the famous Sanasarean school of Karin (Erzurum) and in Zurich (1900–07). On his return, he became the superintendent of the Armenian school in Alexandria (1907), and in Adana from 1908 to his death. Wrote satirical short stories.

Collections

Žołovatzu erkeri. (Tiflis, 1905).

Texts (prose)

Všti tzitzał. (Tiflis, 1905; Erevan, 1947, 1961).
P'rkichner. (Alexandria, 1907). (Play).
M, 1886/3852, 314–15.
Murč, 1901/8, 104–10. 1902/1, 31–48; 3, 106–12; 5, 160–73. 1903/2, 125–49. 1905/2–3, 5–23. 1906/1, 5–13.

Translations (Russian)

"Greben' dlia borody." *KHAN,* 2, 162–75. Also published in *RAN,* 125–37.

Criticism

Hakobjanyan, A. *Aṙandzar.* (Erevan, 1972).
Na. "Aṙandzar, Všti tzitzałĕ, Tiflis, 1905." *Murč,* 1906/1, 146. (Review).
Maḥmuryan, A. "Aṙandzari stełtzagortzut'yunĕ ev ṙealizmi hartser." *L,* 1989/9, 16–24.

ARARATEAN, AŁEK'SANDR (1855–1885)

Born in Šamšulda, a village in Georgia. Educated at the Nersisean School in Tiflis (1868–70). Devoted the best part of his short life to teaching and wrote poetry (some for children), short stories, and plays (including vaudevilles and comedies), mostly about life in Armenian villages.

Texts

Erku t'umb kam Ḥelč siraharner. (Baku, 1877; Tiflis, 1895). (Story).
K'narik mankakan. (Tiflis, 1880). (Poetry).
Giwłakan ḥalfay. (Tiflis, 1883).
P'njik. (Tiflis, 1885). (Poetry).
Himnarkut'iwn gawaṙakan usumnarani. (Tiflis, 1889). (Essays/stories).
Sut čgnawor. (Tiflis, [1891]). (Play).

Criticism

Grich. "Erku t'umb . . . ." *P'ordz,* 1877–78/2, 317–19. (Review).

ARARATEAN, YARUT'IWN (1774–1830s?)

Born in Vałaršapat (now Ējmiatzin), where he lived until 1795. He then moved to Tiflis and joined the Russian army in Transcaucasia (1795–96). Permanently settled in St. Petersburg in 1797. Traveled to Paris in 1817, and after two years in Europe, he went on an extensive tour in the Middle East and North Africa. In 1831, he left St. Petersburg for India and never returned. His autobiography, his only published work, originally written in Armenian, first appeared in Russian.

Texts

Zhizn' Artemiia Araratskago . . . (St. Petersburg, 1813). (Russian).

Translations

Armenian

P[ṙōšeants], P[erč]. *Vałaršapatetsi Yarut'iwn Ararateani keank'ĕ.* (Tiflis, 1892).

ENGLISH

Memoirs of the Life of Artemi, of Wagarschapat, Near Mount Ararat, in Armenia . . . (London, 1822).

Criticism

Chobanyan, P. "Nor nyutʻer Harutʻyun Araratyani kyankʻi u gortzuneutʻyan masin." *PBH,* 1978/1, 81–94.

Danielyan, K. "Harutʻyun Araratyan." *T,* 1958/11, 43–54.

———. "Harutʻyun Araratyani memuarnerĕ." *T,* 1960/3, 47–58.

A[ristakēs] E[piskopos] S[edrakean]. *Yarutʻiwn Ararateani kełtzikʻĕ, parzets A. E. S.* (Baku, 1894).

ARAZI, (1878–1964)

Pen names: Arazi, Fernando.

Born Movses Harutʻyunyan in the village of Šulaver (now Šahumyan, Georgia). Educated in his birthplace, in Tiflis, and in St. Petersburg. Considered to be one of the originators of Soviet Armenian literature. Well-known are his historical novel *Israyel Ōri,* and above all, his short story "Arevĕ" (The sun).

Collections

Erker. Vol. 1. (Erevan, 1937).

Ĕntir erker. (Erevan, 1946).

Ĕntir erker. (Erevan, 1948).

Erkeri žołovatzu. 3 vols. (Erevan, 1955–57).

Texts (short stories and novels)

Patmvatzkʻner. (Tiflis, 1923).

Patmvatzkʻner. (Erevan, 1926).

Traktorĕ. (Erevan, 1926).

Patmvatzkʻner. (Baku, 1928).

Aprołnerĕ. (Erevan, 1929).

Luyserĕ. (Erevan, 1931).

Karmir Karon. (Erevan, 1931).

Pioner Saron. (Erevan, 1931).

Pʻokʻrik šinararnerĕ. (Erevan, 1931).

Ekvornerĕ. (Erevan, 1933).

Ardzak poemner. (Erevan, 1935).

Nor tʻeverov; Lusni šołerov; Jrveži tsolkʻum. (Erevan, 1935).

Heros Karenĕ. (Erevan, 1935, 1957).

Pʻokʻrik herosĕ. (Erevan, 1937).

Anbaḥt orskanner. (Erevan, 1937).

Akunkʻner. (Erevan, 1938).

Mankakan patmvatzkʻner. (Erevan, 1938).

Mišikĕ. (Erevan, 1938).

Ayrvoł horizonĕ. Book 1. (Erevan, 1940).

Ardzak poemner. (Erevan, 1941).

Erekʻ kʻajer. (Erevan, 1942).

Hayrenikʻi kanchĕ. (Erevan, 1942).

Anhałtʻnerĕ. (Erevan, 1944).

Hałtʻakan̦ tziler. (Erevan, 1950).

Mankakan patmvatzkʻner. (Erevan, 1952).
Patmvatzkʻner ev vipakner. (Erevan, 1953).
Israyel Ōri. (Erevan, 1959, 1961 [Books 1 and 2]; Erevan, 1963, 1964).
Arevĕ. (Erevan, 1970, 1981).
Aryunot tzałikner. (Erevan, 1973).
Mankakan patmvatzkʻner. Ardzak poemner. (Erevan, 1984).

Translations

English

WM, 111–20.

French

E (Kara-Sarkissian), 132–33.

Russian

Arsharuni, A. *Povesti i rasskazy.* (Moscow, 1961).
Sukiasian, S. *Izbrannye rasskazy.* (Moscow, 1934; Erevan, 1952).
———. *Tysiachegolovyi. Rasskaz.* (Tiflis, 1935).
Sukiasian, S., et al. *Povesti i rasskazy.* (Erevan, 1960)

Criticism

Hayryan, A. "Arazu drakan kerparnerĕ." *SG,* 1958/3, 121–25.
Sargsyan, Gr. "Proletarakan groł-řevolyutsionerĕ (M. Arazu tznndyan 80-amyaki aṙtʻiv)." *PBH,* 1958/2, 140–50.
Sargsyan, S. "Movses Arazi." *SG,* 1959/7, 123–35.
———. "Ergitzakanĕ Movses Arazu stełtzagortzutʻyan mej." *SG,* 1963/3, 143–45.
———. "Arazin ev hełapʻoḥutʻyunĕ." *SG,* 1978/5, 119–23.
Stepʻanyan, G. *Movses Arazi.* (Erevan, 1954).
Tʻerzipašean, V. "Arazi." *Ani,* 3 (1948–49), 9–10.
———. *Arazi.* (Erevan, 1956). (Russian).

ARŁUTʻEAN, YOVSĒPʻ (1743–1801)

Born in Sanahin, a village in northern Armenia, to a family that traced its descent from the Zakʻarean princely family. Attended the Ējmiatzin seminary, took holy orders, and was consecrated bishop in 1769, at the early age of twenty-six. Served as the primate of the Armenians of Russia (1773) and of the Armenians of Crimea (1780). Played an instrumental role in founding the towns of Nor Naḥijewan (by Armenians from the Crimea) and Grigoriopolis (by Armenians from Moldova and Bessarabia). Initiated and actively pursued political plans to liberate Armenia from Ottoman and Persian yoke with Russian assistance and to revive Armenian statehood under Russian protection. He was elected Catholicos of Armenia in 1800, but died in Tiflis before assuming office.

Texts

Ōrinak handisawor tzanutsman ew ołboy . . . asatseal srbakron teaṙn Yovsepʻay arkʻepiskoposē i mayrakʻałakʻn Ṙōman . . . (Madras, 1790, 1792).
Tetrak hamaṙōt anuaneal duṙn ołormutʻean. (Nor Naḥijewan, 1792). (On the founding of the city of Grigoriopolis).
Kʻaroz. (Nor Naḥijewan, 1795).
Ḥōskʻ asatseal i Yovsepʻay psakazgeats s. arkʻepiskoposē hiwsisayin kołmans ełeal amenayn azgis hayots . . . (Astrakhan, 1796).

Yovsēpʻ katʻołikos Arłutʻean, published in *Diwan hayots patmutʻean,* Vol. 9, edited by Giwt Ałaneants, (Tiflis, 1911).

Criticism

Gevorgyan, P. "Hovsepʻ arkʻepiskopos Arłutʻyaně ev hay tpagrutʻyan gortzě Ṙusastanum 18-rd darum." *EJ,* 1954/9, 45–55; 11, 45–49; 12, 39–45.

Hatityan, A. "Hay azatagrakan šaržumnerě 1780–1800 tʻvakannerin ev Hovsepʻ arkʻeps. Arłutʻyani kyankʻn u gortzuneutʻyuně." *EJ,* 1978/8–9, 72–81.

Lēō. *Yovsēpʻ katʻołikos Arłutʻean,* (Tiflis, 1902).

Mnatsakanyan, As. "18-rd darum grvatz hay-ṙusakan dašnagrayin erku naḥagtzeri gnahatman hartsi šurjě." *BM,* 1958/4, 139–60.

ARMĒN, ENOVKʻ (1883–1968)

Born in Ēfkʻērē (Efkere), a village near Kayseri, Turkey, and educated at the Kedronkan Armenian school and Robert College of Constantinople. A journalist and writer. Edited a number of periodicals and taught for a brief period in Constantinople. From 1931 until his death he lived in Marseilles.

Texts

Kině. (Constantinople, 1906). (Stories).

Tʻrkʻahay grakanutʻiwně mamuli azatutʻean tʻuakanin. (Constantinople, 1909). (About Western Armenian literature in 1908).

ARMEN, MKRTICH (1906–1972)

Pen name: Mkrtich Armen.

Born Mkrtich Harutʻyunyan (also Alikʻyan) in Alexandrapol (later Leninakan and now Gyumri, Armenia). Educated in his birthplace. A graduate of the State Institute of Cinematography in Moscow. He was one of the founders of the short-lived Union of Writers in Leninakan, known as 'Hoktember.' Driven to exile in Siberia with numerous Armenian writers and intellectuals, Armen was one of the few who survived the ordeal and lived long enough to relate his harrowing experiences in his later works.

Collections

Erker. 5 vols. (Erevan, 1966–73).

Texts

Širkanal. (Leninakan, 1925). (Poetry).

Erkatʻavorvoł erkri erger. (Erevan, 1927). (Poetry).

Zubeida. (Erevan, 1928). (Story).

Patmvatzkʻner. (Erevan, 1928). (Stories).

Patmvatzkʻner. Books 1 and 2. (Erevan, 1929). (Stories).

Kʻałakʻě bluri vra. (Erevan, 1930). (Novel).

Gazayin eraz. (Erevan, 1931). (Poem).

Erevan. (Moscow, 1931).

Kino. (Erevan, 1932). (Story).

Skaut No. 89. (Erevan, 1933, 1937). (Novel).

Gagatʻneri ergě. (Erevan, 1933). (Stories and essays).

Hianali sermer. (Erevan, 1934). (Story).

Aṙajin patmvatzkʻner. (Erevan, 1934). (Stories).

Aṙajin patkomner. (Erevan, 1935). (Novel; *Patkom = patani komunar*).

Hełnar ałbyur. (Erevan, 1935, 1936, 1955, 1961; Cairo, 1948). (Novel).
Meržvatzneri handipumĕ. (Erevan, 1936). (Prose).
Uraḥ ōr. (Erevan, 1936). (Story).
Erekʻ siravep. (Erevan, 1936). (Stories).
Errord militsionerĕ. (Erevan, 1937). (Story).
Yasva. (Erevan, 1953). (Novelette).
Karmir ev kapuyt pʻołkapner. (Erevan, 1954). (Novel).
Patmvatzkʻner. (Erevan, 1957). (Stories).
Guynzguyn tʻagavorutʻyun. (Erevan, 1959). (Story).
Oske hndzan. (Erevan, 1959). (Stories).
Vardavan. (Erevan, 1962). (Stories).
Patviretsin handznel dzez. (Erevan, 1964). (Stories).
Indz pʻntroł ałjikĕ. (Erevan, 1965). (Stories).
Žirayr Glents. (Erevan, 1967). (Novel).

Translations

ENGLISH

Botting, T. "A Song about my Town." *SL,* 1966/3, 108–14.
Manning, E. "Sunshine on the Threshold." *SL,* 1961/11, 94–98.

ENGLISH ANTHOLOGIES

WM, 155–57.

FRENCH ANTHOLOGIES

Yéghiaian, A. *E,* 46–49.

GERMAN

Czora, R. "Sonne an der Schwelle." *Sowjetliteratur,* 1961/11, 104–8.

RUSSIAN

Atsvor. (Tiflis, 1935).
Dimitrieva, A. *Iasva. Povest'.* (Moscow, 1954).
Dve povesti. (Erevan, 1956).
Folian, P. *Skaut No. 89. Povest'.* (Tiflis, 1935).
Khachaturian, N. *Rodnik Egnar.* (Erevan, 1984).
Martirosian, E. *Zubeida.* (Moscow and Leningrad, 1930).
Mnatsakanian, P. *Rodnik Egnar.* (Moscow, 1936).
Solntse u poroga. Povesti i rasskazy. (Moscow, 1959).

Criticism

Aharonean, V. "Hełnar ałbiwr." *HK,* 15 (1936–37/4), 169–73.
Ałababyan, S. "Mkrtich Armen." *SG,* 1960/9, 113–27.
Melkʻonyan, M. *Mkrtich Armen.* (Erevan, 1970).
———. *Mkrtich Armen (Kyankʻn u stełtzagortzutʻyunĕ).* (Erevan, 1981).
Ter-Sarkisian, L. "Tri 'Rodnika Egnar'." *BEH,* 1984/1, 243–51.
Zakʻaryan, A. "Mkrtich Armeni 'Hełnar ałbyur' vipaki problematikan." *T,* 1976/9, 23–30.

ARPʻIAREAN, ARPʻIAR (1851–1908)

Pen names: Haykak, Hracheay, Hrazdan, Hrpet, Skeptik.
Born aboard a ship (near Samsun, Turkey) bound for Constantinople to a family originally from Apucheḥ, a village near Akn (Eğin, now Kemaliye, Turkey).

Received elementary education in Constantinople and pursued studies at the Murat Rapʻayēlean school in Venice. On his return to the Ottoman capital in 1870, he found employment in the Armenian Patriarchate and private business. Contributed to *Mšak* of Tiflis for almost three decades, promoting closer relations between the Eastern and Western Armenians. Was instrumental in launching in 1884 of three important periodicals: *Arewelkʻ, Masis,* and *Hayrenikʻ*. That same year, he visited Tiflis and Eastern Armenia to cover for *Arewelkʻ* the election of a new catholicos of Armenia in Ējmiatzin. By now he was known not only as a bright writer and journalist, but also as the leader of a new breed of writers, the Realists. Following a brief incarceration for political activities, like so many of his colleagues, he fled the Ottoman capital, which had been stained with Armenian blood during the Armenian massacres of the mid-1890s, and settled in London in 1896. He then lived in Paris, Venice, and, eventually, Cairo, where a third attempt on his life proved fatal.

Collections

Patmuatzkʻner u vipakner. (Paris, 1931).
Stepʻanyan, G. *Ĕntir erker.* (Erevan, 1951).
Galayčean, A. *Ambołjakan erker.* (Jerusalem, 1972). (Only the first volume has been published).
Sahakyan, S. *Erker.* (Erevan, 1987).

Texts

Noravēpkʻ. (Constantinople, 1885). (Stories).
Apušě. (Conseantinople, 1886). (Story).
Simonakan tērtērě. (Constantinople, 1889). (Story).
Karmir žamuts. (Varna, 1909; Constantinople, n.d., 1909; Cairo, 1950; Venice, 1956; Beirut, 1956, 1966). (Novelette).
Datapartealě ew Erazi mě gině. (Cairo, 1928). (Stories).
Ḥndamolik ałjikě. (Constantinople, 1928). (Story).
Katak mě. (Cairo, 1929). (Story).
Patmutʻiwn ŽTʻ daru Turkʻioy hayots grakanutʻean. (Cairo, 1943). (History of nineteenth-century Western Armenian literature).

Works in periodicals

M, 1884/3729, 5–11. "Raffi ew hay vipasanutʻiwně." 1884/3734, 129–31; 3736, 191–95; 3737, 215–17; 3739, 263–64. 1884/3747, 463–74. 1889/3928, 69–84; 3930, 112–19; 3931, 129–35; 3926, 45–48; 3931, 129–35. 1890/3932, 149–51; 3935, 191–98; 3938, 239–42; 3940, 276–77; 3938, 244–48; 3939, 256–64; 3940, 278–80; 3943, 321–24; 3945, 352–53; 3944, 343–44; 3945, 356–64; 3947, 389–96.
Širak, 1905/1, 20–35; 3, 191–94; 4, 293–99; 5, 355–72; 7, 17–30; 8, 123–42; 9, 161–80; 10–11, 339–55. 1906/1, 1–11, 40–52, 60–64; 2, 92–97, 101–7, 108–22; 3, 129–46, 161–70, 181–85; 4, 193–209, 231–35, 250–56; 5, 257–66, 274–89, 310–20. 1907/6, 338–43, 349–60; 7, 380–85; 8, 462–65, 473–88; 9, 506–9, 514–25.

Translations

English

Pilibosian, H. "For Pleasure." *Armenian Mirror-Spectator,* October, 12 and 26, 1963.

Russian

Ter-Akopian, Kh. "Karmir zhamuts (Krasnaia lepta)." *Rus. Mysl'* (Moscow), 1905/8, 71–120.

Criticism

Bžikean, Ł. "Arpʻiar: 1850–1908." *B,* 69 (1911), 89–93, 146–54.
Chōpanean, A. "Arpʻiar Arpʻiarean." *ANA,* 3 (1901), 33–55.
Ḥachikyan, G. "Arpʻiar Arpʻiaryanĕ kʻnnadatakan ṙealizmi tesaban." *L,* 1988/8, 33–34.
Kʻasim, "Tʻłtʻaktsutʻiwn, azgayin nišer." *AM,* 1889, 273–78.
Kiwrčean, M. "Arpʻiar Arpʻiarean." *HK,* 10 (1931–32/6), 110–27; 7, 105–19.
Mnatsakanyan, L. "Arpʻiar Arpʻiaryanĕ kʻnnadat." *BEH,* 1981/2, 163–72.
Muradyan, L. "Raffi ev Arpʻiar Arpʻiaryan." *PBH,* 1986/3, 57–66.
———. "Arpʻiar Arpʻiaryanĕ hraparakaḥos." *PBH,* 1989/1, 79–94.
———. "Arpʻiar Arpʻiaryanĕ kʻnnadat ev grakanutʻyan patmaban." *L,* 1990/2, 29–41.
Šahpaz, S. *Arpʻiar Arpʻiarean.* (Beirut, 1987 [cover says 1988]). (Makes use of some of Arpʻiarean's papers).
Stepʻanyan, G. "Arpʻiar Arpʻiaryani grakanagitakan hayatskʻnerĕ." *T,* 1948/12, 39–61.
———. *Arpʻiar Arpʻiaryan.* (Erevan, 1955).
Tayean, Ł. "Arpʻiar Arpʻiarean." *B,* 67 (1909), 228–37.
Vratsean, S. "Arpʻiar Arpʻiarean." *HK,* 9 (1930–31/11), 79–95.
Yušardzan ołbatseal Arpʻiar Arpʻiareani. (Constantinople, 1911).
Zōhrap, G. "Tzanōtʻ dēmkʻer–Arpʻiar Arpʻiarean." *M,* 1892/3969, 226–27.

ARŠAKEAN, HERANOYŠ (1887–1905)

Born in Constantinople. Attended local Armenian schools but was unable to complete her studies because of her rapidly failing health. Died of consumption. Only a small part (twenty-four poems) of her literary output has been published posthumously.

Poetry

Nazareants, H. *Heranoyš Aršakean, ir keankʻĕ ew banastełtzutʻiwnnerĕ.* (Constantinople, 1910).
Yakobean, S. *Heranoyš Aršakean, keankʻn u banastełtzutʻiwnnerĕ.* (Vienna, 1922).
Hoginerun artsunkʻĕ. (Erevan, 1956).

Translations

Kelikian, H. "On the Verge of Death." *Ararat,* Fall, 1962, 41–42.

Criticism

Gabrielyan, V. "Heranuš Aršakyan." *PBH,* 1972/1, 115–26.

ARSĒN DPIR KOSTANDNUPŌLSETSI (18th c.)

Arsēn is known to have been a student of Patriarch Yakob Nalean (c1706–64) of Constantinople. His only known work is an encyclopedic compilation.

Text

Girkʻ sahmanats yognadimi irołutʻeants. (Constantinople, 1749).

ASAPOV, (17th c.)

No biographical details are available for this poet, who is presumed to have lived in Nor Jułay (New Julfa), Isfahan, in the seventeenth century.

Texts

"Ov loyseram dask' k'ahanayits lusatesil mankants pantzali . . ." *HA,* 45 (1931), 528–29. Also published in *HA,* 49 (1935), 309–10.

SUM, 2, 297–305.

Criticism

Akinean, N. "Asapov, 17. daru (1670) tałasats mě." *HA,* 45 (1931), 527–31.

ASAR SEBASTATSI (16th–17th c.)

It is thought that the author was a sixteenth- or seventeenth-century physician from Sivas.

Texts

"Yałags manḫulia hiwandut'ean." *B,* 39 (1881), 36–37. Also published in *PHG,* 506–07. (Medical text).

Karapetyan, D. *Girk' bžškakan arhesti (XVI–XVII dd.).* (Erevan, 1993).

Criticism

Tzovakan, N. "Asar Sebastatsi." *S,* 1963, 116–18.

ASATUR, ZAPĒL (1863–1934)

Pen names: Anahit, Ōriord Alis, Sipil (i.e., Sibyl).

Born Zapēl Ḫančean in Constantinople and educated in local French and Armenian schools. One of the earliest Armenian women to write poetry in the modern period. Began writing verse and prose at an early age. Played a particularly significant role in founding the "Azganuēr hayuheats ěnkerut'iwn" (1879–95, 1908–15), a society whose primary task was to set up girls schools in the Armenian provinces. After her first husband's death, she was married to Hrant Asatur (1862–1928) and collaborated with him on highly acclaimed textbooks of Armenian language and literature.

Collections

K'ert'vatzner. (Erevan, 1935).

Ambołjakan gortzě K'ert'uatzner, Vol. 1, (Istanbul, 1939). (Cover reads *Ambołjakan hawak'atzoy K'ert'uatzner,* 1940).

Banastełtzut'iwnner. (Venice, 1955).

Erker. (Erevan, 1965).

Texts

Ałjkan mě sirtě. (Constantinople, 1891). (Novel).

Tsolk'er. (Constantinople, 1902). (Poetry).

Knoj hoginer. (Constantinople, 1905). (Stories).

Magnis. (Constantinople, 1909). (Poetry; written with Alp'aslan).

Harsě. (Boston, 1938). (Play).

Other works

Gortznakan k'erakanut'iwn ardi ašḫarhabari. 3 vols. (Constantinople, 1877, 1899, 1902).

Gortznakan dasěnťatsk' franserēnē hay ťargmanuťean. First year. (Constantinople, 1902).

Asatur Z., and Asatur, H. *Ťangaran hatěntir hatuatzneru, ardzak ew otanawor.* (Constantinople, 1908, 1911).

Translations

ENGLISH ANTHOLOGIES

AP, 195–200.

FRENCH

"La Vierge du couvent," "La Malade," "Sur le point de passer." *La Patrie,* 1909/24, 172–74.

FRENCH ANTHOLOGIES

APA, 93–96.

GERMAN ANTHOLOGIES

ALG, 126–27.

ITALIAN ANTHOLOGIES

LPAM, 175–87.

RUSSIAN ANTHOLOGIES

BPA, 447–50.

VAM, 178–80.

SPANISH ANTHOLOGIES

APAS, 159–62.

Criticism

Aharonean, A. "Tikin Sipil." *Murč,* 1905/1, 110–18.

Azatean, Ť. *Žamanakakits dēmk'er, 1: Zapēl ew Hrant Asatur.* (Constantinople, 1937).

Čanašean, M. "Sipil." *B,* 100 (1942), 66–72.

Čiwhērean, E. "Žamanakakits ťrk'ahay banastełtzner, Sipil." *AM,* 1906, 196–200.

Galstyan, L. "Sipili poezian." *T,* 1964/3, 41–48.

Hyusyan, M. "Menagruťyun Sipili masin." *SG,* 1981/3, 140–42.

K'ēšišean, H. "Tesaktsuťiwn mě Sipili het." *AM,* 1905, 281–82.

Mařk', H. *Zapēl (Sipil) Asatur.* (Constantinople, 1949).

Minasyan, A. *Sipil–Zapel Asatur.* (Erevan, 1980).

Step'anean, K. " 'Tsolk'er' ew ir k'nnadatnerě." *AM,* 1902, 776–82.

Yaruťiwnean, A. "Grakan dimastuerner, Sipil." *M,* 1899/16–17, 505–7.

———. "Nor girk'er." *AM,* 1902, 566–71. (On *Tsolk'er).*

Zardarean, Ṙ. "Ťrk'ahay banastełtzuťiwně, *Tsolk'er'.*" *AM,* 1902, 691–98.

Zōhrap, G. "Tzanōť dēmk'er–Sipil." *M,* 3966 (1892), 179–80.

ASATUREAN, YAKOB (1903–)

Pen name: Mažaktsi.

A native of Çomaklı, a village near Kayseri in Turkey. Educated in the local Ḥrimean elementary school. Writer, singer, and musicologist. Survived the Armenian massacres and deportations of 1915, and fled the Syrian desert, finding shelter in the orphanage set up by the Armenian General Benevolent Union in Jerusalem. He permanently settled in New York in 1920.

Texts

Andastan: kʻertʻuatzner. Antasdan, Poems in Armenian. (New York, 1946).
Komitas vardapet ew hay ergě. (New York and Beirut, 1962). (Komitas and the Armenian song, a study).
Yovakimi tʻoṙnerě. The Grandchildren of Joachim: Short Stories in Armenian. (Beirut, 1965; Erevan, 1974).
Kʻari ew hoɫi patmutʻiwn. Stories of Stone and Earth. (New York and Beirut, 1969). (Impressions of a visit to Soviet Armenia).
Paroyr Sewaki het. (Beirut, 1971).
Hariwrameak: handipumner, yušer. (New York and Beirut, 1978). (Reflections on the Komitas centennary in Erevan).
To, lač tnawer. Thou, Homeless Lad. (New York, 1986).

ASLANEAN, LUIZA (1906–c1945)

Pen name: Las.

Born in Tabriz. Studied in her birthplace, Tiflis, and later in Paris, after moving to France with her husband in 1923. Was active in Armenian communal life in Paris and, later, in the French Resistance. In July, 1944, she and her husband were arrested by the Nazis, taken to a concentration camp, and never seen again. Aslanean's literary output consists of a novel and a few short stories. A considerable number of her manuscripts as well as her diaries were confiscated by the Nazis.

Texts

Hartsakani uɫinerov. 2 vols. (Paris, 1936; Erevan, 1959).
Gtzits durs. (Beirut, 1956).

Translations (Russian)

"Boloto." *PCN,* 76–89. Also published in *KNS,* 98–112.

Criticism

Chōpanean, A. "Erekʻ hay herosakan nahatakner (Geɫam Atʻmačean, Misakʻ Manušean, Luiza Aslanean)." *ANA,* 12/1 (1946), 1–9.
Hatityan, G. "Luiza Aslanyani patmvatzkʻnerě." *SG,* 1980/12, 137–45.
Vahē-Vahean. "Las–Luiza Aslanean." *Ani,* 5 (1952/6–7), 373–79.

ASLANYAN, MKRTICH (1906–)

Born in the village of Kopʻ near Bulanık, northwest of Van. A novelist and short story writer. Emigrated to Eastern Armenia in 1914 and settled in Tiflis thereafter. Twice headed the Armenian radio program in Tbilisi (1935–41, 1956–72).

Texts (novels and short stories)

Pʻotʻorik. (Erevan, 1947).
Kʻoɫarkvatz hetkʻerov. (Erevan, 1950).
Anerevuytʻ čakat. (Erevan, 1954).
Ašḥen Satʻyan. (Tbilisi, 1955).
Erjankutʻyan arahetov. 2 vols. (Tbilisi, 1960–61).
Erb sksvum ē dznhalě. (Erevan, 1963).
Anhangist bnavorutʻyunner. (Erevan, 1967).
Havasarum chors anhaytov. (Tbilisi, 1973).

Kesgišerits ants. (Tbilisi, 1977).
Čakatagrer u čampʻaner. (Tbilisi, 1979).

AŠOT, GUSAN (1907–)

Pen name: Gusan Ašot.

Born Ašot Dadalyan in Goris, Armenia. After receiving his elementary education in Baku, he briefly returned to his native Zangezur in the late 1920s and permanently settled in Erevan. Continued the tradition of Armenian minstrelsy in Soviet Armenia.

Texts (poetry)

Ašułakan erger. (Erevan, 1946).
Gusani serě. (Erevan, 1955, 1958 [with musical notation]).
Siro krakner. (Erevan, 1971).
Srti nvagner. (Erevan, 1979).
Tzovastłiks. (Erevan, 1982).
Leřnerě kanchum en. (Erevan, 1988).

ASTUATZATUR, (16th c.?)

Author known for his only published poem, "Ayn ařajin žamanakin."

Poetry

"Ayn ařajin žamanakin," *B,* 33 (1875), 216–17. Also published in *KNZ,* 2, 41–45; 3, 63–66; *SUM,* 1, 71–78.

Translations (French)

Astvatzatour. "Louange du verger." *LPA,* 128–30.

ATʻMAČEAN, MAŘI (c1909–)

Born in Bafra, Turkey. Sister of A. Sema (q.v.). She grew up in orphanages, following her father's murder during the Armenian massacres and deportations of 1915. In 1926 she settled in France permanently. Her first poems appeared in A. Sema's literary journals *Jankʻ* and *Mšakoytʻ.*

Texts (poetry)

Tēgrēšēntō. (Paris, 1939). (Play).
Gołgotʻayi šušanner: kʻertʻuatzner. (Paris, 1948).
Astełakʻał: kʻertʻuatzner. (Paris, 1951).
Yawitenakan ułiner: kʻertʻuatzner, 1950–56. (Paris, 1956).
Gałtʻašharhi erger: kʻertʻuatzner, 1956–61. (Paris, 1961).
Oski gełōn: kʻertʻuatzner, 1960–67. (Paris, 1967).
Hrełen aštarak. (Erevan, 1970). (Selections from previous collections).
Verjaloysēn ařaj: kʻertʻuatzner, 1967–74. (Paris and Beirut, 1974).
Yaweržakan ułinerov: tzałkakʻał. (Paris and Beirut, 1974).

Criticism

Ełivard. "Fransahay banastełtzuhi Maři Atʻmačean." *S,* 1974, 372–75.
Tayean, A. *Kʻertʻołuhi Maři Atʻmačeani 35ameay grakan berkʻin ařjew.* (Beirut, 1975).
Vahē-Vahean. " 'Astełakʻał' Maři Atʻmačeani." *Ani,* 5 (1952/2), 111–12.

ATRPET, (1860–1937)

Pen name: Atrpet.

Born Sargis Mubayeajean in Kars. A prolific and multifarious writer. Having been educated in Kars and Constantinople, he lived mostly in Transcaucasia, wandering from one city to another (Alexandrapol, Tiflis, Akhalkalak, Baku, etc.), and in Tabriz. In the mid-1890s he was incarcerated by the Russian government for his political activities in the ranks of the Hnchakean party. Toured Europe in 1905–06, and spent the rest of his life in Alexandrapol (Leninakan, now Gyumri, Armenia). Many of his works are still scattered in Armenian periodicals.

Collections

Erkeri žołovatzu. 10 vols. (Tabriz, 1904–1911). (Vol. 9, Alexandrapol, 1911; vol. 10, Tiflis, 1911).

Erker. (Erevan, 1964).

Texts

Ḥew Karapet. (Tiflis, 1889). (Novel).

Almast. (Tiflis, 1890; Moscow, 1891; Tabriz, 1905). (Novel).

Šušan. (St. Petersburg, 1890). (Play).

Sarraf. (Tiflis, 1893). (Drama).

Šḥnots. (Nor Naḥijewan, 1898). (Short novel).

K'oṙ-Ełik. (Tiflis, 1898). (Novel).

Bersai Aṙak'ēlě. (Nor Naḥijewan, 1899). (Short novel).

T'ulumbajiner. (Nor Naḥijewan, 1899). (Story).

Žaṙangner. (Nor Naḥijewan, 1899). (Story).

Ōrinakan žaṙang. (Tabriz, 1903).

Dimakner. (Tabriz, 1904).

Jawahir. (Tabriz, 1904). (Novel).

Vipakner. (Tabriz, 1904). (Stories).

Čarahat. (Tabriz, 1905).

Kareli ē sirel [?]. (Tabriz, 1905).

Vičak. (Tabriz, 1905).

Čiwałě. (Tiflis, 1911).

Irani patuhasnerě. (Tiflis, 1911).

Ltzkannern ew vampirě, aṙak. (Alexandrapol, 1912). (Prose).

Agṙawneri t'asibě. (Alexandrapol, 1912). (Story).

Višapamayr. (Alexandrapol, 1912). (Story).

Tžvžik. (Erevan, 1938; Aleppo, 1945; Erevan, 1948, 1964, 1969, 1975).

Other works

Ḥalifat'. (Nor Naḥijewan, 1899).

Imamat'. (Alexandrapol, 1906).

Hołatirut'iwně Kovkasum. (Alexandrapol, 1906).

Hay t'agaworneri ew k'ałak'neri dramnerě naḥnakan žamanaknerits minchew Trdat. (Tiflis, 1913).

Čoroḥi awazaně. (Vienna, 1929)

Translations (Russian)

"Zharekha iz oserd'ia." *KHAN,* 1, 6–66. Also published in *RAN,* 53–58.

Criticism

Eremean, S. "Atrpet." *B,* 61 (1903), 251–56.

M. "Atrpet, Hołatirut'iwně Kovkasum, Alek'sandrapol, 1906." *Murč,* 1906/7, 108.

Mar., Yar. "Atrpet, K'oṙ Ełik, Tiflis, 1898; Šḥnots, N. Naḥijewan, 1898; Žaṙangner, N. Naḥijewan, 1899; Bersayi Aṙak'ēlĕ, N. Naḥijewan 1899; T'ulumbajiner, N. Nahijewan, 1899." *Murč,* 1900/1, 83–90.
S. T'. "Atrpetean, S. *Šušan,* Peterburg [1890]." *Murč,* 1893/4, 622–29.
T. H. "Atrpet, Erkeri žołovatzu, hator 1, T'awriz, 1904." *Murč,* 1904/6, 147–51.

AVAGYAN, ABIG (1919–1983)

Born in Teheran, Iran. A novelist. Educated in Armenian, Persian, and French schools, and the American College in his native city. Served as a pilot in the Iranian Air Force from 1939 to 1941. Became a permanent resident of Soviet Armenia in 1946, and subsequently attended special courses in literature in Moscow.

Texts (short stories and novels)

Vałĕ. (Erevan, 1951).
Šikatsatz hoł. (Erevan, 1955).
Nazeli Dalaryan. (Erevan, 1959).
Patmvatzk'ner. (Erevan, 1962).
Bend gyułi verjin mardĕ. (Erevan, 1963).
Patmvatzk'ner. (Erevan, 1965).
Patmvatzk'ner. (Erevan, 1966).
Haravayin tend. (Erevan, 1971).
Ełel ē, chi ełel. (Erevan, 1973).
Harvatz. (Erevan, 1979).
Mardĕ anapatum. (Erevan, 1981).

Translations

English
WM, 221–33.

French
"Notre quartier pierreux." *OO,* 123 (March 1969), 134–37.

Russian
Shakhatuni, A., and Adamian, N. *Raskalennaia zemlia.* (Erevan, 1956).
Shakhre-shad, veselyi gorod. Rasskazy. (Moscow, 1968).

AYVAZEAN, EŁIŠĒ (1890–1993)

Born in "Araratean dašt" (the plain of Ararat, in Eastern Armenia). Educated at the Nersisean school in Tiflis (1907–10) and at the Gēorgean seminary in Ējmiatzin (1912–14). Attended courses at the Sorbonne. He lived alternately in Paris and Istanbul. Wrote prose and poetry.

Texts

Patmuatzk'ner ew ardzak ējer. (Istanbul, 1960). (Stories).
Anezratsum. (Istanbul, 1974). (Verse).

AYVAZYAN, BAGRAT (1862–1934)

Peṅ name: Ṙašid.
Born in Tiflis. Graduated from the Nersisean school in 1882 and taught in Armenian schools in Transcaucasia (1882–97). He subsequently held administrative

positions as an archivist and secretary within the Armenian Church and community in Georgia, while producing his short stories, novelettes, and historical novels. He died in Tiflis.

Texts (stories and novels)

Muṫ ḩoršerits: patker nerkay keankʻits. (Tiflis, 1888).
Ašot Erkaṫ: patmakan vēp. 2 parts. (Tiflis, 1893–94, 1900; 1903; Cairo, 1936; Beirut, 1940; Teheran, 1959; Erevan, 1964).
Tanjankʻi bovits: vēp irakan keankʻits. (Tiflis, 1895).
Hiwsisi artziwě: patmakan vēp. (Tiflis, 1901).
Sew yałṫanak: vēpik. (Tiflis, 1903).
Anin tzaḩuetsaw. (Paris, 1905; Tiflis, 1910; Beirut, 1960, 1972; Erevan, 1964). (Also widely known as *Anii kortzanumě*).
Sasuně ayrwum ē. (Tiflis, 1913).

AYVAZYAN, SUREN (1915–1981)

Ḩndzoresk, a village in the region of Goris, Armenia, is the birthplace of this novelist. Having studied pedagogy in Goris, Ayvazyan specialized in Armenian language and literature at the State University of Baku (1942), fought in the ranks of the Red Army in World War II, and as a journalist worked in the Armenian daily *Komunist* of Baku (1945–52). Settled in Erevan permanently in 1953.

Texts (stories and novels)

Anavart gorgě. (Baku, 1947).
Ḩoradzortsikʻ. (Baku, 1951).
Leṙntsiner. (Erevan, 1955).
Ḩiłčě. (Erevan, 1957).
Tur dzeṙkʻd, kyankʻ. 2 parts. (Erevan, 1959, 1961, 1962).
Anšej krakneri kłzin. (Erevan, 1960).
Koltntesuṫyan naḩagahě. (Erevan, 1960).
Hovivě. (Erevan, 1963).
Bari aṙavot. (Erevan, 1964).
Jrałatsi čanaparhin. (Erevan, 1964).
Čakatagirn hayots. (Erevan, 1967).
Bardzunkʻi vra. (Erevan, 1969).
Ka ev hetmahu kyankʻ. (Erevan, 1971).
Garuns dzyuneri tak. (Erevan, 1972).
Aṙavot luso. (Erevan, 1976).
Ḩndzoresk. (Erevan, 1982).
Asur, hey Asur. (Erevan, 1985).

Translations

English

WM, 102–10.

Russian

Dolukhanian, V. *Predvestie zari: Roman o [Kh. Aboviane].* (Moscow, 1983).
Gevorkian, M. *Zangezurskie rasskazy.* (Erevan, 1957).
Nersesian, G. *Dobroe utro. Rasskazy.* (Moscow, 1969).

Tadeosian, A. *Protiani ruku, zhizn'*. (Erevan, 1963).
Sud'ba armianskaia. (Erevan, 1980).

Criticism

Amirḥanyan, H. "Ayo, ka ev hetmahu kyank‘." *SG,* 1971/10, 127–30.
Grigoryan, L. "Gyułĕ Suren Ayvazyani stełtzagortzut‘yunnerum." *SG,* 1986/1, 137–40.
Łazanjyan, V. "Čakatagirn hayots." *SG,* 1967/9, 108–13.

AZARIA JUŁAYETSI (16th c.?)

Possibly a sixteenth-century author. He is often confused or identified with Azaria I, Jułayetsi, Catholicos of Sis (1534–1601).

Poetry

"Ararich hayr erknayin." *KNZ,* 4, 31–32. Also published in *PHA,* 1, 42–43.
"K‘ēēn minchew i yaybn." *KNZ,* 4, 34–36. Also published in *PHA,* 1, 44–45.
"Ołb Adamay" ["Adam nstel duřĕn draḥtin"] *MKH,* 139–40. Also published as "Tał Adamay merkanal" in *KNZ,* 4, 32–34, and in *PHA,* 1, 41–42. (According to H. Anasyan, this poem is by Yovhannēs Pluz Erznkatsi).
SUM, 1, 285–98.
"Tał vasn ginwoy yAzariayē asatseal" ["Ararich tēr k‘ałtsratsaw i yAdamay"]. *KNZ,* 4, 29–31. Also published in *PHA,* 1, 39–40.

AZARIA SASNETSI (d. 1628)

Also known as "Hlu" (i.e., "good-natured, obedient"), Azaria was from Sasun, but he spent most of his life wandering in Asia Minor and Constantinople. He is known for his works dealing with astronomy and the calendar. His literary fame rests on his poem on the ravages of the Jelalis, during which most of his close relatives perished. He himself was captured by the Jelalis but somehow managed to flee. He was buried at sea, but his body was reportedly washed ashore near Tripoli (Lebanon) and interred by pious Maronites.

Texts

"Azariayi Sasnetswoy Ołb i veray haruatzots arewelean gawařatsn ew ašḥarhin hayots i dzeřats Čelaleants." *HA,* 50 (1936), 325–27. Also published in *SUM,* 2, 240–55.
"Yišatakaran sakawuk‘ arareal Azariayi banasiri" ["Gut‘n ararchakan ḥnamotsn Astutzoy . . . "]. *HA,* 50 (1936), 320–24.
SUM, 2, 350–87.

Criticism

Akinean, N. "Azaria v. Sasnetsi, astłagēt, tōmaragēt ew tałachap." *HA,* 50 (1936), 297–325. Also published in *AMH,* 4, 241–308.
"Vasn Azaria p‘ilisop‘ayin." *Žamanakagrut‘iwn Grigor vardapeti Kamaḥetswoy kam Daranałtswoy.* (Jerusalem, 1915), 90, 410–13, 431–32.

BABKENTS, (1860–1917)

Pen names: Babkents, Gabriēl-Mačkal.
Born Gabriēl Mnatsakanean in the village of Davalu (now the city of Ararat, Armenia). A novelist and journalist. Educated in Erevan and Tiflis. Pursued

his higher studies at the University of Odessa. Wrote short stories and novels from rural life, and as a journalist, he looked into the economic problems of the peasantry (e.g., lack of arable lands, inadequacy of irrigation systems). Died in Erevan.

Texts

Murč, 1894/5, 682–90. 1894/11–12, 1524–34.
Norek: vēp. (Tiflis, 1897; Erevan, 1961). (Novel).

BAGRATUNI, ARSĒN (1790–1866)

Arsēn Komitas Bagratuni, also known by the surname Antʻimosean, was born in Constantinople. Poet, grammarian, and translator. Was sent to St. Lazarus at age eleven and took the orders there in 1810. After visits to Paris, Rome, and Russia, spent a quarter of a century (1831–56) in Constantinople as the chaplain of the famous Tiwzean family (commonly pronounced and better known as the Duzian family). Returned to St. Lazarus permanently in 1856. Still of some significance are a few of his linguistic-grammatical works and translations into Classical Armenian from Greek and Latin authors. He also published several historical texts and the Bible. But the crown of his literary writings remains his epic poem "Hayk Diwtsazn" (Hayk the hero).

Texts

Tałkʻ Mhitʻarean vardapetats, 3 vols. (Venice, 1852–54), Vol. 1 published as *Tałkʻ teaṙn h. Arsēni Komitasay Bagratunwoy vardapeti Mḥitʻareants, ew or pačučeal anuamb Aṙan Sisakean.* (Venice, 1852). (Poetry).
Hayk Diwtsazn, vēp. (Venice, 1858). (Poem).
"Eruand, ołbergutʻiwn." *B,* 27 (1869), 47–53, 86–90, 143–46, 185–89, 218–21. (Drama).
"Artašēs." *B,* 37 (1879), 23–37, 125–39.

Other works

Kʻerakanutʻiwn gałłiakan. (Venice, 1821).
Tarerkʻ hayerēn kʻerakanutʻean, dpratants tłots hamar. (Venice, 1846, 1848, 1850, 1856, 1860, 1864, 1869, 1874–75).
Hayerēn kʻerakanutʻiwn i pēts zargatselots. (Venice, 1852).
Yałags hnchman L ew Ł taṙits. (Venice, 1852).
Skzbunkʻ ułił ḥorheloy ew barwokʻ keloy. (Venice, 1857).

Translations (Italian)

Porane, Episodio del Poema eroico HAIK. (Venice, 1859).
Tesa, E. *Le due sorelle, frammenti dal poema epico Haig.* (Venice, 1925).
Teza, E. *Kʻorkʻ erkokʻin.* (Venice, 1905). Armenian and Italian. (Possbily a first edition of the above).

Criticism

Biwzandatsi, N. "Hayr Arseni Bagratunwoy Ułłutʻiwnkʻ ĕntʻertsuatzots i girs patmutʻean Pʻawstosi Biwzandatswoy." *HA,* 1983, 357–70.
Čanašean, M. "Bagratunii 'Hayk Diwtsazn'ĕ." *B,* 105 (1947), 49–55, 120–27, 149–57.
———. "Bagratuni ew Ōšakan." *B,* 106 (1948), 197–210; 107 (1949), 67–76.
Eremean, S. "H. A. Bagratuni." *B,* 69 (1911), 404–15, 465–75, 510–30.

Garagašean, K. "Bagratunii 'Hayk Diwtsazn'i masin." *B,* 122 (1964), 274–82.
Harutʻyunyan, E. "Arsen Bagratunu pʻilisopʻayakan hayatskʻnerě." *T,* 1964/7, 67–76.
Łazikean, A. "Aknark mě Bagratunwoy kenats ew gortzots vray." *B,* 58 (1900), 24–27.
———. "H. A. K. Bagratuni ew Homeri Iliakanin tʻargmanutʻiwně." *B,* 58 (1900), 65–72, 161–70.
Ṙštuni, Ē. "Induktiv metʻodi himnavorumě Arsen Bagratunu tramabanakan usmunkʻum." *PBH,* 1967/4, 243–49.
Štikyan, S. "Arsen Bagratuni." *SG,* 1966/12, 171–72.
Tayean, Ł. "Diwanakan nōtʻer Bagratunean 'Hayk Diwtsazn'i masin." *B,* 107 (1949), 111–13.
Tēr-Nersēsean, N. "H. Arsēn Bagratuni, Astuatzašunchi metz vastakaworě." *B,* 124 (1966), 344–46.

BAKUNTS, AKSEL (1899–1937)

Pen name: Aksel Bakunts.

Born Alekʻsandr Tʻevosyan in Goris, Armenia. Interrupted his studies at the Gēorgean seminary in Ējmiatzin to fight in the ranks of Armenian volunteers in fateful battles in Erzurum, Kars, and Sardarapat. He then studied at the polytechnic insitute in Tiflis and the agricultural institute in Kharkov and worked in Goris until 1926, when he settled in Erevan. An agromonist by profession, he increasingly became active in literary circles, and overnight he established himself as an exquisite master of the short story. He also wrote screenplays for a number of Armenian films. Just as his genius began to bloom, Bakunts became a victim of the Stalinist purges: He was arrested in August, 1936, and is believed to have been put to death in July, 1937.

Collections

Patmuatzkʻner. (Paris, 1938, 1941).
Andzrewě, Tzirani pʻołě. (Beirut, 1954).
Ambołjakan gortzě erekʻ hatorov. 2 vols. (Beirut, 1955, 1956).
Erker. (Erevan, 1955).
Ełbayrutʻyan ěnkuzeninerě. (Erevan, 1959).
Grakanutʻyan masin. (Erevan, 1959).
Erker. 2 vols. (Erevan, 1964).
Alpiakan manušak. (Erevan, 1969).
Patmvatzkʻner. (Erevan, 1975).
Erker. 4 vols. (Erevan, 1976, 1979, 1982, 1984).
Mirhav. (Erevan, 1971).
Sełbosyan, L. *Erker.* (Erevan, 1985).
Kʻišoyan, A. *Erker.* (Erevan, 1986).

Texts (short stories)

Galusti vikě. (Erevan, 1926).
Hovnatʻan March. (Erevan, 1927).
Mtʻnadzor. (Erevan, 1927).
Patmvatzkʻner. (Erevan, 1928).
Spitak dzin. (Moscow, 1929).

Ḥachatur Abovyani "anhayt batsakayumě". (Erevan, 1932).
Sev tseleri sermnatsaně. (Erevan, 1933).
Andzrevě. (Erevan, 1935).
Ełbayrutʻyan ěnkuzeninerě. (Erevan, 1936).
Sev tseleri sermnatsaně. (Erevan, 1936).
Kʻeṙi Davon. (Erevan, 1936).
Muroyi zrutsě. (Erevan, 1960).
Alpiakan manušak. (Erevan, 1962).
Muroyi zrutsě. Namak ṙusats ťagavorin. (Erevan, 1969).
Andzrevě. (Erevan, 1970).
Tʻevosyan, H. "Aksel Bakuntsi norahayt namakneřě." *BEH,* 1987/3, 83–85.

Translations

English

Apresyan, S. "Cyclamens." *Nor ašḫarh,* 1959/27, 4; 28, 4; 29, 4. Also published in *Lraber,* July 12, 1960, 4; July 14, 1960, 4; July 16, 1960, 4.
Wixley, A. "This Is Javo Speaking from her Flat." *IL* (later *SL*), 1936/5, 21–24.
———. "The Mountain Cyclamen." *SL,* 1966/3, 67–74.

English Anthologies

WM, 12–21.

French

Butkiewicz, L. "Les Violettes des Alpes." *OO,* 123 (March 1969), 27–35.

German

Hofmaier, H. "Das Alpenveilchen." *Sowjet-Literatur,* 1966/3, 72–80.

Russian

Al'piiskaia fialka: Roman. Rasskazy. (Moscow, 1981).
Povesti i rasskazy. (Moscow, 1962).

Russian Anthologies

AASL, 154–67.
RAN, 305–41.

Spanish

Bernal, E. "Violeta alpina." *Literatura Sovietica,* 1966/3, 69–77.

Bibliographies

Išḫanyan, Ṙ. *Aksel Bakunts, kensagrut'yun ev matenagrut'yun.* (Erevan, 1960).

Criticism

Adamyan, A. "Alekʻsandr Bakuntsi ašakertakan gortzě." *T,* 1958/1, 93–96.
Adonts, N. "Ḥachatur Aboveani vaḫčaně." *Vēm,* 1 (1933/1), 5–13. (On Bakunts's *Ḥachatur Abovyani "anhayt batsakayumě"*).
Aharonean, V. "Aksel Bakunts." *HK,* 14 (1935–36/9), 121–33.
"Aksel Bakunts." *HK,* 31 (1953/2), 42–52; 3, 49–58.
Aksel Bakuntsi stełtzagortzutʻyuně (hodvatzneri žołovatzu). (Erevan, 1959).
Ałababyan, S. "Žołovrdakan kerparnerě Aksel Bakuntsi patmvatzkʻnerum." *PBH,* 1957/3, 136–49.
———. *Aksel Bakunts.* (Erevan, 1959).
———. "Škʻeł tałandě." *SG,* 1959/10, 82–93.
———. *Aksel Bakunts.* (Erevan, 1963).
———. "Aksel Bakunts." *PBH,* 1963/4, 203–10.

———. *Aksel Bakunts, ocherk tvorchestva.* (Moscow, 1965).
———. *Aksel Bakunts.* (Erevan, 1971).
———. "Aksel Bakunts: kyankʿi ev stełtzagortzutʿyan ējerě." *SG,* 1979/7, 17–38.
———. "Aksel Bakuntsi 'Mtʿnadzor' žołovatzun." *PBH,* 1979/2, 3–16.
Ananyan, V. "Bakuntsi het." *SG,* 1963/7, 91–95.
Atʿabekyan, S. "Aksel Bakuntsi lṙutʿyuně." *SG,* 1981/10, 131–37.
Atʿayan, Ṙ. "Kʿnarakan Akselě." *SG,* 1977/10, 136–47.
Gasparyan, D. "Aksel Bakuntsě inchpes or ē." *SG,* 1986/1, 131–36.
Hakobyan, P. "Abovyaně ev Bakuntsě." *BEH,* 1980/2, 47–61.
Hambardzumean, V. "Aksel Bakunts." *HK,* 33 (1955/8), 1–12.
Ḥanzadyan, S. "Aksel Bakuntsi het." *SG,* 1979/7, 4–16.
———. "Sev tseleri sermnatsaně." *SG,* 1974/7, 114–24.
Ḥechumyan, V. "Šołšołun tałandě." *SG,* 1969/5, 150–54.
Išḥanyan, Ṙ. *Aksel Bakunts, kensagrutʿyun ev matenagrutʿyun.* (Erevan, 1960).
———. "Žołovurdneri ełbayrutʿyan gałapʿarě Aksel Bakuntsi stełtzagortzutʿyunnerum." *T,* 1961/5, 39–48.
———. "Erb hušě daṙnum ē nerka (Aksel Bakuntsi stełtzagortzutʿyan mi karevor aṙandznahatkutʿyan masin)." *SG,* 1962/2, 143–53.
———. "Aksel Bakuntsi mi antip stełtzagortzutʿyuně." *SG,* 1965/3, 113.
———. "Aksel Bakuntsi gełjkakan kerparnerě." *BEH,* 1967/3, 183–92.
———. "Pʿastakani ev gełarvestakani sahmanagtzum." *SG,* 1973/11, 129–39.
———. *Bakuntsi kyankʿn u arvestě.* (Erevan, 1974).
———. *Bakuntsi lezvakan arvestě.* (Erevan, 1974).
———. "Metz barekamutʿyun (Charents ev Bakunts)." *BEH,* 1977/3, 117–28.
———. "Aksel Bakunts." *L,* 1979/6, 93–101.
———. "Hay gełarvestakan ardzaki ḥošoraguyn demkʿě (Aksel Bakuntsi 90-amyakin)." *L,* 1989/8, 3–15.
Łazaḥetsyan, V. "Aksel Bakuntsě ev Hayastani ōgnutʿyan komiten (HŌK-ě)." *L,* 1979/6, 102–5.
Mikirtichian, L. "Aksel Bakounts as the Champion of the True Concept of the Popular Basis of Literature in Soviet Armenia." *CR,* 7 (1958), 66–90; 8 (1959), 41–69.
Mkrtchean, L. *Aksel Bakuntsě orpēs anḥardaḥ žołovrdaynutʿean aṙajamartik ḥorhrdahay grakanutʿean mēj.* (Munich, 1959).
Mkrtchyan, H. *Aksel Bakunts.* (Erevan, 1958).
Ōhanyan, V. "Hušer Bakuntsi masin." *SG,* 1979/10, 94–99.
Ōhanyan, Z. "Bakuntsyan noveli mi kʿani aṙandznahatkutʿyunnerě." *SG,* 1974/1, 136–40.
Patrik, A. "Mi drvag Bakuntsi usanołakan tarinerits." *SG,* 1965/3, 114–16.
Šahnazaryan, N. *Aksel Bakuntsi stełtzagortzutʿyan usutsman im pʿordzě.* (Erevan, 1989).
Sanasar, Pʿ. "Sew tseleri sermnatsaně." *HK,* 13 (1934–35/9), 157–60.
Swenyan, A. "Axel Bakunts." *SL,* 1966/3, 170–76.
Tʿamrazyan, H. "Bakuntsi stełtzagortzutʿyan gnahatutʿyan šurjě." *SG,* 1974/11, 98–109.
Tonoyan, Ē. "Gogolyan avandnerě ev Bakuntsi 'Provintsiayi mayramutě'." *BEH,* 1982/3, 179–84.
Zakʿaryan, A. "Bakuntsi mutkʿě grakanutʿyan mej." *PBH,* 1959/4, 140–44.
———. "Aksel Bakuntsě ev grakanutʿyan hartserě." *T,* 1969/11–12, 27–34.

BARḤUDAREAN, GĒORG (1835–1913)

A native of Tiflis. A writer, translator (especially from German), and teacher. Attended school in Tiflis and continued his education at Dorpat (now Tartu, Estonia). Taught in Armenian schools in Transcaucasia, and contributed to the principal periodicals of the time, particularly *Hiwsisapʻayl* of Moscow. His poems express a concern with social injustice and promote patriotism and unity.

Texts

Barepašt mardik. (Tiflis, 1889). (Play).
Banastełtzutʻiwnner. (Tiflis, 1897). (Poems).

BARSEŁEAN, GEŁAM (1883–1915)

Pen names: Gełō, Net, Ōšin-Zartʻōnkʻ.
Born and educated in Constantinople. A writer and journalist. With Šawarš Misakʻean (c1884–1957) and Vahram Tʻatʻul (q.v.), published the literary weekly *Azdak* (Constantinople, 1908–09); became one of the editors of *Azatamart* (Constantinople, 1909–15) and a supporter of the periodical *Mehean* (Constantinople, 1914). He was arrested and put to death during the initial stages of the Armenian genocide of 1915. Wrote short stories, short prose pieces, and lyrical impressions.

Texts

Ambołjakan gortzĕ. (Paris, 1931). (Stories).

Criticism

Sasuni, K. "Gełam Barsełeani ambołjakan gortzĕ." *HK,* 10 (1931–32/1), 170–74.

BAŠALEAN, LEWON (1868–1943)

Pen names: Menik, Tʻapʻaṙik, Tzitzeṙnak, Armēn Zarparean (a collective pen name shared with Vahan Tʻēkʻēean and Surēn Partʻewean), L. Zartʻumean.
Born and educated in Constantinople. A writer of short stories. Joined the ranks of the Hnchakean party and collaborated closely with A. Arpʻiarean in editing the *Hayrenikʻ* daily. Fled the Armenian massacres of the mid-1890s, settled in Europe in 1896, and subsequently published *Nor keankʻ* in London. Financial hardship compelled him to work for a French oil company in Baku, from about 1903 to 1920. He then settled in Paris, became absorbed in the activities of the Armenian National Delegation, the Central Commitee for the Armenian Refugees, and the Armenian General Benevolent Union. Visited Soviet Armenia in 1924 to organize the construction of settlements, schools, and hospitals in Erevan and its suburbs, with financial assistance provided by the Armenian General Benevolent Union. Died in Vichy.

Collections (stories)

Dakʻesyan, V. *Ĕntir erker.* (Erevan, 1962).
Noravēper ew patmuatzkʻner. (Paris, 1939).
Patmuatzkʻner. (Aleppo, 1945).

Works in periodicals

M, 1889/3927, 62–64. 1890/3935, 188–90; 3937, 231–32; 3939, 255–56; 3951, 62–64.
"Tsełin dzaynĕ." *ANA,* 1 (1898–99), 34–37.

"Erku kiner." *Murč,* 1902/2, 5–8.
"Kovkastsi hay išḥani mě kartzikʻnerě." *Širak,* 1907/6, 333–37.
Zarparean, A. "Taragir veryušumner. Gišeruan pahě." *AM,* 1908, 1109–13.

Translations

English

Andreassian, K. M. "The Voice of the Race." *Armenia* (Boston), 2 (1906/8), 36–43. Also in *The New Armenia,* 8 (1916/12), 189–91.
A. S. "Yuletide." *Armenia* (Boston), 2 (1905/2, 3), 36–41. Also published in *Armenia* (Boston), 4 (1911/8), 1–3.
Mahtesian, A. "Yuletide in Armenia." *The New Armenia,* 8 (1916/4), 54–55.
Serpouhie. "The New Suit." *Kochnak,* September 8, 1917, 1101–02.

Russian

"Poprannyi obet." *RAN,* 186–90.

Criticism

Čanašean, M. "Lewon Bašalean." *B,* 105 (1947), 278–79.
Kamsarakan, T. "Lewon Bašaleani grakan gortzě." *ANA,* 5 (1934/5–6), 90.
Manukyan, S. *Levon Bašalyan.* (Erevan, 1969).
Parikean, H. *Lewon Bašalean.* (Aleppo, 1970).

BAŠINJAŁEAN, GĒORG (1857–1925)

Born in Słnaḥ, Georgia. Studied the art of painting in Tiflis (1876–78) and St. Petersburg (1879–83) and spent most of his life in Tiflis. Toured Italy and Switzerland (1884), briefly resided in Paris (1899–1901), and mounted successful exhibitions of his paintings (mainly landscapes) in numerous cities. An accomplished artist, he also took a keen interest in literature and wrote short stories, plays, travel notes, and some literary criticism. Died in Tiflis.

Collections

Erker. (Erevan, 1966).

Texts

Nkarchi keankʻits. (Petersburg, 1903).
Usanołner. (Tiflis, 1912).
Ēskʻizner. (Tiflis, 1913).
Nkarchi keankʻits. (N.p., 1914 [includes second impression of vol. 1 1903, 370–90]; Erevan, 1950).

Translations

Russian

KHAN, 2, 141–46. ("*Iz dnevnika dvorianina.*")

Criticism

Gayfejyan, V., and Sargsyan, A. *Gevorg Bašinjałyan.* (Erevan, 1957).
Samuēlean, Ḥ. "Mi stełtzagortzutʻean patmutʻiwn: Druagner Raffu ew Bašinjałeani stełtzagortzakan hamagortzaktsutʻiwunits." *HA,* 1987 (special issue, 1887–1987), 947–49.
Sargsyan, M. *Gevorg Bašinjałyan: kyankʻě ev gortzuneutʻyuně.* (Erevan, 1957).
Bashindzhagian, Z. G. *30 let otdannye Saiat-Nova.* (Erevan, 1963).

BES, GAREGIN (1910–1986)

Pen name: Garegin Bes.

Born Garegin Sarinyan in Šuši, Artsaḥ (Karabagh); and educated at Stepʻanakert, Tiflis, and at the State Univsersity of Erevan. From 1944 to 1947 he was the secretary for the literary journal *Sovetakan grakanutʻyun,* and later he worked for the Armenian Theatrical Society in Erevan. A novelist and dramatist, he chose his themes from contemporary Armenian and Soviet life.

Collections

Erker. 3 vols. (Erevan, 1976, 1978, 1981). (Vol. 3 has title "erekʻ grkʻov"; vols. 1 and 2 have title "erekʻ hatorov").

Texts (stories and novels)

Kyankʻi ergĕ. (Erevan, 1930).
Jorji Tenli. (Erevan, 1931).
Viškanerĕ bardzranum en. (Erevan, 1932).
Paykʻar. (Erevan, 1932).
Ardzak banasteltzutʻyunner. (Erevan, 1933).
Herosneri stverum. (Erevan, 1939).
Krak. (Erevan, 1944).
Harazatner. (Erevan, 1946).
Petunts Galon. (Erevan, 1947).
Novelner. 2 vols. (Erevan, 1954).
Novelner. 2 vols. (Erevan, 1960–63).
Ašikn u Mašikĕ. (Erevan, 1962).
Ašḥarhn indznov ē sksvum. (Erevan, 1962). (Play).
Nkarchi nverĕ. (Erevan, 1964).
Ayrvatz všter. (Erevan, 1967).
Tznund. (Erevan, 1971).
Hobelyanĕ. (Erevan, 1973).
Gołatsvatz arevĕ. (Erevan, 1974).
Tʻaterakan novelner. (Erevan, 1976).
Im Charentsĕ. (Erevan, 1979).
Ergĕ kanchum ē. (Erevan, 1982).
Kyankʻi kenatsĕ. (Erevan, 1984).
Hušanovelner. (Erevan, 1985).

Translations

Russian

Arsharuni, A., and Glebova A. *Mir nachinaetsia s menia.* (Moscow, 1961).
Mnatsakanian, An. *Selskii deputat.* (Moscow, 1966).
Novelly. (Erevan, 1956).
Vozvrashchenie. (Erevan, 1952).

Criticism

Babayan, A. "Garegin Besi novelnerĕ." *SG,* 1965/8, 135–42.
Verdyan, B. "Tznndavayri neršnchankʻov." *SG,* 1985/2, 138–40.

BIWRAT, SMBAT (1862–1915)

Pen names: Hayk-Lewon, Leṙnordi, Mtrak, Smbat Biwrat, Tʻab.

Born Smbat Tēr-Łazarents in Zēytʻun (now Süleymanlı, Turkey) and educated at the Armenian seminary in Jerusalem. He sat in on courses in pedagogy at the Sorbonne and earned a living teaching in Armenian schools in various cities: Marash, Zēytʻun, Sis (Kozan), Samsun, Constantinople, Alexandria, Cairo, etc. As a member of the Armenian intelligentsia, he was arrested and murdered during the initial stages of the Armenian massacres and deportations in 1915. His novels, elaborating contemporary and past Armenian political activities and aspirations, were enormously popular at the turn of the twentieth century. The list below of his works is considerably incomplete.

Texts

Banastełtzakan erker. Vol. 1. (Constantinople, 1909). (Poetry).
Awarayri aṙiwtzě kam Vardanankʻ. (Constantinople, 1909). (Play).
Vełarawor herosě kam Bartʻołimēos v. Tʻakʻačean. (Constantinople, 1909).
Zeṫuntsi vardapetě kam Grigoris tz. v. Abardeants. (N.p., c1910).
Innsun vets: ariwni mējēn. 6 vols. (Constantinople, 1911). (Novel).
Sasunēn etkʻě. 1. Diakaputnerě. (Constantinople, 1911). (Novel).
Sasunēn etkʻě. 2. Dēpi Eěltěz. (Constantinople, 1911). (Novel).
Bantē bant. 5 vols. (Constantinople, 1910). (Novel).
Eěltězē Sasun. (Constantinople, 1912). (Novel).
Verjin berdě. (Constantinople, 1914). (Drama).
Ariwni dzorě. (Constantinople, 1919). (Story).

Criticism

Eremean, S. "Smbat Biwrat." *B,* 90 (1932), 74–76, 129–32, 301–3.
Smbat-Biwrat. "Leṙnakani mě yušatetrě (inkʻnakensagrutʻiwn)." *B,* 93 (1935), 36–41, 91–100, 205–9, 246–51; 94 (1936), 106–14; 95 (1937), 82–89, 300–4; 96 (1938), 211–15, 306–11.

BORYAN, GURGEN (1915–1971)

Born in Šuši, Artsaḥ (Karabagh). A poet, dramatist, and translator. He pursued his higher studies at the M. Gorky Institute for Literature in Moscow; edited *Grakan tʻertʻ* (1938–41); and twice acted as secretary to the Union of Soviet Writers of Armenia (1938–41, 1950–54). In the years 1958–68, he first became the editor of *Literaturnaia Armeniia,* then that of *Sovetakan grakanutʻyun.* From 1968 to his death, he was the deputy minister of culture in the Armenian SSR.

Collections

Hatěntir. (Erevan, 1953).
Ěntir erker. (Erevan, 1966).
Nuyn harki tak. (Erevan, 1972). (Collection of plays).
Erker. (Erevan, 1982).

Texts

Banastełtzutʻyunner. (Erevan, 1937). (Poetry).
Arevi hambuyrě. (Erevan, 1939). (Poetry).
Čanaparh depi tzově. (Erevan, 1940). (Poetry).
Martiki erdumě. (Erevan, 1941).
Krake lezvov. (Erevan, 1942). (Poetry).
Mankakan banastełtzutʻyunner. (Erevan, 1942). (Poetry).
Hratsolkʻ. (Erevan, 1945). (Poetry).

Tzałkep̔unj. (Erevan, 1946). (Poetry).
Erevanyan lusabats. (Erevan, 1947). (Poetry).
Bardzunk̔nerum. (Erevan, 1949). (Play).
Ayo ev och. (Erevan, 1955).
Banasteltzut̔yunner. (Erevan, 1957). (Poetry).
Čočanak. (Erevan, 1958).
Nuyn harki tak. (Erevan, 1958).
Orn ē lavě [?] (Erevan, 1958).
Inchu [?] (Erevan, 1959).
Erek̔ drama. (Erevan, 1963). (Plays).
Es, du, na. (Erevan, 1965).
Dem aṙ dem. (Erevan, 1968).
Antaṙi p̔esatsun. (Erevan, 1969). (Play).
Im dzin. (Erevan, 1984).
Karusel. (Erevan, 1990).

Translations

Russian

Davidova, A. *Moi kon'.* (Moscow and Leningrad, 1950).
Erevanskie rassvety. (Moscow, 1948).
Ginzburg, L. *Dorogi.* (Moscow, 1958).
[Gonchar, N.], *Na mosty.* (Moscow, 1964).
Ia, ty, on. (Erevan, 1956).
Izbrannoe. (Erevan, 1952).
Kliatva boitsa. Sbornik stikhov. (Erevan, 1942).
Ognennym iazykom. Stikhi. (Moscow, 1944).
Sarkisian, P. *Da i net. Stikhi.* (Moscow, 1955).
Serebriakov, B. *Frontovye stikhi.* (Erevan, 1943).
Stikhi. (Erevan, 1956).
Tadeosian, A. *Dve dramy.* (Moscow, 1960).
[Tadeosian, A.], *Pod odnoi kryshei.* (Moscow, 1959).

Criticism

"Gurgen Boryani tznndyan 60-amyaki aṙt̔iv, 'Du kdimanas'." *SG,* 1975/9, 110–11.

CHAMCHEAN, MIK̔AYĒL (1738–1823)

A native of Constantinople. An eminent historian, linguist-grammarian, and theologian. Joined the Mekhitarists of Venice in 1757 and took holy orders in 1762. For six years he was the pastor of the Armenian Catholics of Basra, Iraq, where he was in ill health. Returned to Venice in 1775 and completed his monumental *History of Armenia,* published in 1784–86. In 1795 he took up residence in Constantinople to recuperate and to organize a Mekhitarist school. There he was personally involved in the unofficial and unauthorized unity talks between the Armenian Apostolic and Armenian Catholic communities, which bore no fruit. Died and was buried in Constantinople.

Texts

K̔erakanut̔iwn haykazean lezui (Venice, 1779, 1801, 1831, 1833, 1843; Calcutta, 1823, 1830; Tiflis, 1826; Šuši, 1833, 1839). (Grammar of Classical Armenian).

Patmutʻiwn hayots. 3 vols. (Venice, 1784–86). (History of Armenia).
Nuagaran ōrhnutʻeants, yorum meknin awag ōrhnutʻiwnkʻ Sałmosaranin meroy. (Venice, 1801).
Hrahang eōtʻneki, eōtʻneak eōtʻambkʻ dasaworeal. (Venice, 1802).
Patker tōnits surb Astuatzatzni. (Venice, 1805).
Ḥraḥčan patmutʻean hayots. (Venice, 1811; Calcutta, 1824). (History of Armenia).
Kiwlzari tʻēvariḥ. Hay millētʻinē tayir hikʻeayēlēr ilē tōnanmiš. Chamchean hayr Mikʻayēl vardapetin łayrētʻi ilē. (Venice, 1812, 1850, 1862). (This is a Turkish version in Armenian characters of the preceding title).
Meknutʻiwn sałmosats. 10 vols. (Venice, 1815–1823).
Sełan ḥnkots. (Venice, 1816).
Patmutʻyun hayots. (Erevan, 1984). (A facsimile reproduction in three volumes of the original title as published in Venice in 1784–86).

Translations

Avdall, J. *History of Armenia.* 2 vols. (Calcutta, 1827). (Abridged).

Criticism

Babikean, A. *Hamaṙōt yayt yandimanutʻiwn erkuts čšmartutʻeants ĕnddēm erkuts molar drutʻeants. Aṙajinn V.H. Mikʻayēli Chamchean, tʻē Ōdznetsin itsē imastasēr hayrapetn Hayots, vkayealn i srbots harts merots. Erkrordn V.H. Mkrtchi Awgerean tʻē tetrakn Ōdznetswoyn itsē ułłapʻaṙ vardapetutʻiwn ew grutʻiwn veroygreal Imastasiri.* (Vienna, 1817).
Čemčemean, S. "H. Mikʻayēl Chamchean ew ir Hayots patmutʻiwnĕ." *B,* 1981/3–4, 300–56.
———. "1809-i Polsoy miutʻenakan šaržumĕ ew H. Mikʻayēl Chamchean." *HA,* 1987/1–12, 897–910.
"H. Mikʻayēl Chamchean." *Mḥitʻar. Yišatak Mḥitʻarean yobelinin.* (Venice, 1901). pp. 76–86.
Mḥitʻarean, Y. M. "H. M. Chamcheani derĕ hayots lezui šarahiwsutʻean zargatsman gortzum." *B,* 127 (1969), 217–24; 128 (1970), 256–62.
Utʻujyan, A. "Grigor Daranałetsin M. Chamchyani Patmutʻyan ałbyur." *L,* 1975/2, 81–89.
———. "Hovhannisik Tzaretsin (16-rd dar) orpes Mikʻayel Chamchyani Patmutʻyan ałbyur." *BEH,* 1976/2, 195–200.
———. "Mikʻayel Chamchyani patmagitakan hayatskʻneri gnahatman hartsi šurjĕ." *BEH,* 1981/2, 144–51.
———. "Mikʻayel Chamchyan." *L,* 1988/9, 71.
Utʻunjyan, A. [sic] "Polsahay hamaynkʻneri miutʻyan ḥndirĕ ev M. Chamchyanĕ." *BEH,* 1978/3, 201–13.

CHARĔG, ARAM (1874–1947)

Pen name: Vtarandi.

Born in Karin (Erzurum). A poet, translator, and teacher. Educated at the Artznean school of his birthplace, at the Gēorgean seminary in Ējmiatzin, and in the Nersisean school of Tiflis. He also audited courses in Leipzig, Paris, and Switzerland. He led a wandering life, teaching in Constantinople, Smyrna, and Eastern Europe, before settling in France. In 1946 he was invited to take part in the second conference of the Union of Soviet Armenian writers in Erevan. Died in Moscow, reportedly of an illness.

Texts

Banastełtzuťiwnner. (Venice, 1900). (Poetry).
Vitōši bazēn. (Geneva, 1906).
Ḥorhrdayin metz Hayastan. (Paris, 1945).

Translations (Russian anthologies)

BPA, 509.

Criticism

E[remean], S. "Aram Charĕg." *B,* 93 (1935), 84–88.

CHARENTS, EŁIŠE (1897–1937)

Pen name: Ełiše Charents.

Born Ełiše Sołomonyan in the Western Armenian city of Kars (now in Turkey) and educated in the local Armenian and Russian schools. In 1915 he joined the Armenian volunteers supporting the Russian war effort on the Russo-Ottoman front in World War I. Took to arms a second time in 1918–19 to support the Red Army in the civil war. Settled in Erevan in the early 1920s, and along with G. Abov and A. Vštuni (q.q.v.), he issued the famous "Declaration of the Three" in June of 1922, which rejected the old and called for a new Armenian literary tradition. In the wake of his return from an extensive tour in Europe, he founded a union of writers, named "Noyember," and worked for the state publishing house from 1928 to 1935. The termination of his position in this establishment marked the beginning of an orchestrated campaign to denounce him and his literature. By this time, he had become addicted to drugs, and the circumstances under which his life came or was brought to an end two years later are still somewhat uncertain.

Collections

Erkeri žołovatzu. 2 vols. (Moscow, 1922).
Žołovatzu poemneri. (Tiflis, 1927).
Erker. (Erevan, 1932).
Poemner. (Erevan, 1936).
Hatĕntir. (Beirut, 1953).
Ĕntir erker. (Erevan, 1954).
Lenin (poemner ev banastełtzuťyunner). (Erevan, 1954).
Ĕntir erker. (Erevan, 1955).
Ambołjakan gortzĕ. Vol. 1. (Beirut, 1955).
Grakanuťyan masin. (Erevan, 1957).
Ĕntir erker. (Erevan, 1957).
Erkeri žołovatzu. 6 vols. (Erevan, 1962–68).
Poemner. (Erevan, 1966).
Ǩnarergakan, arvest ǩerťołuťyan, girǩ imastuťyan, tałer ev ḥorhurdner, ergitzakan, p̌rkvatz patar̃ikner. (Erevan, 1967).
Ĕntir erker. (Erevan, 1973).
Banastełtzuťyunner, poemner, balladner. (Erevan, 1976).
Ĕntir erker. (Erevan, 1977).
LXXX: Hatĕntir. (Erevan, 1977).

Muradyan, Ṙ. *Erker.* (Erevan, 1983).
Gamałelyan, T., et al. *Erker.* (Erevan, 1985).
Charents, A. *Erkeri žołovatzu.* 4 vols. (Erevan, 1986–87).
Jrbašyan, Ēd., and Charents, A. *Hatĕntir.* (Erevan, 1987). (Illus. by G. Ḥanjyan).

Texts (verse)

Erekʻ erg tḥradaluk ałjkan. (Kars, 1914).
Kaputacheay hayrenikʻ. (Tiflis, 1915).
Dantʻēakan aṙaspel. (Tiflis, 1916; Beirut, 1954).
Tziatzanĕ. (Moscow, 1917).
Soma. (Tiflis, 1918).
Ambohnerĕ ḥelagaruatz. (Tiflis, 1919; Beirut, 1954; Erevan, 1967, 1975).
Bolorin, bolorin, bolorin. (Erevan, 1920).
Poēzozuṙna. (Moscow, 1922).
Ṙomans ansēr. (Moscow, 1922).
Kapkaz tʻamaša. (Tiflis, 1923).
Poemner. (Constantinople, 1923).
Komalmanaḥ. (Moscow, 1924).
Mačkal Sakʻoyi patmutʻyunĕ. (Erevan, 1924, 1936).
Stambol. (Constantinople, 1924).
Erekʻ pʻokʻrik poēm 'Lenin' šarkʻits. (Berlin, 1925).
Myur de Federe. (Erevan, 1925).
Leninn u Alin. (Erevan, 1925, 1969).
Erkir Nairi. (Erevan, 1926, 1934, 1977). (Novel).
Hišołutʻyunner Erevani ułłich tnits. (Tiflis, 1927). (Impressions of life in the Erevan correction house).
Ṙubayatʻ. (Tiflis, 1927).
Chors ballad. (Moscow, 1929).
Ēpikʻakan lusabats. (Erevan, 1930).
Girkʻ čanaparhi. (Erevan, 1933 [1934]; Aleppo, 1946 [selections], 1954, 1959; Beirut, 1950, 1959).
Boris Dzneladze. Ballad gndapet Tomsoni, komerit tłi ev gortzaduli masin. (Erevan, 1934).
Ḥmbapet Šavarš. (Erevan, 1961).
Es im anuš Hayastani. (Erevan, 1967, 1970 [in 12 languages]).
Komitas. (Erevan, 1969).
Ballad Vladimir Ilyichi, mužiki ev mi zuyg košiki masin. (Erevan, 1982).
Ananyan, G. *Poemner, banastełtzutʻyunner.* (Erevan, 1984).
Charents, A. "Charentsi antip namakĕ M. Šahinyanin (1933tʻ. dekt. 1-in)." *PBH,* 1987/2, 226–30. (Text in Russian).

Other works (letters and unpublished manuscripts)

"Antip ējer." *SG,* 1962/6, 3–11.
"Navzike (hatvatzner)." *SG,* 1963/2, 3–9.
"Komitasi hišatakin." *SG,* 1964/1, 73–85.
Zakʻaryan, A. "Ełiše Charentsi antip namaknerits." *PBH,* 1964/1, 163–72.
"Ispania," *SG,* 1965/6, 3–4.
"Antip banastełtzutʻyunner." *SG,* 1972/6, 15–17.
Ananyan, G. "Ełiše Charentsi erku namakĕ." *BEH,* 1974/1, 184–86.

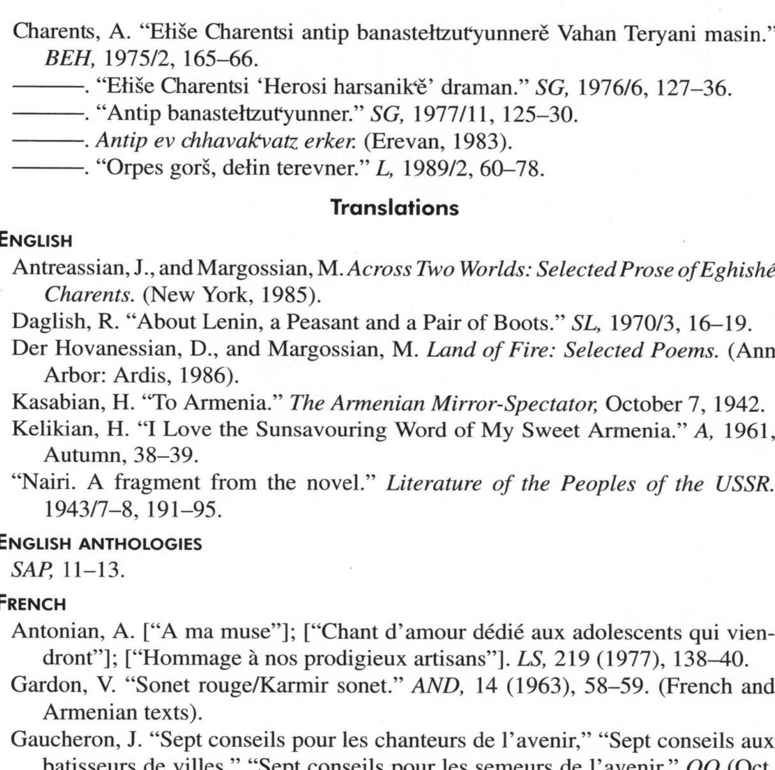

Charents, A. "Ełiše Charentsi antip banastełtzutʻyunnerě Vahan Teryani masin." *BEH,* 1975/2, 165–66.

———. "Ełiše Charentsi 'Herosi harsanikʻě' draman." *SG,* 1976/6, 127–36.

———. "Antip banastełtzutʻyunner." *SG,* 1977/11, 125–30.

———. *Antip ev chhavakʻvatz erker.* (Erevan, 1983).

———. "Orpes gorš, dełin terevner." *L,* 1989/2, 60–78.

Translations

ENGLISH

Antreassian, J., and Margossian, M. *Across Two Worlds: Selected Prose of Eghishé Charents.* (New York, 1985).

Daglish, R. "About Lenin, a Peasant and a Pair of Boots." *SL,* 1970/3, 16–19.

Der Hovanessian, D., and Margossian, M. *Land of Fire: Selected Poems.* (Ann Arbor: Ardis, 1986).

Kasabian, H. "To Armenia." *The Armenian Mirror-Spectator,* October 7, 1942.

Kelikian, H. "I Love the Sunsavouring Word of My Sweet Armenia." *A,* 1961, Autumn, 38–39.

"Nairi. A fragment from the novel." *Literature of the Peoples of the USSR.* 1943/7–8, 191–95.

ENGLISH ANTHOLOGIES

SAP, 11–13.

FRENCH

Antonian, A. ["A ma muse"]; ["Chant d'amour dédié aux adolescents qui viendront"]; ["Hommage à nos prodigieux artisans"]. *LS,* 219 (1977), 138–40.

Gardon, V. "Sonet rouge/Karmir sonet." *AND,* 14 (1963), 58–59. (French and Armenian texts).

Gaucheron, J. "Sept conseils pour les chanteurs de l'avenir," "Sept conseils aux batisseurs de villes," "Sept conseils pour les semeurs de l'avenir." *OO* (Oct. 1967), 95–99.

———. "Roubayats." *OO,* 123 (March 1969), 5.

———. "Les foules sont devenues folles", "Du cycle 'Octaves au soleil'." *OO,* 160 (April 1972), 136–41.

Juin, H. "L'adolescent aux cheveux bouclés," "Méditation." *AND,* 17 (n.d.), 26–29.

———. "Vers l'avenir," "Pour le soleil," "Art poétique." *AND,* 17 (n.d.), 128–32.

———. "Monument"; "Mefisto" *AND,* 18 (n.d.), 81–82.

———. "Louange de l' Arménie," "Etrange automne," "Vahakn." *AND,* 11 (1960), 38–40.

———. "Vahakn/Vahagn." *AND,* 15 (1964), 39–40.

Lénine et Ali. (Erevan, 1967).

Marcel, L.-A. *Choix de poèmes.* (Beirut, n.d.).

———. "Sonet rouge/Karmir sonet," "Pour le soleil/Arewin." *AND,* 10 (n.d.), 38–41. (French and Armenian on facing pages).

Mardirossian, L. "Hymne à la nature." *OO* (Oct. 1967), 93–95.

Ter-Sarkissian, P. *La maison de rééducation.* (Marseilles: Editions Parenthèses, 1992).

FRENCH ANTHOLOGIES

APA, 233–34.

CPA, 215–53.
E, 58–71.
FPA, 52, 61–63.
LPA, 246–85.

Russian

Akhmatova, M. et al. *Izbrannoe.* (Erevan, 1987).
Izbrannoe. (Moscow, 1956).
Izbrannoe. (Erevan, 1967).
Khachatriants, Ia. *Strana Nairi.* (Erevan, 1960).
Kocharian, S. *Leniniana. Stikhotvoreniia i poemy.* (Erevan, 1980).
Maksimov, M. *Dedushka Lenin. Poema.* (Moscow, 1969).
———. *Lenin i Ali.* (Erevan, 1970).
Moiu Armeniiu liubliu. (Erevan, 1967).
Pavlova, A., et al. *Leniniana. Stikhotvoreniia, poemy.* (Erevan, 1987).
Poemy i ballady. (Erevan, 1960).
Stikhi. (Moscow, 1980).
Stikhotvoreniia i poemy. (Leningrad, 1973).
Strana Nairi. (Moscow and Leningrad, 1926; Moscow, 1933, 1935).
Strani Nairi.–Stefan Zorian: Predsedatsel' revkoma; Devushka iz biblioteki. (Moscow, 1964).
Tri poemy o Lenine. (Moscow, 1955).

Spanish anthologies

APAS, 265–69.

Multilingual

Es im anuš Hayastani. (Erevan, 1967). (12 languages).

Bibliography

Jrbašyan, Ē. *Ełiše Charents, 1897–1937. Bibliografia.* (Erevan, 1957).

Criticism

Agababian, A. *Egishe Charents: Ocherk tvorchestva.* (Moscow, 1982).
Aharonean, V. "Ełišē Charents. Girk' čanaparhi." *HK,* 15 (1936–37/2), 172–76.
———. "Ełišē Charentsě erb ē hiast'ap'uel hamaynavarut'iwnits." *HK,* 30 (1952/12), 83–90.
Ałababyan, A. "Ełiše Charentsě ev ṙusakan simvolizmě." *SG,* 1984/6, 115–28.
———. "Puškinyan poetikan ap'erum (Charentsi poeziayi, depi puškinyan poeziayi avandnerě ułłvatzut'yan masin)." *BEH,* 1984/2, 42–60.
———. "Antzanot' šerter E. Charentsi 'ṙusakan kołmnorošumnerits'." *SG,* 1986/2, 126–34.
Ałababyan, G. "Gełarvestakan žamanaki artahaytman skzbunk'nerě (E. Charentsi) 'Erkir Nairi' vepum." *SG,* 1983/3, 97–106.
Ałababyan, S. "Ełiše Charentsi stełtzagortzakan kyank'i aṙajin šrjaně, (1912–17)." *T,* 1957/9, 3–28.
———. "Ełiše Charentsi hoktemberyan poemnerě." *PBH,* 1962/4, 25–42.
———. "Ełiše Charentsi 'Tałaraně'." *PBH,* 1967/2–3, 167–78.
———. "Hayrenik'i t'eman Ełiše Charentsi naḥahoktemberyan stełtzagortzut'yan mej." *BEH,* 1970/2, 43–60.
———. "Hogevark'its depi hełap'oḥut'yun." *SG,* 1970/5, 141–60.
———. "Charentsi artasahmanyan čanaparhordut'yuně." *PBH,* 1972/2, 17–30.

———. *Ełiše Charents*. 2 vols. (Erevan, 1973, 1977).
———. "Ełiše Charentsi gełagitakan davanankʻě." *SG,* 1973/6, 130–43.
———. "Čanaparhi girkʻě." *SG,* 1975/11, 128–43; 12, 127–38.
———. "Charentsi tʻargmanakan arvestanotsě." *SG,* 1976/12, 113–23.
———. "Ketsutʻyan ev arvesti davanankʻě, ěst 'Girkʻ čanaparhi'." *SG,* 1977/11, 131–45.
Ałabekyan, K. "Charentsi 'Erkir Nairi' vepi avandnerě." *SG,* 1979/5, 117–23.
Amirḥanyan, H. "Banastełtzn u martikě." *SG,* 1975/5, 112–17.
Ananian, G. *Charents i russkaia literatura.* (Erevan, 1983).
Ananyan, G. "Hełapʻoḥutʻyan ogešunch ergichě." *BEH,* 1967/3, 123–33.
———. "Charentsě ev Nekrasově." *BEH,* 1978/1, 61–70.
———. *Ełiše Charentsě ev ṙus grakanutʻyuně.* (Erevan, 1979).
———. *Charentsi het.* Erevan, 1980).
———. "Patmutʻyan gełagitakan ěmbṙnumě ev ardiakanutʻyuně." *BEH,* 1984/1, 57–73.
———. *Ełiše Charents.* (Erevan, 1987).
Avagyan, Ṙ. "Avetikʻ Isahakyani ev Ełiše Charentsi dimankarnerě Hayastani foni vra." *SG,* 1984/8, 109–25.
Aznavuryan, G. "Ełiše Charentsi gortzuneutʻyaně veraberoł pʻaster ev tʻver." *T,* 1957/9, 129–31.
———. "Ełiše Charentsi 'Komitasi hišatakin' poemi anhayt lriv tarberakě." *SG,* 1964/1, 72.
Babayan, A. *Charentsě ev Hoktemberě.* (Erevan, 1967).
———. "Hoktemberě Charentsi stełtzagortzutʻyan mej." *PBH,* 1976/2–3, 141–56.
Bes, G. "Charentsyan masunkʻner." *SG,* 1974/2, 123–33.
———. *Im Charentsě.* (Erevan, 1979).
Biwzand, Ē. "Ełišē Charents ew kině." *HK,* 43 (1965/3), 1–12.
Brutyan, G. "Ełiše Charentsi pʻilisopʻayakan ṙubayinerě." *T,* 1954/12, 3–14.
Charents, A. "Ełiše Charentsi komitasyan stełtzagortzutʻyunnerě." *SG,* 1969/10, 114–27.
———. "Charentsě ev Puškině." *BEH,* 1974/1, 140–47.
———. *Charentsi dzeṙagreri ašḥarhum.* (Erevan, 1978).
———. "Ełiše Charentsi inkʻnagir tetraknerě." *SG,* 1982/10, 123–32.
Charentsyan ěntʻertsumner. (Erevan, 1957–1988). (5 volumes).
Dabałyan, N. *Ełiše Charents.* (Erevan, 1954).
Darbinyan, M. " 'Kaputachya hayrenikʻi' aṙełtzvatzě." *SG,* 1976/11, 143–49.
———. "Ełiše Charentsi banastełtzakan mutkʻě." *L,* 1979/3, 11–12.
Daštents, Ḥ. *Ěłdzyal aygabatsi ergichě (ḥoskʻ ev hušer E. Charentsi masin).* (Erevan, 1967).
Davtʻyan, Ṙ. *Ełiše Charentsě ev tʻatroně.* (Erevan, 1984).
———. *Ełiše Charentsě ev kerparvestě.* (Erevan, 1986).
Dzhanpoladian, M. "E. Charents–perevodchik poezii Gorkogo." *BEH,* 1972/3, 67–79.
Edoian, G. *Poetika Charentsa.* (Erevan, 1986).
Edoyan, H. *Ełiše Charentsi poetikan.* (Erevan, 1986).
Ełiazaryan, A. "Erku banastełtzakan hamakarg: Charents-Mayakovski ḥndri šurjě." *SG,* 1977/11, 150–58.
"Ełiše Charentsi tznndyan 90-amyakin nvirvatz gitakan nstašrjan." *L,* 1987/6, 93–94.

Felekʻyan, H. "Charentsě ev mamulě." *BEH,* 1972/2, 127–37.

———. "Ełiše Charentsi ēpigramnerě." *SG,* 1974/4, 156–63.

Gabrielyan, S. "Ełiše Charentsi gełagitakan skzbunkʻneri zargatsman aṙandznahatkutʻyunnerě." *L,* 1987/2, 11–21.

Gaissarian, S. "Eguiche Tcharents." *LS,* 219 (1977), 134–37.

Gasparyan, D. "Dasakan arvesti čanaparhov." *SG,* 1977/10, 123–35.

———. *Ełiše Charentsi ev 1920-akan tʻvakanneri sovetahay poezian.* (Erevan, 1983).

———. "V. Mayakovskin ev E. Charentsi stełtzagortzutʻyuně 1920-akan tʻvakanneri aṙajin kesin." *L,* 1984/1, 3–13.

———. "Hay ergi patmakan ułin ev hay ergchi čakatagirě." *L,* 1989/2, 57–60. (On Charents's "Orpes gorš, dełin terevner . . .").

Gevorgyan, A. "Lenini kerparě Ełiše Charentsi stełtzagortzutʻyunnerum." *L,* 1980/4, 19–26.

Grigoryan, A. "Ṙevolyutsiayi ev arvesti tʻeman Charentsi poeziayum 1917–1929 tʻvakannerum." *T,* 1956/12, 33–50.

———. "Ełiše Charentsě ev Alekʻsandr Blokě." *T,* 1957/9, 29–46.

———. "Ełiše Charents." *SG,* 1959/5, 130–43.

———. "Gełarvestakan mi kʻani traditsianeri hałtʻaharumě Charentsi vał šrjani poeziayum." *SG,* 1961/4, 125–36.

———. *Poeziia Egishe Charentsa.* (Erevan, 1961).

Ḫachikyan, Ya. "Eliše Charentsi ēstʻetikan." *PBH,* 1967/2–3, 157–66.

Hakobyan, G. "Ełiše Charentsě grakan hamalsarani dasaḫos." *BEH,* 1985/2, 102–16.

Hakobyan, H. "Gyotʻe ev Charents." *SG,* 1974/8, 126–29.

Harutʻyunyan, G. "Charentsyan ěntʻertsumner." *BEH,* 1978/1, 216–21.

Harutʻyunyan, H. "Charentsi očakan bazmerangutʻyuně." *BEH,* 1984/3, 68–81.

Hayrapetyan, N. *Charentsě ev girkʻě.* (Erevan, 1987).

Hovhannisyan, E. *Hišołutʻyunner Ełiše Charentsi masin.* (Erevan, 1961).

———. *Hušer Ełiše Charentsi masin.* (Erevan, 1986).

Hovsepʻyan, G. *Charentsi poezian.* (Erevan, 1969).

Hušer Ełiše Charentsi masin. (Erevan, 1986). (Reminiscences by S. Zoryan, G. Mahari, Hṙ. Połosyan, H. Siras, M. Šahinyan, Ḫ Daštents, Ałavni, S. Kaputikyan, G. Ēmin, and V. Norents).

Išḫanyan, Ṙ. "Charentsi lezvi ułin." *BEH,* 1972/3, 52–66.

———. "Metz barekamutʻyun (Charents ev Bakunts)." *BEH,* 1977/3, 117–28.

Jrbašyan, Ēd. "Grakan očavorman problemě ev Charentsi sayatʻnovyan tałerě." *SG,* 1963/9, 98–111.

———. "Ełiše Charentsi ḫmbagratz aṙajin žołovatzun." *SG,* 1976/10, 145–47.

———. "Mi masunkʻ Ełiše Charentsits." *SG,* 1977/1, 114–22.

———. "Aršak Chopanyani hodvatzě Ełiše Charentsi masin." *BEH,* 1977/3, 135–42.

———. "Dari banastełtzě." *SG,* 1977/11, 110–14.

———. *Chors gagatʻ, Tumanyan, Isahakyan, Teryan, Charents.* (Erevan, 1982).

Kʻalantʻaryan, Ž. "Ełiše Charentsi 'Atʻilla' poemi stełtzagortzakan patmutʻyuně." *BEH,* 1978/3, 168–74.

Karinyan, A. *Ełiše Charents (hodvatzner, hušer).* (Erevan, 1972).

Kʻekʻlikean, H. "Charents." *S,* 1960, 201–6.

Kirakosyan, V. "Ayr šnorhyal i verust." *EJ,* 1987/8, 27–33.
K'ot'anjyan, K. et. al. "Hišołut'yunner Ełiše Charentsi masin: K. K'ot'anjyan, H. Połosyan, A. Sahradyan." *SG,* 1967/9, 19–32.
Kotzinyan, S. *Ełiše Charents: tznndyan 60amyaki ar̄t'iv, 1897–1957. Met'odakan nyut'er gradaranneri hamar.* (Erevan, 1957).
Kubat'ian, G. "Pasternak perevodit Charentsa." *BEH,* 1990/1, 70–76.
Łazaḥetsyan, V. "Ełiše Charentsě Erevani ułłich taně." *Banber Hayastani arḥivneri,* 1990/2, 113–26. (Documents).
Madoyan, G. "Ełiše Charentsi grakan arḥivě." *BEH,* 1979/1, 136–40.
Mahari, G. "Kině Ełiše Charentsi erkerum." *SG,* 1967/9, 43–45.
———. *Charents-name.* (Erevan, 1968).
Manukyan, S. "Hangutsayin hartseri skzbunk'ayin k'nnut'yun." *SG,* 1982/8, 142–44. (On Ēd. Jrbašyan's *Chors gagat', . . .*).
Marut'yan, A. Ełiše Charentsě ev hay grakan lezvi zargatsman hartserě." *SG,* 1962/1, 122–29.
———. "Norabanut'yunnerě Ełiše Charentsi chap'atzoyi bar̄apašarum." *SG,* 1964/8, 126–34.
———. *Ełiše Charentsi chap'atzoyi lezun ew očě.* (Erevan, 1979).
Mat'evosyan, V. "Charents-Kojoyan ('Girk' čanaparhi')." *SG,* 1967/9, 33–42.
Mazmanyan, M. "Charentsi het." *SG,* 1960/8, 94–112.
Melik'set'yan, S. "Aha t'e inch ē nšanakum Ełiše Charents." *SG,* 1977/1, 105–13.
Mesropyan, A. "Charentsě Komitasi masin." *EJ,* 1959/6, 29–34.
Mnatsakanyan, V. "Charentsě polemist." *SG,* 1979/4, 95–111.
Movsisyan, H. "Ełiše Charentsi erkeri t'argmanut'yunnerě Iranum." *PBH,* 1977/4, 99–102.
Muradyan, A. "Ełiše Charentsi poeziayi bar̄apašarě." *T,* 1964/3, 27–40.
N. H. "Tant'ē ew Charents." *B,* 123 (1965), 364–65.
Nawasardean, V. *Charents (yušer ew ḥorhrdatzut'iwnner).* (Cairo, 1957).
Norents, V. "Bolor žamanakneri banastełtzě." *SG,* 1967/9, 4–10.
Ōšakan, Y. "Ełišē Charents." *HK,* 3 (1924–25/2), 52–67; 3, 45–62; 4, 41–50.
P'anyan, Yu. "Charentsě ev Bryusově." *PBH,* 1974/4, 61–71.
———. "Banastełtzakan žanreri hartserě Charentsi gełagitut'yan mej." *L,* 1974/8, 16–26.
Partizuni, V. "Vahan Teryaně ev Ełiše Charentsě." *SG,* 1966/2, 139–59.
Sahakyan, P. "Puškini 'Płndze mardě' ev Charentsi 'Chugune mardě'." *SG,* 1974/5, 111–18.
Sak'apetoyan, Ṙ. "Charentsě lezvi masin." *BEH,* 1970/2, 61–72.
———. "Žołovrda-ḥosaktsakan tarrerě Ełiše Charentsi 'Erkir Nairi' vepum." *PBH,* 1972/3, 116–38.
Salakhian, A. *Egishe Charents.* (Erevan, 1956). (Russian).
Šarabḥanyan, P. "Hangi mi k'ani ar̄andznahatkut'yunner Charentsi erkerum." *BEH,* 1969/2, 153–63.
Sargsyan, G. "Charentsě Hoktemberi botsašunch ergich." *PBH,* 1959/2–3, 177–89.
Shakaryan, R. "Eghishe Charents." *SL,* 1966/3, 165–69. (English).
Sigua, A. "Na ayrvum ēr poeziayi hrov." *SG,* 1977/11, 159–61.
Simēōneants, A. "K'ani mě veryišumner Ełišē Charentsi masin." *HK,* 28 (1950/1), 106–11.

Slivniak, D. "Ełiše Charentsi 'Tałarani' kařutsvatzkʻi mi kʻani hartser." *BEH,* 1977/3, 129–34.
Snapean, P. *Andrširimean dzayner: patasḥan Gurgēn Maharii.* (Beirut, 1960).
Šušanyan, V. "Ełiše Charentsi masin (Tpvatz 1923tʻ. sept. Kahirei *Nor šaržum* šabatʻatʻertʻum)." *L,* 1989/10, 77–83.
Tʻamrazyan, H. "Ełiše Charentsě ev sovetahay poezian." *SG,* 1958/1, 99–110.
———. "Charentsi mahvan tesilnerě." *SG,* 1972/6, 18–34.
———. *Eritasard Charentsě.* (Erevan, 1974).
———. "Charentsi yotʻ ḥorhurdě."*SG,* 1977/3, 128–38.
———. "Ełiše Charentsi 'Erkir Nairi' vepě." *PBH,* 1977/4, 23–42.
———. "Charentsi 'šełumnerits' mekě." *SG,* 1977/11, 115–24.
———. *Ełiše Charents.* (Erevan, 1981, 1987).
Tʻeřlik, G. "Ełiše Charentsi 'Sasuntsi Davitě'." *SG,* 1971/9, 140–45.
———. "Charentsi erevanyan mayisě." *SG,* 1975/7, 158–64.
Tʻuršyan, H. " 'Erkir Nairii' erku kerpari naḥatiperě." *SG,* 1967/9, 46–48.
———. "Charentsi mi banastełtzutʻyan hetkʻerov." *SG,* 1971/5, 152. (Mahvan tesil).
Yakobean, S. *Ełišē Charents, grakan kʻnnadatakan verlutzutʻiwn.* (Vienna, 1924).
Zakʻaryan, A. "Ełiše Charentsi banastełtzakan mutkʻě." *SG,* 1972/6, 35–44.
———. "Hełapʻoḥutʻyan tarineri Charentsi banastełtzakan šrjadardzě." *L,* 1977/11, 72–87.
———. "E. Charentsi 1920 tʻ. banastełtzakan šarkʻeri hetkʻerov." *SG,* 1981/10, 104–18.
———. "E. Charentsě verjin angam hayreni Karsum." *L,* 1982/2, 13–24.
Zakʻaryan, G. "Ełiše Charentsi 'Dantʻeakan ařaspelě'." *L,* 1990/4, 3–13.
Zakʻaryan, M. "Ełiše Charentsě 20akan tʻvakanneri grapaykʻarum." *SG,* 1973/5, 131–34.
———. "Hełapʻoḥutʻyan tʻeman E. Charentsi poeziayum." *L,* 1980/10, 3–14.
———. "E. Charentsi hušagrutʻyuně ('Erevani ułłich tnits')." *BEH,* 1982/1, 159–67.
———. *Kʻałakʻatsi banastełtzě.* (Erevan, 1985).
"Žamanakakitsnerě Charentsi masin." *SG,* 1967/3, 3–10.
Zoryan, S. "Charents." *SG,* 1977/8, 150–60. (Written in 1941).

CHARḤUTEAN, NUPAR (1920–)

Born in Marash (Kahramanmaraş, Turkey), Charḥutean grew up in Aleppo. He lived in Damascus until the late 1940s and subsequently moved to Beirut, where he taught French and French literature. Initially, he wrote in French, but in the early 1950s he began writing both prose and verse in Armenian. He moved to California in 1986.

Texts (in Armenian)

Kayēn anmełě. (Beirut, 1954). (Novel).
Ōrōr diakneru hamar. (Beirut, 1955). (Poetry).
Ardarnerun očirě. (Beirut, 1961). (Poetry).
Unaynutʻean apʻerě. (Beirut, 1975). (Novel).
Mahapartě. (Los Angeles, 1991). (Novel; first in a projected cycle of four novels, under the general title *Ařants astłi čamban*).

K'ałak'ĕ ur Narek chkar. (Los Angeles, 1993). (Novel).

Texts in French (verse)

Poèmes. (Beirut, 1941).
Salomé. (Damascus, 1949).
Berceuses pour des cadavres. (Beirut, 1953).

CHĒŌKIWREAN, TIGRAN (1884–1915)

Pen name: Mehekan.

Born in Gümüşhane, Turkey. Lost his parents at an early age and grew up in orphanages in Constantinople. Graduated from the famous Pērpērean school of Constantinople in 1907. Taught and engaged in public activities. Published the periodical *Ostan* (Constantinople, 1911–12) with Mik'ayēl Šamtančean (1874–1926). Published some of his short stories and novelettes separately, but his poems are still scattered in the periodical press. Along with numerous colleagues, he was arrested and slain during the deportations and massacres in 1915.

Collections

Erker. (Erevan, 1984).

Texts

Hayreni dzayner. (Constantinople, 1910).
Vank'ĕ. (Constantinople, 1914; Erevan, 1962). (Story).
Vank'ĕ. Herosĕ. (Paris, 1933). (Stories).

Translations (French)

Ter-Sarkissian, P. *Le Monastère, journal d'un religieux.* (Marseilles: Editions Parenthèses, 1988).

Criticism

Ełišē, T'. "Tigran Chēōkiwrean." *VER,* 5 (1921), 24–25.
Eremean, S. "Tigran Chēōkiwrean." *B,* 90 (1933), 208–12.
Ḥachatryan, T'. "Tigran Chyokuryanĕ k'nnadat." *BEH,* 1985/3, 160–64.
Hyusyan, M. "Hay ardzaki gluḫgortzotsnerits mekĕ." *SG,* 1963/1, 129–34.
K'[iwfēčean], Y[akob]. "Girk'er-Vank'ĕ Tigran Chēōkiwreani." *Mehean,* 1914/2, 30.
Sargsyan, G. "Tigran Chyokuryanĕ grakan k'nnadat." *L,* 1985/10, 49–57.
Sewan, A. "Tigran Chēōkiwrean." *HK,* 8 (1929–30/11), 43–72.

CHERAZ, MINAS (1852–1929)

Born in Constantinople to parents originally from the village of Cheraz, near Akn (Eğin, now Kemaliye, Turkey). A public and political figure, teacher, and writer. Educated in his birthplace. Taught at various Armenian schools, and was principal of the Kedronakan school (1886–89) in Constantinople. As secretary and interpreter, he accompanied the unofficial Armenian delegation to the Congress of Berlin (1878) in pursuit of the Armenian Question, which he continued to promote with British and Russian politicians. In 1889 he fled Constantinople and settled in London, where he published *L'Arménie-Armenia* to propagate the Armenian cause. He also lived in Paris (1898–08, 1910–18), Constantinople (1908–10), and Marseilles (from 1918 to his death).

Texts (literary)

Grakan p̕ordzer. (Constantinople, 1874). (Verse, speeches, criticism).
Nouvelles orientales. (Paris, 1911). (Stories in French).
Dambaran. (New York, 1920). (Prose; written with E. Tēmirčipašean).

Other works (political, polemical, and philological)

Azgayin dastiarakut̕iwn. (Constantinople, 1876).
Inch šahetsank̕ Perlini vehažołovēn? (Constantinople, 1878).
Hayastan ew Italia. (Constantinople, 1879).
Grich ew sur. (Constantinople, 1881).
Haykakan ḥndir. (Venice, 1917).
Azgayin ḥndirner: patasḥan aṙ Aršak Alpōyačean. (Paris, 1927).
Kensagrakan miwsionner. (Paris, 1929).

Translations

English

"Armenaki." *The Oriental World* (New York) 1914/4, 113–16. (Translated from the French). Also published in *Armenia* (Boston), 7 (1914/4), 113–16.
"The Beggar." *Nor ašḥarh* (New York), 1963/25, 4.
"Dangoudy." *Armenia* (Boston), 7 (1913/1), 14–17. (From *Nouvelles orientales*). Also published in *The New Armenia,* 8 (1916/15), 232–34.
"Deunme Emine." *Armenia* (Boston), 4 (1911/10), 8–11. (From *Nouvelles orientales*).
"The Last Dance." *Armenia* (Boston), 4 (1911/11), 5–6. Also published in *The Armenian Mirror,* December 1, 1933, 2, 4; and *The New Armenia,* 8 (1916/10), 151.
"Loxandra Pandelis. A Story Founded on Fact." *Armenia* (Boston), 3 (1907/4), 18–24.
"The Mendicant. An Armenian Legend." *Armenia* (Boston), 6 (1913/6), 181–82.
"New Year's Day in Armenia." *Armenia* (Boston), 5 (1912/6), 166–67. Also published in *The New Armenia* (Boston), 10 (1918/1), 4–5.
"The Old Mountaineer." *Armenia* (Boston), 6 (1913/8), 244–45.
"The Pasha and His Wives." *Armenia* (newspaper), January 1, 1894, 2–3.
"Sooren's Revenge." *The New Armenia* (Boston), 8 (1916/9), 136–37.

French

"Armenaki." *L'Arménie* (newspaper), 1906/206, 4.
"La dernière danse." *L'Arménie,* 1904/191, 1–2.
"Lévon." *L'Arménie,* 1905/205, 4.
"Le pacha à quarante femmes." *L'Arménie,* 1894/63, 2–3. Also published in *La Patrie* (Constantinople), 1911/129, 205.
"Le vieux montagnard." *L'Arménie,* 1902/170, 1–2.

Criticism

Alpōyačean, A. *Minas Cheraz, ir keank̕ě ew gortzě.* (Cairo, 1927).
Marshall, A. "Minas Tcheraz, a Biographical Sketch." *Armenia* (Boston), 6 (1913/8), 240–43.
Minas Cherazi vat̕snameay hanrayin gortzunēut̕ean yobelean, 1865–1925. (Paris, 1928).
"Minas Tcheraz." *The New Armenia* (Boston), 21 (1929/3), 40–41.

Yovhannēsean, A. *Minas Cheraz, Arewelean vēpikner, usumnasirutʻiwn.* (Paris, 1927).

CHIFTʻĒ-SARAF, ŌNNIK (1874–1932)

Pen names: Kʻotakʻ; Yovh. Tohmik; Yovhannēs Aspet.

Born Yovhannēs Abisołomean Aspet in Constantinople. A journalist and writer of short stories. Educated at the Kedronakan of his birthplace. In 1920, he was in Corfu looking after Armenian orphans. Spent the last decade of his life teaching in Marseilles and Geneva (1928 to his death). Most of his works, appearing in many periodicals, including *Masis* (Constantinople, 1901, 1903, 1904, etc.) and *Hay grakanutʻiwn* (Smyrna, 1911–12), have not yet been collected.

Collections

Erker. (Erevan, 1981).

Texts (prose)

Miamiti mě arkatznerě (erb amuri ēr). (Constantinople, 1908).
Tʻurkʻ tʻēṙōri ōrerēn, im bantarkutʻiwns. (Constantinople, 1909).

Criticism

Akopdzhanian, A. *Chifte Saraf.* (Erevan, 1983).
Chōpanean, A. "Mah Yovhannēs Aspeti." *ANA,* 1932/1–2, 180–82.
Ēsačanean, L. "Yovhannēs Aspet." *HK,* 11 (1932–33/11), 130–32.
Esayean, Z. "Vipakan aruestě mer mēj—'Miamiti mě arkatznerě'." *M,* 1908/12–13, 239–43.
Gamēr, "Urvagitzner–Chiftʻē-Saraf." *M,* 1903/37, 585.
Hakobjanyan, H. "Ōnnik Chiftʻe-Sarafi grakan-kʻnnadatakan žaṙangutʻyuně." *PBH,* 1981/4, 167–81.
Parsamean, M. "Gałapʻarner u zgayutʻiwnner." *AM,* 1905, 236–39.
———. "Grakan kʻronik. 'Miamiti mě arkatznerě'." *AM,* 1907, 1285–87.
Yarutʻiwnean, A. "Vičabanutʻiwn mě." *AM,* 1906, 442–45. (On Chiftʻē-Saraf and others).
———. "Dēmkʻer, Chiftʻē-Saraf." *AM,* 1907, 1087–92.
———. "Grakan kʻronik, aṙaspel mě." *AM,* 1908, 216–21.
———. "Grakan kʻronik, anbaroyakan grakanutʻiwn." *AM,* 1908, 703–6.

CHŌPANEAN, ARŠAK (1872–1954)

Born in Constantinople and educated at the local Kedronakan school. A poet, playwright, literary critic, publicist-journalist, and translator. Taught in Armenian schools, published his writings in the periodical press, and briefly edited the periodical *Tzałik,* before making Paris home in 1895. There, he soon established extensive and close contacts with leading French and European intellectuals. In 1898, he launched his celebrated perodical *Anahit* (1898–1911, 1929–40, 1946–49), and a short-lived monthly, *Veratznund* (1917–21). To the very end of his life, he tirelessly propagated Armenian culture, concerns, and aspirations through translations into French and the publication of literary texts and anthologies.

Collections

Norents, V., and Tarontsi, S. *Erker.* (Erevan, 1966).
Erker. (Erevan, 1988).

Texts

Aršaloysi dzayner. Parts 1 and 2 (Constantinople, 1891). (Prose and verse).
Tułťi ṗaṙkĕ; hogebanakan vipak. (Constantinople, 1892, 1924). (Story).
Trťṙumner: hawakatzoy banastełtzuťean. (Constantinople, 1892). (Poetry).
Gťuťiwn: ḱerťuatz. (Constantinople, 1892). (Poem).
Horizonĕ. (Paris, 1905).
Ḱerťuatzner: Aršaloys, Žamerun karawanĕ, Andzkuťiwn, Tesilner, Gišerin mēj, Blurin vray. (Paris, 1908). (Poetry).
La vie et le rêve. Poèmes en prose, contes, fantaisies. (Paris, 1913).
Offrande poétique à la France. (Paris, 1917).
Hayastanĕ ťurḱ lutzin tak. (Boston, 1918). (Armenian version of his *L'Arménie sous le joug turc*).
Tłu hoginer. (Paris, 1923). (Stories).
Hayreni ḱnar. (Paris, 1925). (Verse and prose).
Patkerner. (Paris, 1940). (Essays).
Keanḱ ew eraz: ardzak banastełtzuťiwnner, hēḱeaťner, ḱmatzin ējer. (Paris, 1945). (Prose).
Banastełtzuťiwnner. (Paris, 1949 [cover, 1950]). (Poetry).
Bambasanḱ. (Paris, 1950). (Play).
Hrašḱĕ. (Beirut, 1952). (Play).
Pasmačean, G. *Antip namakner A. Chōpaneanēn.* (Cairo, 1973). (Letters).
Namakani. (Erevan, 1980).
Vardanyan, V. "Aleḱsandr Abelyani namaknerĕ Aršak Chopanyanin." *L,* 1982/5, 89–98.

Other works and translations by Chōpanean

Les massacres d'Arménie. (Paris, 1896).
L'Arménie; son histoire, sa littérature, son rôle en Orient. (Paris, 1897).
Le peuple arménien, son passé, sa culture, son avenir. (Paris, 1913).
L'Arménie sous le joug turc. (Paris, 1916).
Hayastanĕ ťurḱ lutzin tak. [Armenian version of the above]. (Boston, 1919).
La France et le peuple arménien. (Paris, 1917).
La femme arménienne. (Paris, 1918).
Dēmḱer. 2 vols. (Paris, 1924, 1929).
Erkrašaržĕ artasahmani mēj. (Boston, 1926).
Hay azgĕ "meławor" chē. (Paris, 1926).
Mer grakanuťiwnĕ. (Paris, 1926).
Victor Hugo, Chateaubriand et Lamartine dans la littérature arménienne. (Paris, 1935).
La nation arménienne et son œuvre culturelle. (Paris, 1945).
Les arméniens ne sont nullement pourchassés en France. (Paris, 1947).

Translations

Aghassi. *Zeitoun.* (Paris, 1897).
Poèmes arméniens, anciens et modernes. (Paris, 1902).
Chants populaires arméniens. (Paris, 1903). [Bibliothèque arménienne].
Trouvères arméniens. (Paris, 1906).
La roseraie d'Arménie. 3 vols. (Paris, 1918–1929).

English

"Before the Manger." *Armenia* (Boston), 5 (1911/5), 133–34.

Blackwell, A. "Lullaby for Mother Armenia." *The New Armenia,* 8 (1916/15), 237–38.
———."Within My Heart," "The Wind." *Armenia* (Boston), 5 (1912/8), 237.
"The Epic of Armenia." *The Armenian Herald,* May, 1918, p. 317.
Gregory, M. *The People of Armenia: Their Past, Their Culture, Their Future.* (London, 1914).
S[afrastian], A. "She Walks Where the Dewy Sunset," "White Dove, Why Do You through the Day . . ." *Ararat* (London), 1 (1914/8), 270–71.
S. E. "The Trouvère, Like a Wingless Bird," "My Heart Is like a Child that Cries." *Ararat* (London), 1 (1914/9), 309–10.
———. "Comrade, Do Not Despond," "With Slippers that so Lightly Tread." *Ararat* (London), 1 (1914/8), 269–71.
"What Shall I Do With My Soul?" *Armenia* (Boston), 6 (1913/10), 302–3.
J. G. M. "What Can I Do with the Spirit?" *The Armenian Review,* 6 (1953/2), 111–12.

English anthologies

ALP, 118.
AP, 175–85.

French

"Berceuse pour notre mère l'Arménie." In *Hommage à l'Arménie,* (Paris, 1919), 19–22.
Chobanean, A. "A l'Arménie." *L'Arménie* (newspaper), 1898/116, 4.
———. "L'Aventure du petit paysan d'Arménie." *Mercure de France* (Série moderne), 29/111 (March, 1899), 605–11.
"Il faut mourir." *La Patrie* (Constantinople), 1909/25, 186–87.
"Le bonheur present.–Rêve." *La Patrie* (Constantinople), 1909/33, 286.
H. "Poésies." *La Patrie* (Constantinople), 1908, 5–8, 106. 1909, 186, 286, 399, 421–22.
———. "Tes yeux dans mes yeux," "Une jeune fille en prière," "Attente." *La Patrie* (Constantinople), 1909/31, 262.
———. "A une jeune fille." *La Patrie* (Constantinople), 1909/44, 380–81.
———. "La douleur d'Adam," "Un monstre," "Vieux souvenir." *La Patrie* (Constantinople), 1909/46, 399.
———. "O mère . . ." *La Patrie* (Constantinople), 1909/49, 421–22.
———. "Ode à la France." *Šant‘,* 1919/15, 170.
"Le messager divin." *La Patrie* (Constantinople), 1908/8, 95–96.
Minassian, J. "Hais-moi mais ne m'oublie pas." *La Patrie* (Constantinople) 1908/1, 12–13.
O. "Éctrennes." *La Patrie* (Constantinople), 1908/9, 106.
———. "Voyez-vous celui qui travaille là?" *La Patrie* (Constantinople), 1908/2, 25.
"Sonnet." *La Patrie* (Constantinople), 1908/5, 58.
Tchobanian, A. *La sœurette lointaine et autres histoires d'enfants.* (Paris, 1926).
La vie et le rêve. (Paris, 1913).

French anthologies

APA, 133–39.
FPA, 49–51.
LPA, 198–99.

German anthologies

AD, 22–23.

Russian anthologies

BPA, 457–58.

VAM, 172–75.

Spanish anthologies

APAS, 197–200.

Criticism

Abełean, A. "Mijnadarean hay banastełtzutʻiwnĕ ew Aršak Chōpanean." *Z* (amsōreay), 1 (1938/6), 43; 1 (1938/7), 52.

Alekʻsanean, T. *Aršak Chōpanean.* (Athens, 1939).

Andrikean, N. "Aršak Chōpanean." *B,* 66 (1908), 220–22.

Armēn, E. *Aršak Chōpanean–keankʻĕ ew grakan u hasarakakan gortzunēutʻiwnĕ.* (Constantinople, 1913).

"Aršak Chōpanean," *Ani,* 4 (1950–51/9), 515–19.

Atʻmačyan, M. "Hušer Aršak Chopanyani kyankʻin verjin šrjanen." *SG,* 1972/6, 119–22.

Avetisyan, Y. " 'Tzałik' handesĕ Aršak Chopanyani ḥmbagrutʻyamb." *BEH,* 1986/2, 137–45.

Baluean, H. "Aršak Chōpanean." *Z* (amsōreay), 1 (1938/5), 33.

Čanašean, M. "Aršak Chōpanean." *B,* 114 (1956), 252–56.

Dallakʻyan, K. *Aršak Chopanyan.* (Erevan, 1987).

Fēnērčean, G. *Aršak Chōpanean. Kensagrakan ew matenagrakan nōtʻer.* (Paris, 1938).

Fntkʻlean, G. "Erekʻ banastełtz–Mihran Yovhannēsean, 'Irakan keankʻi nuagner'; Aršak Chōpanean, 'Tʻrtʻrumner'; Mkrtich Ačēmean, 'Garnan hover'." *M,* 1965 (1892), 159–64.

Gabrielyan, V. "Aršak Chopanyanĕ sovetahay grakanutʻyan kʻnnadat." *BEH,* 1989/1, 33–46.

Hapēšean, H. *Aršak Chōpanean: kensagrakan gtzer.* (Paris, 1924).

Inčikyan, A. "Isahakyani ev Chopanyani namakagrutʻyunĕ." *BEH,* 1970/2, 157–76.

Kʻalantʻaryan, Ž. "Aršak Chopanyanĕ spʻyurkʻahay grakanutʻyan kʻnnadat." *BEH,* 1989/3, 26–36.

Khayadjian, E. *Archag Tchobanian et le mouvement arménophile en France.* (N.p., n.d.; possibly Marseilles, 1986).

Kostanyan, A. "Metz žařangutʻyun." *SG,* 1966/10, 126–31.

Marshall, A. "Arshag Tchobanian. A biographical sketch." *Armenia* (Boston), 6 (1913/10), 298–301.

Muratean, S. *Aršak Chōpanean, hamařōt kensagrakan mĕ.* (Paris, 1902).

Nazariantz, H. *Arsciak Ciobanian nella sua vita e nelle sue pagine migliori.* (Bari, 1917).

Norents, V. "Aršak Chopanyan." *SG,* 1964/9, 111–19.

———. "Hay mšakuytʻi metz eraḥtavorĕ." *SG,* 1972/6, 93–97.

Ōšakan, Y. "Aršak Chōpanean." *S,* 1952, 316–21.

Šakʻlean, A. "Tułtʻi pʻařkʻ." *AM,* 1892, 415–22.

Saruḥan, "Aršak Chōpaneani yobeleanĕ." *HA,* 39 (1925), 80–87.

Siruni, H. "Aršak Chopanyanĕ inchpes or ē." *SG,* 1972/6, 106–18.

Sivadjian, J. *Archag Tchobanian.* (Paris, n.d.).
Step'anyan, G. "Aršak Chopanyan." *PBH,* 1972/2, 129–42.
T'op'chyan, S. "Aršak Chopanyani namakneri žołovatzun." *SG,* 1981/3, 131–34. (On *Namakni,* Erevan, 1980).
Zak'aryan, A. "Połos Makintsyani namaknerě Aršak Chopanyanin." *L,* 1981/3, 93–96.
Zaroyean, P. "A. Chōpaneani p'ařk'ě." *Z* (amsōreay), 1 (1930/5), 35.

ČUŁURYAN, HARUT'YUN (1864–1938)

Pen names: Giwłatsi, Set'.

Born in Ḫašt'ařak, a village in Ijevan, Armenia. Graduated from the Nersisean school in Tiflis in 1890 and was ordained a married priest in 1898. Taught in Armenian schools in Tiflis, in his birthplace, and in other villages in Ijevan. In his prose encompassing life in Armenian villages, he focused on social-political concerns and criticized men of religion. The entire run of his *Chatoyi baḫti aniwě* (Chato's wheel of fortune) was confiscated and destroyed by the czarist censorship. Moved to Erevan in 1923, abandoned the priesthood, and resumed his teaching career in Soviet Armenia. Died in Erevan.

Texts (stories and novels)

Mořatsuatz ašḫarh. Books 1 and 2. (Tiflis, 1895). Book 3 (Tiflis, 1896). (Erevan, 1935, 1968).
Ała surb Sargisě ew Malak' tati hawatě. (Tiflis, 1899).
Ałk'ati halě. (Tiflis, 1902).
Giwłi ayrin. (Tiflis, 1902).
Chatoyi baḫti aniwě. (Tiflis, 1908).
Širinants Naḫšuně. (Tiflis, 1911, 1931).

Criticism

Ałbalean, N. "Čułurean Y. sarkawag, Mořatsuatz ašḫarh, 3. girk', Tiflis, 1896." *Murč,* 1896/12, 1597–99.
———. "Čułurean Y. k'ahanay, Ała surb Sargisě ew Malak' tati hawatě, Tiflis, 1899." *Murč,* 1899/2–3, 288–91.
M. L. "Čułurean Y. sarkawag, Mořatsuatz ašḫarh, 1. girk', Tiflis, [1895]." *Murč,* 1895/2, 285–87.

DARBINYAN, MAT'EVOS (1891–1937)

Pen names: For a complete list, see B. Melyan's *Mat'evos Darbinyan (kensamatenagitut'yun),* Erevan, 1970, pp. 309–11.

Born in the village of T'ovuz, in the region of Šamšadin (now Tauš), Armenia. Wrote short stories, plays, poetry, and literature for children. Received his elementary education in his native village. Graduated from the Nersisean school of Tiflis (1908) and subsequently taught at Armenian schools in Transcaucasia. In 1922, with Hakob Hakobyan (q.v.), he founded the Armenian section of the Association of Proletarian Writers of Georgia. In the years 1930–32, he was head of the Armenian programs broadcast by radio Tiflis. His life was cut short during the Stalinist purges.

Collections

Payazat, S. *Erker.* (Erevan, 1959).

Texts

Ministrner. Komedia. (Tiflis, 1924). (Comedy).
Vlastě.-Komdezě.–K'ot'ot'ě. (Tiflis, 1925). (Stories).
Tsarn u Murčě. (Tiflis, 1925). (Story).
Šah-Zadei abasin. (Tiflis, 1927), (Tale).
Čutiknerě. (Tiflis, 1928).
Kikosě: vipak. (Erevan, 1929). (Novella; introduction by E. Charents).
Norě. (Tiflis, 1929). (Stories).
Jałatspan Antoně. (Erevan, 1930). (Novelette).
Komsomol: hakakronakan komedia. (Tiflis, 1930). (Comedy).
P'arsadan. (Tiflis, 1930). (Story).
Zart'noł gyułě. (Erevan, 1930). (Stories).
Kolḥozayin. (Tiflis, 1931). (Stories).
Člkutě (čahčutě). (Erevan, 1931).
P'ok'rik komunarě. (Erevan, 1931).
Oske t'eler. (Tiflis, 1932). (Stories).
Verjině. (Tiflis, 1934). (Novel).
P'ok'rik herosner. (Tiflis, 1934). (Stories).
Suldin u Buldin. (Erevan, 1936). (First published in Georgian).
Ḥalicha. (Tiflis, 1936). (Poetry).
Tzavikn u hatikě. (Erevan, 1937).

Translations

RUSSIAN

Korganova, M. *Pugovitsa.* (Tiflis, 1932).
Shamtsian, M. *Kikos.* (Moscow, 1966).

Bibliographies

Melyan, B. *Mat'evos Darbinyan (kensamatenagitut'yun).* (Erevan, 1970).

Criticism

Eremean, A. "Matt'ēos Darbinean." *ANA,* 2 (1931/5–6), 130–31.

DARBNI, ARŠAVIR (1910–1980)

Pen name: Aršavir Darbni.

Born Aršavir Mnatsakanyan in the village of Getašen, in the Ḥanlar region of Azerbaijan. Fabulist, poet, and playwright. Worked at the Armenian theater of Baku after his graduation from the institute of cinematography in Moscow. In the wake of World War II, he moved to Erevan and briefly held the position of secretary to the Union of Soviet Writers of Armenia (1949–50).

Collections

Erker. (Erevan, 1972). (Intended to be 3 vols., but vols. 2 and 3 have not been published).
Banastełtzut'yunner. (Erevan, 1978).

Texts

Erb batsvum ē manušakě. (Baku, 1948). (Play).

Mrgašati lusabatsě. (Erevan, 1952). (Prose).
Arakner. (Erevan, 1952, 1955, 1959; Beirut, 1957). (Fables in verse).
P'isikě kinoyum. (Erevan, 1957). (Poem).
Kamurj. (Erevan, 1958).
Tzaɫikner ev šaɫikner. (Erevan, 1959).
P'ok'rik bžškuhin. (Erevan, 1962).
Balikner ev tzaɫikner. (Erevan, 1963).
Arevits paytzar anun. (Erevan, 1966).
Aɫvesě draḥtum. (Erevan, 1969). (Poetry).
Mankut'yuně chi tzeranum. (Erevan, 1981).

Translations

French

Gaucheron, J. *E.*
LPA, 329–30.

Russian

Ginzburg, L. *Basni.* (Erevan, 1952).
———. *Neobyknovennaia vezhlivost'. Basni i stikhi.* (Erevan, 1956).
———. *Solovei v ambulatorii. Basni i stikhi.* (Moscow, 1959).
Rassvet v Mrgashate. (Erevan, 1952).
Vanshenkin, K., and Ginzburg, L. *Kotenok v kino. Basni i stikhi dlia mladsh. vozrasta.* (Moscow, 1959).

Criticism

Gasparyan, Ṙ. "Aršavir Darbnu araknerě." *SG,* 1960/2, 156–59.
Sargsyan, S. "Aršavir Darbni." *SG,* 1970/2, 135–38.

DARFI, GĒORG (1907–1964)

Pen name: Gēorg Darfi.
Born Gēorg Yovhannisean-Ḥudoyean in Saramerik, a village near Salmas, Iran. Dramatist. Following his studies in Tiflis (1915–17) and in a French school in Tabriz, he engaged in teaching.

Texts (dramas)

Siauš ew Sudabē. (Teheran, 1936).
Ardarut'ean čanaparhin. (Teheran, 1955).
Oɫjoyn k'ez, Milano. (Teheran, 1960).
Mesrop Maštots. (Teheran, 1963).
Ariwnot t'agě. (Teheran, 1964).
Ank'awelin. (Teheran, 1964).
Vahan ew Ṙazmduḥt. (Teheran, 1964).

DARYAN, ZARZAND (1912–1984)

Pen name: Zarzand Daryan.
Born Zarzand Movsisyan in the village of Kop' (near Bulanık, northwest of Lake Van). A novelist and a writer of short stories and plays. Graduated from Erevan State University and worked as a journalist.

Collections

Erker. 2 vols. (Vol. 1, Erevan, 1976).

Texts

Patmvatzkʻner. (Erevan, 1938). (Stories).
Patmvatzkʻner. (Erevan, 1946). (Stories).
Im aṙavotě. (Erevan, 1949). (Prose).
Garun. (Erevan, 1949).
Ałbyur. (Erevan, 1951). (Prose).
Kʻnnutʻyun. (Erevan, 1953). (Story).
Mayis. (Erevan, 1957). (Novel).
Ardzagankʻ. (Erevan, 1959).
Garnan ałmuk. (Erevan, 1959). (Plays).
Sayatʻ-Nova. 2 vols. (Erevan, 1960–63, 1978). (Novel).
Kʻasał. (Erevan, 1962). (Collection of short stories and essays).
Artziv Vaspurakani. (Erevan, 1965, 1988). (Novel).
Verjin tʻṙichkʻě. (Erevan, 1967). (Prose).
Hasmik. (Erevan, 1969).
Dzmṙan mi gišer. (Erevan, 1969). (Play).
Ays hin ašḥarhě. (Erevan, 1974). (Prose).
Šušan. (Erevan, 1975). (Prose).
"Arevě tzagum ē tzovits." *SG,* 1980/9, 6–49.
Kʻaṙułiner. 2 books. (Erevan, 1981–82). (Novel).
Askʻ Nga [i.e., the old Province of Nig, Armenia] (Patma-hayrenagitakan aknark). (Erevan, 1983).
Mer hamr, mer hazaralezu hołě. (Erevan, 1985). (Essay).
Aydpisi ser. (Erevan, 1986). (Stories).
Arevagal. (Erevan, 1990). (Novels, dramas).

Bibliography

Petrosyants, V. *Zarzand Daryan.* (Erevan, 1988).

Translations (Russian)

Barkhudarian, A. *Moe utro–V nashem sele.* (Erevan, 1952).

DAŠTENTS, ḤACHIK (1910–1974)

Pen name: Ḥachik Daštents.

Born Ḥachik Tonoyan in Daštadem (a village in the region of Bitlis). Novelist, poet, and translator (principally from English, and the works of Shakespeare in particular). Survived the Armenian massacres of 1915; was given shelter and education by American organizations in Alexandrapol (Leninakan, now Gyumril, Armenia). Graduated from the State University of Erevan and studied English at the Institute of Foreign Languages in Moscow (1940). Taught at various institutions: Erevan State University (1940–41), the Briusov Institute for Foreign Languages in Erevan (1941–48), and the Polytechnic Institute (1960–66). Worked at the Institute of Art (1965–74).

Texts

Ergeri girkʻ. (Erevan, 1932). (Poetry).
Garnanayin erger. (Erevan, 1934). (Poetry).
Bots. (Moscow and Erevan, 1936). (Poetry).
Ay du žulik Msra Melikʻ. (Erevan, 1940).

Tigran Metz. (Erevan, 1947). (Drama).
Ḥodedan. (Erevan, 1950, 1956, 1960). (Novel).
Leṙan tzaɫikner. (Erevan, 1963). (Poetry).
Fayton Alekʻě. (Erevan, 1967, 1982). (Poem).
Ṙanchparneri kanchě. (Erevan, 1979, 1984).

Other works

Bayroně ev hayerě. (Erevan, 1959).
Ěɫdzyal aygabatsi ergichě. (ḥoskʻ ev hušer E. Charentsi masin). (Erevan, 1967).

Translations

RUSSIAN

Baiandur, A. *Zov pakharei. Roman-epopeia.* (Moscow, 1984; Erevan, 1986).
Tadeosian, A. *Khodedan. Roman.* (Erevan, 1961).

Criticism

Aharonean, V. "Ḥachik Daštents." *HK,* 18 (1939–40/11), 72–81.
Alekʻsanyan, E. "Ḥachik Daštentsi vepě." *SG,* 1984/9, 136–44. (*On Ṙanchparneri kanchě*).
Esayan, V. "Daštentsi het." *SG,* 1980/7, 142–43.
Muradyan, N. "Ḥachik Daštents." *SG,* 1980/7, 133–41.
Vahē-Vahean. " 'Ḥodedan' Ḥachik Daštentsi." *Ani,* 4 (1950–51/8), 527–30.

DAVTʻYAN, MARGAR (1910–1964)

Born in Šoṙotʻ, a village in Naḥijevan, and educated at the Pedagogical Institute in Erevan and at the State Universityof Baku. Worked for the Armenian daily *Komunist* (Baku), and for the Armenian literary journal *Grakan Adrbejan* (Baku, 1957–64). President of the Armenian section of the Union of Writers of Azerbaijan, from 1939 to his death.

Texts (novels and stories)

Dzorě. (Baku, 1933).
Aṙajin kině. (Erevan, 1934).
Verjin čichě. (Baku, 1935).
Erjankutʻyun. (Baku, 1939).
Uɫiɫ čakatin. (Baku, 1942).
Tzirani tzaṙ. (Baku, 1944).
Veradardz. (Baku, 1946).
Mer gyuɫum. (Baku, 1948).
Uṙenu tak. (Erevan, 1949).
Mer kʻaɫakʻum. (Baku, 1950).
Lusavor uɫi. (Baku, 1952).
Erb tzagum ē arevě. (Baku, 1954).
Vazě. (Baku, 1955).
Patmvatzkʻner. (Baku, 1957).
Aṙajin šivě. (Baku, 1960).
Hapʻštakvatz ser. (Baku, 1960).
Haveržakan ktak. (Erevan, 1965).
Kyankʻn ir hunov. (Baku, 1966).

Translations

RUSSIAN

Boiskunskii, E. *Zaria nad gorodom.* (Baku, 1964).

Kasparov, S. *Vinogradnaia loza. Povest'.* (Baku, 1958).

Pod ivoi. Povest'. ([Baky], 1950).

DAWITʻ BAŁIŠETSI (d. 1673)

Born in Bałēš (Bitlis). Became a celibate priest in 1647 and *vanahayr* (father-superior) of the Ḥndrakatar monastery in 1651. Known for his *Chronicle* and the manuscripts he himself copied or had copied. He was buried on the islet of Lim, Lake Van.

Texts

"Dawtʻi banasiri Bałišetswoy tzałkakʻał arareal i bazum patmagrats [zaz]gn Yabetʻi ew suł inch zSem[ay] ew zKʻamay ěstoyg gtakaw bazum ašḥatutʻeamb ěntrelov zlawn ew zpitanin ansḥalapēs šnorhōkʻ Kʻristosi Astutzoy meroy" in *Manr žamanakagrutʻyunner,* vol. 2, (Erevan, 1956), 300–65. (Chronicle).

Secondary texts

Abrahamyan, A. "Davitʻ Bałišetsu taregrutʻyuně ev nra aržekʻě hay matenagrutʻyan hamar." *EJ,* 1946/8–10, 55–59; 11–12, 35–42.

Kiliketsi. "Dawitʻ Bałišetsi." *A,* 1898, 120–24.

DAWITʻ SALADZORETSI (17th c.)

Dawitʻ is believed to have been a seventeenth-century poet from the village of Saladzor in Erzurum. No other details are known of him save that he was an orphan ("orbik") who may have become a priest after the death of his wife and daughter.

Poems

"Govasankʻ tzałkants." *Mełu Hayastani,* 1858, 21–23. Also published in *Arewelean mamul,* 1884, 137–39, 177–79; Sruandzteants, G. *Hamov hotov* (Constantinople, 1884), 278–85; *KNZ,* 2, 66–75; *Banasēr,* 2–3 (1901), 87–97.

"Dawitʻ Saladzoretswoy Ołb i mahn dster iwroy," *HA,* 50 (1936), 499–501. Also published in *AMH,* 4, 359–62; *Z* (amsōreay), 1 (1938/4), 28; *S,* 1961, 305–6.

"Łaripin sirtn ē i sukʻ, dartn ē ḥorun." *MPT,* 35–36.

Translations

FRENCH

"La louange des fleurs." *RA,* 3, 185–93; *LPA,* 140–46.

RUSSIAN

"Voskhvalenie tsvetov." *AAP,* 296–99.

Criticism

Akinean, N. "Dawitʻ erets Saladzoretsi tałasats." *HA,* 50 (1936), 495–501. Also published in *AMH,* 4, 353–62.

Avetikyan, G. "Davitʻ Saladzoretsu 'Govasankʻ tzałkantsě'." *Grakan tʻertʻ,* January 1, 1941.

Biwzandatsi, N. "Kʻnnutʻiwn anuants tzałkants yišatakelots i Dawtʻē Saladzoretswoy." *Banasēr,* 2–3 (1901), 97–129.

K'iwrtean, Y. "Niwt'er mijnadarean hay tałasatsut'ean hamar: Dawit' Saladzoretswoy Ołb i mah dster iwroy (noragiwt ew aweli ěndardzak tarberak mě; ir kensagrut'ean masin niwt'er)." *Z* (amsōreay), 1 (1938/4), 28.
Sahakyan, H. "Davit' Saladzoretsi." *PBH,* 1972/1, 161–73.

DEMIRČYAN, DERENIK (1877–1956)

Born Derenik Demirčōłlean, in Aḥalk'alak', Georgia. Novelist, poet, and playwright. Educated at the Nersisean school (1897) and the University of Geneva (1905–10). Settled in Erevan in 1925. Elected to the Armenian Academy in 1953. In recognition of his contributions, the Derenik Demirčyan State literary prize for prose writings was established in Soviet Armenia in 1980.

Collections

Erkeri žołovatzu. Vol. 1. (Erevan, 1931).
Erker. Vol. 1. (Erevan, 1946).
Ĕntir patmvatzk'ner. (Erevan, 1950).
Erkeri žołovatzu. 6 vols. and 2 supplementary vols. (Erevan, 1955–63).
Antzanot' ējer. (Erevan, 1974).
Ĕntir patmvatzk'ner. (Erevan, 1974).
Erkeri žołovatzu. 14 vols. (Erevan: Vol. 1, 1976; Vols. 2, 3, 1977; Vol. 4, 1978; Vol. 5, 6, 1982; Vols. 7, 8, 9, 13, 1983; Vols. 10, 11, 12, 1985; Vol. 14, 1987).
Erker. 2 vols. (Erevan, 1977). (Short stories, short pieces, satire).

Texts

Banastełtzut'iwnner. (Tiflis, 1899). (Poetry).
Uḥtaworner. (Tiflis, 1904). (Prose).
Och ays ašḫarhits. (Tiflis, 1905). (Poetry).
Banastełtzut'iwnner. (Tiflis, 1913). (Poetry).
Dēpi tiezerk'. (Tiflis, 1913). (Poetry).
Garun. (Tiflis, 1920). (Verse).
Tzanot'ner. (Erevan, 1927). (Stories).
Patmvatzk'ner. (Erevan, 1928). (Stories).
K'aj Nazar. (Erevan, 1929, 1941, 1956, 1973; Beirut, 1957). (Comedy).
Nrants žpitě. (Erevan, 1929). (Stories).
Chors erg. (Erevan, 1934). (Verse).
Puypuy mukikě. (Erevan, 1934, 1936, 1946, 1955, 1958, 1974, 1986). (Verse).
Nigyar. (Erevan, 1936). (Prose).
Ṙašid. (Erevan, 1936). (Prose).
Tzteri kolektivě. (Erevan, 1937). (Verse).
Patmvatzk'ner. (Erevan, 1938). (Stories).
Ĕnkerner. (Erevan, 1942). (Play).
Vardanank'. 2 vols. (Erevan, 1943–46, 1951, 1954, 1968, 1987; Cairo, 1956). (Novel).
Arjuk-lrjuk. (Erevan, 1944; Aleppo, 1945). (Verse).
Avelordě. (Erevan, 1945, 1962). (Story).
Banastełtzut'yunner. (Erevan, 1945). (Verse).
Tsavatz ser. ([Erevan], 1945). (Novelette).
Tztapar. (Erevan, 1947). (Verse).
Mankakan ašḫarh. (Erevan, 1949).

Patmvatzkʻner. (Erevan, 1955). (Stories).
Krasnarmeytsě. (Erevan, 1968). (Stories).
Tʻumanyani het. (Erevan, 1969). (Reminiscences about Y. Tʻumanean).
Girkʻ tzałkants. (Erevan, 1985). (Story).
Sargsyan, V. "Kʻaj Nazar." *BEH,* 1989/1, 94–105. (Demirčyan's incomplete novel.)

Translations

English

Apresean, S. "Chargah." *Lraber,* August 20, 1960, 4; August 25, 1960, 4; August 27, 1960, 4. Also published in *Nor ašharh,* 1959/14, 4; 15, 4; 16, 4; 17, 4; 18, 4; 19, 4.
Chrakian, E. "The Armenian." *The Armenian Mirror-Spectator,* March 30, 1957, 1, 3.
"King Aram." *The Armenian Review,* 11 (1958/3), 95–100.
"Lenin, Hero of Folklore: Notes on a Train Ride in Armenia." *International Literature* (later *SL*), 1935/6, 46–48.
Pyman, A. "Merkeh." *SL,* 1966/3, 60–64.
———. "Miniatures." *SL,* 1966/3, 65–66.
Wixley, A. "Two Comrades." *International Literature* (later *SL*), 1941/5, 7–24.

English anthologies

ALP, 73.
WM, 22–43.

French

B. du Crest. "De trop." *OO,* 123 (March 1969), 36–54.
Kirazian, D., and Gordon, V. *Vartananc.* (Paris, 1963).

French anthologies

APA, 123–24.
Gamarra, P. *E.* 114–24.
Kirazian, T. *E.* 124–32.

German

Einhorn, E. "Merké." *Sowjet-Literatur,* 1966/3, 66–71.

German anthologies

ALG, 129.
AN, 117–23.

Russian

Balasan, V. *Izbrannoe.* (Short stories and tales). (Erevan, 1950).
Chargai. Rasskazy. (Erevan, 1956).
Khachatariants, Ia. *Khrabryi Nazar.* (Moscow and Leningrad, 1940).
Khrabryi Nazar. P'esa.–Rasskazy. (Moscow, 1937).
Rasskazy. (Moscow, 1954).
Spendiarova, T. *Myshonok Pui-Pui. Skazka.* (Erevan, 1984).
Tadevosian, A. *Vardanank.* (Moscow, 1956, 1961 [Books 1 and 2]; Erevan, 1985).
Ter-Arakelian, V. *Rashid. Povest'.* (Tiflis, 1935).
Vo imia zhizni. (Short stories). (Erevan, 1954).
Vo imia zhizni. Rasskazy. (Moscow, 1964).

Spanish

Kostiukovskaia, A. "Merké." *Literatura Sovietica,* 1966/3, 63–68.

Spanish anthologies

APAS, 185–87.

Bibliographies

Mirzabekyan, Z. *Derenik Demirčyan: matenagrutʻyun, matenagitutʻyun.* (Erevan, 1977).

Muradyan, Hr. *Derenik Demirčyan, 1877–1956, bibliografia.* (Erevan, 1957).

Criticism

Adamyan, A. "Vaveragrer Derenik Demirčyani masin." *T,* 1957/6, 115–17.

Adamyan, H. "Derenik Demirčyanĕ ev ṙus grakan mitkʻĕ." *SG,* 1978/10, 153–57.

Ałababyan, S. "Derenik Demirčyan." *PBH,* 1977/2, 13–26.

———. *Derenik Demirčyan: tznndyan l00amyakĕ.* (Erevan, 1977).

———. "Derenik Demirčean" *HA,* 1983, 179–98.

Alekʻsanyan, E. "Demirčyan ev Gogol." *SG,* 1974/9, 129–37.

Ananyan, G. "Demirčyanĕ ev patmutʻyunĕ." *BEH,* 1977/1, 112–25.

Antʻabyan, Pʻ. "Derenik Demirčyan." *EJ,* 1956/11–12, 117–19.

Antonean, A. "Derenik Demirčean, Banastełtzutʻiwnner." *M,* 1899/15, 484–87.

Arzumanyan, S. "Metz čanaparhi hanragumarĕ." *SG,* 1962/6, 157–63.

Avagyan, M. "Derenik Demirčyani ergitzankʻi lezvaočakan arvesti hetkʻerov." *SG,* 1975/3, 135–46.

Avetisyan, Z. "Erkaḥosutʻyunn u menaḥosutʻyunĕ Demirčyani 'Vardanankʻum'." *SG,* 1979/2, 122–27.

———. " 'Vardanankʻi' hłatsman ev poetikayi hogebanutʻyan mi kʻani hartser." *SG,* 1977/4, 117–28.

Baḥchinyan, H. "Vipasani gałtnikʻĕ." *SG,* 1971/5, 150–51. (On *Vardanankʻ*).

Bałdasaryan, A. "Derenik Demirčyani 'Vardanankʻi' dzeṙagrerĕ." *PBH,* 1964/2, 289–92.

———. "Derenik Demirčyani anavart ev antip erkerĕ." *PBH,* 1965/1, 231–36.

———. "Derenik Demirčyani erkeri stełtzagortzakan patmutʻyunits." *BEH,* 1971/2, 230–37.

———. " 'Kyankʻi tesil' poemi patmutʻyunits." *SG,* 1971/12, 154–57.

———. "Banastełtzakan patkeri oronman čanaparhin." *SG,* 1973/9, 147–51.

———. *Derenik Demirčyani stełtzagortzakan ašḥatankʻĕ ev varpetutʻyunĕ.* (Erevan, 1973).

———. "Demirčyani manrapatumnerĕ." *SG,* 1977/4, 129–32.

Bałdasaryan, G. "Sundukyanĕ Demirčyani hayatskʻov." *SG,* 1976/5, 111–16.

Biwzand, Ē. "Derenik Demirčean." *HK,* 43 (1965/1), 10–21; 2, 23–29.

Davtʻyan, Ṙ. "Mayreni lezvi makʻrutʻyan u harstatsman hartserĕ Derenik Demirčyani hodvatznerum." *BEH,* 1976/3, 145–48.

———. "Demirčyanĕ ev arvesti mi kʻani hartser." *BEH,* 1981/2, 191–97.

———. "Derenik Demirčyanĕ mamuli ḥndirneri masin." *BEH,* 1983/2, 186–91.

———. "Ergitzankʻĕ D. Demirčyani 1920–1930-akan tʻvakanneri stełtzagortzutʻyunnerum." *L,* 1983/3, 31–37.

"Derenik Demirčean–Šawarš Misakʻean." *B,* 115 (1957), 45.

Gasparyan, V. "Kensapʻilisopʻayakan hartserĕ 'Vardanankʻ patmavepum." *BEH,* 1979/1, 10–20.

Gonchar, N. "Gogol' i tvorchestvo D. Demirchiana." *Gogol' i literatura narodov Sovetskogo Soiuza,* (Erevan, 1986), 248–71.

Haḥumyan, T. *Derenik Demirčyani dramaturgian.* (Erevan, 1958).

Ḥachatryan, M. "Derenik Demirčyani feliotonnerě." *L,* 1980/2, 24–31.
———. "Derenik Demirčyani katakergutʻyunnerě." *L,* 1985/7, 22–31.
Hovhannisyan, H. "Haverž eritasard ogin." *SG,* 1977/4, 111–16.
———. "Hušer Demirčyani masin." *SG,* 1967/2, 141–45.
Hunanyan, A. "Demirčyani dramaturgiakan mutkʻě." *SG,* 1977/4, 133–45.
Kʻalantʻaryan, Ž. "Demirčyani grakanagitakan hayatskʻnerě sovetakan grakanutʻyan dzevavorman šrjanum." *BEH,* 1977/1, 126–39.
Łazarean, P. "Varpetě ew ir sanerě." *Ani,* 1 (1946), 243–45.
Melikʻsetʻyan, S. "Demirčyani het." *SG,* 1974/12, 73–83.
Melikʻyan, M. "Derenik Demirčyani kʻaṙyaknerě." *L,* 1978/7, 53–59.
Mkrtchian, V. *Derenik Demirchian: Tvorcheskii put': lit. sotsiol. estet. kontseptsii.* (Erevan, 1982).
Mkrtchyan, V. "Antsman hakasutʻyunneri mej." *SG,* 1960/9, 128–45.
———. "Derenik Demirčyani poetakan žaṙangutʻyuně." *PBH,* 1960/4, 104–15.
———. *Derenik Demirčyani Vardanankʻě: problematikan ev poetikan.* (Erevan, 1977).
Muradyan, H. *Derenik Demirčyan.* (Erevan, 1954, 1961).
Nalbandyan, V. *'Vardanants paterazmě' ev D. Demirčyani 'Vardanankʻě'.* (Erevan, 1955).
Orbuni, Z. "Derenik Demirčean." *AND,* 6–7 (n.d.), 185–92.
Oganesian, A. "Rasskazy A. P. Chekhova v perevodakh D. Demirchiana." *BEH,* 1987/2, 151–57.
Sargsyan, Ḥ. "Derenik Demirčyani manrapatumneri masin." *T,* 1947/1, 77–88.
Sarinyan, S. "Patmavepi ardiakanutʻyuně." *SG,* 1978/6, 115–19. (On *Vardanankʻ*).
Tʻamrazyan, H. *Derenik Demirčyan.* (Erevan, 1977).
Tonoyan, Ē. " 'Napoleon Korkotyan' ergitzankʻi mi kʻani aṙandznahatkutʻyunneri masin." *SG,* 1984/23, 138–41.
———. "D. Demirčyani ergitzakan ardzakě 30-akan tʻvakannerin." *BEH,* 1986/1, 122–25.
Tʻopʻchyan, Ē. "Derenik Demirčyan." *T,* 1954/7, 3–18.
———. "Derenik Demirčyan." *SG,* 1972/4, 114–24.
Zakʻaryan, A. "Derenik Demirčyan." *T,* 1961/4, 3–19,
———. "Derenik Demirčyan." *L,* 1977/5, 3–13.

DEW, (1901–1976)

Pen name: Dew.

Born Margar Łarabegean in Teheran. Poet and artist. Educated in his birthplace and Nor Jułay (New Julfa, Isfahan). His lyric poetry first appeared in the Armenian periodical press in the Middle East and the United States. Engaged in cultural activities and teaching.

Collections

Hatěntir. (Erevan, 1973).

Texts (poetry)

Im ergerě. Banastełtzutʻiwnneri aṙajin girkʻ. (Teheran, 1947).
Ays erkar čampʻan. (Erevan, 1963).
Srti dzayner (banastełtzutʻiwnneri žołovatzu, III). (Teheran, 1974).

Criticism

Allahverdean, H. *Dew–Margar Łarabegean ew ir poēzian.* (New Julfa, 1972).
"Iranahay anvani banastełtz-nkarchi het." *SG,* 1963/8, 99–102.
Sarean, A. *Yušamatean banastełtz-nkarich Dewi.* (Teheran, 1974).

DODOḤEAN, GĒORG (1830–1908)

Born in Simferopol. A single poem, "Tzitzeṙnak" (Swallow), which may in fact be a translation or an adaptation, brought immediate and lasting fame to this poet. Attended the Lazarean Institute in Moscow, studied painting in St. Petersburg and law and economics at the University of Dorpat (now Tartu, Estonia). Taught in St. Petersburg and in Armenian schools in northern Caucasus and the Crimea. A considerable part of his verse and prose is still unpublished.

Collections

Beglarov, I. *Erker.* Vol. 1. (Tiflis, 1939).

Translations

English anthologies

ALP, 111–12.
AP, 130–31.

French anthologies

PA, 141–43.

Russian anthologies

BPA, 285.
VAM, 86–87.

Criticism

Davtʻyan, Ṙ. "Gevorg Dodoḥyani ev nra 'Tzitzeṙnak' banastełtzutʻyan masin." *BEH,* 1984/1, 12–13.
"Gēorg Dodoḥean." *A,* 1908, 627–28.
Pʻ[ēchikean], E. "Dodoḥeani 'Tzitzeṙnak'ĕ." *B,* 90 (1932), 33–34.
Šahaziz, E. "Gevorg Dodoḥyanĕ ev nra 'Tzitzeṙnak'ĕ." *EJ,* 1947/1–2, 59–64; 1947/3–4, 44–60.

DUREAN, EŁIŠĒ (1860–1930)

Born Mihran Durean in Constantinople. Poet and scholar. Brother of Petros Durean (q.v.). Took the vows of celibacy and was renamed Ełišē, in accordance with the traditions of the Church of Armenia, in 1879. Taught and held administrative positions in Partizak (Bahçecik, Turkey), at the seminary of Armaš (near Izmit, Turkey), and in Constantinople. Armenian Patriarch of Constantinople, 1909–11; Armenian Patriarch of Jerusalem, 1921–30.

Collections

Ambołjakan erker. 9 vols. (Jerusalem, 1933–36).
Srbazan kʻnar. (Jerusalem, 1936). (Complete works, 9).

Texts (literary)

Hovuakan sring: krōnakan kʻertʻuatzner, (1904–1907). (Smyrna, 1909). (Poetry).
Druagner Manuk Yisusi keankʻēn. (Jerusalem, 1926, 1950).

Other works

Ĕntir asatsuatzkʻ ōtarazgi akanawor andzants . . . (Constantinople, 1882).
Patmutʻiwn hay matenagrutʻean. (Constantinople, 1885). (Complete works 1).
Baṙagitutʻiwn kam utʻ masunkʻ bani hayerēn kʻerakanutʻean. (Jerusalem, 1926, 1961).
Ĕntʻatskʻ i grots barbaṙ. 3 vols. (Jerusalem, 1927–29).
Aybubēnkʻ hayerēn banasirutʻean. (Jerusalem, 1928).
Hayots hin krōnĕ kam Haykakan ditsabanutʻiwn. (Jerusalem, 1933). (Complete works, 2).
Azgayin patmutʻiwn. (Jerusalem, 1934). (Complete works, 3).
Hamaṙōt patmutʻiwn pʻilisopʻayutʻean. (Jerusalem, 1934). (Complete works, 4).
Dasakan matenagrutʻiwn. [Jerusalem, 1935]. (Complete works, 5).
Usumnasirutʻiwnkʻ ew kʻnnadatutʻiwnkʻ. (Jerusalem, 1935). (Complete works, 6).
Krōnneru patmutʻiwn. (Jerusalem, 1935). (Complete works, 7).
Baroyagitutʻiwn. (Jerusalem, 1936). (Collected works, 8; essentially a translation).

Translations

ENGLISH

Manukean, M. "The Travellers of Emmaus." *S,* 1971, 330–32.

FRENCH ANTHOLOGIES

APA, 81–87.

Criticism

Abrahamyan, H. "Eresun tari aṙaj." *EJ,* 1960/2, 21–22.
B[aluean], H. "Nšmarner–Mah Durean patriarkʻi." *Z,* 1 (1929–1930), 375.
Chōpanean, A. "Banastełtzĕ Durean srbazani mēj." *ANA,* 1 (1930/5), 1–5.
Eremean, S. "Ełišē Durean." *B,* 87 (1930), 234–37.
Gabamačean, S. "Ełišē episkopos Durean." *AM,* 1904, 769–75.
Golančyan, E. "Ełiše arkʻ. Duryan (hušer ev notʻer)." *EJ,* 1954/11, 37–42.
Gušakean, Tʻ. *Ełišē patriarkʻ Durean (ir kʻahanayutʻean yisnameay yobelianin aṙtʻiw).* (Jerusalem, 1932).
Ḥachaturean, G. *Ełišē srbazan Durean II Šnorhali.* (Istanbul, 1960).
Kiwlēsērean, B. *Kensagrutʻiwn norin amenasrbutʻiwn T. Ełišē s. arkʻep. Durean.* (New York, 1929).
Mšakn u vardzkʻĕ, yobelinakan hratarakutʻiwn. (Jerusalem, 1931).
Naroyan, M., et al. "Kartzikʻner Ełiše arkʻepiskopos Duryani masin." *EJ,* 1960/2, 16–18.
Simkʻēšean, E. "Ełišē patriarkʻ Durean." *Z* (amsatʻertʻ), 4 (1960/7–8), 3.
Siruni, H. "Ełiše patriarkʻ Duryan." *EJ,* 1960/1, 41–49; 1960/2, 23–30; 1960/3, 23–28; 1960/4, 28–37.
Tziatzan, Š. "Grakan kendanagirner–Ełišē episk. Durean." *M,* 1905/7, 101–3.
Vardanean, G. "Ełišē arkʻ. Durean." *HK,* 8 (1929–30/1), 75–77.
Yovhannēsean, V. "Ełišē Durean ir banastełtzutʻiwnnerun mēj." *B,* 118 (1960), 297–301.

DUREAN, PETROS (1851–1872)

Born Petros Zĕmpayean in Constantinople. Poet and playwright. Brother of Ełišē Durean (q.v.). Educated at the Armenian school of Scutari. Upon graduation, he engaged in acting and journalism. Some of the historical plays he wrote were performed in the Armenian theaters of Constantinople. His genius shone in the few poems he wrote in the last few years of his short life. Died of consumption.

Collections

Tałkʻ ew ťatrerguťiwnkʻ. (Constantinople, 1872).

Tałkʻ ew ťatrerguťiwnkʻ, namakani, dambanakan yōduatzkʻ dzeřagir, otanawor, tapanagir. (Constantinople, 1893).

Banastełtzuťiwnner. (Baku, 1900; Vałaršapat, 1904).

[*Tałer*]. (Šuši, [1903]).

Erger ew tałer. (Constantinople, 1908).

Tałkʻ ew namakani. (New York, 1918).

Ĕntir kʻerťuatzner. (Vienna, 1922).

Kʻerťuatzner. (Beirut, 1926).

Alazan, V., and Norents, V. *Tałer.* (Erevan, 1932, 1936).

Tałer, namakner, dambanakan. (Beirut, 1940).

Ĕntir kʻerťuatzner. (Aleppo, 1945).

Tałer-namakner (hatuatzner). (Venice, 1945, 1959).

Ačařyan, H. *Erker.* (Erevan, 1947).

Kʻerťuatzner ew namakner. (Beirut, 1952, 1956).

Tarontsi, S. *Tałer.* (Erevan, 1954).

Norents, V. *Tałer.* (Erevan, 1963, 1967).

Galayčean, A. *Tałkʻ Petros Dureani, ṗordz mě bnagrayin verakangnumi.* (Jerusalem, 1967).

———. *Namakani Petros Dureani.* (Jerusalem, 1968).

Sevak, P. *Erkeri žołovatzu.* 2 vols. (Erevan, 1971–1972).

Šaruryan, A. *Erker.* (Erevan, 1981).

Erker. (Anťilias, 1987).

Texts

Aspatakuťiwnkʻ parskats i Hays kam Awerumn Ani mayrakʻałakʻin Bagratuneats. (Constantinople, 1908). (Drama).

Sew hołer kam Yetin gišer araratean. (Constantinople, 1908). (Drama).

Translations

English

Blackwell, A. "My Rest." *Armenia* (newspaper), 93 (1896), 2.

Miller, F. "My Pain." *Armenia,* 2 (1905/1), 19. Corrected version, *Armenia,* 2/2–3 (1905), 29.

English anthologies

ALP, 18–19, 50, 82–84, 121.

AP, 13–38, 214–18.

German anthologies

AD, 12–18.

ALG, 125–26.

French

"Je t'ai aimée." *L'Arménie* (newspaper), 77 (1895), 4.

"Nouveaux jours noirs." *L'Arménie,* 84 (1895), 4.

O. "Le Lac," "Ma mort." *La Patrie,* 1908/3, 34–35.

Panossian, A. "Ma mort." *Šanť,* 1912/21, 341–42.

"Petit lac." Tchéraz, M. *Conférence arménienne à Amsterdam.* (Amsterdam, n.d.), 23–24.
"Plaintes," "Repentir." *L'Arménie,* 88 (1896), 3.
"Souhaits à l'Arménie." *L'Arménie,* 83 (1895), 4.
Tchobanian, A. "Elle," "Que dit-on?," "Murmures," "Sur la tombe du très cher Vartan Loutfian," "Gémissements," "Ma peine." *REArm,* 2 (1922), 337–41.

French anthologies

APA, 75–79.
JM, 138–49.
LPA, 176–80.
PA, 1–79.
PAAM, 80–81.

Italian

Bazardjian, R. "Il mio dolore." *LArmenia. Conferenza.* (Milan, 1917), 21.
Lucini, G. "Il fanciullo all croce." *Šanť,* 44 (1913), 303.
———. "Il mio dolore." *Šanť,* 51 (1913), 35.
———. "Lamenti." *Amenun taretsoytsě,* 1914, 55–57.
Nazariantz. *I Miserabili, Drama in cinque atti.* (Milan, 1916).

Italian anthologies

LPAM, 121–34.
Nazariantz, H. *Bedros Turian, poeta armeno. Dalla sua vita e dalle sue pagine migliore, con cenno sull' arte armena.* (Bari, 1915).

Russian anthologies

AAP, 397–402.
BPA, 440–44, 493.
IZAP, 9–16.
SHAP, 65–70.
VAM, 163–71.

Spanish

APAS, 145–52.

Criticism

Alekʻsandryan, M. "Petros Duryani 'Artašes I' tʻatergutʻyuně." *SG,* 1971/9, 117–19.
Arpʻiarean, T. "Meṙatz gragētner." *M,* 1966 (1892), 176–79.
Atrušan. *Petros Durean: kʻnnakan aknark mě ir keankʻin ew gortzin vray.* (Constantinople, 1911).
Čałaryan, A. *Petros Duryan, demkʻi verakangnumě.* (Erevan, 1971).
Čanašean, M. "Petros Durean." *B,* 130 (1972), 99–113.
———. *Petros Durean dar mě etkʻ.* (Venice, 1974).
———. "Verlutzumi pʻordz mě Petros Dureani tʻatrergutʻiwnnerun." *B,* 131 (1973), 107–22, 167–83.
Chōpanean, A. *Petros Durean: kensagrakan ew kʻnnadatakan usumnasirutʻiwn.* (Tiflis, 1894; Erevan, 1967).
Davtʻyan, V. "Hančareł trtunj." *SG,* 1972/1, 115–18.
Danielyan, K. "Petros Duryan" *SG,* 1983/5, 114–26.

Durean, E. "Bołok‘ mě (Petros Dureani gortzerě)." *S,* 1930, 150–51. (Written in 1874).

Ē. B. "Dureani mahě." *M,* 3998 (1893), 404–8.

Ēk‘sērčean, B. *Dureani ěndardzak kensagrut‘iwně.* (Constantinople, 1893).

———. "Petros Dureani tpeal ew antip gortzerě." *AM,* 1892, 288.

Erkat‘, A. "Petros Durean." *HK,* 32 (1954/10), 1–7.

Gyulyan, G. "Petros Duryan." *SG,* 1967/2, 139–40.

Hrand. "Dureani patkerě ew ir nkarichě." *M,* 3995 (1893), 360–62.

K‘iparean, K. "Petros Durean." *B,* 79 (1922), 271–73, 335–38.

Łanalanyan, A. *Petros Duryan.* (Erevan, 1957).

Navarean, A. "Durean." *AM,* 1898, 414–17.

Nazariantz, H. *Bedros Turian, poeta armeno. Dalla sua vita e dalle sue pagine migliori, con cenno sull' arte armena.* (Bari, 1915).

Orberean, Ṙ. "Dureanin 'Lčakě'." *M,* 1900/16, 247–49.

Pachalian, L. "Le cinquantenaire de la mort du poète arménien Bèdros Tourian." *REArm,* 2 (1922), 327–30.

Poyačean, Z. "Petros Durean ew Čon K‘its." *HK,* 16 (1937–38/9), 83–87.

Ṙubeni, A. "Hetzetzank‘neri ergichě, Petros Durean." *Murč,* 1903/3, 112–36.

Sargsyan, H. *Petros Duryan.* (Erevan, 1959).

Šaruryan, A. "Tek‘stabanakan ditołut‘yunner Petros Duryani banastełtzut‘yunneri masin." *PBH,* 1966/2, 165–72.

———. "Nyut‘er Petros Duryani kyank‘i ev stełtzagortzut‘yan veraberyal." *BEH,* 1967/1, 164–81.

———. "Petros Duryani namakneri banasirakan k‘nnut‘yuně." *PBH,* 1967/4, 213–18.

———. "Namakner Petros Duryani masin." *BEH,* 1968/1, 142–54.

———. "Petros Duryani grakan žaṙangut‘yan hetk‘erov." *BEH,* 1968/2, 205–13.

———. "Patmakann u stełtzakaně Petros Duryani ołbergut‘yunnerum." *PBH,* 1968/4, 159–69.

———. "Petros Duryani 'Trtunjk‘ě'." *SG,* 1970/10, 141–48.

———. "Petros Duryani stełtzagortzakan čanaparhi skizbě." *BEH,* 1971/1, 72–84.

———. "Petros Duryan." *PBH,* 1972/2, 31–44.

———. *Petros Duryan: kyank‘ě ev gortzě.* (Erevan, 1972).

———. *Petros Duryaně vaveragrerum ev žamanakakitsneri hišołut‘yunnerum.* (Erevan, 1982).

Sevak, P. "Mer k‘narergut‘yan Vahagně," *SG,* 1972/1, 111–14.

Siruni, H. "Čanchnalu hamar Duryaně," *SG,* 1972/1, 119–25.

Step‘anean, Y. "Petros Durean." *HK,* 8 (1929–30/3), 55–69.

Tchobanian, A. "Bédros Tourian. Sa vie, son œuvre." *REArm,* 2 (1922), 330–41.

T‘erzibašyan, V. *Petros Duryan.* (Erevan, 1959).

Yakobean, S. "Arewmtahay banastełtzner, Petros Durean: nra keank‘n u erkerě. Grakan-k‘nnakan verlutzut‘iwn." *HA,* 35 (1921), 417–21, 511–22, 619–33; 36 (1922), 40–55, 158–81. (Reprinted separately, Vienna, 1922).

Zēk‘iean, L. "Petros Dureani k‘narergut‘ean ent‘aḥawě ew k‘ert‘ołi nerašḥarhě." *B,* 131 (1973), 247–61.

ĒGAZ, ŁUL (d. 1734)

According to the scarce biographical information available for Ēgaz, he was one of the earliest representatives of the Nor Jułay (New Julfa, Isfahan) school of Armenian minstrels. He died and was buried in New Julfa.

Poetry

EPA, 6–11.
SHA, 71–84.
THG, 45–46.

Criticism

Eremean, A. *Parskahay ašułner.* (Tiflis, 1930), 2–11.

EŁIA KʻAHANAY (16th or 17th c.)

An anonymous history depicting the tribulations of Ełia, a Jacobite priest, at the hands of Turks in Ḥarberd (Harput, Turkey).

Texts

Ačařean, Hracheay. *Patmutʻiwn Ełia kʻahanayi* (*ŽZ dar?*). (Vałaršapat, 1908; also previously published in *A,* 1908).

B[asmadjian], K. "Patmu[tʻ]i[wn] t[ē]r Ełieay kʻahannayi, Ḥarbertʻtsoy." (Histoire du Père Elie de Kharpout). *ROC,* 16 (1911), 55–67.

Translations

French

Basmadjian, K. "Histoire du Père Elie de Kharpout." *ROC,* 15 (1910), 337–49. (A translation of Basmadjian's text).

EŁIA MUŠEŁEAN (1689–?)

Also known as Ełia Karnetsi or Ełia Astuatzaturean Mušełean.

Born to a wealthy Armenian family in the village of Krman in Ḥotorjur (near Erzurum). Received a semi-religious education in Karin (Erzurum). There, he converted to Catholicism and helped the Catholic missionaries, but he soon turned to trade as his lifelong profession. His wide travels in Iran, southern Russia, Armenia proper, Transcaucasia, and Europe; his close connections with the Catholic missionaries and the ruling circles of the region; and his still nebulous plans for the liberation of Armenia add a touch of mystery to his life. He was the French consul in Meshad shortly before his arrest in 1734 by the Russians, who accused him of spying for Persia and incarcerated him for almost twelve years. Ełia passionately blamed the Catholic missionaries for his misfortune, and for the mistrust and mistreatment, with which he was treated by the Armenians, the Russians, the Persians and the Ottoman Turks. He spent his last years in obscurity in Erzurum.

Texts

Ełia Karnetsu divaně: nyutʻer Merdzavor Arevelkʻi ev Andrkovkasi patmutʻyan. (Erevan, 1968).

Erevanli, Akʻper. "Ełia Mušełyani grakan žařangutʻyunits." *PBH,* 1972/1, 103–14.

Criticism

Oskean, H. "Ełia Astuatzaturean Mušełean ew ir grakan artadrutʻiwnnerě." *HA,* 41 (1927), 28–36, 126–38, 237–49, 367–76, 493–501. (Reprinted separately, Vienna, 1927).

Sobranie aktov otnosiashchikhsia k obozreniiu istorii armianskogo naroda. Vol. 1, (Moscow, 1833), 363–64. (A description of Mušełean's archive).

EŁIAYEAN, BIWZAND (1900–1995)

Born in Adana. Educator, historian, and writer. Survived the Armenian massacres of Adana and the genocide of 1915. Educated at St. Paul's at Tarsus and at the International College in Smyrna. Fled Smyrna in the early 1920s and pursued his studies at the School of Religion in Athens and at the Institut de Hautes Etudes Internationales in Geneva. Taught in various schools and institutions in the Middle East. From 1931 to his retirement and move to the United States in the early 1970s, he taught at the Seminary of the Catholicosate of Cilicia in Antilias, Lebanon.

Texts (stories)

Spʻiwṙkʻ. (Beirut, 1950).

Karawaně. (Beirut, 1979).

Other works

Krōnkʻ ew keankʻ. (Jerusalem, 1932).

Melgonean krtʻakan hastatutʻiwn. (Beirut, 1957).

Azuniyēi hay bužaraně. (Antʻilias and Beirut, 1960).

Serundi mě dastiarakutʻiwně. (Antʻilias and Beirut, 1962).

Mankavaržakan dasaḥōsutʻiwnner. (Antʻilias and Beirut, 1965).

Atanayi hayots patmutʻiwn. (Antʻilias and Beirut, 1970).

Hay Katʻolik ew Awetaranakan yaranuanutʻeants bažanumě 19. darun. (Antʻilias and Beirut, 1971).

Kʻnnakan patmutʻiwn surbgrakan žamanakneru. 5 vols. (Antʻilias and Beirut, 1972–76).

Žamanakakits patmutʻiwn Katʻołikosutʻean hayots Kilikioy, 1914–1972. (Antʻilias and Beirut, 1975).

EŁIVARD, (1910–1990)

Pen name: Ełivard.

Born Ełiazar Tērtērean in the village of Kaynimiran (to the south of Lake Van). Brought to Jerusalem as an orphan after the genocide of 1915. Completed his studies at the Armenian seminary in Jerusalem and became a celibate priest in 1932 and renamed Ełišē. Held numerous positions within the Armenian Patriarchate of Jerusalem and was the Armenian Patriarch of the Holy City from 1960 to his death. He wrote verse and prose.

Collections

Ěntir ējer. (Jerusalem, 1973).

Texts

Magdałinēn mełramomē. (Jerusalem, 1941). (Poetry).

Ḥortakman gišerner. (Jerusalem, 1943).
Leran vrayēn eraniner. (Jerusalem, 1945).
Antsordě. (Jerusalem, 1946). (Verse).
Akełdama. (Jerusalem, 1948). (Poem).
Vardanankʻ (ťateraḥał vets ararov). (Jerusalem, 1951). (Play).
Surb Mesrop. (Jerusalem, 1962). (Poem).
Ōtarakaně. (Jerusalem, 1966). (Prose).
Heťanosats aṙakʻealě. (Jerusalem, 1975). (Prose).
Karmir Zōravarě. (Jerusalem, 1975).
Lusamatean. (Brussels, 1980).

Other works

Narekě hay grakanuťean mēj. (Jerusalem, 1947).
Hayastaneayts Ekełetsin erek ew aysōr. (Jerusalem, 1948).

Criticism

"Amenapatiw t. Ełišē s. arkʻeps. Tērtērean. . . . (kensagrakan)." *S,* 1960, 126–27.
Margarean, M. "Norits mi paytzaṙ zōrawor grich." *S,* 1976, 162–66, 186–90, 237–45.

ĒMIN, GEVORG (1919–1998)

Pen name: Gevorg Ēmin.

Born Gevorg (renamed Karlen at a very young age) Muradyan in Aštarak, Armenia. Awarded the USSR State Prize for literature (1951 and 1976) and the Charents Literary Prize (1979). Specialized in hydraulic engineering at the Erevan Polytechnic Institute (1940), worked briefly at the Matenadaran, and took special courses in literature in Moscow (1949–50, 1954–56). Edited *Literaturnaia Armeniia* (1968–72) and worked at the Institute of Art in Erevan for many years. Visited the United States on a number of occasions.

Collections

Erkeri žołovatzu. 2 vols. (Erevan, 1975, 1977).
Erkeri žołovatzu. 3 vols. (Erevan, 1985–86).

Texts (poetry)

Naḥašavił. (Erevan, 1940).
Ḥałałuťyan tzḥamorčě. (Erevan, 1942).
Norkʻ. (Erevan, 1946).
Nor čanaparh. (Erevan, 1949, 1953).
Šakʻe. (Erevan, 1949, 1951, 1965).
Saryakneřě. (Erevan, 1952).
Ḥosir, Hayastan. (Erevan, 1952).
Balladner ev poemner. (Erevan, 1955).
Oronumner. (Erevan, 1955).
Erevani luyseřě. (Erevan, 1957).
Minchev aysōr. (Erevan, 1959, 1962).
Erku čampʻa. (Erevan, 1962).
Yoť erg. (Erevan, 1962).
Ays tarikʻum. (Erevan, 1968).
Haykakan simfonia. (Erevan, 1969).

Ballad dzknorsi masin. (Erevan, 1970, 1984).
Girkʻ hayrenašunch. (Erevan, 1970).
Mer aybubenĕ. (Erevan, 1970).
XX–rd dar. (Erevan, 1970).
Yotʻ erg Hayastani masin. (Erevan, 1970).
Sasuntsineri parĕ. (Erevan, 1975, 1979).
Čampʻabažan. (Erevan, 1979).
Haverži čampʻordĕ. (Erevan, 1980).
Aḥ, ays Masisĕ. (Erevan, 1980).
Yotʻ erg Hayastani masin. Girkʻ hayrenašunch. (Erevan, 1981).
"Anavart hušer (banasteɫtzuhi Vera Zvyagintsevayi masin)." *SG,* 1982/4, 119–28. (Reminiscences about Vera Zviagintseva).
" 'Abu-lala-Mahari' poemi ev Isahakyani greladzevi mi kʻani aṙandznahatkutʻyunneri masin." *SG,* 1983/12, 127–34.
"Heɫapʻoḥutʻyan patgamaḥosĕ." *SG,* 1983/7, 3–6.
Girkʻ tʻargmanutʻyants. (Erevan, 1984). (Translations by Ēmin).
Maštotsits minchev mer ōrerĕ; mtorumner hay grakanutʻyan masin. (Erevan, 1984). (Articles and essays on Armenian literature).
Haverži čampʻordĕ. (Erevan, 1985). (Verse and prose).
Zinvori ōragrits. (Erevan, 1985).
Haverži čampʻordĕ. (Erevan, 1987). (Essay; in Russian, English, German, and French).
Elkʻ Egiptosits (banasteɫtzutʻyunner). (Erevan, 1989).

Translations

English

"Ah, that Massis." *L,* May 14, 1963, 4.
Botting, T. ["Armenia mine–how deep a love for you I feel"]. *SL,* 1973/4, 125–26.
———. "Letter from My Loved One." *SL,* 1973/4, 129.
———. "Portrait of a Painter." *SL,* 1973/4, 126.
Der Hovanessian, D. *For You on New Year's Day.* (Athens, Ohio, 1985).
Johnstone, A. "Revelation." *SL,* 1954/10, 126.
Pyman, A. ["I dreamt: A monastery on the Sevan"]. *SL,* 1973/9, 129–30. (Also published in *SL,* 1980/6, 50–51).
Robbins, M., and Sonentz-Papazian, T. *Land, Love, Century.* (Washington, DC, 1988).
Rottenberg, D. "To Moscow." *SL,* 1954/10, 126–27.
———. "Songs of Armenia." *SL,* 1966/3, 5–24.
———. ["Tell me, who can . . ."]. *SL,* 1966/3, 148. Also published in *SL,* 1972/11, 48.
———. ["The smell of grapes pervades the village air"] *SL,* 1973/4, 125.
———. "To a Woman with Sea-Green Eyes." *SL,* 1973/4, 127–28.
———. *Songs of Armenia.* (Moscow, 1979). (Selected poems; English and Russian texts).
Soghikian, M. *Seven Songs About Armenia.* (Moscow, 1981).
Tempest, P. ["What's the meaning of life?"; "For around two months not a word I wrote," "Why ponder death," "I Love all Languages," "My Love Is," "Tonight let us feast," "To you, my Love"]. *SL,* 1977/8, 153–57.
———. ["I want to write words to the music of the rain"]. *SL,* 1979/7, 96.

———. "I Love all Languages." *SL,* 1980/6, 49–50.

English anthologies

SAP, 40–42.

French

Antonian, A. ["En quoi consiste le sens de la vie?," "Création," "La mort? Je m'en moque," "J'aime toutes les langues," "Le cep de vigne," "Allons, festoyons cette nuit"]. *LS,* 223 (1977), 133–38.

"Chants de l'Arménie." *OO,* 123 (March 1969), 6–25.

Falk, C. ["J'ai fait un rêve: dans le monastère"]. *OO,* 177 (Sept. 1973), 146.

"Funérailles." *OO* (April 1962), 103–4.

Gaucheron, J. "En ce temps." *OO,* 123 (March 1969), 76.

———. ["Qu'est-ce qui est plus fort que l'homme?"]. *OO,* 167 (Nov. 1972), 54–55.

Martirossian, L. "Le disparu." *OO* (June 1963), 136.

———. "A l'avenir," "Penche sur des manuscrits anciens," "Crois-moi, dis 'Bonjour' à tous nos chers vieux," "Le Piano," "Tes mains," "Je désire écrire des paroles," "Le Cantique des cantiques," "En ce monde il n'est plus riche que moi." *LS,* 249 (1979), 109–15.

———. "A l'avenir," "Je désire écrire des paroles," "Crois-moi, dis 'Bonjour' à tous nos chers vieux." *LS,* 258 (1980), 62–63.

French anthologies

Gaucheron, J. *E,* 94–97.

LPA, 356–60.

German

"Armenien, mein Land. . . ." *Sowjet-Literatur,* 1966/3, 6–27.

Movsessian, L. "Kranichlied." *Armenische Grammatik* (Vienna, 1959), 286–88.

Osterreicher, S. "Sag, wer stärker mag sein." *Sowjet-Literatur,* 1966/3, 146–47.

Russian

Gambarian, A. *Sem' pesen ob Armenii. Ocherk.* (Moscow, 1967, 1981).

Izbrannaia lirika. (Moscow, 1968).

Lastochka iz Ashtaraka. (Moscow, 1988).

Mech i lemekh. Stikhi. (Moscow, 1958).

Muzyka dozhdia. (Moscow, 1986).

Novaia doroga. (Moscow, 1951).

Novaia doroga. (Moscow, 1951).

Oboldusev, G. *Stikhi.* (Moscow, 1947).

Ostrogorskaia, V. *Ogni Erevana. Ocherki.* (Moscow, 1956).

Pered chasami. Stikhi. (Moscow, 1962).

Pesnia mira. (Erevan, 1952).

Sel'vinskii, I. *Tri pesni. Stikhi.* (Moscow, 1957).

Sem' pesen ob Armenii. (Erevan, 1979).

Spendiarova, T. *Skvortsy. Stikhi.* (Moscow, 1961).

Stikhi. (Moscow, 1963).

V nashem dome. (Moscow, 1954).

Vesennie vody. (Moscow, 1953).

Zviagintseva, V., and Ginzburg, L. *Shake. Poema. Pererab. i dop. avtorom dlia russk. izd.* (Moscow and Leningrad, 1952).

Spanish

Canovas, M. "Canciones de Armenia." *Literatura Sovietica,* 1966/3, 6–26.
Silvestre, L. "Quein es mas fuerte que el hombre?" *Literatura Sovietica,* 1966/3, 148.

Bibliographies

Hovhannisyan, Ē., and Babayan, Ē. *Gevorg Ēmin, Kensamatenagitakan tsank.* (Erevan, 1982).

Criticism

Aristakesyan, A. "Gevorg Ēmin." *SG,* 1960/12, 156–65.
Gasparyan, D. "Banastełtzi žamanakě." *SG,* 1980/7, 147–53.
"Gevorg Ēmin." *SL,* 1977/8, 151–53.
Hovakimyan, V. *Gevorg Ēmin.* (Erevan, 1986).
Téléouké, V. "Guévorg Emine." *LS,* 249 (1979), 107–8.

ĒMIN, YOVSĒPʻ (1726–1809)

Born in Hamadan, Iran. Left for England in 1751, and having received military training there, he saw action in the Seven Years' War. He then devoted himself to the cause of liberating Armenia. Approached the British first, then turned to the Russians, and later tried to forge an Armeno-Georgian alliance for the same purpose. His efforts bore no fruit. Spent his remaining years in India, after settling there in 1783.

Text

The Life and Adventures of Joseph Emin, an Armenian. Written in English by Himself. (London, 1792; Calcutta, 1918 [2d ed.]).

Criticism

Aslanyan, M. "Angliakan memuarayin grakanutʻyan avanduytʻnerě ev Hovsepʻ Ēmini inkʻnakensagrutʻyuně." *L,* 1980/1, 64–78.
Giwzalean, G. "Yovsēpʻ Ēmin ew Yovnan vardapet." *HK,* 26 (1948/10), 50–59; 11, 72–80; 12, 89–96; 27 (1949/3), 66–75.
Hovhannisyan, A. "Ēdmond Běrkě Hovsepʻ Emini masin." *T,* 1960/12, 61–65.
Ioannisyan, A. R. *Iosif Emin,* (Erevan, 1945).

EREMIA chēlēpi KʻĒŌMIWRČEAN (1637–1695)

Born in Constantinople. Studied at the feet of an Armenian priest. Apparently completed his education through self-instruction as he is believed to have had a good command of Greek and Latin in addition to his mother tongue and Turkish. After his marriage in 1657, he briefly held the position of secretary at the Armenian Patriarchate of Constantinople (late 1650s–early 1660s). He traveled to Palestine, Syria, Asia Minor, and Eastern Armenia and was intimately involved in Armenian national affairs in the turbulent decades of the second half of the seventeenth century.

Texts

Govabanutʻiwn tnōrinakan tełeats yErusałēm. (Constantinople, 1678).
ANA, 11 (1903), 188–92. (5 poems).

T'orgomean, V. *Eremia chēlēpii K'ēōmiwrčean Stampōloy patmut'iwn.* 3 vols. (Vienna, 1913, 1932, 1938). (History of Istanbul).

"Eremia chēlēpwoy Gandz ew ołb i veray Yakob kat'ołikosi." *HA,* 47 (1933), 589–95. (Verse).

Akinean, N. *Eremia chēlēpi K'ēōmiwrčean, keank'n ew grakan gortzunēut'iwnĕ.* (Vienna, 1933). (Texts, pp. 193–263).

Nšanean, M. *Ōragrut'iwn Eremia chēlēpi K'ēōmiwrčeani. Yaweluatz: a) t'ułt'er, b) ułerdzner, g) gandzer ew ołber.* (Jerusalem, 1939).

Sahakyan, H. "Eremia chelepi K'yomurčyani mi antip poemĕ." *BM,* 6 (1962), 409–26. ("Vasn ēk'mēk'či ařnawut Timōyi umemn . . .").

Sahakyan, H. *Eremia K'yomurčyan.* (Erevan, 1964). (Texts, pp. 129–63).

K'iwrtean, Y. "Nor niwt'er Eremia chēlēpi K'ēōmiwrčeani masin." *B,* 124 (1966), 175–82; 125 (1967), 88–94, 143–49. (Texts).

Vasn sut margarēin or kochiwr Sapēt'ayi Sewi. (Constantinople, n.d.).

Tałaran p'ok'rik ew gełetsik, ergetseal i banastełtzitsn imastasirats i ḥraḥčans mankantsn Siōni, ew i p'ařs amenametzin Astutzoy. (N.p., n.d.). (7 poems).

Texts (in anthologies)

SUM, 2, 444–501.

Translations

ENGLISH

Sanjian, A., and Tietze, A. *Eremya Chelebi Kömürjian's Armeno-Turkish Poem "The Jewish Bride."* (Wiesbaden, 1981).

FRENCH

Marcel, L.-A. "Chant d'amour." *AND,* 14 (1963), 56–57.

FRENCH ANTHOLOGIES

CPA, 107–8.

TA, 233–38.

RUSSIAN

EPA, 217.

TURKISH

Andreasyan, H. *Eremya Çelebi Kömürcüyan, Istanbul tarihi, XVII. asırda Istanbul.* (Istanbul, 1952).

Criticism

Akinean, N. "Eremia chēlēpi K'ēōmiwrčean: keank'n ew grakan gortzunēut'iwnĕ." *HA,* 46 (1932), 510–36; 624–77; 47 (1933), 94–114. (Revised, updated, and reprinted separately, Vienna, 1933).

Erem[ean], S. "E. chēlēpi, taregrakan patmut'iwn." *B,* 60 (1902), 367–69, 473–79.

K'iwrtean, Y. "Nor niwt'er Eremia chēlēpi K'ēōmiwrčeani masin." *B,* 124 (1966), 175–82; 125 (1967), 88–94, 143–49.

Nšanean, M. "Eremia chēlēpwoy Gandz ew ołb i veray Yakob kat'ołikosi." *HA,* 47 (1933), 589–95.

O. K. "Tzanōt'ut'iwnk' inch zvaruts Eremeay chēlēpwoy yeranelwoyn Komitasay yełbōre iwrmē." *B,* 83 (1926), 197–98.

Ōšakan, Y. "Eremia Chēlēpi." *S,* 1939, 331–38, 367–69; 1940, 30–35, 71–74, 103–9, 142–45, 194–98.

Sahakyan, H. *Eremia K'yomurčyan.* (Erevan, 1964).

Schütz, E. "Jeremia Čelebis türkische Werke." *Studia Turcica,* (Budapest, 1971), 401–30.
Ter-Łevondyan, A. "E. Chelepin orpes Munajjim Bašii ałbyurnerits mekě." *T,* 1960/7–8, 143–51.

ERKATʻ, ARSĒN (1893–1969)

Pen name: Arsēn Erkatʻ.

Born Arsēn Šamlean in Amasia (Amasya, Turkey). Educated in the local Armenian school and in the Galustean school in Cairo. Sat in on courses at the Sorbonne. Resided in Egypt for almost six decades, and moved to Montreal in 1966. Numerous poems by this poet, who also wrote in French, are still scattered in the periodical press.

Texts (verse)

Ergetsi . . . nor serundin. (Constantiople, 1911).
Hncheakneru girkʻě. (Marzuan, 1912).
Artzatʻē tsolkʻer. (Marzuan, 1912).
Antzanōtʻ stuerner. (Marzuan, 1912).
Eraz u višt (herosakan patmuatzkʻner). (Cairo, 1915). ("Heroic stories").
Hayastan. (Cairo, 1916).
Hayrenikʻis daptʻninerě. (Cairo, 1916).
Ališan-Raffi (ołberguṫiwn). (Venice, 1919).
Tsaygatʻitʻeṙě. (Venice, 1920).
Arewi ew mahuan erger. (Cairo, 1922).
Astuatzneru verjaloysě. (Venice, 1925).
Kuzik-Petōn (hēkʻeatʻ). (Cairo, 1933). (Tale).
Sonatʻner. (Cairo, 1946).
Egiptakankʻ. (Cairo, 1956, 1960; Beirut, 1969).
Ardzak ējer: yušagrutʻiwnner ew patmuatzkʻner. (Cairo, 1957). (Prose).
Kʻertʻuatzner, 1945–1960. (Cairo, 1961).

Translations

French

Les Cypres embrasés, suivis des Stances à Astrée. (Paris, 1930).

Italian anthologies

LPAM, 273–76.

ERUḤAN, (1870–1915)

Pen names: Ašuł, E. Gałtʻakan, Eruḥan.

Born Eruand Srmakʻēšḥanlean in Constantinople and educated in his birthplace. Joined the editorial board of *Arewelkʻ* (1890), but fled to Bulgaria during the Armenian massacres of the mid-1890s. There as well as in Egypt (where he arrived in 1904), he continued teaching and published his short stories and novelettes in the Armenian periodical press. Returned to Constantinople in 1908 and assumed the editorship of *Arewelkʻ*. Settled in Harput in 1913 to teach at the Armenian school in nearby Mezre. Like most of his colleagues, he and his family were arrested and slain during the Armenian genocide of 1915.

Collections

Patmuatzkʻner žołovrdakan keankʻē. (Paris, 1942).
Tʻopʻchyan, Ēd. *Novelner.* (Erevan, 1946).
Harazat ordi ew Patmuatzkʻner. (Aleppo, 1953).
Hovhannisyan, S. *Novelner.* (Erevan, 1965).

Texts (stories and novels)

Keankʻin mēj. (Constantinople, 1911).
Harazat ordi. (Constantinople, 1913; Alexandria, 1936).
Amirayin ałjikě. (Constantinople, 1929, 1942; Erevan, 1949; Beirut, 1971). (Novel; first serialized in the periodical press).

Texts in periodicals

ANA, 1 (1898–99), 275–78; 1907/6–9, 120–27.
HG, 1 (1911/1), 8–15.
Nawasard, 1914, 75–83.
SG, 1964/11, 110, 113–19.

Translations

English

Ashjian, S. "In Return for the Fish." *Nor Ašḥarh,* March 16, 1963, 4; March 23, 1963, 4; March 30, 1963, 4; April 6, 1963, 4.

German

S. M. "Die Liebe des Fischers." *Sowjet-Literatur,* 1946/4, 67–70.

German anthologies

AN, 22–28.

Russian

KHAN, 1, 21–25; 2, 136–40.

Criticism

Hovhannisyan, S. "Eruḥan." *SG,* 1964/11, 111–12.
———. "Eruḥan." *L,* 1966/8, 55–69.
———. *Eruḥan: kyankʻě ev gortzuneutʻyuně.* (Erevan, 1970).
———. "Eruḥani grakan hayatskʻnerě." *PBH,* 1970/3, 235–42.
———. "Eruḥani novelneri gełarvestakan aṙandznahatkutʻyunnerě." *PBH,* 1974/4, 123–32.
Siruni, H. "Gitzer Eruḥani kyankʻen." *SG,* 1970/8, 126–45.

ESAYAN, ZAPEL (1878–1943)

Pen name: Šahan.

Born Zapēl Yovhannēsean in Constantinople. Attended local schools and the Sorbonne. After her marriage in 1900, she led a wandering life between Paris, Constantinople, and Transcaucasia. Escaped the arrest and subsequent slaughter of her colleagues in 1915 and actively helped shelter Armenian orphans. After a visit to Soviet Armenia in 1926, she settled in Erevan permanently (1933). Taught French literature at Erevan State University, but her career and life were cut short by the Stalinist regime.

Collections

Erkeri žołovatzu. (Erevan, 1937).
Erker. (Erevan, 1959).
Erker. (Beirut, 1972).
Avetisyan, A. *Zapel Esayan, namakner.* (Erevan, 1977).
Erker. 2 vols. (Antʻilias, 1987).

Texts

Šnorhkʻov mardik. (Constantinople, 1907). (Stories).
Kełtz hančarner. (Constantinople, 1909). (Novelette).
Aweraknerun mēj. (Constantinople, 1911). (Prose on the Armenian massacres in Adana).
Tʻrkʻahay žamanakakits grołner. (Tiflis, 1916). (On contemporary Armenian writers).
Murati čampʻordutʻiwně Suazēn Batʻum. (Boston, 1920). (On Murad [Sebastatsi, 1874–1918] and his activities).
Hogis akʻsoreal. (Vienna, 1922). (Prose).
Andzkutʻean žamin. (Salonica, 1924). (Prose).
Verjin bažakě. (Constantinople, 1924). (Prose).
Erb aylews chen sirer. (Constantinople, 1925). (Prose).
Nahanjoł užerě. (Erevan, 1926). (Novel).
Meliha Nuri haněm. (Paris, 1928). (Story).
Promētʻēos azatagruatz. (Marseilles, 1928). (Impressions of Soviet Armenia).
Krake šapik. (Erevan, 1934). (Autobiographical story).
Silihtari parteznerě. (Erevan, 1935; Cairo, 1950). (Prose reminiscences).
Barpa Ḥachik. (Erevan, 1966). (Novel).
"Zapēl Esayeaně ew Vahram Alazaně Vahan Tʻēkʻēeanin." *Haykazean hayagitakan handēs,* 10 (1982–84), 299–308.
Avetisyan, A. "Zapel Esayani antip namaknerits." *PBH,* 1986/3, 204–11.

Texts in periodicals

"Skiwtari verjaloysner." *AM,* 1905, 253–56, 326–32, 421–27, 468–72, 561–66, 615–20.
"Molorumě." *M,* 1907, 557–61, 633–36, 655–58, 676–79, 696–700.
"Varžapetě." *HG,* 1 (1911–12/9), 21–26; (1911–12/10), 6–10; (1911–12/11), 21–25. 2 (1912–13/1), 25–29.

Translations

English

Baliozian, A. *The Gardens of Silihdar & Other Writings.* (New York, 1982).
Exerjian, V. "The Mother's Narration." *Lraber,* June 29, 1965, 4.
Serpouhi. "The Idiot." *Kochnak,* May 12, 1917, 601–2.
"The Yashmak." *Armenia,* 4 (1911/9), 19–20.

English anthologies

ALP, 17.

French

[Fantôme]. *Humanité nouvelle,* January, 1899.
"Sa vengeance." *La Patrie* (Constantinople), 1908/6, 75–76.

Tchobanian, A. "Le bain de sang." *La femme arménienne* (Paris, 1918), 67–69.

Criticism

Arzumanyan, S. *Zapel Esayan, kyankʻě ev gortzě.* (Erevan, 1964).

Avchyan, S. "Irakan patkerneri artatsolumě Zapel Esayani hogebanakan ētyudnerum." *SG,* 1983/12, 134–38.

Chiftʻē-Saraf. "Aruestagēt amolě." *AM,* 1906, 257–61.

———. "Aruestagēt amolin šurjě." *AM,* 1906, 329–35.

———. "Verjin ḥōskʻs." *AM,* 1906, 510–14.

Esayan, H. "Im mayrikě." *SG,* 1978/3, 84–95.

Gamēr. "Uruagitzner–Tikin Zapēl Esayean." *M,* 1903/14, 217.

Kʻiriščean, L. "Grakan nišer." *AM,* 1904, 293–96.

Tōminō. "Tikin Zapēl Esayean." *M,* 1907/20, 391–96.

———. "Zapēl Esayeani šurjě." *M,* 1907/37, 752–54.

Ułurlean, M. "Nor girkʻer, 'Šnorhkʻov mardik'." *AM,* 1907, 607–12.

Yarutʻiwnean, A. "Vičabanutʻiwn mě." *AM,* 1906, 442–45. (On Esayan and others).

———. "Grakan kʻronik, anbaroyakan grakanutʻiwn." *AM,* 1908, 703–6.

ESAYEAN, ĒMMANUĒL (1839–1907)

Born in Constantinople. Poet and playwright. Educated in his birthplace and at the Murat-Ṙapʻayēlean school in Venice. Teaching paid his bills. Of his trilogy "Aršak B.–Gnēl–Ołimpia," only the first play, which is perhaps his best extant work, was published.

Texts

Aršak. (Constantinople, 1870). (Drama).

Hṙipʻsimē. (Constantinople, 1872). (Drama).

Metzadzori neršnchmunkʻ, ōragrutʻiwnkʻ Ēmmay (1891–1892). (Constantinople, 1893). (Verse).

Criticism

Galayčean, A. "Ēmmanuēl Esayean: moṙtsuatz hay groł mě." *S,* 1971, 129–32.

FARMAN MANUK

A medieval love poem of uncertain origin. Its only extant text is in Armenian.

Texts

Hanelukkʻ kam Aṙełtzuatzkʻ srboyn Nersisi Šnorhalwoy. . . . Ayl ew katareal patmutʻiwn Farman manukin. (Constantinople, 1724).

Makʻlēr, F. "Patmutʻiwn Farmani Asmani." *ANA,* 6 (1904), 63–66, 92–95, 102–4, 133–34, 151–54, 169–71. 7 (1905), 37–38, 72–73, 112–14, 135–37, 170–72, 192–95.

Nazaryan, Š. *Patmutʻiwn Farman Mankann (mijnadaryan poem).* (Erevan, 1957).

Translations

French

Macler, F. "Histoire de Pharmani Asman." *ANA,* 6 (1904), 63–66, 92–95, 102–4, 133–34, 151–54, 169–71. (Incomplete).

———. "Histoire de Pharmani Asman." *Revue des Traditions Populaires,* 21 (1906), 417–40, 481–500.

Criticism

Andrikean, N. "Azgayin vēperēn . . . Farmani Asmani . . ." *B,* 64 (1906), 299–303.

Poturean, M. "Fr. Maglēr ew Farmani Asman." *B,* 65 (1907), 188–90.

GALĒMKʻEAREAN, ZARUHI (1874–1971)

Pen names: Ewterpē, G. Zaruhi, S. Zaruhi.

Born and educated in Constantinople. Her initial writings, both poetry and prose, appeared in Armenian periodicals of both Constantinople and New York, where she spent the latter part of her life.

Collections

Haskakʻał. (Erevan, 1965).

Texts

Nuagkʻ Ewterpeay. (Constantinople, [1892]).
Zarṫōnkʻ. (Constantinople, [1892]).
Mrmunjkʻ. (Constantinople, 1894).
Tʻoṙnikis girkʻě. (Istanbul, 1936). (Travel account).
Keankʻis čambēn. (Beirut and Antʻilias, 1952). (Prose).
Ōrer ew dēmkʻer. (Jerusalem, 1965). (Prose).

Translations (French anthologies)

APA, 113–14.

Criticism

G. Y. "Tikin Zaruhi Galēmkʻeareani het." *B,* 109 (1951), 30–35.

Maṙkʻ, H. *Zaruhi Galēmkʻearean (keankʻn u gortzunēutʻiwně).* (Istanbul, 1950).

GAPASAḤALEAN, GRIGOR (1740–1808)

Born in Kayseri. Poet; also known for his works on Armenian music. Received his education at the monastery of Surb Karapet, Kayseri, and in Constantinople, where he settled at an early age.

Texts

Grkʻoyk or kochi nuagaran. (Constantinople, 1794).
Girkʻ eražštakan. (Constantinople, 1803).
Grkʻoyks kochetseal ergaran. (Constantinople, 1803).
Nuagaran eražštakan. (Constantinople, 1803).
"Hamaṙōtutʻiwn eražštakani gitutʻean . . ." *BM,* 11 (1973), 291–334.

Poetry

PHA, 2, 184–92.

Criticism

Aṙakʻelyan, A. "Grigor Gapasaḥalyan." *EJ,* 1972/11, 58–63.

Atʻayan, Ṙ. "Grigor Gapasakalyaně ev ḥazabanutʻyuně." *BM,* 5 (1960), 165–5.

GAṘŌNĒ, ARAM (1905–1974)

Pen name: Aram Gaṙōnē.

Born Aram Bałdasarean in Tabriz. Poet; studied in his native city. Taught in France (1928–32) and in Iran (1932 to his death).

Texts (verse)

Banastełtzutʻiwnner. (Paris, 1924).
Ara ew Šamiram. (Tabriz, 1926).
Arewahas. (Teheran, 1942).
Tzałikner, tzałikner . . . (Teheran, 1942).
Ašnanamut. (Teheran, 1948).
Ašnan tzałikner. (Teheran, 1960).
Ardarutʻean čanaparhov. (Teheran, 1962). (Story).
Iriknamut. (Teheran, 1972).

GĒORG MḤLAYIM (18th c.)

Little is known about this *vardapet,* save that he studied in Paris (possibly at the Collège Louis-le-Grand), spent some time in Rome (as a visitor and as a prisoner), and had a good command of a number of languages. Most probably, he was a native of Constantinople, where he spent most of his life. His books were written in passionate defense of the doctrines of the Church of Armenia.

Texts

Girkʻ vičabanutʻean ĕnddēm erkabnakats. (Constantinople, 1734).
Čšmarit nšanakutʻiwn katʻułikēutʻean. (Constantinople, 1750). (This is a second, separate edition of this work first published in the book above).
Čaṙ vasn tznndean Teaṙn meroy Yisusi Kʻristosi. ([Constantinople], n.d.). (Several subsequent editions published in Constantinople in 1787, 1793, 1804).
Vkayutʻiwnkʻ hayrapetats yałags mioy bnutʻean Kʻristosi, žołovealkʻ i grotsn latinatswots. (Constantinople, n.d.).

Criticism

Ter-Stepʻanyan, A. "Gevorg Mḥlayim." *EJ,* 1984/5, 36–44.

GRAŠI, AŠOT (1910–1973)

Pen name: Ašot Graši.
Born Ašot Grigoryan in Baku, and educated at the State University of Erevan. Poet; from 1933 to 1946, the date of his final return to Erevan, Graši worked in Baku as a librarian and journalist and was at one point secretary of the Armenian Section of the Union of Writers of Azerbaijan.

Collections

Erker. 2 vols. (Erevan, 1965).

Texts (verse)

Mutkʻ. (Baku, 1934).
Žołovrdi het. (Baku, 1938).
Kʻnarakan. (Baku, 1939).
Ṙazmi kʻnar. (Baku, 1942).
Kṙunk. (Baku, 1944).
Ampaberd. (Baku, 1945).
Im garunĕ. (Erevan, 1946).

Ełbayrut'yan astłi tak. (Erevan, 1949).
Ergĕ t'ṙchum ē ašḥarhov. (Erevan, 1952).
Im siro poemĕ. (Erevan, 1954).
Sareri sringĕ. (Erevan, 1957).
Tziatzani yot' ergĕ. (Erevan, 1961).
Ur es siro molorak [?] (Erevan, 1968).
Arevi k'uyrĕ. (Erevan, 1972).
K'ṙunkneri ałbyur. (Erevan, 1976).
Im siro legendĕ. (Erevan, 1983).

Translations

ENGLISH

Zelikoff, L. "My Hills." *SL,* 1966/3, 137.

FRENCH

Mardirossian, L. ["O monde, tu n'es qu'un vaste mystère."] *OO,* 123 (March 1969), 36.

GERMAN

Leschnitzer, F. "Gäbs nicht euch . . ." *Sowjet-Literatur,* 1966/3, 135.

RUSSIAN

Derev'ia meniaiut listvu. Lirika 1934–1964. (Moscow, 1965).
Gory poiut. Stikhi. (Moscow, 1946).
Imenem pravdy. Stikhi. (Moscow, 1952).
Karabakhskaia vesna. Stikhi. (Moscow, 1941).
Kupriianov, V. *Kolybel' radug. Stikhi.* (Moscow, 1980).
Lirika. 1934–1956. (Moscow, 1956).
Pyl-Pugi. (Moscow, 1960).
Sem' pesen radugi. (Moscow, 1959).
Shuba Pyl-Pugi. (Moscow, 1956).
Soldaty mira. (Moscow, 1950; Erevan, 1952).
Stikhi. (Moscow, 1960).
Stikhotvoreniia. (Moscow and Leningrad, 1950).
Vesenniaia galaktika. (Moscow, 1969).

SPANISH

Alberti, R., and Leon, M. T. "Atlas montañas." *Literatura Sovietica,* 1966/3, 137.

Criticism

Bałdasaryan, A. "Ašot Graši." *SG,* 1962/6, 164–68.
Rostovtseva, I. "Achot Grachi, La flûte montagnarde, Moscou, 1977." *LS,* 234 (1978), 173–75.

GRIG, GEVORG (1893–1987)

Pen name: Gevorg Grig.

Born Gevorg Grigoryan in Vałaršapat (Ējmiatzin). Poet; went to schools in his native town, Erevan, and Tiflis. Taught in various schools in Eastern Armenia and in other parts of Transcaucasia. Retired in 1951 after losing his eyesight.

Texts (verse)

Erkat'i ergĕ. (Tiflis, 1925).
Gyułatsin u gaylĕ. (Tiflis, 1927). (Tale).

Banasteltzutʻyunner. (Tiflis, 1929).
Haltʻanaki ulinerov. (Tbilisi, 1956).
Hayrenikʻi hamar. (Erevan, 1959).
Elbayrutʻyan tzalkepʻunj. (Tbilisi, 1963).
Im tzaliknerě. (Erevan, 1965).
Ser. (Erevan, 1978).
Siro varder. (Tbilisi, 1979).
Kʻare anun. (Erevan, 1983).

GRIGOR DARANAŁTSI or KAMAḤETSI (1576–1643)

Born in Kamaḥ (Kemah, Turkey). Historian and scribe. Studied at the celebrated monasteries of Mount Sepuh, near his birthplace, and in other religious centers in Armenia. Led a turbulent life, traveling widely and participating in Armenian communal and national affaris. For a while he shared the Patriarchate of Constantinople with two other bishops, but then he became the primate of the Armenians of Rodosto (Tekirdağ), where he seems to have spent his last years.

Text

Nšanean, M. *Žamanakagrutʻiwn Grigor vardapeti Kamaḥetswoy kam Daranaltswoy,* (Jerusalem, 1915).

Texts (secondary)

Perperean, H. "Grigor Daranałtsii džuarimats mēk hatuatzin masin." *S,* 1951, 273–74.

———. " 'Alii dašnagirě' Grigor Daranałtsii 'Žamanakagrutʻean' mēj." *S,* 1951, 302–4, 330–31.

Utʻujyan, A. "Grigor Daranałtsin M. Chamchyani Patmutʻyan ałbyur." *L,* 1975/2, 81–89.

GRIGOR ŌŠAKANTSI (c1756–1798)

Born in Ōšakan, Armenia. Poet and celibate priest. Member of the Ējmiatzin Brotherhood. Toured Armenian monasteries as the nuncio ("nuirak") of the Catholicos of Armenia. Died and buried in Erzurum.

Poetry

HA, 78 (1964), 15–27; 142–54; 311–22 (18 poems). Reprinted in H. Oskean's *Chors hay tałasatsner ew anonts tałerě.* (Vienna, 1966), 61–136.

MPT, 66–72. (Four poems also published in the above sources).

Criticism

Nazaryan, Š. "Grigor Ōšakantsu kyankʻn u stełtzagortzutʻyuně." *PBH,* 1964/4, 101–15.

Oskean, H. "Grigor arkʻep. Ōšakantsi." *HA,* 78 (1964), 7–28, 141–54, 311–22.

GRIGOR ŠŁTʻAYAKIR (1669–1749)

Grigor (also referred to as *Širuantsi*) studied at the "university" of Amrdol (also Amrtol or Amlordi) in Bałēš (Bitlis) and later became the Abbot General of the Monastery of Surb Karapet of Tarōn (northwest of Muš) from 1710 to 1715. In

1717 he was appointed patriarch of Jerusalem, where he arrived only in 1721, after launching a campaign to repay the enormous debts of the patriarchate. He bore a chain for nearly a decade, until the successful conclusion of his campaign; hence his soubriquet *šłtʻayakir* ("The Chainbearer"). He spent four years in Constantinople (1736–40) defending the rights of the Armenian community in the perennial conflicts with the Greeks and Latins over the Holy Places. Died in Jerusalem.

Texts

"Storagrutʻiwn ułeworutʻean t. Grigori Šłtʻayakri Patriarkʻi S. Atʻoṙoys, yErusałemē i K. Pōlis." *S,* 1866, 122–27; 141–43; 184–89. (Account of his visit to Constantinople).

"Hayagitakan ayl ew aylkʻ. Grigor Šłtʻayakri mi namakě Yovhannēs Kolotin." *A,* 1915, 211–18. (A letter).

Anasyan, H. "Grakan nmušner Grigor Šłtʻayakrits." *EJ,* 1950/3–4, 39–46. Also published in *S,* 1950, 299–307; *B,* 1980/1–4, 290–94. (Literary samples).

———. "Grigor Šłtʻayakri patmakan metz yišatakaraně." *HA,* 1980/1–12, 2–11.

Galayčean, A. "Namakani Grigor Šłtʻayakir patriarkʻi." *S,* 1971, 351–55, 422–33; 1972, 61–75, 149–50, 370–80, 464–77; 1973, 41–50, 145–61, 259–74. (Letters).

Criticism

G[abikean], G. "Grigor Šłtʻayakir patriarkʻi šinararakan gortzě." *S,* 1950, 326–31.

———. "Šłtʻayakri patriarkʻutʻean naḥěntʻatsě ew Amrtoli dprevankʻě." *S,* 1950, 313–24.

Mušean, Y. "Šłtʻayakir artʻun pahakě." *S,* 1950, 310–12.

N. vrd. [Połarean]. "Grigor Šłtʻayakir, patriarkʻ Erusałemi." *S,* 1950, 288–91.

"Šłtʻayakirě." *S,* 1950, 277–82.

Tzovakan, N. [Połarean]. "Grigor Šłtʻayakri tznołkʻě." *S,* 1978, 263.

———. "Žamanakagrutʻiwn Grigor Šłtʻayakiri." *S,* 1977, 88–92.

Vrtʻanēsean, P. "Grigor patriarkʻ Šłtʻayakir." *S,* 1950, 307–10.

GRIGOR VANETSI

Vanetsi is thought to have been a sixteenth- or seventeenth-century author.

Text

Mnatsakanyan, A. "16.-17. dareri moṙatsvatz banastełtz Grigor Vanetsin ev nra antip tałerě." *EJ,* 1975/10, 40–45. (Poems).

Works in anthologies

SUM, 1, 386–96.

GRIGORYAN, SAMVEL (1907–1987)

Born in the village of Šušikʻend, Artsaḥ (Karabagh). Poet. Graduated from Erevan State University. Grigoryan was the director of the Armenian radio program in Baku (1928–57), editor-in-chief of the Armenian literary journal *Grakan Adrbejan* (Baku, 1957–79), and secretary to the Armenian section of the Union of Writers of Azerbaijan.

Collections

Erker erku hatorov. 2 vols. (Baku, 1968–69).
Hatĕntir. (Baku, 1977).

Texts (verse)

Lirikakan huyzer. (Baku, 1934).
Hayrenikʻi hamar. (Baku, 1939).
Ḥizaḥ artzivĕ. (Baku, 1942).
Mor sirtĕ. (Baku, 1944).
Liuťyun. (Baku, 1949).
Kaspiakani aṙavotĕ. (Baku, 1954).
Jinj horizonner. (Baku, 1955).
Krakner. (Erevan, 1958).
Tzałkir, azat im hayrenikʻ. (Baku, 1961).
Toł aydpes lini. (Erevan, 1965).
Singara. (Baku, 1965).
Mayramuti krakner. (Baku, 1973).
Nvirakan anunner. (Baku, 1974).

Translations (Russian)

Derzanie. (Baku, 1958).
Ogni. Stikhi. (Moscow, 1963).

GURJI-NAVĒ, (d. 1840)

An Eastern Armenian *ašuł.*

Poetry

MKH, 446–47, 467–68.
PHA, 2, 75–97.
THG, 92–98.

GUYUMČEAN, YAKOB (1904–1961)

Born in Mersin, Turkey. Poet and novelist. Survived the Armenian carnage of 1915, but his parents and brothers did not. Returned to Adana for a few years (1919–22) and emigrated to Philadelphia (1924) via the Middle East.

Texts (verse)

Ayspēs ē Amerikan. (Philadelphia, 1934).
Leninean erger. (New York, [1935]).
Poťorik. (New York, 1936).
Egiptos (poēm) ew ardzak banastełtzuťiwnner. (New York, 1938).
Grigor M. Siwni, eražštagētĕ ew mardĕ. (Philadelphia, 1943). (Biography).
Čełkʻuatz sirt. (Philadelphia, 1947).
Oskełen hundzkʻ. (Philadelphia and New York, 1948).
Hayrenakan hamanuag. 1st cycle. (Philadelphia and New York, 1948). 2d cycle (New York, 1948). 1st and 2d cycles (Philadelphia, 1948).
Aha kʻezi Amerikan, iravēp. Vol. 1. (Boston, 1949). (Novel).
Ariwnot anapat, irakan keankʻ. (Boston, 1949). (Novel).

Ōrerus ergě. (New York, 1949).
Erewanean erger, banasteltzutiwnner. (Philadelphia, 1957).
Araratean tzałikner. (Philadelphia, 1960).

Criticism

Eremean, A. *Yakob Guyumčean ew ir grakanutiwně.* (Boston, 1958).
Stepʻanyan, K. "Hakob Guyumčyan." *SG,* 1958/5, 154–58.

GYULNAZARYAN, ḤAŽAK (1918–)

Born in Erevan. Literary critic and writer of prose. Obtained doctorate in literature in 1972 and was awarded the Armenian State Prize for literature for the children's and young adult fiction he wrote. Employed at the Institute of Literature since 1950.

Collections

Ěntir erker 2 hatorov. (Erevan, 1989–90).

Texts (stories and novels)

Char bazei mahě. (Erevan, 1938).
Tzuyli verjě. (Erevan, 1940).
Dašti tererě ev hyurerě. (Erevan, 1951).
Ov inch gite. (Erevan, 1952).
Lav čanaparhordnerě. (Erevan, 1953).
Bolorinn ē. (Erevan, 1954).
Kʻałakʻi aṙavotě. (Erevan, 1956).
Kesōr. (Erevan, 1957).
Naziki sirelinerě. (Erevan, 1958).
Šarkʻerum. (Erevan, 1959).
Ōreri čanaparhě. (Erevan, 1962, 1982).
Bari luys, mayrik. (Erevan, 1964).
Oski oronołnerě. (Erevan, 1964).
Inch-or teł verjanum ē horizoně. (Erevan, 1966).
Meṙatz ašḫarhi akama bnakichnerě. (Erevan, 1968).
Patmvatzkʻner Artutiki masin. (Erevan, 1970).
Patvo kʻarě. (Erevan, 1970).
Nṙani. (Erevan, 1971).
Zarmanali hekʻiatʻner. (Erevan, 1974).
Chułarkvatz namakner. (Erevan, 1975).
Sibir. (Erevan, 1976).
Sinantrop-Pitekantrop. (Erevan, 1977).
Deṙ dprots chenkʻ gnum. (Erevan, 1979).
Moṙatskot tzerunu hekʻiatʻě. (Erevan, 1980).
Hetkʻer getni vra ev getni tak. (Erevan, 1984).
Girkʻ anaknkal. (Erevan, 1985).
Deṙ dprots chenkʻ gnum. (Erevan, 1987).
Im nkarich Goṙě. (Erevan, 1988).
Jrałats. (Erevan, 1989).

Other works

Grakan hartserě naḥaṙevolyutsion šrjani hay bolševikyan mamulum. (Erevan, 1954).
Aknarkner hay mankakan grakanuťyan patmuťyan. (Erevan, 1961).
Vaḥťang Ananyan. (Erevan, 1963).
Hakob Hakobyani kyankʿi ev gortzuneuťyan taregruťyun. (Erevan, 1965). (Co-written with S. Manukyan).
Aťabek Ḥnkoyan. (Erevan, 1968).
Hay kʿnnadatakan mitkʿě 1920–akan ťvakannerin. (Erevan, 1971).

Translations

English

Yefremova, D. "The Silver Ribbon," "Written Specially for You," "Garsevan." *SL,* 1963/3, 102–6.

English anthologies

WM, 158–62.

Russian

Ai-Artian, M. *Doroga dnei. Roman.* (Moscow, 1964).
Aiartian, M., and Aiartian, G. *Sledy na zemle i pod zemlei.* (Erevan, 1987).
Kafrieliants, R. *Kak ia poterialsia.* (Moscow, 1969).
Mnatsakanian, M. *Khoroshie puteshestvenniki.* (Moscow, 1961).

Bibliographies

Karapetyan, L. *Ḥažak Gyulnazaryan.* (Erevan, 1980).

HAČEAN, MKRTICH (1915–1985)

Born in Geyve (Turkey), and educated at the famous Kedronakan school in Constantinople. Poet and writer of short stories. Also wrote numerous articles dealing with music, painting and literary criticism. Spent the last three decades of his life in Mexico.

Texts

Knateatsě. (Istanbul, 1949). (Play).
Botser: kʿerťuatzner. (Beirut, 1973). (Verse).
Hołēn erkinkʿ: kʿerťuatzner. (Los Angeles, 1977). (Verse).

ḤACHATUR ĒRZRUMETSI (1666–1740)

Also known by the surname Aṙakʿelean. Born in Constantinople. Studied at the College of Propaganda and held pastoral-religious positions in Constantinople and Venice. Wrote in both Latin and Armenian on philosophical, theological, religious, and moral themes.

Texts

Girkʿ kʿerakanuťean. (Livoṙno, 1696).
Hamaṙōt meknuťiwn Ergoy ergotsn Sołomoni. (Constantinople, 1700).
Hamaṙōtuťiwn baroyakani astuatzabanuťean. (Venice, 1709, 1736).
Bankʿ ew kʿarozkʿ yałags tērunakan tōnits. 2 vols. (Venice, 1710).
Hamaṙōtakan imastasiruťiwn. 2 vols. (Venice, 1711).

Čartasanutʻiwn. (Venice, 1713).
Astuatzabanutʻiwn ĕndardzak. Liakatar astuatzabanutʻiwn . . . 2 vols. (Venice, 1729–1734).
Neratzutʻiwn aṙ kʻristoneakan katarelutʻiwn. (Venice, 1733).
Karčarōtaguneł hamaṙōtutʻiwn ĕndhanrakani astuatzabanutʻean. (Venice, 1736).

Criticism

Tʻahmizyan, N. K. "Ḥachatur Ērzrumetsin orpes mijnadaryan hay eražštutʻyan tesaban." *L,* 1966/11, 66–74. (Includes text of "Yałags eražštutʻean" reproduced from *Hamaṙōtakan imastasirutʻiwn,* vol. 2, pp. 529–35).
Nazaryan, Š. "Ḥachatur Ērzrumetsu usutsołakan banastełtzutʻyunnerě." *PBH,* 1969/4, 206–19.

ḤACHATUR EWDOKATSI (16th–17th c.)

Birthplace presumed to be Tokat. Visited Italy, where he had some bitter experiences. Wrote a history of Venice, the first two editions of which were attributed to Ḥachatur Etʻovpatsi.

Text

Ališan, Ł. "Yarmareal patmutʻiwn Vanatikoy pʻokʻr i šatē i Ḥachatur iritsuē Etʻovpatswoy ĕst kari ew ĕst tkar mtats, orum akanates ełakʻ ew och akanjalur leal gretsi zsa . . ." *B,* 5 (1847), 172–77.
Chōpanean, A. "Yarmareal patmutʻiwn Vanatikoy. . . ." *ANA,* 1903/2–3, 31–37.
"Patmutʻiwn Vēnētikoy kʻałakʻin." *Patmutʻiwn Pʻarēzi ew Vennayi (mijnadaryan aspetakan siravep), Patmutʻiwn Venetik kʻałakʻin (chapʻatzo),* K. Melikʻ-Ōhanjanyan, (Erevan, 1966, pp. 253–86).

ḤACHATUR ḤASPĒK ERĒTS KAFATSI (1610–1686)

Born in Caffa, Crimea. A poet, scribe, teacher, and married priest. Spent most of his life in Crimea.

Poetry

"Tał i veray vardin ew anušahot tzałkants i Ḥaspekē asatseal." *Girkʻ dprutʻean ew Tałaran* (Constantinople, 1714, pp. 214–16). Also published in *TH,* 119–20; and in *KNZ,* 2, 11–14.
"Tał siroy ew uraḥutʻean" ("Ek, sireli uraḥastsukʻ"). *KNZ,* 3, 12–15.

Works in anthologies

SUM, 2, 128–52.

Criticism

Akinean, N. "Ḥachatur Ḥaspēk erēts Kafatsi." *Ditsawan,* 1923, Book 1, pp. 138–42.
———. "Ḥachatur Ḥaspēk erēts Kafatsi tałasats (1610–1686)." *HA,* 49 (1935), 336–44. (Reproduced in *AMH,* 4, 173–89).

ḤACHATUR JUŁAYETSI

An eighteenth-century historian whose work contains detailed information on Iran and the Armenians of Iran in the eighteenth century.

Text

Patmutʿiwn parsits. (Vałaršapat, 1905).

ḤACHATUR KAFAYETSI (c1592–1659?)

Born Ḥachgṙuz in Caffa, Crimea. Renamed Ḥachatur on his ordination into married priesthood in 1624. Remembered for his chronicle regarding Crimea and its Armenian community.

Text

"Ḥachatur Kafayetsu taregrutʿyunĕ (XVII d.)." Hakobyan, V. *Manr žamanakagrutʿyunner,* Vol. 1 (Erevan, 1951, pp. 205–36).

Anthologies

SUM, 2, 125–27.

Translations

German

Schütz, E. "Eine armenische Chronik von Kaffa aus der ersten Hälfte des 17. Jahrhunderts." *AO,* 29 (1975) fasc. 2, pp. 133–86.

Criticism

Abgaryan, G. "Ḥachatur Kafayetsu Žamanakagrutʿyan germaneren tʿargmanutʿyunĕ ev Matenadarani no. 7709 tałaranĕ." *L,* 1977/6, 65–78.

Abrahamyan, A. "Ḥachatur erets Kafayetsu Taregrutʿyunĕ." *EJ,* 1944/1, 39–51.

HAKOBYAN, HAKOB (1866–1937)

Pen name: Proletar.

Born in Elizavetpol (Kirovabad, and now Ganja, Azerbaijan). Generally recognized as the principal founder of Armenian Marxist-Proletarian poetry. Discontinued his education at his birthplace, moved to Tiflis in 1886, and sought employment in a variety of occupations. In 1921 he was appointed the "komisar" of all banks in Tiflis. In 1922, with some other colleagues, he founded the Armenian branch of the Association of Proletarian Writers of Georgia and edited its organ, *Darbnots.*

Collections

Nor aṙavot. (Erevan, 1931).
Banastełtzutʿyunner. (Erevan, 1935).
Ĕntir erker. (Erevan, 1936).
Banastełtzutʿyunner. (Erevan, 1948).
Erker. (Erevan, 1951).
Erker chors hatorov. (Erevan, 1955–58).
Im ašḥarhĕ. (Erevan, 1956).
Banastełtzutʿyunner ev poemner. (Erevan, 1958).
Banastełtzutʿyunner, poemner. (Erevan, 1966).

Texts (verse)

Banastełtzutʻiwnner. (Tiflis, 1899).
Ašḥatankʻi erger. (Tiflis, 1906).
Yełapʻoḥakan erger. (N.p., 1907).
Nor ařawōt. (Tiflis, 1910).
Yełapʻoḥakan erger. (Tiflis, 1917).
Yišatakin kʻsanvets komunarneri. (Tiflis, 1919).
Karmir alikʻ. (Tiflis, 1921).
Yełapʻoḥakan bem. (Tiflis, 1922).
Erku poem. (Tiflis, 1923).
Baylševik ē Šir-kanalě. (Tiflis, 1925).
Banastełtzutʻyunner. Vol. 1. (Tiflis, 1926).
Agitatori hušerits. (Tiflis, 1927).
Leningradyan poem. (Tiflis, 1931).
Nor erger. (Tiflis, 1936).

Translations

Russian

Asatrian, A., et al. *Sochineniia. V odnom tome.* (Moscow, 1956).
Izbrannoe. (Erevan, 1948).
Izbrannoe. (Moscow, 1951).
Pesni truda i revoliutsii. Stikhotvoreniia. (Tiflis, 1932).
Stikhi. (Moscow, 1938).
Stikhi. (Moscow, 1966).
Stikhi i poemy. (Erevan, 1960).
Stikhotvoreniia i poemy. (Leningrad, 1961, 1981).

Bibliographies

Hovhannisyan, Ē. *Hakob Hakobyan (1866–1937), matenagitutʻyun.* (Erevan, 1967).
Manukian, S. *Akop Akopian: Kritiko-biogr. ocherk. (Per. s arm. M. Malkhazovoi).* (Moscow, 1980).

Criticism

Asatryan, A. *Hakob Hakobyan.* (Erevan, 1947). Erevan, 1955.
Azatyan, A. *Hakob Hakobyan.* (Erevan, 1955).
Gyulnazaryan, Ḥ., and Manukyan, S. *Hakob Hakobyani kyankʻi ev gortzuneutʻyan taregrutʻyuně.* (Erevan, 1965).
Harutʻyunyan, L. "Ṙomantizmi hastatumě Hakobyani poeziayum." *SG,* 1963/6, 142–48.
Hovakimyan, B. "Mi banastełtzutʻyan patmutʻyuně." *SG,* 1978/11, 165–68. ("Tikin N. N.-in").
Manukyan, S., and Gyulnazaryan, Ḥ. "Hakob Hakobyani paykʻarě buržuakan natsionalizmi dem." *T,* 1953/5, 17–28.
———. "Hakob Hakobyani ardzakě." *T,* 1955/9, 3–18.
Manukyan, S. "Hakob Hakobyani grakan usumnasirutʻyan ułin." *L,* 1970/9, 22–33.
———. *Hakob Hakobyan (kyankʻě ev gortzě).* (Erevan, 1975).

Sargsyan, G. *Hakob Hakobyan.* (Erevan, 1955).
———. "Ṙevolyutsioner banastełtzi ardzakě." *SG,* 1958/1, 111–20.
———. *Hakobyani kyankʻě: hamaṙot aknark.* (Erevan, 1966).
Vardanyan, A. "Hełapʻoḥutʻyan šepʻoraharě." *SG,* 1966/5, 115–19.

HAMASTEŁ, (1895–1966)

Pen names: Hamasteł, Ōhan Tzopʻetsi.

Born Hambardzum Kēlēnean in the village of Pʻērchēnč, near Ḥarberd (Harput, Turkey), and educated in Mezirē (or Mezrē), in the same region. In 1913, he settled in the United States (Boston) and wrote about the indelible memories of his birthplace. Some of his work is still scattered in the periodical press, notably in *Hayrenikʻ* of Boston.

Collections

Erker. Vol. 1. (Beirut, 1966). (*Giwłě* ew *Andzrew*).
Sevan, G. *Hayastani leṙneru srngaharě.* (Erevan, 1989).

Texts (stories)

Giwłě. (Boston, 1924; Beirut, 1955).
Andzrew. (Paris, 1929).
Spitak dziaworě. 2 vols. (Los Angeles, 1952). (Novel).
Kʻajn Nazar ew 13 patmuatzkʻner. (Cairo, 1955).
Ałōtʻaran. (Beirut, 1957).
Aytzetomar ew uriš banastełtzutʻiwnner. (Cairo, 1960). (Verse).
Patmuatzkʻner u hēkʻeatʻner. (Istanbul, 1963).
Aṙajin sērě. (Beirut, 1966).
"Gurgen Maharu ev Hamasteḷi namakagrutʻyuně." *SG,* 1983/8, 90–98.

Translations

English

Mandalian, J. "The Kiss." *The Armenian Review,* Summer, 2 (1949/2), 3–23.
———. "The Pigeons." *The Armenian Review,* Autumn, 4 (1951/3), 3–20.

Criticism

Alikʻyan, A. "Hay gyuḷi annman srngaharě." *EJ,* 1966/5, 36–39.
Antonean, Ṙ. "Hamasteḷi 'Giwł'in mēj ew 'Andzrew'in tak." *B,* 124 (1966), 339–43.
Baluean, H. "Hamasteḷi 'Andzrewě'." *Z,* 1 (1929–30?), 83–85.
Čanašean, M. "Hamasteł ew ir gortzě." *B,* 124 (1966), 325–36; 125 (1967), 12–16.
Hamasteł, 1895–1966 (yisnameay yobelean Hamasteḷi grakan gortzunēutʻean). (New York, [1967]).
Kurtikyan, S. "Hamasteḷi ašḥarhě." *SG,* 1985/6, 104–14.
Šahinean, G. *Hamasteł.* (Beirut, 1961).
———. "Hamastełě ew ir ašḥarhě." *HK,* 39 (1961/5), 9–13; 6, 17–21; 7, 43–47; 8, 57–61; 9, 47–54; 10, 48–53.
Sōfean, V. "Hamastełě." *HK,* 16 (1937–38/3), 85–88.
Tēr Łazarean, E. "Hamasteł giwłagir." *B,* 124 (1966), 337–38.

ḤANENTS, GALUST (1910–1998)

Pen name: Galust Ḥanents.

Born Galust Ḥanean in Teheran and educated in Armenian and French schools in the same city. Poet, teacher, and translator of Persian literature into Armenian.

Texts (verse)

Ambołj srtov. (Teheran, 1957).
Hrašali zōrutʻiwn. (Teheran, 1972).
Barew kʻez, mard. (Beirut, 1974).

ḤANZADYAN, SERO (1915–1998)

Born in Goris, in the region of Zangezur, Armenia. Studied pedagogy at his birthplace and taught in the region until the outbreak of World War II. Fought in the ranks of the Red Army, and later recorded his experiences in his *Erekʻ tari 291 ōr,* which won him the Armenian State Literary Prize in 1977. In the 1970s and 1980s, he was a consultant to the Union of Writers of Armenia and held various political positions. He has visited the Armenian communities of the Middle East and the United States.

Collections

Erkeri žołovatzu. 5 vols. (Erevan, 1967–70).
Erkeri žołovatzu. 6 vols. (Erevan, 1981–83).

Texts (stories and novels)

Mer gndi mardik. (Erevan, 1950, 1987).
Hołě. 2 vols. (Erevan, 1954–55, 1957, 1969).
Lal Hamazě. (Erevan, 1955, 1970).
Orotani kirčum. (Erevan, 1956).
Karmir šušanner. (Erevan, 1958).
Kʻarandzavi bnakichnerě. (Erevan, 1961, 1979).
Harstutʻyuně leṙnerum. (Erevan, 1961).
Mḥitʻar Sparapet. (Erevan, 1961; Cairo, 1962; Beirut, 1962; Erevan, 1963, 1988).
Depkʻer leṙnerum. (Erevan, 1962).
Koratz arahetner. (Erevan, 1964).
Kʻajaran. (Erevan, 1964).
Ayrvatz tuně. (Erevan, 1965).
Matyan ełelutʻyants. (Erevan, 1966).
Andzrevits heto. (Erevan, 1969).
Inchu, inchu. (Erevan, 1970).
Erekʻ tari 291 ōr. (Erevan, 1972).
Sevani lusabatsě. (Erevan. 1974).
Avandatun: hekʻiatʻner, ałvesagirkʻ, zruytsner. (Erevan, 1976).
Ḥosekʻ, Ḥayastani leṙner. (Erevan, 1976, 1980).
Tʻaguhin hayots. (Erevan, 1978).
1971, amaṙ. (Erevan, 1979).
Hayrenapatum. (Erevan, 1980).
Hayrenapatum. 1929–1970. 4 vols. to 1989. (Erevan, 1980, 1981, 1984, 1989).
"Libananyan ułegrutʻyun." *SG,* 1982/3, 11–52.
"Hovhannes Širaz." *SG,* 1985/1, 76–86.
Arakʻsě płtorvum ē. (Erevan, 1985).

Hovhannisyan, H. "Zruyts Sero Ḥanzadyani het." *SG,* 1985/11, 4–15.
Hors het ev ařants hors. (Erevan, 1986).
Inchpes hišum em. (Hušer). (Erevan, 1988).
Pělě Pułi. (Erevan, 1988).
Andranik. (Erevan, 1989).

Translations

English

Efremova, D. "The Gorge Is Not What It Used to Be." *SL,* 1966/3, 97–107.

English anthologies

WM, 163–68.

French

Lusternik, H. "Fleur des montagnes." *OO,* 123 (March 1969), 77–87.

French anthologies

Yéghiaian, A. *E.* 155–61.

German

Einhorn, E. "Eine Schlucht verändert sich." *Sowjet-Literatur,* 1966/3, 105–15.

Russian

Aleksanian, E. *Doroga v gorakh. Rasskazy.* (Moscow, 1967).
Aleksanian, E., and Kafrieliants, R. *Poteriannye tropy: Rasskazy.* (Erevan, 1986).
Izbrannye proizvedeniia. 2 vols. (Moscow, 1985).
Kafrieliants, R. *Povesti i rasskazy.* (Moscow, 1986).
———. *Tri goda 291 den': Frontovoi dnevnik.* (Moscow, 1984).
Kafrieliants, R., and Manasian, G. *Mkhitar Sparapet.* (Moscow, 1982). ("Dopolnitel'ny tirazh," 1983).
———. *Tsaritsa armianskaia. Roman.* (Moscow, 1984).
Kananova, E. *Govorite, gory Armenii.* (Erevan, 1987).
Mnatsakanian, M. *Liudi nashego polka. Roman.* (Erevan, 1956).
Moi rodnye i sosedi. Rasskazy. (Moscow, 1959).
Sadovskii, A. *Zemlia. Roman.* 2 vols. (Erevan, 1956–57).
Sluchai v gorakh. Rasskazy. (Moscow, 1960). Erevan, 1989.
Strana semi dolin. (Moscow, 1968).

Criticism

[Armēn, A.] "Mḥitʻar Sparapetě." *HK,* 42 (1964/5), 67–71; 6, 59–71; 7, 63–73.
Ḥachatryan, A. "Sero Ḥanzadyan." *SG,* 1959/10, 107–18.
Hayryan, G. "Metz hayrenakani patumnerits." *SG,* 1974/3, 98–111.
———. *Sero Ḥanzadyan.* (Erevan, 1979).
Łukasyan, Z. " 'Mḥitʻar Sparapet' patmavepě." *T,* 1965/6, 69–78.
Mahari, G. "Mtorumner 'Kʻajaran' vepi masin." *SG,* 1966/1, 122–26.
Minasyan, N. "Ardzakagri lezun: Sero Ḥanzadyani gyułě patkeroł erkeri ōrinakov." *SG,* 1972/6, 149–55.
———. "Sero Ḥanzadyani stełtzagortzakan lezvi kʻerakanakan ařandznahatkutʻyunnerě." *L,* 1972/9, 82–89.
Petrosyan, Tʻ. "Ḥčankar depi hamaynapatker." *SG,* 1983/8, 139–43.
Sarinyan, S. "Patmutʻyan gełarvestakan ěnkalman ułinerum." *SG,* 1977/9, 141–49. (On *Ḥosekʻ, Hayastani leřner*).
Sołomonyan, S. "Sero Ḥanzadyani 'Mḥitʻar Sparapetě'." *SG,* 1961/11, 161–74.

ḤATISEAN, MARIAM (1845–1914)

Born Mariam Marisean in Tiflis. Headed "Kovkasi hayuheats baregortzakan ěnkeruťiwn," a charitable-cultural society, from 1882 to 1907. Her novels and novelettes deal mainly with women's social status and role.

Texts

Hełinē. Vēp. ([Tiflis], 1890). (Novel).
Nor čanaparhi vray: vēpik. (Petersburg, 1894). (Story).
P'esay orsołner. (Tiflis, 1894). (Story).
Džbaḥt kin. Vēp. (Tiflis, 1899). (Novel).

Criticism

Yovakimean, H. "Miriam Ḥatisean." *A,* 1914, 948–56, 1047–54.

HAVASI, GUSAN (1896–1978)

Pen name: Gusan Havasi.
Born Armenak Markosyan in Ayazma, a village in the region of Tzalka, Georgia. Lost his eyesight to an illness at the age of three. Began his apprenticeship in minstrelsy early in his life and before long emerged as a leading *gusan.* Spent the last three decades of his life in Erevan.

Collections

Ergeri žołovatzu. (Erevan, 1958).

Texts (verse)

Burmunk'. (Erevan, 1950).
Im k'narě. (Erevan, 1961).
K'ařyakner. (Erevan, 1966).
Hasmik. (Erevan, 1975).

Criticism

Aťayan, Ṙ. *Gusan Havasu kyank'ě ev stełtzagortzuťyuně.* (Erevan, 1963).

HAYK, VAHĒ (1896–1983)

Pen name: Vahē Hayk.
Born Vahē Tinčean in Ḥarberd (Harput, Turkey). Graduated from Euphrates College and continued his studies in Constantinople (1915–20). Settled in the United States in 1920. For many years he engaged in journalism, both as an editor and writer.

Collections

Hayreni tzḥan. (Erevan, 1960).

Texts (stories)

Hayreni tzḥan, ardzakner, hēk'eaťner, patmuatzk'ner. 1st series (Fresno, 1930). 2d series (Fresno, 1941). 3d series (Boston, 1946). 4th series (New York, 1954). 5th series (Beirut, 1970).

Other works

Hazar hing hariwrameak Vardanants paterazmin. (Fresno, 1952).
Ḥarberd ew anor oskełēn daště. (New York, 1959).
Lusawor dēmk'er mer ōrerun vray. (Beirut, 1972).

Hayastani mankakan ašḥarhĕ ew anor mankakan grakanutʻyunĕ. (Fresno, 1974).

Translations

English

TFA, 49–62.

French

Kara-Sarkissian. *E.* 142–46.

Russian

KNS, 25–40.

PCN, 15–17.

Criticism

Baluean, H. "Ḥarberd ew anor oskełēn daštĕ." *Z* (amsatʻertʻ), 4/1–2 (1959), 13–14.

Grigoryan, H. "Vahe Hayk." *SG,* 1959/9, 127–34.

Taturyan, Š. "Vahe Hayk." *SG,* 1966/3, 108–13.

HAYKAZ, ARAM (1900–1986)

Pen name: Aram Haykaz.

Born Aram Chekʻemean in Šapin-Garahisar (Šebinkarahisar, Turkey). Took part in the defense of the city, and by professing Islam, he survived the genocide and World War I, in the service of Turks stationed in the mountains of Kurdistan (1915–19). Fled to Constantinople in 1919 and emigrated to the United States in the early 1920s. His prose reflects life in Western Armenia, Kurdistan, and the United States.

Collections

Aprēkʻ ereḥēkʻ. (Beirut, 1973).

Texts (stories)

Tsełin dzaynĕ. 2 vols. (New York, 1949; Beirut, 1954).

Chors ašḥarh. (New York and Beirut, 1962).

Pandok. (New York and Beirut, 1967).

Karōt: ardzak aprumner. (Beirut, 1971).

Chors tari Kʻiwrtistani leṙnerun mēj. (Beirut, 1972).

Erjankutʻiwn. (Beirut, 1978).

Other works

Šapin Garahisar u ir herosamartĕ. (New York and Beirut, 1957).

Criticism

Aram Haykaz: keankʻn u gortzĕ. (Beirut, 1962).

Baluean, H. "Šapin Garahisar u ir herosamartĕ." *Z* (amsatʻertʻ), 3 (1959/11–12), 13.

Yobelenakan handisutʻiwn Aram Haykazi yisnameay grakan gortzunēutʻean. (New York, 1972).

HAYKUNI, ARMENAK (1835–1866)

Pen name: Armenak Haykuni.

Born Armenak Čizmēčean (or Chizmēčean) in Constantinople. Novelist, poet, and journalist. Educated in the local Armenian schools and at the Theological

Seminary at Bebek, founded by C. Hamlin in 1840. Published the first Armenian theatrical periodical, *Musaykʻ Maseats* (1857–58), and founded with G. Chilinkirean (1839–1923) the periodical *Tzałik* (1861). Wrote one of the earliest novels in modern Armenian literature and a number of poems and plays that are still scattered in the periodical press. His attempts to explain biological, social, and political phenomena in a scientific manner, as well as his anti-clerical views, were vigorously opposed by the Armenian Church. His books listed under "other works" deal with such themes.

Texts

Ēliza kam Verjin Arewelean paterazmi žamanak tełi unetsatz irakan dēpkʻ mě. (Smyrna, 1861). (Novel).

Other works

Bnakan ḥnamatatzutʻiwn kam Aṙachnord marts amenaharkawor mēk partakanutʻeanĕ. (Constantinople, [1859?]).
Tʻurfanta tikin ew iwr gałapʻarĕ amerikatsi Eritsakan kʻarozchats vrayōkʻ. (Constantinople, 1860).
Płaton i Vosbor, ĕnddēm dimakawor 'Bari mard ew bari kʻristoneay' anun grkʻin. (Constantinople, 1860).
Garnan tzałikner kam Eritasardats ew ōriordats ardi vičakĕ. (Constantinople, 1863, [1871?]).
Gałtnikʻ bnutʻean kam Skzbunkʻ mardkayin tznndakanutʻean ewropatsi imastasirats ardi drutʻean hamemat. (Constantinople, 1863, [1871], 1895).
Čermak kam Paron S. Pʻapʻazean ew iwr Žamanakĕ. (Constantinople, 1863).
Gerezmankʻ eritasardats kam Tṙpʻakan hiwandutʻiwnkʻ, Ewropioy imastasirats ardi drutʻeanĕ hamemat. (Constantinople, 1863, [1869?], [1871?]).
Usumnakan zbōsanats tʻułtʻ. [Constantinople, 1864?]. (Armenian history).
Hamaṙōt patmutʻiwn ew ašḫarhagrutʻiwn hayots. (Constantinople, 1864). (History and geography of Armenia).
Mah Ołimpiadayi tʻaguhwoyn hayots. (Constantinople, [1864?]).
Gałtnikʻ kłerakanutʻean kam Ariwnalits viheru nkaragrutʻiwnĕ. (Constantinople, 1864).
Ašnan terewner kam Gałtnikʻ eritasardats ew pataneats. (Constantinople, n.d.).

Criticism

Hayrapetyan, S. "Armenak Haykunu hasarakakan-kʻałakʻakan hayatskʻnerĕ." *PBH,* 1967/4, 230–35.
———. "Armenak Haykunu 'Ēliza' vepĕ." *L,* 1967/5, 93–102.
Ōšakan, V. "Armenak Haykuni: arewmtahay aṙajin naḥaṙomantʻikʻnerēn." *Haykazean hayagitakan handēs,* 1970, 172–83.
Stepʻanyan, G. "Armenak Haykuni." *T,* 1955/11, 43–58.

HAYRAPET, ABDIN ŌŁLI (18th c.)

This *ašuł* (minstrel) is believed to have lived in Julfa in the second half of the eighteenth century.

Poetry

EPA, 35–39.
MPT, 85.

PHA, 1, 17–18.
SHA, 154–59.

Criticism

Eremean, A. *Parskahay ašułner.* (Tiflis, 1930), 33–39.

HAYRAPETYAN, HAYRAPET (1874–1962)

Born in Tanakert a village in Naḥijevan. Translator, author of school textbooks, writer of poetry for children, teacher, and journalist for many decades. Received elementary education in Zakʻatʻala, Georgia. Studied at the Nersisean school of Tiflis. Settled in Erevan in the 1930s.

Collections

Ĕntir erker. (Erevan, 1957).
Erkeri žołovatzu. 2 vols. (Erevan, 1965).

Texts (verse)

Mełuneri komunan. (Erevan, 1931).
Mer getě. (Erevan, 1931).
Hasmiki namakě. (Erevan, 1931).
Kolḥozi hamar. (Erevan, 1934).
Tʻrchunner. (Erevan, 1935, 1936).
Uraḥ Hrayrě ev sagi saylě. (Erevan, 1936).
Napastaki ev ałvesi hekʻiatʻě. (Erevan, 1938).
Im ergerě. (Erevan, 1939).
Tsołikn u Šołikě. (Erevan, 1941).
Kapavorě. (Erevan, 1942).
Gayl Vahan. (Erevan, 1943).
Ḥizaḥ leřntsin. (Erevan, 1943).
Čagarn u ałvesě. (Erevan, 1945).
Kovn u čagarě. (Erevan, 1947).
Pʻnjik. (Erevan, 1948).
Im ergerě: Im hayrenikʻě, Bnutʻyan erger. (Erevan, 1951).
Anhnazand ulikě. (Erevan, 1953).
Hušer manuk ōrerits. (Erevan, 1956).
Gurgenikě, Aran u es. (Erevan, 1958).
Ḥann u hovivě. (Erevan, 1959).
Balikneri hamar. (Erevan, 1961).
Akʻlori, lusni ev aregaki hekʻiatʻě. (Erevan, 1962).
Pʻisiki dasě. (Erevan, 1966).
Tzitn u tłan. (Erevan, 1971).
Ḥabvatz tzitikě. (Erevan, 1983).

ḤECHUMYAN, VIGEN (1916–1975)

Born Vidok Ḥechumyan in Erevan. A graduate of Erevan State University (1940). Worked at the Matenadaran (1938–40, 1943–56); served in the Red Army in World War II (1940–43). In the mid-1950s, he began working as a journalist for the literary periodical *Sovetakan grakanutʻyun.*

Texts (stories and novels)

Chatu ḥani patmutʻyuně. (Erevan, 1943).

Zvartʻnots. (Erevan, 1945).
Tzałkoři ordin. (Erevan, 1954).
Mez mot, haravum. (Erevan, 1955).
Girkʻ pandḫtutʻyan. (Erevan, 1959).
Šikatsatz avazi vra. (Erevan, 1962; Teheran, 1966).
Guyner ev erangner. (Erevan, 1962).
Gluḫ-gortzotsě. (Erevan, 1964).
Girkʻ linelutʻyan. 2 vols. (Erevan, 1966, 1971).
Girkʻ makʻar̄man. (Erevan, 1968).
Girkʻ grots. (Erevan, 1978).

Translations

ENGLISH ANTHOLOGIES

WM, 127–44.

FRENCH

Champenois, J. "Le faiseur de flutiaux." *OO*, 123 (March 1969), 117–21.

FRENCH ANTHOLOGIES

Yeghiaian, A. *E*. 162–66.

GERMAN

M. S. "Ownan der Miniator." *Sowjet-Literatur*, 1946/4, 61–67.

GERMAN ANTHOLOGIES

AN, 177–99.

RUSSIAN

Kniga stranstvii. Rasskazy. (Moscow, 1958).
Nersesian, G. *U nas na iuge. Roman*. (Moscow, 1956).

SPANISH

Kantorovskaia, A. "El libro de las peregrinaciones." *Literatura Sovietica*. 1966/3, 110–24.

Criticism

Bałdasaryan, G. "Askʻ mijnadari masin." *SG*, 1972/2, 148–52.

HĒKʻIMEAN, SRAPION (1832–1892)

Born in Constantinople and educated at the Murat-Rapʻayēlean school in Venice. Wrote poetry and drama, almost exclusively in Classical Armenian. Played an instrumental role in founding the first Armenian professional theater in Constantinople.

Texts

Tałkʻ, kʻertʻuatzkʻ ew tʻatrergutʻiwnkʻ. (Constantinople, 1857). (Poems and plays).
Yulianē. (Constantinople, 1864). (Play).

Criticism

Tēr-Yakobean, Y. "Ēj mě hay gra-tʻaterakan keankʻēn." *AM*, 1901, 643–46.

HISAREAN, YOVHANNĒS (1827–1916)

Born and educated in Constantinople. A teacher by profession, he wrote prose and poetry. Founded the periodical *Banasēr* (1851–52, 1859), in which he published his *Ḥosrov ew Makʻruhi,* reckoned to be the first novel in modern Western Armenian literature.

Texts

Ḥosrov ew Makʻruhi. In *Banasēr,* 1851/1, 22–28; 2, 81–88; 3, 122–33; 4, 169–76; 5, 216–23; 6, 252–66; 7, 317–28; 8, 359–72; 9, 406–14; 10, 461–70. (Novel; reference possibly incomplete).
Neṙn kam kataratz ašḫarhi. (Constantinople, 1867). (Novel).
Diwan, or ē tałaran. (Constantinople, 1871, 1910 [expanded]). (Verse).

Other works

Karčaṙōt patker Nabolēon Ponabartʻēin varutsě. (Constantinople, 1847).

ḤNKO-APER (1870–1935)

Pen name: Ḥnko-Aper.
Born Atʻabek Ḥnkoyan in the village of Łaraboya (renamed Ḥnkoyan after him, in the region of Spitak, Armenia). A writer of children's literature (poems, tales, fables) and author of Armenian language textbooks for schools. Studied in his birthplace and in Alexandrapol (Leninakan, now Gyumri, Armenia). Taught at various schools throughout Transcaucasia. Settled in Erevan permanently in the early 1920s.

Collections

Ěntir erker. (Erevan, 1940).
Žołovatzu. (Erevan, 1945).
Hatěntir. (Erevan, 1950).
Aṙakner. (Erevan, 1953).
Manuknerin. (Erevan, 1954).
Ěntir ējer. (Erevan, 1961).
Hekʻiatʻner u patmvatzkʻner. (Erevan, 1967).
Žołovatzu. (Erevan, 1979).
Ḥnkoyan, V. *Erker.* (Erevan, 1980).
Gasparyan, M. *Erker.* (Erevan, 1984).

Texts (verse and prose)

Banastełtzakan pʻordzer. (Alexandrapol, 1890).
Giwłatsin ew arjě. (Tiflis, 1909; Erevan, 1959).
Ałuēsn u arjě. (Tiflis, 1910; Erevan, 1941, 1970).
Goł makʻin. (Tiflis, 1911; Erevan, 1941, 1949).
Ki-ki-li-ki. (Tiflis, 1911).
Tzitn u orberě. (Tiflis, 1912).
Kʻrunkn u ałuēsě. Ěnkerě ułił pētkʻ ē lini. (Tiflis, 1912).
Pʻesatsu mukě. (Tiflis, 1912).
Firdusi (925–1020). (Tiflis, 1912).
Napastaki tuně. (Tiflis, 1913).
Kʻaratsatz kʻuyrer. (Tiflis, 1916).
Aṙakner. (Tiflis, 1917).
Gyułatntes-anasnabuytzě ev ir agrozruytsě. (Erevan, 1926).
Metz Hoktember. Patkomnerin. (Erevan, 1927).
Tʻḫsamerě. (Erevan, 1929).

Aṙakner. (Erevan, 1930).
Erkatʻuɫi Erevan-Tʻiflis. (Erevan, 1930).
Pioner Hrachě. (Erevan, 1930, 1931).
Mardn inchov e campʻordum[?] (Erevan, 1931).
Motzakě. (Erevan, 1931).
Dzoragēs. (Paris, 1934).
Tramvayě Erevanum. (Erevan, 1934, 1936).
Mknern inchpes kṙvetsin katvi dem. (Erevan, 1936).
Aṙakner. (Erevan, 1937).
Banasteɫtzutʻyunner. (Erevan, 1937).
Es. (Erevan, 1939).
Mrgastan. (Erevan, 1939).
Girkʻ. (Erevan, 1940).
Ḥozn u agṙavě. (Erevan, 1940).
Gayln u gaṙě. (Erevan, 1941).
Ki-ki-li-ki akʻlorn em. (Erevan, 1941).
Papn u šaɫgamě. (Erevan, 1941).
Tzaɫikner. (Erevan, 1943).
Katun, akʻlorn u aɫvesě. (Erevan, 1948).
Mkneri žoɫově. (Erevan, 1957, 1964, 1972, 1979).
Gayln u katun. (Erevan, 1957).
Žantaḥtě. (Erevan, 1966).
Tzaɫkatz tzov. (Erevan, 1970).
Meɫu. (Erevan, 1971).
Safrazyan, K. *Aṙakner.* (Erevan, 1985).
Bklik dzknik. (Erevan, 1986).
Napastaknerě (aṙak). (Erevan, 1987).

Translations (Russian)

Saakian, M., et al. *Petukh i krysha: Stikhi, basni, skazki.* (Erevan, 1987).

Bibliographies

Melyan, B. *Atʻabek Ḥnkoyan. Kensagrutʻyun ev matenagrutʻyun.* (Erevan, 1969).

Criticism

Gyulnazaryan, Ḥ. *Atʻabek Ḥnkoyan.* (Erevan, 1968).
Melyan, B. *Atʻabek Ḥnkoyan. Kensagrutʻyun ev matenagrutʻyun.* (Erevan, 1969).
Sargsyan, S. "Atʻabek Ḥnkoyan." *SG,* 1970/10, 134–40.

HOVHANNISYAN, HOVHANNES (1864–1929)

Born in Vaɫaršapat (Ējmiatzin). His verse paved the way for some new trends and traditions in modern Eastern Armenian poetry. Studied in Erevan, at the Lazarean (Lazarevskii) Insitute in Moscow, and Moscow University (1884–88). Taught for many years at the Gēorgean seminary in Ējmiatzin. Later in his life, he held administrative positions in the fields of education and culture in Baku and in Soviet Armenia.

Collections

Zaryan, Ṙ. *Erkeri žoɫovatzu.* Vol. 1. (Erevan, 1937).
Hatěntir. (Erevan, 1939).

Zaryan, Ṙ. *Ĕntir banastełtzutʻyunner.* (Erevan, 1945).
Banastełtzutʻyunner. (Erevan, 1949).
Hatĕntir. (Erevan, 1953).
Erker, mihatoryak. (Erevan, 1959).
Erkeri žołovatzu. 4 vols. (Erevan, 1964–68).
Hatĕntir: kʻertʻvatzner. (Erevan, 1971).

Texts (verse)

Banastełtzutʻiwnner. (Moscow, 1887).
Banastełtzutʻiwnner. (Vałaršapat, 1908).
Banastełtzutʻiwnner. 1882–1912 yobelenakan hratarakutʻiwn. (Vałaršapat, 1912).
Vahagni tznundĕ: kʻertʻvatz ev nkar. (Erevan, 1972, 1981).

Translations

English

"Hast Thou Seen My Country?" *The Oriental World,* 1914/3, 76.

English anthologies

AP, 190–94.
ALP, 20, 60–61, 77.

French anthologies

APA, 97–100.
LPA, 181–82.

German anthologies

AD, 32–33.
ALG, 124–25.

Russian

Arsharuni, A. *Izbrannoe.* (Moscow, 1949).
Lirika. (Moscow, 1963).
Rozhdestvenskii, V. *Stikhotvoreniia.* (Erevan, 1940).

Criticism

Abełean, M. "Uruagtzer hayots grakanutʻean patmutʻiwnits: Yovhannēs Yovhannisean." *A,* 1912, 347–63, 515–24.

———. "Yovhannēs Yovhannisean." *HK,* 8 (1929–30/3), 40–53.

Akinean, N. "Yovhannēs Yovhannisean (mahuan aṙtiw)." *HA,* 44 (1930), 237.

Asmaryan, L. *Hovhannes Hovhannisyan.* (Erevan, 1963).

Avdalbegyan, Tʻ. *Hovhannes Hovhannisyan, grakan-patmakan verlutzutʻyun.* (Erevan, 1934).

Avetisyan, A. "Hovhannes Hovhannisyanĕ Moskvayum." *PBH,* 1963/2, 257–60.

Aznavuryan, G. "M. Nalbandyanĕ Hovhannes Hovhannisyani antip stełtzagortzutʻyunnerum." *T,* 1955/1, 95–96.

B[aluean], H. "Yovhannēs Yovhannēsean." *Z,* 1 (1929–30?), 332.

Balasanean, G. "Yovhannēs Yovhannisean." *HA,* 23 (1909), 135–41.

Berberean, M. "Sgawor idēalist." *A,* 1908, 380–95.

E. G. "Y. Yovhanniseani 'Banastełtzutʻiwnneri' mi kʻnnadatutʻean aṙitʻov." *Ardzagankʻ,* 1887/45, 708–11.

———. "Yovhannēs Yovhannisean, Banastełtzutʻiwnner, Moskua, 1887." *Ardzagankʻ,* 1887/26, 386–87.

Gevorkian, T. "Lermontov i tvorchestvo Ioannesa Ioannisiana." *BEH,* 1989/3, 16–25.

Hovsepʻyan, G. *Hovhannes Hovhannisyan.* (Erevan, 1957).
———. "Žołovrdakan banastełtzě." *PBH,* 1964/2, 17–30.
Kʻalantʻar, A. "Yovhannēs Yovhanniseani banastełtzutʻiwně." *Murč,* 1889/7, 1078–93.
Karinyan, A. "Hovhannes Hovhannisyan." *SG,* 1958/1, 92–98.
Khitarova, S. *Poeziia Ioannisiana.* (Moscow, 1968).
Łanalanyan, H. *Hovhannes Hovhannisyan.* (Erevan, 1946).
Malḥasean, Y. *Yovhannēs Yovhannisean, siroy ew gałapʻari ergichě.* (Tiflis, 1913).
Melikʻyan, M. "Hovhannes Hovhannisyaně tʻargmanich." *L,* 1976/9, 33–45.
Makʻsapetyan, M. "Banastełtz-tʻargmanchi gełarvestakan pʻordzě." *SG,* 1981/3, 146–49.
Muradyan, N. *Hovhannes Hovhannisyani arvestě.* (Erevan, 1964).
Połosyan, M. "Hovhannes Hovhannisyani Bakʻvi šrjani gortzuneutʻyuně." *SG,* 1964/9, 106–10.
Tēr-Margarean, Y. "Banastełtz Yovhannēs Yovhanniseani 30ameay yobeleaně." *HA,* 26 (1912), 329–32.
Tērtērean, A. *Yovhannēs Yovhannisean, siroy ew karektsutʻean ergichě.* (Erevan, 1912).
Vardanyan, V. "Hay grołneri ev mšakuytʻi gortzichneri norahayt namakneře Hovh. Hovhannisyanin." *L,* 1990/3, 88–98.
———. *Hovhannes Hovhannisyaně žamanakakitsneri hušerum.* (Erevan, 1990).
"Yovhannēs Yovhannisean." *B,* 66 (1908), 348–51.
Yovhannēsean, V. "Yovhannēs Yovhannisean." *B,* 87 (1930), 90–91.
Yovhannisean, A. "Yovhannēs Yovhanniseani tun-tʻangaraně." *Ani,* 2 (1947–48), 29–31.

HOVHANNISYAN, HRACHYA (1919–1998)

Born in the village of Šahab (now Mayakovski, in the region of Abovyan, Armenia). Poet. Educated in Erevan. He was twice editor-in-chief of *Grakan tʻertʻ* (1955–59, and from 1978 to the early 1980s). Awarded the Armenian State Literary Prize in 1979.

Collections

Banastełtzutʻyunner. 2 vols. (Erevan, 1971–72).
Ĕntir erker. 2 vols. (Erevan, 1989–1990).

Texts (verse)

Im kyankʻi ergě. (Erevan, 1948).
Erkrord handipum. (Erevan, 1951).
Hrašali aygepan. (Erevan, 1956).
Tzovi lřutʻyuně. (Erevan, 1964).
Vayri vard. (Erevan, 1968).
Surě dapʻnu vra. (Erevan, 1970).
Anmahutʻyun. (Erevan, 1970).
Hayrakan erg. (Erevan, 1977).
Arevot kłzu ergě. (Erevan, 1980).
Iriknayin łołanj. (Erevan, 1982).
Oske amp. (Erevan, 1984). (Prose; part 2 published in *SG,* 1982/9, 3–90).
Mštadalar tzařě. (Erevan, 1985). (Articles and essays).

Paterazmi demkʻě. (Erevan, 1986). (Part 2 published in *SG,* 1984/12, 3–74).
"Čavčavadzei hayrenikʻě im achkʻerov." *SG,* 1987/11, 80–91.
Charentsi lapterě. (Erevan, 1988).

Other works

Motikn u heṙun (aknarkneri ev hodvatzneri žołovatzu). (Erevan, 1967).
Žamanaki šunchě. (Erevan, 1976).

Translations

English

Evans, G. "Drinking Songs." *SL,* 1966/3, 142.
Jacque, V. "The Call of Love." *SL,* 1973/9, 128.
Rottenberg, D. ["A gardener's hand–it must be hard and rude."] *SL,* 1972/11, 113–14. Also published in *SL,* 1980/6, 116–17.
Tempest, P. ["Death's terrifying just to those. . . ."] *SL,* 1979/9, 93. Also published in *SL,* 1980/6, 117.

English anthologies

SAP, 33–35.

French

Antonian, A., and Alikian, A. ["Hommes, je ne peux vivre sans vous"], "La chagrin de la terre," ["J'ai dispersé tous les biens de ma vie"], ["Les années passeront mais jamais notre cœur"], ["Vie, ce que j'attends de toi?"], "Mes yeux," ["Je ne cherche en ce monde ni trésor"], ["Que faire? Mon cœur est devenu si délicat"], "Testament." *OO,* 170 (Feb. 1973), 5–12.
———. "Vie, ce que j'attends de toi?." *LS,* 258 (1980), 140.
Galin, M. "L'appel." *OO,* 177 (Sept. 1973), 144–45.
———. ["Qu'elle soit calleuse, la main du jardinier."] *OO,* 167 (Nov. 1972), 131.
Gaucheron, J. ["Les années s'en vont, pourtant, impossible"], *OO,* 123 (March 1969, 88.
———. "Qu'elle soit calleuse, la main du jardinier." *LS,* 258 (1980), 139.
Yoccoz, D. "Seul craint la mort celui." *SL,* 247 (1979), 103.

German

Leschnitzer, F. "Ich giess in den Becher mir güldenen Wein." *Sowjet-Literatur,* 1966/3, 140.

Russian

Chudesnii sadovnik. Stikhi. (Moscow, 1960).
Chudesnii sadovnik. (Erevan, 1970).
Dikaia roza. (Moscow, 1980).
Moim tovarishcham po schast'iu. Stikhi. (Moscow, 1952).
Molchanie moria. Stikhi. (Moscow, 1966).
Rozhdenie liubvi. (Erevan, 1956).
Tatosian, G. *Zvezdy moei iunosti: Memuarnaia povest' v 2kh ch.* (Erevan, 1988).

Spanish

Alberti, R. y Maria Teresa Leon. "Levanto mi copa." *Literatura Sovietica,* 1966/3, 141.

Criticism

Jrbašyan, Ēd. "Serndi dzaynov." *SG,* 1972/10, 97–105.
Sołomonyan, S. "Hrachya Hovhannisyan." *SG,* 1959/4, 121–34.

ḤRIMEAN, MKRTICH (1820–1907)

Born in Van. He was one of the most popular religious-national figures of his time. Took the vows of celibacy in 1854 and became the abbot of the monastery of Varag (near Van) and the primate of Muš (Tarōn) in 1862. Established the first printing press in Western Armenia and published *Artzui Vaspurakani* (1858–64), the first Armenian periodical to appear in the region. In 1868, he was created bishop in Ējmiatzin, and a year later, he was elected Patriarch of Constantinople (1869–73). In his capacity as the formally recognized head of the Armenians in the Ottoman Empire, he initiated and submitted to the Porte, a detailed report documenting oppression and misgovernment in the Armenian provinces. In 1878, he headed an unofficial Armenian delegation to the Congress of Berlin to advance Armenian aspirations, and he served as the primate of Van (1879–85) soon after his return from Germany. The radical conclusion he drew from the Congress of Berlin, bitterly articulated in a famous sermon, promoted the legitimacy of self-defense among Armenians. Exiled to Jerusalem in 1890, he was elected Catholicos of all Armenians (1893–1907). His new position brought him into conflict with the Russian authorities, notably in 1903, when he and his subordinates, acting on instructions from him, defied the czar's order calling for the confiscation of Armenian Church property and the closure of Armenian schools. His flock had long since venerated him as "Hayrik" (i.e., "father" with the endearing diminutive *ik*) in recognition of his selfless dedication to his people and homeland. His verse and prose reflect his patriotism, along with his religious, moral, social, and political concerns.

Collections

Ambołjakan erker. (New York, 1929).
Erker. (Ant'ilias, 1989).

Texts (prose and verse)

Hrawirak araratean. (Constantinople, 1850, 1876).
Hrawirak Erkrin aweteats. (Constantinople, 1851; Jerusalem, 1892).
Margarit ark'ayut'ean erknits. (Constantinople, 1866, [1876], 1887; Vałaršapat, 1894).
Draḥti ĕntanik'. (Constantinople, 1876, 1887, 1911; Tiflis, 1893).
Ḥachi čaṙ. (Constantinople, 1876, 1887; Vałaršapat, 1894).
Yisusi verjin šabat'. (Constantinople, 1876, 1887; Vałaršapat, 1894).
Žamanak ew ḥorhurd iwr. (Constantinople, 1876, 1909; Tiflis, 1895).
Vangoyž. (Constantinople, 1877, 1908).
Haygoyž. (Constantinople, 1877, 1908).
Sirak' ew Samuēl. (Constantinople, 1878, 1887; Tiflis, 1892, 1893).
Papik ew T'oṙnik. (Vałaršapat, 1894; Beirut, 1957).
Tagaworats žołov. (London, 1915). (English and Armenian).
Ḥōsk' hražarman Ḥrimean s. Patriark'i Hayots Azgayin eresp'oḥanakan žołovoy 64rd patmakan nistin mēj or tełi unetsaw 1873 Ōgostos 3-in. ([Constantinople, 1873]; Constantinople, 1910).
Verjaloysi dzayner. (Cairo, 1901).
Ołbatsoł Ḥorenatsin. (Vałaršapat, 1902).
Tzragir barenorogmants. (Constantinople, 1909).

Translations

ENGLISH

Tonapetean, P., and Binyon, L. *The Meeting of the Kings.* (London, 1915). (Armenian and English texts).

ENGLISH ANTHOLOGIES

AP, 201–13.

Criticism

Ačaṙyan, H. "Mkrtich katʻołikos Ḥrimyan." *EJ,* 1944/4–5, 15–20.

Ačēmean, H. *Ḥrimean Hayrik, 1820–1920.* (Ējmiatzin, 1920; Tabriz, 1929). *(Hayots Hayrik. 1. Kensagrutʻiwn).*

Amenayn Hayots Hayrik. (Boston, 1957).

Čanašean, M. "Ḥrimean Hayrik." *B,* 128 (1970), 303–11.

Durean, E. et al. "Kartzikʻner Ḥrimyan Hayriki masin." *EJ,* 1957/11, 34–37.

Eremean, M. "Ḥrimean Hayrik." *B,* 70 (1912), 136–42, 214–19.

Frangean, E. *Hay mitkʻě: Vani imastasērě–Ḥrimean Hayrikě.* Book 1 (Teheran, 1919). Book 2 (Cairo, 1925).

Gabriēlean, M. *Ḥrimean Hayrik.* (New York, 1892).

Giwrjean, A. "Ḥrimean Hayriki yišatakin." *Lumay,* 3–4 (1908), 62–72.

Giwzalean, G. "Ḥrimean Hayriki krōnakan ašḥarhayetsołutʻiwně. *HK,* 30 (1952/3), 49–60.

———. *Ḥrimean Hayrik: gałapʻarneri ašḥarhě.* (Beirut, 1954).

G[ušakean], Tʻ. *Ḥrimean Hayrik* (*ir tznndean hariwrameakin aṙtʻiw*). (Paris, 1925).

Hatityan, A. "Vaspurakani Artzivě." *EJ,* 1957/11, 3–6.

"Ḥrimyan Hayrik ev nergałtʻě." *EJ,* 1946/2–3, 24–25.

Kʻiwrtean, Y. "Ḥrimean Hayrik ew Ējmiatznay tačarin nkarnerě." *HK,* 35 (1957/1), 83–101.

Ł. M. "Hayots Hayrikě hay grakanutʻean asparizum." *A,* 1900, 178–86.

Manuēlean, H. *Ḥrimeani kensagrakan tesutʻiwn, patkerov.* (Tiflis, 1892).

Natʻanean, M. "Hayrik." *Širak,* 9 (1907), 489–500.

Nersisyan-Pʻanikyan, H. "Ḥrimyan Hayriki 'Draḥti ěntanikʻě'." *EJ,* 1976/7, 26–30.

Palčean, K. [later Vazgēn I, Catholicos of Armenia]. *Ḥrimean Hayrik orpes dastiarak.* (Bucharest, 1943; 2d ed. published under Vazgēn A., New York, 1987).

———. "Ḥrimyan Hayrik orpes dastiarak." *EJ,* 1971/2, 5–10.

Pʻolatean, A. *Ḥrimean Hayrik.* (New York, 1957).

Poturean, M. "Ḥrimean Hayrik." *B,* 65 (1907), 562–66; 66 (1908), 55–58, 189–91.

Ṙuben vrd. "Hayrenasirutʻyuně Ḥrimyani erkerum." *EJ,* 1945/3–4, 25–30; 1945/8–10, 26–31.

Siamantʻo. "Ḥrimyan Hayrik." *EJ,* 1971/2, 52–53.

Sion arkʻep. *Hayots Hayrik (1820–1907).* (Buenos Aires, 1957).

Siruni, Y. "Ḥrimean gragētě." *Vēm,* 2 (1934/1), 17–37.

Širvanzadē, "Ḥrimean Hayrik." *HK,* 2 (1923–24/10), 33–37.

Tēr-Yakobean, N. "Ḥrimean Hayrik (tpaworutʻiwnner)." *S,* 1930, 29–30.

Tʻērzipašean, A. *Artziwě ir boynin mēj.* (Paris, 1938).

Tʻumanyan, H. "Erku hayr." *EJ,* 1971/2, 46.

Vahē-Vahean. "Hayots Hayrikě." *Ani,* 2 (1947–48), 393–95.

Vazgēn A. *Ḥrimean Hayrik orpēs dastiarak.* (New York, 1987; 2d ed., cf. *supra,* K. Palčean).
"Vehapʻaṙ Hayrapeti tznndean 80-rd taredardzě." *A,* 1900, 163–68.
"Vkayutʻyunner Ḥrimyan Hayriki masin." *EJ,* 1971/2, 24–32.
Zawēn vrd. "Gragētě Hayots Hayrik M. Ḥrimeani mēj." *S,* 1957, 305–9.
Zohrabyan, H. "Ḥrimyan Hayriki mahě." *EJ,* 1971/2, 40–45.

HURYAN, TʻATʻUL (1912–1942)

Pen name: Tʻatʻul Huryan.

Born Tʻatʻul Ḥachatryan in Tʻajrlu, a village in Surmalu, Russia (now in the easternmost part of Turkey). Poet. Studied in Baku and pursued his higher studies in Moscow. Killed in action in World War II, fighting in the ranks of the Red Army. He was posthumously awarded the E. Charents and N. Ostrovskii literary prizes.

Collections

Graši, A. *Astł.* (Baku, 1943).
Banastełtzutʻyunner ev poemner. (Erevan, 1949).
Erkri het. (Baku, 1951).
Banastełtzutʻyunner. (Erevan, 1956).
Hušardzan. (Baku, 1970).
Duryan, L. *Lusapsak.* (Erevan, 1982).

Texts (verse)

Hołi aryuně. (Erevan, 1932).
Dnepr. (Baku, 1933).
Hasak. (Baku, 1934).
Poemner. (Baku, 1941).
Frik. (Erevan, 1945). (Play).

Translations

RUSSIAN

Balasan, V. *Stikhi.* (Erevan, 1950).
———. *Stikhi i poemy.* (Erevan, 1952).

Criticism

Akopian, Zh. *Zhizn' i tvorchestvo Tatula Guriana.* (Erevan, 1986).
Hakobyan, Ž. "Grchov ev zenkʻov." *BEH,* 1985/3, 173–77.

INTRA, (1875–1921)

Pen name: Intra (i.e. Indra).

Born Tiran Chrakʻean in Constantinople. Studied at the celebrated Pērpērean school and taught at local schools. Traveled to Paris and Geneva (1897) and Egypt (1898). Symptoms of his mental imbalance progressed in the wake of World War I, and he turned to zealous preaching. In 1921, the Kemalists arrested him and sent him into exile. According to one of his companions, Intra went insane during the long march from Konya to the interior and died shortly after crossing the Tigris near Diyarbakir.

Collections

Erker. (Erevan, 1981).

Texts

Nerašḥarh. (Constantinople, 1906; Beirut, 1955). (Prose).
Nočastan. (Constantinople, 1908; Beirut, 1958). (Verse).

Texts in periodicals

AM, 1904, 826–32. 1906, 147–52.
Širak, 1905/1, 46–52; 2, 93–100; 3, 188–90; 8, 109, 110; 9, 181–82; 10–11, 300.
"Grakan dēmkʻer." *HK,* 5 (1926–27/6), 58–65; 7, 39–45; 8, 53–58.

Translations

ITALIAN

LPAM, 167–72.

Criticism

Baluean, H. "Tiran Chrakʻeani 'Nerašḥarhĕ' ew notʻer ir keankʻin masin." *Z* (taregirkʻ), 1937, 1–7.
Ḥanamirean, G. "Intra ew ir grelakerpĕ." *Z,* 1 (1929–[30]), 102–4, 184–85.
"Intrayi girkʻĕ." *SG,* 1982/7, 143–44.
Kʻiparean, K. "Intrayi 'Nočastan'-ĕ." *B,* 1981/3, 289–99.
Kirakosyan, V. "Intrayi stełtzagortzutʻyan grapatmakan aržekʻĕ." *BEH,* 1972/3, 209–15.
Mušeł vardapet. "Nerašḥarh kam Intra." *AM,* 1902, 687–90.
Nikołosean, A. "Intrai Nerašḥarhĕ." *M,* 1906/2, 32–34; 1906/3, 54–56; 1906/4, 70–74.
Ōšakan, Y. "Tiran Chrakʻean, Intra." *Z* (taregirkʻ), 1937, 54–63.
Samikean, Ṙ. "Grakan vayrkeanner–Intrai 'Nerašḥarhĕ'." *M,* 1906/20, 308–11.
Sargisean, A. "Tiran Chrakʻean (Intra), yušer ew tpaworutʻiwnner." *Ani,* 2 (1947–48), 361–67, 425–32.
Setʻean, Y. "Nerašḥarh–hełinak Intra." *Širak,* 1906/3, 173–80.
Simkʻēšean, E. "Intrayi mistʻikʻakanutʻiwnĕ. *Z* (taregirkʻ), 2 [1944], 121–25.
Veniws. "Intra." *AM,* 1907, 1290–94. (On *Nerašḥarh*).

ISAHAKEAN, ISAHAK (1893–1916)

Born in Łazarapat (now Isahakyan, in the region of Ani, Armenia). Poet; nephew of Avetikʻ Isahakyan (q.v.). Educated in Alexandrapol (Leninakan, now Gyumri, Armenia) and at the military school in Tiflis. Killed in action on the Russo-Turkish front in World War I.

Collections

Hekʻiatʻ arevi tak. (Erevan, 1974).

Texts

Hēkʻeatʻ arewi tak. (Alexandrapol, 1912). (Poem).

Poetry

Gevorg Afrikyan, Isahak Isahakyan, Art. Ter-Martirosyan, erekʻ kʻnar. (Erevan, 1963), 71–153.

ISAHAKYAN, AVETIKʻ (1875–1957)

Born in Alexandrapol (Leninakan, now Gyumri, Armenia). Studied in his native city, at the Gēorgean Seminary in Ējmiatzin (1889–92, where H. Hovhannisyan was one of his teachers), and audited courses at the universities of Leipzig (1893) and Zurich (late 1890s). Returned home in 1902. After a second term of incarceration for anti-government activities, he went back to Europe in 1911 and lived in France, Italy, Switzerland, Austria, and Germany. He resided in Soviet Armenia, 1926–30, and then moved to Europe for a last time (Paris, 1930–36), before he permanently settled in Erevan in 1936. A member of the Academy of Sciences of the Armenian SSR (1943) and a winner of the USSR State Prize for literature (1946). From 1944 to his death, he was president of the Union of Soviet Writers of Armenia. In recognition of his contributions to Armenian verse, the Avetikʻ Isahakyan literary prize for poetry was established in Erevan in 1980.

Collections

Ĕntir erker. 2 vols. (N.p., 1939–40).
Hatĕntir. (Erevan, 1943).
Ardzak ējer. (Erevan, 1945).
Ĕntir erker. (Erevan and Moscow, 1948).
Erkeri žołovatzu. 4 vols. (Erevan, 1950–51).
Hušer ev hodvatzner. (Erevan, 1951).
Ardzak ējer. (Erevan, 1955).
Banastełtzutʻiwnner. (Beirut, 1955).
Erger ev ṙomansner. (Erevan, 1955, 1975).
Erker. (Erevan, 1955).
Hatĕntir. (Erevan, 1958).
Erker. 4 vols. (Erevan, 1958–59).
Awetikʻ Isahakeani namaknerĕ V. Nawasardeanin, Ṙ. Darbineanin, E. Khatʻanaseanin, V. Aharoneanin. (Cairo, 1959).
Hayduki erger. (Beirut, 1960).
Patmvatzkʻner, legendner. (Erevan, 1962).
Ardzak ējer. (Erevan, 1963).
Lirika. (Erevan, 1968).
Erker. (Erevan, 1970).
Ardzak. (Erevan, 1973).
Erkeri žołovatzu. 6 vols. (Erevan, 1973–79).
Hatĕntir. (Erevan, 1975).
Sełbosyan, L. *Erker.* (Erevan, 1980).
Matʻevosyan, G. *Ardzak stełtzagortzutʻyunner.* (Erevan, 1985).
Isahakyan, Av. *Erker.* (Erevan, 1987).
Inčikyan, A. *Tzanotʻ ev antzanotʻ ējer.* (Erevan, 1988).

Texts

Erger u vērkʻer. (Alexandrapol, 1897). (Verse).
Hin-nor erg u vērkʻerits. (Baku, 1902). (Verse).
Banastełtzutʻiwnner. (Baku, 1903). (Verse).
Erger u vērkʻer. (Tiflis, 1908). (Verse).
Abu-lala-Mahari. (Constantinople, 1911, 1918, 1920, 1926, 1936 (*—ew ir veradardzĕ*), 1945; Boston, 1922; Erevan, 1929, 1971, 1975, 1984; Beirut, 1939, 1953, 1957; Buenos Aires, 1945; Cairo, 1961). (Poem).
Ała Nazar. (Constantinople, 1912; Beirut, 1939). (Prose).
Hayreni ałbiwrits. (Boston; 1920). (Poetry).

Ašnan tzałikner. (Venice, 1922). (Poetry).
Ardzak ējer. Vol. 1. (Constantinople, 1922). (Stories).
Sasmay Mher. (Vienna, 1922; Erevan, 1938; Beirut, 1952). (Verse).
Lilit'.—Arevelyan tesilner. (Tiflis, 1927). (Stories).
Hamberank'i chibuḥě. (Erevan, 1929). (Stories).
Banastełtzut'yunner. (Erevan, 1930). (Verse).
Nrank' drōšak unin. (Paris, 1932). (Story).
Kak'avn u ałvesě. (Erevan, 1940).
Arjn u ōdzě. (Erevan, 1941).
Arkatzaḥndirnerě. (Fresno and New York, 1943). (Prose).
Alagyazi maniner. (Erevan, 1945, 1954). (Verse).
Hanun hayrenik'i ev kulturayi paštpanut'yan. (Erevan, 1945).
Aṙakner. (Erevan, 1946).
Im hušerits. (Erevan, 1946; Beirut, 1955). (Reminiscences).
Garibaldiakaně. (Erevan, 1948, 1970). (Story).
Sgavor aragilě. (Erevan, 1948). (Prose).
Usta Karō ew Ōrt'e Yarut'. (Teheran, 1959). (Incomplete novel).
Nukim k'ałak'i ḥelok'nerě. (Erevan, 1962). (Story).
Mer gri anmah p'aṙk'ě. (Eevan, 1969). (On Tumanyan).
Ktak. (Erevan, 1973).
Lṙut'yan aspetě. (Erevan, 1973). (Prose and verse).
Aṙakner. (Erevan, 1974).
Lilit'. (Erevan, 1974).
Grigoryan, S. *Banastełtzi sirtě.* (Erevan, 1975). (Isahakyan's letters to Anna Beroyan).
Inčikyan, A. *Hišatakaran.* (Erevan, 1977). (Grakan žaṙangut'yun, 10). (Diary).
Naryan, M. *K'aj zinvorě.* (Erevan, 1980). (Verse and prose).
Hamberank'i chibuḥě. (Erevan, 1982). (Story).
Arevi mot. (Erevan, 1983). (Tales).
"Ējmiatzni patmakan derě." *EJ,* 1983/11–12, 56–58. (Hodvatzě grvatz ē 1955t'. Vazgen A-i ěntrut'yan ev ōtzman aṙt'iv).
Hovhannisyan, J. "Avetik' Isahakyani norahayt namakě." *L,* 1985/8, 74–75.
Isahakyan, Av. *Hayduki ergě.* (Erevan, 1990).

Translations

Bibliography of Translations

Nazikyan, A. "Avetik' Isahakyani stełtzagortzut'yunneri t'argmanut'yunnerě (matenagitakan tsank)." *PBH,* 1975/3, 219–36.

English

Boyajian, Z. *Abu Lala Mahari.* (New York, 1948; n.p. 1958).
Chrakian, E. *Scent, Smile and Sorrow, Selected Verses (1891–1957) and Jottings from Notebooks.* (Watertown, MA, 1975).
Darbinian, Ṙ. "Ousta Karo." *Armenian Review,* Summer, 1958, 15–22.
Kudian, M. *The Muse of Sheerak.* (London, 1975).
———. *Selected Poetry and Prose.* (Moscow, 1976).
Mangouni, N. "Illusion." *Lraber,* October 26, 1961, 4.
Manukean, M. "Abu Lala Mahari." *S,* 1973, 211–12, 337–38. 1974, 36–37, 132–33, 256–57. 1975, 114–15, 204–5.
"My Land Is an Orchard in Bloom." *Lraber,* January 12, 1957, 4.

Rottenberg, D. "To My Mother"; ["In the heart of the far Himalayas"]; "Bingyol"; "The Roll-Call." *SL,* 1975/8, 118–20.

Tempest, P. ["In my garden there's a weeping"]; ["A star of brightest magnitude"]; "Bell of Freedom"; ["From distant seas and desert grim"]; "To My Homeland"; ["Tonight beneath midsummer skies that glow"]; ["I would that death"]; "Omar Khayam Quarrels with Allah"; "The Death of a Nightingale." *SL,* 1975/8, 115–17, 121–22.

Varandyan, E. "If You Wish"; "I Will Give You My Soul"; "Homeless Nights"; "Night Descends with Cool Velvet Steps"; "O, Young Age, O, Full-Blooded Age"; "Oh, Impatient Heart, Wait"; "Oh, Homeland, Beloved Motherland." *Hoosharar,* 1956/15, 4–6.

———. "Before the Mother Star of the Skies"; "I Am a Bard, Singer of the Spring"; "The Leaves Fell from Wan Trees." *Hoosharar,* 1956/19, 10.

———. "Abu Lala Mahari." *Nor ašḥarh,* 1963/37, 4; 38, 4; 39, 4; 40, 4.

English anthologies

ALP, 6, 11, 29–30, 42.

AP, 249.

SAP, 5–7.

WM, 44–47.

French

Antonian, A. ["Toutes les nuits dans mon jardin"]; ["A maman"]; ["Une étoile est tombée des nues"]; ["Cloche de liberté"]; ["Des lointaines mers, des déserts arides"]; ["A l'heure qu'il est, aux confins des cieux"]; ["A ma patrie"]; ["Par une tranquille et bleue nuit d'été"]; ["Bingole"]; ["Cri de guerre"]; ["Quand viendra la mort"]; ["Ou Omar Khayyam polémique avec dieu"]; ["La mort du rossignol"]. *LS,* 200 (1975), 146–54.

Arax, "Le dernier printemps de Saadi." *LS,* 207 (1976), 129–32.

Makotinskaïa, "Le dernier printemps de Saadi." *La littérature soviétique,* 1946/12, 36–38.

Mardirossian, L. "A Avik"; "Mon pays." *OO* (Dec. 1960), 192–93.

Martirossian, L. "A Ravenne." *La littérature soviétique,* 1957/1, 3.

Minassian, J. *Abou-lala Mahari.* (Paris, 1952).

French anthologies

APA, 157–60.

Gamarra, P. *E.* 47–50.

FPA, 45–46.

LPA, 200–3.

German

"Das Gluck des Lebens. (Reden der Schriftsteller und Kunst, schaffenden)." *Sowjet-Literatur,* 1949/11, 227–29.

"Meiner Mutter." *Mitteilungen uber Armenien,* 160 (1958), 7.

Noeren, H., and Nazariantz, L. "Abul Ala Mahari." *Der neue Orient,* 6 (1919/2), 77–83.

Schick, M. "Du begreifst mich nicht"; "Dem ewigen Gedenken S.G. Sagijans." *Sowjet-Literatur,* 1946/4, 75–76.

German anthologies

AD, 38–40.

ALG, 129–30.

ITALIAN ANTHOLOGIES

LPAM, 247–54.

RUSSIAN

Isaakian, Avik, A. *Ia upodobil serdtse nebu.* (Erevan, 1988).
Izbrannoe. (Erevan, 1952).
Izbrannoe. (Moscow, 1970).
Izbrannoe. (Erevan, 1974).
Izbrannye proizvedeniia. (Moscow, 1952).
Izbrannye sochineniia. 2 vols. (Moscow, 1956).
Izbrannye stikhi. (Moscow, 1945).
Khachatriants, Ia. *Izbrannaia proza.* (Erevan, 1947).
———. *Znamia nadezhdy. Rasskazy.* (Moscow, 1948).
Khitarova, S. *Umniki goroda Nukima: Skazki.* (Erevan, 1985).
Mger iz Sasuna. (Erevan, 1939; Moscow, 1939).
Pesni. (Moscow, 1907). ("Tsvety Araza," vyp.1).
Stikhotvoreniia i poemy. (Moscow, 1960).

SPANISH

Agayan, H. *Abu Lala Mahari.* (Buenos Aires, 1929).
"La felicidad de la vida." *Literatura Sovietica,* 1949/11, 206–7.

Bibliographies

Babaian, A. *Avetik Isaakian: Bibliogr. 1899–1976.* (Moscow, 1980).
Ḥanzadyan, P̀., et al. *Avetikʻ Isahakyan (1875–1957), kensamatenagitakan tsank.* 2 parts. (Erevan, 1976, 1977).
Mkrtchian, L. *Avetik Isaakian na russkom iazyke.* (Erevan, 1964).
[Nazikyan, A.] "Avetikʻ Isahakyani stełtzagortzutʻyunneri tʻargmanutʻyunnerě (matenagitakan tsank)." *PBH,* 1975/3, 219–36.

Criticism

Abełyan, H. "Avetikʻ Isahakyaně haykakan žołovrdakan ēposi masin." *L,* 1970/9, 42–53.
———. "Avetikʻ Isahakyani 'Sasma Mher' poemi stełtzagortzakan patmutʻyunits." *L,* 1972/9, 41–49.
———. "Avetikʻ Isahakyani 'Sasma Mher' vipergi anavart errord tarberakě." *PBH, 1972/4,* 111–22.
———. *Isahakyaně ev žołovrdakan ēposě.* (Erevan, 1975).
Adamyan, A. "Avetikʻ Isahakyani ašakertakan gortzě." *T,* 1956/10, 99–100.
Afrikyan, G. "Erku huš." *SG,* 1975/8, 142–45.
Aharonean, V. "Aw. Isahakeani 'Im yušerits' hatorě." *HK,* 26 (1948/2), 106–7.
Ałababyan, S. "Av. Isahakyani vał šrjani kʻnarergutʻyuně." *SG,* 1984/7, 126–29.
Alekʻsanyan, E. "Isahakyani ergitzakan liro-ēposě. 'Usta Karo' vepi masin." *SG,* 1975/4, 126–31.
Ananyan, G. "N. Ałbalyani namaknerě Av. Isahakyanin." *BEH,* 1989/2, 57–64.
Aṙakʻelyan, V. *Avetikʻ Isahakyani poeziayi lezva-očakan aṙandznahatkutʻyunnerě.* (Erevan, 1954).
Aramean, H. "Veryišumner Awetikʻ Isahakeani pʻarizean keankʻēn." *Z* (amsatʻertʻ), 2/1–10 (1958), 4.
Arveladze, B. "Avetikʻ Isahakyaně ev vrats grakanutʻyuně." *SG,* 1975/10, 140–44.
Asatryan, A. *Avetikʻ Isahakyani kyankʻě ev stełtzagortzutʻyunnerě.* (Erevan, 1940).

At'ayan, Ṙ. "Ditołut'yunner 'Avetik' Isahakyanĕ ev hay ergĕ' hartsi aṙt'iv." *EJ,* 1975/11, 33–36.

———. "Ork'an šat ban t'ołets na . . ." *SG,* 1975/2, 104–12.

Avagyan, Ṙ. "Avetik' Isahakyani ev Ełiše Charentsi dimankarnerĕ Hayastani foni vra." *SG,* 1984/8, 109–25.

"Awetik' Isahakean." *B,* 66 (1908), 351–54.

Bagarat. "Ṙusahay grakanut'enēn. Awetis Isahakeants." *AM,* 1900, 115–23. (On *Erger u vērk'er*).

Baluean, H. "Awetik' Isahakean." *Z* (amsat'ert'), 2 (1958/9–10), 1–2.

Berberean, M. "Tḥur mełediner. (H. Haynē–Aw. Isahakean–Š. Kurłinean)." *A,* 1908, 157–64.

Chōpanean, A. "Awetik' Isahakean." *ANA,* 7 (1936/4), 49–57.

Darbinyan, V. "Šarzman patkerĕ 'Abu-Lala-Mahari' poemum." *SG,* 1976/11, 149–52.

Demirčyan, D. "Avetik' Isahakyani stełtzagortzut'yan žołovrdaynut'yunĕ." *T,* 1955/11, 3–12.

Dzhanpoladian, M. "O legende Isaakiana 'Lilit'." *BEH,* 1975/2, 31–42.

Eremean, A. *Akademikos Awetik' Isahakeani pōēziayi himnakan gtzerĕ.* (New Julfa, 1946).

———. *Isahakeani het Venetikum (usanołakan yušer).* (Teheran, 1946).

Evgenov, S. "Banastełtzneri avagaguynĕ." *SG,* 1964/10, 112–19.

Gabrielyan, H. "Handipumner Avetik' Isahakyani het." *BEH,* 1975/2, 51–54.

Gaïssarian, S. "Avétik Issahakian." *LS,* 200 (1975), 140–45.

———. "Avetik Issahakian." *SL,* 1975/8, 108–14. (English).

Grigorian, K. *Avetik Isaakian. Ocherki tvorchestva.* (Moscow, 1954).

———. *Tvorcheskii put' Avetika Isaakiana.* (Moscow, 1963).

Grigoryan, A. "Isahakyani banastełtzut'yunnerĕ sp'yuṙk'ahay kompozitorneri stełtzagortzut'yunnerum." *PBH,* 1975/3, 50–76.

Gullakyan, S. "Avetik' Isahakyani 'Ała Nazarĕ'." *SG,* 1965/10, 88–93.

Ḥachatryan, A. "Azatagrakan payk'arĕ Av. Isahakyani k'narergut'yan mej." *L,* 1985/9, 30–39.

———. *Avetik' Isahakyani sirergut'yunĕ.* (Erevan, 1985).

———. *Avetik' Isahakyani hayrenasirakan poezian.* (Erevan, 1987).

Haḥverdyan, L. *Isahakyani kyank'n u gortzĕ.* (Erevan, 1975).

———. "Isahakyani sirayin k'narĕ." *SG,* 1975/10, 103–9.

Hakobyan, N. "P'ok'r Mherĕ Avetik' Isahakyani vipergum." *BEH,* 1975/2, 43–50.

Hambardzumyan, H. "Handipumner Varpeti het." *SG,* 1975/2, 112–16.

Harut'yunyan, H. "Žołovrdakan baṙ u bani harstut'yunĕ." *SG,* 1975/10, 132–35.

Harut'yunyan, S. "Isahakyan." *SG,* 1983/9, 106–21.

Ḥoršidyan, T. "Avetik' Isahakyani stełtzagortzut'yunnerĕ Zabel Boyajyani t'argmanut'yamb." *PBH,* 1975/3, 65–69.

Hovhannisyan, G. *Avetik' Isahakyani ardzakĕ.* (Erevan, 1963).

———. *Isahakyani stełtzagortzakan ašḥarhĕ.* (Erevan, 1969).

———. *Avetik' Isahakyan.* (Erevan, 1975).

———. "Isahakyani stełtzagortzakan ułu skizbĕ." *PBH,* 1975/1, 23–32.

———. "Hay grakanut'yunn u arvestĕ Avetik' Isahakyani gnahatmamb." *L,* 1975/10, 20–27.

Hovhannisyan, H. "Handipumner." *SG,* 1975/10, 64–69.

Hovnan, G. *Avetikʻ Isahakyan.* (Erevan, 1976).
Hovsepʻyan, Ē. "Inchpes ē Isahakyann ĕnkalel u marmnavorel vipakan Mheri kerparĕ." *Banber Hayastani arḥivneri,* 1986/2, 95–106.
Hunanyan, A. "Avetikʻ Isahakyani kʻnarakan patmvatzkʻneri kaṙutsvatzkʻayin aṙandznahatkutʻyunnerĕ." *PBH,* 1976/3, 139–44.
Inčikyan, A. *Avetikʻ Isahakyan.* (Erevan, 1944, 1955, 1977).
———. "Avetikʻ Isahakyanĕ ev hay klasik grakanutʻyan traditsianerĕ." *T,* 1955/11, 13–24.
———. *Avetik Isaakian.* (Erevan, 1956). (Russian).
———. A. "Metz banastełtzn u hayrenaserĕ." *SG,* 1958/10, 90–98.
———. " 'Abu Lala Mahari' poemi naḥnakan tarberakĕ." *PBH,* 1968/4, 111–24. (Im kʻaravanĕ).
———. "Avetikʻ Isahakyani 'Hišatakaranĕ'." *PBH,* 1977/2, 99–104.
Isaakian, Avik. "Iz istorii russkikh perevodov poezii Isaakiana." *PBH,* 1987/1, 40–54.
———. *Avetik Isaakian i Rossiia.* (Moscow, 1988).
Isahakyan-100. Hobelyanakan taregrutʻyun. (Erevan, 1978).
Isahakyan, Abas. *Avetikʻ Isahakyani masin (ašḥarhi mtavorakanneri namaknerits).* (Erevan, 1971).
Isahakyan, A. V. "Isahakyanĕ ev Blokĕ." *PBH,* 1983/4, 58–68.
Isahakyan, Avik. "Žołovrdi anpartutʻyan artatsolumĕ Isahakyani ardzakum." *SG,* 1972/12, 151–58.
———. "Avetikʻ Isahakyanĕ ṙusakan poeziayi tʻargmanich." *SG,* 1978/10, 143–52.
———. "Isahakyanĕ ev Tolstoyĕ." *SG,* 1981/3, 119–28.
———. *Avetikʻ Isahakyanĕ ev ṙus grakanutʻyunĕ.* (Erevan, 1984).
Išḥanyan, Ṙ. "Isahakyani stełtzagortzutʻyan lezvakan zargatsumĕ." *BEH,* 1975/2, 13–30.
Jrbašyan, Ēd. "Avetikʻ Isahakyani 'Abu-lala Maharin' ev ṙomantikakan poemi avanduytʻnerĕ." *PBH,* 1975/3, 43–64.
———. "Avetikʻ Isahakyani kʻnarergutʻyan herosĕ." *SG,* 1975/10, 70–91.
———. *Chors gagatʻ, Tʻumanyan, Isahakyan, Teryan, Charents.* (Erevan, 1982).
Kanayan, Ḥ. *Avetikʻ Isahakyani lezun.* (Erevan, 1940).
Kankava, G. *Avetik Isaakian i gruzinskaia literatura. [Na pravakh rukopisi].* (Erevan, 1960).
Kʻaramyan, M. "Avetikʻ Isahakyanĕ Vrastanum." *SG,* 1965/10, 84–87.
Karapetyan, T. "Avetikʻ Isahakyanĕ ev Vrastanĕ." *SG,* 1975/8, 133–41.
Kirakosyan, L. "Avetikʻ Isahakyani hušagrutʻyunĕ." *SG,* 1968/5, 130–36.
———. "Avetikʻ Isahakyani naḥasovetakan šrjani hraparakaḥosutʻyunĕ." *PBH,* 1969/1, 163–70.
Kʻiwfēčean, Y. "Ṙusahay grakanutʻenēn–Awetis Isahakean." *HG,* 1912/11, 31–37.
Łanalanyan, A. "Žołovrdakan avandutʻyunneri isahakyanakan mšakumnerĕ." *PBH,* 1975/4, 63–75.
Łanalanyan, H. *Isahakyani lirikan.* (Erevan, 1940).
———. *Avetikʻ Isahakyan.* (Erevan, 1955, 1985).
———. *Avetikʻ Isahakyan: hušer.* (Erevan, 1975).
———. "Hay dasakan poeziayi jahakirĕ." *SG,* 1975/10, 126–31.
Łaribjanyan, G. *Avetikʻ Isahakyan.* (Erevan, 1985).

Manukyan, S. "Hangutsayin hartseri skzbunk'ayin k'nnut'yun." *SG,* 1982/8, 142–44. (On Ēd. Jrbašyan's *Chors gagat',* . . .).

Melk'onyan, H. "Bar̄imastov paymanavorvatz očakan gortzuneut'yunĕ Av. Isahakyani ardzakum." *L,* 1984/3, 10–17.

———. "Kirar̄akan olortov paymanavorvatz očakan gortzatzut'yunnerĕ Av. Isahakyani gełarvestakan ardzakum." *BEH,* 1984/1, 205–11.

Mirza-Avakian, M. "Rabota A. Bloka nad perevodami stikhov Isaakiana." *PBH,* 1960/4, 179–95.

Mkrtchian, L. *Avetik Isaakian i russkaia literatura.* (Erevan, 1963, 1975).

———. "Avetik Isaakian i simvolizm." *T,* 1965/10, 25–36.

Mkryan, M. *Isahakyani humanizmĕ.* (Erevan, 1975).

———. "Mardasirut'yan poezian." *BEH,* 1975/2, 3–12.

Mnatsakanyan, V. "Isahakyani sḥrank'ĕ." *SG,* 1973/10, 127–37. (On his decision to repatriate).

———. "Metz banastełtzn u k'ałak'atsin." *SG,* 1975/10, 92–102.

———. "Serundneri metz žamanakakitsĕ." *L,* 1975/10, 3–19.

Motalova, L. "Mi k'ani ditołut'yunner Avetik' Isahakyani bar̄apašari masin." *T,* 1965/6, 43–50.

Movsisyan, H. "Avetik' Isahakyani erkeri t'argmanut'yunnerĕ Iranum." *PBH,* 1975/3, 77–82.

Mušełyan, A. "Murč kam zndan." *BEH,* 1979/2, 140–52.

———. "Avetik' Isahakyani patanekan banastełtzut'yunnerĕ." *SG,* 1980/6, 115–21.

———. "Av. Isahakyani layptsigyan tarineri k'narergut'yunĕ." *L,* 1980/9, 17–30.

———. *Avetik' Isahakyan. Vał tariner: 1875–1898.* (Erevan, 1983).

Nazikyan, A. "[A. Isahakyanĕ] ōtar lezunerov." *SG,* 1975/10, 144–45.

Oganian, Z. "Aleksandr Blok kak perevodchik poezii Isaakiana." *PBH,* 1973/4, 137–42.

Ōšakan, Y. "Metz varpeti Awetik' Isahakeani yobeleani ar̄it'ov." *S,* 1946, 89–93.

Oskerchyan, A. "Avetik' Isahakyanĕ ev r̄usakan hełap'oḥut'yunĕ." *SG,* 1981/9, 104–18.

Partizuni, V. "Isahkyanĕ Teryani ĕnt'ertsmamb." *SG,* 1975/6, 122–34.

Pēšikt'ašlean, N. "Awetik' Isahakeanĕ uriš grołneru masin." *HK,* 41 (1963/4), 20–22.

[Pōyačean, Z.] "Zapel Poyačyani antip namaknerĕ Avetik' Isahakyanin." *SG,* 1986/9, 121–24.

R̄uḥkyan, H. *K'san tari varpeti het.* (Erevan, 1975).

Salakhyan, A. "Re-reading Isaakyan." *SG,* 1966/3, 162–64.

Sarinyan, S. "Avetik' Isahakyan." *PBH,* 1975/3, 27–42.

———. "Nor ḥosk' isahakyanagitakan bnagavar̄um." *SG,* 1970/9, 116–20.

Siras, H. *K'sanmek tari Avetik' Isahakyani het.* (Erevan, 1984).

Slovo ob Avetike Isaakiane. Sbornik statei. (Erevan, 1975).

Smirnova, V. "Avetik Isaakyan." *SL,* 1956/7, 178–80. (English).

T. N. "Awetik' Isahakeani yišatakin." *B,* 115 (1957), 237–39.

T'adevosyan, R̄. "Isahakyanĕ ev Lermontovĕ." *SG,* 1975/10, 135–40.

Tiḥonov, N. "Avetik' Isahakyan." *SG,* 1975/10, 9–19.

T'orosyan, Š. "Zruyts Isahakyani het." *SG,* 1975/10, 30–40.

Tzałkuni, Z. *Awetik' Isahakean.* (Cairo, 1946).

Vauni, S. *Ob Avetike Isaakiane.* (Erevan, 1971).
Vershiny: Aleksandr Blok—perevodchik Avetika Isaakiana. (Erevan, 1980). (In Russian and Armenian).
Zaryan, N. "Varpeti het." *SG,* 1975/10, 41–59.
Zaryan, Ṙ. *Avetikʻ Isahakyan.* (Erevan, 1974).

IŠḤAN, MUŠEŁ (1913–1990)

Pen name: Mušeł Išḥan.
Born Mušeł Čēntērēčean in Sivrihisar, Turkey. Poet, novelist, playwright. Education in Armenian schools in Damascus, Cyprus (Melkonian, spelled Melgonean) and Beirut. His higher studies at the University of Brussels (1938–40) were interrupted due to World War II. Returned to Beirut in 1940, and for many years he taught at the Nšan Pʻalančean Čemaran, one of the leading Armenian high schools in Beirut.

Texts

Tunerun ergě. (Beirut, 1936). (Verse).
Krakě. (Beirut, 1938, 1959). (Verse).
Hayastan. (Aleppo, 1946; Teheran, 1961). (Verse).
Keankʻ u eraz. (Beirut, 1949). (Verse).
Erekʻ metz hayer. (Beirut, 1951).
Hatsi ew loysi hamar. (Beirut, 1951, 1974). (Novel).
Mušeł Mamikonean. (Beirut, 1951).
Hatsi ew siroy hamar. (Beirut, 1956). (Novel).
Ołjoyn kʻez, keankʻ. (Beirut, 1958). (Verse).
Oski ašun. (Beirut, 1963). (Verse).
Taṙapankʻ. (Beirut and Antelias, 1968). (Verse).
Meṙnilě orkʻan džuar ē. (Beirut, 1971). (Play).
Mnas barov, mankutʻiwn. (Beirut, 1974). (Autobiography).
Spasum. (Beirut, 1977). (Story).
Saṙnaranēn elatz mardě. (Beirut, 1979). (Play).
Tateraḥałer. (Beirut, 1980). (Plays).

Other works

Ardi hay grakanutʻiwn. 3 vols. (Beirut, 1973–75).

Criticism

Baluean, H. "Grkʻeru mōt—1. Tunerun ergě: banastełtzutʻiwnner Mušeł Išḥani." *Z* (amsōreay), 1 (1937/2), 12–13.
Farman, S. "Tunerun ergě." *HK,* 15 (1936–37/7), 175–76.
Garačean, E. *M. Išḥani 'Oski ašuně'.* (Beirut, 1964).
Parsamean, M. "Nor vēp mě—'Hatsi ew loysi hamar." *HK,* 30 (1952/5), 111–12.

IWAN (1800–1865)

Pen name: Iwan.
Yovhannēs Sargsean Sargseants was a minstrel (*ašuł*) from Astrakhan.

Poetry

THG, 142–46.

JAVAḤETSI, (1874–1937)

Pen name: Javaḥetsi.

Born Łazaros Tēr-Grigorean in the village of Gandza (Bogdanovka, Georgia). Brother of Vahan Tērean (q.v.). Graduated from the Nersisean school of Tiflis and taught in Armenian schools. Life in the countryside, especially its social aspects, is a predominant theme in his short stories.

Texts (stories)

Jawaḥkʻi ałētě. (Tiflis, 1900).
Krakě. (Tiflis, 1903).
Patkerner. Book 1. (Tiflis, 1905).
Patkerner. (Erevan, 1930).
Patkerner. (Erevan, 1936).

JIWANI, (1846–1909)

Pen name: Ašuł Jiwani.

Born Serovbē Lewonean in the village of Karzaḥ, in the region of Aḥalkʻalakʻ, Georgia. A distinguished *ašuł.* Mastered his art through apprenticeship and self-instruction. Moved to Tiflis in the mid-1860s. In 1868 he settled in Alexandrapol (Leninakan, now Gyumri, Armenia), but he traveled extensively throughout the region. Lived in Tiflis from 1895 until his death.

Collections

Ergeri žołovatzu. (Erevan, 1936).
Sahakyan, A. *Jivanu kʻnarě.* (Erevan, 1959).
Kʻnar. Liakatar hawakʻatzu inkʻnuroyn ew pʻoḥadrakan erkasirutʻiwnneri. Otanaworner ew ardzak. 2 vols. Vol. 1 (Tiflis, 1900). Vol. 2 (Vałaršapat, 1904).
Sahakyan, A. *Erger.* (Erevan, 1988).

Texts (verse)

Ašěł Jiwanu ergerě. (Alexandrapol, 1882, 1886, 1893; Tiflis, 1912).
Ašěł Łaribi hěkʻeatʻě, handerdz ergerov. Pʻoḥadrutʻiwn. (Alexandrapol, 1887; Tiflis, 1897; Constantinople, 1922).

Translations

English anthologies

AP, 121, 261–62.

French

Tchobanian, A. *Les plus belles chansons de Djivani, le grand poète populaire arménien.* (Paris, 1919).
———. "Quelques chansons de Djivani." *REArm,* 1 (1921), 426–31.

French anthologies

RA, 2, 297–311.
TA, 279–91.

Russian anthologies

AAP, 350–56.
BPA, 265–66.
SHAP, 29–30.

Criticism

Sahakyan, A. *Hayrenašunch kʻnar.* (Erevan, 1965).

———. "Žołovrdneri barekamut'yan ergichě." *T,* 1959/8, 65–76.
Stepʻanean, Y. "Ašuł Jiwanin ew ir stełtzagortzutʻiwnĕ." *HK,* 22 (1944/3), 38–48.

KAMSARAKAN, TIGRAN (1866–1941)

Pen names: Antsord, Aseł, B. Tēr-Zakʻarean, Molorak, Net Nestor, Ōvkʻitē, Pʻiwnik, Šołegrich, Z, ZZZ.

A native of Constantinople, educated in the local Aramean school. At the age of twenty, he became a literary celebrity thanks to his novel *Varžapetin ałjikě,* which was acclaimed after a good deal of initial controversy. He rarely contributed to Armenian literature after fleeing Constantinople during the Armenian massacres of the mid-1890s. He first settled in Egypt (1895–1919) and then moved to Paris for good in 1919. Died in Vichy.

Texts

Varžapetin ałjikě. (Constantinople, 1888, 1921, 1930; Cairo, 1941; Erevan, 1956). (Novel).
Sargsyan, Ṙ. *Erker.* (Erevan, 1984). (Includes works by Kamsarakan and Tigran Chēōkiwrean).

Other works

Širvanzadē ew ir gortzě. (Constantinople, 1911).

Texts in periodicals

ANA, 3 (1932/5–6), 43–47; (1934/5–6), 90; (1935/1–2), 55–58; (1938/5–6), 1–9.
M, 1886/3813, 779–84. 1889/3927, 51–55. 1892/3956, 11–18; 3957, 35–38; 3959, 71–76; 3972, 279–82.
SG, 1966/7, 123–26.

Translations (French)

J. "Haro." *La Patrie* 1908, 113 (Constantinople).

Criticism

Chiftʻē-Saraf, Ō. "Siruatz dēmkʻer–Tigran Kamsarakan." *M,* 1901/48, 755–56.
Galayčean, A. "Tigran Kamsarakan." *S,* 1966, 10–13.
Kotʻikyan, A. "Tigran Kamsarakan." *SG,* 1966/7, 118–22.
Margaryan, H. "Tigran Kamsarakani grakan žařangutʻyan šurjě." *T,* 1961/4, 33–46.
———. *Tigran Kamsarakan, kyankʻě ev stełtzagortzutʻyuně.* (Erevan, 1964).
Ōšakan, Y. "Tigran Kamsarakan." *S,* 1941, 65–73.
P[řōšean], P. "Kamsarakan, T. Varžapetin ałjikě, K. Polis, 1888." *Murč,* 1889/5, 790–93.
Šahnur. "Tʻłtʻaktsutʻiwn." *AM,* 1888, 483–85. (On *Varžapetin ałjikě* and others).

KAPUTIKYAN, SILVA (1919–)

A native of Erevan and a winner of the USSR literary prize (1952). Poet; early in her career she wrote poetry for children. Completed her training in Armenian language and literature at the State University of Erevan (1936–41), and studied at the Gorky Institute for literature (1949–50). Her frequent travels abroad have taken her to the Middle East, Europe, the United States, Canada, and Japan, resulting in two travel books.

Collections

K'ert'uatzner. (Aleppo, 1954).
Banastettzut'iwnner. (Beirut, 1963).
Hatĕntir. (Beirut, 1963).
Erkeri žołovatzu. 2 vols. (Erevan, 1973).
Hatĕntir. (Erevan, 1979).
Erker. 3 vols. (Erevan, 1984–85).

Texts (verse)

Hatutsum. (Erevan, 1942).
Saryakner. (Erevan, 1942).
Erku zruyts manukneri het. (Erevan, 1943).
Vahaniki erazĕ. (Erevan, 1943).
Ōreri het. (Erevan, 1945).
Zangvi ap'in. (Erevan, 1947).
Ays im erkirn ē. (Erevan, 1949).
P'ok'rik Ara, akanj ara. (Erevan, 1950, 1971).
Depi Moskva. (Erevan, 1951).
Im harazatnerĕ. (Erevan, 1951, 1953).
Mer lalikĕ-p'ok'rik sirun mer balikĕ. (Erevan, 1952, 1955, 1957).
Tanĕ, bakum, p'ołotsum. (Erevan, 1953).
Srtabats zruyts. (Erevan, 1955).
Bari ert'. (Erevan, 1957).
Mi tarov ēl metzatsank'. (Erevan, 1958).
Arden gitem nkarel. (Erevan, 1959).
Mtorumner čanaparhi kesin. (Erevan, 1961, 1977).
Menk' ōgnum enk' mayrikin. (Erevan, 1961).
K'aravannerĕ deṙ k'aylum en. (Erevan, 1964, 1973). (Account of a visit to the Middle East).
Mer p'ošekul mek'enan. (Erevan, 1964).
Yot' kayaranner. (Erevan, 1965).
Im ējĕ. (Erevan, 1968).
Erg ergots. (Erevan, 1970).
P'ok'rik Ara, akanj ara. (Erevan, 1971, 1981).
Depi ḥork'ĕ leṙan. (Erevan, 1972).
Ḥčankar hogu ev k'artezi guynerits. (Erevan, 1976). (Account of a visit to North America).
Im žamanakĕ. (Erevan, 1979).
Lilit'. (Erevan, 1981).
Dzmeṙ ē galis. (Erevan, 1983).
Tzałkanots. (Erevan, 1984).
"Hayastan-Kipros ert'ułiov. Ułegrut'yun." *SG,* 1984/8, 53–96.
Girs mna hišatakoł. (Erevan, 1988).

Bibliographies

Išḥanyan, Ṙ. *Silva Kaputikyan.* (Erevan, 1987).

Translations

English

Kelikian, H. "Words to My Son." *Ararat,* Autumn, 1961, 39.

Mesrobian, P. "My Majestic Sayat-Nova." *L,* November 2, 1968, 4.
Rottenberg, D. "My Sources." *SL,* 1966/3, 140. Also published in *SL,* 1980/6, 69.
———. "Welcome." *SL,* 1969/1, 138–39. Also published in *SL,* 1972/11, 62–63.
———. "Motherhood." *SL,* 1975/3, 123.
Tempest, P. "Song of Songs." *SL,* 1979/7, 93. Also published in *SL,* 1980/6, 68.
Vynott, J. "Welcome." *SL,* 1960/1, 121.
Wettlin, M. "Song of the Stones." *SL,* 1973/9, 125–26.
Zheleznova, I. "Song of Spring"; ["You're gone"]; "A Mother's Lullaby." *Lraber,* June 5, 1956, 4.
———. "Partings." *SL,* 1969/1, 139.

English anthologies

SAP, 36–39.

French

Antonian, A. "A la mère." *LS,* 195 (1975/3), 128–29.
Falk, S. "Chant des pierres d'Arménie." *OO,* 177 (Sept. 1973), 142.
Gaucheron, J. "Mes sources." *OO,* 167 (Nov. 1972), 76. Also published in *LS,* 258 (1980), 82–83.
Karvovski, A. "Ton monument." *OO,* 135 (March 1970), 100.
Martirossian, L. "La Marseillaise en Arménie." *La litterature sovietique,* 1954/7, 132–33.
———. "Si mon amour . . ."; "La plaine de l'Ararat." *OO* (Dec. 1960), 133–34. Also published in *OO,* 167 (Nov. 1972), 78.
———. "Quand le telephone se tait." *OO,* 123 (March 1969), 60. Also published in *OO,* 167 (Nov. 1972), 77.
Yoccoz, D. "Cantique des cantiques." *LS,* 247 (1979), 102–3. Also published in *LS,* 258 (1980), 83–84.

French anthologies

Gaucheron, J. *E.* 93–94.
LPA, 361–64.

German

Leschnitzer, F. "Mein Woher." *Sowjet-Literatur,* 1966/3, 139.
Remané, M. *Kleine Gäste.* (Berlin, 1961).
Schaginjan, M. "In Zachnadsor, in Zachnadsor . . ." *Leben und Leute in Armenien.* (Berlin, 1947), 67.

Russian

Chasy ozhidaniia: Stikhi. (Moscow, 1983).
Ia, Alesha i Ali. [Stikhi. Dlia doshk. vozr.]. (Moscow, 1957, 1965).
Izbrannaia lirika. (Moscow, 1956).
Izbrannye proizvedeniia. 2 vols. (Moscow, 1989).
Krovlia Armenii. (Moscow, 1981).
Liricheskie stikhi. (Moscow, 1955).
Lirika. (Moscow, 1964).
Masha risuet. [Stikhi. Dlia doshk. vozr.]. (Moscow, 1960).
Mazmanian, M., and Fima, G. *Karavany eshche v puti.* (Moscow, 1969; Erevan, 1970).
Moi rodnye. Stikhi. (Moscow, 1951, 1952).
Moi rodnye. Stikhi. (Moscow, 1952).

Moia stranitsa. (Moscow, 1970).
Moia tropka na dorogakh mira. (Moscow, 1989).
Ogonek v okne. (Moscow, 1961).
Pamiatki: Izbrannoe. (Erevan, 1988).
Razdum'ia na polputi. Stikhi. (Moscow, 1962).
Rozovye kamni. Stikhi. (Moscow, 1959).
Smolianskaia, T. *Meridiany karty i dushi.* (Moscow, 1982).
———., et. al. *Vstrechi bez rasstavanii.* (Erevan, 1987).
Spendiarova, T. *Masha ne plachet.* [Stikhi. Dlia doshk. vozr.]. (Moscow, 1954).
———. *Masha obedaet.* [Stikhi. Dlia doshk. vozr.]. (Moscow, 1957, 1958, 1959, 1960).
———. *Masha rabotaet.* [Stikhi. Dlia doshk. vozr.]. (Moscow, 1963).
Stikhi. (Moscow, 1947).
Stikhotvoreniia. (Moscow, 1959).
Tokmachev, I., and Spendiarov, T. *Maminy pomoshchnitsy.* (Odessa, 1987).
Tokmakov, I. *Posidi, poslushai.* [Stikhi. Dlia doshk. vozr.]. (Moscow, 1969).
Tokmakova, I. and Akim, E. *Tsvetnik: Stikhi.* (Erevan, 1988).
Trevozhnyi den': Stikhi. (Moscow, 1985).
V dobryi put'. (Moscow, 1954).
V Moskvu. [Stikhi dlia doshk. vozr.]. (Moscow and Leningrad, 1951).
Zdravstvuite, druz'ia. Stikhi. (Erevan, 1952).
Zhivu ia serdstem. (Erevan, 1963).

SPANISH

Alberti, R. y Maria Teresa Leon. "Mis origenes." *Literatura Sovietica,* 1966/3, 139.

Criticism

Aristakesyan, A. "Silva Kaputikyani sirerguťyuně ev sirayin lirikayi mi k'ani hartser." *SG,* 1966/3, 88–101.
———. "K'ałak'atsiakan motivnerě Silva Kaputikyani stełtzagortzuťyan mej (1955–65)." *L,* 1966/10, 30–41.
Galstyan, H. "Nor pahanjneri hamemat." *SG,* 1974/8, 130–38. (Also discusses P. Sevak, V. Davťyan).
Jrbašyan, Ēd. "Žamanaki ev taratzuťyan hanguytsnerum." *SG,* 1977/4, 151–60. (On *Ḥčankar hogu . . .*).
Manukyan, S. "Silva Kaputikyan." *SG,* 1959/8, 134–35.
Meželaytis, Ē. "Hogu ev k'artezi mijōreakanner." *SG,* 1980/5, 151–55.

KARAPET BAŁIŠETSI (c1475–c1520?)

A poet and scribe who hailed from Bałēš (Bitlis). He was a celibate priest (*vardapet*), and at some point he may have become the father superior of the monastery of Aṙak'elots in Muš.

Texts (verse)

"Tał ašḥarhatsoyts gełetsik." *B,* 38 (1880), 97–100. Also published under the title "Tał araratzots asatseal i Karapetē" in *HA,* 51 (1937), 328–38.
"Ołb i veray aršawanats Šah Ismayēli." *REArm,* 1 (1920), fasc. 2, 94–101. Also published in *HA,* 51 (1937), 338–43.

"Tał vasn vardin" ("Pulpuln ē hager i yotěn kōšik"). *MKH,* 246. Also published in *TH,* 72–73, and *KNZ,* 2, 14–15.

"I hrahang hambagē jahasaneann lerinn. Erg inch sa tařěndzeřeal bařiwk'n haykakan, oro katseal tałiwk'n homerakan ogeal očiw ew barařnakan kocheal zmasuns hnazandakan" ("Amenayni ěskizbn es em"). *BEH,* 1975/2, 185–92.

Anthologies

SUM, 1, 17–41.

Translations (French)

Macler, F. "Ołb i veray aršawanats Šah Ismayēli." *REArm,* 1 (1920), fasc. 2, 101–6.

Criticism

Ḥachatryan, P. *Hay mijnadaryan patmakan ołber (ŽD–ŽĒ dd.).* (Erevan, 1969), pp. 92–106.

KAŘVARENTS, GĒORG (1892–1946)

Pen name: Gēorg Kařvarents.

Born Gēorg Arapačean in Bolu (northwest of Ankara, south of Zonguldak, Turkey) and educated in Smyrna and at the American College in Partizak (Bahçecik, Turkey). Taught in Constantinople until World War I. Survived the Armenian massacres and deportations of 1915 and resumed teaching in Greece (1922–43). Died in Milan and was buried at St. Lazarus, Venice.

Texts (verse)

Gerezmani tzałikner. (Constantinople, 1921).
Tawił ewolean. (Athens, 1931).
Banastełtzut'iwn. (Venice, 1977).

Criticism

T'. B. "Tawił ewolean." *HK,* 11 (1932–33/2), 173–75.

K'ICHIK'-NŌVAY, (18th c.)

No biographical information is available for this *ašuł,* save that he lived in Tiflis in the eighteenth century.

Poetry

MKH, 534–35.
SHA, 307–26.
THG, 51–53.

KIWRČEAN, MELK'ON (1859–1915)

Pen names: Awō, Hrand, Pontatsi, Šahēn, Šawasp, T'łt'akits i Pontos.

Equally well known by his real name and his pen name, Hrand. A journalist and writer of short stories. Born in the village of Hawaw (near Palu, Turkey). Attended Armenian educational institutions in the Ottoman capital and taught in Armenian schools in both Constantinople and Rodosto (Tekirdağ). Fled the Armenian massacres of the mid-1890s and took refuge in Varna, Bulgaria. On his return to Constantinople in 1898, he was arrested at the port and banished to Kastamonu. He returned to Constantinople ten years later and resumed his literary activities. Put to death by the Young Turks during the Armenian massacres and deportations of 1915.

Collections

Ambołjakan erker. 1. Panduḥti keank'ēn. (Paris, 1931).

Texts in periodicals

M, 1890/3944, 339–42; 3945, 354–56; 3946, 376–79; 3951, 61–62. 1892/3972, 282–84. 1893/3982, 154–57; 3987, 231–33; 3989, 267–70; 3991, 300–2; 3993, 326–28; 3995, 360–62; 3997, 397–99.

HG, 1911/4, 10–15; 6, 8–13. 1913/10–11, 8–17.

Nawasard, 1914, 113–30.

HK, 30 (1952/5), 11.

Criticism

Azatean, D. "Ambołjakan erker (Hrand)." *HK,* 9 (1930–31/9), 93–95.

Gevorgyan, J. "Melk'on Kyurčyani ergitzank'ě." *PBH,* 1977/2, 119–27.

Sargsyan, G. "Melk'on Kyurčyan." *PBH,* 1985/2, 93–102.

Siruni, H. "Melk'on Kyurčyan." *SG,* 1971/9, 83–100.

KIWRČEAN, MIK'AYĒL (1879–1965)

Pen names: Arsēn Molar, Ditak, E. M. Kiwrōt (with E. Ōtean), Hamširak A., K'antak, Mēn Kēn, Mḥit'ar Pontatsi, Paroyr, Petros Agat'an, Pont, Srčep' A., Zarmayr Sahakean.

Born in Constantinople and educated in the local Nersēsean and Pērpērean schools (1891–95). Settled in Alexandria, Egypt, in 1896, where he worked as a clerk in courts and as an employee of the Ottoman Bank. He was one of the founders of the literary periodical *Širak* (1905) and the newspaper *Arew,* which he edited from 1920 to 1923. Wrote a number of comedies jointly with E. Ōtean, but a considerable part of his prose is still scattered in the periodical press, including his best work, *Martik Ała,* serialized in *Nor Keank'* of London, 1898–99, under the pen name "Paroyr," but never completed.

Collections

Anunin gišerě ew ayl patmuatzk'ner polsahay bark'erē. (Cairo, [1963]).

Texts

Frank'ō-t'rk'akan paterazmě kam Charšělě Art'in ała. (Cairo, 1903). (Comedy; written with E. Ōtean).

Herosaḥał. (Cairo, 1928; Beirut, n.d.). (Play; written with E. Ōtean).

I ḥorots srti ḥōsk' ěnd paštelwoyn. (Beirut, 1960).

K'san tari etk'. (Beirut, 1961).

K'OCHAR, HRACHYA (1910–1965)

Pen name: Hrachya K'ochar.

Born Hrachya Gabrielyan in K'umlibujał, a village near Alaškert (Eleşkirt, Turkey), and orphaned in the Armenian massacres of 1915. Novelist and short story writer. He took refuge in Eastern Armenia and settled in Erevan in 1927.

Fought in World War II in the ranks of the Red Army. From 1946 to 1951, he was the secretary to the Union of Soviet writers of Armenia and editor of the literary periodical *Sovetakan grakanut'yun.* In 1954, he briefly became editor of *Ozni,* a satirical monthly. He was posthumously awarded the first Armenian State Prize for Literature in 1967.

Collections

Erkeri žołovatzu. 6 vols. (Erevan, 1964–72).
Ĕntir erker. 2 vols. (Erevan, 1975, 1977).
K'ochar, M. *Erker.* (Erevan, 1980).

Texts (stories and novels)

Vahan Vardyan. (Erevan, 1934).
Ōgsen Vaspuri čanaparhordut'yunĕ. (Erevan, 1937).
Žamanakner. (Erevan, 1941).
Herosneri tznundĕ. (Erevan, 1942).
Naḫōryakin. (Erevan, 1943).
Srbazan uḫt. (Erevan, 1946).
Grakanut'yun ev kyank'. (Erevan, 1949).
Barekamut'yun. (Erevan, 1950).
Metz tan zavaknerĕ. Book 1. (Erevan, 1952). Books 1 and 2 (Erevan, 1959).
Vipakner ev patmvatzk'ner. (Erevan, 1956).
Metz taregrut'yan ējerits. (Erevan, 1957).
Lusni sonatĕ. (Erevan, 1963).
Spitak girk'ĕ. (Erevan, 1965).
Gndapeti patmatzĕ. (Erevan, 1967).
Ep'rati kamurjin. (Erevan, 1971).
Nahapetĕ. (Erevan, 1986).
"Erku namak." *SG,* 1980/7, 134–37. (Two letters addressed to Nairi Zaryan).

Translations

English

"Sister." *Armenian Tribune,* December 14, 1946, 1, 4; December 21, 1946, 1, 3.
Talmy, V. "Naapet." *SL,* 1966/3, 75–96.

English anthologies

WM, 121–26.

French

Yeghiaian, A. *E.* 150–54.

German

M. S. "Die Schwester des Generals." *Sowjet-Literatur,* 1946/4, 70–74.
Wrazek, I. "Naapet." *Sowjet-Literatur,* 1966/3, 81–104.

Russian

Deti bol'shogo doma. (Erevan, 1954, 1955, 1962 [2 books]; Moscow, 1955, 1956, 1966 [2 books]).
Frontovye ocherki. (Erevan, 1944).
Iz stranits velikoi letopisi [V. I. Lenin i bol'sheviki Armenii]. (Erevan, 1970).
Lunnaia sonata. [Sbornik povestei i rasskazov]. (Moscow, 1959).
Mat'. (Rasskazy). (Moscow, 1961).
Rasskazy. (Erevan, 1950).
Salakhian, A., and Baiandur, A. *Naapet: Povest.* (Erevan, 1989).

SPANISH

Alberdi, M. "Naapet." *Literatura Sovietica,* 1966/3, 78–102.

Criticism

Grigoryan, A. "Hrachya K'ochari lezvakan arvestĕ." *T,* 1948/12, 25–38.
Hamazaspyan, V. "Hrachya K'ocharĕ im hušerum." *SG,* 1980/7, 127–33.
Łazanjyan, V. "Hayrenakan paterazmĕ metz ktavi vra." *SG,* 1960/1, 134–35.
Margaryan, A. "Hrachya K'ochari patmvatzk'nerĕ ev vipaknerĕ." *T,* 1954/6, 3–32.
Matinyan, G. "Hrachya K'ochari ōragrut'yunĕ." *SG,* 1969/5, 112–16.
———. "Azgayin čakatagri imastavorumĕ." *SG,* 1971/11, 137–45.
———. "Hrachya K'ochari grakan k'nnadatut'yunĕ." *SG,* 1973/11, 147–51.
Mḥit'aryan, A. "Hrachya k'ochar." *SG,* 1966/5, 122–28.
Nazaryan, Š. *Hrachya K'ochar.* (Erevan, 1962).
Noruni, Y. *Hracheay K'ochari 'Spitak girk'ĕ.'* (Beirut, 1967).
Sołomonyan, S. "Hrachya K'ochar." *SG,* 1962/8, 105–25.
T'at'ikyan, Š. "Im lavaguyn barekamĕ." *SG,* 1980/10, 104–9.
Vardanyan, E. "Hrachya K'ochari stełtzagortzut'yunneri bar̄apašarĕ." *L,* 1975/8, 21–30.

KORYUN, MKRTICH (1913–1984)

Pen name: Mkrtich Koryun.

Born Koryun Mkrtchyan in the village of Łzlchaḥchaḥ, in the region of Kars (now in Turkey). A poet, fabulist, and writer of children's literature. Fleeing the Armenian massacres of 1915, Koryun's family first moved to Alexandrapol (renamed Leninakan under the Soviets, now Gyumri) and later settled in Erevan. Acquired his education in Leninakan and Erevan, graduating from Erevan State University in 1937.

Collections

Hatĕntir. (Erevan, 1976).
Mihatoryak. (Erevan, 1976).
Anmeł katakner. (Erevan, 1980).

Texts

Temperi herosnerĕ. (Erevan, 1932). (Verse).
Kyank'i ev siro erger. (Erevan, 1937). (Verse).
Tzałikn u mełun. (Erevan, 1937). (Verse).
Charikn u K'ajarikĕ. (Erevan, 1938). (Tale).
Hanelukner. (Erevan, 1938). (Riddles).
Ḥorhrdavor gorgĕ. (Erevan, 1938). (Riddles, stories).
Tzałkadzor. (Erevan, 1938). (Verse).
Hek'iat'ner. (Erevan, 1941). (Tales).
Mer patasḥanĕ. (Erevan, 1941). (Verse).
Partizanĕ. (Erevan, 1942). (Verse).
Mankakan piesner. (Erevan, 1944). (Plays for children).
Ar̄akner, hek'iat'ner, patmvatzk'ner. (Erevan, 1945). (Fables and stories).
Kamo (Patmakensagrakan vipak). (Erevan, 1947, 1955, 1958 [revised and expanded]). (Story of Kamo [Simon Ter-Petrosyan, 1882–1922]).
Im nverĕ. (Erevan, 1954).
Manukneri het. (Erevan, 1956). (Verse).
Karmir gat'a. (Erevan, 1959, 1969).

Mankakan erker. (Erevan, 1959). (Verse).
Hanelukner. (Erevan, 1961). (Riddles).
Hekʻiatʻner, piesner. (Erevan, 1961). (Tales and plays).
Aŕakner. (Erevan, 1964). (Fables).
Dasĕnker. (Erevan, 1967).
Hanelukner. (Erevan, 1970). (Riddles).
Im ĕntʻertsaranĕ. (Erevan, 1971).
Aŕakner. (Erevan, 1973). (Fables).
Anmeł katakner. (Erevan, 1980).
Mankakan ašharh. (Erevan, 1982).
"Suren Spandaryan." *SG,* 1982/12, 106–16. (A passage from a novel of the same title).
Dprotsakan tʻatron. Piesner. (Erevan, 1984).
Tʻoŕan ev papi achkʻerov. (Erevan, 1986).

Translations

Russian

Basni. (Erevan, 1952; Moscow, 1958).
Chuzhoi uspekh. (Moscow, 1962).
Gaikovich, B. *Istoricheskaia cherepakha. Basni.* (Moscow, 1978).
———., and Il'in, M. *Sil'nee l'va: Miniatiury s natury.* (Moscow, 1980).
Ioanisian, T. *Charik i kadzharik.* (Leningrad, 1954).
Kamo. (Erevan, 1970).
Mikhalkov, et al. *Solovei po shtatu.* (Erevan, 1987).
Gaikovich, B. *Tevan-lezheboka: Po motivam arm. nar. skazok.* (Moscow, 1982). ["Vypusk dopolnitel'nyi," 1983].

Criticism

Melyan, B. *Mkrtich Koryun.* (Erevan, 1973).

KOSTANDEAN, YARUTʻ (1909–1979)

Born in Bushire (Bushehr), Iran, and educated at an English school in Bombay. Poet. After a brief sojourn in Italy and England (1926), he resided in France from 1927 until his death.

Texts (verse)

Ōreri imastutʻiwnĕ. (Paris, 1935).
Banasteltzutʻeamb. (Beirut, 1974).
Ōreri imastutʻyunĕ. Banasteltzutʻyunner; ardzak. (Erevan, 1988). (Verse and prose).

Criticism

Sanasar, Pʻ. "Y. Kostandean, Ōreri imastutʻiwnĕ." *HK,* 14 (1935–36/8), 172–74.

KŔANEAN, BIWZAND (1912–)

Pen name: Biwzand Kŕanean.

Born Biwzand Chēkʻičean in Aintab (Gaziantep, Turkey). Poet and novelist. Fled his birthplace and spent a decade or so in Egypt. In the 1930s, he studied agriculture at the State University of New York. He moved to Los Angeles in the mid-1950s.

Collections

Tpaworutʻiwnner, Mer aruestagētnerě, Hastatumner. (Beirut, 1975). (His Ambołjakan erker, vol. 1).

Banastełtzutʻiwnner: Keankʻě mern ē hima, Ḥentutʻiwn srbazan, Ardzak paher, Nerkʻin dzayner. (Los Angeles, 1980). (His Ambołjakan erker, vol. 2).

Texts

Keankʻě mern ē hima. (Cairo, 1948). (Verse).

Ḥentutʻiwn srbazan. (Cairo, 1955). (Verse).

Haykakan katakergutʻiwn. (Beirut, 1967). (Novel).

Hayastan ew hayě. (Los Angeles, 1977). (Impressions of a visit to Soviet Armenia).

Translations (English)

Baliozian, A. *My Land, My People.* (Los Angeles, 1978).

———. *Selected Poems, 1936–1982.* (New York, 1983).

KURŁINYAN, ŠUŠANIK (1876–1927)

Born Šušanik Pʻopolčyan in Alexandrapol (Leninakan, and now Gyumri). Poet. Attended a Russian and an Armenian women's school (Arłutʻean) in her native city; played an active social and political role in the Armenian communities of the Caucasus. Recognized as one of the founders of Armenian Marxist-proletarian poetry.

Collections

Kurłinyan, A. *Hatěntir.* (Erevan, 1939).

Mkrtchyan, H. *Erkeri žołovatzu.* (Erevan, 1947).

Mirzabekyan, J. *Banastełtzutʻyunner.* (Erevan, 1971).

Hatěntir. (Erevan, 1978).

Banastełtzutʻyunner, ardzak ējer, piesner, namakner. (Erevan, 1981).

Texts

Aršaloysi łōłanjner. (Nor Naḥijewan, 1907). (Poetry).

Translations

English

Kelikian, H. "Roving Brother, Come to My House." *Ararat,* Autumn, 1961, 40.

English anthologies

ALP, 51.

AP, 247–48.

French

Tchobanian, A. "Je tresserai des chants." *La femme arménienne,* (Paris, 1918), 70–71.

French anthologies

APA, 163–66.

LPA, 204–5.

Russian anthologies

BPA, 405.

SHAP, 49–62.

Criticism

Abazyan, G. "Šušanik Kurłinyan." *SG,* 1966/8, 81–84.
Berberean, M. "Tḥur mełediner. (H. Haynē–Aw. Isahakean–Š. Kurłinean)." *A,* 1908, 157–64.
Łazaryan, H. "Šušanik Kurłinyani stełtzagortzakan verelkʿě ṙusakan aṙajin ṙevolyutsiayi žamanakašrjanum." *T,* 1953/1, 73–100.
———. *Šušanik Kurłinyan.* (Erevan, 1955).

KURTIKYAN, STEPʿAN (1908–1986)

Born in Bursa, Turkey. Journalist and writer of short stories. Educated in his birthplace and at the Anatolia College in Thessaloniki. In 1927 he went to Erevan as a student, but he became a permanent resident and continued his education at the Abovyan Pedagogical Institute, the Institute for Foreign Languages, and the Institute of Marxism-Leninism. From 1946 to 1962, he was an assistant editor to the literary monthly *Sovetakan grakanutʿyun,* and he was its chief editor from 1962 to the early 1980s.

Texts (stories)

Alpyan arotnerum. (Erevan, 1935).
Metz aršavum. (Erevan, 1935).
Herosuhinerě. (Erevan, 1943).
Arevot ṫerakłzum. (Erevan, 1947).
Mi pʿokʿrik kyankʿi patmutʿyun. (Erevan, 1947).
Leṙnašḥarhi dustrě. (Erevan, 1948).
Herosneri mot. (Erevan, 1950).
Hetaḥuyzner. (Erevan, 1950).
Erevan. (Erevan, 1952, 1960).
Zruytsner ḥaruyki šurjě. (Erevan, 1954).
Hayreni legendner. (Erevan, 1957).
Meḥanizatori kyankʿi ułin. (Erevan, 1958).
Hayreni hołi vra. (Erevan, 1960).
Žamanakner ev mardik. (Erevan, 1962).
Andaluzyan leṙnerum. (Erevan, 1966).
Komitasyan łołanjner. (Erevan, 1969).
Prolomyan hovtašušanner. (Erevan, 1969).
Lusašḥarh hanim zim gutʿan. (Erevan, 1974).
Veratznund. (Erevan, 1977).
"Zevsi ev Homerosi erkrum." *SG,* 1981/11, 112–28; 12, 100–47.
Artasahmani hay grołneri het. (Erevan, 1984).
Im kyankʿi chanaparhin. (Erevan, 1984).
"Hamastełi ašḥarhě." *SG,* 1986/5, 104–14.
Gndakaharekʿ, es ochinch chgitem . . . (Erevan, 1985).

Other works

KIM-i antsatz ułin. (Erevan, 1931). (KIM: Kommunisticheskii internatsional molodezhi).
Komeritmiutʿyuně ašnanatsani frontum. (Erevan, 1931).
Mayor Mamikon Ḥachanyan. (Erevan, 1945).
Sovetakan Miutʿyan heros gvardiayi avag leytenant Ṙuben Hakobyan. (Erevan, 1945).

Sovetakan Miutʻyan heros Hunan Avetisyan. (Erevan, 1945).
Milionater koltntesutʻyunnerum. (Erevan, 1951).
Zootehnikě. (Erevan, 1958).
Herosutʻyan ułiov. (Erevan, 1961).
Aṙatutʻyan hamar. (Erevan, 1962).
Dašnaktsutʻyan paragluhnerě imperializmi tzaṙayutʻyan mej. (Erevan, 1964).
Daniel Varužan. (Erevan, 1976).

Translations

English

Ghazarian, V. "The Bell of the Armenians." *Lraber,* April 12, 1960, 4.
Herald, L. "Xenophonian Villages Depart." *Youth,* August 29, 1935/2–3.
Kooyoomdjian, H. "The Blue Lake." *Lraber,* July 19, 1960, 4.

French

Der-Melkonian, C. "Le Temple de la lumière." *Contes et legendes arméniens.* (Beirut, 1964), 61–64. (Adapted).

Russian anthologies

AASL, 273–76.
RAN, 412–14.

ŁAZAR, BAŁĒR ŌŁLI (18th c.)

Łazar, an *ašuł,* was presumably a native of Nor Jułay (New Julfa, Isfahan).

Poetry

BM, 2 (1950), 187–90.
SHA, 104–43.
THG, 33–36.

Criticism

Allahverdean, A. "Ašuł Bałer Ōłli." *HK,* 11 (1932–33/7), 114–21.
Eremean, A. "Ašuł Bałer Ōłli Łazar." *B,* 106 (1948), 55–67.

ŁAZAR JAHKETSI (d. 1751)

Łazar was nuncio of Ējmiatzin in Smyrna when he was elected Catholicos of all Armenians in 1738. Briefly ousted in 1748, he was reinstated to office in 1749 and held it until his death. Theological and religious themes dominate his works, some of which were written specifically in defense of the doctrinal positions of the Church of Armenia.

Texts

Girkʻ a[stua]tzabanakan or kochi draht tsankali. (Constantinople, 1735).
Girkʻ noraboys or kochi ergaran. (Constantinople, 1737, 1744).
Girkʻ ałōtʻits or kochi Astuatzałers. (Constantinople, 1742; St. Petersburg, 1786; New Nakhijevan, 1792, 1793).

ŁAZAR SEBASTATSI (16th–17th c.)

An author who lived in the sixteenth and seventeenth centuries.

Texts (poems)

Sruandzteants, G. "Tał siroy ew urahutʻean" ("Tzov achkʻ, am kʻani nayis holorov"). *Mananay,* (Constantinople, 1876), 272–74. Also published in *KNZ,* 2, 23–27; 3, 56–62.

Ter-Step'anyan, A. "Łazar Sebastatsu tałerě." *BEH,* 1977/3, 193–205. (7 poems).

Works in anthologies

SUM, 1, 96–108.

Translations

French anthologies

LPA, 123–25.
TA, 215–21.

Russian

AAP, 243.

Criticism

Gazančean, Y. "Mijnadarean sirerguner." *Nawasard,* 1914, 225–31. (Includes excerpts from "Tał siroy").

LEO, (1860–1932)

Pen names: Gawaṙatsi, H. A. G., Hrahat, Lēō, Ṙusahay.

Born Aṙak'el Babaḥanean in Šuši, Artsaḥ (Karabagh). Historian, writer, literary critic, and journalist. Received his education in his native Šuši, and as a contributor and later as secretary (1895–1906), he forged a close association with the celebrated periodical *Mšak* of Tiflis. Taught at the Gēorgean Seminary in Ējmiatzin for one year (1906–07), and at the State University of Erevan, from 1924 until his death.

Collections

Gełarvestakan erker. (Erevan, 1959). (*Meliki' ałjikě ev Osku žḥori mej*).
Erkeri žołovatzu 10 hatorov. (Erevan, 1966–). (9 vols. to 1989).

Literary texts (Stories)

Skayordi. Nor tsaw. (Šuši, 1885).
Koyri ałjikě. (Šuši, 1888).
Panduḥt. (Baku, 1888).
Tzayrer. (Šuši, 1888).
Vahan Mamikonean. (Šuši, 1888).
Koratzner. (Šuši, 1889).
Arnagin. (Tiflis, 1890, 1897).
Spanwatz hayrě. (Šuši, 1891).
Verjin vērk'erě. (Tiflis, 1891).
Tat'aḥman gišerě. (Šuši, 1892; Tiflis, 1903).
Aḥtahanut'iwn. (Baku, 1893).
Anzugakaně. (N.p., [1893]).
Melik'i ałjikě. (Tiflis, 1898, 1905; Boston, 1933; Beirut, 1938). (Novel).
Aytzaratzě. (Baku, 1904).
Karmir gtakě. (Baku, 1904).
Vardanank'. (Tiflis, [1916]). (Drama).

Other works

Uḥtawori yišatakaraně. (Šuši, 1885).
Vēp t'ē patmut'iwn. (Šuši, 1887).
Dawit' ew Mher. (Moscow, 1891).

Im yišatakaranē. (Šuši, 1891).
Ereweli mardik. (Baku, 1894).
Gladstōn. (Tiflis, 1899).
Haykakan tpagrutiwn. 3 vols. (Tiflis, 1901–02, 1904 [revised]).
Grigor Artzruni. 3 vols. (Tiflis, 1902–05).
Stepʻanos Nazarean. 2 vols. (Tiflis, 1902).
Yovsēpʻ katʻołikos Arłutʻean. (Tiflis, 1902).
Ṙusahayots grakanutʻiwnĕ skzbits minchew mer ōrerĕ. (Venice, 1904, 1928).
S. Mesrop. (Tiflis, 1904; Erevan, 1962). (*Mesrop Maštots).*
Hayots hartsĕ. (Tiflis, 1906).
Eresnameak Hayots baregortzakan ĕnkerutʻean Kovkasum, 1881–1911. (Tiflis, 1911).
Hay grkʻi tōnĕ. (Tiflis, 1912, 1913).
Patmutʻiwn Erewani hayots tʻemakan hogewor dprotsi 1837–1912. (Tiflis, 1914).
Patmutʻiwn Łarabałi hayots tʻemakan hogewor dprotsi 1838–1913. (Tiflis, 1914).
Hayots hartsi waweragrerĕ. (Tiflis, 1915).
Vani tʻagaworutʻiwnĕ. (Tiflis, 1915; Fresno, 1950). (*Vani Urartu tʻagaworutʻiwnĕ).*
Hay hayrenikʻĕ. (Tiflis, 1916).
Hayots patmutʻiwn. (Tiflis, 1917 [vol. 1]; Erevan, 1946–47 [vols. 2, 3]).
Hay herosner. Jraberd. (Erevan, 1920).
Antsyalits: hušer, tʻłtʻer, datumner. (Tiflis, 1925).
Ḫojayakan kapitalĕ ev nra kʻałakʻakan-hasarakakan derĕ hayeri mej. (Erevan, 1934).
Tʻiwrkʻahay yełapʻoḫutʻean gałapʻarabanutʻiwnĕ. 2 vols. (Paris, 1934–35).
Ani. (Erevan, 1946, 1963).
Kazandzhian, A. "Maloizvestnye stat'i Leo." *Banber Hayastani arḫivneri,* 1986/2, 33–46.

Criticism

A. Babaḫanean–"Lēō." *Kensagrakan-grakan aknark nra 25ameay yobeleani aṙtʻiw.* (Tiflis, 1908).
Andrikean, N. "Lēō." *B,* 68 (1910), 6–9, 69–75, 107–14, 159–66, 194–204. 69 (1911), 69–75, 107–14, 159–66, 194–204.
Awetisean, A. "Lēōi grakan yobeleanĕ." *HA,* 22 (1908), 129–32.
E. "Lēō." *B,* 66 (1908), 145–57.
Eremean, S. "Lēō." *B,* 90 (1933), 513–15.
Ōhanyan, A. "Leoyi gełarvestakan ardzakĕ." *SG,* 1962/11, 106–12.
———. "Hayreni erkri antsyaln u nerkan Leoyi ułegrutʻyunnerum." *SG,* 1964/12, 130–36.
———. *Leoyi gełarvestakan stełtzagortzutʻyunĕ.* (Erevan, 1970).
Snḫchyan, I. "Leoyi mi antip ašḫatutʻyunĕ." *L,* 1979/12, 58–64.
Tiwrean, K. "Lēō." *HA,* 18 (1904), 1–9. (Part of the series "Ṙusahayots grakanutʻiwnĕ").

LEṘ KAMSAR (1888–1965)

Pen name: Leṙ Kamsar.

Born Aram Tʻovmasyan (also Ter-Tʻovmasyan) in Van and educated at the Gēorgean Seminary in Ējmiatzin (1909). Satirist. Participated in the defense of

Van and subsequently settled in Eastern Armenia. As a satirist, he contributed to the daily *Ḥorhrdayin Hayastan* (later *Sovetakan Hayastan*) from 1921 to 1935. Survived banishment during the Stalinist purges.

Collections

Połosyan, Ḥ. *Mihatoryak.* (Erevan, 1980).
Žpit, ťiw 5. (Beirut, 1980). (Collection includes two pieces by L. K.).
Erker. (Erevan, 1988).

Texts (prose)

Anvaver meṙelner. (Erevan, 1924).
Azgayin aybbenaran. (Erevan, 1926; Beirut, 1954 [selections]).
Vripatz artsunkʻner. (Erevan, 1934).
Grabar mardik. (Erevan, 1959).
Mardě tanu šorerov. (Erevan, 1965).

Criticism

Margaryan, V. "Leṙ Kamsari ergitzankʻi mi kʻani aṙandznahatkutyunnerě." *SG,* 1976/2, 147–50.

LEṘENTS, (1866–1939)

Pen names: Awō, Leṙents.

Born Awetis Nazarbēk (also Nazarbēkean) in Tiflis. Poet, translator, and one of the founders, along with his wife, Marō Nazarbēk (née Vardanean, 1864–1941, a resdient of Tiflis, 1918–41, marriage ended, 1904) of the Social Democratic Hnchakean Party (Sotsial Demokrat Hnchakean Kusaktsuťiwn). Educated in local schools. Pursued higher studies at St. Petersburg, Paris, and Geneva. One of the founders of the official organ of the party, *Hnchak* (1887). Collaborated with Marxists in European capitals. In 1923, he left Paris for the United States and joined the ranks of the American Communists. Traveled to Moscow and became a member of the Communist Party of the Soviet Union in 1934. Nothing is known about him beyond this point, except that he died in 1939.

Texts (verse)

Azat žamer. (Tiflis, 1883). (Verse).
Banastełtzuťiwnner. (Petersburg, 1890). (Verse).
Ṗaḥstakaně. (N.p., 1891). (Poem).
Awazakě. (Athens, 1892). (Poem).
Martum. (Athens, 1893). (Verse).
Nwag u mełedi. (London, 1895). (Verse).
Darbnewor. (Rusjuk, 1904).

Translations (English)

Elton, L. *Through the Storm: Pictures of Life in Armenia.* (London, 1899).

ŁUKAS KARNETSI (c1722–1799)

Born in the town of Kełi (or Kʻłi, now Kığı, Turkey), southwest of Karin (Erzurum, Turkey). Studied in Ējmiatzin and took the vows of celibacy in 1751. Served as the nuncio of the Mother See of Ējmiatzin in Rumeli and Crimea. He was created bishop in 1763 by Simēon Erewantsi (q.v.), who had just ascended the throne of Ējmiatzin. Primate of the Armenians of Smyrna, 1764–75. Succeeded his mentor, Simēon Erewantsi, as Supreme Patriarch and Catholicos of Armenia (1780). Renovated Ējmiatzin and commissioned the celebrated artist Yovnatʻan Yovnatʻanean (1730s–c1802) to paint murals and pictures for the cathedral. Died in office.

Texts

Łukas katʻułikosi kondakner. In *Diwan hayots patmutʻean, Łukas katʻułikos (1780–1800),* G. Ałaneants, Vol. 4, Tiflis, 1899.

Grigoryan, V. "Łukas Karnetsu mi antip erkasirutʻyunĕ." *BM,* 6 (1962), 429–34. (Text: "Patmutʻiwn galstean ḥoyetswots ew naḥchuantswotsn yerkirs Erewanu . . .").

ŁUKASYAN, HOVHANNES (1919–)

Born in Tabriz, Iran and educated in the local Armenian school. Novelist and poet. Settled in Soviet Armenia permanently in 1946.

Collections

Erkeri žołovatzu. 3 vol. (Erevan, 1972–76).
Ĕntir erker. 2 vols. (Erevan, 1989–90).

Texts

Aṙakner ew banastełtzutʻiwnner. (Tabriz, 1944). (Fables and poems).
Banastełtzutʻiwnner, hēkʻiatʻner ew balladner. (Tabriz, 1944). (Verse).
Berdi Yišatakaran (M. Nalbandean). (Tabriz, 1944).
Zoya. (Tabriz, 1944). (Poems).
Jauanšir. (Tabriz, 1945). (Verse).
Ṙubayiner. (Tabriz, 1945). (Verse).
Katʻilner. (Tabriz, 1945).
Ałbiwr. (Tabriz, 1945).
Hayrenadardz. (Erevan, 1947). (Verse).
Ḥavari ašḥarhum. (Erevan, 1950). (Prose).
Pʻokʻrik vrižaṙuner. (Erevan, 1950, 1979). (Prose).
Arakʻsi ayn apʻin. (Erevan, 1951). (Prose).
Hasani hišatakaranĕ. (Erevan, 1953). (Prose).
Garnanayin patmutʻyun. (Erevan, 1955).
Vipakner. (Erevan, 1957). (Stories).
Anhangist patanekutʻyun. (Erevan, 1959, 1987).
Erekʻ patmvatzkʻ. (Erevan, 1962). (Stories).
Oskan Erevantsi. (Erevan, 1962, 1965, 1988). (Novel).
Karčatesi arkatznerĕ. (Erevan, 1964).
19 patmvatzkʻ. (Erevan, 1966). (Stories).
"Ḥaṙnaypʻntʻur" ōratsuyts. (Erevan, 1966). (Story).
Deṙ spasum en. (Erevan, 1969).
Bogdan Saltʻanov. 2 vols. (Erevan, 1980, 1985). (Novel).
Im 'Lusałbyurĕ'. (Erevan, 1981).
"Tagnapi ev hskumi gišerner." *SG,* 1988/6, 119–39. (Story).

Translations

RUSSIAN

Almazova, L., and Khechumian, V. *Vesenniaia povest'.* (Moscow, 1963).

Barkhudarian, A. *Zapiski Gasana.* (Moscow and Leningrad, 1953).
———., and Cherkasova, V. *Vremia-zoloto. Povest'.* (Moscow, 1960).
Malen'kie mstiteli. (Rasskaz Gasana). (Moscow and Leningrad, 1950, 1952; Moscow, 1954; Saratov, 1954; Tashkent, 1954).

Criticism

Aramyan, Ṙ. "Hovhannes Łukasyan." *SG,* 1967/4, 135–37.
Melkʻonyan, M. "Hovhannes Łukasyan." *SG,* 1987/10, 122–28.

ŁUL ARZUNI (17th–18th c.)

No biographical details are available about this *ašuł.*

Poetry

EPA, 19–32.
PHA, 1, 263–66.
SHA, 85–103.
THG, 17–20.

Criticism

Eremean, A. *Parskahay ašułner.* (Tiflis, 1930), 12–32.

ŁUNKIANOS KARNETSI (d. 1841?)

Łunkianos left his native Karin (Erzurum, Turkey) at an early age. Traveled to Iran and went on to Lebanon to become a monk, but he gave up his religious plans and moved to Egypt, where he engaged in commercial pursuits. Suffered losses in his mercantile activities, went to Aleppo, and wandered on to the Crimea, Eastern Armenia, and the village of Varevan in Ahalkʻalakʻ, where his family had settled after fleeing Karin in the aftermath of the Russo-Ottoman War of 1828–29. Spent the last days of his destitute life in the village. Wrote poetry in both Armenian and Turkish.

Texts (verse)

"Kʻerduatzkʻ Łunkianosi ergchi Karnetswoy." *B,* 41 (1883), 238–46, 332–40. 42 (1884), 50–57, 137–42, 212–16, 322–28. 43 (1885), 38–43, 123–31, 217–26. (Reprinted separately, Venice, 1886, 1893).
"Kʻałuatzkʻ Łunkianos ergchi Karnetswoy, Ilahikʻ." *M,* 3748 (1884), 493–94. (Reprinted from *B*).
"Kʻertʻuatzkʻ Łunkianos ergchi Karnetswoy—Tiwrkʻmanikʻ." *M,* 3760 (1885), 779–80. (Reprinted from *B*).
"Łunkianos ergchi Karnetswoy." *M,* 3790 (1885), 229. (Reprinted from *B*).

Translations

French

TA, 265–78.

Russian

RPA, 237–38.

Criticism

H. A. T[iroyean], "Łunkianos ergich Karnetsi." *B,* 41 (1883), 97–110.
Harutʻyunyan, A. "Łunkianos Karnetsi." *L,* 1973/4, 71–78.

MAHARI, GURGEN (1903–1969)

Pen name: Gurgen Mahari.

Born Gurgen Ačemyan in Van. Novelist and poet. Fled his native Van during the Armenian genocide of 1915 and found a home in orphanages in Dilijan and Erevan. Completed his studies at the State University of Erevan and devoted himself entirely to literature. Survived an eleven-year banishment in Vologda, to the north of Moscow, during the Stalinist era. Died in Lithuania but was buried in Erevan.

Collections

Erker. (Erevan, 1954).
Erkeri žołovatzu. 5 vols. (Erevan, 1966–90).

Texts

3 agit ōperet. (Erevan, 1924). (Verse).
Titanik. (Leninakan, 1924). (Verse).
Erku poem. (Erevan, 1926). (Verse).
Erku mayr. (Erevan, 1927). (with Mkrtich Armen).
Kesgišerits minchev ar̄avot. (Erevan, 1927). (Poem).
Bardinerě. (Erevan, 1927). (Poem).
Siro, ḥandi ev Nitstsayi partizpanneri masin. (Erevan, 1929). (Stories).
Mankutʻyun ev patanekutʻyun. (Erevan, 1930). (Prose).
Zigzagnerum, Ełia Chubarin. (Moscow, 1931). (Prose).
Zruyts Noyemberi masin. (Erevan, 1932).
Mrgahas. (Erevan, 1933). (Verse).
Eritasardutʻyan semin. (Erevan, 1956). (Prose).
Hndzanner. (Erevan, 1959). (Prose).
Lr̄utʻyan dzayně. (Erevan, 1962; Beirut, 1963). (Stories, essays, reminiscences).
Sev mardě. (Erevan, 1964). (Prose).
Ayrvoł aygestanner. (Erevan, 1966). (Novel).
Charents-name. (Erevan, 1968). (Reminiscences about Charents).
Ays hmut, hančareł lor̄etsin. (Erevan, 1971). (On Y. Tʻumanean).
Hovhannes Širazi masin. (Erevan, 1974). (Written with S. Ałababyan, H. Tʻamrazyan, and M. Sargsyan).
"Gurgen Maharu ev Hamastełi namakagrutʻyuně." *SG,* 1983/8, 90–98.
Tzałkatz pʻšalarer. (Erevan, 1988).
"Iz pisem Gurgena Maari L. S. Pervomaiskomu." *BEH,* 1989/1, 80–93.

Translations

English

Mesrobian, P. "Return." *Lraber,* November 7, 1963, 4.

English anthologies

SAP, 21–23.

French

Champenois, J. "Le kantar"; "Nchan-aga." *OO,* 123 (March 1969), 100–107.
Ter-Sarkissian, P. *Les Barbelés en fleurs.* (Paris: Messidor, 1990).

French anthologies

LPA, 309–13.

Russian

Detstvo i otrochestvo. [Povest']. (Erevan, 1956).

Lidin, V. *Istoriia starogo sada.* (Moscow, 1959).
———. *Iunost'. Povest'.* (Moscow, 1966).
Makintsian, P. *Detstvo.* ([Tiflis], 1931).
Ogni Nairi. [Stikhi]. (Moscow, 1962).

Criticism

Ačemyan, G. "Mrgahasits aṙaj." *SG,* 1973/8, 136–41.
———. "Maharin poeziayi kʻnnadat." *SG,* 1975/2, 130–36.
———. "Maharin ev Eseninē." *SG,* 1976/6, 154–60.
———. "Gurgen Maharin namaknerum." *SG,* 1978/1, 135–44.
Ałababyan, S. *Gurgen Mahari.* (Erevan, 1959).
———. "Kendani Charentsē hušerum." *SG,* 1968/8, 126–27.
———. "Kyankʻi ev stełtzagortzutʻyan ējer." *SG,* 1983/8, 72–89.
Ałabekyan, K. *Gurgen Mahari.* (Erevan, 1975).
Alikʻsanean, A. "Ardzakagir Maharin." *AND,* 14 (1963), 25–27.
Baluean, H. "Gurgēn Mahari." *Z,* 2 [1931], 37–39.
———. "Mrgahas. Banastełtzutʻiwnner G. Maharii, Erewan, 1932." *Z* (taregirkʻ), 1 (1937), 209–10.
Bodosyan, S. *Gurgen Mahari.* (Erevan, 1981).
Gonchar-Khandzhian, N. "Iz pisem Gurgena Maari L. S. Pervomaiskomu." *BEH,* 1989/1, 80–93.
Kareyan, S. "Taṙapankʻi ev žpiti aspetē (Hartsazruyts G. Maharu knoj: A. Maharu het)." *SG,* 1983/8, 99–101.
Madoyan, A., and Nersisyan, V. "Gurgen Maharu 'Ayrvoł aygestanner' vepi kʻnnarrkumē." *BEH,* 1967/2, 257–62.
Marutʻyan, L. "Gurgen Mahari." *SG,* 1962/2, 121–31.
Mḥitʻaryan, M. "Grołē ev patmakan čšmartutʻyunē." *L,* 1967/10, 108–15. (On *Ayrvoł aygestanner*).
Šahinean, G. *Gurgēn Mahari vatʻsuni hangruanin.* (Beirut, 1964).

MALĒZEAN, VAHAN (1871–1967)

Pen name: Zepʻiwṙ.

Born in Sulina (Rumania), but brought up in Constantinople, where he studied law. Poet. Spent his life in different parts of the world: Cairo (1898–1923), Brussels (1923–27), Paris-Marseilles (1927–45), New York (1945–48), before settling in Nice in 1948. In Cairo, he was one of the founders of the Sahmanadrakan Ṙamkavar Party, which later merged with other organizations to form the Ṙamkavar Azatakan Kusaktsutʻiwn (Armenian Democratic League). Held administrative positions within the Armenian General Benevolent Union, founded in Cairo in 1906.

Collections

Hanganak hatĕntir kʻertʻuatzneru. (Beirut, 1961).

Texts

Mrmunjkʻ. (Constantinople, 1890).
Anitzealē. (Constantinople, 1892).
Yušardzan Arpʻiareani. ([Cairo], 1911).
Keronner, 1891–1911. (Cairo, 1912).

Taragri mě yušatetrě. (Cairo, 1915).
Antsatz ōrer: yušamatean Gatěkʻēōyi grakan erekoytʻneru, 1892–1894. (Paris, 1927).
Karapi ergě. (Paris, 1949).
Hogii dzayner. (Paris, 1949).
Metz hayrs Y. Malēzean patueli. (Paris, 1949).
Čambus vray: yušakʻał. (Paris, 1950).
Čambus tzayrě. 2 vols. (Paris, 1954–55).

Translations

FRENCH

Navarian, A. *La corbeille fleurie.* (Paris, n.d.).

FRENCH ANTHOLOGIES

APA, 141–48.

RUSSIAN ANTHOLOGIES

BPA, 461–62.
VAM, 176–77.

SPANISH ANTHOLOGIES

APAS, 201–5.

Criticism

Dzōnamatean Vahan Malēzeani 85ameakin artʻiw (1871–1956). (Paris, 1956).
Pahri, Z. *Vahan Malēzeani keankʻn u gortzě: yušamatean ir utʻsunameakin artʻiw, 1871–1951.* (Paris, 1951).
Parsamean, M. "Grakan dēmkʻer–Vahan Malēzean." *M,* 1904/24, 370–74.

MAMIKONYAN, NIKOŁAYOS (1860–1937)

A native of Gandzak, Kirovabad (now Ganja, Azerbaijan). Studied law at the university of Odessa. From 1917 until his death in Kirovabad, he lived and practiced law in Tiflis. His novels and short stories reflect country life.

Texts

Hazarits mēkě. (Tiflis, 1895). (Novelette).
Chhasutʻiwn. (Tiflis, 1899). (Novel).
Višap. (Tiflis, 1908). (Story).

MAMUREAN, MATTʻĒOS (1830–1901)

Pen names: Aprsam, M. M., Šahnur, V., Vroyr.

Born in Smyrna. Journalist, writer, translator, and educator. Studied at the Muratean school in Padua (1845–50) and sat in on courses at Cambridge (1856–57). Briefly resided in Constantinople and held clerical positions in the Armenian Patriarchate. Returned to his birthplace in 1865 and devoted himself to literature, journalism, and teaching. In 1871, he launched his celebrated monthly *Arewelean mamul* (1871–1909, 1919–22), which rapidly became one of the most influential Armenian periodicals.

Collections

Łazaryan, H., and Połosyan, H. *Erker.* (Erevan, 1966). (Includes *Ankliakan namakani . . .* and *Haykakan namakani*).

Texts

[Vroyr]. *Haykakan namakani.* (Smyrna, 1872). (Prose).

Angłiakan namakani kam Hayu mě čakatagirě. (Smyrna, 1880, 1881, as *Ankliakan namakani kam Hayu mě čakatagirě*). (Novel).

Tunēn durs. (Smyrna, 1882). (Play).

Sew leṙin mardě. (Smyrna, 1909; Athens, 1932). (Novel).

Works in periodicals

"Sew leṙin mardě." *AM,* 1871, 513–20; 561–66. 1872, 145–50; 193–97; 307–12; 443–49; 498–505. 1873, 66–75; 168–73; 400–96. 1874, 58–64; 108–12. 1875, 71–76; 89–97; 313–17; 397–99; 471–77. 1876, 217–22; 269–73; 370–74; 471–75. 1878, 164–68; 239–47; 284–88. 1879, 348–52; 396–406; 440–48; 490–93. 1879, May, 34–40; June, 86–93; August, 181–90; October, 273–83. 1880, March, 521–27; April, 563–69; May, 67–71; June, 138–43; August, 270–81; September, 343–50; November, 483–97; December, 545–52. 1881, March, 96–103.

AM, 1873, 484–86. 1876, 257–67; 281–93; 329–42. 1880, 418–31. 1882, 358–73. 1883, 331–43. 1884, 208–12; 509–15. 1885, 308–14; 335–36. 1887, 135–42. 1888, 482–85. 1891, 278–83. 1893, 190–92; 223–34; 342–44. 1894, 513

"Tirayr kam Metz mardě," *AM,* 1885, 369–76; 417–24; 465–72. 1886, 41–48; 88–96. 1891, 359–61; 404–05.

"Imastasēr mankik mě." *AM,* 1893, 8–11; 74–77; 126–29; 232–37; 425–31; 529–33. 1894, 256–58; 490–93. 1897, 276–80; 393–96; 628–31; 722–24. 1898, 387–91; 949–52.

"Im yušagrerēs, Mankakan ōrer." *AM,* 1895, 22–24; 55–59; 89–94; 121–25; 151–57; 216–20; 250–54; 279–84; 343–49; 378–83; 411–15; 443–45; 475–78; 540–44; 569–72; 637–40; 699–702; 757–61. 1897, 65–69; 146–48; 253–56; 363–67; 437–40; 527–34; 691–94; 820–23. 1898, 275–80; 430–35; 595–600; 791–97; 872–76. 1899, 210–13; 371–73.

Other works

Hamaṙōt ěndhanur patmutʻiwn dprotsats hamar. Hin patmutʻiwn arewelean žołovrdots. Vol. 1 (Smyrna, 1875; Constantinople, 1884). Part 2 (Smyrna, 1877). Part 3 (Smyrna, 1878). Vol. 2 (N.p., n.d.; Smyrna, 1900). Vol. 3 (Smyrna, 1878).

Manr vēper u daser kʻałuatz manr tłots hamar. (Smyrna, [1876]).

Banali hayerēn šaradrutʻean. (Smyrna, 1878, 1884, 1887).

Chorrord ěntʻertsaran kam Gitelikʻ u partikʻ tłayots. (Smyrna, 1879, 1885, 1887, 1899; Constantinople, 1882, 1895).

Gitelikʻ u partikʻ tłayots. (Smyrna, 1879, 1885, 1887, 1887; Constantinople, 1882, 1895).

Nor ěntʻertsaran tłayots hamar. (Smyrna, 1879; Constantinople, [1885]).

Hamaṙōt patmutʻiwn hayots minchew mer ōrern. (Smyrna, 1887).

Aṙajin ěntʻertsaran. (Constantinople, 1889, 1892; Smyrna, 1900, 1902).

Aṙtnin tntesutʻiwn. (Constantinople, 1891).

Erkrord ěntʻertsaran. (Constantinople, 1893 [5th printing], 1897; Smyrna, 1900).

Errord ěntʻertsaran. (Smyrna, 1900 [7th printing]).

Criticism

Ačaṙyan, H. "Mattʻeos Mamuryan." *EJ,* 1959/8–9, 36–42.

Argos. "Mamureani derě ibr hraparakagir ew gragēt." *M,* 1900/2, 17–22.
Eremean, S. "Matt'ēos Mamurean ew iwr grakan yobeleanē." *B,* 57 (1899), 493–95.
———. "Matt'ēos Mamurean." *B,* 69 (1911), 359–67.
Gasparyan, G. "Mat'evos Mamuryani p'ilisop'ayakan hayatsk'nerě." *T,* 1959/1, 43–52.
Hakobyan, M. "Matt'eos Mamuryani anhayt tzatzkanuně." *PBH,* 1984/2, 52–60.
Ḥaṙatyan, A. "M. Mamuryani baroyagitakan hayatsk'nerě." *L,* 1975/7, 39–51.
Karinyan, A. "M. Mamuryaně mšakuyt'i patmut'yan masin." *T,* 1962/3, 19–36.
L. "Grakan korustner." *Murč,* 1901/4, 260–70.
Łazaryan, H. "M. Mamuryani hasarakakan-k'ałak'akan hayatsk'nerě 1860–70 t'vakannerin." *T,* 1957/3, 83–100.
———. "Matt'eos Mamuryani 'Sev leṙin mardě' vepi gałap'arakan bovandakut'yuně." *T,* 1960/9, 37–52.
———. *Matt'eos Mamuryan.* (Erevan, 1961).
"Matt'ēos Mamurean, ink'nuroyn gruatzk'ner, t'argmanut'iwnner." *A,* 1901, 180–81. (Includes bibliography).
Nalbandean-K'alant'ar, V. "Matt'ēos Mamurean orpēs k'ałak'akan groł." *HK,* 5 (1926–27/4), 130–38.
Orberean, Ṙ. "Mamureani verjin ōrerě." *M,* 1901/4, 57–59.
Sargsyan, S. "Matt'eos Mamuryani mardabanakan hayatsk'neri šurj." *L,* 1988/11, 24–33.
Sołomonyan, M. "Matt'eos Mamuryani hakakronakan hayatsk'neri dzevavorman himk'erě." *BEH,* 1989/2, 134–39.
Varpetean, Ł. "Mamureani keank'ēn." *M,* 1904/6, 81–83.
Yarut'iwnean, A. "Grakan dimastuerner, M. Mamurean." *M,* 1901/3, 33–35.
———. "Grakan dimastuerner. Matt'ēos Mamurean." *AM,* 1904, 124–29.

MANUĒL DPIR KOSTANDNUPOLSETSI (18th c.)

Manuēl also called himself Srmak'ēš, Kesarean, Karčik, and P'ok'r. His parents were from Kayseri, but he was born in Constantinople. Most of his writings, some of which are compilations, are polemical, written in defense of the dogmas and traditions of the Church of Armenia.

Texts

Tetrak or kochi gawazan krknazōr. (Constantinople, 1750).
Ergaran hakirč. (Constantinople, 1752).
Girk' or kochi lutzich tarakusanats. (Constantinople, 1755).
Tetrak or kochi aknots achats srti. (Constantinople, 1780).
Girk' or kochi akn lusatu. (Constantinople, 1782). (Turkish in Armenian characters).
Girk' or kochi himn stugut'ean. (Constantinople, 1783).

MANUĒL KIWMIWŠḤANATSI (1768–1843)

Born Step'anos in Gümüşhane, Turkey. Received his education in his birthplace and in Karin (Erzurum). Became a celibate priest in 1796. Engaged in teaching and held office in several Armenian communities in Eastern Europe, Eastern Armenia, and Crimea, where he died. His writings, some of which are still unpublished, deal mostly with Armenian affairs of his time.

Texts

Patmutʻiwn antsits antselots Sēwanay vanuts. (Vałaršapat, 1871). (History; first published in *A,* 1871).

Lutz armatoyn meroy. (Constantinople, 1841).

Andznakan patmutʻiwn Manuēl Kiwmiwšhanatsi vardapeti, Altʻuneani kam Šahinovi. In *Diwan hayots patmutʻean,* Vol. 12: *Manuēl Kiwmišhanetsi, masn I.,* G. Ałaneants (Tiflis, 1917). (Autobiography).

MANUĒLEAN, LEWON (1864–1919)

Born in Nerkʻin Agulis in Naḥijevan. Poet, playwright, and novelist. Received his elementary education at Verin Agulis, Naḥijewan, where Raffi was one of his teachers. Studied at the University of Moscow (1886–90) and taught at the Gēorgean seminary in Ējmiatzin, at the Nersisean school in Tiflis, and in Alexandrapol (later Leninakan, now Gyumri).

Collections

Ěntir erker. (Erevan, 1955).

Texts

Chalabineri aršawankʻě. (Tiflis, 1891). (Story).

Tigranuhi. (Tiflis, 1892). (Drama).

Ḥortakuatz keankʻ. (Tiflis, 1897–99). (Novel).

Banasteltzutʻiwnner ew poemaner. Book 1. (Baku, 1899). Book 2 ([Baku], 1907). (Verse).

Dōktōr Eruand Bošayean. (Baku, 1900). (Play).

Dēp i ver. (Petersburg, 1902). (Poem).

Nkarich Taščean. (Tiflis, 1903). (Play).

Ōtarutʻean mēj. (Tiflis, 1903).

Translations

GERMAN ANTHOLOGIES

AD, 37–38.

RUSSIAN ANTHOLOGIES

UDS, 71–75.

VAM, 96–98.

MANUĒLEAN, SURĒN (1906–1980)

Pen name: Siran Mihran.

Born in Słam, a village near Palu, Turkey. Survived the massacres and deportations of 1915, and in 1926 he found his way to New York, via the Middle East, the Balkans, and France.

Texts

Barak larer. ([Boston], 1946).(Essays).

Argawand akōsner: patmuatzkʻner. (Boston, 1949). (Stories).

Dgal mě šakʻar. (Jerusalem, 1965). (Stories and impressions of a visit to Soviet Armenia).

MANUKEAN, MARTIROS (1846–1922)

Born and educated in Nor Jułay (New Julfa, Isfahan). A merchant by profession and an *ašuł*. Lost his eyesight at the age of twenty-seven. It is believed that at some point he traveled to Calcutta.

Poetry

EPNA, 84–101.

Criticism

Eremean, A. *Parskahay noragoyn ašułner.* (Vienna, 1925), 75–101.

MANUŠEAN, MISAKʻ (1906–1944)

A native of Adıyaman, Turkey, Manušean escaped the fate of his parents, who were killed during the Armenian massacres and deportations of 1915. Spent a few years in an orphanage in Lebanon and settled in France in 1925. In Paris he published the periodicals *Jankʻ* (1930–31) and the weekly *Zangu* (1935–37), the former jointly with A. Sema (q.v.). A poet and a well-known leader in the French Resistance, Manušean was executed in Paris by the Nazis.

Texts

Banastełtzutʻiwnner. (Paris, 1946; Erevan, 1956, as *Im ergě*). (Verse).

Translations

French Anthologies

Gaucheron, J. *E,* 83–85.
FPA, 41.
LPA, 324–36.

Criticism

Chōpanean, A. "Erekʻ hay herosakan nahatakner (Gełam Atʻmačean, Misakʻ Manušean, Luiza Aslanean)." *ANA,* 12 (1946/1), 1–9.

MANVELYAN, MIKʻAYEL (1877–1944)

Born in Nerkʻin Agulis, Naḫijewan. Actor and writer of short stories and plays. Studied acting in Moscow (1903–05). Appeared in leading roles in Western, Russian, and Armenian plays staged by Armenian theater groups in Tiflis. Visited Constantinople (1909) with the celebrated Abelean-Armēnean theater troupe. From 1922 until the end of his life, he was employed by the Armenian State theater (later named after Gabriēl Sundukean) in Erevan.

Collections

Erkeri žołovatzu. (Tiflis, 1917).
Ěntir erker. (Moscow, 1936).
Patmvatzkʻner. (Erevan, 1945, 1954).
Ěntir erker. (Erevan, 1947).
Erker. (Erevan, 1955).
Erker. (Erevan, 1959).

Texts

Ēskʻizner. (Baku, 1903). (Prose).
Ēskʻizner. (St. Petersburg, 1905). (Prose).

Patmuatzkʻner. (Alexandrapol, 1906). (Stories).
Dramatikakan ētiwdner. Book 1. (Baku, 1909). (Prose).
Patmuatzkʻner. (Tiflis, 1912). (Stories).
Victus vos salutat. (Tiflis, 1912). (Verse).
Čakatagir. (Tiflis, 1913). (Story).
Spitak tzałikner. (Baku, 1913).
Varžuhin (patmuatzkʻ). (Tiflis, 1913). (Story).
Hēkʻiatʻ. (Tiflis, 1914). (Tale).
Hrabuḥ (drama). (Tiflis, 1916). (Play).
Haryur čipot (hin zinvori hušatetrits). (Łarakʻilisa [now Vanadzor], 1926). (Story).
Gortzadul. (Erevan, 1927). (Prose).
Žamankakits melodram. (Erevan, 1927). (Prose).
Sev kʻałakʻě. (Erevan, 1927). (Stories).
Mi glḥarki patmutʻyun. (Erevan, 1929). (Prose).
Ašnan čančer (patmvatzkʻner). (Erevan, 1931). (Stories).
Anapatě ktzałki. (Erevan, 1933). (Novelette).
Patkerner tsarakan banakits. (Erevan, 1934). (Prose).
Tokioyits Kioto (čaponakan hekʻiatʻ). (Erevan, 1938). (Japanese tale).
Zartʻonkʻ. (Erevan, 1939). (Novel).
Mankakan patmvatzkʻner. (Erevan, 1939). (Stories for children).
Tʻertʻikner im kyankʻits. (Erevan, 1950). (Reminiscences).
Tʻtʻenin. (Erevan, 1971).

Translations

German anthologies

AN, 170–76.

Russian anthologies

AASL, 73–77.
KHAN, 1, 87–91.

Criticism

Bagdasaryan, A. "Mikʻayel Manvelyani sovetakan šrjani stełtzagortzutʻyuně." *T,* 1956/1, 11–24.
———. *Zhizn i tvorshestvo Mikaela Manveliana.* (Erevan, 1954).
H. T. "Manuēlean, M. Ēskʻizner, Bakʻu [1903]." *Murč,* 1903/12, 170–72.

MARGAR, (1880–1944)

Pen name: Margar.

Born Margar Awetisean, in Nor Bayazēt (now Kamo, Armenia). A novelist and short story writer. Educated at the Nersisean school in Tiflis. Taught in Teheran, Baku, and Tiflis, where he spent the last years of his life.

Texts (stories and novels)

Eraḥtikʻ. (Baku, 1904).
Halatzankʻi tznundě. (Alexandrapol, 1905).
Hogewarkʻi tzitzałě. (Baku, 1906).
Gołě (zinuori yišatakaranits). (Tiflis, 1910).
Ḥikar imastun. Płndzē kʻałakʻi zroytsnerě. (Tiflis, 1911).
Vēpikner. (Tiflis, 1913).

Tasnamya t̕oṙnikner. (Tiflis, 1930).
Zoranotsum (patmvatzk̕ner). (Erevan, 1934).
Hrełen alik̕ner. Vol. 1. (Tiflis, 1934).
Meržum. (Tiflis, 1935).
Chalik. (Tiflis, 1936).

MARGARYAN, MARO (1915–1999)

Born in Šulaver (now Šahumyan, Georgia) and educated in local schools. Pursued her higher studies at the State University of Erevan, graduating in 1938. For many years she worked at the Committee for Cultural Relations with the Armenians Abroad.

Collections

Hatěntir. (Erevan, 1985).

Texts (verse)

Mtermut̕yun. (Erevan, 1940).
Banastełtzut̕yunner. (Erevan, 1945).
Mor dzayně. (Erevan, 1950).
P̕šateni. (Erevan, 1954).
Lirikakan lusabats. (Erevan, 1957).
Lirika. (Erevan, 1962).
Dznhalits heto. (Erevan, 1965).
Ltsvatz lṙut̕yun. (Erevan, 1972).
Ōreri ḥork̕its. (Erevan, 1975).
Banastełtzut̕yunner. (Erevan, 1978).
Nvirumner. (Erevan, 1982).
Banastełtzut̕yunner. (Erevan, 1984).
Siro erger. (Erevan, 1985).

Translations

English

Jacque, V. ["Little and eager the girl sped"]. *SL,* 1973/9, 130.
Kelikian, H. "My Rockridden Country." *Ararat,* Autumn, 1961, 39.
Rottenberg, D. ["The poppies laugh"]. *SL,* 1966/3, 141.

English anthologies

SAP, 30–32.

French

Galin, M. ["Dans la plaine infinie"], *OO*, 177 (Sept. 1973), 146.

French anthologies

Loriol, P. *E,* 92.
LPA, 352–55.

German

Leschnitzer, F. "Es lacht der Mohn." *Sowjet-Literatur,* 1966/3, 137.

Russian

Golos materi. Stikhi. (Moscow, 1952).
Gornaia doroga. [Stikhi]. (Moscow, 1962).
Iz ognia liubvi i pechali. (Moscow, 1989).

Lirika. (Moscow, 1960).
Netel'. (Erevan, 1983).
Razdum'e. [Stikhi]. (Erevan, 1956).
Stikhotvoreniia. (Moscow, 1955).

SPANISH

Alberti, R. y Maria Teresa Leon. "Rien las amapolas." *Literatura Sovietica,* 1966/3, 140.

Criticism

Armen, M. "Tʻur ḥoher tʻrutʻyan masin." *SG,* 1967/4, 126–34.
Arzumanyan, S. "Nurb ev ankełtz kʻnar." *SG,* 1958/4, 143–52.
———. "Šitak kardal banastełtzutʻyunĕ." *SG,* 1967/8, 117–22.
Parsamyan, A. "Tʻank karotner." *SG,* 1985/10, 140–42.

MAṘKʻ, HAYKANOYŠ (c1883–1966)

Born and educated in Constantinople. Writer, teacher, and journalist. She edited the periodicals *Tzałik* (1905–07) and *Hay kin* (1919–32). Most of her prose is still available only in periodicals.

Collections

Haykanoyš Maṙkʻi keankʻn u gortzĕ. (Istanbul, 1954).

Texts

Tzulutʻean paherēs. (Constantinople, 1921).

Criticism

Baluean, H. "Haykanoyš Maṙkʻ, ir grakan yisnameay yobeleanin aṙtʻiw." *Z* (amsatʻertʻ), 1 (1956/9), 1.
Haykanoyš Maṙkʻi keankʻn u gortzĕ. (Istanbul, 1954).

MARKOSEAN, ḤACHIK (1894–1977)

Pen name: M. Ḥachuni.
Markosean was born in Tłmadzor, a village near Tercan, Turkey, and educated in Marzuan (Merzifon, 1900–07). He then worked in Samsun (1907–13) and emigrated to the United States in 1913.

Texts

Topʻumner: kʻertʻuatzner ew ardzak ējer. (New York, 1938). (Verse and prose).
Ałberak: inkʻnatip kʻertʻuatzner ew tʻargmanutʻiwnner. (New York, 1960). (Poems and translations).
Ašnan berkʻ: ĕntir kʻertʻuatzner. (New York, 1972). (Poems).

MARTIROS ḤARASARTSI (16th c.?)

No biographical details are known about this author.

Texts (poems)

"Aysōr tōnemkʻ, dzez awetis." *Čṙakʻał,* 1859, 45–46. Also published in *MKH,* 428–30, and *KNZ,* 2, 49–52. (Both reprinted from *Čṙakʻał*).
"Aysōr ḥmenkʻ kʻałtsr ew yordor." *B,* 33 (1875), 106.

"Tał harsaneats ew uraḥutʻean ĕntir ew gełetsik," "Tał ew ōrhnutʻiwn uraḥutean," "Astuatz ōgnē mer knkʻahōrn." *KNZ,* 4, 17–23.
"Tał i tes sireleats ew heṙaworats." *TH,* 103–4. Also published in *KNZ,* 4, 24–26.
Sahakyan, H. "Martiros Ḥarasartsu tałerĕ." *BM,* 10 (1971), 315–55. (Introduction and the texts of 15 poems).

Anthologies

SUM, 1, 145–78.

MARTIROS ŁRIMETSI (d. 1683)

Also known as Kʻefetsi Tʻatʻar Martiros and Martiros Kafatsi. Born in Kafa, Crimea. Studied at the local Surb Nšan monastery, at Tokat, and at the feet of Astuatzatur Tarōnetsi, who later became patriarch of Jerusalem and ordained Martiros into celibate priesthood. Patriarch of Constantinople for one year (1659–60). Created bishop c1661 by Catholicos Yakob IV, Jułayetsi, of Ējmiatzin, just before his departure for Crimea as the primate of the Armenian community. Closely involved in the controversies of the time and particularly known for his long, bitter opposition to Ełiazar Ayntʻaptsi, who challenged the supremacy of the Mother See of Ējmiatzin. Patriarch of Jerusalem for two short and turbulent terms (1677–80, 1681–83). Died in Egypt on his way to Jerusalem from Constantinople. Eremia chēlēpi Kʻēōmiwrčean is believed to have briefly studied under Martiros, who, apart from his literary work, is also remembered as a scribe and a sponsor of scribes.

Works in periodicals and anthologies

"Govest surb Astuatzatznay vanatsn yAnkurioy, ogeal i Martiros vardapetē Łrimetswoy." *KNZ,* 4, 26–29.
Kʻiwrtean, Y. "Martiros Łrimtsi kam Kafatsii tałerĕ Tʻrakioy ew Pulkarioy hayots vrayōkʻ." *B,* 86 (1929), 283–87. 87 (1930), 114–17, 264–68. (5 poems).
"Martiros Łrimetsu tałerĕ." *Vēm,* 1934/5, 47–54; 6, 60–66. (9 poems).
Martirosyan, A. *Martiros Łrimetsi, usumnasirutʻyun ev bnagrer.* (Erevan, 1958).
Nawasard (Bucharest), 1923, by M. Poturean. (6 poems).
Oskean, H. "Karg ew tʻiw tʻagaworatsn hayots i Martiros vardapetē Łrimetswoy." *HA,* 79 (1965), 31–50. (Reprinted in *Chors hay tałasatsner ew aṇonts tałerĕ.* H. Oskean [Vienna, 1966], 191–210).
Poturean, M. *Martiros Łrimetsi ew ir kʻertʻuatznerĕ.* (Bucharest, 1924).
S, 1930, 350–51, 384–86. 1931, 146–47. 1932, 121–22, 252–54. 1941, 85–86, 126–27. (9 letters).
Šrjik (Siruni). "Mer hin tērtērnerĕ." *Azdarar,* 1929, 911–2. (2 poems by Martiros on priests).
"Yałags kʻałakʻin Amasiu." *KNZ,* 1, 38–41.

Translations (French)

"Liste rimée des souverains de la petite Arménie." *RHC,* 1, 681–87.

Criticism

Kʻiwrtean, Y. "Martiros Łrimetsii tałerun Kʻiwrtean hawakʻatzoyi ōrinakĕ." *B,* 118 (1960), 65–71.
Martirosyan, A. "Martiros Łrimetsu mi chapʻatzo anetzkʻi masin." *BM,* 4 (1958), 241–46.

———. *Martiros Łrimetsi, usumnasirutʻyun ev bnagrer.* (Erevan, 1958).
Oskean, H. *Chors hay tałasatsner ew anonts tałerě.* (Vienna, 1966), pp. 179–90.

MEHEAN, KARŌ (1898–1984)

Pen names: Karō Mehean, Sōseats Tłan.

Born Karō Łazarosean in Rodosto (Tekirdağ, Turkey) and educated in local schools. Survived the Armenian massacres and deportations of 1915 and resided in Bulgaria until World War II. After the establishment of the Communist regime in Bulgaria, he was arrested and exiled to the Soviet Union. Lived in Paris after his release from the Soviet Union in the mid-1950s. Wrote short stories and plays.

Texts

Mayramuti hoginer. I. Verjaloysi tak. (Sofia, 1926).
Veratznundi ōrerēn. (Sofia, 1927).
Imastutʻeants ułiov: hēkʻeatʻner ew awandutʻiwnner. Vol. 1 (Paris, 1959). Vols. 1 and 2 (Cairo, 1962; Beirut, 1973).
Akʻsorakani mě yušerēn. (Beirut, 1969).
Aletzuptʻ jurer. (Patmuatzkʻner ew awandutʻiwnner). (Beirut, 1973).
Orpēs eraz ankrkneli. (Beirut and Antʻilias, 1980). (Stories).

Criticism

Yobelean grakan ew krtʻakan 50ameay gortzunēutʻean. (Paris, 1975).

MELIKʻ-ŠAHNAZARYAN, KOSTANDIN (1856–1940)

Pen name: Tmblachi Ḥachan.

Born in Šuši, Artsaḥ (Karabagh), and educated in the local Armenian school and at the Gēorgean seminary in Ējmiatzin. Went to Montpellier, France, and Switzerland in the early 1880s to study agriculture and cheesemaking. After his return, he worked as an agriculturalist in Transcaucasia, and from 1919 until his death, in Armenia. He wrote extensively on agriculture, but listed below are his short prose writings (essays and short stories) written in a satirical vein, in the Armenian dialect of Artsaḥ.

Texts

Łělětsē knanots pěně-pʻešakě. (Tiflis, 1882).
Šōšvay łalin ḥērn u šaṙě. (Tiflis, 1887).
Pʻšrankʻ. (Šuši, 1888).
Zuṙna-Tmbla. 3 vols. (Baku, 1900–01).
Zuṙna-Tmbla. 3 vols. (Vałaršapat, 1907–08).
Pʻnjik. (Baku, 1907).

Criticism

Kostandin Karapeti Melikʻ-Šahnazaryan (grakan 50–amya ev gyułatntesakan 40–amya gortzuneutʻyuně). (Erevan, 1924).

MELIKʻ-ŠAHNAZARYANTS, SOŁOMON (1862–1942)

Born in Šuši, Artsaḥ (Karabagh). A teacher by profession. Educated in his birthplace and at the Gēorgean seminary in Ējmiatzin. His prose writings deal with life in the countryside.

Texts

Hay giwłatsu sew ōrě. (Tiflis, 1890).
Gortzakatar Martirosě. (Tiflis, 1913).

MELKʻO, ŠAMCHI (18th–19th c.)

Pen name: Šamchi Melkʻo.

Born Melkʻo Gulkʻaneants. An *ašuł*. Lived in Georgia (possibly Tiflis) in the second half of the 18th century and the first half of the 19th century. He was a wax-chandler by profession and seems to have had close connections with the Georgian court. Wrote in Armenian, Georgian, and in what is now referred to as Azeri Turkish.

Poetry

Melikʻsetʻ-Bek, L. *Šamchi-Melkʻon ev nra hayeren ḥałerě.* (Erevan, 1958). *MKH,* 564–65.
Sahakyan, H. "Šamchi Melkʻoyi mi banastełtzutʻyuně." *T,* 1957/12, 85–92. *SHA,* 271–306.
Tēr Ałekʻsandrean, G. *Tʻiflisetsots mtawor keankʻě.* Vol. 1, (Tiflis, 1886), 36–37, 40–43.
THG, 39–42.

Criticism

Asatur, G. "Šamchi-Melkʻo." *Patmutʻyan ev grakanutʻyan instituti tełekagir.* (Erevan, 1938). (Unverified).
Hovh[annisyan], G. "Ašuł-banastełtz Šamchi-Melkʻo." *Proletar* (Tiflis), 10 March, 1936.
Melikʻsetʻ-Bek, L. *Šamchi-Melkʻon ev nra hayeren ḥałerě.* (Erevan, 1958).

METZARENTS, MISAKʻ (1886–1908)

Pen names: Misakʻ Metzarents, Šawasp Tziatzan.

Born Misakʻ Metzaturean in the village of Benkean (or Binkean) near Akn (Eğin, now Kemaliye, Turkey). Poet. Attended the local Armenian school, an Armenian school in Sebastea (Sivas, 1894–96), and the Anatolia College in Marsovan (1896–1901). Resumed his studies when he and his parents settled in Constantinople in 1902, but he was unable to finish the Kedronakan school, due to his rapidly worsening consumption, which soon claimed his life.

Collections

Tziatzan ew Nor tałer. (Constantinople, 1924).
Oski arišin tak. (Ardzak erkeru hawakʻatzoy). (Constantinople, 1934).
Tziatzan, Nor tałer ew Kʻertʻuatzner. (Beirut, 1954).
Alazan, V., and Norents, V. *Erkeri žołovatzu.* (Erevan, 1956).
Čanašean, M. *Banastełtzutʻiwnner: Tziatzan, Nor tałer.* (Venice, 1959).
———. *Kʻertʻuatzner, babaḥumner, ardzak ējer, inkʻnadatutʻean pʻordz mě.* (Venice, 1960).
Akʻasianeru šukʻin tak. (Erevan, 1969).
Irikvan dzayner. (Erevan, 1974).
Šaruryan, A. *Erkeri liakatar žołovatzu.* (Erevan, 1981).
Ambołjakan erker. (Antʻilias, 1986).
Šaruryan, A. *Erker.* (Erevan, 1986).

Texts

Nor tałer. (Constantinople, 1907).
Tziatzan. (Constantinople, 1907).

Translations

English

Kelikian, H. "Unnamed of Nameless." *Ararat,* Autumn, 1961, 42–43.

French

Marcel, L. A. "Astuatzamōr/A la Vierge," "Jrtukʻ/L'Arrosage." *AND,* 10 (n.d.) 20–25.

French anthologies

APA, 225–26.
LPA, 240–43.
PAM, 190–96.

German anthologies

ALG, 133–34.

Italian anthologies

DLA, 11–13.
LPAM, 191–204.

Russian anthologies

AAP, 523–26.
BPA, 471–72.
IZAP, 21–34.
Zimniaia noch'. (Erevan, 1987).

Spanish anthologies

APAS, 253–55.

Criticism

Armēn, E. "Grakan nor hosankʻi pʻordz mě." *M,* 1907/47, 837–42.
———. "Čšmartutʻean varagoyrě." *AM,* 1908, 337–41.
———. " 'Kʻapōtʻēn'nerě." *M,* 1908/14–15, 273–82.
Ašrafean, Y. "Metzarentsi grakan naḥakʻaylerě." *B,* 122 (1964), 133–47, 226–33.
Azatean, Tʻ. *Misakʻ Metzarents: ir keankʻě.* (Constantinople, 1922).
Baluean, H. "Misakʻ Metzarents." *Vēm,* 2 (1934/2), 21–40.
Chēōkiwrean, T. "Tziatzan – Misakʻ Metzarentsi." *M,* 1907/28–29, 581–83.
Fēnērčean, G. "Misakʻ Metzarents." *ANA,* 1931/3–4, 154–58.
Gazančean, V. "Hayeatskʻner banastełtzutʻean vray ew Metzarentsi 'Tziatzaně'." *AM,* 1907, 697–703.
Hyusyan, M. "Misakʻ Metzarents." *SG,* 1966/2, 111–17.
Jrbašyan, Ēd. *Misakʻ Metzarents.* (Erevan, 1958, 1977 [expanded edition]).
Kirakosyan, V. "Misakʻ Metzarents." *EJ,* 1986/6, 42–47.
Łanalanyan, H. *Misakʻ Metzarents.* (Erevan, 1958).
Metzaturyan, Z. "Hišołutʻyunner Misakʻ Metzarentsi mankakan kyankʻēn." *SG,* 1978/3, 133–39.
"Misakʻ Metzarents." *A,* 1908, 628–31.
"Misakʻ Metzarentsi mahuan yissnameaki [sic] tōnakatarutʻiwně Pʻarizi mēj." *Z* (amsatʻertʻ), 3 (1959/8–10), 12–13.
Mnatsakanyan, L. "Metzarentsě žamanaki poeziayi kʻnnadat." *BEH,* 1986/2, 129–33).

Mrmĕrean, Y. "Nor tałeru aṙtʻiw." *AM,* 1907, 1267.
Mułnetsyan, Š. "Misakʻ Metzarentsi gełarvestakan patkerneri mi kʻani aṙandznahatkutʻyunnerĕ." *PBH,* 1980/1, 166–79.
Ōšakan, Y. "Misakʻ Metzarents." *HK,* 2 (1923–24/7), 49–65; 8, 43–57.
Oskerichean, V. "Anhetatsołin etewēn, Misakʻ Metzarents." *AM,* 1908, 691–93.
Parsamean, M. "Misakʻ Metzarents." *HK,* 30 (1952/10), 63–76.
Pʻaylak. "Kanḥahas Zatik." *M,* 1908/20, 424–26.
Ṙštuni, H. "Simvolizmĕ ev Misakʻ Metzarentsi arvestĕ." *PBH,* 1984/1, 67–79.
———. *Misakʻ Metzarents.* (Erevan, 1986).
———. "Misakʻ Metzarents." *PBH,* 1986/2, 3–16.
Šahbazyan, P. "Hayastanyayts ekełetsin ev Misakʻ Metzarentsi grakan žaṙangutʻyunĕ." *EJ,* 1967/7, 45–52.
Šaruryan, A. "Erku pʻast Misakʻ Metzarentsi masin." *L,* 1975/8, 83–84.
———. "Misakʻ Metzarentsi 'Tziatzan' žołovatzui stełtzagortzakan patmutʻyunits." *PBH,* 1976/3, 89–94.
———. Misakʻ Metzarentsĕ ev žamanaki grakan kʻnndatutʻyunĕ." *BEH,* 1979/1, 21–37.
———. "Misakʻ Metzarentsi usumnaṙutʻyunĕ." *PBH,* 1979/2, 102–12.
———. *Misakʻ Metzarents.* (Erevan, 1983).
———. *Misakʻ Metzarentsĕ ev Daniel Varužanĕ žamanakakitsneri hušerum.* (Erevan, 1986).
Siruni, Y. "Gitzer Misakʻ Metzarentsi keankʻēn." *HK,* 1 (1922–23/10), 57–68.
Surenyan, K. "Inch arbetsutʻyamb." *EJ,* 1990/8–9, 57–63.
Tʻutʻunjyan, H. "Misakʻ Metzarentsi banastełtzakan ĕmbṙnman mi aṙandznahatkutʻyun." *T,* 1959/3, 43–48.
Yarutʻiwnean, A. "Grakan kʻronik: nor banastełtz mĕ." *AM,* 1907, 672–78.
Yovhannēsean, A. "Ṙ. Sewaki kartzikʻnerĕ Metzarentsi masin." *HK,* 17 (1938–39/9), 110–13.

MḤITʻAR SEBASTATSI (1676–1749)

Born in Sebastea (Sivas), christened Manuk. As a monk, he founded the Mekhitarist Congregation (*Mḥitʻarean miabanutʻiwn*) at San Lazzaro, Venice. At the age of fifteen, he entered the monastery of Surb Nšan in his native town, embarking on the arduous life of a celibate priest. Traveled widely and preached extensively both before and after converting to Catholicism in 1695. In 1703, he launched his religious order in Constantinople, but he sought refuge in Methone to escape the increasing intolerance of the Armenian Patriarchate of Constantinople and the Ottoman authorities. On the eve of the Ottoman attack on Morea in 1715, he fled to Venice with his disciples. The Senate of Venice in 1717 responded favorably to Mḥitʻar's request, and the islet of San Lazzaro was offered to his order. Choosing the Benedictine rules for his congregation, Mḥitʻar taught and organized the brotherhood on solid foundations. By the time he died, his disciples had attained noteworthy cultural accomplishments.

Texts

Ḥokumn varuts. (Constantinople, 1705 [published anonymously]; Venice 1753, 1810).

Lutzmunkʻ džuarimatsits ew tarakusanats banits Alpertin. (Venice, 1716). (Published as a supplement to *Hamaṙōtutʻiwn astuatzabanutʻean,* by Albert Metzn, Venice, 1715).
Krtʻutʻiwn ałōtʻits. (Venice, 1718, 1772).
Ricorso fatto nell'anno MDCC-XVIII. (Rome, 1718).
Aybbenaran ew girkʻ Kʻristonēakani vardapetutʻean. (Venice, 1725).
Duṙn kʻerakanutʻean ašḫarhabaṙ lezuin hayots, šaradretseal tačkakanaw lezuaw . . . (Venice, 1727). (Grammar of Modern Armenian in Turkish).
Girkʻ Kʻristonēakani vardapetutʻean šaradretseal ašḫarhabaṙiw lezuaw ěnd orum ew ergkʻ tałits. (Venice, 1727, 1732, 1771 [includes an additional section "ałōtʻkʻner."]).
Hartsumn ew patasḫani zkʻerakanutʻenē ew zmasants norin. (Venice, 1730, 1759).
Kʻerakanutʻiwn grabaṙi lezui haykazean seṙi. (Venice, 1730). (Grammar of Classical Armenian).
Tōmar karčaṙōt. (Venice, 1733, 1747, 1748, 1771, 1786, 1789, 1807).
Meknutʻiwn Grots Žołovołin. (Venice, 1736).
Kʻristonēakan vardapetutʻiwn or i gortz atzi i mekneln zpatkers i žamanaki ḫałaloy. (Venice, 1737, 1775).
Meknutʻiwn srboy Awetarani teaṙn meroy Yisusi Kʻristosi or ěst Mattʻēosi. (Venice, 1737).
Baṙgirkʻ haykazean lezui. 2 vols. (Venice, 1749, 1769). (Dictionary).
Dzayn Kʻristosi ew hawatatseal hogwoyn. (Venice, 1753, 1810).
Ałōtʻkʻ i pēts iwrots ašakertats. (Venice, 1832).
"Ančaṙ anhas stełtzoł goyutʻeants bnawits." *MKH,* 105.
Patčaṙkʻ orkʻ aṙberin ěnddēm notsin orkʻ asen tʻē och erbēkʻ part ē gnal ułłapʻaṙats i žamn Hayots. (Smyrna, 1879).
Hatkʻ i banits ew i grots Mḫitʻaray Abbahōr. (Venice, 1900).
Namakani. 2 vols. (Venice, 1961, 1962). (Letters).
Mtatzutʻiwnkʻ i veray banits Pʻrkchin ew i niwtʻ krtʻutʻean. (Venice, 1969).
"Namak aṙ tēr Isahak vrd. aṙajnord Ērzrumi." *B,* 135 (1977), 33–36.
"Kʻerakanutʻiwn ašḫarhabar lezuin hayots." *B,* 137 (1979), 194–261.

Translations (Italian)

Frasson, G. *Sei inni sacri.* (Venice, 1977).

Criticism

Agonts, S. *Patmutʻiwn kenats ew varuts teaṙn Mḫitʻaray Sebastatswoy rabunapeti ew abbayi.* (Venice, 1810).
Akinean, N. "Mḫitʻar Sebastatsi, keankʻn ew gortzuneutʻiwně." *HA,* 63 (1949) 371–434. (Reprinted separately, Vienna, 1950. [Festschrift]).
———. "Mḫitʻar Abbayi Mattʻēi Awetaranin meknutʻiwně." *B,* 107 (July–December 1949), 289–95. (A special issue).
Ałačanean, G. P. "Mḫitʻar Abbahayr ew Ḫachatur Vardapet." *B,* 107 (July–December 1949), 30–45. (In Armenian and French; a special issue).
Amaduni, G. "Mekhitar le réformateur du monachisme arménien." *B,* 107 (July–December 1949), 175–221. (A special issue).
Bardakjian, K. *The Mekhitarist Contributions to Armenian Culture and Scholarship.* (Cambridge, MA, 1976).
Čemčemean, S. "Mḫitʻar Abbahōr hratarakchakan aṙakʻelutʻean goharnerě." *B,* 135 (1977), 37–96.

———. "Mhitʻar Abbahōr hratarakchakan arakʻelutʻiwnĕ." *B,* 135 (1977), 437–81. 137 (1979), 5–180. (Reprinted separately, Venice 1980).
———. "Yovhannēs Patkerahan. Mhitʻar Abbahayr ev Yovhannēs Patkerahan." *B,* 1986/1–4, 272–81.
Chantʻayean, Y. "Mhitʻar Abbahayr ułewor Venetikēn Hrom." *B,* 135 (1977), 112–38.
Fērhatʻean, B. *Mhitʻar Metz Sebastatsin.* (Beirut, 1949).
Fēyti, F. "Andradardzutʻiwnner Mhitʻar Abbahōr Bararanin šurj." *B,* (107, July–December 1949), 308–12. (A special issue).
Fokolean, Ł. "Mhitar Abbahayr ew Transilvanioy Mhitʻarean arakʻelutʻean arajin šrjanĕ." *B,* 135 (1977), 139–65.
Fokolean, Ł. "Mhitar Abbahayr ew Transilvanioy Mhitʻarean arakʻelutʻean erkrord šrjanĕ (1723–1736)." *B,* 1977/1–2, 139–65. 1985/3–4, 267–93. 1986/1–4, 59–91.
Gełuni nuiruatz eranašnorh Mhitʻar Abbahōr mahuan B. daradardzin, 1749–1949. (Venice, 1950). (Keghouni, Armenian Illustrated Review Dedicated to the Bicentenary of the Death of the Ven. Abbot Mekhitar).
Hamelean, P. "Mhitʻar Abbahōr 'Yałags matʻematʻikʻayi' dasagirkʻĕ ew anor nšanakutʻiwnĕ." *B,* 107 (July–December 1949), 222–29. (A special issue).
Hofmann, G. "Investigationes ad Vitam Servi Dei Mechitar spectantes." *B,* 107 (July–December 1949), 159–74. (A special issue).
Inglisian, V. *Der Diener Gottes Mechitar von Sebaste, Stifter der Mechitaristen und Kulturapostel des armenischen Volkes.* (Vienna, 1929).
———., et al. *Mhitʻar Sebastatsi.* (Vienna, 1949).
Kasangian, A. "Mechitar Architetto del proprio Monastero." *B,* 107 (July–December 1949), 399–421. (A special issue).
Kehiayan, N. "Brevis Dissertatio Abbatis Mechitar de SS.ma Communione Eucharistica." *B,* 107 (July–December 1949), 361–85. (A special issue. Armenian text with Latin translation).
Kʻiparean, K. "Dastiaraki dimagitzĕ Mhitʻar Abbahōr mēj." *B,* 107 (July–December 1949), 230–44. (A special issue).
Matteucci, G. "Mons. Pier Battista Mauri e il Ven. Abate Mechitar (1720–1730)." *B,* 107 (July–December 1949), 113–46. (A special issue).
Mhitʻar, Yušardzan lusanorog Mhitʻar Abbayi mahuan erkrord daradardzin (1749–1949), batsarik "Bazmavēp"i, Yulis-Dektember, 1949. (Mekhitar, numéro spécial de la Revue arménienne Pazmaveb publié à l'occasion des Célébrations Commémoratives du Deuxième Centenaire de la mort du Vén. Abbé Mekhitar (1749–1949). (Venice, 1950). (Some of the articles in this special issue are listed separately in this section).
Mhitʻarean, G. "Mhitʻar ew ir npastĕ hay mšakoytʻin." *HK,* 28 (1950/7), 37–43.
Muyldermans, J. "Mechithar de Sébaste et les Méchitharistes." *LM,* 43 (1930), 117–32.
Nazaryan, Š. "Mhitʻar Sebastatsin ev 18—rd dari grakan šaržman mi kʻani hartser." *SG,* 1976/8, 111–18.
Nourikhan, M. *Le serviteur de Dieu abbé Mekhitar de Sebaste.* (Venice, 1922).
Połosyan, P. "Mhitʻar Sebastatsin ibrev čartasan ev mankavarž." *BEH,* 1983/2, 207–12.
Raes, A. "Una risposta di Mechitar a Quesiti Liturgici." *B,* 107 (July–December 1949), 356–60. (A special issue).

Šahbazyan, P. "Mḥit'ar Sebastatsi." *EJ,* 1977/9–10, 70–76.
Sek'ula, Aw. "Mḥit'ar Abbahōr S. Grk'i hratarakut'ean aržēk'ĕ." *B,* 107 (July–December 1949), 296–307. (A special issue).
T'ahmizyan, N. "Mḥit'ar Sebastatsin ew veranorogut'ean šaržumĕ hay hogewor ergaruestum." *B,* 135 (1977), 205–14.
T'aščean, M. *Hamaṙōt kensagrut'iwn Mḥit'ar Abbahōr.* (Venice, 1967).
Tēr-Nersēsean, N. "Mḥit'ar Abbahayr himnadir hay astuatzabanakan veratznundin." *B,* 107 (July–December 1949), 245–88. (A special issue).
———. "Mḥit'ari npastĕ ašḥarhabari kazmut'ean." *B,* 135 (1977), 482–542. 136 (1978), 302–27. 137 (1979), 183–261 (includes introduction and text of Mḥit'ar's "K'erakanut'iwn Ašḥarhabar lezuin hayots," 195–261). 1981/1–2, 95–128.
———. "Mḥit'ari loysĕ." *B,* 135 (1977), 13–32.
T'ērzean, M. "Mḥit'ar Abbahayr ew Abraham Artziwean." *B,* 107 (July–December 1949), 147–58. (A special issue).
Tisserant, E. "Un défenseur de Mekhitar à Rome, Khatchatour Vartapet Arakelean. *B,* 107 (July–December 1949), 19–29. (A special issue).
T'orosean, Y. *Vark' Mḥit'aray Abbayi Sebastatswoy.* (Venice, 1901).
Vita del servo di Dio Mechitar. (N.p., n.d.).
Willebrands, J. "Mechitar e l'Unione dei Cristiani." *B,* 135 (1977), 395–436. (In Armenian and Italian).

MIK'AYĒLEAN, P'AYLAK (1905–1936)

A native of Erzinjan, Turkey. Poet and short story writer. His parents perished during the Armenian massacres of 1915, and he was adopted by a Turkish family. After 1918, he found shelter in orphanages in Constantinople and Greece. Spent the last years of his short life in France.

Texts

Ewa (ardzakurdi batsikner). (Paris, 1930; Beirut, 1956).
Arew, arew . . . (Paris, 1933). (Novel).
Hetk'er srti vra. (Erevan, 1963).

MIK'AYELYAN, KAREN (1883–1942)

A native of Verin Agulis, a village in Naḥijewan. Novelist, short story writer, and translator. Attended the Nersisean school in Tiflis, sat in on courses at the University of Moscow, and studied philosophy at Jena, Germany. In the years 1925–27, he visited Europe and the United States to organize assistance for Soviet Armenia as a member of the Armenian Red Cross and the Committee for Relief for Armenia (HŌK = Hayastani ōgnut'ean komitē, 1921–37). His writings focus on social issues and the Armenian Dispersion.

Collections

Ketstsen hałt'vatznerĕ. (Erevan, 1961).

Texts (prose)

Zrkank'i yoyzer (patmuatzk'neri ew patkerneri žołovatzu). Vol. 1. (Tiflis, 1907).
Dzmran ereko (erkeri žołovatzu). Vol. 2. (Moscow, 1912).
Anmahakan kaytz (p'oḥadrut'yun). (Moscow, 1924).

Gyułakan heṙaḥos. (Paris, 1926). (Drama).
Majestic. Amerikyan karč patmvatzkʻner. (Moscow, 1928).
Guyneri kṙivě. Book 4. (Moscow, 1929).

Other works

Hay žołovrdakan harstutʻyunnern artasahmanum. (Moscow, 1928).

Translations (Russian)

Ter-Martirosian, A., et al. *Novelly.* (Moscow and Leningrad, 1930).
Otdalennye rasskazy. (Moscow, 1936). (Stories).

MINAS AMDETSI (c1630–1704)

Born in Diyarbakır, Turkey. Took the vows of celibacy in 1655, and in 1666 he was created bishop in Jerusalem by his close collaborator, Ełiazar Ayntʻaptsi. Copied some manuscripts, such as Samuēl Anetsi's chroncile, Mḥitʻar Gōš's *Datastanagirkʻ,* and published, for the first time, Grigor Narekatsi's *Book of Lamentations.* From 1698 to 1702 he was the patriarch of Jerusalem. Died in office.

Texts

Azgabanutʻiwn tʻagaworatsn hayots yordwots yordis, hamaṙōteal i Movsisē Ḥorenatswoy. (Constantinople, 1784). (Genealogy of Armenian kings; 2d edition published as *Azgabanutʻiwn hayots,* Vałaršapat, 1870).
"I Markos vardapets ē asatseal govest bani i Minasē." *AMH,* 6, 123–44.
"Minasay Amdetswoy Tʻułtʻ ōrhnutʻean aṙ mayrakʻałakʻatsisn Uṙhayi." *AMH,* 6, 145–55.
"Yakob katʻułikosin tzaṙay Minas." *AMH,* 6, 118–22.

Criticism

Ačaṙean, H. "Hayerēn nor baṙer Minas Hamdetsowy mēj." *B,* 75 (1917), 314–16.
Akinean, N. "Minas Amdetsi, patriarkʻ hayots Erusałēmi." *AMH,* 6, 91–155.
Amatuni, K. "Minas vardapet Amdetsi, patriarkʻ Erusałēmi, 1630–1704 noyemb. 24." *HA,* 1983, 27–82.
Gēorgean, G. "Čštumner Minas Amtʻetsii masin." *B,* 124 (1966), 193–97.

MINAS, ČĒRĒAN ŌŁLU (1730–1813)

A native of Ḥarberd (Harput, Turkey). A blind, itinerant *ašuł* who traveled throughout Armenia. Died while on a visit to Constantinople.

Poetry

SHA, 336–50.

Criticism

Azatean, Tʻ. "Hay ašułner ew žołovrdakan ergichner." *Astłaberd,* 1951/2, May, 41–45. (Unverified).

MINAS, LUTʻFI (1892–1957)

A native of the village of Kʻēsrik near Ḥarberd (Harput, Turkey), the poet Minas emigrated to Boston, Massachusetts, in 1912. He was a graduate of Brown University.

Texts (verse)

Aygerg. (Boston, 1918).
Garun. (Boston, 1935).
Arpiakan. (Boston, 1947).
Pšruatz bažak. (Los Angeles, 1953).

Criticism

"Mahagrutiwn–Lutfi Minas." *Z* (amsatert‘), 2 (1958/11–12), 13.

MINAS TOḤATETSI (c1510–?)

Born in Tokat, Turkey. Minas emigrated to Poland in the 1540s, where he was employed as a secretary at the Armenian Cathedral in Lvov.

Texts (poems)

"Tał siroy" or "Tał gełetsik i žam uraḥut‘ean erku lezuē." *Girk‘ dprutean ew Tałaran* (Constantinople, 1714), 209–11. Also published under the title "Tał karōtov aṙ surb Lusaworich" in *Grk‘uks or kochi tałaran* (Constantinople, 1740), 310–12.

"Ołb i veray Olaḥats erkrin hayerun . . ." *Nšḥark‘ matenagrut‘ean hayots,* K‘. Patkanean, (Petersburg, 1884), 53–58. Also published in *M,* 3832 (1886), 1090–91; 3834, 28–29; 3835, 43–44; 3836, 62–63; 3837, 76–78. Also in *HA,* 2 (1888), 37–40, 62–63. Critical edition by N. Akinean published in *AHPT,* 85–102.

"Govasank‘i Grigor vardapetn." *AM,* 1885, 123. Also published in *AHPT,* 111–12.

"Tał ew govasank‘ herisi." *AM,* 1886, 18–19. Also published in *S,* 1874, 132–35; *KNZ,* 1, 50–56; *HA,* 35 (1921), 159–62. Critical edition published in *AHPT,* 102–11.

"Tułt‘ hayots Lovay aṙ Mik‘ayēl kat‘ołikos Ējmiatzni." *Kamenits, taregirk‘ hayots Lehastani ew Ṙumenioy,* Ł. Ališan, (Venice, 1896), 228–31. (Attribution uncertain).

"Tał i veray ĕndunaynut‘ean ašḥarhi" or "Tał i veray mahuan" ("Tesēk‘ duk‘ zarmatsk‘ bazum . . ."). *AHPT,* 113–14. (Attribution uncertain).

Works in anthologies

SUM, 1, 426–63.

Translations

German

Dan, D. *Die Verfolgung der Armenier in der Moldau vom Jahre 1551, beschrieben vom Diakon Minas aus Tocat.* (Czernowitz, [1894]).

Rumanian

Buiucliu, G. *Cânt de Jâlire asupra Armenilor din tara Vlahilor de diaconul Minas Tokatti.* (Bucharest, 1895). (Traducere din limba armean, cu o introducere de Grigore M Buiucliu).

Criticism

Akinean, N. "Minas dpir T‘oḥat‘etsi." *Hing panduḥt tałasatsner* (Vienna, 1921), 57–114. (Previously published in *HA*).

Gazančean, Y. "Minas sarkawag T‘oḥat‘etsi." *Iris* (Eudochia), 1912, 85–86.

Pĕyĕk‘lean, G. "Minas T‘oḥat‘etswoy Ołb i veray hayots Ašḥarhin Ulaḥats." *HA,* 9 (1895), 97–103, 131–37. (An Armenian translation of the same author's article listed under Rumanian translations above).

MINASEAN, SEPUH (1825–1887)

Born in Constantinople. Playwright. Educated at the Murat-Rapʻayēlean school (1838–41) in Venice. Worked for the imperial Ottoman mint, except for the years 1863–68, which he spent in Paris as secretary to the Ottoman ambassador to France.

Texts

Helēnē. (Venice, 1920).
Aršak Erkrord. (Venice, 1921).

Criticism

Sargisean, B. *Sepuh Minasean ew ir grakan erkasirutʻiwnnerě.* (Venice, 1904).

MIRAKʻYAN, VAHAN (1866–1942)

Born in Šulaver, a village in Georgia. Poet; educated at the Surb Astuatzatzin monastery in Sanahin and in the town of Gori (Georgia). Taught in various parts of Eastern Armenia, the Caucasus, and Erevan (from 1924 on). Also wrote plays, most of them unpublished, and stories for children. His fame rests principally on his popular long poem "Lalvari orsě," about village life. Died in Tbilisi and buried in Erevan.

Texts

Aṙants lareri. (Tiflis, 1897). (Verse).
Laluari orsě. (Tiflis, 1901; Erevan, 1929, 1935, 1936, 1948, 1963, 1967). (Poem).
Manuši harsanikʻě. (Erevan, 1927). (Play).
Nor gyułi šemkʻin. (Erevan, 1927). (Verse).
Ḥozaratzi kině. (Erevan, 1928). (Play).
Sev katʻ. (Erevan, 1938).

Translations (Russian)

Adamian, N. *Okhota na Lalvare.* (Erevan, 1942).

Criticism

Balasanean, G. "Vahan Mirakʻean ew nra 'Laluari orsě.' *Banasēr,* 5 (1903), 295–304.
Batikyan, L. "Grołě ev žołovrdakan banaḥyusutʻyuně." *SG,* 1964/5, 150–53. (On "Lalvari orsě").
———. " 'Lalvari orsi' stełtzagortzakan patmutʻyunits." *T,* 1963/5, 55–68.
———. *Vaan Mirakian.* (Erevan, 1964). (Russian).
———. *Vahan Mirakʻyan.* (Erevan, 1968).
———. "Vahan Mirakʻyani antip ējerě." *PBH,* 1963/2, 254–57.
Chobanyan, S. "Ējer Vahan Mirakʻyani kyankʻits." *L,* 1966/10, 51–64.
———. "Vahan Mirakʻyan." *SG,* 1967/4, 143–45.
Eremean, A. "Banastełtz Vahan Mirakʻean." *ANA,* 1 (1930/6), 66–69.

MISKIN-BURJI, (1810–1847)

This *ašuł* was a native of old Naḥijewan, but he spent most of his life in Gandzak (Elizavetpol, Kirovabad, now Ganja, Azerbaijan).

Poetry

MKH, 211–12; 396–97; 448–49; 466–67.
THG, 86–91.

MNDZURI, YAKOB (1886–1978)

Pen name: Yakob Mndzuri.

Born Yakob Tēmirčean in the village of Armtan (Armudan, west of Erzinjan), Turkey. Spent the years 1897–1907 in Constantinople, where he attended an Armenian school and, briefly, Robert College. Returned to his birthplace (1907–14) but settled in Constantinople for good on the eve of World War I.

Collections

Nadryan, S. *Erker.* (Erevan, 1986).

Texts (stories)

Kapoyt loys. (Istanbul, 1958; Erevan, 1968).
Armtan. (Istanbul, 1966).
Kṙunk, usti kugas [?] (Istanbul, 1974).
Aznavuryan, G. "Antip namakner Hakob Mndzuruts." *BEH,* 1983/1, 107–29.

Translations (Russian anthologies)

KNS, 121–140.

Criticism

Baluean, H. "Erekʻ yobeleanner–Yakob Mndzuri." *Z* (amsatʻertʻ), 3 (1959/8–10), 15.

Galfayan, H. "Arevmtahay gyułagrutʻyunĕ ev Hakob Mndzurin." *SG,* 1980/9, 133–40.

Sevan, G. *Hakob Mndzuri.* (Erevan, 1981).

MURATSAN, (1854–1908)

Pen name: Muratsan.

Born Grigor Tēr-Yovhannēsean in Šuši, Artsaḥ (Karabagh). Attended local schools. Taught for two years in his birthplace, toured his native province and the region of Siwnikʻ, and settled permanently in Tiflis in 1878. Employed as an accountant, Muratsan wrote his plays, short stories, novelettes, and novels at his spare time. Although initially acclaimed, Muratsan received much wider recognition after his death.

Collections

Muratsani erkasirutʻiwnnerĕ. 2 vols. (Tiflis, 1904, 1910).
Ĕntir erker. 4 vols. (Erevan, 1936–40).
Erker. (Erevan, 1980).
Erker erku grkʻov. (Erevan, 1970–72).
Erkeri žołovatzu. 5 vols. (Erevan, 1951–54).
Erkeri žołovatzu. 7 vols. (Erevan, 1961–65).
Erkeri žołovatzu. 3 vols. (Erevan, 1975–76).

Texts

Ṙuzan kam Hayrenasēr ōriord. (Tiflis, 1882; Erevan, 1944 [2d ed.]). (Drama).

Hay bołokʻakani ĕntanikʻĕ. (Tiflis, 1883). (Novelette).

Noyi agṙawĕ. (Tiflis, 1889; Erevan, 1933, 1947 [published with *Aṙakʻyalĕ,* see below]). (Novelette).

Gēorg Marzpetuni. (Tiflis, 1912; Cairo, 1940; Boston, 1952; Erevan, 1957, 1960, 1977, 1982, 1988). (Novel).

Patmvatzkʻner. (Erevan, 1939). (Stories).
Andrēas Erēts. (Cairo, 1941). (Novel).
Aṙakʻyalě. Noyi agṙavě. (Erevan, 1947). (Novel and novelette).

Translations

ENGLISH

Mandalian, J. *Gevorg Marzpetouni. Armenian Review,* 1952/1, 142–57; 2, 142–56; 3, 141–56; 4, 127–47. 1953/1, 141–58; 2, 146–59; 3, 147–57; 4, 141–57. 1954/1, 143–55; 2, 147–60; 3, 146–57; 4, 144–54. 1955/1, 144–56; 2, 144–56; 3, 135–44. (Novel; abridged).

RUSSIAN

Amirov, R. *Sviashchennik Andrias.* (Baku, 1907).
Apostol. (Erevan, 1950).
Ioannisian, A. *Georg Marzpetuni.* (Moscow, 1945; Erevan, 1984; Moscow, 1990).
Karumian, I. *Kazhdodnevnye besedy.* (Erevan, 1968).
Korganov, K. *Georg Marzpetuni.* (Erevan, 1940).
Ter-Akopian, N. *Noev voron.* (Moscow, 1961).

RUSSIAN ANTHOLOGIES

ARAS, 1, 106–70.
RAN, 41–52.

Criticism

Abełean, A. "Muratsani yišatakarani skizbě." *HA,* 44 (1930), 710–18.
Ałaneants, G. "Erku sarsapʻneri patasẖan." *Lumay,* 1910/7–8, 78–89.
———. *Muratsaně ew nra kʻnnadatutʻiwně.* (Tiflis, 1910).
Avetisyan, Z. "Žamanaki kategorian 'Gevorg Marzpetuni' vepum." *L,* 1979/4, 68–78.
Awdalbegean, Tʻ. "Hoři viště Muratsani erkerum. Patmakan-grakan verlutzutʻiwn." *A,* 1911, 864–67, 949–53, 1027–36.
Chrakʻean, Kʻ. "Muratsan, 1854–1908." *B,* 67 (1909), 89–91.
H[ambarean], H. "Muratsan (1854–1908)." *Lumay,* 1 (1909), 57–61.
———. "Muratsan." *HA,* 23 (1909), 6–8.
Gyulbudałyan, V. "Muratsani grakan žařangutʻyuně A. Terteryani gnahatutʻyamb." *BEH,* 1980/2, 148–56.
"Muratsan (Grigor T. Yovhannisean)." *A,* 1908, 836–38.
Partizuni, V. " 'Andreas erets' vipaki patmakanutʻyuně." *T,* 1955/1, 13–30.
———. *Muratsani kyankʻn u stełtzagortzutʻyuně.* (Erevan, 1956).
———. "Hanun bardzraržekʻ tʻargmanutʻyan." *SG,* 1969/4, 122–24. (On translations of Muratsan).
L. "Muratsan, Ṙuzan kam Hayrenasēr ōriord." *Murč,* 1901/3, 194–201.
———. "Erku ẖōskʻ." *Murč,* 1901/7, 260–63. (Reply to a letter by Muratsan published in *Murč,* 1901/7, 255–60).
Šahnuri barekamě. "Dēpkʻer u dēmkʻer." *AM,* 1903, 787–92.
Sarinyan, S. "Aṙakʻelutʻyan gałapʻarě Muratsani ṙomantizmi hamakargum." *BEH,* 1968/3, 81–95.
———. "Muratsani ṙomantikakan patmahayetsutʻyuně." *PBH,* 1969/1, 15–28.
———. "Muratsani ṙomantizmi sotsiologian." *SG,* 1969/2, 122–33.
———. *Muratsan: tipabanutʻyuně, ētʻikan.* (Erevan, 1976).
Stepʻanean, Y. "Muratsaně." *HK,* 30 (1952/10), 43–59.

Tērtērean, A. *Muratsanĕ orpēs mtatzoł ew gełagēt.* (Petersburg, 1913).
———. *Muratsan.* (Erevan, 1971).

NAHAPET K'UCHAK (16th century?)

The texts, mostly *hayrēns,* listed below have been erroneously attributed to this author, of whom very little is known. History has recorded the names "Nahapet" and "K'uchak," but they apparently refer to two different individuals. One such K'uchak (more than one person bore this name) hailed from the village of Ḥaṙakonis, in the region of Van. In a seventeenth-century colophon, a K'uchak referred to his great-grandfather as "Nahapet varpet," who was, he added, also known as "Ašěł K'uchak." More recently, the enigmatic name "Nahapet K'uchak" has surfaced. Although there is no unanimity among scholars, Nahapet K'uchak is now considered the author of ten poems, most of them in Turkish.

Texts (verse)

"Hayreni kargaw." *KNZ,* 3, 44–53.
Chōpanean, A. *Nahapet K'uchaki diwanĕ. Siroy erger, ḥratakan ew aylabanakan erger, panduḥti erger, k'nnakan usumnasirut'eamb mĕ.* (Paris, 1903).
———. "Nahapet K'uchaki antip tałikner." *ANA,* 1907/10–12, 184–89; 1909/1–2, 32; 1909/5–6, 108.
"K'uchakean k'ert'uatz mĕ", "Tał". *B,* 67 (1909), 400. (Attribution uncertain).
Chōpanean, A. *Hatĕntir ējer k'uchakean tałašark'ēn.* (Paris, 1926).
"Antip hayren k'aṙeakner." *Z,* 1 (1929–1930?), 224.
Chōpanean, A. " 'Hayren'neru burastanĕ." *ANA,* 2 (1930/1), 3–13.
———. "K'uchakean tałer." *ANA,* 2 (1930/1), 14–17; 2 (1930/4), 1–11; 2 (1931/5–6), 165–66, 3 (1931/1–2), 8–16; 3 (1931/5–6), 165–66; 4 (1932/1–2), 28–39; 6 (1935/1–2), 11–15.
K'iwrtean, Y., ed, "Nahapet K'uchaki kam 'Hayren'nerun burastanin aṙjew." *B,* 87 (1930), 518–23. (Texts and criticism).
K'iwrtean, Y. "K'uchakean nor tałašark' mĕ." *B,* 90 (1932), 464–72.
Akinean, N. "K'uchakean tałeru nor šark' mĕ." *ANA,* 1933/3–4, 96–102. 1934/5–6, 19. 1935/1–2, 11–14; 3–4, 18–19; 5, 5–6, 26–27. 1936/1–3, 34–36; 4, 23–24. 1937/1–2, 26–27; 3–4, 32–33.
K'iwrtean, Y. "K'uchakean erek' nor tałašark'er." *B,* 94 (1936), 91–93.
———. "K'uchakean siroy tałeru nor šark' mĕ." *HK,* 15 (1936–37/5), 58–62.
———. "K'uchakean tałašark'er (noragiwt ew antip k'aṙeakner)." *HK,* 31 (1943/2), 57–75.
Hayreni kargav. (Erevan, 1957).
Ēganyan, Ō. "Nahapet K'uchaki hayataṙ t'urk'eren tałerĕ." *BM,* 5 (1960), 465–81. (7 poems in Armeno-Turkish, i.e., Turkish in Armenian characters; with Armenian translations).
Haryur u mek hayren. (Erevan, 1975). (Armenian and Russian; Russian title: *Sto i odin airen*).
Haryur u mek hayren. (Erevan, 1979). (Armenian and English on facing pages; translation by Ewald Osers; English title: *A Hundred and One Hayrens*).
Haryur ev mek hayren. (Erevan, 1987). (In Armenian, German, and Russian).

Translations

ENGLISH ANTHOLOGIES

ALP, 4–5, 31.

AP, 242.
A Hundred and One Hayrens. (Erevan, 1979). (Translated by Ewald Osers; see *Haryur u mek hayren* above).

French

Tchobanian, A. "Les chants de Nahabed Koutchak: chants d'amour, chants d'émigré, chants gnomiques." *ANA,* 4 (1902), 123–25.
Marcel, L. A. "Lune déserté glissant là-haut," "O inconnue qui m'a aimé." *AND,* 15 (1964), 104.

French anthologies

CPA, 97–100.
LPA, 108–14.
RA, 2, 179–94.
TA, 21–80.

German

Die armenische Nachtigall: Lieder des Nahabed Kutschak. (Berlin, [1924]).
Bischoff, G. "Liebeslieder von Nahabed Koutchak." *AND,* 5 (n.d.), 115–17.
Haryur ev mek hayren. Hundert und ein Hairen. (Erevan, 1987). (Text in Armenian, German, and Russian).

Russian

Ambartsumian, A. *Pesni liubvi.* (St. Petersburg, 1904).
Grebnev, N. *Aireny.* (Erevan, 1968).
Haryur ev mek hayren. Sto i odin airen. (Erevan, 1987). (Text in Armenian, German, and Russian).
Mkrtchian, L. *Lirika "aireny."* (Moscow, 1972).
Osers, E., and Mkrtchian, L. *A Hundred and One Hayrens, Nahapet Kuchak.* (Erevan, 1979). (English and Armenian).
Stepane, A. *Stikhotvoreniia.* (Erevan, 1941).
Sto i odin airen. (Erevan, 1975). (See *Haryur u mek hayren* above).
Zviagintseva, V. *Lirika.* (Moscow, 1961).

Russian anthologies

AAP, 284–89.
PPA, 203–13.

Criticism

Abełean, A. "Nahapet K'uchakĕ germanerēn lezuov." *ANA,* 9 (1938/1–3), 4–13.
Abełyan, M. *Hin gusanakan žołovrdakan erger.* (Erevan, 1967), 11–280. (Vol. 2 of his *Erker*).
Akinean, N. "Noragoyn kartzik'ner 'K'uchakean k'ařeakneru' masin." *Z,* 1 (1929–1930?), 292–95.
Akopova, A. "Naapet Kuchak v russkom perevode." *L,* 1976/5, 34–48.
Amirkhanian, M. "O russkikh perevodakh trekh airenov Naapeta Kuchaka." *BEH,* 1970/1, 186–92.
Chōpanean, A. "Nahapet K'uchaki ergerĕ." *ANA,* 4 (1902), 117–21.
———. "Nahapet K'uchaki šurj." *ANA,* 1907/6–9, 97–111.
Grigoryan, Š. "Ov ē, i verjo, Nahapet K'uchakĕ [?]." *L,* 1984/7, 34–42.
K'iwrtean, Y. "K'uchakean tałašark'eru hnagoyn tpagrut'iwnner (niwt'er mijnadarean hay tałachaput'ean hamar)." *Vēm,* 2 (1934/2), 41–53.

Mnatsakanyan, A. "Hayrenneri ev Nahapet K'uchaki masin." *PBH,* 1958/2, 211–57.
P'aṙnak, G. "Nahapet K'uchaki diwanĕ." *ANA,* 4 (1902), 250–54. 5 (1903/1), 22–23; 5 (1903/2–3), 27–30.
Pazil. "Nahapet K'uchaki diwanĕ." *B,* 69 (1911), 230–33.
Pērpērean, H. "K'uchak." *S,* 1939, 398–99.
S. "Nahapet K'uchaki diwanĕ . . ." *Lumay,* 1903/2, 213–16.
T'adēosean, Y. "K'uchak Nahapeti ergerĕ." *Lumay,* 1902/3, 257–59; 4, 208–15; 5, 165–83. (Reprinted separately, Tiflis, 1903).

NALBANDEAN, MIK'AYĒL (1829–1866)

Pen names: Dōn Ēmmanuēl, Koms Ēmmanuēl, Simēōn Manikean.

Born in Nor Naḥijewan (Rostov na Donu, Russia). A writer and revolutionary activist. Complemented the elementary education he received in his birthplace with self-instruction. Abandoned his plans for priesthood, moved to Moscow in 1853, and audited medical courses at Moscow University (1854–58). Briefly taught Armenian at the Lazarean (Lazarevskii) Institute. In 1858, he collaborated with S. Nazarean (1812–79) in founding and editing, for a year or so, the famous periodical *Hiwsisap'ayl* (i.e., the northern lights, *aurora borealis,* 1858–64). Visited Europe (Warsaw, Berlin, Paris, London) and Constantinople in 1859. Shortly after his return from a second tour abroad (1860–62, a long journey to India with numerous sojourns), he was arrested on charges of clandestine activities and collaboration with emigré-Russian revolutionaries residing in the West. He was imprisoned in St. Petersburg (1862–65) and later banished to Kamyshin (1865), where he died of tuberculosis. His remains were interred at the Surb Ḥach (Holy Cross) Armenian monastery in Nor Naḥijewan.

Collections

Erkerĕ. 2 vols. (Ṙōstov Dōn [Rostov-na-Donu], 1903–06).
Šahaziz, Ye. *Divan Mik'ayel Nalbandyani.* (Erevan, 1932).
Hovhannisyan, A. *Antip erker.* (Moscow and Erevan, 1935).
Muradyan, N. *Erkeri liakatar žołovatzu.* 4 vols. (Erevan, 1940–49).
Muradyan, N. *Banastełtzut'yunner.* (Erevan, 1941).
Ĕntir erker. (Erevan, 1953).
Banastełtzut'yunner. (Erevan, 1954).
Erker. (Erevan, 1979).
Daronyan, S. *Erkeri liakatar žołovatzu.* 6 vols. (Erevan, 1982–).
Muradyan, Ṙ. *Erker.* (Erevan, 1985).
Hakobyan, S. *Erker.* (Erevan, 1987).

Texts

Minin ḥōsk', miwsin harsn. (Moscow, 1858 [printed but not distributed]; Erevan, 1971). (Novel).
Erku toł. Čšmartut'iwnĕ krōn ē, noran miayn ḥndretsēk', isk noranits ochinch. Robert Owen. (Paris, 1861; Erevan, 1939 [includes *Azgayin t'švaṙut'yun,* see below]). (Polemical writing).
(Under Simēōn Manikean) *Erkragortzut'iwnĕ orpēs ułił čanaparh.* (Paris, 1862; Boston, 1910; Erevan, 1930). (Socio-economic political study).
Hayrenasēri tałerĕ. (Geneva, 1903). (Poems).

Berberean, Ṙ. "M. Nalbandeantsi antip erkerě." *Vēm,* 4 (1936/2), 38–65.
Erku toł. Azgayin ťšvaṙuťyun. (Erevan, 1939).
Kritika 'Sos ev Vardiťer' azgayin vipasanuťyan P. Pṙošyants. (Erevan, 1940). (Criticism of P. Pṙōšean's *Sos ew Vardiťer*).
Abrahamyan, H. "Nalbandyanin verabervoł arḫivayin vaveragrer." *BM,* 1 (1941), 195–205.
Abrahamyan, Ṙ. "Erku nor vaveragir M. Nalbandyani Hndkastanum kataratz ašḫatankʻi masin." *BM,* 4 (1958), 247–49.
Madoyan, G. "Nor vaveragrer Mikʻayel Nalbandyani masin." *PBH,* 1981/2, 104–32.
Hakobyan, P. "Nalbandyani antzanotʻ inkʻnagirě (Surb grkʻi hin hayeren ťargmanuťyan bnagri usumnasiruťyan nyuťerits)." *E,* 1989/8, 38–47.
———. "Pataṙikner Mikʻayel Nalbandyani 'Arkatzkʻ naḫahorn' poemi naḫnakan tarberakits." *PBH,* 1990/1, 95–110.

Translations

English

"Our Fatherland." *Ararat* (London), 1915/19, 234.

English anthologies

ALP, 12–13.
AP, 39–42.

French

"Liberté." *L'Arménie* (London), 1894/65, 3.

French anthologies

APA, 39–44.
LPA, 168–69.
PA, 145–47.

Italian

"Liberta." *Armenia* (Torino), 1916/7, 10.

Italian anthologies

LPAM, 91–94.

Russian

Arsharuni, A. *Stikhotvoreniia.* (Moscow, 1967).
Izbrannoe. (Erevan, 1979).
Khachaturian, A. *Izbrannye filosofskie i obshchestvenno-politicheskie proizvedeniia.* (Moscow, 1954).
Sarkisian, Kh. *Izbrannye sochineniia.* (Erevan, 1941).
Sochineniia. 2 vols. (Erevan, 1968–70).

Spanish anthologies

APAS, 119–21.

Criticism

Abrahamyan, A. "Mikʻayel Nalbandyani hayatskʻnerě lezvi bnuytʻi, deri ev nra mšakman masin." *PBH,* 1980/1, 96–114.
Abrahamyan, Ṙ. "Bengaliayi tzayraguyn datarani včiṙě Mikʻayel Nalbandyani kołmits ktakagumarnerě šahelu masin." *L,* 1979/11, 105–09.
A-dō. *Mikʻayēl Nalbandeani keankʻi hetakʻrkʻir mi ējě ew Bakunini nran gratz namaknerě.* (Erevan, 1908).

Ałuzumtsyan, V. *Mikʻayel Nalbandyani sotsial-tntesakan hayatskʻnerě.* (Erevan, 1955).
Asatryan, A. "Mikʻayel Nalbandyani stełtzagortzutʻyan norahayt ējerits mekě." *PBH,* 1960/2, 85–94.
Atʻanasyan, Ł. "Im handipumě Mikʻayel Nalbandyani het Erevanum." *EJ,* 1954/12, 18–19.
Avdalbegyan, Tʻ. *Mikʻayel Nalbandyan.* (Erevan, 1928).
Aznavuryan, G. "Mikʻayel Nalbandyaně Hovhannes Hovhannisyani antip stełtzagortzutʻyunnerum." *T,* 1955/1, 95–96.
Bagdasarian, A. *Mikael Nalbandian.* (Erevan, 1980).
Barsełyan, Ḥ. "Sovetakan nalbandyanagitutʻyan nvačumnerě." *L,* 1979/11, 29–40.
Bazyan, S. *Mikʻayel Nalbandyan.* (Erevan, 1955).
Berberean, M. "Grakanutʻiwn ew keankʻ." *Lumay,* 2 (1902), 163–74.
Berberean, Ṙ. "Mikʻayel Nalbandean." *HK,* 7 (1928–29/10), 78–90; 11, 87–95; 12, 118–25. 8 (1929–30/1), 79–91; 2, 78–91; 3, 70–81; 4, 92–106; 6, 129–42; 7, 91–103; 8, 137–47; 9, 120–34.
———. "Nalbandeants ew G. v. Ayvazovski." *ANA,* 1932/1–2, 92–101.
Chrakʻean, Kʻ. "Mikʻayēl Nalbandean." *B,* 60 (1902), 73–78.
Chubar, G. "Mikʻayel Nalbandean." *ANA,* 1930/5, 99–104.
Danielyan, M. "Mikʻayel Nalbandyani ētʻikakan hayatskʻneri masin." *T,* 1955/3, 3–18.
Daronian, S. *Mikael Nalbandian.* (Moscow, 1963).
———. *Mikael Nalbandian i russkie revoliutsionnye demokraty.* (Moscow, 1967).
———. "Mikʻayel Nalbandyani 'Minin ḥoskʻ, myusin harsn' norahayt vipakě." *SG,* 1968/11, 139–48.
———. "Mikʻayel Nalbandyani 'Minin ḥoskʻ, myusin harsn'i odisakani avartě." *SG,* 1972/8, 139–40.
———. *Mikael Nalbandian: problemy tvorchestva i literaturnykh sviazei.* (Erevan, 1975).
———. "Gogolskie traditsii v tvorchestve M. Nalbandiana." *L,* 1979/9, 24–35.
———. "M. Nalbandian i tainoe obshchestvo 'Zemlia i Volia'." *PBH,* 1979/3, 21–37.
———. *Mikʻayel Nalbandyan.* (Erevan, 1979).
Daronyan, S. "Azatutʻyan ergichě." *SG,* 1979/11, 147–53.
———. "Mikʻayel Nalbandyani artasahmanyan aṙajin ułevorutʻyan hartsi šurjě." *SG,* 1983/3, 138–44.
———. "Nalbandyani kełtzanunneri hartsi šurj." *L,* 1984/2, 30–40.
Doluḥanyan, A. "Mikʻayel Nalbandyaně ev Łazar Pʻarpetsu 'Tʻułtʻě'." *BEH,* 1980/3, 142–45.
Gabrielyan, Ṙ. *Nalbandyaně ev bnagitutʻyuně.* (Erevan, 1967).
Galamdaryan, V. "Nor nyutʻer Mikʻayel Nalbandyani masin." *EJ,* 1955/3, 43–47.
Galoyan, G. "Mikʻayel Nalbandyani ašḥarhayatskʻi internatsionalizmě." *L,* 1979/11, 18–28.
Grigor'ian, K. "Neizvestnaia stat'ia Mikaela Nalbandiana, napechatannaia v gazete 'Molva'." *T,* 1954/79–83.
———. *Mikael Nalbandian.* (Leningrad, 1966).
Grigoryan, Š , "Sayatʻ-Novayin tvatz Nalbandyani mi gnahatakani šurj." *SG,* 1962/3, 114–20.

Ḥachaturyan, A. *Mik'ayel Nalbandyan.* (Erevan, 1987).
Hakobyan, M. "Mik'ayel Nalbandyani 'Italatsi ałjka ergi' skzbnałbyuri šurjě." *SG,* 1978/2, 145–48.
———. "Mamuli ev hraparakaḥosut'yan nalbandyanakan ěmbřnumě." *L,* 1979/10, 21–31.
Hakobyan, P. "Petropavlovyan berdum Mik'ayel Nalbandyani ěnt'ertsatz grk'erits mekě." *L,* 1969/12, 61–62.
———. "Mik'ayel Nalbandyani norahayt ink'nagirě." *L,* 1979/11, 41–43.
———. "M. Nalbandyani chirakanatsvatz mtahłatsumnerě." *PBH,* 1989/2, 75–88.
———. "Nalbandyani antzanot' ink'nagirě." *EJ,* 1989/8, 38–47.
———. "Patařikner Mik'ayel Nalbandyani 'Arkatzk' naḥahōrn' poemi naḥnakan tarberakits." *PBH,* 1990/1, 95–110.
Harut'yunyan, G. "Kensagrakan nyut'er Mik'ayel Nalbandyani masin." *EJ,* 1948/5–6, 51–61; 1948/10–12, 48–55.
Hovhannisyan, A. "Mik'ayel Nalbandyani kensagrut'yan anhayt mi ējě." *T,* 1954/6, 95–100.
———. "Mik'ayel Nalbandyani šrjadardzě idealizmits depi materializm." *T,* 1954/11, 3–18.
———. *Nalbandyaně ev nra žamanakě.* 2 vols. (Erevan, 1955–1956).
Ḥudoyan, S. *Mik'ayel Nalbandyan.* (Erevan, 1956).
Inčikyan, A. *Mik'ayel Nalbandyani kyank'i ev gortzuneut'yan taregrut'yuně.* (Erevan, 1954, 1980 [revised]).
———. *Mik'ayel Nalbandyan.* (Erevan, 1957).
———. "Nalbandyani anhayt erkern u ankatar mtahłatsumnerě." *PBH,* 1966/4, 19–40.
———., and Harut'yunyan, G. *Mik'ayel Nalbandyan: Vaveragreri žołovatzu.* (Erevan, 1956).
Jrbašyan, Ēd. "Mik'ayel Nalbandyaně ev žołovrdakan banahyusut'yuně." *PBH,* 1957/2, 67–96.
———. "Mik'ayel Nalbandyani ardzaki gełarvestakan hamakargě." *PBH,* 1979/3, 3–20.
———. "Nalbandyaně ev ardiakanut'yuně." *SG,* 1979/11, 130–39.
———. " 'Ułił čanaparhi' metz oronołě." *BEH,* 1983/2, 48–74.
———. *Mik'ayel Nalbandyaně ev ardiakanut'yuně.* (Erevan, 1984).
Karinyan, A. *Mik'ayel Nalbandyaně ev XIX dari 60—akan t'vakanneri řus ařajavor gortzichnerě. Hodvatzner.* (Erevan, 1949, 1979).
Kazarian, M. "Ob odnom psevdonime, pripisyvaemom Nalbandianu." *PBH,* 1959/4, 244–48.
Kusikean, K. "Mik'ayēl Nalbandean." *Murč,* 1906/1, 61–86.
Łanalanyan, A. "Mik'ayel Nalbandyaně ev žołovrdakan banahyusut'yuně." *PBH,* 1959/1, 71–80.
Łaribjanyan, G. "Mik'ayel Nalbandyaně hay mark'sistakan mtk'i gnahatmamb (naḥahoktemberyan šrjan)." *L,* 1979/11, 3–17.
Łazaryan, A. "Mik'ayel Nalbandyani lezvabanakan hayatsk'nerě." *T,* 1954/11, 37–50.
Łazaryan, M. "Nalbandyani ev Patkanyani gałap'arakan hakamartut'yan hartsi šurjě." *PBH,* 1959/4, 249–87.
Łurłanyan, K. "Mik'ayel Nalbandyani hetk'erov." *SG,* 1979/11, 159–60.

Madoyan, G. "Petropavlovyan amrotsi kalanavorě." *SG,* 1979/11, 140–46.
———. "Nor vaveragrer Mikʻayel Nalbandyani masin." *BEH,* 1981/2, 104–32.
Makaryan, A. *Mikʻayel Nalbandyaně ev arevmtahay demokratian.* (Erevan, 1946).
———. "Mikʻayel Nalbandyani ev St. Oskani pʻoḥharaberutʻyan hartsi šurjě." *T,* 1955/4, 81–104.
Margaryan, A. *Mikʻayel Nalbandyani lezvagitakan gortzuneutʻyuně.* (Erevan, 1957).
———. "Mikʻayel Nalbandyanin veragrvoł mi hodvatzi masin." *T,* 1954/11, 79–82.
Mḥitʻaryan, M. "M. Nalbandyani šurjě arevelahay mamulum tzavalvatz mi polemika." *T,* 1976/4, 73–80.
———. "M. Nalbandyani tzatzkanunneri šurj." *L,* 1986/3, 59–69; 1986/5, 63–73.
Mkrtchian, A. *Mikael Nalbandian.* (Erevan, 1955).
Muradyan, H. *Mikʻayel Nalbandyani tznndavayrum.* (Erevan, 1980).
Muradyan, M. "Mikʻayel Nalbandyaně ev eražštutʻyan hartserě." *T,* 1963/5, 31–44.
Muradyan, N. *Mikʻayel Nalbandyan.* (Erevan, 1954).
———. "Ḥoher Nalbandyani masin." *SG,* 1966/4, 84–90.
———. *Nalbandyan, kyankʻě ev gortzě.* (Erevan, 1980).
Osipova, V. "M. Nalbandian o probleme determinizma i svobody voli." *T,* 1956/8, 33–42.
Ovsepian, O. "Gosudarstvenno-pravovye vozzreniia revoliutsionera-demokrata Mikaela Nalbandiana." *PBH,* 1980/2, 87–97.
Palean, E. *Mikʻayēl Nalbandeani tntesakan tʻēōrian.* (Baku, 1911).
Pʻechikean, E. "Gamaṙ-Kʻatʻipa ew Mikʻayēl Nalbandean." *B,* 87 (1930), 484–89.
Pʻiloyan, H. "Kronakan baroyakanutʻyan kʻnnadatutʻyuně M. Nalbandyani erkerum." *BEH,* 1982/1, 176–81.
Ṙštuni , H. "Mikʻayel Nalbandyani 'Kritikan' ev pṙošyanagitutʻyan ḥndirnerě." *SG,* 1979/11, 154–58.
Šahaziz, E. *Mikʻayēl Łazari Nalbandeants: kensagrutʻiwn.* (Moscow, 1897).
———. "Mikʻayēl Nalbandeantsě S. Peterburgum (1862–1865)." *Lumay,* 1902/4, 113–83.
———. "Ḥorēn arkʻepiskopos Galfayeaně ew Nalbandeantsi 'Ałtsmikʻě'." *Lumay,* 1903/2, 139–52; 3, 45–81; 4, 59–83; 5, 101–48; 6, 102–48.
———. "Mikʻayēl Nalbandeantsě Hndkastanum." *Lumay,* 1904/2, 141–58; 3, 72–94; 4, 101–23; 5, 46–77.
———. "Nalbandeantsi noragiwt hnagoyn namakneri aṙtʻiw." *Lumay,* 1905/1, 79–92; 2, 93–95.
Sargisian, Kh. *Mikael Nalbandian i voprosy iazyka.* (Erevan, 1955).
Sargsyan, Ḥ. *Nalbandyani grakan stełtzagortzutʻyuně.* (Erevan, 1959).
———. "Mikʻayel Nalbandyan." *PBH,* 1966/2, 3–12.
———, and Grigoryan, K. "Nor nyutʻer Mikʻayel Nalbandyani masin." *T,* 1954/7, 81–110. (In Russian).
Sarinyan, S. "Nalbandyanagitutʻyuně nor ḥndirneri aṙaj." *SG,* 1976/2, 134–39.
Simonyan, K. "Nalbandyan kam azatutʻyan aspetn u nahatakě." *SG,* 1982/11, 3–72.
Simonyan, P. "Mikʻayel Nalbandyani andznakan gradaraně." *T,* 1954/11, 83–98.
Simonyan, Š. *Mikʻayel Nalbandyani hogebanakan hayatskʻnerě.* (Erevan, 1969).

Step'anyan, G. "Mik'ayel Nalbandyani 'Erku tołum' hišatakvatz mi azganvan ałavałman šurjě." *T,* 1952/6, 105–16.

———. "Mik'ayel Nalbandyani 'Azatut'yun' banastełtzut'yan haryuramya kyank'ě." *T,* 1954/11, 59–78.

———. "Nalbandyani arevmtahay barekamneri masin." *T,* 1961/8, 91–96.

Step'anyan, H. "Mik'ayel Nalbandyani ułevorut'yunnerě." *T,* 1956/10, 95–100.

Step'anyan, Ž. *Mik'ayel Nalbandyani ēst'etikakan hayatsk'nerě.* (Erevan, 1967).

Štikyan, S. "Mik'ayel Nalbandyani 'Hišatakarani' 1945 t'. hratarakut'yan mi k'ani tzanot'agrut'yunneri masin." *PBH,* 1979/3, 129–34.

———. "Dardzyal M. Nalbandyani 'Hišatakarani' masin." *PBH,* 1981/4, 230–41.

Tēr Astuatzatrean, H. *Mik'ayēl Nalbandeants.* (Tiflis, 1908).

Tērtērean, A. *Mik'ayēl Nalbandean, azgut'ean hraparakaḥōsě.* (Alexandrapol, 1910 [cover says 1911]).

Tovmasian, St. "M. L. Nalbandian i russkaia revoliutsionno-demokraticheskaia estetika." *T,* 1954/11, 19–36.

NALEAN, YAKOB (c1706–1764)

Born in the village of Zimara, somewhere near or between the towns of Divriği and Akn (Eğin, now Kemaliye), Turkey, but exact location unknown. Yakob was taken to Constantinople around 1720 and enrolled in the school set up by Patriarch Yovhannēs Bałišetsi Kolot (1715–41). Became a *vardapet* in 1728. Consecrated bishop in Ējmiatzin the following year. Succeeded Kolot to the patriarchal seat of Constantinople in 1741, but he was dethroned in 1749. Briefly served as patriarch of Jerusalem, until his re-election as patriarch of Constantinople in 1752. Died in office.

Texts

Girk' kochetseal vēm hawatoy. (Constantinople, 1733).

Girk' kochetseal k'ristonēakan usaneli ew kam k'ristonēits varžich. (Constantinople, 1737, 1747, 1806).

Girk' meknut'ean ałōt'its srboyn Grigori Narekatswoy. (Constantinople, 1745–46).

Grk'uks kochetseal hogešah erkuts čaṙits srboyn Yohannu Oskeberanin yAndriandeay grk'oy errord ew chorrord čaṙitsn otanaworeal. (Constantinople, 1746; Nor Nakhijewan, 1794).

Grk'uks kochetseal črag čšmartut'ean. (Constantinople, 1756).

Girk' kochetseal zēn hogewor. (Constantinople, 1757, 1787, 1820, 1844). (Parts 2 and 3 in Turkish in Armenian characters).

Girk' kochetseal gandzaran tzanutsmants. (Constantinople, 1758).

Girk' ałōt'its amenayn andzants harkawor. (Constantinople, 1760).

Tetrak zunaynut'enē kentsałoys, otanaworeal i hogeloys Yakob astuatzaban patriark'ē Kostandnupolsoy . . . (Constantinople, 1805). (Nalean's writing only 10 pages long).

"Ołb mōr i wałameṙik ordin." *MKH,* 141.

"Im aregakěn ḥawaretsaw." *MKH,* 142.

Criticism

Nazaryan, Š. "Hakob Nalyaně ev nra chap'aberakank'ě." *PBH,* 1984/1, 80–84.

NAR-DOS (1867–1933)

Pen name: Nar-Dos.

Born Mikʻayēl Yovhannisean in Tiflis. Received his elementary education in the local Armenian schools. Worked as editor and administrator for several Armenian papers, particularly *Nor-Dar* (1890–1906) and *Surhandak* (1913–18), and devoted what little spare time was left to writing novels and short stories. Died in Tiflis.

Collections

Ĕntir patmvatzkʻner. (Erevan, 1934).
Erker. (Erevan, 1977).
Erker chors hatorov. 2 vols. (Erevan, 1989).
Zaryan, Ṙ. *Erkeri liakatar žołovatzu.* 8 vols. (Erevan, 1938–50).
Erkeri žołovatzu. 3 vols. (Erevan, 1955).
Połosyan, Ḥ., and Batikyan, L. *Erkeri žołovatzu.* 5 vols. (Erevan, 1968–71).

Texts

Anna Saroyean: ētiwd. (Tiflis, 1889, 1906; Erevan, 1933; Teheran, 1955). (Novelette).
Spanuatz aławni. (Baku, 1901; Erevan, 1929 [revised], 1986). (Short novel).
Tantirojs ałjikĕ. (Tiflis, 1902). (Story).
Ṅoratzin manukĕ. (Vałaršapat, 1904). (Story).
Nor ōrerits mēkĕ. (Tiflis, 1904 [cover says 1905]). (Story).
Paykʻar. (Tiflis, 1911; Cairo, n.d.; Erevan, 1957 [published with *Mahĕ*]). (Novel).
Mahĕ. (Tiflis, 1912; Moscow, 1934; Erevan, 1957 [published with *Paykʻar*]). (Novel).
Mer ťałĕ: patmvatzkʻner. (Erevan, 1926, 1952, 1982). (Stories).
Erku bolševik: St. Šahumyan, S. Spandaryan. (Erevan, 1935). (Written with A. Širvanzade).
Sakʻuln uḥt gnats. Inchpes bžšketsin. (Erevan, 1938). (Stories).
Grakan žaṙangutʻyun. Vol. 1 (Erevan, 1961). (Letters of A. Tzaturean and Nar-Dos).
Kʻnkʻuš larer. Zazunyan. Spanvatz ałavni. (Erevan, 1971). (Novels).
Patmvatzkʻner. (Erevan, 1985). (Stories).

Translations

English

Ashjian, S. "The Interest on the Black Coins." *Nor Ašḥarh* (New York), December 29, 1962, 4.

German Anthologies

AN, 29–46.

Russian

Anna Saroian. Ubity golub'. Bor'ba. (Erevan, 1960).
Arsharuni, A. *Ubity golub'.* (Moscow, 1960).
Balasan, V. *Nash kvartal.* (Erevan, 1985).
Ia i on. (Erevan, 1963).
Levonian, G. *Anna Saroian.* (Tiflis, 1902).
Poslednie mogikane. (Tiflis, 1935).
Povesti i rasskazy. (Moscow, 1955).

Povesti i rasskazy. (Moscow, 1956).
Rasskazy i povesti. (Erevan, 1949).
Rasskazy i povesti. (Erevan, 1952).
Ter-Martirosian, A. *Smert'.* (Moscow and Leningrad, 1931).

RUSSIAN ANTHOLOGIES

AASL, 23–29.
ARAS, 1, 280–324.
KHAN, 1, 31–42.
RAN, 81–100.

Criticism

Eremean, A. "Zroyts vipagir Nar-Dosi het." *ANA,* 1929/5, 42–44.
Harutʻyunyan, T. *Nar-Dosi 'Mahě' vepě.* (Erevan, 1961).
Hovakimyan, H. "Nar-Dosě ev tʻatroně." *SG,* 1967/3, 140–41.
Hovhannisyan, G. "Nar-Dosi 'Mer tʻałě' novelneri masin." *T,* 1957/2, 35–46.
———. "Nar-Dosi 'Paykʻar' vepě." *T,* 1958/3, 51–60.
———. *Nar-Dos.* (Erevan, 1959).
Hovsepʻyan, G. *Nar-Dos.* (Erevan, 1961).
Kʻaloyan, A. "Nor herosě Nar-Dosi vał šrjani vipaknerum." *L,* 1990/6, 64–69.
Marguni, H. "Nar-Dosi novelneri syužen." *PBH,* 1966/3, 171–76.
Ṙštuni, H. "Nar-Dos." *PBH,* 1967/4, 11–24.
Sargsyan, G. "Hay ṙealistakan ardzaki varpetě." *SG,* 1958/7, 154–63.
Sarinyan, S. "Nar-Dosi stełtzagortzutʻyuně." *SG,* 1967/9, 85–95.
Stepʻanean, Y. "Nar-Dos." *HK,* 18 (1939–40/4), 16–26; 5, 127–33; 6, 97–105; 8, 125–32.
Tērtērean, A. *Nar-Dosi stełtzagortzutʻiwně.* (Tiflis, 1913).
Zaryan, Ṙ. "Nar-Dos." *SG,* 1959/2, 96–103.
Zoryan, S. "Nar-Dos." *SG,* 1967/3, 138–39.

NARDUNI, ŠAWARŠ (1898–1968)

Pen name: Šawarš Narduni.

Born Askʻanaz Ayvazean in Armaš, near Izmit, Turkey. Attended school in his birthplace. Completed his medical studies in Paris (1927) after his suspension from the University of Istanbul for political reasons. Contributed to Armenian periodicals on numerous topics, including literature, philology, and history. Also published *Hay boyž,* a popular medical journal, from 1934 to 1967.

Collections

Nardean patarag. (Beirut, 1968).
Grakan tsolkʻer. (Beirut, 1975).

Texts (prose)

Alpōm hēkʻeatʻneru. (Athens, 1927).
Mełediner, mełediner . . . hēkʻeatʻ ew banastełtzutʻiwn. (Paris, 1933).
Erusałēm, Erusłēm . . . vipergutʻiwn. (Paris, 1938).
Baner, baner inch baner . . . ardzak banastełtzutʻiwn ew hēkʻeatʻ. (Paris, [1941]).
Vardamatean (hēkʻeatʻner ew patmuatzkʻner). (Paris, 1951).
Nizakamart Šawaršanay daštin vray. (Paris, 1956).
Lusamatean (hēkʻeatʻner ew banastełtzutʻiwn). (Paris, 1966).

Other works

Nardean širer kanach bažakov. (Paris, 1945).
Jrvēž. (Paris, 1950).
Es tesay žołovurdě. (Teheran, 1954).
Gragētě, or ir žołovurdě pntřelu elatz ē. (Teheran, 1954).
Ogin haykazants. (Cairo, 1954).
Mełuin čařě. (Paris, 1960).
Aha es čankers layn batsatz. (Paris, 1966).
Mer hołerě, mer hołerě . . . (Beirut, 1966).
Yanun Mesrop Maštotsi. Paštpanutiwn hay lezui. 2 vols. (Paris, 1967; Beirut, 1969).

Criticism

B[aluean], H. "Mełediner, mełediner . . . grets Šawarš Narduni." *Z* (taregirkʻ), 1 (1937), 208.
———. "Girkʻeru mōt: Erusałēm, Erusałēm . . . viperguṫiwn Š. Nardunii." *Z* (amsōreay), 1 (1938/6), 45.
Mḥitʻarean, G. "Š. Narduni ew ir hēkʻeatʻneru 'Alpōmě'." *Z* (1929–[30]), 78–80.
Parsamean, M. *Šawarš Narduni.* (Paris, 1933).
Vahē-Vahean. "Šawarš Narduni." *Ani,* 6 (1954), 50–53.

NARPĒY, ḤORĒN (c1831–1892)

Pen names: Narpēy, Lusinean (Lusignan), and others.
Born Ḥorēn Galfayean in Constantinople. Brilliant orator and a highly acclaimed poet, playwright, and translator (mainly from French). Became a member of the Mḥitʻarean Congregation after completing his training at St. Lazarus. Along with two other Mekhitarist monks (Sargis Tʻēodorean and Gabriēl Ayvazean or Ayvazovski, brother of the famous painter), he severed his ties with the order (1856) and returned to the Church of Armenia. Consecrated bishop in Ējmiatzin, in 1867. A member of the unofficial Armenian delegation to the Congress of Berlin (1878). Denuded of his glory and withdrawn from public life by the mid-1880s, he was ungraciously suspended from all religious activities in 1892 by patriarch Ḥorēn Ašěgean of Constantinople (1888–94). Allegations that he was poisoned on orders from Abdulhamid II are unsubstantiated.

Texts

Aršak Erkrord. (Theodosia, 1861). (Drama).
Alafranka. (Theodosia, 1862). (Comedy).
Vardenikʻ. (Theodosia, 1863). (Verse).
Kʻnar pandḥtin. (Constantinople, 1868). (Verse).
Stuerkʻ haykakankʻ. (Constantinople, 1874). (Verse).

Other works

Pōlsoy 'Mełuin' 160 tʻuoyn mēk hatuatzin patasḥan. [Constantinople, 1862].
Hayots Ekełetsin ew Andraleṙnakankʻ. (Constantinople, 1870).
Naḥakrtʻaran franserēn lezui. (Constantinople, 1873).
Naḥnakan kʻristonēakan ěst vardapetutʻean Hayastaneayts S. Ekełetswoy. (Constantinople, 1877, 1890).
Krtʻakan kʻristonēakan ěst vardapetutʻean Hayastaneayts S. Ekełetswoy. (Constantinople, 1877, 1887).
Naḥnakan srbazan patmutʻiwn. (Paris, 1896).

Translations

ENGLISH

"Vahan Mamigonian. Words and Music by Corène de Lusignan." *Armenia* (newspaper), July 1, 1894, 2.

ENGLISH ANTHOLOGIES

AP, 43–59, 219–23.

FRENCH

Archag II. (Paris, 1864).

"A ma sœur Rosa," "Annitza." *L'Arménie* (London), 1893/52, 4.

"Si l'on me donnait . . ." *L'Arménie* (London), 1893/53, 1. (Reprinted in *L'Arménie,* 1894/66, 4).

Tchobanian, A. "A Victor Hugo." *V Hugo, Chateaubriand et Lamartine dans la littérature arménienne.* (Paris, 1935), 1–2.

"Vahan Mamigonian. Paroles et musique de Corène de Lusignan." *L'Arménie* (London), 1894/69, 2.

FRENCH ANTHOLOGIES

APA, 47–58.

PA, 149–51.

SPANISH ANTHOLOGIES

APAS, 131–34.

Criticism

"Bischof Khohren Narbegh Lucinian." *Der christliche Orient,* 7 (1906), 149–60.

Eremean, S. "Narpēy." *B,* 71 (1913), 42–44, 57–64.

Hatsuni, V. *Norakert hay Lusineanner.* (Venice, 1953).

Šahaziz, E. "Ḥorēn ark'episkopos Galfayeanĕ ew Nalbandeantsi Ałtsmik'ĕ." *Lumay,* 5 (1903), 101–48; 6 (1903), 102–48.

Siruni, H. "Antzanot' ējer Ḥoren Narpeyi kyank'en." *PBH,* 1970/1, 175–86.

NAT'ALI, ŠAHAN (1884–1983)

Pen names: Nemesis, Šahan, Šahan Nat'ali.

Born Yakob Tēr Yakobean in Hiwsenik, a village near Ḥarberd (Harput, Turkey). Attended the local Armenian elementary school. Orphaned when his father was killed during the Armenian massacres of the mid-1890s. Continued his studies at the Pērpērean school in Constantinople (1897–1901). Taught in his native village (1901–04) and emigrated to the United States in 1904. He was one of the chief organizers of the assassination, soon after World War I, of some of the principal Young Turk Ottoman leaders, who had masterminded the Armenian genocide of 1915.

Texts

Šant'er. (Boston, 1907) (Verse).

Amper. (Constantinople, 1909). (Verse).

Ōrēnk'i ew ĕnkerut'ean zoherēn. (Boston, 1909). (Stories).

K'awut'ean erger. (Boston, 1911). (Verse).

Sēri ew atelut'ean erger. (Boston, 1915). (Verse).

Mardĕ. (Smyrna, 1912). (Play).

Aslan bēg. (Boston, 1918). (Play).

Vrēži awetaran. Vol. 2. (Boston, 1918). (Verse).

K'ezi. (Boston, [1920]). (Verse).
Nšmar Šahan Nat'alii grakan, hasarakakan yisnameay keank'in. ([Boston], 1953). (Includes poetry).

Other works

Kargawor 'hayrer'. (New York, 1917).
T'urk'erě ew menk' (veragnahatumner). (Athens, 1928; [Boston], 1931).
Alek'sandrapoli dašnagrēn 1930i kovkasean apstambut'iwnnerě (veragnahatumner). 2 vols. (Marseilles, 1934, 1935).
Erewani hamadzaynagirě. (Boston, 1941).
Girk' matutsman ew hatutsman. I. Ayspēs spannetsink'. II. Yaweluatz. ([Boston], 1949).
'Verstin yaweluatz' Alek'sandrapoli dašnagri 'inchpēs'n u 'inchu'n paštōnakan vaweragreru ew yušagrakan vkayut'iwnneru loysin tak. (Boston, 1955).

Criticism

Nšmar Šahan Nat'alii grakan, hasarakakan yisnameay keank'in. ([Boston], 1953).

NAZANI, (1870–1912)

Pen name: Nazani.
Ōhanēs Tēr-Martirosean, an *ašuł,* lived in Alexandrapol (Leninakan, now Gyumri).

Poetry

THG, 246–49.

NERSĒS MOKATSI (c1575–c1625)

Also known as "Bełlu" and "Vanetsi" (i.e., from Van). Nersēs was born in the village of Asknjaws, reportedly located in the old Armenian region of Mokk', south of Lake Van. Acquired his education at the famous school of the monastery of Amrtōl (also Amrdol or Amlordi), in Bałēš (Bitlis). From 1616–21 he taught at the celebrated "Siwneats Anapat" hermitage, near Tat'ew in Eastern Armenia. The Hermitage of Lim, which he founded on the islet of Lim in Lake Van, played a significant role in the revival of monastic life and Armenian culture in the seventeenth century.

Texts (verse)

"Vičabanut'iwn erkni ew erkri." *B,* 5 (1847), 331–32.
"Nšḥar p'aytin or šnorhetsaw." *B,* 20 (1862), 232.
Tzovakan, N. "Mijnadaryan tałasatsner (Nersēs vard. Mokatsi)." *EJ,* 1944/10–12, 32–35. (Includes texts and criticism).
Doluḥanyan, A. *Nerses Mokatsi, banasteltzut'yunner.* (Erevan, 1975, 1985).

Criticism

Akinean, N. *Bałēši dprotsě, 1500–1704.* (Vienna, 1952), 92–115. ("Nersēs v. Bełlu Mokatsi").
Doluḥanyan, A. "Nerses Mokatsun verabervoł mi dzeṙagri masin." *L,* 1970/7, 92–93.
———. *Nerses Mokatsi, banasteltzut'yunner.* (Erevan, 1975 [5–33], 1985).

NIRANI, (1822–?)

Pen names: Nirani, Šahri.

Yovhannēs Šaramanean, a native of Vałaršapat (Ējmiatzin), was a self-taught *ašuł*.

Poetry

MKH, 571.
THG, 105–9.

NOR-AYR, (1912–1981)

Pen name: Nor-Ayr.

Born Norayr Harutʻyunyan in the village of Mawrak in the region of Kars. Novelist. Educated in Leninakan (now Gyumri) and Nor Bayazet (now Kamo, Armenia). Completed special courses in journalism (1931) under the auspices of the Communist party of Armenia and edited a number of local periodicals. Held various cultural and administrative positions, and from 1957 to 1974 he was the secretary to the Kirovakan (now Vanadzor) section of the Union of Soviet Writers of Armenia.

Texts (stories and novels)

Čartarapetuhin. (Erevan, 1932).
Pʻrkutʻyan pʻaros. (Erevan, 1938).
Hyuranotsi ałjikě. (Erevan, 1946).
Olortnerum. (Erevan, 1947).
Novelner ev vipakner. (Erevan, 1949).
Luyser. (Erevan, 1950).
Antaṙi ergě. (Erevan, 1959).
Metz Parni. (Erevan, 1961).
Loṙva astłer. (Erevan, 1962).
Nvirakan srter. (Erevan, 1965).
Anapati aṙavotě. (Erevan, 1968).
Aram. (Erevan, 1970).
Patmutʻyun grvatz kʻari vra. (Erevan, 1978).

Translations (Russian)

Aram. (Moscow, 1970).

NOR TETRAK OR KOCHI YORDORAK ŠARADRETSEAL SAKS STʻAPʻELOY ERITASARDATSN, EW MANKANTS HAYKAZANTSN I VEHEROTEAL EW I HEŁGATSEAL TʻMRUTʻENĒ KʻNOY TZULUTʻEAN

This important book reflects aspects of Armenian political thought, especially the views of some leaders of the Armenian community in India in the closing decades of the eighteenth century. It is a patriotic exhortation intended to awaken the timid and indolent Armenian youth and to prompt readers with the prospect of a future Armenia, revived through self-reliance. It reviews Armenian history and the causes for the collapse of Armenian political power and analyzes a number of favorable economic and geographic factors meant to inspire optimism. Author uncertain. Originally, it was attributed to Yakob Šahamirean, and later to Movsēs Bałramean. Some believe it was a collective effort.

Texts

Nor tetrak or kochi yordorak šaradretseal saks st'ap'eloy eritasardatsn, ew mankants haykazantsn i veheroteal ew i hełgatseal t'mrut'enē k'noy tzulut'ean. (Madras, 1772–73).

Criticism

Mnatsakanyan, A. "Ov ē 'Nor tetrak, or kochi yordorak . . .' grk'i hełinakě?" *PBH,* 1962/2, 131–42.

Połosyan, S. "Azatagrakan gałap'araḥosut'yuně 'Nor tetrak or kochi yordorak' grk'um." *BEH,* 1972/2, 86–100.

NORENTS, VAŁARŠAK (1903–1973)

Pen name: Vałaršak Norents.

Born Vałaršak Eritsean in Šēnik, a village in the region of Sasun (south of Muš, Turkey). Poet. Received his elementary education in his native village. Survived the Armenian massacres of 1915. Grew up in orphanages in Tiflis and Leninakan (now Gyumri). Attended the Nersisean school and settled in Erevan. In 1925, he participated in the founding of "Noyember" (November), a literary society, which soon merged with its rival, "Hayastani proletarakan grołneri asotsiatsia" (Association of Proletarian Writers of Armenia), to form a new union of writers, "Hayastani proletarakan grołneri miut'yun" (Union of Proletarian Writers of Armenia). Survived many years of exile under Stalin.

Collections

Erker. (Erevan, 1963).
Erkeri žołovatzu. 3 vols. (Erevan, 1971–76).

Texts (verse)

Ōreri čamp'in. (Dilijan, 1925).
Irikun. (Erevan, 1926).
Erkrord girk'. (Erevan, 1930).
Lirikakan front. (Erevan, 1932).
Banastełtzut'yunner. (Erevan, 1936).
Girk' k'narakan. (Erevan, 1954).
Čanaparhner. (Erevan, 1956).
Im ašḥarhě. (Erevan, 1958).
P'še šapik. (Erevan, 1959).
Dareri avand. (Erevan, 1968).

Other works

Tasnerku tari (Sovetakan Hayastani 1920–32) mšakut'ayin kyank'i not'agrut'yun. (Erevan, 1933). (Written with Vahram Alazan).
Hušer ev ardzagank'ner. (Erevan, 1968). (Reminiscences and literary articles).

Translations

French anthologies

Rebec, J. P. *E,* 81–82.
LPA, 314–15.

Russian

Altaiskii K., and Pen'kovskii, L. *Lirika.* (Erevan, 1956).

Izbrannye stikhi. (Moscow, 1936).
Stikhotvoreniia. (Moscow, 1957).

Criticism

"Argasavor čanaparh." *SG,* 1963/9, 116–19.
Hatityan, G. "Vałaršak Norents." *SG,* 1961/5, 130–36.

NURIKEAN, BENIAMIN (1894–1988)

Born in the village of Hiwsenik, near Ḥarberd (Harput, Turkey). Received his elementary education at the village school and at the school founded by Tʻlkatintsi (q.v.) in Ḥarberd. Arrived in the United States in 1913. Graduated from Columbia University in 1920 and received his M. A. from the same institution the following year. One of the founders and editors of *Nor gir,* a journal of literature and the arts, published in New York (1936–54).

Texts (stories)

Aygekutʻkʻ. (New York, 1937).
Panduḥt hoginer. (Erevan, 1958).
Karot hayreni. (Erevan, 1978).

Translations (anthologies)

Kara-Sarkissian. *E,* 138–42.
KNS, 81–87.
PCN, 127–14.

Criticism

Baluean, H. "Aygekutʻkʻ; ardzak ējer B. Nurikeani." *Z* (amsōreay), 1 (1938/5), 39.
B[aluean], H. "Panduḥt hoginer." *Z* (amsatʻertʻ), 4 (1960/11–12), 14.
Selyan, P. "Beniamin Nurikyan." *SG,* 1958/1, 183–85.
Taturyan, Š. "Beniamin Nurikyan." *SG,* 1974/12, 97–105.

ŌHAN KARŌ (1890–1933)

Pen name: Ōhan Karō.
Born Yovhannēs Karapetean in Nor Giwł, a village in the region of Van. A teacher by profession; educated at Ałtʻamar in Lake Van. Joined the Armenian volunteers in the Caucasus during World War I. Settled in Paris permanently after 1920. Most of his writings (prose and poetry) are still scattered in the periodical press.

Collections

Ḥrčitʻnerēn minchew ḥorhrdaran: ardzak ējer ew kʻertʻuatzner. (Paris, 1933). (Prose and poetry).

ORBEREAN, ṘUBĒN (1874–1931)

Pen name: Ṙubēn Alikʻean.
Born in Malatʻia (Malatya), Turkey. Educated at the Euphrates College in Ḥarberd (Harput). Moved to Constantinople in the early 1890s. Taught, for a decade or so, in Smyrna and Constantinople. Went into business in Djibouti, 1903–20. Correspondent for *The Daily Mail* of London and *The New York Herald* during the Russo-Japanese War. In 1920, he took up permanent residence in Paris. A good deal of his prose and poetry is still buried in periodicals.

Collections

Petrosyan, E. *Erker.* (Erevan, 1963).

Texts

Yišatakats tzaɫikner, otanawor ew ardzak gruatzkʻ. (Constantinople, 1893). (Prose and poetry).

Ovasis (ardzak ew otanawor). (Paris, 1920). (Prose and poetry).

Works in periodicals

AM, 1896, 555–57, 563–66, 630–32, 656–57, 662–64, 698–700. 1897, 283–84, 318, 654. 1898, 189–91, 545–46, 672–73, 712–13, 781–82. 1899, 35–36, 359–60, 438–41, 532, 626–27, 764, 908–11, 957–58. 1900, 19–21, 901–3, 940–43. 1901, 11–13, 458–62, 579–84. 1902, 29–30, 205–9, 565–66, 921–25. 1904, 440–42. 1905, 302–5, 493–94, 1097–102. 1907, 8–10. 1908, supplement 1, 85. 1909, 870–71.

M, 1900/6, 82–83; 8, 116–17; 12, 183; 16, 247–49; 24, 376–78; 30, 467; 31, 487–88; 38, 604–5. 1901/4, 57–59. 1902/6, 84–87; 37, 557–59.

Nawasard, 1914, 19–20.

Translations (French anthologies)

APA, 149–56.

Criticism

Ēsačanean, L. "Ṙubēn Orberean." *HK,* 11 (1932–33), 123–27.

Gabrielyan, V. "Ṙ. Orberyanĕ ev spʻyuṙkʻahayutʻyan hamahavakʻĕ." *T,* 1964/1, 51–60.

———. "Ṙ. Orberyan." *SG,* 1964/5, 146–49.

———. *Ṙuben Orberyan: kyankʻĕ ev grakan gortzuneutʻyunĕ.* (Erevan, 1964).

Pēšiktʻašlean, N. "Ṙubēn Orbereanĕ." *HK,* 41 (1963/6), 44–47.

ORBUNI, ZAREH (1902–1980)

Pen names: Heraz, Zareh Orbuni.

Born Zareh Ēōkʻsiwzean in Ordu (Turkey). Novelist. His father was killed during the genocide of 1915, but he and his mother managed to flee to Simferopol. Attended the Pērpērean school during a short stay in Constantinople (1919–22). Sailed for France, lived in Marseilles for two years, then in Paris (1924–30) and Strasbourg (1930–37). Editor, jointly with Petros Zaroyean (1903–), of two short-lived periodicals: *Nor hawatkʻ* (1924) and *Lusabats* (1938–39). A prisoner of war in Germany from 1940 to 1945. Although most of his novels and short stories have been published separately, some of his verse and prose writings are still scattered in periodicals, and some are still in manuscript form.

Collections

Ev eɫev mard. (Erevan, 1967). (Includes *Pʻordzĕ, Ev eɫev mard* and 8 short stories).

Texts (stories and novels)

Pʻordzĕ. (Marseilles, 1929; Beirut, 1958).

Vardzu seneak. (Paris, 1946).

Dēpi Erkir. (Paris, 1947).

Andzrewot ōrer. (Paris, 1958).

Ew eɫew mard. (Paris, 1965).

Patmuatzkʻner. (Beirut, 1966).
Tʻeknatzun. (Beirut, 1967).
Asfaltʻě. (Istanbul, 1972).
Sovorakan ōr mě. (Beirut, 1974).

Works in periodicals

ANA, 1 (1930/6), 76–78; 2 (1930/2), 31–33; 2 (1930/3), 31–32; 2 (1930/4), 40. 3 (1931/4), 40; 2 (1931/5–6), 79–92; 3 (1931/1–2), 154. 8 (1937/1–2), 45–54. 9 (1938/1–3), 15–19. 11 (1940/4), 17–21.
AND, 1 (1952), 25–32. 3 (1953), 76–84. 11 (1960), 17–29. 12 (1961), 24–32. 13 (1962), 49–61. 15 (1964), 48–56. 16 (1965), 12–16. 18 (n.d.), 58–64.
Ani, 1 (1946), 8–12, 59–64, 183–85, 306–8. 2 (1947–48), 6–7, 225–26, 406–8, 457–62. 4 (1950–51/10), 535–37. 4 (1950–51/11–12), 591–96. 5 (1952), 4–6. 6 (1954/2), 81–89.

Translations (Russian anthologies)

KNS, 171–75.
PCN, 35–47.

Criticism

Chinchinean, Z. "Z. M. Orbunii Andzrewot ōrerě." *Z* (amsatʻertʻ), 3 (1958/4–5), 12.
Fēnērčean, G. "Halatzuatznerě, A. Pʻordzě, Z. M. Orbuni." *Z,* 1 (1929–30), 301–2.
Ter-Yakobean, Y. "Z. Orbunii 'Andzrewot ōrer'ě." *Z* (amsatʻertʻ) 3 (1958/4–5), 12.
Vahē-Vahean. " 'Dēpi Erkir' Z. M. Orbunii, Pʻariz, 1948." *Ani,* 2 (1947–48/11), 613–14.
Yakobean, A. "Z. M. Orbunii 'Pʻordzě'." *Z,* 2 [1931], 65–67.

ŌŠAKAN, YAKOB (1883–1948)

Pen names: Gełjuk, Yakob Ōšakan, Yakob Yovhannēsean.
Born Yakob Kʻiwfēčean in Sēōlēōz, near Bursa. Writer, critic, and teacher. After elementary school in his birthplace, he attended the Armaš seminary for a year. Began his lifelong teaching career in Bursa; moved on to Malgara and Constantinople. There, jointly with Kostan Zaryan and Gełam Barsełean (q.q.v.), he launched the periodical *Mehean* (1914). With some luck and adroitness, he managed, unlike most of his colleagues, to escape death in 1915, by fleeing to Bulgaria disguised as a German officer. Returned to Constantinople after the Armistice of Mudros and published the periodical *Bardzravankʻ* (1922), with a few old friends and confrères who had survived the butchery of 1915. He and his colleagues left Constantinople for the last time in 1922. Taught in Bulgaria, Cairo, Cyprus (Melkonian), and lastly at the St. James Armenian seminary in Jerusalem. Died in Aleppo.

Collections

Kʻałhankʻ. (Jerusalem, 1946).
Snapean, P. *Erker.* [Beirut and Antʻilias, 1973]. (Includes *Tzak ptukě, Hači Murat,* and *Hači Aptullah*).
Kurtikyan, S. *Erker.* (Erevan, 1979).

Literary works

Ḥonarhnerě. Vol. 1. (Constantinople, 1920; Beirut, 1958). (Stories).
Ḥorhurdneru meheaně. (Constantinople, 1922). (Tales).
Erb patani en. (Constantinople, 1926). (Story).
Mnatsordats. 3 vols. (Cairo, 1932–34; Ant'ilias, 1988). (Incomplete novel).
Step'anos Siwnetsi (k'naraḥał mijin darerēn). (Paris, 1938). (Play).
Erb mer̄nil gitenk'. (Jerusalem, 1944). (Play).
Ōrn ōrerun: ḥorhurd (mer žamanaknerēn). (Jerusalem, 1946 [cover says 1947]). (Play).
Kayserakan yałt'erguťiwn. Hinēn u norēn. Erb pztik en. (Beirut, 1983). (Stories).
K'naraḥałer. (Beirut, 1983). (Plays in verse).
Minchew ur [?]. (Beirut, 1983). (Play).
Namakani. Vol. 1. (Beirut, 1983). (Letters).
Erknk'i čambov (ḥał mer žamanaknerē, druag mě mer taragrut'enēn). (Beirut, 1985). (Play).
Sahak Pargewean. Vēp. (Ant'ilias, 1985). (Novel).
Siwlēyman Ēfēnti. (Ant'ilias, 1985). (Novel).
Erek' ťateraḥałer: Nor psakě; Knk'ahayrě; Ak'loramartě. (San Francisco, 1990).

Other works

Hay grakanut'iwn. (Jerusalem, [1942], 1966 [3d ed.]). (A textbook of modern Armenian literature).
Sp'iwr̄k'ě ew iraw banastełtzut'iwně. (Jerusalem, 1945). (On V. T'ēk'ēean).
Hamapatker arewmtahay grakanut'ean. 10 vols. (Vols. 1–5, Jerusalem, 1945, 1953, 1954, 1956, 1962, respectively; Vol. 6, Beirut, 1968; Vols. 7–10, Ant'ilias, 1979, 1980, 1980, 1982, respectively). (A history of Western Armenian literature).
Vkayut'iwn mě. (Aleppo, 1946). (On A. Tzar̄ukean's poem "Hēy jan Erewan").
Arewelahay banasirut'iwně ew Ējmiatzin: Garegin kat'ołikos Yovsēp'ean. (Beirut and Ant'ilias, 1948). (On Eastern Armenian philology and Garegin Yovsēp'ean).
Hrašk'ě. (Ant'ilias, 1984). (A polemical defense of the religious and spiritual aspects of the Armenian ethos against communist materialism in Soviet Armenia).
Vahan T'ēk'ēean. (Beirut, 1985).
Mer matenagirnerě. (Ant'ilias, 1987). (On Sahak Part'ew, P'awstos Buzand, Łazar P'arpetsi, Ełišē, Movsēs Kałankatuatsi, Yovhannēs Drasḥanakerttsi, Nersēs Šnorhali, and Nersēs Lambronatsi).

Works in periodicals

HK, 2 (1923–24/4), 6–29; 5, 18–38. 3 (1924–35/10), 1–17. 4 (1925–26/4), 34–35. 41 (1963/4), 1–8.
Z, 1 (1929–[30]), 15–18; 67–69. *Z* (taregirk'), 1 (1937), 54–63. *Z* (amsōreay), 1 (1937/1), 1. *Z* (er̄amseay), 1947/2, 109. *Z* (amsat'ert'), 4 (1960/9–10), 3; 4 (1960/11–12), 5. (Incomplete).
"Erknk'i čambov." *HK*, 14 (1935–36/6), 8–27; 7, 50–66; 8, 48–54; 9, 10–30. (Play).
"Minchew ur [?]" *HK*, 17 (1938–39/3), 1–14; 4, 39–57; 5, 54–69. (Play).
AND, 5 (n.d.), 61–62. 6–7 (n.d.), 65, 192.

Criticism

Andrēasean, A. "Ōšakani 'Datum'in vripankʻě." *Ani,* 1 (1946), 275–82.
B[aluean], H. "I patiw Yakob Ōšakanin (–Ōšakan kʻnnadatě)." *Z* (amsōreay), 1/2 (1937), 12.
———. "Yakob Ōšakan." *Z* (eṙamseay), 1948/3, 233–36.
Chakʻěrean, G. "Yakob Ōšakan." *HK,* 28 (1950/12), 33–47.
Hamasteł. "N. Ałbaleani ew Y. Ōšakani masin." *HK,* 27 (1949/12), 22–26.
Mḥitarean, G. "Yakob Ōšakan." *HK,* 26 (1948/3), 84–89.
Parsamean, M. "Yakob Ōšakan aruestagētě." *Z* (amsatʻertʻ), 1 (1956/4), 1; 1 (1956/5–6), 6–7; 1 (1956/7), 4.
———. "Yakob Ōšakan grakan kʻnnadat." *AND,* 12 (1961), 113–18.
Tʻašean, B. "Mayrineru šukʻin tak, grakan zroyts mě Y. Ōšakani het." *HK,* 10 (1931–32/5), 125–38; 7, 151–60.
———. "Hanrayin gitzě Ōšakani grakanutʻean mēj." *Z* (taregirkʻ), 1 (1937), 86–89.
Vahē-Vahean. "Yakob Ōšakan." *Ani,* 2 (1947–48), 368–70.

OSTANIK (1896–1954)

Born Ostanik Yovhannēsean in Ołm, a village near Van. Attended Armenian schools in Van, Ałtʻamar, Ējmiatzin, and Erevan. Joined the ranks of Armenian volunteers during World War I and remained in Eastern Armenia until 1921. Worked as an editor and taught in the first Republic of Armenia. Crossed the border into Iran when Armenia became Soviet. Spent the next decade or so in Paris. Taught in Teheran from 1934 until his death.

Collections

Erker. (Teheran, 1972).

Texts

Hekekankʻner. (Erevan, 1913).
Ziwlfi erger. (Tabriz, 1921).
Arewelkʻēn arewmutkʻ. (Paris, 1932).
Erg ergots. (Teheran, 1934).
Šahēni ḥrčiṙě. (Teheran, 1935).
Nerašḥarh. (Teheran, 1942).

ŌTEAN, ERUAND (1869–1926)

Pen names: E. M. Kiwrōt (with Mikʻayēl Kiwrčean), Erōt, Vahram, Vahram Vahramean, S. Žirayr.

Born in Constantinople. Satirist, novelist, journalist, and translator. Left the Pērpērean school after a year or so and was tutored privately. Contributed to Armenian papers and published numerous periodicals, most of them short-lived (e.g., *Azat ḥōskʻ, Krak, Kaṙapʻnat, Sew katu, Ignat ała,* etc.). The Armenian massacres of the mid-1890s marked the first phase of his wandering life. He fled the Ottoman capital and lived in Athens, Vienna, London, Paris, and visited India (1904) before temporarily settling in Alexandria (1902–09). Returned to Constantinople after the Young Turk coup. He was deported to the Syrian desert in 1915, but survived and returned to his birthplace immediately after World

War I. Left Constantinople in 1922 and lived in Bucharest and various parts of the Middle East. Died in Cairo.

Collections

Erkeri žołovatzu. (Erevan, 1934).
Manukyan, A. *Erker.* (Erevan, 1956).
Makaryan, A. *Erkeri žołovatzu.* 6 vols. (Erevan, 1960–63).
Erker. (Erevan, 1978).
Ĕntir erker. (Erevan, 1988).

Texts (novels and prose)

Frankʻō-ṫrkʻakan paterazm kam Charšĕlĕ Arṫin ała. (Constantinople, 1909). (Comedy; written with Mikʻ. Kiwrčean).
Zavallĕn. (Constantinople, 1909, 1928; Beirut, 1961). (Vaudeville).
Aṙakʻeluṫiwn mĕ i Tzaplvar. (Constantinople, 1911; Venice, 1959). (Part of *Ĕnker Ṗanjuni*).
Aptiwl Hamit ew Šerlōkʻ Holms. (Constantinople, 1911; Beirut, 1937). (Novel).
Saliha hanĕm kam Banakĕ Bṙnaworin dēm: vēp ōsm. yełaṗoḥakan keankʻē. (Constantinople, 1912. 1931; Beirut, 1938). (Novel).
Pōłos ṗaša Nupar (kensagrakan nōṫer). (Constantinople, 1913). (Biography).
Ĕnker Ṗanjuni (ir nor aṙakʻeluṫiwnĕ Vaspurakani mēj ew ir ašḥarhayeatskʻnerĕ). (Constantinople, 1914). (Part of *Ĕnker Ṗanjuni*).
Ĕnker Ṗanjuni Vaspurakani mēj. Ĕnkervarakan namakani ĕnker B. Ṗanjuniē. (Constantinople, 1914). (Part of *Ĕnker Ṗanjuni*).
Ariwnot yišatakner. (Constantinople, 1920).
Čepĕnṫats noratzinĕ. (Constantinople, 1920; Alexandria, 1928).
Chakʻĕr Avram kam Grigorin vrēžĕ. (Constantinople, 1920).
Ergitzabanakan taretsoyts. (Constantinople, 1920).
Yełaṗohuṫean makaboytznerĕ. (Constantinople, 1920). (Stories).
Datastanakan ḥorhurdin aṙjew kam Berayi gayṫakłuṫiwnnerĕ: ergitzakan vēp polsakan keankʻē. (Constantinople, 1921). (Novel).
Ergitzakan taretsoyts: 1922. (Constantinople, 1921).
Tʻałakanin knikĕ. (Constantinople, 1921). (Novel).
Matnichĕ: vēp azgayin yełaṗoḥakan keankʻē. (Constantinople, 1922; Beirut, 1940). (Novel).
Tasnerku tari Polsēn durs. 1896–1908. (Constantinople, 1922). (Reminiscences).
Kaṙkʻi arkatz mĕ. (Constantinople, 1924).
Azgayin barerar. (Cairo, 1926). (Novelette).
Es drsetsi chem aṙner. (Constantinople, 1926 [cover says 1927]). (Novel).
Herosaḥał. (Constantinople, 1928). (Play; written with Mikʻ. Kiwrčean).
Ĕntanikʻ, patiw, baroyakan: vēp polsahay azgayin keankʻē. (Constantinople, 1929). (Novel).
Mijnord tēr papan: ergitzakan vēp polsahay keankʻē. (Constantinople, 1930). (Novel).
Ĕnker Ṗanjuni. (Paris, 1935). (Includes Tzaplvar, Vaspurakan, Ašḥarhayeatskʻnerĕ, Pahpanołakanĕ). (Novel).
Ĕnker Ṗanjuni i Tzaplvar ew Vaspurakan. (Cairo, 1938). (Ill. by A. Saruḥan; part of *Ĕnker Ṗanjuni*).
Paterazm ew . . . ḥałałuṫiwn. (Ĕntanekan namakani). (Paris, 1938). (Prose).
Ĕnker Ṗanjuni taragruṫean mēj ew Ĕnker Ṗanjunii ašḥarhayeatskʻnerĕ. (Cairo, 1939). (Ill. by A. Saruḥan; part of *Ĕnker Ṗanjuni*).

Tēr-Minasean, A. *Ōteani namakner, ergitzakan vaweragrer. 1. šrjan.* (Constantinople, 1946).
Hambardzum ała. (Erevan, 1956). (Story).
Ĕnker P'anjuni Vaspurakani mēj. (Venice, 1959; 1962). (Part of *Ĕnker P'anjuni*).
Ĕnker P'anjuni taragrut'ean mēj and *Paterazm ew hałałut'iwn.* (Venice, 1960). (The first title is part of *Ĕnker P'anjuni*).

Translations

English

Antreassian, J. *Comrade Panchoonie.* 2 parts. (New York, 1977). (Part 1: Dsablvar; part 2: Vasbouragan).
"Comrade Panchoonie." *Ararat,* Summer 1961, 23. (Excerpts of a satirical prose narrative).
Mandalian, J. "A Mission to Dzablvar." *The Armenian Review,* Summer, 1952, 3–27.

French

Cavezian, Z. *Une mission à Dzablvar; lettres socialistes du citoyen P. Pantchouni.* (Smyrna, 1922).
Feydit, F. *Une mission à Dzablvar.* (Venice, 1961).

French anthologies

Yéghiaian, A. *E,* 108–13.

German anthologies

AN, 47–56.

Russian anthologies

KHAN, 1, 43–52; 2, 147–61.
RAN, 138–59.

Criticism

Feydit, F. "La Comédie et la satire en Arménie: Baronian et Odian." *B,* 118 (1960), 167–78; 119 (1961), 24–30.
Maḥmuryan, A. "Ergitzank'i drsevorman aṙandznahatkut'yunnerĕ Er. Ōtyani 'Ĕnk. P'anjuni' vepum." *BEH,* 1989, 120–25.
Makaryan, A. "Ervand Ōtyanĕ ibrev k'nnadat." *T,* 1947/1, 49–60.
———. *Ervand Ōtyan.* (Erevan, 1957).
———. *Ervand Ōtyan.* (Erevan, 1965).
———. "Ervand Ōtyani namaknerĕ A. Chopanyanin." *L,* 1966/6, 72–81.
———. "Metz ergitzabanĕ." *SG,* 1969/12, 114–17.
Manukyan, S. "Hay metz ardzakagir-ergitzabanĕ." *PBH,* 1979/3, 117–29.
———. "K'ałak'akan ergitzavepi varpetĕ." *L,* 1979/12, 3–15.
Pušlikean, Y. "Eruand Ōtean (tznndean 100ameakin aṙit'ov)." *B,* 127 (1969), 287–96; 128 (1970), 55–59, 268–75.
Siruni, Y. "Gitzer Eruand Ōteani keank'ēn." *HK,* 5 (1926–27/8), 45–52; 9, 37–45.
———. "Ervand Ōtyan." *SG,* 1969/12, 118–36.
Titanyan, N. "Ervand Ōtyani patmvatzk'neri kaṙutsvatzk'ĕ ev lezun." *L,* 1979/10 13–20.

PAŁTASAR DPIR (c1683–c1768)

Also referred to as Grigorean, after his father; Kesarean, after his father's native city, Kayseri; and Kostandnupolsetsi, after his birthplace. Born in Constantinople.

Poet, teacher, and publisher. Studied at the feet of Bishop Astuatzatur Jułayetsi, a nuncio of the Catholicos of All Armenians. Until his death, he taught and supervised at the Kum Kapu school of the Armenian Patriarchate, founded by Patriarch Yakob Nalean (q.v.). Many of those who studied under him later became distinguished men of letters or leaders (including Simēon Erewantsi and Petros Łapʻantsi q.q.v.). Pałtasar is credited with the publication of several old Armenian texts of importance (e.g., Aṙakʻel Siwnetsi, *Adamgirkʻ*; Grigor Tatʻewatsi, *Girkʻ hartsmants,* etc.). Died in Constantinople.

Texts

Grguks šahawēt, uni yinkʻean bazum inch hawakʻetseal asti ew anti. Yałags ōgti orots mits unin ew lselis. (Constantinople, c1715–25; c1750).

Pu patmutʻiwn girkʻi ōltur kʻi, Grigorios surb Lusaworichin ēvēlintēn aẖērēnatakʻ patmutʻiwnunu vē pu Hayots azgĕn nē sēpēptēn kʻristonēakan hawatkʻna kēlip lusaworel ōlmasĕnĕ, tiynēyēnē nagl ētēr. (Constantinople, n.d.; 1820, 1831, 1841, 1850; Jerusalem, 1867, 1884, 1889, 1901, 1909, 1928). (The story of Grigor Lusaworich and the conversion of Armenia; in Armeno-Turkish).

Parzabanutʻiwn kʻerakanutʻean karčaṙōt ew diwrimats. Yałags nor ekelots i usumn grots gitutʻean. 2 vols. (Constantinople, 1736, 1771; Madras, 1791). (A grammar of Classical Armenian in Classical Armenian).

[“Krtʻutʻiwn kʻristonēakan”] *Pu girkʻ ōlturkʻi kʻristonēakan hawatkʻēmĕza igtizalĕ kerēkʻ ōlan pir gach ēōyrēnilēčēkʻlēr hayča pilmēyēn kʻristoneay ełbayrlarĕmĕz ichin tʻiwrkʻče šaradrel oluntu, vē atĕnĕ Krtʻutʻiwn kʻristonēakan tētikʻ.* (Constantinople, 1742, 1777, 1816, 1816, 1820). (In Armeno-Turkish.)

Ōrinakkʻ barewagrats norapēs šaradretseal. (Constantinople, 1752, 1786, 1807, 1827).

Anuamb Astutzoy Hōr ew Ordwoy ew Hogwoyn Srboy. Grkʻoyk or kochi Tsank girkʻ Nor Ktakaranin. Or parunakē yinkʻean zbans omans erewelis edeal ĕst aybbenakan kargin handerdz hamaratʻuov glẖotsn ew hamaratsn tĕnatmants . . . (Constantinople, 1753).

Girkʻ kʻerakanutʻean. (Constantinople, 1760). (A grammar of Classical Armenian in modern Armenian).

Tałaran pʻokʻrik Pałtasar Dprē asatseal zanazan gunov (Constantinople, 1768). (3d ed.; 1st and 2d eds. supposedly published in 1723 and 1734). (Verse).

Tałaranik siroy ew karōtanats ew ayl i Pałtasar Dprē i veray zanazan gunits. (Constantinople, 1768). (Verse).

[*Tałaran*]. (Constantinople, 1768). (Verse; published untitled).

[*Tałaran*]. (Constantinople, n.d.). (Verse; published untitled).

[*Žamanakagrutʻiwn*] (“Abgar hawatats i Kʻristos i tʻuin Kʻristosi 40 . . .”). *Manr žamanakagrutʻyunner XIII–XVIII dd.,* V. A. Hakobyan, Vol. 1 (Erevan, 1951), 333–49. (Chronicle).

Tałikner siroy ew karōtanats. (Erevan, 1958). (Verse; ed. by Š. Nazaryan and As. Mnatsakanyan).

Nazaryan, Š. *Tałikner.* (Erevan, 1985).

“Tałer Pałtasar Dpri.” *CHE,* 91–102. (14 poems).

“Erg uraẖutʻean.” *MKH,* 373–74. (Poems).

“Garunn ē batsuer.” *MKH,* 374–75. (Poems).

“I nnjmanēd arkʻayakan.” *MKH,* 469.

"Zis k'o siroyn, ov nazeli." *MPT,* 56–57.
"Šat siro k'ez barew . . ." *MPT,* 57–58.
"Zandzn im ayspēs achk' yartasus." *MPT,* 58.

Translations

FRENCH

LPA, 149–50.
RA, 2, 264–83.

RUSSIAN

AAP, 313–14.

Criticism

Baḥchinyan, H. "Bałdasar Dpirě orpes banastełtz." *PBH,* 1990/1, 127–38.
Nazaryan, Š. *Pałtasar dpir.* (Erevan, 1985).
———. "Narekatsiakan šaržumě 18–rd darum Pałtasar dpri k'narergut'ean mēj." *B,* 1986/1–4, 202–35.
Poturean, M. "Pałtasar Dpir." *B,* 70 (1912), 334–39.

P'ANOSEAN, AŁEK'SANDR (1859–1919)

Pen name: Alp'aslan.
Born in Constantinople and educated at the Nupar-Šahnazarean Armenian school there. Poet and translator; wrote children's literature and comedies. Also wrote in French.

Texts

Šołer u tsołer. (Constantinople, 1884). (Verse).
T'eknatzuner. (Constantinople, 1901). (Comedy).
Aygekut'. (Constantinople, 1908). (Verse).
Azat k'nar. (Constantinople, 1908). (Verse).

Criticism

Ałek'sandr P'anosean, 1859–1919, yobeleani yišatak. (Constantinople, 1919).
Arminē. "K'ert'ołut'ean ṙahviray mě." *M,* 1900/39, 615–17.
Gamēr. "Uruagitzner–Ałek'sandr P'anosean." *M,* 1903/33, 521.

P'ANOSEAN, SMBAT (1909–)

Born in Tiflis. Orphaned at a very young age and raised in orphanages. Moved, along with hundreds of other orphans, to Jerusalem in 1922. Graduated from the Melkonian Educational Institute of Cyprus (1926–30). Following a sojourn in Beirut (1930–33), he permanently settled in Latakia, Syria. His novels and short stories reflect realities of the Armenian Dispersion of the Middle East.

Texts

Anardzagang k'ayler. (Beirut, 1949).
Or mrrkaw ēin zatuatz. (Beirut, 1953).
Sērě or gin chunēr. (Beirut, 1968).
Vark' Komitas Kutinatsii. (Beirut, 1970).
Zandzn im p'aṙaworeal. (Ant'ilias, 1989).

PAPAYAN, ARAMAŠOT (1911–)

Added to his first name, Ašot, that of his deceased brother, Aram. Playwright. Born in Batum and educated in the local shools. Attended the pedagogical institute in Rostov-Na-Donu. Worked as an actor in northern Caucasus (1931–40) and Soviet Armenia (1941–42). Took special courses at the Gorky Institute for literature (1951).

Collections

Piesneri žołovatzu. (Erevan, 1950).
Katakergutʻyunner. (Erevan, 1962).
Ašḫarhn ayo šuṙ ē ekel. (Erevan, 1972).
Artasahmanyan pʻesatsu. Piesneri žołovatzu. (Erevan, 1982).
Metz harsanikʻ. (Erevan, 1987).

Texts

Ššmetsutsich harvatz. (Erevan, 1955).
Metz harsanikʻ. (Erevan, 1960).
Tzitzał. (Erevan, 1965).
Ašḫarhn, ayo, šuṙ ē ekel. (Erevan, 1968).

Translations

English

Parlakian, N. *Be Nice, I'm Dead.* (New York, 1990).

Russian

Da, mir perevernulsia: P'esy. (Moscow, 1988).
Lukovskii, I. *Smotreny. Komediia v 1 d.* (Moscow, 1958).

Criticism

Hunanyan, A. "Uraḫ ev kensahastat katakergutʻyun." *SG,* 1984/7, 23–26.

PʻAPʻAZEAN, VRTʻANĒS (c1866–1920)

Pen names: Aprō, Vardgēs, Vrtʻanēs.

Born in Van. Writer, literary critic, historian, teacher, and translator. Taught and trained at schools in Agulis, Naḫijewan; Tabriz (1875–78); the Gēorgean Seminary in Ējmiatzin (1878–79); and Geneva University (1891–94). His peregrinations, mainly as a teacher, took him to numerous cities in many a region: Transcaucasia (Erevan, Tiflis, Baku, Šuši); Russia (northern Caucasus, Astrakhan, Moscow); Western Armenia (Van, Erzurum); Iran (Teheran, Tabriz); and many other cities. Fled Russia in 1912, traveled abroad (Bucharest, Bursa), but was back in Transcaucasia by 1915 and settled in Ējmiatzin in 1919. Died at a hospital in Erevan.

Collections

Ĕntir erker. 2 vols. (Erevan, 1939–40).
Patmvatzkʻner ev zruytsner. (Erevan, 1946).
Ĕntir erker. (Erevan, 1951).
Patmuatzkʻner. (Beirut, 1955).
Erkeri žołovatzu. 5 vols. (Erevan, 1958–59).
Erkeri žołovatzu. 3 vols. (Erevan, 1972–73).
Korsvatz ardarutʻyun. (Erevan, 1981).

Tsamak'yan, A. *Erker.* (Erevan, 1981).
Sargsyan, Ṙ. *Erker.* (Erevan, 1987).
Ōhanyan, A. *Vana katun.* (Erevan, 1988).
Nanumyan, Ṙ. *Vrt'anes P'ap'azyanĕ grakanut'yan masin.* (Erevan, 1962).

Texts (stories, essays, novels, plays)

Enicheri. (Tiflis, 1889).
Ḫat'-saba. (Hay bošaneri keank'its). (Tiflis, 1890).
Lalō. (Tiflis, 1890).
Parskakan zroytsner. (Tiflis, 1890).
T'ōp'al. (Tiflis, 1890).
Čgnawor Ełō. (Moscow, 1891).
Ginegortzi ałjikĕ. (Tiflis, 1891).
Patkerner t'iwrk'ahayeri keank'its. (Moscow, 1891).
Anyagĕ. (Tiflis, 1892, 1919).
Sasuntsi Ōhan. (Moscow, 1892).
K'rk'ijner. (Paris, 1893).
Erek' patker. (Baku, 1894).
Turisti yišołut'iwnner. (Tiflis, 1895).
Sant'ō. (Hay bošaneri keank'its). (Tiflis, 1898; Constantinople, 1910).
Hay bošaneri vrannerum. (Tiflis, 1899).
Hay bošaner. (Azgagrakan usumnasirut'iwn). (Tiflis, 1899).
Gtzer keank'its. (Tiflis, 1899).
Ēmma: vēp žamanakakits bark'erits. (Tiflis, 1901).
Patmuatzk'ner. (Tiflis, 1901).
Korsuatz ardarut'iwn. (Chinakan legenda). (Baku, 1902).
Abałayi daštum. (Baku, 1903).
Asi (vēp parskakan keank'its). (Tiflis, 1903).
Aspet. (Tiflis, 1903).
T'ṙchoł ḥozĕ. (Baku, 1903).
Ḥent'ĕ ew uriš patmuatzk'ner. (Tiflis, 1903).
Lur-da-lur. (Baku, 1903; Erevan, 1937; Beirut, 1954).
Višap (zroyts). (Baku, 1903; Erevan, 1940).
Alēmgir. (Tiflis, 1904).
Ḥelōk' ak'ałałner ew Draḥt. (Tiflis, 1904).
Metz p'akank' ew Aṙiwtzi mahĕ. (Tiflis, 1904).
Patmuatzk'ner t'iwrk'ahayeri keank'its. (Tiflis, 1904).
Paytaṙi hogin ew Ankełtz ĕntzay. (Tiflis, 1904).
Višap ew uriš zroytsner. (Tiflis, 1904).
Azrfēza: (vēp parskakan keank'its). (Tiflis, 1905).
Erku t'ṙchun. (Tiflis, 1905).
Žayṙ. (Tiflis, 1907; Erevan, 1946).
Patmut'iwn hayots grakanut'ean. Vol. 1 (Erevan, 1907; Tiflis, 1910; [Constantinople, 1931]), Vol. 2 (Constantinople, 1913, [1947]).
Haji bēk. (Constantinople, 1909).
Mšuš. (Tiflis, 1909).
Patkerner. (Trebizond, 1909).
Artašēs Erkrord. (Baku, 1910).
Gagik Erkrord. (Baku, 1910).

Lewon Erkrord. (Baku, 1910).
Sahak ew Mesrop. (Baku, 1910).
T'oros Išḫan. (Baku, 1910).
Vardanants paterazmě. (Baku, 1910).
Zroytsner. (Šuši, 1911).
Giwłits: patkerner. (Tiflis, 1913).
T'ł'ē nawakits minchew tzařě: (mankakan patmuatzk'). (Tiflis, 1917).
Gařnukě (mankakan piesa). (Tiflis, 1918; Constantinople, 1930).
Tpaworut'iwnner Nuḫuts. Drut'iwně Nuḫay ew Areši gawařnerum. (Tiflis, 1919).
Erasḫi vrayov. (Erevan, 1945).
Mankut'ean yušerēn. (Beirut, 1950, 1959). (Translated from Eastern Armenian into Western Armenian by L. Šant').

Translations

ENGLISH

Antreassian, K. "The Secret of his Strength." *Armenia,* 4 (1901/5), 12–13.
Ashjian, S. "Loor-ta-loor." *Nor Ašḫarh.,* 1963/26, 4; 1963/27, 4.
"Drops of Blood." *Armenia,* 6 (1912/5), 143–47.
"The Pathometer." *Armenia,* 5/5, 156–57.
Torossian, P. "The Lost Justice." *The New Armenia,* 8 (1916/11), 173.

FRENCH

D'Hérminy, S. *Santho.* (Paris, 1920). (Préface de Frédéric Macler).

RUSSIAN

Babiian, V., and S. *Lur-da-lur (kurdskaia poema).—Nogoi dervish.* (Simferopol, 1904).
Bagaturova, N. *Piatna krovi i drugie rasskazy.* (Moscow, 1911).
Dilanian, A. *Pravednik Eggo: rasskazy.* (Moscow, 1968).
Giul'-Nazarov, F. *Drakon.* (Petersburg, [1906]).
Poteriannaia spravedlivost'. (Erevan, 1972).

RUSSIAN ANTHOLOGIES

KHAN, 1, 104–6.
RAN, 59–63.

Criticism

Davt'yan, H. "V. P'ap'azyani stełtzagortzut'yuně řusakan ařajin řevolyutsiayi žamankašrjanum." *T,* 1955/7, 23–38.
Hunanyan, A. "Hełap'oḫakan tramadrut'yunnerě V. P'ap'azyani zruytsnerum." *L,* 1977/4, 14–23.
Karinyan, A. "Vrt'anes P'ap'azyan." *L,* 1986/9, 82–85.
Muradyan, L. "V. P'ap'azyaně grak'nnadat." *L,* 1970/1, 73–78.
———. "V. P'ap'azyaně hay grakanut'yan patmaban." *PBH,* 1970/2, 216–22.
———. "V. P'ap'azyaně řus ev evropakan grakanut'yan masin." *BEH,* 1970/2, 239–45.
Nanumyan, Ř. "V. P'ap'azyani grakan gortzuneut'yan vał šrjaně." *T,* 1954/6, 51–62.
———. *Vrt'anes P'ap'azyan.* (Erevan, 1956).
———. "Vrt'anes P'ap'azyan." *SG,* 1966/4, 91–94.
Ōhanyan, A. "V. P'ap'azyaně 'Šavił' t'ert'i ḫmbagir." *SG,* 1975/9, 1 152–58.
———. *Vrt'anes P'ap'azyan.* (Erevan, 1976).
Serobyan, G. "Vrt'anes P'ap'azyani grakan ułłut'yan masin." *SG,* 1984/12, 113–18.

PARONEAN, YAKOB (1843–1891)

Born in Edirne. Satirist, journalist, and teacher. Received some schooling in the Armenian and Greek schools in his birthplace. Lived in Constantinople from the early 1860s to his death. Engaged in acting and several other occupations before taking up accounting and journalism as his lifelong professions. Editor and/or publisher of a number of periodicals: *P̔oł ar̄awōtean* (1870), *Mełu* (1872–74), *T̔atron* (1874–77), *Tiyatro* (1874–75, possibly longer), *T̔atron barekam mankants* (1876), and *Ḥikar* (1884–88), where most of his writings were first published. Contributed to some Eastern Armenian periodicals (e.g., *P̔ordz, Ardzagank̔, P̔aros Hayastani*), thereby avoiding Abdulhamid II's censorship, gaining wide fame but little fortune. Died of consumption in Constantinople.

Collections

Hoshosi dzer̄atetrě; Ptoyt mě Pōlsoy t̔ałerun mēj; Ḥikari gušakut̔iwnk̔. (Tiflis, 1892, 1900).
Taretsoyts ew gušakut̔iwnk̔ Ḥikari. (Tiflis, 1892; Cairo, 1936).
Erkasirut̔iwnner. 3 vols. (Tiflis, 1899–1900).
Ergitzabanakan hatuatzner. (Alexandrapol, [1904]).
Ambołj erker. 4 vols. (Constantinople, 1910–11).
Atamnaboyžn arewelean; Erku tērov tzar̄ay mě; P̔r̄oyg. (Constantinople, 1910).
Metzapatiw muratskanner and *Ksmit̔ner.* (Constantinople, 1910).
Arevelyan atamnabuž; Pałtasar ałbar; K̔ałak̔avarut̔yan vnasnerě. (Moscow, 1927).
Azgayin jojer; Hoshosi dzer̄atetrě; Tzitzał. (Moscow, 1927).
Metzapativ muratskanner; Ptuyt mě Polso t̔ałerun mej. (Moscow, 1927).
Erkeri liakatar žołovatzu. 11 vols. (Erevan, 1931–48).
Ḥndalov . . . (Boston, 1947).
Erkeri žołovatzu. 2 vols. (Erevan, 1954–55).
Erker. (Erevan, 1958).
Metzapatiw muratskanner, K̔ałak̔avarut̔ean vnasnerě, Ar̄tnin tesaranner ew Pałtasar ałbar. (Istanbul, 1961).
Azgayin jojer and *Ptoyt mě Pōlsoy t̔ałerun mēj.* (Istanbul, 1962).
Erkeri žołovatzu. 10 vols. (Erevan, 1962–1979).
Madoyan, G. *Anhayt ējer ev aforizmner.* (Erevan, 1964).
Erker. (Erevan, 1969).
Metzapatiw muratskanner, Ptoyt mě Pōlsoy t̔ałerun mēj. (Beirut, 1970).
Erker. (Erevan, 1979).
Bołaryan, H. *Erker.* (Erevan, 1987).

Texts

Atamnaboyžn arewelean. (Constantinople, 1868; Tiflis, 1899. (Comedy).
Azgayin jojer. (Constantinople, 1880, 1904, 1924; Tiflis, 1891, 1896). (Satire).
Ptoyt mě Pōlsoy t̔ałerun mēj. (Constantinople, 1880; Tiflis, 1892). (Satire).
Tzitzał. (Constantinople, 1883). (Allegorical satire).
Metzapatiw muratskanner. (Constantinople, 1888; Tiflis, 1891, 1895, 1900; Sofia, 1933; Erevan, 1934, 1936, 1950; Beirut, 1955; Venice, 1955; Cairo, 1962). (Satirical novel).
K̔ałak̔avarut̔ean vnasnerě. (Tiflis, 1900; Erevan, 1934, 1959, 1976; Cairo, 1954). (Satire).
Pałtasar ałbar. (Constantinople, 1910). (Comedy).

Šołokʻortʻě. (Constantinople, 1920, 1954). (Comedy).
Pstik kʻitʻ ev franseren lezu. (Erevan, 1927). (Satirical prose).
Mžłuk, tʻmbuk. (Erevan, 1977). (Satirical prose).

Translations

ARABIC

Khalīlī, Nizār *al-Mutasawwilūn al-shurafā'.* (Aleppo, n.d.).

ENGLISH

Antreassian, J. *The Honorable Beggars.* (New York, 1980).
Kudian, M. *Honourable Beggars.* (London, 1978).
Megerditchian, E. *Gentleman Beggars.* (Boston, 1930).
———. *Uncle Balthazar.* (Boston, 1933).

FRENCH

Ohannessian, Z., and Gressent, M. "Les honorables gueux; Le poète." *Humanité nouvelle,* February, 1899, 144–49.
Silnitzky, J. *Maître Balthasar.* (Paris, 1913).

GERMAN

Hagop-Krikor. *Herr Baltasar* and *Der Schmeichler.* (Gstaad, 1971).

GERMAN ANTHOLOGIES

AN, 57–66.

RUSSIAN

Balasan, V. *Vysokochtimye poproshaiki.* (Erevan, 1982).
Khachatrian, Ia. *Vysokochtimye poproshaiki.* (Moscow, 1937).
———. *Diadia Bagdasar.* (Moscow, 1937).
———. *Izbrannoe.* (Moscow, 1950).
Khodzhik, E. *Izbrannoe.* (Erevan, 1965).

Criticism

Abovyan, S. "Hakob Paronyan ev evropakan divanagitutʻyuně." *SG,* 1972/11, 143–46.
Aleksanian, E. "Gogol' i Paronian." *Gogol' i literatura narodov Sovetskogo Soiuza.* (Erevan, 1986), 272–88.
Arpʻiarean, T. "Yišataknerēs—Paroneani amusnutʻiwně." *M,* 3973 (1893), 7–9.
Asatryan, A. "Hakob Paronyaně ev Harutʻyun Sěvačyaně." *T,* 1964/5, 3–16.
Asatur, H. "Mełun Paroneani ḥmbagrutʻean ōrov." *M,* 3972 (1892), 275–79.
———. "Yakob Paroneani 'Tʻatroně'." *Taretsoyts Nšan-Papikeani* (Constantinople), 2 (1906), 111–36.
Bardakjian, K. "Baronian's *Tiyatro.*" *Klatzor(Gladzor) Armenological Review,* 2 (1986/1), 57–64.
Bazyan, S. "Hakob Paronyan." *T,* 1946/11–12, 113–24.
Darbinyan, V. "Hakob Paronyani tʻatergutʻyunnerě." *L,* 1972/5, 73–80.
Eremean, S. "Yakob Paronean." *B,* 71 (1913), 151–59.
Ěrłatʻbašyan, M. "Hakob Paronyani norahayt ergitzavepě." *L,* 1978/12, 41–46.
Feydit, F. "La comédie et la satire en Arménie: Baronian et Odian." *B,* 118 (1960), 167–78. 119 (1961), 24–30.
Gljyan, A. "Hakob Paronyani ařajin stełtzagortzutʻyunnerě." *BEH,* 1990/3, 82–87.
Grigoryan, A. "Hakob Paronyaně mankakan mamuli himnadir u mankagir." *SG,* 1964/5, 131–32.

Hakobyan, H. *Hay hełapʿoḥakan-demokratneri pʿilisopʿayakan hayatskʿnerě.* (Erevan, 1989). (On Paronean, Raffi, and Yarutʿiwn Sěvačean).

Ḥaṙatyan, A. "Hakob Paronyani ašḥataktsutʿyuně 'Asia' tʿertʿin." *L,* 1989/12, 49–56.

———. "Hakob Paronyani 'Erkeri žołovatzui' tzanotʿagrutʿyunneri masin." *PBH,* 1988/2, 112–23.

Hattēčean, Ṙ. *Yakob Paroneani mtermutʿean mēj.* (Istanbul, 1965).

Karinyan, A. "Metz humanist-groł Hakob Paronyaně." *T,* 1964/7, 3–14.

Kotʿikyan, A. "Metz ergitzabaně." *SG,* 1964/5, 108–17.

Łanalanyan, A. "Žołovrdakan banahyusutʿyan derě H. Paronyani ergitzankʿi mej." *T,* 1954/3, 53–62.

Madoyan, G. "Hakob Paronyani žaṙangutʿyan šurjě." *SG,* 1958/6, 151–55.

———. *Hakob Paronyan.* (Erevan, 1960).

———. "Hakob Paronyani 'Epʿratʿ ergitzatʿertʿě." *SG,* 1966/7, 149–53.

Makaryan, A. " 'Azgayin jojeri' grakan naḥapʿordzerě." *SG,* 1985/6, 136–42.

———. *Hakob Paronyani 'Azgayin jojerě'.* (Erevan, 1988).

———. "Irakani ev gełarvestakani haraberaktsutʿyuně 'Azgayin jojeri' kerparnerum." *BEH,* 1985/1, 165–70.

———. "Molierě ev Paronyaně." *L,* 1972/3, 35–42.

Mamurean, M. "Y. Y. Paronean." *AM,* 1891, 278–83.

Manukyan, A. *Hakob Paronyan, tznndyan 120—amyaki aṙtʿiv.* (Erevan, 1964).

Marguni, H. "Paronyani novelneri syužetayin kaṙutsvatzkʿě." *T,* 1964/12, 37–48.

Mkryan, M. "Hakob Paronyan." *PBH,* 1964/2, 3–16.

Ōšakan, Y. "Yakob Paronean, verjaban: Paroneani derě mer grakanutʿean mēj." *ANA,* 13 (1947/2), 19–26. 14 (1948/1), 33–35; 14 (1948/2), 31–34. 15 (1949/1), 6–9.

[Paronean, Ašot]. "Yakob Paroneani keankʿēn antip druagner." *Mšakoytʿ-azgagrakan taregirkʿ.* (Istanbul, 1948), 93–98.

Partagčean, G. *Yakob Paroneani aylabanakan karg mě erkerun patmakan dēmkʿern u dēpkʿerě.* (Boston, 1980).

Pasmajean, M. "Usumnasirutʿiwn Paroneani erkasirutʿeants." *B,* 58 (1900), 219–23, 273–76, 311–14.

Šahnur. "Tʿłtʿaktsutʿiwn." *AM,* January, 1880, 420–31. (On *Azgayin jojer, Ptoyt mě,* and others).

———. "Tʿłtʿaktsutʿiwn." *AM,* October, 1880, 418–19. (General information on Paronean).

———. "Tʿłtʿaktsutʿiwn." *AM,* 1884, 208–12. (On *Ḥikar* and others).

———. "Tʿłtʿaktsutʿiwn." *AM,* 1884, 509–15.

———. "Tʿłtʿaktsutʿiwn." *AM,* 1893, 190–92. (On *Azgayin jojer*).

Setʿean, Y. "Y. Paroneani mēk kʿani yatkanšakan kołmerě." *Yišatakaran,* V. Zardarean, (Cairo, 1933–39), part 5, 43–44.

Stepʿanyan, G. *Hakob Paronyan.* (Erevan, 1956).

———. "Hakob Paronyani 'Tʿiyatʿro' tʿurkʿeren parberakaně." *T,* 1962/9, 65–74.

———. "Hakob Paronyanin veragrvoł mi kʿani tzatzkanunneri masin." *PBH,* 1963/3, 137–46.

———. "Antzanotʿ ējer Hakob Paronyani grakan žaṙangutʿyunits." *SG,* 1964/5, 118–30.

———. "Hakob Paronyani 'Tʿatron' ergitzatʿertʿě." *PBH,* 1964/1, 57–72.

———. *Hakob Paronyan: kyakʻě ev stełtzagortzutʻyuně.* (Erevan, 1964).
———. "Hakob Paronyani 'Azgayin jojerě'." *T,* 1965/9, 75–112.
———. "Hakob Paronyani 'Azgayin jojeri' stełtzagortzakan patmutʻyuně." *T,* 1965/8, 18–40.
———. "Hakob Paronyani norahayt ergitzavepě." *PBH,* 1971/3, 17–34.
Terteryan, A. "Paronyani gełagitakan hayatskʻnerě." *SG,* 1941/1, 52–76; 2, 52–60; 3, 58–72; 5–6, 118–30. Reprinted in *Hay klasikner* (Erevan, 1944), 258–465.
V. B. "Yakob Paronean." *Murč,* 1905/4, 114–46.
Vałinak. "Paronean ew Adamean." *Ardzagankʻ,* 1891/7, 103–7; 1891/14, 214–15.
"Yakob Paronean (1842–1891)." *Yišatakaran,* V. Zardarean, (Cairo, 1933–39), part 5, 40–45.
Y. Y. "Yakob Paronean (kensagrakan aknark)." *Arakʻs* (Petersburg), 8/1 (1898), 89–95.
Zardarean, V. *Yušatōni grkʻoyk anmah ergitzaban Y. Paroneani.* (Istanbul, 1965).

PARSAMEAN, MERUŽAN (1883–1944)

Born in Apucheḥ, a village near Akn (Eğin, now Kemaliye, Turkey). Poet. Entrusted to his grandfather's care when his father was killed during the Armenian massacres of the mid-1890s. Studied at Armaš (near Izmit, Turkey). Published the periodical *Šantʻ* (1911–15) in Constantinople. Made Paris his home in 1919, where he and his younger brother, Mkrtich Parsamean (1886–1966), published the periodical *Keankʻ ew aruest* (1931–40). Also wrote in French.

Texts (verse)

Anrjankʻ. (Constantinople, 1904).
Patrankʻi tzałikner. (Constantinople, 1907).
Epʻratin zoherě. (Constantinople, 1908).
Kʻrizantʻēm. (Constantinople, 1908).
Marmnergutʻiwn. (Paris, 1919).
Mardkayin. (Paris, [1938]).

Translations

Navarian, A. *Les deux morts.* (Constantinople, 1913). (Poem).

Criticism

Dawitʻean, M. " 'Patrankʻi tzałiknerě' Meružan Parsameani." *AM,* 1908, 379–81.
Eremean, S. "Meružan Parsamean." *B,* 93 (1935), 17–20, 79–84, 193–95.
K[iwrčean], M. "M. A. Parsamean—Anrjankʻ." *Širak,* 3 (1905), 221–26.
Zardarean, Ṙ. "Anrjankʻ." *AM,* 1904, 1044–49.
Zawēn, T. "Parsamean, M. A. Anrjankʻ, K. Polis, 1904." *Murč,* 1905/5, 159–66.

PARTʻEWEAN, SURĒN (1876–1921)

Pen name: Surēn Partʻewean.

Born Sisak Partizpanean in Constantinople. Attended the Pērpērean and Kedronakan schools in his birthplace. Took refuge in Paris during the Armenian massacres of the mid-1890s and audited courses at the Sorbonne. Returned to Constantinople in 1908. Edited a number of periodicals (e.g., *Vałuan dzayně, Dašinkʻ, Dzayn hayreneats, Azg,* and others), and published collections of his short stories. Fled Smyrna in the early 1920s and spent his last days in Egypt. Died in Alexandria.

Texts

Ḥarazan. (Paris, 1901).
Kilikean arhawirkʻě. (Constantinople, 1909).
Kʻaykʻayum. (Smyrna, 1910).
Hayuhin. (Constantinople, 1911).
Ariwnin mateaně. (Cairo, 1915).

Other works

Egiptahay taretsoytsě. (Cairo, 1914).

Translations (English)

Antreassian, K. "A Drop of Water." *The New Armenia,* 8 (1916/18), 283–86.

Criticism

Grigoryan, A. "Suren Partʻevyani namaknerits." *SG,* 1974/8, 154–57.
———. "Hayrenasirutʻyan ev azgayin azatagrutʻyan gałapʻarnerě Suren Partʻevyani erkerum." *PBH,* 1985/4, 117–25.
Ōhanyan, A. "Daraskzbi hay azatagrakan šaržumneri ardzagankʻnerě Suren Partʻevyani ardzakum." *SG,* 1970/6, 140–44.

PATKANEAN, GABRIĒL (1802–1889)

Born in Tiflis. Father of Ṙapʻayēl Patkanean (q.v.). A prolific writer, teacher, translator, and journalist. Grew up in Astrakhan (1805–27). Launched his teaching career in Nor Naḫijewan (Rostov-na-Donu, 1827–46), where he set up a private school (1834–46). While in Nor Naḫijewan, he became a married priest, but he was defrocked, jailed in Rostov (1853–60), and banished to the interior of Russia on false charges of plotting to assassinate the mayor of Nor Naḫijewan. Returned from exile in 1863 and lived in St. Petersburg, where he resumed his teaching activities. Listed below are his literary works only.

Texts

Šawarš B. (St. Petersburg, 1863).
Hṙipʻsimē kam Pʻrkutʻiwn Hayastani. (Rostov-on-Don, 1875).
Mrmunjkʻ Yisusi. (Rostov-on-Don, 1875).
Anušawan. (Smyrna, 1875).
Mah Parēti. (Smyrna, 1875).
Sanduḫt. (Constantinople, 1876).
Zawan. (Smyrna, 1877).
Pʻaṙnak. (Smyrna, 1877).
Paroyr. (Smyrna, 1876).

Criticism

A, 1879, 233.
Eremean, S. "Gabriēl tēr Patkanean." *B,* 71 (1913), 193–203.
Ḥalatʻean, G. "Tēr Gabriēl Patkaneani dzeṙagirneri masin." *A,* 1902, 174–81.
Nazaryan, Š. *Gabriel Patkanyani kyankʻn u grakan-hasarakakan gortzuneutʻyuně (1830–60akan tʻvakanner).* (Erevan, 1956).
Sałyan, M. *Patkanyanner.* (Erevan, 1982). (History of the Patkanyan family).

“T'agawor kayser šnorhatz nerumn dadaratz k'ahanay Gabriēl Patkaneanin.” *A,* 1879, 100.

PATKANEAN, ṘAP'AYĒL (1830–1892)

Pen names: Aḥtamerkean, Ašuł Karapet, Čankov Mamuk, Gamaṙ-K'at'ipa, Ḥamchi, Ḥěči-ała, Nštrak, Siwliwk, M. Vayelchean, and others.

Born in Nor Naḥijewan (Rostov-na-Donu) to a well-known family of intellectuals, whose traditions found their fullest expression in Ṙap'ayēl's literary output. Educated in his father's school in his birthplace. Irregularly attended the Lazarean (Lazarevskii) Institute (1843–49), the University of Dorpat (now Tartu, Estonia, 1851–52), and the University of Moscow (1852–54), and completed his higher studies at the University of St. Petersburg (1855–60). In 1852, he founded, with two fellow students (Gēorg K'ananean and Mnatsakan T'imurean), a literary coterie that they named *Gamaṙ-K'at'ipa* (by inserting an *a* between the initial letters of their first names, GaMaṘ, and combining the first two letters of their last names), and which Patkanean later assumed as a pen name. He returned to his birthplace in 1867 and became a teacher. During these years he also wrote novels and short stories.

Collections

Ěntir ašḥatasirut'iwnk'. 3 vols. (Vols. 1 and 2, Petersburg, 1893; Vol. 3, Nor Nakhijewan, 1904).
Banastełtzut'yunner. (Erevan, 1941).
Mankakan banastełtzut'yunner. (Erevan, 1941).
Mankakan erger. (Erevan, [1944]).
Erkeri žołovatzu. Ardzak. (Erevan, 1946).
Erker. (Erevan, 1955).
Erkeri žołovatzu. 8 vols. (Erevan, 1963–74).
T'op'chyan, S. *Erker.* (Erevan, 1980).
Papoyan, Ō. *Erker.* (Erevan, 1984).

Texts

Gamaṙ-K'at'ipayi ardzak ew chap'aberakan ašḥatut'iwnnerě. 5 vols. (Petersburg, 1855–57). (Prose and poetry).
Gamaṙ-K'at'ipayi banastełtzut'iwnk'ě. (Moscow, 1864). (Verse).
Patmuatzk'ner Nor-Naḥijewani očov. (Petersburg, 1875). (Stories).
Azat erger. (Tiflis, 1878; Geneva, 1903). (Verse).
Pampulios. (Rostov-on-Don, 1879). (Play).
Nor Naḥijewani k'nar. (Rostov-on-Don, 1879). (Verse).
Mankakan erger. (Tiflis, 1880). (Verse).
Gamaṙ-K'at'ipayi banastełtzut'iwnk'ě. (Moscow, 1881). (Verse).
Tikin ew nažišt. (Tiflis, 1884). (Novelette).
Šaterēn mēkě. (Nor Nakhijewan, 1905). (Story).
Chaḥu. (Tiflis, 1909; Erevan, 1946, 1951). (Story; tr. from Nakhijewan dialect by S. Lisitsean).
Garun. (Erevan, 1941).
Tzitzeṙnak. (Erevan, 1941).
Hovhannes, D. *Astłikner.* (Erevan, 1981).
Berberean, Ṙ. “Ṙ. Patkaneani antip namaknerě.” *Vēm,* 1 (1933/1), 39–52.

Translations

ENGLISH

Arnot, R. "Sweet Lady, Whence the Sadness in your Face?" *The New Armenia,* 1929/1, 11–12.

Blackwell, A. "Let the Wind Blow." *The New Armenia,* 1916/11, 173.

Boyajian, Z. "Leretz amberi." *Armenia,* 1913/10, 294.

"The Tears of Araxes." *Šołakatʻ,* 1961/67.

ENGLISH ANTHOLOGIES

AL, 48, 49–54.

AP, 66–94, 250.

FRENCH

"Le jeune Vaniote." *L'Arménie* (London), 1893/54, 3.

"Les larmes de l'Araxe." *L'Arménie* (London), 1894/64, 1.

"Les larmes de l'Araxe." *Le Feu,* 1919/4, 63.

FRENCH ANTHOLOGIES

APA, 23–31.

LPA, 170–73.

PA, 81–113.

PAAM, 84–88.

GERMAN

Leist, A. *Drei Erzählungen.* (Leipzig, n.d.). (Mein Nachbar; Der verodete Hof; Ich war verlobt).

GERMAN ANTHOLOGIES

AD, 24–29.

ITALIAN ANTHOLOGIES

LPAM, 97–104.

RUSSIAN

Chalkhush'ian, G. *Armianskaia poeziia v litse Rafaila Patkaniana.* (Rostov-on-Don, 1886), 41–58.

Pevets grazhdanskoi skorbi. Izbrannye stikhotvoreniia. (Moscow, 1904).

Vermishev, I. *Nozhichek.–Rasskaz vodovoza.* (Tiflis, 1889).

RUSSIAN ANTHOLOGIES

AAP, 374–82.

ABS, 347–409.

ARPO, 143–44.

BPA, 271–82.

RAN, 15–25.

VAM, 25–54.

SPANISH ANTHOLOGIES

APAS, 109–14.

Criticism

Abełyan, H. "Patkanyani ev Sundukyani grakan mtermutʻyunĕ." *T,* 1964/1, 35–50.

Abovyan, S. *Azatagrakan paykʻari motivĕ Ṙ. Patkanyani stełtzagortzutʻyunnerum.* (Erevan, 1984).

Aleksanian, E. "Gogolevskoe v satire R. Patkaniana." *L,* 1975/1, 31–41.

Bałdasaryan, A. "Ĕntʻertselov groł namaknerĕ." *SG,* 1980/10, 118–22.

Berberean, Ṙ. "Gamaṙ K'at'ipa." *HK,* 10 (1931–32/2), 86–96; 3, 147–53; 4, 137–45; 5, 79–86; 6, 147–57; 7, 129–34; 8, 135–41; 9, 127–37; 10, 117–22; 11, 103–10; 12, 130–40.
Chalkhush'ian, G. *Armianskaia poeziia v litse Rafaila Patkaniana.* (Rostov-on-Don, 1886).
Chilingarian, E. "Rafael Patkanian i tvorchestvo nekotorykh basnopistsev." *L,* 1983/2, 55–65.
———. "Patkanian i Nekrasov: tipologiia tvorchestva." *L,* 1986/1, 31–40.
Geanjetsean, A. "Gamaṙ-K'at'ipayi 'Meznits šat aṙajě'." *Lumay,* 1 (1904), 111–17.
Hovnan, G. *Mayr Arak'si ap'erov . . . 'Arak'si artasuk'i' mijazgayin ardzagan-k'nerě.* (Erevan, 1990).
Inčikyan, A. "Ṙap'ayel Patkanyani ev 1850–80akan t'vakanneri hay azgayin-azatagrakan šaržumneri gnahatut'yan hartsi šurjě." *PBH,* 1961/1, 122–44.
Išḥanean, B. *Hasarakakan gałap'arnerě Ṙ. Patkaneani ew S. Šahazizi banastełtzu-t'iwnneri mēj.* (Tiflis, 1910).
Kusikean, K. "Banastełtz k'ałak'atsi." *Murč,* 1894/5, 661–74; 6, 804–26.
Łulean, A. "Grakanakan mi tgeł erewoyt'i aṙit'ov." *Murč,* 1892/10, 1516–17.
Madat'ean, E. "Azgi ergichě." *Murč,* 1892/10, 1469–81; 11, 1660–70; 1893/4, 606–21.
Malḥasean, S. "Ṙafayēl Patkanean." *Murč,* 1892/9, 1354–59.
Mkrtchyan, V. *Ṙap'ayel Patkanyan. (Hamaṙot menagrakan aknark).* (Erevan, 1966).
Muradyan, H. *Ṙap'ayel Patkanyan.* (Erevan, 1956).
———. "Ṙap'ayel Patkanyanin trvatz mi sḥal gnahatakani aṙt'iv." *PBH,* 1958/3, 214–39.
Muradyan, L. "Rafayel Patkanyani stełtzagorrtzut'yuně žamanaki grakan k'nna-datut'yan gnahatmamb." *PBH,* 1980/4, 32–44.
"Namakner Patkanyanin." *SG,* 1980/10, 123–25.
Ōhanyan, A. "Ṙap'ayel Patkanyaně ev ašḥarhabarě." *BEH,* 1974/2, 225–32.
———. "Sotsial-tntesakan hartserě Ṙap'ayel Patkanyani hraparakaḥosut'yan mej." *L,* 1974/5, 22–31.
———. *Ṙafayel Patkanyani hraprakaḥosut'yuně.* (Erevan, 1981).
P'echikean, E. "Gamaṙ-K'at'ipa ew M. Nalbandean (irents 100–ameakin aṙit'ov)." *B,* 87 (1930), 484–89.
Šahaziz, E. "Arak'si artasuk'ě." *EJ,* 1951/4–6, 68–69.
Sałyan, M. "Ṙafayel Patkanyan." *L,* 1980/12, 35–44.
———. "Ṙafayel Patkanyaně ev ṙus vat'sunakannerě." *PBH,* 1980/4, 18–31.
———. *Ṙafayel Patkanyan. Kyank'ě ev gortzě.* (Erevan, 1980).
———. *Patkanyanner.* (Erevan, 1982). (History of the Patkanyan family).
Sarinyan, S. "Ṙafayel Patkanyani grakan davanank'ě." *PBH,* 1980/4, 3–17.
Simonyan, Ṙ. "Patkanyani ardzakě." *SG,* 1968/11, 149–58.
Širvanzadē. "Gamaṙ-K'at'ipa." *HK,* 2 (1923–24/6), 36–47.
Štikyan, S. "Patkanyani tohmatzaṙě." *L,* 1966/8, 106–12.
Tcheraz, M. "Kamar-Katiba." *Great Thoughts,* 8 (1897/202), 312.
Tēr-Mkrtchean, G. "Ṙap'ayēl Patkaneani yišatakin." *A,* 1901, 465–67.
T'op'chyan, S. "Ṙap'ayel Patkanyan." *SG,* 1980/10, 110–17.
Tzaturean, A. "Gamaṙ-K'at'ipayi t'arm širmi aṙaj." *HGP,* 5 (1894), 332–36.
Vardanyan, V. "Azgayin metz banastełtz Ṙap'ayel Patkanyaně." *EJ,* 1956/3 48–54.
Yovhannisean, T. "Namak ḥmbagrin." *Murč,* 1890/5, 772–74.

PATMUTʻIWN ŁAPʻANTSWOTS

A history of the wars fought in the 1720s by Dawitʻ Bēk and his companions. Believed to have been written by Fr. Łukas Sebastatsi Stepʻanosean (1709–52), a Mekhitarist monk, who based his narrative on the eyewitness accounts of Stepʻan Šahumean (18th c.) and Tēr Awetikʻ (18th c.), both of whom had been close collaborators of Dawitʻ Bēk.

Texts

Stepʻanosean Gulamireants, A. *Ĕntir patmutʻiwn Dawitʻ Bēgin ew paterazmats hayotsn Ḥapʻanu orkʻ ełen ĕnddēm tʻurkʻats i merum žamanaki, ayn ē yami Tearn 1722, ew hayots 1171.* (Ējmiatzin, 1871).

Aramean, S. *Dawitʻ Bēk kam "Patmutʻiwn Łapʻantswots."* (Venice, 1978). (A critical edition of Stepʻanosean's text).

Criticism

Čemčemean, S. "H. Łukas Sebastatsi (1709–1752) hełinak Dawitʻ Bēki Patmutʻean." *B,* 130 (1972), 491–501.

Łltčean, A. "Niwtʻer Dawitʻ Bēki patmutʻean verabereal." *A,* 1905, 382–87.

Pʻēchikean, E. " 'Dawitʻ Bēk'i patmakan ałbiwrnerĕ ew Mḥitʻareankʻ." *B,* 96 (1938), 172–87.

PATMUTʻIWN PʻARĒZI EW VENNAYI

An adaptation of a text by Yovhannēs Tērzntsi (16th–17th c.), a well-known publisher and translator. J. -P. Mahé has maintained that the European source of Tērzntsi's version is an Italian translation of the original Catalan (*Paris E Viana*; cf. R. H. Kévorkian, *Catalogue des "incunables" arméniens . . .* Genève, 1986, p. xiii). However, some scholars believe that the original (*Paris et Vienne*) was penned in French by Pierre de la Cépède of Marseilles in 1342. A Turkish translation made by Eremia chēlēpi Kʻēōmiwrčean (1637–95) from an Armenian version (which Kʻēōmiwrčean maintained was derived from a Latin original) appeared in Constantinople in 1871, under the title *Hikʻeayēi Faris vē Vēna, tʻēēlif ōlunmuš latʻin lisanĕnta vē tʻērčēmē ōlunmuš hay lisanĕna, pir ēhli mēarif zatʻ marifētʻiylē, Homeros istʻillahi ilē, vē tʻēkʻrar tʻērčēmē ōlunmuš lisani tʻiwrkʻiyē, mēvzun vē mugaffa ōlarag, Eremia Chēlēpi Kʻēōmiwrčeants marifētʻiylē . . . .*

Text

Melikʻ-Ōhanjanyan, K. *Patmutʻiwn Pʻarēzi ew Vennayi (mijnadaryan aspetakan siravep); Patmutʻiwn Venetik kʻałakʻin (chapʻatzo).* (Erevan, 1966), 91–234. (Text and study).

PAYAZAT, SERGO (1909–1971)

A native of Alexandrapol (Leninakan, now Gyumri), Payazat was educated in Tiflis and worked as a journalist in Erevan. Wrote prose, verse, and plays.

Texts

Erku erg gyułerin. (Tiflis, 1926).
Hołašen. (Tiflis, 1929).
Manr mardik. (Erevan, 1931).
Kałnuti siraharnerĕ. (Erevan, 1948).
Getĕ varder ē berum. (Erevan, 1981).

Other works

A. P. Chekhov. (Erevan, 1960).

PAYTZAṘĒ, (1859–1904)

Pen name: Paytzaṙē.

Born Varšam Trdateants in the village of Giwlagarak (now in Loṙi, Armenia). An *ašuł*. Spent most of his life in Alexandrapol (Leninakan, now Gyumri).

Poetry

Ašuł Paytzaṙēi (Varšam Trdateants) ergerě. (Tiflis, 1895).
THG, 201–5.

PĒRPĒREAN, ṘĒTʻĒOS (1848–1907)

Born in Constantinople and educated at the local Nersēsean school. A celebrated educator and poet. In 1876 he founded his own school, the Pērpērean, destined to become a prestigious institution, where generations of Armenians and a host of prominent Armenian intellectuals were educated. The school moved to Cairo in 1924 and was closed in 1934.

Literary texts (verse)

Aṙajin terewkʻ. (Constantinople, 1877).
Ḥohkʻ ew yuškʻ. (Venice, 1904).

Other works

Mardik ew irkʻ. (Constantinople, 1886).
Dastiaraki mě ḥōskʻerě. (Vienna, 1901).
Dprots ew dpruṫiwn. (Vienna, 1907).

Criticism

Ačaṙyan, H. "Haytni mankavarž Ṙetʻeos Perperyan." *EJ,* 1950/11–12, 64–69.
Eremean, M. "Ṙētʻēos Pērpērean." *B,* 70 (1912), 326–34.
"Ṙētʻēos ēf. Pērpērean." *A,* 1907, 436.
"Ṙētʻēos Pērpēreani kʻsan ew hing ameay gortzunēutʻean yobeleaně." *A,* 1901, 441–42.

PĒŠIKTʻAŠLEAN, MKRTICH (1828–1868)

Pen name: Hrant.

Born in Constantinople. Received his education at the Mekhitarist school in the district of Pera in his birthplace. Pursued his studies at the Muratean school in Padua (1839–45). Upon his return, he taught and was intimately involved in community affairs, distinguishing himself by his artistic gifts and patriotic zeal to promote unity and enlightenment among his fellow countrymen. He was one of the first Romantic authors. Composed verse and wrote drama in both Classical and Modern Armenian. He is also remembered for founding and acting in the Armenian theater of Constantinople. He died of conumption, which had much earlier claimed the lives of his parents and his brother, and which eventually killed his sister.

Collections

Matenagituṫiwnkʻ M. Pēšikṫašleani. (Constantinople, 1870).

Tałer. (Tiflis, 1903).
Chōpanean, A. *Mkrtich Pēšikt‘ašleani k‘ert‘uatznern u čaṙerě.* (Paris, 1904).
Tałk‘ ew t‘atergut‘iwnk‘. (New York, 1917).
Inčikyan, A. *Tałer.* (Erevan, 1947).
Banastełtzut‘iwnner, čaṙer: hatuatzner. (Venice, 1956).
Tałer. (Erevan, 1961).
Manukyan, A. *Erkeri liakatar žołovatzu.* (Erevan, 1987).

Texts (plays)

Erek‘ k‘ajer. (Tiflis, 1885). (Comedy).
Awazakats. (Constantinople, 1909). (Comedy).
Aršak. (Constantinople, 1909). (Drama).
Vahan Mamikonean. (Constantinople, 1910). (Drama).
Vahē. (Constantinople, 1910). (Drama).
Manukyan, A. "Mkrtich Pešikt‘ašlyani norahayt namaknerě." *PBH,* 1983/1, 197–207. (Letters).

Translations

ENGLISH

Miller, F. "The Lyre of the Virgin." *Armenia,* 1905/2–3, 27–28.

ENGLISH ANTHOLOGIES

AL, 47, 48–49.
AP, 60–65.
ALP, 89.

FRENCH

Besse, L. "La bonne nouvelle." *L'Arménie* (London), December 1, 1897.

FRENCH ANTHOLOGIES

APA, 33–37.
LPA, 166–67.
PAAM, 86–91.

GERMAN

Leist, A. "Zieh hin o meine Lieder," "Ach, möchte ich ein Lüftchen sein," "Frühling." *Litterarische Skizzen,* A. Leist. (Leipzig, n.d.), 61–64.

GERMAN ANTHOLOGIES

AD, 18–21.
ALG, 121.

ITALIAN ANTHOLOGIES

LPAM, 75–87.

RUSSIAN ANTHOLOGIES

ABS, 2, 523–27.
BPA, 431–36.

Criticism

Adonts, N. "Pēšikt‘ašlean ew ktsord ḥndirner." *HK,* 9 (1930–31/6), 79–94.
Alt‘unean, G. "M. Pēšikt‘ašlean." *Murč,* 1902/11, 123–41.
Arp‘iarean, T. "Mer patkerě–Mkrtich Pēšikt‘ašlean." *M,* 3986 (1893), 217–19.
Bampuk‘čean, G. "Norayayt p‘šrank‘ner Mkrtich Pēšikt‘ašleanēn." *S,* 1970, 243–45.
Chōpanean, A. "M. Pēšikt‘ašlean." *Murč,* 1905/5, 77–88; 6, 36–46; 7, 5–13.

———. "Pēšikťašlean ew ťatronē hayots mēj." *Lumay,* 7–8 (1906), 5–45.
———. *Mkrtich Pēšikťašleani keank'n u gortzē.* (Paris, 1907).
———. "Mkrtich Pēšikťašlean." *B,* 94 (1935), 280–88.
Eremean, S. "Baŕ u k'nar." *B,* 87 (1930), 269–70.
Eritsean, S. "Im tzanōťuťiwnē p. Pēšikťašleani het." *P'ordz,* 1877/4, 186–97.
Hin ew nor nšanawor dēmk'er, 13: *Mkrtich Pēšikťašlean.* (N.p., n.d.).
Mirzabekyan, J. "Erkeri liakatar žołovatzu." *L,* 1988/1, 82–85.
P'echikean, E. "Mkrtich Pēšikťašlean." *B,* 87 (1930), 524–31.
Pipēŕčean, A. *Yušardzan M. Pēšikťašleani. Metz banastełtzin keank'n u gortzerē.* (Constantinople, 1914).
Safaryan, V. "Erb ē grvel Pešikťašlyani 'Kořnak' piesē?" *L,* 1966/1, 75–82.
———. "Mkrtich Pešikťašlyanē ev 'Hamazgeats ěnkeruťyunē." *PBH,* 1966/4, 197–206.
———. "Pešikťašlyanē ev hay nor eražštuťyunē." *L,* 1967/1, 55–61.
———. "Mkrtich Pešikťašlyan." *PBH,* 1968/4, 185–92.
———. "Mkrtich Pešikťašlyanē ev 50—akan ťvakanneri azgayin-hayrenasirakan ergē." *SG,* 1968/12, 124–31.
———. *Mkrtich Pešikťašlyan, kyank'ē ev gortzuneuťyunē.* (Erevan, 1972).
Sewean, S. "Lalli Ťōlēntal. Charls Uōlf. Mkrtich Pēšikťašlean." *B,* 81 (1924), 51–52.
Siruni, Y. "Aruestagētē Mkrtich Pēšikťašleani mēj." *HK,* 11 (1932–33/8), 100–110.
Štikyan, S. "Mkrtich Pešikťašlyani ergitzakan mi banastełtzuťyan masin." *PBH,* 1989/2, 61–70.
V. K. "Mkrtich Pēšikťašlean, dasakanuťenēn dēpi řomanťizm." *B,* 126 (1968), 330–56.
Yaruťiwnean, Y. "Mkrtich Pēšikťašlean: patmakan-k'nnadatakan tesuťiwn." *A,* 1912, 49–53, 840–57.

PĒŠIKŤAŠLEAN, NŠAN (1898–1972)

A native of Constantinople and a resident of France. Received his incomplete elementary education in his birthplace. Although his fame rests upon his satire, Pēšikťašlean was a prolific author of plays, verse, and prose writings, some of which are still strewn in the periodical press while others are still in manuscript form.

Texts

Ěnker Šahnazar, ergitzavēp. (Paris, 1927; Sofia, 1937).
Sidonna. (Paris, 1928).
Ŕappi (k'naravēp). (Constantinople, 1931).
Ergitzakan. (Paris, 1933).
Hiwandtes. (Paris, 1937).
Tzałrankarner. (Paris, 1938).
Hay ałbrtik'. (Paris, 1941).
Ergitzavēper. (Paris, 1942).
Luluti (hrašavēp biwzandakan šrjanēn). (Paris, 1942).
Tzirani gōti. (Paris, 1945).
Zēnuzard. (Paris, 1946).

Mer partēzēn. (Paris, 1947).
Yakob Ōšakan. (Paris, 1947).
Mer draḥtēn. [Paris, 1948].
Grigor Narekatsi ew Smbat II (patmakan ťateraḥał). (Paris, 1950).
Yuzumě. (Beirut, 1953).
Momianer: noragoyn tzałrankarner. (Paris, 1954).
Sadayēlin pochin tak u šukʻin: vēp. (Cairo, 1954).
Lusaberd. (Paris, 1956).
Yisusi dimankarě. (Cairo, 1957 [cover says 1958]).
Hrašagortz hayě. (Beirut, 1957, 1972).
Mełkʻi kʻarě. (Beirut, 1960).
Erknayin zroyts. (Beirut, 1961).
Bžiškner ew hiwandner. (Beirut, 1964).
Hrašalur patmuťiwn hayots: Bagratunikʻ ew Ṙubineankʻ, Ašot I.ēn minchew Heťum I, 859–1270. (Beirut, 1972).
Hndkahawer. (Beirut, 1973).

Other works

Ťaterakan dēmkʻer. (Beirut, 1969).

Criticism

Azatean, D. "Nšan Pēšiktʻašlean, 'Ṙappi'n." *HK,* 10 (1931–32/4), 120–22.
Baluean, H. " 'Sidonna', hełinak Nšan Pēšiktʻašlean, patmuťean ew aruesti nkatařmamb." *Z,* 1 (1929–[30]), 30–36.
Chōpanean, A. "Yisus ew Nšan Pēšiktʻašleani eřankarě." *ANA,* 3 (1931/3–4), 88–116. (On "Ṙappi," including "Nardos," "Dziťeni',"and "Sidonna").
Vehazat, A. "Pʻoḥan graḥōsakani." *AND,* 4 (1953), 130–32.
Yovhannisean, A. *Nšan Pēšiktʻašlean: usumnasiruťiwn.* (Paris, 1928).

PETROS DI SARGIS GILANENTS (d. 1724)

Biographical information regarding this author is sketchy. He spoke a number of languages and participated in the Armenian liberation movement in the first quarter of the eighteenth century. Stimulated Russian interest and influence in northwestern Iran by supplying the Russians with vital information about the region and by forming an "Armenian squadron" to fight alongside the Russians. Killed in action in Resht. His only surviving work is a chronicle that covers the years 1722–23.

Text

"Žamanakagruťiwn Petros di Sargis Gilanēntsi jułayetswots barbařov gratz." *Kʻřunk hayots ašḥarhin,* 1863, pp. 81–112, 181–212.

Translations

English

Minassian, C. *The Chronicle of Petros de Sarkis Gilanentz.* (Lisbon, 1959).

Russian

"Dnevnik osady Ispagani afganami, vedennyi Petrosom di Sarkis Gilanents v 1722 i 1723 godakh. Materialy dlia istorii Persii. Perevod i ob'iasneniia K. Patkanova." (St. Petersburg, 1870). (Prilozhenie K XVII-mu tomu Zapisok Imp. Akad. nauk, no. 3).

Turkish

Andreasyan, H. *Osmanlı-Iran-Rus Ilişkilerine ait iki Kaynak. I. Petros di Sarkis Gilanentz'in Kronolojisi. II. Nadir Şah Devrine ait bir Anonim Kronoloji.* (Istanbul, 1974). (Petros di Sargis Gilanents text, pp. 1–52).

Criticism

Hovannissian, A. "Pétros di Sargis Gilanentz, Notes biographiques et historiques." *REArm.* N. S. 1 (1964), 217–32. (A translation of article below).

Yovhannisean, A. "Petros di Sargis Gilanents." *A,* 1916, 105–28. (Reprinted separately, Ējmiatzin, 1916).

PETROS ŁAPʻANTSI (d. 1784)

Petros was from the region of Łapʻan (Siwnikʻ) and as a nuncio or primate he spent most of his long life in Constantinople and the neighboring cities. He died in Nicomedia (Izmit, Turkey).

Texts (verse)

Grkʻoyk kochetseal ergaran. (Constantinople, 1772).

MKH, 106–8; 388; 390–91; 417–26. (4 poems).

"Ałałak ḥorhrdabar aṙ bardzrealn Astuatz . . ." ("Erdnum arewt arkʻayakan, vard, vard.") *TH,* 82–84.

Nazaryan, Š. *Petros Łapʻantsi.* (Erevan, 1969).

———. *Banastełtzutʻyunner.* (Erevan, 1990).

Translations

French

LPA, 151–53.

Criticism

Asatur, H. "Moṙtsuatz banastełtz mě." *AM,* 1904/1, 16–20.

Eremean, A. "Petros Łapʻantsii mi ergi antip pʻopʻoḥakě." *S,* 1910, 138–39.

Kʻiwrtean, Y. "Antzanōtʻ hay tałachap mě." *Kochnak Hayastani,* 20 (1920), 795–96.

Nazaryan, Š. *Petros Łapʻantsi.* (Erevan, 1969), 5–225.

———. "Petros Łapʻantsin ev nra azatasirakan ergerě." *PBH,* 1966/1, 229–38.

PETROSYAN, MADATʻ (1867–1944)

Born in the village of Kotʻi (or Kotʻigeł, renamed Šavaršavan, now in Noyemberyan, Armenia). A writer of short stories. Worked as a mechanic for a while and was active in social and public activities in Tiflis.

Texts

Patmuatzkʻner. (Tiflis, 1906).

Patmuatzkʻner, grkʻuyk 2–rd. (Tiflis, 1911).

Nor darbnots. (Tiflis, 1925).

Patmvatzkʻner. (Tiflis, 1928).

Patmvatzkʻner. (Erevan, 1930).

Patmvatzkʻner. (Erevan, 1931).

Mišt patrast. (Erevan, 1932).

Pionerě hngamyakum. (Tiflis, 1932).

P'ok'rik mek'enavarě. (Tiflis, 1934).
Patmvatzk'ner. (Tiflis, 1935).
Mankut'yun. (Tiflis, 1935).
Mankakan patmvatzk'ner. (Erevan, 1940).
Patmvatzk'ner. (Erevan, 1949).

P'ŌLATEAN, KARAPET (1914–1986)

Born in Marash (Kahramanmaraš, Turkey). Novelist and poet. Miraculously survived the Armenian massacres and deportations of 1915 and found shelter in Aleppo, where he received his elementary education. Taught in Addis Ababa (1929–31) and moved to Marseilles permanently in 1931.

Texts

Arewelk'i tłak'ě. (Paris, 1946; Beirut, 1978).
Kě hražarim hayut'enē . . . (Paris, 1949; Beirut, 1979).
Veradardz. (Cairo, 1955).
Artziwnerě anapatin mēj. (Paris, 1958).
Loyser. (Paris, 1964).
Krakē šapikě. (Beirut, 1966). (Continuation of *Artziwnerě anapatin mēj*).

Other works

Zroyts. 5 vols. (Paris, 1952; Cairo, 1961; Beirut, 1966, 1971, 1979).
Haykakan sp'iwřk'ě ir derakatarnerov. (Beirut, 1973). (1st vol. of a supposedly multi-volume work).

Criticism

Baluean, H. "Artziwnerě anapatin mēj." *Z* (amsat'ert'), 3 (1959/11–12), 14.
Mḥit'arean, G. "Kě hražarim hayut'enē." *HK,* 29 (1951/5), 103–9.

POŁOSYAN, HṘIP'SIME (1899–1972)

Połosyan (Asilyan) was born and educated in Tiflis and attended the Transcaucasian University. Poetess and translator, mostly from Russian into Armenian. Wrote poetry principally for children. She was active in Sergei Gorodetski's "Tsekh poetov" and published her first poem in Russian in 1919. Worked as a literary editor for the monthly *Mankakan tziler* of Tiflis (1930–31). In 1934 she moved to Erevan, where she briefly headed the children's literature section (1937–38) of the Union of Soviet Writers of Armenia.

Texts

Banastełtzut'yunner. (Tiflis, 1930).
Metak's. (Tiflis, 1931).
Mek'enaneri ert'ě. (Tiflis, 1932).
Mayrakan. (Erevan, 1936).
Lusni vra. (Erevan, 1936).
Margartatzałki ev lusatitiki hek'iat'ě. (Erevan, 1937).
P'ok'rik pioneri ev p'ołkapi masin. (Erevan, 1939).
Banastełtzut'yunner. (Erevan, 1942).
Ordineri het. (Erevan, 1942).
Ḥndut'yun. (Erevan, 1948).

Banastełtzuťyunner. (Erevan, 1950).
Karda ays girkʻě–tes inch ē dařnum mirgě. (Erevan, 1951).
Hušardzan. (Erevan, 1951).
Im tzałikě. (Erevan, 1953).
Havatarmuťyun. (Erevan, 1954).
Andzrevits heto. (Erevan, 1958).
Anťařamě. (Erevan, 1961).
Astłayin čampʻordě. (Erevan, 1963).
Ereko. (Erevan, 1966).
Ardzagankʻ (hušer). (Erevan, 1973).

Translations

English

Evans, G. "From the Dim Ages." *SL,* 1966/3, 143.

French anthologies

Gamara, P. *E*, 71–72.
LPA, 286–87.

German

Leschnitzer, F. "Aus Zeitentiefe." *Sowjet-Literatur,* 1966/3, 141.

Russian

Rodnye liudi. Stikhi. (Moscow, 1960).
Snegova, I. *Nasha ulitsa. Stikhi.* (Erevan, 1952).
Vernost'. (Erevan, 1956).
Vo imia mira. Stikhi. (Erevan, 1952).

Spanish

Alberti, R. y Maria Teresa Leon. "De los sigolos lejanos." *Literatura Sovietica,* 1966/3, 142.

Bibliographies

Muradyan, M. *Hřipʻsime Połosyan: matenagituťyun.* (Erevan, 1976).

PŌYAČEAN, EDUARD (1915–1966)

Pen names: Alpaťros, E. Sarean, Vazgēn Tiranean, E. Tzovikean.

A native of the village of Ḥētěr Beg (Musa Dagh, Turkey). Educated in his birthplace and at the Čemaran in Beirut, 1930–35. He taught in Beirut until his death. Numerous writings of his, both in prose and verse, are still scattered in periodicals.

Collections

Erker. (Beirut, 1972).

Texts (prose and verse)

Sēr ew višt. (Beirut, 1944).
Hołě. (Beirut, 1948).
Tułť zawaknerus. (Beirut, 1960).
Tomar taragri. (Beirut, 1963).
Erku namakner. (Beirut, 1964).
Other works: Dēmkʻer. (Beirut, 1967).

PṘŌŠEAN, PERČ (1837–1907)

Pen names: Pahlawuni, Perč Pr̄ōšeants, Yovhannēs Pr̄ōš Aštaraketsi.

Born Yovhannēs Tēr-Ar̄ak'elean in Aštarak, Armenia. He was educated in his birthplace and the Nersisean school of Tiflis (1852–55), following which he worked as a teacher, photographer, and a charcoal dealer in various cities of the Caucasus (Tiflis, Šuši, Agulis, etc.) and southern Russia (Astrakhan). He briefly contributed to the influential *Mšak* and later to *P'ordz,* and he settled permanently in Tiflis in 1887, when he was invited to teach Armenian at the Nersisean school. Towards the end of his life, Pr̄ōšean made a short trip to Europe. He died in Baku but was buried in Tiflis.

Collections

Erker. 2 vols. (Erevan, 1939–41).
Erkeri žołovatzu. 3 vols. (Erevan, 1953–54).
Erkeri žołovatzu. 7 vols. (Erevan, 1962–64).
Erkeri žołovatzu. 3 vols. (Erevan, 1974–75).
Sargsyan, L., et al. *Erker.* (Erevan, 1982).
Sahakyan, P. *Erker.* (Erevan, 1984).
Sarinyan, S. *Erker.* (Erevan, 1987).

Texts

Sōs ew Vardit'er. (Tiflis, 1860, 1888, 1903; Erevan, 1887, 1953; Baku, 1905). (Novel).
Ałasi. (Tiflis, 1863). (Play).
Kr̄uatzałik. (Tiflis, 1878). (Novel).
Hatsi ḥndir. (Tiflis, 1880, 1900; Baku, 1904; Erevan, 1940, 1968). (Novel).
Šahēn. (Tiflis, 1883; Baku, 1905). (Novel).
Tsetser. (Tiflis, 1889). (Novel).
Błdē. (Tiflis, 1890). (Novel).
Skizbn erkants. (Tiflis, 1892). (Novel).
Yušikner. I šrjan. (Tiflis, 1894).
Ak'tsizchin. (Tiflis, 1896). (Story).
Mik'ēl Ałents Abdulě. (Tiflis, 1896).
Na. (Tiflis, 1896). (Story).
Ezidi Mkrtchents tuně. (Tiflis, 1899). (Story).
Mer Ḥechon. (Tiflis, 1899). (Story).
Yunōn. (Tiflis, 1901). (Novel).
Hušer. (Erevan, 1940).
Adamyan, A. "Nor nyut'er Perč Pr̄ošyani masin." *BM,* 4 (1958), 251–64.
"Perč Pr̄ošyani mi k'ani zekutsagrern u haytararut'yunnerě (1879–1883)." *Banber Hayastani arḥivneri,* 1988/2, 42–53.

Translations

German

Lalajan, J. *Sako.* 2 vols. (Leipzig, n.d.). (Armenische Bibliothek, 5 and 6).

Russian

Ioannisian, A. *Iz-za khleba. Roman.* (Moscow, 1950; Erevan, 1952; Moscow, 1955).

Russian Anthologies

ABS, 1, 42–83.

Criticism

Babayan, A. *Perč Přošyan.* (Erevan, 1962).
———. *Perch Proshian (zhizn i tvorchestvo).* (Erevan, 1963).
Berberean, M. "Perč Přōšeants." *A,* 1907, 1065–76.
Chōpanean, A. "Perč Přōšeants." *ANA,* 1 (1898–99), 230–32.
Darbinyan, H. "Perč Přošyan." *PBH,* 1987/4, 5–16.
Davtʻyan, Ṙ. *Perč Přošyanĕ ev tʻatronĕ.* (Erevan, 1988).
Ērukʻyan, Ž. "Perč Přošyani hušagrakan žařangutʻyunĕ." *BEH,* 1969/1, 202–7.
Gevorgyan, G. *Přošyani tun-tʻangaranĕ.* (Erevan, 1960).
Hakobyan, M., and Mikʻayelyan, M. "Perč Přošyani tznndyan 150—amyakĕ." *L,* 1987/10, 98–99.
Hakobyan, P. "Nyutʻer Perč Přošyani kensagrutʻyan hamar." *L,* 1970/3, 83–8.
Harutʻyunyan, G. *P. Přošyan.* (Erevan, 1972).
Hovhannisyan, H. *Perč Přošyani tun-tʻangaranĕ Aštarakum. Ułetsuyts.* (Erevan, 1980).
Kʻaramean, N. "Perč Přōšeants ew nora vēperĕ." *Murč,* 1889/1, 127–32; 2, 284–300; 3, 459–75.
Łanalanyan, A. *Přošyanĕ ev zołovrdakan banahyusutʻyunĕ.* (Erevan, 1938).
Manukyan, S. *Perč Přošyan.* (Erevan, 1964, 1987).
Muradyan, H. *Přošyani kyankʻĕ.* (Erevan, 1937).
"Niwtʻer p. Perč Přōšeantsi kensagrutʻean hamar." *Ardzagankʻ,* 1890/10, 4.
Perč Přōšeani hamařōt kensagrutʻiwnĕ. (Tiflis, 1899).
Poturean, M. "Perč Přōšeants ew Smbat Šahaziz." *B,* 66 (1908), 84–86.
Širvanzadē. "Perč Přōšeants." *HK,* 2 (1923–24/8), 60–64.
Terteryan, A. *Perč Přošyan.* (Erevan, 1955).
Tēr-Yarutʻiwnean, A. *Přōšean ew nra grakan gortzunēutʻean aržēkʻĕ.* (Nor Naḥijewan, 1908).

RAFFI, (c1835–1888)

Pen names: Melikʻzadē, Pʻawstos, Raffi.

Born Yakob Melikʻ-Yakobean in the village of Pʻayajuk, near Salmas (northwestern Iran). Educated in the local elementary school, at a private school, and at the Russian school in Tiflis. In 1856 he abandoned his studies in Tiflis and returned to his birthplace to attend to the family business, which was on the brink of collapse. In 1857–58 he traveled through Iran and historic Armenia, gaining profound impressions that had wide implications for his outlook and writing. In the early 1870s, Raffi began a long-lasting association with Grigor Artzruni (1845–92), in whose *Mšak* he published some of his novels in eagerly awaited installments. During the same decade, he also taught at Tabriz (1875–77) and Agulis (1877–79). The Raffi-Artzruni collaboration, beneficial to both parties and Armenian letters in general, was disrupted in 1884, and afterwards Raffi contributed to other well-established periodicals such as *Ardzagankʻ.* Died in Tiflis.

Collections

Pʻunj. 2 vols. (Tiflis, 1874).
Psak. (Tiflis, 1884).
Ḥentʻ[ĕ] ew Jalalēddin. (Moscow, 1890; Vienna, 1905; Athens, 1931).
Vēpikner ew patkerner. 2 vols. (Tiflis, 1892, 1893).

Ḥamsayi mēlikʿutʿiwnnerě; Łarabałi astłagētě; Gałtnikʿ Łarabałi. (Vienna, 1906). (2d title by P. Zubov).
Tʿamazyan, A. *Chors patmvatzkʿ.* (Erevan, 1941).
Mkryan, M., et al. *Erkeri žołovatzu.* 3 vols. (Erevan, 1949).
Tʿopʿchyan, Ē., et al. *Erkeri žołovatzu.* 10 vols. (Erevan, 1955–59).
Karapetyan, L. *Grakanutʿyan masin.* (Erevan, 1958).
Erkeri žołovatzu. 10 vols. (Erevan, 1962–64).
Ḥentʿě ev Ḥachagołi hišatakaraně. (Erevan, 1978).
Erkeri žołovatzu. 12 vols. projected. (Erevan, 1983–). (1st 9 vols. published through 1987).

Texts

Ḥentʿě. (Šuši, 1881; Moscow, 1890; Vienna, 1905, 1966; Boston, 1937). (Novel).
Dawitʿ bēk. (Tiflis, 1881, 1891; Vienna, 1903, 1963; Beirut, 1935; Athens, 1935; Erevan, 1941, 1980). (Novel).
Ḥamsayi mēlikʿutʿiwnnerě. (Tiflis, 1882, 1895; Vienna, 1906).
Oski akʿałał. (Tiflis, 1882; Vienna, 1903, 1956; Baku, 1903; Constantinople, 1922; Erevan, 1927, 1980; Alexandria, 1937; Beirut, 1966). (Short novel).
Ḥachagołi yišatakaraně. (Tiflis, 1883–84, 1895; Vienna, 1905; Constantinople, 1922; Cairo, 1936; Boston, 1936; Paris, 1937; Erevan, 1981, 1989). (Novel).
Kaytzer. 2 vols. (Tiflis, 1883 [Vol. 1], 1887 [Vol. 2], 1893; Vienna, 1900, 1904, 1954–56; Beirut, 1934; Alexandria, 1937; Erevan, 1947). (Novel).
Jalalēddin. (Moscow, 1884, 1890; Vienna, 1905; Teheran, 1959). (Short novel).
Samuēl. (Tiflis, 1888; Vienna, 1898, 1906; Athens, 1936; Erevan, 1940, 1957, 1984; Beirut, 1956, 1979 [abridged]). (Novel).
Hay kině and *Hay eritasardutʿiwně.* (Tiflis, 1889). (Articles).
Mině ayspēs, miwsn aynpēs. (Tiflis, 1890; Vienna, 1930). (Incomplete novel).
Artziw Vaspurakani ("nuēr Vaspurakan Artzwoyn"). (Tiflis, 1893). (Poem).
Paroyr Haykazn. (Tiflis, 1894). (Story).
Ov ēr meławor. (Tiflis, 1895). (Story).
Tačkahaykʿ. (Tiflis, 1895; Vienna, 1913).
Zahrumar. (Tiflis, 1895; Vienna, 1930). (Novel).
Salbi. (Vienna, 1911). (Novel).
Parskakan patkerner. (Vienna, 1913; Erevan, 1961 [selections]). (Stories and essays).
Samuēl. (Boston, 1924). (Play; adapted by H. Bagratuni).
Jalaleddin. Ḥentʿ. (Erevan, 1982).
Patmvatzkʿner ev vipakner. (Erevan, 1986).

Translations

English

Andreassian, K. "Jelaleddin." *Armenia* (Boston), 2 (1906/9), 16–28; 2 (1906/10), 24–31; 2 (1906/11), 35–40; 2 (1906/12), 29–33; 3 (1906/1), 19–29; 3 (1906/2), 28–33; 3 (1906/3), 41–48.
Basil, H. "Fire-Sparks." *Ara* (Calcutta), 2 (1893/1), 23–32; 2 (1893/2), 73–84; 2 (1893/3), 107–14; 2 (1893/4), 153–50; 2 (1893/5), 193–200; 2 (1893/6), 261–76; 2 (1893/7–8), 313–20; 2 (1893/9), 361–68; 2 (1893/10–11), 441–56; 2 (1893/12), 489–96; 3 (1894/1), 33–40; 3 (1894/2), 73–80; 3 (1894/3), 113–28; 3 (1894/4), 145–60; 3 (1894/5), 185–200; 3 (1894/6–7), 225–40.

Boyajian, Z. "The Araxes." *Ararat* (London), 1913/2, 35.

Pyrantz, J. "The Golden Rooster." *The Armenian* (Calcutta), 2 (1908/4–5), 35–36; 2 (1909/8–9), 63–67; 3 (1909/1), 4–5; 3 (1909/2) [page unknown].

Tashjian, J. *Samuel. The Armenian Review,* Winter, 1948, 131–39; Spring, 1948, 144–58; Summer, 1948, 143–58; Autumn, 1948, 143–57. Spring, 1949, 142–57; Summer, 1949, 142–55; Autumn, 1949, 142–5; Winter, 1949–50, 136–51. Spring, 1950, 135–54; Summer, 1950, 139–56; Autumn, 1950, 140–55; Winter, 1950–51, 131–55. Spring, 1951, 146–55; Summer, 1951, 138–55; Autumn, 1951, 146–58; Winter, 1951, 142–55.

Wingate, J. *The Fool.* (Boston, 1950).

English anthologies

ALP, 78, 86–88, 103–5, 114–17.

AP, 124, 243–46.

French

Altiar and Kibarian. *Samouël.* 2 vols. (Paris, 1924).

Ioannisian, A. *Contes persans; Bibi-Scharabani; Les khaz-pouches.* (Paris, 1902).

Tchobanian, A. "Djelaleddin." *Revue des revues* 1896/23, 457–65; 1896/24, 462–69. 1897/1, 73–81; 1897/2, 158–66; 1897/3, 270–78.

German

Rubenli, L. *Bilder aus Persien und Türkisch-Armenien.* (Leipzig, n.d.).

Russian

Bogaturova, N. *Dzhalaleddin.* (Moscow, 1911, 1915).

Dubrovina, A., and Kusikian, I. *Samvel.* (Erevan, 1958, 1959, 1960).

Iskry. (Erevan, 1986).

Kara-Murza, N. *Zolotoi petukh.* (Tiflis, 1892).

———. *Khent.* (Tiflis, 1901, 1908; Erevan, 1957, 1962, 1969).

———. *Son Vardana.* (Moscow, 1915). (From *Ḥenťě*).

Khachaturian, E. *Samvel.* (Erevan, 1982).

Khitarova, S. *Zolotoi petukh.* (Moscow, 1959).

———. *Garem i drugie rasskazy.* (Erevan, 1966).

———. *Zolotoi petushok.* (Erevan, 1980).

Lisitsian, S. *Zolotoi petukh.* (Erevan, 1948).

Terian, V., et al. *Iskry.* (Erevan and Moscow, 1949).

Ter-Karapetov, A., and Erevantsian, I. *Samvel.* (Moscow, 1946).

Vermisheva, I. *Bibi-Sharabani.* (Tiflis, 1889).

Russian anthologies

ABS, 1, 129–343.

SBAL, 7–14; 100–8.

Spanish

Agemian, B. *Las memorias del Hurtacruz.* (Buenos Aires, 1949).

Criticism

Afťandilean, A. *Raffi; patkerner Raffii keankťits.* (Alexandrapol, 1904).

Aharonean, A. "Raffi." *HK,* 2 (1923–24/11), 47–64.

Aharonean, V. "Raffii keankťě." *HK,* 16 (1937–38/4), 76–87; 6, 119–24; 7, 125–32; 8, 144–50; 9, 125–29; 10, 143–49; 11, 132–38; 12, 127–33. 17 (1938–39/1), 135–44.

Aŕakʻelean, H. "Raffin ibrew hasarakakan gortzich ew hraparakaḥōs." *Ardzagankʻ,* 1888/16, 218–20.

Arpʻiarean, A. "Raffi ew hay vipasanutʻiwnĕ." *M,* 3734 (1884), 129–31; 3736, 191–95; 3737, 215–17; 3739, 263–64.
Avetisyan, Z. "Raffin ev vepi tesutʻyan hartserĕ." *PBH,* 1985/4, 17–27.
Babaḥanyan, A. "Aveli, kʻan tʻyurimatsutʻyun." *SG,* 1963/9, 149–51 (On "Letters" from Constantinople).
Berberean, Ṙ. "Erb ē, uremn, tznuatz Raffin?" *HK,* 16 (1937–38/8), 114–19.
———. "Raffii hančarĕ ew irakan mtʻnolortĕ." *HK,* 16 (1937–38/1), 58–73.
Chōpanean, A. "Raffi." *ANA,* 8 (1937/5–6), 27–58.
Chugaszyan, B. "Raffin parsits mšakuytʻi ev grakanutʻyan masin." *L,* 1987/1, 19–26.
Danielyan, K. "Raffi–Hakob Melikʻ-Hakobyan." *L,* 1985/12, 3–15.
Darbinyan, H. *Raffin ev Ṙusastanĕ.* (Erevan, 1986).
Davtʻyan, Ṙ. "Raffu hraparakaḥosutʻyunĕ 19–rd dari 80–akan tʻvakannerin." *L,* 1987/6, 24–32.
Esayean, Y. *Raffi, nra keankʻĕ ew grakan gortzunēutʻiwnĕ.* (Tiflis, 1903).
Ezekyan, L. "Herosneri anhatakanatsman lezvakan mijotsnerĕ Raffu 'Samvel' vepum." *BEH,* 1969/2, 225–30.
———. "Raffin ev grakan ašḥarhabarĕ." *BEH,* 1977/1, 168–77.
Gabamačean, S. *Raffi: kensagrutʻiwn.* (Constantinople, 1914).
Gasparyan, G. "Raffu erkeri akademiakan hratarakutʻyan masin." *PBH,* 1985/4, 216–19.
Gevorgyan, S. "Raffin ev knoj azatagrman hartsĕ." *L,* 1974/10, 38–45.
Gṙuzean, E. "Raffi ew hay vipagrutʻiwnĕ." *B,* 95 (1937), 161–72.
Hakobyan, H. *Hay hełapʻoḥakan-demokratneri pʻilisopʻayakan hayatskʻnerĕ.* (Erevan, 1989). (On Raffi, Paronean, and Yarutʻiwn Sĕvačean).
Hamasteł. "Šrjanĕ ew Raffin." *HK,* 17 (1938–39/3), 49–59.
Harutʻyunyan, G. *Raffin mankavarž.* (Erevan, 1990).
Haykazuni, H. *Raffii sgali mahĕ ew kensagrutʻiwnĕ.* (Tiflis, 1888).
Hayruni, A. "Raffin ev žołovrdakan banahyusutʻyunĕ." *BEH,* 1980/3, 108–13.
Ḥudinyan, G. "Raffu azgayin azatagrakan gałapʻaraḥosutʻyan usumnasirutʻyan patmutʻyunits." *BEH,* 1985/3, 33–43.
Ḥuršidyan, T. "Raffu ĕntanikʻĕ Londonum." *PBH,* 1985/4, 94–102.
Hovhannisyan, A. "Artzrunu ev Raffu gałapʻarakan nerhakutʻyan akunkʻĕ." *BEH,* 1968/1, 15–31.
Išḥanyan, Ṙ. "Raffu lezvi gnahatman šurjĕ." *BEH,* 1974/2, 170–91.
Jamalean, A. "Raffi arewelean hayots ṙusakan ōrientasioni masin." *HK,* 15 (1936–37/9), 70–85; 10, 105–19; 11, 90–109; 12, 83–106.
Karapetean, B. *Hariwr taruay erkḥōsutʻiwn.* (Teheran, 1986).
Karapetyan, A. "70–80akan tʻvakanneri hay buržua-demokratakan azgayin-azatagrakan paterazmnerĕ ev Raffin." *SG,* 1961/1, 142–65.
Karinyan, A. "Raffin ev ir ṙeaktsion kʻnnadatĕ." *T,* 1954/6, 39–50.
Łazaryan, L. "Raffu 'Kaytzer' vepĕ ev nra aṙajin ĕntʻertsołnerĕ." *BEH,* 1985/3, 22–32.
———. "Raffu stełtzagortzutʻyunĕ ōtarazgi ĕntʻertsołneri ĕnkalmamb (1980–1910—akan tʻvakanneri)." *L,* 1987/5, 57–62.
Makaryan, L. "Raffu lusavorakan-demokratakan hayatskʻnerĕ." *BEH,* 1986/2, 123–28.
———. "Raffin orpes azgayin-azatagrakan šaržman gałapʻaraḥos." *BEH,* 1990/1, 159–64.

Manukyan, S. *Raffii Jalaleddini tzagumě.* (Erevan, 1932). (Comparison with *Die Räuber*).

Mkryan, M. "Raffii 'Kaytzer' vepi hratarakutʻyan aṙtʻiv." *T,* 1951/11, 79–85.

Muradyan, L. "Raffi ev Arpʻiar Arpʻiaryan." *PBH,* 1986/3, 57–66.

Nahapetyan, M. "Raffin banastełtz." *SG,* 1969/12, 107–13.

Pʻechikean, E. " 'Dawitʻ Bek'i patmakan ałbiwrner ew Mḫitʻareankʻ." *B,* 95 (1937), 172–87.

Petrosyan, E. "Raffu 60akan tʻvakanneri stełtzagortzutʻyunnerě." *T,* 1954/8, 63–80.

———. *Raffi, kyankʻě ev stełtzagortzutʻyuně.* (Erevan, 1959).

———. "Anbareḫłčutʻyan ptułnerě." *SG,* 1961/5, 120–29. (Takes issue with A. Karapetyan's "70–80akan tʻvakanneri . . ." *SG,* 1961/1, 142–65).

Raffi: keankʻě, grakanutʻiwně, yišołutʻiwnner. (Paris, 1937).

"Raffu namakneri masin." *A,* 1913, 198–203.

Raffi (Yakob Melikʻ-Yakobean). *Loys ěntzayuatz tznndean hariwrameakin aṙtʻiw (1835–1937).* (Boston, 1938).

Sagayean, E. "Hayots Raffin ew fransatswots Žiwl Verně." *ANA,* 6 (1935/1–2), 52–54.

Sahakyan, S. *Raffu hay azgayin-azatagrakan šaržman gałapʻaraḫosutʻyuně.* (Erevan, 1990).

Samvelyan, Ḥ. *Raffi (Hakob Melikʻ-Hakobyan): hamaṙot aknark.* (Erevan, 1957).

———. "Mi banasirakan čštum." *SG,* 1977/2, 146–48.

———. "Druagner Raffu ev Nazaryani barekamutʻean patmutʻiwnits." *HA,* 1983, 435–42.

———. "Mi ēj Raffu 'Kaytzeri' stełtzagortzakan patmutʻyunits; Aršak Raffu antip namakě; Raffu chhratarakvatz dzeṙagrerits." *SG,* 1985/12, 100–28.

———. *Raffin žamanakakitsneri hušerum. Žołovatzu.* (Erevan, 1986).

———. *Raffi. Stełtzagortzakan ułin.* (Erevan, 1987).

———. "Mi stełtzagortzutʻean patmutʻiwn: druagner Raffu ew Bašinjałeani stełtzagortzakan hamagortzaktsutʻiwnits." *HA,* 1987/1–12 (*Yušamatean, Festschrift, 1887–1987*), 947–49.

Sanasar, Pʻ. "Jalalēddin. Raffin ibrew patmoł." *Z* (amsatʻertʻ), 1 (1955/1), 3; 1 (1955/2), 3; 1 (1955/3), 3.

Sarinyan, S. *Raffi.* (Erevan, 1957).

———. "Havaknot ḥizaḥutʻyun." *SG,* 1961/4, 113–24. (Takes issue with A. Karapetyan's "70–80akan tʻvakanneri . . ." *SG,* 1961/1, 142–65).

———. "Mardu problemě Raffu stełtzagortzutʻyan gełarvestakan hamakargum." *SG,* 1985/12, 87–99.

———. *Raffi: Gałapʻarneri ev kerparneri hamakargě.* (Erevan, 1985).

Širmazanean, A. "Paron Raffii 'Pʻunj' banastełtzutʻean veray." *A,* 1874, 291–306.

Tʻamrazyan, H. "Raffu kʻnnadatakan hayatskʻnerě." *BEH,* 1985/3, 3–21.

Tchobanian, A. *Raffi, le grand romancier arménien.* (N.p., 1896).

Tērtērean, A. "Nkatołutʻiwnner Raffii masin: ašḫarhayeatskʻě." *Banber Hayastani gitakan instituti,* 1–2 (1921–22), 35–67.

Tʻopʻchyan, S. "Raffin orpes patmavepi tesaban." *PBH,* 1965/2, 157–64.

———. *Raffu ēstʻetikakan hayatskʻnerě.* (Erevan, 1971).

Varandean, M. "Raffi." *HK,* 7 (1928–29/7), 67–80; 8, 72–86; 9, 155–62; 10, 102–9.

Vardanyan, G. " 'Mṙayl dasakargi' tiperě Raffu erkerum." *L,* 1988/11, 34–40.

Veratzin, M. "Raffii ew ir ĕntanikʻin šurjĕ." *HK,* 16 (1937–38/5), 141–48.
Vr[atsean], S[imon]. "Raffi." *Vēm,* 5 (1937/3), 59–78.
Zakʻaryan, H. "Astrahanahay lusavorakan gortzichĕ (H. H. Pʻaremuzyanĕ) Raffu masin." *BHA,* 1986/1, 71–3.

ŠAHAZIZ, SMBAT (1840–1907)

The youngest of six brothers, Šahaziz was born in the town of Aštarak, in Eastern Armenia. He was educated at the Lazarean school in Moscow (1851–62) and taught at his alma mater until his retirement in 1897. Following the publication of his two verse collections in the 1880s, Šahaziz wrote little poetry, devoting himself instead to teaching and journalism.

Collections

Inčikyan, A. *Ĕntir banastełtzutʻyunner.* (Erevan, 1941).
Šahaziz, E. *Erker.* (Erevan, 1947).
Erker. (Erevan, 1961).

Texts

Azatutʻean žamer. (Moscow, 1860).
Lewoni vištĕ. (Moscow, 1965).
Avetisyan, A. "Smbat Šahazizi antip namaknerits." *PBH,* 1981/1, 234–62.
Melikʻyan, M. "Šahazizi Smb. antip namaknerits." *PBH,* 1988/3, 180.

Other works

Hraparakahōs dzayn. (Moscow, 1881).
Tzitzałi toprak. (Tiflis, 1892).
Amaṙnayin namakner. (Moscow, 1897).
Yišołutʻiwnner Vardanants tōni aṙtʻiw. (Moscow, 1901).
Mi kʻani hōskʻ im ĕntʻertsołnerin. (Moscow, 1903).

Translations

English

Boyajian, Z. "I Heard." *Armenia,* 3 (1907/4), 34.
———. "My Beloved Children." *Armenia,* 3/4, 32–33.

Anthologies

ABS, 2, 499–507.
AD, 35–36.
ALG, 123–24.
ALP, 46.
APA, 59–62.
APAS, 127–29.
BPA, 289–94.
PAAM, 82–83.
VAM, 55–85.

Criticism

A. A. "Šahazizean, S. Amaṙnayin namakner, Moskua, 1897." *Murč,* 1897/7–8, 1070–77.
Arashanean, A. "Erku hōskʻ." *Murč,* 1892/1, 132–34.
Balasanean, G. "Smbat Šahaziz." *Banasēr,* 6 (1904/3–4), 74–83.

———. "Smbat Šahaziz." *HA,* 23 (1909), 161–64, 297–300; 24 (1910), 100–5.
Berberean, M. *Siroy ew všti ergichě.* (Vałaršapat, 1908).
Berberean, Ṙ. " 'Lewoni viště' ew S. Šahazizeani andznakan tṙamě." *HK,* 16 (1937–38/10), 61–74; 11, 118–31; 12, 112–26. 17 (1938–39/1), 105–12; 2, 83–91; 3, 74–81.
Grasēr. "Smbat Šahaziz." *HK,* 42 (1964/12), 14–21.
Ḥachatryan, I. "A. S. Puškině Smbat Šahazizi stełtzagortzutʻyan mej." *BEH,* 1975/3, 178–84.
Hovasapʻyan, H. *Smbat Šahaziz.* (Erevan, 1960).
Išḥanean, B. *Hasarakakan gałapʻarnerě Ṙ. Patkaneani ew S. Šahazizi banastełtzutʻiwnneri mēj.* (Tiflis, 1910).
Kusikean, K. "Hiwsisapʻayl ew S. Šahazizeani banastełtzutʻiwně." *Murč,* 1895/7–8, 1094–104. 1898/5, 684–97; 1898/9, 1241–64.
L. "Šahazizean, S. Yišołutʻiwnner Vardanants tōni aṙitʻov, Moskua, 1901." *Murč,* 1901/1, 219–22.
Madatʻean, E. "Smbat Šahazizean banastełtz-hraparakaḥōs." *Murč,* 1891/3, 367–74; 1891/5, 632–45; 1891/7–8, 906/12; 1891/12, 1557–67. 1892/1, 119–31.
Manukyan, A. *Smbat Šahaziz.* (Erevan, 1959).
Šahaziz, E. *Smbat Šahazizi kensagrutʻyuně.* (Erevan, 1934).
Šahnazareants, S. *Banastełtz-kʻałakʻatsin dprotsakan nwirakan uḥti asparizum.* (Moscow, 1908).
Tzaturean, A. "Azgayin banastełtz Smbat Šahazizeantsin." *HGP,* 1 (1888), 192.
Veselovskii, Iu. *Armianskii poet Smbat-Shakh-Aziz.* (Moscow, 1902, 1905).

ŠAHEN, GUSAN (1909–1990)

Pen name: Gusan Šahen.

Born Šahen Sargsyan in Łurdubulał (a village later renamed Krasar, in Łukasyan, Armenia). A minstrel and professional singer.

Texts

Gusan Hayastani. (Erevan, 1964, 1976).

SAHINYAN, ANAHIT (1917–)

A native of the village of Vardablur (Stepʻanavan, Armenia). A novelist. She graduated from the State University of Erevan in 1941. From 1942–47 and 1953–58, she headed the children's section at Haypethrat (Hayastani petakan hratarakchutʻyun), one of the major state publishing houses in Soviet Armenia. For several years starting in 1969, she was editor of the monthly *Pioner.*

Collections

Ĕntir erker. 3 vols. (Erevan, 1987–88).

Texts

Vayelkʻ. (Erevan, 1942).
Barekamner. (Erevan, 1944).
Ḥachułiner. (Erevan, 1946, 1958, 1962, 1979).
Tzarav. (Erevan, 1955, 1959, 1980).
Veradardzi arahetnerov. (Erevan, 1960).
Gełetsik linelu gałtnikʻě. (Erevan, 1965).

Ušatsatz žamadrutʻyun. (Erevan, 1965).
Karot. (Erevan, 1975, 1981).
Keṙmanner. (Erevan, 1976).
Septʻakan otnahetkʻerov. (Erevan, 1984).
Hekʻiatʻ ḥṙovkanneri hamar. (Erevan, 1985).
Hey čamptʻaner, čamptʻaner. (Erevan, 1986). (Travel writing).

Translations

RUSSIAN

Atarov, N., and Dol'tseva, M. *Puti-dorogi. Roman.* (Moscow, 1963).
Smolianskaia, T., and Khitarova, S. *Toska. Roman.* (Erevan, 1983; Moscow, 1990).
[Ter-Minasian, L., and Ostrogorskii, V.] *Zhazhda. Roman. Kn. 1.* (Erevan, 1956).
Zhazhda. (Moscow, 1986).

Criticism

Arzumanyan, S. "Groɫi azniv havatkʻě." *SG,* 1976/3, 125–32.
Parsamyan, A. "Liaryun kyankʻi tzaravov." *SG,* 1983/7, 131–32.
Sarinyan, S. "Anahit Sahinyan." *SG,* 1961/7, 107–18.
———. "Hayrern u ordinerě." *SG,* 1978/11, 169–75. (On *Ḥachuɫiner*).

ŠAHNAZARYAN, ARŠAK (1872–1942)

Born and educated in Aštarak, Armenia. A writer of short stories and a professional teacher. Taught at various cities in Transcaucasia.

Collections

Arevi čamptʻin. (Erevan, 1939).

Texts

Ḥawar ašḥarhum. (Erevan, 1909).
Azatararě. (Erevan, 1926).
Haram-katʻnaker aɫjikě. (Erevan, 1926).
Errordutʻyan gaɫtnikʻě. (Erevan, 1929).
Gyuɫakan patkerner. (Erevan, 1933).
En sev ōrerits. (Erevan, 1936). (Poem).
Melikʻi aɫjikě. (Erevan, 1944).

Criticism

Tʻumanyan, H. "A. Šahnazaryan." *SG,* 1963/6, 152–53.

ŠAHNUR, ŠAHAN (1903–1974)

Pen names: Šahan Šahnur, Armen Lubin (in French writings).
Born Šahan Kʻerestʻēčean in Constantinople. Graduated from the Pērpērean school in 1921. In 1923, he left for France, where he and a number of writers initiated a literary movement, "Menkʻ," and launched a periodical bearing the same name (1931–32), with a view to shaping a new tradition. Both the movement and its organ were short-lived. By this time Šahnur had established himself as a famous, if controversial, novelist with his first novel, *Nahanjě aṙants ergi.* In the late 1930s, Šahnur's fragile health deteriorated rapidly. He spent the better part of the last

two decades of his life undergoing treatment in hospitals in France. Curiously, most of Šahnur's prose writings are in Armenian, while most of his poetry is in French. Of this issue, he once commented, "Pourquoi j'utilise l'arménien en prose et le français en poésie? Je ne le sais pas. C'est venu ainsi," (cf. his posthumous collection, *Les logis provisoires,* p. 7).

Collections

Alajajyan, S. *Erker.* (Erevan, 1962).
Erker. 2 books. (Erevan, 1982–85).

Texts

Nahanjĕ ařants ergi. (Paris, 1929; Beirut, 1959).
Yaralēzneru dawačanutʻiwnĕ. (Paris, 1933, 1971).
Tʻertʻis kiraknōreay tʻiwĕ. (Beirut, 1958).
Zoyg mĕ karmir tetrakner. (Beirut, 1967).
Azatn Komitas. (Paris, 1970).
Bats tomarĕ. (Paris, 1971).
Krakĕ kołkʻis. (Paris, 1973).
"Šahan Šahnuri namaknerĕ Vahan Tʻekʻeyanin." *SG,* 1984/9, 128–34.

Works in periodicals

Z, 1 (1929–[30]), 338–42. 2 [1931], 18–22.
ANA, 3 (1932/5–6), 50–56.
Ani, 2 (1947–48), 186–88.
SG, 1965/6, 108–9. 1977/9, 150–57.

Works in French

Fouiller avec rien. (Paris: René Debresse, 1942).
Le passager clandestin. (Paris: Gallimard, 1946).
Sainte patience, poèmes. ([Paris]: Gallimard, [1951]).
Transfert nocturne. (Paris: Gallimard, [1955]).
Les hautes terrasses; poèmes. (Paris: Gallimard, [1957]).
Feux contre feux. (Paris: Grasset, 1968).
Les logis provisoires. ([Montemart]: Rougerie, [1983]).

Translations

English

Amirian, L. "Flight Without Song." *Ararat,* Summer, 1977, 28.
Kudian, M. *Retreat Without Song.* (London, 1982).
———. *The Tailor's Visitors.* (London, 1984).

Russian anthologies

KNS, 3–19.
PCN, 153–64.

Criticism

Alikʻyan, A. "Šahan Šahnuri 'Gišerayin pʻoḥadrum' girkʻĕ." *SG,* 1963/8, 123–25.
Chōpanean, A. "Ařołjn u vatařołjn Šahan Šahnuri grakanutʻean mēj." *ANA,* 10 (1939/1–2), 79–93.
Fēnērčean, G. "Nahanjĕ ařants ergi, Šahan Šahnur." *Z,* 1 (1929–[30]), 302–4.
Grigoryan, H. "Šahan Šahnur." *SG,* 1960/6, 121–30.
Ḥ. A. "Yaralezneru dawačanutʻiwnĕ." *HK,* 12 (1933–34/8), 158–60.

Misakʻean, A. "Šahan Šahnur." *AND,* 5 (n.d.), 121–23.
Mułnetsyan, Š. *Nahanji ahazangĕ.* (Erevan, 1984).
Pērpērean, M. "Šahan Šahnur." *HK,* 32 (1954/4), 45–59.
"Šahan Šahnur." *SG,* 1963/8, 116–18.
Šahinean, G. *Kensagrutʻiwn ew matenagitutʻiwn Šahan Šahnuri.* (Antʻilias, 1981).
———. *Šahan Šahnur: akʻsor ew aruest.* (Antʻilias, 1985).
Šahnurean ĕntʻertsumner. (Beirut, 1983).
T. N. "Nahanjĕ aṙants ergi." *HK,* 8 (1929–30/2), 158–62.
Tʻopʻchyan, S. "Šahan Šahnuri ḥostovanutʻyunĕ." *SG,* 1963/8, 119–22.
———. "Ētyud Šahnuri masin." *SG,* 1985/1, 115–29.
Tʻoranean, Tʻ. *Verstin kardalov Šahan Šahnurĕ.* (Aleppo, 1971).
Vahē-Vahean. "Šahan Šahnur." *Ani,* 2 (1946–47), 184–85.

ŠAHRIAR (1855–1918)

Pen name: Šahriar.

Born Hambardzum Aṙakʻelean, in Šuši, Artsaḥ (Karabagh). A journalist, novelist, and short story writer. Educated in his birthplace, Tabriz, Baku, and briefly in Moscow. Taught in Baku. Settled in Tiflis and formed a life-long association with Grigor Artzruni (1845–92) and his *Mšak* as an editor and member of the editorial board. In 1915 he organized a committee to help the Armenian survivors of the genocide. He was assassinated in Tiflis.

Texts

Jhuk-Kʻušan, vēp Parskastani keankʻits. (Tiflis, 1902). (Novel).
Ełōi kʻoṙ baḥtĕ. (Tiflis, 1903). (Story).
Tasn ew erku patmuatzkʻ. (Tiflis, 1909). (Stories).

SAHYAN, HAMO (1914–1993)

Pen name: Hamo Sahyan.

Born Hmayak Grigoryan in Lor, a village in Sisian, Armenia. Took up residence in Baku in 1927 and studied at the local pedagogical institute (1935–39). Became a journalist following his discharge from service in the Soviet Navy during World War II. From 1965 to 1967, he was the editor-in-chief of the literary weekly *Grakan tʻertʻ* (organ of the Union of the Soviet Writers of Armenia). His verse collection, "Sezam, batsvir," won him the Armenian State Award for poetry in 1975.

Collections

Erker. 2 vols. (Erevan, 1967–69).
Erkeri žołovatzu. 2 vols. (Erevan, 1975–76).
Erker. 2 vols. (Erevan, 1984).

Texts (verse)

Orotani ezerkʻin. (Erevan, 1946).
Aṙagast. (Baku, 1947).
Slatskʻi mej. (Baku, 1950).
Tziatzanĕ tapʻastanum. (Erevan, 1953).
Bardzunkʻi vra. (Erevan, 1955).
Nairyan dalar bardi. (Erevan, 1958).

Hayastanĕ ergeri mej. (Erevan, 1962).
Mayramutits ar̄aj. (Erevan, 1964).
K'arap'neri ergĕ. (Erevan, 1968).
Tariners. (Erevan, 1970).
Sezam, batsvir. (Erevan, 1972).
Kanche, kr̄unk. (Erevan, 1973).
Iriknahats. (Erevan, 1977).
Žayr̄its masur ē kat'um. (Erevan, 1979).
Azgi kanchĕ. (Erevan, 1981).
Kanach-karmir ašun. (Erevan, 1981).
Dałdzi tzałik. (Erevan, 1986).

Translations

English

Evans, G. "On the Height." *SL,* 1966/3, 144.
Jacque, V. "Sunset in the Mountains." *SL,* 1973/9, 127.
Katibian, J. "After All I Am a Man." *Lraber,* 1965/23, 4.
———. "Boundaries." *Lraber,* November 30, 1965, 4.
———. "The Sunset Is Late on the Summit." *Lraber,* October 5, 1965, 4.
Mesrobian, P. "My Sayat-Nova." *Lraber,* November 14, 1963, 4.
Tempest, P. "Like Water." *SL,* 1979/7, 95.

English anthologies

SAP, 27–29.

French

Antonian, A. "Comme l'eau." *LS,* 247 (1979), 104–5.
———, and Alikian, A. "Le crepuscule." *OO,* 177 (Sept. 1973), 144.
Hékimian, G. "Homme." *Notre Voix,* 1965/96, 1.
Mardirossian, L. "Vivre ainsi." *OO,* 123 (March 1969), 55.

French anthologies

Gamara, P. *E,* 89–91.
LPA, 346–51.

German

Österreicher, S. "Auf der Höhe." *Sowjet-Literatur,* 1966/3, 142.

Russian

Dudin, M. *Pozdnie iagody: Stikhi.* (Leningrad, 1981, 1983).
Gody moi. (Erevan, 1970).
Lirika. (Erevan, 1989).
Makintsian, A. *Stikhi.* (Moscow, 1986).
Na vysotakh. (Erevan, 1956).
Pered zakatom. Stikhi. (Moscow, 1969).
Zelenyi topol' Nairi. Stikhi. (Moscow, 1959).
Zelenyi topol'. Stikhi. (Baku, 1950). (Includes "Blagodarnost' " and "Na beregakh Vorotana").
Zviagintseva, V. *Blagodarnost'. Stikhi.* (Erevan, 1952).

Spanish

Alberti, R. y Maria Teresa Leon. "En lo alto." *Literatura Sovietica,* 1966/3, 143.

Criticism

Ałababyan, S. "V. Mnatsakanyan, H. Sahyan, kʻnnadatneri u banastełtzneri erkaḥosutʻyunĕ." *SG,* 1970/9, 101–7.
Aninski, L. "Čšmartutʻyan ezrerĕ: Hamo Sahyanĕ ev žamanakakits kʻnarergutʻyunĕ." *SG,* 1973/8, 152–58.
Davtʻyan, Š. "Žamanaki zgatsołutʻyunĕ Hamo Sahyani poeziayum." *SG,* 1973/10, 157–59.
Dymshits, A. "The World of Amo Sagiyan." *SL,* 1973/1, 129–32.
Felekʻyan, H. "Hamo Sahyan." *SG,* 1961/8, 114–23.
Hayrapetyan, A. "Banastełtzi kochumĕ." *SG,* 1974/5, 124–29.
Hovhannisyan, H. "Hamo Sahyani poeziayi jiłĕ." *SG,* 1984/4, 8–13.
Karapetyan, G. "Banastełtzakan patkeri hnchyunayin ev gunayin dzevavorumĕ Hamo Sahyani poeziayum." *L,* 1985/8, 15–23.
Mayilyan, H. "Hamo Sahyani 1960—akan tʻvakanneri poezian." *L,* 1973/9, 3–10.
Mkrtchyan, L. *Zruytsner banastełtzi het.* (Erevan, 1984).
Mkrtchyan, V. *Hamo Sahyani banastełtzakan bnapʻilisopʻayutʻyunĕ.* (Erevan, 1987).
Mnatsakanyan, V. "Hinn u norĕ orn ē [?]" *SG,* 1968/9, 139–56.
Papoyan, A. "Lezvi žołovrdaynutʻyan mi kʻani drsevorumner Hamo Sahyani chapʻatzoyum." *BEH,* 1971/1, 220–29.
———. "Hamo Sahyani banarvesti mi kʻani hartser." *SG,* 1975/8, 146–55.
———. *Chapʻatzoyi lezvakan arvesti hartser. Hamo Sahyan ev Vahagn Davtʻyan.* (Erevan, 1976).
Ulubabyan, B. "Banastełtzi ašḥarhĕ." *SG,* 1984/4, 3–8.
Zoryan, S. "Sahyanĕ gnalu čanaparh uni." *SG,* 1974/5, 119–32.

ŠAKʻLYAN, ARIS (1900–1959)

Pen names: A. Š., Varužnak Aris.

Born and educated in Dörtyol (Turkey). Taught in the Armenian schools of Alexandretta (Iskenderun) and Damascus and edited the periodical *Epʻrat* (1929, 1931–32, 1936–37, 1943–45) before settling in Soviet Armenia in 1947.

Texts

Dełin erger. (Aleppo, 1927).
Mijinkʻ. (Aleppo, 1943). (Verse).
Kar u chkar. (Aleppo, 1946). (Stories).
Mer Hayastann ē. (Erevan, 1949).
Hēkʻiatʻner. (Aleppo, 1950). (Tales).
Baḥtn u ašḥatankʻĕ. (Erevan, 1956). (Tales).
Indznits kʻez ḥrat. (Erevan, 1957). (Tales).
Fellahner. (Erevan, 1958). (Novel).
Hekʻiatʻner. (Erevan, 1960). (Tales).

SAŁATʻELYAN, LEVON (1884–1968)

The village of Kʻuchak (in Aparan, Armenia) is the birthplace of this dramatist, who graduated from the Gēorgean Seminary of Ējmiatzin in 1908 and from the Institute of Commerce in Moscow in 1916. He worked as a professional economist in various parts of Armenia.

Collections

Dramatikakan erker. (Erevan, 1954).
Dramatikakan erker. (Erevan, 1961).

Texts

Mi ktor hoŀi hamar. (Tiflis, 1924; Erevan, 1931).
Dramaner. (Erevan, 1947).
Apʻsos baderě. (Erevan, 1954, 1958).
Batsvatz varaguyrě. (Erevan, 1965).

SANDAL, (1858–1922)

Pen name: Sandal.

Born Alekʻsandr Petrosean in Tiflis and educated at the local Nersisean school. Belonged to a group of Armenian writers who focused their work on the countryside. He was a teacher by profession and briefly taught in Western Armenia (Muš, 1883–84). In the late 1880s he found clerical employment in Moscow and St. Petersburg, but he spent his last days in Tiflis in utter poverty.

Texts

Višap. (Tiflis, 1884). (Stories).
Pʻokʻrik astł. (Moscow, 1892). (Novel).

Criticism

Łarajyan, G., [and Arkomed, S. T.] *Sandalě ev nra veperě.* (Tiflis, 1929 [cover says 1930]).

ŠANTʻ, LEWON (1869–1951)

Pen name: Lewon Šantʻ.

Born Lewon Nahašpetean in Constantinople and later changed his name to Sełbosean, after his father, Sełbos. Educated in the famous Scutari College, at the Gēorgean Seminary in Ējmiatzin (1884–91), and in various German universities (1893–99). A playwright, novelist, and poet. Taught in Armenian schools in the Caucasus (1906–11) and in Constantinople (1911–13), and left for Europe in 1913, fortuitously escaping the fate of his colleagues, who were slain in 1915. He returned to the Caucasus in 1915, but left just after the Bolshevik Revolution, only to return to the region in the following year. He engaged in political activities on behalf of the Armenian Republic (1918–20) and was incarcerated in Erevan following the establishment of Soviet regime in Eastern Armenia. After spending the years 1921–26 in Europe, and following a brief stay in Egypt, he settled in Beirut in 1929. There he became one of the founders of the Čemaran (renamed Nšan Pʻalančean čemaran in 1950), a well-known secondary school.

Collections

Lewon Šantʻi erkerě. 9 vols. (Beirut, 1946–47).
Davtʻyan, M. *Ěntir erker.* (Erevan, 1968).
Lewon Šantʻi erkerě. 2 vols. (Los Angeles, 1988).
Tʻopʻchyan, S. *Erker.* (Erevan, 1989).
Erker. (Antʻilias, 1990).

Texts

Leṙan ałjikě. (Tiflis, 1893, 1904). (Poems).

Dursetsiner: vēp. (Tiflis, 1896). (Novel).
Eraz ōrer. (Tiflis, 1896). (Prose diary).
Veržin. (Tiflis, 1898; Constantinople, 1911). (Novel).
Dardz: vēp. (Tiflis, 1899; Constantinople, 1924). (Novel).
Erger. (Tiflis, [1904]). (Verse).
Hin astuatzner. (Constantinople, 1912; Boston, 1917). (Play).
Čambun vray. (Constantinople, 1914). (Play).
Uriši hamar. (Tiflis, 1914). (Play).
Kaysr, ťaterak biwzandakan darerēn. (Tiflis, 1916). (Play).
Šłťaywatzě (ḥał mer mijnadarēn). (Constantinople, 1921; New York, 1922; Teheran, 1922). (Play).
Kině. (Constantinople, 1924 [2d ed.]). (Story).
Derasanuhin. (Constantinople, 1924 [2d ed.]). (Novel).
Hoginerě tzarawi: vēp. (Beirut, 1945). (Novel).
Aznavuryan, G. "Levon Šantʻi namaknerě Hovhannes Tʻumanyanin." *PBH,* 1982/1, 201–17.

Translations

ENGLISH

Mandalian, J. "The Woman." *Armenian Review,* 2 (1949/5), 3–26.
Baytarian, H. *The Princess of the Fallen Castle.* (Boston, [1929]).

FRENCH ANTHOLOGIES

APA, 115–18.

ITALIAN

Monico, G. *Gli Antichi Dei.* (Milan, 1917).

SPANISH ANTHOLOGIES

APAS, 175–76.

Bibliographies

Lewon Šantʻ, 1869–1969. (Beirut, 1969). ("Matenagitutʻiwn Lewon Šantʻi," pp. 53–96).

Criticism

Aharonean, V. "Lewon Šantʻě ir masin." *HK,* 38 (1960/2), 1–8; 3, 17–22; 4, 24–34; 5, 29–31.
Aršaruni, A. "Šłťayuatzi datavarutʻiwně." *HK,* 30 (1952/11), 19–22.
B. A. "Lewon Šantʻi gełaruestakan gortzerě." *HK,* 26 (1948/4), 10–12.
Banean, G. "Lewon Šantʻ." *HK,* 30 (1952/1), 23–32.
Chtʻchyan, A. "Levon Šantʻě ev Gaspar Ipʻekyaně 'Hamazgayin' mšakutʻayin miutʻyan gortzichner." *L,* 1990/3, 57–65.
Dilanean, G. "Lewon Šantʻ ew 'Hin astuatzner'." *HK,* 18 (1939–40/12), 147–55.
Ēdilean, G. "Šantʻ, 'Hin astuatzner'." *A,* 1913, 234–63.
———. *Hin astuatzner Šantʻi.* (Vałaršapat, 1913).
Gełard, Y. *Lewon Šantʻ.* (Beirut, 1969).
"Hin astuatznerě." *Nawasard,* 1914, 263–65. (An account of discussions and criticisms of the work).
Pessimist. "Ditołutʻiwnner L. Šantʻi 'Hin astuatzner' dramayi masin: patmakan, tełagrakan, kentsałakan tesakētits." *HA,* 39 (1925), 312–16, 504–7, 598–602.
Šahinean, G. *Dziwnern i ver: menagrutʻiwn L. Šantʻi masin.* (Beirut, 1967).

Sargsyan, Ḥ. *Levon Šant'.* (Erevan, 1930).
Sarinyan, S. "Levon Šant'i krt'ut'yan tesut'yuně." *L,* 1990/6, 13–18.
T'ašean, B. "Lewon Šant' ew ir 'Kaysr'ě." *Z,* 1 (1929–30?), 115–18, 180–83.
———. "Šant'i 'Kaysr'ě." *HK,* 8 (1929–30/2), 56–77.
Tayk', K. "Lewon Šant'i gełarwestakan erkerě." *Vēm,* 3 (1935/1), 27–34; 2, 15–26.
Tēr-Pōłosean, G. *Lewon Šant'i 'Hin astuatznerě' ew Step'annos vanakani yišatakaraně.* (Šuši, 1913).
Tēr Ṙubinean, G. *L Šant', nra erkern ew Hin astuatzner draman.* (Tiflis, 1913).
Tērtērean, A. "Lewon Šant', seṙi ew dasalk'ut'ean ergichě." *A,* 1913, 352–75, 437–68. (Reprinted separately, Vałaršapat, 1913).

SARAFEAN, NIKOŁOS (1905–1972)

Born aboard a ship bound for Varna from Istanbul, Sarafean grew up and received his elementary education in Varna, Bulgaria. Spent the years 1914–17 in Rumania, Odessa, Rostov, and Novorossiysk, and, fleeing the region, then ablaze with the flames of World War I and the Bolshevik Revolution, returned to Varna. Moved to Constantinople with his family after the Armistice of 1918 and attended the Kedronakan. Within a few years he left for France via Marseilles and settled in Paris in 1923.

Collections

Chap'atzoy erker. (Ant'ilias, 1982).
Erker. (Erevan, 1988).

Texts

Anjrpeti mě grawumě. (Paris, 1928).
14. (Paris, 1933).
Išḫanuhin (vēp). (Paris, 1934). (Novel).
Tełatuut'iwn ew makěnt'atsut'iwn. (Paris, 1939).
Mijnaberd. (Paris, 1946).
Mijerkrakan. (Beirut, 1971).
Vēnsēni antaṙě. (Paris, 1988).

Works in periodicals

Z, 1 (1929–[30]), 10, 145–52. "Łukas aypanelin." 1 (1929–[30]), 257–68, 344–49, 391–96, 424–29. 2 [1931], 8–13, 73–78. *Z* (taregirk'), 1937, 8–10. *Z* (eṙamseay), 1948/3, 184–95.

ANA, 2 (1930/3), 38–49. 1933/3–4, 30–31. 9 (1938/4), 61–82; 9 (1938/5–6), 34–43.

HK, 9 (1930–31/1), 1–18. 10 (1931–32/3), 1–5; 10/5, 1–8. "Ḥarisḥēn heṙu (vēp)," 10 (1931–32/11), 1–46; 11, 13–32; 12, 71–100. "Hskum," 11 (1932–33/12), 1–27; 12 (1933–34/1), 58–74. 12 (1933–34/12), 87–88. 24 (1946/3), 19–22. 6, 1–24. 25 (1947/3), 1–11; 4, 29–38.

AND, 1 (1952), 14–18, 65–71. 3 (1953), 2–6. 6–7 (n.d.), 27–28.

Translations

French anthologies

Drézian, A. *Le Bois de Vincennes.* (Marseilles: Editions Parenthèses, 1993).
LPA, 318–21.

Italian anthologies

LPAM, 301–6.

Criticism

A. "Dasaḥōsutʻean mě aṙitʻov." *AND,* 3 (1953), 123–24.
Baluean, H. "N. Sarafeani 'Anjrpeti mě grawumě'." *Z,* 1 (1929–[30]), 81–82.
Sanasar, Pʻ. "Išḥanuhin, vēp Nikołos Sarafeani." *HK,* 13 (1934–35/6), 150–51.
———. "Nikołos Sarafean, Anjrpeti mě grawumě." *HK,* 14 (1935–36/8), 169–72.
Tʻopʻchean, A. "Nikołayos Sarafean, kam Spʻiwṙkʻi banadzevumě." *HA,* 1988/1–12, 251–56.

SARGIS APUCHEḤTSI

A seventeenth-eighteenth century author from the village of Apucheḥ near Akn (Eğin, now Kemaliye, Turkey).

Texts and criticism

Mkrtchyan, M. *Sargis Apucheḥtsi, usumnasirutʻyun ev bnagrer.* (Erevan, 1971).

SARKAWAG BERDAKATSI

Presumed to be a sixteenth-century author, Sarkawag is known by a single poem, "Ḥałoł zkʻez govel piti."

Poetry

KNZ, 1, 46–47; 3, 67–69.
S, 1968, 370–72.
SUM, 1, 281–84.

Translations

FRENCH

Marcel, L.-A. "Eloge du vin." *AND,* 17 (n.d.), 125–27.

FRENCH ANTHOLOGIES

CPA, 104–6.
RA, 3, 155–63.
TA, 181–85.

SARMEN, (1901–1984)

Pen name: Sarmen.
Born Armenak Sargsyan in Paḥuankʻ, a village in the ancient Armenian region of Ṙštunikʻ, south of Lake Van. His parents were killed during the genocide of 1915, and he was raised in orphanages. Completed his studies at the State University of Erevan (1932). He wrote the national anthem of Soviet Armenia.

Collections

Hatěntir. (Erevan, 1951).
Erker. 2 vols. (Erevan, 1966–67).

Texts (verse)

Dašterě žptum en. (Leninakan, 1925).
Tṙichkʻ. (Moscow, 1935).
Sepʻo. (Erevan, 1939).
Ergastan. (Erevan, 1940).
Herosakan mah. (Erevan, 1940).
Astłer. (Erevan, 1942).

Hayrenik̒. (Erevan, 1944).
Tzałkunk̒. (Erevan, 1945).
Srti dzaynov. (Erevan, 1947).
Yot̒ erjanikner. (Erevan, 1950).
Tzałkadzor. (Erevan, 1952).
Koratz dzeřk̒er. (Erevan, 1954).
Gagat̒neri karotě. (Erevan, 1954).
Hayreni tun. (Erevan, 1955).
Karoti krakner. (Erevan, 1957).
Ḥosoł tzałikner. (Erevan, 1958).
Erger. (Erevan, 1959).
Hayots sirt. (Erevan, 1960).
Banastełtzi ałbyurě. (Erevan, 1961).
Kenats bažak. (Erevan, 1963).
Tzałkavor dzmeř. (Erevan, 1964).
Erazank̒. (Erevan 1969).
Im hayreni ałjiknerě. (Erevan, 1971).
Manukneri ašḥarhum. (Erevan, 1972).
K̒yořołli. (Erevan, 1974).
Hayos u K̒art̒los. (Erevan, 1979).
Hayi achk̒er. (Erevan, 1980).
Sirt. (Erevan, 1981).
K̒yořōłli. (Erevan, 1981). (Poem).
Mesrop Maštots. (Erevan, 1982). (Poem).
Huysi hasmikner. (Erevan, 1987).

Translations

English

Wettlin, M. "The Children's World." *SL,* 1973/9, 128–29.

French

Antonian, A., and Alikian, A. "Dans le monde des enfants." *OO,* 177 (Sept. 1973), 145.

French anthologies

Gaucheron, J. *E,* 78–79.
LPA, 298–99.

Russian

Gorokhov, N. *Vershiny. Stikhi.* (Moscow, 1980).
Radost̒ i slava. (Erevan, 1952).
Rodnye gory. Stikhi. (Moscow, 1959).
Semero schastlivykh. Stikhi. (Moscow and Leningrad, 1952).
[Tushnova, V.] *Rodnik poeta.* (Erevan, 1956).
Zima v tsvetakh. Stikhi i poemy. (Moscow, 1970).

Bibliographies

Manukyan, A. *Sarmen-80.* (Erevan, 1983).

Criticism

Arzumanyan, S. "Sarmeni poezian." *SG,* 1960/1, 122–33.
Daryan, Z. *Baru ergichě (hodvatzner).* (Erevan, 1981).

Hyusyan, M. *Sarmen.* (Erevan, 1970).
Kurtikyan, S. "Karoti krakner." *SG,* 1958/6, 119–28.
Sołomonyan, S. "Banastełtzi ułin." *SG,* 1963/11, 128–37.
V[ahē-]V[ahean]. "Banastełtz k'ałak'atsin." *Ani,* 1 (1946), 42–43.

SARYAN, GEŁAM (1902–1976)

Pen name: Gełam Saryan.

Born Gełam Bałdasaryan and educated in Tabriz. Emigrated to Soviet Armenia in 1922. At first he settled and taught in Leninakan (Gyumri, 1922–26), but he later moved to Erevan and worked as a journalist. From about 1935 until his death, Saryan devoted himself entirely to literature. In 1970, his collection of poems titled "K'rizant'em" won him the Armenian State Prize for literature.

Collections

Hatĕntir. (Erevan, 1945).
Hatĕntir. (Erevan, 1951).
Erker. (Erevan, 1956).
Erker. 2 vols. (Erevan, 1961).
Ĕntrvatz ējer. (Erevan, 1965).
Erker. 5 vols. (Erevan, 1969–72).
Ĕntir erker. (Erevan, 1974).
Saryan, N. *Banastełtzut'yunner ev poemner.* (Erevan, 1982).

Texts (verse)

Širaki harsanik'ĕ. (Leninakan, 1925).
Yunkersi ḥortakumĕ. (Leninakan, 1926).
Patmvatzk'ner. (Erevan, 1928). (Stories).
Ōtar mardĕ. (Erevan, 1929). (Story).
Erkir ḥorhrdayin. (Erevan, 1930).
Erkat'e otnadzayner. (Erevan, 1933).
Erek' erg. (Erevan, 1935).
Gyulnara. (Erevan, 1935).
Mijōre. (Erevan, 1935).
Ispaniayi patani herosnerĕ. (Erevan, 1936).
Banastełtzut'yunner. (Erevan, 1940).
Tłan u mahĕ. (Erevan, 1941).
Hayrenik'i hamar. (Erevan, 1942).
Pahakĕ. (Erevan, 1942).
Balladner. (Erevan, 1944).
P'ar̄k'i tačarĕ. (Erevan, 1944).
Banastełtzut'yunner. (Erevan, 1947).
Hrašali serund. (Erevan, 1950).
Banastełtz. (Erevan, 1954).
Balladner. (Erevan, 1957).
Ḥałĕnkerner. (Erevan, 1957).
Manukn u dzyunĕ. (Erevan, 1958).
Sayat'-Nova. (Erevan, 1964).
Hatutsum. (Erevan, 1966).
Grigor Derin. (Erevan, 1967). (Play).

K'rizant'em. (Erevan, 1968).
Bažak ełbayrut'yan. (Erevan, 1970).
Mterim ējer. (Erevan, 1972).
Ur gnal [?] (Erevan, 1984).

Translations

English

Evans, G. "Where, Little Cloud?," *SL,* 1966/3, 145.

English anthologies

SAP, 18–20.

French

Mardirossian, L. "Le nuage." *OO,* 123 (March 1969), 36.

French anthologies

FPA, 54–56.
Gamarra, P. *E,* 79–81.
LPA, 300–6.

German

Sinner, N. "Vom Taubengefieder verstreut . . ." *Sowjet-Literatur,* 1966/3, 143.

Russian

Adalis, A. et al, *Izbrannye stikhi.* ([Moscow], 1936).
Ballady. ([Moscow], 1945).
Izbrannoe. (Erevan, 1941).
Stikhotvoreniia. (Moscow, 1948, 1956).
Stikhotvoreniia i poemy. (Moscow, 1952, 1958; Erevan, 1959).
Zviagintseva, V. and Smeliak, Ia. *Chudesnoe pokolenie. Poema.* (Moscow, 1950).

Spanish

Alberti, R. y Maria Teresa Leon. "Nube pequenita." *Literatura Sovietica,* 1966/3, 144.

Criticism

Aławni, "Orn ē banastełtzě[?]" *Ani,* 1 (1946), 44–46.
Bazyan, S. *Erek' urvagitz—Nairi Zaryan, Širaz, Gełam Saryan.* (Erevan, 1941).
Darbni, V. "Ašḥarh, es ēl mi ašḥarh em . . ." *SG,* 1982/12, 117–20.
H. A. "Erkat'ē otnadzayner." *HK,* 13 (1934–35/6), 143–45.
Manukyan, S. *Gełam Saryan.* (Erevan, 1954).
Mnatsakanyan, V. "Kardalov Gełam Saryanin." *SG,* 1959/12, 104–23.
———. *Gełam Saryani poezian.* (Erevan, 1963).
Ṙštuni, H. *Gełam Saryan.* (Erevan, 1958).
Sołomonyan, S. "Gełam Saryan." *SG,* 1962/12, 88–95.
T'amrazyan, H. "Žołovrdi het, žołovrdi hamar." *SG,* 1960/11, 161–72.

ŠAYBON, AŠOT (1905–1982)

Pen name: Ašot Šaybon.

Born Ašot Gasparyan in Tiflis and educated at the Nersisean school. He was one of the first Armenian writers to write science fiction; he also wrote poetry and drama. Gave up his teaching career and interrupted his studies at the State University of Erevan in 1936 to study cinematography in Moscow.

Texts

Dinamo nvag. (Tiflis, 1925).
Karmir kʻałakʻi šrjmolikě. (Tiflis, 1925).
Nairi kʻucha. (Tiflis, 1925).
Zrahavor garun. (Erevan, 1931). (Prose).
Brigadirikě. (Erevan, 1932).
Pʻokʻrik leṙnagortzner. (Erevan, 1932).
Verelkʻi erger. (Erevan, 1932).
Kovkas. (Tiflis, 1935).
Allo, lsum ekʻ [?], menkʻ hyusisum enkʻ. (Erevan, 1938).
Hayrenakan lirika. (Erevan, 1944). (Verse).
Spitak stverneri ašḫarhum. (Erevan 1951, 1963). (Science fiction).
Gišerayin tziatzan. (Erevan, 1954, 1959, 1981). (Science fiction).
Tiezerakan ōvkianosi kapitannerě. (Erevan, 1955, 1986). (Science fiction).
Erkir moloraki gałtnikʻnerě. (Erevan, 1960). (Science fiction).
Ansovor patmutʻyun. (Erevan, 1965). (Novel).

Translations

RUSSIAN

Karagezian, L. *Suvorovtsy.* (Erevan, 1952).
[Tadeosian, A.] *Pobediteli t'my. Nauch. fantast. roman.* (Erevan, 1952).

Criticism

Abovian, A. *Ashot Shaibon.* (Erevan, 1980).

SAYEATʻ-NŌVAY, (1722?–1795)

This celebrated *ašuł* (minstrel), born in Tiflis, was originally named Arutʻin or Yarutʻiwn. Wrote and sang in Armenian, in Georgian and in what is now known as Azeri-Turkish. He was initiated into the minstrelsy in the tradition of Armenian *ašuls:* by seeking divine grace at the monastery of Surb Karapet in Muš. His talent soon brought him wide recognition, royal patronage at the Georgian court, and a good deal of misery in matters of the heart. His latter years are not well documented. At one point he became a married priest and was renamed Stepʻanos. But in the wake of his wife's death in 1768, he joined the brotherhood of the monastery of Hałbat in northern Armenia as a celibate priest. According to many accounts, he was killed by the Persians invading Tiflis for declining apostasy.

Collections

Baḥchinyan, H. *Ḥałeri žołovatzu.* (Erevan, 1987). (Armenian, Azeri, and Georgian poems).

Texts

Aḥverdean, G. *Gusankʻ. 1. Sayeatʻ-Nōvay.* (Moscow, 1852).
Sayeatʻ-Nōva, azgayin ergich (ašuł). (Tiflis, 1882).
Sayeatʻ Nōvay. (Tiflis, 1914).
Sayeatʻ-Nōvay. (Baku, 1914).
Sayatʻ-Nova: hayeren ḥałeri žołovatzu. (Erevan, 1931).
Sayatʻ-Nova: tałer. (Beirut, 1931).
Levonyan, G. *Hayeren ḥałeri liakatar žołovatzu.* (Erevan, 1935).

Abrahamean, R. *Sayeatʻ-Novayi tałerě.* (Teheran, 1943).
Matean imastutʻean, gełetskutʻean ew anmatoyts siroy. (Alexandria, 1944).
Hasratʻyan, M. *Hayeren, vratseren, adrbejaneren ḥałeri žołovatzu.* (Erevan, 1945, 1959, 1963).
Sayatʻ-Nova. (Erevan, 1946).
Połpatean, E. *Sayeatʻ-Nōvay.* (Beirut, 1952).
Ḥałer: nmanahanutʻyun. (Erevan, 1963).
Kʻaṙatołer. (Erevan, 1963).
Payazat, S. *Ḥałer.* (Erevan, 1969).
Sayatʻ-Nova, siroy ew ardarutʻean ergichě. 2d ed. (Beirut, 1969).
Baḥchinyan, H. *Hayeren ḥałer.* (Erevan, 1984).

Translations

English anthologies

ALP, 14, 35, 74, 85, 110.
AP, 119–20.

French

Arsenian, M. *Quelques poèmes et pensées.* (Paris, 1977).
Gardon, V. ("Ce sacré monde est une fenêtre.") *AND,* 16 (1965), 76–77.
Martirossian, L. ["Sagesse en toi . . ."; "Tel un rossignol . . ."]. *OO* (Sept. 1963), 141–44.

French anthologies

LPA, 155–58.
PA, 115–39.
PAM, 183–87.
TA, 251–61.

Italian

Gianascian, M. *Sayath-Nova, Canzoniere.* (Venice, 1964).

Russian

Briusov, V., Verkhovskii, Iu., et. al. *Pesni.* (Moscow, 1939).
Lirika. (Moscow, 1963).
Saiat-Nova v perovodakh V. Ia. Briusova. (Erevan, 1963).
Sbornik armianskikh, gruzinskikh i azerbaidzhanskikh pesen. (Erevan, 1945, 1963).
Stikhotvoreniia. (Leningrad, 1961, 1982).

Russian anthologies

AAP, 333–39.
ARPO, 59–77.
BPA, 227–36.
SHAP, 17–26.

Multilingual

Harutʻyunyan, S. *Sayatʻ-Nova, 1712–1962: kʻertʻvatzner tʻargmanvatz zanazan lezunerov.* (Erevan, 1963).

Bibliographies

Nazikyan, A. "Sayatʻ-Novan ōtar lezunerov: matenagitakan tsank." *SG,* 1963/10, 155–58.
———. "Sayatʻ-Novayi tałerě evropakan lezunerov." *EJ,* 1963/7–8, 54–60.

Criticism

A. H. "Sayeat‘ Novayi mahwan šurjě." *Vēm,* 4 (1936/3), 110–14.

Abov, G. "Hay žołovrdi metz banastełtzě." *PBH,* 1963/3, 3–16.

———. *Siro ev ardarut‘yan metz ergichě Sayat‘-Novan.* (Erevan, 1945).

Abrahamyan, A., et al, *Sayat‘-Nova: gitakan ašḥatut‘yunneri žołovatzu.* (Erevan, 1963).

———. "Sayat‘-Novayi ‘Ayběbiměn’ ḥaŕi tzatzkagrut‘yan vertzanut‘yuně." *PBH,* 1979/3, 207–11.

Ałbalean, N. "Ditołut‘iwnner Sayat‘-Novayi masin." *HA,* 38 (1924), 259–70, 360–68.

———. *Sayat‘-Novayi het.* (Beirut, 1966). (Vol. 2 of Collected Works).

Ananyan, G. *Sayat‘-Novan banastełtzneri ergerum.* (Erevan, 1963).

———. "Sayat‘-Novayi kerparě poeziayum." *T,* 1963/10, 115–22.

Anasyan, H. "Sayat‘-Novayi tałerě: matenagitakan tesut‘yun." *SG,* 1963/10, 130–54.

Andreasean, S. *Hay ergi erku hskaner–Sayat‘-Nova ew Komitas vardapet.* (Chicago, 1979).

Astero. "Saiat-Nova na iazykakh narodov Evropy." *Literaturnaia Armeniia,* 1963/10, 89–92.

Avetisyan, A. "Sayat‘-Novayi erkeri aŕajin hratarkut‘yan ardzagank‘nerě." *SG,* 1960/8, 169–72.

———. "Metz gusani haytnagortzołě." *SG,* 1963/9, 112–16.

———. "Aŕajin sayat‘novagetě. " *SG,* 1987/10, 101–4. (On G. Aḥverdean).

Baḥchinyan, H. "Sayat‘-Novayi erek‘ tzatzkagri vertzanut‘yuně." *PBH,* 1975/4, 169–75.

———. "Ditołut‘yunner Sayat‘-Novayi Davt‘ari veraberyal." *PBH,* 1976/3, 209–21.

———. "Sayat‘-Novayi hayeren ḥałeri tesaknerě ev tałachap‘ut‘yuně." *L,* 1976/6, 60–72.

———. "Sayat‘-Novayi kensagrut‘yan erku hartsi šurjě." *BEH,* 1977/2, 162–75.

———. "Sayat‘-Novayi hayeren ḥałeri grut‘yan t‘vakannerě." *L,* 1984/6, 52–61.

———. "Sayat‘-Novayi tzatzkagrerě." *HA,* 1987/1–12 (*Yušamatean, Festschrift,* 1887–1987), 833–39.

———. *Sayat‘-Nova. Kyank‘ě ev gortzě.* (Erevan, 1988).

———. "Sayat‘-Novayi vratseren ḥałeri lezun." *L,* 1987/12, 21–26.

———. "Sayat‘-Novan ev arevelyan vipašḥarhě." *SG,* 1987/10, 82–91.

Bałdasaryan, V. "Lsenk‘ Sayat‘-Novayin." *SG,* 1975/2, 148–51.

———. "Sayat‘-Novayi Davt‘ari ev mi k‘ani ḥałeri masin." *PBH,* 1979/1, 233–44.

———. "Sayat‘-Novayi adrbejaneren łarahejaneri masin." *PBH,* 1980/3, 280–85.

Baramidze, A. "Sayat-Nova po gruzinskim istochnikam." *T,* 37–44.

Bašinjałyan, Z. "Mišt Sayat‘-Novayi het." *T,* 1963/10, 89–102.

———. *30 let otdannye Saiat-Nova.* (Erevan, 1963).

Bayramyan, H. "Sayat‘-Novayi vratseren ḥałeri gnahatut‘yan šurj." *BEH,* 1986/2, 116–22.

Čanašean, M. *Sayat‘-Nova.* (Venice, 1964).

Ch. M. "Saiat Nova, sa vie et ses chansons." *Journal of the Royal Asiatic Society,* July, 1893, 497–508.

Daryan, Z. "Daravor oronumner." *SG,* 1959/11, 135–51.

Dulyan, B. *Sayatʻ-Nova.* Vol. 1 (Erevan, 1990).
Durgaryan, K. "Sayatʻ-Novayi azdetsutʻyunĕ antsyali hay ašułneri ev banastełtzneri vra." *SG,* 1963/10, 111–14.
———. "Sayatʻ-Novayi hangaranĕ." *T,* 1963/10, 69–78.
———. "Sayatʻ-Novayi hayeren ḥałeri tałachapʻutʻyunĕ." *PBH,* 1963/3, 67–78.
Enikolopov, I. "Gurgen-khan i Saiat-Nova." *L,* 1971/2, 108–12.
Eremean, A. "Sayeatʻ-Novayi erkeri ēakan yatkanišnern ew aruestĕ." *HA,* 78 (1964), 181–84.
Erevanli, A. "Andrkovkasyan žołovrdneri harazat šunchĕ." *SG,* 1963/10, 115–18.
Gaisarian, S. *Saiat-Nova; zametki o zhizni i tvorchestve velikogo armianskogo poeta.* (Moscow, 1963).
———. "A Minstrel of Old Armenia." *SL,* 1963/9, 145–50.
Gazančean, R. "Sayeatʻ-Novayi banastełtzutʻiwnĕ (verlutzakan pʻordz)." *B,* 121 (1963), 218–23.
Gevorgyan, Kʻ. "Sayatʻ-Novayi kensagrutʻyunĕ." *EJ,* 1961/9–10, 51–60.
Gevogyan, N. "Sayatʻ-Novayi aliflamaneri ev łarahejaneri masin." *PBH,* 1982/1, 98–108.
———. "Sayatʻ-Novayi ḥałeri mi kʻani patkerneri meknabanutʻyan masin." *PBH,* 1984/4, 199–207.
Grigoryan, S. "Sayatʻ-Novayi kyankʻi hałbatyan šrjani masin." *PBH,* 1971/3, 95–114.
Ḥachikyan, H. "Sayatʻ-Novayi gełagitakan hayatskʻneri bnutʻagrman šurj." *PBH,* 1963/3, 45–52.
Hakobyan, P. "Sayatʻ-Novayi Hałbati vankʻum linelu hartsi šurjĕ." *PBH,* 1969/3, 209–25.
———. "Dardzyal Sayatʻ-Novayi Hałbati vankʻum gtnvelu masin." *PBH,* 1973/4, 157–71.
Harutʻyunyan, G. "Sayatʻ-Novayi 'Geln u chobanĕ' ḥałi mi nor variantĕ." *EJ,* 1947/ 5–6, 55–56.
Harutʻyunyan, S. *Ergi hančarĕ: Sayatʻ-Novan.* (Erevan, 1963).
Hasratʻyan, M. "Sayatʻ-Novayi Davtʻarĕ." *T,* 1963, 3–32; 1963/11, 3–22.
———. "Prof. A. G. Abrahamyani hodvatzi aṙitʻov." *PBH,* 1979/3, 212–13.
Hovhannisyan, N. "Sayatʻ-Novayi hayeren ḥałeri aṙandznahatkutʻyunnerĕ." *L,* 1990/9, 48–56.
Hovhannisyan, S. "Sayatʻ-Novayi aržekʻavorman patmutʻyunits." *SG,* 1987/10, 92–100.
Kʻochoyan, A. *Sayatʻ-Novayi hayeren ḥałeri baṙaran.* (Erevan, 1963).
———. "Sayatʻ-Novayi hayeren ḥałeri baṙayin kazmĕ." *PBH,* 1963/1, 259–61.
Łanalanyan, A. "Sayatʻ-Novan haykakan avandutʻyunnerum." *PBH,* 1963/3, 79–90.
———. *Sayatʻ-Novayi stełtzagortzutʻyan žołovrdakan akunkʻnerĕ.* (Erevan, 1963).
———. "Žołovrdakan banarvesti artatsolumĕ Sayatʻ-Novayi ergerum." *PBH,* 1982/1, 17–25.
Madoyan, G. "G. Aḥverdyanĕ sayatʻnovagitutʻyan himnadir." *T,* 1963/10, 59–68.
Melikʻsetʻ-Bek, L. "Vratsakan ałbyurnerĕ Sayatʻ-Novayi masin." *PBH,* 1963/3, 17–43.
Mirzoyan, I. "Sayatʻ-Novayi ḥałerum ōgtagortzvatz mi šarkʻ ōtarazgi baṙeri meknabanman pʻordz." *L,* 1967/3, 79–91.

Mkryan, M. "Sayat‘-Novayi stełtzagortzut‘yan gełarvestakan metzut‘yunĕ." *SG,* 1963/10, 88–96.

Muradean, H. *Sayat‘-Nova.* (Beirut, 1960; Erevan, 1963).

Muradyan, P. *Sayat‘-Novan ĕst vratsakan ałbyurneri: banasirakan prptumner ev nyut‘er.* (Erevan, 1963).

———. "Sayat‘-Novayi stełtzagortzut‘yan derĕ vrats grakanut‘yan mej." *PBH,* 1963/3, 91–98.

———. "Vrats sayat‘novagitut‘yan patmut‘yunits." *T,* 1963/10, 77–88.

Nalbandyan, G. "Sayat‘-Novayi tzatzkagir tałeri vertzanman hartsi šurjĕ." *BEH,* 1968/3, 131–46.

———. "Sayat‘-Novayi tzatzkagir tałeri vertzanman šurjĕ." *BEH,* 1976/2, 158–66.

Nalbandyan, V. *Sayat‘-Nova.* (Erevan, 1987).

———. "Sayat‘-Nova ev Grigor Narkatsi." *SG,* 1988/4, 137–44.

Naryan, M. "Ditołut‘yunner Sayat‘-Novayi hayeren ḥałeri lezvi masin." *PBH,* 1963/3, 53–55.

———. "Mi k‘ani baṙ ergchi ḥałerits. *SG,* 1963/10, 119–24.

———. "Sayat‘-Nova ev H. T‘umanyan." *T,* 1963/10, 103–14.

———. "Banasirakan ditołut‘yunner Sayat‘-Novayi mi k‘ani ḥałeri kapaktsut‘yamb." *PBH,* 1974/4, 81–88.

———. "Sayat‘-Novayi gortzatzatz mi k‘ani artahaytut‘yunneri masin." *L,* 1974/2, 44–49.

Nazikyan, A. "Sayat‘-Novan ōtar lezunerov: matenagitakan tsank." *SG,* 1963/10, 155–58.

———. "Sayat‘-Novayi tałerĕ evropakan lezunerov." *EJ,* 1963/7–8, 54–60.

Nersisyan, V. "Mi ułłum sayat‘novyan bnagrum." *PBH,* 1987/4, 194–95.

Ovakimian, B. "Istoriia pervogo izdaniia pesen Saiat-Novy." *Literaturnaia Armeniia,* 1963/10, 79–88.

Połosyan, Ḥ. "Metz banastełtz-humanistĕ." *SG,* 1963/8, 126–37.

Sahakyan, H. "Mijnadaryan hay tałergut‘yan avandnerĕ ev Sayat‘-Novan." *PBH,* 1964/2, 85–96.

Šahazizyan, A. *Sayat‘-Nova, tznndyan 250—amyakĕ.* (Erevan, 1963).

Šahsuvaryan, A. "Sayat‘-Novan ev parskakan mšakuyt‘ĕ." *SG,* 1963/10, 125–29.

Sargsyan, H. *Sayat‘-Nova.* (Erevan, 1963).

"Sayat‘-Novayi tznndyan 250—amyaki aṙt‘iv." *L,* 1987/11, 95–98.

Seiidov, Mirali. *Pevets narodov Zakavkaz'ia.* (Baku, 1963).

Šems, H. *Sayeat‘-Nova.* (Alexandria, 1944).

Sevak, P. "Sluga naroda, pevets liubvi." *Literaturnaia Armeniia,* 1963/10, 51–65.

———. "Erb ē tznvel Sayat‘-Novan [?]" *PBH,* 1966/2, 85–114.

———. *Sayat‘-Nova.* (Erevan, 1969, 1987).

Sevoyan, H. "Erb ē tznvel Sayat‘-Novan [?]" *PBH,* 1966/3, 119–30.

———. *Nor ējer Sayat‘-Novayi kyank‘its.* (Erevan, 1989).

T‘ahmizyan, N. "Sayat‘-Novayi hayeren ergeri ełanakneri masin." *T,* 1963/10, 33–58.

———. "Sayat‘-Novan ev nor šrjani haykakan eražštakan gełagitakan mtk‘i skzbnavorumĕ." *PBH,* 1988/1, 80–92.

T‘at‘osyan, G. "Sayat‘-Novan ṙuseren." *SG,* 1962/6, 151–56. (General history of his Russian translations).

Tēr-Alēkʻsandrean, G. "Sayeatʻ-Novayi yišatakin." *Ardzagankʻ,* 1 (1885), 3–4. (Includes two unpublished poems).
Tʻumanyan, H. *Sayatʻ-Nova.* (Erevan, 1945, 1963).
———. *Sayatʻ-Novan: hodvatzner ev čaṙer.* (Erevan, 1963).
Zawrean, Y. "Sayeatʻ Nova." *Vēm,* 1 (1933/1), 28–38; 2, 32–48. 2 (1934/1), 38–49; 2, 12–20; 3, 18–28; 4, 38–53.

SEMA, A. (c1910–1940)

Pen name: A. Sema.

Born Gełam Atʻmačean in Bafra (Turkey). Having lost his father and other members of the family to the Armenian massacres of 1915, Sema sought shelter in orphanages. He then lived in Istanbul (1919–24), Aleppo (1924–25), and eventually settled in France (1926). Took up residence in Paris in 1928 and attended courses in literature, history, and social sciences at the Sorbonne. Began publishing his poetry and prose in this period, and launched two literary periodicals: *Jankʻ* (1930), jointly with M. Manušean (q.v.), and *Mšakoytʻ* (1935–37). He was killed fighting for France in May, 1940.

Texts

Zrahawor garun. (Paris, 1936, 1946). (Verse).
Paron Kaluni. (Paris, 1937). (Play).
Šamiram. (Paris, 1938). (Play).
Atʻmačean, M. *Lusamatean banastełtz A. Semayi (Gełam Atʻmačean, 1910–1940) yišatakin.* (Paris, 1970).

Translations

ITALIAN

LPAM, 309–11.

RUSSIAN

"Bez rodiny." *PCN,* 142–52.

Criticism

Chōpanean, A. "Erekʻ hay herosakan nahatakner (Gełam Atʻmačean, Misakʻ Manušean, Luiza Aslanean)." *ANA,* 12 (1946/1), 1–9.
Stepʻanyan, S. "Spʻyuṙkʻahay kyankʻi ējerě." *SG,* 1966/10, 132–36.
Vahē-Vahean. "A. Sema." *Ani,* 4 (1950–51), 94–95.

ŠERAM, GUSAN (1857–1938)

Pen name: Gusan Šeram.

Born Grigor Talean in Alexandrapol (Leninakan, now Gyumri). A popular *ašuł* (minstrel) with no formal education. Subsequently settled in Tiflis (1915–35), but he spent the last three years of his life in Erevan.

Texts

Ergich Grigor Taleantsi kʻnarě. (Alexandrapol, 1902).
Gangati šantʻer. (Alexandrapol, 1905).
Sēr ew kṙiw. (Alexandrapol, 1907).
Anjur partēz. (Alexandrapol, 1913).
Anzusp aršaw. (Alexandrapol, 1915).

Erger. (Erevan, 1946).
Siro erger. (Erevan, 1948). (Includes score).
Erger. (Erevan, 1959). (104 songs with scores).
Erger. (Erevan, 1969).
Erger. (Erevan, 1979).
Siro erger. Tḥur antsyalits. Ergitzakan. (Erevan, 1981).

Criticism

Brutyan, Ts. "Šeram." *SG,* 1960/6, 169–72.
Daryan, Z. "Hayrer ev zavakner." *SG,* 1971/8, 137–45. (On Šeram and the folklorist Bense, i.e., Sahak Movsisyan, 1867–1939).
Eremean, A. *Ašuł Grigor Talean.* (Venice, 1930).
Talyan, V. "Šeram.' *SG,* 1967/3, 146.
———. "Šeram." *SG,* 1986/8, 71–77. (A short story on Šeram).

SETʻEAN, YOVHANNĒS (1853–1930)

Pen name: Eosēy Vanantʻnseh.
Born in Constantinople. Poet. Studied at the Kedronakan and taught in Armenian schools in his birthplace. Fled the Armenian massacres of the mid-1890s and settled in Cairo permanently.

Collections

Arsaloysēn verjaloys. (Cairo, 1912).

Texts

Grakan zbōsankʻ. (Constantinople, 1882).
Yuzman žamer. (Constantinople, 1888).
Blurn i ver. ([Constantinople], 1896).
Taragrin kʻnarě. ([Cairo], 1912).

Criticism

Alpʻiar, Y. "Yovhannēs Setʻean." *HG,* 12 (1913), 28–31.
Eremean, S. "Yovhannēs Setʻean (dimagitz)." *B,* 87 (1930), 157–59.
Tēr-Margarean, Y. "Yovhannēs Setʻeani yobeleanĕ." *HA,* 26 (1912), 563–64.
Yovhannēs Setʻean. (Constantinople, 1913).

SEVUNTS, GAREGIN (1911–1969)

Pen name: Garegin Sevunts.
Born Garegin Grigoryan, in Ḥndzoresk, a village in Goris, Armenia. Novelist. Studied Armenian language and literature and received military training in Baku. Worked for the Armenian newspaper *Komunist* (Baku, 1935–38) and edited the Armenian monthly *Ḥorhrdayin groł* (Baku, 1938–41). After active service in the Soviet Army (1941–45), he resided permanently in Erevan. In Armenia, Sevunts pursued journalism and adminstrative work.

Collections

Erker. 5 vols. (Erevan, 1963–65).

Texts (novels)

Depi erkir. (Baku, 1935).
Tzovaḥoršum. Book 1. (Baku, 1938).

Višapasari ałjikě. (Baku, 1945).
Azatutʻyan połota. (Erevan, 1947).
Aṙajin šarkʻ. (Erevan, 1947).
Iranakan notʻer. (Erevan, 1949).
Tʻehran. 2 vols. (Erevan, 1952, 1953 [Vols. 1 and 2], 1973 [Vols. 1 and 2]; Beirut, 1954 [Vol. 1]).
Danubits Ganges. (Erevan, 1957).
Geriner. (Erevan, 1958).
Vietnami garuně. (Erevan, 1960).
Petakan gałtnikʻ. (Erevan, 1967).
Chika. (Erevan, 1968).
Ayn ōrerin. (Erevan, 1979).
Kjankʻě tʻeveri vra. (Erevan, 1984).

Translations

Russian

Asoiants, T. *V'etnamskaia vesna. Putevye ocherki.* (Moscow, 1963).
Barkhudarian, A. *V pervom riadu.* [Rasskazy dlia detei]. (Erevan, 1952).
Rusalka. Rasskazy. (Moscow, 1969).
Sadovskii, A., and Tadeosian, A. *Tegeran. Roman.* 2 vols. (Moscow, 1952, 1953, 1956, 1959).
Sevunts, A. *V bukhte. Roman.* (Moscow, 1970).
Taronian, A., and Zuev, A. *Plenniki. Roman.* (Erevan, 1960).

SEWAK, ṘUBĒN (1885–1915)

Pen name: Ṙubēn Sewak.

Ṙubēn Chilinkirean was born in Silivri (Turkey) and educated in his birthplace as well as at the American school in Partizak (Bahçecik, Turkey) and the Pērpērean school of Constantinople. Studied (1905–11) and practiced medicine in Lausanne. Returned to Constantinople with his Swiss-born wife in 1914. Made a name for himself as a leading poet and writer of short stories and as a highly respected professional. He was tortured to death near Çankırı (northeast of Ankara), soon after the collective arrest of Armenian intellectuals in April, 1915.

Collections

Karmir girkʻě, Siroy girkʻě, Tsriw kʻertʻuatzner. (Jerusalem, 1944).
Bžiškin girkʻēn pʻrtsuatz ējer ew Kʻertʻuatzner. (Paris, 1946).
Erker. (Erevan, 1955).
Tʻopʻchyan, A. *Erker.* (Erevan, 1985).
Erker. (Antʻilias, 1986).

Texts

Karmir girkʻě. (Constantinople, 1910). (Poems).
Bžiškin girkʻēn pʻrtsuatz ējer. (Salonica, 1925; Jerusalem, 1943). (Prose).
Tʻopʻchyan, A. "Sevaki antip banastełtzutʻyunnerits." *SG,* 1985/4, 18–19.

Translations

French Anthologies

APA, 213–20.
LPA, 229–30.

RUSSIAN ANTHOLOGIES

AAP, 530–38.
DILS, 37–54.
IZAP, 75–92.

SPANISH ANTHOLOGIES

APAS, 247–52.

Criticism

Aznavuryan, G. "Anhayt ēǰer hay nahatakneri grakan žaṙangutʻyunits." *EJ,* 1965/2–4, 43–57. (Previously unpublished letters and other material by Komitas, G. Zōhrap, D. Varužan, Siamantʻō, Tʻlkatintsi, Ṙ. Zardarean, and Ṙ. Sewak).

Jrbašyan, Ēd. *Ṙuben Sevak, stełtzagortzutʻyan hamaṙot aknark.* (Erevan, 1965).

Karapetean, Y. "Ēǰ mě akʻsori yišataknerēs." *Z* (amsatʻertʻ), 2 (1957/1–2), 6; 2 (1957/3–4), 2; 2 (1957/5–6), 6.

Kirakosyan, V. "Ṙuben Sevaki azgayin-kʻałakʻakan poezian." *PBH,* 1965/1, 63–74.

———. "Ṙuben Sevaki stełtzagortzutʻyuně." *T,* 1965/12, 65–72.

———. *Ṙuben Sevak (kyankʻě ev stełtzagortzutʻyuně).* (Erevan, 1972).

Sewan, A. "Ṙubēn Sewak." *HK,* 9 (1930–31/1), 43–60; 2, 62–83.

Yovhannēsean, A. "Kʻałakʻakan gortziché Ṙ. Sewaki mēǰ." *HK,* 17 (1938–39/8), 83–87.

———. "Ṙ. Sewaki kartzikʻnerě Metzarentsi masin." *HK,* 17 (1938–39/9), 110–13.

SĒYEAD, (1810–1872)

Pen name: Sēyead.

Petros Tēr Yovsēpʻean Madatʻeants was a minstrel born in Artsaḥ (Karabagh) and educated at the Nersisean school of Tiflis. Little else is known about him save that he rose to the rank of captain in the Russian cavalry and spent the last part of his life in Constantinople.

Poetry

ANA, 1929/5, 25–26.

Čṙakʻał, 1859, 415–16. 1860, 34. 1861, 263, 275–76, 292, 308–9, 326–27, 341–42, 356–58, 365–67, 383.

MKH, 115–16, 257–61, 366–67, 395–96, 405–15, 465–66, 483–84, 495–97, 513–14, 530–34, 539–41, 568–69, 572–78.

THG, 79–85.

Criticism

MKH, 590.

SEYRANYAN, BENIK (1913–)

Born in Kotʻi, a village renamed Šavaršavan (in Noyemberyan, Armenia). Educated in Tiflis, where he resided from an early age. In 1958 he received his first degree in education from the Ḥ. Aboyvan Pedagogical Institute of Erevan (by correspondence). For many years from the early 1930s onward he worked as a journalist for the daily *Sovetakan Vrastan* (previously *Proletar*) and headed the Armenian section of the Union of Soviet Writers of Georgia. His literary works consist of prose and plays.

Texts

K'arapi katzanĕ. (Tiflis, 1935).
Tziranak'ar. (Erevan, 1945). (Stories).
Tzałkatz hušardzan. (Erevan, 1946). (Stories).
Lefnayin byureł. (Erevan, 1949). (Stories).
Dzularani kraknerĕ. (Erevan, 1950). (Stories).
Ałbyurner. (Erevan, 1953).(Stories).
Astłeri hovit. (Tbilisi, 1959). (Novel).
Astładzor. (Erevan, 1963). (Novel).
Lefnerum. (Erevan, 1963). (Stories).
Ayn ałmkot garnan. (Erevan, 1967). (Stories).
Čamp'aner ev čakatagrer. (Erevan, 1968). (Novel).
Siro luys. (Erevan, 1974). (Stories).
Karoti krakner. (Erevan, 1976). (Stories).
Ełbayr k'ałak'nerĕ. (Tbilisi, 1976).
Tzovahavk'i kanchĕ. (Tbilisi, 1976). (Stories).
Aršaluysits verjaluys. (Erevan, 1979). (Prose).
Gugark'i urah zruytsner. (Erevan, 1982).
Es k'ez kgtnem. (Erevan, 1988).
Masruti ełnikĕ. (Erevan, 1988).

Translations

RUSSIAN

Golubaia pesnia: Povesti, rasskazy, novelly. (Moscow, 1984).
Perim, A. *Puti i sud'by: roman.* (Tbilisi, 1982).

SEZA, (c1903–1973)

Pen name: Seza.

Born Siranoyš Zarifean in Constantinople. A writer of short stories and sister of the poet Matt'ēos Zarifean (q.v.). Educated at the American College for Girls in Constantinople, which she left for Beirut in the early 1920s. Pursuing her higher studies at Columbia University (late 1920s through early 1930s), she obtained an M.A. in journalism and literature. Back in Beirut, she launched her well-known monthly *Eritasard hayuhi* (1932–34, 1946–68).

Texts

Ogii užov. (Beirut, 1954).
Patnēšĕ. (Beirut, 1959).
Meławoruhin. (Beirut, 1960; Erevan, 1967). (Selections).
Hēk'eat'neru ašharhēn. (Beirut, 1973).

Criticism

K'asuni, Ž. "Siran Seza (kensagrakan gitzer). *Širak* (Beirut), 16 (1973/9–10), 89–92.

SIAMANT'Ō (1878–1915)

Pen name: Siamant'ō.

Born Atom Earčanean in Akn (Eğin, now Kemaliye, Turkey). Studied in Akn and Constantinople and sought safety in Europe during the Armenian massacres of the mid-1890s. In Paris, he attended literature classes at the Sorbonne, and shortly after his return to Constantinople in 1908, he sailed for Boston on a visit to the United States that lasted until 1911. In 1913–14 he visited Tiflis and Eastern Armenia (most memorably Ējmiatzin and the village of Ōšakan), and returned to the Ottoman capital via Geneva. He was one of the intellectuals rounded up in Constantinople in April and murdered in the interior in mid-1915.

Collections

Ambołjakan erker. (Beirut, 1974).
Ambołjakan erker. (Anťilias, 1989).
Ambołjakan gortzer. (Paris, 1902).
Ambołjakan gortzě. (Boston, 1910). (Includes "Hayreni hrawēr").
Ambołjakan gortzě. (Delmar, NY: Caravan Books, 1979). (A reproduction of the 1910 Boston edition).
Ěntir erker. (Erevan, 1957).
Siamanťo, Daniel Varužan, Erker. (Erevan, 1979).

Texts

Diwtsaznōrēn. (Paris, 1902).
Hayordiner. 1st cycle. (Geneva, 1905).
Hogewarki ew yoysi jaher. (Paris, 1907).
Hayordiner. 1st and 2d cycles. (Paris, 1908; Constantinople, 1908).
Hayordiner. 3d cycle. (Paris, 1908).
Karmir lurer barekamēs. (Constantinople, 1909; Beirut, 1969).
Surb Mesrop. (Constantinople, 1913).

Translations

English

Blackwell, A. "My Native Fountain." *Armenia*, 4 (1910/1), 3.
———. *The Song of the Knight.* (Constantinople, 1912).
———. "The Dance." *The New Armenia,* 8 (1916/24), 373–74.
———. "Fountain of My Fatherland," "Tears," "The Song of the Knight." *The New Armenia,* 20 (1928/4), 57–59.

English Anthologies

AP, 141–67.

French

Tchobanian, A. "Je veux mourir en chantant." *Hommage à l'Arménie* (Paris, 1919), 32–33.

French Anthologies

APA, 171–79.
Gaucheron, J. *E,* 50–52.
FPA, 64–65.
JM, 58–71.
LPA, 206–14.

German Anthologies

ALG, 131–32.

Italian

Bazardjian, R. "Casa paterna." *Armenia: Confernza* (Milano, 1917), 22.
"Caucazo!" *Armenia* (Torino), 1917/5, 5.

"Noi dobbiamo lottare," "Lutto," "Il sogno d'una madre." *Armenia* (Torino), 1916/11, 12.

Italian anthologies

DLA, 13–16.
LPAM, 207–11.

Russian anthologies

AAP, 527–29.
ARPO, 193–98.
BPA, 474–78.
DILS, 11–16.
IZAP, 55–70.
Shatova, M. *Loza gneva.* (Erevan, 1987).

Spanish anthologies

APAS, 225–28.

Criticism

Aharonean, V. "Handipumner Siamantʻōyi het." *HK,* 20 (1942/2), 55–61.
Aznavuryan, G. "Anhayt ējer hay nahatakneri grakan žaŕangutʻyunits." *EJ,* 1965/2–4, 43–57. (Previously unpublished letters and other material by Komitas, G. Zōhrap, D. Varužan, Siamantʻō, Tʻlkatintsi, Ṙ. Zardarean, and Ṙ. Sewak).
Bekʻmezyan, H. "Siamantʻoyi bnapaštutʻyuně." *PBH,* 1977/3, 115–20.
Chōpanean, A. "Atom Earčanean, 'Diwtsaznōren'." *ANA,* 4 (1902), 50–54.
———. "Atom Earčanean, Hogewarkʻi ew yoysi jaher." *ANA,* 1907/3–5, 87–94.
Ṙštuni, H. "Siamantʻoyi poeziayi žołovrdakan akunkʻnerě." *PBH,* 1968/4, 170–84.
———. "Siamantʻoyi kʻertʻutʻyan arvestě." *SG,* 1968/9, 119–31.
———. *Siamantʻo.* (Erevan, 1970).
———. "Lavatesutʻyan akunkʻnerě Siamantʻoyi banastełtzakan ašḫarhum." *PBH,* 1974/3, 93–104.
———. "Makʻaŕman ergichě." *SG,* 1978/8, 138–45.
Sargsyan, G. "Azgayin taŕapankʻi, makʻaŕman ev huysi ergichě." *PBH,* 1978/2, 45–54.
Sasuni, K. "Siamantʻō." *HK,* 33 (1955/4), 11–23.
Širvanzadē. "Siamantʻon." *HK,* 3 (1924–25/2), 50–52.
Tʻamrazyan, H. "Siamantʻo." *SG,* 1964/6, 109–42.
Varduni. "Siamantʻō ew ir grakan gortzě." *HA,* 74 (1960), 595–604.
V[aružan], D. *Grakan asulisner, Atom Earčanean.* (Constantinople, 1913).
———. "Surb Mesrop." *Nawasard,* 1914, 254.
V. K. "Ěntʻertsum 'Diwtsaznōrēn'i." *B,* 127 (1969), 210–16.
———. *Siamantʻoyi 'Diwtsaznōrēn'i masin grakan ḫoher.* (Venice, 1974).
Zawēn, T. "Siamantʻō, Hayordinerě, Žěnew, 1905." *Murč,* 1905/6, 137–41.

SIMĒON APARANETSI, "METZN" (d. 1615?)

Born in the village of Aparankʻ in the southern part of Lake Van. Studied in the famous monastic schools of Bałēš (Bitlis) and Ostan. Took the holy orders and taught at various monasteries in Armenia proper. Died in Van.

Texts (verse)

Vipasanutʻiwn saks Pahlawuneatsn zarmi ew Mamikoneantsn seŕi. (Vałaršapat, 1870).

"Ołbankʻ." *TH,* 151–63. ("Ołbatsēkʻ anloytz sěgov/ Ekełetsis Hayastaneats . . .").
Sukʻiasyan, K. *Banastełtzutʻyunner.* (Erevan, 1976).

Translations

French anthologies

LPA, 126–27.
RA, 2, 167–77.

Criticism

Akinean, N. "Simēon v. Aparanetsi." *HA,* 33 (1919), 79–96.
———. "Simēon v. Aparanetsi 'Metzn'." *Bałēši dprotsě, 1500–1704,* by N. Akinean (Vienna, 1952), 122–50.
Sargisean, B. "Simēon Aparanetsi ew kełtz Sebēosi ařełtzuatzě." *B,* 73 (1915), 1–9, 33–39.
Sukʻiasyan, K. "Simeon Aparantsu Vipasanutʻyan ałbyurnerě." *L,* 1970/8, 30–38.
———. "Simeon Aparantsu 'Vipasanutʻyuně'." *BEH,* 1970/2, 246–50.
Sukʻiasyan, K. "Simeon Aparantsun patkanatz dzeřagrerě." *BM,* 10 (1971), 373–77.

SIMĒON I, EREWANTSI (d. 1780)

A native of Erevan, Simēon received instruction in religious studies in Ējmiatzin. He became a *vardapet* in 1747 and was created bishop in 1754. As nuncio of the Catholicos of Ējmiatzin, he visited many parts of Western Armenia and Armenian communities in other parts of the Ottoman Empire. Elected Catholicos of All Armenians in 1763, a position he held to his death. One of his several memorable initiatives was the founding of the printing press in Ējmiatzin in 1771.

Texts

Girkʻ handisutʻeants tōnits kayserakanats. (Ējmiatzin, 1771, 1833, 1915).
Girkʻ ałōtʻits or kochi zbōsaran hogewor. (Ējmiatzin, 1772).
Tałaran pʻokʻrik. (Ējmiatzin, 1772, 1777).
Karg tʻałman hayrapetats, episkoposats ew kʻahanayits. (Ējmiatzin, 1777).
Girkʻ or kochi partavčar. (Ējmiatzin, 1779–83).
MKH, 59–63. (2 poems).
Jambř. (Vałaršapat, 1873).
"Epʻrem katʻołikos, Yišatakaran. Simēon katʻołikos." *A,* 1875, 333–40. (Texts and criticism).
"Tsutsak dzeřnadrelotsn i Simēon katʻołikosē." *A,* 1876, 171–77. (Includes two poems).
"Lutzmunkʻ artakʻnots." *A,* 1888, 155–58.
"Simēon katʻołikosi yišatakaraně." *Diwan hayots patmutʻean,* by G. Ałaneants, vols. 3, 8, 11 (Tiflis, 1894, 1908, 1913).
"Mejberumner Simeon Erevantsi katʻołikosi matenagrakan vastakits." *EJ,* 1972/12, 18–20.
MPT, 59–63. (3 poems).

Criticism

Gevorgyan, P. "Simeon katʻołikos Erevantsu jankʻerě hayots ekełetsu miasnutʻyan ev hay žołovrdi azgapahpanman gortzum." *EJ,* 1972/12, 35–41.

Hatityan, A. "Simeon Erevantsi" *EJ,* 1972/12, 21–34. (Includes a list of unpublished works).
"Simēon katʻołikosi kensagrutʻiwnĕ." *A,* 1896, 495–500. (Colophon).
Tēr-Mkrtchean, K. (On finding a collection of Simēon's sermons in the German Royal Library). *A,* 1894, 154.
"Vkayutʻyunner Simeon Erevantsi katʻołikosi masin." *EJ,* 1972/12, 8–17.

SIMĒON JUŁAYETSI (d. 1657)

Simēon was as a child among the Armenians forcibly deported from Jułay (Julfa) to Isfahan at the turn of the seventeenth century. In Nor Jułay (New Julfa), Simēon studied under Ḥachatur Kesaratsi and collaborated with him closely. He taught at various monasteries and universities in Iran and Eastern Armenia and wrote works concerning grammar and philosophy. Died in Tokat.

Texts

Girkʻ or kochi kʻerakanutʻiwn. (Constantinople, 1725).
Girkʻ tramabanutʻean. (Constantinople, 1728, 1794).
"Yar̄ajaban Meknutʻean Prokłi (hatuatz)." *PHG,* 523.
"Es ēi azat azgi." *MPT,* 39–42.

Anthologies

SUM, 2, 260–66.

Criticism

Mḫitʻaryan, H. "S. vrd. Jułayetsu matenagrakan ev kʻerakanagitakan vastakĕ." *EJ,* 1968/7, 35–44.
Mirzoyan, H. "Simeon Jułayetsu kyankʻĕ ev gortzuneutʻyunĕ." *PBH,* 1966/2, 189–98.
———. "Hogu ev marmni pʻoḫharaberutʻyan hartsn ĕst Simeon Jułayetsu." *BEH,* 1967/1, 231–36.
———. *Simeon Jułayetsi.* (Erevan, 1971).
———. "Simeon Jułayetsi ev Oskan Erevantsi." *BEH,* 1978/3, 186–93.
Tzar̄ukyan, V. "Šarahyusakan hartserĕ Simeon Jułayetsu kʻerakanakan erkum." *PBH,* 1974/4, 133–42.

SIMĒON LEHATSI (c1584–?)

Born in Zamostsa (Zamosc), Poland (hence, he is also referred to as Zamostsatsi), to parents who had emigrated to this Polish city from Kafa, Crimea. In 1608, he embarked on an extensive tour which took him to Italy, Armenia proper, and the Near East. Upon his return from his voyage in 1618, he married, settled in Lvov in 1624, and taught in the local school. He opposed the Roman Catholic N. Tʻorosovich (Torosowicz) in the religious strife that bedeviled the Armenian community and eventually led to its assimilation into Polish society. It is believed that Simēon made a second trip to the Middle East in 1632–36, but nothing is known of him after 1639.

Texts

"Vipasanutʻiwn Nikolakan" [incomplete]. *Kamenits, taregirkʻ hayots Lehastani ew R̄umenioy,* by Ališan (Venice, 1896), 202–14.
Akinean, N. *Simēon dpri Lehatswoy Ułegrutʻiwn, taregrutʻiwn ew yišatakarankʻ.* (Vienna, 1936). (Previously published in *HA,* 1932, 1933, 1934, 1935).

———. "Simēon dpir Lehatswoy erku yišatakarank'." *HA,* 50 (1936), 246–58.
K'iwrtean, Y. "Simēon dpir Lehatsii yišatakaranov dzeragirk' Nor Jułayi Amenapṙkich matenadaranē." *B,* 96 (1938), 313–16.

Anthologies

SUM, 2, 91–118.

Translations

Russian

Darbinian, M. *Putevye zametki.* (Moscow, 1965).

Criticism

Abełean, A. "Simēon dpir ew ir ułegrutʻiwnē." *HK,* 16 (1937–38/6), 97–104; 11, 104–17. 17 (1938–39/2), 78–83; 3, 105–12; 4, 160–65.
Dashkevich, Y. "Simeon dpir Legatsi–kto on?." *Ksiega pamiatkowa ku czci Eugeniusza Sluzkiewicza.* (Warsaw, 1974), 67–77.
———. "Siméon dpir Lehatsi. Qui est-il?" *REArm.* 12 (1977), 347–64.
———. "Le second voyage de Siméon de Pologne en Orient et les questions relatives à l'étude ultérieure de son héritage littéraire." *REArm,* 13 (1978–79), 251–57.
Schütz, E. "The Turkish Loanwords in Simēon Lehatsi's Travel Accounts." *Acta Orient. Hungarica,* tomus XX, fasc. 3, 1967, 307–24.

SIMONEAN, SIMON (1914–1986)

A native of Aintab (Gaziantep, Turkey). A journalist and novelist. Educated in his birthplace and, after his family's deportation, at Krtʻasirats Elementary School and other schools in Aleppo. Was one of the first students to graduate from the newly founded seminary in Antʻilias, Lebanon (1930–35). He taught in Aleppo (1935–46) and at the Antʻilias seminary (1946–55), while also acting as editor of *Hask,* of the Armenian Catholicosate of Cilicia. Set up the Sewan publishing house in 1955, and three years later launched his well-known weekly *Spʻiwṙkʻ* (1958–74).

Texts (stories)

Kě ḥndrui . . . ḥachadzewel. (Beirut, 1965). (Satirical prose).
Ḥmbapet Aslani ałjikě. (Beirut, 1967).
Sipʻanay kʻajer. 2 vols. (Beirut, 1967, 1970).
Leṙnakanneru verjaloysě. (Beirut, 1968).
Leṙ ew čakatagir. (Beirut, 1972). (Includes some new stories and revised selections from *Sipʻanay kʻajer* and *Leṙnakanneru verjaloysě*).
Anžamandros. Vēp. (Beirut, 1978). (Novel).

Other works

Arewelahay grakanutʻiwn: ěntir ējer, kensagrutʻiwnner, gortzerě, baṙaran, matenagitutʻiwn. (Beirut, 1965).
Hin hay matenagrutʻiwnē orpēs entʻahoł ardi hay grakanutʻean. (Beirut, 1975).

SIRAS, HMAYAK (1902–1983)

Pen name: Hmayak Siras.
Hmayak Oskanean was born and educated in Karakilise (northwest of Alaškert, i.e., Eleşkirt), Turkey. A novelist and short story writer. Following a seven-year

sojourn in Tiflis (1914–21), he put down roots in Erevan. Studied at the State University of Erevan and held administrative positions in party organizations before his admission into Moscow University as a journalism student. Siras was the editor of *Ḥorhrdayin* (later *Sovetakan) grakanutʻyun* (1938–40, 1954–57) and a secretary to the Union of Soviet Writers of Armenia (1938–41, 1946–48).

Collections

Erker. (Erevan, 1956).
Erkeri žołovatzu. 4 vols. (Erevan, 1958–61).
Erkeri žołovatzu. 5 vols. (Erevan, 1976–80).

Texts (stories and novels)

Hartsrekʻ nrants. (Moscow, 1931).
Kyankʻi karotě. (Erevan, 1934).
Mamen u Ašen. (Erevan, 1934).
Latʻife. (Erevan, 1935).
Asmar. (Erevan, 1936).
Chgrvatz ōrenkʻ. (Erevan, 1936).
Tʻalisman. (Erevan, 1936).
Sasuntsi Davitʻ. (Erevan, 1939).
Anahit. (Erevan, 1940, 1964).
Chariki erazě. (Erevan, 1941).
Hayr ev ordi. (Erevan, 1946).
Hayr ev ordi. (Erevan, 1947).
Ararat. (Erevan, 1950, 1955, 1967).
Ełbayrutʻyun. (Erevan, 1952).
Naḥōryakin. (Erevan, 1954).
Ananun ałjik. (Erevan, 1969).
Hayreni ašḥarh. (Erevan, 1974, 1978).
Žamanaki hanguytsnerum. Askʻ. (Erevan, 1982).
Kʻsanmek tari Avetikʻ Isahakyani het. Hušer. (Erevan, 1984). (Reminiscences about Avetikʻ Isahakyan).

Translations

RUSSIAN

Anait. (Moscow, 1949, 1958).
Ararat. Roman. (Moscow, 1956, 1962). (2d ed. "Pererabot. i dop. izd.").
Devushka bez imeni. Povesti. Rasskazy. Legendy. (Moscow, 1968).
Khitarova, S., and Petrosian, A. *Nakanune. Roman.* (Moscow, 1965).
[Tadeosian, A., and Musatov, A.] *Pesnia.* (Erevan, 1952).

Criticism

Manukyan, S. "Hmayak Siras." *SG,* 1962/2, 159–68.

ŠIRAZ, HOVHANNES (1915–1984)

Pen name: Hovhannes Širaz.

Born Ōnik Karapetean in Alexandrapol (Leninakan, now Gyumri). His father was killed during the Turkish onslaught in 1920, and his childhood was unhappy. After a brief teaching career in his birthplace, Širaz moved to Erevan and completed his studies at the State University of Erevan (1937–41). He was awarded the Armenian State Literary Prize in 1975.

Collections

Hatěntir. (Erevan, 1949).
Hatěntir. (Erevan, 1954).
Hatěntir. (Erevan, 1971).
Erker. 4 vols. (Erevan, 1981–86). (5 vols projected).
Uměršatyan, U. *Mi pʻetur im artziv kyankʻits.* (Erevan, 1984).

Texts

Garnanamut. (Erevan, 1935).
Siamantʻo ev Ḥajezare. (Erevan, 1935, 1947, 1955, 1957, 1970, 1978; Beirut, 1955, 1957).
Arevi erkir. (Erevan, 1938).
Beveṙi aṙumě. (Erevan, 1938).
Pʻokʻrik hovivě. (Erevan, 1938, 1943).
Bronze artzivě. (Erevan, 1940).
Erg Hayastani. (Erevan, 1940).
Banastełtzi dzayně. (Erevan, 1942).
Ergeri girkʻ. (Erevan, 1942).
Lirika. (Erevan, 1946).
Girkʻ ḥałałutʻyan ev siro. (Erevan, 1950).
Im ěnker Lorikě. (Erevan, 1950, 1960).
Ṙustʻavtsi Šotʻan ev Tʻamarě. (Erevan, 1952; Beirut, 1952).
Ōdzn u mełun. (Erevan, 1953).
Banastełtzutʻyunner. (Erevan, 1954).
Kʻnar Hayastani. Books 1–3. (Erevan, 1958, 1964, 1974).
Šłtʻayvatz mełediner. (Erevan, 1962).
Hayots Dantʻēakaně. (Beirut, 1965, 1978, 1985; Erevan, 1990).
Hušardzan mayrikis. (Erevan, 1968, 1972, 1980; Beirut, 1968).
Siraname. (Erevan, 1969).
Banastełtzutʻyunner. (Erevan, 1971).
Yotʻnapatum. (Erevan, 1977).
Aṙaks zinch tsutsane . . . (Erevan, 1978).
Ḥałałutʻyun amenetsun. (Erevan, 1982). (Poem).

Translations

ENGLISH

Botting, T. ["A woman's heart so crystal clear"]. *SL,* 1973/9, 130–31.
Rottenberg, D. "Water-vendor." *SL,* 1966/3, 147.
Tempest, P. ["You, cherished homeland, in my heart . . ."]. *SL,* 1979/7, 95.

ENGLISH ANTHOLOGIES

SAP, 24–26.

FRENCH

Antonian, A. "Tu es dans mon cœur, ô Patrie sacrée." *LS,* 247 (1979), 104.
Falk, C. ["Qu'est-ce qu'un cœur de femme? Un verre de cristal"]. *OO,* 177 (Sept. 1973), 147.
Malkhassian, L. *Poème biblique.* (Paris, 1964).

Martirossian, L. “Poèsies: Les colombes ont fui . . . ; Mes enfants m’appellent . . . ; Qu’elle est triste la demeure . . .” *LS,* 1958/3, 153–54.
———. “Ma mère.” *OO* (Dec. 1960), 130.
———. “A ne pas lire les poètes.” *OO,* 123 (March 1969), 55.

French anthologies

Gaucheron, J. *E,* 87–88.
FPA, 66–67.
LPA, 340–45.

German

Movsessian, L. “Leist diese Welt.” *Armenische Grammatik* (Vienna, 1959), 282.
Österreicher, S. “Der Wasserverkäufer.” *Sowjet-Literatur,* 1966/3, 145.

Russian

Adamian, N. *Moi tovarishch Lorik.* (Erevan, 1952).
Izbrannoe. (Erevan, 1956).
Pamiatnik materi: Stikhi i poema. (Moscow, 1981).
Spendiarova, T. *Rodnik. Stikhi.* (Moscow, 1945).
———., et al. *Lirika.* (Erevan, 1986).
Stikhi. (Moscow, 1939, [1952]).
Stikhi i poemy. (Moscow, 1960).
Stikhotvoreniia i poemy. (Moscow, 1956).
Tarkovskii, A. *Siamanto i Khadzhezare. Poema-skazka.* (Moscow, 1956). Erevan, 1960.

Spanish

Silvestre, L. “El aguador.” *Literatura Sovietica,* 1966/3, 145.

Bibliographies

Melyan, B. *Hovhannes Širaz (kensamatenagitutʻyun).* Part 1. (Erevan, 1989).

Criticism

Ałababyan, S. “Hovhannes Širazi čanaparhě.” *SG,* 1964/10, 120–38.
———. *Hovhannes Širaz.* (Erevan, 1984).
Alekʻsanyan, V. “Širazi poeziayi patkeravorutʻyan mi kʻani dzeveri masin.” *SG,* 1964/4, 145–50.
———. “Hovhannes Širazi ‘Bnutʻyan gluḫgortzotsě’ poemi lezva-očakan aṙandznahatkutʻyunnerě.” *T,* 1965/2, 17–30.
Aṙakʻelean, A. “Yovhannēs Širaz.” *Z* (amsatʻertʻ), 1 (1957/10–11), 1; 1 (1957/12), 4.
Atʻabekyan, S. “Seri ev tzałki metaforě Hovhannes Širazi kʻnarergutʻyan mej (‘Ergeri erg’, ‘Lirika’).” *SG,* 1974/4, 129–35.
———. *Hovhannes Širazi kʻnarergutʻyuně.* (Erevan, 1979).
Barsełyan, Ḥ. *H. Širaz. (Hušanovelner, masunkʻner).* (Erevan, 1986).
Batikyan, L. “ ‘Siamantʻo ev Ḥjezare’ poemě nor mšakumov.” *SG,* 1972/2, 124–32.
———. *Hovhannes Širazi mayrakaně.* (Erevan, 1976).
Bazyan, S. *Erekʻ urvagitz—Nairi Zaryan, Širaz, Gełam Saryan.* (Erevan, 1941).
Grigoryan, A. *Patumner Širazi masin. (Hušer).* (Erevan, 1987).
Ḥanzadyan, S. “Hovhannes Širaz.” *SG,* 1985/1, 76–86.
Hayrapetyan, Ł. “Banastełtzi het.” *SG,* 1982/3, 106–11.

Hovhannisyan, Hr. "Širazi fenomenĕ." *SG,* 1984/3, 107–09.
Hovsepʻyan, G. "Žamanakin aržani hncheɫutʻyun." *SG,* 1975/5, 153–57.
Karapetyan, G. "Banasteɫtzakan patkeri kařutsvatzkʻĕ Hovhannes Širazi poeziayum." *L,* 1983/11, 55–61.
Ɫaribjanyan, G. "Handipumner Hovhannes Širazi het Leninakanum (1960—akan tʻtʻ)." *Banber Hayastani arḥivneri,* 1989/2, 207–22.
Mahari, G. "Ḥoher Hovhannes Širazi masin." *SG,* 1970/6, 108–14.
———., et al. *Hovhannes Širazi masin.* (Erevan, 1974).
Melkʻonyan, S. "Geɫarvestakan lezvi bařapašari harstatsumĕ Hovhannes Širazi steɫtzagortzutʻyunnerum." *L,* 1977/2, 25–36.
Sahakyan, P. "Hovhannes Širaz." *SG,* 1962/4, 115–23.
Soɫomonyan, S. "Sovetahay akanavor banasteɫtzĕ." *PBH,* 1964/3, 43–58.
Tʻamrazyan, H. "Hovhannes Širaz." *SG,* 1974/4, 115–28.

ŠIRIN (1827–1857)

Pen name: Širin.

Yovhannēs Karapetean, a popular *ašuɫ,* was a native of Koɫb, a village near Erevan. He lost his eyesight at the age of two and served his apprenticeship with minstrels in Alexandrapol (Leninakan, now Gyumri) and Karin (Erzurum). Spent his short life as an itinerant *ašuɫ,* writing and singing in both Armenian and what is now called Azeri-Turkish.

Poetry

Hovhannisean (sic), Oskan, Erewantsi. *Zanazan ergkʻ paron Hovhannēsi* [*sic*] *Karapetean ašĕg Širin makanwaneloy.* (Moscow, 1856).
MKH, 197–98, 251–52, 404–5, 436, 464–65, 527–29, 570, 579–80.
M, 1885/3770, 1021; 3773, 1093; 3792, 279–80.

Criticism

MKH, 588–89.

ŠIRVANI (20th c.)

Pen name: Širvani.

An early twentieth-century author whose original name was Ɫewond Ḥachpanean.

Poetry

Ɫewond Yarutʻiwnean-Ḥachpaneani ergerĕ, "Širvani." (Vaɫaršapat, 1905).
THG, 256–64.

ŠIRVANZADE (1858–1935)

Pen name: Širvanzade.

Alekʻsandr Movsisean was born and educated in Šamaḥi (Shemakha, now in Azerbaijan). Went to Baku and worked as a clerk in the local government (1875–78), as an accountant for oil companies (1878–81), and as a librarian for the Mardasirakan Armenian Society of Baku (1881–83). He then lived in Tiflis (1883–1905) and was briefly employed as a secretary to the weekly *Ardzagankʻ* (1885–90). He spent the years 1905–10 in Paris, and from 1911–19 in the Caucasus.

Went abroad for a final time (1919–26) before returning permanently to Erevan in 1926. Died in Kislovodsk and interred in Erevan.

Collections

Žołovatzu erkeri. 4 vols. (Tiflis, 1903 [Vols. 1–3]; 1912 [Vol. 4]).
Havakʻatzu pʻokʻrik erkeri. (Erevan, 1930).
Erkeri liakatar žołovatzu. 8 vols. (Erevan, 1930–34).
Ĕntir erker. (Erevan, 1939).
Erkeri liakatar žołovatzu. 9 vols. (Erevan, 1950–55).
Erkeri liakatar žołovatzu. 10 vols. (Erevan, 1958–62).
Erker. 2 vols. (Erevan, 1971).
Tsamakyan, A. *Erker.* (Erevan, 1982).
Felekʻyan, H. *Erker.* (Erevan, 1983).
Tʻamrazyan, H., et al. *Erker.* 5 vols. (Erevan, 1986 [Vols. 1 and 2], 1987 [Vols. 3 and 4], 1988 [Vol. 5]).

Texts

Gortzakatari yišatakaranits . . . ew Hrdeh nawtʻagortzaranum. (Tiflis, 1884). (Stories).
Ḥnamatar. (Tiflis, 1885). (Novelette).
Namus. (Tiflis, 1885, 1901; Constantinople, 1920; Erevan, 1937). (Novel).
Arambin. (Tiflis, 1888). (Novel).
Zur yoyser. (Tiflis, 1890). (Novel).
Tasnuhing tari antsatz. (Tiflis, 1890; Erevan, 1937 [published with "Fatʻman ev Asadĕ"]). (Story).
Arsēn Dimakʻsean. (Tiflis, 1893). (Novel).
Vēpikner. (Tiflis, 1894). (Stories).
Krak. (Baku, 1896; Erevan, 1937). (Stories).
Tsawagarĕ. (Tiflis, 1897). (Story).
Kʻaos. (Baku, 1898; Erevan, 1926, 1934, 1944, 1975). (Novel).
Melania. (Tiflis, 1899; Erevan, 1938). (Novelette).
Artistĕ. (Tiflis, 1903; Tiflis, 1911; Erevan, 1934, 1938, 1946, 1951, 1959, 1964). (Story).
Ewginē. (Tiflis, 1903). (Drama).
Patui hamar. (Tiflis, 1905; Constantinople, 1920). (Drama).
Awerakneri vray. (Tiflis, 1911). (Drama).
Tsawagarĕ ew Jhudi akanjĕ. (Tiflis, 1911). (Stories).
Šaṙlatanĕ. (Tiflis, 1912). (Comedy).
Char ogi. (Tiflis, 1914; Constantinople, 1923; Erevan, 1934, 1937). (Drama).
Kortzanuatzĕ. (Tiflis, 1914). (Drama).
Armenuhi. (Tiflis, 1916). (Drama).
Eotʻ patmuatzkʻner. (Boston, 1920). (Stories).
Artistĕ. Fatʻman ew Asatĕ. Ōriord Liza. (Boston, 1924). (Stories).
Kyankʻi bovits. 2 parts. (Erevan, 1930–32). (Autobiography).
Morgani ḥnamin. (Erevan, 1930, 1934). (Comedy).
Vardan Ahrumyan. (Erevan, 1934, 1955). (Novel).
"Niwtʻer Širvanzadēi masin." *Vēm,* 3 (1935/4), 89–99. 4 (1936), 93–100.
Hrdeh navtʻagortzaranum. (Erevan, 1937, 1956). (Story).
Im kyankʻits. (Erevan, 1938, 1953).
Išḥanuhi. (Erevan, 1948). (Drama).

Herosi veradardzĕ. (Erevan, 1949). (Story).
Ĕnkernerĕ. (New York, 1959). (Story).
Fatman ev Asadĕ. (Erevan, 1960). (Story).
Orn ē mayrĕ. (Erevan, 1963). (Story).
Kyanki bovits. Hišołutyunner. (Erevan, 1982).
"Širvanzadei antip namaknerĕ." *SG,* 1985/8, 102–14.
Madoyan, G. "Širvanzadei namaknerĕ Raffu masin." *Banber Hayastani arḫivneri,* 1986/2, 63–76.
Patmvatzkner. (Erevan, 1986).
"Sarıłamiši čakatamarti skizbĕ." *BEH,* 1990/1, 101–6.

Translations

English

Kooyoomdjian, H. "Fire at the Oil Wells." *Alexander Shirvanzade, Eminent Armenian Dramatist and Novelist . . .* (New York), 11–16. (Extract).
Parlakian, N. *For the Sake of Honor.* (New York, 1976).
———. *Evil Spirit.* ([New York], 1980).

French

D'Herminy, S. *L'Artiste.* (Paris, 1909).
———. "Fatma et Assad." *Les Milles Nouvelles Nouvelles,* 22 (n.d.), 97–122.
Tchobanian, A. *La possédée.* (Paris, 1910).

French Anthologies

Tchalikian, A. *E,* 106–8.

German Anthologies

AN, 82–113.

Russian

Adonts, G. *Khaos.* (Moscow and Leningrad, 1930).
Aivazian, S. *Khaos.* (Tiflis, 1936).
Chest'. (Tiflis, 1902; Moscow, 1912; Moscow and Leningrad, [1927], 1929, 1930).
Goian, G. *P'esy.* (Moscow, 1958).
Khachatriants, Ia. *Izbrannoe.* (Moscow, 1947, 1949).
———. *Khaos.* (Moscow, 1956; Erevan, 1983).
———. *Zloi dukh. Povesti i rasskazy.* (Moscow, 1959).
Khatisov, Al. *Liza.* (Tiflis, 1891).
Korneev, B. *Namus.* (Tiflis, 1935).
Iz gornila zhizni. (Tiflis, 1932).
Iz-za chesti. (Moscow and Leningrad, 1941).
Izbrannoe. (Moscow, 1952).
Izbrannye proizvedeniia. 2 vols. (Moscow, 1958).
Izbrannye sochineniia. 3 vols. (Tiflis, 1936–38).
Melik-Karakozova, M. *Pozhar na neftianom zavode.* (Tiflis, n.d.).
Ogon'. (Erevan, 1939).
Povesti. Rasskazy. (Erevan, 1958).
Sobranie sochinenii. 3 vols. (Moscow, 1957).
Sochineniia. 3 vols. (Tiflis, 1935 [Vol. 1]).
Ter'ian, V. *Zloi dukh. Povest'.* (Moscow and Leningrad, 1929; Tiflis, 1934; Moscow, 1959).

Bibliographies

T'amrazyan, H. *Alek'sandr Širvanzade (1858–1958), bibliografia.* (Erevan, 1959).

Criticism

Aharonean, V. "Gtzer Širvanzadēi keank'its." *HK,* 14 (1935–36/1), 117–24.
Antonean, A. *Širvanzadē.* (Constantinople, 1911).
Awdalbegean, T'. "Širvanzadēi vēperi niwt'ĕ." *A,* 1910, 358–75, 437–41.
Babayan, A. "Metz groŀi čšmartatsi dimankarĕ." *SG,* 1962/1, 137–42.
Bebutov, G. "K tvorcheskoi istorii romana Shirvanzade 'Namus'." *T,* 1957/6, 111–14.
Chōpanean, A. "Širvanzadēi 'Ewginēn'." *ANA,* 4 (1902), 128–31.
———. "Širvanzadē." *ANA,* 1909/7–8, 145–49.
Eng. G. " 'Ḥnamatar' Širvanzadēi." *Ardzagank',* 1885/7, 101–5.
———. "Hin tsaw." *HGP,* 1 (1888), 252–65. (On "Ōriord Liza").
Gyulbudaŀyan, S. *Alek'sandr Širvanzadei lezvakan mšakuyt'ĕ.* (Erevan, 1966).
Hay. "Širvanzadē (kensagrakan aknark)." *Lumay,* 7–8 (1910), 64–77.
Hovakimyan, H. "Širvanzaden ev t'atronĕ." *T,* 1964/8, 11–18.
K'alant'aryan, Ž. "Alek'sandr Širvanzadei steŀtzagortzut'yunĕ sovetakan šrjanum." *BEH,* 1984/1, 36–45.
Kamsarakan, T. *Širvanzadē ew ir gortzĕ.* (Constantinople, 1911).
K'iparean, K. "Širvanzadēi vēperĕ." *B,* 84 (1927), 114–18.
Kiwlō, S. "Handipumner Alek'sandr Širvanzadēi het." *Ani,* 5 (1952), 629–42.
Ł. E. *K'nnakan hayeatsk' Širvanzadēi 'Arsēn Dimak'sean' vēpi masin.* (Tiflis, 1893).
Łazaryan, H. "Širvanzaden sovetakan tarinerin." *PBH,* 1964/2, 233–37.
Malḫas, G. *Širvanzatē ew ir erkĕ.* (Constantinople, 1911).
Mat'evosyan, V. "Alek'sandr Širvanzadei ēst'etikakan hayatsk'nerĕ." *SG,* 1958/10, 116–24.
Melik'set'yan, S. *Mtermakan Širvanzaden.* (Erevan, 1965).
Melik'yan, S. "Teryanĕ Sundukyani ev Širvanzadei t'argmanich." *SG,* 1964/10, 139–45.
Mkrtchyan, V. "Širvanzadei ṙealistakan arvesti mi k'ani bnoroš gtzerĕ." *PBH,* 1959/1, 144–53.
Mnatsakanyan, L. "Širvanzadei payk'arĕ ṙealizmi hamar." *BEH,* 1983/3, 39–48.
Muradyan, H. "Buržuakan bark'eri k'nnadatut'yunĕ Širvanzadei memuarnerum." *L,* 1968/10, 73–80.
Norents, V. "Erku eluyt'." *SG,* 1958/11, 75–80.
Ōšakan, Y. "Širvanzatē t'ateragir." *Bardzravank',* 1 (1922), 26–32; 3, 95–101.
Partizuni, V. "Alek'sandr Širvanzade." *PBH,* 1958/3, 18–40.
Sahakyan, P. *Konfliktĕ Širvanzadei 'K'aos' vepum.* (Erevan, 1962).
Sarinyan, S. "Širvanzaden ev ṙealizmi zargatsumĕ hay grakanut'yan mej." *T,* 1959/2, 47–64.
Saryan, S. "Širvanzaden novelist." *PBH,* 1960/1, 159–66.
Sevunts, G. "Metz ṙealistĕ" *SG,* 1958/12, 106–15.
Širvanzadē ew ir gortzĕ. (Constantinople, 1911).
Širvanzadei steŀtzagortzut'yunĕ (hodvatzneri žoŀovatzu). (Erevan, 1959).
Step'anyan, G. "Alek'sandr Širvanzadei dramaturgian arevmtahay bemum." *SG,* 1958/11, 81–95.
T'amrazyan, H. *Alek'sandr Širvanzade.* (Erevan, 1956).

———. *Dramaturgiia Shirvanzade.* (Erevan, 1956).
———. *Širvanzade: hamaṙot aknark.* (Erevan, 1958).
———. "Traditsiayi užě." *T,* 1958/10, 11–18.
———. "Širvanzaden ev nra naḥordnerě." *SG,* 1960/7, 123–42.
———. *Širvanzade, kyankʿě ev gortzě.* (Erevan, 1961).
———. *Shirvanzade, zhizn' i tvorchestvo.* (Erevan, 1962).
———. *Tałandi tznundě (Širvanzadei kyankʿits).* (Erevan, 1971).
———. " 'Kʿaosě' ev hay ṙealizmě." *SG,* 1983/4, 87–103.
Tērtērean, A. *Širvanzadē, hay ěntanikʿi ew inteligenti vipasaně.* (Tiflis, 1911).
———. "Širvanzadei tipakan arvestě." *T,* 1946/8, 3–30.
———. "Širvanzadei tiperi ēpoḥan." *T,* 1947/2, 3–28.
———. *Širvanzadei grakan tiperi hanragitaraně.* (Erevan, 1959).
Tʿopʿchyan, S. "Širvanzaden ṙealizmi ev tipakanutʿyan masin." *SG,* 1958/9, 163–72.
———. "Gełetsikě ev čšmaritě." *SG,* 1962/7, 148–50. (On Širvanzade's conception of realism).
———. *Širvanzadei ēstʿetikan.* (Erevan, 1963).
———. "Širvanzaden arevmtaevropakan 'Nor arvesti' kʿnnadat." *PBH,* 1963/1, 3–14.
———. "Širvanzaden ṙealizmi tesaban." *T,* 1963/4, 45–60.
———. "Širvanzadei patmvatzkʿnerě." *SG,* 1983/4, 104–12.
Tʿotʿovents, V. *Širvanzade (kensagrutʿyun).* (Erevan, 1930).
Vahanyan, G. "Alekʿsandr Širvanzaden ev gełarvestakan ḥoskʿi varpetutʿyan hartserě." *SG,* 1958/11, 96–105.
Vanandetsi, G. *Širvanzadei stełtzagortzutʿyan himnakan gtzerě.* (Erevan, 1930).
Verdyan, G. "Tarber bnuytʿi naḥadasutʿyunnerě Al. Širvanzadei dramatikakan erkerum." *BEH,* 1984/2, 170–77.
Yakobean, S. *Širvanzadē, grakan-kʿnnakan usumnasirutʿiwn.* (Tiflis, 1911).
———. "Širvanzadē: nra grakan gortzunēutʿean eresnameaki aṙitʿov." *HA,* 25 (1911), 321–34.
Zoryan, S. "Širvanzade." *SG,* 1958/11, 63–74.

SITAL, KARAPET (1891–1972)

Pen name: Karapet Sital.

Karapet Šahinean was born in Kašt (or Kačet), a village near Šataḥ, south of Lake Van. Poet; educated in local schools and in American institutions in Van and Tabriz. Lived in Philadelphia from 1914 until his death. Was a staunch supporter of and a frequent traveler to Soviet Armenia, where some of his books were published. He used Armenian and Kurdish folklore extensively in his poems.

Collections

Lusabats. (Erevan, 1936).
Paykʿari erger. (Erevan, 1953).
Dyutsaznakan. (Erevan, 1957).
Oske hundz. (Erevan, 1962).

Texts (verse)

Gusanerger. (New York, 1919).
Gišerēn minchew lusabats. (Philadelphia, 1931).

Lusabatsi erger. ([Philadelphia], 1933).
Giwłn im heṙawor. ([Philadelphia], 1936).
Sasna tzṙer. (Philadelphia, 1939).
Kašti kʻajer. (Philadelphia, 1942).
Hazaran blbul. ([Philadelphia], 1946).
Mam u Zin. (Philadelphia, 1951).
Hoviw Azon. (Philadelphia, 1954).

Other works

Tesa mer erkri arewtzagě. (New York, 1948). (Impressions of Soviet Armenia).
Hayastani lusapʻaṙ arewtzagě ew Vratseani marol dzēṙi čragě. (New York, 1949).

Translations

ENGLISH

"From America to Armenia." *Armenian Affairs,* 1 (1950/2), 159–66. (Excerpt from book).

FRENCH ANTHOLOGIES

Gaucheron, J. *E,* 54.

Criticism

Eremean, A. *Karapet Sitali keankʻn u stełtzagortzuṙiwnnerě.* (Philadelphia, 1957).
Selyan, P. *Karapet Sital.* (Erevan, 1961).

ŠITANEAN, ARMĒN (1870–1932)

Born in Aliwr, a village near Van. Novelist and playwright. Studied at the Kedronakan of Constantinople. Fled to Bulgaria during the Armenian massacres of the mid-1890s and taught at Plovdiv and Burgaz. Died in Varna.

Texts (novels)

Tiapartě kam Vanakaně. (Varna, 1902–03, 1910; Constantinople, 1910, 1911, 1912; Athens, 1933; Beirut, 1936, 1965).
. . . Karip aḥpēr . . . (Varna, 1908).
Akʻsorakaně. (Constantinople, 1911; Beirut, 1937).
Andranik. (Varna, 1911).
Awazakapetě. ([Constantinople, 1911], Constantinople, 1912, 1913; Athens, 1932; Beirut, 1937, 1959, 1972).
Tapʻaṙakan hayu ordin. ([Constantinople, 1911]; Beirut, 1938, 1961).
Vašḥaṙun. (Constantinople, 1911).
Sulṫan Hamid. (Varna, 1913).
Tapʻaṙakan hayě. ([Constantinople, 1914]; Varna, 1925; [n.p.], 1934; Alexandria, 1938; Beirut, 1956).
Faṫma. (Varna, 1925).
Nētēlkʻa. (Sofia, 1928).
Paterazmě. (Sofia, 1929).
Kaḥałanēn etkʻě. (Cairo, 1930).
Matnichě. (Alexandria, 1938).

SRAPEAN, ARAMAYIS (1910–1969)

Born in Geyve (southeast of Izmit, Turkey). After his father was slain during the 1915 massacres, Srapean grew up in orphanages in Constantinople and Corfu.

Educated at the Murat Rapʻayēlean school (1925–29) of Venice, where he and some other orphans had been sent in 1923. Specialized in medicine in Milan and served in the Italian Army in France and the Balkans. Resided permanently in Milan. Wrote both prose and poetry.

Collections

Anavart ertʻ. (Erevan, 1971).

Texts

Handipumner Musayin het. (Venice, 1949).
Azoloyēn Venetik. (Venice, 1953).
Zēnkʻi tak. (Venice, 1956).
Alpean ṙazmikneru het. (Paris and Venice, 1959).

SRUANDZTEANTS, GAREGIN (1840–1892)

Pen names: Garegin Sruadzteants, Vard.
Born Ōhannēs Sandents in Van and educated at the seminary of the monastery of Varag near Van. Ethnographer, folklorist, teacher, and writer. Toured certain parts of historic Armenia (1860–61) in the company of his mentor, (Mkrtich) Ḥrimean Hayrik (q.v.), and took the vows of celibacy in Karin (Erzurum) in 1864. In 1878 he was commissioned by Nersēs Varžapetean (1837–84), Patriarch of Constantinople, to tour Western Armenia to report on his fellow countrymen. As on his previous visits, Sruandzteants recorded, thus preserving, fragments of a rich tradition that all but perished in 1915. He was created bishop in Ējmiatzin in 1886. Served as primate of the Armenians of Trebizond and of Tarōn and as father-superior of the monastery of Surb Karapet in Muš. Spent the last few years of his life in Constantinople.

Collections

Erker. 2 vols. (Erevan, 1978 [Vol. 1], 1982 [Vol. 2]).

Texts (literary)

Šušan Šawaršana. (Constantinople, 1875). (Play).

Texts (folklore)

Grots u brots ew Sasuntsi Dawitʻ kam Mheri duṙ. (Constantinople, 1874).
Hnots ew norots. (Constantinople, 1874).
Manana. (Constantinople, 1876).
Tʻoros Ałbar Hayastani čambord. 2 vols. (Constantinople, 1879, 1884).
Hamov-hotov. (Constantinople, 1884; Tiflis, 1904; Paris, 1949–50).

Translations

ENGLISH

Andreassian, K. "The Martyrs of Avarair." *Armenia,* 4 (1910/7), 14.
"Avarair." *The Armenian Church,* 1962/11, 5.
Wingate, J. "God Gives to the Giver." *Armenian Affairs,* 1 (1949–50/1), 82–83.

ENGLISH ANTHOLOGIES

ALP, 25–26.
AP, 253–54.

Criticism

Ačaṙyan, H. "Garegin epis. Srvandztyants." *EJ,* 1950/5–6, 29–32.

Bdoyan, V. "Hayrenik'ě Garegin epis. Srvandztyantsi erkerum. Hayrenasirut'yuně Garegin episkopos Srvandztyantsi erkerum." *EJ,* 1944/2–3, 38–46; 1944/4–5, 27–36.

———. "Garegin Srvandztyantsě orpes azgagraget." *EJ,* 1946/1, 37–42.

Eremean. M. "Garegin Sruandzteants." *B,* 70 (1912), 4–11, 50–59.

Kostandyan, Ē. "Garegin Srvandztyants." *BEH,* 1970/1, 127–37.

———. "Garegin Srvandztyantsě ev arevmtahay azgayin azatagrakan šaržumnerě." *L,* 1970/1, 18–25.

———. "Garegin Srvandztyantsi lusavorakan gortzuneut'yuně." *PBH,* 1970/1, 187–96.

———. "Garegin epis. Srvandztyants." *EJ,* 1972/3, 27–36.

———. *Garegin Srvandztyants: kyank'ě ev gortzuneut'yuně.* (Erevan, 1979).

Łanalanyan, A. "Hay banahyusut'yan metz erahtavorě." *PBH,* 1966/1, 17–32.

Petrosyan, H. "Mšo Gełami namaknerě Garegin Srvandztyantsin." *BEH,* 1977/1, 181–96.

STEP'ANOS DAŠTETSI (17th–18th c.)

A widely traveled native of Isfahan, Step'anos was educated in Nor Jułay (New Julfa) and Isfahan. Many of his writings are still unpublished, including those of a theological and religious nature that he wrote from a Roman Catholic viewpoint.

Texts (verse)

"Jułayetswots hayreni parz lezun ay, zor ku partzenan." *Lumay,* 4 (1899), 275–76.

Chōpanean, A. "Otk' šaradreal i veray ayleway1 irats." *ANA,* 10 (1939/1–2), 3–11.

Abrahamyan, A. "Step'anos Daštetsu haneluknerě." *EJ,* 1947/1–2, 46–54.

Simonean, S. "Hayewar t'ajnis Step'ani." *Z* (eṙamseay), 1 (1948/3), 205.

Abrahamyan, Ṙ. "Step'anos Daštetsi." *T,* 1956/12, 101–17. (Includes several texts).

Criticism

Simonean, S. "Step'anos Daštetsi, norayayt ašuł mě." *ANA,* 10 (1939/3), 51–68.

"Step'anos Daštetsi." *Z* (eṙamseay), 1 (1948/3), 203–5.

Melik'-Bahšyan, S. "Step'anos Daštetsu mi žamanakagrut'yan masin." *Gitakan ašhatut'yunner,* V. M. Molotovi anvan Erevani petakan hamalsaran. Vol. 47 (Erevan, 1955), 117–32. (Includes text of "Karg t'agaworats Hěndkats," 129–32.)

STEP'ANOS ṘŌŠK'A (1670–1739)

Step'anos, noted for his chronicle, was born in Kamenits (Kamenets-Podolsk) and was also known as Kamenetsatsi or Kamentsi. He studied in Rome, and as a man of religion, he served the various Armenian communities in Poland.

Texts

Oskean, H. *Step'anosi Ṙōšk'ay Žamanakagrut'iwn kam tarekank' ekełetsakank'.* (Vienna, 1964).

Criticism

Čanašean, M. "Step'anos Ṙōšk'eani baṙaraně." *B,* 113 (1955), 129–38, 185–91, 249–55.

Dachkévytch, Ya. *REArm,* n.s. 3 (1966), 471–77. (Review of Oskean's article listed below).
"Step'anos Ṙošk'a." *B,* 43 (1885), 247.
Ł. M. "Tesut'iwn i Gandz lezuin hayots kam i Step'anean bar̄aran." *B,* 10 (1852), 86–95.
Oskean, H. *1. Step'anos v. Ṙōšk'a. 2. Matt'ēos v. Jułayetsi.* (Vienna, 1968).

STEP'ANOS, T'OḤAT'ETSI (1558–?)

Born in Tokat. Married at age nineteen and became a priest in 1580. Fled native town after the Jelali onslaught in 1602. Arrived in Constantinople in 1603 and went on to Crimea, where he taught and copied manuscripts. Returned to Tokat in 1621, but nothing is known of him after this date.

Texts (verse)

"Gangat i veray lvanun ew čančerun." *PHG,* 486–88.
"Govasanut'iwn Kafayu k'ahanayits veray." *Azgagrakan handēs,* 9 (1902), 71–72.
"I veray čanči." *KNZ,* 1, 62–64.
"Ołb ew otanawor tał i veray Ewdokia metzi k'ałak'in . . ." *Hayapatum,* 605–8.
"Patmakan yišatakaran Šaraknotsin . . ." in *Yoys* (Armaš), 4 (1870), 126–27.
T[ayean], Ł. "Bank' mḥit'arakank' Step'anos v.-i T'oḥat'etswoy." *B,* 79 (1922), 129–32. (Prose).
———. "Step'anos T'oḥat'etswoy Ołb i veray vałamer̄ik ełbor iwroy Yakob k'ahanayi Ewdokeatswoy." *B,* 79 (1922), 161–66. (Followed by an untitled poem).

Anthologies

SUM, 1, 501–30.

Criticism

Akinean, N. "Step'anos T'oḥat'etsi." *AHPT,* 117–37.

STEP'ANYAN, ANŽELA (1917–)

A native of Tiflis. Novelist; educated at the State University of Erevan. Taught German (1942–46), worked for the Committee for Cultural Relations with Armenians Abroad (1969–74), and worked for some years for the monthly *Sovetakan grakanut'yun* beginning in 1975.

Texts (novels and stories)

K'uyrer. (Erevan, 1947).
Oske medal. (Erevan, 1952, 1958).
Tat'eviki čanaparhordut'yunĕ. (Erevan, 1955).
Amar̄namut. (Erevan, 1959, 1979).
Antzanot' tzanot'ner. (Erevan, 1964).
Gunavor k'ayler. (Erevan, 1967).
Erb ijnum ē erekon. (Erevan, 1974).
Mormok'. (Erevan, 1982).

Translations

RUSSIAN

Chailakhian, T. *Zolotaia medal'. Povest'.* (Moscow, 1954, 1956).

Criticism

Margaryan, A. " 'Amaṙnamut' vepi lezun." *SG,* 1960/6, 131–40.

SUNDUKEAN, GABRIĒL (1825–1912)

Pen names: Hadid, Hamal.

Born in Tiflis; educated at the University of St. Petersburg (1846–50). Had a good command of a number of Western and Middle Eastern languages and held administrative positions within the Russian bureaucracy. Began to write rather late in life. Spent all of his life in Tiflis except for the years 1854–58, when he was banished to Derbend (Dagestan, Russia).

Collections

Ěntir erker. (Erevan, 1938).
Harutʻyunyan, S. *Erkeri liakatar žołovatzu.* (Erevan, 1934).
Zaryan, Ṙ. *Erkeri liakatar žołovatzu.* 4 vols. (Erevan, 1951–61).
Erkeri žołovatzu. 3 vols. (Erevan, 1973–75).
Hatěntir. (Erevan, 1976).
Erker. (Erevan, 1980).
Petrosyan, J. *Erker.* (Erevan, 1984).

Texts

Gišeruan sabrě ḥer ē. (Tiflis, 1866, 1901, 1908).
Kʻandatz ōjaḥ. (Tiflis, 1873, 1882, 1905).
Pēpō. (Tiflis, 1876, 1901, 1903, 1904, 1906, 1920; Erevan, 1933, 1950, 1971; Venice, 1960). (Literary E. Armenian by L. Sewumean-Arzumanean).
Ḥaṙabalay. (Tiflis, 1881, 1904).
Ēli mēk zoh. (Tiflis, 1884, 1888, 1902).
Amusinner. (Tiflis, 1893, 1896, 1897, 1905).
Ōskan Petrovichn ēn kinkʻumě. (Tiflis, 1899, 1906).
Ew ayln kam Nor Dioginēs. (Tiflis, 1907).
Bałněsi boḥchay. (Tiflis, 1908).
Sēr ew azatuṙiwn. (Tiflis, 1910).
Gabriēl Sundukeantsi ktakě. (Tiflis, 1912).
Hamali maslahaṙnirě. (Tiflis, 1912).
Varinki vecherě: vepik. (Erevan, 1976).

Translations

English

Megerditchian, E. *Bebo.* (Boston, 1931).

English anthologies

AL, 81–142. ("The Ruined Family").

German

Rubenli, L. *Die ruinierte Familie.* (Leipzig, n.d.).

Russian

Izbrannoe. (Moscow, 1953).
P'esy. (Moscow and Leningrad, 1941, 1949).
Suprugi. (Tiflis, 1897).
Tsaturian, A., and Veselovskii, Iu. *Pepo.* (Moscow, 1896).

Russian anthologies

Ter'ian, V. *SBAL*, 11–62. (*Pepo*).
Veselovskii, Iu., and Berberian, M. *ABS*, 2, 348–410, 411–27. (Selections from *Pepo* and *Razorennaia sem'ia*).

Bibliographies

Babayan, M., et al. *Gabriel Sundukyan (1825–1912): kensamatenagitakan tsank*. (Erevan, 1976).

Criticism

Abov, G. *Gabriel Sundukyan*. (Erevan, 1953).
———. *Gabriel Sundukian*. (Erevan, 1956). (Russian).
Alekʻsanyan, E. "Ōstrovsku ev Sundukyani dramaturgiakan kaperits." *SG*, 1973/5, 102–7.
———. "Gabriel Sundukyani grakan metʻodi mi kʻani aṙandznahatkutʻyunnerě." *PBH*, 1975/4, 58–62.
Arveladze, B. *Sundukyaně ev vrats irakanutʻyuně*. (Erevan, 1976).
Asmaryan, L. "Gabriel Sundukyan." *L*, 1976/5, 3–13.
———. *Gabriel Sundukyan. Kyankʻě ev stełtzagortzutʻyuně*. (Erevan, 1980).
Babayan, A. "Gabriel Sundukyani vał šrjani tʻateragrutʻyuně." *L*, 1982/1, 22–28.
———. " 'Ḥatʻabala' katakergutʻyan stełtzman patmutʻyunits." *BEH*, 1982/1, 152–58.
———. " 'Pepoyi' stełtzman patmutʻyunits." *BEH*, 1983/2, 142–49.
———. *Gabriel Sundukyani stełtzagortzutʻyuně*. (Erevan, 1988).
Bałdasaryan, G. "Sundukyaně Demirčyani hayatskʻov." *SG*, 1976/5, 111–16.
Bašayan, Ṙ. " 'Pepon' Polsum." *SG*, 1976/5, 117–21.
Bazyan, S. "Sundukyani stełtzagortzutʻyunnerě." *L*, 1970/8, 37–62.
Demirčean, D. "Sundukeani stełtzagortzutʻiwně." *Ani*, 4 (1950–51), 253–56.
Eremean, A. " 'Pēpō'i aṙajin nerkayatsumě." *Z* (*amsōreay*), 1 (1938/4), 30–31.
Gyuli-Kʻevḥyan, H. *Gabriel Sundukyan*. (Erevan, 1944).
Ḥalatʻyan, L. " 'Amusinneri' veradardzě tʻatron." *SG*, 1974/9, 138–45.
Harutʻyunyan, S. *Gabriel Sundukyani kyankʻn u stełtzagortzutʻyuně*. (Erevan, 1934).
———. "Vaveragrer Gabriel Sundukyani tznołneri čort linelu masin." *EJ*, 1950/11–12, 76–80. 1951/1–3, 54–57.
———. *Gabriel Sundukyan*. (Erevan, 1960).
———. "Hay metz dramaturgě." *PBH*, 1975/4, 45–57.
———. *Gabriel Sundukyan*. (Erevan, 1975).
Hovnan, G., and Harutʻyunyan, N. *Žamanakakitsnerě Gabriel Sundukyani masin*. (Erevan, 1976).
Janibekean, G. "Hay irapašt tʻateragrutʻean himnadirě." *Ani*, 4 (1950–51), 163–71.
Jrbašyan, Ēd. "Gabriel Sundukyani ('Varinki vecher') miak patmvatzkʻě." *PBH*, 1981/4, 52–57.
Karapetian, O. "Perevod komedii 'Pepo' na russkii iazyk." *L*, 1976/12, 59–65.
Kʻochoyan, A. "Tʻbilisii barbaṙi hnchyunayin kaṙutsvatzkʻě Gabriel Sundukyani erkerum." *T*, 1957/6, 65–76.
———. "Gabriel Sundukyani lezvi baṙayin kazmi kʻnnutʻyuně." *T*, 1958/10, 85–94.
Łahramanyan, N. "Sundukyani ev Ōstrovsku stełtzagortzakan aṙnchutʻyuně." *SG*, 1970/3, 129–32.

Madoyan, G. "Gabriel Sundukyanĕ ev vrats grakanutʻyunĕ." *SG,* 1976/5, 105–8.
Mḥitʻaryan, A. "Gełarvestakan ĕndhanratsumĕ Gabriel Sundukyani dramaturgiayum." *BEH,* 1976/1, 43–55.
———. "Patmakan aṙakʻelutʻyamb." *SG,* 1976/5, 96–99.
Mkryan, M. "Gabriel Sundukyan." *PBH,* 1976/2, 29–38.
N., H. "Tantʻē ew Sundukean." *B,* 123 (1965), 362–63.
Naryan, M. "Sundukyani chapʻatzon." *PBH,* 1976/2, 89–98.
———. *Sundukyan ev Sayatʻ-Nova.* (Erevan, 1976).
Šahaziz, E. *Gabriel Sundukyan: kensagrakan nyutʻer.* (Erevan, 1927).
Sargsyan, G. *Hay metz dramaturgĕ.* (Erevan, 1976).
Širvanzadē. "Gabriēl Sundukeants." *HK,* 2 (1923–24/7), 69–73.
Sundukyants, E. "Im hišołutʻyunnerĕ hors masin." *SG,* 1976/5, 101–4.
Tiwrean, K. "Gabriēl Sundukeants." *HA,* 2 (1888), 125–27, 136–38.
Zawrean, Y. "Gabriēl Sundukean." *Vēm,* 4 (1936/5), 1–23.

ŠUŠANEAN, VAZGĒN (1903–1941)

Pen name: Yovhannēs Tʻrakatsi.

Ōnnik Šušanean was born in Rodosto (Tekirdağ, Turkey) to a well-to-do family. Survived the genocide of 1915, which claimed the lives of his parents, sister, and brother. Ended up in France in 1922, after short stays in his birthplace, Armenia, and Istanbul. Lived in various parts of France, studying and working as an administrator in the French educational system in Nemours (1933–35) and Rouen (1935–40). Died in a hospital in Paris, and his remains were interred in an unidentified spot. A considerable part of his work is still scattered in the Armenian periodical press.

Collections

Tʻopʻchyan, Al. *Erkir hišatakats.* (Erevan, 1966).

Texts (prose and novels)

Garnanayin (siroy hez namakner). (Paris, 1928; Beirut, 1956).
Amran gišerner. (Cairo, 1930).
Mtʻin patanutʻiwn. (Beirut, 1956). (First published in *HK,* 18 (1939–40/7), 115–29; 8, 24–37; 9, 13–28; 10, 41–55; 11, 19–31; 12, 29–41. 19/1 (1940–41), 32–38.
Siroy ew arkatzi tłakʻĕ. (Beirut, 1957). (First published in *HK,* 6 (1927–28/3), 1–24; 4, 41–53; 5, 28–39; 6, 30–43; 7, 29–42; 8, 33–51.
Siroy ew mełkʻi partēz. (Beirut, 1958).
Mahuan aṙagastĕ and *Aṙajin sērĕ.* (Beirut, 1959).
Čermak Varsenik. (Beirut, 1960).

Works in periodicals

HK, 2 (1923–24/2), 17–19; 6, 14–18; 9, 53–55; 10, 17–26. 3 (1924–25/4), 1–20; 5, 34–35; 12, 1–23. 4 (1925–26/2), 22; 4, 1–34, 37.
"Ōrerĕ gełetsik chen." 7 (1928–29/8), 1–37; 9, 37–64; 10, 25–43; 11, 34–62. 8 (1929–30/4), 22–45; 5, 49–66; 6, 66–84; 7, 46–65; 8, 68–82; 9, 64–85. "Daṙn hatsĕ." 18 (1939–40/1), 7–26; 2, 8–30; 3, 22–33.
"Ōragirs." 20 (1942/4), 1–11; 5, 18–23; 6, 13–18. 21 (1943/1), 8–16; 2, 14–21; 3, 36–41. 26 (1948/12), 28. 40 (1962/11–12), 11–22. 42 (1964/3), 23–25.

Ani, 3 (1948–49), 301–4.
AND, 10 (n.d.), 79. 12 (1961), 17–20. 15 (1964), 18–22. 16 (1965), 7–11. 17 (n.d.), 32. 18 (n.d.), 103–4.

Bibliographies

"Abmołjakan tsankě Vazgēn Šušaneani grakan ašḥatank'neru." *HK,* 21 (1943/3), 111–12.

Criticism

Addarean, G. *Vazgēn Šušanean, ḥōsk' mahuan 25ameakin.* (Beirut, 1966).
Azatean, D. "Amran gišerner." *HK,* 9 (1930–31/9), 95–97.
Minasean, P. "Vazgēn Šušanean." *Ani,* 3 (1948–49), 297–301, 377–82.
Sevan, G. *Vazgen Šušanyan (kyank'n u stełtzagortzut'yuně).* (Erevan, 1968).
Simk'ēšean, E. "Vazgēn Šušanean." *Z* (amsat'ert'), 3 (1959/8–10), 8.

T'ADĒOS T'OḤAT'ETSI (16th c.?)

No biographical information is available on this poet, who is believed to have written in Armenian and in Turkish.

Texts

Pourean, M. "Mijnadarean tałasats T'at'os T'oḥat'etsi." *B,* 68 (1910), 207–8, 273–82. (Study and texts).
K'iwrtean, Y. "Mijnadarean hay tałasats T'at'os sarkawag T'oḥat'etsi." *HK,* 13 (1935/11), 74–82.

Anthologies

SUM, 1, 464–98.

Criticism

Akinean, N. "T'adēos v. Kołoniatsi, T'oḥat'etsi ew T'adēos erēts Sebastatsi tałasatsner." *HA,* 67 (1953), 53–71.
K'iwrtean, Y. "T'adēos v. Kołoniatsi, T'oḥat'etsi ew T'adēos erēts Sebastatsi tałasatsner." *B,* 112 (1954), 70–77.

T'AŁIADEAN, MESROP (1803–1858)

Born in Dzoragiwł, near Erevan. Sent to the seminary at Ējmiatzin, he was ordained a deacon, but he never became a priest. In the early 1820s, he left Armenia for India, returning to Ējmiatzin in 1831 after completing his studies at the Bishop's College in Calcutta. Lived briefly in Nor Jułay (New Julfa, Isfahan, 1834–36), where he met his first wife; in Tabriz (1837–38); and in Constantinople (1838). From the Ottoman capital he was banished to Trebizond for suspected Protestant sympathies. After an adventurous escape, he returned to India, married for a second time (1841), and roamed Calcutta as a peddlar. His business enterprise failed, and he set up a school and published *Azgasēr* (1845–52; later *Azgasēr araratean*). Following the death of his second wife, and in view of unending conflicts with the community, he sold his printing press and set off for home. He never completed his journey; he died and was buried in Shiraz.

Collections

Gełarvestakan erker. (Erevan, 1965).

Nanumyan, Ṙ. *Ułegrutyunner, hodvatzner, namakner, vaveragrer.* (Erevan, 1975).
Aščean, M. *Diwan Mesrop D. Tałiadean: antip ōragrutiwnner erker ew kertuatzner, vaweragrer, namakner.* (New Julfa, 1979).

Texts

Astuatzasēr ew azgasēr hasarakutean hayots pṙkeal kałakin Erewanay srbakrōn kahanayits, baretznund išḥanats ew hamayn barepaštōn žołovrdots. (Calcutta, 1828).
Vēp Vardgisi T[eaṙ]n Tuhats. (Calcutta, 1846).
Čanaparhordutiwn Mesrovbay D. Tałiadeants V. A. sarkawagi srboy Ējmiatzni i Hays. (Calcutta, 1847).
Sōs ew Sondipi. (Calcutta, 1847; Constantinople, 1871).
Tutak Tałiadeants. (Calcutta, 1847).
Vēp Varsenkan skayuhwoy ałuanits: i hnuteants hayreneats pọheats yardi oč ew gir M. D. (Calcutta, 1847).
Ełerergutiwn yōrhas Tankay Tałiadeants. (Tiflis, 1893).

Other works

Ditsabanutiwn. (Calcutta, 1830).
Mesrovbean aybbenaran. (Calcutta, 1840).
Mesrovbean šaradrich hay ew angłiakan lezuats. Child's First Attempt at English and Armenian Composition. (Calcutta, 1840).
Patmutiwn hin Hndkastani yanyišatak daruts anti tsyardzakumn mahmetakanats. History of Ancient India, From the Earliest Ages to the Invasion of the Mahomedans. (Calcutta, 1841).
Patmutiwn parsits. (Calcutta, 1846).
Zuarčaḥōs aṙakk parsits. Targmaneal handerdz yaweluatzovk. (Calcutta, 1846).
Čaṙ dastiarakutean ōriordats. (Calcutta, 1847).
Karg ew kanonk surb Sanduḥt dprotsi ōriordats ew paronkats. (Calcutta, 1847).
Mesrovbean aṙajnord mankants. (Calcutta, 1847).
Vkayabanutiwn srboyn Sandḥtoy. (Calcutta, 1847).

Criticism

Ačēmean, H. *Mesrob Tałiadean: yušardzan mahwan hariwrameakin aṙtiw.* (Teheran, 1958).
Amatuni, L. "Mesrop T'ałiadyan." *EJ,* 1956/4–5, 93–96.
Ēd., Š. "Mesrop T'ałiadyan." *EJ,* 1947/1–2, 55–58.
Grigoryan, G. "Mesrop T'ałiadyani ašḥarhayatsk'i himnakan gtzerě." *T,* 1963/2, 53–64.
Harut'yunyan, G. "Norahayt nyut'er Mesrop T'ałiadyani masin." *EJ,* 1947/3–4, 31–43.
Mirzabekyan, J. "Mesrop T'ałiadyaně hay banasirut'yan mej." *T,* 1960/12, 39–46.
———. "Mesrop T'ałiadyani 'Vep Vardgisi' stełtzagortzut'yan tzagumě." *T,* 1961/7, 69–72.
———. "Mesrop T'ałiadyani grakan žaṙangut'yan šurjě." *T,* 1962/11, 61–66.
———. *Mesrop Tałiadyan.* (Erevan, 1971).
Mkrean, Y. *Kensagrutiwn Mesrovbay Dawtean Tałiadeants Erewantswoy.* (Tiflis, 1886).
Nanumyan, Ṙ. *Mesrop Tałiadyan.* (Erevan, 1948).
———. "Mesrop T'ałiadyani ōragrerě." *SG,* 1980/6, 134–38.

Sargsean, Y. *Ditołagir i veray kensagrut'ean Mesrovbay D. Tałiadeantsi.* (Constantinople, 1888).
Sēt'ean, M. *Grich oskegrich matenagrin Mesrovbay Dawt'ean Tałiadeants ew Kensagrakan aknark.* (Venice, 1926).
T'amrazyan, H. "Ējer hay k'nnadatut'yan patmut'yunits." *BEH,* 1986/2, 11–23.

T'AP'ALTSYAN, K'RISTAP'OR (1910–1967)

Born in Kop', a village near Bulanık, northwest of Van. Novelist; educated in Leninakan (now Gyumri), at the State University of Erevan, and at the Gorky Institute for Literature in Moscow. Worked as a journalist, editor, and in administrative positions in the field of education.

Texts (novels and short stories)

Viktoria. (Erevan, 1937).
Kyank'i aršaluysě. (Erevan, 1939, 1957).
Hayrenik'. (Erevan, 1942).
Paterazm. 4 vols. (Erevan, 1946–65).
Oske hovit. (Erevan, 1955).
Azniv hovivnerě. (Erevan, 1958).
Patani kombaynavarě. (Erevan, 1958).
Hayrenašen. 2 books. (Erevan, 1963, 1973).
Kyank'i aršaluysě; Viktorya. (Erevan, 1981).

Translations

RUSSIAN

Nersesian, G. *Zolotaia dolina.* (Moscow, 1959).
Tadeosian, A. *Airenashen.* (Moscow, 1966).
Za tebia Moskva. (Erevan, 1956).

T'ARGYUL, LYUSI (1905–1955)

Born in Van. Left her native city for Eastern Armenia in 1914. Educated in the Yovnanean school in Tiflis and graduated from the State University of Erevan in 1929. Wrote short stories and novels.

Texts

Čanker. (Erevan, 1931). (Story).
Čakatum. (Erevan, 1932). (Novel).
Azatarar ałjikě. (Erevan, 1937).
Ēdiki ařajin hamergě. (Erevan, 1937).
Iskapes haneluk. (Erevan, 1937).
Hskaneri šark'um. (Erevan, 1937). (Novel).
Mankakan erkat'ułi. (Erevan, 1938).
Depi Ispania. (Erevan, 1939). (Novelette).
Erku mayr. (Erevan, 1939).
Ułti parě kamrji vra. (Erevan, 1940).
Eražiště. (Erevan, 1942).
Iskakan paterazm. (Erevan, 1942).
Mayrer. (Erevan, 1942).
P'ok'rikneri metz gortzě. (Erevan, 1942).

Lusni sonat. (Erevan, 1944).
Te inchu ḥozi ktin erkate ōł hagtsrin. (Erevan, 1947).
Tzałkavan. (Erevan, 1948).
Pionerakan ḥostum. (Erevan, 1952).
Patmvatzkner. (Erevan, 1954).
Třchoł tzałikner. (Erevan, 1955).
Komitas. (Erevan, 1956).

TARONTSI, SOŁOMON (1905–1971)

Pen name: Sołomon Tarontsi.

Born Sołomon Movsisyan in Kop' (a village near Bulanık, northwest of Lake Van). Emigrated to Eastern Armenia with his parents in 1914. Studied at the State University of Erevan (1930). Wrote both verse and prose; also worked as a translator and journalist.

Collections

Novelner. (Erevan, 1962).
Erker. 2 vols. (Erevan, 1964–65).
Kamrjvoł apter. (Erevan, 1973).
Mełraget. (Erevan, 1980).

Texts (poetry and prose)

Ařavot. (Erevan, 1930).
Křiv Dnepri het (ěst Maršaki). (Erevan, 1932).
Serundneri ergě. (Erevan, 1933).
Dareri legendě. (Erevan, 1934).
Astłaptuš. (Erevan, 1934).
Adavia. (Erevan, 1936).
Hopop. (Erevan, 1938).
Banastełtzutyunner. (Erevan, 1940).
Tzuyl tłan. (Erevan, 1940).
Agřavě. (Erevan, 1941).
Erjankutyan etevits. (Erevan, 1941).
Ṙazmi šeptor. (Erevan, 1941).
Krak. (Erevan, 1942).
Paterazm. (Erevan, 1942).
Mi tupt lutsku hamar. (Erevan, 1942).
Zruyts šataker Šreyteri, zinvor Piki ev mi aklori masin. (Erevan, 1942).
Aspet Liparit. (Erevan, 1944).
Krake kařułinerov. (Erevan, 1944).
Davti ergě. (Erevan, 1946).
Ampropits heto. (Erevan, 1948).
Chłjikě. (Erevan, 1948).
Stalingrad. (Erevan, 1951). (Verse).
Metz ařōrya. (Erevan, 1953).
Banastełtzutyunner. (Erevan, 1954). (Verse).
Kapuyt heřuner. (Erevan, 1956).
Aveli luys. (Erevan, 1958).

Zruyts arevi tak. (Erevan, 1959).
Oskedar. (Erevan, 1960).

Translations

French anthologies

Faure, L. *E,* 82–83. (Adaptation).
LPA, 316–17.

Russian

Kniga schast'ia. (Erevan, 1952).
Stikhi. (Erevan, 1956).

Criticism

Hunanyan, A. "Stełtzagortzakan ink'nahastatman čanaparhov." *SG,* 1971/6, 113–21.
Muradyan, H. "Ḥohakan k'narerguťyun." *SG,* 1985/9, 137–38.
Norents, V. "Bazmabełun vastak." *SG,* 1965/1, 115–17.
Yuzbašyan, B. "Sołomon Tarontsi." *SG,* 1960/2, 130–37.

TATREAN, ATRINĒ (1915–)

Born in Çorum, Turkey. A novelist, playwright, and poet. Educated in Armenian and French schools in Constantinople. Her higher studies in Germany and Austria were interrupted by World War II. Later, she resided in France. Some of her early plays and stories are for children.

Texts

Aniin gandzanakĕ. (Istanbul, 1946). (Play).
Gołtsuatz ałjikĕ. (Istanbul, 1946). (Story).
Anerewoyť ōdanawordnerĕ. (Istanbul, 1947). (Story).
Koyr ałjkan ĕnkerĕ. (Istanbul, 1948). (Story).
Dzknorsin ałjikĕ. (Istanbul, 1950). (Play).
Šušikin kałandĕ. (Istanbul, 1952). (Play).
Zarťik hōrk'urin tunĕ. (Istanbul, 1953). (Play). (Written with B. Ťewean).
Ayspēs metztsan anonk'. (Istanbul, 1954). (Play).
Mayťerun vray. (Istanbul, 1955). (Novel).
Miranta ew Žirōnta. (Istanbul, 1956). (Story).
Vanō ew Marō. (Istanbul, 1957). (Play).
Patēn kaḥuatz košiknerĕ. (Istanbul, 1963). (Story).
Gehēni čambun vray. (Istanbul, 1966). (Novel).
Hrdeh kay . . . maretsēk': banastełtzuťiwnner. (Istanbul 1968). (Verse).
Chorrord mĕ kĕ p̄ntřui. (Istanbul, 1971). (Nòvel).
Hełinak, ketsir. (Istanbul, 1980). (Novel).

TATREAN, VAHRAM (1900–1948)

Born in Çorum, Turkey. Novelist. Survived the Armenian massacres and deportations of 1915 and safely arrived in Constantinople in 1919. Emigrated to the United States in 1936 and settled in Fresno, California.

Texts

Dēpi anapat (p̄rtsuatz ējer ōragrēs). (New York, 1945). (Diary).

Gerezmanneru mējēn (p̒rtsuatz ējer ōragrēs, 2. šark‘). (New York, 1945). (Novel).
Sew hogin (ezrap̒akum). (New York, 1945). (Novel).
Ir antsealě (noravēp polsahay keank‘ē). (New York, 1946). (Novelette).
K‘oyr Anna (noravēp polsahay keank‘ē). (New York, 1946). (Novelette).
Nelli Pella (noravēp polsahay keank‘ē). (New York, 1946). (Novel).
Hing t‘aterahałer ew tsruatz ējer. (Boston, 1950). (Plays and essays).
Gabiki arkatznerě. (Fresno, 1947). (Humorous stories).
Chawartatz hamanuagě. Ariwnot matnahetk‘erě ew Hrabuhi vray. (Boston, 1952). (3 detective stories).

T‘AT‘UL, VAHRAM (1887–1943)

Pen name: Vahram T‘at‘ul.
Born Vahram Garagašean in Constantinople. Poet. Had his schooling, and studied architecture, in his birthplace, but devoted himself to teaching and literary activities. Spent the latter part of his life in France.

Texts (verse)

Amenayn zgušut‘eamb: k‘ert‘uatzner. (Paris, 1941).
Hin u nor tałer, 1907–1940. (Paris, 1941).

Criticism

Metzarents, M. "Antip banastełtz mě." *AM,* suppl. 1, 1908, 92–99.
Ułurlean, M. "Karč patasḥan mě." *AM,* 1908, 574–75.

TATUREAN, AHARON (1886–1965)

Pen name: Aharon.
Born in the village of Ōvačěk‘ (Ovacık, near Izmit, Turkey). Educated in Constantinople and in the Murat Ṙap‘ayēlean school in Venice (1907–09). Survived the Armenian massacres and deportations of 1915. After a brief sojourn in Constantinople and Bulgaria, he pursued his studies in Prague (1923–28) and settled in France in the late 1920s.

Texts

Magałat‘ner. (Paris, 1938 [cover says 1937]).
Pohemakank‘. (Paris, 1939).
Sōseats antaṙ. (Paris, 1948 [cover says 1949]).
Erkner erkir. (Paris, 1957).
Baginnerus krakin dēm. (Paris, 1958).
Karmir awetaran. (Paris, 1959).
Ankrkneli aprumner. (Cairo, 1971).
Hin k‘ert‘uatzner. (Beirut, 1971).
Verjin kat‘ilner. (Beirut, 1971).

Translations (Italian anthologies)

LPAM, 279–83.

Criticism

A. S. V. "Pohemakank‘ (Aharon Taturean, 1939)." *S,* 1939, 270–72.
Čanašean, M. "Aharon Taturean." *B,* 123 (1965), 34–61. Reprinted separately, Venice, 1965.
T[ērtērean], E. "Magałat‘ner (Aharon Taturean, 1937–38)." *S,* 1938, 303–04.

T'ĒK'ĒEAN, VAHAN (1878–1945)

Pen names: Aspatak, Asup, B. K. M., Bikmalion, Hamširak B., Ḥorēn Orotum, Iskuhi Hovean, Nšan Hartsakan, Skayordi, Surēn Tiranean, Tat'ew, V. T., V. Tiranean, Vahan Tiranean, Vēt'ō, Yovhannēs Karapet.

Born in Constantinople. Attended the Pērpērean and Kedronakan schools in his birthplace. Spent several years in Europe (Liverpool, Marseilles, Hamburg) working for various businesses. Arrived in Egypt in 1903, and with a number of colleagues, he founded the literary periodical *Širak* (1905) and *Arew* (1915). Returned to Constantinople in 1908, visited Eastern Armenia in 1910, and went back to Egypt in 1914. As a member of the Armenian National Delegation based in Paris, T'ēk'ēean traveled to Armenia in 1919 and spent the next two years in Constantinople. During these years he was actively involved in efforts to locate and shelter Armenian orphans. Under his leadership, the Ṙamkavar and Azatakan parties merged in 1921. Wandered far and wide in the years 1922–24, before settling permanently in Egypt. Died in Cairo and is buried next to A. Arp'iarean and E. Ōtean.

Collections

Ambołjakan erker. (Cairo, 1949–50). (Only vols. 3, 4, 5, 7, 8, and 9 have appeared).
Hatěntir. (Beirut, 1954).
Erker. (Erevan, 1958).
Hayerguťiwn ew Hatěntir k'erťuatzner. (Beirut, 1958).
Hatěntir. (Beirut, 1978).
Irikvan ḥorhurdner: sēr, ḥoh, hayerguťyun. (Erevan, 1978).

Texts (verse)

Hoger. (Paris, 1901).
Hrašali yaruťiwn (1901–1914). (Constantinople, 1914).
Kēs-gišerēn minchew aršaloys (1914–1918). (Paris, 1919).
Sēr: k'erťuatzner, 1919–33. (Paris, 1933).
Hayerguťiwn ew ayl k'erťuatzner (tpagreal ew antip). (Cairo, 1943).
Tałaran (šark' k'erťuatzneru). (Cairo, 1944).
Vahan T'ēk'ēeani namaknerě Lewon Zawēn Siwrmēleanin [ew] Loys zuarť. (New York and Paris, 1950; Beirut, 1972). (Letters to Z. Siwrmēlean).
Sančean, A. *Vahan T'ēk'ēean. Namakani.* (Los Angeles, 1983).
Łazarean, V. *Mamuli mēj tpuatz ev antip erker u namakner Vahan T'ēk'ēeanēn.* (Beirut, 1987).

Translations

English

Asadian, A. "Ode to Vardan." *The Fifteen-Hundredth Anniversary of Saint Vardan the Brave.* V. Haig, (New York, n.d.), 39–40.
Chrakian, E. "Meditation on Vardanantz." *The Armenian Mirror-Spectator,* April, 20, 1963, 2.
Der Hovanessian, D., and Margossian, M. *Sacred Wrath: The Selected Poems of Vahan Tekeyan.* (New York, 1982).
Essefian, S. "Armenian Church." *The Fifteen-Hundredth Anniversary of Saint Vardan the Brave.* V. Haig (New York, n.d.), 39–40.
Natalie, S. "Armenian Church." *The Armenian Guardian,* 14 (1960/6), 11.

French

Sahakian, S. "Ta main," "Prière du soir," "Ave." *AND,* 11 (1960), 44–66.
Simkechian, E. "Au large." *AND,* 12 (1961), 147.

French anthologies

APA, 167–69.
Tʻēkʻēean. *E,* 52–54.
FPA, 53.
JM, 78–106.
LPA, 215–17.

German anthologies

ALG, 132.

Italian anthologies

LPAM, 257–64.

Russian anthologies

BPA, 465–67.
IZAP, 97–110.

Spanish

Agemian, B. "La Iglesia Armenia." *El Mundo,* 1960, set 11, suppl. 4.

Spanish anthologies

APAS, 135–38, 219–23.

Criticism

Ałababean, S. "Vahan Tʻēkʻēeani kʻnarě." *HA,* 91 (1977), 239–52.
———. "Vahan Tʻekʻeyani kʻnarě." *SG,* 1978/11, 132–37.
Alpōyačean, A. *Vahan Tʻēkʻēean ibr hanrayin mard ew hraparakagir.* (Beirut, 1988).
Asmaryan, L. *Vahan Tʻekʻeyan: kyankʻě ev stełtzagortzutʻyuně.* (Erevan, 1971).
———. "Vahan Tʻekʻeyan." *PBH,* 1978/2, 74–80.
Baluean, H. "Vahan Tʻēkʻēean." *Z,* 1 (1929–[30]), 97–101.
Chōpanean, A. "Vahan Tʻēkʻēean, 'Hoger'." *ANA,* 3 (1902), 45–50.
———. "Vahan Tʻēkʻēean [čaṙ]." *ANA,* 1933/3–4, 109–11.
Eremean, S. "Vahan Tʻēkʻēean." *B,* 90 (1933), 497–512.
Grigoryan, H. "Vahan Tʻekʻeyani stełtzagortzakan ułin." *PBH,* 1958/2, 151–61.
Łazarean, I. *Vahan Tʻēkʻēean.* ([Los Angeles], 1984).
Łazarean, V. "Vahan Tʻēkʻēeaně žamanakakitsneru namaknerun mēj." *Haykazean hayagitakan handēs,* 1981/9, 225–34.
———. "Vahan Tʻekʻeyani kyankʻi u stełtzagortzutʻyan aṙajin šrjaně." *BEH,* 1982/3, 62–75.
Mḥalean, G. "Vahan Tʻēkʻēeani grakan gortzunēutʻiwně." *S,* 1934, 45–52.
Mḥitʻarean, G. "Vahan Tʻēkʻēeani namaknerě." *HK,* 29 (1951/5), 110–12. (Review).
Ōšakan, Y. *Spʻiwṙkʻě ew iraw banastełtzutʻiwně (V. Tʻēkʻēeani aṙitʻov).* (Jerusalem, 1945).
Parsamean, M. "Vahan Tʻēkʻēean." *Vēm,* 1 (1933/2), 47–54. 2 (1934/1), 50–61.
———. *Vahan Tʻēkʻēean.* (Beirut, 1985).
L. S. "Tʻēkʻēean Vahan, Hoger, Pʻariz, 1901." *Murč,* 1901/11, 221–23. (Review).
Vahē-Vahean. "Vahan Tʻēkʻēean." *Ani,* 1 (1946), 170–71.
———. "Vahan Tʻēkʻēean." *Ani,* 2 (1947–48), 452.

———. "Vahan Tʻekʻeyan." *SG,* 1976/11, 112–28.
Yobelean Vahan Tēkʻēeani kʻaṙasnameay grakan gortzunēutʻean. (Paris, 1933).

TĒMIRČIPAŠEAN, EŁIA (1851–1908)

Pen names: A. Azataḥohean, Čgnawor, Čin Yakob, Grasēr Atom, Z. Ḥaytʻuni, Hur Hayran, Melania, Monazn, Mšak, Nurania, Šaržeants or Šaržents, Tʻewaniō, and others.

Born in Constantinople. Received his elementary education at the local Nersēsean and Šahnazarean schools. In the 1870s, he briefly studied at Marseilles and worked for the Ottoman bureaucracy as an interpreter. In the 1880s, he taught in Armenian schools, contributed to numerous Armenian periodicals, launched the periodical *Grakan ew imastasirakan šaržum* (1883–88), and edited *Erkragunt* (1884–88). Overwhelmed by consumption and ever-worsening mental and emotional disturbances, Tēmirčipašean committed suicide.

Collections

Nazareants, H. *Namakkʻ sirayin Ełia Tēmirčipašeani, 1886–1889.* (Constantinople, 1910).
Ardzak ējer, namakner, kʻertʻuatzner. (Paris, 1955).
Sargsyan, Ṙ. *Erker.* (Erevan, 1986).

Texts

Šahnazareani mě ḥłčin parz kʻnnutʻiwně. (Constantinople, 1870).
Dambaran. (Constantinople, 1878; New York, 1920). (Includes pieces by M. Cheraz).
Nor keankʻ. A. Azgayin lezu, paštpanutʻiwn Minas Cherazi ěntrołakan ašḥarhabarin. (Constantinople, 1879).
Pitzak. (Constantinople, 1879).
Pʻilisopʻayakan baṙaran. 2 vols. (Constantinople, 1879).
Hatěntir ěntʻertsuatzkʻ. (Constantinople, 1881).
Ałjkants dastiarakutʻean vray čaṙ. (Constantinople, 1890).
Šrjagayutʻiwn im tʻałis mēj. (Constantinople, 1890).
Tarerkʻ patmutʻean imastasirutʻean. (Constantinople, 1891).
Grpani baṙaran hayerēně gałłierēn, 25000 baṙ. (Constantinople, 1894).

Works in periodicals

AM, 1885, 337–38, 392–95, 500–02, 550–51. 1894, 747–48. 1906, 1040–41. 1907, 23.
ANA, 1929/1, 21–22. 1931/3–4, 14–17.
AND, 14 (1963), 82.
EJ, 1976/4, 48–49.
M, 1892/3957, 28–29; 3959, 71; 3962, 117–18. 1893/3978, 101; 3981, 136–41; 3982, 146–48. 1899/7, 204–7; 8–9, 247–50; 10, 300–303, 313–14. 1901/8, 113–15; 11, 166–68; 12, 179; 13, 193–95; 15, 232–33; 17, 260; 20, 309–11; 21, 324–25; 23, 355; 24, 369–71; 26, 403; 29, 454–55. 1902/26, 408–9; 29, 460–61. 1906/1, 5; 2, 26; 3, 43; 4, 64. 1907/3, 57–58; 6–7, 111; 9, 169; 15, 293; 23–29, 576. 1908/9, 179; 12–13, 238.
Z, 1 (1929–[30]), 11. 200.

Translations

ENGLISH

Turpanjian, M. "The Prayer of a Desperate Mother." *The Armenian Herald,* February–April, 1919, 231–32.

ENGLISH ANTHOLOGIES

ALP, 98–100.

FRENCH ANTHOLOGIES

APA, 67–73.

ITALIAN ANTHOLOGIES

LPAM, 137–48.

SPANISH ANTHOLOGIES

APAS, 139–44.

Criticism

Antonean, A. "Bats namak Ełia Tēmirčipašeanin." *M,* 1899/8–9, 262–64.

Armēn, E. "Ełia Tēmirčipašeani keank'ēn." *ANA,* 1 (1929/2), 40–43.

Atrušan, "Ełia Tēmirčipašean." *HG,* 1 (1911–12/2), 5–9; 4, 4–8; 8, 16–21; 9, 15–19; 11, 8–12; 2 (1912–13/1), 14–18; 3, 22–26; 5, 31–34; 8, 11–15; 9, 6–9.

Chift'ē-Saraf. "Ełiayin muralě." *M,* 1907/28–29, 567–69.

"Ełia Tēmirčipašean." *A,* 1908, 631–32.

Ēsačanean, L. *Ełia Tēmirčipašean.* (Constantinople, 1909).

Fēnērčean, G., and Petrosean, H. *Ełia Tēmirčipašean, ir keank'ě ew ir gortzě.* (Constantinople, 1921).

Galēmk'earean, Z. "Ełia Tēmirčipašean." *ANA,* 2 (1931/5–6), 17–112.

Harut'yunyan, S. "Imastut'yan tesut'yan hartserě Ełia Temirčipašyani erkerum." *BEH,* 1972/2, 207–13.

———. "Ełia Temirčipašyani kyank'n u gortzuneut'yuně." *L,* 1972/6, 90–94.

Kamsarakan, T. "Ełia Tēmirčipašean." *M,* 1892/3956, 11–18.

Kostanyan, A. "Ełia Temirčipašyan." *SG,* 1970/9, 132–43.

Mamurean, M. "Tałaran T'evanioyi." *AM,* 1885, 335–36.

Orberean, Ṙ. "Erkuk'i bažnuatz, 1. Ełia Tēmirčipašean." *M,* 1902/6, 81–87.

Ōtean, G. "Azniw Tēmirčipašean." *Z* (eṙamseay), 1947/2, 94–96. (2 letters from G. Ōtean).

Parsamean, M. "Ełia Tēmirčipašean." *AND,* 14 (1963), 65–81.

Šahnur. "Tłt'aktsut'iwn." *AM,* 1882, 364–73.

———. "Tłt'aktsut'iwn." *AM,* 1887, 135–42.

———. "Tłt'aktsut'iwn." *AM,* 1893, 342–44.

Samikean, Ṙ. *Ełia Tēmirčipašean, 1880–1908.* (Constantinople, 1909).

Tayean, Ł. "Ełia Tēmirčipašean." *B,* 66 (1908), 57–73.

Yarut'iwnean, A. "Grakan dimastuerner, Ełia Tēmirčipašean." *M,* 1899/15, 473–76.

———. "Grakan dimastuerner, Ełia Tēmirčipašean." *AM,* 1902, 243–53.

Zōhrap, G. "Ełia Tēmirčipašean." *M,* 1907/38, 759–62.

T'ĒŌLĒŌLEAN, MINAS (1913–1997)

Pen names: Armēn Amatean, Nočeats Tłan, Vazgēn Vanandean.

Born in Partizak (Bahçecik, Turkey). Writer, teacher, literary historian, and a prolific journalist. Educated in Armenian schools in Istanbul. Lived and taught in Bulgaria (1936–37) and Rumania (1937–38). In 1944, he moved to Aleppo where he co-edited the daily *Arewelkʻ* (1946–56) and taught at and became first principal of the Karen Jeppe secondary school (1947–56). After brief sojourns in Egypt (1956–57) and Lebanon (1957–60), he settled in Boston in 1960, where he served as the Armenian Revolutionary Federation's executive secretary (1960–66) and edited the daily *Hayrenikʻ* from 1966 to his retirement in 1978.

Texts

Naḥergankʻ. (Sofia, 1937). (Poems).
Mṫnolort. (Aleppo, 1945). (Verse and prose poems).

Other works

Kʻerakanuṫiwn. (Aleppo, 1950). (2 parts; elementary grammar).
Dar mĕ grakanuṫiwn. 2 vols. (Cairo, 1955–56; Boston, 1977–82 [revised and expanded]). (Anthology with biographical and literary introductions to Western, Soviet, and Diaspora Armenian writers, 1850–1950).
Haykakan artasahmanĕ ew Azgayin sahmanadruṫiwnĕ. (Beirut, 1968). (On the Armenian National Constitution of 1863 and its role in Diaspora).
Hayastaneayts ekełetsin ew hay ekełetsakanuṫean kochumĕ. (Montreal, 1986). (Articles previously published in *Hayrenikʻ*).

TER-GRIGORYAN, GRIGOR (1916–1981)

Born in Erevan. Dramatist. After a brief teaching career (1931–34), he studied construction at the Erevan Polytechnic Institute (1939), a profession he practiced for only a few years. Studied history at the Ḥachatur Abovyan Pedagogical Institute of Erevan (1947). Held administrative and political positions within the Soviet Air Force, the government, and the Communist party. From 1951 to 1955, he was the secretary of the Union of Writers and editor of *Grakan ṫerṫ*. From 1955 to his death, was editor in chief of *Ozni,* the only Soviet Armenian satirical periodical.

Texts

Ays astłerĕ mern en. (Erevan, 1950). (Written with Levon Karagyozyan, 1913–86).
Garnan andzrev (piesneri žołovatzu). (Erevan, 1962).
Tasĕ tari. (Erevan, 1969).
Im ḥełč Portos. (Erevan, 1977).
Amen inch kam ochinch (Piesner). (Erevan, 1987).

Translations

RUSSIAN

Dramy i komedii. (Erevan, 1981).
Pogodin, N. *Eti zvezdy nashi.* (Moscow and Erevan, 1949; Moscow, 1950; Erevan, 1952).

Criticism

Avagyan, Ḥ. *Grigor Ter-Grigoryan.* (Erevan, 1983).

TĒR KARAPETEAN, GEŁAM (1865–1918)

Pen names: Asołik, Mšoy Gełam, Tatrak.
Born in the village of Ḥēybian on the plain of Muš. Educated in the venerated monastery of Surb Karapet and the Armenian school in the town of Muš. For many

years, though with some interruptions (e.g., working for the Armenian church in Diyarbakır, 1894–97), he worked as a secretary in the Armenian church in Muš. Elected to the Ottoman Parliament in 1908, he moved to Constantinople in early 1909. A selection from Tēr Karapetean's short stories and novelettes previously published in the periodical press in Constantinople was published posthumously.

Texts

Tarōni ašḥarh. (Paris, 1931).

Criticism

Sasuni, K. "Gełam Tēr Karapetean (keank'n u gortzě)." *HK,* 9 (1930–31/12), 109–22.

Petrosyan, H. *Gełam Ter-Karapetyan (Mšo Gełam): kyank'ě ev stełtzagortzut'yuně.* (Erevan, 1983).

TER-MARTIROSYAN, ARTAŠES (1892–1937)

Born in Alexandrapol (Leninakan, now Gyumri, Armenia). A poet and literary critic. After graduating from the Institute of Commerce in Moscow (1917), he became a Bolshevik revolutionary and was incarcerated twice, once in Tiflis and once in Erevan, for his participation in the May rebellion against the Armenian Republic. Resided in Moscow from 1924 until his death.

Texts (verse)

Ašnut. (Alexandrapol, 1912).

Poetry

Gevorg Afrikyan, Isahak Isahakyan, Art. Ter-Martirosyan, erek' k'nar. (Erevan, 1963), 157–203.

TĒR SARGSENTS, SEDRAK (c1853–1941)

Pen name: Tewkants (brother of Aristakēs *vardapet* Tevkants).

Born and educated in Van. A novelist and poet. Found employment in Constantinople as a private tutor and teacher, but he returned to Vaspurakan, the region around his native Van, to teach. After a visit to Transcaucasia in 1884, he settled in Europe, residing mainly in England and France. Died in Nice.

Texts

Vařarani m'kaytzer. (Constantinople, 1875). (Verse).
Šahēnn i Sipir kam Gałt'akan hayě. (Constantinople, 1877, 1911). (Novel).
Manukneru ark'ayut'iwn. (Constantinople, 1878).

TĒR-STEP'ANEAN, MIHRAN (1899–1964)

Born in Dörtyol (now Turkey) and educated in the local Armenian school and the Pēzazean school in Constantinople. Survived the genocide of 1915 and worked as an interpreter for the French administration in Cilicia. After the French withdrawal from the region, he took up residence in Syria and held a high-ranking position in the Syrian bureaucracy. In his birthplace he edited, with Martiros Tēr Step'anean, the short-lived periodical *Nuik* (1914), and with Aris Šak'lyan (q.v.), the weekly *Sisuan* (1920–21). Contributed to a number of Armenian periodicals, especially the daily *Zart'ōnk'* of Beirut, Lebanon. Wrote verse and prose.

Texts

Yoysi ḥaroykner. (Beirut, 1959). (Prose).
Erker. (Beirut, 1967). (Verse and prose).

TĒR-YOVHANNISEAN, GABRIĒL (1837–1920)

Pen name: K'ajberuni.

Born in Uzunt'ala, a village in Ijevan, Armenia. Novelist. After graduating from the Nersisean school of Tiflis, he studied medicine in Moscow. He has also written ethnographic and travel accounts.

Texts

Ter Sargis. Surb Georgi łulĕ. (Erevan, 1938).

Criticism

Bałdasaryan, H. " 'Ter Sargsi' hełinakĕ. *SG,* 1975/7, 164–66.

TĒREAN, VAHAN (1885–1920)

Pen name: Vahan Tērean.

Born Vahan Tēr-Grigorean in Gandza, a village in Georgia. Educated in Aḥalk'alak' (Akhalkalaki, Georgia), Tiflis, the Lazarean (Lazarevskii) Insititute in Moscow, the University of Moscow, and the University of St. Petersburg, where he studied under N. Marr. Supported the Bolshevik Revolution and held administrative positions within the "Commissariat for Armenian Affairs" based in Moscow. His fragile health deteriorated seriously, and he died in Orenburg on his way to Central Asia.

Collections

Makintsyan, P. *Erkeri žołovatzu.* 4 vols. (Constantinople and Erevan, 1923–25).
100 otanavor. (Tiflis, 1930).
Banastełtzut'yunner. (Erevan, 1936).
Isahakyan, A. *Banastełtzut'yunneri liakatar žołovatzu.* (Erevan, 1940).
Ĕntir k'ert'uatzner. (Aleppo, 1945).
Erkeri žołovatzu. Vol. 1. (Erevan, 1950).
Vahan Tērean. (Beirut, 1953). (Poems).
Łazaryan, H. *Erker.* (Erevan, 1956).
Mt'nšałi anurjner, Gišer ew yušer, Oski hēk'iat', Veradardz, Oskē šłt'ay, P'šē psakĕ, Erkir Nayiri. (Venice, 1956).
Partizuni, V. *Erkeri žołovatzu.* 3 vols. (Erevan, 1960–63).
Erker chors hatorov. (Erevan, 1972–79).
Namakner. (Erevan, 1972).
Jrbašyan, Ēd. *Banastełtzut'yunner. Liakatar žołovatzu.* (Erevan, 1985).
Simonyan, G. *Erker.* (Erevan, 1989).

Texts

Mt'nšałi anurjner. Book 1 (Tiflis, 1908; Beirut, 1939).
Banastełtzut'iwnner. Vol. 1 (Moscow, 1912).
Banastełtzut'yunner. (Erevan, 1980).
P'anoyan, Ō. *Banastełtzut'yunner.* (Erevan, 1982).
Banastełtzut'yunner. Vol. 1 (Erevan, 1985). (Facsimile edition of author's manuscripts).
Davt'yan, V. *100 banastełtzut'yun.* (Erevan, 1985).

Translations

English

Abelian, D. "Automn Melody." *The Armenian Mirror-Spectator,* January 19, 1963, 2.

Evans, G. ["Glory to you, rubescent . . ."] *SL,* 1966/3, 11.

English anthologies

SAP, 8–10.

French anthologies

APA, 207–11.

Loriol, P. *E,* 57–58.

JM, 111–32.

LPA, 231–36.

German anthologies

ALG, 130.

Italian anthologies

DLA, 3–4.

LPAM, 237–44.

Russian

Borian, G., and Vartazarian, R. *Izbrannoe.* (Erevan, 1952).

Lirika. (Erevan, 1985).

Partizuni, V. *Stikhi.* (Moscow, 1950).

Pirverdiev, S. *Armianskii poet Vagan Terian.* (Alexandrapol, 1917).

Rozhdestvenskii, V., and Grigor'ian, K. *Stikhotvoreniia.* (Moscow and Leningrad, 1960).

Stikhotvoreniia. (Leningrad, 1973).

Terian, N., and Ioannisian, A. *Neizdannye pis'ma.* (Erevan, 1970).

Uspenskii, L. *Izbrannoe.* (Erevan, 1941).

Bibliographies

Melikian, S. *Vaan Ter'ian na russkom iazyke: bibliografiia perevodov i kriticheskoi literatury.* (Erevan, 1956).

Spanish anthologies

APAS, 241–46.

Criticism

Aharonean, V. "Vahan Tērean." *HK,* 23 (1945/2), 44–52; 3, 88–92; 4, 102–6.

Ałababyan, S. "Vahan Teryan." *PBH,* 1975/1, 8–22.

———. "Vahan Teryan." *PBH,* 1985/1, 7–20.

Aliḥanyan, S. "Vahan Teryanĕ Hoktemberyan sotsialistakan metz ṙevolyutsiayi gałapʻarneri propagandist." *T,* 1955/2, 13–28.

———. *Vahan Teryani petakan gortzuneutʻyunĕ.* (Erevan, 1955).

Alikhanian, S. *Vaan Terian: obshchestvenno-politicheskaia i gosudarstvennaia deiatel'nost'.* (Erevan, 1960).

Arveladze, B. *Vahan Teryanĕ ev Vrastanĕ.* (Erevan, 1985). (Translated by M. Sahakyan).

Baburyan, M. " 'Vagrenavor'i naḥergankʻi Teryani tʻargmanutʻyunĕ." *PBH,* 1966/4, 187–92.

B[aluean], H. "Nšmarner–Vahan Tērean." *Z,* 1 (1929–[30]), 376.

Bolšakov, L. *Vahan Teryani verjin gortzułumě.* (Erevan, 1985). (Translated from Russian by F. Meloyan). (Essay).
———. "Verjin gortzułumě." *SG,* 1985/5, 135–44.
Daronian, S. "Vaan Ter'ian i russkii simvolizm." *Briusovskie chteniia 1980 goda [sbornik statei],* (Erevan, 1983), 185–97.
Engibarean, G. " 'Mtʻnšałi anurjner' Vahan Tēreani." *Lumay,* 7–8 (1909), 81–85.
Erkatʻ, A. "Vahan Tērean." *B,* 79 (1921), 340–43; 80 (1922), 8–10.
Grigor'ian, K. *Vaan Ter'ian: ocherk zhizni i tvorchestva.* (Moscow, 1957).
Grigoryan, A. "Teryanakan miaynutʻyan patkeri kařutsvatzkʻě." *SG,* 1973/10, 138–45.
Grigoryan, K. *Vahan Teryan.* (Erevan, 1956).
———. "Vahan Teryaně ev Simvolizmě." *T,* 1956/1, 25–42.
———. "Vaan Terian v peterburgskom universitete." *L,* 1970/1 96–105.
———. *Vahan Teryan (kyankʻn u stełtzagortzutʻyuně).* (Erevan, 1983).
Harutʻyunyan, Z. "Blok ev Teryan." *SG,* 1974/7, 157–61.
Ḥotsanyan, M. *Teryaně leninyan erkeri propagandist ev tʻargmanich.* (Erevan, 1985).
Išḥanyan, Ṙ. "Vahan Teryaně ev hay grakanutʻyan lezvi hartserě." *BEH,* 1970/2, 26–42.
———. "Vahan Teryani 'Mtʻnšałi anurjnerě' lezvakan ařumov." *L,* 1971/1, 58–67.
———. "Tʻumanyan-Teryan hartsi šurj." *PBH,* 1971/2, 125–43.
———. "Teryani erekʻ serě." *SG,* 1979/2, 138–42.
———. "Teryani ḥohě, aprumě, serě." *BEH,* 1985/1, 42–57.
Jrbašyan, Ēd. "Vahan Teryaně ev Lermontovi poezian." *PBH,* 1974/2, 3–17.
———. *Chors gagatʻ, Tʻumanyan, Isahakyan, Teryan, Charents.* (Erevan, 1982).
Kʻiparean, K. "Vahan Tērean." *B,* 84 (1927), 49–52, 82–85.
Kirakosian, L. *Na perelome.* (Erevan, 1989).
Łanalanyan, H. *Vahan Teryan.* (Erevan, 1960).
———. "Inchpes en stełtzvel ergern ays poeti." *SG,* 1983/6, 120–26.
———. *Hay kʻnari kaḥard ergichě.* (Erevan, 1985).
Manukyan, S. "Hangutsayin hartseri skzbunkʻayin kʻnnutʻyun." *SG,* 1982/8, 142–44. (On Ēd. Jrbašyan's *Chors gagatʻ . . .*).
Melikian, S. "Perevody Vaana Teriana dlia 'Poezii Armenii'." *PBH,* 1963/4, 241–48.
———. "Teryaně Sundukyani ev Širvanzadei tʻargmanich." *SG,* 1964/10, 139–45.
———. "Perevody Vaana Ter'iana iz russkoi literatury." *PBH,* 1965/3, 239–45.
Minasyan, K. "Vahan Teryaně Lenini masin." *SG,* 1987/11, 127–28.
Mkrtchyan, A. *Tałandi dzevavorman akunkʻnerum.* (Erevan, 1981).
———. "Teryani stełtzagortzutʻyan ařandznahatkutʻyunneri mi kʻani hartser." *L,* 1988/7, 32–42.
Mkrtchyan, V. "Vahan Teryaně Javaḥkʻum." *SG,* 1960/8, 113–16.
Oganian, Z. "Obshchnost' poezii A. Bloka i V. Teriana." *PBH,* 1976/1, 159–68.
Ōhanyan, A. "Teryani 'Kʻnarakan poemi' herosě." *L,* 1988/2, 22–39.
Partizuni, V. *Vahan Teryaně žamanakakitsneri hušerum.* (Erevan, 1964).
———. "Vahan Teryan." *PBH,* 1965/2, 61–76.
———. "Vahan Teryaně ev Ełiše Charentsě." *SG,* 1966/2, 139–59.
———. " 'Tʻumanyan ev Teryan' problemi šurjě." *PBH,* 1970/2, 137–58.

———. "Ējer V. Teryani 'skzbnakan krt'ut'yan' patmut'yunits." *L,* 1982/6, 32–42.
———. *Teryani kensapatumě.* (Erevan, 1984).
———. " 'Mt'nšaŀi anurjneri' aṙajin ardzagank'nerě." *SG,* 1985/5, 117–27.
———. *Vahan Teryani het.* (Erevan, 1989).
Ṙštuni, H. "Teryaně ev dari grakan mt'nolortě." *SG,* 1985/5, 128–34.
Sahaṙuni, S. "Vahan Tēreani tuně." *HK,* 32 (1954/12), 85–87.
Sargsyan, G. "Myasnikyaně ev Teryaně." *SG,* 1975/3, 125–34.
Sargsyan, Ḥ. *Vahan Teryan.* (Erevan, 1926).
Sarinyan, S. "Vahan Teryani haytnut'yuně." *L,* 1985/5, 39–50.
Sedrakyan, M. *Teryani Gandzan.* (Erevan, 1986).
Simēōneants, A. "Yušer Vahan Tēreani ew ir ěnkerneri masin." *HK,* 24 (1946/4), 80–89.
Suk'iasyan, S. *Ējer Vahan Teryani kyank'its.* (Erevan, 1959).
T'amrazyan, H. *Vahan Teryan.* (Erevan, 1985).
Taragir, "Handipumner V. Tēreani het." *HK,* 10 (1931–32/1), 87–96.
Ter-Grigoryan, N. "Vahan Teryani mankut'yuně." *SG,* 1964/8, 80–98.
Terian, N. "Dva pis'ma Vaana Teriana." *BEH,* 1972/1, 169–71.
Tērtērean, A. *Vahan Tērean, tsnork'i tzarawi ew haštut'ean ergichě.* (Tiflis, 1910).
T'op'chyan, Ē. *Vahan Teryan.* (Erevan, 1945).
T'umanyan, N. "Teryaně ev T'umanyaně." *T,* 1950/9, 77–80.
V. K. "Tērean, Verlēn ew urišner" and "Tērean ew Potlēr." *B,* 127 (1969), 313–21; 128 (1970), 127–40.
Yakobean, S. *Vahan Tērean: grakan-k'nnadatakan verlutzut'iwn.* (Berlin, 1923).
Zak'aryan, A. "Vahan Teryani žaṙangut'yuně." *SG,* 1964/11, 145–59.

T'ĒRZEAN, T'OVMAS (1840–1909)

Born in Constantinople to an Armenian father and an Italian mother. A poet and playwright. Educated at the Murat-Ṙap'ayēlean school in Venice (1852–58) and became a teacher upon his return. Wrote the libretto for *Aršak II* (in both Armenian and Italian), the first Armenian opera, which was based on the accounts of both P'awstos Buzand or *Buzandaran patmut'iwnk',* i.e., *The Epic Histories,* and Movsēs Ḥorenatsi. It was put to music by Tigran Chuḥačean (1837–98) in 1868 and remains popular today.

Collections

Banasteŀtzut'eants amboŀjakan hawak'atzon. 2 vols. (Venice, 1929).

Texts (plays)

Sanduḥt. (Constantinople, 1862; Venice, 1871; Jerusalem, 1881 [includes French text]).
Aršak II. (Constantinople, 1871).
Yovsēp' Geŀetsik. (Venice, 1872).

Other works

Banali hay-gaŀŀierēn k'erakanut'ean Ōllēntorfi drut'eamb. (Constantinople, 1868).
Nor k'erakanut'iwn gaŀŀierēn lezui Ōllēntorfi drut'eamb. (Constantinople, 1868).
Gortznakan k'erakanut'iwn franserēn lezui. (Venice, 1873, 1879, 1882, 1886, 1891, 1896, 1899).
Erkrordakan krt'ut'iwn. (Constantinople, 1878–79).

Mtamarzutʻiwn ěst Bēlisiēi. 2 vols. (Constantinople, 1879, 1885 [Vol. 1]).
Hrahangkʻ. (Venice, 1882). (Exercises for *Gortznakan . . .* above).
Kʻerakanutʻiwn ašḫarhabar lezui. (Constantinople, 1882, 1884).
Naḫnakan ěntʻertsaran patkerazard. (Constantinople, 1884).

Translations

ENGLISH ANTHOLOGIES

ALP, 44–45.
AP, 128–29.

FRENCH

Fēruḫḫan, M. *Sanduḫt.* (Jerusalem, 1881). (Armenian text with French translation).

FRENCH ANTHOLOGIES

APA, 63–66.

ITALIAN ANTHOLOGIES

LPAM, 107–18.

Criticism

Chōpanean, A. "Tʻovmas Tʻērzean." *ANA,* 1909/1–2, 35–39.
———. "Tʻovmas Tʻērzean." *B,* 94 (1936), 289–93.
Dawtʻean, S. "Tʻovmas Tʻērzean." *AM,* 1903, 509–13.
Eremean, S. "Kʻnarakan Tʻērzeaně." *B,* 88 (1931), 80–84.
Gamēr, "Uruagitzner–Tʻovmas Tʻērzean." *M,* 1904/15, 233.
Iskandaryan, S. "Tʻovmas Tʻerzyani kʻnnadatakan žaṙangutʻyuně." *L,* 1982/11, 29–37.
———. "Tʻovmas Tʻerzyaně žamanaki kʻnnadatutʻyan gnahatmamb." *BEH,* 1983/2, 158–65.
———. "Tʻovmas Tʻerzyani dramaturgian." *PBH,* 1984/4, 99–107.
———. "Tʻurkʻakan bṙnapetutʻyan ḫarazanumě Tʻovmas Tʻerzyani stełtzagortzutʻyan mej." *L,* 1988/3, 33–40.
Mamikonyan, K. "Tʻovmas Tʻerzyani stełtzagortzutʻyuně." *L,* 1974/9, 44–55.
Yarutʻiwnean, A. "Grakan dimastuerner, Tʻovmas Tʻērzean." *AM,* 1903, 825–30.

TIWSAB, SRBUHI (c1841–1901)

Born Srbuhi Vahanean to a well-to-do family in Constantinople. Educated privately. One of her tutors was Mkrtich Pēšiktʻašlean (q.v.). Her deteriorating health compelled her to seek treatment in Paris (1889–91). Her daughter's untimely death in 1891 shattered her, and she spent her remaining years in total seclusion.

Collections

Łazaryan, H. *Erker mi hatorov.* (Erevan, 1959).
Erker. (Erevan, 1981).

Texts

Mayta. (Constantinople, 1883).
Siranoyš. (Constantinople, 1884 [cover says 1885], 1925).
Arakʻsia kam Varžuhi. (Constantinople, 1887 [cover says 1886]).

Criticism

Ačaṙyan, H. "Tikin Srbuhi Tyusab." *EJ,* 1971/1–3, 41–45.

Alpōyačean, A. "Usumnasirutʻiwn Srbuhi Tiwsabi." *B,* 58 (1900), 359–63, 466–75, 552–58. Reprinted separately, Venice, 1901.
A[rpʻiarean], T. "Ōruan maherě." *M*, 1901/2, 30–32.
L. "Tikin Srbuhi Tiwsab." *Murč,* 1901/6, 283–87.
[Mamurean, M.] "Mayta." *AM,* 1883, 339–43.
Mērsētēs. "Gragētn u hasarakutʻiwně (Tikin Tiwsabi mahuan aṙtiw)." *M,* 1901/2, 17–22.
N. S. "Andznakan yišatakner Tikin Tiwsabi u Dprotsasēr Tiknants vray." *M,* 1901/6, 89–91.
Šahnur. "Tʻłtʻaktsutʻiwn." *AM,* 1883, 331–39. (On *Mayta*).
Šaruryan, A. "Knoj dati paštpaně." *SG,* 1960/8, 164–68.
———. "Srbuhi Tyusab." *PBH,* 1961/3–4, 166–80.
———. "Srbuhi Tyusaběbanastełtz u hraparakaḥos." *T,* 1961/9, 69–80.
———. *Srbuhi Tyusab: kyankʻě ev stełtzagortzutʻyuně.* (Erevan, 1963). (Includes bibliography, pp. 215–45).
Zōhrap, G. "Mayta." *Erkragunt,* 10 (1883), 305–12.

TʻLKATINTSI, (c1860–1915)

Pen names: Pʻaṙnak, Tʻlkatintsi.

Born Yovhannēs Yarutʻiwnean in the village of Tʻlkatin (Ḥuylu, near Harput, Turkey). Moved to Harput at an early age and studied at the local Smbatean school. After teaching in a numbr of schools, he became permanently associated with the Kedronakan school of Harput, which attained prestige as one of the finest schools in the Armenian provinces under his directorship. At the outbreak of the Armenian massacres of 1915, Tʻlkatintsi went into hiding at the home of a Muslim friend, but he was caught and imprisoned. He was killed outside Harput, after having learned of the deportation of his second wife, his only son, and his six daughters, who were never seen again.

Collections

Tʻlkatintsin ew ir gortzě. (Boston, 1927).
Gyułi kyankʻě. (Erevan, 1966).

Texts

Or mēkun etewēn[?] (Boston, 1912).

Works in periodicals

M, 1899/8–9, 239–40. 1905/13, 201–3. 1906/18, 273–75; 19, 292–93. 1908/10, 198; 11, 216; 12–13, 244; 17, 352; 18, 373.
AM, 1908, 942–44, 1058–62. Suppl. 2, 170–82. Suppl. 3, 369–78. 1909, 760–66.
ANA, 1909/11–12, 272–76. 1929/3, 19–20.
Nor gir (New York). 12 (1950/3–4), 207–56.

Criticism

Aznavuryan, G. "Anhayt ējer hay nahatakneri grakan žaṙangutʻyunits." *EJ,* 1965/2–4, 43–57. (Previously unpublished letters and other material by Komitas, G. Zōhrap, D. Varužan, Siamantʻō, Tʻlkatintsi, Ṙ. Zardarean, and Ṙ. Sewak).
Gasbarean, M. (Jrvēž). *Tasě tari Tʻlkatintsiin šunchin tak ew dēmkʻer u dēpkʻer.* (Fresno and Beirut, 1968).
Gisak. "Tʻlkatintsin (mankutʻean yišataknerēs)." *M,* 1900/39, 612–13.

Hamasteł. "Gawaṙě ew T'lkatintsin." *HK,* 6 (1927–28/6), 49–57; 7, 63–72.
Ḥantsean, G. "Tḥur patker mě." *AM,* 1901, 873–78.
Karapetyan, L. "T'lkatintsin ev 'Vałvan' grakanut'yuně." *T,* 1965/8, 41–52.
———. *T'lkatintsi.* (Erevan, 1966).
Parsamean, M. "Gawaṙi harazat dēmk'ě T'lkatintsin." *Z* (amsat'ert'), 2 (1957/1–2), 9, 12.
Šahinean, G. "Tandē ew T'lkatintsi." *AM,* 1902, 334–35.
———. "Tant'ē ew T'lkatintsi." *B,* 123 (1965), 360–61.
Step'anyan, K. "T'lkatintsi." *SG,* 1968/2, 142–44.
Yarut'iwnean, A. "T'lkatintsin." *AM,* 1904, 463–65.
———. "Grakan k'ronik." *AM,* 1908, 626–28.
———. "T'lkatintsin." *AM,* 1908, 574.
Žamkochean, H. *Mer aržēk'nerě. T'lkatintsin ew ir k'ronikneře.* (Cairo, 1949).

T'NKĚREAN, SŌNA (1918–1986)

Born Sōna Tēr Margarean in Constantinople. Short story writer. Educated at the celebrated Esayean and Kedronakan Armenian schools of her birthplace. Taught and held administrative positions in the local Armenian schools. She lived in the United States for the last five years of her life.

Texts (stories)

Keank'i mējēn. (Istanbul, 1950).
Keank'in het. (Istanbul, 1968–69).

T'ŌP'ALEAN, BIWZAND (1902–1970)

Born in Aintab (Gaziantep, Turkey). A survivor of the genocide, he took up permanent residence in France in the 1930s. Set up a printing press in Paris ("Arak's") and published the literary periodical *Andastan* (1952–69). His artistic talent found expression in both poetry and painting.

Collections

Arevagal. (Erevan, 1968).
B. T'ōp'alean. (Paris, 1970). (Includes "Miayn 1500 tołov" and *Matenašar žamanakakits sp'iwṙk'ahay banastełtsut'ean*).
Hatěntir. (Paris, [1970]).

Texts

Aygahandēs: k'ert'uatzner, 1924–29. (Aleppo, 1930).
Arewagal (k'ert'uatzner). (Paris, 1936).
Hamaynakan sēr. (Paris, 1950).
Hraḥałut'iwn. (Paris, 1953).
Ardzanagir. (Paris, 1960).
Daštankar. (Paris, 1976).

Translations

French anthologies

LPA, 307–8.

Italian anthologies

LPAM, 293–98.

Criticism

Baluean, H. "Aygahandēs: k'ert'uatzner B. T'ōp'aleani." *Z,* 2 (1931), 35.

———. "Arewagal: banastełtzut'iwnner Biwzand T'ōp'aleani." *Z* (taregirk'), 1 (1937), 211–12.

Taturyan, Š. "Byuzand T'op'alyan." *SG,* 1970/8, 146–48.

T'ORGOMYAN, TZERUN (1896–1986)

Pen name: Tzerun T'orgomyan.

Born Tzerun Dełtrikyan in Van. Received his elementary education in his native city, which he fled amid death, destruction, and deportation, finding his way to Tiflis. Became a journalist and published the literary almanac *Hrazdan* (Tiflis, 1918), along with *Ardzagank'* and *Karmir astł* (both in Krasnodar, 1918–21). Blinded in the early 1930s due to an accident.

Collections

Erkeri žołovatzu. Vol. 1. (Tiflis, 1926).

Erker. (Erevan, 1948).

Texts (novels and stories)

Ałayi p'ešk'ešě. (Tiflis, 1930).

Patmvatzk'ner. (Tiflis, 1930).

Hordzank'um. (Erevan, 1931).

Mřayl ōrer. (Tiflis, 1935).

Kanach bardzunk'ner. (Tiflis, 1935).

Kaputak jreri mot. (Erevan, 1936).

Žptatsoł kyank'ě. (Erevan, 1936).

Ḥndut'yun. (Tiflis, 1936).

Bnut'yan grkum. (Erevan, 1939).

Artzat'e žapaven. (Erevan, 1940).

Bldan jurě. (Erevan, 1940).

Harazat larer. (Erevan, 1947).

Patmvatzk'ner. (Erevan, 1951).

Anmar krakner. (Tbilisi, 1953; Erevan, 1955, 1959).

Herosi mahov. (Tbilisi, 1956).

Patmvatzk'ner. (Erevan, 1956).

Hušer. (Erevan, 1962).

Alekotz tzově. (Erevan, 1965).

Anmořats ōrer. (Erevan, 1967).

Patmvatzk'ner. (Erevan, 1973).

Hoget'ov huyzer. (Tbilisi, 1975).

Andznver martikě. (Tbilisi, 1978).

Aletzup' srter. (Erevan, 1981).

Translations

RUSSIAN

Mililova, A. *Rodnye struny. Rasskazy.* (Tbilisi, 1961).

Criticism

Štikyan, S. "Hušeri čanaparhov." *SG,* 1983/11, 124–26.

T'OT'OVENTS, VAHAN (1894–1938)

Born and educated in Mezre (Harput, Turkey). Left his birthplace in 1909, went to Paris and New York, and studied at the University of Wisconsin (1912–15). As a volunteer, he participated in the self-defense of Van and Erzurum. Spent the years 1917–20 in Transcaucasia and visited the United States a second time (1920–22), before returning to Armenia permanently in 1922. The Stalinist purges claimed his life.

Collections

Hayreni patmuatzk'ner. (Beirut, 1939).
Erker. (Erevan, 1957).
Kapuyt tzałikner. (Erevan, 1972).
Erker. 2 vols. (Erevan, 1988, 1989). (3 vols. projected).

Texts

Awerak. (Constantinople, 1906, 1908).
Sring. (Constantinople, 1909).
Ołb anmahut'ean. (Tiflis, 1917). (Poem).
Tonon. (Tiflis, 1917; Beirut, n.d.). (Story).
Arewelk'. (Tiflis, 1918). (Poem).
Ařawōtin mēj. (Tiflis, 1921).
Garunin sirtě. (Constantinople, 1921).
Hayastani Ton-K'išot'ě. (Constantinople, 1921).
Patmuatzk'ner, ařajin šark'. (Constantinople, 1921). (Stories).
Patmuatzk'ner. (Boston, 1921). (Stories).
Doktor Burbonyan. (Vałaršapat, 1923). (Satirical novel).
Mahvan bataleon. (Erevan, 1923). (Play).
Połpate čaš. (Erevan, 1924). (Play).
Sełbosě. (Erevan, 1924).
Im horak'uyrě. (Erevan, 1925). (Stories).
Nor Byuzandion. (Erevan, 1925; Beirut, 1958). (Play).
Sasma tzřer. (Erevan, 1925). (Play).
Kritiko-tzitzał. (Erevan, 1927).
Nyu-York'. (Erevan, 1927). (Prose).
Amerika. (Erevan, 1929). (Stories).
Asatur ev Kleopatra. (Erevan, 1929). (Story).
Lao-ho. (Erevan, 1929, 1930).
Bak'u. 3 vols. (Erevan, 1930–34). (Novel).
Erku sur. (Erevan, 1930). (Play).
Širvanzade. (Erevan, 1930). (Biography).
Hay azgi "p'rkich" dašnakneře. (Moscow, 1931).
Kyank'ě hin hřovmeakan čanaparhi vra. (Erevan, 1933, 1966, 1979; Beirut, 1956). (Prose).
Ałavniner. (Erevan, 1934, 1957, 1966). (Story).
Hovnat'an ordi Eremiayi. (Erevan, 1934). (Story).
Hrkizvatz t'łt'er. (Erevan, 1934). (Story).
Bats-kapuyt tzałikner. (Erevan, 1935). (Story).
Moḥrakuyt. (Erevan, 1936). (Play).

Translations

English

Kudian, M. *Scenes from an Armenian Childhood.* (New York, 1962).
———. *Tell Me, Bella.* (London, 1972).
———. *Jonathan, Son of Jeremiah.* (London, 1985).

French

Verdun, P. *Une enfance arménienne.* (Paris: Julliard, 1985). ("Traduit de l'anglais," "revu par Jean-Pierre Mahé").

Russian

Zhizn' na staroi rimskoi doroge. Povesti i rasskazy. (Moscow, 1970).

Criticism

Arzumanyan, S. "Kyank'ě p'ok'r ktavi vra." *SG,* 1960/10, 168–89.
———. *Vahan T'ot'ovents.* (Erevan, 1961).
———. "Vahan T'ot'ovents." *SG,* 1966/6, 124–25.
Gevorgyan, A. "T'ot'oventsi arvesti k'narakanut'yuně." *SG,* 1974/11, 126–30.
———. "Vahan T'ot'oventsi steltzagortzakan ulu hartserits." *SG,* 1978/11, 161–65.
Ḥaṙatyan, A. "Vahan T'ot'oventsě Andraniki masin." *PBH,* 1990/1, 3–14.
Manukyan, S. "Vahan T'ot'ovents." *SG,* 1958/6, 139–49.
———. "Vahan T'ot'oventsi ergitzakan erkerě." *T,* 1958/7, 17–26.
———. *Vahan T'ot'ovents.* (Erevan, 1959).
Melik'set'yan, S. "Mer T'ot'oventsě." *SG,* 1971/11, 156–59.
T'oranean, T'. "Mer niwt'ě T'ot'oventsn ēr." *AND,* 17 (n.d.), 137–41.
Zak'aryan, M. "V. T'ot'oventsi 'Kyank'ě hin hṙomeakan čanaparhi vra' vipakě." *SG,* 1984/8, 137–41.

T'UMANEAN, YOVHANNĒS (1869–1923)

Born in the village of Dseł (Loṙi, Armenia). Received an incomplete education in Jalalōłli (now Step'anavan, Armenia) and the Nersisean School in Tiflis (1883–87). Resided permanently in Tiflis and was closely involved in community affairs. Such activities brought him into conflict with the Russian authorities, who incarcerated him twice, in 1908–09 and 1911–12. Founded (with others) and headed the Union of Armenian Writers in Tiflis (1912–21). From 1915–22, he actively organized relief for orphans and refugees fleeing the Armenian genocide and sought support for the Armenian state. Visited Constantinople in 1921 and underwent serious surgery upon his return. Died at a hospital in Moscow on his way to Berlin for treatment. He was buried in Tiflis.

Collections

Banasteltzut'iwnner. (Constantinople, 1922 [cover says 1923]).
Erkeri žołovatzu. (Erevan, 1926).
Makintsyan, P. *Ĕntir grvatzk'ner.* (Erevan, 1929).
Hek'iat'ner. (Erevan, 1930).
Poemner. (Erevan, 1933).
Charents, E. *Gełarvestakan erker.* (Erevan, 1934).
Legendner, balladner, erger. (Erevan, 1934).
Tērn u tzaṙan ew uriš patmuatzk'ner. (Bucharest, 1934).
Patmvatzk'ner. (Erevan, 1937).

Banastełtzut'yunner. (Erevan, 1938).
Erger. 5 books. (Erevan, 1938).
Hek'iat'ner. 2 vols. (Erevan, 1938).
Kendanineri keank'its. (Erevan, 1938).
T'umanyan, N. *Erker.* (Erevan, 1938).
———. *T'umanyanĕ k'nnadat.* (Erevan, 1939).
Hatĕntir. (Erevan, 1940).
Sahakyan, S., et. al. *Erkeri žołovatzu.* 6 vols. (Erevan, 1940–59).
Ĕntir erker. 2 vols. (Erevan, 1940–41).
Erger, k'ar̄eakner . . . hēk'iat'ner. (Venice, 1944).
Hek'iat'ner. (Erevan, 1944).
P'ēchikean, E. *Žołovrdakan erger, poēmner.* (Venice, 1944).
Mankakan erger. (Erevan, 1945).
Patmuatzk'ner u hēk'iat'ner. (Cairo, 1945).
P'njik (erkeri žołovatzu). (Stuttgart, 1947).
K'ałuatzoyk'. (Cairo, 1948).
Patmvatzk'ner. (Erevan, 1948).
Ĕntir erker. (Erevan, 1953).
Erker. 2 vols. (Erevan, 1958).
Hatĕntir. (Erevan, 1959).
Hek'iat'ner. (Erevan, 1967).
Akhverdian, L. *O Rossii i russkoi kul'ture: stat'i i pis'ma.* (Erevan, 1969).
Erkeri žołovatzu. 4 vols. (Erevan, 1969).
Hatĕntir. (Erevan, 1969).
Safrazbekyan, I. *Arvesti masin.* (Erevan, 1969).
———. *Šek'spiri masin.* (Erevan, 1969).
Šahazizyan, A. *Asuyt'ner, t'evavor ḥosk'er, kensagrakan ev matenagitakan tełekut'yunner.* (Erevan, 1969).
Ĕntir erker. (Erevan, 1978).
Erker. (Erevan, 1980).
Karmenyan, K. *Banastełtzut'yunner ev legendner.* (Erevan, 1981).
Haḥverdyan, L. *Ĕntir erker.* 2 vols. (Erevan, 1985).
Safrazyan, K. *Banastełtzut'yunner, k'ar̄yakner, poemner, legendner ev balladner.* (Erevan, 1986). (In Armenian and Russian).
K'ar̄yakner ev balladner. (Erevan, 1987).
Erkeri liakatar žołovatzu. (Erevan, 1988–). (6 vols. to 1994; 10 vols. projected).
Hek'iat'ner. (Erevan, 1988).

Texts (verse, stories, and tales)

Banastełtzut'iwnner. 2 vols. (Moscow, 1890, 1892).
Dašnakner. (Tiflis, 1893, 1896 [revised]).
Lor̄etsi Sak'on. (Tiflis, 1896).
Banastełtzut'iwnner, 1892–1899. (Tiflis, 1899).
Yovhannēs T'umaneants. (Tiflis, 1899).
Banastełtzut'iwnner. (Tiflis, 1903).
Hazaran-Blbul. (Tiflis, 1903).
Anoyš. (Tiflis, 1904, 1916; Constantinople, 1921 [with *T'mkaberdi ar̄umĕ*], 1922, 1959; New York, 1923; Aleppo, 1925; Beirut, 1935 [with *T'mkaberdi ar̄umĕ*], 1953; Cairo, 1946; Erevan, 1952).

Legendner. (Tiflis, 1904).
Sasuntsi Dawiťě. (Tiflis, 1904; Erevan, 1934, 1936, 1941, 1943, 1950; Cairo, 1939; Istanbul [n.d.]).
Gikʻorě. (Tiflis, 1907, 1908; Erevan, 1924, 1936; Istanbul, 1939 [in Western Armenian], 1960; Beirut, 1970). (Story).
Kakʻawi ergě. (Tiflis, 1908).
Šunn u katun. (N.p. 1908; Tiflis, 1909; Erevan, 1927, 1935, 1942, 1948, 1982; Paris, 1969).
Ałuēsě. (Tiflis, 1909; Erevan, 1939).
Anbaḥt vačařakanner. ([Tiflis, 1909]; Erevan, 1949; Paris, 1969).
Anyałť akʻlorě. ([Tiflis], 1909; Erevan, 1976).
Gařnik aḥper. (Tiflis, 1909; Erevan, 1946).
Mi kaťil mełr. (Tiflis, 1909, 1911; Erevan, 1936, 1948; Paris, 1969 [in Western Armenian]).
Ťmkaberdi ařumě. (Tiflis, 1909; Constantinople, 1921; Erevan, 1958, 1959 [with "Anuš"]; Paris, 1969).
Tzitě. ([Tiflis], 1909).
Ulikě. (Tiflis, 1909).
Ḥōsoł dzukě. ([Tiflis], 1910).
Tērn u tzařan. (Tiflis, 1910; Erevan, 1925, 1936, 1985).
Oski kʻałakʻě: hndkakan hēkʻiať. (Tiflis, 1911; Erevan, 1985).
Kʻēf anołin kʻēf chi paksil (arewelean patmuatzkʻ). (Tiflis, 1911; Erevan, 1941, 1973, 1985).
Pʻokʻrik dzknorsě. (Tiflis, 1912).
Kʻaj Nazarě. (Tiflis, 1912; Erevan, 1931, 1937, 1944, 1985; Istanbul, 1963; Paris, 1969).
Hayrenikʻis het. (Tiflis, 1916).
Nałaš Yovnaťaně ew nra, Kʻuchak Nahapeti u Sayeať-Novayi sērě. (Tiflis, 1916).
Kʻařeakner. (Tiflis, 1920; Erevan, 1934, 1938).
Gēlě. (Erevan, 1925, 1983).
Ełjerun. (Erevan, 1928).
Arjavors. (Erevan, 1929).
Gabo bidzu šeramapahuťyuně. (Erevan, 1935).
Chari verjě. (Erevan, 1937, 1948, 1966, 1975, 1982, 1987).
Kałnu tnvornerě. (Erevan, 1938).
Ťřchuni mtatzmunkʻě. (Erevan, 1939).
Čampʻordner. (Erevan, 1939).
Pʻisiki gangatě. (Erevan, 1941, 1983).
Pʻokʻrik erkragortzě. (Erevan, 1944).
Połos-Petros. (Erevan, 1945).
Sayať-Nova. (Erevan, 1945, 1963). (Essays and lectures).
Motzakn u mrjyuně. (Erevan, 1948).
Pʻarvana. (Erevan, 1949; Istanbul, 1960 [in Western Armenian]; Erevan, 1966; Paris, 1969).
Tzałikneri ergě. (Erevan, 1950).
Chaḥchaḥ ťagavorě. (Erevan, 1957).
Sutasaně. (Erevan, 1958).
Aḥťamar. (Erevan, 1959).

Katsin aḥper. (Erevan, 1959).
Osku karas. (Erevan, 1959).
Sutlik orskanĕ. (Erevan, 1960, 1981, 1983).
Zarmanali ašułĕ. (Erevan, 1969).
Aławnu vank'ĕ ew Ḥōsoł dzukĕ. (Paris, 1970).
Irikun. (Erevan, 1976).
Bzezi dprotsĕ. (Erevan, 1983).
"Ējer Hovhannes T'umanyani antip namaknerits." *BEH,* 1984/3, 130–40.
Sutasanĕ. (Erevan, 1984).
"Tałov ekav . . ." *SG,* 1987/10, 80.
"Hovh. T'umanyani mi antip hodvatz." *PBH,* 1988/2, 201–11.

Translations

English

Abeghian, A. "Kiko's Death." *Hairenik Weekly,* May 3, 1956, 6, 8.
Kudian, M. *The Bard of Loree.* (London, 1970). (Poems and tales).
Hamalian, L. "Before a Painting by Ayvazovsky." *Ararat,* Spring, 1963, 61.
Mangouni, N. "The Big Jar of Gold." *Lraber,* August 19, 1961, 4.
———. "The Handless Girl." *Lraber,* August 24, 1961/4; August 26, 1961, 4.
———. "The Master and the Servant." *Lraber,* August 29, 1961, 4.
———. "The Talking Fish." *Lraber,* September 9, 1961, 4.
Manukean, M. "Homesickness." *S,* 1971, 417.
———. "Parvana." *S,* 1971, 227–30.
Mesrobian, P. *Gikor.* (Erevan, 1950).
Rottenberg, D., and Bean, B. *Hovhannes Toumanian: A Selection of Stories, Lyrics and Epic Poems.* (New York: T&T Publishers, 1971).
Tempest, P. "Far from Home." *SL,* 1969/9, 165.
———. "The Kitten's Complaint." *SL,* 1969/9, 165.
Tolegian, A. *David of Sassoun.* (New York, 1961).
T'orikean, Y. *T'umaneani Sasuntsi Dawit'.* (New York, 1971). (Armenian and English).

English Anthologies

AFT, 27–31, 43–62, 137–41.
ALP, 62, 79–80.
AP, 186–89.
SAP, 1–4.
WM, 59–62.

French

Champenois, J. *Œuvres choisies.* (Moscow, 1969).
D'Herminy, S. "Anouche." *REArm,* 10 (1930/1), 85–116.
"Dans les montagnes d'Arménie," "L'Adieu de Sirius," "La vieille bénédiction," "Illusion," "Descente." *AND,* 18 (n.d.), 97–102.
Gaspard, A. *La geste de David le Sassouniote.* (Geneva, [1945]).
Hekimian, G. "Requiem." *Notre voix,* 1965/7, 1.
"A minuit, suspendue au ciel . . ." *Pour les peuples d'Orient.* 1913/16, 9–12.
Portookalian, V. "La Saule." *Šinarar,* 1960/47, 16.
Tchobanian, A. "Parmi les montagnes d'Arménie," "Appel." *Hommage à l'Arménie.* (Paris, 1919), 16–18.

French anthologies

APA, 107–12.
Gamara, P. *E,* 43–47.
FPA, 47.
LPA, 191–97.

German

"Das Licht des Herrn. (Gedichte)." *Armenier und Armenien.* (Sofia, 1941), 57.
Das Taubenkloster. (Berlin, 1972).

German anthologies

AD, 40–44.
ALG, 128.
AN, 67–71.

Italian

"Tra le montagne d'Armenia," "Appello." *Armenia,* 2 (1916/11), 7.

Italian anthologies

LPAM, 151–63.

Russian collections

Akhverdian, L., and Mkrtchian, L. *Izbrannye proizvedeniia.* 3 vols. (Erevan, 1969).
Gorodetskii, S. *Izbrannye stikhotvoreniia.* (Tiflis, 1919).
Grebnev, N. *Chetverostishiia.* (Erevan, 1968).
[Grigor'ian, K.] *Stikhotvoreniia i poemy.* (Leningrad, 1958, 1969).
Izbrannoe: stikhi i proza. (Tiflis, 1937).
Izbrannye proizvedeniia. (Moscow, 1937).
Khachatriants, Ia., et al. *Skazki.* (Erevan, 1985).
Khitarova, S. *Izbrannye proizvedeniia.* (Moscow, 1946).
Legendy i skazki. (Erevan, 1948).
Lirika. (Moscow, 1969).
Madatian, A. *Skazki.* (Erevan, 1948).
[Mkrian, M.] *Izbrannye sochineniia.* (Erevan, 1956).
Ovnan, G. *Izbrannoe.* (Erevan, 1969).
Safrazyan, K. *Banastełtzut'yunner, k'ar̄yakner, poemner, legendner ev balladner.* (Erevan, 1986). (Russian and Armenian).
Shaginian, M. *Izbrannye sochineniia.* (Erevan and Moscow, 1950).
Shervinskii, S. *Izbrannoe.* (Erevan, 1941).
Tumanian, N. *Izbrannye proizvedeniia.* (Moscow, 1952).
———, and Indzhikian, A. *Izbrannye proizvedeniia.* 2 vols. (Moscow, 1960).

Spanish anthologies

APAS, 167–72.

Multilingual

Połosyan, A. *Hayots ler̄nerum.* (Erevan, 1969). (Armenian text with translations in 13 languages, including English, French, German, Russian).
Safrazbekyan, Ṙ. *Aḥt'amar.* (Erevan, 1969). (Armenian text with translations in 14 languages including English, French, Russian).

Bibliographies

Babaian, A. *Ovanes Tumanian: bibliografiia russkikh perevodov (1893–1968).* (Erevan, 1969).

Ishkhanian, R. *Ovanes Tumanian na iazykakh narodov SSSR i inostrannykh iazykakh.* (Erevan, 1983).
Jrbašyan, Ēd. *Hovhannes Tʻumanyan (1869–1923): Matenagitutʻyun.* (Erevan, 1961).
Šahazizayan, A. *Hovhannes Tʻumanyan (1869–1969). Asuytʻner, tʻevavor ḥoskʻer, kensagrakan ev matenagitakan tełekutʻyunner.* (Erevan, 1969).
Tʻaščyan, L. *Hovhannes Tʻumanyanĕ SSHM žołovurdneri ev ōtar lezunerov. Matenagit. (1893–1983).* (Erevan, 1983).

Criticism

Abełyan, H. "Nor ējer Hovhannes Tʻumanyani banastełtzakan žaṙangutʻyunits." *PBH,* 1977/1, 111–16.
Aharonean, V. "Amenayn hayots banastełtzĕ." *HK,* 14 (1935–36/2), 125–32; 3, 126–39; 4, 126–37; 5, 137–50; 6, 140–54; 7, 144–55; 8, 114–24.
———. *Yovhannēs Tʻumanean, mardĕ ew banastełtzĕ.* (Boston, 1936).
Akhverdian, L. "Hovhannès Toumanian (1869–1923)." *OO,* 123 (March 1969), 170–73.
———. "Hovanes Tumanian." *SL,* 1969/9, 160–64. (In English).
———. *Mir Tumaniana. Put' poeta.* (Moscow, 1969).
———. *Tumanian.* (Erevan, 1969).
Ałababyan, S. "Hovhannes Tʻumanyanĕ ev ardiakanutʻyunĕ." *L,* 1979/9, 7–19.
———. "Norovi ĕntʻertsvatz Tʻumanyanĕ." *SG,* 1966/9, 138–44.
Ałbalean, N. "Y. Tʻumaneani 'Aławnu vankʻĕ'." *HK,* 25 (1947/3), 66–72.
———. "Nikol Ałbalyani namaknerĕ Hovh. Tʻumanyanin (1902–1912 tʻtʻ.)." *PBH,* 1989/4, 198–220.
Aṙustamyan, S. *Hovh. Tʻumanyani stełtzagortzutʻyan usutsman im pʻordzĕ.* (Erevan, 1980).
Arveladze, B. "Hovhannes Tʻumanyanĕ vrats mtavorkanutʻyan gnahatmamb." *SG,* 1969/9, 116–21.
Asmaryan, L. "Tʻumanyanĕ grakan kʻnnadat." *L,* 1979/9, 35–41.
Atabekian, M. *Ovanes Tumanian—literaturnyi kritik.* (Erevan, 1946).
Avdalbegyan, Tʻ. *Hay gyułĕ Hovhannes Tʻumanyani erkerum.* (Erevan, 1925).
Avetisyan, Ṙ. "Šałkapavor kapaktsutʻyamb homaniš bard storadasakan naḥadasutʻyunnerĕ Tʻumanyani stełtzagortzutʻyan mej." *L,* 1978/6, 27–34.
Avetisyan, Z. "Baṙĕntrutʻyunĕ ev baṙōgtagortzumĕ Tʻumanyani poeziayum." *PBH,* 1968/3, 169–74.
———. "Kensakan pʻordz ev mtahłatsum." *SG,* 1969/9, 148–51.
———. *Tʻumanyani stełtzagortzakan laboratorian.* (Erevan, 1973).
———. "Tʻumanyani stełtzagortzakan mtatzołutʻyan hartserits." *L,* 1979/8, 42–48.
Ayvazyan, L. "Hovhannes Tʻumanyanĕ ṙus ĕntʻertsołin." *SG,* 1969/9, 96–101.
Babayan, A. "Hovhannes Tʻumanyani gradaranĕ." *BEH,* 1977/2, 199–204.
Bałdasaryan, E. "Tʻumanyani erkeri ketadrakan aṙandznahatkutʻyunnerĕ." *L,* 1979/11, 86–91.
Baluean, H. "Yovhannēs Tʻumaneani 'Anuš'ĕ." *Z* (amsatʻertʻ), 1 (1955/1), 2; 2, 2; 3, 4; 4, 7.
———. "Yovhannēs Tʻumaneani Anuš ōpʻeran ew Armēn Tigranean." *Z* (amsatʻertʻ), 4 (1959/1–2), 1–4.
Berkov, R. "Poet i narod v khudozhestvennom soznanii Tumaniana." *L,* 1979/8, 49–62.

Čanašean, M. "Yovhannēs Tʻumanean–tznndean 100ameakin aṙitʻov." *B,* 127 (1969), 273–77.

Čiwmpiwšean, A. *Yušahandēs Yovhannēs Tʻumaneani tznndean hariwrameaki.* (Istanbul, 1969).

Čšmarityan, Ž. "Hovhannes Tʻumanyani ʻGikʻorěʼ patmvatzkʻi lezvaočakan aṙandznahatkutʻyunnerě." *BEH,* 1974/2, 82–95.

Danielyan, K. "Hovhannes Tʻumanyani kʻaṙyaknerě." *SG,* 1984/12, 102–13.

Darbinyan, H. "Hay ev adrbejanakan žołovurdneri barekamutʻyuně Tʻumanyani erku patmvatzkʻum." *L,* 1972/1, 11–18.

———. "Tʻumanyaně ev žołovurdneri barekamutʻyuně." *L,* 1972/5, 3–14.

Darbinyan, V. "Erki hogebanakan mšakumě Tʻumanyani mot." *T,* 1957/1, 41–60.

———. "Bnagrin hamazor tʻargmanutʻyunner." *PBH,* 1969/3, 37–48.

———. "Mankan hogebanakan ēvolyutsian Hovhannes Tʻumanyani ʻIm ěnker Nesonʼ patmvatzkʻum." *L,* 1979/9, 42–46.

———. "Mankakan hogebanutʻyuně Hovhannes Tʻumanyani ʻGikʻorumʼ." *L,* 1979/10, 43–56.

———. "Knoj kerparě Hovhannes Tʻumanyani erkerum." *PBH,* 1984/4, 108–16.

Demirčyan, D. *Tʻumanyani het.* (Erevan, 1969).

Dzhanpoladian, M. "Peredacha natsional'nogo svoeobraziia v perevodakh Ov. Tumaniana iz russkogo i serbskogo eposa." *BEH,* 1968/1, 94–109.

———. "Armianskii narodnyi epos v obrabotke Tumaniana." *BEH,* 1979/2, 48–61.

Dzhrbashian, E. *Poeziia Tumaniana.* (Moscow, 1969). (Translation from Armenian).

Ełiazaryan, A. "Baṙě poeziayum (Tʻumanyan, Isahakyan, Teryan)." *PBH,* 1979/1, 75–87.

———. "Kerpari žołovrda-ēpikakan himkʻě Tʻumanyani stełtzagortzutʻyan mej." *PBH,* 1983/2, 89–99.

———. "Mardě ev žołovrdi baroyakan aržekʻnerě Hovh. Tʻumanyani stełtzagortzutʻyan mej." *L,* 1983/4, 45–53.

———. "Ašḥarhi patkerě Tʻumanyani stełtzagortzutʻyan mej." *L,* 1987/11, 59–69.

———. *Tʻumanyani poetikan ev nra žołovrdakan akunkʻnerě.* (Erevan, 1990).

Eremean, A. *Yovhannēs Tʻumanean.* (Fresno, 1957).

———. "Yovhannēs Tʻumanean ibrew giwłi banastełtz." *HA,* 37 (1923), 350–60, 433–45.

Eremean, S. "Yovhannēs Tʻumanean." *B,* 72 (1914), 233–36.

Erznkyan, A. "Hušer Tʻumanyani masin." *SG,* 1963/3, 133–42.

Galstyan, H. "Tʻumanyani kʻaṙyaknerě." *SG,* 1969/9, 136–42.

Ganalanian, O. *Charodei armianskoi poezii.* (Erevan, 1969).

———. *Ovanes Tumanian.* (Moscow, 1969).

Gasparyan, G. "Hovhannes Tʻumanyani baṙaranagrakan ditołutʻyunnerě." *PBH,* 1979/4, 65–76.

Gevorgyan, V. "Hovhannes Tʻumanyani kʻnarergutʻyan mi kʻani gtzer." *PBH,* 1967/4, 206–12.

Grigorian, K. "Pavlo Tichina i Ovanes Tumanian." *T,* 1946/11–12, 125–32.

———. *Ovanes Tumanian, 1869–1923.* (Leningrad, 1950; Moscow, 1953; Erevan, 1969).

Grigoryan, Š. *Hovhannes Tʻumanyan.* (Erevan, 1969).

Gullakyan, S. "Hovhannes T'umanyani 'K'aj Nazar' hek'iat'i gałap'arakan imastě." *T,* 1965/9, 113–20.
Gyulnazaryan, Ḥ. "Hovhannes T'umanyani antip banastełtzut'yunnerě." *L,* 1979/1, 26–36.
Ḥachikyan, Ya. "Ṙealistakan arvesti anḥonj jatagově." *PBH,* 1969/3, 15–24.
Haḥverdyan, L. "Banastełtzě ev žamanakě." *SG,* 1963/3, 103–22.
———. *T'umanyan.* (Erevan, 1969).
———. *T'umanyani ašḥarhě.* (Erevan, 1966).
Hakobyan, P. "T'umanyani verjin t'argmanut'yunnerits mekě." *BEH,* 1990/1, 14–21.
Ḥanjean, H. "Y. T'umanean." *HK,* 18 (1939–40/5), 58–67.
Harut'yunyan, G. "Mi 'partk''i patmut'yun." *EJ,* 1948/2, 68–73.
———. "T'umanyanakan vaveragir." *SG,* 1974/4, 154–55.
Hayrapetyan, A., et al. *Hovhannes T'umanyani andznakan gradaranĕ Erevanum.* Vol. 1: *Hayeren grk'er ev parberakan hratarakut'yunner.* (Erevan, 1987). Vol. 2: *Ṙuseren grk'er.* (Erevan, 1989).
Hovakimyan, B. "T'umanyani mi anhayt stełtzagortzut'yan masin." *SG,* 1976/10, 147–49.
Hovakimyan, H. "T'umanyann u t'atroně." *SG,* 1963/3, 130–32.
Hovhannes T'umanyan: hamamiut'enakan mijhamalsaranakan gitakan konferansi nyut'er. (Erevan, 1969).
Hovhannes T'umanyaně ev ṙus grakanut'yuně. (Erevan, 1956).
Hovhannisyan, Ṙ. "T'umanyaně ṙus grakanut'yan masin." *SG,* 1969/9, 92–95.
Hovhannisyan, S. "Hovhannes T'umanyaně ev Hay grołneri kovkasyan ěnkerut'yuně." *L,* 1983/10, 40–50.
———. "T'umanyaně ev hay-vratsakan barekamut'yuně." *PBH,* 1989/2, 63–74.
Inčikyan, A. "Hovhannes T'umanyaně ev haykakan hamalsaraně." *BEH,* 1967/2, 185–97.
———. *Hovhannes T'umanyan.* (Erevan, 1969).
———. "T'umanyani mankut'yuně." *L,* 1969/1, 40–58.
———. "Hovhannes T'umanyani aṙajin žołovatzun ev nra ardzagank'nerě." *BEH,* 1979/1, 73–89.
———., and Hakobyan, P. *T'umanyaně žamanakakitsneri hušerum.* (Erevan, 1969).
Inčikyan, A., and Jrbašyan, Ēd. *T'umanyan: usumnasirut'yunner ev hraparakumner.* (N.p., 1969).
Isahakean, A. "Yušer: Yovhannēs T'umanean." *Ani,* 2 (1947–48), 505–12.
———. *Mer gri anmah p'aṙk'ě, Hovhannes T'umanyan.* (Erevan, 1969).
Išḥanyan, Ṙ. "T'umanyaně hay gełarvestakan grakanut'yan lezvi masin." *BEH,* 1969/2, 33–47.
———. "T'umanyani k'aṙyakneri lezvakan ev tałachap'akan aṙandznahatkut'yunnerě." *PBH,* 1976/2, 109–20.
———. "T'umanyani lezvi zargatsman ułin." *BEH,* 1977/1, 33–51.
Janp'oladyan, M. "Puškini balladnerě T'umanyani t'argmanut'yamb." *BEH,* 1974/1, 131–39.
———. *T'umanyaně ev žołovrdakan ēposě.* (Erevan, 1969).
Jrbašyan, Ēd. "T'umanyani erkeri akademiakan hratarakut'yan masin." *SG,* 1961/5, 149–55.

———. "Hovhannes T'umanyani ergitzakan poemě." *PBH,* 1963/3, 123–36.
———. "Kyank'i ev mahvan aṙełtzvatzi handep." *SG,* 1964/2, 133–47.
———. *T'umanyani poemnerě.* (Erevan, 1964, 1986 [revised ed.]).
———. "Koratz stełtzagortzut'yan hetk'erov." *SG,* 1965/2, 156–58.
———. "Tek'stabanakan ditołut'yunner Hovhannes T'umanyani stełtzagortzut'yan masin." *BEH,* 1968/3, 110–12.
———. "Hayrenik'i metz ergichě." *BEH,* 1969/2, 3–18.
———. "T'umanyaně ev žołovrdaynut'yan problemě." *PBH,* 1969/3, 3–14.
———. *T'umanyani balladnerě.* (Erevan, 1969).
———. "Ołbergakan t'emayi zargatsumě T'umanyani k'narergut'yan mej." *BEH,* 1973/2, 78–93.
———. "Hovhannes T'umanyaně ev 1910—akan t'vakanneri grakan k'nnadatut'yuně." *PBH,* 1979/2, 28–44.
———. *Chors gagat', T'umanyan, Isahakyan, Teryan, Charents.* (Erevan, 1982).
———. "T'umanyani ardzaki skzbunk'nerě." *PBH,* 1983/2–3, 21–40.
———. *T'umanyan. Stełtzagortz. problemner.* (Erevan, 1988).
———. "Ałayan-T'umanyan: grakan žaṙangut'yan hartsi šurjě." *PBH,* 1990/2, 41–61.
Karapetyan, H. "Ṙusastaně ev ṙus žołovurdě Hovhannes T'umanyani hraparakagrut'yan mej." *SG,* 1978/10, 135–42.
Karapetyan, L. "Hovhannes T'umanyani antip namakneri masin." *PBH,* 1977/3, 107–14.
———. "Nyut'er Hovhannes T'umanyani hasarakakan gortzuneut'yunits." *PBH,* 1979/3, 147–54.
Karapetyan, M. "Hovhannes T'umanyaně haykakan kotoratzneri masin (1918–1919 t't')." *PBH,* 1987/2, 240–43.
Karapetyan, T. "Hovhannes T'umanyaně ev Vrastaně." *SG,* 1969/9, 122–26.
———. *Lusavor hayatsk'ov.* (Erevan, 1969).
———. "T'umanyaně žołovurdneri barekamut'yan jatagov." *PBH,* 1969/2, 31–42.
Karinyan, A. *Hovhannes T'umanyan (hušer, hodvatzner).* (Erevan, 1971).
Kogean, S. "Yovhannēs T'umanean (banaḥōsut'iwn)." *HA,* 37 (1923), 269–78. Reprinted separately, Vienna, 1923.
Kostanyan, A. "T'umanyani p'aṙk'ě." *SG,* 1969/9, 80–91.
Łanalanyan, A. *Hovhannes T'umanyani lirikan.* (Erevan, 1948).
Łanalanyan, H. *T'umanyani lirikan.* (Erevan, 1954).
Łazaryan, H. *Anuši stełtzagortzakan patmut'yuně.* (Erevan, 1975).
Łazaryan, M. "Neršnchoł kerparner." *PBH,* 1969/4, 49–64.
Łukasyan, V. "Haynen T'umanyani ev Teryani t'argmanut'yamb." *L,* 1969/9, 47–52.
Madoyan, G. "Hayrenašunch banastełtzn u k'ałak'atsin." *EJ,* 1969/9, 19–25.
Mahari, G. *Ayt hmut, hančareł Loṙetsin.* (Erevan, 1971).
Manukyan, S. "Hangutsayin hartseri skzbunk'ayin k'nnut'yun." *SG,* 1982/8, 142–44. (On Ēd. Jrbašyan's *Chors gagat'* . . .).
Margar, A., and Hambardzumyan, H. "Ardzanagrut'yun." *SG,* 1974/4, 155–56.
Melik'-P'ašayan, K. V. "T'umanyaně ev azgagrut'yuně." *PBH,* 1969/3, 77–84.
Melk'onyan, S. "Hovhannes T'umanyani lezvagitakan hayatsk'nerě." *T,* 1959/6, 71–82.
———. "T'umanyani stełtzagortzakan laboratoriayits." *SG,* 1960/2, 138–48.

———. *Hovhannes T'umanyani poeziayi lezun ev ocě.* (Erevan, 1969).
———. " 'Loṙetsi Sak'on' poemi stełtzagortzakan patmut'yan mi k'ani hartser." *SG,* 1975/3, 163–67.
———. "Hovhannes T'umanyaně ev hay gełarvestakan grakanut'yan lezvi zargatsumě." *L,* 1977/9, 23–40.
———. "Hovhannes T'umanyani lezvi ēvolyutsian 80–90akan t'vakannerin." *L,* 1979/8, 26–37.
———. *Hovhannes T'umanyaně ev arevelahay gełarvestakan grakanut'yan lezun.* (Erevan, 1986).
Melk'umyan, M. "Metz mankagir Hovhannes T'umanyaně ev nra mi k'ani traditsianerě." *SG,* 1959/2, 167–77.
———. *Hovhannes T'umanyaně krt'ut'yan ev dastiarakut'yan masin.* (Erevan, 1969).
Melyan, B. *T'umanyani ōrerě Mankakan gradaranum.* (Erevan, 1969).
Miasnikean, A. *Yovhannēs T'umaneani stełtzagortzut'ean sotsialakan aržēk'ě.* (Tiflis, 1923).
Mkryan, M. *Hovhannes T'umanyani stełtzagortzut'yunnerě.* (Erevan, 1981).
Narovchatov, S. *Velikii poet i grazhdanin.* (Erevan, 1970).
Nazinyan, A. "Metz banastełtzě ev žołovrdakan banahyusut'yuně." *PBH,* 1979/3, 25–36.
Ōšakan, Y. "Yovhannēs T'umanean ew ir gortzě." *HK,* 1 (1922–23/10), 40–56.
Ovanes Tumanian. Materialy Vsesoiuz. mezhuniversitetskoi nauch. konferentsii. (Erevan, 1979).
P'ap'azyan, V. "Hovhannes T'umanyan." *L,* 1969/9, 5–6.
Partizuni, V. "Hovhannes T'umanyan ev V. Teryan." *SG,* 1965/2, 107–30.
Petrosyan, E. "Ṙomantikakaně T'umanyani poeziayum." *L,* 1979/9, 30–34.
Petrosyan, L. "Hovhannes T'umanyani lezvi ev oči mi k'ani aṙandznahatkut'yunnerě." *PBH,* 1961/1, 72–81.
———. *Hovhannes T'umanyani gełarvestakan erkeri baṙaran.* (Erevan, 1976).
Połosyan, H. "Anmoṙats handipumner." *SG,* 1969/9, 127–30.
Ṙubinyan, Ṙ. "T'umanyan ev Šek'spir." *SG,* 1969/9, 131–35.
Safrazbekian, I. *Traditsii mirovoi literatury i formirovanie esteticheskikh vzgliadov Ovanesa Tumaniana.* (Tiflis, 1982).
Safrazbekyan, I. "Čaponakan hek'iat'nerě T'umanyani t'argmanut'yamb." *T,* 1961/11, 87–96.
———. "Hovhannes T'umanyani t'argamanakan hek'iat'nerě." *T,* 1962/12, 93–104.
———. "Ṙusakan hek'iat'nerě T'umanyani t'argmanut'yamb." *SG,* 1963/3, 123–29.
———. "Hovhannes T'umanyaně serbakan ēposi t'argmanich." *SG,* 1967/3, 134–37.
———. "Tumanian i angliiskaia poeziia." *BEH,* 1972/3, 190–200.
———. "T'umanyaně ev Arevelk'ě." *SG,* 1975/2, 144–48.
———. "T'umanyaně ev germanakan poezian." *SG,* 1973/6, 144–49.
Sahakyan, A. "Hovhannes T'umanyani kyank'ě." *EJ,* 1969/9, 29–35.
Sargsyan, H. "T'umanyani k'aṙyaknerě." *PBH,* 1959/4, 69–85.
Sargsyan, K. "Hovhannes T'umanyani kolektsiayits." *Banber Hayastani arḫivneri,* 1989/2, 237–39.

Sarinyan, S. "T'umanyanĕ ev hay žołovrdi ṙusakan kołmnorošman hartsĕ." *PBH,* 1978/3, 87–97.

Sarkisian, Kh. "Mir i chelovek v tvorchestve Tumaniana." *L,* 1969/9, 20–29.

Simēōneants, A. "Yuš mĕ Yovhannēs T'umaneani verjin ōreru masin." *HK,* 27 (1949/10), 87–89.

Simonyan, G. "Hovhannes T'umanyani derĕ hay mankakan grakanut'yan zargatsman gortzum." *L,* 1982/4, 34–40.

Siruni, H. "Bari šunchĕ, or mez berav T'umanyan." *SG,* 1968/6, 160–71.

T'amrazyan, H. "Hovhannes T'umanyan." *SG,* 1969/9, 20–46.

———. "T'umanyanĕ k'nnadat." *BEH,* 1979/2, 19–32.

Tatetsian, G. "Vospitatel'nye motivy basennoi poezii I. A. Krylova i Ov. Tumaniana." *BEH,* 1988/1, 177–82.

Tērtērean, A. "Yovhannēs T'umanean, hayreni ezerk'i k'narergun." *A,* 1911, 498–502, 592–605, 692–700, 775–86, 854–60, 937–48, 1012–26; 1912, 38–48. (Reprinted separately, Ējmiatzin, 1911).

T'irabyan, N. "T'umanyanĕ Zoryani gnahatmamb." *BEH,* 1982/2, 173–78.

T'op'chyan, S. "T'umanyani ēst'etikakan hayetsut'yunĕ." *SG,* 1979/9, 102–15.

T'umanyan. (Erevan, 1964). (Essays by various authors).

T'umanyan 100 hobelyanakan taregrut'yun. (Erevan, 1972).

T'umanyan: usumnasirut'yunner ev hraparakumner. (Erevan, 1969–). (4 vols. to 1985; periodical devoted to studies on T'umanean).

T'umanyan, N. *T'umanyani mankut'yunĕ ev patanekut'yunĕ.* (Erevan 1938, 1946, 1955).

———. *Hovhannes T'umanyan.* (Erevan, 1939).

———. *Hovhannes T'umanyan.* (Erevan, 1955).

———. *Hovhannes T'umanyan ev ṙus grakanut'yunĕ.* (Erevan, 1956).

———. *T'umanyani mankut'yunĕ.* (Erevan 1983).

———. *Hušer ev zruytsner.* (Erevan, 1987).

Vardanyan, A. "Hovhannes T'umanyani hek'iat'neri sevagir pataṙiknerĕ." *L,* 1978/11, 41–52.

———. "Žołovrdakan hek'iat'nerĕ Hovhannes T'umanyani stełtzagortzakan tesadaštum." *L,* 1980/4, 52–64.

———. *Hovhannes T'umanyani hek'iat'nerĕ.* (Erevan, 1986).

Vardanyan, Ṙ. "Bnut'yunĕ T'umanyani patmvatzk'nerum." *BEH,* 1979/2, 62–67.

Viadro, S. "Ovanes Tumanian i Ukraina." *L,* 1972/3, 65–75.

Yovhannēs T'umaneani 100—ameak. (Beirut, 1969).

Zak'aryan, A. "T'umanyani poemnern avandnerov ev žanrayin hatkanišnerov." *SG,* 1965/1, 143–48.

Zarean, Ṙ. "Yovhannēs T'umaneani erkeri gitakan hratarakut'iwnĕ." *Ani,* 5 (1952), 490–96.

Zoryan, S. *Im T'umanyanĕ.* (Erevan, 1969).

T'UMANYAN, HENRIK (1916–1982)

Born in Aštarak, Armenia. A poet and journalist. Pursued his higher studies at the Gorky Institute for Literature in Moscow. Served in the Soviet Army in World War II and worked as a journalist for various daily newspapers and journals in Soviet Armenia.

Texts

Garnanayin. (Erevan, 1932).
Kaṙutsołnerě. (Erevan, 1933).
Arevatzag. (Moscow, 1936).
Hayrenik'is het. (Erevan, 1939).
Aštarak. (Erevan, 1948).
Mer tuně. (Erevan, 1952).
Hayreni vtak. (Erevan, 1955).
Ergi tznundě. (Erevan, 1960).
Erdum havatarmut'yan. (Erevan, 1964).
Siro hrašk'ě. (Erevan, 1967).
Serě chi tzeranum. (Erevan, 1971).
Čakatagir. (Erevan, 1975).
Tarineri mijov. (Erevan, 1978).

Translations

RUSSIAN

Chudo liubvi. (Moscow and Leningrad, 1969).
Rodnoi pritok. (Erevan, 1956).
Stikhi. (Moscow, 1958).

T'URINJ, (1790–1875)

Pen name: T'urinj.
Born T'oros Mart'ałean, in K'ark'anj (Shemakha, Azerbaijan). A minstrel (*ašuł*). Spent most of his life in Astrakhan.

Poetry

Čŕak'ał, 1 (1858), 38–39.
MKH, 447–48, 450–51, 470–71.
THG, 61–69.

TZAṘUKEAN, ANDRANIK (1913–1989)

Pen names: A. Tzaṙ, Arsēn Bagratean, V. Ḥažak, Vazgēn Tērunean.
Born in Gürün, Turkey. When his father was slain during the genocide, he sought shelter in orphanages in Aleppo. Educated in Aleppo and continued his studies at the Čemaran (a well-known high school later renamed Nšan P'alančean) in Beiurt. Returned to Aleppo in the mid-1930s and taught. Launched his popular periodical *Nayiri* in Aleppo in 1941, relocated to Beirut in the early 1950s, and published as a weekly until the early 1980s. Together with S. Simonean's *Sp'iwṙk'* and a few other periodicals, *Nayiri* is a valuable chronicle of Armenian literary, cultural, political, and social realities.

Texts

Ełerabaḥt k'ert'ołner. (Beirut, 1932). (Armenian poets who were killed or died young).
Moḥramaně. (Beirut, 1935). (Humorous prose).
Aṙagastner. (Aleppo, 1939). (Verse).
Tułt' aṙ Erewan. (Aleppo, 1945, 1946, 1948; Cairo, 1945; Beirut, 1950; Boston, 1954, 1954). (Poem).

Mankutʻiwn chunetsoł mardik. (Beirut, 1955, 1980; Erevan, 1959). (Stories).
Hin erazner, nor čambaner . . . (Beirut, 1960). (Essays and reflections).
Erazayin Halēpě. (Beirut, 1980). (Stories and reflections).
Verjin anmełě. (Beirut, 1980). (Novel).
Nor Hayastan, nor hayer. (Beirut, 1983).
Mankutʻyun chunetsoł mardik. Erazayin Halepě. (Erevan, 1985).
Sērě ełeṙnin mēj. (Beirut, 1987). (Novel).

Translations

ENGLISH

Bayizian, E., and Margossian, M. *Men Without Childhood.* ([New York], 1985).
Margossian, M., and Der Hovanessian, D. "Chronicler of Chaos." *Ararat,* Spring, 1979, 24–29.

FRENCH

Boghossian, S. *Des hommes sans enfance.* (Paris, 1977).

Criticism

Vanandean, V. "Andranik Tzaṙukeani 'Hey jan Erewan'ě." *HK,* 24 (1946/3), 110–12; 4, 105–7.

TZATUREAN, AŁEKʻSANDR (1865–1917)

Pen names: Artziwean, Šitakean, Slakʻean, and others.

Born and educated in Zakʻatʻala (Zakataly, Azerbaijan). After the death of his parents, he moved to Tiflis (1881) to pursue his education. But both the Nersisean school of Tiflis and the Gēorgean Seminary at Ējmiatzin denied him admission. He became a private tutor in 1886 and moved to Moscow permanently in 1888. There he translated Russian poets into Armenian and helped Russian writers publish anthologies of Armenian literature. His health deteriorated rapidly, and he headed south for treatment and recuperation. He died soon after his arrival in Tiflis in early 1917.

Collections

Ěntir banastełtzutʻyunner. (Erevan, 1937).
Mkrtchyan, H. *Erker.* (Erevan, 1948).
Banastełtzutʻyunner. (Erevan, 1958).
Grakan žaṙangutʻyun, 1. (Erevan, 1961). (Letters of Tzaturean and Nar-Dos).

Texts

Banastełtzutʻiwnner. 2 vols. (Moscow, 1891, 1898).
Smbat Šahazizeani eresnameay yobeleaně (1862–1892). (Moscow, 1894).
Eresun ew hing tari. (Moscow, 1898). (Also dealing with S. Šahazizean).
Grchi hanakʻner. (Moscow, 1901).
"Alekʻsandr Tzaturyani namaknerě K. Kusikyanin." *L,* 1980/2, 100–5.

Translations

ENGLISH ANTHOLOGIES

ALP, 43.

FRENCH ANTHOLOGIES

APA, 121–22.

German anthologies

ALG, 127–28;

Russian collections

Polonskaia, E. *Izbrannoe.* (Erevan, 1940).

Stikhotvoreniia. (Moscow, 1958).

Russian anthologies

AAP, 414–20.

BPA, 313–20.

SBAL, 113–16.

Sovremennye armianskie poety. (Moscow, 1903), 51–66.

Veselovskii, Iu. *Stikhotvornye perevody.* (Moscow, 1898), 39–57.

Criticism

Antonean, A. "Ałek'sandr Tzaturean, Banastełtzut'iwnner, 2 hator (1892–98), Moskua." *M,* 1898/10, 304–13.

Aramyan, A. "Ałek'sandr Tzaturyanĕ Puškini t'argmanich." *L,* 1972/4, 44–50.

Bežanyan, A. *Ałek'sandr Tzaturyan.* (Erevan, 1960).

Čałarbegean, Y. "Ałek'sandr Tzaturean. Banastełtzut'iwnner, erkrord hator." *Lumay,* 2 (1899), 282–302.

Felek'yan, H. *Ałek'sandr Tzaturyan.* (Erevan, 1965).

Ḥaṙatyan, A. "Ałek'sandr Tzaturyani mi anhayt banastełtzut'yan masin." *SG,* 1965/2, 152.

Inčikyan, A. *Tzaturyani kyank'ĕ.* (Erevan, 1940).

Mḥit'aryan, M. "Ałek'sandr Tzaturyanĕ žamanakaktsi hušerum." *L,* 1973/2, 43–50.

S. L. "Tzaturean, Ał. Grchi hanak'ner, Moskua, 1901." *Murč,* 1901/6, 208–9.

TZERENTS, (1822–1888)

Pen name: Tzerents.

Born Yovsēp' Šišmanean in Constantinople. Studied with the Mekhitarists at St. Lazarus, Venice (1837), but later specialized in medicine in France (1848–1853). Believed that Armenian solidarity transcended religious loyalties, and he was intimately involved in communal affairs, particularly in the so-called Hasunean conflict that rent the Armenian Catholic community apart. After his wife's death, he was posted to a medical position in Cyrprus (1876–78), but lived in Tiflis thereafter. He frequently traveled to Armenia and Constantinople. Suffered devasting grief over the untimely loss of his daughter in 1885 and never quite recovered; he died and was buried in Tiflis.

Collections

Erker. (Erevan, 1957, 1968).

Sełbosyana, L., and Nersisyan, V. *Erker.* (Erevan, 1983).

Sargsyan, Ṙ. *Erker.* (Erevan, 1985).

Texts (historical novels)

T'oros Lewoni. (Constantinople, 1877, 1911; Tiflis, 1881, 1902; Boston, 1917; Aleppo, 1933; Beirut, 1935, 1956).

Erkunk' T. daru. (Tiflis, 1879; Constantinople, 1911, Beirut, 1936; Cairo, 1940; Boston, 1944).

T'ēōdoros Ṙštuni. (Tiflis, 1881; Constantinople, 1911; Beirut, 1936; Cairo, 1941).

Other works

Ewropakan kʻałakʻakanutʻean nerkay žamanaknerus hay azgin vray ěratz azdetsutʻiwně. (Constantinople, 1873). (About the influence of European politics on Armenians).

Translations

English

Toros Levoni. Armenian Stories. (Boston, 1917).

Russian

Ioannisian, A. *V mukakh rozhdeniia.* (Erevan, 1961, 1969). (Published with *Toros Syn Levona*).

Khachaturian, N. *Toros Syn Levona.* (Erevan, 1969). (Published with *V mukakh rozhdeniia*).

———., and Ioannisian, A. *V mukakh rozhdeniia; Toros, Syn Levona.* (Erevan, 1981).

Criticism

Adamyan, A. "Tzerentsi ašḥarhayatskʻi zargatsman ěntʻatskʻě." *BEH,* 1986/2, 92–100.

Arpʻiarean, A. *T. Zakʻarean, H. Asatur, Y. Šišmanean.* (Cairo, 1946).

Avetisyan, Z. "Tzerentsě ev hay patmavepi skzbnavorumě." *BEH,* 1982/2, 47–59.

———. "Tzerentsi patmavepi fabulan, syužen ev kompozitsian." *L,* 1982/3, 27–35.

Gełamean, Y. "Erkunkʻ T. daru, Tʻiflis, 1879." *Pʻordz,* 1880/8–9, 199–225.

Grich. "Tʻoros Lewoni, K. Polis, 1878." *Pʻordz,* 1879/2, 126–45.

Nanumyan, Ṙ. *Tzerents.* (Erevan, 1961).

———. "Tzerents." *AND,* 14 (1963), 112–16.

———. *Tzerents. Kyankʻě ev gortzě.* (Erevan, 1986).

Ōtean, E. "Yovsēpʻ Šišmanean (Tzerents)." *M,* 3997 (1893), 387–90.

Šamlyan, V. "Tzerentsě orpes hraparakaḥos." *L,* 1966/11, 39–56.

———. "Tzerentsě ev patmakan antsyalě." *L,* 1970/5, 63–67.

Sarinyan, S. "Tzerents." *PBH,* 1972/3, 28–36.

Šaruryan, A. "Tzerentsi 'To'ros Levoni' vepi patmakan himkʻě." *BEH,* 1975/2, 193–97.

VAHĒ-VAHEAN, (1907–1998)

Pen name: Vahē-Vahean.

Born Sargis Aptalean in Gürün, Turkey. Survived the carnage of 1915 and spent a few years in Aintab (Gaziantep, Turkey) and Aleppo, attending local Armenian schools, before settling in Beirut, Lebanon. Graduated from the engineering school of the American University of Beirut (1930), but gave himself over to teaching and cultural activities. Taught at the celebrated Melkonian Educational Institute in Cyprus (1935–46), at the A. G. B. U. Daruhi Yakobean High School for Women in Beirut, and at the Eruand Hiwsisean Armenian Studies Program. From 1946 to 1955, he published the literary monthly *Ani.*

Collections

Oski kamurj. (Erevan, 1958).

Matyan siro ev mormokʻi. (Erevan, 1971).

Hatěntir. (Beirut, 1986).

Texts

Arew-andzrew: kʻerťuatzner, 1930–32. (Beirut, 1933). (Verse).
Oski kamurj: kʻerťuatzner (1933–45). (Beirut, 1946). (Verse).
Yaralēznerun haštuťiwnĕ, hayrenakan yušer. (Beirut, 1953). (Impressions of a visit to Soviet Armenia).
Matean siroy ew mormokʻi: kʻerťuatzner, 1945–68. (Beirut, 1968). (Verse).
Yušardzan Vahramis. (Beirut, 1977). (Verse).
Berkʻahawakʻ. 2 vols. (Beirut, 1978–87).

Translations

French anthologies

Viguier, M. *E,* 85–86.
LPA, 327–38.

Italian anthologies

LPAM, 287–90.

Criticism

B[aluean], H. "Girkʻeru mōt: Arew andzrew, banastełtzuťiwnner Vahē-Vaheani." *Z* (amsōreay), 1 (1938/6), 45; 7, 53.
"Hogevin barekamĕ gełetsiki ev ardari . . . (hartsazruyts)." *SG,* 1981/5, 125–29.
Kurtikyan, S. "Tałandavor kʻnarergun." *SG,* 1959/5, 144–51.
Taturyan, Š. "Vahe-Vahyan." *SG,* 1968/1, 132–38.

VARUŽAN, DANIĒL (1884–1915)

Pen name: Daniēl Varužan.

Born Varužan Chpugkʻearean in Brgnikʻ, a village near Sebastea (Sivas, Turkey). Educated in the Mekhitarist schools in Constantinople (1896–1902) and the Murat Ṙapʻayēlean of Venice (1902–05). Pursued his higher studies at the University of Ghent, Belgium (1905–09). Upon his return home, he taught in Armenian schools in Sebastea (1909–11), Tokat (1911–12), and Constantinople (1912–15). He was among the Armenian intellectuals arrested on the night of 24 April 1915. A little later in the year, he was brutally murdered in the interior.

Collections

Heťanos erger. Hatsin ergĕ. (Venice, 1944). (Selections).
Sarsuṙner. Tsełin sirtĕ. (Venice, 1944). (Selections).
Ĕntir erker. (Aleppo, 1946).
Tarontsi, S. *Erker.* (Erevan, 1946).
———. *Ambołjakan erker.* (Erevan, 1955).
———. *Banastełtzuťyunner.* (Erevan, 1955).
Namakani. (Erevan, 1965).
Erker. (Erevan, 1969).
Banastełtzakan erker. (Antʻilias, 1986).
Asmaryan, L., et al. *Erkeri liakatar žołovatzu.* 3 vols. (Erevan, 1986, 1986, 1987).

Texts

Sarsuṙner. (Venice, 1906, 1927; Jerusalem, 1950).
Jardĕ. (Paris, 1908).
Tsełin sirtĕ. (Constantinople, 1909; Jerusalem, 1953).
Heťanos erger. (Constantinople, 1912; Jerusalem, 1953).

Hatsin ergě. (Constantinople, 1921; Jerusalem, 1950; Erevan, 1964).
Harčě. (Erevan, 1946; Aleppo, 1946; Beirut, 1952; Erevan, 1977).

Translations

English

X. "When God Wept." *Kilikia,* 9 (1965/1), 64.

English anthologies

AP, 168–74.

French

Godel, V. *Le Chant du pain.* (Paris, 1959).
———. *Le Chant du pain.* (Marseilles: Editions Parenthèses, 1990). (Bilingual edition).
———. "Vahagn/Vahak." *AND,* 10 (n.d.), 42–50. (Armenian and French on facing pages).
Marcel, L.-A. "Les coquelicots." *Hayastan,* 1964/61, 3.
———. "Ov Lalagē/O Lalake," "Ōrhneal es du i kanays/Tu es benie entre toutes les femmes," "Guřě/L'abreuvoir." *AND,* 10 (n.d.), 26–37. (French and Armenian on facing pages).
———., and Poladian, G. "Le Pâtre." *AND,* 15 (1964), 105–10.
Minassian, J. *La Concubine.* (Constantinople, 1914; n.p. 1955).
Simkechian, E. "A la statue de Van Artévelde." *B,* 97 (1939), 172.
———. "A la statue de beauté." *AND,* 12 (1961), 148.
T. A. "Les Montagnes natales." *La Revue des amitiés franco-etrangères,* 1916/4, 31–33. Also in *Hommage à l'Arménie.* (Paris, 1919), 42–44.
Varuzan, D. "Poème arménien." *B,* 97 (1939), 131–32.

French anthologies

APA, 197–206.
CPA, 129–212.
JM, 14–54.
LPA, 218–28.
PAM, 197–210.

German anthologies

ALG, 132–33.

Italian

"Armenia," "La terra rossa." *Armenia,* 2 (1916/4), 8.

Italian anthologies

DLA, 5–9.
LPAM, 221–34.

Russian anthologies

AAP, 517–22.
ARPO, 154–92.
BPA, 481–84.
DILS, 19–34.
IZAP, 39–50.

Criticism

Aharonean, V. "D. Varužani inkʻnakensagrutʻiwně." *HK,* 4 (1925–26/3), 46–50.
Ałababyan, S. "Daniel Varužan." *PBH,* 1984/2, 3–17.

Andrikean, N. "Daniēl Varužani banastełtzutʻiwnĕ." *B,* 64 (1906), 221–26.
Aznavuryan, G. "Anhayt ējer hay nahatakneri grakan žaṙangutʻyunits." *EJ,* 1965/2–4, 43–57. (Previously unpublished letters and other material by Komitas, G. Zōhrap, D. Varužan, Siamantʻō, Tʻlkatintsi, Ṙ. Zardarean, and Ṙ. Sewak).
———. "Anhayt ējer Daniel Varužani žaṙangutʻyunits." *BEH,* 1969/3, 145–63.
Balagyan, L. "Daniel Varužanĕ ḩałałutʻyan ergich." *SG,* 1984/6, 107–9.
B[aluean], H. "Daniēl Varužan ew ir 'Hatsin ergĕ'." *Z* (amsōreay), 1 (1938/6), 42; 1 (1938/7), 50.
Chōpanean, A. "Grakan kʻronik." *ANA,* 1906/6–7, 97–113.
Čizmečean, D. *Daniēl Varužan: dprotsakan keankʻĕ, antip namaknerĕ, grakanutʻiwnĕ.* (Cairo, 1955).
———. "Dasĕnkers Daniēl Varužan." *HK,* 39 (1961/2), 69–70.
Daniēl Varužani 'Hetʻanos ergerĕ'. (Constantinople, 1913).
Davtʻyan, V. "Aṙnakan taṙapankʻ, aṙnakan ser u erazankʻ." *SG,* 1974/4, 102–7.
Eremean, S. "Daniēl Varužan." *HK,* 5 (1926–27/5), 51–55.
———. "Daniēl Varužan." *B,* 88 (1931), 328–31, 442–47, 489–99.
Ēsačanean, L. *Daniēl Varužan (keankʻn ew ir gortzĕ).* (Constantinople, 1919).
Gabrielyan, V. "Daniel Varužani grkʻeri stełtzman patmutʻyunits." *PBH,* 1975/4, 103–16.
———. "Daniel Varužani 'Sarsuṙner' žołovatzui naḩnakan kazmĕ." *BEH,* 1976/2, 177–89.
———. "Kinĕ Varužani 'Hetʻanos ergerum'." *L,* 1977/12, 15–24.
———. "Banastełtzi inkʻnutʻyunĕ." *BEH,* 1978/1, 44–60.
———. *Daniel Varužan.* (Erevan, 1978).
———. "Daniel Varužani gełagitakan hayatskʻnerĕ." *L,* 1978/4, 24–33.
———. "Taṙapołneri zayruytʻĕ ev taṙapankʻi gełetskutʻyunĕ: Daniel Varužani 'Gołgotʻayi tzałikner' šarkʻĕ." *SG,* 1978/5, 148–56.
———. *Daniel Varužani stełtzagortzutʻyunĕ.* (Erevan, 1982).
———. "Daniel Varužani ardzakĕ." *BEH,* 1984/3, 56–67.
Galiončean, S. "Bnazdi astuatzatsumĕ–D. Varužani 'Hetʻanos ergeru' hratarakutʻean aṙtʻiw." *HG,* 1913/9, 21–24.
Gasparyan, H. "Grakan mi ušagrav iradardzutʻyan šurjĕ." *SG,* 1964/4, 113–19.
Gazazean, Z. "Grakan verlutzumner." *HG,* 1913/2, 28–32. (On *Tsełin sirtĕ* and *Hetʻanos erger*).
Ḩachatryan, A. "Hayreni všti ev paytzaṙ galikʻi ergichĕ." *L,* 1984/5, 12–22.
Jrbašyan, Ēd. "Daniel Varužani verjin matyanĕ." *L,* 1975/4, 3–14.
Karapetean, Y. "Ēj mĕ akʻsori yišataknerēs." *Z* (amsatʻertʻ), 2 (1957/1–2), 6; 2 (1957/3–4), 2; 2 (1957/5–6), 6.
Kirakosyan, V. "Banastełtzutʻyan aspetĕ." *SG,* 1984/6, 99–107.
Kiwfēčean, Y. "Mer banastełtznerĕ—Daniēl Varužan (Tsełin sirtĕ u Hetʻanos erger)." *HG,* 1912/12, 4–14. 1913/1, 8–14; 2, 6–12; 3, 5–12; 4, 14–18; 5, 28–31.
Kurtikyan, S. *Daniel Varužan.* (Erevan, 1976).
Łanalanyan, H. *Daniel Varužan.* (Erevan, 1961).
Madoyan, A. *Daniel Varužan.* (Erevan, 1976).
Madoyan, G. "Daniel Varužani aṙajin grkʻuykĕ." *SG,* 1972/9, 151–53.
———. "Ējer Daniel Varužani kensagrutʻyunits." *SG,* 1974/2, 160–67.
Manukyan, A. "Daniel Varužani 'Hetʻanos ergerĕ'." *PBH,* 1960/1, 167–78.

Matt'evosyan, V. "Erkeri liakatar žołovatzu." *B,* 1989/1–4, 437–39.
Movsisyan, H. "Daniel Varužanĕ parskeren." *SG,* 1984/6, 110–11.
Narduni, Š. "Ent'akayakan ew tsełayin larĕ hay žamanakakits banastełtzut'ean mēj ew Daniēl Varužan." *Z* (amsōreay), 1 (1938/6), 41; 7, 50.
Nersēsean, N. "Varužan dardzeal Pelčik'ayi mēj." *B,* 116 (1958), 39–40.
Patrik, A. "Ogekochumner (usutschis Varužani yišatakin)." *Z* (amsōreay), 1 (1938/6), 42; 7, 51; 2 (1939/8), 60.
———. *Daniel Varužann im hušerum.* (Erevan, 1965). Beirut, 1968.
Pēšikt'ašlean, N. "Daniēl Varužanĕ ew k'ert'ołikĕ." *HK,* 41 (1963/5), 32–35.
Petrosyan, E. "Daniel Varužani banastełtzut'yunneri ařajin antip žołovatzun." *L,* 1974/6, 59–64.
———. "P'uši akosner." *SG,* 1974/4, 108–10.
———. *Daniel Varužan.* (Erevan, 1987).
P'ōlatean, K. *Yušamatean Daniēl Varužani (1884–1915).* (Paris, 1958).
Poturyan, M. "Daniel Varužan. (Hušer)." *EJ,* 1958/8, 35–37.
Ṙštuni, H. *Daniel Varužan.* (Erevan, 1961).
———. "Daniel Varužani poezian." *PBH,* 1965/1, 69–84.
———. "Het'anos hosank'ĕ ev Daniel Varužani poezian." *PBH,* 1982/3, 73–84.
Sargsyan, G. "Varužani stełtzagortzakan ułin." *SG,* 1959/5, 120–31.
———. "Varužanĕ žamanakakitsneri gnahatut'yamb." *BEH,* 1984/2, 27–41.
Sarinyan, S. "Daniel Varužan." *PBH,* 1974/3, 21–34.
Šaruryan, A. "Daniel Varužanĕ Sebastiayum." *SG,* 1980/10, 149–51.
———. *Daniel Varužani kyank'i ev stełtzagortzut'yan taregrut'yun.* (Erevan, 1984).
———. *Daniel Varužani stełtzagortzut'yunĕ.* (Erevan, 1984).
———. *Misak' Metzarentsĕ ev Daniel Varužanĕ žamanakakitsneri hušerum.* (Erevan, 1986).
Siruni, Y. "Dēpi ałbiwrĕ loysin." *Nawasard,* 1914, 220–24. (On *Het'anos erger*).
———. "Gitzer Daniēl Varužani keank'ēn." *HK,* 2 (1923–24/1), 33–52.
———. "Mḥit'areank' Daniēl Varužani mēj." *B,* 94 (1936), 305–19.
———. *Daniēl Varužan.* (Bucharest, 1940).
Tonyan, Ṙ. "Brgniki luysĕ." *SG,* 1984/6, 109–10.
T'op'chyan, S. "Daniel Varužani 'Tsełin sirtĕ' žołovatzun." *PBH,* 1968/1, 165–73.
———. "Daniel Varužani 'Het'anos ergerĕ'." *SG,* 1968/3, 141–54.
———. "Daniēl Varužan." *AND,* 18 (n.d.), 121–24. (Mispaginated).
Vardanyan, Ḥ. "Daniel Varužani 'Het'anos ergeri' gnahatman šurj." *L,* 1987/8, 25–35.
———. "Varužani 'Het'anos' mtatzołut'yan barešrjumĕ." *BEH,* 1990/1, 31–45.
Varduni, "Varužan ew ir grakan gortzĕ." *HA,* 74 (1960), 435–43.
Zēk'ean, L. "Daniēl Varužan banastełtz ew aruestagēt: banastełtzut'ean nkaragirĕ ew aruestin kazmaworumĕ." *B,* 1984/1–2, 10–25.

VERDYAN, BOGDAN (1919–1993)

Born in Elizavetpol (Kirovabad, now Ganja). A novelist and linguist. In 1941, he graduated from the Pedagogical Institute in Erevan (later named after Ḥachatur Abovean) and obtained a doctoral degree in 1970. Following his discharge from the Red Army after World War II, he served his alma mater in a number of teaching and administrative positions.

Texts

K'ez hamar, Leningrad. (Erevan, 1951).
Leṙneri ordin. (Erevan, 1952).
Inchpes ē galis erjankut'yunĕ. (Erevan, 1958).
Tzałikners mnatsin heṙvum. (Erevan, 1969, 1990).
Errord kursĕ. (Erevan, 1975).
Ayrvoł alik'ner. (Erevan, 1977). (Book 1 of trilogy).
Erkḥosut'yun. (Erevan, 1980). (Book 2 of trilogy).
Artakarg despanner. (Erevan, 1985). (Book 3 of trilogy).
"Na gtnum ē iren." *SG,* 1985/12, 3–30.

Other works

Bard storadasakan naḥadasut'yan šarahyusut'yun. (Erevan, 1970).

Translations

Russian

Dolukhanian, V. *Ognennye volny. Roman.* (Moscow, 1980).
Ioannisian, A. *Rozhdennyi v gorakh. Roman.* (Moscow, 1965).

VESPER, (1893–1977)

Pen name: Vesper.

Born Martiros Dabałyan in Van. Educated in the local Eramean school. Fled to safety in Eastern Armenia in 1915. Taught and worked primarily as a journalist and translator. His literary output consists of poetry, short stories, and novelettes.

Collections

Hatĕntir. (Erevan, 1973).

Texts

Kayaranner. (Tiflis, 1925).
Kendani ev krake mardkants het. (Tiflis, 1931).
Paytzaṙut'yun. (Erevan, 1936).
Manukneri het. (Erevan, 1937).
T'elikn u Melikĕ. (Erevan, 1938).
Ełevni. (Erevan, 1939).
Uraḥ im dzi. (Erevan, 1939).
Vets harvatz. (Erevan, 1940).
Mayisyan varder. (Erevan, 1941).
Nkarich hayriki ḥostumĕ. (Erevan, 1942).
Aygn ē batsvum. (Erevan, 1944).
Hišatak. (Erevan, 1948).
Aṙajin ašun. (Erevan, 1956).
Andzrev ev arev. (Erevan, 1957).
Hrazdan. (Erevan, 1959).
Horełbor sring. (Erevan, 1960).
Ardzak ējer. (Erevan, 1963).
Mayreni erger. (Erevan, 1965).
Šušani šap'rakner. (Erevan, 1968).
Mer k'aj Džikon. (Erevan, 1972).

Translations

Russian anthologies

AAP, 620–21.

AASL, 127–28.

Criticism

Avetisyan, S. "Vastakavor hobelyarĕ." *SG,* 1963/11, 143–45.

VRT‘ANĒS SṘNKETSI (16th c.)

Born in the village of Gilan (the town of Azagiran in Nakhichevan, now in ruins) in Eastern Armenia. Emigrated to Poland and later became bishop of the Armenians of Kafa in Crimea.

Texts

"Mēk mard mi črag vaṙer, Bardzr i teł drer . . ." *Maseats aławni,* 1863, 264–65. (Also published in *HA,* 34 [1920], 360–63, and in *AHPT,* 31–37, titled "I Vrt‘anēs vardapetē asatseal bank‘s ays, Omn metzatun unēr . . .").

"Astuatz, Hayr erknawor, zk‘ēn gohanam, Tēr . . ." *HNV,* 396–400. (Also published in *AHPT,* 47–53, titled "Tał nor nahatakin K‘ristosi, surb Paron Lusin.").

"Hayastaneayts hazar t‘ĕvin . . ." *HNV,* 401–8. (Also published in *AHPT,* 38–47, titled "Tał Vrdanēs vardapeti asatseal yałags nor vkayin K‘ristosi surb Paron Lusin . . .").

"Vkayabanut‘iwn Paron Loys Kafatswoy." *HNV,* 386–94. (Prose; titled "Paron Loys Kafatsi").

"Aybēn minchew i k‘ēn k‘ez gohut‘iwn, Tēr, Bareats k‘ots gohanamk‘ yawitenits Tēr . . ." *HA,* 34 (1920), 359. (Also published in *AHPT,* 29–30, titled "Tał azniw ew gełetsik . . .").

"Aybēn minchew i k‘en K‘ristos mełay k‘ez, Bazum ḥṙovut‘eants hetewetsay es . . ." *HA,* 34 (1920), 283–84. (Also published in *AHPT,* 15–16, titled "Vrt‘anēs vardapeti, Vasn haštut‘ean . . .").

"Aybēn minchew i k‘ēn govetsi zk‘ez, Aybēn minchew i k‘ēn ełbayr mełay k‘ez . . ." *HA,* 34 (1920), 284–85. (Also published in *AHPT,* 16–18, titled "Norin Vrt‘anisi asatseal").

"Aybēn minchew i girn verjin mełay asem es K‘ristosin, Bazum baniw ḥṙovut‘eants hetewetsak‘ i het charin . . ." *HA,* 34 (1920), 285–88. (Also published in *AHPT,* 18–23, titled "Otanawors norin Vrt‘anisi asatseal ē").

"Ays sut kentsałoys veray es miayn šutov ḥabetsay . . ." *HA,* 34 (1920), 288–92. (Also published in *AHPT,* 23–29, titled "Norin Vrdanisi").

Anthologies

SUM, 1, 223–50.

Translations

French

Verthanès Kafayetsi. "Les dits du prêtre Verthanès (Extraits)." *LPA,* 131–33.

Criticism

Akinean, N. "Vrt‘anēs Sṙnketsi, Episkopos Kafayi." *AHPT,* 3–53.

"Vrt‘anēs Sṙnketsi (1500?–1570?)." *PHG,* 457–59.

VŠTUNI, AZAT (1894–1958)

Pen names: Azat, Azat Vštuni, Karap, Karapet Ṫaščyan, Seyid Ēl Nur.

Born Karapet Mamikonean in Van. Poet; received his education in the local Eramean school, at the Kedronakan of Constantinople (1908–11). Audited courses at the Sorbonne (1911–14). Spent the years 1914–1918 in Tiflis, and after a brief stay in the Crimea (1919–20) he traveled to Iran and Iraq to organize the repatriation of Armenians to Soviet Armenia. Became the first chairman of the Association of Writers of Soviet Armenia, the first literary organization to be founded in the Second Republic of Armenia. He was one of the writers making up the famous group known as the "Three" (along with E. Charents and G. Abov, q.q.v.), who rejected the past and advocated forging a new Armenian culture that would befit the new socialist society.

Collections

Erker. (Erevan, 1935).
Ĕntir erker. (Erevan, 1941).
Hatĕntir. (Erevan, 1944).
Erkeri žołovatzu. (Erevan, 1947).
Erker. (Erevan, 1956).
Erker. 2 vols. (Erevan, 1960–61).
Ĕntir erker. (Erevan, 1971).

Texts

Kamawori yušatetrits. (Baku, 1915).
Srtis lareren. (Baku, 1915).
Banastełtzuṫiwnner. (Tiflis, 1918).
Huzank̇ u zang. (Alexandrapol, 1923).
Neo Orientana (zarṫnoł Arewelk̇i erger). (Erevan, 1923).
Salamname. (Tiflis, 1924).
Arewelk̇ĕ hur ē hima. (Erevan, 1927).
Banastełtzuṫyunner. (Erevan, 1929).
Ḥosum ē ṙadio Alžirĕ. (Erevan, 1931).
Ṙam-Ṙoy. (Erevan, 1936).
Lusademin. (Erevan, 1939).
Nor serundĕ. (Erevan, 1941).
Villi Volf. (Erevan, 1941).
Erb kaytzakĕ ṗaylatakum ē. (Erevan, 1942; Aleppo, n.d.).
Mankakan ṙazmaḥał. (Erevan, 1942).
Mankikn u katvikĕ. (Erevan, 1944).
Ser ev ateluṫyun. (Erevan, 1946).
Mankuṫyan ōrer. (Erevan, 1953).
Banastełtzuṫyunner ev poemner. (Erevan, 1954).
Girk̇ manukneri hamar. (Erevan, 1972).

Translations

French Anthologies

FPA, 57–58
LPA, 244–45.

Russian

Kreitan, G. *Govorit radio-Alzhir. Poema-satira.* ([Tiflis], 1933).
Izbrannye stikhi. (Moscow, 1937).
Novy Vostok. Stikhi. (Moscow and Leningrad, 1930).
Stikhi. (Erevan, 1952).
Stikhi i poemy. (Tiflis, 1936; Erevan, 1951).

Criticism

Alazan, V. "Azat Vštunu het, hayrenaser artistn u grołĕ." *SG,* 1962/7, 106–13.
———. "Zart'noł Arevelk'i ḥandavaṙ ergichĕ." *SG,* 1964/8, 135–36.
Hovhannisyan, H. "Arevelk'i ergichĕ." *SG,* 1974/7, 125–31.
Hovhannisyan, Y. "Banastełtzi ułin." *SG,* 1984/7, 84–88.
———. "A. Vštunu mi grakan tzatzkanvan masin." *L,* 1984/11, 61–62.
Łazaryan, H. *Azat Vštuni.* (Erevan, 1959).
Ṙštuni, H. "Azat Vštuni. *SG,* 1959/3, 124–32.
Solaḥyan, A. "Azat Vštunin im hušerum." *SG,* 1969/7, 117–18.

YAKOB KARNETSI (1618–?)

Born in Karin (Erzurum). Historian. He was ordained a priest in Ējmiatzin in 1641, and is believed to have spent most of his life in his native city.

Texts

"Hakob Karnetsu Žamanakagrut'yunĕ." *Manr žamanakagrut'yunner,* Vol. 1, (Erevan, 1951), 237–44.
"Patmut'iwn S. Astuatzatzin ekełetswoyn Karnoy." *Tełagir Verin Hayots: yišatakaran ŽĒ daru,* Yakovb Karnetsi, (Vałaršapat, 1903), 53–61.
"Patmut'iwn vasn hōrn merum Gēorga k'ahanayin ē . . ." *Manr žamanakagrut'yunner,* Vol. 1, (Erevan, 1951), 246–49.
"Šinuatz Karnoy k'ałak'in, or kochetsaw T'ēudupōlis, or ayžm Arzrum veraydzaynial kochi." *Manr žamanakagrut'yunner,* Vol. 2, (Erevan, 1956), 548–82. (Critical edition of "Hakob Karnetsi, 'Tełagir Verin Hayots' ").
Yakovb Karnetsi. *Tełagir Verin Hayots: yišatakaran ŽĒ daru.* (Vałaršapat, 1903).

Translations

French

Hakovb Karnétsi. *Erzeroum ou topographie de la Haute-Arménie.* Traduit et annoté par F. Macler (tirage à part du *J.As.*). (Paris, 1919).

YAKOB SSETSI (17th c.)

Yakob was a priest who took the vows of celibacy upon his wife's death.

Texts (verse)

"Angin gohar." *Erkragunt,* 1884, 424–25. (Also published in *KNZ,* 4, 9–11).
Tzovakan, N. "Yakob erēts Ajpan Ssetsi ew iwr patmakan mēk otanaworĕ." *Hask,* 14 (1945/1–2), 28–31. ("Šaradrut'iwn vardapetats hayots i Gōšay hetē otiw chap'eal, ĕst anuan ergołi ew chap'ołi.").
"Vasn paḥarakeloy ōrinazantsitsn." *BM,* 2 (1950), 193–95.
K'iwrtean, Y. "Yakob erēts Ssetsi tałasats." *S,* 1965, 362–67. (A study and texts including "Šaradrut'iwn . . . ," first published by N. Tzovakan in *Hask*).

Anthologies

SUM, 2, 267–76.

Criticism

Sahakyan, H. "XVII dari banastełtz Hakob Ssetsi." *PBH,* 1968/1, 184–92.

YAKOB TʻOḤATʻETSI (c1560–1660s)

Born in Tokat. Spent most of his life in Moldavia and Poland. Also known as Batʻuk (or Batʻukents) Yakob erēts; he was a priest and a man of letters, a scribe, and a translator.

Texts (verse)

"Norin Yakobi asatseal i veray Erusałēmi . . ." *HA,* 23 (1909), 371–74. (Published under the title "Yakob erēts Kesaratsi, ŽĒ daru tałasats" by N. Akinean, who concluded [cf. *AMH,* 4, 7, footnote 2, and *HA,* 44 (1930), 368–69] that he wrongly attributed this poem to Yakob erēts Kesaratsi).

"Ołb i veray erkrin Ōlaḥats." *AMH,* 4, 13–21.

"Ołb i veray Ewdokia kʻałakʻin or ayžm asi Tʻoḥatʻ." *Hayapatum,* 608–10.

"Tał vasn kenats mardkan." *Hambawaber Ṙusioy,* 1863/40–43, 7–8. Also published in *B,* 23 (1865), 208–11.

Anthologies

SUM, 1, 531–73.

Criticism

Akinean, N. "Yakob erēts Tʻoḥatʻetsi, 1573–1680." *HA,* 35 (1921), 273–85, 374–85, 472–85. (Reprinted in *AHPT,* 141–202).

———. "Yakob Tʻoḥatʻetswoy Ołb i veray erkrin Ōlaḥats." *AMH,* 4, 3–21.

YAKOBEAN, ŽAG (1917–)

Born in Jerusalem. Moved to Cairo with his family at an early age and was educated in local Armenian schools. Traveled to Beirut (1938) for medical studies, but World War II forced him to continue his studies in pharmacology in Cairo. Graduated in 1942 and served three years in the Egyptian Army as a chemist. He then lived two years in Melbourne, Australia (1949–51), five years in Cairo (1951–56), ten years in Beirut (1956–65), two more years in Melbourne (1965–67), before making Los Angeles his home in 1967. Since the 1960s, religious themes have been predominant in his verse.

Texts (verse)

Gałtni čamban. (Cairo, 1938).
Mełralusin. (Cairo, 1943).
Mesropašunch. (Cairo, 1946).
Mard mě meṙaw . . . (Cairo, 1947).
Veratznund. (Cairo, 1949).
Yisus, Kiraki, Hayastaneayts Ekełetsi. (Beirut, 1959).
Masisatzin. (Beirut, 1963).
Jahertʻ. (Beirut, 1964).
Yisusaboyr. (Beirut, 1965; Pasadena, 1994).
Žagapʻunj. (Beirut, 1969). (Includes some prose).
Hayatropʻ. (Beirut, 1970).
Hrašadar. (Pasadena, 1978).
Ulunkʻašar. (Pasadena, 1983).
Kṙunkě kě kanchē. (Pasadena, 1986).

Hogin haykakan. (Cairo, 1987). (Selections).
Ogin aprilean. (Cairo, 1990). (Selections).
Hayagoyn. (Pasadena, 1991).
Hołašnchum. (Pasadena, 1991).
Tēr-Zōr dełin. (Pasadena, 1991).
Hayrenatropʻ. (Cairo, 1992). (Selections).
Hay žołovurdi ogełēn zoyg bardzunkʻnerě. (Cairo, 1993). (Selections).
Mesropatropʻ. (Cairo, 1993). (Selections).
Eōtʻnōreay mah. (Pasadena, 1995).
Anmaš hritak. (Cairo, 1995). (Selections).
Aprileankʻ kʻsanchorsi. (Cairo, 1995). (Selections).
Harsnagnats eram. (Pasadena, 1996).

Translations (English)

Selected Poems. (Cairo, 1988; Pasadena, 1993).

YARTʻUN ŌŁLI (c1760–1840)

A native of Asdabad (Chahar Mahall, Isfahan, Iran). An *ašuł.* Was instructed in the art of minstrelsy by both Amir Ōłli and Łul Yovhannēs (q.q.v.). Made the traditional pilgrimage to the monastery of Surb Karapet in Muš to seek divine grace in the art, a long-standing custom for Armenian minstrels.

Poetry

Eremean, A. *Ašuł Yartʻun Ōłli.* (New Julfa, 1920; Teheran, 1946).
THG, 59–60.
SHA, 213–64.
Eremean, A. "Antip tałer ašuł Yartʻun Ołluts." *HA,* 79 (1965), 525–28.
———. "Antip ējer Yartʻun Ōłlu ašułakan ełanaknerits." *S,* 1971, 68–71.

YARUTʻIWNEAN, ARTAŠĒS (1873–1915)

Pen names: Karō, Manišak, Pan, Šahēn-Kar, Uruakan.

Born and educated in the town of Malgara, Turkey. A poet and literary critic. In 1912, he moved with his family to Constantinople, taught in Armenian schools, and worked for a French insurance company. He was among the Armenian intellectuals slain in 1915.

Collections

Ardzak ējer ew kʻertʻuatzner. (Paris, 1937).
Gišervan čampʻordě. (Erevan, 1968).

Texts

Lkʻuatz kʻnar. (Constantinople, 1902).
Erkunkʻ. (Constantinople, 1906).
Nor kʻnar. (Constantinople, 1912).

Criticism

Avetisyan, A. "Artašes Harutʻyunyan." *PBH,* 1989/2, 215–19.
Gazančean, Y. "Matenaḥōsakan." *AM,* 1903, 223–36. (On *Lkʻuatz kʻnar*).

Mnatsakanyan, L. "Artašes Harutʻyunyani grakʻnnadatakan hayatskʻnerě." *BEH,* 1974/3, 191–99.
Nahapetyan, A. "Artašes Harutʻyunyaně grakʻnnadat." *PBH,* 1982/2, 81–88.
Pʻaylak, "Artašēs Yarutʻiwneani 'Nor kʻnarě'." *HG,* 1912/2, 29–34.
Šamlyan, V. "A. Harutʻyunyani poezian." *L,* 1977/6, 24–34.
Yarutʻiwnean, V. "Artašēs Yarutʻiwneani kensagrutʻiwně." *ANA,* 10 (1939/4–5), 1–17.

YOVASAPʻ SEBASTATSI (c1510–?)

Born in Sebastea (Sivas). A deacon of the Armenian Church. Instructed by his father, who was a scribe and a poet. Emulating his father, he copied manuscripts and wrote poems of love, religion, and history in spoken Armenian.

Texts (verse)

"Tał urahutʻean, siroy." *TH,* 109–16. (Published anonymously; "Yayn ařajin žamanaki").
"Dardzeal hayerēn." *CHE,* 32–35. (Published under the name Yovasapʻ Piwstatsi)
"Tēr im gtʻatz, Astuatz bari . . ." *A,* 1918, 267.
Gevorgyan, V. *Hovasapʻ Sebastatsi, Banasteltzutʻyunner.* (Erevan, 1964).

Translations

French

LPA, 115–17.
RA, 2, 137–49; 3, 139–46.

Russian

AAP, 290–92.

Criticism

Gevorgyan, V. *Hovasapʻ Sebastatsi, Banasteltzutʻyunner.* (Erevan, 1964). (Study and texts).
Yovsēpʻean, G. "Yovasapʻ Sebastatsi." *A,* 1918, 226–61. (Study and texts; reprinted separately, Vałaršapat, 1918).

YOVHANNĒS JUŁAYETSI (1643–1715)

Born in Nor Jułay (New Julfa, Isfahan, Iran). Also known by the sobriquet "Mrkʻuz" or "Mrguz." Took his holy orders as a *vardapet* (a celibate priest) in 1669. Had a good command of Arabic and Persian and used the latter in some of his works, many of which are still unpublished. He wrote mainly on philosophical and theological themes and was often involved in theological disputes with Catholic missionaries and Muslim theologians and rulers.

Texts

Girkʻ hamařōt vasn iskapēs ew čšmarit hawatoy ew dawanutʻean ułłapʻař katʻołikē ew ěntʻhanur [sic] Hayastaneayts ekełetswoy. (Nor Jułay, 1688; Constantinople, 1713 [two editions]).
Hamařōt kʻerakanutʻiwn ew tramabanutʻiwn. (Amsterdam, 1711).
Girkʻ patmutʻean. (Calcutta, 1797).
Girkʻ or kochi srbaznagortzutʻiwn. (Madras, 1812).

Criticism

Mirzoyan, H. "Hovhannes Jułayetsu 'Girkʻ srbaznagortzutʻean" erki tpagrutʻyan šurjě." *BEH,* 1980/3, 58–68.

YOVHANNĒS KAMENATSI (16th–17th c.)

No biographical information is available on this author, whose written history depicts the Polish-Ottoman War of 1621.

Text

Anasyan, H. *Patmutʻiwn paterazmin Ḫotʻinu.* (Erevan, 1964).

Translations (Russian)

Iuzbashian, K. "Istoriia Khotinskoi voiny, proiskhodivshei vo vremena turetskogo sultana Osmana, kogda armianskim katolikosom v sviatom Echmiadzine byl Melkhisedek." *PBH,* 1958/2, 262–86.

Criticism

Anasian, A. "Ottolski bitv pri Khotine (1621 g.) v armianskikh istochnikakh." *Velikaia druzhba. Sbornik posviaschenny 300—letiiu vossoedineniia Ukrainy s Rossiei.* (Erevan, 1954), 225–38.

YOVHANNĒS KARNETSI (c1755–c1820)

No biographical details are available on this poet, save that he was born in Karin (Erzurum) and was a teacher and a scribe. He wrote in both Armenian and Turkish and rendered poetical works from Armenian into Turkish and vice versa.

Texts

"Yałags metzi sovoyn ew słutʻean . . ." *B,* 42 (1884), 118–22.

"Patmutʻiwn Děvněktsi nahatakatsn . . ." *A,* 1895, 445–52.

"Yałags umemn Msěr kochetseal Sahak mankan . . ." *HNV,* 572–601. (Under "Sahak Msěr Karnetsi").

"Karnetsi omn Yarutʻiwn anun eritasard nahatakeal i yIzmir . . ." *HNV,* 620–26. (Published as "Yarutʻiwn Karnetsi").

"Yałags umemn Vaṙvaṙ anun ariasirt ałjkan . . ." *HNV,* 646–73. ("Patmutʻiwn Děvněktsi nahatakatsn" is a shorter version of this poem).

Nazaryan, Š. *Hovhannes Karnetsi, Tałaran.* (Erevan, 1962).

Oskean, H. *Chors hay tałasatsner ew anonts tałerě. Yovhannēs Karnetsi, Grigor arkʻep. Ōšakantsi, Movsēs dpir Karnetsi ew Martiros v. Łrimetsi.* (Vienna, 1966). (Biographical sketches and texts).

YOVHANNĒS ŁRIMETSI (d. 1848)

Little is known about this author, who is also referred to as Yovhannēs Sureneants Pʻōtʻišantsi. As a secretary and translator, he was active in Ējmiatzin and helped draft the preliminary version of the *Polozhenie* ("Statute," promulgated in 1836), which regulated the affairs of the Armenian Church in the Russian Empire. He was the prelate of the Armenians of Nor Jułay (New Julfa, Isfahan, Iran) from the early 1840s until his death.

Text

Oskean, H. *Yovhannu Łrimetswoy patmutʻiwn hṙchakawor vanits Hałbatay s. Nšanin.* (Vienna, 1965). (History of Surb Nšan in Hałbat).

Translations (Russian)

Brosset, M. "Opisanie monastyrei Akhpatskago i Sanaginskago, arkhimandrita Ioanna Krymskago" (Description des monastères arméniens d'Haghbat et de Sanahin, par l'archimandrite Jean de Crimée, avec notes et appendice par M. Brosset. VIIe Série, tome VI, no. 6, St. Pétersbourg, 1863; an abridged version of the original).

YOVHANNĒS, ŁUL (c1740–1834)

Birthplace uncertain. An architect and builder by profession, he turned into an itinerant *ašuł* after making the traditional pilgrimage to the monastery of Surb Karapet in Muš, where Armenian minstrels went to seek divine grace in the art. Died in Nor Jułay (New Julfa, Isfahan, Iran).

Poetry

B, 86 (1929), 48.
Eremean, A. *Ašuł Łul Yovhannēs.* (Venice, 1929).
SHA, 160–212.

Criticism

Eremean, A. *Ašuł Łul Yovhannēs.* (Venice, 1929).
———. "Nor Jułayi 18–19 darešrjani kʻałakʻakan dēpkʻerě ew ašuł Łul Yovhannēsi patmakan antip tałerě." *Ditsawan,* 1 (1923), 124–36.

YOVHANNĒS SEBASTATSI (d. 1830)

Presumably born in Sebastea (Sivas, Turkey). Birthdate unknown. Took the vows of celibacy as a *vardapet* in 1797. Primate of the Armenians of Sebastea from 1809 to 1829. Wrote a history of Sebastea and a number of poems.

Texts

Nerbołakan nuagergutʻiwnkʻ yōrineal i srbazan Yovhannēs arkʻepiskopos Sebastatswoy . . . (Tiflis, 1825).
"Yōhannēs Sebastatsi patmich." *Diwan hayots patmutʻean,* G. Ałaneants, Vol. 10 (Tiflis, 1912), 385–438. (Excerpts from his "History of Sebastea.")
Chugaszyan, B. *Patmutʻiwn Sebastioy.* (Erevan, 1974). (A critical edition of the above).

Criticism

Pērpērean, H. "Hamematutʻiwn Ananun Sebastatsii (ŽG dar) ew Yovhannēs Sebastatsii (ŽĚ-ŽTʻ dar) kʻani mě hatuatznerun mijew." *Hask,* 1957, April–May, 146–51.

YOVHANNĒS VANANDETSI (1772–1840)

Pen name: Yovhannēs Vanandetsi.
Born Amirzadē Mirzayean in Van. Educated at the Ktuts monastery on the islet of Ktuts in Lake Van, and in Constantinople, where he resided briefly from 1792 to

1798. Moved to Smyrna, married in 1802, and became a priest in 1817. From the time of his arrival in Smyrna until his death, he taught at the celebrated Mesropean school that was founded in 1799.

Texts (poems)

Arṗiakan Hayastani. (Constantinople, 1836).
Kerakur kʻahanayits. (Ējmiatzin, 1841).
Oski dar Hayastani. (Smyrna, 1841).
Čaṙ nerbołakan i surb ḥachn Kʻristosi. (Moscow, 1853).
Tesaran handisits Haykay, Aramay ew Arayi. (Smyrna, 1856).

Criticism

Oski dar Hayastani, (Smyrna, 1841), 1–16. (Biography).

YOVHANNĒSEAN, SARGIS DPIR (c1735–1805)

Born in Constantinople. Also known as Sargis dpir Saraf Yovhannēsean. He was a teacher by profession and wrote a number of books, some of a historical-descriptive nature, most of which are still in manuscript form.

Texts

Kʻiwrtean, Y. "Kanonkʻ ew sahmankʻ Palatʻu sb. Hreštakapetats ekełetswoyn (1778ēn noragiwt vaweragrutʻiwn mě Sargis dpir Saraf Yovhannēseanē)." *Šołakatʻ,* 1952, 112–16.

Vipagrutʻiwn Kostandnupolis mayrakʻałakʻin. (Jerusalem, 1967). (Previously published in *Sion*; a description of Constantinople).

Criticism

Bampukʻčean, G. "Sargis dpir Yovhannēsean ew ir antip tapanagirn u norayayt 'Kʻristonēakan'ě." *S,* 1969, 38–49.

YOVHANNĒSEAN, VAHAN (1894–1977)

Born in the village of Tzḥaltʻṗila (Akhaltsikhe, Georgia). Joined the Mekhitarist Congregation of Venice in 1908, and having completed his studies in Rome (1916–22), he took the vows of celibacy in 1922. Supervised or taught at Mekhitarist schools in Italy (1922–29), France (1931–37) and Aleppo (1948–55). At the outbreak of World War II, he was principal of the Armenian school in Addis Ababa. Drafted into the Italian Army as a chaplain and was captured by the British. He was released in 1946, returned to Venice, and founded the monthly *Mḥitʻarean ěntanikʻ* in 1947. Primarily a poet, but he also wrote short stories and plays.

Texts

Hayreni krakaran. (Venice, 1930).
Srteru ergě–Vankʻi tzałikner. (Venice, 1939).
Haykakan giwłě. (Venice, 1948).
Ḥełč mardkutʻiwn. (Venice, 1948).
Maremakan. (Venice, 1954).
Aniēn kʻar mě ber. (Venice, 1957, 1970).
Arginayi zangaknerě. (Venice, 1957, 1970).
Tawrosi aṙiwtzě. (Venice, 1959).

Es u du. (Venice, 1960).
Dēpi Awarayr. (Venice, 1962).
Inchpēs tesay Hayastanĕ. (Venice, 1962).
Maštotsakan. (Venice, 1963).
Šušan Vardeni. (Venice, 1964).
Trtmutʻean erger. (Venice, 1964).
Hogineru hangruanĕ. (Venice, 1970).
Šemkʻori aṙin–Manukneru yełapʻoḥutʻiwnĕ. (Venice, 1970).
Smbati gandzerĕ. (Venice, 1970).
Gayianēi vrežĕ. (Venice, 1971).
Leṙneru ergĕ. (Venice, 1971).
Bakin pztikĕ. (Venice, 1973).
Lezun or kĕ meṙni. (Venice, 1973).
Erazneru kłzin Surb Łazar. (Venice, 1974).
Sewanēn Surb Łazar. (Venice, 1979).

Translations (Italian)

Baslini, F. *Poesie.* (Venice, 1947).

Criticism

Tēr-Nersēsean, N. "H. Vahan vrd. Yovhannēsean (1894–1977)." *B,* 137 (1979), 356–400. (Includes a detailed bibliography, 384–400).

YOVHANNISIK TZARETSI (c1560–?)

Very little is known of this priest, also known as Yohanisik Vardapet, whose chronicle reflects historical events in Transcaucasia between 1572 and 1600.

Texts

"Yohanisik vardapeti Hamaṙōt patmutʻiwn antsits antselots i verin kołmans Hayastani ĕst kargi žamanakagrutʻean—skseal i ṘIA tʻuakanēn hayots ts ṘḤTʻ (ayn ē yami Teaṙn 1572 ts 1600)." *Čṙakʻał,* 3 (1859), 69–76; 4, 105–12; 6, 195–99; 7, 227–30.

Samuēli kʻahanayi Anetswoy Hawakʻmunkʻ i grots patmagrats yałags giwti žamanakats antselots minchew i nerkays tzayrakʻał arareal. A. Tēr-Mikʻelean, (Vałaršapat, 1893), 185–200. (Reprint of above).

"Patmutʻiwn Ałuanits ašḥarhin arareal Tzaretsi Yovhannēs vardapetin." *Patmutʻiwn Aṙakʻel vardapeti Dawrižetswoy* (Vałaršapat, 1896), 605–19. (Another version of the above text).

"Hovhanisik Tzaretsu žamanakagrutʻyunĕ (XVI d.)." *Manr žamankagrutʻyunner.* Vol. 2, (Erevan, 1956), 235–55. (Third edition of above text).

YOVNATʻAN NAŁAŠ (1661–1722)

Born in the village of Šoṙotʻ in the region of Naḥijewan. A poet and artist. Acquired some formal education at the monastery of Surb Tʻovma in Agulis, but was basically self-taught. Traveled widely, and for a while in the 1710s he was the favorite poet in the Georgian court. Just as vivid as his portraits and murals, his poetry encompassed themes of nature and love, merrymaking and satire.

Texts

"Tał urahutʻean." *Čṙakʻał*, 1861, 216.
"Tał i veray katui, zor mknern tanin tʻałel." *MKH*, suppl., 45.
"Ōrhnutʻiwn gełatsi iritsi." *MKH*, suppl., 46.
"Tał i veray Tʻiflisu." *TH*, 122–23.
"Gawaṙakan erger. Ginergutʻiwnkʻ Nałaš Yovnatʻani." *M*, 3755 (1885), 657–58 (Includes four poems).
"Tał Nałaš Yovnatʻanē asatseal." *M*, 3789 (1885), 208.
"Jułayetsikʻ ankʻ, ku partzenkʻ." *Lumay*, 1899, 275–76.
"Grem kʻartes yoyž ołbali." *Lumay*, 1899, 276–80.
"Govem srtiw urahakan." *Lumay*, 1899, 280–82. ("Govasankʻ Gurjustanoy").
Chōpanean, A. *Nałaš Yovnatʻan ašułě ew Yovnatʻan Yovnatʻanean nkarichě*. (Paris, 1910).
Mkryan, M. *13–18 dareri hay ašharhik grakanutʻyun*. (Erevan, 1938), 235–70.
Mnatsakanyan, A., and Nazaryan, Š. *Banastełtzutʻyunner*. (Erevan, 1952, 1961).
Nazaryan, Š., and Mnatsakanyan, A. "Nałaš Hovnatʻani antip tałerě." *T*, 1954/7, 71–80.
Mkrtchyan, M. "Nałaš Hovnatʻani mi antip tałě." *T*, 1955/8, 101–4.
Abrahamyan, Ṙ. "Nałaš Hovnatʻani mi anhayt banastełtzutʻyuně." *T*, 1956/1, 95–100.
Minasean, L. "Erku tał Nałaš Yovnatʻanits ew Tʻohatʻetsi Sēpʻil Palits." *S*, 1970, 263–64.
Mnatsakanyan, A. *Tałer*. (Erevan, 1983).

Translations

French

CPA, 109.
LPA, 147–48.
RA, 2, 283–95.
TA, 24–47.

Russian

AAP, 304–12.
BPA, 218–21.

Criticism

Akinean, N. "Yovnatʻan ew Nałaš Yovnatʻaneankʻ ew irents banastełtzakan ew nkarchakan ašhatutʻiwnkʻ." *HA*, 25 (1911), 211–31, 390–410. (Reprinted separately, Vienna, 1911).
Avdalbegyan, M. "Hay nor grakanutʻyan nahanšannerě XVI–XVII dareri tałergutʻyan mej ew Nałaš Hovnatʻaně." *PBH*, 1962/1, 84–93.
Dr. Bazil. "Yovnatʻan Nałaš." *B*, 69 (1911), 476–78.
Hovhannisyan, N. "Bayakan haradrutʻyunnerě Nałaš Hovnatʻani tałerum." *L*, 1984/9, 36–41.
———. "Nałaš Hovnatʻani tałeri šaraharutʻyamb bard nahadasutʻyunnerě." *PBH*, 1985/2, 138–44.
———. "Neł barbaṙayin baṙer Nałaš Hovnatʻani tałerum." *L*, 1987/4, 56–61.
Išhanyan, Ṙ. "Nałaš Hovnatʻani stełtzagortzutʻyan lezvakan bnutʻagirě." *L*, 1972/1, 40–50.
Łazaryan, M. "Nałaš Hovnatʻani norahayt ktavě." *L*, 1968/7, 56–61.

Mkrtchyan, M. *Nałaš Hovnat'an.* (Erevan, 1957).
Oganesian, N. *Iazyk poezii Nagasha Ovnatana kak proiavlenie rannego ashkharabara.* (Erevan, 1988).

ZAK'ARIA AGULETSI (1630–c1691)

A merchant born in Agulis, Nakhijevan, Zak'aria kept a detailed diary of his travels in the Middle East and Western Europe.

Text

Aguletsu Oragrut'yunĕ. (Erevan, 1938). (Diary).

Translations (Russian)

Dnevnik Zakariia Agulisskogo. (Erevan, 1939).

Criticism

Avdalbegyan, M. "Nyut'er Z. Aguletsu 'Oragrut'yun' ev A. Erevantsu 'Patmut'yun paterazmatsn' grk'eri hratarakman patmut'yan veraberyal." *PBH,* 1974/1, 224–38

ZAK'ARIA, EPISKOPOS GNUNEATS (16th c.)

Born in the village of Ḥžiž on the shores of lake Van, hence his sobriquet, "Ḥžěžetsi." Also identified as "Lmetsi," for his possible religious and educational association with the island of Lim in Lake Van, and as Zak'aria "Gnuntsi" for having briefly been bishop of the ancient Gnuneats province north of Lake Van. He is believed to have studied at Ałt'amar, where he may have mastered the art of copying and illuminating manuscripts. It appears that he visited Rome. He was in Constantinople in the 1540s, but no other details are known about the latter part of his life.

Texts (verse)

"Ařajin mardoy nman es . . ." *TH,* 78–81.
Akinean, N. "Zak'aria ep. Gnuneats ew iwr tałerĕ." *HA,* 23 (1909), 231–38, 279–88, 341–45. (Reprinted separately, Vienna, 1910).
Poturean, M. "Tał surb Astuatzatznin." *B,* 68 (1910), 155–60. (Includes 4 other poems).
"I k'ēn tēr haytsem, hayr gt'akan." *MPT,* 20–22.

Translations (French anthologies)

RA, 2, 123–32.

ZAK'ARIA K'ANAK'EṘTSI (1627–c1699)

Born in K'anak'eř (now a northern suburb of the Armenian capital). Studied at Yovhannavank' (near Aštarak, Armenia). A deacon of the Armenian Church. Devoted his life to teaching. His history seems to be his only written work.

Text

Zak'areay Sarkawagi patmagrut'iwn. 3 vols. (Vałaršapat, 1870).

Translations (Russian)

Darbinian-Melikian, M. O. *Zakarii Kanakertsi, Khronika.* (Erevan, 1969).

Criticism

Mḥitʻareants, Abēl. "Kensagrutʻiwn Zakʻariay patmagri Sarkawagi Yovhannavanats." *A,* 1870/5, 151–55.

ZARDAREAN, HRACH (1892–1986)

Born in Harput, Turkey. Son of Ṙubēn Zardarean (q.v.). Attended some of the distinguished Armenian schools of the time: Sanasarean (Karin), Kedronakan (Constantinople), and when he escaped his father's fate and found safety in Transcaucasia, he resumed his studies at the Nersisean of Tiflis, the Gēorgean seminary at Ējmiatzin, and the district school in Erevan. Took up residence in Paris, attended courses at the Sorbonne, and eventually specialized in dentistry. Numerous short stories and other writings by him are still scattered in the periodical press.

Texts

Mer keankʻě. (Paris, 1934).

Orbatsoł mardik. (Paris, 1953).

Žamanak ew ḥorhurdkʻ iwr. (Paris, 1955).

Tʻopʻchyan, Al. *Mer kyankʻě.* (Erevan, 1982). (Articles).

Works in periodicals

HK, 2 (1923–24/2), 31–34; 9, 10–25. 3 (1924–25/3), 9–12; 4, 31–34; 6, 22–25. 4 (1925–26/3), 1–22. 5 (1926–27/10), 1–13. 6 (1927–28/6), 14–28. 12 (1933–34/10), 1–21.

ANA, 2 (1930/4), 89–94. 1933/3–4, 106–8. 6 (1935/12), 35–36.

Z, 1 (1938/3), 17; 4, 27; 5, 37.

Ani, 2 (1947–48/11), 569. 3 (1948–49), 337–45, 456–60. 4 (1950–51), 3–7.

AND, 1 (1952), 49–51. 2 (1952), 28–32. 4 (1953), 3–12. 11 (1960), 4–8. 12 (1961), 49–78. 15 (1964), 12–17. 16 (1965), 5–6, 41–52. 18 (n.d.), 3–8.

ZARDAREAN, ṘUBĒN (1874–1915)

Pen names: Achkʻ Ehovayi, Aslan, Ēztahar, and others.

Born in Siverek, Turkey; educated in Harput. Taught in Armenian schools. Incarcerated in 1903 for suspected political activites. Fled to Plovdiv, Bulgaria, in 1905, and published the periodical *Ṙazmik* (1906–09). Returned to Constantinople in 1909 and launched the daily *Azatamart* (1909–15). In this period, journalism and political activities absorbed most of his attention and left him with no time to add to his small but fine literary writings. Participated in the Congress of the Armenian Revolutionary Federation (Dašnaktsutʻiwn), held in Erzurum in 1914. He was arrested by the Young Turk regime on the night of 24 April 1915, and was put to death a little later in the year.

Collections

Ambołjakan erker, 1. Ardzak ējer ew hekʻeatʻner. (Paris, 1930).

Texts

Tsaygaloys (ardzak ējer). (Constantinople, 1910; Venice, 1945). (Selections; Antʻilias, 1977).

Mełraget. (Constantinople, 1914).

Tsaygaluys. (Erevan, 1959).

Works in periodicals

M, 1893/3979, 108–9. 3995, 364–66. 1898/1, 22. 1899/3, 75. 1900/40, 629–32. 1901/16, 249–52. 1902/9, 131–35.

AM, 1901, 904–8. 1902, 63–73, 201–9, 309–12, 521–26, 691–98, 806–10, 845–51. 1904, 367–71, 631–33, 662–65, 701–5, 725–30, 925–28, 1044–49. 1905, 83–88, 118–21, 139–41, 167–70, 537–41, 573–78.

Širak, 1905/1, 15–18; 3, 182–87; 5, 321–32; 10–11, 262–67.

ANA, 12 (1911/9–12), 195–96; 1 (1929/2), 29–3; 5, 6–9. 1934/5–6, 20–22.

Nawasard, 1914, 7–18.

HK, 16 (1937–38/6), 117–18; 27 (1949/5), 18–22.

AND, 15 (1964), 9–11.

Translations

English

Ashjian, S. "A Sultan in His Heart." *Nor ašḫarh,* January 19, 1963, 4; January 20, 1963, 4; February 2, 1963, 4; February 9, 1963, 4.

"The Bride of the Lake." *The Oriental World,* 1914/5, 142. (Also published in *The New Armenia,* 9 [1917/4], 59).

Keljik, B. "How Death Came to Earth." *Armenia,* 4 (1910/1), 4–5.

Mangouni, N. "The Bride of the Lake." *Lraber,* September 16, 1961, 4.

———. "The Truthful Boy." *Lraber,* September 21, 1961, 4.

———. "When Men Did Not Die." *Lraber,* October 28, 1961, 4; October 31, 1961, 4.

French

"L'Arbre solitaire." *Hayastan,* June 24, 1965, 4.

"La mort n'existait pas . . ." *Hayastan,* June 13, 1965, 4; July 8, 1965, 4.

Tchobanian, A. "La fiancée du lac," "Fleurs! Rouges fleurs!," "Les petrifiés." *Mercure de France,* 18 (1896), 202–4.

———. *Clarté nocturne.* (Paris, 1913).

Italian

"La fidanzata del lago." *Armenia,* 1916/5, 6.

Russian

"Ulitsa." *KHAN,* 1, 26–30. (Also published in *RAN,* 76–80).

Criticism

Antonean, Y. "Ṙubēn Zardarean." *HK,* 10 (1931–32/6), 107–10.

Aznavuryan, G. "Anhayt ējer hay nahatakneri grakan žaṙanguťyunits." *EJ,* 1965/2–4, 43–57. (Previously unpublished letters and other material by Komitas, G. Zōhrap, D. Varužan, Siamanťō, Tlkatintsi, Ṙ. Zardarean, and Ṙ. Sewak).

Baluean, H. "Ṙ. Zardareani ambołjakan gortzě." *Z,* 2 [1931], 32–35.

Kostanyan, A. "Ṙubēn Zardarean." *EJ,* 1965/2–4, 136–39.

Kurtikyan, S. "Hayrenikʻi bnašḫarhi ergichě." *SG,* 1974/12, 87–96.

Mḫiťarean, G. "Y. Ōšakani 'Ṙ. Zardareaně'." *HK,* 6 (1927–28/7), 165–66.

Orberean, Ṙ. "Vaḫ, es meṙnēi." *AM,* 1902, 205–9. (Criticism of work of the same title).

Ōšakan, Y. "Ṙubēn Zardarean." *HK,* 4 (1925–26/11), 14–20; 12, 29–36. 5 (1926–27/1), 89–96; 2, 57–60; 3, 50–63; 11, 49–58; 12, 52–57. 6 (1927–28/1), 68–74; 2, 53–58; 3, 53–56.

Ṙubēn Zardareani 'Tsaygaloysě'. (Constantinople, 1913).

Sargsyan, G. "Ṙuben Zardaryanĕ ev ir noraveperĕ." *PBH,* 1989/2, 89–100.
Siruni, Y. "Ṙubēn Zardarean." *HK,* 3 (1924–25/3), 28–44.
Stepʻanean, K. "Bats namak aṙ Ṙubēn Zardarean." *AM,* 1902, 135. (On "Vaḥ, es meṙnēi").
Zardarean, H. "89ameak tznndean Ṙubēn Zardareani." *AND,* 15 (1964), 9–11.

ZARIFEAN, MATTʻĒOS (1894–1924)

A native of Constantinople. Brother of Seza (q.v.). Studied at the Pērpērean school and taught for one year in Adana (1913). Served in the Ottoman Army in World War I, but soon symptoms of tuberculosis confined him to a military hospital. In 1919, he worked as an interpreter for the British Army and briefly taught at his alma mater. Two collections of lyric poetry had already earned him fame, when consumption overpowered this young man of considerable athletic abilities.

Collections

Ambołjakan gortzer. (Beirut, 1956).
Ĕntir kʻertʻuatzner. (Aleppo, 1946).
Erger. (Erevan, 1965).
Erker. (Antʻilias, 1990).

Texts

Trtmutʻean ew ḥałałutʻean erger. (Constantinople, 1921; Jerusalem, 1951).
Keankʻi ew mahuan erger. (Constantinople, 1922; Jerusalem, 1951).

Works in periodicals

Z (taregirkʻ), 1937, 19.

Translations

French anthologies

APA, 229–31.

Italian anthologies

LPAM, 267–70.

Spanish anthologies

APAS, 261–64.

Criticism

Avagyan, A. "Kyankʻ, aprvatz ayrumov." *SG,* 1975/12, 116–21.
Kapents, P. "Namak ḥmbagrutʻean." Z (amsōreay), 1 (1938/3), 27, 29.
Oskean, S. "Mattʻēos Zarifean." *Vēm,* 2 (1934/5), 41–46.
Yapʻujyan, S. "Mattʻeos Zarifyan." *SG,* 1974/6, 153–56.

ZARKEAR, (1824–1874)

Pen name: Zarkear.

Abraham, whose surname is unknown, was born in Shemakha (now in Azerbaijan). An *ašuł* who resided in Baku for most of his life.

Poetry

Zarkeari kʻnarĕ. (Baku, 1909).
THG, 165–72.

ZARYAN, KOSTAN (1885–1969)

Born Kostan Ełiazaryan in Šamaḫi (i.e., Shemakha), now in Azerbaijan. Educated in a Russian school in Baku (1890–95). Pursued his higher studies in Paris (1895–1901), and in Brussels (1901–04). Learned Armenian in Venice (1910–13); went to the Ottoman capital; and published, jointly with colleagues such as Yakob Ōšakan (q.v.), the short-lived periodical *Mehean.* Fortuitously escaped the fate of his colleagues, slaughtered in 1915 on orders from the Young Turk ruling circles, and lived in Italy for a while. Returned to Constantinople after World War I and published another short-lived periodical, *Bardzravank‘* (1922) jointly with V. T‘ēk‘ēean, Y. Ōšakan and others. Took up residence with his family in Soviet Armenia in 1922, but returned to the West, having taught for three years at the University of Erevan. From 1925 to his second and final return to Soviet Armenia in 1961, he lived in Italy, France, the United States, and the Middle East. Published *The Armenian Quarterly* (1946) in the United States and lectured on Armenian studies at Columbia University (1944–46). Despite recent publications, some of his work still lies buried in periodicals.

Collections

Erker. (Beirut and Ant‘ilias, 1975). (Includes "Antsordē ew ir čamp‘an," "Arewmutk‘," and "K‘ałak‘ner").

Girk‘ diwtsaznergut‘ean. (Jerusalem, 1978).

Erker. (Erevan, 1985).

Texts

Ōreri psakē. (Constantinople, 1922; Beirut, 1971). (Verse).

Tatragomi harsē. (Boston, 1930; Erevan, 1965). (Poem).

Erek‘ erger aselu hamar vištē erkri ew vištē erknk‘i. (Vienna, 1931). (Verse).

Nawē leran vray. (Boston, 1943; Erevan, 1963 [revised ed.]). (Novel).

Bankōōpē ew mamut‘i oskornerē. (Ant‘ilias, 1987).

Works in periodicals

Nawasard, 1914, 132–33.

HK, 4 (1925–26/2), 23–33; 4, 40–41; 7, 7–9; 11, 10–12. 7 (1928–29/11), 1–12. 8 (1929–30/2), 55. 6, 1–44.

ANA, 1929/1, 8–13; 4, 37–38.

Z, 1 (1929–[30]), 2–4, 51–53. *Z* (amsōreay), 1 (1938/3), 19. *Z* (eṙamseay), 1947/2, 103–7. *Z* (amsat‘ert‘), 1 (1955/1), 1. 1 (1956/8), 3. 2 (1957/1–2), 5. 3 (1959/8–10), 1. 4 (1959/1–2), 5. 4 (1960/5–6), 1–2.

"Bankōōpē ew mamut‘i oskornerē." *HK,* 10 (1931–32/1), 1–22; 2, 10–26; 3, 6–29; 4, 39–56; 5, 11–30; 6, 52–69; 7, 26–46; 8, 28–45; 9, 13–27; 10, 48–61; 11, 33–48; 12, 58–70. 11 (1932–33/1), 19–34; 2, 32–43; 3, 68–71; 4, 29–42; 5, 55–68; 6, 44–57; 7, 32–47; 8, 65–78; 9, 26–41; 10, 29–32; 11, 14–26; 12, 29–41. 12 (1933–34/1), 25–41; 2, 42–55.

"Erkirner ew astuatzner." *HK,* 13 (1934–35/12), 1–18. 14 (1935–36/1), 75–91; 14/2, 45–60; 14/3, 38–54; 14/4, 39–53; 14/5, 44–60; 14/6, 47–60; 14/7, 67–83; 14/8, 55–72; 14/9, 33–49, 84-85; 14/10, 1–15; 14/11, 25–40; 14/12, 41–57. 15 (1936–37/1), 36–52; 15/2, 41–56; 15/3, 51–67; 15/4, 45–57; 15/5, 42–56; 15/7, 29–44; 15/9, 27–42; 15/11, 53–63; 15/12, 43–49. 16 (1937–38/1), 37–44; 2, 42–51; 3, 59–70; 4, 59–66; 5, 89–99; 6, 17–21. 26 (1948/11), 1–15; 12, 8–19. 27 (1949/3), 1–5; 7, 1–20; 12, 1–9. 28 (1950/1), 10–19.

Ani, 1 (1946), 57.
"Kłzin ew mi mard." *HK,* 33 (1955/2), 1–10; 3, 16–24; 4, 24–31; 5, 9–21; 6, 17–29; 7, 23–32; 8, 14–24.

Translations

ENGLISH

Amirian, L. "The Builders." *The Armenian Student,* 5 (1934/3), 19–25.
Baliozian, A. *The Traveller & His Road.* (New York, 1981).
———. *Bancoop & the Bones of the Mammoth.* (New York, 1982).
———. *The Island & a Man.* (Toronto, 1983).
Kanayan, M. "How It Rained on Sevan." *Hayrenik Weekly,* August 16, 1956, 6. (Excerpts).

FRENCH ANTHOLOGIES

LPA, 237–39.
Ter-Sarkissian, P. *Le Bateau sur la montagne.* (Paris: Editions du Seuil, 1986). (Translation of the original 1943 edition).

RUSSIAN

Korabl' na gore. (Moscow, 1969, 1974). (Translation of the revised edition).

Criticism

Aharonean, A. "Kostan Zarean." *HK,* 8 (1929–30/9), 57–62; 10, 109–20; 11, 36–42; 12, 40–48.
Akhverdian, L. "Kostan Zarian: 'Le Navire sur la montagne'." *OO,* 139 (July 1970), 166–68.
"Kostan Zaryan." *SG,* 1969/12, 151–52.
Melikʻsetʻyan, S. "Kostan Zaryan: tʻṙutsik ḥoskʻ." *SG,* 1979/12, 126–27.
Snapean, P. *Awazaḥratz nawě.* (Beirut, 1964).
Tʻaščean, B. "Kostan Zarean." *Z* (amsatʻertʻ), 4 (1960/7–8), 2–3.

ZARYAN, NAIRI (1900–1969)

Pen name: Nairi Zaryan.

Hayastan Ełiazaryan was born in Ḥaṙakonis, a village near Van. Losing his parents to the horrors of 1915, he fled to Eastern Armenia and found shelter in orphanages in Dilijan and Erevan. Participated in the defense of Eastern Armenia against the Turkish onslaught of 1918. Graduated from the State University of Erevan (1927), pursued his higher studies in Leningrad, and practiced journalism for a while. President of the Union of Soviet Writers of Armenia, 1944–46. He also held various political positions (deputy, etc.) in local party and government organizations, traveled abroad extensively, and was decorated on numerous occasions.

Collections

Erker. 5 vols. (Erevan, 1945–56).
Hatěntir. (Erevan, 1951).
Mihatoryak. (Erevan, 1959).
Erkeri žołovatzu. 6 vols.; 1 supp. vol. (Erevan, 1962–65).
Mihatoryak. (Erevan, 1975).
Erker. 4 vols. (Erevan, 1984–85).

Texts (verse, prose, and plays)

Hranušě. (Erevan, 1925).

Jrantsk'i kapuyt erkrum. (Erevan, 1926).
Noyemberyan ōrerin. (Tiflis, 1926).
Chin ałjik. (Erevan, 1926).
Ṙušani k'arap'ě. (Erevan, 1930, 1932, 1936).
Harvatzner. (Erevan, 1933).
Ōdachu Hanrin. (Erevan, 1934).
Amrots. (Erevan, 1935).
Sak'o Mikinyan. (Erevan, 1935, 1936).
Hatsavan. (Erevan, 1937 [incomplete], 1947, 1949 [revised], 1955, 1960, 1977).
Haveržakan gagat'ner. (Erevan, 1939).
Dyutsaznagirk'. (Erevan, 1940).
Mankakan. (Erevan, 1940).
Aršak ev Šapuh. (Erevan, 1941, 1943).
Martakoch. (Erevan, 1941).
Vrež. (Erevan, 1942).
Tsasman zavakě. (Erevan, 1942).
Lsek', darer. (Erevan, 1943).
Dzayn hayrenakan. (Erevan, 1943).
Šikatsatz hogov. (Erevan, 1943).
Hitlerě zooparkum. (Erevan, 1944).
Ara Gełetsik. (Erevan, 1946, 1968; Paris, 1960; Beirut, 1966).
Amenagazan. (Erevan, 1947).
Tnamerdz aygi. (Erevan, 1947).
Ałbyuri mot. (Erevan, 1950).
Armenuhi. (Erevan, 1950).
Ułegrut'yunner. (Erevan, 1953).
Arev u stver. (Erevan, 1957).
Paron Petros u ir naḥararnerě. (Erevan, 1958).
Ser ev gžtut'yun. (Erevan, 1960).
Du indz kp'ntres. (Erevan, 1965).
Sasna Davit'. (Erevan, 1966).
Spasum em k'ez. (Erevan, 1968).
Hayreni tun. (Erevan, 1970).
Erkrord kyank'. Ink'napatum. (Erevan, 1982).

Translations

English

Zelikoff, L. "Flowers." *SL,* 1966/3, 139.

English Anthologies

SAP, 14–17.

French

Mardirossian, L. "Mes petits-enfants." *OO,* 123 (March 1969), 26.

French Anthologies

Gamarra, P. *E,* 72–78.
LPA, 288–97.

German

Leschnitzer, F. "Blumen." *Sowjet-Literatur,* 1966/3, 138.

RUSSIAN

Antokol'skii, P. *Vechnye vershiny. Stikhi.* (Moscow, 1940).
Ara Prekrasnyi. (Moscow, 1947).
Aramuni. Poema. (Moscow, 1953).
Atsavan. Roman. (Erevan, 1952).
David Sasunskii. Povest' po motivam arm. eposa. (Moscow, 1968).
Geroi Sovetskogo Soiuza kapitan N.G. Stepanian. (Erevan, 1943).
Golos rodiny. (Erevan, 1944).
Dudintseva, V., and Taronian, A. *Gospodin Petros i ego ministry.* (Moscow, 1961).
Ia doma. Stikhi i poemy. (Moscow, 1960).
Izbrannoe. (Moscow, 1949).
Izbrannoe. ([Moscow], 1954).
Izbrannye stikhi. (Moscow, 1937).
Izbrannye proizvedeniia. (Moscow, 1947).
Opytnoe pole. (Moscow, 1956).
Otchii dom. Izbr. stikhi i poemy. ([Moscow], 1958).
Rushanskaia skala. Poema. (Moscow, 1935).
Stikhi. (Moscow, 1963).
Serebriakov, K. *Tam tsvela vishnia. Iapon. ocherki.* (Moscow, 1965).

SPANISH

Silvestre, L. "Aprem-chaprem." *Literatura Sovietica,* 1966/3, 146.

Criticism

Ałababyan, S. *Nairi Zaryan.* (Erevan, 1954).
———. "Kyankʻi hordzanutum." *SG,* 1977/5, 155–56.
———."Nairi Zaryani ułegitzě." *SG,* 1980/12, 104–25.
Avagyan, M. *Nairi Zaryani stełtzagortzutʻyan lezun ev očě.* (Erevan, 1961).
Bazyan, S. *Erekʻ urvagitz–Nairi Zaryan, Širaz, Gełam Saryan.* (Erevan, 1941).
Daronyan, S. "N. Zaryani 'Ara Gełetsikě' ev dasakan ołbergutʻyan avanduytʻnerě." *PBH,* 1981/4, 58–71.
———. *Nairi Zaryan.* (Erevan, 1982).
Ēmin, G. "Nairi Zaryan." *SG,* 1976/1, 123–26.
Manassian, G. "L'œuvre de Nairi Zarian." *OO* (Nov. 1961), 166–69.
Matoyan, Ch. "Nairi Zaryaně ev kʻṙdakan irakanutʻyuně." *SG,* 1980/12, 126–29.
Muradyan, H. "Bṙnakalutʻyan ev azatasirutʻyan bahumě." *SG,* 1962/1, 130–36.
Oskerchyan, A. "Nairi Zaryani 20—akan tʻvakanneri stełtzagortzutʻyan masin (ditołutʻyunner)." *T,* 1954/5, 41–60.
Petrosyan, Z. "Nairi Zaryan." *SG,* 1961/3, 133–44.
Safaryan, V. "Martakochi ergichě." *SG,* 1975/5, 146–52.
———. *Nairi Zaryan.* (Erevan, 1985).
Sargsyan, G. "Mer žamanaki harazat dzayně." *PBH,* 1961/3–4, 149–65.
Zaryan, Ṙ. "Nairi Zaryan, Paruyr Sevak." *SG,* 1975/6, 81–96.

ZŌHRAP, GRIGOR (1861–1915)

Born in Constantinople. Educated in Armenian elementary and secondary schools. Studied engineering and law at higher institutions in his native city. Eminently active in public life as a writer, a journalist, a brilliant and audacious lawyer, and an illustrious professor of law. Elected to the Ottoman Parliament in 1908 and distinguished himself as an eloquent orator and a dedicated public figure. Stood up for his fellow countrymen and was stunned by the carnage in Adana, coming so soon after the dawn of freedom and fraternity as proclaimed by the Young Turks. Instrumental in reviving the Armenian Question in the early 1910s. He was arrested on 20 May 1915, a few weeks after the collective round-up of Armenian intelligentsia on 24 April 1915, and was brutally murdered in the interior a few weeks later.

Collections

Tzanōtʻ dēmkʻer u patmuatzkʻner. (Paris, 1932).
Hyusyan, M. *Novelneri liakatar žołovatzu.* (Erevan, 1954).
Ambołjakan hawakʻatzoy noravēperu ew patmuatzkʻneru. (Constantinople, 1959).
Gamałelyan, T. *Novelner.* (Erevan, 1961, 1987).
Erkeri žołovatzu. 2 vols. (Erevan, 1962).
Ambołjakan erker. 2d ed. (Beirut, 1971).
Hyusyan, M. *Grakanutʻyan masin.* (Erevan, 1973).
Gasparyan, M. *Novelner.* (Erevan, 1978).
Erker. (Antʻilias, 1988).

Texts

Anhetatsatz serund mě. (Constantinople, 1887, 1924; Beirut, 1957, 1971 [published with *Pʻotʻorikě*]). (Novel).
Ḥłčmtankʻi dzayner. (Constantinople, 1909; Beirut, 1958, 1977). (Stories).
Keankʻě inchpēs or ē. (Constantinople, 1911; Beirut, 1959, 1975). (Stories).
Luṙ tsawer. (Constantinople, 1911; Beirut, 1956, 1971). (Stories).
La Question arménienne à la lumière des documents. (Paris, 1913). (Published under the pseudonym Marcel Léart).
Ējer ułewori mě ōragrēn. (Smyrna, 1922; Beirut, 1959). (Travel notes).
Pʻotʻorikě. (Constantinople, 1924). (Story).
Mer keankʻēn . . . (Constantinople, 1945).
Haykakan hartsě pʻastatʻułtʻeru loysin tak. (Beirut, 1973). (Armenian version of French original).
Šaruryan, A. "Grigor Zohrapi hraparakaḥosakan aṙajin eluytʻnerě." *BEH,* 1980/3, 120–35.
Erekʻ novel. (Erevan, 1988).

Translations

English

Andreassian, K. "Submission." *Armenia,* 4 (1911/12), 16.
Antreassian, J. *Voice of Conscience: The Stories of Krikor Zohrab.* (New York, 1983).
Baliozian, A. *Zohrab: An Introduction.* (Kitchener, Ontario, Canada and Cambridge, MA, 1985).
"Sister Emily." *The Armenian Review,* 6 (1953/2), 30–34.

French

"Ayinga." *La Patrie* (Constantinople), 1909/27, 207–8.
Panossian, A. "Résignation." *M,* 1901/30, 467.
"Le retour." *La Patrie* (Constantinople), 1909/33, 285; 1909/34, 296–97; 1909/35, 308; 1909/36, 317; 1909/37, 322–23; 1909/39, 343.

German

AN, 5–21.

Russian

Iuzbash'ian, M., et al. *Novelly.* (Erevan, 1986).
Salakhian, A. *Novelly.* (Moscow, 1962).

Russian anthologies

DILS, 57–152.
KHAN, 1, 3–20; 2, 3–26.
RAN, 26–40.

Criticism

Alpōyačean, A. *Anhetatsoł dēmkʻer: Grigor Zōhrap (ir keankʻě ew ir gortzě.)* (Constantinople, 1919).

Apʻinyan, A. "Grigor Zohrapě ev Stepʻan Zoryaně." *PBH,* 1987/1, 112–23.

Aznavuryan, G. "Anhayt ējer hay nahatakneri grakan žaṙangutʻyunits." *EJ,* 1965/2–4, 43–57. (Previously unpublished letters and other material by Komitas, G. Zōhrap, D. Varužan, Siamantʻō, Tʻlkatintsi, Ṙ. Zardarean, and Ṙ. Sewak).

———. "Ējer Grigor Zohrapi odisakanits." *BEH,* 1977/3, 179–92.

Chiftʻē-Saraf. "Siruatz dēmkʻer–Grigor Zōhrap." *M,* 1901/20, 307–9.

Chōpanean, A. "Grigor Zōhrap." *ANA,* 2 (1930/3), 1–9.

———. "Žēōn–tʻurkʻeru yałtʻanakě ew Grigor Zōhrap." *ANA,* 9 (1938/4), 1–7.

Ēpliłatʻean, M. "Grigor Zōhrapi keankʻēn." *HK,* 29 (1951/10), 38–53.

Gamēr. "Uruagitzner–Gr. Zōhrap." *M,* 1903/51, 802–3.

Hakobyan, G. "Novelayin dzeveri skzbnavorumě Grigor Zohrapi poetikayum." *L,* 1986/9, 39–47.

Hambaryan, A. "Haykakan hartsě pʻastatʻłtʻeri luysi tak." *SG,* 1979/9, 129–32.

Hovhannisyan, S. "Hełinaki, patmołi ev herosi ḥoskʻi aṙandznahatkutʻyunnerě Gr. Zohrapi noraveperum." *L,* 1981/3, 15–25.

Hyusyan, M. "Hamematutʻyuně Grigor Zohrapi stełtzagortzutʻyan mej." *T,* 1956/5, 65–80.

———. *Grigor Zohrap: kyankʻě ev stełtzagortzutʻyuně.* (Erevan, 1957).

———. "Grigor Zohrapi lezvi patkeravorutʻyan mijotsnerě." *T,* 1959/11–12, 61–72.

———. "Grigor Zohrap." *T,* 1961/8, 65–68.

———. "Grigor Zohrapi gełagitakan hayatskʻnerě." *SG,* 1961/6, 116–26.

———. "Pʻoḥharaberutʻyuně Grigor Zohrapi stełtzagortzutʻyan mej." *PBH,* 1961/2, 150–59.

———. *Grigor Zohrapi arvestě.* (Erevan, 1964).

———. "Chmoṙatsvoł anunner." *EJ,* 1965/2–4, 71–75.

Kʻiwfēčean, Y. "Mer vipasannerě–Grigor Zōhrap." *HG,* 2 (1912–13/1), 6–14.

Kurtikyan, S. "Anzugakan mer Zohrapě." *SG,* 1961/6, 110–15.

Mamurean, H. "Masis ew A. Mamul." *AM,* 1900, 494–95.

M[amurean], M. "Mitʻē patasḥan [ē]?" *AM,* 1900, 650–52.

Ot'ian, E. "Ha smertnom puti: Zorab i Vardges." *L,* 1989/2, 79–82.

Šahpaz, S. "Grigor Zōhrap—uruagtzołě." *B,* 113 (1955), 198–206.

———. "Grigor Zōhrap—yełapʻoḥakaně." *Z* (amsatʻertʻ), 2 (1957/7–8), 5–6.

———. *Grigor Zōhrap.* (Beirut, 1959).

Šaruryan, A. "Grigor Zohrapi hraparakaḥosakan eluytʻnerě." *BEH,* 1980/3, 120.

———. "Grigor Zohrapi erkeri hratarakut'yunneri patmut'yunits." *PBH,* 1988/2, 92–100.
Serinkyulyan, H. "Hušer Grigor Zohrapi masin." *EJ,* 1965/2–4, 130–32.
Step'anean, K. "Grigor Zōhrap, Marapetě -P'ot'urlěn." *AM,* 1900, 448–50.
———. "Marapetin u P'ot'urlěin aṙt'iw." *AM,* 1900, 515–19.
———. "Verjin arar." *AM,* 1902, 547–51. (On Zōhrap's style).
Terteryan, A. "Zohrapi arvestě." *T,* 1946/1, 3–31.
Tziatzan, Š. "Grakan kendanagirner—G. Zōhrap." *M,* 1905/12, 188–90.
Yarut'iwnean, A. "Grakan k'ronik, anbaroyakan grakanut'iwn." *AM,* 1908, 703–6.

ZORYAN, STEP'AN (1889–1967)

Pen names: St. Roffor, Step'an Zoryan.

Born Step'an Aṙak'elyan, a native of Łarak'ilisa (Kirovakan under the Soviets, but renamed Vanadzor following Armenia's independence). Educated locally. Moved to Tiflis in 1906 and worked mainly as a journalist. From 1919 until his death, he lived in Erevan, holding numerous academic, cultural, editorial, journalistic, administrative, and political positions locally and in some all-Union organizations. Elected to the Academy of Sciences of the Armenian SSR, 1965. An annual state prize named after him, for translations from or into Armenian, was established in 1980.

Collections

Novelner, erkeri žołovatzu. Vol. 1. (Erevan, 1931).
Patmuatzk'ner. (Paris, 1939).
Erkeri žołovatzu. 6 vols. (Erevan, 1940–54).
Erkeri žołovatzu. 10 vols. (Erevan, 1960–64).
Erkeri žołovatzu. 12 vols. (Erevan, 1977–90).
Patmvatzk'ner. (Erevan, 1980).

Texts (prose)

Ṭhur mardik. (Tiflis, 1918). (Patmuatzk'ner, vol. 1).
Tsankapat. (Erevan, 1923, 1926). (Patmvatzk'ner, vol. 2).
Erkat'ułin. (Moscow, 1925).
Gradarani ałjikě. (Erevan, 1925, 1934, 1954 [with *Hełkomi naḥagahě*], 1958).
Hazaran blbul. (Erevan, 1925, 1937, 1981).
Paterazm. (Erevan, 1925). (Patmvatzk'ner, vol. 3).
Hełkomi naḥagahě. (Erevan, 1926).
Tzovaně. (Moscow, 1926).
Elektrakan lampě. (Erevan, 1927).
Krak. (Erevan, 1927). (Patmvatzk'ner, vol. 4).
Ḥužan Aršon. (Erevan, 1928).
Aṙajin ōrer. (Erevan, 1930, 1967). (Patmvatzk'ner, vol. 5).
Chalankě. (Erevan, 1930).
Vardadzori komuně. (Erevan, 1930).
Mi gišer antaṙum. (Erevan, 1931).
Heros komunarě. (Erevan, 1932).
Karmir aragil. (Erevan, 1932, 1970).
Spitak k'ałak'. (Erevan, 1932).
Dzmṙan gišer. (Erevan, 1935).

Mi kyank'i patmut'yun. Vol. 1. (Erevan, 1935).
Sev Set'on. (Erevan, 1935).
P'ordzank'. (Erevan, 1936).
Ḥałoħi aygum. (Erevan, 1937).
Šamon. (Erevan, 1937).
Tnōrhnek' ev uriš patmvatzk'ner. (Erevan, 1937).
Vanušě. (Erevan, 1938).
Mi kyank'i patmut'yun. 2 vols. (Erevan, 1939, 1955, 1988).
Šunn u katun. (Erevan, 1940).
Mi kyank'i patmut'yun. Vol. 1. (Erevan, 1940). (Revised edition for young readers).
Hek'iat'ner. (Erevan, 1941; Aleppo, 1950).
Smbat Bagratuni. (Erevan, 1941).
Pap t'agavor. (Erevan, 1944, 1957, 1989; Paris, 1950–51 [3 parts]; Aleppo, 1951).
P'ok'rik patmvatzk'ner. (Erevan, 1944).
Hrašali sringě. (Erevan, 1945; Cairo, 1960).
Parz hoginer. (Erevan, 1945).
Mełk'ě. (Cairo, 1946).
Sarašeni tłanerě. (Erevan, 1951).
Mer tzanot'nerě. (Erevan, 1952, 1977).
Čanaparhord Jekon. (Erevan, 1957, 1978).
Hek'iat'ner. (Erevan, 1957).
Hušeri girk'. (Erevan, 1958).
Hayots berdě. (Erevan, 1959; Beirut, 1960).
Savaṙnoł droš. (Erevan, 1960).
Varazdat. (Erevan, 1967).
Hin tzanot'ner. (Erevan, 1969).
Im T'umanyaně. (Erevan, 1969).
"Step'an Zoryani namaknerě." *SG,* 1983/3, 112–28. (Letters to K. Mik'ayelyan).
T'irabyan, N. "Step'an Zoryani namaknerě Misak' Ēp'rikyanin." *BEH,* 1985/3, 116–33.
"Ḥełč kině." *SG,* 1988/4, 129–31.

Translations

English

"A Mother." *International Literature* (later *SL*), 1943/6, 43–45.
Ingman, A. "The Orchard." *SL,* 1966/3, 25–59.

English anthologies

WM, 63–101.

French

Butkiewicz, L. "Les Pigeons." *OO,* 123 (March 1969), 56–59.

French anthologies

Yéghiaian, A. *E,* 134–37.

German

Löffler, G. *Sterne hinter den Bergen.* (Berlin, 1962). (Slightly abridged).
Wrazek, I. "Der Apfelgarten." *Sowjet-Literatur,* 1966/3, 29–65.

German anthologies

AN, 124–69.

RUSSIAN

Babaian, A. *Devushka iz biblioteki.* (Moscow and Leningrad, 1930).
———. *Devushka iz biblioteki.* (Erevan, 1939).
Ioannisian, A. *Tsar' Pap. Ist. roman.* (Moscow, 1946; Erevan, 1967).
Izbrannye novelly. (Erevan, 1948).
Izbrannye proizvedeniia. (Moscow, 1956).
Izbrannye rasskazy. (Tiflis, 1934).
Khachatriants, Ia. *Belyi gorod.* (Moscow, 1933).
———. *Iablonevyi sad. Povesti i rasskazy.* (Moscow, 1948).
Krylatoe znamia. (Moscow, 1954).
Musatov, A. *Noch' v lesy. [Rasskazy].* (Moscow, 1955, 1958).
Obitateli belogo doma. Rasskazy i povesti. (Erevan, 1937).
Povesti i rasskazy. (Moscow, 1952).
Predsedatel' revkoma. Rasskaz. (Tiflis, 1934).
Rasskazy dlia detei. (Erevan, 1946, 1952).
Sukiasian, S. *Istoria odnoi zhizni.* (Moscow and Leningrad, 1949, 1950; Moscow, 1955, 1961).
Tadeosian, A. *Sem'ia Amirianov.* (Moscow, 1967).
Ter-Martirosian, A. *Rasskazy.* (Moscow and Leningrad, 1930).
U kolodtsa. Smert' Oana. (Tiflis, 1934).
Zimniaia noch'. (Tiflis, 1936).

SPANISH

Talon, V. "El manzanar." *Literatura Sovietica,* 1966/3, 27–62.

Criticism

Abgaryan, Ṙ. "Patmavipasani očakan arvestě." *SG,* 1984/5, 122–26.
Ałababyan, S. *Step'an Zoryan.* (Erevan, 1955).
———. *Stepan Zorian.* (Erevan, 1956). (Russian).
———. "Step'an Zoryan." *SG,* 1961/4, 103–12.
———. "Step'an Zoryani patmaveperě." *PBH,* 1973/2, 77–88.
———. "Step'an Zoryan." *PBH,* 1980/4, 57–71.
Alek'sanyan, E. "Cheḥově ev Zoryaně." *SG,* 1977/12, 125–31.
Amirḥanyan, V. "St. Zoryani patmakan novelnerě." *SG,* 1981/3, 149–51.
———. *Step'an Zoryani p'ok'ratzaval ardzakě.* (Erevan, 1985).
Ap'inyan, A. "Step'an Zoryaně ṙus k'nnadatut'yan gnahatmamb." *BEH,* 1984/1, 74–87.
———. "Step'an Zoryaně ev Anton Cheḥově." *L,* 1985/4, 22–29.
———. "Step'an Zoryaně ev Mak'sim Gorku avanduyt'nerě." *BEH,* 1985/1, 96–107.
———. "Step'an Zoryaně ev grakan avanduyt'i hartserě." *L,* 1986/8, 33–40.
———. "Grigor Zohrapě ev Step'an Zoryaně." *PBH,* 1987/1, 112–23.
———. *Step'an Zoryaně ev ṙus grakanut'yuně.* (Erevan, 1988).
———. "Step'an Zoryani ardzaki ṙit'mě." *BEH,* 1990/1, 65–78.
———. "Step'an Zoryani banarvesti mi k'ani hartser." *PBH,* 1990/3, 3–17.
Hovhannisyan, H. "Zoryann im achk'erov." *SG,* 1975/6, 97–104.
Hovsep'yan, G. *Step'an Zoryani stełtzagortzut'yuně.* (Erevan, 1951).
Hunanyan, A. "Nor mardu kazmavorumě Step'an Zoryani patmvatzk'nerum." *SG,* 1978/6, 140–44.
Mkrtchyan, H. *Step'an Zoryan.* (Erevan, 1954).

———. "Step'an Zoryan." *SG,* 1965/9, 99–102.
———. "Hay hin gyułě Step'an Zoryani patmvatzk'nerum (Tsankapat)." *SG,* 1967/5, 119–33.
———. "Hełap'oḥut'yuně ev k'ałak'atsiakan kṙivnerě Step'an Zoryani erkerum." *SG,* 1977/6, 125–35.
Nalbandyan, V. "Chorrord dari hay irakanut'yuně ev Step'an Zoryani patmaveperě." *PBH,* 1968/2, 57–80.
———. "Grołě ev patmut'yuně." *SG,* 1968/6, 128–44.
———. "Zoryan-patmavipasani gełarvestakan varpetut'yan mi k'ani hartser." *L,* 1968/7, 15–32.
Šahinean, G. "Step'an Zōreani 'Hayots berdě'." *HK,* 38 (1960/7), 95–99.
Sargsyan, Ḥ. "Step'an Zoryani erku patmvatzk'i masin." *T,* 1957/l, 25–40.
———. "Step'an Zoryan." *PBH,* 1960/2, 76–84.
———. *Step'an Zoryan, tasakan t'vakanner.* (Erevan, 1960).
———. *Step'an Zoryan.* (Erevan, 1961).
———. "Step'an Zoryani nor vepě." *SG,* 1964/8, 118–25. (On *Amiryani ěntanik'ě*).
———. "Step'an Zoryan." *SG,* 1970/9, 107–15.
Sargsyan, M. "Srti ḥosk'." *SG,* 1980/10, 130–32.
Šat'iryan, H. "Hnaravor ē, ardyok', verstełtzumě." *SG,* 1976/12, 124–29.
Ter-Sarkisian, L. "Sintaksis originala i perevod: (Roman S. Zor'iana "Tsar' Pap" v perevodakh na rus. iazyk." *BEH,* 1989/1, 205–12.
T'irabyan, N. "T'umanyaně Zoryani gnahatmamb." *BEH,* 1982/2, 173–78.
Zak'aryan, M. "Step'an Zoryani 'Mi kyank'i patmut'yan' stełtzagortzakan akunk'nerě." *L,* 1982/7, 34–41.

3

Bibliographies and Reference Literature

General Bibliographies of Armenian Literature

Bibliographies of bibliographies

Išḥanyan, Ṙ. *Matenagitutʻyun haykakan matenagitutʻyan (ułetsuyts).* (Erevan, 1963).

History of bibliography

Išḥanyan, Ṙ. *Hay matenagitutʻyan patmutʻyun.* 3 vols. (Erevan, 1964, 1968, 1966). (A history of Armenian bibliography).

Other bibliographies

Abrahamyan, G. "Matenagitakan tsank Kayserakan ṙusakan ašḥarhagrakan ěnkerutʻyan kovkasyan bažanmunkʻi parberakannerum hraparakvatz hayagitakan hodvatzneri." *PBH,* 1973/3, 246–52.

Anasyan, H. *Haykakan matenagitutʻyun.* Vol. 1: *A-Aṙakʻel Saladzoretsi.* (Erevan, 1959). Vol. 2: *Aṙakʻel Siwnetsi-Bēatrikē Hṙomayetsi.* (Erevan, 1976).

———. *Matenagrakan bnagrer ev dzeṙagratsutsakner.* (Erevan, 1959). (Off-print from vol. 1 of his *Haykakan matenagitutʻyun*).

———. *Hay hnatip grkʻi matenagitakan tsutsak, 1512–1800.* (Erevan, 1963).

———. "Hayots molorakan hamarvatz grkʻern ěst latinakan mi hin tsutsaki." *EJ,* 1975/10, 27–39.

Antonyan, H., et al. *Patma-banasirakan handes. Matenagitakan tsank, 1958–1982.* (Erevan, 1983).

Armianskie perevody proizvedenii pisatelei russkikh i drugikh narodov Rossii (1843–1920): Bibliograficheskii ukazatel'. (Erevan, 1984).

Armianskie sovetskie pisateli. Spravochnik. (Erevan, 1956).

Avakian, A. *Armenia and the Armenians in academic dissertations.* (Berkeley, CA, 1974, 1987 [suppl.]).

Avanesyan, H. *Matenagitutʻyun 'Hasker' amsagri, 1905–1917, 1922.* (Erevan, 1981).

Aznavuryan, G. *Ułetsuyts Grakanutʻyan ev arvesti ṫangarani grakan fonderi, Haykakan SSṘ.* (Erevan, 1962).

Babadzhanian, R. *Armeniia i armianskaia kul'tura v dorevoliutsionnykh izdaniiakh Akademii nauk SSSR (bibliografiia).* (Erevan, 1974).

Babayan, A. *Armianskie literaturnye sviazi (1920–1960). Materialy k bibliografii.* (Erevan, 1960).

Babloyan, M. *Hay parberakan mamulě: matenagitakan hamahavakʻ tsutsak (1794–1980).* (Erevan, 1986).

Barsełyan, Ḥ., et al. *'Arevelyan mamul' handesi matenagitutʻyun (1871–1909).* (Erevan, 1976).

Churchill, S. "A List of Works Printed in Persia in the Armenian Language." *Ind. Antiquary,* 17 (1888), 116.

Daniēlean, Ž. "Aknark libananahay mamuli patmutʻean." *Haykazean hayagitakan handēs,* 4 (1973), 237–82.

———. "Hay parberakan mamuli hartser." *Haykazean hayagitakan handēs,* 6 (1977–78), 267–319.

———. "Spʻiwṙkʻahay nor parberakan mamulě 1967–1980 tʻtʻ.un." *Haykazean hayagitakan handēs,* 8 (1980), 301–23.

———. *Hay nor parberakan mamulě, 1967–1981.* (Beirut, 1984).

Davtʻyan, H. *Ašḥarhabar girkʻě hay tpagrutʻyan skzbits minchev 1850 tʻvakaně: aṙajaban ev matenagitakan tsutsak.* (Erevan, 1964).

———. *Hay girkʻě 1801–1850 tʻvakannerin: matenagitutʻyun.* (Erevan, 1967).

Dwight, H. G. O. "Catalogue of all works known to exist in the Armenian language of a date earlier than the seventeenth century." *JAOS,* 3 (1853), 241–88.

Eganyan, Ž., et al. *Al. F. Myasnikyani anvan hanrapetakan gradaranum chełatz sovetahay grkʻeri tsutsak (1917–1967).* (Erevan, 1969).

Ěndhanur gratsutsak Mḥitʻarean gravačaṙanotsi: Tʻriest, Vienna, Plovdiw (Filipē), Gahirē ew Pēyrutʻ, 1776–1972). (Vienna, 1972).

Eriksson, T.-E. *Die armenische Büchersammlung der Universitätsbibliothek zu Helsinki.* (Helsinki, 1955).

Erevani petakan hamalsarani hratarakutʻyunneri bibliografia. Erevan, 1964–. Gasparyan, L., part 1, 1922–63 (Erevan, 1964; continued under *Erevani petakan hamalsarani hratarakutʻyunneri matenagitutʻyun*); Kʻalantʻaryan, E., part 2, 1964–70 (Erevan, 1980); Kʻalantʻaryan, E., part 3, 1971–1975, (Erevan, 1984); Kʻalantʻaryan, E., part 4, 1976–80 (Erevan, 1985); Kʻalantʻaryan, E., part 5, 1981–85 (Erevan, 1989).

Ferhatʻean, P. *Tsutsak hayagitakan hratarakutʻeants yEwropa.* (Vienna, 1919).

Galayčean, A. "Tsutsak ew yišatakaranner Erusałēmi Kiwlpēnkean matenadarani hay hnatip girkʻeru (1512–1800)." *S,* 1967, 52–61, 156–70, 253–64, 331–43, 446–58, 557–68. 1968, 73–86, 176–90, 264–78, 384–97, 481–93. 1969, 64–79, 167–83, 245–62, 370–89, 476–89. 1970, 188–94, 272–89, 355–70, 478–87, 567–77. 1971, 72–81, 183–90, 373–77, 462–77. 1972, 81–91.

Galēmkʻearean, G. *Patmutʻiwn hay lragrutʻean i skzbanē minchew mer žamanakě.* Vol. 1. (Vienna, 1893).

Gratsutsak Mḥitʻarean tparanin, 1700–1978. (Venice, 1978).

Grigorean, M. "Matenagitakan ditołutʻiwnkʻ hay hnatip grkʻeru masin." *HA,* 79 (1965), 51–64.

Grkʻi taregir. (Erevan, 1936–).

Ḥachatryan, F. *Matenagitutʻyun 'Ałbyur' amsagri.* (Erevan, 1987).

Ḥachatryan, H. *Grakan tełekatu (Hayastani sovetakan grołneri miutʻyan andamner, 1934–1974).* (Erevan, 1975, 1980, 1986 [revised, expanded]).

Hakobyan, G., and Išḥanyan, Ṙ. *Girkʻě Sovetakan Hayastanum: matenagitutʻyun. Hator 1* (1920–1930). Vol. 1. (Erevan, 1978).

Hakobyan, M., and Tzerunyan, Ž. *'Arevelkʻ' (1855–1856) ev 'Arevmutkʻ' (1859, 1864–65) handesneri anotatsvatz matenagitutʻyun.* (Erevan, 1980).

Haykakan SSH Gitutʻyunneri akademiayi hratarakutʻyunneri matenagitutʻyun. Grigoryan, A., *1962–63* (Erevan, 1966); *1964* (Erevan, 1966); *1965–66* (Erevan, 1970); *1967–68* (Erevan, 1973). Tʻadevosyan, L., *1969–73,* (Erevan, 1978); *1976–1977 tʻtʻ* (Erevan, 1980); *1978–1979 tʻtʻ* (Erevan, 1981); *1980–1981 tʻtʻ* (Erevan, 1984); *1982–1983 tʻtʻ* (Erevan, 1984); *1984* (Erevan, 1985); *1986* (Erevan, 1988). See also Vlasyan, E., et al., *Armfani ev Haykakan SSṘ Gitutʻyunneri akademiayi hratarakutʻyunneri bibliografia (1935–56),* (Erevan, 1957).

Kʻalašyan, V., et al. "Sovetakan Hayastani arḫivneri harstutʻyunnerě." *PBH,* 1961/1, 212–21.

Karmenian, V., et al. *Bibliografiia izdanii Akademii nauk Armianskoi SSR. Knigi i stat'i. 1935–49.* (Erevan, 1950).

Kʻatsaḫyan, K. *Matenagitutʻyun 'Murč' amsagri (1889–1907).* (Erevan, 1977).

———. *Matenagitutʻyun 'Pʻordz' handesi, Tʻiflis (1876–1881).* (Erevan, 1978).

———. *Matenagitutʻyun 'Azgagrakan handesi'. (1896–1916). (Šuši-Tʻiflis).* (Erevan, 1985).

———. *Matenagitutʻyun 'Ēminyan azgagrakan žołovatzu'i (1901–1913).* (Erevan, 1985).

———. *Matenagitutʻyun* [bibliographies-indices of nine Soviet Armenian periodicals]. (Erevan, 1986).

———. *Matenagitutʻyun 'Luma' handesi, Tʻiflis, 1896–1912.* (Erevan, 1988).

Kévorkian, R. *Catalogue des "incunables" arméniens (1511/1695) ou chronique de l'imprimerie arménienne.* (Geneva, 1986).

Kirakosyan, A. *Hay parberakan mamuli matenagitutʻyun (1794–1967), hamahavakʻ tsank.* (Erevan, 1970).

Korkotyan, Kʻ. *Hay tpagir girkʻě Kostandnupolsum (1567–1850 tʻtʻ).* (Erevan, 1964).

Kotzinyan, S. *Matenagitutʻyun 'Ararat' amsagri [1868–1919].* (Ējmiatzin, 1970).

———. *Matenagitutʻyun 'Ējmiatzin' amsagri, [1944–1973].* (Ējmiatzin, 1975).

Łazikean, A. *Haykakan nor matenagitutʻiwn ew hanragitaran hay keankʻi.* 3 parts, *A–M:* Venice, 1909–12; *M–N:* [N.p., 1913]. (Subtitle: *Nouvelle bibliographie arménienne et encyclopédie de la vie arménienne, 1512–1905*).

Lewonean, G. *Hayots parberakan mamulě. Patmakan tesutʻiwn skzbits minchew mer ōrerě (1794–1894).* (Alexandrapol, 1895).

———. *Hayots parberakan mamulě. Liakatar tsutsak hay lragrutʻyan skzbits minchev mer ōrerě (1794–1934).* (Erevan, 1934).

Macler, Fréd. "Les livres imprimés arméniens de la bibliothèque de l'université d'Amsterdam." *REArm,* 6 (1926), 71–146.

Muradyan, L., and Ananyan, N. *Hay kʻnnadatakan mtkʻi patmutʻyan matenagitutʻyun (1794–1920).* (Erevan, 1987).

Nazigian, A. *The Armenian Literature in Foreign Languages: a Bibliography.* (Yerevan, 1971).

Nersessian, V. *An Index of Articles on Armenian Studies in Western Journals.* (London, 1975).

———. *Catalogue of Early Armenian Books, 1512–1850.* (The British Library, 1980).

———. "Bibliographical Spectrum on Modern Armenian Literature." *Review of National Literatures: Armenia.* Ed. A. Paolucci and V. Oshagan, Vol. 13. (New York: Griffin House Publications, 1984), 214–37.

Oskanyan, N., et al. *Hay girkě 1512–1800 ťvakannerin. Hay hnatip grkʻi matenagituťyun.* Vol. 1. (Erevan, 1988).
Oskean, H. "Viennayi Mḥitʻareanneru Triesti mēj hratarakatz hayerēn u hayataṙ tačkerēn grkʻerě." *HA,* 81 (1967), 225–44, 289–312, 449–76.
Paštpanvatz disertatsianer (hasarakakan gituťyunneri gtzov): matenagitakan gitainformatsion byuleten 3. (Erevan, 1971).
Patcanian, M. "Catalogue de la littérature arménienne depuis le commencement du IV. siècle jusque vers le milieu du XVII." *MA,* 4 (Petersburg, 1860), 75–134.
Petrosyan, H. *Hay hin ev mijnadaryan grakanuťyan hamaṙot bibliografia (V–XIX dar).* (Erevan, 1941).
———. *Sovetahay gełarvestakan grakanuťyan bibliografia.* (Erevan, 1949).
———. *Hay grakanuťyan bibliografia (XIX darits minchev Hayastanum sovetakan kargeri hastatumě).* (Erevan, 1953).
———. *Hay parberakan mamuli bibliografia.* 2 vols. Vol. 1, 1794–1900 (Erevan, 1956). Vol. 2, 1900–1956 (Erevan, 1957).
———. *Hay gitnakanner, hraparakaḥosner, žuṙnalistner (kensabibliografiakan tzanoťagruťyunnerov).* (Erevan, 1960).
Poturean, M. *Hay mamulě tasnewhing tarun mēj, 1894–1909.* (Venice, 1909).
Pratt, I. *Armenia and the Armenians: A List of References in the New York Public Library.* (New York, 1919).
Salmaslian, A. *Bibliographie de l'Arménie.* (Paris, 1946; Erevan, 1968 [revised ed.]).
Silvanyan, H. *Hamašḥarhayin grakanuťyan hayeren ťargmanuťyunnerě (1512–1920). Matenagitakan ułetsuyts. Prak aṙajin. Ṙus ev Ṙusastani ayl žołovurdneri grołneri erkeri hayeren ťargmanuťyunnerě (1843–1920).* Part 1. (Erevan, 1984).
———. *Hamašḥarhayin grakanuťyan hayeren ťargmanuťyunnerě (1512–1920). Matenagitakan tsank. Prak erkrord. Artasahmanyan grakanuťyan hayeren ťargmanuťyunnerě (1708–1920).* Part 2. (Erevan, 1985).
———. *Hamašḥarhayin grakanuťyan hayeren ťargmanuťyunnerě (1512–1920). Matenagitakan tsank. Prak errord. Artasahmanyan grakanuťyan hayeren ťargmanuťyunnerě (1587–1920).* Part 3. (Erevan, 1986).
Siruni, H. "Pour une bibliographie arménienne." *Studia et Acta Orientalia,* 1 (1957), 348–50.
Sovetahay gradaranagitakan bibliografian 40 tarum. (Erevan, 1962).
Stepʻanyan, H. *Hayataṙ ťurkʻeren grkʻeri matenagituťyun, 1727–1968.* (Erevan, 1985).
———. *Hayataṙ ťurkʻeren parberakan mamul (matenagituťyun).* (Erevan, 1987).
Stepʻanyan, Y. *Hay kʻartezagrakan hratarakuťyunnerě 260 tarum, 1695–1955, hamaṙot aknark.* (Erevan, 1957).
Stone, M. "Early Armenian Printings in the National and Universal Library, Jerusalem." *S,* 1968, 473–80.
Tēr Ḥachaturean, A. "Libananahay mamuli yisun tarin, 1921–71 ťť." *Haykazean hayagitakan handēs,* 1971, 203–96.
———. "Suriahay mamuli patmuťiwn." *Haykazean hayagitakan handēs,* 3 (1972), 195–230.
Vlasyan, E., et al. *Armfani* [Armfan = Armianskii filial Akademii nauk SSSR] *ev Haykakan SSṘ Gituťyunneri akademiayi hratarakuťyunneri bibliografia (1936–56).* (Erevan, 1957). *1957–61* (Erevan, 1963).

Yovsēpʻeants, S. *Ĕndhanur tsank niwtʻots yisnameay Bazmavipats, 1843–1893.* (Venice, 1896).

Zarphanalean, G. *Haykakan matenagitutʻiwn [1565–1883]. (Aybubenakan tsutsak tpagrutʻean giwtēn minchew aṙ mez ełatz hayerēn hratarakutʻeants.* (Venice, 1883).

———. *Matenadaran haykakan tʻargmanutʻeants naḫneats (dar 4.–13).* (Venice, 1889).

———. *Usumnasirutʻiwnkʻ hay lezui ew matenagrutʻean yArewmuts 13–19 dar.* (Venice, 1895).

General Reference Works on Armenian Literature

Does not include works listed under "Studies of shorter periods," or titles in the sections devoted to special topics.

Abełean, A. "Hayagitutʻiwně yetpaterazmean Germaniayum." *Vēm,* 1 (1933/2), 55–67. (Armenian studies in postwar Germany).

Abełyan, M. *Erker.* 8 vols. to 1985. (Erevan, 1966–). (Collected works).

Ałbalean, N. *Patmutʻiwn hayots grakanutʻean.* (Beirut, 1944). (History of Armenian literature).

Anasyan, H. *Haykakan matenagitutʻyun.* Vol. 1: *A-Aṙakʻel Saladzoretsi* (Erevan, 1959). Vol. 2: *Aṙakʻel Siwnetsi-Bēatrikē Hṙomayetsi* (Erevan, 1976). (Exhaustive bibliography of manuscripts and texts).

———. *Manr erker.* (Los Angeles, 1987). (Covers a wide range of topics in Armenian studies to the eighteenth century).

Armianskaia literatura (bibliograficheskii ukazatel'). Vol. 1, ed. H. Adamian, E. Nersisian, N. Khoetsian (Erevan, 1972). Vol. 2, ed. S. Kotsinian and M. Nersisian (Erevan, 1974). (A bibliographic guide to Armenian literature).

Avetisyan, Yu. "Mijnadaryan hay grakanutʻyuně 'Anahit' handesum." *BEH,* 1990/1, 143–49. (Medieval Armenian literature in A. Chōpanean's *Anahit* in the years 1898–1911).

Baumstark, A. *Das christliche Schrifttum der Armenier und Georgier,* Sammlung Göschen, 527 and 529 (Leipzig, 1911).

Berbérian, H. "Littérature arménienne." *Histoire des littératures,* ed. R. Queneau, Vol. 1 (Paris, 1955), 791–802.

Chugaszyan, B. *Hay-iranakan grakan aṙnchutʻyunner.* (Erevan, 1963). (Armenian-Iranian literary relations).

Doluḥanyan, A. *Hogu ev marmni problemě mijnadari hay kʻnarergutʻyan mej.* (Erevan, 1987). (About the soul and the body in medieval Armenian lyric poetry).

Durean, E. *Patmutʻiwn hay matenagrutʻean.* (Jerusalem, 1933). (History of Armenian literature).

———. *Usumnasirutʻiwnkʻ ew kʻnnadatutʻiwnkʻ.* (Jerusalem, 1935). (Studies).

Ferhatʻean, P. *Tsutsak hayagitakan hratarakutʻeants yEwropa (1896–1910).* (Vienna, 1919). (Catalogue of publications on Armenian studies in Europe, 1896–1910).

Finck, F. "Geschichte der armenischen Literatur." *Geschichte der christlichen Literaturen des Orients,* ed. C. Brockelmann, et al. (Leipzig, 1907), 75–130.

Ganalanian, O. *Poeziia Armenii v perevodakh i otsenke V. Ia. Briusova.* (Erevan, 1963). (Armenian poetry translated and evaluated by Briusov).

Gazančean, Y. *Patmutʻiwn hay grakanutʻean: skizbēn minchew mer ōrerě.* 2 vols. (Beirut, 1970). (History of Armenian literature from its beginning to 1960s).

Grigorian, K. *Iz istorii russko-armianskikh literaturnykh i kulturnykh otnoshenii (X-nachalo XX vv).* (Erevan, 1974). (Russian and Armenian literary and cultural relations, from the tenth century to the early twentieth century).

Hakobyan, G. *Skevṙayi grakan-mšakutʻayin dprotsě.* (Erevan, 1988). (About the literary and cultural school of Skewṙay).

Hay mšakuytʻi nšanavor gortzichnerě, V–XVIII darer. (Erevan, 1976). (Notable characters of Armenian culture).

Haykakan sovetakan hanragitaran. 12 vols. (Erevan, 1974–86). (Soviet Armenian encyclopedia). *Sovetakan Hayastan. Haykakan sovetakan hanragitaran.* (Erevan, 1987). (A supplementary volume devoted to Soviet Armenia).

Hayrapetean, S. *Hay hin ew mijnadarean grakanutʻean patmutʻiwn.* (Los Angeles, 1986). (A history of classical and medieval Armenian literature).

Inglisian, V. "Die armenische Literatur." *Handbuch der Orientalistik,* 1. Abteilung, 7. Band, ed. G. Deeters, et al. (Leiden and Cologne, 1963), 156–272.

Kʻalantʻaryan, Ž. *Hay grakan kʻnnadatutʻyan kʻrestomatia.* 2 vols. (Erevan, 1981–84). (An anthology of Armenian literary criticism from the ninth century to the nineteenth century).

———. *Hay grakanagitutʻyan patmutʻyun (V–XIX darer).* (Erevan, 1986). (A history of Armenian literary criticism to the nineteenth century).

Łazikean, A. *Haykakan nor matenagitutʻiwn ew hanragitaran hay keankʻi.* 3 parts. *A–M* (Venice, 1909–1912); *M–N,* (n.d. [1913]; subtitle: *Nouvelle bibliographie arménienne et encyclopédie de la vie arménienne,* 1512–1905).

Madoyan, A. *Mijnadaryan haykakan poemě (ŽA–ŽZ darer).* (Erevan, 1985). (On Armenian poems of the eleventh–sixteenth centuries).

Malḫasyants, S. *Banasirakan hetazotutʻyunner.* (Erevan, 1982). (Philological studies on early Armenian literature).

Mkrtchyan, H. " 'Płndze kʻałakʻi patmutʻyan' arabakan ev haykakan tarberaknerě." *PBH,* 1986/2, 130–38. (Arabic and Armenian versions of the story of the City of Copper).

Mkryan, M. *Grakanutʻyan patmutʻyan hartser.* (Erevan, 1982). (Aspects of literary history).

———. *Erker.* 2 vols. (Erevan, 1987). (Vol. 1 deals with the literary history of the old period; vol. 2 covers medieval and modern periods).

Mnatsakanyan, A. *Ałvanits ašḫarhi grakanutʻyan hartseri šurjě.* (Erevan, 1966). Russian version, *O literature kavkazskoi Albanii* (Erevan, 1969). (On Caucasian Albanian literature).

Mułnetsyan, H. " 'Gołtʻan ergeri' gełagitakan hamakargě." *PBH,* 1981/3, 174–86. (The aesthetic system of the Gołtʻn songs).

Nalbandyan, V., et al. *Uroki armaianskoi drevnosti.* (Erevan, 1985). (Articles mainly on early Armenian literature and its echoes in the Soviet period).

———. *Hay mijnadaryan grakanutʻyun. Hamaṙot patmutʻyun.* (Erevan, 1986). (A concise history of Armenian literature to the eighteenth century).

———. *Armianskaia srednevekovaia literatura: Kratkaia istoriia.* (Erevan, 1986). (A concise history of Armenian literature to the eighteenth century).

Nersessian, V. *An Index of Articles on Armenian Studies in Western Journals.* (London, 1975).

Nersisyan, V. and Baḫchinyan, H., eds. *Hay mijnadaryan grakanutʻyan žanrer.* (Erevan, 1984). (On genres in medieval Armenian literature).

Nersisyan, V. "Manuk Abełyanĕ ev hayots hin grakanutʻyan azgayin yurahatkutʻyan hartsĕ." *PBH,* 1990/1, 88–94. (Manuk Abełyan and the issue of the national particularity of old Armenian literature).

Neuman, K. *Versuch einer Geschichte der armenischen Literatur.* (Leipzig, 1836). Supplement: *Beiträge zur armenischen Literatur.* (Munich, 1849).

Nève, F. *L'Arménie chrétienne et sa littérature.* (Louvain, 1886).

Orbeli, I. *Izbrannye trudy.* (Erevan, 1963). (Selected works).

Ōšakan, Y. *Mer matenagirnerĕ.* (Antʻilias, 1987). (On Sahak Partʻew, Pʻawstos Buzand, Łazar Pʻarpetsi, Ełišē, Movsēs Kałankatuatsi, Yovhannēs Drasḥanakerttsi, Nersēs Šnorhali, and Nersēs Lambronatsi).

Pʻapʻazean, V. *Patmutʻiwn hayots grakanutʻean skzbits minchew mer ōrerĕ.* (Tiflis, 1910; Constantinople, 1931). (History of Armenian literature from the beginning to modern times).

Petrosyan, H. *Hay hin ev mijnadaryan grakanutʻyan hamaṙot bibliografia.* (Erevan, 1941). (Brief bibliography of ancient and medieval Armenian literature).

Połarean, N. *Hay grołner, V–XVII dar.* (Jerusalem, 1971). (Covers Armenian authors from fifth–seventeenth centuries).

Połosyan, S., et al. *Hayagitutʻyunĕ 50 tarum.* Part 1. (Erevan, 1971). (Armenian studies in the last fifty years).

Review of National Literatures: Armenia. Ed. A. Paolucci and V. Oshagan, Vol. 13. (New York: Griffin House, 1984).

Russkaia i armianskaia srednevokovye literatury. (Leningrad, 1982). (Studies on classical and medieval Armenian literature and certain aspects of Armenian-Russian literary relations).

Salmaslian, A. *Bibliographie de l'Arménie.* (Paris, 1946; Erevan, 1969 [revised ed.]).

Somal, S. *Quadro della storia letteraria d'Armenia.* (Venice, 1829).

Srapyan, A. "Aṙaki žanrayin ĕmbṙnumĕ mijnadarum." *L,* 1981/9, 61–70. (Medieval Armenian perceptions of fables as a genre).

Tʻamrazyan, H. *Hay kʻnnadatutʻyun.* 3 vols. (Erevan, 1983–92). (The origins and history of Armenian literary criticism to the nineteenth century).

———. *Gełarvestakan lezvi ev bovandakutʻyan ĕmbṙnumnerĕ hayots mijnadarum.* (Erevan, 1988). (Perceptions of idiom and content in medieval Armenian literature).

Ter-Grigoryan, Ṙ. "Aṙatzneri ev asatsvatzkʻneri tʻargmanutʻyan hartsi šurj." *BEH,* 1981/3, 116–26. (On translating proverbs and sayings).

Ter-Łevondyan, A. "Mušełi vepĕ arab patmagrutʻyan mej." *L,* 1986/6, 52–58. (Mušeł Mamikonean's story of anti-Arab rebellion in the 770s in Arab historiography).

Ter-Petrosyan, L. *Hay hin tʻargmanakan grakanutʻyun.* (Erevan, 1984). (Old translations into Armenian).

———. *Drevnearmianskaia perevodnaia literatura.* (Erevan, 1984). (Old translations into Armenian).

———. *Hay hin tʻargmanakan grakanutʻiwn. Ancient Armenian Translations.* (New York, 1992). (In Western Armenian and English).

Thorossian, H. *Histoire de la littérature arménienne, des origines jusqu'à nos jours.* (Paris, 1951).

Zarbhanalean, G. *Patmutʻiwn hayerēn hin ew nor dprutʻeants.* Vol. 1: *Hin dprutʻiwn, 4–13 dar* (Venice, 1865, 1897, 1932). Vol. 2: *Nor dprutʻiwn, 14–18 dar,* (Venice, 1878, 1915). (History of Armenian literature; see also the section on bibliographies).

Studies of Shorter Periods

1500–1920

Abełean, A. *Dorpati hay usanołuťiwně.* (Vienna, 1942). (Armenian students at Dorpat University, Estonia).

Abełyan, M. *Hayots hin grakanuťyan patmuťyun.* 2 vols. (Erevan, 1944, 1946; Beirut, 1955, 1959). Vol. 1 translated into Russian as *Istoriia drevnearmianskoi literatury,* (Erevan, 1975). (History of ancient Armenian literature).

———. "Uruagtzer 19-rd daru hayots grakanuťean patmuťiwnits." *A,* 1908, 890–904, 1103–15; 1909, 257–70, 321–34, 417–38, 722–33. (Sketches of a history of nineteenth-century Armenian literature).

Abrahamyan, A. "Mer mijnadaryan grichnerě." *EJ,* 1944/2–3, 58–62; 1944/4–5, 42–45. (Medieval scribes).

———. *Haykakan tzatzkagruťyun.* (Erevan, 1978). (On Armenian cryptography).

Ačaṙean, H. *Patmuťiwn hayots nor grakanuťean.* 3 parts. (Vałaršapat, 1906; Nor Naḥijewan, 1910, 1912). (A history of modern Armenian literature).

Ačemyan, V. *Grakan arevmtahayereni dzevavorumě.* (Erevan, 1971). (Formation of the modern Western Armenian literary standard).

Akinean, N. *Bałēši dprotsě (1500–1700).* (Vienna, 1952). (On the Bitlis School, 1500–1700).

Ałababyan, S. *Grakan herkerum.* (Erevan, 1974). (Articles on modern and Soviet Armenian literature).

———. "P̕aṙk' patmuťyan musanerin." *SG,* 1978/6, 120–25. (On the historical novel).

———. *Hodvatzner, dimankarner, hušer.* (Erevan, 1982). (Articles and reminiscences about Armenian authors of the late nineteenth and the twentieth centuries).

———. *XX dari hay grakanuťyan zugaheṙakannerum.* 2 vols. (Erevan, 1983–1984). (Articles on twentieth century Armenian literature).

———. *Dasakanner ev žamanakakitsner.* (Erevan, 1986). (On classic and contemporary Armenian authors, from Ḥ. Abovean to the 1980s).

Aławnuni, M. "Naḥnik' oronts oewē mēk gortzě tpagruatz ē s. Aťoṙoys tparanin mēj." *S,* 1934, 52–55. (Works by early writers printed at the Armenian Patriarchate of Jerusalem).

Alek'sanyan, S. *Hay lusavorakan ṙealizmě.* (Erevan, 1980). (On Armenian realism).

Aloyan, L. *Grakanutʻyan, arvesti ev lusavorutʻyan hartserě 1892–1905 tʻtʻ. ʻMšakʼ lragrum.* (Erevan, 1989). (Literature, art, and issues of enlightenment in the periodical *Mšak* from 1892–1905).

Ananyan, G. "Hay grołneri ěnkerutʻyun himnelu mi pʻordzi masin." *PBH,* 1966/4, 193–96. (On an attempt to found a society of Armenian writers in the 1890s).

Ananyan, N. "Arevmtahay sentimental vipagrutʻyuně ev Hovh. Hisaryaně." *L,* 1969/10, 55–61. (Western Armenian sentimental novel and the novelist Yovhannēs Hisarean).

Anasean, Y. *Manr erker.* (Los Angeles, 1987). (Covers a wide range of topics in Armenian studies to the eighteenth century).

Andrēasean, A. *Grakanutʻean ew grołneru masin.* (Los Angeles, 1988). (On nineteenth- and twentieth-century Armenian authors).

Antonean, Ṙ. "Imastasirakan tarrer hay veratznundi patmutʻean mēj (H. Arsēn Bagratuni)." *B,* 125 (1967), 210–15; 127 (1969), 158–67. (Philosophical elements in the modern Armenian renaissance and Arsēn Bagratuni's work).

Aprsam, "Kʻnnadatakan uruagrer." *AM,* 1882, 358–69. (On Western Armenian literature).

———. "Grakan zroytsner." *AM,* 1896, 124–27. (On Western Armenian women writers).

———. "Grakan zroytsner." *AM,* 1898, 554–58. (On Western Armenian literature).

Areshian, S. *Armianskaia pechatʼ i tsarskaia tsenzura.* (Erevan, 1957). (On the Armenian press and czarist censorship).

Arevelyan ałbyuragitutʻyun. Studies in Oriental Sources. Vol. 1.—(Erevan, 1988–). (Covers mainly Middle Eastern topics).

Armēn, E. *Tʻrkʻa-hay grakanutʻiwně mamuli azatutʻean tʻuakanin.* (Constantinople, 1909). (Western Armenian literature in 1909).

———. *Hay nor banastełtznerě.* (Constantinople, 1911). (On the new Armenian poets).

Armianskie perevody proizvedenii pisatelei russkikh i drugikh narodov Rossii (1843–1920): Bibliograficheskii ukazatelʼ. (Erevan, 1984). (Armenian translations of the works of Russian writers and writers of other nationalities in Russia. A bibliographical guide).

Arpʻiarean, A. *Patmutʻiwn 19. daru Turkʻioy hayots grakanutʻean.* (Cairo, 1944 [title page says 1943]). (A history of nineteenth-century literature of the Armenians of Turkey).

Asatryan, A. *Hay grakanutʻyuně ev ṙusakan aṙajin ṙevolyutsian.* (Erevan, 1956). (Armenian literature and the first Russian revolution).

Asatur, H. *Dimastuerner.* (Constantinople, 1921). (Portraits of Armenian authors).

Asmaryan, L. *Hay grakan kʻnnadatutʻyuně XIX dari 70-80akan tʻvakannerin.* (Erevan, 1979). (Armenian literary criticism in the 1870s and 1880s).

Avagyan, S. *Nyutʻer Łarabałi naḥasovetakan šrjani mamuli patmutʻyunits.* (Erevan, 1969). (The periodical press in pre-Soviet Łarabał).

Avdalbegyan, M. *Mijandaryan hay ardzaki tzagumn u zargatsumě.* (Erevan, 1970). (On the origin and development of medieval Armenian prose).

Avetisyan, Yu. "Mijnadaryan hay grakanutʻyuně ʻAnahitʼ handesum." *BEH,* 1990/1, 143–49. (Medieval Armenian literature in *Anahit,* in 1898–1911).

Avetisyan, Z. *Hay patmavepi poetikan.* (Erevan, 1986). (The art of Armenian historical novels).

Awagean, Y. *Grakan dēmk'er.* (New York, 1925). (Modern Western and Eastern Armenian writers).

Awger, Y. "Latin lezun ew grakanut'iwnĕ naḫneats k'ov." *B,* 67 (1909), 59–66, 145–60; 68 (1910), 556–69. (Latin language and literature in the work of early Armenian writers).

Azatean, E. *Grakan, gełaruestakan seweṙumner.* (La Verne, California, 1988). (Articles and reviews of nineteenth- and twentieth-century authors and artists).

Aznavuryan, G. "Anhayt ēјer hay nahatakneri grakan žaṙangut'yunits." *EJ,* 1965/2–4, 43–57. (Previously unpublished letters and other material by Komitas, G. Zōhrap, D. Varužan, Siamant'ō, T'lkatintsi, Ṙ. Zardarean, and Ṙ. Sewak).

Baḫchinyan, H. "17-rd dari hay azgayin-hayrenasirakan banastełtzut'yunĕ." *PBH,* 1990/3, 26–42.

Barsełyan, Ḥ. *'Mšak'i t'łt'akitsneri ev ašḫatakitsneri vertzanvatz tzatzkanunnerĕ.* (Erevan, 1962). (Real names of contributors to the periodical *Mšak* of Tiflis).

Bek'mezyan, A. *Vipaki žanrĕ hay nor grakanut'yan mej.* (Erevan, 1984). (The short novel in modern Armenian literature).

Berberean, Ṙ. *Hayots noragoyn banastełtznerĕ.* Book 1. (Rostov-on-Don, 1898). (Contemporary young Armenian poets).

Bežanyan, A. "Hay gyułagrut'yan mi k'ani hartser." *T,* 1962/12, 31–40. (Some issues regarding literature about the countryside).

Bžikean, Ł. "Mer ardi grakanut'iwnĕ." *B,* 66 (1908), 59–63, 458–60, 508–12, 566–69. 67 (1909), 223–27, 378–80. 68 (1910), 353–58. (Modern Armenian literature).

Čanašean, M. *Patmut'iwn ardi hay grakanut'ean, (Veratznundi šrjanēn minchew mer ōrerĕ).* Vol. 1. (Venice, 1953). (A history of modern Armenian literature from the Armenian renaissance to the mid-twentieth century).

———. "Hay banastełtzut'iwnĕ 1900-i semin." *B,* 114 (1956), 193–99. (Armenian poetry on the eve of 1900).

———. *Hay grakanut'ean nor šrjani hamaṙōt patmut'iwn (1701–1920).* (Venice, [1973]). (A concise history of modern Armenian literature, 1701–1920; a revised version of the 1953 edition).

Chalatiantz, B. *Die armenische Literatur des 19. Jahrhunderts.* (Heidelberg, 1905).

Chōpanean, A. *Dēmk'er.* 2 vols. (Paris, 1924, 1929). (Portraits of Armenian writers).

Chrak'ean, K'. *Hay matenagirner XIX daru.* (Venice, 1904). (Nineteenth-century Armenian authors).

Chugaszyan, B. "Norahayt namakner." *SG,* 1973/3, 146–59. (Newly found letters by various Western Armenian writers).

Čingozyan, K. "Ējer 19-rd dari 50-60-akan t'vakanneri zmyuṙnahay grakan šaržman patmut'yunits." *PBH,* 1982/2, 61–67. (Some aspects of literary activities in Smyrna, 1850s–1860s).

Danielyan, K. *Hay memuarayin grakanut'yan patmut'yunits.* (Erevan, 1961). (Sketches of the genre of memoirs in Armenian literature).

———. "Haykakan ṙomantizmě patmakan lusabanutʻyamb." *SG,* 1966/10, 113–21. (Armenian romanticism from a historical viewpoint).

———. *Hay gyułagirnerě 19-rd darum.* (Erevan, 1973). (nineteenth-century writers on country life).

———. *Grakan mšakner.* (Erevan, 1977). (Secondary realist writers, 1860–90).

———. " 'Gyułagir' termini masin." *L,* 1988/8, 54–56. (On the term "giwłagir," which denotes an author writing on village life).

———. *Grakanutʻyan patmutʻyan luysě.* (Erevan, 1989). (On nineteenth- and twentieth-century Armenian authors).

Danielyan, S. " 'Mehyan' handesi grakan havatamkʻě." *L,* 1980/3, 14–26. (Literary creed of journal *Mehean* [Constantinople]).

———. *Heṫanosakan grakan šaržman patmutʻyunits.* (Erevan, 1988). (Aspects of the "pagan" literary movement in Western Armenian literature in the early twentieth century).

Davtʻyan, A. " 'Armianskie belletristy' hratarakutʻyan patmutʻyunits, 1893–1894 tʻtʻ." *SG,* 1969/2, 134–42. (On the history of the publication of *Armianskie belletristy,* a Russian anthology of Armenian writers).

Davtʻyan, L. "L. Manvelyani 'Ṙusahay grakanutʻyan patmutʻyuně'." *PBH,* 1968/3, 163–68. (L. Manuēlean's History of Eastern [Russian] Armenian literature).

Doluḥanyan, A. " 'Graṙajkʻnerě' hay mijnadaryan matenagrutʻyan mej." *L,* 1975/12, 66–74. ("Prefaces" in medieval Armenian literature).

———. *Hogu ev marmni problemě mijnadari hay grakanutʻyan mej.* (Erevan, 1987). (On the soul and the body in medieval Armenian lyric poetry).

Eremean, S. *Azgayin dēmkʻer, gragēt hayer.* 9 vols. (Venice, vols. 2–8, 1913–14; vol. 1, 1920; vol. 9, 1931).

———. "Grakan patmutʻiwn. Uruagitz, 1850–1910." *B,* 72 (1914), 13–26, 59–69, 97–112. (Outline of literary history, 1850–1910).

Esayean, Z. "Vipakan seṙi vray." *AM,* 1904, 1110–14. (On prose).

Fēnērčean, G. "Šrjan mě, 1900–08." *Bardzravankʻ,* 1922/3, 82–87; 1922/4, 122–28. (General criticism on the literature of the period 1900–1908).

Frangean, E. *Hay hasarakakan mitkʻě: Abovean, Nazarean, Nalbandean, Patkanean, Ḥrimean Hayrik.* (Cairo, 1928). (Armenian social thought and Ḥachatur Abovean, Stepʻanos Nazarean, Mikʻayēl Nalbandean, Ṙapʻayēl Patkanean and Mkrtich Ḥrimean).

Gabrielyan, V. "Polsahay grakan kyankʻě 1918–1922 tʻvakannerin." *BEH,* 1973/3, 214–23. (Armenian literary life in Constantinople in 1918–22).

———. *Arevmtahay banastełtzner: grakan dimagtzer.* (Erevan, 1974). (Western Armenian poets of the turn of the twentieth century).

Ganalanian, O. *Poeziia Armenii v perevodakh i otsenke V. Ia. Briusova.* (Erevan, 1963). (Briusov's translations and evaluation of Armenian poetry).

———. *Poety Armenii XVIII–XX vekov.* (Erevan, 1976). (Armenian poets of eighteenth–twentieth centuries).

Gasparyan, H. "Hay u evropatsi mšakutʻayin gortzichneri namakagrutʻyuně." *SG,* 1972/10, 145–59. (Correspondence between Armenian and European intellectuals).

Gazančean, Y. "Tʻrkʻahay grakanutʻiwně 1905-in." *AM,* 1906, 65–70. (Western Armenian literature in 1905).

———. "Ṫrk'ahay grakanuṫiwnĕ 1906-in." *AM,* 1907, 11–14, 49–52, 73–79. (Western Armenian literature in 1906).

———. "Ṫrk'ahay grakanuṫiwnĕ 1907-in." *AM,* 1908, 25–29, 49–52, 73–80. (Western Armenian literature in 1907).

———. "Ṫrk'ahay grakanuṫiwnĕ 1908-in." *AM,* 1909, 9–12, 56–59, 101–5. (Western Armenian literature in 1908).

Gevorgyan, E. "Hungarahayeri grakan stełtzagortzuṫyunĕ 'Armenia' amsagri ējerum (1887–1907)." *BEH,* 1974/3, 78–91. (Hungarian-Armenian literary works in the monthly *Armenia,* 1887–1907).

Gevorgyan, L. "Hay gełarvestakan grakanuṫyunĕ ev k'nnadatuṫyunĕ 'Murč' amsagri ējerum, 1901–1907 ṫṫ." *BEH,* 1980/3, 146–54. (Literature and literary criticism in the monthly *Murč,* 1901–07).

Gljyan, A. "Gełagitakan hartserĕ arevmtahay grakan lezvi zargatsman hamar młvoł payk'arum (19-rd dari erkrord kes)." *BEH,* 1980/2, 115–21. (Aesthetic issues in the effort to promote a Western Armenian literary standard in the second half of the nineteenth century).

———. "Azgayin grakanuṫyan hartserĕ arevmtahay k'nnadatuṫyan mej." *L,* 1980/8, 14–24. (Issues concerning national literature in Western Armenian criticism).

Gonchar-Khandzhian, N. *Armianskaia literatura v russkoi sovetskoi kritike: bibliografiia. Stat'i.* (Erevan, 1989). (Armenian literature in Soviet Russian criticism; bibliography and articles).

Grakan stełtzagortzuṫyun. (Erevan, 1983). (On the methods and principles of analyzing the works of nineteenth- and twentieth-century Armenian authors).

Grigoryan, K. "Vatikani dem młvatz payk'ari artatsolumĕ arevmtahay grakanuṫyan mej." *L,* 1973/12, 82–89. (The reflections of the anti-Vatican struggle in Western Armenian literature, 1850s–1870s).

Gyulnazaryan, Ḥ. "Grakanuṫyan mi k'ani hartser ev naḥaṙevolyutsion šrjani hay bolševikyan mamulĕ." *T,* 1954/3, 27–52. (The pre-revolutionary Armenian Bolshevik press and some literary issues).

———. *Aknarkner hay mankakan grakanuṫyan patmuṫyan.* (Erevan, 1961). (A sketch of children's literature).

Ḥachatryan, P. *Hay mijnadaryan patmakan ołber (XIV–XVII darer).* (Erevan, 1969). (Historical laments, fourteenth–seventeenth centuries).

Haḥumyan, T. *Hušer.* (Erevan, 1987). (Reminiscences about nineteenth- and twentieth-century Armenian authors).

Haḥverdyan, L. *Hay ṫatroni patmuṫyun (1901–1920).* (Erevan, 1980). (A history of Armenian theater, 1901–20).

———. *Mtorumner.* (Erevan, 1984). (Reflections on nineteenth- and twentieth-century authors).

Hakobjanyan, A. "Daraskzbi arevmtahay grakan šaržman patmuṫyunits." *SG,* 1965/1, 124–32. (Notes on the Western Armenian literary movement at the turn of twentieth century).

Hakobyan, M. "Teteyanneri mšakuṫayin-lusavorakan gortzuneuṫyunĕ (Zmyuṙniayum)." *L,* 1982/10, 47–57. (The cultural activities of the Tētēean [i.e. Dedeyan] family in Smyrna).

———. *Zmyuṙnahay parberakan mamulĕ (1839–1860 ṫṫ).* (Erevan, 1984). (The Armenian periodical press in Smyrna, 1839–60).

Hakobyan, P. "Arevelyan Hayastani azatagrumĕ ev hayots nor grakanutʻyunĕ." *L,* 1978/10, 21–38. (Liberation [i.e. annexation to Russia] of Eastern Armenia and the new Armenian literature).

———. "Naḥaabovyanakan hay ardzaki mi norahayt ēj." *BEH,* 1982/2, 117–64. (A newly discovered, pre-Abovean work of prose).

Ḥaṙatyan, A. "Gełarvestakan grakanutʻyunn 'Arevelyan mamul' parberakanum." *PBH,* 1979/1, 88–102. (Belles lettres in the periodical *Arewelean mamul* of Smyrna).

Harutʻyunyan, A. "Mijnadaryan mi kʻani tałeri masin." *PBH,* 1965/3, 223–38. (On some medieval poems).

Harutʻyunyan, B. *XIX–XX dareri hay tʻatroni taregrutʻyun (1801–1922).* Vol. 1: *1801–1900* (Erevan, 1980); Vol. 2: *1901–1911* (Erevan, 1980); Vol. 3: *1912–1922* (Erevan, 1981). (A chronological record of nineteenth- and twentieth-century Armenian theater).

Hay nor grakanutʻyan patmutʻyun. 5 vols. (Erevan, 1962, vols. 1–2; 1964, vol. 3; 1972, vol. 4; 1979, vol. 5). (A history of modern Armenian literature).

Haykakan ṙealizmi tesutʻyan ev patmutʻyan hartser. (Erevan, 1987). (Armenian realism and some realist writers, such as Y. Paronean and Y. Tʻumanean).

Haykakan sovetakan hanragitaran. 12 vols. (Erevan, 1974–86). (Soviet Armenian encyclopedia). *Sovetakan Hayastan. Haykakan sovetakan hanragitaran.* (Erevan, 1987). (A supplementary volume devoted to Soviet Armenia).

Hayrapetyan, S. "Dimankari žanrĕ arevmtahay grakanutʻyan mej." *BEH,* 1972/1, 205–10. (The genre of the literary portrait in Western Armenian literature).

———. *Hay hin ew mijnadarean grakanutʻean patmutʻiwn.* (Los Angeles, 1986). (A history of classical and medieval Armenian literature).

Hnasēr, G. "Hay grakanutʻiwnĕ tapanakʻareru vray." *B,* 85 (1928), 208–15, 264–69, 339–45. 86 (1929), 17–22, 43–46, 149–51, 229–32, 310–12. (Armenian literature on tombstones).

Hovhannisyan, H. *Tʻatronĕ mijnadaryan Hayastanum.* (Erevan, 1978). (Theater in medieval Armenia).

Hovhannisyan, Ṙ. "Hay grołnerĕ ev azatagrakan šaržumnerĕ XIX dari 70-80-akan tʻvakannerin." *SG,* 1965/9, 120–27. (Armenian writers and liberation movements in the 1870s and 1880s).

Hovhannisyan, S. "Hay grołneri Kovkasyan ĕnkerutʻyan himnadrman patmutʻyunits." *PBH,* 1984/2, 43–51. (Some aspects of the history of the founding of the Caucasian Society of Armenian Writers).

———. "Grakan kʻnnadatutʻyan ev tesutʻyan hartserĕ hay grołneri kovkasyan ĕnkerutʻyan erekuytʻnerum." *L,* 1985/6, 18–27. (Issues of literary criticism and theory as topics of discussion at literary evenings of the Caucasian Society of Armenian Writers).

Hovhannisyan, Y. " 'Vernatun' grakan ḫmbakĕ." *SG,* 1979/6, 145–47. (The literary coterie "Vernatun" of Tiflis).

Hrpet. "Tʻurkʻioy hayots grakanutʻiwnĕ (1880–1900)." *B,* 60 (1902), 321–28. (Western Armenian literature, 1880–1900).

Hunanyan, A. "XX dari skzbi arevelahay patmvatzkʻi žanrayin aṙandznahatkutʻyunnerĕ." *PBH,* 1976/4, 136–46. (The short story and its characteristics as a genre in Eastern Armenian literature at the turn of the twentieth century).

———. *Dramaturgia ev t'atron.* (Erevan, 1980). (Modern dramaturgy and theater).

Hyusyan, M. *Metz ełeřni zoh grołnerě.* (Erevan, 1965). (Armenian writers slaughtered during the 1915 genocide).

———. *Ējer arevmtahay grakanut'yan patmut'yunits.* (Erevan, 1977). (Sketches of a history of Western Armenian literature).

Irazek, Y. "Hay andranik t'atrergut'iwnē ('Ḥtradimay džrołut'ean')." *Vēm,* 1 (1933/2), 1–18. (The first Armenian play).

———. "Ews mi hin t'atrergut'iwn." *Vēm,* 2 (1934/4), 21–37. (On "Leyli," Calcutta, 1932).

———. "Ov ē 'Ḥtradimay'-i hełinakě." *Vēm,* 2 (1934/6), 121–24. (On the authorship of the play "Ḥtradimay džrołut'ean").

———. *Patmut'iwn hndkahay tpagrut'ean.* (Ant'ilias, 1986). (A history of Armenian printing in India).

Išḥan, M. *Ardi hay grakanut'iwn.* Vol. 1: *Zart'ōnk'i šrjan* 1850–1885 (Beirut, 1973); Vol. 2: *Irapašt šrjan* 1885–1900 (Beirut, 1974); Vol. 3: *Gełapašt šrjan* 1900–1915 (Beirut, 1975). (A history of modern Armenian literature, from 1850–1915).

Išḥanyan, Ṙ. "Ašḥarhabar banastełtzut'yan akunk'neri mot." *BEH,* 1971/1, 57–71. (On the earliest poetic works in Eastern Armenian).

———. "Erb ē skzbnavorvel hay nor grakanut'yuně [?]." *SG,* 1974/9, 155–59. (When did modern Armenian literature begin?).

———. "Amenalavě amenačištn ē (grapayk'ari masin)." *SG,* 1975/12, 124–29. (About the complex struggle in the nineteenth century to make modern Armenian the national standard).

Jrbašyan, Ēd. *Ašḥarhayatsk' ev varpetut'yun: grakanut'yan tesut'yan ev patmut'yan hartser.* (Erevan, 1967). (Modern Eastern and Soviet Armenian writers; literary theory and history).

———. " 'Didaktik poemnerě' hay grakanut'yan mej." *PBH,* 1968/1, 53–66. (Didactic poems in Armenian literature).

———. "Hay grakanut'yan hosank'nerě XX dari skzbin." *PBH,* 1977/1, 31–48; 1977/2, 47–66. (Armenian literary currents at turn of twentieth century).

———. "XX dari skzbi hay grakanut'yan žanrayin kazmě." *BEH,* 1977/2, 51–63. (Genres in Armenian literature at the beginning of the twentieth century).

———. *Gełagitut'yun ev grakanut'yun.* (Erevan, 1983). (Aesthetics, literature, and some nineteenth- and twentieth-century Armenian literary traditions and authors).

———. "Hay klasitsistakan poemi žanrayin taratesaknerě." *L,* 1988/9, 18–27. (The variations of genre in Armenian poems of the era of classicism).

———. *Grołě ev žołovurdě: dasakan ev žamanakakits grakanut'yan masin.* (Erevan, 1989). (On aspects of nineteenth- and twentieth-century Armenian literature; literary portraits of some Armenian and Russian writers).

———. *Poetika i literaturnoe razvitie.* (Trans. by N. Gonchar-Khandzhian and L. Kazarian). (Erevan, 1985). (On aspects of literary theory and Armenian writers of the nineteenth–twentieth centuries).

K'alant'aryan, Ž. *Hay grakan k'nnadatut'yan k'restomatia.* 2 vols. (Erevan, 1981–1984). (An anthology of Armenian literary criticism).

———. *Hay grakanagitut'yan patmut'yun (X–XIX darer).* (Erevan, 1986). (A history of Armenian literary criticism from the tenth century to the nineteenth century).

Karinean, A. *'Ḥent'ě' ew 'Abełan': ṙusahay grakanut'iwně ew ṙusahay mtaworakanut'iwně.* (Paris, 1926). (On Eastern Armenian literature and intelligentsia).

———. *Grakan-patmakan aknarkner.* (Erevan, 1982). (On some nineteenth- and twentieth-century authors).

Karō. "Batsatrut'iwn mě vałuan grakanut'ean masin." *AM,* 1899, 351–64. (On tomorrow's Armenian literature).

Kirakosyan, V. "Ṙealizmi skzbnavorumě arevmtahay poeziayum." *SG,* 1976/8, 138–45. (On the genesis of realism in Western Armenian poetry).

———. *Arevmtahay banastełtzut'yuně, 1890–1907 t't'.* (Erevan, 1985). (On innovative trends in Western Armenian poetry, 1890–1907, particularly in the works of A. Chōpanean, Intra, and M. Metzarents).

Kostanyan, A. "Noravepi žanrě 90-akan t'vakanneri arevmtahay grakanut'yan mej." *T,* 1963/3, 41–54. (The short story–i.e., the "noravēp"–in Western Armenian literature in the 1890s).

Kusikean, K. *Grakan dēmk'er.* (Moscow, 1912). (Contemporary Eastern Armenian writers).

Łanalanyan, H. *Hamastełut'yun.* (Erevan, 1984). (Articles on P. Durean, D. Varužan, A. Isahakyan, M. Metzarents, V. Tērean, and E. Charents).

Łazaryan, H. *Hay poezian 1917–1920 t'vakannerin.* (Erevan, 1958). (Armenian poetry, 1917–20).

Łazinyan, A. "Dimaṙnut'yuně mijnadaryan hay banastełtzut'yan mej." *L,* 1974/5, 32–41. (Personification in medieval Armenian poetry).

Leist, A. *Literarische Skizzen (R. Patkanian, G. Sundukiantz, M. Bechiktashlian, L. Alishan).* (Leipzig, 1886).

Lēō. "Ṙusahay vipagrut'iwn." *B,* 61 (1903), 287–308, 354–62, 393–403, 482–92. 62 (1904), 5–14, 101–13, 315–21. (Eastern Armenian prose).

———. *Ṙusahayots grakanut'iwně skzbits minchew mer ōrerě.* (Venice, 1904). (A history of Eastern Armenian literature from origins to present).

Łukasyan, Z. " 'Garun' almanaḥě." *SG,* 1976/2, 150–59. (The literary collection 'Garun' [3 vols., Moscow, 1910–12]).

Madoyan, A. "Nerses Metzi tesilě mijnadaryan hay poeziayum." *PBH,* 1969/4, 237–42. (On the vision of Nersēs the Great in medieval Armenian poetry).

———. *Mijnadaryan haykakan poemě (ŽA-ŽZ darer).* (Erevan, 1985). (Medieval Armenian poems of the eleventh–sixteenth centuries).

Madoyan, G. "Hay grakanut'yan korustnerě." *EJ,* 1965/2–4, 76–84. (On Armenian writers killed in the 1915 genocide).

Makintsyan, P. *Dimagtzer.* (Erevan, 1980). (On Sayeat'-Nōvay; nineteenth- and twentieth-century Armenian authors and some non-Armenian writers).

Mamikonyan, K. "Arevmtahay banastełtzut'yuně 19-rd dari 70-80-akan t'vakannerin." *SG,* 1974/9, 150–55. (Western Armenian poetry in the 1870s and 1880s).

Manuēlean, L. *Ṙusahay grakanut'ean patmut'iwn.* 4 parts. (Alexandrapol, 1909, part 1; Tiflis, 1910, parts 2–3; Tiflis, 1911, part 4). (A history of Eastern Armenian literature).

Manukyan, S., and Asmaryan, L. *Aknarkner hay grakanut'yan patmut'yan.* (Erevan, 1984). (Some aspects of modern Armenian literary history).

Mḫit'arean, G. *K'ařord dar grakanut'iwn.* (Cairo, 1946). (Modern Armenian and Diaspora writers).

Mḫit'aryan, A. *Vrastani sovetahay grakanut'yunĕ.* (Erevan, 1966). (Armenian literature in Soviet Georgia).

Mḫit'aryan, M. "Kovkasi grak'nnakan komitei nyut'erits." *PBH,* 1974/3, 105–12. (Russian censorship committee materials in the Caucasus).

Mik'ayelyan, V. "17 dari Kafayi hay banastełtznerĕ." *SG,* 1966/3, 133–38. (Seventeenth-century Armenian poets in Kafa [Theodosia, Crimea, Ukraine]).

———. "Bnut'yan, siro ev hayrenik'i ergichnerĕ: 17-rd dari łrimahay tałasatsnerĕ." *SG,* 1974/5, 163–67. (Seventeenth-century Armenian poets of Crimea).

Misak'ean, Š. "Tomser." *AM,* 1907, 1007–9, 1127–29, 1246–50. (Western Armenian literature).

Mkrtchyan, A. *Nyut'er 10-18rd dareri hayots grakanut'yan patmut'yan hamar.* 2 vols. (Erevan, 1949). (Materials for the history of Armenian literature from the tenth to the eighteenth centuries).

Mkryan, M. *Ējer hay vipasanut'yan patmut'yunits.* (Erevan, 1959). (Mainly on modern Armenian prose).

———. *Grakanut'yan patmut'yan hartser.* (Erevan, 1982). (Armenian authors from the tenth through the twentieth centuries).

———. *Erker.* 2 vols. (Erevan, 1987). (On the Armenian literary tradition and authors from its origins to the twentieth century).

Mnatsakanyan, A. "Hin tałarannerum katarvatz mi šark' ałavałumneri masin." *BM,* 1 (1941), 171–77. (Textual corruption in ancient poem collections).

———. *Haykakan mijnadaryan žołovrdakan erger.* (Erevan, 1956). (Medieval popular songs).

———. *Hay mijnadaryan hanelukner (V–XVIII dd).* (Erevan, 1980). (Armenian riddles, from the fifth to the eighteenth centuries).

Mnatsakanyan, L. *Arevmtahay k'nnadatakan mtk'i patmut'yunits.* (Erevan, 1982). (Aspects of Western Armenian literary criticism).

———. *Grakan k'nnadatut'yunĕ 'Navasard' ev 'Mehean' parberakannerum.* (Erevan, 1988). (Literary criticism in the periodicals *Nawasard* [1914] and *Mehean* [1914], both published in Constantinople).

Mnatsakanyan, V. "Ašḫarhabari orpes grakan lezvi paštpanut'yan p'ordzeri masin." *BEH,* 1986/2, 45–55. (Pre-Abovean attempts to promote modern Armenian as the literary standard).

Muradyan, L., and Ananyan, N. *Hay k'nnadatakan mtk'i patmut'yan matenagitut'yun (1794–1920).* (A bibliography of Armenian literary thought and criticism).

Mušeł vardapet. "Verlutzumner." *AM,* 1903, 169–73, 193–99, 218–22, 241–46. (On Western Armenian and anti-clerical literature).

Nalbandyan, V. *Hay mijnadaryan grakanut'yun. Hamařot patmut'yun.* (Erevan, 1986). (A concise history of Armenian literature to the eighteenth century).

———. *Armianskaia srednevekovaia literatura: Kratkaia istoriia.* (Erevan, 1986). (A concise history of Armenian literature to the eighteenth century).

Nanumyan, Ř. "1810–20-akan t'vakanneri hndkahay grakan šaržman patmut'yunits." *L,* 1989/5, 27–36. (Armenian literary activities in India in the 1810s–1820s).

Nazaryan, Š. "Gełarvestakan grakanut'yunĕ 'Ałbyur' amsagrum." *L,* 1967/6, 57–64. (Belles lettres in the monthly *Ałbiwr* [Tiflis, 1883–1918]).

———. "XVIII d. veranorogvoł hay gełarvestakan grakanutʻyan bnoroš gtzerě." *L,* 1979/8, 46–57. (Characteristics of eighteenth-century Armenian literature).
———. "Veranoroguoł gełaruestakan grakanutʻiwně ew hay-ṙusakan yaraberutʻiwnneri artatsolkʻě nranum." *B,* 1982/3–4, 241–69. (The reflection of Armeno-Russian relations in the regenerate Armenian literature).
———. "ŽĚ dari gełaruestakan lezui ěndhanur patkerě." *B,* 1985/1–2, 7–37. (A sketch of the literary idiom in the eighteenth century).
———. "Narekatsu ołbi ardzagankʻnerě 18-rd dari banastełtzutʻyan mej." *PBH,* 1989/2, 133–46. (Echoes of Grigor Narekatsi's *Matean ołbergutʻean,* Book of prayers or lamentations, in eighteenth-century Armenian poetry).
Nersisyan, V. "Makdirě XIII–XVI dareri hay tałergutʻyan mej." *BEH,* 1970/3, 190–97. (Epithet in Armenian poetry, thirteenth–sixteenth centuries).
———. *Hay mijnadaryan tałergutʻyan gełarvestakan mijotsnerě, XIII–XVI darer.* (Erevan, 1976). (Artistic and literary techniques in medieval poetry, thirteenth–sixteenth centuries).
Nersisyan, V., and Baḫchinyan, H., eds. *Hay mijnadaryan grakanutʻyan žanrer.* (Erevan, 1984). (Genres in medieval Armenian literature).
O. "Poètes arméniens: Pierre Tourian; Pierre Atamian; Bechgueturian; M. Oughourlian; Sybille." *La Patrie,* 1908, 34–35, 47–48, 62–63. 1909, 101, 114–15, 172–74. (Petros Durean and some secondary poets).
Ōšakan, V. "Arewmtahay patmuatzkʻi tzagumě -aknark-." *Haykazean hayagitakan handēs.* (N.p., 1971), 205–25. ("The Origins of the West Armenian Short Story").
———. "L'Ecole des traducteurs arméniens des Smyrne au XIXe siècle." *Haykazean hayagitakan handēs,* 4 (1973), 199–216.
———. "Cosmopolitanism in West Armenian Literature." *Review of National Literatures: Armenia.* Ed. A. Paolucci and V. Oshagan, Vol. 13. (New York: Griffin House, 1984), 194–213.
Ōšakan, Y. *Hamapatker arewmtahay grakanutʻean.* 10 vols. (Vols. 1–5, Jerusalem, 1945, 1953, 1954, 1956, 1952; vol. 6, Beirut, 1968; vols. 7–10, Antʻilias, 1979, 1980, 1980, 1982). (A history of Western Armenian literature).
———. *Hay grakanutʻiwn.* (Jerusalem, 1966 [3d ed.]). (A textbook with general analyses of Western Armenian authors and poems).
Oskanyan, N., et al. *Hay girkʻě 1512–1800 tʻvakannerin. Hay hnatip grkʻi matenagitutʻyun.* Vol. 1 (Erevan, 1988). (A bibliography of old Armenian books, 1512–1800).
Pʻapʻazean, V. *Vtak: grakan-banasirakan žołovatzu.* (Tiflis, 1901). (Creative and critical contributions by modern writers).
Parsamyan, A. "Siro hogebanutʻyan batsahaytman gełarvestakan mijotsnerě hayrennerum." *BEH,* 1977/1, 197–202. (Techniques of expressing amorous sentiments in "hayrēn" poems).
Partizuni, V. *Paytzaṙ hamastełutʻyun.* (Erevan, 1987). (Articles on nineteenth- and twentieth-century Armenian literature).
Petrosyan, E. " 'Hetʻanosakan' grakan hosankʻě arevmtahay grakanutʻyan mej." *PBH,* 1971/4, 121–32. (The pagan movement in Western Armenian literature).
———. *Grakan demkʻer.* (Erevan, 1977). (On Siamantʻō, Ṙ. Zardarean, Eruḥan, Chiftʻē-Saraf, Ṙ. Orberean, and A. Chōpanean).
Połosyan, P. "Hayots lezvi očakan hamakargi ěmbṙnumě XVII–XIX dareri

čartasanakan ašḥatutʻyunnerum." *L,* 1976/1, 98–106. (The stylistic system in rhetorical works from the seventeenth through the nineteenth centuries.

Poturean, M. "Mijin daru hay krōnakan banastełtzutʻiwnĕ." *B,* 63 (1905), 556–69. (Armenian religious poetry of the Middle Ages).

———. "Mijnadarean hay banastełtzner." *B*, 68 (1910), 417–21, 499–504, 558–59. (Medieval Armenian poets).

Pōyačean, E. *Dēmkʻer.* Book 1. (Beirut, 1966). (Ancient, modern, and Diaspora writers).

Ṙado, D. "Hay grakanutʻyunĕ Hungariayum." *T,* 1960/11, 70–81. (Armenian literature in Hungary).

Review of National Literatures: Armenia. Ed. A. Paolucci and V. Oshagan, Vol. 13. (New York: Griffin House Publications, 1984).

Russkaia i armianskaia srednevekovye literatury. (Leningrad, 1982). (Studies on classical and medieval Armenian literature and aspects of Armeno-Russian literary relations).

Sahakyan, H. *Uš mijnadari hay banastełtzutʻyunĕ (XVI–XVII dd).* (Erevan, 1975). (Armenian poetry in sixteenth–seventeenth centuries).

Šahinean, G. *Hatĕntir: verlutzakan yōduatzner.* (Beirut, 1962). (On some Western Armenian and Diaspora writers).

Sałyan, M. *Hyusisapʻayli poezian.* (Erevan, 1956). (Poetry published in the periodical *Hiwsisapʻayl* [Moscow, 1858–62, 1864]).

Sargsyan, A. *Arevelahay ev arevmtahay grakan lezunerĕ.* (Erevan, 1985). (The Eastern and Western Armenian literary standards).

Sarinyan, S. *Kʻnnadatakan ṙealizmi skzbnavorumĕ hay grakanutʻyan mej.* (Erevan, 1955). (The beginnings of realism in Armenian literature of the 1850s and 1860s).

———. *Haykakan ṙomantizm.* (Erevan, 1966). (Armenian romanticism in the nineteenth century).

———. " 'Grakan nor šaržman' hartserĕ 'Mehyan' ev 'Navasard' handesnerum." *L,* 1973/7, 9–22. (The new literary movement in the periodicals *Mehean* and *Nawasard,* [Constantinople, 1914]).

———., ed. *Grakan demkʻer.* (Erevan, 1976). (On A. Haykuni, Intra, L. Manuēlean, and V. Pʻapʻazean).

———. *Serunder ev avandner.* (Erevan, 1984). (Some nineteenth- and twentieth-century authors, literary criticism, and literary trends and traditions).

———., ed. *Hay kʻnnadatutʻyan patmutʻyun.* (Erevan, 1985). (A history of Armenian literary criticism in the nineteenth and the early twentieth centuries).

———. *Hayots grakanutʻyan erku darĕ.* 2 vols. (Erevan, 1988–89). (Two centuries [nineteenth–twentieth] of Armenian literary-critical traditions and authors).

Sasuni, K. *Patmutʻiwn arewmtahay ardi grakanutʻean.* (Beirut, 1951, 1963). (History of Modern Western Armenian literature).

Sewan, A. *Nahatak grołner.* Book 1. (Sofia, 1931). (On T. Chēōkiwrean and Ṙ. Sewak, victims of the Armenian genocide of 1915).

———. *Nahatak banastełtzner.* (Buenos Aires, 1961). (T. Chēōkiwrean, Ṙ. Sewak and others, slain in the genocide of 1915).

Simkʻēšean, E. *Jahakirnerĕ.* (Istanbul, 1973). (Modern Western Armenian writers).

Simonean, P. "Verlutzumi ew gnahatumi p'ordz Hayastani eritasardakan banasteł-tzut'ean masin." *Haykazean hayagitakan handēs,* 1971, 227–61. (An analysis of the works of Armenia's young generation of poets).
Simonyan, H. *Hay mijnadaryan kafaner, X–XVI dd.* (Erevan, 1975). (Medieval Armenian poems of the genre known as "kafa," tenth through the sixteenth century).
Simonyan, P. *Žamanakakitsneri hušerě hay dasakan grołneri masin.* (Erevan, 1975). (Reminiscences of major Armenian writers by their contemporaries).
Siruni, H. "Erb garun ēr 1913-in." *SG,* 1966/10, 137–49; 1966/11, 129–41. (Armenian literary activities in Constantinople in 1913).
———. "Ējer arevmtahay grakanut'yan patmut'enen." *PBH,* 1972/1, 35–47. (Armenian literature in Constantinople and the Armenian provinces of the Ottoman Empire).
Sōlōvean, Y. *K'nnadatakan tesut'iwnner. 1. Žamanakakits hay k'narergut'ean p'ilisop'ayut'iwně.* (Tiflis, 1912). (Philosophy of contemporary Armenian lyric poetry).
Srapyan, A. *Hay mijnadaryan zruytsner.* (Erevan, 1969). (Medieval tales).
———. "Banasirakan čšgrtumner." *PBH,* 1972/4, 137–45. (Literary notes on various writers form Erzinjan).
Step'anean, K. "Hay grołneru trtunjě." *AM,* 1900, 677–84. (On Armenian literature in general).
Step'anyan, G. *Urvagitz arevmtahay t'atroni patmut'yan.* 3 vols. (Erevan, 1962, 1969, 1975). (A history of Western Armenian theater).
Step'anyan, H. *Hayatař t'urk'eren grk'eri matenagitut'yun, 1727–1968.* (Erevan, 1985). (A bibliography of books in Armeno-Turkish [Turkish in Armenian characters]).
———. *Hayatař t'urk'eren parberakan mamul (matenagitut'yun).* (Erevan, 1987). (A bibliography of Armeno-Turkish periodicals, 1840s–1940s).
Štikyan, S. *Hay nor grakanut'yan žamanakagrut'yun, 1801–1850.* (Erevan, 1973). (A chronology of modern Armenian literature, 1801–50).
———. *Hay nor grakanut'yan žamanakagrut'yuně, 1850–1865).* (Erevan, 1983). (A chronological record of modern Armenian literature, 1850–65).
T'adevosyan, M. "Grakan žanreri problemě haykakan klasitsizmi tesut'yan mej." *PBH,* 1972/2, 61–76. (The problem of genres in the theory of Armenian classicism).
———. "Gełetsikě ev vehě haykakan klasitsizmi tesut'yan mej." *BEH,* 1972/3, 80–91. (The beautiful and the sublime in the theory of Armenian classicism).
———. *Haykakan klasitsizmi tesut'yuně.* (Erevan, 1977). (The theory of Armenian classicism).
T'amrazyan, H. *Grakan ułinerum.* (Erevan, 1962). (Modern Armenian literature).
———. *Poezian patmut'yan k'ařułinerum.* (Erevan, 1971). (On nineteenth- and twentieth-century Armenian poetry).
———. *Hay k'nnadatut'yun.* 3 vols. (Erevan, 1983–1992). (The rise of literary thought and criticism from the fifth to the nineteenth centuries).
———. *Ĕntir erker.* (Erevan, 1986). (On G. Narekatsi, P. Durean, Y. T'umanean, M. Metzarents, Siamant'ō, A. Isahakyan, V. Tērean, and E. Charents).
———. *Gełarvestakan lezvi ev bovandakut'yan ěmbřnumnerě hayots mijnadarum.* (Erevan, 1988). (Medieval Armenian perceptions of literary idiom and content).

Tavušetsi, B. "Nahatak hay mtavorakanneri tzatzkanunnerě." *EJ,* 1965/ 10, 31–36; 1966/2, 52–57. (Pen names assumed by Armenian intellectuals killed in the 1915 genocide).

Tchobanian, A. "The Armenian Poetry." *Armenia* (Boston), 4 (1910/1), 2–3; 2, 9–10; 3, 8–9; 4, 14–15.

T'ēōlēōlean, M. *Dar mě grakanut'iwn.* 2 vols. (Cairo, 1955, 1956). 2d ed., 2 vols. (Boston, 1977). (An anthology of Modern Western Armenian literature, with biographical sketches and literary analyses).

Tēr-Łazarean, G. "Ṙusahay grakanut'iwně 1916 t'uin." *A,* 1917, 176–92. (Eastern Armenian literature in 1916).

Tēr-Mkrtchean, K. "Mer mamulě." *A,* 1903, 448–63. (Reflections on the press and modern poets).

Tēr-Yakobean, Y. "T'rk'ahay vipagrut'iwn." *AM,* 1901, 385–90. (The Western Armenian novel).

Terteryan, A. *Nkatołut'yunner mer gyułagirneri masin.* (Erevan, 1927). (Notes on writers of the countryside).

———. *Hay hayrenaser grołner.* (Erevan, 1942). (Y. T'umanean and Ł. Ałayean).

———. *Hay klasikner.* (Erevan, 1944). (Modern Armenian classics).

———. *Erker.* (Erevan, 1980). (A collection of some of his essays and articles on modern Armenian literature).

T'op'chyan, Ēd. *Žołovrdaynut'yun ev ṙealizm.* (Erevan, 1980). (Marxist and Armenian literary traditions of the nineteenth and twentieth centuries).

T'op'chyan, S. *Anhuni andradardzě.* (Erevan, 1982). (Articles and reviews on nineteenth- and twentieth-century authors, literary issues, and theory).

———. *Kerp ev iskut'yun.* (Erevan, 1987). (On E. Tēmirčipašean, Širvanzade, Nar-Dos, Ṙ. Sewak, and Š. Šahnur).

U. S. "Kovkasean grak'nnut'iwně." *A,* 1912, 684–95. (About governor G. Golytsin and Russian censorship in the Caucasus).

Vardanyan, Ḥ. "Daraskzbi arevelahay grakan šaržman patmut'yunits." *BEH,* 1982/3, 168–78. (Trends in the Eastern Armenian literature at the turn of the twentieth century).

Veselovskii, Iu. *Ocherki armianskoi literatury, istorii i kul'tury.* (Erevan, 1972). (On Armenian literature, history, and culture).

Vṙam. "Aknarkner." *AM,* 1900, 405–8. (On Western Armenian poetry).

Yarut'iwnean, A. "Grakan nor šaržumě." *Mehean,* 1914/5, 68–69. (The new literary movement; the periodical *Mehean* of Constantinople, its founders and followers).

———. "P'ntṙumner." *Mehean,* 1915/6, 81–82. (Contemporary literature).

Yerkat, Tigran. "Le mouvement littéraire arménien." *Revue des revues,* August 15, 1896.

Yovsep'ean, G. "Žołovrdakan banahiwsut'ean hetk'er mijnadarean tałarannerum." *A,* 1898, 544–51. 1899, 44–47. (Traces of folk poetry in collections of medieval poetry).

Zak'aryan, A. *XX dari skzbi hayots banastełtzut'yuně.* 2 vols. (Erevan, 1973, 1977). (Armenian poetry at the beginning of twentieth century).

———. *Ṙus grołnerě Andrkovkasum ev hay grakan kyank'ě (1914–1920).* (Erevan, 1984). (Armenian literary life and Russian writers in Transcaucasia, 1914–20).

———. *Grakanutʻyan ev patmutʻyan ěntʻatskʻnerě.* (Erevan, 1989). (On nineteenth- and twentieth-century Armenian authors).
Zardarean, Ṙ. "Barekami ḫōskʻer." *AM,* 1901, 904–8. (Armenian provincial literature).
———. "Mer banastełtzutʻiwně." *AM,* 1902, 521–26. (Western Armenian poetry).
———. "Takawin kě šarunakē." *AM,* 1902, 806–10. (Armenian provincial literature).
Zaryan, Ṙ., ed. *Šekʻspirakan: haykakan šekʻspiryan taregirkʻ (Shakespearakan, an Armenian Yearbook of Shakespeare).* 7 vols. to 1985. (Erevan, 1966, 1967, 1970, 1974, 1975, 1980, 1985).
Zēkʻiean, L. *Hay tʻatroni skzbnakʻaylerě ew hay veratznundi šaržumě: hamadrakan hayeatskʻ.* (Venice, 1975). ("Les premiers pas du théâtre arménien et le mouvement de la renaissance arménienne").
Zōhrap, G. "Ṙusahay grakanutʻiwně." *AM,* 1892, 472–75. (On contemporary Eastern Armenian literature).

Soviet Armenian literature

Abajyan, G. "Mořatsvatz ējer." *SG,* 1960/12, 166–77. (On Soviet Armenian proletarian writers).
Adalyan, N. "Sovetahay patmvatzkʻě 1920–30akan tʻvakannerin." *PBH,* 1965/3, 185–94. (The Soviet Armenian short story in the 1920s and 1930s).
———. "Ařajin hamašḫarhayin paterazmi artatsolumě sovetahay patmvatzkʻum." *T,* 1965/8, 53–63. (Reflection of World War I in Soviet Armenian short stories).
———. "Sovetahay patmvatzkʻi drakan tiperě." *SG,* 1965/11, 145–55. (Positive characters in Soviet Armenian short stories).
———. *Sovetahay patmvatzkʻě.* (Erevan, 1969). (A study of the Soviet Armenian short story).
———. "Sovetahay balladě." *SG,* 1970/8, 117–25. (A study of the genre of ballad in Soviet Armenian poetry).
———. "Mer nor ardzaki hartserits." *SG,* 1972/5, 143–49. (Problems of contemporary Soviet Armenian prose).
———. "Žamanakě ev banastełtzutʻyuně." *SG,* 1979/12, 132–61. (Time and poetry).
Ałababyan, S. "Sovetahay ardzakě etpaterazmyan žamanakašrjanum." *T,* 1952/6, 63–88. (Post-World War II Soviet Armenian prose).
———. "Sovetahay grakanutʻyan patmutʻyan usumnasirutʻyan mi kʻani hartser." *SG,* 1959/7, 93–103. (Problems in the study of history of Soviet Armenian literature).
———. "Ardzakě 20-akan tʻvakannerin." *SG,* 1960/5, 158–82. (Prose in the 1920s).
———. "Sovetahay poezian 20-akan tʻvakannerin." *PBH,* 1961/1, 57–71. (Soviet Armenian poetry in the 1920s).
———. "Žołovrdi herosakan ogu dzayně." *SG,* 1962/10, 122–40. (Soviet Armenian literature during and about World War II).
———. "Kyankʻi ev patmutʻyan ułinerum." *SG,* 1963/6, 90–107; 1963/7, 114–29. (The contemporary Soviet Armenian novel).
———. "Notes on Prose." *SL,* 1966/3, 149–61.
———. "Žamanakakits ardzaki ḫndirnerits." *SG,* 1967/1, 109–38. (Problems of contemporary prose).

———. "Sovetahay vepi ułin." *SG,* 1967/6, 131–41. (The Soviet Armenian novel).

———. "Ardi banastełtzutʻyan hartserits." *SG,* 1969/5, 117–38. (Issues in contemporary poetry).

———. "Hay grakanutʻyan gełagitakan nor orakĕ." *SG,* 1971/1, 109–21. (The new aesthetic quality of Armenian literature).

———. "Hay sovetakan grakanutʻyan patmutʻyan nor ḥndirnerĕ." *L,* 1971/7, 3–16. (New challenges in the study of history of Soviet Armenian literature).

———. *Hodvatzner, dimankarner, hušer.* (Erevan, 1982). (Articles, literary portraits, and reminiscences about late nineteenth- and twentieth-century authors).

———. *XX dari hay grakanutʻyan zugaheṙakannerum.* 2 vols. (Erevan, 1983–84). (On twentieth century Armenian literature).

———. *Dasakanner ev žamanakakitsner.* (Erevan, 1986). (On writers from Ḥ. Abovean to the 1980s).

———. *Hay sovetakan grakanutʻyan patmutʻyun.* Vol. 1. (Erevan, 1986). (Covers the history of Soviet Armenian literature in the 1920s and 1930s).

———. "Hay kʻnnadatutʻyunĕ ev grakanagitutʻyunĕ 1920–30-akan tʻvakannerin." *PBH,* 1980/1, 16–37. (Armenian literary criticism and theory in the 1920s and 1930s).

———. "Hušayin veraprumner." *SG,* 1980/5, 128–46. (Reminiscences about D. Demirčyan, S. Zoryan, G. Mahari, A. Inčikyan, and Ḥ. Sargsyan).

———., et al. *Sovetahay grakanutʻyan patmutʻyun.* Vol. 1, 1917–41; Vol. 2, 1941–64. (Erevan, 1961, 1965). (A history of Soviet Armenian literature).

———. *Istoriia armianskoi sovetskoi literatury.* (Moscow, 1966). (History of Soviet Armenian literature).

Ałabekyan, K. "Žamanakakits herosi oronumner." *SG,* 1975/1, 111–16. (In quest of contemporary characters in prose).

Aleksanian, E. *V poiskakh geroia i stilia.* (Erevan, 1984). (Contemporary Soviet Armenian prose).

Alekʻsanyan, V. "Sovetahay poeziayi lezvakan mi kʻani aṙandznahatkutʻyunneri masin." *PBH,* 1965/3, 203–10. (Aspects of idiom in Soviet Armenian poetry).

Amirḥanyan, H. *Sovetahay grakanutʻyan zargatsumĕ Adrbejanum.* (Baku, 1949). (Soviet Armenian literature in Azerbaijan).

Amiryan, S. "Hay grakanutʻyunĕ ṙus kʻnnadatutʻyan gnahatmamb 1920-akan tʻvakannerin ev 1930-akanneri skzbin." *L,* 1979/12, 14–28. (Evaluation of Armenian literature by Russian criticism in the 1920s and the early1930s).

"Ampʻopʻelov banavečĕ." *SG,* 1973/2, 150–55. (Summary of the discussion on contemporary poetry).

Ananyan, G. *Hodvatzner.* (Erevan, 1981). (On Soviet Armenian authors).

Andrēasean, A. *Grakanutʻean ew grołneru masin.* (Los Angeles, 1988). (On literature and writers, including Soviet Armenian authors).

Aṙakʻelyan, G. " 'Pravdan' ev hay grakanutʻyunĕ." *SG,* 1977/6, 113–24; 7, 119–33; 8, 137–49. (*Pravda* and Armenian literature).

Aristakesyan, A. "Siro erekʻ inkʻnartahaytutʻyun." *SG,* 1970/6, 115–32. (Love theme in three authors' works).

———. *Banstełtzneri ev banastełtzutʻyan masin.* (Erevan, 1971). (On poets and poetry).

Arzumanyan, L. "Arevelkʻi gełarvestakan patkerman patmutʻyunits (20–30-akan tʻvakanner)." *BEH,* 1983/1, 138–44. (The East as an anti-imperialistic element in Soviet Armenian literature of the 1920s and 1930s).

Arzumanyan, S. "Vepě kyankʻi ḥtatsvatz patkern ē." *SG,* 1960/7, 143–59. (On the Soviet Armenian novel).

———. "Aknarkě kyankʻi masnakits." *SG,* 1961/11, 142–51. (On the essay and its role).

———. "Avandakann u norě." *SG,* 1963/6, 119–32. (The traditional and the new in the short story).

———. "Patmahełapʻoḥakan vepě 20–30akan tʻvakannerin." *SG,* 1967/4, 90–98. (The historical-revolutionary novel in the 1920s and 1930s).

———. *Sovetahay vepě.* 3 vols. (Erevan, 1967–86). (On the Soviet Armenian novel).

———. "Antsyali tʻematikan ev ardiakanutʻyuně." *SG,* 1968/6, 121–31. (Relevance of themes of the past to the present).

———. "Sovetahay ardi ardzakě." *SG,* 1971/5, 123–34. (Contemporary Soviet Armenian prose).

———. "Ardi ardzaki hogserits." *SG,* 1975/12, 97–105. (Problems of modern prose).

———. "Arvesti kensakan erakě." *SG,* 1979/4, 112–32. (On the Soviet Armenian novel).

Asryan, A. *Hay grołneri hraparakaḥosutʻyuně Hayrenakan paterazmi tarinerin.* (Erevan, 1972). (Journalism articles by Armenian authors in World War II).

Avetisyan, Z. *Hay patmavepi poetikan.* (Erevan, 1986). (On the historical novel as a genre, and the historical novels of Tzerents, Raffi, Muratsan, D. Demirčyan, and S. Zoryan).

Azatean, E. *Grakan, gełaruestakan seweṙumner.* (La Verne, California, 1988). (Articles and reviews on nineteenth- and twentieth-century authors and artists).

Azroyan, L. "Hay grakanutʻyuně vratsakan 'Mnatʻobi' handesum." *L,* 1967/2, 41–52. (Armenian literature in *Mnatʻobi,* a Georgian periodical).

Babayan, A. *Hayrenakan metz paterazmi šrjani sovetahay grakanutʻyan mi kʻani bnoroš gtzerě.* (Erevan, 1952). (Some characteristics of Soviet Armenian literature written during World War II).

Bodosyan, S. "20-akan tʻvakanneri hay ergitzakan mamulě." *T,* 1961/10, 37–46. (Satire in the periodical press in the 1920s).

———. *Sovetahay ergitzankʻě 20-akan tʻvakannerin.* (Erevan, 1963). (Soviet Armenian satire in the 1920s).

———. *Lirika desiatiletiia, 1958–1968.* (Erevan, 1970). (Lyric poetry, 1958–68).

Boryan, G. "Literature of the New Armenia." *SL,* 1956/7, 145–51.

Charentsyan ěntʻertsumner. 5 vols. to 1988 (Erevan, 1973–88). (Studies on Charents).

Danielyan, G. "Poezia–1970-akan tʻvakanner." *SG,* 1977/7, 134–45. (Poetry in the 1970s).

Danielyan, K. *Grakanutʻyun ev irakanutʻyun.* (Erevan, 1986). (Various aspects of Soviet Armenian literature from the 1960s to the 1980s).

Davtʻyan, V. "Dasakan avandnern u aysōrva poezian." *SG,* 1976/7, 108–20. (Classical traditions and contemporary poetry).

Ełiazaryan, A. "Ardzaki nor ułinerě." *SG,* 1972/9, 123–29. (Prospects for Soviet Armenian prose).

———. "Mardkants poezian." *SG,* 1978/5, 134–41. (On poetry).

———. "Kyankʻě, or patmum ē ir masin." *SG,* 1979/6, 127–37. (Modern prose).

Ēmin, G. "Mtorumner poeziayi čampʻin." *SG,* 1970/1, 126–43. (Reflections on poetry).

"The Fourth Congress of Soviet Armenian Writers." *CR,* 8 (1959), 110–12.

Gabrielyan, V. "Sovetakan grakanutʻyan bazmazg bnuytʻě." *BEH,* 1983/1, 45–55. (The multinational nature of Soviet literature).

Galstyan, G. "Banastełtzutʻyan ěmbṙnumě." *SG,* 1970/6, 133–39. (On Soviet Armenian poetry).

———. "Sovetahay banastełtzutʻyan etpaterazmyan šrjani patmutʻyunits." *SG,* 1971/4, 138–42. (On the history of Post–World War II Soviet Armenian poetry).

———. "Ardi patma-hełapʻoḥakan vepi hartserits." *SG,* 1977/3, 139–47. (Modern historical-revolutionary novel).

———. "Och hartʻagrutʻyun, och bardagrutʻyun, ayl mardagrutʻyun." *SG,* 1978/5, 124–33. (Modern poetry).

Galstyan, H., and Gasparyan, D. *Sovetahay grakanutʻyan taregrutʻyun, 1957–75.* (Erevan, 1977). (A chronology of Soviet Armenian literature, 1957–75. An earlier volume, covering the years 1917 to 1956, was compiled by H. Łazaryan, et al., *Sovetahay grakanutʻyan taregrutʻyun,* Erevan, 1957).

Gasparyan, A. " 'Norkʻ' handesě ev antsyali grakan žaṙangutʻyan gnahatutʻyuně." *L,* 1969/3, 37–46. (Evaluation of the old literary tradition in the journal *Norkʻ*).

Gasparyan, D. "Banastełtzakan kaṙutsvatzkʻi hartser." *SG,* 1973/5, 120–30. (Questions of structure in poetry).

———. "Baṙeri gałtnikʻě, dyutʻankʻn u dzandzruytʻě: mtorumner 1973 tʻvakani poeziayi šurj." *SG,* 1974/4, 136–46. (Reflections on poetry produced in 1973).

———. "Aṙajadrvoł grakanutʻyuně ev žamanaki aṙajadrankʻě." *SG,* 1978/4, 142–52. (Issues of contemporary prose).

———. *Sovetahay poeziayi tałachapʻutʻyuně.* (Erevan, 1979). (Prosody of Soviet Armenian poetry).

———. *Banastełtzutʻyan ogin.* (Erevan, 1980). (Charents and later Soviet Armenian writers).

———. "Sovetahay grakan šaržumě 1920-akan tʻvakanneri erkrord kesin." *L,* 1980/7, 3–14. (Soviet Armenian literary trends in the mid and late-1920s).

———. *Žamanak ev šaržum.* (Erevan, 1984). (Contemporary Soviet Armenian literature and literary criticism).

———. *Helikoni astłě.* (Erevan, 1988). (On Soviet Armenian literary criticism, theory and some authors).

———. *Hay ḥorhrdayin grakanutʻyan patmakan zargatsman ułin.* (Erevan, 1989). (A brief survey of Soviet Armenian literature).

———. *Poezian ev kyankʻi čšmartutʻyuně.* (Erevan, 1990). (On H. Širaz, H. Sahyan, S. Kaputikyan, G. Ēmin, N. Zaryan, G. Saryan, M. Margaryan, and others).

———., et al. *Hay sovetakan poeziayi patmutʻyun, 1920–1970.* (Erevan, 1987). (A history of Soviet Armenian poetry, 1920–1970).

———., et al. *Gełarvestakan metʻod ev grakan protses.* (Erevan, 1990). (On Soviet Armenian literary history, criticism, and theory).

Gaisaryan, S. "Armenian Poetry Today." *SL,* 1973/9, 119–23.

Gevorkian, T. "Nekotorye zhanrovye osobennosti sovremennoi sovetskoi prozy." *L,* 1983/9, 12–22. (On some aspects of genres in contemporary Soviet Armenian literature).

Gilavyan, M. *Žamanakě ev poezian.* (Erevan, 1990). (Soviet Armenian poetry of the 1950s and 1960s in relation to Soviet poetry in general).

Gonchar-Khandzhian, N. *Armianskaia literatura v russkoi sovetskoi kritike: bibliografiia. Stat'i.* (Erevan, 1989). (Armenian literature in Soviet Russian criticism; bibliography and articles).

Grakan stełtzagortzutʻyun. (Erevan, 1983). (On literary analysis and the works of nineteenth- and twentieth-century Armenian authors).

Grakanutʻyuně ev žamanakě. Sovetahay grakanutʻyan hartser. (Erevan, 1980). (Various aspects of Soviet Armenian literature and its history).

Grigoryan, A. "Intelektualizmě žamanakakits poeziayum." *SG,* 1968/2, 126–34. (Intellectualism in contemporary poetry).

———. "Poezian ev žamanakě: 70-akan tʻvakanneri gełarvestakan oronumnerě." *SG,* 1978/3, 98–104. (Experiments in Soviet Armenian poetry of the 1970s).

Grigoryan, S. *Žamanakakits ḥorhrdahay poemě (1960–1980-akan tʻvakanner).* (Erevan, 1990). (Soviet Armenian poems of 1960s–80s).

Grigoryan, V. "Sovetahay dramaturgiayi kazmavorman patmutʻyunits (1920–30 tʻtʻ)." *PBH,* 1973/3, 85–93. (Beginnings of Soviet Armenian dramaturgy).

Gyulnazaryan, Ḥ. "Ditołutʻyunner sovetahay mankakan grakanutʻyan masin." *SG,* 1959/12, 130–40. (Remarks on Soviet Armenian children's literature).

Ḥachatryan, H. *Grakan tełekatu.* (Erevan, 1981, 1986 [revised]). (A bio-bibliographical directory, listing only Armenian members of the Union of Soviet Writers of Armenia and the Writers' Union of the USSR who wrote in Armenian).

Haḥumyan, T. *Hušer.* (Erevan, 1987). (Reminiscences about some nineteenth- and twentieth-century authors).

Haḥverdyan, L. *Mtorumner.* (Erevan, 1984). (Reflections on nineteenth- and twentieth-century authors).

Hambardzumyan, V. "Ardzakagirě ev gełarvestakan ḥoskʻi inkʻnatiputʻyuně." *SG,* 1978/2, 125–34. (Style and diction in modern prose).

Ḥanjyan, A. *Mer grakanutʻyan ḥndirnerě.* (Erevan, 1934). (Challenges facing Soviet Armenian literature).

Harutʻyunyan, S. "Sovetahay mankakan grakanutʻyuně." *SG,* 1967/12, 117–25. (Soviet Armenian children's literature).

Hatityan, G. "Noraguyn banastełtzutʻyan dzgtumneri masin." *SG,* 1970/3, 123–28. (On new trends and aspirations in contemporary Soviet Armenian poetry).

Hay sovetakan tʻatroni patmutʻyun. (Erevan, 1967). (History of Soviet Armenian theater).

Haykakan sovetakan hanragitaran. 12 vols. (Erevan, 1974–86). (Soviet Armenian encyclopedia). *Sovetakan Hayastan. Haykakan sovetakan hanragitaran.* (Erevan, 1987). (A supplementary volume devoted to Soviet Armenia).

Hayryan, G. *Nor herosi oronman čanaparhin.* (Erevan, 1965). (On Soviet Armenian literature of the 1920s).

Hoktemberě ev hay grakanutʻyuně (hodvatzneri žołovatzu). (Erevan, 1967). (The October Revolution and Armenian literature).

Hovhannisyan, H. "Grakan nor serndi ašḥarhě." *SG,* 1966/2, 121–38. (On young writers).

———. "Sovetahay grakanutʻyan hisun tarin." *SG,* 1971/1, 99–108. (The first fifty years of Soviet Armenian literature).

———. "Grakanutʻyan mayrułin." *SG,* 1979/9, 91–100. (Modern literature).

Hovsepʻyan, G. *Grakan dimagtzer.* (Erevan, 1981). (Literary portraits of D. Varužan and some Soviet Armenian writers).

Hunanyan, A. *Ardi hay draman.* (Erevan, 1964). (Modern Soviet Armenian drama).

———. *Dramaturgia ev tʻatron.* (Erevan, 1980). (Modern Armenian dramaturgy and theater).

Išḥanyan, Ṙ. "Hay nor banastełtzutʻyan lezvi zargatsman ułinerě." *SG,* 1971/6, 122–35. (Forging an idiom for new poetry).

Istoriia armianskoi sovetskoi literatury, ed. S. Ałababyan, et al. (Moscow, 1966). (History of Soviet Armenian literature).

Jrbašyan, Ēd. *Poemi žanrě sovetahay grakanutʻyan mej (patmutʻyuně ev tesutʻyuně).* (Erevan, 1955). (The history and theory of the genre of poem in Soviet Armenian literature).

———. "Žamanakakits poemi ułinerě." *SG,* 1966/6, 129–44. (Prospects for the genre of contemporary poem).

———. "Nor oronumneri čanaparhin: avanduytʻnern u norararutʻyuně žamanakakits hay poeziayum." *SG,* 1972/6, 45–60; 7, 90–103. (Traditions and innovation in contemporary Soviet Armenian poetry).

———. *Poetika i literaturnoe razvitie.* Trans. by N. Gonchar-Khandzhian and L. Kazarian. (Erevan, 1985). (On some aspects of literary theory and some nineteenth- and twentieth-century Armenian writers).

———. *Grołě ev žołovurdě.* (Erevan, 1989). (On aspects of nineteenth- and twentieth-century Armenian literature; literary portraits of Armenian and Russian writers).

Kʻalantʻaryan, Ž. "Noveli žanrě sovetahay grakanutʻyan mej (20-akan tʻvakannerin)." *BEH,* 1973/1, 197–202. (The Soviet Armenian novel in the 1920s).

Karinyan, A. *Grakan-patmakan aknarkner.* (Erevan, 1982). (On some nineteenth- and twentieth-century Armenian authors).

Kirakosyan, L. "Šaržman ułłutʻyunnerě." *SG,* 1978/1, 114–19. (Trends in Soviet Armenian prose).

———. *Cherty vremeni: Literaturno-kriticheskie stat'i.* (Erevan, 1985). (On Soviet Armenian writers).

Kontseptsiia lichnosti v literature razvitogo sotsializma. (Moscow, 1980). (A collection of articles examining Soviet Armenian literature from a Marxist literary perspective).

Kostanyan, A. "Žamanakneri kapě." *SG,* 1966/4, 146–56. (On the history of Soviet Armenian Writers Congresses).

Lalaḥanyan, S. *Sovetahay mankakan ardzakě etpaterazmyan šrjanum (1946–1980 tʻtʻ).* (Erevan, 1980). (Soviet Armenian children's prose literature, 1946–80).

Łanalanyan, H. *Hamastełutʻyun.* (Erevan, 1984). (On P. Durean, D. Varužan, A. Isahakyan, M. Metzarents, V. Tērean, and E. Charents).

Łazanchyan, V. "Grakan aṙajěntʻatsi kazmakerpman patmutʻyunits." *SG,* 1974/9, 146–50. (The Party, literature, and literary movements in the 1920s and 1930s).

Łazaryan, H., et al. *Sovetahay grakanutʻyan taregrutʻyun (1917–1956).* (Erevan, 1957). (Chronology of Soviet Armenian literature, 1917–56; a volume recording literary events from 1957 to 1975 was compiled by H. Galstyan and D. Gasparyan, *Sovetahay grakanutʻyan taregrutʻyun, 1957–1975,* Erevan, 1977).

Łazaryan, H. "Sovetahay grakanutʻyan skzbnavorumě." *L,* 1970/11, 42–49. (Origins of Soviet Armenian literature).

———. *Grołě ev irakanutʻyuně.* (Erevan, 1981). (Literature and some Soviet Armenian authors from a Marxist perspective).

Łukasyan, Z. *Žamanakakits sovetahay vepě.* (Erevan, 1964). (On the contemporary Soviet Armenian novel).

———. *Sovetahay grakanagitutʻyuně 1920–1930-akan tʻvakannerin.* (Erevan, 1981). (Soviet Armenian literary criticism in the 1920s and 1930s).

Makintsyan, P. *Dimagtzer.* (Erevan, 1980). (On Sayeatʻ-Nōvay, nineteenth- and twentieth-century Armenian authors, and some non-Armenian writers).

Manukyan, A. "Gitafantastik grakanutʻyan hartser." *SG,* 1975/9, 137–41. (Soviet Armenian science fiction).

———. "Gitafantastikakan žanri zargatsman ułiov." *SG,* 1978/3, 127–33. (Soviet Armenian science fiction).

Manukyan, S. *Žołovurdneri barekamutʻyan artatsolumě sovetahay grakanutʻyan mej.* (Erevan, 1956). (Reflections of international friendship in Soviet Armenian literature).

Matoyan, Ch. *Kʻrdakan banahyusutʻyan mšakumnerě sovetahay grakanutʻyan mej.* (Erevan, 1980). (Adaptations of Kurdish folklore in Soviet Armenian literature).

Melikʻsetʻyan, S. *Urvagitz sovetahay tʻatroni patmutʻyan.* (Erevan, 1960). (An outline of the history of Soviet Armenian theater).

Melkʻonyan, M. *Hayrenakan metz paterazmě sovetahay ardzakum.* (Erevan, 1985). (World War II as reflected in Soviet Armenian prose).

———. *Och miayn hatsiv.* (Erevan, 1987). (A Marxist perspective on literature and some Soviet Armenian writers).

Mḥitʻaryan, A. "Gełarvesti aṙandznahatkutʻyan mi kʻani hartserě ev sovetahay poeziayi nor erkerě." *SG,* 1965/3, 127–36. (On contemporary poetry).

———. "Sovetahay grakan kyankʻě Tʻbilisium." *SG,* 1967/9, 114–32. (Soviet Armenian literary life in Tbilisi).

———. "Tʻbilisahay grakan kyankʻě 1920-akan tʻvakannerin." *BEH,* 1968/3, 154–61. (Armenian literary life in Tiflis in the 1920s).

———. "Sovetahay grakanutʻyuně Vrastanum." *PBH,* 1972/4, 29–36. (Armenian literature in the Georgian SSR).

———. *Armianskaia literatura v Gruzii.* (Erevan, 1980). (Armenian literature in the Georgian SSR).

Mkrtchyan, H. "Ḥoher eritasardakan ardzaki masin." *SG,* 1972/7, 104–16. (Reflections on young prose writers).

Mkryan, M. *Erker.* 2 vols. (Erevan, 1987). (The Armenian literary tradition and authors from its origins to the twentieth century).

Mnatsakanyan, V. "Tałand ev žamanak." *SG,* 1963/9, 124–30. (Modern poetry).

———. "Barov ekʻ ekel, ov norer." *SG,* 1969/3, 161–71. (On young writers).

Muradyan, N. "Sovetahay grakanutʻyan kes darĕ." *EJ,* 1967/10–11, 32–42. (The first fifty years of Soviet Armenian literature).

Nalbandian, V. *Uroki armianskoi drevnosti.* (Erevan, 1985). (Articles on early Armenian literature and its echoes in the Soviet period).

Nazarean, A. *Sovetahay grakanutʻean yatkanišerĕ ew hay žołovrdi miasnakanutʻiwnĕ.* (Paris, 1954). (Characteristics of Soviet Armenian literature and the unity of the Armenian people).

Nurikean, B. "Grakan hamagumarin aṙtʻiw." *Ani,* 2 (1947–48), 46–48. (On the occasion of the Congress of Soviet Armenian Writers).

Orbuni, Z. "Grakan hamagumarin aṙtʻiw." *Ani,* 2 (1947–48), 48. (On the occasion of the Congress of Soviet Armenian Writers).

Palatʻon, S. *Sovetahay grakanutʻiwn.* (Latakia, 1958). (Soviet Armenian literature).

Połosyan, V. "Žołovrdakan banahyusakan nyutʻeri ev lezvamijotsneri ōgtagortzumĕ 20–30-akan tʻvakanneri Vrastani sovetahay ardzakum." *BEH,* 1976/3, 154–59. (Use of popular folklore in Armenian literature of the 1920s and 1930s in the Georgian SSR).

Safaryan, V. "Oronumneri ev verakaṙutsman čiger." *SG,* 1970/7, 157–63. (On young poets).

Sahakyan, Ṙ. "Žamanakakits hay poemi tesaknerĕ." *BEH,* 1974/2, 241–48. (Different poem genres in contemporary Soviet Armenian poetry).

Sahakyan, Y. "Banastełtzutʻyunĕ ser ē." *SG,* 1970/10, 110–12. (Modern poetry).

Sarian, S. *Poslevoennaia armianskaia sovetskaia literatura, 1945–55.* (Erevan, 1956). (Post–World War II Soviet Armenian literature).

———. "Ob armianskom sovetskom rasskaze." *T,* 1958/10, 35–46. (The Soviet Armenian short story).

———. *Sovetahay ardi patmvatzkʻĕ.* (Erevan, 1959). (The modern Soviet Armenian short story).

———. *Sovetskaia armianskaia literatura, 1941–1960.* (Erevan, 1964). (Soviet Armenian literature, 1941–60).

Sarinyan, S. "1957 tʻvakani ardzakĕ." *SG,* 1958/4, 124–42. (Soviet Armenian prose in 1957).

———. *Hayots grakanutʻyan erku darĕ.* 2 vols. (Erevan, 1988–89). (Nineteenth- and twentieth-century Armenian literary tradition and authors).

Sevak, P. "Džvarĕ irenits hasun lineln ē." *SG,* 1970/4, 161–66. (On contemporary poetry).

Simonean, P. "Verlutzumi ew gnahatumi pʻordz Hayastani eritasardakan banastełtzutʻean masin." *Haykazean hayagitakan handēs,* 1971, 227–61. (An analysis of the works of Armenia's young generation of poets).

Simonyan, D. *Hayastani grakanutʻyunĕ.* (Erevan, 1934). (The literature of Soviet Armenia).

"The Sixth Congress of Young and New Authors in Armenia." *CR,* 6 (1958), 146–47.

Sołomonyan, S. *Ardi poeziayi mi kʻani hartser.* (Erevan, 1960). (Modern Soviet Armenian poetry).

———. *Žamanakakits hay banastełtzner.* 2 vols. (Erevan, 1965–67). (Contemporary Soviet Armenian poets).

Sovetahay grakanutʻyan patmutʻyun, ed. S. Ałababyan, et al., 2 vols. Vol. 1: *1917–41.* Vol. 2: *1941–64.* (Erevan, 1961, 1965). (History of Soviet Armenian literature).

"Sovetahay grakanutʻyan taregrutʻyunits." *SG,* 1966/7, 138–48. (The chronology of events in the history of Soviet Armenian literature).

Sovetakan grakanutʻyan poetikan. (Erevan, 1980). (Soviet literary theory, Socialist realism, and the works of a few Soviet Armenian writers).

Spʻyuṙkʻi grołnerě sovetahay grakanutʻyan masin. (Erevan, 1980). (Writers of the Armenian Diaspora on Soviet Armenian literature).

Tʻamrazyan, H. "Žołovrdi poeziayi argasavor ułin: sovetahay poeziayi patmutʻyunits." *SG,* 1960/2, 101–21. (The evolution of Soviet Armenian poetry).

———. *Grakan ułinerum.* (Erevan, 1962). (Soviet Armenian literature).

———. "Žamanakakits hay poeziayi zargatsman mi kʻani hartser." *SG,* 1967/2, 130–38; 3, 115–33. (Contemporary Soviet Armenian poetry).

———. "Hełapʻoḥutʻyuně ev azgayin poezian." *BEH,* 1971/1, 3–12. (The Bolshevik Revolution and national literature).

———. "Hayrenakan paterazmě ev hay grakanutʻyuně." *SG,* 1975/9, 112–36. (World War II and Armenian literature).

———. *Sovetahay grakanutʻyan patmutʻyun.* (Erevan, 1980, 1984 [revised]). (A history of Soviet Armenian literature to the 1940s).

———. *Ěntir erker.* (Erevan, 1986). (On G. Narekatsi, P. Durean, Y. Tʻumanean, M. Metzarents, Siamantʻō, A. Isahakyan, V. Tērean, and E. Charents).

Terteryan, A. *Erker.* (Erevan, 1980). (A collection of essays and articles on modern Armenian literature).

Tʻopʻchyan, A. "Poetakan nor serund, mifě ev irakanutʻyuně." *SG,* 1970/10, 103–9. (Myths and realities in contemporary poetry).

———. *Baṙi sahmannerě.* (Erevan, 1978). (On Soviet Armenian and Diaspora authors and literary issues).

Tʻopʻchyan, Ēd. *Žołovrdaynutʻyun ev ṙealizm.* (Erevan, 1980). (Marxist and Armenian literary traditions of the nineteenth and twentieth centuries).

Tʻopʻchyan, S. *Anhuni andradardzě.* (Erevan, 1982). (Articles and reviews on nineteenth- and twentieth-century authors, literary issues, and theory).

Yovhannēsean, V. "1960-i banastełtzakan artadrutʻiwně Ḥorhrdayin Hayastani mēj." *B,* 119 (1961), 20–22, 74–80. (Soviet Armenian poetry in 1960).

Zakʻaryan, A. *Sovetahay grakanutʻyan antsatz ułin.* (Erevan, 1957). (The accomplishments of Soviet Armenian literature).

———. "Grapatmakan irołutʻyunneri hetkʻerov." *L,* 1988/12, 14–28. (Of literature, politics, and biographical documentation of the lives of V. Tērean, E. Charents, D. Demirčyan, S. Zoryan and A. Bakunts in the 1920s and 1930s).

———. *Grakanutʻyan ev patmutʻyan ěntʻatskʻnerě.* (Erevan, 1989). (Studies on nineteenth- and twentieth-century Armenian authors).

Literature of the Post-Genocide Dispersion

Addaryan, G. "Orpeszi spʻyuṙkʻahay grakanutʻyuně goyatevi u zargana." *SG,* 1966/5, 141–45. (The future of Diaspora literature).

Andrēasean, A. *Grakanutʻean ew grołneru masin.* (Los Angeles, 1988). (On nineteenth- and twentieth-century authors, including some Diaspora writers).

"Aṙajadimakan grołneri ambioně." *SG,* 1959/7, 156–59. (On progressive Lebanese-Armenian writers).

Azatean, E. *Grakan, gełaruestakan seweṙumner.* (La Verne, California, 1988). (Articles and reviews on nineteenth- and twentieth-century authors and artists).

Babloyan, M. *Sp'yuṙk'ahay mamuli patmut'yunits, 'Ani' 1946–55*. (Erevan, 1965). (A history of the literary periodical *Ani,* Beirut, 1946–55).

Baluean, H. "P'arizahay grakan berk'ě: p'ordz hamadrut'ean." *Z* (amsat'ert'), 3 (1958/4–5), 6, 10; 3 (1959/6–7), 13–14. (A survey of French Armenian literature in the past three decades).

———. "Polsahay ardi k'ert'ołut'iwně." *Z* (amsat'ert'), 3 (1959/8–10), 13. (Contemporary Armenian poetry from Istanbul).

———. "Parskahay ardi grakanut'iwně." *Z* (amsat'ert'), 4 (1960/3–4), 4; 4 (1960/5–6), 10. (Modern Iranian Armenian literature).

Dallak'yan, K. "Grakanut'yuně 'Haṙaj'i ev 'Haṙaj grakan'i ējerum." *SG,* 1964/3, 127–34. (Belles lettres in the periodicals *Yaṙaj* and *Yaṙaj grakan,* Beirut).

Danielyan, S. "Sp'yuṙk'ahay grakanut'yan hartserin nvirvatz erkrord gitažołově." *L,* 1989/8, 92–94. (On the conference of Armenian Dispersion literature, held in Erevan).

———. *Amerikahay vipagirner.* (Erevan, 1990). (On Hamasteł, Y. Asaturean, and A. Andreasean).

Gabrielyan, V. *Dimankarner: sp'yuṙk'ahay grołner.* (Erevan, 1976). (On K. Zaryan, Y. Mndzuri, Š. Šahnur, V. Šušanean, and V. Hayk).

———. *Sp'yuṙk'ahay grakanut'yun (patmut'yan aknarkner).* (Erevan, 1987). (A history of the literature of the Armenian Dispersion).

Galstyan, G. "Arevmtahay gyułě sp'yuṙk'i grakanut'yan mej." *BEH,* 1974/1, 22–24. (Reflection of Western Armenian village life in Diaspora literature).

Grigoryan, H. "Eresnakan t'vakanneri sp'yuṙk'ahay grakan zart'onk'ě." *T,* 1962/2, 3–18. (Survey of Armenian literature in France, the Middle East, and the United States in the 1930s)

Guyumjyan, G. "Amerikahay grakan šaržman patmut'yunits." *SG,* 1978/1, 144–51. (The Armenian-American literary movement as reflected in journals).

Hačean, M. "Polsoy nor grakanut'iwně." *Z* (amsat'ert'), 3 (1959/11–12), 11. (The new Armenian literature in Istanbul).

Haḥverdyan, L. *Mtorumner.* (Erevan, 1984). (Reflections on nineteenth- and twentieth-century authors, including Diaspora writers such as A. Tzaṙukean and V. Mavean).

Hamaynapatker hanrapetakan šrjani Istanpulahay grakanut'ean. (Istanbul, 1957). (Panorama of Armenian literature in Republican Turkey).

Hatityan, G. "Sp'yuṙk'ahay grakanut'yan lusabanman hartserits." *SG,* 1973/2, 156–60. (General reflections on literature of the Armenian Dispersion).

Haykakan sovetakan hanragitaran. 12 vols. (Erevan, 1974–86). (Soviet Armenian encyclopedia). *Sovetakan Hayastan. Haykakan sovetakan hanragitaran.* (Erevan, 1987). (A supplementary volume devoted to Soviet Armenia).

Hayryan, G. "Sp'yuṙk'ahay grakanut'yan usumnasirut'yan mi k'ani hartser." *SG,* 1986/3, 139/41. (Some issues on the study of literature of the Armenian Dispersion).

———., et al. *Sp'yuṙk'ahay grołner.* Book 1. (Erevan, 1990). (On Beniamin Nurikean, Vahē Hayk, and Lewon-Zawēn Siwrmēlean).

"Iranahay ardi grakanut'yuně." *SG,* 1979/10, 114–25. (An interview with the writer G. Ḥanents on contemporary Iranian-Armenian literature).

Iranahay ardi grołner. Book 1. (Teheran, 1964). (An anthology of modern Iranian-Armenian writers, with biographies).

Jrbašyan, Ēd. *Grołē ev žołovurdě.* (Erevan, 1989). (On aspects of nineteenth- and twentieth-century literature; literary portraits of some Russian and Armenian authors, including a few Diaspora writers).

Kurtikyan, S. "Payk'ari u hałt'anaki havatov (not'er sp'yuṙk'ahay grakanut'yan)." *SG*, 1961/2, 122–39. (Armenian writers in France, the Middle East, and the United States).

———. "Polsahay grakanut'yan erekn u aysōrě." *SG,* 1964/1, 115–30. (Survey of Armenian literature in Istanbul from 1918 to the present).

———. "Sp'yuṙk'ahay grakanut'yun." *SG,* 1965/8, 125–35. (A survey of the literature of the Armenian Dispersion).

———. "Mtorumner sp'yuṙk'ahay grakanut'yan šurj." *SG,* 1966/7, 127–37. (Reflections on literature of the Armenian Dispersion).

———. "Leninyan gałap'arnerě ev artasahmani hay grakanut'yuně." *SG,* 1970/4, 148–72; 1970/5, 110–40. (Leninism and literature of the Armenian Dispersion).

Mḥit'arean, G. *K'aṙord dar grakanut'iwn.* (Cairo, 1946). (Modern Armenian and Diaspora writers of the preceding twenty-five years).

———. "Sp'iwṙk'i hay grakanut'iwně verjin 25-ameakin." *HK,* 31 (1953/12), 1–15. (Literature of the Armenian Dispersion of the preceding twenty-five years).

Mułnetsyan, S. "Hayrenik'i t'eman etpaterazmyan libananahay poeziayum." *L,* 1975/2, 21–29. (The theme of the homeland in post–World War II Lebanese-Armenian poetry).

Ōšakan, Y. *Hay grakanut'iwn.* 3d edition. (Jerusalem, 1966). (A textbook with analyses of Western Armenian authors and works).

Oshagan, V. "Literature of the Armenian Diaspora." *World Literature Today,* 60 (1986/2), 224–28.

Pōyačean, E. *Dēmk'er.* Book 1. (Beirut, 1966). (Ancient, modern, and Diaspora writers).

Šahinean, G. *Hatěntir: verlutzakan yōduatzner.* (Beirut, 1962). (On Western Armenian and Diaspora writers).

Sevan, G. *Sp'yuṙk'ahay grakanut'yan patmut'yan urvagtzer.* (Erevan, 1980). (A history of the literature of the Armenian Dispersion).

———. *Hayrenik'-Sp'yuṙk' grakan kaperě.* (Erevan, 1988). (Literary relations between Soviet Armenia and the Armenian Dispersion).

"Sp'iwṙk' ew grakanut'iwně." *S,* 1947, 193–97, 225–28, 258–60, 289–92, 369–71, 401–5. (Reflections on literature of the Dispersion).

Step'anyan, G. *Aknarkner sp'yuṙk'ahay t'atroni patmut'yan. 1 Fransahay t'atron.* (Erevan, 1982). (A history of the French-Armenian theater of the Armenian Dispersion).

Step'anyan, H. *Hayataṙ t'urk'eren grk'eri matenagitut'yun, 1727–1968.* (Erevan, 1985). (A bibliography of books in Armeno-Turkish, Turkish in Armenian characters).

———. *Hayataṙ t'urk'eren parberakan mamul (matenagitut'yun).* (Erevan, 1987). (A bibliography of Armeno-Turkish periodicals, 1840s–1940s).

T'op'chean, E. "Artasahmanean žamanakakits hay grakanut'iwně." *Ani,* 1 (1946), 476–84. (A survey of contemporary Diaspora literature).

T'op'chyan, A. *Baṙi sahmannerě.* (Erevan, 1978). (On some Soviet Armenian and Diaspora writers and literary issues).

T'op'chyan, S. "Erazank'i, korsti ev oronman čanaparhin." *SG,* 1967/5, 134–43. (On Diaspora literature in general and H. Zardarean and V. Šušanean in particular).

———. *Anhuni andradardzě.* (Erevan, 1982). (Articles and reviews on nineteenth- and twentieth-century authors, literary issues, and theory).

———. *Kerp ev iskut'yun.* (Erevan, 1987). (On E. Tēmirčipašean, Širvanzade, Nar-Dos, Ṙ. Sewak, and Š. Šahnur).

———. *Apagayi nerkayut'yamb.* (Erevan, 1988). (On Ṙ. Sewak, Š. Šahnur, and V. Šušanean, among others).

Yovhannēsean, V. "Mer nor banastełtznerě." *B,* 95 (1937), 187–92. (On the latest poetry of some Diaspora poets).

4

Anthologies

Anthologies in Armenian

Bibliographies

Ṙubinyan, Ṙ. *Sovetahay grakan gełarvestakan žołovatzuner.* 2 vols. (Erevan, 1964 [Vol. 1, 1924–60], 1966 [Vol. 2, 1961–65]).

Anthologies

Ałayean, Ł., et al., *Hay grołner.* Vol. 1. (Tiflis, 1909, 1914).
Akinean, N. *Hing panduḥt tałasatsner.* (Vienna, 1921).
Alazan, V., and Norents, V. *Arevmtahay banastełtzner.* (Erevan, 1930).
Ardi hay grakanutʻiwn. Vol. 1: *Artasahmani grołner* (Paris, 1939). Vol. 2: *Artasahmani grołner* (Paris, 1941). Vol. 3: *Hayastani grołner* (Paris, 1941).
Artzruni, V. *Glḥawor matenagirner haykakan dprutʻean 4–20 dar.* (Alexandria, 1944).
Avdalbekyan, M., et al. *Ējer hay mijnadaryan gełarvestakan ardzakits.* (Erevan, 1957).
Awagean, Y., and Yovnanean, P. *Goharner hay grakanutʻean.* (New York, 1916).
Aznavuryan, G. *Arevmtahay grołneri namakani.* (Erevan, 1972).
Basmadjian, G. *Armenian-American Poets: A Bilingual Anthology.* (Detroit, 1978).
Čanašean, M. *Tzałkakʻał ardi hay grakanutʻean.* 2 vols. (Venice, 1957, 1963).
Čašak nor grakanutʻean. Vol. 1. (Constantinople, 1904).
Chōpanean, A. *Hay ējer. Mer naḥneats banastełtzutʻiwnn u aruestě.* (Paris, 1912).
———. *Hayrenneru burastaně.* (Paris, 1940).
Danielyan, V. *Moṙatsvatz ašḥarh.* (Erevan, 1983).
Dew. *Iranahay ardi grołner.* Vol. 1. (Teheran, 1964).
Duryan, L., and Karčikyan, H. *Nor dzayner: kʻertʻvatzner.* (Erevan, 1975).
Ěntir ējer hay grakanutʻyan. (Erevan, 1946).
Ěntir noravēper: hawakʻatzoy. (New York, 1918).
Eresun garun (grakan-gełarvestakan almanaḥ). (Baku, 1950).
Etmekjian, J. *An Anthology of Western Armenian Literature.* (Delmar, New York, 1980).
Gabrielyan, V. *Spʻyuṙkʻahay banastełtzutʻyun.* (Erevan, 1981).
Galstyan, H. *Sovetahay poezia.* (Erevan, 1986).
Gapʻamačean, M. *Hawakʻatzoy ěntir grwatzots azgayin ew ōtar matenagrutʻeants.* 2 vols. (Constantinople, 1890, 1892, 1901 [Vol. 2, revised]).
Gaziyan, A. *Hay azgayin zinvorakan erger.* (Erevan, 1989). (Martial songs).
Gełuni, L. *Yaṙaji sanerě: tzałkepʻunj.* (Paris, 1939).

Girkʻ siro. (Erevan, 1975). (Love poems).
Grakan almanaḥ (Adrbejani hay grołneri stełtzagortzutʻyunnerits). (Baku, 1951).
Grakan gełarvestakan žołovatzu. (Berlin, 1943).
Grigoryan, H., and Tʻopʻchyan, Ē. *Artasahmanyan žamanakakits hay grołner. Žołovatzu.* (Erevan, 1946).
Grigoryan, Ṙ. *Hay žołovrdakan ōrorotsayin ev mankakan erger.* (Erevan, 1970).
Guyumčyan, H. *Kʻani arev ka: spʻyuṙkʻahay grołner.* (Erevan, 1971).
Hakobyan, G., and Mirijanyan, L. *Hay kʻnarergutʻyun. Antik šrjanits minchev Ĕ dar.* (Erevan, 1981). (Armenian lyric poetry from antiquity to the eighth century).
Hakobyan, V. *Manr žamanakagrutʻyunner XIII–XVIII d.d.* 2 vols. (Erevan, 1951, 1956).
Hay grakanutʻiwn: patmuatzkʻner. (Beirut, 1978).
Hay grołnerĕ ev banahyusutʻyunĕ ĕnddem kroni: atʻeistakan kʻrestomatia. (Erevan, 1976).
Hay hin ev mijnadaryan kʻnarergutʻyun. (Erevan, 1986).
Hisun garun. (Baku, 1971). (Armenian writers from Artsaḥ-Karabagh).
Hovnan, G. *Haveržutʻyun: hay banastełtznerĕ Ṙusastanin.* (Erevan, 1978).
Iranahay ardi grołner. Vol. 1. (Teheran, 1964).
Kʻalantʻaryan, Ž. *Hay grakan kʻnnadatutʻyan kʻrestomatia.* 2 vols. (Erevan, 1981–84).
Koryun, M., and Sevan, H. *Pʻunj: sovetahay mankakan grakanutʻyun.* (Erevan, 1961).
Kostaneants, K. *Tzałkakʻał ardzak ew chapʻatzoy banits, i pēts varžaranats.* 3 parts. (Tiflis, 1881).
———. *Nor žołovatzu: mijnadarean hayots tałer ew otanaworner.* 4 parts. (Tiflis, 1892 [parts 1–2], 1896 [part 3]; Vałaršapat, 1903 [part 4]).
Lenini masin: balladner. (Erevan, 1967).
Leṙnayin nvagner: Leṙnayin Łarabałi banastełtzneri stełtzagortzutʻyunnerĕ. (Baku, 1973). (Armenian writers of Nagorno-Karabagh, in Armenian and Azeri).
Macler, F. *Chrestomathie de l'arménien moderne.* (Paris, 1932).
Madoyan, A., and Nersisyan, V. *Oskepʻorik: nmušner hay hin ev mijnadaryan ardzakits.* (Erevan, 1977).
Margaritner hay kʻnarergutʻyan. Vol. 1: hnaguyn šrjanits minchev 18. dar. Vol. 2: *nor šrjan.* (Erevan, 1974).
Markosean, M. *Nor gir ew ir ašḥatakitsnerĕ: ĕntir ējer.* (New York, 1984).
Melikʻ-Ōhanjanyan, K. *Ējer hay mijnadaryan gełarvestakan ardzakits.* (Erevan, 1957).
Mkrtchyan, L., and Madoyan, A. *Hay dasakan kʻnarergutʻyun.* 2 vols. Vol. 1: 5th–12th centuries (Erevan, 1986); Vol. 2: 13th–18th centuries (Erevan, 1986 [cover says 1987]). (Classical lyric poetry).
Mkrtchyan, M. *Hay mijnadaryan pandḥtutʻyan tałer (XV–XVIII dd.).* (Erevan, 1979).
Nawasard 66: grakan žołovatzoy. (Beirut, 1966).
Nazareants, Y. *Ĕntir hatuatzner.* Vol. 1: ardzak. (Tiflis, 1889).
Nersisyan, V., and Madoyan, A. *Hayots hin ev mijnadaryan ardzaki kʻrestomatia.* (Erevan, 1981). (Classical and medieval prose).
Nor garun. (Erevan, 1973). (Young Armenian poets).

Norents, V., and Harutʻyunyan, M. *Sovetahay grakanutʻyan ĕntir ējer: poezia.* (Erevan, 1960).
Oskean, H. *Chors hay tałasatsner ew anonts tałerĕ: Yovhannēs Karnetsi, Grigor arkʻeps. Ōšakantsi, Movsēs dpir Karnetsi ew Martiros v. Łrimetsi.* (Vienna, 1966).
Palean, T. *Hay ašułner, žołovrdakan hay ergichner ew tałasatskʻ.* 2 vols. (Smyrna, 1911, 1914).
Patkanean, Kʻ. *Nšḥarkʻ matenagrutʻean hayots.* (Petersburg, 1884).
Patmuatzkʻneru žołovatzoy: arewmtahay grołner. (Beirut, 1938).
Piesneri žołovatzu. 4 vols. (Erevan, 1946–51).
Pipērčean, S. *Čašak ardi hay matenagrutʻean.* 2 vols. (Constantinople, 1888, 1910).
Sahakyan, H. *Uš mijnadari hay banastełtzutʻyunĕ (XVI–XVII dd.).* 2 vols. (Erevan, 1986–87).
Sahakyan, S. *Hay dramaturgia.* (Erevan, 1985).
Sałyan, M. *ʻHyusisapʻayliʼ poezian: žołovatzu.* (Erevan, 1957).
Sarmen, and Tʻapʻaltsyan, Kʻ. *Eritasard groł, almanaḥ.* Part 2 (Erevan, 1951). (For Part 1, see H. Siras).
Sasuni, K. *Grakan goharner, mijnadarean ašḥarhabar grakanutʻean ew žołovrdakan banahiwsutʻean.* (Beirut, 1949).
Šavił. (Abḥaziayi hay grołneri ardzak gortzerĕ). (Sukhumi, 1962).
Sevan, G., and Gabrielyan, V. *Spʻyuřkʻahay patmvatzkʻ.* Vol. 1. (Erevan, 1984).
Simonean, S. *Arewelahay grakanutʻiwn: ĕntir ējer, kensagrutʻiwnner, gortzerĕ, bařaran, matenagitutʻiwn.* (Beirut, 1965).
Simonyan, D. *Hayastani grołnerĕ tasnhingamyakin, gełarvestakan žołovatzu.* (Erevan, 1935).
Siras, H., and Vahuni, S. *Eritasard groł, almanaḥ.* Part 1. (Erevan, 1950). (For Part 2, see Sarmen).
Sovetahay dramaturgia, piesneri žołovatzu. (Erevan, 1959).
Srapyan, A. *Hay mijnadaryan zruytsner.* (Erevan, 1969).
Tʻamazyan, A. *Hay gyułagirner.* (Erevan, 1950).
———. *Psak. Hayrenakan metz paterazmum zohvatz hay grołneri stełtzagortzutʻyunneri žołovatzu.* (Erevan, 1944).
Tēmirčipašean, E. *Dar: hawakʻatzoy azgayin grakan ew gitnakan hatuatzots.* (Constantinople, 1889).
Tʻēōlēōlean, M. *Dar mĕ grakanutʻiwn.* 2 vols. (Cairo, 1955, 1956); 2d ed., 2 vols. (Boston, 1977).
Tēōšēmēčean, V. *Hawakʻatzoy arewmtahay grołneru.* Three vols. (Istanbul, 1971, 1972, 1973).
Tevkants, A. *Hayerg: mełedikʻ, tałkʻ ew ergkʻ.* (Tiflis, 1882).
Toneryan, E. *Hay řevolyutsion poezia (1900–1920).* (Erevan, 1961).
Tontsean, A. *Andastan iranahay banastełtzutʻean.* (Beirut, 1963).
Tʻoranean, Tʻ. *Hayastani 8 eritasard ardzakagirner.* (Beirut, 1969).
Tʻořnean, Tʻ. *Hatĕntir ĕntʻertsuatzkʻ i matenagrutʻeants naḥneats handerdz tzanōtʻutʻeambkʻ.* (Vienna, 1893).
Vahē-Vahean. *Hay grakanutʻiwn. Patmuatzkʻner.* Vol 1. (Beirut, 1978). (Short stories by nineteeth and early twentieth-century authors).
———. *Tzałkakʻał ardzaki hay grołnerē.* 3 vols. (Beirut, 1984, 1985, 1988).

Vantsean, G. *Hay hełinakner.* 3d ed. (Tiflis, 1908).
Vardanyan, H. *Karmir aragil.* (Erevan, 1977). (Stories by Soviet Armenian writers).
Zangakner. (Erevan, 1974). (Soviet Armenian poetry for young people).

Anthologies in Translation

Antologiia armianskoi sovetskoi literatury. (Erevan, 1958).
Antreassian, J. *Tales from the Armenian.* (New York, 1955).
Armianskaia klassicheskaia lirika. 2 vols. (Erevan, 1977).
Armianskaia literatura. 2 vols. (Erevan, 1955).
Arsharuni, A. *Pod chuzhim nebom.* (Moscow, 1967).
Arutiunian, S., and Kirpotin, V. *Antologiia armianskoi poezii s drevneishikh vremen do nashikh dnei.* (Moscow, 1940).
Ashjian, S. *Classical Armenian Short Stories.* (Beirut, 1959). (Nineteenth- and twentieth-century authors).
———. *Great Armenian Short Stories.* (Beirut, 1959). (Nineteenth- and twentieth-century authors).
Basmadjian, G. *Armenian-American Poets: A Bilingual Anthology.* (Detroit, 1978).
Blackwell, A. *Armenian Poems.* (Boston, 1896, 1917; New York, 1978).
Boghossian, S., et al. "Littérature arménienne." *Europe,* (February–March, 1961), 1–207. (Selections from thirty-three writers in French translation).
Boyajian, Z. *Armenian Legends and Poems.* (London, 1916; London and New York, 1958).
Bratstvo. Literaturno-khudozhestvennyi sbornik pisatelei Zakavkaz'ia. (Erevan, 1957).
Briusov, V. *Lirika i epos.* (Tiflis, 1935).
———. *Poeziia Armenii.* (Moscow, 1916; Erevan, 1966 [revised], 1987).
Gianascian, M. *La poesia Armena moderna.* (Venice, 1963).
Glagoleva, F. *We of the Mountains.* (Moscow, 1972).
Godel, V. *La Poésie arménienne, du Ve siècle à nos jours.* (Paris: Editions de La Difference, 1990).
Gorodetskii, S. *Dzheiran.* (Batum, 1919).
Gullakian, S. *Skazki armianskikh pisatelei.* (Erevan, 1988).
Der Hovannessian, D., and Margossian, M. *Anthology of Armenian Poetry.* (New York, 1978).
Dinolov, K. *Armenska poeziia.* (Sofia, 1942)
Dzhanpoladian, M., et al. *Armianskie poety novogo vremeni.* (Leningrad, 1983).
Ganalanian, O. *Poeziia Armenii. V perevodakh i otsenke V. Ia. Briusova.* (Erevan, 1963).
Gor'kii, M. *Sbornik armianskoi literatury.* (Petersburg, 1916).
Izbrannaia armianskaia sovetskaia poeziia. (Vilnius, 1982).

Izbrannye stranitsy sovetskoi armianskoi literatury. Proza. (Erevan, 1960).
Karapetian, A. *Sovremennye armianskie povesti.* (Moscow, 1981).
Khachatriants, Ia. *Armianskie novelly.* 2 parts. (Moscow, 1945, 1948).
Khitarova, S. *Tsvet abrikosa. Povesti i rasskazy armianskikh pisatelei.* (Erevan, 1981).
Kudian, M. *Soviet Armenian Poetry.* (London, 1974).
Leist, A. *Armenische Dichter.* (Dresden and Leipzig, 1898).
Lerena Acevedo de Blixen, J. *Antologia de poetas armenios.* (Montevideo, 1943).
Melik, R. *Poésie arménienne: anthologie des origines à nos jours.* (Paris, 1973).
Misakian, B. *Au Jardin des Muses de la littérature arménienne.* (Venice, 1961).
Mkrtchian, L. *Srednevekovaia armianskaia poeziia.* (Moscow, 1981).
———. *Ot "Rozhdeniia Vaagna" do Paruira Sevaka: Antolog. sbornik armianskoi liriki.* 2 vols. (Erevan, 1983).
Mnogogolosie. Armianskaia poeziia v perevodakh russkikh poetov. (Erevan, 1978).
Navarian, A. *Anthologie des poètes arméniens.* (Paris, 1928).
Rachian, Kh. *Armianskie novelly.* (Erevan, 1962).
Safrazbekian, I. *Komochek nezhnogo serdtsa.* (Erevan, 1973).
Sarkisian, I. *Armianskaia literatura (rasskazy v perevode).* (Tiflis, 1912).
Sevan, G. *Antologiia armianskoi sovetskoi detskoi literatury.* (Erevan, 1981).
Sharti, S. *Armianskie poety.* (Tiflis, 1917).
Shervinskii, S. *Iz armianskoi poezii.* (Erevan, 1966).
Shklovskii, V. *Armianskie rasskazy.* 2 vols. (Erevan, 1953).
Sovetskaia armianskaia literatura. Sbornik poezii i prozy. (Erevan, 1953).
Sovremennaia armianskaia literatura. Part I. (Moscow, 1906).
Spendiarova, T. *Izbrannye perevody.* (Erevan, 1971).
Tchéraz, M. *Poètes arméniens.* (Paris, 1913). (A prose rendition of modern poetry).
Tchobanian, A. *Poèmes arméniens anciens et modernes.* (Paris, 1902).
———. *Chants populaires arméniens.* (Paris, 1903).
———. *Les trouvères arméniens.* 2d ed. (Paris, 1906).
———. *La Roseraie d'Arménie.* 3 vols. (Paris, 1918, 1923, 1929).
Ter-Akopian, A. *Iz zapadnoarmianskoi poezii.* (Erevan, 1979).
Tikhonov, N. *Dni otkrytii. Kniga ob Armenii.* (Erevan, 1970).
Tolegian, A. *Armenian Poetry Old and New.* (Detroit, 1979).
Umanets, L., and Dervish, A. *Sovremennye armianskie poety.* (Moscow, 1903).
Veselovskii, Iu. *Stikhotvornye perevody.* (Moscow, 1898).
———., and Berberian, M. *Armianskie belletristy. Sbornik.* 2 vols. (Moscow, 1893–94).
———., and G. Khalatiants. *Armianskaia muza. Sbornik.* (Moscow, 1907).
Zviagintseva, V. *Moia Armeniia.* (Erevan, 1964).

5

Special Topics

Ašułs (Minstrels)

Some significant *ašułs* are included in part 2. This section includes general reference works on Armenian *ašułs*. Listed under *Collections* are works containing poems by Armenian minstrels (such collections often list poetry by other authors as well). Found under *Texts* are collections of some of the *ašułs* who are not listed in part 2. The section on *Criticism* includes secondary literature on *ašułs* and the *ašułakan* genre.

Collections

Aḥverdean, G. *Hay ašułner. Gusankʻ A. Sayeatʻ-Nōvay.* (Moscow, 1852).

———. *Gusankʻ B. Hay ašułner.* (Tiflis, 1903). (Published by M. Aḥvērdean).

Brutean, A. *Ṙamkakan mrmunjner.* (Alexandrapol, 1895, 1897, 1901).

Chōpanean, A. *Hay ējer, mer naḥneats banastełtzutʻiwnn u aruestě.* (Paris, 1912).

Eremean, A. *Ašuł Yartʻun Ōłli. I: Pʻšrankʻner ašułakan grakanutʻiwnits.* (Nor Jułay, 1920). Part 2: *Parskahay ašułner. I-Amir Ōłli. II-Łul Ēgaz. III-Abdin Ōłli Hayrapet.*

———. *Parskahay noragoyn ašułner.* (Vienna, 1925).

———. *Parskahay ašułner.* (Tiflis, 1930).

———. "Pʻšrankʻner hay ašułakan grakanutʻiwnits (19 dar)." *B,* 115 (1957), 274–79. 116 (1958), 26–31, 91–96.

———. "Pʻšrankʻner ašułakan grakanutʻiwnits." *S,* 1968, 465–67.

———. "Ējer hay ašułakan grakanutʻiwnits." *S,* 1969, 232–34.

Kostaneants, K. *Nor žołovatzu, mijnadarean hayots tałer u otanaworner.* 4 parts. (Tiflis, 1892 [parts 1–2], 1896 [part 3], 1903 [part 4]).

Lewonean, G. *Hay ašułner.* (Alexandrapol, 1892).

Mḥitʻareants, A. *Tałer u ḥałer.* (Alexandrapol, 1900).

Miansareants, M. *Kʻnar haykakan.* (Petersburg, 1868).

Minasean, L. *Pʻeriayi hay ašułnerě: irents hamaṙōt kensagrakannerov ew stełtzagortzutʻeants nmoyšnerov.* (Teheran, 1964).

Mkrtchyan, M. *Hay mijnadaryan pandḥtutʻyan tałer (XV–XVIII dd.).* (Erevan, 1979).

Nazariantz, H. *I Trovieri dell'Armenia nello loro vita e nei loro canti. Con cenno sui canti populari armeni.* (Bari, 1916).

Palean, T. *Hay ašułner, žołovrdakan hay ergichner ew tałasatskʻ.* 2 vols. (Smyrna, 1911–14).

Sahakyan, H. *Hay ašułner, XVII–XVIII dd.* (Erevan, 1961).

Širaki hay ašułnerě. (Erevan, 1986).

T'arsiwni, T'. *Nor ergaran.* (Tiflis, 1898).
T'arverdyan, G. *Hay ašułner.* (Erevan, 1937).
———. *Hay gusanner.* (Erevan, 1957).
T[ēr] Gēorgean-Yovhannisean, O. *Nor k'nar Hayastani.* 5 parts. (Moscow, 1855–59).
Tevkants, A. *Hayerg: mełedik', tałk' ew ergk'.* (Tiflis, 1882).

TEXTS

Ašěł Haziri ergerě. (Moscow, 1892).
Ašěł Sazayi. *Amrah ew Salvi.* (Nor Payazit, [1890]).
Ašuł T'aṙi. (Tabriz, [1921]).
Eremean, A. "Ašuł Aṙak'el Yarut'iwnean." *B,* 118 (1960), 72–78; 125–30.
Ergich Jamalu k'narakan ergerě. (Alexandrapol, 1892).
Minasean, L. *Ergasats Tēr-Karapet: keank'n u hayerēn ergerě.* (Teheran, 1967).
Mnatsakanyan, As. "17-rd dari ergich K'osa Eretsě ev nra ergerě." *BM,* 3 (1956), 265–76.

CRITICISM

Amiryan, Ḥ. "T'rk'alezu hay ašułnerě ev M. F. K'yop'rulyun." *SG,* 1976/3, 151–57.
Eremean, S. "Hay ašułner." *B,* 61 (1903), 362–66; 431–36; 62 (1904), 81–84.
Gevorkian, N. "K voprosu ob ashugskoi poetike." *L,* 1982/7, 82–92.
Grigoryan, S. *Hayots hin gusanakan ergerě.* (Erevan, 1971).
Hakobjanyan, A. "Gusana-ašułakan poeziayi mi k'ani hartser." *SG,* 1972/7, 161–64.
Kurtikean, S. "T'rk'agēt hay banastełtzner ew ašułner." *Taretsoyts Azgayin hiwandanotsi.* 1935, 116–27.
K'ocharyan, A. *Hay gusanakan erger.* (Erevan, 1976).
Levonyan, G. "Hay žołovrdakan ev ašułakan ergerě, hamematakan tesut'yun." *Tełekagir git. ev arvesti inst.* 4 (1929), 160–78.
———. *Ašułnerě ev nrants arvestě.* (Erevan, 1944).
Macler, F. *Quatre conférences sur l'Arménie.* (Paris, 1932).
Muratean, M. "Sasnoy ašułnerě." *B,* 92 (1934), 462–63.
Narduni, Š. "Npast mě hay ew t'urk' ašułakan grakanut'ean hamematakan usumnasirut'ean." *Vēm,* 3 (1935/1), 45–56; 2, 78–81; 4, 30–36.
"S. Ējmiatzině hay ašułneri ergerum." *A,* 1903, 511–20.
Tēr Łazarean, Y. "Hay ašułakan grakanut'iwně." *B,* 90 (1933), 263–67.

Folklore

Armenian texts

PRINCIPAL COLLECTIONS

Ēminean azgagrakan žołovatzu. 9 vols. Vol. 1 (Moscow and Alexandrapol, 1901). Vol. 2 (Moscow and Vałaršapat, 1901). Vol. 3 (Moscow and Vałaršapat, 1902). Vol. 4 (Moscow and Vałaršapat, 1902). Vol. 5 (Moscow and Vałaršapat, 1903). Vol. 6 (Moscow and Vałaršapat, 1906). Vol. 7 (Moscow, 1908). Vol. 8 (Moscow and Nor Naḫijewan, 1911). Vol. 9 (Tiflis, 1913). (Particularly relevant are vols. 1, 2, 4, 5, 6).

Nawasardeants, T. *Hay žołovrdakan hēkʻiatʻner: žołovatzu.* 10 vols. Vol. 1 (Vałaršapat, [1882]). Vol. 2 (Erivan, 1882). Vol. 3 (Tiflis, 1884). Vol. 4 (N.p., n.d.). Vol. 5 (Tiflis, 1889). Vol. 6 (Tiflis, 1890). Vol. 7 (Tiflis, 1891). Vol. 8 (Tiflis, 1893). Vol. 9 (Tiflis, 1902). Vol. 10 (Tiflis, 1903). (Armenian folktales).

Ōrbeli, H., [et al.]. *Hay žołovrdakan hekʻiatʻner.* 13 vols. to 1985. (Erevan, 1959 [Vols. 1–2]; 1962 [Vol. 3]; 1963 [Vol. 4]; 1966 [Vol. 5]; 1973 [Vol. 6]; 1979 [Vol. 7]; 1977 [Vol. 8]; 1968 [Vol. 9]; 1967 [Vol. 10]; 1980 [Vol. 11]; 1984 [Vol. 12]; 1985 [Vol. 13]). (Armenian folktales).

OTHER COLLECTIONS

Abgareants, T. "Nor Jułayi ařatznerě." *HA,* 78 (1964), 549–54. 79 (1965), 111–20, 283–90, 395–404. (New Julfa proverbs).

Abełyan, M. *Gusanakan žołovrdakan tałer, hayrenner yev antuniner.* (Yerevan, 1940). (Popular traditional songs).

Ačēmean, H. "Tzałkakʻał Vaspurakani hay žołovrdakan banahiwsutʻean. Mokats Mirza. (Bun ergě Moksi barbařov). Karos Ḫach. (Bun ergě Vani barbařov)." *A,* 1917, 543–68. (Samples of the oral tradition from Vaspurakan, east of Van).

Akinean, N. "Erekʻ harsanekan tałer hin žołovrdakan banahiwsutʻenēn." *HA,* 46 (1932), 223–27. (Three old wedding poems).

Ařakʻelyan, B., et al. *Hay azgagrutʻyun ev banahyusutʻyun: nyutʻer ev usumnasirutʻyunner.* 11 vols. to 1980. (Erevan, 1970 [Vol. 1]; 1971 [Vol. 2]; 1972 [Vol. 3]; 1973 [Vols. 4–5]; 1974 [Vol. 6]; 1975 [Vol. 7]; 1978 [Vols. 8–9]; 1980 [Vols. 10–11]). (Considerable folkloric material found in these volumes).

Ayvazean, G. *Hazar ew mi ařakawor bankʻ, azgayinkʻ ew ōtar.* (Constantinople, 1874). (Collection of allegorical sayings, Armenian and non-Armenian).

Azgagrakan handēs. 26 books from 1895 to 1917. Vol. 1 (Šuši, 1895). All subsequent volumes published in Tiflis. Vol. 2 (1897); Vol. 3, bks. 1–2 (1898); Vol. 4, bk. 5 (1899); Vol. 5, bk. 6 (1900); Vol. 6, bks. 7–8 (1901); Vol. 7, bk.

9 (1902); Vol. 8, bk. 10 (1903); Vol. 9, bk. 11 (1904); Vol. 9, bk. 12 (1905); Vol. 9, bk. 13, (1906); Vol. 10, bk. 14 (1906); Vol. 10, bks. 15–16 (1907); Vol. 11, bks. 17–18 (1908); Vol. 12, bks. 19–20 (1910); Vol. 13, bk. 21 (1911–12); Vol. 14, bks. 22–23 (1912); Vol. 15, bk. 24 (1913); Vol. 15, bk. 25 (1914); Vol. 16, bk. 26 (1916–17). (Ethnographic journal; considerable folkloric material found in this periodical).

Berger, W. *Beiträge zur armenischen Foklore. Unedirte Redensarten und Sprichwörte aus Turkisch Armenien.* (Kolozsvar, 1883).

Čulartean, S. *Aŕatzkʻ azgayinkʻ.* (Venice, 1880). (Proverbs).

Eremean, A. *Chaharmahali hay žołovrdakan banahiwsutʻiwnĕ.* (Vienna, 1923). (Armenian folklore in Chaharmahal, Iran).

———. "Pʻšrankʻner hay žołovrdakan banahiwsutʻiwnits." *HA,* 42 (1928), 536–52. (Samples of Armenian folklore).

———. *Pʻšrankʻner jułahay ew hndkahay banahiwsutʻiwnits. (Tałer ew žołovrdakan erger), 17–19 dar.* (Vienna, 1930). (Folksongs of Armenians in New Julfa and India).

———. "Charmahali žołovrdakan banahiwsutʻiwnits." *B,* 124 (1966), 109–16. (Folklore in Chaharmahal, Iran).

———. "Antip ējer Charmahali žołovrdakan aŕaknerits ew sramtutʻiwnnerits." *B,* 125 (1967), 154–59, 269–72. (New proverbs and humourous sayings from Chaharmahal, Iran).

———. "Ējer žołovrdakan banahiwsutʻiwnits." *S,* 1971, 345–50. (Samples of folklore).

Garegin Sarkawag. *Pʻšrankʻner žołovrdakan banahiwsutʻiwnits.* (Tiflis, 1892). (Samples of folklore).

Harutʻyunyan, S. *Hay žołovrdakan hanelukner.* 2 vols. (Erevan, 1960, 1965). (Riddles).

Haykuni, S. "Ōhan Ōtzeli." *A,* 1898, 412–14. (Folktale; transcribed by S. Haykuni and narrated by Kʻrsetsi Arewšat-Saribek).

———. "Barak šah, anuš šah ew tiwliwn šah." *A,* 1901, 375–82. (A folktale in the dialect of Mokkʻ, south of Van).

Grigoryan-Spandaryan, M. *Leŕnayin Łarabałi banahyusutʻyunĕ.* (Erevan, 1971). (Folklore in Łarabał).

Kostaneants, Y. *Širaki legendanerits ew žołovrdakan keankʻits.* (Traditions in Širak, Eastern Armenia).

Lalayeants, E. *Jawaḥkʻi burmunkʻ.* (Tiflis, 1892). (Folklore from Jawaḥkʻ, northwest of Armenia, now in Georgia).

———. *Vaspurakan: banahiwsutʻiwn.* Part 2. (Tiflis, 1914). (Folklore from Vaspurakan, east of Lake Van).

Łanalanyan, A. *Aŕatzani.* (Erevan, 1960). (Proverbs).

———. *Avandapatum.* (Erevan, 1969). (Folkloric traditions).

Lisitsean, S. *Sovatz gaylĕ. Žołovrdakan hēkʻiatʻ.* (Tiflis, 1909). (A folktale).

Margaritner hay banahiwsutʻean. 2 vols. (Tiflis and Ējmiatzin, 1914). (Gems of Armenian folklore).

Martirosean, N. "Nšḥarkʻ Tarōnoy." *S,* 1968, 354–65, 435–45. (Folklore from Tarōn, northwest of Lake Van).

Melikʻ-Ōhanjanyan, K. *Ējer hay mijnadaryan gełarvestakan ardzakits.* (Erevan, 1957). (Proverbs and tales).

Minasean, M. "Nmoyšner K'ēsapi žołovrdakan ḥałiknerēn." *Haykazean hayagitakan handēs.* 1982–84, 287–98. (Popular traditional songs from Kesab, in northwestern Syria).

Mnatsakanyan, As. *Haykakan mijnadaryan žołovrdakan erger.* (Erevan, 1956). (folksongs and poems).

———. *Hay mijnadaryan hanelukner.* (Erevan, 1980). (Medieval riddles).

Moskofean, Y. "Nmoyšner Sebastioy žołovrdakan banahiwsut'enēn." *HA,* 51 (1937), 351–59. (Folklore from Sivas).

P'ork'šeyan, Ḥ. *Nor Naḥijevani hay žołovrdakan banahyusut'yunĕ.* (Erevan, 1965). (Folklore from Nor Naḥijewan).

Šahinyan, Š. "Nyut'er Ṙostovi marzi haykakan gyułeri žołovrdakan banahyusut'yunits." *L,* 1970/9, 71–74. (Armenian folklore in the rural areas in the region of Rostov).

———. *Daravor armatner.* (Erevan, 1980). (Armenian folklore from Nor Naḥijewan).

Sasuni, K. *Grakan goharner mijnadarean ašḥarhabar grakanut'ean ew žołovrdakan banahiwsut'ean.* (Beirut, 1949). (Folklore and medieval literature).

Srapyan, A. *Hay mijnadaryan zruytsner.* (Erevan, 1969). (Study and texts of tales).

Sruandzteants, G. *Hnots ew norots.* (Constantinople, 1874). (Folktales and traditions).

———. *Grots u brots ew Sasuntsi Dawit' kam Mheri duṙ.* (Constantinople, 1874). (Folktales and the first recorded version of the epic *Sasuntsi Dawit'*).

———. *Manana.* (Constantinople, 1876). (Folktales and traditions).

———. *T'oros Ałbar Hayastani čambord.* 2 vols. (Constantinople, 1879, 1884). (Folktales and traditions).

———. *Hamov-hotov.* (Constantinople, 1884). (Folktales and traditions).

Tigranean, G. *Aṙatzk', asatsuatzk' ew zroytsk' Nor Naḥijewani.* (Rostov, 1892). (Proverbs and tales from Nor Naḥijewan).

T'oṙlak'yan, B. "Pataṙikner hamšenahayeri ev Trapizoni žołovrdakan banahyusut'yunits." *BEH,* 1972/2, 182–92. (Folklore from Trebizond).

T'umačyan, M. *Hayreni erg u ban.* 3 vols. (Erevan, 1972 [Vol. 1], 1983 [Vol. 2], 1986 [Vol. 3]). (Folklore).

Vardanean, V. *Mardn u namardĕ–hek'eat'.* (Tiflis, 1912). (Folktale).

Varžapetean, M. *Čermkuk meṙelĕ, awandavēp.* (Marzuan, 1913). (Tale).

Zeyt'un, S. *Musa leṙan žołovrdakan hēk'iat'ner.* (Beirut, 1973). (Folktales from Musa Dagh).

Armenian texts in translation

Larger collections

Boiadzhian, L., et al. *Armianskie narodnye skazki.* (Erevan, 1986).

Djélali. *Contes et chants arméniens.* (Paris, 1899).

Downing, C. *Armenian Folk-Tales and Fables.* (London, 1972).

[Ganalanian, A.]. *Armianskie narodnye skazki.* (Erevan, 1965).

———. *Armianskie narodnye skazki.* (Erevan, 1983).

Hoogasian-Villa, S. *One Hundred Armenian Tales and Their Folkloristic Relevance.* (Detroit, 1966).

Karapetian, G. *Armianskii fol'klor.* (Moscow, 1967).

———. *Doroga Mgera: Armianskie legendy i predaniia.* (Moscow, 1990).

Khachatrianz, I. *Armenian Folk Tales.* (Philadelphia, 1946).

Kurtikian, S. *Sinee oko: Armianskie legendy, skazaniia.* Trans. from the Armenian by A. Tadeosian and I. Safrazbekian. (Erevan, 1980).
Macler, F. *Contes arméniens.* (Paris, 1905).
———. *Contes et légendes de l'Arménie.* (Paris, 1911).
———. *Contes, légendes et épopées populaires d'Arménie.* 2 vols. Vol 1: *Contes* (Paris, 1928); Vol. 2: *Légendes* (Paris, 1933).
Mourier, J. *Contes et légendes du Caucase.* (Paris, 1888). (Includes *Contes géorgiens, Contes mingréliens, Contes arméniens*).
Nicolaides, J. *Contes licencieux de Constantinople et de l'Asie Mineure recueillis.* (Paris, 1906).
Roszko, K. *Les contes des arméniens polonais de Kutz. Textes et traduction.* (Cracow, 1960).
Seklemian, A. *The Golden Maiden and Other Folk Tales and Fairy Stories Told in Armenian.* (Cleveland and New York, 1898).
Surmelian, L. *Apples of Immortality: Folktales of Armenia.* (London, 1968).
Tchéraz, M. *L'Orient inédit. Légendes et traditions arméniennes, grecques et turques recueillies et traduites.* (Paris, 1912).
Tchobanian, A. *Chants populaires arméniens.* (Paris, 1903).
Wlisiocki, H. *Märchen und Sagen der Bukowinaer und Siebenbürger Armenier.* (Hamburg, 1892).

Shorter collections and individual works

Edwards, G. "Items of Armenian Folklore collected in Boston." *Journal of American Folklore,* 12 (1899), 97–107.
Goodspeed, E. "Tertag and Sarkis. An Armenian Folk-Tale." *American Antiquarian and Oriental Journal,* 28 (1906), 123–40.
Hedwig, A. *Fedai und Christ. Erzählung aus den Wan-Bergen.* (Frankfurt/Main, 1906).
Popescu, I. "Les Contes de fées, récits et traditions arméniennes de Transylvanie." *REArm,* 4 (1967), 377–93.
Seklemian, A. "The Fisherman's Son. An Armenian Fairy Tale." *Armenia* (New York), 4 (1910/5), 7–11.
———. "The Water-child and the Wolf-child." *Armenia* (New York), 4 (1910/7), 9–12.
———. "The Wicked Stepmother. An Armenian Folk-Tale." *Journal of American Folk-lore,* 10 (1897), 135–42.
Ter-Akobian, S. "Das armenische Märchen vom 'Stirnauge'." *Globus,* 44 (1908), 205–6.
Wingate, J. "Armenian Stories: 1. The Bride of the Fountain. 2. The Wise Weaver." *Armenia* (Boston), 4 (1910/6), 11–12.
———. "Armenian Folk-Tales." *Folk-Lore* (London), 21 (1910), 217–22, 365–71, 507–11. 22 (1911), 77–80, 351–61, 476–84. 23 (1912), 94–102, 22–23.
———. "Armenian Riddles." *Folk-Lore* (London), 23 (1912), 471–72.

Secondary literature

Abeghian, M. *Der armenische Volksglaube.* (Leipzig 1899).
Abełyan, M. *Hayots mijnadaryan ar̄aknerĕ u sotsialakan haraberutʻyunnerĕ nrants mej.* (Erevan, 1935). (Medieval Armenian proverbs and the social relations they reflect).

Andrikean, N. "Azgayin vēperēn." *B,* 64 (1906), 298–303, 341–47, 509. (On "Płndzē k'ałak'ĕ," "Farmani Asmani," and "Hartsmunk' ałjkan").
———. "Ditołut'iwnner gołt'an ergeru vray." *B,* 64 (1906), 105–7. (On various aspects of Gołt'n songs).
Aršaruni, A. *Hay žołovrdakan t'aterahałer.* (Erevan, 1961). (Traditional plays and performances).
Bouchor, M. "Coup d'œil sur le folklore de l'Arménie." *Revue des traditions populaires,* May–June 1949, 149–57.
Čałarbēgean, Y. *Banahiwsut'ean tesut'iwn.* (Tiflis, 1894). (On folklore).
Ēsapalean, H. "Harsanekan t'agaworĕ." *HA,* 58 (1944), 36–56. (On the groom in folklore).
Gaziian, A. "Ustnoe narodno-poeticheskoe tvorchestvo Artsakha." *L,* 1990/7, 27–36. (Oral popular traditions of Artsaḥ Karabagh).
Gevorgyan, T'. "Loṙu patmaazgagrakan šrjani banahyusut'yunĕ." *PBH,* 1980/4, 291–95). (Folklore in the region of Loṙi).
Grigoryan, G. *Sovetahay vipergern u patmakan ergayin banahyusut'yunĕ.* (Erevan, 1965). (Soviet Armenian epic poems and ancient recitative folklore).
———. *Hay žołovrdakan banahyusut'yun.* (Erevan, 1967). (Armenian folklore).
———. *Hay žołovrdakan vipergerĕ ev patmakan ergayin banahyusut'yunĕ.* 2 vols. (Erevan, 1972–81). (Epic poems and old, recitative folklore).
Gullakian, S. "Armianskie skazki na stranitsakh russkikh dorevoliutsionnykh izdanii." *L,* 1976/9, 46–55. (Armenian folktales in pre-revolutionary Russian publications).
———. *Ukazatel' motivov armianskikh volshebnykh skazok.* (Erevan, 1983). (Motifs in Armenian folktales).
Hakobyan, N., and Sahakyan, A. "Haykakan žołovrdakan hek'iat'neri žanrayin tarberakman hartsi šurj." *BEH,* 1978/1, 127–38. (On distinguishing Armenian folktales by genre).
———. "Hay žołovrdakan hek'iat'neri graṙman patmut'yunits." *BEH,* 1986/1, 126–33. (On the process of transcribing folktales).
Harut'yunyan, S. "Azizbekovi šrjani žołovrdakan banahyusut'yan nmušner." *SG,* 1958/1, 178–82. (Various aspects of folklore in Azizbekov, Armenian SSR, now Vayk', Armenia).
———. "Žołovrdakan hanelukneri mi k'ani aṙandznahatkut'yunnerĕ." *PBH,* 1959/l, 163–72. (On the peculiarities of riddles).
———. "Haykakan hanelukneri kapĕ banahyusut'yan myus žanreri het." *T,* 1959/4, 55–68. (On the relevance of riddles to other genres of folklore).
———. "Hanelukneri gełarvestakanut'yan šurjĕ." *SG,* 1959/8, 127–33. (On the literary merits of riddles).
———. *Dastiarakchakan gałap'arnerĕ žołovrdakan hek'iat'nerum.* (Erevan, 1959). (The edifying concepts of folktales).
———. *Hay žołovrdakan hanelukner (usumnasirut'yun).* (Erevan, 1960). (A study of Armenian riddles).
———. " 'Karos Ḥach' vipergi mi mijnadaryan patum." *L,* 1975/8, 87–93. (A medieval version of the poem "Karos Ḥach").
———. "Mahvan patkeratsumnerĕ haykakan anetzk'nerum." *L,* 1985/12, 53–65. (Death as envisioned in Armenian curses; i.e., maledictions).

———. "Hndevropakan tałachapʻutʻyan mi kʻani ařandznahatkutʻyunneri drsevorumnerě hay hin banastełtzutʻyan ev banahyusutʻyan mej." *PBH,* 1987/4, 48–60. (Particulars of Indo-European prosody in old Armenian poetry and folklore).

Łanalanyan, A. *Tʻšnamu kerparě hin hay banahyusutʻyan mej.* (Erevan, 1943). (The enemy in Armenian folklore).

———. "Žołovrdakan banahyusutʻyuně hasarakakan mtkʻi tarber hosankʻneri gnahatutʻyamb." *T,* 1953/5, 29–48. (The interpretation of folklore by diverse currents of social thought).

———. "Hay žołovrdakan hekʻiatʻnerě." *PBH,* 1965/3, 35–48. (On Armenian folktales).

———. "Mesrop Maštoc' dans la tradition arménienne." *REArm,* N.s. 3 (1966), 359–67. (A translation of an essay from *Mesrop Maštots,* Erevan, 1963, pp. 325–41).

———. "Žołovrdakan avandutʻyunneri žanrayin ařandznahatkutʻyunneri masin." *BEH,* 1968/2, 73–88. (On the peculiarities of genre in popular traditions).

———. "Sovetahay banagitutʻyuně 50 tarum." *PBH,* 1970/3, 14–32. (Soviet Armenian folklore studies in the past fifty years).

———. *Hay grakanutʻyuně ev banahyusutʻyuně.* (Erevan, 1986). (Armenian literature and the traditions of Armenian folklore).

Łaziyan, A. "Łarabałi zvarčaḥos Pěl Pułin." *L,* 1978/9, 60–69. (On Pěl Pułi, a traditional comic character in Łarabał).

Macler, F. *Quatre conférences sur l'Arménie.* (Paris, 1932).

Margaryan, H. "Vipakan tarrerě 10–12-rd dareri hay patmagrutʻyan mej." *PBH,* 1987/4, 5–16. (Epic elements in Armenian historiography of the tenth through the twelfth centuries).

Mkrtchyan, H. "Hay-arabakan banahyusakan kaperi patmutʻyunits." *L,* 1987/3, 54–60. (Aspects of Armeno-Arab folklore).

Nazinyan, A. *Sovetahay žołovrdakan banahyusutʻyuně.* (Erevan, 1957). (Soviet Armenian folklore).

———. "Sovetahay banagitutʻyan antsatz ułin." *PBH,* 1967/2–3, 87–94. (On Soviet Armenian folklore studies).

Petrosyan, A. "Gayli paštamunkʻě hay žołovrdakan havatalikʻnerum." *BEH,* 1989/2, 72–80. (The cult of wolves in popular beliefs).

Sargsyan, S. "Ergitzankʻě hay žołovrdakan ařakneri mej." *SG,* 1968/12, 132–39. (Satire in Armenian fables).

Svazlyan, V. "Ṙostovi marzi hay žołovrdakan banahyusutʻyuně." *T,* 1961/10, 107–12. (Armenian folklore in the region of Rostov).

———. "Musa leřan hay žołovrdakan banahyusutʻyuně." *PBH,* 1969/1, 201–6. (Armenian folklore of Musa Dagh).

T[ēr]-S[ahakean], K. "Gołtʻan erger, banasirakan tesakitiw." *B,* 60 (1902), 502–9; 61 (1903), 403–8. (Gołtʻn songs from a philological viewpoint).

Tʻořlakʻyan, B. *Hamšenahayeri azgagrutʻyuně.* (Erevan, 1982). (Ethnography of the Armenians of Hamšen).

Vardanyan, S. "Banahyusakan nyutʻer Leřnayin Łarabałits." *L,* 1971/8, 88–93. (On folkloric material from Nagorno Karabagh).

Yovsēpʻean, G. "Žołovrdakan banahyusutʻyan hetkʻer mijnadarean tałarannerum." *A,* 1898, 544–51. 1899, 44–47.

Literary Influences

Listed here are texts dealing with (a) the relationships between Armenian literature and other national literatures, and (b) the influence of non-Armenian writers on Armenian literature.

Abuladze, I. "Nor hušardzanner vrats ev hayots grakan haraberutʻyunneri masin antsyalum (16–17 dd.)." *BM,* 4 (1958), 377–423.
Agaian, G. *Fadeev i armianskaia literatura.* (Erevan, 1985).
Agaian, Ts., et al. "Ob armiano-vengerskikh istoricheskikh i kul'turnykh sviaziakh i zadachakh ikh izucheniia." *L,* 1969/5, 39–56.
Aivazian, M. *Chekhov i armianskaia kul'tura.* (Erevan, 1981).
Akopian, E. *Armenovedenie v Rossii: Voprosy filologii.* (Erevan, 1988).
Ałababyan, S. "Ṙus grakanutʻyan haykakan ardzagankʻneri dinamikan." *PBH,* 1978/3, 77–86.
Alekʻsanyan, E. *Haykakan ṙealizmě ev ṙus grakanutʻyan pʻordzě.* (Erevan, 1977).
———. "19th Century Armenian Realism and Its International Relations up to 1915." *Review of National Literatures: Armenia.* Ed. A. Paolucci and V. Oshagan, Vol. 13. (New York: Griffin House Publications, 1984), 45–63.
Amirian, S. *Armiano-ukrainskie literaturnye sviazi.* (Erevan, 1972).
———. "Hay-ukrainakan grakan kaperi erekn u aysōrě." *SG,* 1973/10, 161–63.
———. *Armiano-ukrainskie literaturnye sviazi (bibliografiia).* (Erevan, 1976).
———. *Russkaia khudozhestvennaia literatura ob Armenii.* (Erevan, 1983).
———. "Armianskie znakomstva Tarasa Shevchenko." *PBH,* 1984/2, 123–31.
Amirkhanian, A. *L. N. Tolstoi i armianskaia deistvitel'nost'.* (Erevan, 1985).
Antonyan, G. *Nizamin ev hay grakanutʻyuně.* (Baku, 1947).
Aṙakʻelyan, V. "Kalidasayi 'Amp-averaber' poemi šarahyusakan kaṙutsvatzkʻi mi aṙandznahatkutʻyan masin." *PBH,* 1980/2, 110–20.
———. "Hasarakakan baṙapašari artahaytman mijotsnerě Ṙigvedayi hayeren tʻargmanutʻyan žamanak." *PBH,* 1985/3, 123–35.
Arevelyan ałbyuragitutʻyun. Studies in Oriental Sources. (Erevan, 1988). (Covers mainly Middle-Eastern sources).
Armianskie perevody proizvedenii pisatelei russkikh i drugikh narodov Rossii (1843–1920): Bibliograficheskii ukazatel'. (Erevan, 1984).
Arsharuni, A. "K voprosu ob armiano-arabskikh literaturnykh sviaziakh." *T,* 1960/5–6, 185–90.
Aslanyan, M. "Angliakan memuarayin grakanutʻyan avanduytʻnerě ev Hovsepʻ Ēmini inkʻnakensagrutʻyuně." *L,* 1980/1, 64–78.
Avagyan, Ṙ. "Sergey Esenini haykakan kaperě." *SG,* 1972/7, 136–43.
Avagyan, S. "Hayeri ev vratsineri grakan-kulturakan kaperě." *SG,* 1961/2, 147–49.

Babayan, A. "XIX dari hay grołnerě ev Šillerě." *PBH,* 1958/3, 168–82.
———. *Šillerě hay grakanut'yan mej ev t'atronum.* (Erevan, 1959).
———. "Shiller v armianskoi literature." *T,* 1960/5–6, 219–30.
———. "Háy grołnerě ev Danten." *SG,* 1974/1, 140–44.
Bagdasarian, R. "Nikolai Tikhonov i armianskaia literaturnaia zhizn'." *L,* 1986/6, 21–30.
———. "Pis'ma Nikolaia Tikhonova deiateliam literatury i iskustva Armenii." *Banber Hayastani arḥivneri,* 1986/1, 93–96.
Baḥchinyan, H. "Bodlerě hay irakanut'yan mej." *SG,* 1972/9, 154–55.
Bek'aryan, A. "Bayroně ev Mḥit'aryannerě." *PBH,* 1988/2, 34–47.
———. "Nerbołner Bayronin hay banastełtznerits." *BEH,* 1989/3, 127–32.
Boyajian, Z. "Armenian and English Poetry: Some Parallels." *The Contemporary Review,* 1926/666 (June), 801–10.
Briusov i Armeniia. 2 vols. (Erevan, 1988–89).
Chekhov i literatura narodov Sovetskogo Soiuza. (Erevan, 1982).
Čingozyan, K. *Hay-bułłarakan grakan kaperi patmut'yunits.* (Erevan, 1966).
———. "Hay-bułłarakan haraberut'yunneri patmut'yunits." *PBH,* 1973/1, 3–22.
Danielyan, S. *Lermontově ev hay mšakuyt'ě.* (Erevan, 1960).
Daronian, Iu. "Armeniia v publitsistike i proze S. Gorodetskogo." *L,* 1982/4, 41–52.
———. "Drevnearmianskaia kul'tura v osveshchenii S. Gorodetskogo." *L,* 1983/1, 33–40.
Daštents, Ḥ. *Bayroně ev hayerě.* (Erevan, 1959).
Deich, E. *Dusha, otkrytaia liudiam: O Vere Zviagintsevoi. Vospominaniia, stat'i, ocherki.* (Erevan, 1981).
Dzhanpoladian, M. "N. Grebnev-perevodchik Kuchaka i Tumaniana." *BEH,* 1981/3, 192–205.
Ep'remyan, L. *Hay-mongolakan grakan kaper, 1945–1980. Matenagitakan tsank.* (Erevan, 1982).
Etmekjian, J. *The French Influence on the Western Armenian Renaissance, 1843–1915).* (New York: Twayne Publishers, 1964).
———. "Western European and Modern Armenian Literary Relations up to 1915." *Review of National Literatures: Armenia.* Ed. A. Paolucci and V. Oshagan, Vol. 13. (New York: Griffin House Publications, 1984), 64–92.
Gachev, G. *Natsional'nye obrazy mira: Obshchie voprosy. Russkii. Bolgarskii. Armianskii.* (Moscow, 1988).
Galstyan, P., and Simonyan, I. *Hay-t'urk'menakan grakan kaper, 1944–1982. Matenagitakan tsank.* (Erevan, 1983).
Gasparyan, G. "Poeziia Viktora Giugo i armianskaia literatura." *T,* 1960/5–6, 205–18.
———. *Viktor Hyugon hay grakanut'yan mej.* (Erevan, 1963).
Gevorgyan-Bagi, Ē. *Hay-hungarakan grakan ar̃nchut'yunnerě ev 'Armenia' amsagirě.* (Erevan, 1979).
Gilavyan, M. "Simvolizmi hartserě arevelahay grak'nnadatut'yan mej." *SG,* 1981/12, 148–50.
Golubeva, L. *Vzaimosviazi i vzaimodeistvie literatur narodov SSSR: Bibliograficheskii ukazatel'.* (Moscow, 1983).

Gonchar-Khandzhian, N. "Dukhovnoe porodnenie (o tvorcheskikh sviaziakh L. Pervomaiskogo s Armeniei i armianskoi literaturoi)." *BEH,* 1982/3, 31–39.

———. *Armianskaia literatura v russkoi sovetskoi kritike: bibliografiia. Stat'i.* (Erevan, 1989). (Armenian literature in Soviet Russian criticism; bibliography and articles).

Gorodetskii, S. *Hayastani ev hay kulturayi masin.* (Erevan, 1980).

Grigorian, R. *Maiakovskii i armianskaia literatura.* (Erevan, 1956).

Grigoryan, Š. "Arevelkʻi ev hay banastełtzakan arvesti ařnchutʻyunneri hartsi šurjě." *PBH,* 1965/2, 192–96.

Grišašvili, I., and Leonidze, G. *Hayastani ev hay kulturayi masin.* (Erevan, 1983).

Hakobyan, P. "Mijnadaryan hay kʻnarergutʻyan mutkʻě germanakan irakanutʻyan mej." *SG,* 1984/6, 115–22.

Hambardzumyan, L. "Hay-germanakan grakan kaperi patmutʻyunits." *SG,* 1978/3, 140–41.

Harutʻyunyan, B. *Hay-řusakan tʻaterakan kaper.* (Erevan, 1955).

Hay grakanutʻyan mijazgayin kaperě. Vol. 1 (Erevan, 1983). (3 vols. projected).

Hay grołnerě gełarvestakan tʻargmanutʻyan masin. (Erevan, 1985).

Hay-latišakan grakan kaperě (1945–78): matenagitakan tsank. (Erevan, 1978).

Hayrapetyan, K. "Hay-bułłarakan grakan kaperě XIX dari verjum ev XX dari skzbin." *BEH,* 1972/1, 100–8.

———. "Mi kʻani drvag hay-bułłarakan grakan kaperi patmutʻyunits." *SG,* 1976/1, 96–97.

Hovnan, G. *Makʻsim Gorkin ev hay kulturan.* (Erevan, 1940).

———. *N. V. Gogolě ev hay grakanutʻyuně.* (Erevan, 1952).

———. *N. A. Nekrasově ev hay poezian.* (Erevan, 1956).

———. "N. A. Dobroliubov i armianskaia literaturno-obshchestvennaia mysl' XIX veka." *T,* 1960/5–6, 95–112.

———. *Řus-hay grakan kaperě XIX–XX darerum.* 2 vols. (Erevan, 1960–61).

———. *Lui Aragoně Hayastani ev hay mšakuytʻi masin.* (Erevan, 1984).

Khachatryan, R. "Rol' russkoi istoricheskoi literatury v russko-armianskom sblizhenii." *L,* 1984/2, 34–47.

Khudozhestvennyi perevod: Voprosy teorii i praktiki. (Erevan, 1982).

Kubat'ian, G. "Mesto armianskoi temy v tvorchestve O. Mandel'shtama (Uroki Armenii)." *BEH,* 1989/2, 11–20.

Łaribjanyan, G. "N. G. Černiševskin ev 19. dari 60–80-akan tʻvakanneri hay ařajavor gortzichnerě." *L,* 1978/7, 12–27.

Literaturnye sviazi. 2 vols. (Erevan, 1973, 1977).

Literaturnye sviazi. (Erevan, 1981).

Łukasyan, Z. *Řus-hay grakan kaperě nahařevolyutsion šrjanum.* (Erevan, 1961).

Madoyan, G. "Hay-vratsakan grakan kaperě sovetakan šrjanum." *T,* 1961/12, 51–60.

Mamedov, S. "Iz istorii literaturnykh vzaimootnoshenii azerbaidzhanskogo i armianskogo narodov." *PBH,* 1965/3, 246–52.

Margaryan, A. "Hay-řus grakan kaperi usumnasirman šurjě." *SG,* 1961/4, 136–45.

Melikʻsetʻ-Bek, L. "Hay-vratsakan grakan kaperi patmutʻyunits." *EJ,* 1957/7–8, 39–42.

Melikʻsetʻyan, S. "Henrik Ibseně hay mšakuytʻi kyankʻum." *SG,* 1978/4, 161–63.

Mezhelaitis, E. *Armianskii fenomen [stikhi, stat'i, zametki]*. Trans. from the Lithuanian by F. Fikhman. (Erevan, 1982).

Minasyan, A. "Firdusu hay t'argmanichnerě." *L,* 1980/4, 74–80.

Mkhitarian, A. *Armianskaia literatura v Gruzii.* (Erevan, 1980). (Armenian literature in Soviet Georgia).

———. *Armiano-gruzinskie literaturnye vzaimosviazi. Armianskaia sovetskaia literatura v Gruzii.* (Tbilisi, 1982).

Mkrtchian, K. "Chetyre 'Nosa' [Povesti N. V. Gogolia 'Nos'-original i chetyre armianskikh perevoda]." *BEH,* 1980/3, 162–74.

———. " 'Zapiski sumashedshego' i ikh armianskii perevod." *BEH,* 1983/2, 175–85.

———. *Peterburgskie povesti N. V. Gogolia v armianskikh perevodakh.* (Erevan, 1984).

Mkrtchian, L. *Esli by v Vavilone byli perevodchiki: stat'i, razmyshleniia, zametki.* (Erevan, 1987).

Mkrtchyan, H. " 'Płndze k'ałak'i patmut'yan' arabakan ev haykakan tarberaknerě." *PBH,* 1986/2, 130–38.

———. "Hay-arabakan banahyusakan kaperi patmut'yunits." *L,* 1987/3, 54–60.

Mkryan, M. "Nekrasově ev hay grakanut'yuně." *PBH,* 1971/4, 17–26.

———. "Gełetsiki idealě Gorku stełtzagortzut'yan mej ev hay grakanut'yuně." *SG,* 1978/10, 128–34.

Movsisyan, H. "Mi ēj 19. dari hay-parskakan grakan ar̄nchut'yunneri patmut'yunits." *PBH,* 1970/3, 243–48.

———. " 'K'alile ev Demnei' (ar̄akagrk'i) ev nra erku anhayt gluḥneri šurj." *Merdzavor ev Mijin Arevelk'i erkrner ev žołovurdner.* Vol. 11 (Erevan, 1982), 224–46.

Muradyan, P. "Hay-vratsakan grakan-mšakut'ayin p'oḥharaberut'yunneri patmut'yunits." *T,* 1964/10, 55–68.

———. "Hay-vratsakan grakan-mšakut'ayin p'oḥharaberut'yunneri patmut'yunits." *EJ,* 1966/11–12, 51–58.

———. *Armiano-gruzinskie literaturnye vzaimootnosheniia v 17. veke.* (Erevan, 1966).

Nanumyan, Ṙ. *Hay-r̄us grakan kaperi šurjě (hamar̄ot aknark).* (Erevan, 1945).

Oshagan, V. *The English Influence on West Armenian Literature in the Nineteenth Century.* (Printed at Cleveland State University, Cleveland, Ohio, 1982. Distributed by Caravan Books).

Oskerchyan, A. *Ṙus ev hay grakanut'yan hartser.* (Erevan, 1982).

Ovnan, G. N. A. *Dobroliubov i armianskaia literaturno-obshchestvennaia mysl'.* (Erevan, 1986).

Paronikian, E. "Dorevoliutsionnye perevody dramaticheskikh proizvedenii A. S. Pushkina na armianskii iazyk." *BEH,* 1982/1, 147–51.

P'art'amyan, V. "Sviftě hay grakanut'yan mej." *SG,* 1965/10, 104–7.

———. *Hay-angliakan grakan ar̄nchut'yunnerě.* (Erevan, 1975).

Petrosyan, Ē. "Klasitsizmi šrjani hay-fransiakan grakan kaperi šurjě." *T,* 1946/7, 51–68.

———. "Bayroně ev hay kulturan." *T,* 1947/3, 47–76.

Review of National Literatures: Armenia. Ed. A. Paolucci and V. Oshagan, Vol. 13. (New York: Griffin House Publications, 1984).

Rozov, N. "K izucheniiu russko-armianskikh kul'turnykh sviazei drevneishego perioda." *BEH,* 1970/2, 197–203.
Russkaia i armianskaia srednevekovye literatury [sbornik statei]. (Erevan, 1982).
Saakian, A. *I. S. Turgenev v armianskoi literature (v perevodakh i kritike).* (Tbilisi, 1980).
Safrazbekyan, I. "Ivan Buninĕ ev hay poezian." *SG,* 1965/3, 146–51.
Šahsuvaryan, A. *Avetsinnan ev hay matenagrutʻyunĕ.* (Erevan, 1960).
Samvelyan, L. *Šekʻspirĕ ev hay grakan u tʻaterakan mšakuytʻĕ: naḫasovetakan šrjan.* (Erevan, 1974).
Seferyan, S. "Šekʻspiri aṙajin ašḫarhabar tʻargmanichĕ." *BEH,* 1984/1, 176–79.
Silvanyan, H. *Hamašḫarhayin grakanutʻyan hayeren tʻargmanutʻyunnerĕ (1512–1920). Matenagitakan ułetsuyts. Prak aṙajin. Ṙus ev Ṙusastani ayl žołovurdneri grołneri erkeri hayeren tʻargmanutʻyunnerĕ (1843–1920).* Part 1. (Erevan, 1984).
———. *Hamašḫarhayin grakanutʻyan hayeren tʻargmanutʻyunnerĕ (1512–1920). Matenagitakan tsank. Prak erkrord. Artasahmanyan grakanutʻyan hayeren tʻargmanutʻyunnerĕ (1708–1920).* Part 2. (Erevan, 1985).
———. *Hamašḫarhayin grakanutʻyan hayeren tʻargmanutʻyunnerĕ (1512–1920). Matenagitakan tsank. Prak errord. Artasahmanyan grakanutʻyan hayeren tʻargmanutʻyunnerĕ (1587–1920).* Part 3. (Erevan, 1986).
Simonyan, H. *Hay mijnadaryan kafaner (X–XI dd.).* (Erevan, 1975). (Medieval Armenian kafas from the tenth through the sixteenth centuries).
Stepʻanyan, G. *Hayataṙ tʻurkʻeren hay mamulĕ.* (Erevan, 1963). (Off-print: *Hay parberakan mamuli patmutʻyunits,* Vol. 1, Erevan, 1963).
Stepʻanyan, H. *Hayataṙ tʻurkʻeren grkʻeri matenagitutʻyun, 1727–1968.* (Erevan, 1985).
———. *Hayataṙ tʻurkʻeren parberakan mamul (matenagitutʻyun).* (Erevan, 1987).
Sviazi armianskoi literatury s literaturami narodov SSSR (sbornik statei). (Erevan, 1982).
Tatevosian, R. *Lermontov i armianskaia klassicheskaia poeziia.* (Erevan, 1981).
———. "Trevozhnoe sluzhenie pred idealom krasoty" (k voprosu "Tiutchev i armianskaia literatura"). *BEH,* 1983/1, 56–63.
———. *Lev Tolstoi i armianskaia klassicheskaia literatura.* (Erevan, 1990).
Tayan, A. *Dantei 'Astvatzayin katakergutʻyan' banastełtzakan arvestĕ ev tʻargmanutʻyan problemnerĕ.* (Erevan, 1982).
Tchobanian, A. *Victor Hugo, Chateaubriand et Lamartine dans la littérature arménienne.* (Paris, 1935).
Ter-Łevondyan, A. "Hay ev kʻristonya arabakan matenagrakan aṙnchutʻyunneri patmutʻyunits." *EJ,* 1977/11, 57–63.
———. "Mušełi vepĕ arab patmagrutʻyan mej." *L,* 1986/6, 52–58.
Zakʻaryan, An. "Valeri Bryusovĕ Andrkovkasum ev hay grakan kyankʻĕ." *PBH,* 1983/2–3, 74–88.
———. "Vasili Kamerskin Andrkovkasum ev hay grakan kyankʻĕ." *L,* 1983/7, 14–24.
———. "Sergey Gorodetskin Andrkovkasum ev hay grakan kyankʻĕ (1916–1921)." *L,* 1984/2, 22–33.
———. "Pis'ma Ioanny Briusovoi Tigrany Ioannisianu." *Banber Hayastani arḫivneri.* 1986/1, 97–99.

Zar'ian, R. *Shekspir i armiane.* Trans. by S. Gullakian. (Erevan, 1981).

Zaryan, Ṙ., ed. *Šekʻspirakan: haykakan šekʻspiryan taregirkʻ* (Shakespearakan, an Armenian yearbook of Shakespeare). 7 vols. to 1985. (Erevan, 1966, 1967, 1970, 1974, 1975, 1980, 1985).

Zedgenidze, Ts. *Gruzinskie pisateli ob armianskoi literature.* (Erevan, 1984).

Prosody

Abełyan, M. *Hayots lezvi tałachapʻutʻyun (metrika).* (Erevan, 1933). (See also his *Works,* Vol. 1, Erevan, 1970).

Ařakʻelyan, A. "Haykakan tałachapʻutʻyuně." *EJ,* 1952/2, 26–33.

Bahatʻrean, A. *Hin hayots tałachapʻakan aruestě, kʻnnakan tesutʻiwn.* (Šuši, 1891).

Chōpanean, A. "Haykakan tałachapʻutʻean verabereal hartser." *ANA,* 15 (1949/1), 1–2.

Gabriēlean, S. "Ditołutʻiwnner haykakan tałachapʻutean vray." *HA,* 26 (1912), 97–110.

Gasapean, S. *Tałachapʻutʻiwn ardi hayerēn lezwi, handerdz tzanōtʻutʻeamb chapʻakan ew šešteal otanaworneru vray.* (Constantinople, 1895).

Gasparyan, D. "1941–45 tʻvakaneri sovetahay poeziayi tałachapʻakan ařandznahatkutʻyunnerě." *L,* 1973/5, 83–94.

———. "Hangi drsevorman ařandznahatkutʻyunnerě ardi hay poeziayum." *SG,* 1975/11, 144–53.

———. *Sovetahay poeziayi tałachapʻutʻyun. E,* 1979.

Gray, L. "Les mètres paiens de l'Arménie." *REArm,* 6 (1926), 159–67.

Hiwrm[iwz], E. "Haykakan tałachapʻutʻiwn." *B,* 31 (1873), 97–106.

Jrbašyan, Ēd. "Eřavank chapʻerě 20. dari hay poeziayum." *BEH,* 1975/1, 121–39.

———. "Manuk Abełyaně ev haykakan tałachapʻutʻyan usumnasirutʻyan hartserě." *BEH,* 1968/1, 80–93.

Łulyan, Ṙ. "Hamašešt otanavorě 20-akan tʻvakaneri hay poeziayum." *BEH,* 1971/2, 222–29.

Nazlean, Y. *Kʻnnakan usumnasirutʻiwn ew ěntʻatskʻ bnik-hay tałachapʻutʻean.* (Cairo, 1959).

Palean, M. "Gołtʻan ergeri tałachapʻutʻean masin." *A,* 1901, 99–106. (Meters of the songs from Gołtʻn).

Ṙuben vardapet. "Hetʻanos Hayastani ašḥarhik ergeri tałachapʻutʻyuně ekełetsakan ergerum." *EJ,* 1944/7–9, 27–32.

Sahakean, K. "Ašḥarhabari nor tałachapʻutʻean vray." *B,* 63 (1905), 437–41.

———. "Ašḥarhabari nor tałachapʻutʻiwn mě." *B,* 63 (1905), 500–9.

———. "Azgayin hin tałachapʻutʻean gałtnikʻě." *B,* 65 (1907), 245–54.

———. "Amanakawor chapʻě ew toktʻ. S. M. Gabriēlean." *B,* 67 (1909), 481–88.

Šarabḥanyan, P. "Hangě hay mijnadaryan banastełtzutʻyan mej." *PBH,* 1969/1, 207–16.

Tʻireakʻean, Y. *Haykakan tałachapʻutʻiwn.* (New York, 1918).

Tiroyean, A. "Asorakan ew haykakan tałachap'ut'iwn." *B,* 57 (1899), 12–15, 105–9, 245–53, 345–50, 502–6.

———. "Banastełtzakan lezun ew haykakan chap'in grawatz tełě." *B,* 70 (1912), 433–48.

Y[ovnanean], Ł. "Mijnadarean azgayin tałachap'ut'iwn ṙamkaḥaṙn." *HA,* 9 (1895), 305–10. Continued as "Tałachap'k ew tałk'," *HA,* 10 (1896), 52–55, 115–19. Published separately with N. Akinean's *Yovnat'an Nałaš ew Nałaš Yovnat'aneank'.* (Vienna, 1911).

Indexes

Note to the reader. There are two contemporary literary Armenian standards: Eastern (spoken in the Republic of Armenia, the former soviet dispersion, and Iran, and, in recent decades, notably in Northern America as well) and Western (spoken by the descendants of the survivors of the genocide of 1915, now dispersed throughout the world). Of the many differences between these two standards two are of central relevance to us here: the phonetic and orthographic systems. Eastern Armenian has maintained the phonetic values of Classical Armenian but uses a new spelling system. Western Armenian has maintained the traditional spelling system of Classical Armenian but not all of its phonetic values. The following brief and simplified explanations of the shifts in the phonetic values and of a few fundamental spelling differences are meant to help the reader find an entry for an author in an easier fashion.

1. Basically, the following two columns of consonants have "reversed" their sounds:

	Eastern	Western		Eastern	Western
բ	b	p	պ	p	b
գ	g	k	կ	k	g
դ	d	t	տ	t	d
ձ	dz	ts	ծ	ts	dz
ջ	j	ch	ճ	č	j

The "Western" consonants in the first column are pronounced the same way as the following corresponding aspirated consonants: փ = p'; ք = k'; թ = t'; ց= ts; չ = ch; hence, the "identical" pairs of consonants in Western Armenian and some of the spelling difficulties faced by students of Western Armenian. Here are some examples to illustrate the resulting differences:

Surname	Eastern pronunciation	Western pronunciation
Ծերենց	Tzerents	*Dz* erents
Ճուղուրեան	Čułurean	*J* ułurean
Պարոնեան	Paronean	*B* aronean
Բաշինջաղեան	Bašinjałean	*P* ašin *ch* ałean
Գաբրիէլեան	Gabriēlean	*K* a *p* riēlean
Կամսարական	Kamsarakan	*G* amsara *g* an

Բագրատունի	Bagratuni	*P* a *k* ra *d* uni
Տէմիրճիպաշեան	Tēmirčipašean	*D* ēmir *j* i *b* ašean

The transcription system in this *Guide* follows the Classical/Eastern phonetic system; consequently, the names mentioned above, for instance, should be looked up under the forms listed under "Eastern pronunciation."

2. As for the soviet orthographic reform, one principal change is very important to remember. The system reduced the dual phonetic value of the letter "y" (յ, Յ) to one sound: y. In traditional spelling it is pronounced as an "h" at the beginning of a word and as a "y" in the middle of words (its value in final position is not of much relevance here); thus, Յակոբ is pronounced as "Hakob" or "Hagop" (Western), and այս as "ays." The new system spells this and similar words beginning with a "y" (e.g., Yovhannēs) with an "h" instead (Hovhannes), while leaving the phonetic value of "y" unchanged in middle position. Also, the letter "y" replaced the letter ե = e in the diphthong եա = ea (always pronounced "ya"); hence the "yan" in surnames: Simonyan, as opposed to the traditional Simonean. But this and similar changes, such as the replacement in the middle of words of "ē" with "e," as in "Tērean-Teryan"; of "ō" with "o," as in "Pōłosean-Połosyan"; of "w" with "v," as in "Awetisean-Avetisyan" (the system did away with "w" as a separate, independent letter); of "u+vowel" with "v+vowel," as in "Manuēlean-Manvelyan"; of the diphthong "iw" with "yu" when followed by a consonant in the middle of a word, as in "Yarutʻiwnean-Harutʻyunyan"; etc., are less crucial to this index since they occur in middle or rearward positions in names.

Index I
Principal Authors

This is an author list and an index of all the principal Armenian writers featured, discussed, or referred to in both the narrative and bio-bibliographical parts of this Guide; of their pen names; and of some variant forms of their names (i.e., Armenian forms rendered in accordance with Western Armenian phonetic values, and/or general, "unscientific" rendering of such forms into English, French, Russian, and other languages.) The latter are cross-referenced to names appearing in this index only, but most of these names are found in Index II as well. Such cross references nearly always appear without the Armenian surname endings *ean, ian, yan* (e.g., Hagop. *See* Hakob; Yakob). Authors' real names and pen names are listed, with cross references to the form used as the primary entry. Also listed are individual titles analyzed or referred to in the narrative part of the guide and critical literature by principal authors listed under "Criticism" in the bio-bibliographical section.

Names in bold capital letters are those of the principal authors. Page numbers in bold italics refer to the discussion of the work of an author and/or to the bio-bibliographical entry for the author. Works are listed under the Armenian title; English translations are cross-referenced to the Armenian. Both traditional and new (reformed or "soviet") orthography have been maintained.

Index II
General Names and Subjects

This index is necessarily selective. It is chiefly an index of critics and literary historians whose writings appear under "Criticism" in the bio-bibliographical part and in parts 3, 4, and 5 of this *Guide*. As a general rule, editors and translators have been excluded, but exceptions have been inevitable. This index also includes all critics and authors, Armenian and non-Armenian alike, to whom or to whose works references have been made in the narrative part. This is in addition an index, not always exhaustive, of certain subjects and place names. Only a single reference is made to names occurring more than once on the same page. Armenian clergymen are listed by their first name.

No cross-references are made to Armenian surname endings *ean, ian, yan* (though they are used to distinguish identical Eastern and Western Armenian forms), nor to diacritical marks that do not essentially alter the phonetic value of a letter, nor to inconsistencies in spelling (e.g., P' ē chikean / P' e chikean). Thus, the traditional *Tērtērean*, and the reformed *Terteryan,* are grouped together. Only a few cross-references are given from the variant forms of Armenian names with a view to complementing the extensive list of such references in Index I.

Due mainly to the lack of certain letters in the Russian script, Russian forms of Armenian names pose a major problem. Thus, Hakobyan/Yakobean is rendered as Akopian, Janp'oladyan as Dzhanpoladian, Łazaryan as Kazarian, etc. If the bearer of such a surname writes exclusively or mostly in Russian, and no other authors with the same name are found in the index, no cross-references are given to the corresponding Armenian form of that name (e.g. Agaian / Ałayan). If, however, the author writes solely in Armenian, or in both Armenian and Russian, or his/her Armenian writings are frequently translated into Russian, a cross-reference is made from the Russian form to the main Armenian entry (e.g., Dzhrbashian, E. / Jrbašyan, Ēd.). Diacritical marks and slight variations in spelling and transcription systems (e.g. Armenian "š," "ḥ" = Russian "sh," "kh") are disregarded if both first and last names of the same author are, or appear to be, identical (e.g. T'erzibašyan, V[ahram] / Terzibashian, V[agram]; Gaïssarian, S. / Gaisarian, S.; Ayvazyan / Aivazian; Alek'sanean-Aleksanian-Alek'sanyan; Amirḥanyan / Amirkhanian). A cross-reference is provided if the initial letter or both or either of the last or first names is different in the Russian form (e.g., Khachatrian / Ḥachatryan; Orbeli, I[osif] / Ōrbeli, H[ovsep'].